Microsoft®
Office 2007
in business

Joseph M. Manzo

Dee R. Piziak

CJ Rhoads

PEARSON
Prentice
Hall

Upper Saddle River
New Jersey 07458

Library of Congress Cataloging-in-Publication Data

Microsoft Office 2007 in business, Core / CJ Rhoads, Dee R. Piziak, Joseph M. Manzo, series editor.
  p. cm.
  Includes bibliographical references and index.
  ISBN-13: 978-0-13-156087-1
  ISBN-10: 0-13-156087-5
  1. Microsoft Office. 2. Business--Computer programs. I. Rhoads, CJ. II. Piziak,
Dee R. III. Manzo, Joseph M.
HF5548.4.M525M52497 2008
  005.5--dc22   2006039211

Vice President and Publisher: Natalie E. Anderson
Associate VP/Executive Acquisitions Editor, Print: Stephanie Wall
Executive Acquisitions Editor, Media: Richard Keaveny
Sr. Acquisitions Editor: Melissa Sabella
Product Development Manager: Eileen Bien Calabro
Sr. Editorial Project Manager: Eileen Clark
Development Editor: Jill Rembetski
Editorial Assistants: Becky Knauer, Lora Cimiluca
Executive Producer: Lisa Strite
Content Development Manager: Cathi Profitko
Project Manager, Media: Alana Meyers
Director of Marketing: Margaret Waples
Sr. Marketing Manager: Scott Davidson
Marketing Assistant: Angela Frey
Sr. Sales Associate: Rebecca Scott
Managing Editor: Lynda J. Castillo
Market Development Editors: Karen Misler, Claire Hunter
Production Project Manager: Wanda Rockwell
Production Media Project Manager: Lorena Cerisano
Production Editor: Angelique Amig
Photo Researcher: Andrea Shearer
Manufacturing Buyer: Natacha Moore
Production/Editorial Assistant: Sandra K. Bernales
Design Director: Maria Lange
Art Director/Interior Design: Blair Brown
Front Cover Image: Courtesy of Istockphoto/Ingvald Kaldhussaeter
Back Cover Author Photo: Courtesy of Natasha Berger
Composition: GGS Book Services
Project Management: GGS Book Services
Cover Printer: Phoenix Color
Printer/Binder: Von Hoffmann Press/Jefferson City

Microsoft, Windows, Word, PowerPoint, Excel, Access, Outlook, FrontPage, Visual Basic, MSN, The Microsoft Network, and/or other Microsoft products referenced herein are either trademarks or registered trademarks of Microsoft Corporation in the U.S.A. and other countries. Screen shots and icons reprinted with permission from the Microsoft Corporation. This book is not sponsored or endorsed by or affiliated with Microsoft Corporation.

Credits and acknowledgments borrowed from other sources and reproduced, with permission, in this textbook are as follows or on the appropriate page within the text.

Pages 2, 15, 76, 112, 204, and 245: Getty Images, Inc. -Stone Allstock; pages 5, 167, 314, and 358: Dorling Kindersley Media Library; pages 5, 118, 139, 252, and 308: Getty Images, Inc.- Photodisc.; pages 22, 69, 364, and 337: Pearson Education/PH College; pages 144, 159, 722, and 774: PhotoEdit Inc.; pages 166 and 197: Getty Images, Inc.- Stockbyte; pages 382, 428, 436, 482, 488, and 525: iStockphoto.com; pages 532 and 583: SuperStock, Inc.: pages 590 and 639: Corbis/Bettmann; pages 646 and 658: Masterfile Corporation; pages 664 and 714: Corbis/SABA Press Photos, Inc. pages 782 and 831: John Coletti; pages 838 and 897: Allyn & Bacon; pages 904 and 942: The Image Works; pages 316 and 317: ETM Associates, Inc; and pages 319, 320, 321, 322 and 323: Taijiquan Club.

10 9 8 7 6 5 4 3 2 1
ISBN 0-13-156087-5

For my parents.
As I get older, I have a deeper understanding and appreciation for the commitment and sacrifices they made for me during my childhood.
I hope I have made them proud.

—Joseph M. Manzo

This book is dedicated to
My parents, who made me what I am today.
My children, without whose love and support, I would not be where I am today.
My students, whom I have been privileged to know and teach all these years.

—Dee R. Piziak

I'd like to dedicate this book to my loving and supportive husband, Robert J. Rhoads, as well as to my immediate and extended family who all patiently put up with me while I'm in "furiously writing" mode. I love you all.

—CJ Rhoads

Joseph M. Manzo
**In Business series editor and author of Microsoft® Office Excel 2007 In Business
and Microsoft® Office Access 2007 In Business**

Joseph began his career in a family-owned business in the garment center of New York City where he managed production plans for knitted textiles sold in the domestic market. Since then, he has worked with several U.S. corporations in the manufacturing, retailing, consulting, and finance industries. He has held positions in Strategic Planning, Information Systems, and Merchandise Planning and Buying. The use of Microsoft Excel and Access was an integral part of managing information and making decisions throughout his career. He developed a high level of expertise in these applications and eventually trained business professionals as a manager in the information systems division of a multibillion dollar retail corporation.

Today, Joseph is a teacher and independent consultant. After practicing business for several years, he moved his career into academia by developing and teaching the Excel competency program at Lehigh University's prestigious College of Business and Economics. He also teaches the Introduction to Business class to first-year business students at Lehigh. In his consulting practice, Joseph develops strategic plans for new businesses, and develops desktop IT solutions for business performance reporting and analysis. He received an MBA with a concentration in Information Systems Management from Lehigh University and attended Rutgers University for his undergraduate degree.

Dee R. Piziak
Author of Presenting with Microsoft® Office PowerPoint® 2007 In Business

Dee Piziak is an adjunct faculty member at the University of Wisconsin-Milwaukee and at Concordia University. She teaches various information systems courses at both the undergraduate and graduate level.

Dee holds a B.S. in Computer and Information Science from the University of Florida and an M.S. in Computer Science from the University of Wisconsin-Milwaukee.

In addition to teaching, Dee is an Information Technology professional. She has held sales and marketing positions at IBM Corporation, Ameritech, and EMC Corporation. She is currently an Assistant Director for Field Development Systems at Northwestern Mutual in Milwaukee, Wisconsin.

Chris J. Rhoads
Author of Communicating with Microsoft® Office Word 2007 In Business

Dr. Rhoads ("CJ") is President and CEO for ETM Associates, Inc., which specializes in helping companies make better decisions regarding business management and information technology. She is also Associate Professor in the College of Business at Kutztown University, where she shares her knowledge in a variety of graduate and undergraduate courses. CJ is a dynamic speaker and sought-after guru on improving business through information technology. She has been widely published, including several instructional manuals, and is a regular columnist for several business publications.

CJ developed her extensive knowledge through a combination of startups and Fortune 500 companies in the financial industry. Prior to starting ETM Associates, she served as Chief Technology and Operations Officer for CommerceLinks.Net, a startup specializing in Live Video Customer Service technologies. During the height of the Internet bubble, she utilized her talents as Chief Technology Officer of Millstar, an E-commerce software development company specializing in online catalogues of highly complex product sets for click and mortar companies. Her large company experience was garnered as Vice President of First USA and MBNA, where she provided internal consult to senior management on technology decision-making topics.

CJ started her career by building Computer Educational Services, a highly successful computer training and consulting firm that eventually merged into Verso Technologies, a publicly traded company. She has a doctorate in Educational Technology from Lehigh University and a Master's degree from Temple University.

» Acknowledgments

–Joseph M. Manzo, *Series Editor*

It would have been impossible for me to write these books without the help, support, and extraordinary efforts of so many people. I would first like to thank Melissa Sabella, our senior acquisitions editor, who worked tirelessly to manage all the players, schedules, visions, and events to make this series possible. Melissa, along with Natalie Anderson (vice president and publisher), believed in my vision and I am so grateful that they gave me this opportunity. Scott Davidson, our senior marketing manager, has an infectious excitement and enthusiasm that got the sales force passionate about the series before it was even published.

A critical component of any team is the players. I am very lucky to be working with such a dynamic and talented group of people. Dee Piziak not only carried the vision and all the writing of the PowerPoint books but was also a great person to talk to late at night when I needed to "vent" or laugh during the exhausting process of writing. After my first conversation with Dee, I felt like I had known her for twenty years. CJ Rhoads was a tremendous asset for carrying the vision and all the writing of the Word book. I never met anyone who knows as much about Word as CJ.

Eileen Clark, our senior editorial project manager (and my first trainer in the do's and dont's of textbook writing) kept our books on track and ultimately printed. Cathi Profitko, our product development manager, was instrumental in getting one of the most distinctive features of this product accomplished: the videos. Alana Meyers, media editor, pulled our many resources into an easy to use system for professors and students.

Lynda Castillo leads an amazing production team including Wanda Rockwell and Natacha Moore, who didn't let any obstacles make us pause for even a second. The whole GGS team lead by Kevin Bradley and Doug Bell made the impossible possible by publishing these books despite all the challenges. Blair Brown, art director, took my vision, on the first shot, created a design that makes this a true, easy to use, functional reference text.

I am so fortunate to work with Jill Rembetski, the team's development editor. She is without question a gifted writer and had an outstanding impact with regards to the writing style of these books. She is also one of the best listeners I have ever met; she had to listen to my "soapbox rants" on many occasions.

I would also like to thank people from home who gave me tremendous support over the years of developing the vision and writing of these books. Karen Collins is not only my mentor on writing textbooks but it was also her suggestion that led me to contact Prentice Hall about this vision. Like anything in life, a project of this magnitude certainly has its ups and downs. Karen and her husband, Bill, have been there for me every step of the way with great advice and encouragement. Robert Kendi, Nancy Freeman, and Joan DeSalvatore gave me the freedom and support to develop the Excel and Access competency programs at Lehigh University. Without their support and belief in my skills, I would have never developed the vision that is embodied in this series. Ed Ballinger and John Santamaria were instrumental in refining the very first production of the Excel videos that became the distinctive trait of my vision. They also sat through countless takes so I could get it right (Let's do one more take, Ed!). Finally, I can never give enough thanks to Julie Curran. She has been my friend, companion, cheerleader, proofreader, film critic, and sometimes voice coach through this entire process. I am incredibly lucky to have Julie in my life. I love her dearly.

–Dee Piziak

To Brian Normoyle and Stephanie Wall. My association with Prentice Hall, which began with you, has been one of the most rewarding experiences in my career. I am so grateful to both of you for helping me achieve my goal of authoring a college textbook.

To Melissa Sabella, senior acquisitions editor. You assembled a highly talented group of people to create this series. I cannot thank you enough for asking me to be part of the team and for refusing to take "no" for an answer. It is such a privilege to work with you.

To Joseph Manzo, series editor. I could not have written this book without your vision, mentorship, and encouragement. Even after your most exhausting day (including your Sunday office hours!), you never failed to call to answer questions and make sure things were on track, no matter how late it was. You are an amazing person. Thank you for everything, my friend.

To Jill Rembetski, development editor. This book would not be anywhere near what it is today without your guidance. You are a wonderfully gifted writer and editor and we are so fortunate to have you. You also had the monumental task of handling all the books and chapters, which at any given point in time were in various stages of completion. Thank you for your patience and for skillfully moving us all forward.

To Rita Cheng, Johannes Britz, Tom Walker, Chad Zahrt, Alex Koohang, and David Borst. Thank you for supporting my passion for teaching and for giving me the opportunity to be part of your faculty.

To my former students—Mitchell Braverman, Amir Davis, Larry Gilroy, Heidi Gold, Greg Lampert, Erin Mahoney, Shahab Rahman, Mike Schmackle, Margaret Stern, and Jeanna Winkler. Thank you for contributing your papers for my chapters. Students like you are the reason I teach—you are intelligent, engaging, hard-working, and have tremendous potential. You are going to accomplish many great things in your lives.

This book could not have happened without the support of many people on the home front. With gratitude and deepest regards, I would like to acknowledge each of them.

To Anne Fruchterman Hunt. There are simply not enough words to thank you and Bob for your love, support, and friendship. I would not be where I am today without you.

To Desiree Rosas, who ran my household smoothly and took care of my children so I could write this book.

To Kevin and Patty Whaley, Kevin Gibson and Elizabeth Lentini, Tom and Nancy Backes, Suzy Shaw, Janine Werner, and Cheri Peery. Thank you for welcoming us to your community with open arms and for taking care of carpools and other logistics so that I could use every spare minute to work on this book. You have no idea how much that helped.

To my beloved children, Adriana and Elizabeth. Everything good that's ever happened in my adult life is because of you. You are the hardest working and kindest people I know and I am very proud of you. It is a privilege to be your mother. I love you both dearly.

–CJ Rhoads

As anyone who has their name on the cover of a book knows, no book is written solely by the author. A good book cannot exist without an entire team of people working on it, and it is only by convention and convenience (not to mention space) that not all of those names appear on the cover. They are no less responsible for its birth than I.

First would be Melissa Sabella, our senior acquisitions editor, who worked tirelessly to make this series possible and worked overtime to communicate the series concept and convinced me to join the team. Our series editor, Joseph Manzo, who had the vision, drive and determination to bring the series to reality. Dee Piziak added incredible value in the PowerPoint book, and provided an excellent four-step process for business writing which I unceremoniously adopted for my book as well. Eileen Clark, our senior editorial project manager, patiently put up with my endless questions and suggestions and worked hard to educate me on the way things were done. Kevin Bradley at GGS Book Services was very knowledgeable and extremely helpful.

Jill Rembetski, the team's development editor, is simply an amazing woman. Her ability to keep things moving, provide the exact right amount of feedback, and add the exact right phrase to clarify the essential concept is nothing less than spectacular. Of course I also owe a great deal to Jeff Olson, my wonderful agent, who knows the business of publishing inside and out. Jeff is always there for me, offering to help edit or listening to my complaints or celebrating my successes.

I would also like to thank the faculty and staff of the College of Business (in alphabetical order): Okan Akcay, Dan Benson, Pat Blatt, Henry Check, Donna DeLong, Arifeen Daneshyar, Mark Dinger, Ken Ehrensal, Philip Evans, Tom Grant, Keshave Gupta, David Haas, John Hamrick, Ray Heimbach, Roger Hibbs, Eileen Hogan, Fidel Ikem, Jonathan Kramer, John Kruglinski, Patricia Patrick, Elisabeth Rogol, Paul Sable, Norman Sigmond, David Wagaman. Their encouragement and support enabled me to postpone some of my research and focus on this book over the summer. Additionally, the employees of my business—Kathy and Gene Brown, Elly Hargrave, George Deeble, and Bonnie Taylor who all had to put up with my split focus while I was working on the book. My clients were also helpful and understanding, especially Bob Goodman and Andy Klee.

Furthermore, several people picked up the slack for me in the Pacem In Vita program I developed—a leadership program for kids based on Taijiquan. I must thank Jack Solchurch, Judy Butler, Vicky Lee Levy, Luke Jih, Sandy Wise, and Judd Meinhart. Additionally, the International Taijiquan Forum, held at Confederation College and Lakehead University in Thunderbay, Canada, offered several days of uninterrupted solitude that allowed me to meet all of my deadlines during the conference. In helping with that endeavor I must thank Peng Youlian, Pat Forrest, Brenda Reimer, Oliver Reimer, Jane Taylor, Wayne Bilbrough, Ed Linkewich, Su Jing, Steve Higgins, Ed Cooper, Susan Nash, Jing Shan Tang & Wendy Bons, as well as the masters visiting from China Wu Wenhan, Yang Zhenduo, Chen Zhenglei, Sun Yongtian, Zeng Nailiang, Wu Kwong Yu and Ma Hailong.

Of course none of this would be possible without my many mentors over the years (in alphabetical order): Fred Beste, Mike Bolton, David Bosler, Jack Bradt, Tom Casey, Betsy Chapman, Martin Cheatle, Jim Collins, Vanessa DiMauro, Jonathan Dreazen, Francois Dumas, Marsha Egan, Dale Falcinelli, John Lucht, John MacNamara, Nancy Magee, Ray Melcher, Maggie Newman, Pete Musser, Josephine Painter, Joe Puglisi, Leo Robb, Robert Rubin, Lee Scheele, Steve Sperling, Alan Weiss, and Kevin Wren. Though the amount of time I spent with each varied, each one has given me a gift that has turned out to be of extreme value in my never-ending quest to improve myself.

No list would be complete without my fabulous family; my mother Judith Liffick, and my father Martin Devlin and his wife Jeri, along with my brothers and sisters, Jeffrey Devlin, T. Max Devlin, Eileen Piccolo, and Denise Rankin. I also received a great deal of help and advice from several of my accomplished aunts and uncles, most of whom are authors in their own right: Tom and Barb Liffick, Blaise and Alana Liffick, Kathy Liffick, Mike Lillich, and Anita and Gary Young. All of them patiently put up with my writing on what was supposed to be a family vacation. I wish to thank Marianne Pawlikowski as well—who provided the New Jersey Shore getaway that formed the backdrop of many hours of my writing.

Most important of all, of course, is my patient and loving husband Bob. He is my world, and I am so lucky to have found my soul mate and true love so early in my life. To have spent the past 26 years with a man of his incredible talents would have been a treat to anyone, but to have loved him, and been loved by him all that time is a pleasure of epic proportion.

>> Reviewers

REVIEWER ADVISORY BOARD

Alan Abrahams
The Wharton School, University of Pennsylvania
Philadelphia, PA

Richard D. Blamer
John Carroll University
Cleveland, OH

Gary Donnelly
Casper College
Casper, WY

Thomas Lee
The Wharton School, University of Pennsylvania
Philadelphia, PA

Ruth MacKinnon
Georgia Southern University
Statesboro, GA

Craig J. Peterson
Utah State University
Logan, UT

Brenda Rhodes
Northeastern Junior College
Sterling, CO

Farshad Ravanshad
Montclair State University
Montclair, NJ

Lou Thompson
University of Texas at Dallas
Richardson, TX

REVIEWERS

Dennis Adams
Bauer College of Business, University of Houston
Houston, TX

Bonnie Brinton Anderson
Brigham Young University
Provo, UT

Barbara Bartosiewicz
West Shore Community College
Scottville, MI

Jim Brodzinski
The College of Mount Saint Joseph
Cincinnati, OH

Annie Brown
Hawaii Community College
Hilo, HI

Kuan Chen
Purdue University–Calumet
Hammond, IN

Carey Cole
James Madison University
Harrisonburg, VA

Joseph R. Cullom
University of Northern Colorado
Greeley, CO

Spring W. Davidson
University of Delaware
Newark, DE

Shirley Dembo
Brookdale Community College
Lincroft, NJ

Dawna Travis Dewire
Babson College
Babson Park, MA

Eric Dodge
Hanover College
Hanover, IN

Bill Dorin
Indiana University Northwest
Gary, IN

Giles D'Sousa
University of Alabama
Tuscaloosa, AL

Martin Dumas
Baruch College
New York, NY

Laura Earner
Saint Xavier University
Chicago, IL

Paula N. Ecklund
Duke University's Fuqua School of Business
Durham, NC

Roland Eichelberger
Baylor University
Waco, TX

Gerard Engeholm
Pace University
New York, NY

Jeffrey G. Gaines
San Jose State University
San Jose, CA

Yvonne Galusha
University of Iowa
Iowa City, IA

Laura Galvan
Fayetteville Technical Community College
Fayetteville, NC

Gail Gemberling
University of Texas at Austin
Austin, TX

Candace Gentry
Pierce College
Tacoma, WA

Michael Goeken
Northwest Vista College
San Antonio, TX

Mary Granger
George Washington University
Washington, DC

Kerry Gregoryk
Valley City State University
Valley City, ND

Brandi N. Guidry
University of Louisiana at Lafayette
Lafayette, LA

Matt Harris
Utah State University
Logan, UT

Bobbye Haupt
Cecil Community College
North East, MD

Lourdes Herling
Wayne State College
Wayne, NE

Katherine Hoppe
Wake Forest University
Winston-Salem, NC

Curtis Izen
Baruch College
New York, NY

R. Kent Jackson
Brigham Young University
Rexburg, ID

Keith Jenkins
Judson College
Elgin, IL

Amy Kinser
Indiana University
Bloomington, IN

Jim Kress
Central Oregon Community College
Bend, OR

Joanne Lazirko
University of Wisconsin–Milwaukee
Milwaukee, WI

Vedran Lelas
Plymouth State University
Plymouth, NH

Lynn M. Mason
Lubbock Christian University
Lubbock, TX

Carol Martin
Louisiana State University–Alexandria
Alexandria, LA

Pat Matthews
Mount Union College
Alliance, OH

James McGibany
Marquette University
Milwaukee, WI

Lynn McKell
Brigham Young University
Provo, UT

Margaret Mottola Menna
Bryant University
Smithfield, RI

David Mollura
Reading Area Community College
Reading, PA

Ellen F. Monk
University of Delaware
Newark, DE

James S. Moore
Indiana University–Purdue University
    Fort Wayne
Fort Wayne, IN

Donald Mulder
Trinity International University
Deerfield, IL

Roger Alan Pick
University of Missouri–Kansas City
Kansas City, MO

Janice I. Pitera
Broome Community College
Binghampton, NY

Katie Pittman
Southern Oregon University
Ashland, OR

Michelle Powell
Holmes Community College
Goodman, MS

Paula Ruby
Arkansas State University
Jonesboro, AK

Paul Schwager
East Carolina University
Greenville, NC

Karl L. Smart
Central Michigan University
Mount Pleasant, MI

Evelyn Smith
Lincoln Memorial
Harrogate, TN

Jane L. Smith
Saint Xavier University Graham School of
    Management
Chicago, IL

K. David Smith
Cameron University
Lawton, OK

John Stancil
Florida Southern College
Lakeland, FL

Bernice R. Sutton
Florida Southern College
Lakeland, TX

Cathy Van Landuyt
Missouri State
Springfield, MO

Patricia Weaver
Juniata College
Huntington, PA

Lorna Wells
Salt Lake Community College
Salt Lake City, UT

Teri L. Weston
Harford Community College
Bel Air, MD

Mary Beth White
University of South Florida Saint
    Petersburg
Saint Petersburg, FL

Stephen J. Woytowish
Indiana University of Pennsylvania
Indiana, PA

Dezhi Wu
Southern Utah University
Cedar City, UT

Dmitry Yarushkin
Grand View College
Des Moines, IA

Alec Zama
Grand View College
Des Moines, IA

>> Contents

CHAPTER 5 | Applying the Core Skills 143

Word

CHAPTER 1 | Introduction to Word Basics 165

CHAPTER 2 | Creating a Basic Report 203

CHAPTER 3 | Word Document Enhancements.........251

CHAPTER 4 | Word Sharing Objects and Adding References 313

Excel

CHAPTER 1 | Introduction 363

CHAPTER 2 | Excel Basics 381

CHAPTER 6 | Applying Core Competency Skills: Financial Planning and Accounting 589

Access

CHAPTER 1 | Introduction 645

CHAPTER 2 | The Database Table 663

CHAPTER 3 | Selecting and Summarizing Data from Tables 721

The in business Series

Why I Developed This Series

At Lehigh University, where I teach Intro to Business, we were faced with a challenge–students were coming into our business program with some knowledge of Microsoft® Office, but not enough to make it through the rest of their curriculum. As a result, other business professors had to take the time out of their discipline-specific classes (like Accounting, Finance, Marketing, etc.) to cover software skills.

After talking to other business programs across the country, I realized that–whether they were offering an Office course, stand alone courses in the individual applications, adding coverage of applications to other courses, or not teaching Office at all–we were all struggling to have students understand not just isolated skills or tasks in Office, but how to use the software in business. Because all of the books on the market focus on drilling students on a collection of skills to master and are tutorial-based, business students were missing:

- Exposure to real business files that meet professional standards

- A reference that they can use in later courses and their careers

- An understanding of how to use the software as a tool to accomplish business goals

- Coverage of the core Office skills they will need in business

At Lehigh University I developed a solution to address this need, consisting of a core competency exam that every student needs to pass, and an instructional package that includes a book and practical, illustrative videos. With Prentice Hall's stellar track record of publishing in business and their commitment to developing a series specifically for the business student, it was easy to choose them as my partner to develop this series.

Many professors believed in this product from the start. In addition to invaluable manuscript reviews, we were able to incorporate the experiences of hundreds of their business students across the country who are using preliminary editions. Together, their contributions make me confident that this series will effectively prepare students to get the most out of a valuable tool for business—Microsoft® Office.

–Joseph M. Manzo

Key Features

- **In Practice Author Anecdotes:** Immediately place the student in a real business scenario to consider how they can use the application to solve the business problem with stories from the author's own experience.
- **Real Business Applications:** Exercises using financial accounting statements and comprehensive business plans expose students to the accurate and professional files they will be using in their other business courses and careers.

- **Quick Reference Boxes:** These features break down a skill step-by-step, offering students a valuable resource to quickly relearn or reference a skill in their other courses as well as in their future careers.
- **Immediate Skills Reinforcement:** Students practice and apply their skills as soon as they are introduced; they do not have to wait until end-of-chapter exercises.
- **Video Workshops:** These workshops provide students with immediate access to instruction any time, anywhere, with a demonstration of the companion exercise in the textbook by the author. Some students do better when they can process an exercise visually.
- **Why Do I Need This?:** These exercises answer the questions many students have about how and why they will use the skills and concepts in their professional lives.
- **What's Wrong with This?:** This feature provokes critical-thinking skills by challenging students to evaluate the accuracy and integrity of results produced by Office applications.
- **Common Mistakes Boxes:** Sidebars illustrate typical pitfalls and how to avoid them.
- **Skills Exams:** These exams cover all the skills to assess the execution and understanding of the content learned in the chapter. Other business instructors can be assured that these students are ready for their business courses.
- **Challenge Questions:** These questions present real business situations that require students to choose the appropriate skills learned in the chapter and use them creatively to come up with a solution.

Meeting the Needs of Business

In Business assures business faculty that students have the necessary office skills to complete their degrees. All the content presented in this series was selected and organized by business instructors to ensure students will have success in all their business courses—Accounting, Marketing, Finance, Economics, Management, and Business Communication—by focusing on actual challenges they are likely to encounter in those courses as well as in their careers. Students often enter their core business classes with weak or insufficient Office skills despite their vast experience with computers or even after the completion of an applications course.

Because they are written expressly for the Business student, the core focus of **Microsoft® Office Excel 2007 In Business** and **Microsoft® Office Access 2007 In Business** is how to best use the applications to make decisions and analyze data. All the sample spreadsheets and databases found in the books are from the real-world corporate environment.

Presenting with Microsoft® Office PowerPoint® 2007 In Business focuses on much more than the simple "how-to's" of PowerPoint®—it provides guidance on creating a presentation outline, organizing slides, and delivering a strong presentation, in addition to tackling the skills of using the software. Similarly, **Communicating with Microsoft® Office Word 2007 In Business** focuses on creating professional-looking documents and on using the software's features to enhance efficiency.

Organization of Office 2007 In Business

The new Office 2007 In Business series includes the following:

- **Microsoft® Office 2007 In Business, Core** includes the first six chapters of Excel and Access, five chapters of PowerPoint, and four chapters of Word.

- **Microsoft® Office Excel 2007 In Business, Core** includes Chapters 1–6 of Excel.

- **Microsoft® Office Excel 2007 In Business, Comprehensive** includes Chapters 1–10 of Excel.

- **Microsoft® Office Access 2007 In Business, Core** includes Chapters 1–6 of Access.

- **Microsoft® Office Access 2007 In Business, Comprehensive** includes Chapters 1–10 of Access.

- **Communicating with Microsoft® Office Word 2007 In Business, Core** includes Chapters 1–4 of Word.

- **Presenting with Microsoft® Office PowerPoint® 2007 In Business, Core** includes Chapters 1–5 of PowerPoint.

- **Presenting with Microsoft® Office PowerPoint® 2007 In Business, Comprehensive** includes Chapters 1–8 of PowerPoint.

The Enhanced Instructor's Resource Center on DVD includes the following:

- Additional In Practice Anecdotes for every chapter to highlight the application of office skills to the different disciplines within business including Marketing, Economics, Finance, Accounting, and Management.

- Additional Skills Exams for every chapter to use for assessment with score guides and annotated solutions for grading.

- A Comprehensive Competency Exam for every book provides one project to assess students' mastery of all the core or advanced skills covered in one application. Each exam has score guides and annotated solutions for simple and consistent grading.

- PowerPoint Presentations for each chapter with notes included for online students.

- Lecture Notes that correlate to the PowerPoint Presentations and reference in chapter material.

- Student Data Files.

- Annotated Solution Files.

- Complete Test Bank.

- TestGen Software with QuizMaster.

TestGen is a test generator program that enables you to view and easily edit testbank questions, transfer them to tests, and print in a variety of formats suitable to your teaching situation. The program also offers many options for organizing and displaying testbanks and tests. A random number test generator enables you to create multiple versions of an exam.

QuizMaster, also included in this package, enables students to take tests created with TestGen on a local area network. The QuizMaster Utility built into TestGen enables instructors to view student records and print a variety of reports. Building tests is easy with TestGen, and exams can be easily uploaded into WebCT, BlackBoard, and CourseCompass.

Prentice Hall's Companion Website at www.prenhall.com/inbusiness offers expanded IT resources and downloadable supplements. This site also includes an online study guide for students containing true/false and multiple choice questions and practice projects.

Online Course Cartridges
Flexible, robust, and customizable content is available for all major online course platforms that include everything you need in one place.

www.prenhall.com/webct
www.prenhall.com/blackboard
www.coursecompass.com

 **WebCT**

 myitlab

 **Bb** Blackboard
www.blackboard.com

 CourseCompass

myitlab completes the system with online assessment and training. Students become certified within the core applications with final office exams and they also receive valuable and immediate instruction with the video workshops.

>> Visual Walk-Through

>> Chapter 3

Calculating Data
Formulas and Functions

Chapter Goals

encourage students to consider what they have learned and prepares them with an overview of what they will be learning in the chapter.

Chapter Goals

This chapter introduces the calculating power of Excel through two main objectives. The first is to present the fundamental techniques of creating formulas and functions, which are the primary tools used to calculate data. The second is to show how cell referencing is used within formulas and functions to maximize the dynamic abilities of Excel. In other words, formulas and functions will automatically produce new outputs when the data in one or more cell locations is changed. In business, these dynamic abilities are critical when evaluating what-if scenarios. Chapter 2 introduced the concept of what-if scenarios by demonstrating how to create multiple versions of a worksheet within a workbook. This chapter develops this concept even further by demonstrating how to perform common business calculations and analyses using formulas and functions.

Skill Sets

organizes skills according to their objectives to help students easily find the skills they need.

>> Excel | Skill Sets

Skills

are itemized with page numbers to provide students a quick reference for their later coursework and careers.

73

Excel in **Practice** | Anecdote

My Role as a Consultant

You may *think* that, after you've completed hours of intense research and analysis related to a project, the hard work is over. However, in reality, how you present your findings is just as critical as the quality of the information you present. I learned this lesson quickly when I first began working as a consultant. My primary responsibility was to analyze the performance of a client's business and compare it with other companies within that industry. My results then served as a basis for developing rec- ommendations on ways my clients could improve or grow their business. Although I had piles of written documents to support my findings, my main forum for sharing this information was in front of an audience of business owners or head managers at meetings called progress reviews. These people had busy schedules and little time. The pressure to deliver an accurate, appropriate, and efficient presentation was always an intense challenge.

>> Continued on page 221

in Practice Anecdotes based on actual workplace issues immediately place the student in a real business scenario to consider how they will use the application to solve a business problem.

Screen Shots
are actual learning
tools that illustrate key
concepts described
in the text.

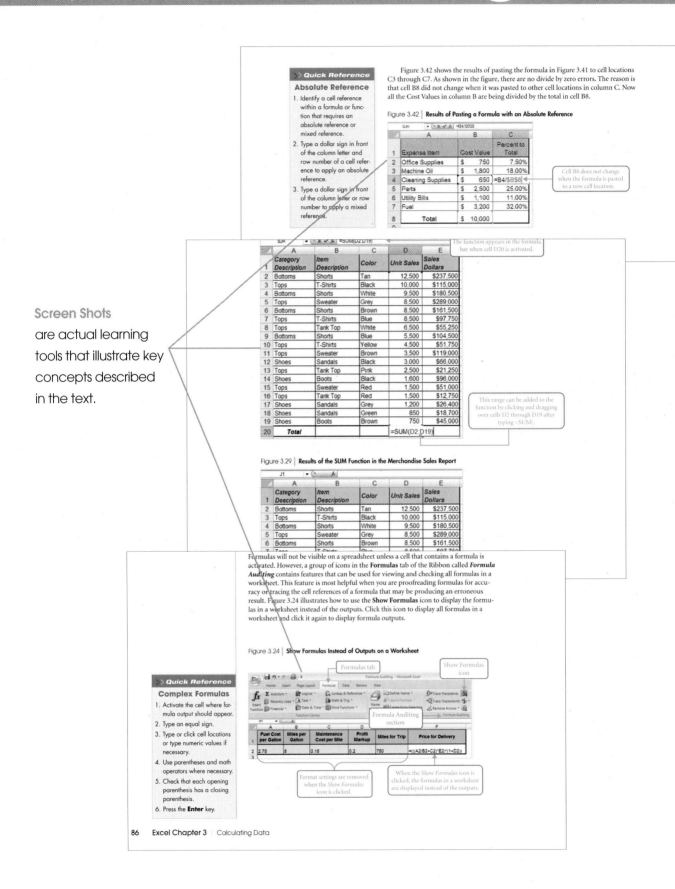

Figure 3.50 | Values in Cells Referenced by the Future Value Function Are Changed

	B6	▼	fx	=FV(B2,B3,-B4,-B5)
	A		B	
1	**Evaluating Investments**			
2	Annual Interest Rate		8%	
3	Number of Years Investing		4	
4	Annual Deposit Amount	$	12.00	
5	Deposits Made at Beginning or End of Year		1	
6	Future Value of Investment		$58.40	
7				

Values in these two cell locations were changed.

Since cell references were used to construct the Future Value function, this output changed when the values in cells B3 and B4 were changed.

COMMON MISTAKES | RATE, NPER, and PMT Arguments

Always check that the **rate**, **nper**, and **pmt** arguments of the **Future Value** function are expressed in equal terms. For example, investments might be made on a monthly basis, but the interest or return rate quoted by a bank or financial institution is expressed on an annual basis. In this case, you would have to define the **rate** argument by dividing the annual interest rate by 12 if the number of months is used to define the **nper** argument and the monthly investment value is used to define the **pmt** argument. The key is to make sure the **rate**, **nper**, and **pmt** arguments are all defined using equivalent terms.

> Quick Reference

Future Value Function

1. Activate the cell where output should appear.

2. Type an equal sign.

3. Type the function name FV or double click **FV** from the function list.

4. Type an open parenthesis (if you double clicked the function from the function list, this will already be added).

5. Define the following arguments:

rate: Interest Rate

nper: Number of Periods or Amount of time

pmt: Payments (must use a negative sign)

[pv]: Present Value

[type]: When payments are made (1 = beginning of year; 0 = end of year)

6. Close the parenthesis.

7. Press the **Enter** key.

The Payment Function

A close relative of the **Future Value** function is the *Payment* or *PMT* function. The **PMT** function is most helpful when calculating the payments of a loan. For example, if you were buying a home and had to borrow $225,000, how much would your monthly payment be if a bank charged 6% interest over a 30-year period? The **PMT** function can be used to answer this question.

Similar to the **Future Value** function, at least three of five arguments must be defined for the **Payment** function to produce an output. Figure 3.51 shows the five arguments of the **Payment** function, which are very similar to the arguments of the **Future Value** function. The following defines each of these arguments:

- **rate**: The interest charged by a lender.
- **nper**: The number of payments or, as in the **Future Value** function, a period of time (i.e., years, months, weeks, etc.).
- **pv**: Present Value; the argument used to define the amount of money being borrowed or the principal of the loan. As in the **Future Value** function, *you must use a negative sign for any values or cell references used for this argument.*
- **[fv]**: Future Value; the argument used when part of a loan is paid off with periodic payments and the balance of the loan is paid off in one lump sum at a future point

Common Mistakes boxes alert students to typical pitfalls and how to avoid them.

Quick Reference boxes break skills down step-by-step, offering students a valuable reference to quickly relearn a skill.

>> Visual Walk-Through

Video Workshop provides students with immediate access to instruction any time, anywhere.

>> Future Value Function

The purpose of this workshop is to review the use and construction of the **Future Value** function. I will be demonstrating the tasks in this workshop in the **Future Value Function** video. Open the file named ib_e03_thetimevalueofmoney before starting the following tasks.

1. **Data Entry (Video: Future Value Function)**
   a. Activate the Periodic Investment worksheet.
   b. Type the following values into the cell locations listed:
      Cell B2: **.08**
      Cell B3: **3**
      Cell B4: **10**
      Cell B5: **1**
   c. Format cell B2 to a percent with 1 decimal place and then format cell B4 to U.S. currency with 2 decimal places.

2. **Calculating the Future Value of a Periodic Investment (Video: Future Value Function)**
   a. Type an equal sign in cell B6, followed by the function name **FV** and an

Why Do I Need This? answers the questions many students have about how and why they will use skills and concepts in their professional lives.

EXERCISE
Why Do I Need This?

>> Financial Planning for Retirement

A potential career goal for a person studying finance might be to work as a financial planner. One of the responsibilities a financial planner might have is to help people plan for retirement. This involves estimating how many years a person will work before they retire and how much money they can contribute to a retirement account. The financial planner's job is to evaluate various scenarios to see how clients can maximize the growth of a retirement account so they can live comfortably when they stop working. In this situation, the **Future Value** function can become a critical tool.

Exercise

Whether you have aspirations of being a financial planner or not, retirement is something everyone will eventually face. The purpose of this exercise is to construct a spreadsheet for a person who is planning to open a retirement account. Your job

n this person needs to
on, this person is age 25
do the tasks listed here,
planning.

w in cell C6. In this sce-
invested in a conservative
ut the potential growth is

n cell C7. In this scenario,
rn is increased to 8%.

and the word **High** in
tial return are high.

ow 25 and is planning to
utions to her retirement

ng of putting $75 a month

7. Copy the function created in cell D6 and use the **Paste Special** command to paste only the function into cells D7 and D8.

8. Given the current contribution of $75 per month, will this person reach her target through any of the scenarios?

9. How much money will she have to deposit in her account per month (approximately) to reach $2 million taking the Aggressive investment scenario?

10. How much money will she have to deposit in her account per month (approximately) to reach $2 million taking the Conservative investment scenario?

11. Save and close your file.

What's Wrong with This Spreadsheet? provokes critical-thinking by challenging students to evaluate the accuracy and integrity of results produced by Office applications.

>> What's Wrong with This Spreadsheet?

Problem

You are the director of a real estate investment firm. An intern has just completed a project for you evaluating a potential investment. You are about to present the results to the president of the firm showing the potential return on property near a growing U.S. city. A recent assessment has shown that similar commercial properties in this area have been increasing in value 15% every six months. You will propose that the firm buy 10 acres of land at a total price of $1,750,000. You will recommend that the land be held for three years and then sold to developers.

You have asked the intern to

1. Evaluate the future value of the investment in three years given the 15% growth rate stated in the problem. The property will be purchased in one lump sum investment at the beginning of the first year.

2. Calculate the monthly payments of this loan considering the following: The company may opt to finance the price of the property through a bank instead of paying for the land in cash. A bank has offered a 15-year loan at a 3.5% interest rate if the company makes a $500,000 down payment. Payments will be made at the end of the month.

Open the file the intern has completed, named ib_e03_realestateresults. Look at the file carefully. Are you comfortable presenting these numbers to the president of the company? Consider the following:

1. Look at the results calculated on the spreadsheet. Do they make sense? What estimates can you quickly do to see if the results are in the "ballpark."

2. Were the arguments in the **PMT** and **FV** functions properly defined?

3. Are the statistics of the investment properly considered in the analysis?

Exercise

Write a short answer for each of the points in the Problem section. Then, make any adjustments or corrections that will improve the reliability of the spreadsheet.

PROBLEM & EXERCISE

Excel in **Practice** | Anecdote

Solution from page 170

Using charts is the key to conducting an effective progress review meeting. A well-constructed chart can explain trends, relationships, and results in a very short period time. Therefore, I converted the data calculated and evaluated in numerous Excel files to a few charts, pasted them into PowerPoint slides, and presented them at progress review meetings. Constructing charts this way not only increased the efficiency of the meetings, but also demonstrated a professional standard that my clients often appreciated.

Assignment

1. The file named Client Research Data contains data for a meeting with the executives of a major corporation.

2. Create a chart that will best display the sales trend by region in the Regional Sales worksheet. This chart should demonstrate how the overall sales of the company have shifted between the regions.

3. Use any annotations, objects, and formatting techniques to highlight changes in the company's sales by region. Note that the total sales for the company by year are in row 8 of the worksheet. Your chart must show these total sales results.

4. Create a PowerPoint slide with the title **Region 4 Provides Future Growth**. Display the chart you created in this slide. This PowerPoint slide as well as the chart should have a professional appearance.

Questions for Discussion

1. Why are charts better to use in presentations as opposed to worksheets?
2. Is it possible to have too much formatting on a chart?
3. What do you need to know to create an effective chart?

Anecdote, Solution challenges students to use the software to solve the business problem presented at the start of the chapter.

>>Visual Walk-Through

Review Questions

tests students on their conceptual understanding of the chapter content with True/False and Fill In the Blank questions.

>>Review Questions

The following questions are related to the concepts addressed in this chapter. There are three types of questions: Short Answer, True or False, and Fill in the Blank. If your answer to a True or False question is False, write a short explanation as to why you think the statement is not true.

1. The _____ is used when creating formulas in Excel that require multiplication.

2. Hold the Shift key and press the number _____ key when using exponents or raising a number to a certain power when creating formulas in Excel.

3. Explain why you should never do computations on a calculator and type the result into an Excel spreadsheet.

4. True or False: In cell referencing, the cell locations in a formula automatically change when you paste them to a new location.

5. When should you use numbers in Excel formulas?

Skills Exam

assesses the recognition and execution of all the skills in the chapter in one comprehensive exam designed for competency testing. Other business instructors can be assured that the students are ready for their business courses.

>>Skills Exam

The following exam is designed to test your ability to recognize and execute the Excel skills presented in this chapter. Read each question carefully and answer the questions in the order they are listed. You should be able to complete this exam in 60 minutes or less.

1. Open the file named ib_e03_skillsexam.

2. Type a **SUM** function in cell B9 that adds the values in cells B3 through B8. Correct any #### signs if necessary.

3. Copy the **SUM** function in cell B9 and paste it into cell C9. Correct any #### signs if necessary.

4. Type a formula in cell D3 to calculate the growth rate. Your formula should subtract the Value Last Year in cell B3 from the Present Value in cell C3 and divide that result by the Value Last Year in cell B3: (Present Value - Value Year) ÷ Value Last Year.

5. Format the result in cell D3 to a percentage with 1 decimal place.

6. Copy cell D3 and paste it into cells D4:D9.

7. Type an **AVERAGE** function in cell B10 that calculates the average of cells B3 through B8.

8. Copy cell B10 and paste it into C10.

9. Calculate the average growth rate in cell D10 using the **SUM** and **COUNT** functions. Follow this example: ((Sum of Present Value C3:C8 ÷ Count of Present Value C3:C8)-(Sum of Value Last Year B3:B8 + Count of Value Last Year B3:B8))/(Sum of Value Last Year B3:B8 ÷ Count of Value Last Year B3:B8).

10. Format the result in cell D10 to a percentage with 1 decimal place. The result in D10 should match the value in cell D9.

11. Type a formula in cell E3 that divides the present value in cell C3 by the total of the present values in cell C9. Place an absolute reference on cell C9.

12. Format the result in cell E3 to a percent with 2 decimals. Then, copy cell E3 and paste it to cells E4 through E8.

13. Use the **Payment** function in cell D14 to calculate the monthly mortgage payments. Your function should use cell A14 for the rate, B14 for the periods, and C14 for the present value. Assume that payments are made at the end of the month.

14. Use the **Payment** function in cell E18 to calculate the monthly lease payments. Your function should use cell A18 for the rate, B18 for the periods, C18 for the present value, and D18 for the future value. Assume payments made at the end of the month.

15. Use the **Future Value** function in cell E21 to calculate the future value of all the investments in two years. Your function should use cell D9 for the rate and the number 2 for the periods. The total present value for all investments in cell C9 should be treated as a one-time lump sum investment. Assume that this investment is made at the beginning of the year. Format the result to U.S. currency with 0 decimal places. Correct any #### signs if necessary.

16. Type a formula in cell E22 that subtracts the total present value of all investments in cell C9 from the future value of all investments in cell E21.

17. Type a formula in cell E23 that multiplies the monthly mortgage payments in cell D14 by 24. Format the result to U.S. currency with 0 decimal places.

18. Type a formula in cell E24 that multiplies the monthly lease payments in cell E18 by 24. Format the result to U.S. currency with 0 decimal places.

19. Type a formula in cell E25 that subtracts the result of adding cells E23 and E24 from cell E22. Format the result to U.S. currency with 0 decimal places. Fix any #### signs if necessary.

20. Sort the range A2:E8 in ascending order based on the values in the Present Value column.

21. Save and close your file.

>> Challenge Questions

The following questions are designed to test your ability to apply the Excel skills you have learned to complete a business objective. Use your knowledge of Excel as well as your creativity to answer these questions. For most questions, there are several possible ways to complete the objective.

1. *Without* using the **Future Value** function, create a worksheet that determines the value of an investment if a person deposits $1,500 into a mutual fund at the beginning of every year for 20 years. Assume that the mutual fund achieves a 6% annual growth rate every year. Your worksheet should show the value of this investment at the end of every year for 20 years. In addition, your worksheet should be flexible to show what the value of the account would be at different deposit amounts or annual growth rates. For example, be able to show the value of the account in 20 years if a person decides to deposit only $1,200 per year but achieves an annual growth rate of 7%. Then, show the value of the account if a person deposits $1,000 per year but achieves an annual growth rate of 8%.

2. Complete question 1 again using the **Future Value** function. However, your worksheet should show only one number indicating the value of the investment in 20 years. Remember to keep your worksheet flexible so a new output will be produced if the annual deposit amount or annual growth rate values are changed.

3. A person asks you for help on an investment she is thinking of making. She wants to invest $5,000 into a medium-term bond that earns 4.5% interest per year. In addition, she wants to add $100 at the beginning of every month into the account. She wants to know what the value of her investment will be after five years. Create a worksheet showing her the value of this investment.

4. If you were going to lease a car, but could afford to pay only *$175 a month*, what would be the maximum price you could pay for a car? Assume the lease will run for four years, the annual interest rate is 3%, and that the car will retain 40% of its value after four years. Create a worksheet that shows the maximum price of the car you can lease.

5. You have an opportunity to invest in residential property that will cost $325,000. A real estate survey has shown that the value of property in this town has been increasing at a rate of 25% per year. However, you will have to take out a loan to be able to purchase the property. You can secure a 30-year loan at an annual interest rate of 6.5%. You will also be making a down payment of $75,000. Your plan is to sell this property after three years. After selling the property, you will pay off the loan. Create a spreadsheet that will calculate how much money you will make on this investment.

Challenge Questions present real business situations that require students to choose the appropriate skills learned in the chapter and use them creatively to come up with a solution.

>> Chapter 1

Introduction

Chapter Goals

This chapter will discuss the importance of presentation skills for business professionals, explain why PowerPoint is an important tool for business communication, and demonstrate how to plan for an effective presentation.

>> **PowerPoint** Skill Sets

Business Communication, Influence, and Decision Making

PowerPoint in **Practice** | Anecdote

My Role as a Sales Engineer

For many years, I was a sales engineer for a Fortune 500 technology corporation. I was the technical partner for several sales representatives and supported over 25 large accounts. In sales organizations, compensation is based on revenue. Salespeople receive an annual "quota," and their monthly compensation is based on how much revenue they generate.

Our team was based out of a remote branch office and reported to an office located in a larger metropolitan area. The area manager or another sales executive would fly in once a quarter and conduct territory reviews to determine how well the sales reps were doing on attaining their quotas. These reviews were seen as inquisitions and struck terror in the hearts of many. Preparing for reviews always caused a huge flurry of activity. Some sales representatives would spend days and days documenting every bit of information about their clients and sales strategies. Others would pull all-nighters and looked like death warmed over the next day. On the day of the reviews, each rep would spend an hour presenting his or her accounts and sales results. When the rep came out, the next rep on the schedule would whisper "How did it go?" Many times it didn't go so well, which I didn't understand. Here were hard-working, high-achieving sales representatives who seemed to be failing miserably at conveying their accomplishments and challenges to management. A fluke accident presented me with the opportunity find out the reason why this was so.

>> Continued on page 15

If information is power, then communication is influence. It has been said that 85% of a person's success in business is determined by his or her ability to communicate effectively with others.

There is a direct relationship between effective communication and a person's ability to influence others and make sound decisions. By presenting information clearly, logically, and appropriately

- You come across as credible and knowledgeable.
- Your level of influence immediately increases.
- You can facilitate productive dialogue and critical thinking, which leads to good decisions.

Good decisions in business lead to success. As you advance in your career, the ability to communicate, influence, and make decisions becomes as important as, if not more important than, your subject matter expertise. Many business professionals don't pay enough attention to this subtle point, and it can slow down their career progress.

Microsoft PowerPoint is the industry standard tool for delivering business information. However, presentations themselves are simply a vehicle for communication and effective decision making. The real skill lies in knowing what information to pull together and how to deliver it. The following sections provide real-life examples of business communication, explain why PowerPoint is such a powerful tool, and demonstrate how to plan for a presentation that "hits the mark" with your audience every time.

High-Impact Communication and Decision Making

Figure 1.1 lists examples of critical information, by profession, that is regularly presented to internal and external audiences, along with examples of the decisions that could be made based on this information. As you can see, many of these decisions could impact the economic well-being of the organization. Even in the most technical fields, there are significant communication requirements and decisions to be made.

Figure 1.1 | **Examples of Information and Decisions by Profession**

Profession	Information	Decision
Accounting	• Financial statements • Cash budgets • Sarbanes-Oxley reporting	• Asset management • Purchase/Lease • Collections management
Actuarial Science	• Risk assessments • Insurance design • Pricing scenarios • Profitability analysis	• New product development • Reserve strengthening • Investment diversification • Re-insurance strategy
Engineering	• Product specifications • Design reviews • Turnover to manufacturing • OSHA compliance • Training documents	• Performance benchmarking • Go/no-go decisions

Continued on next page

Figure 1.1 | **Examples of Information and Decisions by Profession** *(Continued from preceding page)*

Profession	Information	Decision
Finance	• Capital structuring • SEC reporting • Initial Public Offering • Mergers and acquisitions • Business case justifications	• Debt structuring • Refinancing • Corporate growth options • Capitalization
Healthcare Administration	• Patient confidentiality • Managed care profitability • Patient outcomes • Reimbursement analysis	• Fee structure • Capitation • Treatment plans • Formularies • HIPAA compliance
Information Systems	• Requirements management • Systems analysis • Project reporting • End-user training • Total cost of ownership	• Staffing • Project approval • Insourcing/outsourcing • Vendor selection • Risk strategies
Marketing	• Market research • Product launches • Press announcements • Competitive analysis	• Price • Product • Promotion • Place
Operations Management	• Supply chain management • Quality benchmarking • Capacity forecasting • Process performance • Location analysis	• Operations strategy • Six Sigma/ISO 9000 • Facilities layout • Location selection • Process re-engineering

As a new graduate, you will soon be asked to prepare and possibly present this type of information, regardless of your role in the company. Organizations today assume that college graduates are knowledgeable in all the Microsoft Office applications, including PowerPoint, and that you have some level of presentation skills. Many companies do not conduct or pay for PowerPoint training for employees; they assume that you are sufficiently trained. And most corporate Help Desks no longer have staff available to assist with Microsoft Office questions.

PowerPoint: The Electronic Flip Chart and Transparency

Presentation aids have come a long way. Business professionals have been delivering information and facilitating decision making for years. What tools were available to them? Before there was PowerPoint, there were flip charts and overhead transparencies.

Flip charts looked like oversized legal pads attached to a special stand. You handwrote your "charts" using thick magic markers and "flipped" each sheet of paper over the top of the stand as you delivered the presentation. The major disadvantages of flip charts were

- The charts looked only as good as your handwriting and ability to draw.
- To make a change, you had to redo the whole chart on a fresh sheet, remove the old one from the stack, insert the new one, and reattach to the stand.
- They were cumbersome to carry around and even worse to travel with.

- If no flip chart stand was available, the alternative was to tape or pin the charts to the wall, which looked unprofessional.

Then came overhead transparencies. These were 8½" x 11" sheets of clear, thick plastic that came in a box. You wrote your presentations on them using special markers and displayed them using an overhead projector that worked like a slide projector, thereby renaming "charts" to "slides." The best thing about them was that, to make changes, you could simply wipe off the old word or sentence with a damp paper towel. Or you could lick your finger and rub it off! Although transparencies were a huge improvement over flip charts, the downsides were

- The slides still looked only as good as your handwriting and ability to draw.
- You had to be sure that there was an overhead projector in the room.
- If the light bulb in the projector didn't work or blew out in the middle of the presentation, you were out of luck. Many people began carrying extra light bulbs in their briefcases.
- If someone spilled coffee, soda, or water on your transparencies, you were seriously in trouble.

Finally, electronic presentation software became available. You no longer had to write out your presentations by hand; you typed everything into the computer. You could also copy and paste images and artwork into the slides. Changes that previously took minutes now took seconds. Sophisticated deliverables could be created by anyone with a PC and the right software. Slowly but surely, secretaries and administrative assistants stopped creating presentations, and the expectation became that staff would do the work themselves.

Over the years, many presentation software vendors have come and gone. Due to the integration with Microsoft Office, PowerPoint emerged as the industry standard.

PowerPoint Concepts and Terminology

- A PowerPoint presentation consists of individual pages, called *slides*.
- Slides can have *text* and can include *graphics* and *charts*.
- Text is written as short phrases that begin with small dots, squares, dashes, or graphics called *bullets*.
- You can create your own *theme* or use one of the many preformatted *templates* that are included with the software.

Because PowerPoint is part of the larger Microsoft Office suite, you can also share information with Access, Excel, and Word. Another major advantage of PowerPoint comes with the ability to include audio and video clips, link to other presentations or spreadsheets on the fly, or collaborate with your work group, using the same document. Since the presentations are in electronic format, you can e-mail them to others or post to a Web site. The options are almost endless, and you will learn many of them in this text. These are just some examples of why PowerPoint has become an extremely powerful business communication tool.

Many professionals also overuse the features of PowerPoint or use the tool as a crutch instead of a presentation aid. The purpose of this text is to teach you how to use PowerPoint effectively in business situations.

COMMON MISTAKES | Death by PowerPoint

The expression "death by PowerPoint" is used to describe presentations that are so poor that they bore people to death. This can also happen if the presentation has so many bells and whistles that the audience is overwhelmed and does not get the message. Following are some general guidelines to prevent this from happening to you:

1. Make sure the presentation is not too long.

2. Do not read the slides to the audience.

3. Strike a balance between text and graphics and don't go overboard on either.

4. Use appropriate-size text. A rule of thumb is the 6 x 6 guideline—six words per bullet and six bullets on a slide.

5. Don't make the slide busy by using multiple colors or styles.

Plan First, Validate, Then Create

In an academic environment, your presentations are largely informational and will impact your grade. In the business world, you will be educating and/or trying to persuade or gain acceptance from the audience. The stakes are higher: your credibility and standing in the organization are on the line. A well-planned and smoothly delivered presentation will go a long way to advance your cause.

As you move up in an organization, a very interesting thing happens. You are given less time to present more critical information to increasingly impatient and busy audiences. Now is the time to develop good planning skills that will serve you well in your career for years to come.

Planning

This section introduces the four-step process for planning any PowerPoint presentation. It is your responsibility to gather this information. Do not assume that the audience will provide it to you ahead of time. These steps do not take as long to complete as you might think, and your time is well spent. Use this process consistently, and you will create professional presentations every time. Later in this chapter, you will have an opportunity to work through each of these steps in the Video Workshop.

Step 1:   What are the objectives?

- Is this presentation informational only?
- What does the audience need from this presentation?
- Are you trying to convince your audience to take some course of action?
- What is that course of action?

Be sure you are very clear about the objectives and focus on the needs of the audience first. After you have done that, you have earned the right to address your own objectives. You may create the most professional-looking presentation, but if it does not address the audience's concerns first, they will not care.

Step 2:   Who is the audience?

- Are they familiar with your business; that is, do they understand the terminology, or will you need to bring them up to speed first?
- Are they decision makers who typically want high-level summary information, or are they more operational and detail oriented?
- What are their "hot buttons"? Visual aids such as graphics, audio, and video can be used to effectively convey the right level of information to various audience types.

Knowing the makeup of your audience impacts steps 3 and 4. For example, if you have a group of people with a varied understanding of the topic, you will have to spend more time up front in educating and level setting. While that is not necessarily a bad thing, be aware that it takes away from your overall allotted time. If your audience members are not on equal footing with you or each other, you will need to get them there right away.

Step 3:   What are the key messages/decisions?

- List all the things you need and want to get across in order of priority.
- If you are asking your audience to make a decision, then spell it out clearly.

Set the context and sequence for the presentation. Since there is a fixed amount of time, you may not be able to cover all the information in one presentation. That's why you have to address the most important topics first. If there is a decision to be made, put it on the table right away.

Step 4:   How much time do you have?

- Allocate about two to three minutes to deliver each PowerPoint slide and build in the same amount of time for discussion.
- If you anticipate a lot of dialogue from the audience, estimate how much extra time you'll need and subtract that amount from your allotted time.

Time management is an aspect of every presentation that is often overlooked and results in the speaker (you) running out of time with information left to go. Being unable to finish your presentation will leave a poor impression with your audience. The opposite of that is dead time, which is equally bad. If your communication strategy includes audience interaction, try to prevent a situation in which there is no discussion or silence, even if you have to "plant" a few questions with some members of the audience ahead of time. Even though you may have been an excellent speaker, if nobody asked a single question and you ended up doing all the talking, your presentation will not be remembered favorably.

>> **Quick Reference**

Four-Step Planning Process

Step 1   What are the objectives?

Step 2   Who is the audience?

Step 3   What are the key messages/decisions?

Step 4   How much time do you have?

Validating

Before you spend any time creating an outline that ultimately determines the size and scope of your presentation, it is wise to validate your plan. Get in touch with the person who asked you to do the presentation. In an academic environment, this is your instructor. In a business environment, this would be your manager or preferably a key representative of the audience. Spend five to ten minutes reviewing your strategy and your understanding of the objectives, audience, key messages/decisions, and allotted time. If any of these resources are not available, ask someone who you know to be a good presenter to give you feedback.

Do not go into detail unless you discover that you completely misunderstood the requirements. If this happens, spend the necessary time to get back on track.

Validating your thoughts and ideas will save you a lot of time down the road and will also develop your reputation for being results oriented and customer focused.

Creating an Outline

After you've completed the planning process and confirmed that you are on the right track, the next step is to create an outline. If you followed the four-step planning process described previously, creating an outline will go smoothly.

If you haven't learned how to use PowerPoint yet, you may document the outline in Microsoft Word or another tool such as Notepad. If you know how to create a basic presentation, by all means type the outline into PowerPoint right away. This will give you an excellent starting point as you grow and embellish the presentation.

Your outline should have the following five sections:

1. Title
   - Provide the name of the presentation.
   - Be short yet descriptive.

2. Agenda
   - This one-page list indicates what you are going to cover in the given time frame.
   - The agenda sets the tone and expectations for the meeting. If the audience agrees with the agenda, you can go on to deliver the rest of the presentation.
   - However, if the audience wants to modify the agenda, you will have to readjust "on the fly" or stop and regroup for another time. Neither option is desirable.
   - Problems with the agenda are indicators of incomplete or poor planning.
   - This section is sometimes called "Discussion Topics," "Objectives," or "Outline."
   - Even though the agenda page is first in sequence after the title page, it is actually written last—after the body is finalized.

3. Introduction
   - This section explains any background or historical information that the audience needs to know.
   - An introduction gives you the opportunity to make sure the audience is on the "same page" and level of understanding before delving into the details.
   - This section is sometimes called "Background" or "History."

4. Body
   - The majority of your PowerPoint slides will be in this section, and this is where you will spend most of your time with the audience.
   - If you've done a good job in planning, setting the agenda, and explaining the background, your transition into the body will be flawless.
5. Conclusion
   - If your presentation is simply informational, you will want to wrap it up with a "Summary" or "Conclusion" page.
   - If your objective is a call to action, then this section may be named "Next Steps" or "Recommendations."

You should not automatically use these section names as your presentation titles. As you create the presentation, be sure to select titles that reflect and describe the specific topic(s) you are discussing.

COMMON MISTAKES | Spending Too Much Time on the Introduction

The purpose of the introduction section is to bring the audience up to speed—as quickly as possible. Sometimes you can get stuck here, which results in taking time away from the most important section, which is the body. Try to wrap up this section quickly; if someone in the audience insists on getting more background, politely offer to answer all questions "offline," after the presentation is finished.

The PowerPoint Tour

One of the benefits of the Microsoft Office suite is that the applications have a common look and feel, which makes training easier and navigation more intuitive from tool to tool. If you have used Access, Excel, or Word, you will notice that PowerPoint has some of the same basic elements.

When you launch PowerPoint, you will see a blank *presentation* (see Figure 1.2).

Figure 1.2 | **Blank PowerPoint Presentation**

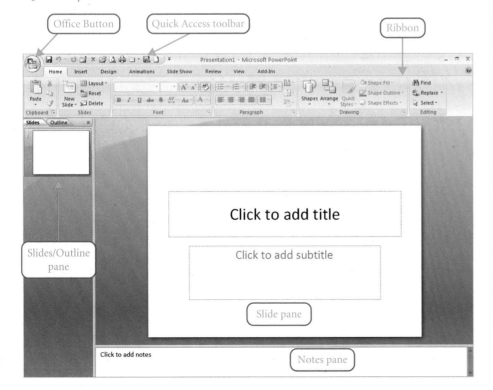

>> *Quick Reference*

Presentation Outline

1. Title
2. Agenda
3. Introduction
4. Body
5. Conclusion

- Quick Access toolbar: The customizable Quick Access toolbar contains a set of commands (icons). PowerPoint comes with a default Quick Access toolbar that contains a few icons. You can add additional icons to the Quick Access toolbar for quick and easy access using the **Office Button**. In Figure 1.2, several additional icons have been added.

- - Save

- - Undo

- - Repeat

- - Close

- - Close Window

- - Open

- - Print Preview

- - Print

- - New Slide

- - Save As

- - New Document

You can also move the Quick Access toolbar to appear above or below the Ribbon. There is no recommended location; its placement is a matter of preference.

- Ribbon: The Ribbon is a panel that organizes all the PowerPoint icons as a set of tabs. Each tab has a group of icons organized in groups. Each tab relates to a specific PowerPoint activity. Some tabs and groups of icons are contextual, which means that they are shown only when needed. For example, on the **Home** tab, selecting a block of text activates the **Font** group of icons. Contextual tabs and groups are hidden or inactive when the objects they work on are not selected.

The two tabs you will most commonly use are **Home** and **Insert**. See Figures 1.3 and 1.4 for an expanded view of each.

- **Home** tab: Contains groups of icons that you will use when creating, modifying, and polishing your slides. From this tab, you can add and delete slides and choose many formatting options.

Figure 1.3 | **Home Tab with the Dialog Boxes**

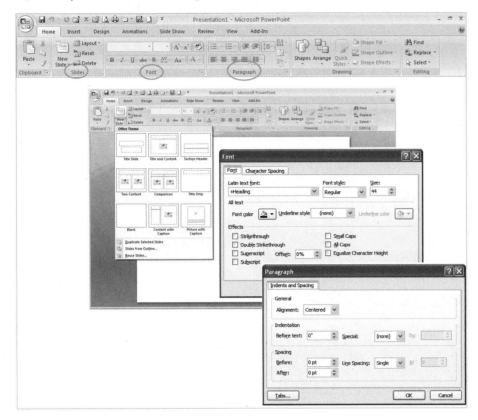

• **Insert** tab: Contains icons that you will use to add items such as tables, pictures, diagrams, and shapes to your slides.

Figure 1.4 | **Insert Tab**

In the **Home** tab, you can use either an icon or the dialog box to complete an activity. Wherever you see a little arrow, it means that a dialog box is available for that activity. There is no right or wrong way to complete an activity; it is a matter of personal preference.

Notice how you can choose **Add Slide** from the **Insert** tab as well as the **Home** tab. The PowerPoint Ribbon is designed to group logically related activities together. **Add Slide** is an example of an icon that needs to be available from multiple places within PowerPoint.

The main PowerPoint panes and tabs that you will be using on a regular basis are as follows:

• **Slide** pane: You will enter information and modify your slides here.

• **Notes** pane: You may enter speaker's notes here. Speaker's notes are discussed in greater detail later in your text.

• **Slides/Outline** pane: This pane allows you to view your slides either as miniature snapshots (**Slides** tab) or text (**Outline** tab). Many people use this pane as a way to keep an eye on how long the presentation is getting as they are creating it or to jump to a specific slide instead of scrolling through the entire presentation. There is no right or wrong way to view the slides; it is a matter of personal preference. (Figures 1.5 and 1.6 illustrate these two different ways of viewing the same presentation.)

Figure 1.5 | **PowerPoint Slides Tab**

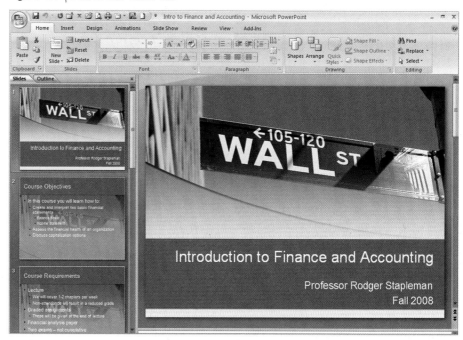

Figure 1.6 | **PowerPoint Outline Tab**

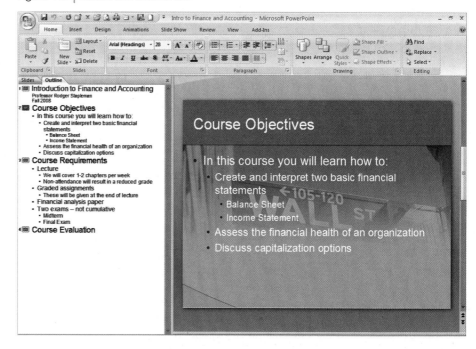

>> Communication and Decision Making

This is the first of several workshops that will be presented in this text. These workshops serve two purposes. The first is to give you an opportunity to practice the skills illustrated in each section of every PowerPoint chapter. The second is to watch the author demonstrate these skills. Many people have an easier time learning skills after they see a demonstration first. You can watch a video demonstration of each workshop by opening the related video file. Each workshop will usually require you to open one or more files to complete the tasks listed.

The purpose of this workshop is to complete the four-step planning process using a real business scenario and create an outline. You will see these skills demonstrated on the following three videos: **Introduction to PowerPoint**, **Planning a Presentation Request and MS Word Review**, and **Create an Outline**. Try completing the workshop on your own before watching the videos.

1. **Introduction to PowerPoint (Video: Introduction to PowerPoint)**
   a. Launch PowerPoint.
   b. Using the default slide, point out the panes and **Slides/Outline** pane.
   c. On the **Home** tab, move your cursor to each option and read the description.
   d. On the **Insert** tab, move your cursor to the **Slides** group and add a new slide.

2. **Planning a Presentation Request and MS Word Review (Video: Planning a Presentation Request and MS Word Review)**
   a. Using Microsoft Word, open the file named ib_p01_email.
   b. Save it as **Chapter1_Email_"lastname"_"firstname"** in your folder.
   c. Read through the e-mail and highlight the key pieces of information that you would need to help you plan a PPT presentation.
   d. Complete the Four-Step Planning process by answering each of these four questions: 1) What are the objectives? 2) Who is the audience? 3) What are the key messages/decisions? 4) How much time do you have? Use the information in both the e-mail and the scenario description contained in the ib_p01_email file.

3. **Create an Outline (Video: Create an Outline)**
   a. Answer each of the four questions from the Four-Step Planning Process questions in detail based on information in ib_p01_email file.
   b. Use your planning answers and create an outline using the format you learned in the Plan First, Validate, Then Create section.

>> Planning a Presentation

This is the first of several exercises that are presented in each section of this text. The purpose of these exercises is to show how you can apply PowerPoint skills to typical situations that you will encounter in school and in the business world.

In the Communication and Decision Making Video Workshop, you learned how to plan for a presentation and create an outline from a simple business e-mail. Long before you enter the corporate world, you will have many opportunities to deliver presentations in school. Following is an example of the type of assignment you would receive as a student. In this exercise you will create an outline only.

Exercise

You are taking an Operations Management class and the professor has given the following assignment:

Most people think of FedEx as simply an overnight shipping company. However, on the company's Web site (http://www.fedex.com/us/about/), it says, "FedEx provides access to a growing global marketplace through a network of supply chain services, transportation services, business and information services." Using the Web site, do a 15-minute presentation on how FedEx expanded its portfolio of services, why it was able to do that, and the impact to its business results.

1. Answer the four questions asked in the planning process.

   1. What is the objective?

   2. Who is the audience? Hint: Is it the professor or the students or both?

   3. What are the key messages?

   4. How much time do you have?

2. Create an outline that covers the scope of the assignment in the allotted time.

>> What's Wrong with This Presentation?

This is the second type of exercise that is presented at the end of each section of every chapter. The purpose of these exercises is to evaluate and/or troubleshoot PowerPoint presentations created by other people, applying the skills you have learned in that chapter. These exercises usually require you to open and evaluate a PowerPoint presentation. This chapter does not include this exercise.

Late one Sunday evening, one of my sales reps, Brian, called me from the local emergency room. He'd been playing basketball with his buddies that weekend, crashed into someone's elbow, and broke his nose. He was going to have reconstructive surgery and would be out of the office for several days. It was the week of the quarterly territory review, and he asked me to find someone to cover for him. "Forget it," I told him. "I'll do it. Take care of your broken nose and don't worry about it."

I didn't have the time to put in hours and hours of preparation, and I certainly didn't want to have a miserable review like so many others always seemed to have. So on Monday, I called the area manager, told him about Brian's situation, and asked if there was an agenda I needed to follow. There was silence on the phone, and he replied, "You are the first person from your office to ever ask me that question. Every time I come up there I get bombarded with tons of information, half of which is irrelevant. I have a limited amount of time to spend in each office, I don't get all of my questions answered, and I never have the opportunity to just chat and get to know the sales teams."

It turns out that he just wanted to know

- What deals were you going to close that quarter?
- Were you on target to make your revenue numbers for the quarter?
- If not, what were the reasons?
- What additional resources could he bring to bear, or what could he personally do to help?
- If you weren't going to make your number, what was your plan to make it up the following quarter?
- What was the customer satisfaction level of your territory?
- What was your satisfaction level with your job?

Using the preceding "hot buttons," I created a PowerPoint template for the entire sales office to use for the upcoming and all future reviews. By using a standard format that met the area manager's objectives, we significantly reduced the prep time going forward. We also had much more pleasant and productive meetings with him.

Assignment

Using the information from the anecdote, create an outline that answers these questions:

1. What are the objectives?
2. Who is the audience?
3. What are the key messages/decisions?
4. How much time do you have?

Questions for Discussion

1. Which planning steps did the sales reps either violate or completely ignore with their original methods?

2. What potentially bad business decisions could have been made by the area manager due to the poor communication in this situation?

3. How will you know if the area manager's objectives or needs change?

4. What other business or academic scenarios can you think of that could benefit from creating a standard, reusable presentation?

The following questions are related to the concepts addressed in this chapter. There are three types of questions: Short Answer, True or False, and Fill in the Blank. If your answer to a True or False question is False, write a short explanation as to why you think the statement is not true.

1. PowerPoint is the industry standard tool for _____ business information.

2. True or False: Many companies regularly conduct PowerPoint training for employees.

3. A PowerPoint presentation consists of individual pages, called _____.

4. You can create your own PowerPoint style or use a preformatted _____.

5. What are the steps in the four-step planning process?

6. What are the five sections in an outline?

7. When you launch PowerPoint, you will see a blank _____.

8. True or False: The **Slides/Outline** pane allows you to view only the text in your slides.

9. True or False: The **Notes** pane allows you to view your slides either as miniature snapshots or as text.

10. The _____ tab contains the icons that you will use the majority of the time when modifying and polishing your presentation.

>> Skills Exam

This section will also be included at the end of each chapter and is used to test your knowledge of executing various skills presented in the text. The primary mission of this book is to explain and demonstrate how PowerPoint is used in professional business situations. However, knowing how to execute key PowerPoint skills is also important. This section will present several skills-based questions which you will have to apply to a PowerPoint presentation. Since skills for creating a PowerPoint presentation have not yet been covered, there is no Skills Exam for this chapter.

>> Challenge Questions

The following questions are designed to test your ability to apply the PowerPoint skills you have learned to complete a business objective. Use your knowledge of PowerPoint as well as your creativity to answer these questions. For most questions, there are several possible ways to complete the objective.

In the Workshop, you created an outline for a 30-minute presentation to the CEO. Suppose you receive a phone call on Sunday evening from your manager saying that you now only have 15 minutes. Answer the following questions:

1. Does this change the objective of the presentation? How?

2. What changes would you make in the agenda, body, and conclusion sections?

3. In what order what would you change these sections?

4. Are there any other sections you would change?

5. How does this change any validation you need to do?

≫ Chapter 2

Creating a Basic Presentation

Chapter Goals

No matter what field of business you are in, creating effective presentations is a critical skill to have. In Chapter 1, you learned how to plan your presentation and create an outline. In this chapter, you will learn how to create a basic presentation using the PowerPoint software.

PowerPoint is a powerful tool that offers a lot of functionality and options. The objective of this chapter is for you to become proficient in the basic features. By the time you finish this chapter, you will know how to select a design, choose the appropriate layout, add text to your slides, and create simple charts and graphics.

≫ **PowerPoint** Skill Sets

PowerPoint in **Practice** | Anecdo

My Role as a Sales Representative

When I was selling information technology to the healthcare industry, I found it very difficult to schedule appointments with physicians, nurses, and other clinicians. Their offices were filled with patients from morning to night, and they were too busy to hear some mumbo-jumbo about how a new system would make their lives easier. After all, they were in the business of patient care, not computers.

When I finally got an audience with the senior physician in a clinic or large practice and went through the product literature, I always got the following question: "Why should I spend hundreds of thousands of dollars to install a system, train my staff, etc., just to submit medical claims electronically when it costs only 39¢ to mail one in? I don't have enough patients at 39¢ a claim to justify the expense of new hardware and software."

A colleague from another part of the country who was enjoying great success in this field shared her secret. It was from her that I learned the impact of presenting information visually. I discovered a technique that I would use to my advantage for years.

>> Continued on page 69

The objective of business presentations is to effectively communicate information and facilitate sound decision making. Regardless of your profession or area of business expertise, how you design your presentation is an important first step in achieving those objectives. This section will show you how to use slide layouts, use a theme and choose alternative themes from Office Online.

Creating a New Presentation

Creating a PowerPoint presentation involves using a blank presentation or choosing a design, adding new slides with layouts, and placing information on the slides. In Chapter 1, you learned the importance of planning and ways to craft an outline. Your outline translates directly into the foundation for your presentation.

The first step you will take when creating a new PowerPoint presentation is to select themes and layouts. Here are some terms to become familiar with:

- **Theme**: This is a prebuilt format that already has design elements (colors, fonts, graphics) applied to it. PowerPoint comes with a large selection of themes. Advantage: When you select a theme, the format is applied to all the slides automatically, which means you have to worry only about content.

- **Layout**: This refers to the way elements are arranged on a slide. A layout contains predetermined placeholders for information.

Recall from Chapter 1 that, when you start PowerPoint, you see a blank unformatted presentation. If you are currently working on a presentation and start a new one, you will also be presented with a blank, unformatted presentation (see Figure 2.1). From this screen, you can design and format your presentation by selecting themes and layouts. It is recommended that you choose your theme first because each theme arranges the elements on a slide (layout) differently. The options you choose will depend on your audience, your company's guidelines, and your objectives.

Figure 2.1 | **Blank Presentation**

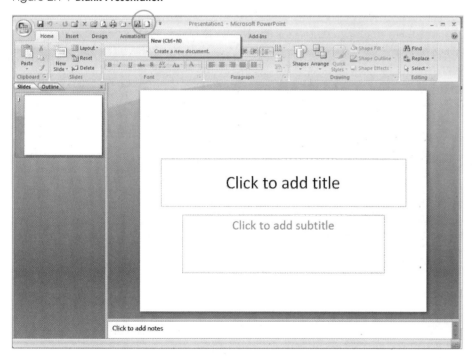

Slide Themes

- **Blank Presentation:** This theme has no formatting and color. You may want to leave your presentation blank at first to start simple and add a design or create your own design later. Advantage: This option allows you to personalize the presentation for your audience. For example, salespeople and consultants often customize their presentations by adding clients' logos or slogans to the slides. This simple technique can be performed quickly and it builds credibility. Some organizations choose to use this option as the final design and do not add any embellishments at all.

- **Built-In Themes:** These are the themes you can access from the **Design** tab. They have been installed on your company's server by a system administrator and are available to everyone. You should expect that they will vary from site to site. To promote consistency, many organizations require that you use specific themes. Sales and consulting organizations often use a standard theme because of the high degree of interaction with clients—for example, IBM, Accenture. This is also the case with companies that have a recognized marketing brand—for example, McDonald's, Proctor & Gamble.

- **Custom Themes:** These are the themes that you have either created or obtained from another source that are installed on your desktop.

- **Browse for Themes:** This option allows you to search for a theme from another computer that you have access to.

- **Microsoft Office Online:** Microsoft.com has a library of hundreds of templates organized by category that you can download and use. If your company does not have a standard template in place, or if you are looking for something different or creative, Office Online is a good resource to turn to.

Figure 2.2 | **PowerPoint Themes**

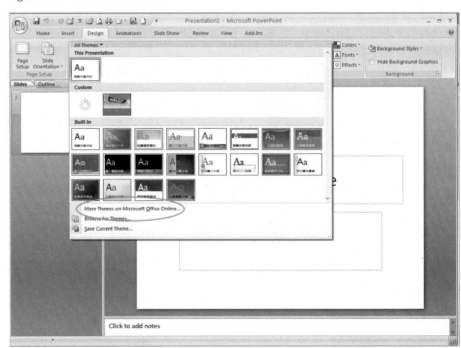

Many default templates come with PowerPoint. Your organization may limit the number of templates or add different ones. Therefore, do not be concerned if you have a different set of templates on your desktop than what you see in this text.

This next section demonstrates how to apply a new or different look to a presentation that is already in progress. Say that the advertising campaign results presentation used in this example was created by a college intern. The marketing manager who will be delivering this presentation to upper management needs to give it a more conservative look and feel. She can simply apply different themes to the existing presentation, and the content remains intact.

To change the appearance of a presentation, follow these steps:

- From the *Design tab*, select the **Themes** drop-down list. All your available themes will be displayed.

- Right click on a theme and select Apply to All Slides. The entire presentation will reflect this theme.

- You can also apply a theme to certain slides in your presentation. To do this, click on the slides you wish to change while holding down the **Ctrl** key from the **Slide Sorter** view. Right click on a theme and then choose a theme. This technique allows you to mix design templates within a presentation.

Figures 2.3–2.6 illustrate how the look of an advertising presentation can be changed quickly by applying a new theme. Notice how the colors and font sizes are changed to fit in with the overall look and feel and proportions of the selected theme.

Figure 2.3 | **Changing the Theme of a Presentation: Before**

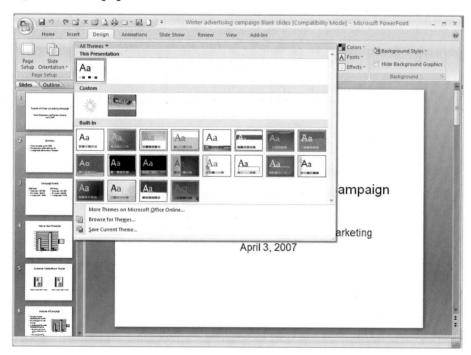

Figure 2.4 | **Changing the Theme of a Presentation: After**

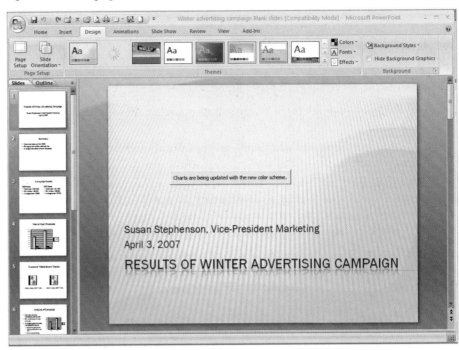

Figure 2.5 | **Changing the Theme of Selected Slides: Before**

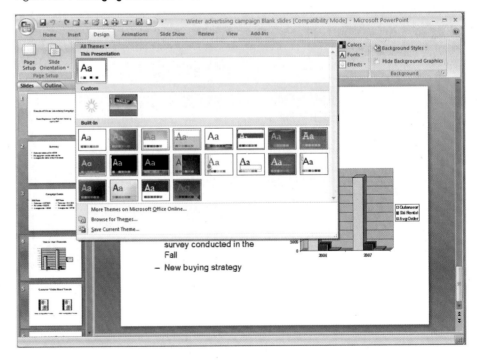

Figure 2.6 | **Changing the Theme of Selected Slides: After**

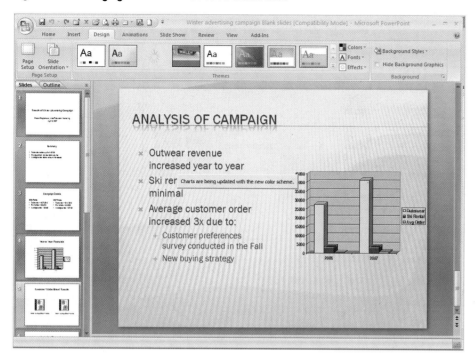

COMMON MISTAKES | Using Multiple Themes in a Presentation

Mixing and matching design templates within a presentation can confuse or throw off the audience. Use multiple themes *only* if you truly need to differentiate a section or subset of slides from the main presentation.

If the themes that come with your installation of PowerPoint do not meet your needs, a large selection is available on Microsoft Office Online. After you download a theme from Microsoft's online library, it will become part of your Custom Themes list.

To access themes on Office Online, go to the **Themes** drop-down list under the **Design** tab and select the More Themes on Microsoft Office Online link (see Figure 2.7).

>> *Quick Reference*

Changing the Appearance of a Presentation

From the **Design** tab, you can apply a design template from one of the following PowerPoint libraries:

1. Select the slides whose theme you wish to change.
   a. Select individual slides from **Slide Sorter** view by using the **Ctrl** key.
   b. You do not have to select any particular slide to change the appearance of the entire presentation.
2. From the **Design** tab, right click on a theme.
3. Select either **Apply to All Slides** or **Apply to Selected Slides**.

Figure 2.7 | **More Themes on Microsoft Office Online Link**

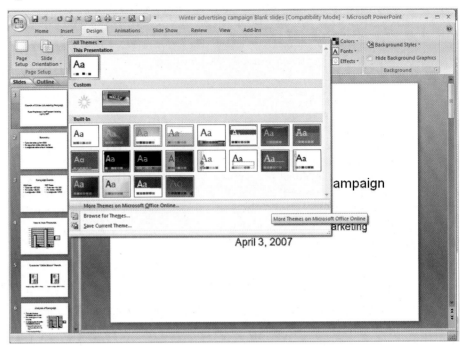

You will be connected to the Microsoft Office Web site. Navigate to the page that lists all the available PowerPoint designs (see Figure 2.8). They are listed by categories of interest.

Figure 2.8 | **PowerPoint Designs on Office Online**

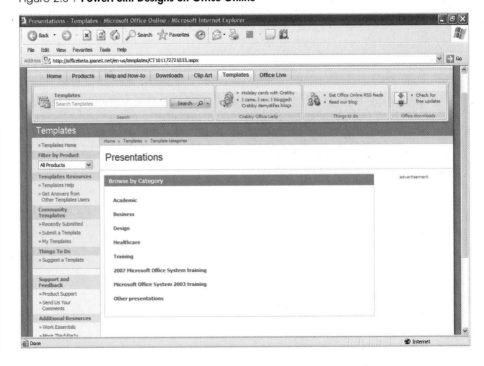

You will see several pages of presentation templates. You can judge the popularity of the design by the number of downloads and its rating (on a five-star (*****)) scale! Find a design that meets your needs and click on the design name.

When you click on **Download Now** (see Figure 2.9), the template downloads, you are launched back into PowerPoint, and a new presentation is created for you. If you were working on a presentation before, it is still active. Some templates even have pre-filled in business content to help you get started on your presentation. If you are creating a presentation from scratch and have no idea how to start, these sample presentations are an excellent aid.

Figure 2.9 | **Download a Template from Office Online**

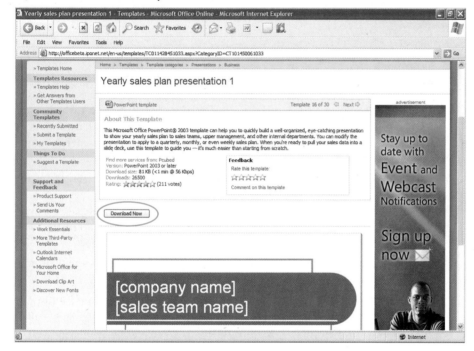

Note: You must be in Microsoft Internet Explorer to download Office Online templates.

Save the new theme by selecting **PowerPoint** Template in the **Save As type** list. See Figure 2.10. This new templete is now in the **Themes** list for future use.

Figure 2.10 | **Save a PowerPoint Theme**

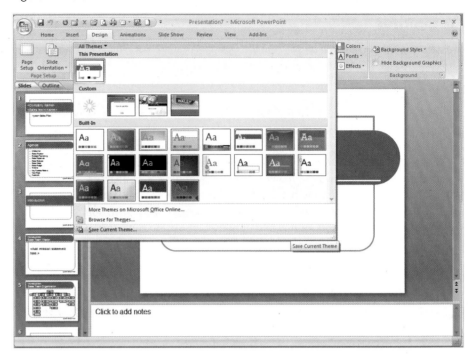

How do you know which theme to use? Here are some guidelines:

- The first time you have to do a presentation for your organization, ask whether everyone uses a standard PowerPoint template. Many organizations have a standard for consistency reasons, especially if their employees create presentations for external customers.

- If no standard exists, ask a senior-level person or someone whose presentations you think are professional if you may use one of his. If the theme resides on the company's network, launch PowerPoint and select **Browse for Themes**. Use it as a starting point and polish it using the skills you learn in this text. By doing this, you don't stand out as the new person or an outsider.

- If there is no existing presentation or one that you like, choose a new theme from Office Online.

- You will rarely use the blank presentation design. Most audiences expect some visual component to any presentation. However, due to the "Death by PowerPoint" syndrome discussed in Chapter 1, some organizations do opt for plain, blank presentations.

COMMON MISTAKES | **Choosing an Inappropriate Design Template**

Select a design template to match the audience profile or corporate culture. When in doubt, be conservative. For example, do not use designs with bubbles or dancing bears if you work for or are presenting to a 110-year-old Fortune 500 firm.

Slide Layouts

When you open a blank presentation in PowerPoint, the default slide layout called Title Slide appears (see Figure 2.11). There are other layouts that you can apply and use as well. Before we discuss additional layouts, there are two terms you should be familiar with:

- *Text*: Letters, numbers, and special characters
- *Content*: Graphics, charts, and diagrams

Figure 2.11 | **Default Slide in a Blank Presentation**

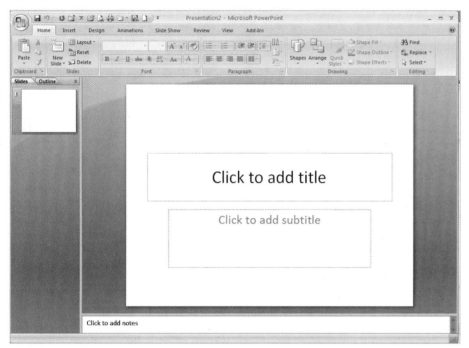

To view additional layouts and/or change the layout of the slide you are working on, position the mouse pointer over the slide in the **Slides** pane or in the **Slides/Outline** pane, right click the mouse button, and select **Layout**. As you move your mouse pointer over the various layouts, the name of the layout appears. Figure 2.12 shows some standard PowerPoint slide layouts; the highlighted one is called Title and Content.

Figure 2.12 | **Standard PowerPoint Slide Layouts**

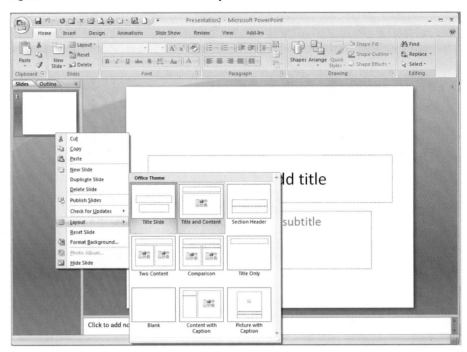

Most of the layouts allow you to enter both text and content. The placeholders in the layout indicate where to put each type of information. Figure 2.13 shows a blank Title and 2-Content layout and its placeholders.

Figure 2.13 | **Title and 2-Content Layout with Placeholders for Text and Content**

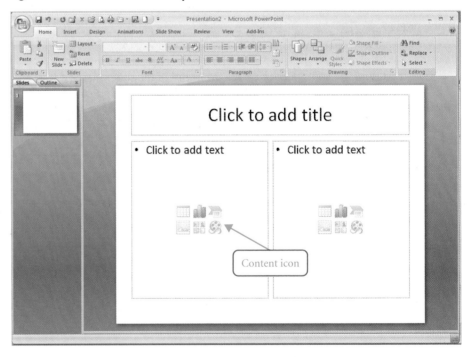

To insert content, click on the appropriate graphic within the **Content** icon (enlarged in Figure 2.14). From there, you can insert the following objects:

- *Pictures*: Digital images in file formats such as .tif, .jpg, .bmp, .png, and so on
- *Charts*: Numerical information that can be presented in several ways, including column, bar, line, and pie charts
- *Tables*: Information presented using rows and columns
- *SmartArt Graphics*: Prebuilt diagrams such as lists, process charts, hierarchies, and pyramids used to represent relationships
- *Movies*: Streaming video files in formats such as .mpg, .avi, and so on
- *Clip Art*: Artwork from a collection

Figure 2.14 | **Content Icon**

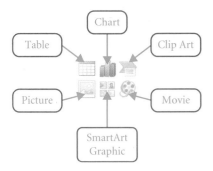

As noted previously, numerous slide layouts exist. PowerPoint comes with a set of standard layouts for blank presentations. If you use any of the other themes to create your presentation (**Built-In, Office Online, Browse for themes**), you will likely inherit additional layouts.

Figures 2.15–2.18 illustrate examples of slides from an advertising campaign presentation. Notice how many different layouts come with this presentation. There are no hard-and-fast guidelines for selecting layouts. Be sure to choose a layout that conveys the information in the most effective manner. For example, if you know that your audience will react well to a presentation that depicts information graphically, you should have more content layouts in your presentation.

All presentations start with a title. Therefore, the first slide in this advertising campaign uses the Title Slide layout.

Figure 2.15 | **Advertising Campaign Title Slide**

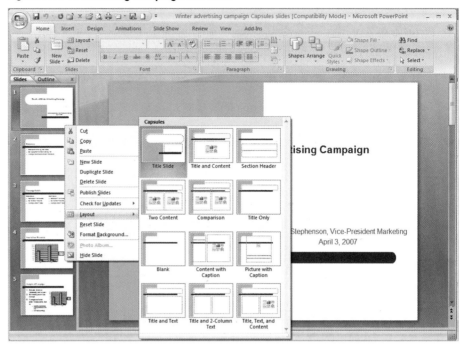

In Figures 2.16–2.18, the placeholders are selected and highlighted so that you can identify and become comfortable with different combinations of title, text, and content.

Figure 2.16 illustrates a slide layout that would be used when information needs to be presented and compared side by side. In this example, sales results are compared from 2006 to 2007.

Figure 2.16 | **Title and 2-Column Text Layout**

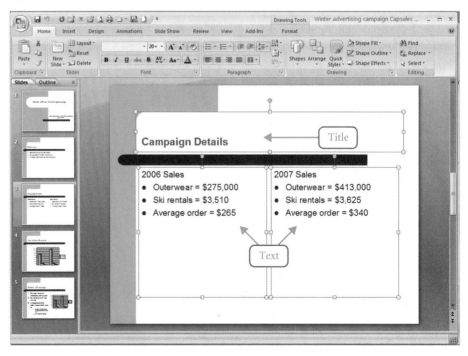

Figure 2.17 illustrates a slide layout that you would choose to present only graphical information. In this example, sales by product line are shown using a bar chart.

Figure 2.17 | **Title and Content Layout**

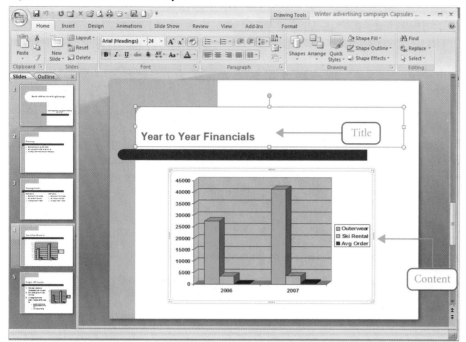

Figure 2.18 illustrates a slide layout that combines text and content. In this example, the advertising campaign results are displayed graphically and combined with a text explanation.

Figure 2.18 | **Title, Text, and Content Layout**

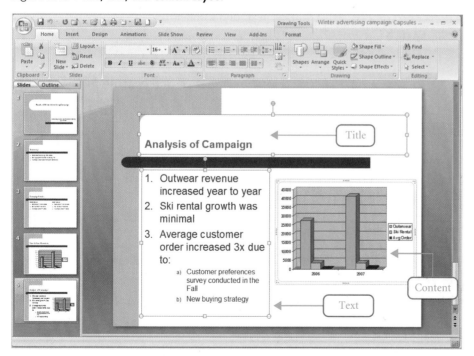

Recall from Chapter 1 the five major sections of a presentation are as follows:

1. Title
2. Agenda
3. Introduction
4. Body
5. Conclusion

Figure 2.19 shows some general slide layout examples for most business presentations. Notice how the layouts for title, agenda, introduction, and conclusion are simple and lend themselves to being "short and sweet." The body is the usual location for most of your text and content; you may want to mix slide layout types in this section. There are certainly exceptions, especially if your presentation is creative and requires more content throughout all the sections (for example, advertising, marketing, entertainment).

Figure 2.19 | **Common Slide Layouts by Presentation Section**

Section	Slide Layout(s)
Title	Title Slide
Agenda	Title and Text
Introduction	Title and Text
	Title and Content
Body	Title and Text
	Title and 2-Column Text
	Title and Content
	Two Content
	Title, Text, and Content
Conclusion	Title and Text, Title and Content

>> *Quick Reference*

Applying a Slide Layout

1. To apply a slide layout to a single slide:
   a. Right click on the slide either from the Slide pane or the **Slide/Outline** pane.
   b. Choose a layout.
2. To apply a slide layout to a multiple slides:
   a. Select a range of slides using the **Shift** key or separate slides using the **Ctrl** key.
   b. Right click on any of the selected slides and choose a layout.

COMMON MISTAKES | Name and Date on the Title Slide

Don't forget to put your name and the date on the Title Slide. These are two of the most often forgotten items. Adding your name and the date is a good practice for keeping track of multiple versions, and if you provide handouts, the audience will remember that this great presentation came from you!

COMMON MISTAKES | Creating a Slide without a Title

Although the slide layouts Title and Content and Content are both used, it is recommended that you use Title and Content because having a title on each slide in your presentation is a good practice.

⟫ Designing Your Presentation

The purpose of this workshop is to demonstrate how to design your presentation using the skills presented in this section of the chapter. You will see these tasks demonstrated in the following five videos: **Starting a New Presentation**, **Selecting a Slide Layout**, **Applying a Theme**, **Finding a Template on the Web**, and **Customizing a Theme**. Try to complete these tasks on your own first before watching the videos.

1. Start a New Presentation (Video: Starting a New Presentation)

   a. Launch PowerPoint.

   b. Close the blank presentation.

   c. Choose the option from the **Quick Access** toolbar (if you customized and added icons to it) or the **File** menu (**Office Home** Button) that tells PowerPoint you are starting a new presentation.

   d. Select a blank presentation.

2. Select Slide Layouts (Video: Selecting Slide Layouts)

   a. Change the default layout of the slide in the **Slide** pane to the following types of layouts:

   Text only; Title, Text and Content; Title and 2-Content

   b. Scroll down and select two layouts at the bottom of the list.

   c. Close the presentation. Do not save it.

3. Apply a Theme (Video: Applying a Theme)

   a. Start a new presentation and select the **Built-In** theme option.

   b. Scroll through the list of available themes and preview three different ones.

   c. Find a theme that has a white background, colored text, and graphics in the background.

   d. Apply this theme to the current slide.

   e. Close the presentation. Do not save it.

4. Find a Template on the Web (Video: Finding a Template on the Web)

   a. Switch your browser to Internet Explorer, if necessary.

   b. Start a new presentation and select the **Office Online** option under **Themes**.

   c. Navigate to the online template library.

   d. Select a business template with a technology theme that is ranked at least three stars.

   e. Download the template and save as `Computer Design`.

>> Designing Your Presentation

In Chapter 1, you learned how to plan your presentation, validate it, and create an outline. After having learned those skills, you know who the audience is, what their objectives are, and the type of information you need to present. Additionally, since you have possibly interacted with a member of the audience already (to obtain validation), the bar has been raised and the audience will be expecting a well-designed presentation.

Exercise

The outline that you created in Chapter 1 has been turned into a shell presentation by a college intern. In the following exercise, you will select an appropriate template, theme, and slide layouts. Use your judgment in choosing design elements that are appropriate to an executive-level audience. Once you master these skills, you can always go back and refine the design as you learn more about the audience and their objectives and if you obtain more information that you want to include in the presentation.

1. Assess a Presentation Design
   a. Open the file named ib_p02_acadiamfgoutline.
   b. Examine the current shell presentation design outline and answer the following questions:
      • How would you describe the profile of an executive-level audience?
      • What is the tone of the message you are delivering?
      • Are the current design elements (template, theme, and layouts) appropriate for this presentation? Why or why not?

2. Modify a Presentation Design
   a. Apply two to four themes until the design is acceptable for the audience and the material that is being presented.
   b. Explain why you chose your final theme.

3. Apply Slide Layouts
   a. Read each slide title and apply an appropriate layout.
   b. Explain why you selected each layout.
   c. Was there more than one layout option? How easily can you go back and change the layout later?

Now that you have created a new presentation for the executive presentation, answer the following questions:

4. What other groups of people might be an audience(s) for this type of presentation? List examples of other audiences and find appropriate design templates for them.

5. How serious is it if you pick the wrong design?

≫ What's Wrong with This Presentation?

Problem

You and a group of classmates are writing a short paper and presenting to your class on the business and financial success of General Electric Corporation. The presentation constitutes 50% of the grade, so it has to be done well. Your instructor has given each team an outline for the presentation and allotted 15 minutes to present. To divide the work, two people are writing the paper, and one person is designing the presentation based on the instructor's outline. Since there won't be much time left after writing the paper, the team needs to set up the presentation shell so that information can be extracted from the paper onto predetermined locations on the slides.

When your team member sends you the slides, it's obvious that either he did not give much thought to how the presentation ultimately needs to look or he does not know too much about the design features of PowerPoint.

Exercise

Open the file named ib_p02_part1_whatswrong and consider the following:

1. Do the slide layouts used indicate what type of information belongs on each slide? How would you change that?

2. Does the presentation look like it was created by one person? Why or why note? Make the necessary changes.

3. Once you hand it in, will the instructor remember who did it?

Write a short answer for each of these points, and fix the presentation for your team member.

≫ Building Your Presentation

Once you have chosen a theme or decided to start with a blank presentation first and add a theme later, you are ready to build your presentation. In this section, you will learn how to insert new slides, add text, use the **Outline** tab, and create bullets and numbered lists.

Adding New Slides and Text

When you start a new presentation, PowerPoint defaults to the **Slides** tab in the **Slides/Outline** tabs. Recall from Chapter 1 that you can choose to work with slides using the **Outline** tab or the **Slides** tab. In this section, we will work with a presentation being developed by a Human Resources director that presents the results of a recent MIS Recruiting Fair. You will learn how to insert new slides and add text to an existing presentation. We will use the **Slides** tab first and then demonstrate how to insert slides and add text using the **Outline** tab.

As mentioned earlier, PowerPoint starts you with the Title Slide slide layout. You are presented with placeholders that prompt you to click and start typing. You can add a new slide in one of two ways:

- In the **Slides/Outline** tabs, place your mouse pointer on the slide after which you want to insert a new one, right click, and select **New slide** (see Figure 2.20). You will get the default slide layout and may have to change it.

Figure 2.20 | **Insert New Slide from the Slides/Outline Tabs**

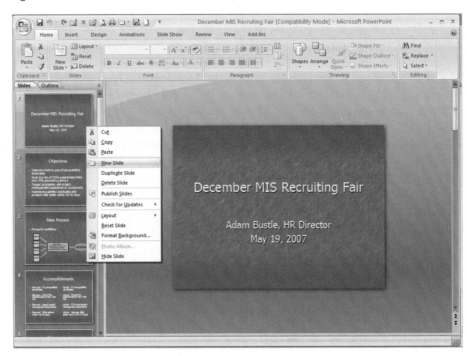

- From the **Home** tab, select **Add Slide**. Click on the bottom of this icon to see the drop-down menu. By doing so, you can add a new slide and choose its layout at the same time (see Figure 2.21).

Figure 2.21 | **Add a New Slide from the Home Tab**

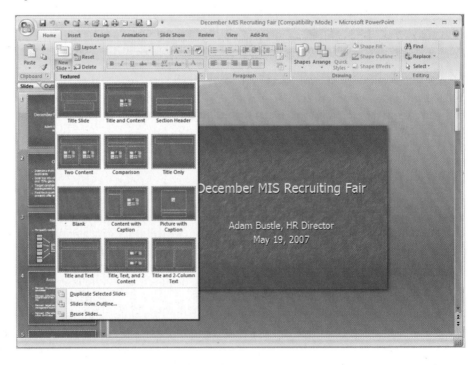

>> Quick Reference

Inserting New Slides

1. From the **Home** tab:
   a. Select **New Slide**. You will be prompted to select the slide layout.
2. From the **Slides/Outline** tabs:
   a. Right click on the slide you wish to insert a new slide after.
   b. Select **New Slide**.
   c. The new slide will inherit the same layout which you may go back later and change.

As you build your presentation by inserting slides, you will see the list of slides growing in the **Slides** tab. Figure 2.22 illustrates the MIS Recruiting Fair presentation with three slides that have different layouts.

Figure 2.22 | **Slides Tab**

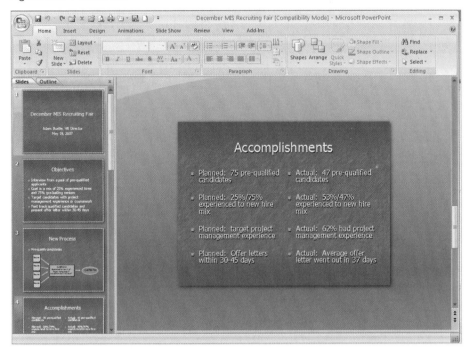

Using the Outline Tab

The next example discusses how to use the **Outline** tab to insert new slides and add text to the MIS Recruiting Fair presentation. Activate the **Outline** tab by simply clicking on the **Outline** tab. Figure 2.23 shows all three slides in this same presentation in a text format instead of a visual format.

Figure 2.23 | **Outline View**

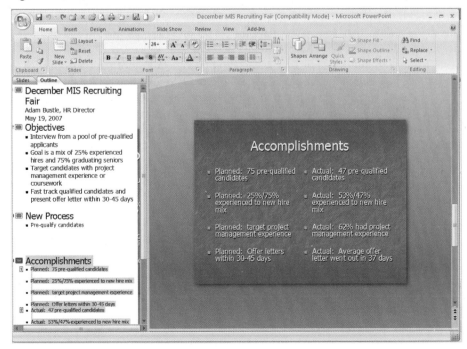

You use the same steps to insert a new slide as you learned before. However, instead of typing the text directly into the blank slide, you type it into the **Outline** tab, and PowerPoint places it on the slide, as shown in Figure 2.24.

Figure 2.24 | **Add Text Using the Outline Tab**

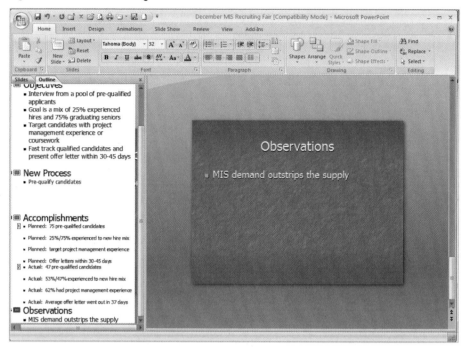

Using the **Slides** tab or the **Outline** tab gives the same result. However, when building a presentation from scratch, most people use the **Slides** tab because it is visually easier to work with.

The **Outline** tab is the preferred method when you want to extract information from a document such as a research paper or memo, for example, and create a presentation. Students use this feature extensively because it allows them to copy and paste from their papers and build a draft presentation without having to retype the information from scratch. Later, they can refine the presentation by changing long sentences into short bullets. Recognize that text format (font, size, color, etc.) does not always match the slide format, so you may have to go back into the presentation and modify or enhance it. You will learn how to do that in Chapter 3.

The next examples (see Figures 2.25–2.26) illustrate how information from a few paragraphs in a student paper can be copied and pasted into a slide with a design template applied. This allows students to quickly create a draft presentation that might then be used to review with their professor for approval before they fill in all the detail. Businesspeople use this technique also to validate their presentation outline with the audience.

Figure 2.25 | **Excerpts from a Student Paper**

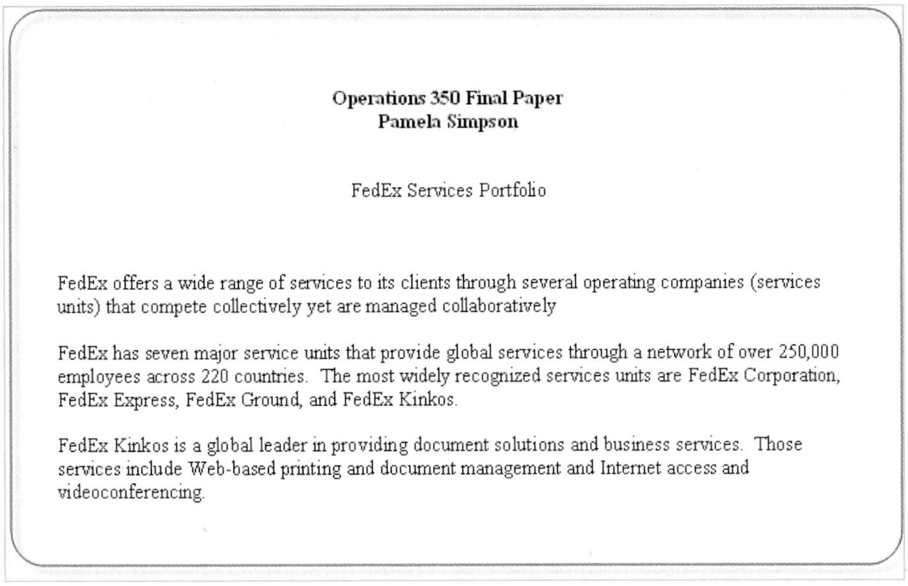

Operations 350 Final Paper
Pamela Simpson

FedEx Services Portfolio

FedEx offers a wide range of services to its clients through several operating companies (services units) that compete collectively yet are managed collaboratively

FedEx has seven major service units that provide global services through a network of over 250,000 employees across 220 countries. The most widely recognized services units are FedEx Corporation, FedEx Express, FedEx Ground, and FedEx Kinkos.

FedEx Kinkos is a global leader in providing document solutions and business services. Those services include Web-based printing and document management and Internet access and videoconferencing.

Figure 2.26 | **PowerPoint Slides Created from Student Paper Excerpts**

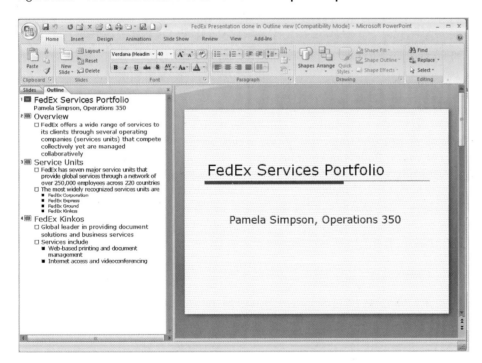

COMMON MISTAKES | Converting from a Document to a Presentation

When creating a presentation from a detailed document such as a research paper, remember to summarize the information and create short sentences. Avoid copying entire paragraphs as this will clutter up the slide and overwhelm the audience.

Bullets and Numbered Lists

Now that you know how to insert text into a presentation, you need to learn some text formatting skills. **Bullets** are used in business presentations to summarize points and list key messages. PowerPoint puts default **bullet points** in front of text placeholders on the slide layouts. Up to now, you have seen how to create a **bulleted list** on your slides by entering text after the bullet points, using the default bullet location and style that came with the slide layout. However, PowerPoint enables you to modify a single bullet, a list of bullets, or all the bullets in a presentation by

- Appearance
- Size
- Color
- Indentation

Instead of bullets, you can use **numbered lists**. Numbered lists work well when you need to explain procedures or present information that has some order or priority associated with it. Numbered lists label items using

- Cardinal numbers (1, 2, 3, etc.)
- Roman numerals (I, II, III, etc.)
- Alphabet (A, B, C, etc.)

For most applications, simple lettering or numbering is best. Avoid Roman numerals unless you have a compelling reason to use them because they are difficult to understand.

COMMON MISTAKES | Incorrect Use of Numbered Lists

Many people forget that the numbered lists imply a sequence. If there is no sequence to the items on the list, use regular bullets.

To change the bullet format, highlight the items you wish to change and select the **Bullets** icon from the **Home** tab. Be sure to click on the down arrow beside the **Bullets** icon and choose **Bullets and numbering**.

Returning to the advertising presentation we discussed earlier in the chapter, the example in Figure 2.27 highlights how and where you would format the bullets and the results:

- A chevron-shaped bullet was chosen from the list to make the bullets stand out more.
- Bullet size was increased from 75% to 100% so that it would be more proportional in size with the bullet text.
- Bullet color was changed from dark blue to teal green to match the color palette.

Figure 2.27 | **Changing Bullet Styles**

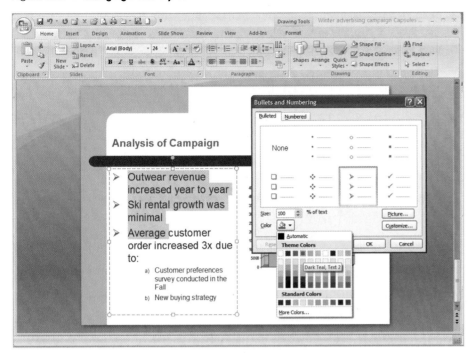

Even though you can choose very interesting and artistic bullets, bullets used in business presentations should be plain.

To change the bulleted list to a numbered list, use the same tab but use the **Numbering** icon instead, as shown in Figure 2.28.

Figure 2.28 | **Changing Bullets to Numbers**

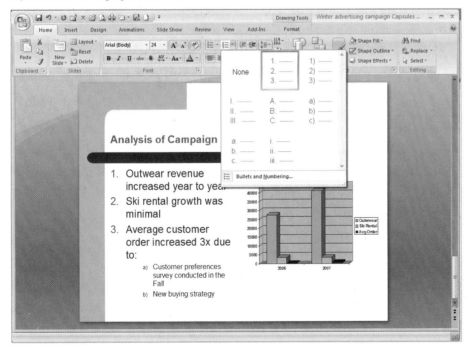

>> *Quick Reference*

Changing Bullet or Numbering Locations on a List

1. To increase list level (move the bullets to the right):

   a. Highlight the bullets you wish to move and select the **Increase List Level** icon.

2. To decrease list level (move the bullets to the left):

   a. Highlight the bullets you wish to move and select the **Decrease List Level** icon.

You can change the location of the bullets by using icons on the **Home** tab:

- *Increase List Level*: Moves the bullet to the right. It also changes the bullet type and text size (usually makes the text smaller in size).
-  Using the **Tab** key also produces the same results.
- *Decrease List Level*: Moves the bullet to the left. It also changes the bullet type and text size (usually makes the text larger in size).
-  Using the **Back Tab** key also produces the same results.

VIDEO WORKSHOP

>> Building Your Presentation

The purpose of this workshop is to demonstrate the presentation-building skills presented in this section of the chapter. We will be opening and saving a presentation, inserting new slides, adding text, and building bulleted and numbered lists. You will see these tasks demonstrated in the video **Inserting New Slides and Adding Text**. Remember to try the tasks on your own first before watching the video.

1. **Insert New Slides and Add Text (Video: Inserting New Slides and Adding Text)**

    a. Launch PowerPoint and open the file named ib_p02_downloadedtemplate. Save the theme as **Computer Theme** and save the file as **ib_p02_buildpresentation**.

    b. On the Title page, type **Corporate Technology Refresh** and the date **June 30, 2007**.

    c. Insert the following slides that just have title and text and type the following information:

Title:	**System Upgrades**
Text:	**100 corporate desktops replaced**
	125 Microsoft Office upgrades
Title:	**Impact to Users**
Text:	**Desktop replacement outage = 2 hours**
	Microsoft Office upgrade downtime = 30 minutes

    d. Insert a Title and 2-Column Text slide and type in the following information:

Title:	**Summary of Improvements**	
	Before Upgrade	**After Upgrade**
	Desktop failure rate of 7/week	**None**
	Memory leakages reported	**One in 3 weeks**
	Software performance slow	**Users report subsecond response**

    e. Change the bulleted lists from step d to numbered lists.

    f. Click on **Title page** and add a new Title and Text page.

g. Switch to **Outline** tab and enter the following information:

Title: `Agenda`

Text: `Summary of System Upgrades`

                   `Impact to Users`

                   `Summary of Improvements`

h. Save and close your file.

>> Building Your Presentation

EXERCISE
Why Do I Need This?

Adding slides, text, and bulleted and numbered lists is essential for creating presentations in PowerPoint. Even if you borrow heavily from other people's presentations, many times you will need to modify their slides. These are the core tasks that every presenter needs to know how to perform.

Exercise

In this exercise, you will create a presentation using the basic skills you learned in Chapter 1 and in the first two sections of this chapter.

1. Open the file named ib_p02_background.

    a. Review the outline and background information

    b. Highlight key pieces of information that might go under each outline element.

2. Open a new presentation and name it **ib_p02_part2acadiamfg**.

    a. Using your judgment, determine the audience profile and tone of message. Select an appropriate template and/or theme.

    b. Build the presentation by adding slides based on the outline and apply the most appropriate layouts for each slide.

    c. Using the **Outline** tab, add the appropriate information to each slide.

    d. Add additional information to the slides if you feel it would enhance the presentation

3. Revisit the bulleted list(s) in your slides.

    a. Are there any lists you would number instead of using bullets?

4. Save your work and close the file.

>> What's Wrong with This Presentation?

PROBLEM &
EXERCISE

Problem

You are a human resources manager for an organization that is implementing a Customer Relationship Management (CRM) system. This new system is seen as a way to strengthen your customer relationships, increase loyalty, and thereby improve sales. Business professionals skilled in CRM are in high demand and are being recruited away from their companies by competitors. In the past 90 days, your firm has lost two key managers who were heavily involved in the project.

You are holding a recruiting open house to attract people who are qualified in this technology. CRM implementations are large, costly, and risky. As a result, many of these projects fail. Being associated with an unsuccessful project can be a career-killer. Potential candidates need to be assured that they are joining a project team that will be on time and on budget.

The operations manager gave you his presentation to use because you don't know much about this key initiative. His presentation was for an internal staff meeting and it's all you have to go with to create your presentation.

Exercise

Open the file you created in the previous exercise named ib_p02_part2_acadiamfg and consider the following points.

1. Does the current presentation in any way address the audience and objectives for the recruiting open house?

2. What parts of the existing presentation are not appropriate for the recruiting fair audience?

3. What parts of the existing presentation can you reuse?

4. What general statements or correlations can you make between audience, design, layout, and content?

Prepare short answers to these questions and modify the PowerPoint presentation to address the issues.

Skill Set

>> Presenting Qualitative and Quantitative Information and Objects

At this point, you are off to a good start by knowing how to create a business presentation using the built-in layouts for text and content. However, as a student or business professional, you will always work with multiple types of of information at the same time, as described here, and you need know how to represent those types of information in PowerPoint:

- *Qualitative*: This is information that is descriptive and narrative. Qualitative information is sometimes considered to be subjective.

- *Quantitative*: Information that is described using numbers and units of measurement. Quantitative information is considered to be objective.

- *Objects*: This is information that in its native form is not computer-ready, but it has been digitized. Examples are media such as graphics, pictures, audio, or video.

One business example of where you would use qualitative and quantitative is for investment decisions. Securities analysts and investors use quantitative information such as ratios (for example, debt-to-equity and price/earnings) as well as financial statements (for example, balance sheets and income statements) to assess the financial position of an organization. However, they also combine qualitative information, such as business practices and management experience, to make final decisions such as "Buy, Hold, or Sell."

A business example of where you might use audio or video is when presenting corporate business results or at employee meetings. A very common use of audio is when the CEO of an organization records a "Thank you for a successful year" message to employees that is embedded into and played from within a presentation.

Audiences have diverse learning styles. Pictures, charts, and diagrams can help convey your message more clearly and bring the audience up to speed more quickly. For example, you can use video to conduct e-learning classes. Audio and video clips, especially if they come from respected sources, can add credibility to your presentations. A subtle advantage of using multiple types of information, especially if it is done well, is that it gives the impression that you are an experienced presenter.

As you move up in an organization, you are given less time to present more critical information to increasingly impatient and busy audiences. Presenting information through a variety of means and media will allow you to convey your message in a shorter period of time.

This section will demonstrate how to use *lines, rectangles,* and *basic shapes* to present qualitative information and tables and charts for quantitative information.

Shapes and Lines

Lines, rectangles, and basic shapes, such as circles and stars, work well when you are presenting qualitative information in a business presentation because they help the audience understand large amounts of information and to grasp it more quickly than if they were just looking at text. Marketing campaigns, business plans, and training materials are just a few examples of presentations that benefit greatly from the use of lines and shapes.

There are no formal guidelines on how and when to present information using lines and shapes. A good rule of thumb is to ask the following question as you create and refine your presentation: "Will my audience understand this information more effectively with a visual instead of text?"

Figure 2.29 | **Shapes**

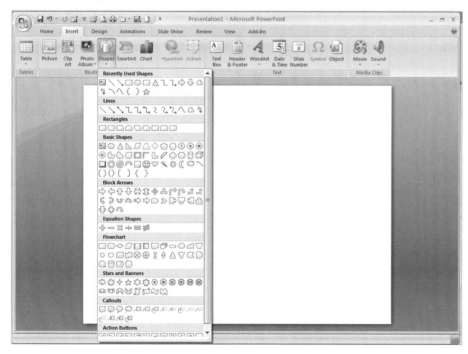

If you click on **Shapes** on the **Insert** tab (see Figure 2.29), you see a large list of shapes that are available to include in your presentation. In this section, we will discuss only Lines, Rectangles, and Basic Shapes.

As you use shapes more and more often, PowerPoint will remember the ones you've used and put them in the section called **Recently Used Shapes**.

To add a shape or rectangle, follow these steps:

- Point to a category and then click the shape you want. Your mouse pointer will turn into a crossbar.

- Position the mouse pointer where you want the shape to appear on the slide. While holding down your left mouse button, drag your mouse to size the shape. Let go of the button when your shape is the size you need it to be.
- Right click on the shape, and you will get a menu of options that include inserting text and formatting the shape.
- If you add text, it becomes a permanent part of the shape. To change the text, right click the shape and select **Edit Text**.

Figure 2.30 illustrates a rectangle and an oval, both with text

Figure 2.30 | **Rectangle and Oval Shapes**

Lines connect shapes and indicate a flow or sequence. There are many line styles, as was shown in Figure 2.29.

To add a line, follow these steps:

- Click on the line style.
- Place the mouse where you want the line to start in the presentation.
- Hold down your left mouse button and drag your mouse until you get the length of line you want.
- Right click on the line to open a list of formatting options (see Figure 2.31)

Figure 2.31 | **Arrow Between Two Shapes**

You can use any combination of shapes to create simple or complex diagrams. Deciding which shapes to use and how to create effective diagrams is more of an art than a science. Your skill in this area will improve with practice and trial and error.

The example in Figure 2.32 shows how three shapes and arrows are used to present a new recruiting process visually instead of using words. Incoming resumes are screened using three specific criteria, and the result is a prequalified pool of candidates. The diagram is so straightforward that the audience can understand the process in a matter of seconds without a great deal of explanation.

Figure 2.32 | **Sample Diagram Using Shapes**

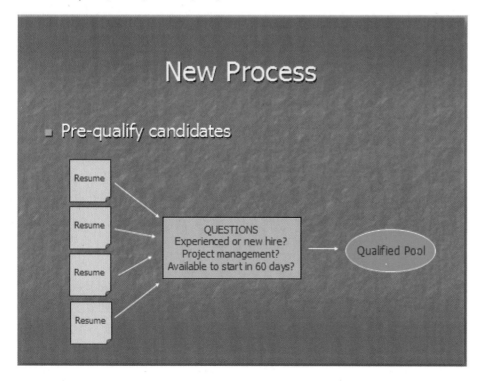

When you finish creating the diagram, a good practice is to ***group*** the shapes, which means to associate them together as one large shape. When you group objects, you can manipulate them (move, rotate, or resize) as though they were a single object. Select the shapes you wish to group by holding down the **Ctrl** key and selecting each shape. Then choose the **Arrange** option under the **Home** tab, as shown in Figure 2.33.

Figure 2.33 | **Grouping Shapes**

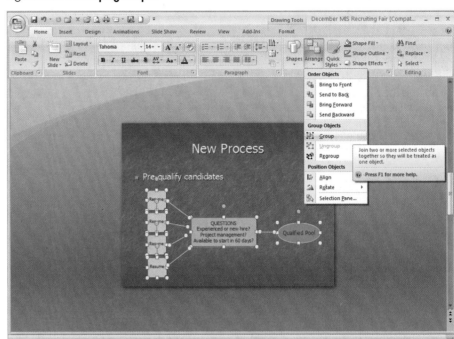

>> **Quick Reference**

Adding a Line

1. From the **Insert** tab, select **Shapes**. Alternately, from the **Format** tab, select a line from the **Insert Shapes** group.

2. Click on a line from the drop-down list.

3. Return to the slide where you want to draw a line. You will see that the cursor has turned into a cross bow.

4. Position the cross bow where you want to start the line. Hold down the left mouse button, slide your mouse until you've drawn the length of line you want or have connected two objects, and release the mouse button.

>> **Quick Reference**

Grouping Shapes

1. Select all the shapes you wish to group.

2. From the **Drawing** group under the **Home** tab, select **Arrange**.

3. Chose **Group** from the drop-down list.

COMMON MISTAKES | Overdoing Graphics

Graphics are meant to clarify and enhance, not replace the text. Because PowerPoint offers a vast array of shapes, pictures, and graphics, many presenters have the tendency to liberally sprinkle these objects all through their presentations. Guard against the tendency to do that. As you do more presentations, your sense of what works and what doesn't work will get better and better.

COMMON MISTAKES | Forgetting to Group Your Shapes

Many people spend hours creating complex diagrams consisting of related shapes and forget to group the objects together at the end. If you do not group your shapes, the slightest movement or adjustment of one could throw the whole diagram off and cause a tremendous amount of rework.

If you want to keep shapes connected, use a connector. A connector is a special type of line that stays attached to the shape when the shape moves. This feature is useful when you are drawing process charts or design diagrams. Three types of connectors can be found in the **Lines** section:

- Line
- Elbow
- Curved

To use a connector, follow these steps:

From the **Shapes** group on the **Insert** tab, choose a connector from the **Lines** options.

Point to the first shape where you want to attach the connector. Click on a red circle (that appears when you place your mouse pointer over the shape); then drag to the other shape and release the mouse button after you point to a red circle on the second shape.

Now, if you move either shape, the connectors remain attached to the shape and move along with it, no matter how and where you move it. To "unlock" the connector, click on it, rearrange it, and then "lock" back on to the shape. You will know if you successfully locked the connector back on when you see the red circles.

Figure 2.34 illustrates a line (that does not connect the rectangle and the oval) and an elbow connector between the rectangle and diamond.

Figure 2.34 | **Lines and Connectors**

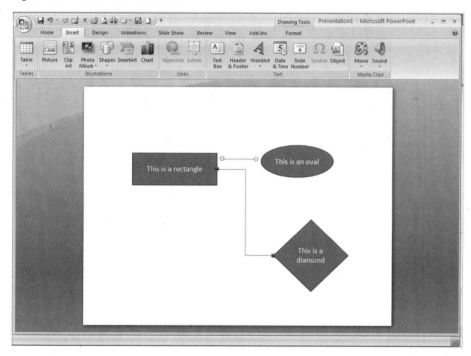

COMMON MISTAKES | Tangling Up Your Connectors

An advantage of connectors is that they adjust and adapt to the movement of the shape. However, if you move the location of the shapes significantly, the connector lines can end up looking like spaghetti, and untangling them will be very labor intensive. Make sure to go back and adjust the connector lines to minimize lines crossing over each other.

Tables and Charts

Tables and charts present quantitative information. In this section, we will discuss tables first.

Tables present information using rows and columns. You can summarize, categorize, and compare information easily using tables; consequently, they are used a great deal in presentations across almost all areas of business. Examples are stock price comparisons, competitive marketing analyses, and employee satisfaction survey results. The list is almost endless. You can create and format a simple table within PowerPoint. You can also create a table in Microsoft Word, Excel, or Access and import it into PowerPoint, thereby saving rework.

PowerPoint tables are used for presenting information only. If, for example, you need to merge names and addresses for a mailing list, perform mathematical calculations, or query a database and import the results into a separate table, the appropriate tools to use are Word, Excel, and Access, respectively.

In this section, you will learn how to create a PowerPoint table that shows the number of prequalified candidates by region as a result of a new recruiting process. Before you begin, you should have an idea of the number of rows and columns you need. Don't worry; if you miscalculate, you can add or delete rows and columns later. Select **Table** from the **Insert** tab. You can either type table dimensions manually or click on the boxes to indicate the number of rows and columns. To type table dimensions manually and see the **Insert Table** dialog box, you must choose **Insert Table** from the drop-down. Both the drop-down and dialog box are shown in Figure 2.35. In this example, the table for the recruiting process requires five columns and two rows.

Figure 2.35 | **Create a Table**

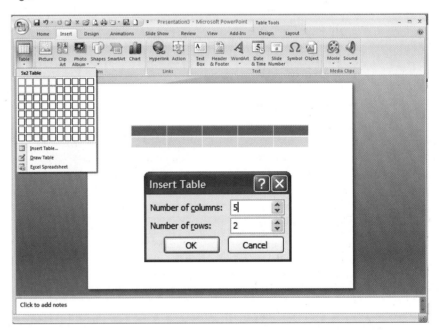

You will then be given a blank five-column, two-row table to fill in and format. Under the **Layout** tab are formatting where you can add and delete rows, or otherwise modify the characteristics of your table. You can also right click on the table itself for formatting choices. Figure 2.36 shows both ways to launch formatting options.

Figure 2.36 | **Table Formatting Options**

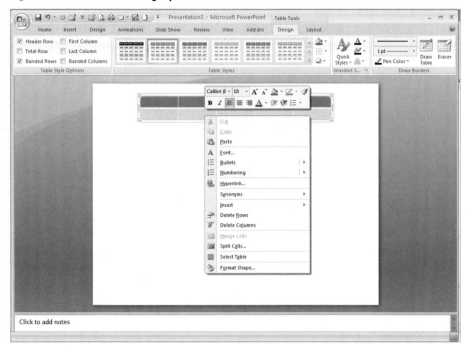

Charts present numerical information visually. You can create a chart from scratch in PowerPoint or import a chart from Excel or Word. PowerPoint charts are preformatted. You can accept the default formats or change almost any aspect to customize it and make it more complex. In this section, you will learn to create simple charts from within PowerPoint. It is assumed that you are familiar with the major chart types summarized in Figure 2.37.

Figure 2.37 | **Commonly Used Chart Types**

Chart Type	Description
Column Chart	This is the default chart type in PowerPoint. Columns are vertical bars that display the values of one or more items. They are used to compare values across items or the value of a single item over time.
Bar Chart	Bar charts are similar to column charts except that they represent values horizontally.
Line Chart	Line charts are used to represent values over a period of time. A line chart is different from a column chart in that values are connected together in a line to show trending.
Pie Chart	Pie charts illustrate the value of each item as a percentage of the total of all values.

The following example creates a chart that visually compares revenue in all four quarters of the year between three regions: East, West, and North. Based on the descriptions of the various chart types in Figure 2.37, a Column chart is a logical choice.

To create a new chart, select **Chart** from the **Insert** tab, or if you selected a Content slide layout, click on the **Chart** icon. You will see the **Create Chart** window. Select the chart type you wish to create, click on **OK**, and PowerPoint will walk you through the process of entering data and creating the chart. Figures 2.38 and 2.39 illustrate how to create a simple Column chart that compares three geographic regions.

Figure 2.38 | **Select a Chart**

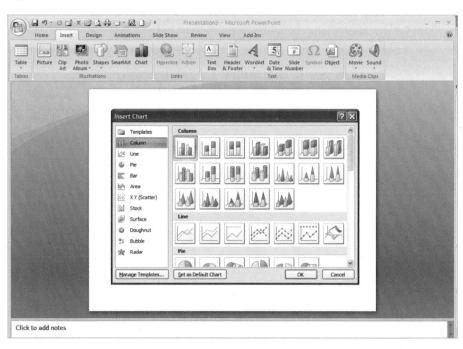

Figure 2.39 | **Enter and Chart the Data for a Column Chart**

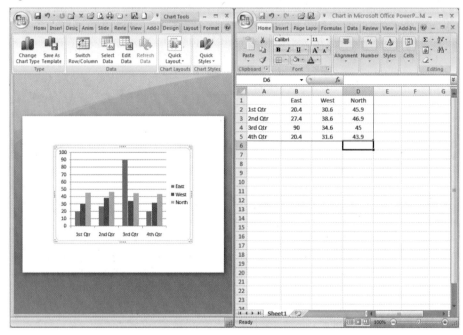

After you select the chart type, PowerPoint launches Excel as your data entry tool. Do not worry—you do not have to be an expert in Excel to use it to create a PowerPoint chart. While you are creating and modifying the chart, you will see PowerPoint and Excel side by side on your screen. Whenever you modify the data on the right side in Excel, you will see the resulting changes in the PowerPoint chart on the left.

Now let's say that you want to focus on the East region and examine its annual revenue more closely. If you want to see how the East region performed by quarter, you may want to use a pie chart. Figures 2.40 and 2.41 show how to select the chart type and enter the data.

Figure 2.40 | **Create a Pie Chart**

Figure 2.41 | **Enter and Chart the Data for a Pie Chart**

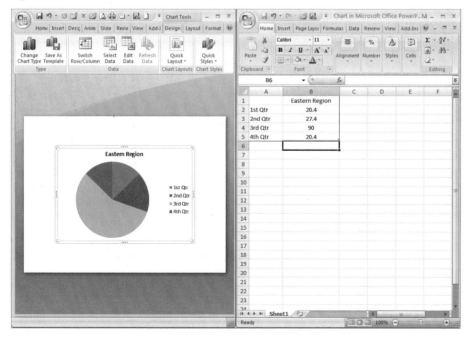

>> **Quick Reference**

Pasting Charts into PowerPoint

1. Activate a chart in an Excel file and click the **Copy** icon.

2. Open a PowerPoint file to a slide where the chart should appear.

3. Click the **Home** tab in the Ribbon.

4. Click the down arrow below the **Paste** icon.

5. Select the **Paste Special** option to open the **Paste Special** dialog box.

6. Select the **Picture (Enhanced Metafile)** option and click the **OK** button in the **Paste Special** dialog box.

7. Adjust the size of the chart by clicking and dragging the sizing handles as needed.

SmartArt

Creating designer-quality graphics and diagrams can be time consuming and challenging, especially if you do not have a background or training in graphic design. SmartArt is a pre-built library of high-end graphics (that comes with PowerPoint) that allows you to convey your ideas visually using extremely professional graphics.

SmartArt layouts are organized into seven categories. Here is a list of those categories and an example of where you would use each layout:

1. *List*: used to show nonsequential information
2. *Process*: used to show steps or a timeline
3. *Cycle*: used to show a continual process
4. *Hierarchy*: used to create an organizational chartor a decision tree
5. *Relationship*: used to show connections
6. *Matrix*: used to show how parts relate to a whole
7. *Pyramid*: used to show proportional relationships with the largest component on the top or bottom

As with many PowerPoint features, the options can be overwhelming and SmartArt is no exception. The most effective way to use SmartArt in your presentations is to first determine what message you are trying to convey to the audience. Then choose a **SmartArt** layout. If it does not look quite right, do not worry. You can switch between layouts and the text will carry over, thereby avoiding rework. Figure 2.42 illustrates how easy it is to get started with SmartArt.

Figure 2.42 | **Launch SmartArt from the Insert Tab**

You are immediately presented with the categories of layouts. As you can see, this is a lengthy list. That is why it makes sense to think about what you are trying to accomplish beforehand to narrow your choices down.

Figure 2.43 | **SmartArt Categories**

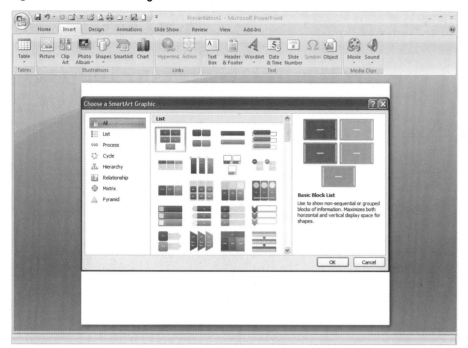

In this example, you have been asked to present an overview of your company's Six Sigma quality initiative to a group of business managers and would like to create a professional diagram.

Six Sigma is a disciplined quality improvement program. It uses a structured methodology to identify defects and systematically eliminates those defects, thereby allowing the organization to deliver its products and/or services at higher levels of quality.

The Six Sigma methodology uses the following repeatable process. With every iteration, additional defects are identified and eliminated.

- *Define*: Formally define the quality goals of the organization.
- *Measure*: Establish the baseline quality measurements.
- *Analyze*: Identify and verify causes of defects and the relationship between those causes.
- *Improve*: Make existing process(es) better based upon the analysis.
- *Control*: Transition to new process(es) continue to measure.

Which SmartArt graphic is an appropriate choice? The methodology is repeatable, so a graphic from the Cycle category would be appropriate. Figure 2.44 shows how you are prompted to enter the text for the diagram.

Figure 2.44 | **Blank SmartArt Diagram**

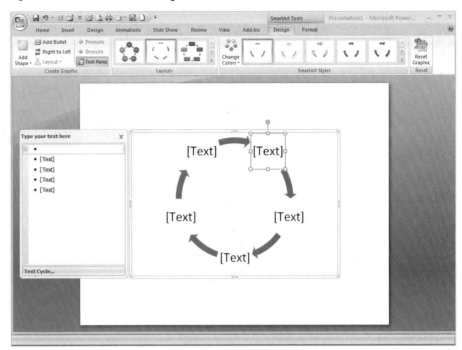

Figure 2.45 shows how the diagram is automatically filled in as you type in the content.

Figure 2.45 | **SmartArt Cycle Diagram**

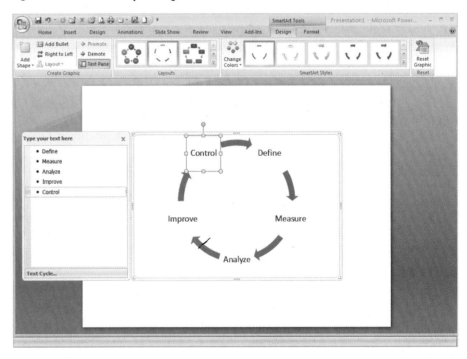

Let's say that you would like to add the definitions of each phase in the process and change the look of the diagram. With SmartArt, you can switch to another layout and retain the text that you already typed in as shown in Figures 2.46 and 2.47.

Right click on the diagram to change the layout or switch to another type of diagram.

Figure 2.46 | **Switch to Another SmartArt Diagram**

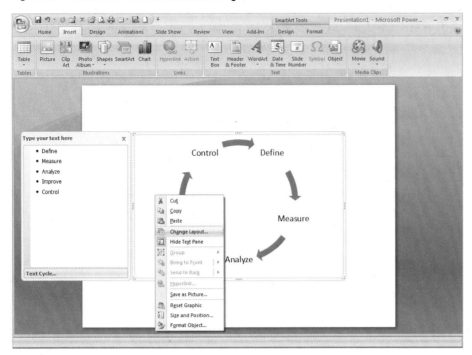

By creating a sub-bullet and typing in additional text in the text box, the diagram now looks different and has more detail.

Figure 2.47 | **Final SmartArt Diagram**

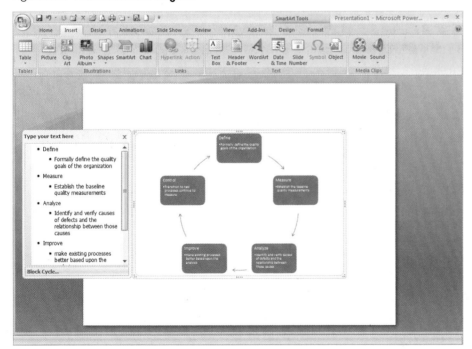

Graphics, Audio, and Video

With the business world becoming increasingly digital, it is now possible to present information electronically where it was not possible before. This section will briefly discuss how to include objects such as graphics, audio, and video into your presentation. All of these features are available from the **Insert** tab.

A few words of caution are due here:

- Remember that the best presentations are usually simple and straightforward. Cluttering your slides up with all sorts of graphics and digital media will overload your audience and detract from your effectiveness. As you have heard before in this text: "Just because you can, doesn't mean you should."

- In this day and age of easy access to digital information, be sure that you are not violating any copyright or intellectual property laws by downloading objects from the Internet and using them in your presentations. You must gain written permission from the creator of the object and acknowledge the source of information in your presentation.

Graphics: Clip Art and Pictures

Two common sources of graphics are your PowerPoint Clip Art library and image files. When PowerPoint is installed on your PC, you get a small library of images called clip art. As you become more proficient in PowerPoint, you can download additional images into your library.

There are two ways to search for and insert clip art into your presentation: (1) from the **Insert** tab or (2) by selecting the **Clip Art** icon from the **Content** icon. As shown in Figure 2.48, type in a keyword that describes the image you are looking for and PowerPoint will search your clip art library and look for matches. Select the one that meets your needs and select **Insert** or drag it into your slide.

Figure 2.48 | **Select Clip Art**

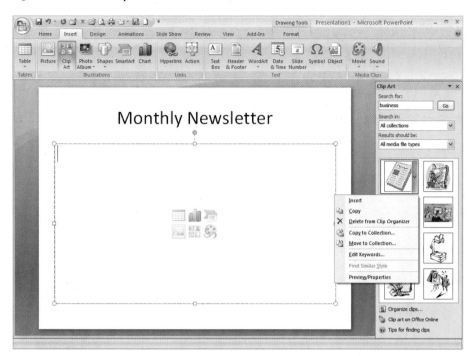

Once the image is on your slide, you can move it to any location you wish. In Figure 2.49, the image is in the upper right hand corner and is part of the slide title.

Figure 2.49 | **Clip Art on a Slide**

If you do not find any clips in your personal library, Office Online offers a vast selection of images that you can copy and paste into your presentation.

>> *Quick Reference*

Insert a Clip into PowerPoint

1. From the **Insert** tab or **Content** icon, select **Clip**.
2. In the **Search** task pane, in the **Search for** box, type a word or phrase that describes the clip you want.
3. Click **Go**.
4. Choose the clip and either drag it into the slide or place it on the slide by using **Insert** on the drop down box.

Inserting a picture into a slide uses a very similar approach as inserting clip art. From the **Insert** tab or from the **Content** icon, select **Insert Picture from File** as shown in Figure 2.50.

Figure 2.50 | **Insert Picture from File**

From the dialog box (Figure 2.51), navigate to the folder where the picture resides. Pictures can be in several formats. The most common formats are:

- JPEG File Interchange format: .jpg
- Portable Network Graphics: .png
- Tag Image File Format: .tif
- Graphics Interchange Format: .gif

Figure 2.51 | **Insert Picture Dialog Box**

Select the file that contains the picture; similar to clip art, you can drag the picture and place it anywhere on the slide. See Figure 2.52.

Figure 2.52 | **Picture on a Slide**

Audio and Video

Inserting audio and video into a PowerPoint slide is also straightforward. From the **Media Clips** group under the **Insert** tab, select **Movie or Sound**. A dialog box similar to the one you saw for **Insert Picture from File** will prompt you to supply the file name. Once you do, a sound or movie icon will appear.

Common video file formats are:

- Windows Media: .asf
- Windows video file: .avi
- Movie file: .mpeg (this is widely used)
- Windows Media Video file: .wmv

Common audio file formats are:

- AIFF audio file: .aiff
- AU audio file: .au
- MIDI file: .midi
- MP3 audio file: .mp3
- Windows audio file: .wav (this is widely used)
- Windows Media Audio file: .wma

You will need to have the appropriate hardware and software installed on your PC to actually run the audio and video clips. In business, organizations typically load the software onto each PC they provide for their employees. Since there are many formats, be sure to check with your system administrator.

≫ Presenting Qualitative and Quantitative Information and Objects

The purpose of this workshop is to demonstrate the commonly used objects and shapes used to present qualitative and quantitative information. We will be creating and inserting charts, tables, and diagrams created from shapes into slides. You will see these tasks demonstrated in the following five videos: **Presenting Qualitative Information**, **Presenting Quantitative Information**, **Using SmartArt**, **Adding Graphics**, and **Adding Sound**. After completing each section of tasks, watch the related video in parentheses. Remember to try the tasks on your own first before watching the videos.

1. **Presenting Quantitative Information (Video: Presenting Quantitative Information)**

   a. Launch PowerPoint and open a blank presentation.

   b. Save it as **ib_p02_part3_video_ws**.

   c. Insert a new slide with the Title and 2-Content layout and name it **Charts and Tables**. For the following steps, leave the PowerPoint default settings:

   > **i.** Create a table that looks like this:

	2005	2006
Revenue (millions)	11	16
Margin (percent)	7.8	4.9

   > **ii.** Create a column chart using the preceding table information.

   d. Insert a new slide with the Title and 2 Content layout and name it **More Charts**.

   > **i.** Create a line chart with the following revenue numbers (in millions): **2004 – 7.4, 2005 – 11, 2006 – 16, 2007 – 20.2**. Click on the legend and delete it.

   e. Save your work and close the file.

2. **Presenting Qualitative Information (Video: Presenting Qualitative Information)**

   a. Launch PowerPoint and open a blank presentation.

   b. Change the default slide layout to Title and Text and title the slide **Shapes and Lines**. For the following steps, leave the PowerPoint default colors and lines:

   > **i.** After the first bullet, type **Annual Employee Performance Review**

   > **ii.** Draw two rectangles, once below the other, and add the text **Self-Review** and **Peer Review** to each of the shapes.

   > **iii.** Using connectors, draw lines that result in the two rectangles converging into an oval entitled **Performance Review:**

    iv. Draw a rectangle to the right of the oval and title it **Review with Manager**.

    v. Draw a circle and label it **Merit Increase.**

  b. Insert a new slide with the Title Only layout and name it **Shapes and Connectors**. For the following steps, leave the PowerPoint default colors and lines:

    i. Connect a trapezoid, right triangle, and hexagon with an arrow and a line (you choose where the line and arrow go).

    ii. Draw a picture illustrating how two documents that are created at the same time are stored on a disk drive.

    iii. Draw a picture of three houses on a curved street; don't forget their front doors.

3. SmartArt (Video: Using SmartArt)

  a. Open a blank presentation and name it **ib_p02_proposedorganization**.

  b. Change the slide layout to Title and Content.

  c. Label the slide title **Proposed Organization Chart**.

  d. Choose a Hierarchy SmartArt category and create an organization chart that reflects the following corporate structure:

    i. CEO and Chairman heads up the organization.

    ii. The CFO and COO report to the CEO.

    iii. The VP of Technology and Director of Accounting report to the CFO.

    iv. The VP of Human Resources reports to the COO.

  e. Save your work and close the file.

4. Graphics (Video: Adding Graphics)

  a. Open the presentation named **ib_p02_proposedorganization** that you created in Step 3.

  b. Find an image that says "Confidential" in your clip art library or on Office Offline and place it in a noticeable position on the slide.

  c. Next to the organization chart box that says CEO, insert the picture of the executive named ib_p02_execpicture.

5. Audio (Video: Adding Sound)

  a. Open the file named ib_p02_monthlynewsletter.

  b. Add a bullet between the first and second that says **Industry reports say that the average income is increased by 45% with a Series 7 license**.

  c. Insert the cash register ring sound file right after the bullet.

≫ Presenting Qualitative and Quantitative Information

There are two major reasons why you need to know how to present qualitative and quantitative information using tables, charts, and diagrams. First, our society is visually oriented; more and more people have this learning style. Second, as you move up in an organization and/or you present information to higher levels of business professionals, using visuals will be the best way to present larger amounts of increasingly complex information in a short period of time.

Exercise

In a real business situation, you will have to make a judgment call as to whether information should be presented as text or a visual. In this exercise, you will be directed to convert information that is in text form to a table, chart, or diagram so that you become more comfortable with these skill sets.

1. Open the file named ib_p02_part2acadiamfg and rename it as **ib_p02_part3acadiamfg**.

2. On the "Background" slide, insert a column chart that represents the Revenue and Headcount information that is expressed in the text.
    a. Change the slide layout.
    b. Notice what happens to the font and the chart legend.
    c. Abbreviate the words if you need to.

3. Create a table in the "Estimated Cost Savings for Other Divisions" slide.

4. Change the written "Recommendations" to a flow diagram using shapes and condense the text.

5. Find a slide that lists the steps in a process and use SmartArt to illustrate those steps.

6. Save your work and close the file.

>> What's Wrong with This Presentation?

Problem

As an acquisition specialist, you analyze companies for potential clients to purchase and make buy/no buy recommendations. If the client goes with one of your recommendations, your firm is chosen to broker the sale and receives a percentage of the purchase price as its commission. These fees can add up to millions of dollars; therefore, the competition in your field is intense.

One of ways you assess the financial health of a company is by analyzing and comparing financial statements and ratios. A potential client is coming to town next week and visiting your companies. You have a short meeting set up in which you will present three acquisition recommendations to her and convince her to choose your firm to handle the deal. The department financial analyst extracted all the pertinent information from detailed financial statements and calculated the ratios. He drafted a few slides for you to review.

Exercise

Open the file named ib_p02_whatswrong3 and consider the following points:

1. Has the analyst used an appropriate approach for presenting this information?

2. What's wrong with the visuals that he used?

3. Is there such a thing as "Death by Charts"?

4. Will this presentation as it looks right now help you gain the client's business?

5. What changes would you make?

Write a short answer for each of the points above. Then, make any adjustments or corrections that will improve the effectiveness of this presentation.

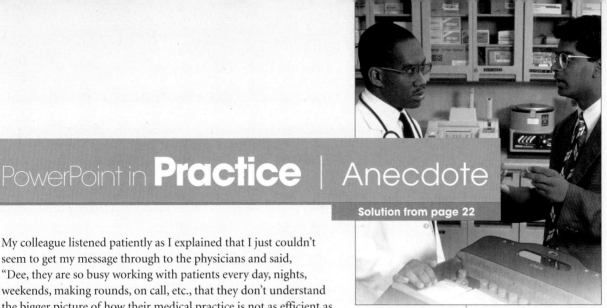

My colleague listened patiently as I explained that I just couldn't seem to get my message through to the physicians and said, "Dee, they are so busy working with patients every day, nights, weekends, making rounds, on call, etc., that they don't understand the bigger picture of how their medical practice is not as efficient as it could be."

My colleague went on to explain that she extracted the key information from our marketing literature and created two time-study diagrams on a single PowerPoint slide that illustrated how long it took to be reimbursed from insurance companies using the 39¢ method versus electronically filing claims once or twice a day. The visual impact of the "Before" and "After" diagrams was amazing. In some cases, the medical office was reimbursed in 157 days when using the old way and in 4 days when using electronically filed claims. My colleague mailed, faxed, and e-mailed these one-page slides with a short and professional cover letter and was getting more phone calls than she could handle.

Assignment

Using the skills you learned in this chapter, do the following:

1. Create a table that compares the "Days to Reimbursement" using the manual method of claims submission and the electronic method.

2. Diagram a sample "Before" and "After" process that depicts the steps in the manual method versus the electronic method.

   a. Manual method: The claim is mailed using the United States Postal Service, takes 5–7 days to arrive at the insurance company, sits in the insurance company mailroom for 3–5 days, is sent to data entry, and is entered by hand. If the claim is correct, it is processed and a check is mailed within 10–15 days to the physician's office.

   b. Electronic method: Claims are sent electronically every night, directly input into the insurance company computer, and processed. A wire transfer for the reimbursement is sent within 3–5 business days to the physician's bank.

Questions for Discussion

1. What slide layouts do you think were used for the time-study slide?

2. Are time-study diagrams an example of qualitative or quantitative information? Or both?

3. Can you think of a non-sales example in which this technique would be effective?

4. What are the limitations of SmartArt?

The following questions are related to the concepts addressed in this chapter. There are three types of questions: Short Answer, True or False, and Fill in the Blank. If your answer to a True or False question is False, write a short explanation as to why you think the statement is not true.

1. _____ refers to the look and feel, color, images, and graphics that form the background for each slide.

2. A _____ contains predetermined "placeholders" for information.

3. A _____ design is typically selected when you want to start simple and add a design or create your own design later.

4. Office Online is located on _____.

5. Text is defined as _____, _____, and _____.

6. Three types of content are _____, _____, _____.

7. True or False: You cannot mix text and content.

8. True or False: It is advisable to mix and match design templates within a single presentation.

9. Design templates on Office Online are rated by _____.

10. Three of the five major sections of a presentation are _____, _____, and _____.

11. The _____ tab displays the slides visually on the left side of the screen.

12. The default slide in which PowerPoint starts each presentation is the _____ slide.

13. What are the two ways to insert a new slide?

14. Outline tab is preferred is for _____.

15. When do numbered lists work better than bullets?

16. _____ is information that is descriptive and narrative.

17. _____ is information that is described using numbers.

18. The most commonly used graphics are _____, _____, _____, and _____.

19. A _____ keeps shapes joined together.

20. A _____ represents information in rows and columns.

21. True or False: Charts are used to present qualitative information.

22. The four most common chart types are _____, _____, _____, and _____.

23. True or False: Smart Art can be a huge productivity tool.

24. A widely used audio file type is _____.

25. Due to the easy access to digital information, be sure that you are not violating any _____ or _____ laws when you include graphics and other objects in your presentation.

>> Skills Exam

The following exam is designed to test your ability to recognize and execute the PowerPoint skills presented in this chapter. Read each question carefully and answer the questions in the order they are listed. You should be able to complete this exam in 60 minutes or less.

1. Open the PowerPoint file named ib_p02_skillsexam.
2. Select the Edge design template.
3. Add overview information about FedEx on the appropriate slide.
4. Use the following revenue numbers for steps 5–8:

    - **FedEx Corporation:**   **$11.2 million**
    - **FedEx Express:**   **$30.6 million**
    - **FedEx Ground:**   **$1.8 million**
    - **FedEx Kinkos:**   **$23.4 million**

5. Change the bulleted list on the "Service Units" slide to a numbered list and sequence the service units by revenue in ascending order.
6. Add a slide that lists HQ Location, CEO, and Revenue by the four Service Units in a table. Locate and include a geographic picture or clip art for each location.
7. Add a slide that shows the revenue of each Service Unit in a column chart.
8. Create a pie chart that compares the revenue contributions listed in step 4.
9. Go to the FedEx Kinko's Web site at http://fedex.kinkos.com/fpfk/index.php? and read through instructions titled "How to Get Started."

    - Draw a diagram using SmartArt that shows the steps involved in using FedEx Kinko's, starting with determining if you have the software.
    - Choose a SmartArt layout that allows you to title the step and include some detail below the title.

» Challenge Questions

The following questions are designed to test your ability to apply the PowerPoint skills you have learned to complete a business objective. Use your knowledge of PowerPoint as well as your creativity to answer these questions. For most questions, there are several possible ways to complete the objective.

PowerPoint offers several prebuilt features: themes, slide layouts, charts. But the tool does not provide prebuilt templates for business scenarios: marketing presentations, new employee orientation.

1. What would be the advantages and disadvantages of having prebuilt business-oriented templates?

2. In what situation(s) would you choose them?

3. What skills have you learned that would assist you in creating such a template?

4. What components or information would be constant from presentation to presentation?

5. What components or information would be different?

6. If you become experienced in creating PowerPoint presentations and develop your library of presentations, what is the advantage of using a prebuilt business template versus using and modifying one of your own?

>> Chapter 3

Enhancing Your Presentation

Chapter Goals

By now, you should know how to use PowerPoint to create a basic business presentation. This chapter builds on those skills by demonstrating advanced PowerPoint customizing and formatting techniques that will enable you to deliver highly polished presentations. By the end of this chapter, you will be proficient in using advanced formatting, sharing content between presentations, and reviewing your slides for accuracy. These techniques comprise the majority of PowerPoint skills you will use as a student and a business professional.

>> **PowerPoint** | **Skill Sets**

My Role as a Global Account Manager

"I went to graduate school to do this?" That was all I could think as I sat hunched over my laptop merging, editing, and cleaning up seven sets of PowerPoint slides on a Sunday afternoon.

As I advanced in my career, I began to manage increasingly more complex engagements for global clients. To complete a project or find a solution to a difficult problem, I often needed to engage subject matter experts who resided in different parts of the world. My job was to create the project plan, divide the work, and assign ownership to the appropriate specialist. The more complex the project, the larger and more spread out the team was. Due to time zone differences, much of the team interaction was done through e-mail. My colleagues did excellent work and created high-quality materials. But at the end of the day, I was the person responsible for pulling together all the information and creating the final deliverable, which was usually an executive presentation.

The good news: Due to our track record of very satisfied clients, the team was getting larger and more visible opportunities to work on. The bad news: I was spending more and more time on combining and cleaning up what everyone sent me (a necessary but not very exciting activity).

I began to realize that before long, the work effort involved in merging and editing the work of my growing team would become overwhelming. I needed to spend the majority of my time organizing the information and making sure we were meeting our clients' needs, not changing colors and fonts. If I didn't, the quality of the final presentation would suffer, and that was unacceptable. There had to be a better way.

>> Continued on page 112

>> Formatting Your Slides

Using prebuilt PowerPoint themes is a good strategy because they are professionally done and save you the time of having to create your own. However, as you become more proficient in PowerPoint or advance in your career, you will likely use a theme as your starting point and then customize it using many of the advanced formatting options you will learn in this chapter.

The decision to customize your business presentation is a judgment call you have to make. There are no hard and fast rules either way. At the beginning of your career, you will probably make simple presentations, and using a prebuilt theme as-is will serve your needs. However, as you gain experience in PowerPoint, work with sophisticated audiences, or deliver high-impact presentations, you will need to add a few customizations. Following are two examples when this might occur:

- When you want to create a presentation that reinforces your marketing brand or identity. When consultants give presentations, every PowerPoint slide contains their firm's logo. This technique is designed to create an automatic "top of mind" association between the topic and the firm. For example, when you think PCs, you think Dell. When you think public accounting, you think Pricewaterhouse Coopers.

- When you need to personalize the presentation for an audience and develop a bond with them. If your audience has a strategic initiative or campaign underway, you may want to include their slogan in your materials. For example, Six Sigma training instructors frequently include "Zero Defects" as a byline in their presentations to remind the audience why they are there. Infosys, a global outsourcer, uses its slogan "Powered by intellect, Driven by values" to instill trust and confidence.

Before we start, a word of caution is due here. PowerPoint offers a seemingly endless array of formatting options. Presentations are not a venue for businesspeople to unleash their repressed artistic desires. Unfortunately, many people do just that. Consequently, their presentations come across as amateurish, and they lose a valuable opportunity to make a connection with or impact on the audience.

Unless you have training or experience in graphic design, or a very good sense of visual aesthetics, use these formatting guidelines:

- Be conservative.
- Be consistent.
- Be minimal (remember, less is better).
- Focus on how the audience will react (it's about them, not you).

There are no predetermined formulas for creating a perfect presentation. The objective of this chapter is to teach you the most commonly used formatting options and practical guidelines around how and when to use them so that you can quickly become expert.

This section will cover the **Clipboard**, **Font**, **Paragraph**, and **WordArt** groups. As shown in Figure 3.1, when you open a new or existing presentation, the following groups are presented on the **Home** tab (the default tab).

- **Clipboard**: This group contains the **Cut**, **Copy**, and **Paste** icons.
- **Font**: These formatting options are applied to text (words, phrases, sentences).
- **Paragraph**: These formatting options are applied to groups or sections of text.

   Word Art is found on the **Insert** tab:
   - **WordArt**: These formatting options allow you to insert text that is formatted as pictures.

Figure 3.1 | **Formatting-Related Groups on the Home and Insert Tabs**

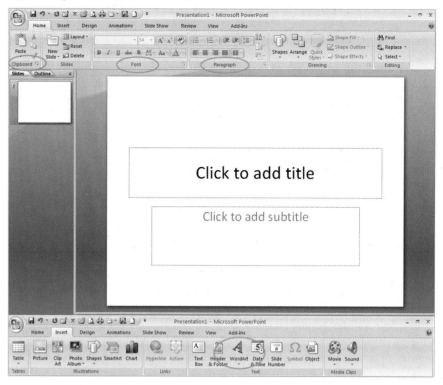

Clipboard Options

The *Cut, Copy,* and *Paste* commands are among the most convenient and commonly used PowerPoint commands. These commands save time when you need to delete, move, or duplicate information on your slides. They are located on the *Clipboard group* under the **Home** tab. Think of the *Clipboard* as a temporary workspace where the information you cut or copied is placed to reuse however many times you would like. Figure 3.2 illustrates the **Cut, Copy,** and **Paste** icons on the **Clipboard** group.

Figure 3.2 | **Clipboard Group: Cut, Copy, and Paste Options**

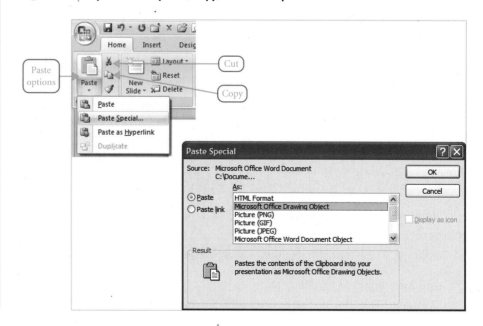

- **Cut:** Removes an object from the slide and places it on the Clipboard for later use. Instead of clicking on the icon, you can also highlight the object (text or graphics) and press **Ctrl + X**.

- **Copy:** Creates a duplicate of the object from the slide and places it on the Clipboard for later use. Instead of clicking on the icon, you can also highlight the object (text or graphics) and press **Ctrl + C**.

- **Paste:** Inserts an object from the Clipboard. Instead of clicking on the icon, you can also highlight the object (text or graphics) and press **Ctrl + V**. *Paste Special* is an extra option under **Paste** that allows you to insert objects and retain the attributes from the tool they were created in.

You would use **Cut**, **Copy**, and **Paste** when modifying, rearranging, or combining text or graphics from slide to slide. These commands can tremendously enhance your productivity because you do not have to delete or retype all the information.

Font Group

The *Font group* on the **Home** tab provides many text formatting options that you can use to make your slides look professional. The list of options may look overwhelming. It helps to remember that you don't have to use them all. As you gain experience in PowerPoint by developing many presentations and develop an "eye" for slide design over time, you will know which ones to use. Figure 3.3 illustrates the **Font** group and the icons that launch each option. Familiarize yourself with each icon and then continue reading to learn how each option works.

Figure 3.3 | **Font Group**

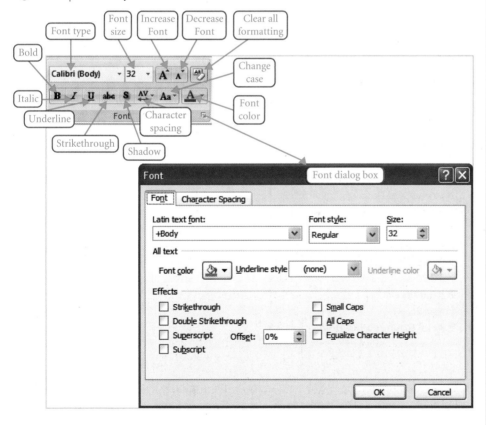

>> **Quick Reference**

Copy and Paste

1. Highlight the text, text box, or icon to be copied.
2. Click the **Copy** icon in the Ribbon.
3. Place the mouse pointer where the copied data should appear.
4. Click the **Paste** icon in the Ribbon.

As you can see, you can choose from many font styles, sizes, and options. So how do you know which ones are most appropriate for your business presentation? If you use a prebuilt theme, all those decisions are made for you. That is one major reason many presenters choose to use themes. Readability and overall look and feel are the key drivers behind changing the default font settings. The following descriptions and figures discuss each option shown on Figure 3.4, with suggestions and examples for when you change the default:

- *Font type*: A *font*, also referred to as a *type* or *typeface*, is a graphic design applied to all numerals, symbols, and alphabetic characters. Fonts fall into one of the following visual categories:
  - *Serif*: These fonts have little curls at the end of each letter. They are used mainly for lengthy documents, such as business reports and white papers.
    - Examples of serif fonts and what they look like: Times New Roman, Garamond, Century Schoolbook, and Book Antiqua.
  - *Sans serif*: These fonts have straight letters. They are crisp and more defined, and they are used in situations in which there is not too much text (titles, phrases, short pieces of text) and where the content needs to be read from a distance. As such, sans-serif fonts are recommended for all text within a PowerPoint presentation.
    - Examples of sans-serif fonts and what they look like: Arial, Tahoma, and Verdana. (see Figure 3.4)

Figure 3.4 | **Font Types**

>> *Quick Reference*

Which Font Should You Use?

1. Serif: Used for documents and situations in which there is a lot of text. Examples are Times New Roman, Garamond, Century Schoolbook, and Book Antiqua.
2. Sans serif: Used to convey short bursts of information, such as presentations. Examples are Arial, Tahoma, and Verdana.

>> *Quick Reference*

How to Select Fonts

1. Highlight the text you wish to change.
2. From the **Font type** drop-down menu, select the new font.
3. The highlighted text font will be changed.

As you develop your presentation, you will most likely need to alter the font size. Headings, for example, lend themselves to larger-sized fonts, while the caption beneath a figure would use a smaller size. Font sizes are determined using points, as shown in Figure 3.5.

To increase or decrease the font sizes in your presentation, use the preset scale of font sizes. Select the text you wish to increase or decrease in size, and each time you click the button, you will either move up or down the size scale.

Figure 3.5 | **Font Sizes and Examples**

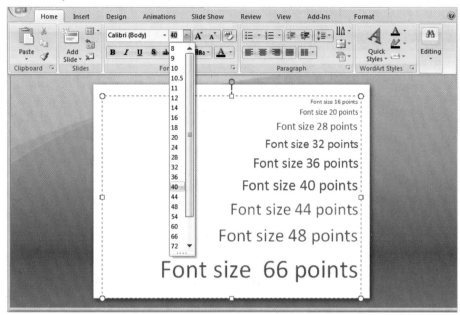

In addition to changing the size of your font, you may perform additional advanced formatting techniques found on the **Font** group. For example, you can choose the following:

- **Clear all formatting**: When you select the text and click on this icon, you will revert back to the PowerPoint default format settings. The default font type in PowerPoint is Calibri. This feature is helpful when you've experimented with different formats and decide to go back to the defaults provided by the template.

- **Bold**: This feature darkens and thickens the selected text. **This is an example of bold.** Select the text you wish to bold and click on the icon. Instead of clicking on the icon, you can also press **Ctrl + B.**

- **Italic**: Italic is a type style in which the characters slant slightly. *This is an example of italics.* Select the text you wish to italicize and click on the icon. Instead of clicking on the icon, you can also press **Ctrl + I.**

- **Underline**: This feature draws a line under the selected text. <u>**This is an example of underlining**</u>. Select the text you wish to underline and click on the icon. Instead of clicking on the icon, you can also press **Ctrl + U.**

  Bold, italic, and underlining are used to draw attention to a specific part of a presentation. The rule of thumb is to use these effects sparingly in a presentation; otherwise, they can cause visual overload and confuse the audience.

- **Text Shadow**: This icon adds a shadow behind the selected text to help it stand out on the slide. When the contrast between the font color and the background color hampers readability, a shadow effect on the text will sharpen the edges and create a better contrast between the text and background. You should use text shadows only to create such contrast where the shadow color is darker than the background.

- **Strikethrough**: This icon draws a line through the middle of the selected text. You would use this feature to draw attention to text that you have purposely deleted and replaced.

- **Character spacing:** This icon allows you to adjust the spacing between characters. You might wish to change character spacing to increase readability. This feature is used for audiences who are far away from the screen. Figure 3.6 lists the options. The default selection is **Normal.**

Figure 3.6 | **Character Spacing**

- **Change case:** This icon allows you to change the selected text to all UPPERCASE, all lowercase, or other common capitalizations. Figure 3.7 lists the options. The default selection is **Sentence case,** which capitalizes the first letter in the sentence and leaves the rest as lowercase. **Capitalize each Word** is used for titles.

Figure 3.7 | **Change Case**

- *Font color:* This feature provides a palette of colors to choose from. Similar to the use of **bold,** *italic,* and underlining options, the rule of thumb with font color is to use it for visual effect and to use it sparingly. Figure 3.8 shows the color palette.

Figure 3.8 | **Font Colors**

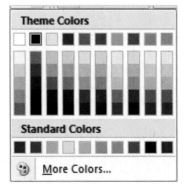

Figure 3.9 provides a few examples of what text looks like when you apply selected formats.

Figure 3.9 | **Font Format Examples**

```
Plain text
Shadowed text
Text with strikeout
Text with tight spacing
Text With Each Word Capitalized
Combining bold, italics, underlining, shadow, and loose
spacing
```

- *Font dialog box:* Instead of clicking on individual icons, you can use this dialog box to apply multiple formats to selected text from one screen.

  You can combine, mix, and match many of the formatting options to suit your needs. But remember: Just because you can doesn't mean you should.

COMMON MISTAKES | Using the Wrong Font

Resist the urge to use a pretty, intricate, or heavy font, such as Comic Sans, Script, or Calligrapher. These fonts may look interesting as you create your presentation, but bear in mind how readable they are from the audience's perspective. Studies have shown that sans-serif fonts are more effective for presentations and result in a higher rate of audience comprehension than serif fonts.

COMMON MISTAKES | Selecting the Wrong Font Size

People think that large font sizes increase readability, but this is not always the case. Large font sizes, such as 40 points or greater, are meant to be used for titles. If they are used in the body of the slide, the text can look awkward and overpower the page. In fact, smaller point sizes can be used with sans-serif fonts because the edges are sharp and crisp. To be absolutely sure what font size to use, find out what the presentation logistics are; that is, what size screen you will have, how many rows of people will be in the audience, and what are the measurements of the audience seating area? If possible, visit the room where you will present and use the Print Preview feature (discussed in this chapter) to gauge the correct font size.

Paragraph Group

While the **Font** group allows you to format individual words or headings in your presentation, the *Paragraph group* (see Figure 3.10) provides many formatting options that are most commonly used to organize multiple lines or *paragraphs* of information. For example, bullets, numbering, and line alignment are all found on the **Paragraph** group. Figure 3.10 illustrates the **Paragraph** group and the icons that launch each option. In this section, you will learn how the formatting techniques available through the **Paragraph** group will help enhance your presentation by organizing large amounts of information in a readable manner.

>> *Quick Reference*

Formatting Data

1. Highlight the text to be formatted.
2. Click the **Home** tab of the Ribbon.
3. Click one of the icons in the **Font** group of the Ribbon or open the **Font** dialog box by clicking the button in the lower-right corner of the **Font** group.
4. If using the **Font** dialog box, click the **OK** button after making a selection.

>> *Quick Reference*

How to Change the Font in the Entire Presentation

1. On the **Home** tab, select **Replace Fonts** from the **Editing** group.
2. When you see the options to change the font type across the entire presentation, make changes as desired.

Figure 3.10 | **Paragraph Group**

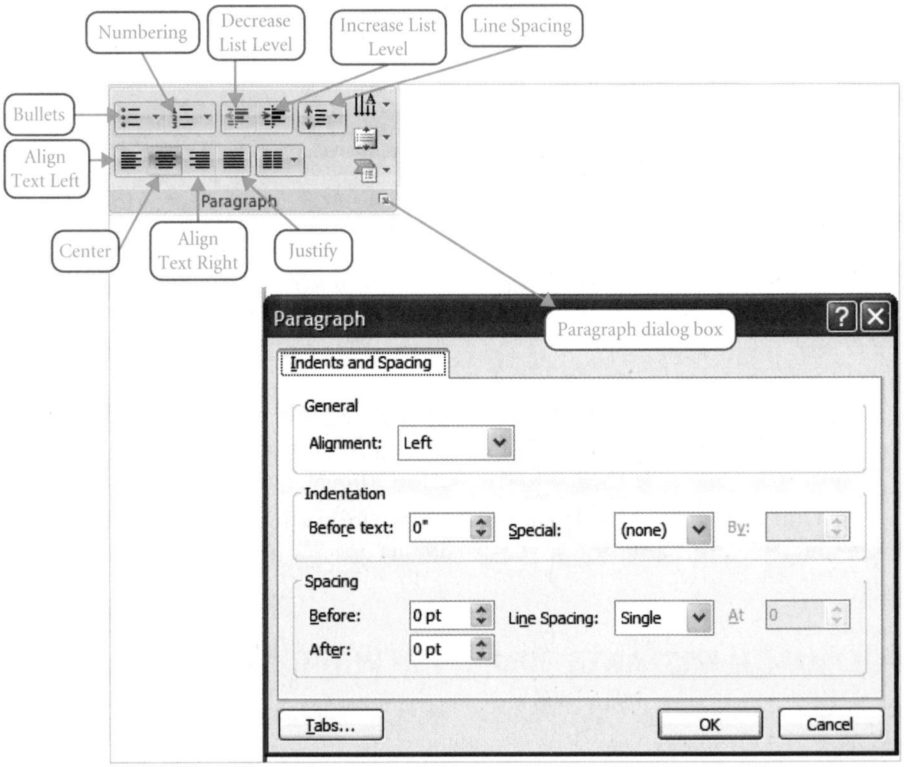

Design templates usually include bulleted lists but not other paragraph formatting options. Here is an explanation of additional and commonly used paragraph options from Figure 3.10:

- **Bullets:** This icon creates a bulleted list of the text you select. Click the arrow to choose different bullet styles.

- **Numbering:** This icon starts a numbered list from the text you select. Click the arrow to choose different numbered formats.

- **Decrease and Increase List Level:** These icons decrease or increase the indentation of bulleted or numbered lists.

- **Line Spacing:** This icon allows you to select a different line spacing value than the default value of **Single** (see Figure 3.11).

FIGURE 3.11 | **Line Spacing Options**

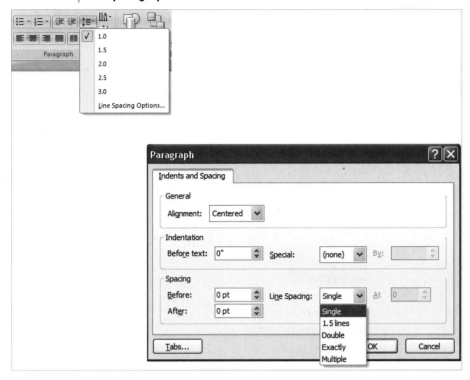

- *Align Text Left*: This icon aligns text and objects to the left edge of the placeholder box. This alignment is usually used with text and paragraphs. Instead of clicking on the icon, you can also press **Ctrl + L**.

- *Center*: This icon places text and objects in the middle of the placeholder box. This alignment is used mainly for headings and titles. Instead of clicking on the icon, you can also press **Ctrl + E**.

- *Align Text Right*: This icon aligns text and objects to the right edge of the place-holder box. Labels commonly use this alignment. Instead of clicking on the icon, you can also press **Ctrl + R**.

- *Justify*: This icon aligns text to both the left and right edges of the placeholder box, adding extra spaces where needed to create the effect.

- Figure 3.12 shows examples of different alignments.

FIGURE 3.12 | **Alignment Examples**

> Left alignment is usually used with text and paragraphs.
>
> Right alignment is commonly used with labels.
>
> Center alignment is used for headings and titles.
>
> The "Justify" alignment creates a clean look along the left and right edge of the placeholder box. Notice where extra spaces have been added in.

- *Paragraph dialog box*: Instead of clicking on individual icons, you can use this dialog box to apply multiple formats to selected text from one screen.

So far, you have learned how to apply formatting by highlighting text and choosing options from the Ribbon. There is another way to format text, called *contextual formatting*.

- Place your mouse pointer where you wish to format text or any other object and right click. PowerPoint will display the formatting options that are appropriate for the object you have chosen. This is known as contextual formatting and is shown in Figure 3.13.

Figure 3.13 | **Contextual Formatting**

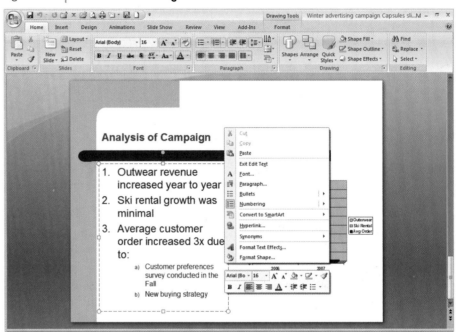

WordArt

WordArt allows to you to apply a colorful, artistic, and graphical look to plain text. WordArt is used for headings or other short phrases (for example, slogans and bylines) that you wish to call attention to in your presentation.

There are two ways to use WordArt:

- From the **Insert** tab, select a WordArt style. PowerPoint will automatically put a placeholder on your slide for you to begin typing your text and activate the **Format** tab (see Figure 3.14).

- Highlight the plain text and select **WordArt Styles** from the **Format** tab. Select the WordArt style; it is applied to all the text you highlighted. See Figure 3.15.

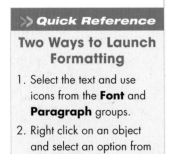

>> *Quick Reference*

Two Ways to Launch Formatting

1. Select the text and use icons from the **Font** and **Paragraph** groups.
2. Right click on an object and select an option from the context menu.

Figure 3.14 | **Add new WordArt**

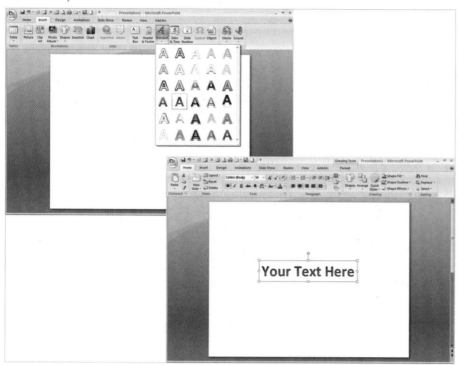

Figure 3.15 | **Convert plain text to WordArt**

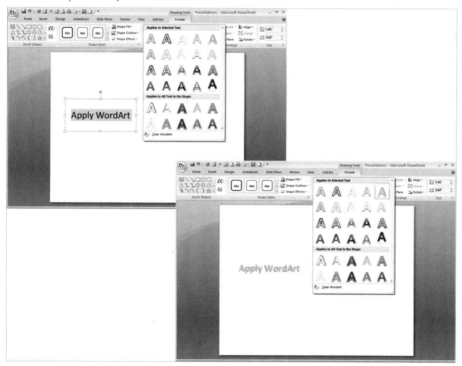

COMMON MISTAKES | Incorrect Use of WordArt

WordArt is used to accentuate headings, titles, or other phrases that require a colorful flair. A common mistake and inappropriate use of WordArt is to use it in the body of the slides because it looks out of context and causes visual overload.

Modifying Slide Masters

When you create a new presentation, PowerPoint automatically presents you with a default Title slide. You can change the default to a theme that has the color scheme and look and feel that is appropriate for your presentation. When you add new slides by selecting New Slide from the **Home** tab, you need to choose the layout from the collection of layouts that belong to that theme. A *layout* is the arrangement of elements (such as title and subtitle text, lists, pictures, tables, charts, shapes, and movies) on a slide.

Figure 3.16 shows two different layouts. Note the elements, location, and size on each layout.

Figure 3.16 | **PowerPoint layouts**

What determines the location, font type and size, color, and so on of these elements? The *slide master* determines all this. For each layout, the slide master is a slide that stores information about the layout and theme, including font styles, *placeholder* sizes and positions, background design, and color schemes.

The slide master controls the overall formatting and object placement for the presentation: font type, size, color, background color, graphics, and so on. If you want to change the look of your presentation, you can make the change(s) on the slide master. Those changes are then reflected on every slide. Some business situations in which you would change slide masters are the following:

- Using your company's or your client's colors for the font (examples: IBM blue, Coca-Cola red)
- Inserting your company's or your client's logo to personalize the presentation
- Placing a "byline" or motto on a slide (example: "This information supplied with permission from the XYZ Company")
- Inserting page numbers for table presentations

The examples given previously are simple changes to the slide master. Examples of more complicated and intrusive changes are these:

- Changing locations of placeholders
- Changing font types, sizes, and colors
- Changing bullet types and sizes

This section will demonstrate how to modify slide masters. You must have the slide layout you wish to modify in the Slide pane. As a working example, you will use a slide that uses the Comparison layout. Select **Slide Master** from the **View** tab to put the slide in slide master "mode," as shown in Figure 3.17.

Figure 3.17 | **Comparison slide layout**

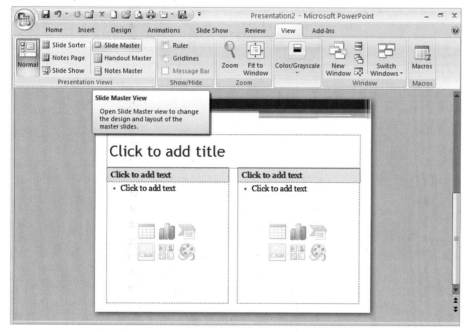

This is what the slide master looks like for the Comparison layout (see Figure 3.18).

Figure 3.18 | **Comparison Slide in Slide Master Mode**

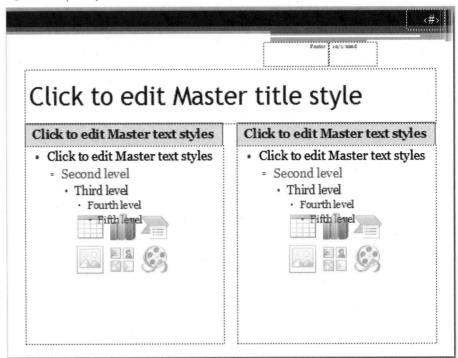

You can change any element by selecting it and using the formatting options on the **Home** tab as though you were working on a regular slide. In this layout, the major elements are a title, two subtitles, and five levels of bullets, and they all use different fonts. If you wish to change the color of the subtitles and make all the fonts the same as the title (Trebuchet MS), the new slide master would look as shown in Figure 3.19.

Figure 3.19 | **Changing the Slide Master**

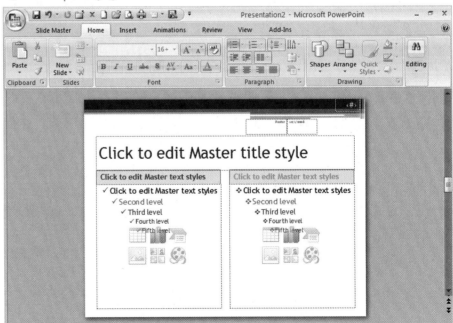

Once you have finished making changes to the slide master, select **Normal** from the **View** tab, as shown in Figure 3.20.

Figure 3.20 | **Select Normal View**

Now any slide that uses the Comparison layout (either existing slides or new ones that you insert) will reflect all the changes you made to the master. Figure 3.21 shows the original slide that now has all the formatting changes. Notice how all the text uses the Trebuchet MS font, the subtitles are different colors, and the bullets are different.

Figure 3.21 | **Slide after Applying Changes to the Slide Master**

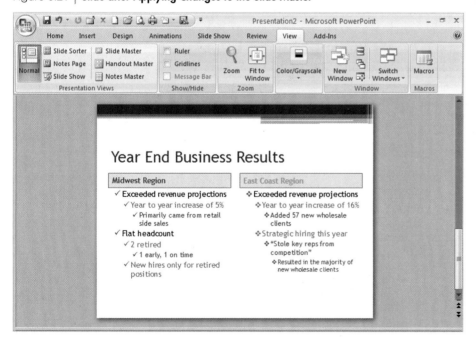

You can also move, delete, and modify placeholders. To move a placeholder, select it and hold the left mouse button down while you drag the placeholder to the new location. To delete a placeholder, select it and either use the **Delete** key on your keyboard or the **Cut** icon from the Clipboard. To modify the font type or size of a placeholder, use the same instructions you learned earlier in this chapter.

In the Comparison layout, note the location of the page number, the footer, and the date. If you would like to move the footer to the bottom center, delete the date, and place the page number at the bottom-right corner, you would go into the slide master and make those changes as though you were working with a regular slide. Figures 3.22 and 3.23 show the "before" and "after" views.

Figure 3.22 | **Slide Master Before Moving the Placeholders**

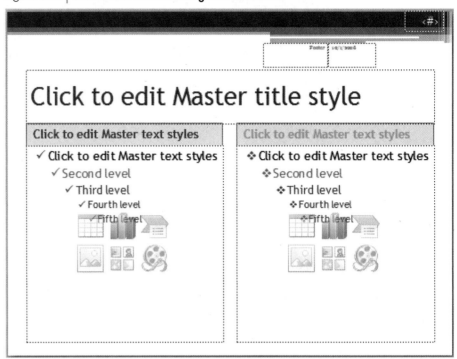

Figure 3.23 | **After Moving and Deleting the Placeholders**

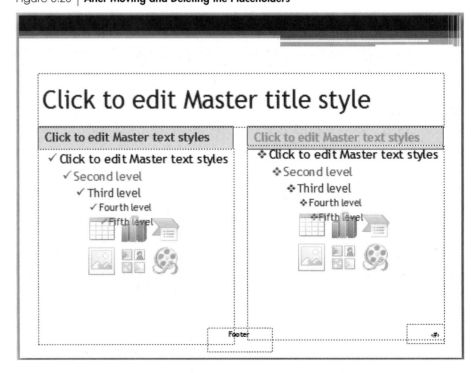

You can also insert graphics, pictures, or other icons. Go into the slide master, insert a picture from the **Insert** tab and drag the object to where you want it placed on every slide. In business presentations, icons are usually placed in the upper-right corner, bottom center, or bottom-right corner. See Figure 3.24.

Figure 3.24 | **Add a Picture to the Slide Master**

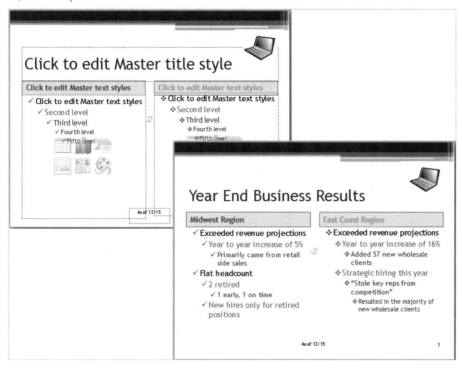

Note: You must modify the slide master for each type of layout used in your presentation.

COMMON MISTAKES | Forgetting to Modify Each Slide Layout Master

Many presenters end up with a disjointed-looking presentation because they forgot to modify the slide master for each type of slide layout used in the presentation. The best way to avoid this is to use the default slide masters and finish assembling your presentation. Then at the end, scroll through your presentation and make any changes to each slide master, slide by slide. This approach saves time and you will be sure to have touched each slide. The other benefit of waiting until the end is that when you actually have content on the slides, you will be able to see right away how the slide looks and make any necessary changes. You may find that not all slide master changes improve the look of your overall presentation.

To put information into a footer and turn page numbering "on," you must select options in the **Header & Footer** dialog box under the **Insert** tab, as shown in Figure 3.25. You can also use the **Header & Footer** dialog box to insert a date and time stamp on each slide. However, use good judgment to be sure that your slides are not getting too "cluttered."

Figure 3.25 | **Header & Footer options**

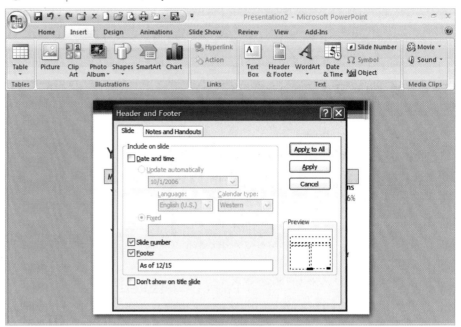

Select Apply to All and every slide in the presentation (existing and new) will now have that footer and a page number (see Figure 3.26). It is a good practice to select the "Don't show on title slide" box because title slides do not have page numbers or footers.

Figure 3.26 | **Footers and Page Numbers**

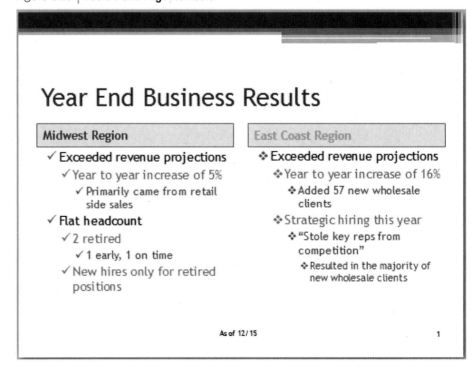

>> Formatting Your Slides

Next to actually creating the presentation, formatting is another area in which you will spend a significant amount of time. The purpose of this workshop is to demonstrate the advanced formatting features presented in this section of the chapter. You will see these skills demonstrated in the following four videos: **Cut, Copy and Paste**; **Font Group Formatting**; **Paragraph Group Formatting**; and **Modifying Slide Masters**. Open the file named ib_p03_formatting before starting this workshop. Try to complete these tasks on your own first before watching the videos.

1. **Cut, Copy and Paste (Video: Cut, Copy and Paste)**
   a. Go to slide 3 and select the fifth bullet item.
   b. Click the **Cut** icon in the **Home** tab of the Ribbon to delete this bullet.
   c. Go to slide 6 and place the cursor at the end of the fourth bullet and press **Enter.**
   d. Click the **Paste** icon in the **Home** tab of the Ribbon to insert "Relax and watch your retirement money grow!" as a new fifth bullet.
   e. Save the presentation.

2. **Font Group Formatting (Video: Font Group Formatting)**
   a. On slide 6 select the three sub-bullets under the second main bullet item.
   b. Use the **Font type** drop-down arrow on the **Home** tab of the Ribbon to change the font type to Calibri.
   c. Increase the font size to 22.
   d. Go to slide 5 and bold the contents of this slide.
   e. On slide 5 apply underlining to the heading title of each column.
   f. Apply the following formatting to the bullets on slide 6:
      i. Give each bullet item a loose character spacing.
      ii. Make the sub-bullet items under "Choose from the following funds" small caps and change their color to red.

3. **Paragraph Group Formatting (Video: Paragraph Group Formatting)**
   a. Go to slide 4 and select all the bullet items.
   b. Use the Numbering icon in the **Paragraph** group on the **Home** tab of the Ribbon to number the bullets.
   c. Go to slide 1 and select the title, then select a WordArt style from the **WordArt Styles** group on the **Format** tab to change the style of the title.
   d. Change the line spacing on slide 2 to 1.5.

4. Modifying Slide Masters (Video: Modifying Slide Masters)

  a. Use the **Header & Footer** dialog box under the **Insert** tab to make the following changes.

  b. Add a slide number to all the slides in the presentation, except the title slide.

  c. Add the footer "Chapter 3 Formatting Workshop" at the bottom to all slides, except the title slide.

  d. Save and close the file.

>> Formatting a Presentation for a Consulting Firm

Presenting information is a task that all business managers will eventually face in their careers. However, for managers working in consulting firms, presentations are a way of life. Consultants will typically conduct a significant amount of research to determine how their clients can improve and grow their business. This research can be a complete waste of time if it is not communicated to the client through an effective presentation. In fact, the professionalism and skills of consultants are often judged by how well they present their research and make recommendations to business executives. The formatting skills you learned in this section are essential for creating a high-quality, effective, and professional presentation. Unless you are presenting someone else's slides, you will always need to apply a variety of formatting techniques to achieve this goal.

Exercise

The purpose of this exercise is to apply formatting techniques to a number of PowerPoint slides that will be presented by the manager of consulting firm. Consulting firms typically use PowerPoint to present research and recommendations to their clients. You will be applying several formatting techniques to transform these slides into a professional presentation. Open the PowerPoint file named ib_p03_consultingpresentation before starting this exercise.

  1. The current font is not appropriate for a serious business presentation. Replace the font style to Calibri and the font color to black in the entire presentation.

  2. For emphasis, change the font style of any quotes in the presentation to italics.

  3. There is inconsistent use of bulleted lists and numbered lists, and numbered lists are used where there is no sequence of events.

   a. Make the lists on each slide bulleted, with the exception of the Recommendations slide.

   b. Convert the sub-bullets on the Recommendations slide to a numbered list.

  4. Change the bullet types so that they are consistent from slide to slide.

   a. Make the first-level and second-level bullets small circles.

  5. Apply the appropriate alignment to the paragraphs, text, and bulleted lists so that they are left aligned.

  6. Using the slide master, change the font size of each slide's title so that it is not truncated.

  7. Delete the title on the title page and replace it with black, shaded, block letter WordArt.

   a. Change the font size of the subtitle to two point sizes lower than the title.

Problem

You are working as an analyst for a large consulting firm. You are approached by a junior coworker on your team who is putting together several PowerPoint slides that will be presented to your clients executive officers next week. The purpose of this presentation is to communicate the research and recommendations you and your team have worked on over the past eight weeks. Tomorrow, you are doing a "dry run" of the presentation to the client sponsor first. Your coworker has just finished a draft of the presentation and asks you to check it over. He attaches an e-mail to the presentation with the following message:

This is what I have for our dry run presentation with your sponsor tomorrow— who, by the way, is a fraternity brother of mine from college. He's a good guy. I need to send a copy of this to our firm's communication director for final approval. I think it looks pretty good, but wanted another set of eyes to take a look at it. Thanks a lot!

Exercise

The presentation your coworker attached to the e-mail is named ib_p03_clientreview Would you be comfortable using these slides to present the team's research and recommendations to the executive officers of your firm's client? Would you even be comfortable using these slides to present to the project sponsor? Consider the following points:

1. Are the formatting techniques in these slides used effectively to guide the audience's attention to the most critical information?

2. Is the presentation appropriate for its intended audience(s)?

3. In your opinion, do these slides appear to be professional quality? Why or why not?

4. Are you comfortable sending these slides to the firm's director (your boss's boss) as a representation of your team's work?

What's wrong with this presentation? Write a short answer for each of the points listed here. Then apply any formatting techniques you think are necessary to produce an effective and professional presentation to your client's executive officers.

>> Sharing Content between Presentations

Skill Set

The ability to delete and rearrange slides after you create your presentation or share content between presentations can tremendously enhance your productivity. These skills will allow you to collaborate with team members easily, divide the work quickly, and then combine everyone's deliverables effectively. As you become more experienced in creating presentations, you will find yourself "borrowing" and reusing slides from your own personal library of presentations. In this section, you will first learn how to delete and rearrange slides; then you will learn how to merge presentations.

Slide Sorter View

A typical business scenario would be to create a small presentation from scratch and then expand it using slides from other presentations in your library or from other people. Up to this point, you have been working with PowerPoint in *Normal view*.

Figure 3.27 illustrates the Winter advertising campaign presentation displayed in **Normal** view. This is the main editing view, where you write and design your presentation. Recall the main working areas from Figure 1.1 in Chapter 1:

- **Outline** tab: Shows your slide text in outline form.

- **Slides** tab: Shows your slides as thumbnail-sized images while you edit. The thumbnails allow you to navigate through your presentation and keep an eye on the presentation as you are adding to it or modifying it. From this tab, you can move, add, or delete slides. The **Outline** and **Slides** tabs are known collectively as the **Slides/Outline** pane.

- You can switch between the **Slides** and **Outline** tabs, depending on which visual representation you are more comfortable with.

- **Slide** pane: Displays a large view of the current slide. This is the place where you add text and other objects.

- **Notes** pane: Allows you to type speaker or instructional notes for the slide that is currently in the **Slide** pane. You can print the notes and use them when you give the presentation or provide them for the audience.

Figure 3.27 | **Normal View panes**

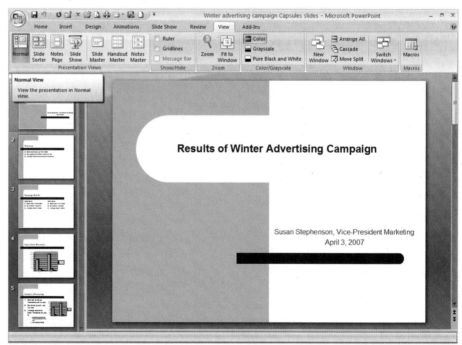

Another way to view your slides is to use the *Slide Sorter* view. **Slide Sorter** view displays all the slides in the presentation in thumbnail form. It is similar to what you see in the **Slides** tab when you are in **Normal** view. To switch the view to **Slide Sorter**, simply click on the **Slide Sorter** icon in the **Presentation Views** group (on the **View** tab), as shown in Figure 3.28, which shows all the slides in the Winter advertising campaign side by side.

The benefits of using **Slide Sorter** view are as follows:

- You can view all the slides in a single presentation in a single panel (as shown in Figure 3.18).

- You can view the slides from multiple presentations side by side (you will see this later in the chapter).

Figure 3.28 | **Slide Sorter View**

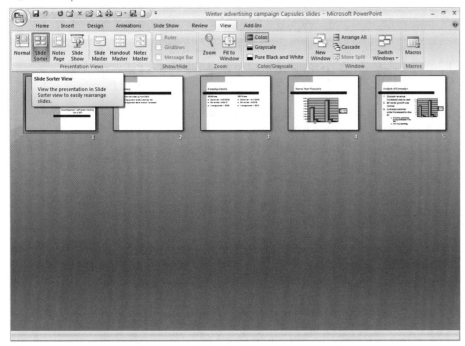

Deleting and Rearranging Slides

You can rearrange slides in a presentation using either the **Normal** view or the **Slide Sorter** view by using the following steps:

- Click the slide you wish to move and hold down the mouse button.
- Drag the slide to the empty space between the two slides where you want to reposition this slide. If you wish to move the slide to the end of the presentation, drag the slide to the empty space right after the last slide.
- Release the mouse button.

You can delete slides in a presentation using either the **Normal** view or the **Slide Sorter** view by using the following steps:

- Click the slide and then press the **Delete** key.
- If you are deleting a sequence of slides, click the first slide, hold down the **Shift** key, and click on the last slide. Release the mouse button and the **Shift** key. The entire sequence of slides will be selected, and you can press the **Delete** key to delete them all.
- If you are deleting a nonconsecutive group of slides, click the first slide. While holding down the **Ctrl** key, click on the other slides you wish to delete. Release the mouse button and the **Ctrl** key. The selected slides will be highlighted, and you can press the **Delete** key to delete them all.

Merging Presentations

There will be many business situations in which you need to merge or use selected slides from other presentations (your own or from others). Following are some common business examples:

- Members of a team are each working on a section of a presentation and the sections will be combined later.

- You need to import slides from an external source of information such as a Web site or from a specialist.
- You are reusing portions of your or another person's presentations.

The most experienced presenters often have such an extensive library of presentations that they create new presentations by merging slides from existing presentations and simply touching up the formats for consistency. Presentations can be merged easily using the **Slide Sorter** view.

To merge or copy and paste slides from one or more presentations, open them and click on *Arrange All* on the **View** tab. This will *tile* the presentations, or arrange them side by side, which makes it easier to perform these tasks. Figure 3.29 shows the Winter advertising campaign you saw earlier tiled next to a plain presentation that has additional slides.

Figure 3.29 | **Tile Multiple Presentations**

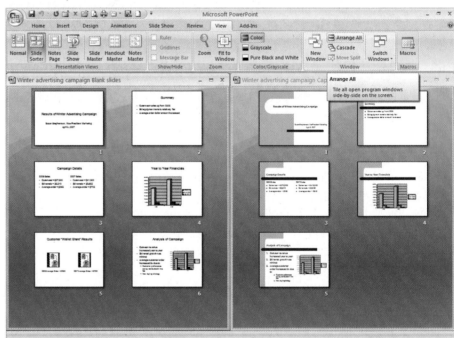

As mentioned, it is a common practice to build your presentation by starting with a few of your own and then copying from other sources. In this example, we will build the Winter advertising campaign by copying slides from a separate presentation.

To copy one slide, follow these steps:

- Select the slide you wish to copy. On the **Home** tab, click the **Copy** icon in the **Clipboard** group. Or you can press **Ctrl + C** instead. See Figure 3.30.

Figure 3.30 | Copy Single Slide

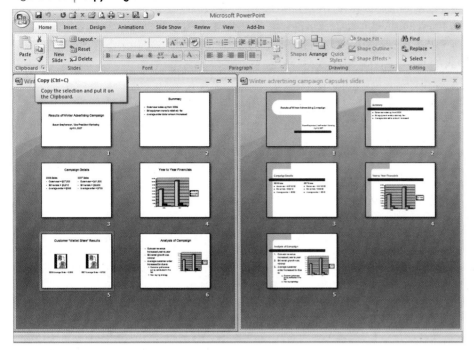

- Select the slide after which you want to place this new slide and click the **Paste** icon in the **Clipboard** group. Alternatively, you may press **Ctrl + V**. Notice the location of the slide and also how it has inherited the theme of the presentation it was pasted into (see Figure 3.31).

Figure 3.31 | Single Slide Copied into a Presentation

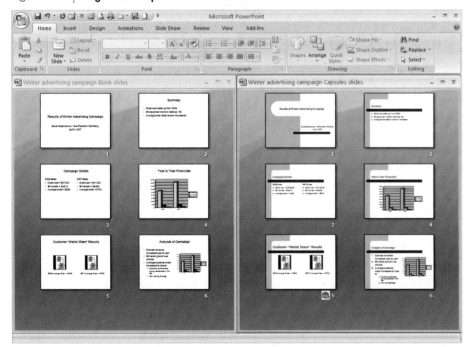

If you are reusing a large percentage of slides from another presentation, you will probably want to copy a large chunk of that presentation. To copy a consecutive sequence of slides from one presentation to another, follow these steps:

- Click on the first slide you wish to copy.
- Hold down the **Shift** key on your keyboard.
- Click on the last slide you wish to copy.
- Click on **Copy**.
- Select the slide after which you want to place all these new slides and click on the **Paste** icon in the **Clipboard** group (see Figure 3.32).

Figure 3.32 | **Copy a Consecutive Sequence of Slides**

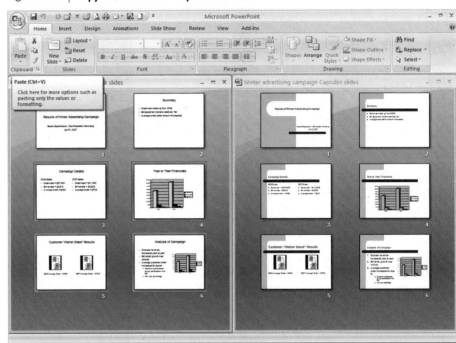

If you are using many sources of information, you will probably be selecting a few slides from each presentation to copy into your own. To copy nonconsecutive slides from one presentation to another, do the following:

- Click on the first slide you wish to copy.
- Hold down the **Ctrl** key on your keyboard.
- Click on the individual slides you wish to copy. In this example, slides 3 and 6 are being copied.
- Click on **Copy**.
- Select the slide after which you want to place all these new slides and click on the **Paste** icon in the **Clipboard** group (see Figure 3.33).

Figure 3.33 | **Copy a Nonconsecutive Sequence of Slides**

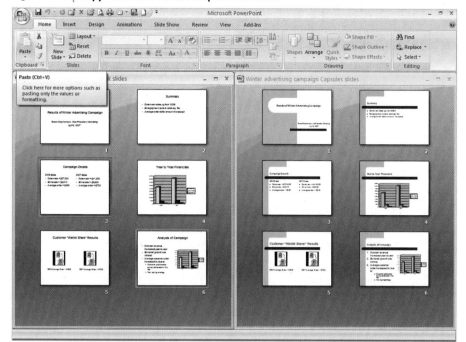

COMMON MISTAKES | Merged Presentations That Look Pieced Together

After merging presentations, go back and make sure all the slides flow together and that the content makes sense. You may have to make changes to the slide titles or content. Spending a few extra minutes to do this will ensure that your presentation looks like it was created by one person using one theme instead of looking as though it was pieced together by different people.

>> Sharing Content between Presentations

The purpose of this workshop is to demonstrate the skills presented in this section of the chapter. We will be opening two existing presentations and rearranging, deleting, and merging presentations. You will see these tasks demonstrated on the following two videos: **Rearrange and Delete Slides** and **Merge Two Presentations**. Try to complete these tasks on your own first before watching the videos.

VIDEO WORKSHOP

1. **Rearrange and Delete Slides (Video: Rearrange and Delete Slides)**

   a. Open the PowerPoint file named ib_p03_presentation1.
   b. Select slide 7.
   c. Use the mouse to drag slide 7 between slides 2 and 3.
   d. Select the "May 2006 MIS Recruiting Plans" slide, then press the **Delete** key, then save the file.

2. Merge Two Presentations Together (Video: Merge Two Presentations Together)

a. Open the PowerPoint file named ib_p03_presentation2. Change the view to **Slide Sorter**.

b. Click Arrange All on the **View** tab of the Ribbon to tile the two presentations so that you can view them side by side.

c. Select slide 1 from Presentation 2, then click the **Copy** icon in the **Home** tab of the Ribbon.

d. Paste slide 1 after slide 2 in Presentation 1.

e. Repeat steps c and d to copy and paste slide 3 from Presentation 2 after slide 2 in Presentation 1.

f. Use the **Shift** key to select slides 4–6 from Presentation 2.

g. Click the **Copy** icon in the **Home** tab of the Ribbon.

h. Return to Presentation 1, then click the **Paste** icon in the **Home** tab of the Ribbon to insert slides 4–6 after the "New Process" slide in Presentation 1.

i. Review the newly merged slides in Presentation 1, slide by slide. Are there issues with the flow? Does the content seem as though this is a presentation created by a single person?

j. Save and close both files.

<table>
<tr><td>EXERCISE
Why Do I Need This?</td></tr>
</table>

>> Creating a Single Presentation from a Team of People

Having the ability to lead and coordinate the efforts of a team is a critical skill you will need in both your academic and professional careers. As a business leader, you will spend most of your day directing and pulling together the efforts of team members and other resources to produce results for your company. When it comes to making presentations or reporting your progress to a company's executive officers, you will likely be pulling together information from a variety of people and sources. As a result, you must know how to manipulate slides within and between presentations. These skills will greatly increase your productivity and prove to be invaluable as you create and work with larger and more complex presentations.

Exercise

The purpose of this exercise is to merge two presentations that were created by different people into one professional and consistent presentation. You will need to open the following two PowerPoint files before starting this exercise: ib_p03_presentation1 and ib_p03_presentation2. Your goal will be to create one seamless presentation that explains the project scope, consulting firm background, findings, recommendations, and results of the project being discussed. The final presentation will be presented to the senior management team at an insurance company.

1. Start ib_p03_presentation1 by discussing the December MIS Recruiting Fair and its objectives. This information will start the presentation on a business-oriented tone.

2. Rearrange the slides in ib_p03_presentation1 so that you have a transition slide to discuss the consulting engagement.

    a. Add two to three bullets on the transition slide that explain why it was necessary to use a consultant.

3. To justify the expenditure to management, you need to explain the consulting firm's credentials. Merge the ib_p03_presentation2 slides that having the following information into the ib_p03_presentation1 slides from the consulting firm:

   a. Company background

   b. Approach to solving the problem

   c. Analysis

   d. Recommendations

4. Bring the conversation back to how the insurance company successfully utilized the consultant's findings. If necessary, rearrange the ib_p03_presentation1 slides so that the next topics discussed are as follows:

   a. How the company implemented one of the recommendations

   b. What the results were

5. You decide that discussing the next recruiting fair is a bit premature, so delete any slides that refer to that future event.

6. You have combined your slides with the consultant's slides, but the presentation needs to appear as though you created it. Go back through all the slides and change any necessary language and formatting (theme, fonts, etc.) so that it's clear the presenter is an employee of the insurance company, not the consultant.

>> What's Wrong with This Presentation?

PROBLEM & EXERCISE

Problem

You are the owner of a small consulting firm that is trying to win the business of a large insurance company where a good friend of yours works. You and your friend have been collaborating on a project, but he agrees to let you make the final presentation to the management team, as long as he can create the accompanying PowerPoint slides. The day of the meeting, he sends you the file.

Exercise

Open the file named ib_p03_sharingwhatswrong. Would you feel comfortable presenting these slides to promote your firm? Consider the following points:

1. Are there any significant issues that appear to be inappropriate when you initially look at the slides?

2. What parts of your friend's presentation are usable?

3. Which slides would you delete and start over?

4. In spite of your friend's enthusiastic support, do you think having him create these slides was an effective strategy? Why or why not?

   What's wrong with this presentation? Write a short answer for each of these points and then make any adjustments you think are necessary to for this presentation.

>> Checking Your Slides

Skill Set

After all the care put into creating your presentation, it is well worth the time to spend a few extra minutes to proofread your work and be sure that your presentation conveys its intended message. Unfortunately, many people skip this step and find misspelled, incorrect, or redundant words for the first time in front of the audience. This can be very embarrassing.

Review Tab

The **Review** tab (shown in Figure 3.34) provides several options for reviewing and checking your work.

FIGURE 3.34 | **Review Tab**

Two features that are used almost religiously by experienced presenters are *Spelling* (sometimes called *Spell Check* or *Spell Checker*) and ***Thesaurus.***

- **Spelling:** If you click on this icon, the entire presentation will be checked word by word, and PowerPoint will present correct spelling(s) for you, as shown in Figure 3.35. If you select **Change**, only that occurrence of the misspelled word will be changed. **Change All** will replace every occurrence of the misspelled word with the selected term in the Suggestions: box.

FIGURE 3.35 | **Check Spelling**

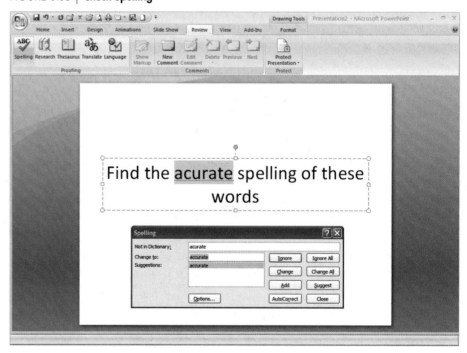

- **Thesaurus:** To make sure you are using the correct word or to avoid using the same word over and over again, use the thesaurus to search for alternatives. Highlight the word you want to change and click on the **Thesaurus** icon. PowerPoint will search for alternate words (synonyms), as shown in Figure 3.36.

FIGURE 3.36 | **Thesaurus**

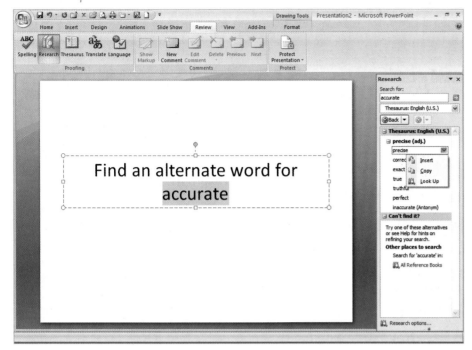

- Select the alternate word and click on **Insert** from the drop-down menu. The new word will replace the old word.

Find and Replace

You can use *Find and Replace* to locate all occurrences of a word or phrase across the presentation. This is a helpful feature to use when you have "borrowed" or merged slides from another presentation into yours and need to delete all references to the original presentation.

To use **Find and Replace**, follow these steps:

- Click on the **Editing** icon in the **Home** tab.
- Enter the word or phrase that you would like to replace under **Find what**.
- Enter the word or phrase to use instead under **Replace with**.
- Select the **Replace All** button. PowerPoint will replace all occurrences of the old with the new and tell you how many changes were made.

Figure 3.37 shows you where **Find and Replace** is located on the **Home** tab and how to enter information into the dialog box.

Figure 3.37 | **Find and Replace**

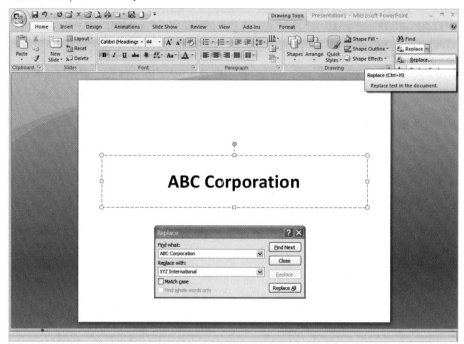

COMMON MISTAKES | **The Find and Replace Function Is Not Perfect**

Never rely on **Find and Replace** to be completely accurate. Go back and read through your entire presentation to be sure that all the words and phrases are written in the right context. Many users also forget to go back and read through the entire presentation as though they were the audience. In doing so, they can potentially catch misspellings, overused words, or inappropriate references.

Print Preview

Print Preview is a quick way to view your slides online to see how the presentation looks to an audience (see Figure 3.38). As you roll through each slide, check for

- All the elements of a presentation you learned about in Chapter 1
- Logical flow of each slide
- Visual appropriateness and appeal (font, font size, color, use of graphics)

Figure 3.38 | **Print Preview**

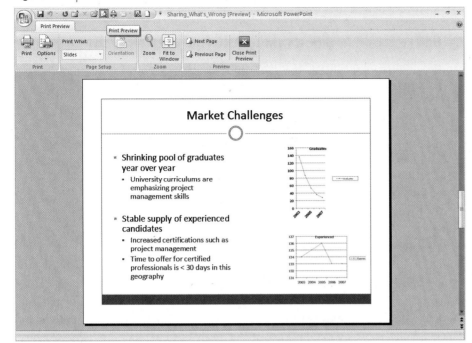

>> Checking for Accuracy

VIDEO WORKSHOP

The purpose of this workshop is to demonstrate the accuracy skills presented in this section of the chapter. You will see these skills demonstrated in the following four videos: **Spell Check the Presentation**, **Use the Thesaurus**, **Use Find and Replace**, and **Print Preview**. Open the file named ib_p03_accuracy before starting this workshop. Try to complete these tasks on your own first before watching the videos.

1. **Spell Check the Presentation (Video: Spell Check the Presentation)**

   a. Click on the **Review** tab and choose **Spelling** to spell check the presentation.

      i. You will quickly notice that in addition to misspelled words, the Spell Checker picks up British spellings of some words. Replace those words with the American versions.

      ii. Use **Change** instead of **Change All** and notice how many occurrences come up that could have been replaced using **Change All** instead.

2. **Use the Thesaurus (Video: Use the Thesaurus)**

   a. The word *organization* is used quite a bit. Using the **Thesaurus** feature, choose an alternate word for the Who We Are slide.

    b. Use the **Thesaurus** to find an alternate word for *reduce* in the Recommendations slide.

3. Use Find and Replace (Video: Use Find and Replace)

    a. Change all occurrences of *Geography* to **Region**.

    b. Save your work as **ib_p03_accuracy_solution**.

4. Print Preview (Video: Print Preview)

    a. Using **Print Preview**, walk through the slides. You will notice that, while the presentation looks a little better, you might still want to improve a few things.

EXERCISE

Why Do I Need This?

>> Creating a Shell

Many companies or departments within an organization deliver standard presentations over and over; the format stays the same, but the content changes. Examples are specialized consulting firms or accounting departments that have to present pro forma financial statements on a quarterly basis. The ability to create a generic presentation (called a *shell*) once and then customize it is a productivity technique used by professional presenters. If you spend time up front in creating a quality shell, you will be able to use the skills learned in this section to quickly create a finished product.

Exercise

In the previous Video Workshop, you cleaned up a presentation and made it ready for general use. The purpose of this exercise is to use the skills learned in this section to customize the presentation for your client.

1. Open the file named ib_p03_accuracy_solution.

2. Reduce the number of times you use the word *university* by using the **Thesaurus**.

3. Make the following replacements on Slide 3:

    a. *region* -> **Midwest**

    b. *Company* -> **Midwest Mutual**

    c. *Sponsor name* -> **Adam Bustle**

4. Save your presentation as **ib_p03_whydo_solution**.

>> What's Wrong with This Presentation?

Problem

You asked an administrative assistant to use the standard corporate presentation on a project involving MIS recruiting and then customize it for another customer. After she completed this presentation, you discovered that the new vice president of Human Resources at this firm had originally worked for another company where your firm had pitched a similar project. You do not want the new vice president to realize that the presentation he sees now is extremely similar to the one he saw while working at the other company.

Exercise

The PowerPoint file the administrative assistant sends you is named ib_p03_accuracy_whatswrong. Knowing that you cannot use a presentation that was used previously for another client, what's wrong with this presentation? Consider the following points.

1. What are the areas in this presentation that are giveaways that this is a reused template?

2. Where are some opportunities to change or add to the presentation? For example,

   a. Is there industry- or region-specific language, or is it too generic?

   b. Are the graphics or charts appropriate for this customer?

   c. Does the content flow for this customer?

   d. Where did **Thesaurus** or **Find and Replace** fall short? Why?

   e. What other recommendations can you make?

   Write a short answer for each of these points and then fix the presentation so it is ready to share with your client.

It occurred to me that sending out a standard format ahead of time and asking everyone to use it might save me a little time on the back end. As our workloads increased and the deadlines became more aggressive, that idea turned out to be very beneficial not only to me, but to the rest of team.

Before creating a standard presentation, I reviewed the slides that my team members sent me and identified the areas that caused me the most rework time. It turns out that the following components were troublesome:

- Different slide layouts: One person would use Title and Text, but another person would use Title and 2 Content.

- Varying font sizes: The font type was not so much an issue because I cleaned up that problem once I merged presentations, but the sizes required a lot of time to review and clean up.

- Inconsistent bullet types, sizes, and indentation: Sometimes there were square bullets, check marks, dashes, and so on.

- Long, winding sentences: I was forever shortening sentences into one-line phrases.

Using the same techniques that you learned in this chapter, I created a shell presentation and a set of instructions on when and how to use it. Every time the team started a new project, I sent out the shell and held a 30-minute conference call to walk through the do's and don'ts. Each time, the team members were only too happy to use it. They had no idea of the amount of time I was spending on redoing their work!

I can honestly say that by simply instituting the standards described here, my rework time was cut in half. No more weekend work or late nights on these excruciatingly boring tasks for me anymore—at least not when it came to PowerPoint!

Assignment

Using the skills you learned in this chapter, do the following:

1. Create a four- to five-slide shell presentation that college instructors in a department might customize each semester and hand out to students to use as their final paper guidelines. Save as ib_p03_anecdote_solution.

2. Write a list of instructions to give the instructors, along with the shell explaining how and where they can format and customize it.

   a. Include areas or sections that may not be modified or omitted and explain why.

Questions for Discussion

1. When creating a shell for business presenters to format and customize later, why is it better to stay simple?

2. How much flexibility and leeway should you give business professionals to add their own customizations and embellishments?

3. How would you address the concern of a fellow business professional that this approach "limits creativity"?

The following questions are related to the concepts addressed in this chapter. There are three types of questions: Short Answer, True or False, and Fill in the Blank. If your answer to a True or False question is False, write a short explanation as to why you think the statement is not true.

1. **Clipboard**, **Font**, and **Paragraph** are found under which tab?

2. The four **Clipboard** options are _____, _____, _____, and _____.

3. What is the difference between **Paste** and **Paste Special**? Give an example illustrating when you would use **Paste Special.**

4. The two categories of fonts are _____ and _____.

5. _____ fonts are used for documents or situations in which there is a lot of text.

6. True or False: Bold, italic, and underlining can be used liberally throughout a presentation.

7. True or False: You can combine, mix, or match formatting options.

8. The four types of text alignment are _____, _____, _____, and _____.

9. True or False: Instead of using the options under the **Home** tab, you can launch formatting by highlighting the text and right clicking your mouse.

10. The _____ determines the location, font type and size, color on a slide.

11. To put information into a footer and turn page numbering "on", you must select options in the _____ dialog box under the _____ tab.

12. True or False: To change elements on a slide master, just add, modify, or delete them as though you were working on regular slide.

13. You can use the _____ view or the _____ view to delete or rearrange slides from a single presentation.

14. You would use the _____ view to share and merge slides between two or more presentations.

15. To copy consecutive slides, you select the _____ slide, hold down the _____ key, and select the _____ slide.

16. To copy nonconsecutive slides, select the _____ slide, hold down the _____ key, and then select _____ slides.

17. **Spelling** and **Thesaurus** are found under the _____ tab.

18. The **Thesaurus** is used to prevent _____ in your presentation.

19. Synonyms and _____ can be found using the **Thesaurus**.

20. The _____ feature saves time when you have to make multiple changes to a word or phrase in an entire presentation.

21. _____ allows you to view the presentation as often as you like without having to print it.

The following exam is designed to test your ability to recognize and execute the PowerPoint skills presented in this chapter. Read each question carefully and answer the questions in the order they are listed. You should be able to complete this exam in 60 minutes or less.

1. Open the ib_p03_skillsexam1 and ib_p03_skillsexam2 presentations.

2. Apply a more business-like theme to the file named ib_p03_skillsexam1 and rename it **ib_p03_skillsexam**.

3. Merge the two presentations by placing the following slides from the file named ib_p03_skillsexam2 to the file named ib_p03_skillsexam after the Title slide:

   - Overview
   - Monetary Policy
   - Control the Money Supply
   - Regulate Bank Reserves
   - Change Interest Rates
   - Questions?

4. Rearrange the slides so that Agenda is the second slide.

5. Replace the word *Fed* with **Federal Reserve** in the entire presentation.

6. Look for an alternative for the word *rate* and replace where appropriate.

7. Create a bulleted list in the Overview slide.

8. Apply consistent bullets to each slide.

9. Select a sans-serif font and apply it throughout the presentation.

10. Make the title on each slide 28 points.

11. Use WordArt for the title of the presentation on the title page.

>> Challenge Questions

The following questions are designed to test your ability to apply the PowerPoint skills you have learned to complete a business objective. Use your knowledge of PowerPoint as well as your creativity to answer these questions. For most questions, there are several possible ways to complete the objective.

1. Recall the discussion about going back and making sure that the presentation looks as though it was created by one person. After completing the steps in the Skills Exam, go back and look for indicators that this presentation was pieced together.

Use the following checklist:

   a. Title on each slide
   b. Footer
   c. Font style and sizes
   d. Text sizes
   e. Is there relevant content on each page?
   f. Does the smiley face on the Questions page reflect the persona of the individual who is delivering this presentation?

2. Identify and remediate areas from the preceding checklist and any others you discover.

3. Are the long and winding sentences appropriate for a presentation? How would you break up the bullets into shorter phrases?

4. If you were the instructor, what additional slide would you look for to know that this presentation was not plagiarized?

5. Open the file named ib_p03_401kplanning.

   a. Check the spelling in the presentation.
   b. Use the **Thesaurus** to suggest alternatives for a word that is highly overused in the slides.
   c. Modify the presentation so that it can be used as a shell presentation for other clients, dates, and 401K funds.

>> Chapter 4

Delivering Your Presentation

Chapter Goals

Conveying information effectively has two dimensions, both of which must be done well: (1) creating the presentation and (2) delivering the presentation. By this point, you have learned advanced formatting techniques to enhance your PowerPoint presentation. You have also learned how to merge presentations created by multiple people into one seamless, professional-looking presentation. Your slide show is ready; you are now ready to tackle the second major objective: delivering your presentation.

>> **PowerPoint** | **Skill Sets**

PowerPoint in **Practice** | Anecdote

My Role as a Senior Manager

As both a college instructor and business professional, I deliver a lot of information through presentations. At the beginning of every term, I ask my students to bring PowerPoint slides from the student resources web site to class for note-taking. At first, the students dislike the idea of carrying yet another stack of paper, but quickly discover the slides reinforce class material and make great study guides. Now they request PowerPoints for each text.

In my corporate life, I lead several large team meetings and work with clients frequently. Several years ago, I started bringing handouts of my slides to business meetings. I knew my colleagues and clients would also like copies for note-taking and future use. I was proud for having thought of such a good idea. At first, the audiences seemed pleasantly surprised, but I soon noticed a couple of things. Sometimes, while presenting, I competed with the sound of paper shuffling or faced a sea of bent heads as my audience read the handouts—this made establishing rapport impossible.

One day, the division manager came to a meeting, picked up a handout, said "This is great, thanks!" and left minutes into a one-hour presentation. I was appalled at his behavior until I realized I had created the problem. There was no incentive to stay for a presentation if they could just read about it later. Now I was in a quandary. If I stopped giving handouts, would those who appreciated them get upset? If I continued would more people simply skip the presentation? Or worse yet, ask me to e-mail them the handouts. I began to realize that maybe this great idea of mine was not so great after all.

>> Continued on page 139

You can deliver your presentation in two ways: either by presenting the slides electronically or using *hard copy*. Hard copy is defined as paper or clear plastic transparencies.

Most presentations today are delivered electronically. Almost every businessperson has his or her own laptop or can easily get access to one. Organizations have **LCD projectors** that connect to the back of the PC and display what is on the screen. An LCD projector is a device utilized for displaying video images or data. It is the modern-day equivalent of a slide projector or overhead projector (described in Chapter 1). The cost and size of LCD projectors have even decreased to the point where many business-people who regularly and frequently deliver presentations buy their own projector and tuck it right into their PC case next to the laptop.

Very rarely are presentations delivered using only paper copies (**handouts**) or transparencies. Following are examples of business situations that call for handouts:

- When no equipment is available or as a backup plan in the event that the equipment fails

- When you are delivering the information in an instructional versus an informational context

Many presenters have a strict policy of never providing handouts so that they can protect their intellectual capital or to force the audience to give their full attention to them and not be distracted by the paper copy. There are no hard and fast guidelines. Use your judgment in each situation, but know that audiences are increasingly more comfortable with electronic-only presentations.

On-Screen (Electronic) Delivery

On-screen (electronic) delivery of your presentation means that you display your slides directly from PowerPoint running on a PC onto a wall, board, or screen. This method is frequently used in business today because it requires little time and additional preparation to go from a finished presentation to delivery.

After you decide that you are going to use this method to give your presentation, you have several options to deliver it:

- Presentation with a live speaker: Presenting in a room in front of an audience by using a monitor or projector. This is the most common way of delivering business presentations.

- Self-running presentation: Setting up a presentation to run unattended in a booth or kiosk at a trade show or convention.

This section will focus on the **Slide Show** and **Animations** tabs, as shown in Figure 4.1a and Figure 4.1b. To deliver your presentation on-screen, you need to learn how to use options under these tabs. On the **Slide Show** tab, you can determine which slides will display and in which order. The **Animations** tab allows you to choose transitions and special effects.

Figure 4.1a | **Slide Show Tab**

Figure 4.1b | **Animation Tab**

Slide Show

As you can see in Figure 4.2, the **Slide Show** tab offers a number of options you can use to deliver your presentation. For example, you may decide to run straight through your slides from beginning to end and take questions at the end. Or your presentation may be more interactive, and you will decide to stop, encourage dialogue from the audience, and then start back up. PowerPoint is flexible in this regard and can support a number of delivery choices. We will discuss the most common: **Start Slide Show** and **Set Up**.

From the **Start Slide Show** tab you can launch and run your presentation in the following ways:

- **From Beginning**: Automatically starts your presentation from Slide 1.
- **From Current Slide**: Automatically starts your presentation from where you are. This option is used in situations in which you need to stop the presentation (to answer questions, etc.) and need to start back up from the point where you stopped.
- **Custom Slide Show**: Allows you to select only those slides that you want to present from a larger set and create "subset" presentations" very quickly. For example, in business **Custom Slide Show** is used in product management. Product managers need to have a comprehensive amount of information regarding their product lines available at all times. If this information is in PowerPoint, the result can be a large slide deck. *Slide deck* is a term commonly used to refer to your set of slides. Depending on the audience (potential clients, engineering teams, executives, cost accountants) and the amount of time allotted, the product manager can select only those slides necessary from the master presentation and give each presentation a different name—for example, "For Accounting," "For Quality Assurance." Whenever the content of a slide changes in one of the presentations, the change is reflected in all the other presentations because each file is linked together.

From the **Set Up** group, an extremely useful feature is the **Hide Slide** icon (see Figure 4.2). **Hide Slide** marks a slide as "do not display" and does not show it as the presenter is rolling through the slide deck. The user is not aware that the hidden slide even exists. After selecting the slides to hide, you would then launch your presentation using any of the **Start Slide Show** options discussed here. To "unhide" the slide, select it and click on the **Hide Slide** icon again.

Figure 4.2 | **Slide Show Tab Options**

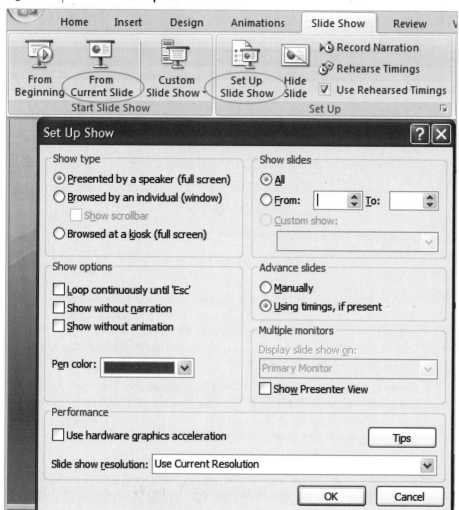

COMMON MISTAKES | Overlooking the Custom Slide Show Option

Many presenters forget about the **Custom Slide Show** feature, so they create multiple, separate presentations for each audience. If you choose to do this, be aware that keeping all your presentations in sync can become labor intensive. If one or two slides change, you have to go back to each individual presentation and update it. Consider using **Custom Slide Show** instead. You will be able to change just the "master" slide, and all the custom slide shows will be updated automatically.

Here are the main options you will use in the **Set Up Show** dialog box under the **Set Up** group. To access this dialog box, shown in Figure 4.3, click on the small arrow in the bottom-right corner of the **Set Up** group.

- **Show type**
  - **Presented by a speaker (full screen):** This option is for presenters who are delivering their presentations in Stand-up mode. The slides take up the entire space on the screen. The speaker has control of the slides and can run the show automatically or manually.
  - **Browsed by an individual (window):** This option is similar to the preceding **Full screen** option except that each slide, when displayed, has a border around it with the presentation title on top, scroll bars on the right side, and the Windows task bar on the bottom.
  - **Browsed at kiosk (full screen):** This option is for a self-running presentation that does not require the speaker to be present. Note: When you select this option, you must set the **Advance Slide** timings under the **Animation** tab (discussed later in this section).

- **Show options**
  - **Loop continuously until 'Esc':** This option causes your presentation to loop and also restricts users from changing it. **Loop continuously** is used with kiosks or at exhibits and trade-show booths. Note: When you select this option, you must set the **Advance Slide** timings under the **Animation** tab (discussed later in this section).
  - **Show without narration** and **Show without animation:** Narration (voice over) and animation (special effects on each slide) are not discussed in detail in this chapter. If your presentation has narration and/or animation and you want to turn off those features, check these boxes. Most users select these options when they are testing the presentation.

- **Show slides:** The **All** option displays the entire presentation (except those slides marked **Hide**). The **From** option allows you to choose a sequential range of slides. The default is **All**.

- **Advance Slides**
  - **Manually:** You must click the left mouse button, press the **Pg Dn** key, or use the arrow keys on the keyboard to advance the presentation forward. This option gives the presentation complete control over the timing. Experienced presenters almost always use this option.
  - **Using Timings, if present:** If you have set the timing for each slide and would like the presentation to run without your intervention, check the **Using timings, if present** box.

Figure 4.3 | **Set Up Show Dialog Box**

Rehearsed Timings

As stated earlier in this section, pre-set timings for slides is recommended only for unattended or kiosk presentations. For those types of presentations, there is often a voice-over or narrator associated with each slide. In order to synchronize the narration with the timing of advancing the slides, the **Rehearse Timings** icon is used. Launch the presentation and select Rehearse Timings (Figure 4.4) under the **Slide Show** tab.

Figure 4.4 | **Rehearse Timings**

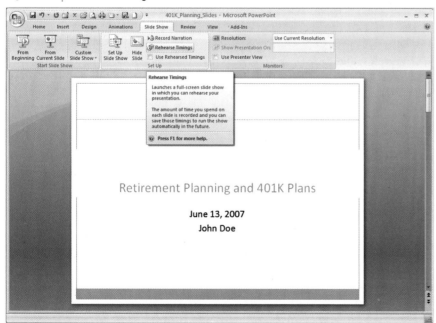

Your presentation will automatically go into Slide Show mode and a timer will display in the upper left hand corner. As you advance from slide to slide, the timer records how much time you spend on each slide. See Figure 4.5.

Figure 4.5 | **Recording slide timings**

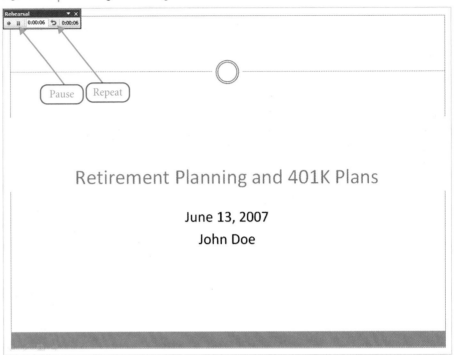

When you finish the presentation, PowerPoint adds up the total amount of time you used, displays it, and asks if you wish to use these timings. If you select "Yes," your presentation is put into Slide Sorter mode and the time spent on each slide is listed as shown in Figure 4.6

Figure 4.6 | **Total slide show time**

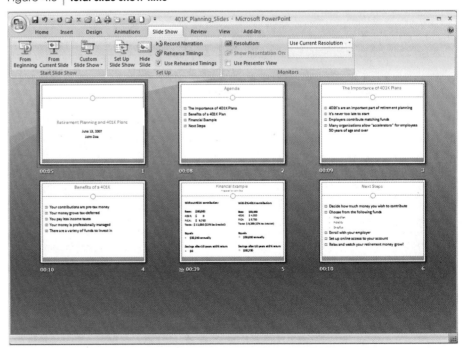

The next time you run a slide show, if you check the **Using timings, if present** box, the slides in your presentation will be advanced using these timings. Only the most recently captured rehearsed timings are used.

A very appropriate application of the Rehearse Timings feature is to use it to make sure your presentation fits within your allotted time frame. Instead of using a stop watch or clock, turn the Rehearse Timings feature and the PowerPoint timer keep track of the time for you. When you actually deliver the presentation, make sure that the Use timings, if present button is not checked.

COMMON MISTAKES | Using Timings Incorrectly

Use preset timings only if the presentation will be run unattended. Some presenters think that they can stay on time if they force the slides (and the audience) to move ahead on a preset schedule. Although this strategy may seem like a good idea on paper, it is usually not well received by audiences. Audience members either feel rushed if they still have questions and PowerPoint automatically moved on to the next slide, or they feel awkward if there is dead silence. All in all, the speaker comes across as inexperienced, and his or her credibility and relationship with the audience is damaged.

Animations and Transitions

In PowerPoint, an *animation* is a special visual or sound effect added to text or an object. For example, you can have your text bullet points fly in from the left, one word at a time, or hear the sound of applause when a picture is uncovered. A *transition* is an effect that specifies how the screen changes as you move from one slide to another.

You can add animations and transitions to emphasize certain points, control the flow of information, and add interest to your presentation.

In this chapter, we will discuss slide transitions. Figures 4.7, 4.8a, and 4.8b show the various options from the **Transitions to This Slide** group. They include

- **Transition effects**: There are several categories of transition effects. Figure 4.7 shows an example of Fades and Dissolves, Wipes, and Push and Cover.
- Slide transition **sound** and **speed**: These options allow you to select the speed associated with a transition and the sound to be played during the transition. See Figures 4.8a and 4.8b.
- **Apply to All**: Highlight a slide (either from **Slide Sorter** view or from the **Slide** pane) and click on this box to apply the transition.

Note: No matter how serious or conservative the presentation topic is, most presenters admit that their favorite part of PowerPoint is "playing around" with the transitions and experimenting with the sounds. Use caution with transitions, especially sounds. Sounds are not recommended for in-person business presentations.

The **Transitions to This Slide** group is also the place where you determine how you will transition from one slide to the next:

- **On Mouse Click**: This option is for manual slide transitions. If you select it, PowerPoint will display the current slide until you click the left mouse button. You can also use the **Pg Dn** key or the **Enter** key to move from one slide to the next.

>> **Quick Reference**

Setting Up a Slide Show

Use the options under the **Slide Show** tab to set up any one of the following slide shows:

1. To show all slides from the beginning to the end:
   a. Select the **From Beginning** icon.
2. To show all slides starting from the one currently on the **Slide** pane to the end:
   a. Select the **From Current Slide** icon.
3. To create a new custom slide show:
   a. Select the **Custom Slide Show** icon.
   b. Select **New** and give the custom slide show a descriptive name.
   c. Select the slides from the **Slides in presentation** list and click the **Add** button to add them to the **Slides in custom show** list. You can select and add the slides one at a time or select a group of them by using the **Shift** or **Ctrl** keys.
   d. Click the **OK** button to save the custom slide show.
4. To show a specific sequence of slides:
   a. Select the **Set Up Slide Show** icon.
   b. Click on the **From** button under **Show Slides** and enter the range of slides you wish to show.

(Continued)

(Continued from preceding page)

>> **Quick Reference**

5. To show all the slides continuously in an unattended mode:

   a. Select the **Set Up Slide Show** icon.

   b. Click on the **Browsed at a kiosk (full screen)** button under **Show type**.

   c. The **Loop continuously until 'Esc'** box directly underneath will automatically be checked and grayed out.

>> **Quick Reference**

Using Rehearse Timings

1. On the **Slide Show** tab, in the **Set Up** group, click **Rehearse Timings**. Be prepared to start delivering your presentation immediately.

2. As you rehearse your presentation:

   a. To move to the next slide, click **Next**.

   b. To temporarily stop recording the time, click **Pause**.

   c. To restart recording the time after pausing, click **Pause**.

   d. To restart recording the time for the current slide, click **Repeat**.

3. After you set the time for the last slide, a message box displays the total time for the presentation and prompts you to do one of the following:

   a. To keep the recorded slide timings, click **Yes**.

   b. To discard the recorded slide timings, click **No**.

4. **Slide Sorter** view appears and displays the time of each slide in your presentation.

• **Automatically After**: This box allows you to set automatic timing in minutes or seconds. Remember to go back to the **Set Up Show** dialog box (under the **Slide Show** tab) and check the **Using timings** box under the **Advance Slides** option.

You will have on opportunity to try out several animation scenarios in the Video Workshop and Exercise.

Figure 4.7 | **Transitions to This Slide Group: Transition Effects**

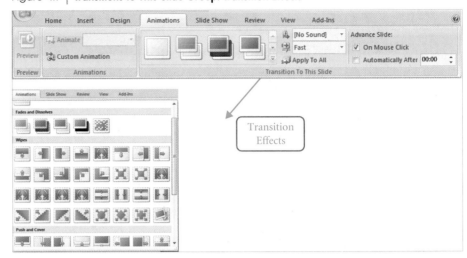

Figure 4.8a | **Transitions to This Slide Group: Sound Options**

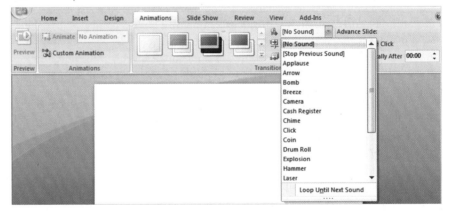

Figure 4.8b | **Transitions to This Slide Group: Speed Options**

COMMON MISTAKES | Specials Effects Overload

Selecting transitions is one of the most fun parts about creating a presentation. However, many speakers forget about the audience and add as many special effects as possible. Having all these special effects overwhelms the audience and causes them to lose track of the content and the objective of the presentation or meeting in the first place. Tip: An overloaded presentation is the sign of an amateur presenter.

COMMON MISTAKES | Setting Automatic Timings

Many presenters guess at setting the **Advance Slide** timings. Often the result is a presentation that runs too fast or too slow. Put yourself in the shoes of the audience members. Review the slides yourself or have another person review them before setting the timings. Remember to adjust the timing for each audience because their needs may be different.

Web Delivery

In today's business environment, employees, customers, suppliers, and other stakeholders are connected to each other through the Internet, an organization's intranet, or the corporate extranet. They all use a common piece of software, called a browser, to access information from each other. Publishing your slides as web pages will allow anyone with a Web browser to view your presentation. They do not have to have the PowerPoint software.

Delivering presentations on the Web is becoming more and more prevalent. Some business examples where this approach is very useful is:

- Webinars—these are "web seminars" that are conducted over the Web. Webinars use PowerPoint slides usually with voice narration to present information. Many training classes and other types of e-learning are now being delivered using this approach because it is very cost-effective.

- Disseminating information to a mobile work force—it is not convenient or feasible for business people who travel or work in remote locations to download PowerPoint presentations. Some of these individuals use PDAs and don't even have PowerPoint loaded on to those devices. They do, however, have Internet access and can log onto a server and view information that way.

In order to view a presentation from a browser, you have to save your PowerPoint presentation in Hypertext Markup Language (HTML) format. From the **Quick Access** toolbar or the Office Button, select Save As and choose one of the two "packaging" options:

- Save as a **Web Page**—this saves the presentation as a single file with an extension of .htm. All supporting material is saved in a separate folder which must be uploaded to a web site to run. This option is good for posting on a site or editing with FrontPage or other HTML editor.
- Save as **Single File Web Page**—this saves the presentation with a file extension of .mht. All the graphics, sounds and animations are packaged together. This option is good for e-mailing your presentation.

Which option should you choose? If you are sending your presentation to someone outside your organization, send it as a Single File Web page so that all the associated objects are packaged together. If you are publishing the presentation within your organization, ask your intranet administrator what his or her preference is but you will most likely convert it to a Web Page (html).

>> *Quick Reference*

Setting Up Slide Transitions

Use the **Transition To This Slide** options under the **Slide Show** tab to set up any one of the following slide shows:

1. Select the slides you wish to apply the transition effect(s) to either from the **Slide Sorter** view or from the **Slides** tab on the left side of the screen.

   a) If you intend to eventually transition all the slides but would like to just test different options on the current slide, you can easily apply your selected transition effects to the entire presentation later.

2. Apply a transition effect from the list.

3. Apply a transition sound and/or transition speed from the pull-down lists.

4. If the presentation is to run unattended, set the timing (in seconds) under **Advance Slide**.

5. If you did not select all the slides in the presentation in step 1, select the **Apply to All** icon.

Figure 4.9 | **Save a presentation as a web page**

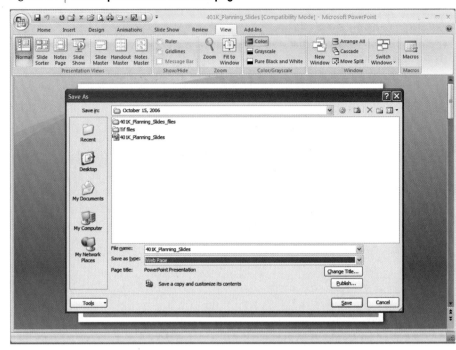

Figure 4.9 shows how to save your presentation as a web page.

To publish the presentation and preview it, select the **Publish** option as shown in figure 4.10

Figure 4.10 | **Publish a PowerPoint presentation in new browser window**

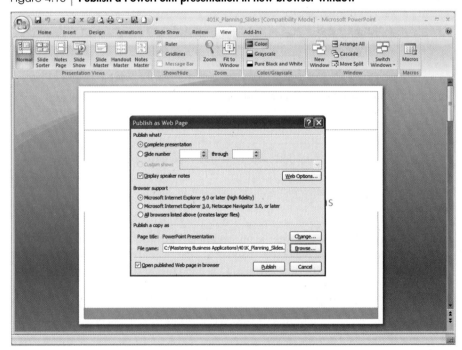

Figure 4.11 illustrates how Internet Explorer is launched and the presentation is displayed.

Figure 4.11 | **Presentation is displayed in Internet Explorer**

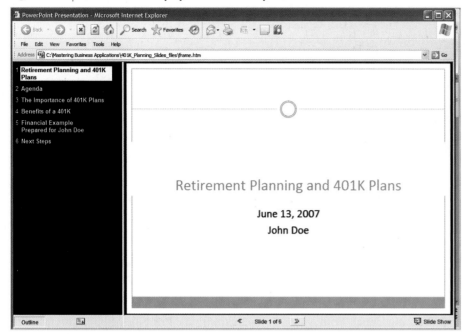

The slide titles are listed on the left hand side. Along the bottom of the screen are scroll forward and scroll backward arrows. When you save your presentation to an HTML format, it is a good idea to bring up your browser and see how the presentation actually "renders." The term "render" refers to how the user will see the slides on the screen.

Hard-Copy Presentations

PowerPoint is a business tool for presenting information. Its primary use is for presentations; it is not intended to be a documentation tool. However, in some situations you will need to print and give out hard (paper) copies of your presentation or create transparencies if on-screen delivery is not possible. To support your presentation, you may want to give your audience handouts (smaller versions of your slides) or *speaker notes* (additional text associated with each slide that can be printed and used for reference). Lastly, when you're working on a presentation, you may prefer to preview it on paper instead of on-screen.

This example will show how a presentation that has been created for students for the first day of a Marketing 101 class can be printed in different ways for a diverse set of audiences.

There are several ways to launch the **Print** function, as shown in Figure 4.12:

- From the **Office** Button
- From the **Quick Access** toolbar (if you have added the **Print** icon, as explained in Chapter 1)
- By pressing **Ctrl+P**
- From **Print Preview**

Figure 4.12 | **Three Methods for Launching the Print Function**

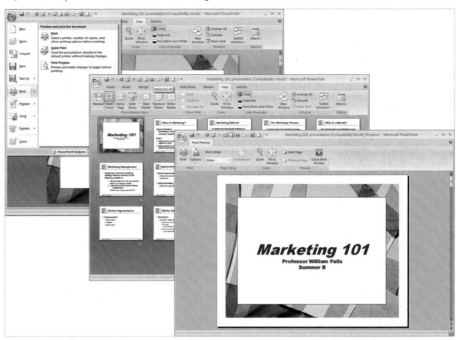

Once you launch **Print**, you are presented with the **Print** dialog box, as shown in Figure 4.7.

Figure 4.13 | **Print Dialog Box**

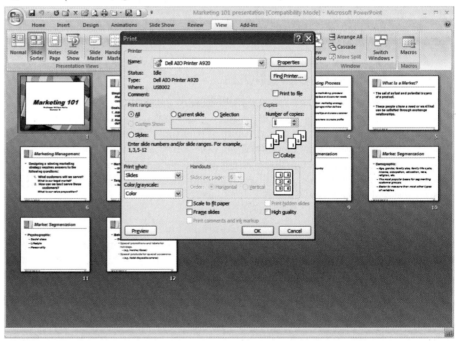

From here, you give PowerPoint the following printing information using the appropriate section of the dialog box:

- **Printer**: Describes the local or network printers available to you. Depending on how the printers have been set up, you will have additional paper and layout options. Because printer configuration options vary widely from computer to computer, refer to your printer's manual or your system administrator for more information on this topic.

- **Print range**: Allows you to select which slides you wish to print.
  - **All**: Prints the slides from beginning to end in the presentation.
  - **Current slide**: Prints a single slide—either the slide that is in the **Slide** pane at the time, or, if you are in the **Slide Sorter** view, the highlighted slide. For example, say you wish to print and hand out just the Agenda page or a particular chart that the audience needs to examine closely.
  - **Selection**: Enables you to highlight a continuous or noncontinuous sequence of slides and print them from the **Slide Sorter** view.
  - **Slides**: Operates similar to **Selection**, except that you have to know the slide numbers.
  - To print different slides, separate the slide numbers with commas (for example, 1, 3, 6).
  - To print a continuous sequence of slides, use a dash (for example, 2–5).
  - To print a combination of individual slides and a sequence, you can also mix and match (for example, 1, 3–5, 10, 14–16).
- **Copies**: Specifies the number of copies you wish to print; if you print more than one copy, be sure to check the **Collate** button; otherwise, you will end up manually sorting the printouts yourself!
- **Print what**: Enables you to select slides, handouts, Notes pages, or the outline to print (see Figure 4.14).
  - **Slides**: Prints one slide per page. Usually, you select this option when you need overhead transparencies made (remember Chapter 1). Many professional presenters still carry transparencies as a backup in case their equipment malfunctions.
  - **Handouts**: Enables you to print handouts, or miniature snapshots of your slides that are condensed onto a page. The use of handouts offers two main benefits: The audience can have something to take with them or jot notes on, and because the slides are captured in snapshots, less paper is used. This is the most widely used **Print What** option.

Figure 4.14 | **Print What Drop-Down: Slides, Handouts, Notes Pages, and Outline View**

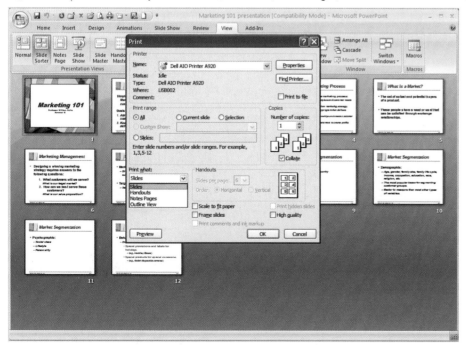

Be careful about providing handouts to your audience. Your key objective is for them to listen to you, not shuffle paper. The rule of thumb is that handouts are appropriate for presentations that are instructional or technical in nature. In those situations, the audience will need to take notes or write down explanations or directions anyway, so the logical place to do that is right next to a picture of the slide. However, presentations that are more marketing-oriented or persuasive in nature should not involve handouts. The audience will need to be focused on the presenter. If somebody wants a copy of the presentation, get his or her email address and send it after the presentation is over.

The options to print handouts are as follows:

- 1 (you are given this option, but it really amounts to the same thing as presenting individual slides).

- 2, 3, 4, 6, or 9 slides per page (3 and 4 per page are the most popular choices for readability reasons). If you select 3 per page, PowerPoint provides a lined area next to each slide to take notes.

The example in Figure 4.15 shows how to print the Marketing 101 presentation as three handouts per page. An appropriate use for this type of printout is for students to take notes during lecture.

Figure 4.15 | **Examples of Handouts: 3 Per Page**

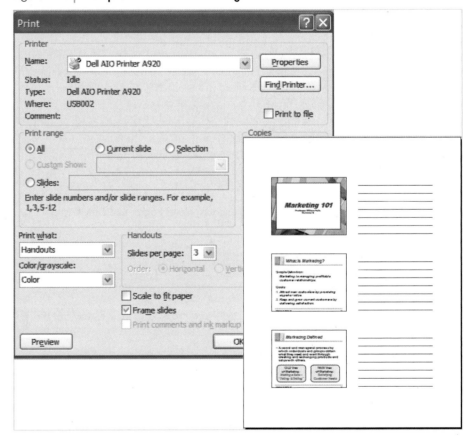

If this professor wanted to show another faculty member what he uses for the first day of class, printing more than three slides per page would be appropriate. His colleague could glance quickly through just a few pages and get a sense of what information was covered, how it was written, and how many slides were used in total. As you can see, a handout with four slides per page is still "readable". However, using six or nine slides per page is rare because the slides can be too small for most people to see. See Figure 4.16 for examples.

Figure 4.16 | **Examples of Handouts: 4, 6, and 9 Per Page**

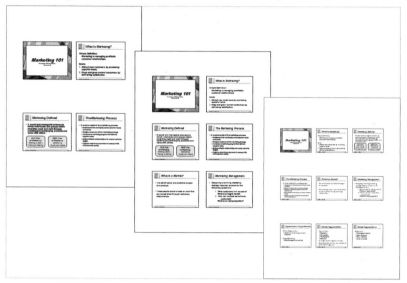

- **Notes Pages:** Chapter 1 briefly touched upon the **Notes** pane. The **Notes** pane is where the presenter can insert speaker's notes or additional information for the audience. If you select to print **Notes Pages**, your slides will print one slide per page as well as the text and any graphics you may have entered from the **Notes** pane below the slide. Let's say that the Marketing 101 professor wanted his teaching assistants to reinforce this information in their discussion sections during the first week of class. Instead of having to provide training to the teaching assistants, he could add notes to this same presentation and provide a "script" for them to follow so that they all consistently deliver the same information. Notice the "frame" around the page in Figure 4.17.

- Notes and Notes pages are also used in business situations. Just a few examples are product announcements, corporate training, canned sales presentations, and new employee training. Notes pages are used whenever a consistent message needs to be delivered.

Figure 4.17 | **Notes Page**

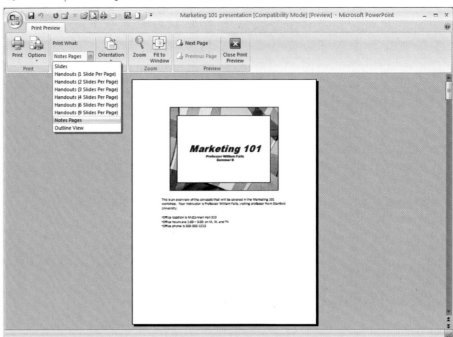

- **Outline View**: Shows only the text from each slide. Generally, you use this option when you want to read the content of the slides and are not concerned with the graphics. This option is not used with audiences because it does not represent all the content in the slides.

You have three color options when printing your slides: **Color**, **Grayscale**, and **Pure Black and White**. The option you choose depends on the impact you are trying to make or the message you are delivering with the audience. While you are still creating and revising, save your money and print black-and-white. However, for the final presentation, if you have to make handouts, try to use color. Studies have shown that color deliverables have a more positive effect on recipients than black-and-white or shades of gray.

- **Color**: Prints your slides as shown on the screen. Color would be a good choice when the presentation includes graphics or when the color of text has a particular meaning. For example, in project reviews, the color green means that an activity or task is on time and on budget. Red means that there is schedule and/or budget variance. An executive could quickly glance through the presentation and focus on the "red areas." If this presentation were not printed in color, all the visual clues would be lost.

- **Grayscale**: Prints color images on a black-and-white printer because it uses shades of gray to convey color differences. Printing in grayscale would be useful when you need to distinguish color differences in some way but do not want the expense of color.

- **Pure Black and White**: Prints with no colors "in between." Even if you choose gray as a color on your slide in PowerPoint, it will print out as black with this option. You might use this option when previewing your slides or printing a draft copy.

Figure 4.18 illustrates the Marketing 101 presentation in these three color schemes.

Figure 4.18 | **Color, Grayscale, and Pure Black-and-White Slides**

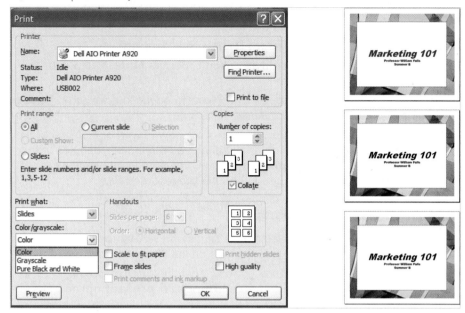

>> Basic Presentation Options

The purpose of this workshop is to demonstrate the on-screen delivery and printing options reviewed in this section. You will see these tasks demonstrated in the following three videos: **Slide Show**, **Transition**, and **Print**. Remember to try the tasks on your own first before watching the video. You will need to open the file named ib_p04_videowkshop.

1. **Slide Show (Video: Slide Show)**

   a. Select **From Beginning** on the **Slide Show** group and run through the entire presentation.

   b. Select slides 2 and 8, then choose **Hide Slide** from the **Set Up** group to hide them; run through the presentation from the beginning.

   c. Unhide slides 2 and 8, select slide 8 as the current slide, and run the slide show again by selecting **From Current Slide** from the **Slide Show** tab.

   d. Select **Custom Slide Show**.
      - Click the **New** button.
      - Name the slide show **Market Segmentation Consultation**.
      - Click slides 2, 6, 7, 9–12 while holding down the **Ctrl** key.
      - Click the **Add** button to group these slides into a custom show.
      - Click the **OK** button.
      - Click the **Show** button to ensure the correct slides were added to the custom slide show.
      - Click **Close.**

e. Click **Set Up Slide Show**.

- From the dialog box, select **Loop continuously until 'Esc'** and run the presentation through two loops.

2. Rehearsed Timing (Video: Rehearsed Timing)

a. Select the **Rehearse Timings** option under the **Slide Show** tab. This will start the presentation.

b. Rehearse the presentation, clicking **Next** to advance each slide, **Pause** to stop, and **Repeat** to continue.

c. Once you complete the presentation, note how PowerPoint has recorded the time spent on each slide. Now when you run the presentation with the **Using timings**, **if present** option, PowerPoint automatically advances to each slide based upon the pre-recorded time.

3. Animations (Video: Animations)

a. In **Slide Sorter** view, select all the slides and set **Advance Slide Automatically After:** to 2 seconds on the **Animations** tab.

b. Go back to the **Slide Show** tab and open the **Set Up Show** dialog box. Make sure the **Using timings, if present** option is selected.

c. Return to the **Animations** tab. Apply one of the following combinations of transition and sound to all the slides:

- Fades and Dissolves   Chime
- Wipes   Cash Register
- Push and Cover   Typewriter
- Stripes and Bars   Wind
- Random   Applause

d. Return to the **Slide Show** tab and run the presentation using the **From the Beginning** option. Press the **Esc** key to stop.

4. Web Delivery (Video: Web Delivery)

a. Select **Save As** and then save as a single file Web page using the same file name (ib_p04_videowkshop), but the file type MHTML.

b. Select the Publish button and launch your browser

c. Scroll through each slide to make sure it renders properly and within the browser window.

5. Print (Video: Print)

a. Launch **Print** from the **Office Button**.

b. In the **Print Range** box, enter 2, 5, 8-12 in the **Slides** box.

c. Select **Pure Black and White**, 2 copies, and check the **Collate** box.

d. Print these slides in each of the following combinations:

- Handouts   3 per page   Grayscale
- Handouts   4 per page   Color

e. In the **Notes** pane for slide 3, type This will be on the quiz.

f. Print the Notes pages in color with only one copy.

>> Customizing a Slide Show

As you gain experience as a business professional, you will be asked to give more presentations to larger audiences. It is important that you learn two techniques to manage your growing library of presentations and your busy speaking schedule. By using a single, master slide deck and "extracting" the necessary slides to create a custom slide show, you can keep your library of presentations down to a small, manageable number. Copying and pasting slides from one presentation to another and managing dozens of PowerPoint files can be very unproductive work. You also don't want to end up with so many files that you forget what you have already created and start from scratch by mistake. Experienced presenters who are highly in demand are also skilled at recognizing when they do and do not have to personally deliver a presentation themselves. If no audience interaction is required, a self-running presentation is an appropriate presentation delivery choice.

Exercise

The purpose of this exercise is to create three targeted presentations from a single deck of slides and select the appropriate on-screen display and printing options. The first presentation will be created for an audience of college business students who are hoping to start their own businesses after graduation. The second presentation is for a group of women entrepreneurs who wish to expand their existing companies by raising capital. The third presentation is for the Student Union kiosk and will run unattended for the rest of the day.

Open the file named ib_p04_entrepreneur.

1. For the student presentation, create a Custom Slide Show named **For Morning Students**.

   a. Assemble the appropriate slides that explain the different types of firms and how to get started.

   b. Print the slides that summarize the organizational structure types and how to get started as handouts on one page.

   c. Print color transparencies as a backup in case the business school equipment fails.

2. For the entrepreneur presentation, hide the slides that do not pertain to financing and create a Custom Slide Show named **For Entrepreneurs**

   a. Print the presenation so that there are lines on the right side of the page to take notes.

   b. Print the financing worksheet on a single page.

3. For the kiosk presentation, create a custom slide show named **For Kiosk** that includes all the slides except the "Financing Worksheet." and has the appropriate title slide.

   a. Select a transition effect that transitions each slide in like a news flash along with the sound of a cash register.

   b. Select an appropriate slide timing that would allow a group of students gathered around the kiosk ample time to read all the bullets on the current slide before it transitions to the next slide.

   c. Run the presentation to test it.

4. Hide the two title slides that have the shorter title names and save the presentation as **ib_p04_entrepreneurweb**.

>> What's Wrong with This Presentation?

Problem

You are the newly hired assistant director of a small business program. Your school has been running a series of popular entrepreneur workshops. There is a long waiting list for additional workshops; however, the program needs additional funding to be able to offer any more workshops this year. You decide to approach the local Rotary Club and ask for financial assistance and their involvement. The Rotary Club is a group of retired former executives who are active in the business community and support initiatives such as yours. The president graciously invited you to be the keynote speaker at the club's golf outing breakfast, just before they hit the greens! The treasurer of the Rotary Club will not be at the outing, but the president promised to send her a copy of your slides to read before the next Rotary Club board meeting, which is scheduled one week from the golf outing.

Because you are new to the organization, you have to borrow your boss's PC to run the presentation. He hurriedly retrieved the PC from the kiosk where the presentation was running and left it on your desk along with the following note:

Sorry I was so late in getting the PC back to the office. The student kiosk was a hit, and we ran later than anticipated. Here is the presentation you will need for your Rotary meeting tomorrow morning. I didn't have time to customize it for those guys, but I put in some notes for you to use to explain the program. Just walk them through the first part of the presentation and skip the financing part. Please do your best to be sure to get on the agenda for their next board meeting. If we don't get funding from them, we will have no more workshops until next year. Feel free to leave behind copies of the presentation. We have a nice color printer in the mailroom you can use. Good luck!

Exercise

The file your boss gives you is named ib_p04_whatswrong. Open the file and run the presentation. What's wrong with this presentation? Would you feel comfortable presenting it before an audience you hope to solicit for program funding? Consider the following:

1. Because the presentation has not been customized, how will you have to verbally position the content on each slide?

2. Are the notes in the Notes pages appropriate?
   a. Are they a mixture of speaker notes and audience notes?
   b. Will you be able to provide the notes as is for the treasurer to read?
   c. If not, how will you have to modify the notes?
   d. Do you think the treasurer will even need notes to understand the context of the presentation?

3. Will this audience require or appreciate handouts? Why or why not?

4. Are the delivery parameters used in the presentation appropriate for the intended audience? Evaluate the following and provide specific recommendations on changes you would make in these areas:
   - Slide theme
   - Slide show
   - Transitions
   - Print setup

Write a short answer for each of the points listed here. Then apply any formatting techniques you think are necessary to produce an effective and professional presentation to the Rotary Club.

Solution from page 118

After the senior manager incident, I decided to discontinue hand-outs in my business presentations. A few people noticed, but they did not insist on having handouts. That was the first surprise because I felt sure there would a noticeable cry from the staff. A few months went by, and I made the following observations:

- The presentations involved less talking on my part and more group discussion.
- We actually got more done in the same time frame.
- My relationship with the management team deepened, and I was asked to work on more strategic initiatives.
- My secretary was much happier now that I was not asking her to make dozens of color copies all the time.

Assignment

One exception to the rule of not providing handouts with presentations occurs when you are presenting recurring information, such as status reports. Audiences like hard copies so that they can file them away, go back and reread them, and see the progress over time. There may also be an instance when you, the presenter, want the audience to pick up the handout, read it quickly, say "thanks," and then leave without interrogating you further. An example of this latter situation is weekly corporate project status reports. Create a short PowerPoint presentation that you could use for a monthly meeting to report on the status of a project to a corporate steering committee. Assume that the audience is the same each time and that they already have the background on the project. Include the following information:

- Name of project, corporate sponsor, and project manager
- Timeline and current status
- Budget and current status
- Risk plan with mitigation strategies and current status
- Staffing issues, if any
- Additional issues for the committee to be aware of

Be sure to apply the following:

- Color or other visual effects.
- Audience notes (not speaker notes). Print out Notes pages and handouts pages.
- Transitions, if appropriate. Explain why or why not.

Questions for Discussion

1. How does the nature of business conversations change when there are no handouts?
2. What can you say about the difference between business presentations and business discussions?
3. If someone insists that he needs a copy of the presentation for the meeting, what should you do?
4. Under what circumstances would you send out the presentation ahead of time?
5. In academic situations, should the practice of giving handouts to the students be discontinued in the interest of facilitating better classroom discussion?

The following questions are related to the concepts addressed in this chapter. There are three types of questions: Short Answer, True or False, and Fill in the Blank. If your answer to a True or False question is False, write a short explanation as to why you think the statement is not true.

1. **Slide Show** determines how the slides _____

2. Animation deals with how the slides _____.

3. Transitions deal with _____.

4. True or False: You can use Rehearse Timings to practice delivering your presentations in the allotted time.

5. True or False: Publishing your slides to the Web is not necessary because most everybody has PowerPoint installed on their computers these days.

6. To view slides that are in HTML format, you only need _____ software.

7. What are the four ways you can print slides?

8. True or False: You can launch the **Print** function using **Ctrl+L**.

9. True or False: Two slides per handout are commonly used for note-taking.

10. The number of slides you can place on a handout (other than one) is ____, ____, ____, ____, and ____.

11. How is **Grayscale** different from **Pure Black and White**?

12. For anything to be included on the Notes page, the presenter must have entered information in the _____.

13. Two ways to advance slides are _____ and _____.

14. True or False: **Hide** and **Unhide Slides** are two separate icons.

15. Loop continuously is used when running presentations in _____.

16. How can you print nonconsecutive slides?

17. You can launch your presentation from the _____ slide or the _____ slide.

18. True or False: Using **Custom Slide Show** requires manual updates to each presentation every time a slide changes.

The following exam is designed to test your ability to recognize and execute the PowerPoint skills presented in this chapter. Read each question carefully and answer the questions in the order they are listed. You should be able to complete this exam in 60 minutes or less.

You are in a situation in which you are educating people in your organization about what e-commerce is and making recommendations on how to use this technology at the same time. Over the next few months, you will be making several presentations to various audiences to champion this cause. Instead of creating several presentations, you decided to create a master presentation and use the appropriate subset of slides for each audience.

Open the file named ib_p04_skillsexam and apply the appropriate **Slide Show, Transitions,** and **Print** options for the following audiences. The objectives for each audience are listed as follows:

1. Corporate planning manager: This is the person who will accept and prioritize your project and allocate funding for it.

   a. Objectives: Explain and justify this initiative from a business perspective. This individual is interested in the scope of your ideas, who will benefit, and what your strategy for implementation is. The corporate philosophy is that upfront investment (training, consulting, etc.) is acceptable, but in the long run, the corporation needs to be self-sufficient. This will be a one-on-one meeting.

2. Information systems development team: This is a team of young programmers and web designers who are coming off a large project and are well versed in current technologies.

   a. Objectives: Convince these individuals that the company is committed to state of the art technology and that there will be exciting and interesting project work for the foreseeable future. This will be a group presentation.

3. Corporate communications: This group publishes the monthly electronic "What's News" newsletter by e-mail to all employees. In a kiosk outside the cafeteria, a corporate "news anchor" reads the current news in broadcast style with the PowerPoint slides in the background.

   a. Objectives: Convey high-level information about corporate initiatives to a wide and diverse employee base. This department does not have an expertise in or knowledge of e-commerce and requires, quite literally, the exact words and language.

4. Outside consultants: There are several of them, and they all want to bid on this project if it is eventually funded.

   a. Objectives: Convey enough information to the consultants about the scope of the initiative so that they can bring the correct resources to bear and start their own planning. However, because the goal of a consultant is to drive as much revenue as possible and "control" the client, you need to manage the details around what information is provided and how it is disseminated.

The following questions are designed to test your ability to apply the PowerPoint skills you have learned to complete a business objective. Use your knowledge of PowerPoint as well as your creativity to answer these questions. For most questions, there are several possible ways to complete the objective.

The first three to five years as a small business owner or entrepreneur are challenging. It is estimated that 50% of businesses fail in the first year and 95% fail within five years. Many small businesses fail because of fundamental shortcomings in their business planning. The business plan must be well thought out, realistic, and based on accurate and current information. In addition, bankers and other business stakeholders require that a sound and up-to-date business plan be in place at all times.

1. Create a PowerPoint presentation of a high-level business plan for a retail store that sells business and game software. The components of the plan may include but are not limited to

    - Description of the business

    - Vision and goals

    - Critical success factors

    - Staffing and skill sets needed

    - Analysis of competition

    - Marketing, advertising, and promotional activities

2. Given the following scenarios, can you reuse the same slides and deliver this presentation for the following audiences? If your answer is yes, explain how you will accomplish this. If your answer is no, explain why.

    a. As an entrepreneur, you are presenting to a potential investor who is evaluating several business opportunities in addition to yours. Your objective is to differentiate yourself from the other presenters, instill confidence, and acquire financial backing.

    b. As the assistant director of the small business program, you are using this presentation for a workshop. Your objective is to use this business plan as an educational tool for the attendees to model their own business plans after.

    c. As the assistant director of the small business program, you are using this presentation to train several workshop facilitators to offer more business planning sessions.

3. Is it even possible to run this presentation unattended? Why or why not?

    a. What general conclusions can you make about how and when to use self-running, unattended presentations?

4. In your opinion, is it better to postpone a presentation until you can be there to personally deliver it yourself?

    a. In what business situations can you send someone the notes and ask that person to deliver your presentation for you?

    b. What are the advantages and risks of having someone else deliver your presentation for you?

 Chapter 5

Applying the Core Skills

Chapter Goals

The purpose of this chapter is to show how the skills covered in this text can be applied to create presentations in two practical situations. As a student, you will be required to present your research papers or project results. As a business professional, you will constantly be asked to synthesize documents that are internal and external to the organization. This chapter brings together all the skills you have learned so far to show you how to convert large amounts of information into a single, time-constrained presentation.

>> **PowerPoint** | **Skill Sets**

Converting Documents into Presentations

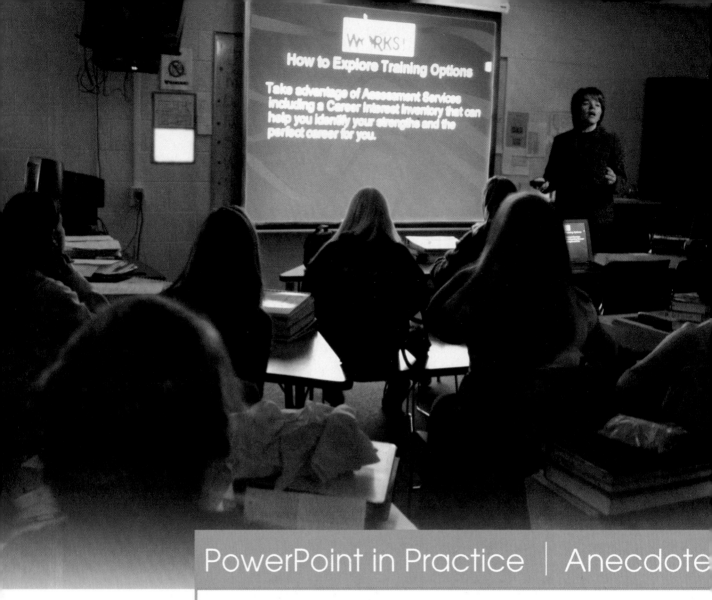

PowerPoint in Practice | Anecdote

My Role as the "RFP Guru"

Imagine taking a 200+ page document and boiling it down into a one-hour presentation. That's exactly what businesspeople who are involved with RFPs have to do.

An RFP, short for *Request for Proposal*, is a document that an organization sends to vendors to solicit competitive bids for products and services. Vendors prepare and submit an RFP response which answers specific questions that the organization asks, details the proposed solution, and includes pricing.

In a typical RFP process, the vendors receive the RFP and have a deadline in which to respond. Depending on the complexity of the situation, an RFP response can be quite large, sometimes up to hundreds of pages. Vendors submit their responses in writing and present their proposal to the decision makers in person. If your organization "makes the cut," you then go on to the next phase of competing for the business. Some RFPs are multiyear and multimillion dollars in size and scope. Because business opportunities of that magnitude don't come along every day, competition is fierce. You have to do your best and be the best every step of the way to win the deal.

Responding to RFPs is grueling and can take hundreds of hours. You have to pull together information from many sources, consult with the experts in your company, and ultimately submit the written response. Everyone hates to work on RFPs and usually tries to delegate the task to the new kid or the youngest member of the team. Early in my career, I got the dreaded task of handling the RFPs that came into the office, and I was not happy about it—until I learned a little secret that earned me the title "RFP Guru."

>> Continued on page 159

>> Converting Documents into Presentations

There are few situations in which you will need to create a PowerPoint presentation completely from scratch. You will almost always have some sort of documentation as a starting point. For example, as a student you may have the following tools:

- Research papers
- Project results
- Lecture notes
- Textbooks
- Web sites

As a business professional, you may have the following documentation to use:

- Internal research
- White papers
- Vendor literature
- Memos
- Project documentation

The main difference between documents such as memos, research papers, white papers, and web sites and PowerPoint presentations is this: Documents and web sites are read by an audience; presentations are delivered to an audience. A subtle difference in accountability takes place. Even though the audience is perfectly capable of reading and understanding the content on the slides, the presenter assumes responsibility for their comprehension. If a person in the audience doesn't understand the message, he or she will not say, "I must not have read that information carefully enough." Instead, that person will say, "That speaker was not very good." That is why it is very important to treat presentations differently and use the right process to create them.

Another major difference is that documents are written using complete sentences and paragraphs. Presentations are written using short, bulleted phrases. Because slides are displayed, attention must also be paid to the "real estate," that is, the amount of space physically available to convey your messages.

So the issue is not necessarily acquiring the information; usually, plenty of written material is available out there. The challenge becomes pulling all the information together into a focused and time-constrained deliverable. Many people think this is an easy task and leave it to the last minute. They couldn't be more wrong. In this section, you will learn an approach to creating a high-quality presentation using existing information. You will also learn presentation delivery techniques to ensure that after all the hard work you put into creating the presentation, you will deliver it like a seasoned professional.

Develop a Road Map

If you were to travel long distance, you wouldn't get into your car, start driving, and hope to arrive at your destination in time (or at all!) without directions. Navigating the endless interstate highways and state roads between your start and finish would be very difficult. Likely, you would use a road map that lists each stop along the way to tell you how to efficiently move from point A to point B. If you were traveling with a friend, by using the road map, each of you could take turns driving (delegation) and get there.

To transform a large amount of information found in documents and web sites (or even other slide decks) into a time-constrained presentation, you need a road map. Recall that, in Chapter 1, you learned how to plan your presentation and create an outline. You learned that creating an outline didn't take as much time as you had thought and that your time was well spent. In this section, you will learn how to create a road map from an outline. Similarly, it doesn't take as much time as you might think and is time well spent.

In this section we will use a paper titled "Motivating Through Leadership and Communication" in two separate examples. In the first example, you (the student) will be asked to present this paper to a class. In the second example, you (the business professional) will use this paper as one of the sources of information for a presentation on the results of an employee satisfaction survey. The figures in this section include excerpts from this paper. You may also open the Word file named ib_p05_managementpaper if you would like to read the entire document.

Consider the following academic scenario. Your group was assigned the topic of employee motivation for an Introduction to Management course. This research paper was written by a leading authority in the field, and your team's objective is to present its contents to the class and instructor. You have 20 minutes in which to present the paper to your class. Let's go back to the basics and create a plan and outline.

As you learned in Chapter 1, the four-step planning process addresses the following questions:

- Step 1: What are the objectives?
- Step 2: Who is the audience?
- Step 3: What are the key messages/decisions?
- Step 4: How much time do you have?

After gathering the planning information, you learned how to create an outline that has the following sections:

- Agenda
- Introduction
- Body
- Conclusion

Figure 5.1 illustrates the planning information and outline for a student presentation.

Figure 5.1 | **Plan and Outline for a Student Presentation**

Planning Process	Presentation Outline
Objectives	1. Title
• This presentation is informational only.	2. Agenda
	3. Introduction
Audience	4. Effective Communication
• Instructor and the class	5. Strong Leadership
	6. Goal Setting
Key Messages/Decisions	7. Teamwork
• Explain the techniques for motivating employees.	8. Participative Management
	9. Summary
Time	10. References
• 20 minutes; there should be 7–10 slides	

To transform your outline into a road map, simply create a table that lists each slide from your outline, the source(s) of content for that slide, and any additional instructions, as shown in Figure 5.2. This approach has the following benefits:

- To create each slide, you know exactly what page(s) in the paper to turn to.
- If you can't identify where in the paper to get the information from, you will know right away that you need another source (such as a textbook, magazine article, or web site).

- By clearly identifying the structure of the presentation and where the information is going to come from, you can delegate the work to other members on your team.

The road map might look like Figure 5.2.

Figure 5.2 | **Road Map for Student Presentation**

Slide	Source of Information
1. Title	➤ Title page of paper: *Motivating Through Leadership and Communication*
2. Agenda	➤ Go back and create this at the end.
3. Introduction	➤ Start with the first phrase in the Dessler textbook, page 283.
	➤ Use paragraph 1 on page 2.
	➤ Add last sentence, first paragraph, page 2.
Body: Employee Motivation Strategies	
4. Effective Communication	➤ Middle of page 2
5. Strong Leadership	➤ Bottom of page 2–first paragraphs of page 3
6. Goal Setting	➤ Page 3 and copy diagram
7. Teamwork	➤ Page 4
8. Participative Management	➤ Page 5
9. Summary	➤ Peter Drucker quote: *"Management is doing things right; leadership is doing the right things."*
	➤ Last paragraph on page 6
10. References	➤ List references from last page.
	➤ Check format in paper against *APA Style Guide.*

As you examine this road map, note the following:

- The speaker organized this presentation into sections.
- Each slide includes specific instructions on where to get the content. Therefore, it would be easy to delegate parts of the presentation to someone else.
- The presenter decided to copy a diagram from the paper in addition to bullets.
- Not all the information for this presentation was available solely in the paper. For example, the Introduction uses information from the student textbook.
- The presenter was not sure about the references formatting and would like to check another source.

Using existing documents as the basis for presentations is common in the business world. Consider the business scenario in this next example: Your department's employee satisfaction survey results were poor, with especially low scores in the employee motivation category. You have been given the task of presenting this information to the department supervisors and creating a plan for improvement. Your manager scheduled a 30-minute time slot at the next department meeting to do this. Your plan, outline, and road map (see Figures 5.3 and 5.4) would be different, but you would still use the approach described for the preceding example.

Figure 5.3 | **Plan and Outline for Business Presentation**

Planning Process	Presentation Outline
Objectives	1. Title
• Summarize the employee satisfaction survey results.	2. Agenda
	3. Introduction
• Present an action plan.	4. Employee Satisfaction Survey
	5. Employee Motivation Strategies
Audience	6. Next Steps
• Department supervisors	7. Action Plan
Key Messages/Decisions	
• Results of survey	
• Discussion of motivational techniques	
• Group buy-in on next steps	
Time	
• 30 minutes and there will be discussion; no more than 10 slides	

Figure 5.4 | **Road Map for Presentation**

Slide	Source of Information
1. Title	➤ *Employee Satisfaction Survey Results*
2. Agenda	➤ Go back and create this at the end.
3. Introduction	➤ Pull the paragraph from page 3 of the annual report that quotes our CEO saying, *"Our people are our competitive advantage."*
Body: Employee Satisfaction Survey	
4. Summary of Survey	➤ First paragraph of VP of Human Resources memorandum
5. Questions Asked	➤ Page 1 of the Employee Satisfaction survey; list the numbered questions
6. Results	➤ Copy the Excel bar chart from the survey results report.
7. Employee Motivation Strategies	➤ Reference the *Motivating Through Leadership and Communication* paper and author credentials.
	➤ Summarize the motivation strategies on 1–2 slides.
8. Next Steps	➤ List the directives from the department head memo.
9. Action Plan	➤ Use this slide to kick off a working session with group.

Notice how, in this scenario, the research paper is one of several sources of information. Business presentations tend to use multiple resources. The reason is that many business initiatives are cross-functional and involve experts and stakeholders from different parts of the organization who provide input. Business presentations also involve the use of external information, such as industry analyst reports or market research information, to facilitate objective decision making.

Assemble Your Presentation

Now that you have the road map, you are ready to assemble your presentation. Notice the use of the word *assemble* instead of *create*. Creating implies that you develop the material from scratch; assembling implies that you are combining existing components.

Assembling existing information for an audience from documents means you will have to do the following:

- Utilize a variety of information sources.
- Convert long sentences and prose into bulleted lists.
- Be cognizant of the available space (real estate) on slides to avoid overcrowding.
- Search for (or create if you have to) graphics and diagrams to convey information visually.
- Acknowledge the use of others' materials through references.

Converting Text into Bullets

To convert text into bullets successfully and not lose valuable content or context, read through the material carefully, identify the key points, and turn sentences into short phrases or sentences. This may sound easy, but it is one of the hardest tasks to do well. For example, while trying to create short bullets, you don't want to shorten the sentences so much that nobody understands what you are saying. Tip: Recognize and accept the fact that you may have to go back several times and tweak the bullets until they look right and convey the right message.

The example in Figure 5.5 from the "Motivating Through Leadership and Communication" paper shows a paragraph that discusses the what, why, and how of employee motivation.

Figure 5.5 | **Sample Paragraph from Research Paper**

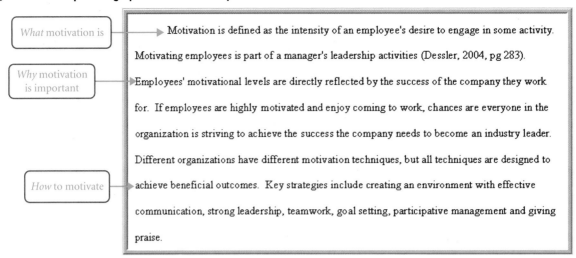

Figure 5.6 shows how this information would be converted into the Introduction PowerPoint slide for the class presentation assignment discussed in the previous section.

Figure 5.6 | **Example of Converting Text into Bullets**

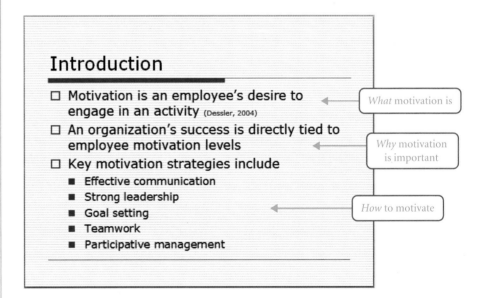

How much information should you put on a slide? A general rule of thumb is no more than six lines per slide for readability reasons. Keep this guideline in mind, but remember that the objective is not to have cluttered slides. Figure 5.6 illustrates how the what, why, and how of employee motivation are converted from a single paragraph into a single slide. Complete sentences from the paragraph are written as shorter sentences or phrases. Long sentences are broken down into smaller bullets.

Presenting Information Visually

Audiences respond well to information that is presented visually (using charts, graphics, diagrams, etc.). Look for opportunities to use this approach to your advantage when converting text from documents into slides. For example, if you received the memo from the Vice President of Human Resources, as shown in Figure 5.7, you might want to represent the information visually as a timeline (graphic), as shown in Figure 5.8.

Figure 5.7 | **Sample Memo**

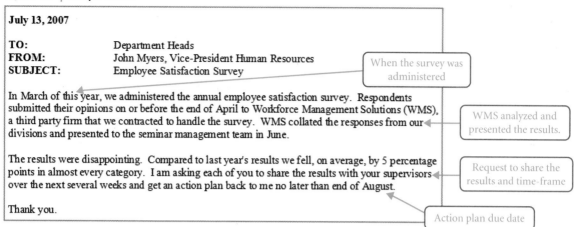

July 13, 2007

TO: Department Heads
FROM: John Myers, Vice-President Human Resources
SUBJECT: Employee Satisfaction Survey

When the survey was administered

In March of this year, we administered the annual employee satisfaction survey. Respondents submitted their opinions on or before the end of April to Workforce Management Solutions (WMS), a third party firm that we contracted to handle the survey. WMS collated the responses from our divisions and presented to the seminar management team in June.

WMS analyzed and presented the results.

The results were disappointing. Compared to last year's results we fell, on average, by 5 percentage points in almost every category. I am asking each of you to share the results with your supervisors over the next several weeks and get an action plan back to me no later than end of August.

Request to share the results and time-frame

Thank you.

Action plan due date

Figure 5.8 | **Converting Text into a Graphic**

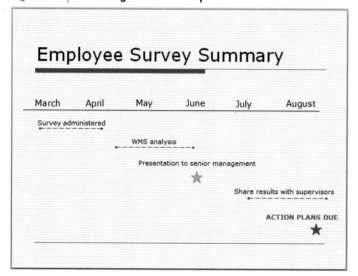

Text from the memo is converted into an activity and its timeline. Notice how color and bold are used to emphasize the point that a significant milestone is coming up in August.

Reference Your Sources

In this day and age when enormous amounts of information are available at your fingertips, be sure to list your sources so that you do not inadvertently violate copyright or permissions laws. References also add credibility to the presentation. In business, for example, you would need to reference the source of information when copying or pasting financial or product information or a quote from an organization's literature.

For example, the Introduction slide from a business presentation that uses the CEO's quote from the annual report might look like the one shown in Figure 5.9.

Figure 5.9 | **Citing References**

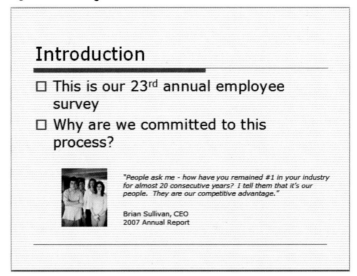

If you have a long list of sources, use a separate page at the end of the presentation or put it in an Addendum section.

COMMON MISTAKES | **Copying Directly from the Source Document**

The author of a presentation has to meet different expectations than the author of a document, memo, or web site does. Inexperienced presenters do not realize, or they forget, that they have to design and assemble a presentation that stays within time constraints, engages the audience, promotes discussion, facilitates a business decision, and so on. To effectively meet these objectives, you must remember that it is not feasible to copy information directly from a source document onto a PowerPoint slide.

Reuse Word and Excel Objects

You can reuse Microsoft Word tables or Excel spreadsheets in your presentations. This strategy will save you time when assembling your presentation. Word and Excel have built-in features that PowerPoint does not have (such as sort, merge, formulas, and charts). Therefore, you may want to use these features to create your object before inserting it into a presentation.

To insert an Excel spreadsheet into a PowerPoint slide, do the following:

- In Excel, highlight the cells you wish to copy and select **Copy** from the **Home** tab.
- In PowerPoint, select **Paste Special** from the **Home** tab and highlight **Microsoft Excel Worksheet Object**.
- Click **OK** and the selected cells will be placed on your slide.

To insert an Excel chart into a PowerPoint slide, follow these steps:

- In Excel, highlight the chart you wish to copy and select **Copy** from the **Home** tab.
- In PowerPoint, select **Paste Special** from the **Home** tab and highlight **Microsoft Office Drawing Object**.
- Click **OK** and the selected cells will be placed on your slide.

The spreadsheet and the resulting chart are treated as two separate Microsoft objects and are imbedded into a slide, as shown in Figure 5.10.

Figure 5.10 | **Insert an Excel Spreadsheet and Chart into a PowerPoint Slide**

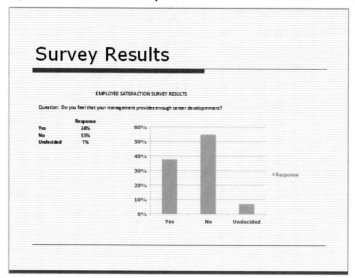

To insert a Word table into a PowerPoint slide, follow these steps:

- In Word, highlight the rows and columns you wish to copy and select **Copy** from the **Home** tab.
- In PowerPoint, select **Paste** from the **Home** tab.
- The rows and columns will be placed on your slide.

Figure 5.11 shows an example of Word table that has been inserted in a slide.

Figure 5.11 | **Insert a Word Table into a PowerPoint Slide**

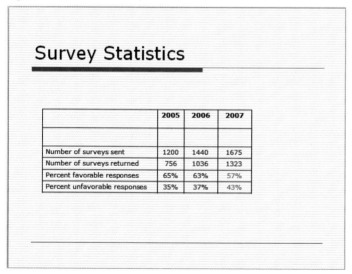

Effective Delivery Techniques

Creating presentations and delivering presentations are two different and equally important skill sets. To deliver the complete package, you really have to be good at both.

Throughout this book, you have learned and been reminded that you don't need to be a graphic artist to create professional business presentations. You will do well by applying the instructions from this textbook, using your good judgment, and practicing. The same is true for delivering presentations. You do not have to take speaking lessons or be a ten-year veteran of Toastmasters International (the world's leading verbal communication

>> *Quick Reference*

Inserting an Excel Spreadsheet or Chart into PowerPoint

1. To insert an Excel spreadsheet into a PowerPoint slide, follow these steps:

   a. In Excel, highlight the cells you wish to copy and select **Copy** from the **Home** tab.

   b. In PowerPoint, select **Paste Special** from the **Home** tab and highlight **Microsoft Excel Worksheet Object**.

   c. Click **OK** and the selected cells will be placed on your slide.

2. To insert an Excel chart into a PowerPoint slide, follow these steps:

   a. In Excel, highlight the chart you wish to copy and select **Copy** from the **Home** tab.

   b. In PowerPoint, select **Paste Special** from the **Home** tab and highlight **Microsoft Office Drawing Object**.

   c. Click **OK** and the selected chart will be placed on your slide.

organization; see http://www.toastmasters.org). By applying the following simple strategies and giving presentations on a regular basis, you will be surprised at how quickly you become an excellent speaker.

Practice, Practice, Practice

Practice is the most important technique, and it cannot be avoided. There are no shortcuts to knowing your presentation inside and out. Many people think that by practicing their presentation, it will appear rehearsed and less than natural. Nothing could be further from the truth.

The reality is that by practicing your presentation, it will become so ingrained in your mind that your self-confidence will be very high. When the time finally comes to deliver it, you will be relaxed and appear highly polished. When you are confident and relaxed, your audience will be confident and relaxed.

Another surprising insight is that by the time you have done the presentation planning, created an outline, developed a road map, and carefully assembled the slide deck, you will have internalized the presentation more than you realize. If you have done all the right things up front, there may not be that much more practicing to do.

How long do you need to practice?

- Until you reach the point at which you only have to glance at the title of the slide and can comfortably turn to the audience and begin discussing the points.

- Until you having the timing down pat. It is never acceptable to go over your allotted time or to end up with a lot of time left over. At most, you should be five minutes under. If, by practicing, you discover that you need more time, either pare back the slides or ask for more time right away. If you discover that you need less time, go back over your outline and road map to make sure you haven't left anything out. Be very careful about asking for less time; it gives people the impression that you are not knowledgeable enough to do a good job.

The Speaking Part

The best presenters don't just present; they "connect" with the audience. Everyone has his or her own style of speaking, but the best practices are

- Use a normal tone of voice.

- Rehearse with someone to be sure you aren't speaking too fast or displaying a nervous habit.

- Make brief eye contact with different members of the audience, moving slowly from left to right and then back the other direction. Do not listen to the advice that says to "stare straight ahead and pretend the audience is not there." You can't connect with people if you do that.

- Don't advance to another slide until you are done with the first. Pause while the slide transitions to the next one and then start speaking again.

- Do not turn your back to the audience.

- Do not stand in front of the slides.

- Try to have someone in the audience give you the "five-minute signal"; that is, have someone let you know when you have only five minutes left. If you've practiced and timed your presentation, you should be wrapping up anyway. If you say something like "We have a only few minutes left, so I'd like to end by saying . . . " you will convey to the audience that you are in control. Audiences like that.

Anticipate and Prepare for Questions

Most business presentations involve discussion either woven into the presentation or at the end. Find out if and when you are going to have questions and prepare for them, both from content and a timing perspective. If the questions come between slides, answer them and then smoothly go back to the presentation. Nothing can

>> **Quick Reference**

Inserting a Word Table into PowerPoint

1. In Word, highlight the rows and columns you wish to copy and select **Copy** from the **Home** tab.

2. In PowerPoint, select **Paste** from the **Home** tab.

3. Click **OK** and the rows and columns will be placed on your slide.

destroy an excellent presentation faster than the presenter not being prepared to answer questions.

Check Out the Logistics

Logistics means room size, arrangement of tables and chairs, acoustics, where the screen is, where you stand, and so on. These details may seem insignificant, but many presentations have been ruined by the presenter's neglecting this aspect. If you cannot inspect the logistics in person, ask someone else to do it and get back to you.

Should You Present Someone Else's Slides?

Do not present someone else's slides unless you are very familiar with the topic or have delivered similar presentations. Most people do not realize the preparation that needs to take place to professionally deliver a presentation. They think you can just launch PowerPoint and read the slides—because that's what they do!

≫ Converting Documents into Presentations

VIDEO WORKSHOP

Having the material you need for a presentation already available gives you a tremendous head start. But remember that documents and other written sources of information need to be converted into a presentation format to be consumed by an audience. The purpose of this workshop is to demonstrate the key skills needed to convert written materials into presentation-ready materials. We will be converting content from a document into slides. You will see these tasks demonstrated in the following three videos: **Convert Text to Bullets**, **Present Information Visually with a Table**, and **Present Information Visually with a Pie Chart**. Try to complete these tasks on your own first before watching the videos.

Open the Word file named ib_p05_managementpaper.

1. **Convert Text to Bullets (Video: Convert Text to Bullets)**
   a. Open PowerPoint and create a new presentation.
   b. Change the first slide to have the **Title and Content** layout and type `Employee Motivation Strategies` as the title.
   c. Make the first bullet `Effective Communication`.
   d. In Word, go to page 2 in the paper and locate the paragraph that explains effective communication.
   e. In PowerPoint, under the first bullet, indent and insert the following sub-bullets
      * `Involves a sender transmitting an idea to a receiver`
      * `Is effective only if the receiver understands the intended information`
      * `Leaders and managers coach, coordinate, and evaluate through this process`

f. Make the definition (the first bullet) a different color than the strategy (the second and third bullets).

g. Save your presentation as **ib_p05_motivation**.

2. **Present Information Visually: Insert a Table (Video: Present Information Visually with a Table)**

   a. Open the presentation named ib_p05_motivation created in step 1.

   b. Insert a new slide after the first slide using the **Title and Content** layout.

   c. Title the slide **Rankings**.

   d. Copy and paste the following Word table that lists the strategies and rankings:

	Rank
Strong leadership	1
Effective communication	2
Goal setting	3
Participative management	4
Teamwork	5

   e. Save your presentation as **ib_p05_motivationv2**.

3. **Present Information Visually: Insert a Pie Chart (Video: Present Information Visually with a Pie Chart)**

   a. Open the presentation named ib_p05_motivationv2. altered in step 2.

   b. Insert a new slide after the second slide using the **Title and Content** layout.

   c. Title the slide **Survey Responses**.

   d. Open the Excel file named Survey Responses. Copy and paste the pie chart that shows the percent response for each motivation strategy.

   e. Save your presentation as **ib_p05_motivationv3**.

EXERCISE

Why Do I Need This?

>> Turning the Road Map into a Project Plan

Many business school programs now include a senior or "Capstone" paper and presentation as a requirement for graduation. The purpose of the Capstone is for students to collect, synthesize, and present the knowledge they have gained throughout the course of their program. Many students do not realize that the Capstone process is similar to what takes place in business.

As you advance in your career and possibly enter into management, you will be responsible for larger projects and teams of people. When projects are completed, you will be required to close them out, usually with a final report and presentation, before moving on to the next one(s). As it happens, the larger the project, the more time it takes, the more paperwork is generated, and the more people are involved. Even if you are highly organized, pulling all the documentation together, organizing the presentation, and delegating the work to the team can be a major event. You'll find out very quickly that closing out your project becomes a mini-project in itself!

Savvy managers recognize the importance of creating a road map. But they also continue to use the road map as a high-level project plan to keep their team on track.

Exercise

The purpose of this exercise is to modify an existing road map based on new requirements and then extend the road map into a high-level project plan and schedule. You will use the skills presented in this section to create a road map and the corresponding PowerPoint presentation. You will need to open the Word file named ib_p05_roadmaptoprojectplan.

The original road map (and corresponding scope of the presentation) was to present the results of the entire survey, facilitate a discussion around employee motivation strategies, and create an action plan for improvement.

1. The CEO was copied on the slides in Figures 5.10 and 5.11 and is absolutely appalled at the poor scores and the steady decline over the past three years. He does not want any discussion on motivation strategies or action plans just yet. He would like a more focused and detailed presentation, by division, on the three survey questions that received the worst scores and the division manager's recommendation on how to improve.

   a. In the Word file named ib_p05_roadmaptoprojectplan, eliminate the slides that are no longer part of the scope of the presentation.

2. There are four divisions (Eastern Seaboard, Southwest, West Coast, and Midwest), and the division managers reside in those geographies.

   a. In the Word file named ib_p05_roadmaptoprojectplan, create a separate section in the road map for each of the four divisions that include the following slides:

   - Division name
   - Question #1 and response
   - Question #2 and response
   - Question #3 and response

3. The CEO would like this information presented by the end of July. Assume that you will send this road map to the division managers on July 15. You need three to four business days to pull together all the results, create a proposed Action Plan and then another two business days to review the data with the Vice President of Human Resources before presenting to the CEO.

   a. In the Word file named ib_p05_roadmaptoprojectplan, add a column to the road map labeled **Due Date**, which is the date the regional managers have to get their information back to you.

   b. Calculate the date that the division managers must get their slides back to you.

   c. Save the document.

4. Create a shell PowerPoint slide deck for the final presentation to the CEO using the road map you modified in steps 1–3. Apply an appropriate theme to this shell (remember the somber nature of this presentation). Save your presentation as **ib_p05_ceopresentation**.

5. Create a set of slides with placeholders that you would send out to the division managers so that they all follow a consistent format in getting their information back to you.

   a. Insert the road map table itself into a slide, highlight the due date and add some explanatory comments.

b. Create the additional slides (listed in step 2a) that are intended to be sent to each division manager with indicators of the information to insert in each slide.

c. Save your presentation as **ib_p05_divisionslides**.

>> What's Wrong with This Presentation?

Problem

You and your classmate meet at the library to finish your term paper on outsourcing for a Global Strategy and Planning class. In the interest of getting the paper and presentation turned in the next day (the due date), it is decided that you will finish the references and she will create the PowerPoint presentation (the time allotted for the presentation is 15 minutes). You are quite surprised when she sends you the PowerPoint file a few hours later with a short e-mail that says, "All done. Here you go . . . that outline view feature in PowerPoint is just GREAT. I'm going out tonight. See you in class tomorrow morning."

Exercise

You have the Word document named ib_p05_outsourcingprosandcons and your friend sent you the PowerPoint presentation named ib_p05_outsourcingprosandcons_presentation. Open both files and compare the presentation with the original source. What's wrong with this presentation? Consider the following:

It is apparent that a great deal of the text from the document was copied directly into the PowerPoint slides. However, as you review each slide, it becomes quite obvious that several guidelines and best practices around creating presentations were completely ignored. Unfortunately, this presentation is not unlike many of the presentations that students (and some business professionals) create.

1. Does the presentation contain information or slides that you would completely delete? Why?

2. If there is so much rework to be done, why would anyone ever use the Outline feature and copy and paste from a document into PowerPoint?

Write a short answer for each of these points; then fix the presentation so that it follows the guidelines presented in this book.

3. Suppose you are the instructor and you know that students tend to overlook the fact that a presentation is different from a document and requires time and techniques to create. Create a checklist to hand out to your students ahead of time to make sure that they don't end up with presentations that look like this. You may have to go back through the text and look for specific recommendations that were made in previous chapters. Organize your checklist as follows:

Sample checklist:

PowerPoint item or feature	Recommendation
1. Slide design	• For business topics, choose a conservative design and color scheme.
2. Real estate	• Do not exceed seven lines per slide.

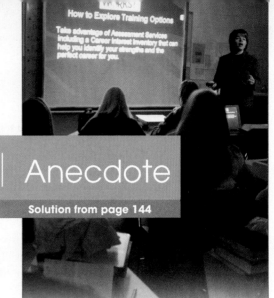

PowerPoint in **Practice** | Anecdote

Solution from page 144

One day I was having lunch with a friend who was the purchasing director at a large company, and I was grumbling about how long it took to respond to an RFP and then how we were expected to present the whole thing in one hour. Her response forever changed the way I viewed the RFP process. She said, "We don't judge vendors on how thick their documents are; in fact, sometimes that's the last thing we consider. We want to partner with companies who demonstrate that they understand our objectives, address all the right points, and respect our busy schedules. I don't know why you people spend so much time generating reams and reams of paper. Half the time nobody reads them."

Armed with that revelation, I immediately began to worry less about having a perfect document and focus more attention on creating a knock-out presentation. I cut my time significantly, and it didn't take long before my team was winning more and more business and I was dubbed the "RFP Guru."

Assignment

Using the skills you learned in this chapter, create a PowerPoint presentation to respond to the following letter your training and e-learning firm received:

Dear Sir or Madam:

Our company, The Frances Group, is accepting proposals from training firms to provide educational services for our sales agents. We invite your firm to submit a proposal to us for consideration. A description of our company, the services needed, and other pertinent information follows:

Background of The Frances Group

- The Frances Group was founded in 1889 to provide insurance and investment opportunities to rural families and businesses. Currently, The Frances Group has 1.4 billion dollars of policies in force, with offices located in 14 states. At the present time, The Frances Group has 1,243 consulting sales agents serving approximately 180,000 clients.

Services to Be Performed

- Your proposal will cover onsite e-learning field office training for the following certifications/licenses:
  1. Chartered Financial Consultant (ChFC)
  2. Chartered Life Underwriter (CLU)
  3. Series 6
  4. Series 7
  5. Series 66

Target Audience

- Entry-level sales agents. These individuals are new hires with little or no previous experience in sales or financial services.

Required Deliverables

- **Courseware:** This will be the primary vehicle for training the agents. The courses must include practice exercises and/or questions with feedback.

- **Mastery tests:** A final test that will establish mastery of subject will be given at the end of each course. Questions will be graded as "correct" or "incorrect," and a final score will be printed.

- **Electronic reference library:** Reference materials for the agents after training has been completed. This will consist of glossaries, quick reference cards, and (5) additional practice tests for each course.

Your Response to This Request for Proposal: Please provide the following information:

1. **Background on Your Firm**
   - Detail your firm's experience in providing these services to companies in the financial services sector, as well as companies of a comparable size to The Frances Group.
   - Describe how and why your firm is different from other firms being considered, and why our selection of your firm is the best decision we could make.
   - Describe your track record in successfully certifying financial services staff.
   - Describe your firm's approach to the resolution of contractual disagreements.

2. **Solution Proposal**
   - Course objectives, descriptions, length of time, and pass/fail criteria
   - Approach to establishing an e-learning presence in each field office
   - Project plan: Activities, resources, and schedule

3. **Cost:** Please provide two pricing models:
   - Fixed price: Training for up to 250 new sales agents
   - Per agent: Please break down cost of training and materials.

4. **References:** Provide the names and contact information for (3) other similarly sized clients.

Questions for Discussion

1. Discuss why organizations require both a written document and a PowerPoint presentation for RFPs.

2. Are the audiences for each different?

3. Are there legal or other business reasons that require a document?

4. Would it be more practical to simply deliver a larger presentation instead of a document *and* a presentation? Why or why not?

>> Review Questions

The following questions are related to the concepts addressed in this chapter. There are three types of questions: Short Answer, True or False, and Fill in the Blank. If your answer to a True or False question is False, write a short explanation as to why you think the statement is not true.

1. Presentations are _____ an audience; documents are _____ an audience.

2. Who bears the responsibility for getting the message(s) across in documents? In presentations?

3. Presentations are written using _____ and _____ phrases.

4. A(n) _____ can help you to transform a large amount of information into a time-constrained presentation.

5. True or False: Business presentations use multiple resources and involve the use of external information.

6. List the three benefits of creating a road map.

7. True or False: Using a road map makes it difficult to delegate the task of assembling presentations.

8. What is the difference between creating and assembling a presentation? List five points you need to keep in mind while assembling existing information for an audience from documents.

9. When converting text into bullets, you must read through the material carefully, identify the _____ _____, and turn sentences into _____ phrases or sentences.

10. True or False: A general rule of thumb is to squeeze as many lines as possible on to a slide.

The following exam is designed to test your ability to recognize and execute the PowerPoint skills presented in this chapter. Read each question carefully and answer the questions in the order they are listed. You should be able to complete this exam in 60 minutes or less.

As a member of an investment analyst team, your responsibility is to conduct a financial analysis of companies under consideration by your firm. You have done due diligence on Allen Bentley Motor Company and now need to present your findings to your management. Open the paper named ib_p05_allenbentleyfinanal.

1. Create a PowerPoint presentation about the company based on the following planning information:

a. Objectives

- Provide a short background on Allen Bentley.

- Summarize the financial ratio categories, the ratios in each category, and their definitions.

- Review the financial ratio and trend analysis.

- Compare Allen Bentley financial performance to industry norms.

- Discuss stock price performance.

b. Audience

- Other seasoned financial analyst professionals on your team

- Financial managers

c. Key messages/decisions

- Financial stability of Allen Bentley

- Growth and financial leadership in the industry

- Buy/Sell recommendation

d. Time: 45 minutes

You are a colleague of the analyst who created the preceding presentation. You have been researching the motorcycle industry and feel that there is competitive marketing information that should be presented to provide a balanced analysis. Make the following changes using information found in the paper named ib_p05_allenbentleymktanal.

2. Modify the presentation created in step 1 to add competitive marketing information.

a. You have only 60 minutes to present both the financial and marketing perspectives.

b. The audience for this presentation will include the firm's competitive marketing analyst.

c. Make a Buy/Sell recommendation and explain why it is the same or different from that of the first analyst.

The following questions are designed to test your ability to apply the PowerPoint skills you have learned to complete a business objective. Use your knowledge of PowerPoint as well as your creativity to answer these questions. For most questions, there are several possible ways to complete the objective.

You are the owner of a bike rider leather apparel company. You have a booth at the Fall Merchandise Mart show, which is sponsored by Allen Bentley and Sazama. In exchange for their sponsorship, you agree to run an informational presentation about each company on your kiosk.

Using the paper named ib_p05_allenbentleymktanal, do the following:

1. Create a self-attended presentation that displays the following information about Allen Bentley and Sazama:

   a. Who They Are
   b. Profile of Their Riders

2. Because both companies are sponsoring your booth, make sure that you present equal information about both of them.

3. Based on their rider/potential rider profile, choose a presentation design, color scheme, transition effects, and timing.

 Chapter 1

Introduction to Word Basics

Chapter Goals

This chapter provides a general overview of Microsoft Word and the reasons why it is a vital tool for business people at all levels in all industries. You will use the basic terminology covered in this chapter throughout the text. The chapter also reviews some basic business writing and word processing skills that are necessary to use Word, although you should have a basic familiarity with both before working with this text.

In business, you must stress the importance of planning ahead. This chapter will help you do that by reviewing the steps for gathering data and organizing your thoughts to start working on a report. Furthermore, you will create and save an outline that normally facilitates organizing the topics in preparation for writing a business document.

>> **Word** | **Skill Sets**

Word in **Practice** | Anecdote

My Role as a Technology Consultant

In 1986, I made the fateful decision to leave teaching, my chosen profession, and start my own technology consulting firm. At the time I had no experience whatsoever in business, but I had talent with technology and a dogged determinism to succeed.

When I first started writing reports for my clients, I often confused quantity with quality. On one hand, creating overly long reports was a good thing because I learned how to deal with long documents in a word processor. Later, that knowledge saved me time and money when I wrote, edited, and printed my 400-page doctoral dissertation. Because typewriters were still more common than word processors back then, my less-knowledgeable classmates were stuck waiting for typists and paying them by the page for each revision.

Furthermore, I developed many techniques to make my reports look highly professional. My clients must have been impressed because my consulting business kept growing. On the other hand, I eventually learned that my clients didn't necessarily always appreciate all the "extra" information my reports included. They sometimes complained that they were too long and too detailed. This was a problem.

>> Continued on page 197

The focus of this text is to illustrate how you can use Microsoft Word to complete a variety of business objectives. First, however, it is important to understand why Word was created and the need it fulfills for business managers. In addition, you need a basic understanding of how to access and activate its commands and features. This section provides a fundamental definition of Word and illustrates its basic functionality. It concludes with the basic preparation steps necessary for authoring good business documents using Word.

Why Are We Here?

In its most basic form, Word is a word processor, which is an electronic version of a *typewriter*. The primary use of any word processor is to display words on a page so that it can be printed on a printer, posted on a Web site, or sent in an e-mail. Before the advent of word processors, all documents were handwritten, typed on a typewriter, or printed on a printing press. An electronic typewriter (seen in Figure 1.1) could type letters on paper, but it could not incorporate graphics or store anything typed.

Figure 1.1 | **A Typewriter**

Let's assume that you typed a 20-page report for your boss. She looks at the report and makes several minor edits for grammatical mistakes and content changes—just a few corrections, but one on every page. You would need to retype the entire 20-page report. A word processor eradicates this additional work.

A traditional computer keyboard is the same one originally developed for the typewriter. You might have wondered why the keys are placed where they are on the QWERTY keyboard (called that because the first five letters in the left corner are Q W E R T and Y). In the early days of manual typewriters, typists could type faster than the mechanical arms could strike the paper, which caused the machine to jam. To avoid this, the keyboard was laid out so that the most commonly used letters were placed far away from each other, whereas less-commonly-used letters were placed in more reachable positions, forcing typists to slow down. Although today's computers could easily keep up with the most nimble of typists, tradition is a very hard thing to break. Because most typists already know how to type using this inefficient keyboard, it would be difficult to change to a more efficient one.

With the innovation of the word processor, a whole new era of **desktop publishing** came about. Instead of sending documents to a typesetter to painstakingly lay out letters on a press to be printed, anyone with a computer and a printer could "typeset" their own newspapers, newsletters, brochures, documents, books, articles, manuals, and so on. Graphics could be inserted right into the electronic file and printed. Instead of waiting weeks for a printer, any business could have a printout of any document within moments. This change truly revolutionized businesses everywhere.

An Overview of Word

When you first launch the Word application, you see a blank document, as shown in Figure 1.2. The term **document** is used to describe a Word file. You can have as many documents open and active as the memory in your computer allows. Each document appears in its own window, which can be minimized, maximized, or resized similar to any other computer program window. There are also scroll bars that appear along the side and bottom that enable you to move within the document (without necessarily moving your cursor).

Figure 1.2 | **Opening Screen of Word 2007**

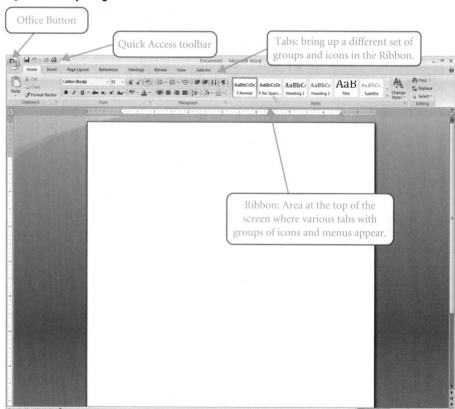

In Figure 1.3, the Word window has three buttons in the upper-right corner. The first button *minimizes* the window, which makes it disappear as a window and appear as a button on the taskbar at the bottom of the screen. The last button *closes* the open file as well as the entire application if there is only one Word file open.

Figure 1.3 | **Minimize, Maximize, and Restore**

Minimize, Restore/Maximize, and Close will allow you to control the window.

The middle button changes depending on the current status of the window. A *maximized* window fills the screen so that you can't see any other windows. If the window is not maximized, the middle button maximizes the window. You can also maximize the window by double-clicking on the *Title bar*, the top line of the window with the document name in the center.

If the window is already maximized, the middle button *restores* the window, making it smaller so that you can see other windows and the desktop underneath. Then you can change the size of the window by grabbing any corner or edge and dragging toward the center to make it smaller or dragging outward to make the window larger.

Figure 1.4 shows the following, from left to right:

- Current page and number of pages
- View controls
- Zoom controls
- Window Resize tool

Figure 1.4 | **More Word Window Controls**

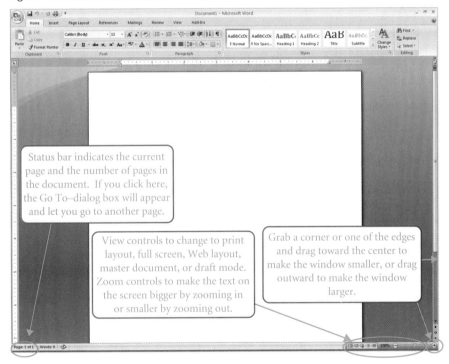

Status bar indicates the current page and the number of pages in the document. If you click here, the Go To–dialog box will appear and let you go to another page.

View controls to change to print layout, full screen, Web layout, master document, or draft mode. Zoom controls to make the text on the screen bigger by zooming in or smaller by zooming out.

Grab a corner or one of the edges and drag toward the center to make the window smaller, or drag outward to make the window larger.

If you click the page number, the **Go To** dialog box appears. You can then enter a page number and click the **Next** button to go to the indicated page. The buttons to the right are the view controls to change to Print Layout, Full Screen Reading, Web Layout, Master Document Tools, or Draft. You most often use the Print Layout view, which shows you the graphics, the headers, and the footers as well as the text; and the Draft view, which shows you only the text (and the hidden formatting marks if you have unhidden them).

Zoom controls make the text on the screen bigger by zooming in or smaller by zooming out. For example, 125% shows the document 25% larger than it will print, and 75% shows the document 25% smaller than it will print. It is important to note that zooming affects only the look of the document on the screen, not the actual size of the document or font.

Ribbon, Tabs, and Icons

The area at the top of the screen called the ***Ribbon*** contains Word commands and features. As shown in Figure 1.4, the Ribbon consists of several ***icons*** arranged in related ***groups*** that are used to activate any Word command. For example, the **Paragraph** group of icons are used to format the spacing, indents, borders, and alignment of each paragraph of text.

Along the top of the Ribbon are several ***tabs***. Each tab opens a separate area of the Ribbon, which contains a different set of icons. Additional tabs are automatically added above the Ribbon if you are working with special objects such as Headers or Footers or Pictures. These context-sensitive toolbar tabs give you access to additional commands and features. The following is a brief description for each of the tabs shown in Figure 1.5:

- **Home**: Contains fundamental commands that are most frequently used when working in Word. Commonly used icons, such as **Copy** and **Paste**, as well as formatting buttons such as **Bold** and **Italics** are found in this tab.

- **Insert**: Used when inserting objects into a document such as Tables, Pictures, Headers or Footers.

- **Page Layout**: Used for accessing commands used to prepare a document for printing.

- **References:** Provides access to Table of Contents, Footnotes, Captions, and other cross-referencing features of Word.

- **Mailings**: Used for accessing features needed to do mail merges, labels, and envelopes.

- **Review**: Used for accessing commands such as Spell Check and Track Changes.

- **View**: Used for adjusting the visual appearance of your Word screen. For example, this tab contains the **Zoom** icon and the **Draft** icon—both useful view alternatives when working with documents.

Figure 1.5 | **Tabs for Ribbons**

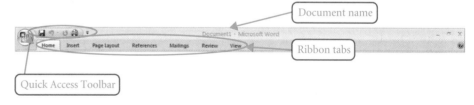

In addition to the Ribbon, the *Quick Access Toolbar* is another way to access Word commands. It contains a few commonly used icons such as **Save** and **Undo**.

You can determine the function of each menu, tab, toolbar, group, and icon by hovering your mouse over the element *without* clicking on it. After a few seconds, a small box appears with the name of the object and a description of what it does as well as a keyboard shortcut. Moving right from the top-left corner, you have the following:

- **Office Button**: Used to access Office commands like Print and Save (details in the next section).
- **Save** icon: Used to save a document in the same place with the same name.
- **Undo** icon: Undoes the last action.
- **Repeat Action** icon: Redoes the last undone action.
- **Print** icon: Prints the document to the printer without displaying the Print dialog box.
- **Customize Quick Access Toolbar**: Used to change the choices on the Quick Access Toolbar
- Name of the document currently open in this Word window
- **Minimize** button: Used to make the window become an icon on the task bar; (already discussed).
- **Restore/Maximize** button: Used to make the window smaller or larger; (already discussed).
- **Close** button: Used to close the document; (already discussed).

File Menu

If you have worked with previous versions of Word, you might have noticed that something was missing when you first looked at the new version. There are no drop-down menus. The drop-down menus have been replaced with the Ribbon system, which provides faster access to the commands you need. However, there is one drop-down menu that does exist in this version of Word, which is the **File** menu. Open the **File** menu by clicking the **Office Button;** it is used for executing tasks such as opening existing documents, creating new documents, or printing documents. Figure 1.6 shows the commands that are accessed through the **File** menu. The **Office Button** provides many of the commands that you need to open a document, save a document, or create a new document.

Figure 1.6 | **File Menu and Office Button**

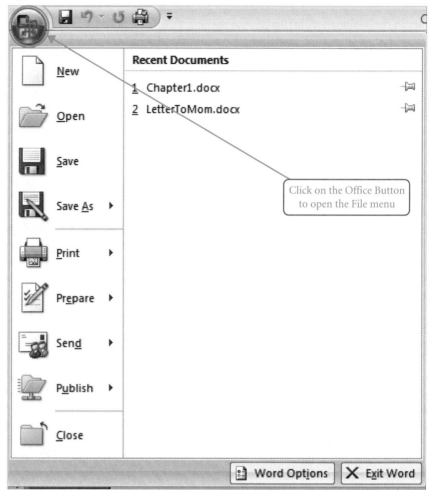

To the right of the menu is a list of the file names of the last few documents that you opened. If you just completed a document called *Background*, for example, that file will appear on the top of the list. You can open these documents again simply by clicking on the file name as long as they haven't been deleted, removed, or renamed. In the bottom-right corner are two buttons:

- **Word Options**: Configures Word the way you want to.
- **Exit Word**: Closes the entire program, including all open Word files. If you made changes to any of the documents, Word asks you if you want to save each document as it closes.

Word 97–2007 File Format

It is important to note that if you are working with people who are using older versions of Word, you need to use the **Save As** command to save your documents in the Word 97–2003 format. Someone who is using Microsoft Office 2003 cannot open a document saved in the 2007 format. Saving documents in the Word 97–2003 format is accomplished as follows:

- Click the **Office Button**.
- Click the *list box* (the triangle on the right side of any button or input text box) next to the **Save As** choice (as shown in Figure 1.7).
- Select **Word 97–2003 Format** on the right side of the **File** menu.
- Navigate to the location and type in the file name.
- Click the **Save** button.

Figure 1.7 | **Save As Word 97–2003**

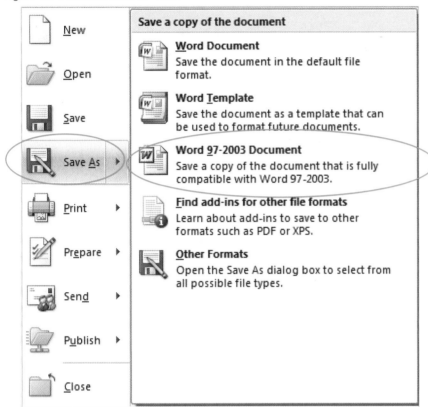

When you open a document in the Word 97–2003 Format using the Word 2007 program, you see the words [**Compatibility Mode**] at the top of the screen next to the document name. This indicates that the document is compatible with older versions of Word. In addition, the **Convert** option appears in the **File** menu list of options. Select this option to convert a document saved in an older version of Word to the 2007 version. Some of the newest features of the Word 2007 program cannot be implemented with older Word formats, so you must use the new format to save the file in some cases.

You can tell whether a document is in the old format or the new format by looking at the *file extension*. Word 97–2003 files have a **.doc** extension, whereas the new version of Word uses a **.docx** extension. If you can't see the file extensions on your computer, you can view them by going into **My Computer** and unchecking the **Hide extensions for known file types** in the **View** tab of the **Folder Options** on the **Tools** menu, as shown in Figure 1.8. Click **Apply to All Folders** if you always want to see the file extensions when you view your files in Windows Explorer or My Computer. If you will be dealing with many files in both the old and new versions of Word, it would be a good idea to be able to see the file extensions in order to confirm which type of file is being opened.

Figure 1.8 | **Viewing File Extensions with My Computer-Tools-Folder Options**

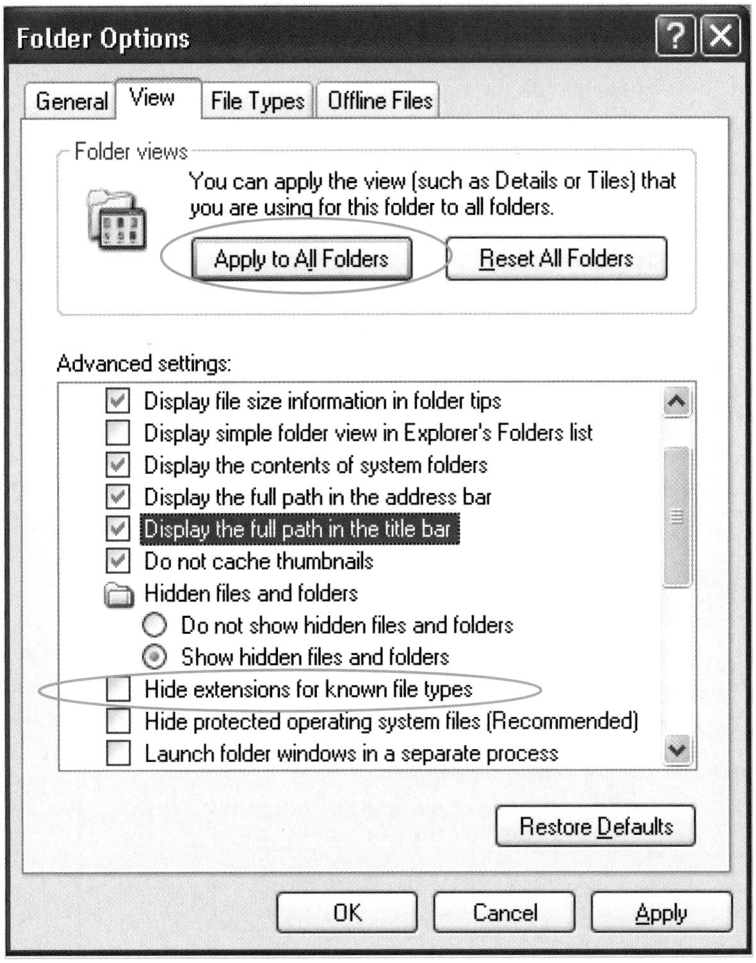

COMMON MISTAKES | Cannot Open Word 2007 Documents in Previous Versions of Word

You cannot open a Word 2007 document using Word 2003 or any other previous version of Word. You must save these documents in the Word 97–2003 format using the Word 2007 program to be able to open them in older versions of Word. The new format is a form of XML (eXtensible Markup Language) and ostensibly makes it easier to post files on Internet servers for viewing on the World Wide Web. The extension for the new Word files is .docx, which actually includes three or four files zipped up together. If you open a .docx file with a compression utility such as PkZip or WinZip, you can see that the underlying files are text in XML format.

Right-Click, Alt Keys, and Control Keys

If you have experience using older versions of Word, you might be accustomed to accessing commands by right-clicking or using Control or Alt keys. All three options are available in the 2007 version of Word.

Right-clicking provides access to a variety of commands, usually referred to as the *option menu* or *context sensitive menu*. Sometimes the commands on the option menu are also available in one of the groups or tabs in the Ribbon, but other times the option menu is the only way to access a particular command. These options change depending upon which object you select when you click with the right mouse button to bring up the option menu.

>> Quick Reference

Saving in Word 97–2003 File Format

1. Click the **Office Button**.

2. Point to the List box (the button with the triangle) on the right side of the **Save As** command. Click the **Word 97–2003 Workbook** option on the right side of the **File** menu.

3. Navigate to the desired folder location using the list box to the right of the **Save in:** text box.

4. Type the file name in the **File name:** text box.

5. Click the **Save** button.

Another way of accessing Word commands is by using keyboard shortcuts. In the earliest version of Office, the **Control (Ctrl)** key was the primary method for accessing commands. A command was activated by holding the **Ctrl** key down on your keyboard and pressing a letter or character. This system can still be used in Office 2007. For several icons in the ribbon there is a corresponding **Ctrl** key combination. In fact, the description for the **Copy** icon that appears when you hover over the icon shows that this command can also be activated by holding the **Ctrl** key down and pressing the letter **c**. Similarly, **Paste** has a shortcut of holding down the **Ctrl** key and pressing the letter **v**. Within this text, these shortcuts will appear with a + sign between them, as in **Ctrl+c** and **Ctrl+v**. Here is a short list of the most commonly used shortcuts (the last one is an **Alt** shortcut):

Undo: Ctrl+z

Copy: Ctrl+c

Cut: Ctrl+x

Paste: Ctrl+v

Print: Ctrl+p

Bold: Ctrl+b

Italic: Ctrl+i

Underline: Ctrl+u

Indent: Ctrl+m

Center: Ctrl+e

Right-Align: Ctrl+r

Left-Align: Ctrl+l

Find: Ctrl+f

Replace: Ctrl+h

Go To Page: Ctrl+g

Repeat Action: Ctrl+y

Save: Ctrl+s

New Document: Ctrl+n

Increase Font Size: Ctrl+>

Decrease Font Size: Ctrl+<

Insert Page Number: Alt+p (Alt+Shift+p)

Another key used to access keyboard shortcuts is the **Alt** key. You can access every tab, icon, and group through the proper **Alt** letter sequence. You can see **Ctrl** shortcuts only when you are hovering over the icon or command, so you must remember the sequence to use it. **Ctrl** shortcuts also require you to press two keys at the same time. On the other hand, you can see the **Alt** letter combinations *on your screen* while you are using it, and you only have to press *one key* at a time. For example, to **Save** a document, instead of pressing **Ctrl+s**, you can press **Alt** and then **ff** and then **s**. If you press the **Alt** key by itself with the **Home** tab on the Ribbon, it looks like the Ribbon in Figure 1.9.

Figure 1.9 | **Alt, Letter Shortcuts for Tabs**

After the **Alt** letter shortcuts appear over the tabs, if you then press one of the letters, that tab becomes active in the Ribbon. Each of the groups and icons has a corresponding shortcut letter, as shown in Figure 1.10. For example, instead of clicking on the **Show/Hide** icon to display the hidden paragraph and formatting marks in the document, you could press **Alt, h, 8**. To change the font, you could press the **Alt** key, then the **h** key, then **ff**, and then press the **a** key to have the font list jump to the first font that starts with **A** (most probably Arial). If you want a different font, just type the font name and it will match each letter as you type until the font you want appears (if it's available on your installation).

Figure 1.10 | **Alt, Letters for the Home Tab on the Ribbon**

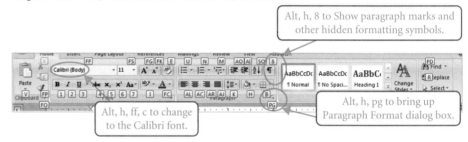

Alt, h, 8 to Show paragraph marks and other hidden formatting symbols.

Alt, h, ff, c to change to the Calibri font.

Alt, h, pg to bring up Paragraph Format dialog box.

COMMON MISTAKES | Starting a New Document—Accidentally

Be careful to press the right keys when using the **Ctrl** key shortcuts. The most common "accidental" key pressed is **Ctrl+n**, which brings up a new document because it is right next to another common shortcut: **Ctrl+b** for bold. When you press **Ctrl+n,** your current document seems to *disappear* from the screen and is replaced with a completely blank document. Many people new to Word don't realize what happened and are horrified, thinking they lost their document. Instead of just closing the new blank document to return to the original, they might start over again by retyping the information, only to have the original appear again on their screen after they save the second document. So, if your document suddenly disappears, don't panic. Just close the blank document, and your original document will return to the screen.

>> **Quick Reference**

Using the Ctrl Shortcuts

1. Hover your mouse over the icon or command to see what the **Ctrl** key shortcut is.

2. Hold down the **Ctrl** key and press the shortcut letter at the same time.

Word Help

Word Help is a tool you can use to get information on various Word commands and features. To open the Word **Help** window, click the **Help** icon, as shown in Figure 1.11.

>> **Quick Reference**

Using the Alt Shortcuts

1. Press the **Alt** key.

2. Press the first letter of the tab that contains the command or icon.

3. Press the letters, in sequence, which appear next to the command or icon.

Figure 1.11 | **Word Help Icon**

To get help, either press F1 or click the Help icon.

To get help, type a question or topic in the input box of the **Help** window and press the **Enter** key or click the **Search** button. You then see a list of links that contain topics related to what you typed in the input box. Click a link to see instructions and information related to your topic, as illustrated in Figure 1.12.

Figure 1.12 | **Help Screen**

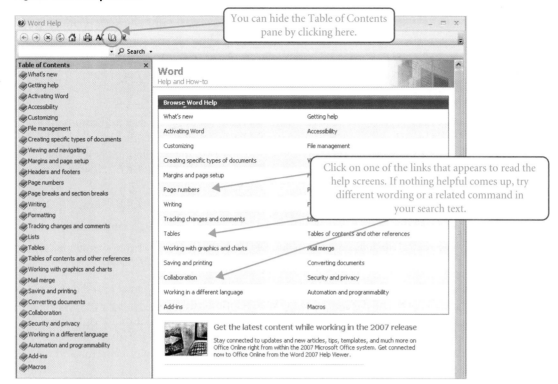

Although Help can be useful, if you don't already know the terminology necessary to find the information you are looking for, it might be less than helpful. If you have tried two or three different terms and still come up blank, try hovering your mouse over each icon on the different tabs on the Ribbon. You can find a term in the description flag for an icon that might be related to what you are looking for, and you can use that to search.

COMMON MISTAKES | Assumed Knowledge and Lagging Help

When there is a new version of a program such as Word 2007, a few problems with the help screens are common. The Help screens sometimes lag behind the actual commands, menus, and buttons. Other times they are inaccurate because the Help screens were written *prior* to finalization of the actual commands, menus and buttons. Just as it takes a few versions of new software for the bugs to be fixed, it often takes a few versions for the Help screens to be complete and accurate. Even then, the assumption is sometimes made that the Word user is already familiar with basic concepts of word processing, so basic information doesn't get emphasized. Help screens often focus on the newest features to the exclusion of old tried-and-true functions.

Settings and the Normal Template

You have the ability to customize the ***Word options*** and ***normal template*** of all new Word documents. A template is a file that *sets up* a new document. A template can set up margins, formatting, fonts, text —anything you can do in Word. The *normal template* is the beginning template, the configuration of any new document in which a template has not been specifically chosen. For example, when you first open Word, all data typed into a worksheet has a Calibri font style with an 11 point font size. You can

>> **Quick Reference**

Using Word Help

1. Click the **Word Help** icon.

2. Type a term into the input box of the **Help** window and then press the **Enter** key or click the **Search** button.

3. Click a link to see instructions and information related to your topic.

change the font style and font type to anything you want for each document, but to change the *default* for all future documents, you need to change the *normal template* and save it in the template directory. The word *default* means "whatever is chosen if nothing else is specified." The following explains how to customize the *normal template*:

- Click the **File** menu.
- Click the **Open** choice.
- Change **Files of Type** to **All Word Templates (dotx).** Word should automatically change the folder to the templates folder. If it doesn't, click the list box to the right of the **Look in** text box and change the folder to the template directory (usually under c:\Documents and Settings*username*\Application Data\Microsoft\Templates).
- Open the document named **Normal.dotx**
- Make the changes you want to the page margins, fonts, styles, and so on.
- Save the **Normal.dotx** template in its original location. Any new documents you create will start with the settings you set up in the *normal template*.

There are other options you can customize in Word 2007. Figure 1.10 shows the options in the Popular section of the **Word Options** dialog box. Notice that there are several other options that you can adjust to customize the settings of your Word screen.

The **Popular** options enable you to input your name and initials so that your name appears in the Author field, as shown in Figure 1.13. You can also turn off the ScreenTips and change the color scheme.

Figure 1.13 | **Word Options: Popular Choices**

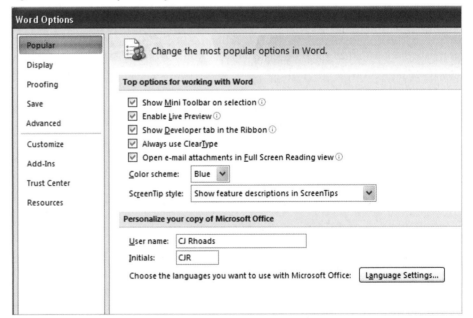

The **Display** options (see Figure 1.14) enable you to choose whether or not to show formatting marks. In several of the exercises of this book you will need to see the codes. You can reveal these hidden codes through an icon on the **Home** tab, but the choice on the **Display** option sets hidden codes on by default for all Word documents. This is also where you determine certain printing options, such as whether or not to print drawings, comments, hidden text, and background colors.

Figure 1.14 | **Word Options: Display Choices**

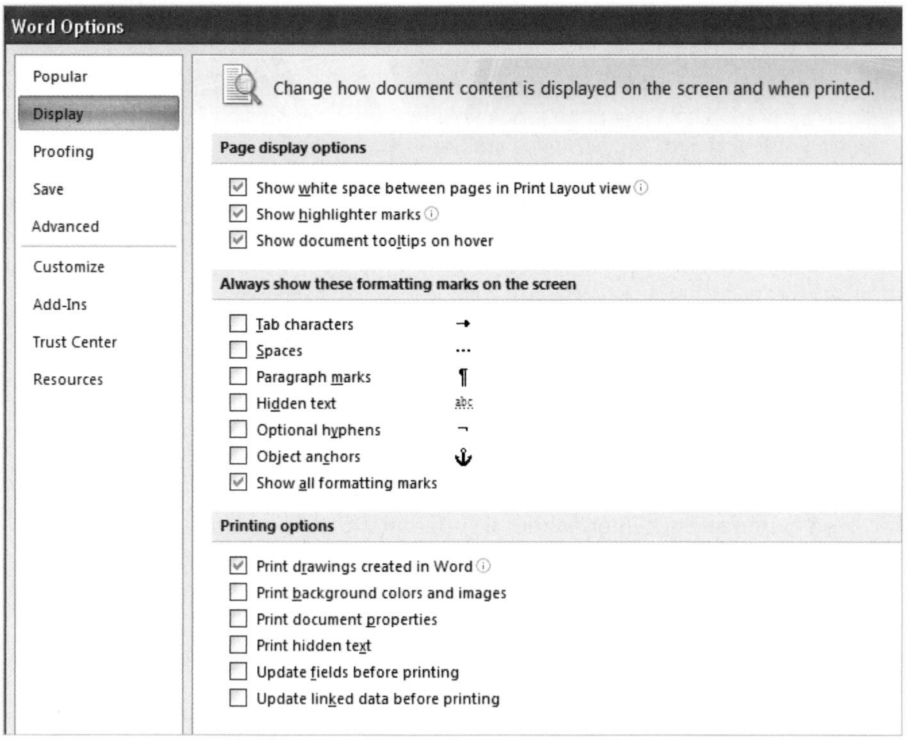

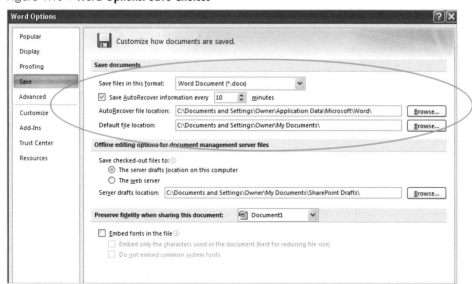

In the **Save** options, you can set Word to save a version of the current document automatically so that if your computer should lose power or your application stops working, you will lose only up to the last *x* minutes of work (*x* being the number of minutes that you set). The default number of minutes is 10 (as you can see in Figure 1.15), but you can change it to any number of minutes. If you are working on a very long document or a document with numerous graphics that can take several minutes to save, you might want to lengthen the time. Otherwise, your typing will be interrupted frequently while the document is saving.

Use the **Save** options to tell Word to always save in an older Word format if you are not yet ready to start using the new XML format. You can also change the default location of where your documents are saved by changing the **Default file location:** folder.

Figure 1.15 | **Word Options: Save Choices**

COMMON MISTAKES | Making the Same Changes Over and Over

If you find yourself constantly changing the defaults, you should set up the *normal template* to your most common page formatting, fonts, and paragraph settings. Many people waste time making the same changes to each new document because they don't realize that they can permanently make these changes in the *normal template*. The changes, however, affect only the current system or user account. If you use more than one computer or account, you must make the changes for each one.

Business Writing

Long before you launch a word processor, you need to plan what you will write and your goals for doing so. In the business world, your ability to gather data and write effectively helps you gain recognition and promotions. You probably already know that business documents must be completely free of typographical errors, misspellings, and incorrect grammar. Such informalities are appropriate when posting on Web pages or talking with friends and family, but business correspondence, even the most informal e-mail, should include proper grammar and spelling. Do not include emoticons or text shortcuts such as IMHO (In My Humble Opinion) or ROTFL (Rolling On The Floor Laughing) in business writing. Such informalities might not be understood, and might give a negative impression to the reader.

Good grammar and formal structures are only a part of the equation, however. The other part is knowing how to gather and present information. Knowing what to write about, and how to write clearly and concisely, are key business skills.

Regardless of your role or position in an organization, you need to write some kind of business document. Business documents can be self-inspired or assigned. A self-inspired document is one that you decide to write without being told. A proposal to your boss to change the way you do your job is one example. A description of a new program you are developing is another. An entrepreneur who writes a business plan is self-inspired. If you are a small business owner, a memo explaining the new dress code to your employees is a self-inspired document.

Most of the time, you write documents that are assigned or expected as part of your responsibilities. If you are a customer service representative, you might be expected to write up a memo on your best or worst clients. If you are the manager of a customer service telephone center, you are probably expected to write a monthly memo on the call statistics. If you are a management consultant, you are expected to write a report of your findings. Regardless of your role in an organization, you are expected to write progress reports. Throughout all businesses, at all levels, there are regularly expected documents that you must write.

Whenever you have writing to do, it is helpful to follow a four-step process to identify what you need to write:

Step 1   What are the objectives?
What does the audience need from this document?
Are you trying to convince your audience to take some course of action?
What is that course of action?

Step 2   Who are the readers?
Are they familiar with the issues? Do they understand the terminology?
Are they decision-makers who typically want high-level summary information or are they more operational and detail-oriented?
What are their "hot buttons?"

Step 3   What are the key messages/decisions?
List all the factors that impact the issue in order of priority.
Spell out the options, the advantages and disadvantages of each.
If you are making a recommendation, spell it out very clearly.

>> Quick Reference

Changing the Default Formatting of Word Documents

1. Click the **Office Button**.
2. Click the **Open** choice.
3. Change **Files of Type** to **Word Template (dotx)**. Word should automatically change the folder to the templates folder.
4. Open the document named Normal.dotx.
5. Make the changes you want to the page margins, fonts, styles, and so on.
6. Save Normal.dotx in the template folder.

>> Quick Reference

Changing Save and Print and Display Options

1. Click the **Office Button** menu.
2. Click the **Word Options** button at the bottom of the dialog box.
3. Choose the option category you want to change.
4. Change the option and click **Save Option**.

Step 4   How long should the document be?

Match the expectations of your readers for document length.

If you don't know the expected length, ask your readers.

Business documents have generally accepted ranges for length, as shown in Figure 1.16. Although documents can vary somewhat from these ranges, most documents fit within these parameters. If you deviate too much from generally expected document length, your reader (who might be your supervisor, your colleague, your customer, your supplier, or your investor) might have a negative reaction. For example, if your boss asks you to write a memo, and you create one that is five pages long, she will probably not be happy. A memo implies a 1–3 page document (and 1 is better than 3). If you write too many or too few pages based on generally accepted ranges of business documents, your writing might be considered unprofessional or you might lose credibility.

Figure 1.16 | **Range of Size Expectations of Business Documents**

Type of Document	Size Range
E-mail	1–2 screen lengths (between 2–8 paragraphs)
Letter	1–2 pages (between 2–15 paragraphs
Memo	1–3 pages (between 2–25 paragraphs
Report	3–25 pages
Whitepaper	5–50 pages
Manual (instructions, documentation, process description, etc.)	15–several hundred pages

After you finish any of these documents, you might want to ask yourself four questions:

- Is the information in the document accurate?
- Is the information in the document clear and concise?
- Does the document meet the readers' requirements?
- Does the document meet your objectives?

If the answer to any of these questions is *no*, revise the document until you can answer *yes* to each of the questions.

COMMON MISTAKES | Too Short or Too Long

Try to clarify the expectation of the reader prior to starting a business document. Although you have learned general document types and their expected sizes in this section, there are many other documents that are not listed. Additionally, the culture or experience of a particular manager in a business might differ from that presented here. The best way to find out how long a document should be and what the topic of the document should be is to *ask the reader*.

Creating, Writing, and Saving a Word Document

Imagine that you are a Retail Division Manager who has been tasked by your boss to create a report outlining various options to solving a problem. You have been through the proper steps of planning and gathering the appropriate information, and are now ready to create an outline to help guide you in writing the report.

To launch Word 2007, you normally choose it from the menu that appears when you click the **Start** button in the bottom-left corner of the screen. You can also click the **Word** button that appears in the **Quick Launch** bar at the bottom middle of the screen or click the **Word** icon on the desktop. After Word is running, you see a blank document (refer to Figure 1.2).

If you are relatively new to word processing, there are a few typing basics that you might find helpful:

- Do not press the **Enter** key at the end of the line within a paragraph. Just keep typing; the word processor wraps your words automatically to the next line.
- Press **Enter** only once at the end of the paragraph. If you want more space between the paragraphs, click the **Space Before** icon on the **Paragraph** group on the **Home** tab instead of pressing the **Enter** key twice.
- If you make a mistake while typing, press the **Backspace** key to delete the letter you just typed (to the left of the blinking cursor).
- If you need to delete a letter to the right of the blinking cursor, press the **Delete** key.
- If your blinking cursor is between two different letters, and you type something, the letters to the right get "pushed over" to make room for what you are typing.
- If you have something selected or highlighted, whatever you type will replace the selection.

Going back to the Retail report outline example, the first topic in your outline would be *background* about the problem. You would:

- Type the word *Background* (but you don't press **Enter** yet).

Because you know that Background will be the first item in the multilevel list, you want a **1.** to appear to the left of the word. The **Multilevel List** icon is on the **Home** tab, so click **Home** if you don't see the Ribbon as shown in Figure 1.17.

When you click the **Multilevel List** icon for the first time in a new document, you get a list of choices for the type of multilevel list. In this example, you would choose the list that starts with a **1.** and then has an **a.** underneath it. (It might be the first one, already in the "current list" choice, although it might also be one of the list types in the bottom half of the dialog box. It depends upon which multilevel list was used previously on that system.)

The **1.** appears at the beginning of the line in which your cursor is located when you click the **Multilevel List** icon. To move to the next line and type the text, do this:

- Press **Enter** to go to the next line.
- Press **Tab**. The **2.** changes to an **a.** for the sublevel.

Pressing the **Tab** key changed the outline to the next level, a sublevel known as a demotion. Normally, if you were ready to type some detailed sublevels under the current outline topic, that would be what you want. But what if the sublevel is not what you want? There won't be a whole lot to the background, so you don't need any sublevels. The next section you type in should be a description of the current situation. Because Current Situation is on the same level as Background, instead of the **a.** you want the outline level to go back to a **2.**, which would be a promotion to a parent level. Do the following:

- Press **Shift+Tab** to change the **a.** to a **2.**
- Type *Current Situation* and press **Enter**.

Figure 1.17 | **Creating an Outline**

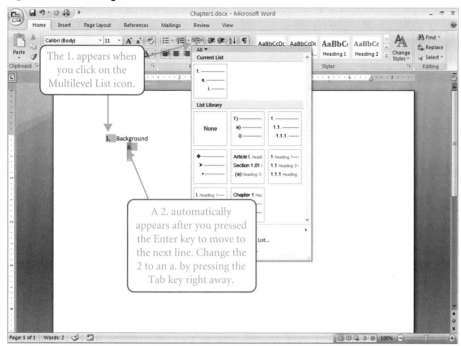

COMMON MISTAKES | **Adding a Space before Tab or Shift+Tab**

To promote or demote an outline level, you must press the **Tab** key or the **Shift+Tab** key immediately after the letter or number of the outline. If you press the space bar, or type a period, or type anything else, the **Tab** key only inserts a tab code; it does not demote or promote the letter or number.

Getting back to your task: after you explain the background and describe the current situation, the only thing left to do is to list the options along with the advantages and disadvantages of each. You already know which options to list from your investigation. Now that you know how to use **Tab** and **Shift+Tab** to change the outline level, you just need to type in each option and put in a section for Advantages and Disadvantages under each one:

- Type *Options* and press **Enter**.
- Press **Tab**, type *Bare Bones Option*, and press **Enter**.
- Press **Tab**, type *Advantages*, and press **Enter**.
- Type *Disadvantages* and press **Enter**.
- Press **Shift+Tab**, type *Middle of the Road Option*, and press **Enter**.
- Press **Tab**, type *Advantages*, and press **Enter**.
- Press **Tab**, type *Disadvantages*, and press **Enter**.
- Press **Shift+Tab**, type *Luxury Option*, and press **Enter**.

Copy and Paste

As you continue the Retail Manager outline example, you notice that you already typed the words *Advantages* and *Disadvantages* and are about to type the words again. A more efficient way to do this is to copy and paste them from the section above. If you click the **Show/Hide** icon on the **Paragraph** group (which looks like a paragraph mark: ¶, it is easier to copy and paste. To copy and paste text, do this:

- Use the mouse to click just to the left of the first line and drag down to the second line to highlight the two lines that say **Advantages** and **Disadvantages**, as shown in Figure 1.18.
- Click the **Copy** icon from the **Clipboard** group (see Figure 1.19).
- Left-click just to the left of the paragraph mark below the words *Middle of the Road Option*.
- Click the **Paste** icon from the **Clipboard** group (see Figure 1.19).

Figure 1.18 │ **Select Two Lines of Text**

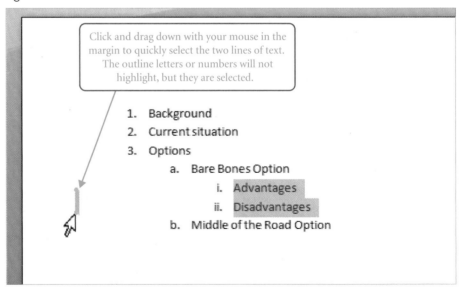

Click and drag down with your mouse in the margin to quickly select the two lines of text. The outline letters or numbers will not highlight, but they are selected.

1. Background
2. Current situation
3. Options
   a. Bare Bones Option
      i. Advantages
      ii. Disadvantages
   b. Middle of the Road Option

Figure 1.19 │ **Copy Icon**

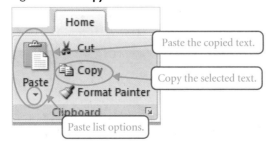

Paste the copied text.

Copy the selected text.

Paste list options.

You can see the entire outline as it would look completed in Figure 1.20.

Figure 1.20 | **Completed Outline Using Multiple Levels**

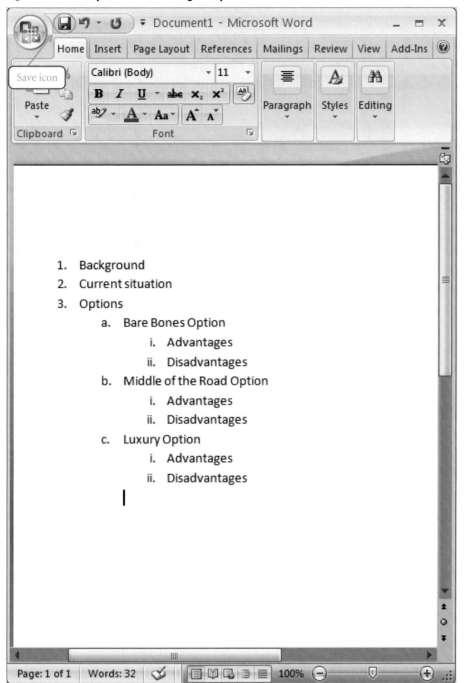

COMMON MISTAKES | Letting Go of the Mouse Too Soon When Dragging

When dragging, don't let go of the mouse until just what you want selected is highlighted. Until you let go of the mouse button when dragging, you can keep moving around to select exactly what you want—even if you select the wrong thing in the meantime. When trying to select text, it is very common to get the line above, get the line below, or even hit the area of the screen that scrolls the selection down very quickly to the bottom or top of the file. Some people instinctively let go if the "wrong" thing gets selected. However, until you let go of the mouse button, nothing has *actually* been selected. Just keep your finger down on the left mouse button and move back until only the text you want selected has been highlighted; then let go.

COMMON MISTAKES | Pasting In an Unexpected Location

Watch where you place your insertion point when copying and pasting. It is common to forget to note whether your blinking cursor has moved when you choose **Paste**. If your cursor isn't where you expect it to be, your pasted text might appear in a strange place—perhaps even in the middle of a word or at the top or bottom of the page. Remember that some ways of scrolling through a document (such as using the **Page Up** or **Page Down** keys) actually move your cursor, whereas others (such as using the scroll bar) move your view, but leave the cursor where it originally was. If you find that you've pasted to the wrong place, simply click **Undo** from the **Quick Access Toolbar** and then place the cursor in the proper location to paste again.

Save the Document

It is a good idea to save a document soon after you create it. Click the **Save** icon (it looks like a floppy disk) from the **Quick Access Toolbar**. The first time a file is saved, the **Save As** dialog box appears regardless of the method of saving you selected. Any subsequent use of the **Save** icon on the **Quick Access Toolbar** does *not* activate the **Save As** dialog box (or any dialog box at all); it simply saves the file with whatever name it currently has.

Get into the habit of using **Save As** instead of just **Save**. By default, Word saves all documents to the **My Documents** folder on the local hard drive, which is not always the best location. If you have a network folder (that you can access from different computers in the same building or campus, for example), you might want to save the documents you create to a folder on the network server. Alternatively, you might want to save the document on a *flash drive* (also called a *USB* drive or memory stick) or maybe even to a floppy disk. To change the location in which the file will be saved, use the **Save As** menu, accessed through the **Office Button**. Then change the location by navigating to the desired folder using the list box at the right side of the **Save In:** text box (as you can see in Figure 1.21).

>> **Quick Reference**

Copy and Paste

1. Select the text you want to copy.
2. Click the **Copy** icon on the **Clipboard** group on the **Home** tab.
3. Place your insertion point where you want the text to be pasted and click to place the blinking cursor.
4. Click the **Paste** icon on the **Clipboard** group on the **Home** tab.

Figure 1.21 | **Save Icon : Saving for the First Time**

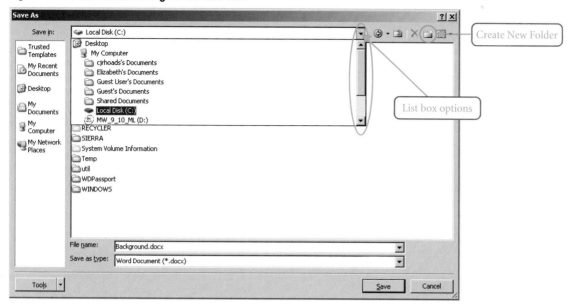

When you click the **Saved In:** list box, a list of all available folders and drives appears. You can save the document in a variety of places:

- Choosing a folder from the C: drive saves the file somewhere on the hard drive inside the computer you are presently using.

- To save to a floppy disk, choose the A: drive.

- To save to a USB drive, choose D: or E: (whichever says "removable drive" or lists the brand name of the type of USB drive you inserted into the USB port of the computer).

- To save to a network drive, choose F: or G: or whichever letter of the alphabet that has been set up on your network.

Alternatively, you might need to choose Network Places and choose the folder from the list that appears.

You might want to create a new folder to hold your Word documents. To create a folder you would:

- Click **Create New Folder**.

- Type in a folder name, such as *WordClassData*, and press the **Enter** key.

- If the name (in this case *Background.docx*) in the **File Name** box, just click **Save**. If not, type the name in and click the **Save** button**.**

Word usually takes the first few words of the document and places them in the **File name:** text box as the default file name. To save the file you just created *inside* the folder you just created, you would make sure the folder name appears in the **Save in:** text box, as shown in Figure 1.22.

Figure 1.22 | **Changing Location to Save a File**

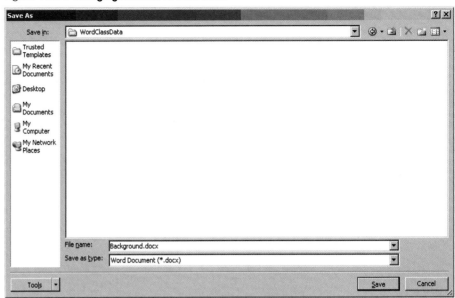

The Ruler

Business documents often follow a specific format. Business articles, for example, often use a first line indent. A list of items in a report might use a hanging indent. Letters often use no indent at all. Quotes within an article would be indented on the left and the right. *Tabs* and *indents* are used to format paragraphs in different ways for these different types of documents. Therefore, to properly format business documents, you must understand tabs and indents.

Do not confuse the use of the word *tab* here with the word *tab* that you click to switch the Ribbon to a different set of groups. The type of *tab* that is found on the **ruler** controls the location of the tab setting used when you press the **Tab** key on the keyboard. The indents set how far from the margin the paragraph should begin and end. The **ruler** shows you which margins, tabs, and indents have been set for the paragraph in which your cursor is currently placed.

The ruler normally appears below the Ribbon (unless you clicked **Hide Ruler** in the **View** group) and it can be used to modify the tab settings and indents of a particular paragraph. In Figure 1.23, you can see a normal paragraph with the words right up against the left margin at 0 inches and stretching all the way across the page to 6.5 inches with the right margin. The page margins are set by clicking the **Page Setup**

>> *Quick Reference*

Saving a Document to a Different Folder or with a Different Name

1. Click the **Save As** command on the **File** menu.
2. The **Save As** dialog box appears.
3. In the **Save In:** text box, click the list box and navigate to the desired location to which to save the document.
4. If necessary, create a folder by clicking the **New Folder** button, typing the new folder name, and clicking **OK**.
5. In the **File name:** text box, type in a file name and click **Save**.

>> *Quick Reference*

Saving a Document Already Named and in the Same Folder

1. Click the **Save** icon on the **Quick Access** menu.

group on the **Page Layout** tab, and the indents are relative to the page margins. If there is no indent, there is no space between the indent tools and the page margins.

Figure 1.23 | **Ruler Showing Normal Paragraph—No Indents or Tabs**

There are two parts to the indent tool on the ruler. The top portion controls the first line indent, and the bottom portion controls the indent for the rest of the paragraph. The little box under both moves both the top and the bottom indents at the same time. In Figure 1.24, you can see that both the top and bottom portions of the indent tool are about one-half inch to the right of the page margin, so the paragraph also starts about one-half inch to the right of the margin, and will wrap at that one-half inch mark all the way to the end. If you change the margin, the indent automatically adjusts. In other words, if the page margin is set at one inch, and the indent is set at one-half inch from that, the paragraph will start at one and one-half inches from the side of the paper. If you change the page margin to two inches, the paragraph will start at two and one-half inches from the side of the paper.

Figure 1.24 | **Ruler Showing Paragraph with Left Indent**

In Figure 1.25, you can see that the top portion of the indent marker is about one-quarter inch to the left of the bottom part of the indent tool. This will give you a hanging indent, in which the first line hangs out farther to the left than the rest of the paragraph. This paragraph formatting is especially helpful when using numbering or outlining. Indeed, if you watch the ruler when you click the **Multilevel List** icon, you notice that Word automatically changes the indent to a hanging indent so the words would wrap to the right of the outline number or letter.

Figure 1.25 | **Ruler Showing Hanging Indent and Right Indent**

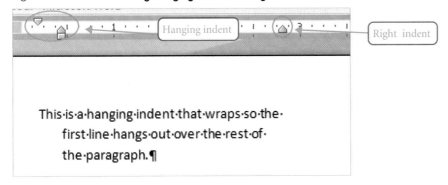

In Figure 1.26 you can see the opposite of a hanging indent. In this paragraph, the first line is indented over a bit to the right, although the rest of the paragraph wraps at the margin.

Figure 1.26 | **Ruler Showing First Line Indent and Right Indent**

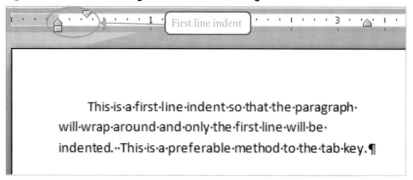

In Figure 1.27, you see a left tab. Unless you indicated that Word should show the formatting marks, you won't see the little arrow that represents the tabs (which is why it is a good idea to reveal these codes while you are working on a document). You set the tab by clicking the ruler where you want the tab. In the old days of the typewriter, secretaries were taught to tab at the beginning of every paragraph. However, using a tab in this way is no longer necessary and might cause formatting problems. Even though it looks the same if you don't reveal the codes, a tab is different from a first line indent.

Figure 1.27 | **Ruler Showing Paragraph with Normal Left Tab**

You can also set tabs to enable words to center around them (as opposed to centering the paragraph with the alignment icons). Wherever the tab is, the words will try to space evenly to the right and the left of the tab (see Figure 1.28).

Figure 1.28 | **Ruler Showing Paragraph with Center Tab**

Similarly, the right tab enables the words to align along the right side—moving the letters over to the left as you type instead of to the right (see Figure 1.29).

Figure 1.29 | **Ruler Showing Paragraph with Right Tab**

There are two other tabs that enable some advanced features. The first is the decimal tab, commonly used with a column of numbers, which aligns all the numbers along the decimal point, wherever that is in the number. You can see this in Figure 1.30.

The last type of tab is known as a bar tab. A bar tab doesn't position text; it inserts a vertical bar at the tab position. Figure 1.31 illustrates a bar tab, along with the markers for all the other types of tabs.

Figure 1.30 | **Ruler Showing Paragraph with Decimal Tabs**

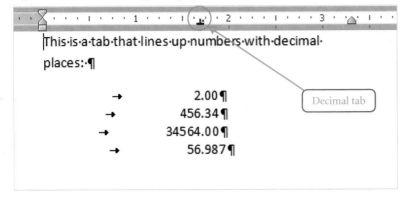

Figure 1.31 | **Ruler Showing Bar Tab**

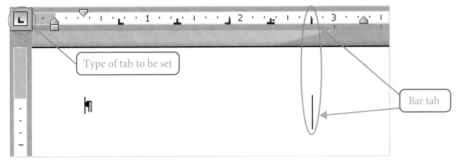

To set the location for the tab, the type of tab you want to set must appear in the far-left corner of the ruler. Clicking this box changes the type of tab through the different types; first line indent, indent, left tab, center tab, right tab, decimal tab, and bar tab. After the type of tab is selected, you just need to click the ruler at the location in which you want that type of tab to appear. After the tab location is set, you use it by pressing the **Tab** key when you are typing in the text.

There is an alternative to using the ruler to set the indents and tabs. If you click the **Dialog Box Launcher** in the lower-right corner of the **Paragraph** group on the **Home** tab (as seen in Figure 1.32), you have more options for setting indents and tabs.

Figure 1.32 | **Dialog Box Launcher**

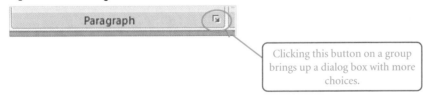

The **Indents and Spacing** tab of the **Dialog Box Launcher** (see Figure 1.33) enables you to set the alignment, the outline level, the amount of indent, and whether there is a first line or hanging indent. You can also set single, 1.5, or double spacing. You can also choose to add more space before or after a paragraph.

Notice that there is a **Tabs** button at the bottom of the dialog box. This button opens the **Tabs** dialog box, which enables you to determine the type of tab to create and the location of the tab. Another way to make the **Tabs** dialog box appear is to double-click an existing tab in the ruler. As can be seen in Figure 1.34, you can enter the location and choose the type of tab.

You can also add a ***leader line*** (a character that automatically fills the space between the last character and the tabbed character), as normally seen in a table of contents. An example is shown in Figure 1.35.

Figure 1.33 | **Paragraph Dialog Box Launcher**

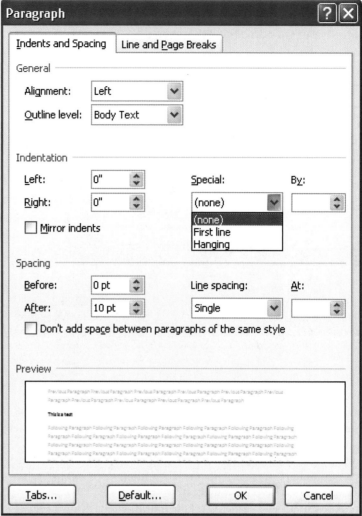

Figure 1.34 | **Setting and Configuring Tabs**

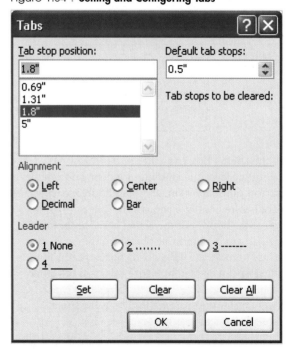

In any case, understanding how tabs are set and their differences from indents is an important concept that underlies many documents that you will be typing as you use Word in business.

Figure 1.35 | **Leader Line Example**

Leader line

Leader line example 1

COMMON MISTAKES | Using Spaces to Locate a Paragraph

Always use indents and tabs to configure paragraphs. People who aren't familiar with paragraph formatting might try to position a paragraph by using spaces. This rarely works because spaces themselves don't have a set "size," so in different venues or different fonts the spacing can be wildly different.

COMMON MISTAKES | Using Tab Instead of Hanging Indent

If you want the first line of a paragraph to hang out over to the left of the rest of the paragraph, use a hanging indent. People who don't know how to set a hanging indent press the **Enter** key at the end of the each line and then press the **Tab** key at the beginning of subsequent lines to start one-half inch over. Although it looks the same as a hanging indent initially (unless you show the hidden codes), if you change even a single word in the paragraph the lines will end up wrapping at the wrong place, creating a mess. Perhaps even more importantly, anyone experienced in Word will know that you don't know how to use tabs and indents, which is an amateurish mistake.

>> *Quick Reference*

Modifying the Indents and Tabs

1. Click and drag one of the **Indent** tools to set the indent.
2. Click the **Tab** tool to the left of the ruler until the type of tab you want to place appears.
3. Click the **Ruler** at the location where you want the tab to appear.
4. Click back into the paragraph and press the **Tab** key to use the tab set.

COMMON MISTAKES | Pressing Tab Multiple Times

Use only one tab at a time. Some people don't understand how to set a tab, so they just keep pressing the **Tab** key and it moves over every one-half inch or so (the default tab setting, which is every one-half inch). If you press the **Tab** key multiple times, when the paragraph formatting changes, nothing will line up, and your text will have unexpected (and decidedly unprofessional-looking) spacing.

≫ Introduction to Word

This is the first of several workshops that will be presented in this text. These workshops serve two purposes. The first is to give you an opportunity to practice the skills illustrated in each section of every chapter. The second is to watch a demonstration of these skills. Many people have an easier time learning software skills after they see techniques and commands demonstrated. You can watch a video demonstration of each workshop by opening the related video file. Most workshops will require you to open a Word file in order to complete the tasks listed, but this workshop starts with a blank Word file.

The purpose of this exercise is to open a blank Word document and examine a few of the basic features that were described in this chapter. We will create a simple outline such as one you might use in a business memo or letter. Try completing each task and then watch the video named **Introduction**.

1. **Open Word (Video: Introduction)**
   a. Launch the Word application.
   b. Click each **Tab** of the Ribbon and view the icons and groups that are shown for each tab. Hover over several of them to read the description and **Ctrl** shortcut keys.
   c. Type in the outline as shown following using the **Multilevel List** icon and pressing **Tab** to demote the level and **Shift+Tab** to promote the level.

```
1. Background
2. Current Situation
3. Options
   a. Bare Bones Option
      i.  Advantages
      ii. Disadvantages
   b. Middle of the Road Option
```

d. Copy the lines with *Advantages* and *Disadvantages* on them and paste them below the *Middle of the Road Option* line.

e. Click the **Office Button**

f. Save your document as **ib_w01_background1v1**.

g. Choose **Save As** to save your document again, but this time with the **Word 97–2003** format. Name the file **ib_w01_background_1v2**.

h. When you return to the document, use the Zoom Slider to increase the Zoom to 140%.

i. Review the **ruler**. With your cursor in one of the lines of text, slide the indent tools and watch their effect on the text. Insert a tab stop on the ruler and watch its effect on the text.

j. Open the **Help** window by clicking the **Help** icon on the Ribbon

k. Change the **Search** option in the Help window to **Word Help – Content from this computer**.

l. Type in the words **Indenting Text** into the input box of the **Help** window and then click the **Search** button. Click some of the links and read the help screens.

m. Close the **Help** window.

n. Close your document and then close Word.

>> An Introduction to Creating an Outline

EXERCISE

Why Do I Need This?

This is the first of several exercises that are presented in each section of this text. The purpose of these exercises is to show how Word skills are applied to typical business situations. The specific Word skills you learned are essential to being able to create and edit documents; copy and paste, creating multilevel outlines, and saving documents to multiple locations.

Exercise

The basic skills of writing clearly and concisely are essential to any business career. Furthermore, communication is enhanced when you understand the general size and expectation of different types of business documents, as well as how to gather data and create an outline based upon that data. To practice these skills, you will create another outline.

You are a supervisor responsible for a number of employees. You will write up an outline for your boss that lists each employee and identifies their strengths and weaknesses.

1. Open the narrative found in the document named ib_w01_empperfrevnotes1.

2. Using the narrative as a basis, create an outline document that might be used for writing an Employee Performance Review report.

3. Within the outline, make sure that you list each employee and have a place for the strengths and weaknesses of each. (Can you use the copy and paste command to save time?)

4. Save the file as **ib_w01_empperfrev1v1**.

>> What's Wrong with This Document?

Problem

A friend of yours is an office manager in a restaurant. She is working on a new menu and is having a hard time editing it after she typed it into Word. She sends the document to you to look at attached to the following e-mail:

"I'm having a hard time with this document. It looked fine at first, but after the margins were changed, the columns got all messed up. Also, when a new entry got added, the numbering of the outline was wrong. Can you help me?"

Exercise

The file the office manager sent you is named ib_w01_dailymenu1. What's wrong with this document? Do you think it is good enough as-is to post or publish in the restaurant? Consider the following points:

- How can you tell what the office manager actually did to create this document?
- Change the margins the way the office manager did to fit this on a one-half sheet of paper (4 inches by 5½ inches). What happened?
- What did she do wrong in lining up the prices?
- What did she do wrong in editing the outline?

Write a short answer to each of these questions and then fix the document. Name the document **ib_w01_dailymenu1v1**.

Word in **Practice** | Anecdote

Solution from page 166

Eventually I learned how to match the expectation of the reader to the amount of information I wrote. I also learned how to clear away all of the "wordiness" and concentrate on just the basics. Using an outline made this much easier for me. If I found myself writing "too much" underneath any one of the items, I knew that I was going off on a tangent and should go back to just the basic information I was trying to convey. I also mastered tabs and indents so that making format changes did not cause headaches with spacing.

Assignment

1. Open up the file named ib_w01_letter1.

2. What do you think the outline for this document would look like?

3. Is there anywhere within this document that the author went off on a tangent?

4. Do you think it really makes a difference if you include unnecessary information in your writing?

5. Which tabs and indents might be appropriate for this document?

6. Make the changes you feel appropriate and save the document as **ib_w01_letter1v1**.

Questions for Discussion

1. What types of mistakes might cause a reader to lower their opinion of an author?

2. What types of careers would use different features and functions of Word more often?

   Which Ribbon tabs would be used more often by clerks and secretaries?

   Which Ribbon tabs would be used more often by authors and professional writers?

   Which Ribbon tabs would be used more often by professional researchers?

   What about graphic designers who develop brochures and marketing documents? Which Ribbon tabs would they use more often?

3. What is the difference between a menu, a toolbar, a tab, a group, a button, an icon, and a dialog box?

4. When should you use indents and when should you use tabs?

5. What difference does it make if you use Word more or less effectively? What advantages do effective Word users have? What disadvantages are there for people who don't use Word effectively?

This section features questions that help you review the key concepts and skills that were presented in the chapter. There will always be a mix of fill in the blank, true or false, or short answer questions. For the true or false questions, if you think an answer is false, provide a short explanation as to why you think the phrase or comment is false.

1. Explain how you would save a document in a different folder on your computer.

2. What can you do if you need to send a Word document to someone who is using the 2003 version of Word?

3. The first step of preparing to write a document is to _____.

4. The second step of preparing to write a document is to _____.

5. The third step of preparing to write a document is to _____.

6. The fourth step of preparing to write a document is to _____.

7. An e-mail should be no more than _____ long.

8. True or False: If your boss were to ask you to write a memo, it is appropriate to prepare a 15-page document.

9. To show the hidden codes such as paragraph marks and tabs in the current document, click the _____ icon on the _____ group on the _____ tab of the Ribbon.

10. To set up an outline in Word, go to the _____ icon on the _____ group on the _____ tab.

11. To change to a sublevel on an outline, press the _____ key when your cursor is _____.

12. To change to the previous level on an outline, press the _____ key when your cursor is _____.

13. To save a document quickly with the same name, click the _____ icon on the _____toolbar.

14. To save a document with a different name or in a different location, click the _____ command and then the _____ menu.

15. True or False: The best way to write a document is to simply start writing and worry about the organization later.

16. You can see the **Ctrl** shortcuts for any applicable buttons by _____ over the button with your mouse pointer.

17. True or False: You can't change the size of the words on the screen without changing the size of the font that prints.

18. True or False: You should always press the **Tab** key to start each paragraph to indent the first line.

19. If you want to line up a column of numbers on the decimal point, use the _____ found on the ruler.

20. If you want to perform a spell check on a document, click the_____ tab.

21. If you want to send letters or e-mail to a few hundred people, you mostly use the _____ tab.

22. If you are writing an article, book, or report that needs to include sources, footnotes, and bibliographies, you are mostly using the _____ tab.

23. If you are enhancing the printing and organization of your document, you are mostly using the _____ tab.

>> Skills Exam

This section, also included at the end of each chapter, is used to test your knowledge of executing various skills presented in the text. As mentioned, the primary mission of this book is to explain and demonstrate how Word is used by business managers to complete business objectives or make business decisions. However, knowing how to execute key skills that are required to operate Word is also important. This section presents several skill-based questions that you have to apply to a Word document. Read each question carefully and answer the questions or perform the tasks in the order they are listed. You should be able to complete this exam in 60 minutes or less.

Open the ib_w01_skillsexam. Complete the following tasks.

1. Identify the objective of the document.
2. Identify who will be reading the document.
3. Describe the key message the document delivers.
4. Does the document fit within expected parameters for documents of its type? What length is inappropriate?
5. In a second document, compose an outline that might have been used to guide the writing of this document.
6. Copy and paste the key steps from the document into your outline. Make sure that they appear at the correct level and indent appropriately for that level.
7. Save the new document with the name **ib_w01_skillsexamv1**.

➤➤ Challenge Questions

This section, which follows the Skills Exam section, features questions that require you to apply the skills you have learned to complete typical business objectives. There is usually no right or wrong method for completing the objectives presented in this section. However, the documents you create must be presentable. This section might also include questions that ask you to identify how wordprocessing might play a role in the success of a business or the decision making process of a business.

1. You have just been promoted to a regional manager in a clothing retail chain store. Compose a memo to introduce yourself to the existing employees and share with them your plans for your first few months as their new manager. Save the file and name it **ib_w01_firstmemov1**.

2. You are the executive manager of a top company in your favorite industry. Create an outline that would be useful for writing a report for the senior leaders of your company on how you intend to trounce your competition. Save the file and name it **ib_w01_reportoutlinev1**.

>> Chapter 2

Creating a Basic Report

Chapter Goals

You've learned to create an outline and become familiar with Word's interface. Now you will be able to take a simple outline and place some professional formatting around it, including page margins, page numbering, headers, and footers. You will also learn about styles and ways they can help you save time when formatting and editing documents.

>> **Word** Skill Sets

Word in Practice | Anecdote

My Role as VP at a Fortune 500 Financial Firm

When I was a student and first started using a word processor, I used it just like a typewriter. I pressed the **Enter** key at the end of each line and pressed the **Tab** key to indent the paragraph. When I wanted space in between paragraphs, I pressed the **Enter** key twice. When I wanted a heading, I clicked on the **B** button to bold-face it and the **U** button when I wanted to underline it. This approach worked fine. . . most of the time.

However, problems did arise. When I went back to edit a document, things didn't work out so well. If I decided to change the look of a heading, It would take hours to go through a long document and modify the formatting for each heading.

The more I used Word, the worse it got. Even after using Word for years, I didn't understand how to apply the style formatting or how to ensure that headers and footers and page numbers appeared where I wanted them. This was a real problem when I started to create long documents like reports.

Eventually, I got a job as a vice president at a Fortune 500 financial firm. The first time I submitted a 45-page report to my boss, (a senior executive vice president), it did not have page numbers, headers, or footers. My boss started reading this long report at his desk just before the meeting in his office. By the time the meeting participants were settled around the conference table, he had gotten the pages completely out of order! It took me ten minutes (which felt like hours because everyone was waiting for the report and my boss looked very annoyed) to put them back in the right order.

There had to be a better way.

>> Continued on page 245

Professional-looking documents include a variety of special formatting. This chapter reviews how to manage the different aspects of a high-quality report such as styles, headers, footers, cover pages, and page numbering. You will start by learning how to convert the outline styles to heading styles automatically. Using this conversion process, you will change the formatting of an outline already written so that you can use the headings to guide your writing in a business report. Although the actual steps are quick and easy, you need to look first at styles to understand the underlying process.

Introduction to Styles

What do you do when you want to boldface a word? Most people would highlight the word and then click on the **Bold** icon in the **Font** group of the **Home** tab on the Ribbon. And to indent it, they would click on the **Indent** icon in the **Paragraph** group of the **Home** tab on the Ribbon. And to add space between paragraphs, they would click on the **Line spacing** icon in the **Paragraph** group of the **Home** tab on the Ribbon. But what if you want all three? And you want all three several times throughout the document?

That's where *styles* come in. A style is a combination of several formatting changes. The best thing about a style is that you can change the formatting after the fact and automatically update all the text that has that style. For example, if you want to change all the text formatted with the **Heading 1** style from boldface to underline, you just modify the style called **Heading 1**, and they all automatically change. No need to go through and adjust each heading individually.

Most businesspeople who use Word never learn how to use styles, which is unfortunate because styles can save you time when you are trying to edit a pre-existing document. Although styles may take more time to set up in the beginning, when you get used to using them, you'll find that styles will save a lot of time.

COMMON MISTAKES | Making Manual Adjustments to Styles

If you want to make a change to text that has a style, make the modification to the style, not the individual information formatted with that style.

If you make a manual format change to just one paragraph that has a style, you would lose the benefits of being able to change the formatting of all the paragraphs by just changing the style. The one with the manual format would not change, and that may cause problems later.

Using styles in long documents such as reports is important because they make formatting consistent and editing easier. Therefore, it makes sense to apply almost all formatting with styles, rather than just making manual changes.

Luckily, Word provides many *built-in styles* that do not require any setup to use. Additionally, many of the built-in styles are used in automated tasks such as an automated table of contents. Furthermore, with styles it is easier to use the "keep together" and "keep with next" feature that will prevent your headings from separating across a page break or from the first paragraph underneath it.

Using Styles to Change an Outline into Headings

You can use these pre-existing styles to turn an outline into a series of headings so that later you can type in the detail information underneath each one, using the headings as a guide. The following example will demonstrate how an outline can serve as the actual headings for a report discussing crisis management options for a food manufacturer dealing with a crisis. Notice the outline in Figure 2.1. Each line of the outline text would serve as a good heading for each section of the report.

Figure 2.1 | **Outline text**

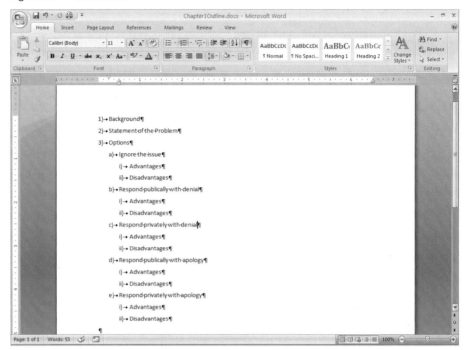

Convert the outline styles into heading styles by following these steps:

- Select all the lines of the outline, as shown in Figure 2.2.
- Click the *Multilevel List* icon in the **Paragraph** group of the **Home** tab of the Ribbon while the text is selected to see all the multilevel list choices.
- Note that a border appears around the outline style used in the paragraph that uses *1)* for the first level, *a)* for the second level, and *i)* for the third level. This list choice also appears under **Current List**.
- Click on the multilevel style that uses *I Heading 1, A Heading 2, and 1. Heading 3.* The border will appear around this choice after it is chosen. Additionally, this choice will appear in the **Current List** and the formats of all the text will change.

Figure 2.2 | **Changing Outline Styles to Header Styles**

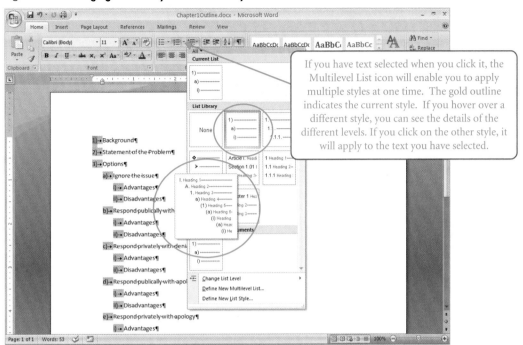

Notice how the fonts in Figure 2.3 have slightly changed? Clicking once on a different outline style in the multilevel lists actually applied three different styles (one for each level). You essentially converted outline levels into heading levels. You can see the first style, **Heading 1**, when your cursor is in the paragraph with the word *Background*, as shown in Figure 2.3.

Figure 2.3 | **See which Style has been applied.**

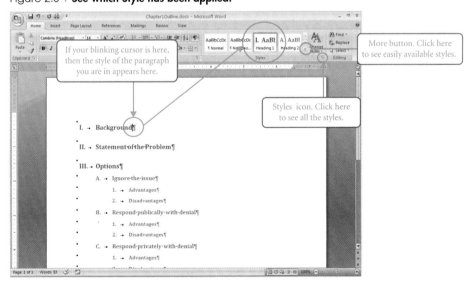

You can see all the existing styles in Word by clicking on the **Styles** launcher button at the right corner of the **Styles** group.

You can also clear the style of any text as follows:

- Select the text where you want to clear the styles.
- Click on the **More** button at the lower corner of the **Styles** group, as shown in Figure 2.4.

- Click *Clear Formatting*.
- The style will revert to the default style, **Normal**.

Figure 2.4 | **List Styles**

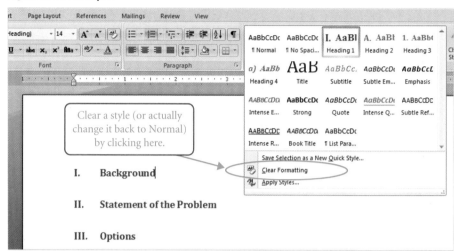

COMMON MISTAKES | Changing a Style When Just Looking

Always know *exactly* where your cursor is before looking at or clicking on the **Styles** group. A common mistake is to *click* on a style to see what it looks like (instead of just hovering over it to preview the style change) only to discover that you've changed the style of whatever paragraph your cursor is in. If your cursor is anywhere in a paragraph, clicking a style changes the entire paragraph to that style.

Creating New Styles

The built-in styles that come with Word are just the beginning. In business you will be writing all sorts of documents: letters, reports, outlines, memos, proposals, instructions, explanations, policies, manuals, e-mails. You will need many more styles than just the ones that already exist in Word. Additionally, sometimes it takes more time to find out which styles are already set up than it would simply to format the text appropriately for the type of document you are writing and create a new style. To create a new style, follow these steps:

- Format some text the way you wish it to be formatted within the style.
- Click on the **More** button in the **Styles** group of the **Home** tab of the Ribbon.
- Click **Selection as a** *New Quick Style* choice, as shown in Figure 2.5.

>> Quick Reference

Convert from One Style to Another Style

1. Select the text.
2. Click on the **Style** icon of the **Styles** group of the **Home** tab of the Ribbon to see the current style, which will be outlined.
3. Click on the style you want to use.

>> Quick Reference

Clear the Style from Text

1. Click on the **More** button in the **Styles** group of the **Home** tab of the Ruler.
2. Click **Clear Formatting**.

Figure 2.5 | **Save As New Quick Style**

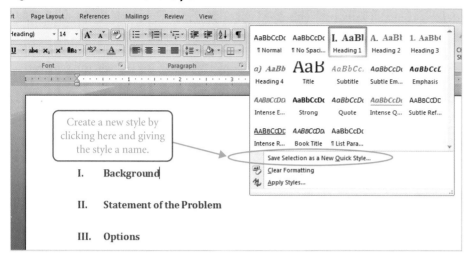

The next example shows the specific steps to set up the formats to create a style for a book proposal (as shown in Figure 2.6). A budding author will make a much better impression on potential publishers if the proposal is professionally formatted with styles.

To select the paragraph, do the following:

1. Click and drag your mouse in the margin of the document in the area to the left of the paragraph.
2. Each of the lines of the paragraph will highlight as you drag your mouse down.
3. Don't release the mouse icon until the exact lines you want selected are highlighted. As long as you don't let go, you can highlight too much or too little; it won't matter until you release the mouse button.

To italicize and indent the text, follow these steps:

1. Italicize by clicking on the **Italics** icon in the **Font** group of the **Home** tab of the Ribbon.
2. Indent by moving the **Left Indent** tool on the ruler over ½ inch to the right and moving the **Right Indent** tool on the ruler over ½ inch to the left.

Figure 2.6 | **Selecting a paragraph**

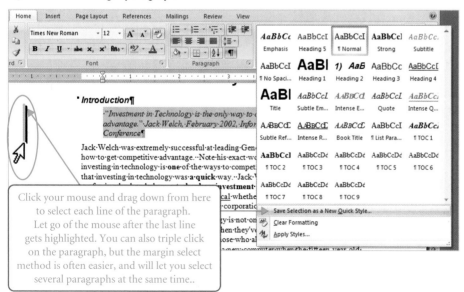

To change the font and font size, do the following:

1. Click on the **Font** list icon in the **Font** group of the **Home** tab. Click on the **Arial** font, as shown in Figure 2.7.

2. Click on the **Font Size** list icon. Either type in the number 14 or choose 14 from the list. If a number size you want does not appear in the list, you can type in the number and press **Enter** to apply it.

Figure 2.7 | **Changing the Font**

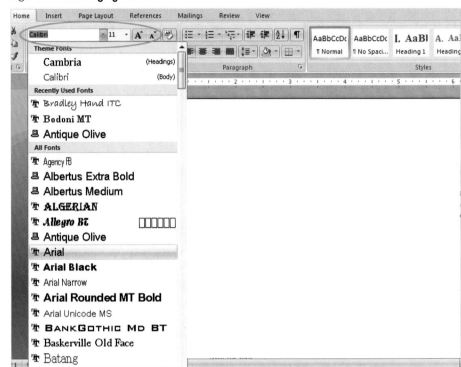

To change space between paragraphs, follow these steps:

1. Click on the **Line Spacing** list icon and choose *Add Space Before Paragraph*, as shown in Figure 2.8.

Figure 2.8 | **Insert spacing between paragraphs**

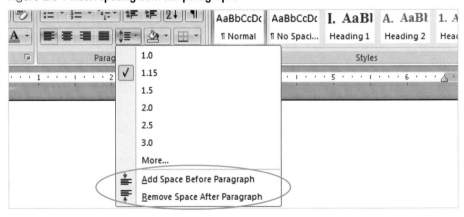

The next change you want to make doesn't appear on any of the icons on the Ribbon, so you have to open the **Paragraph** dialog box to make the change. You will see the effects of some of the other formatting changes you've made on the **Paragraph** dialog box. To make further changes, follow these steps:

1. Click on the **Paragraph** dialog box launcher button at the lower-right corner of the **Paragraph** group of the **Home** tab.
2. In the **Line and Page Breaks** tab, check the *Keep Lines Together* choice of the **Paragraph** dialog box, as shown in Figure 2.9.

Figure 2.9 | **Paragraph Dialog Box**

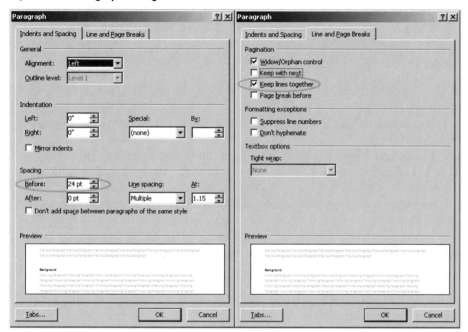

Now that you've made all the formatting choices, you are ready to create the style. To create the style, follow these steps:

1. Select the paragraph (if not still selected from before).
2. Click on the **More** button in the **Styles** group of the **Home** tab of the Ribbon.
3. Click **Selection as a New Quick Style** choice and type BeginQuote as the new style name to save.

In the next section we will discuss in more detail why we made some of these formatting choices.

COMMON MISTAKES | **Changing Font Size and Forgetting to Press Enter**

Don't forget to press **Enter** after typing in a new font size.
If you type in a new number for the font size and then immediately go back to the document by clicking the mouse or selecting something, the font size reverts to the original because you haven't applied the change. Entering the font size is just part of the process; you also need to *apply* the new font size to the selected text by pressing **Enter**.

>> *Quick Reference*

Change Font and Font Size

1. Click on the font name in the **Font** group of the **Home** tab of the Ribbon to change the font.
2. Click on the **Font Size** list icon in the **Font** group of the **Home** tab to change the font size.
3. Choose a font size or type in a new font size and press **Enter**.

>> *Quick Reference*

Placing Extra Space between Paragraphs

1. Click the **Line Spacing** list icon on the **Paragraph** group of the **Home** tab.
2. Choose **Add Space Before Paragraph**.

>> *Quick Reference*

Ensuring the Paragraph Cannot Split across a Page

1. Click on the **Paragraph** dialog box launcher button at the lower-right corner of the **Paragraph** group of the **Home** tab.
2. On the **Paragraph** dialog box, in the **Line and Page Breaks** tab, check **Keep Lines Together**.

>> *Quick Reference*

Create a New Style

1. Select a text paragraph with the formatting you wish to become a style.
2. Click on the **More** button in the **Styles** group of the **Home** tab.
3. Click on **Save Selection as a New Quick Style**.
4. Type in a useful name for the new style.

About Paragraph Formatting, Fonts, and Font Sizes

When you're writing documents for school or family and friends, there is no problem with displaying your creativity by choosing wild fonts and ignoring spacing or paragraph formatting. When you're writing business documents, however, you need to pay attention to several formatting issues.

Having a paragraph split in the middle at the bottom of a page looks unprofessional. In the book proposal example, you wouldn't want an editor to be presented with something that looked unprofessional, so to ensure that the paragraph cannot split across a page, you would check the **Keep Lines Together** option from the **Lines and Page Breaks** tab of the **Paragraph** dialog box.

Having more spacing between the paragraphs than within the paragraphs also gives your document a professional appearance. In the book proposal example, you might have noticed in the **Paragraph** dialog box in Figure 2.9 that the paragraph had 24 points in the **Before** box. Word added **24 pts** when you clicked **Add Space Before Paragraph**. Twenty-four points is about two lines, which is a little much for a book proposal (though probably just fine for a short letter), so for the book proposal, you might want to adjust that to a line and a half or just one line (18 points or 12 points, depending on your font size).

The font that you choose should match the level of formality you want to convey with the document. The font list you have is dependent on the list of fonts installed on your computer. Each program (like Word) adds fonts, so people who have installed a variety of different programs will have more fonts, and those with new computers or few programs will have fewer fonts. You can also purchase and install fonts.

For business documents such as memos and reports, a more conventional font such as Times New Roman, Century Schoolbook, or Bookman Old would be a better choice than some of the progressive, more modern-looking fonts. Especially in conservative businesses such as banking, finance, manufacturing, or retail, you want the content of the document to have the attention, not the font that it is printed in.

A letter can have a "less formal" font than a report or memo. Fonts such as Comic Sans or Script Bold might be appropriate. For a brochure, you might want to choose a font that is associated with the type of product or service. For example, a church might choose an Old English font, whereas a local theater might choose the Playbill font. A flyer for a haunted house might choose the Chiller font.

Newer fonts such as Avante Garde, Batang, Matisse, or Barnhard Fashion convey young, snazzy, or roguish characteristics. These fonts might be more appropriate in younger industries such as fashion, technology, or music.

Courier New is a different kind of font than most others. Courier New is a *fixed width* font. That makes Courier New a good font to use when you want columns of numbers or text to line up—especially in a report or menu or any business document with a list. Because each letter takes up the exact same amount of space in fixed width fonts. For example, an **a** is no wider than an **i**—fixed width fonts line up very easily. However, because Courier New looks like a typewriter font and takes up more room than a variable spaced font, it isn't often used in reports or publications that require reading paragraphs of text.

Fonts are measured by their height in ***points***. There are 72 points in an inch, so a 72-point font is 1-inch tall. This measurement technique is a change from the "old way" when typewriters proliferated. On a typewriter, fonts were measured in ***pitch***, which is determined by how many letters could fit in an inch, a measure of width, not height. With a fixed-pitch font, the larger the number, the *smaller* the font (the exact opposite of points, where the larger the number, the *larger* the font). A Courier New *12-point* font is roughly equivalent to a Courier New *10-pitch* font. At the same time, the Courier New *12-pitch* font is roughly equivalent to a Courier New *10-point* font. (We use Courier New because we can do a comparison such as this only when the width of each letter is exactly the same.)

Applying New Styles

To apply a style after you've created it is simple. In this example of a food manufacturer report, to apply a style you've created, do the following:

- Select the text to which you wish to apply the style.
- Click on the **Style** icon in the **Styles** group of the **Home** tab.
- Choose the style that you wish to apply.

As noted earlier, whether or not you know it, all text has a style applied. The default style is called *Normal*. If you clear a named style, Word actually just applies the **Normal** style to the text. In other words, *no style* and the **Normal** style are synonymous.

Notice the before and after pictures in Figure 2.10 and Figure 2.11. If you look at the style preview area of the **Styles** group of the **Home** tab, when your cursor is in a paragraph without any style, the **Normal** style is outlined in the choices. If you've already created a style called **ReportParagraph** and you just want to apply it, you would do the following:

- Select the paragraph that doesn't have a style.
- Click on the **ReportParagraph** icon in the **Styles** group of the **Home** tab. The formatting of the paragraph will be modified to match the **ReportParagraph** formatting.

Figure 2.10 | **Before ReportParagraph Style is applied.**

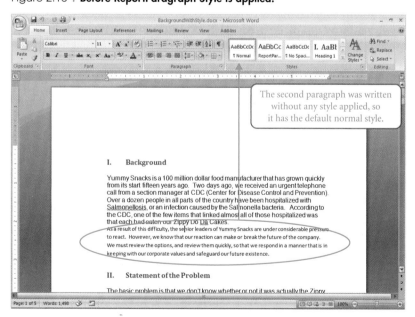

Figure 2.11 | **After ReportParagraph Style Applied**

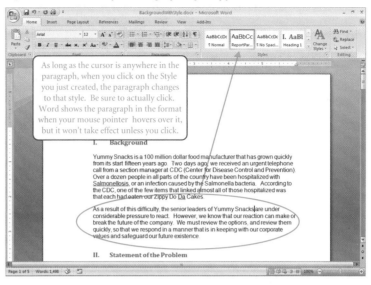

As long as the cursor is anywhere in the paragraph, when you click on the Style you just created, the paragraph changes to that style. Be sure to actually click. Word shows the paragraph in the format when your mouse pointer hovers over it, but it won't take effect unless you click.

COMMON MISTAKES | Not Fully Applying Styles

Make sure you fully click to apply styles because the paragraph will appear to change its format (called **Preview**) before you actually finalize the choice with a click. Often people think the format has changed and go on to their next task without looking to see that as soon as they've moved off the paragraph, the formatting reverts to whatever it was before.

Design Rules: Serifs, Consistency, and Whitespace

You might be asking why anyone should spend time formatting a document. How the page looks doesn't matter, does it? What's important is what is said, right?

Although it is true you can't judge a book by its cover, the fact is people get an impression by how a document looks as well as what it says. Just as you would trust a well-kempt doctor in a white coat more than one who looks slovenly and has dirty hands, you would also think that a financial analysis that crams tiny type onto a marginless page is less credible than the one that separates the paragraphs into headings, has a nice readable font, and has plenty of margin space around the edges. The greatest marketing report in the world will be overlooked and ignored if presented in all capital letters, without breaks or headings. The look of the document provides that first all-important impression to the reader, who might be your boss, your colleague, your client, your customer, or your supplier. Which impression would you like to make?

- Sloppy, inattentive to detail, emotionless, boring
- Bright, exciting, happy, artistic, "wow!"
- Calm, professional, enthusiastic, knowledgeable

Whereas the first one may be an inadvertent or careless impression, and the second one may be appropriate in some limited industries, the third is probably the best option for most business documents.

Correct spelling and grammar are givens, of course. Additionally, certain design rules of thumb exist that convey that you are a highly competent, knowledgeable professional at first sight. In general, keep in mind the following:

1. Serif fonts (fonts such as Times New Roman and Century Schoolbook) of at least 12 points should be used for body text. A serif is the little edge at the ends of the letters, as you can see in Figure 2.12.

>> *Quick Reference*

Applying Styles

1. Place your cursor in the paragraph you want changed or select the text you want changed.

2. Click on the style you wish in the **Styles** group of the **Home** tab.

2. Sans-serif fonts (fonts such as Arial and Helvetica) should be used for headings. Sans serif means "without serifs."

3. A document should have, at most, two or three different fonts.

4. Use headings, subheadings, and subsubheadings as appropriate. Avoid presenting pages and pages of text without any headings.

5. Headings should be bigger than subheadings. Subheadings should be bigger than subsubheadings. All headings should be bigger than body text.

6. At least 30% (and up to 50%) of the page should be whitespace.

7. Each heading should be connected to the text below (no page breaks should appear between the heading and the first paragraph of a new topic).

8. There should be more space before each heading than between the heading and the paragraph below it.

9. Avoid all capital letters (they tend to convey INAPPROPRIATE SHOUTING THAT CAN BE VERY ANNOYING).

10. Avoid all lowercase as well and make sure you use appropriate punctuation (famous poets who do not capitalize or punctuate notwithstanding).

Figure 2.12 | **Serif and Sans-Serif Fonts**

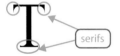

If you break the design rules in most businesses, no one will *say* anything; you will simply appear less professional and credible to your colleagues and superiors. This is especially true in conservative industries such as finance, banking, manufacturing, or retail.

In a few noted industries, these rules can be (and in some cases should be) broken. Fashion, advertising, and music are examples of industries that promote and expect creativity. Knowing how and when to break the normal design rules is encouraged in these newer types of businesses. But astute professionals in those industries *know* the rules that they are breaking, so even when being broken, the rules dominate. (You did realize that e.e. cummings *knew* that names are normally capitalized, didn't you?)

COMMON MISTAKES | Too Little Fonts, Too Little Space

A considerate writer provides reasonably sized text with plenty of whitespace and breaks up the text with an appropriate number of headings so that the reader is guided, calmly, toward the important sections.

In an effort to show off artistic tendencies or simply through ignorance of proper etiquette, some people choose a sans-serif font for the text in long documents. Sans-serif fonts are demonstrably more difficult for people to read, so using a sans-serif font for a document that is longer than a page or two shows a lack of consideration for the reader. Furthermore, a writer might make the font 10 or 11 points instead of 12. Although people with "young eyes" have no problem with 10-point font, many people over the age of 45 cannot read a 10-point font. Or, in an effort to save paper, perhaps, a writer might make the margins very small. Narrow margins will make the page appear cluttered and crowded, and will make a poor impression on the reader.

Paragraph Marks and Styles

Most people type into Word without being aware of invisible codes such as paragraph marks, tabs, and page breaks. Previously, you learned to click on the **Show Paragraph Marks** icon to see the invisible codes. It is a good idea to show these formatting marks at all times.

These invisible codes, especially paragraph marks, become doubly important when you start to use styles. If the style is a ***paragraph-level style***, it is actually stored in that paragraph mark.

Figure 2.13 shows what a blank document might look like with **Show Paragraph Marks** set to On. You can see empty paragraphs, lines with no text in them. However, the style is stored in those empty paragraph marks. If you put your cursor on the *first* line and type text, it would take on the **Normal** style, whereas the *second* line has the **ReportParagraph** style, and the *third* line has the **IntenseReference** style. You can see this in Figure 2.14.

Figure 2.13 | **Empty Paragraph Marks Storing Styles**

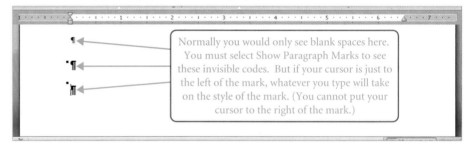

Figure 2.14 | **Text that has been typed into empty paragraph marks**

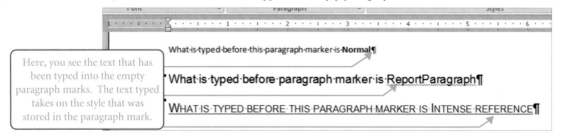

What confuses the issue even more is that a style is ***based on*** another style. If you change a style upon which other styles are based, the other styles change as well. Additionally, each style has a ***following paragraph*** style. When you are at the end of a paragraph and press **Enter** to create a new paragraph, that new paragraph will have the **following paragraph** style, not necessarily the same as the paragraph you were in when you pressed **Enter**.

To see the base and following styles, right click on the style and choose Modify, as shown in Figure 2.15. The **Modify Style** dialog box (as shown in Figure 2.16) will appear.

Figure 2.15 | **Modify Style**

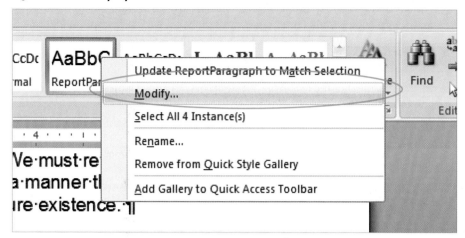

In Figure 2.16, you can see that the **ReportParagraph** style is based on **Normal** style and followed by **ReportParagraph** style. When you press **Enter** at the end of the paragraph with **ReportParagraph** style, the next paragraph will look the same.

Figure 2.16 | **Styles Are Based on Other Styles and Followed by Other Styles**

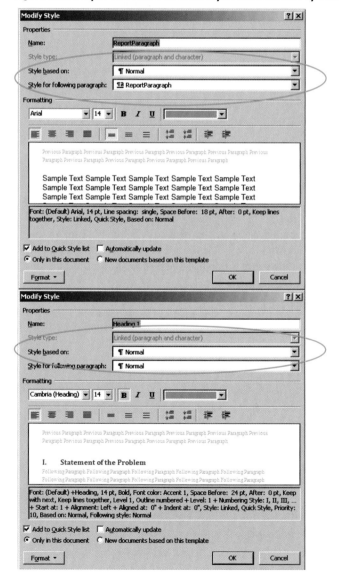

If you are in a paragraph formatted with the **Heading 1** style, however, and you press **Enter**, the **Normal** style appears. In other words, the next paragraph will not look the same. In the food manufacturer report, you can see a specific example in Figure 2.17. If your cursor is at the end of the paragraph with the words "our future existence," which is in the **ReportParagraph** style, when you press **Enter**, the paragraph mark maintains the same style. But if your cursor is at the end of the paragraph with the words "Statement of the Problem" (**Heading 1** style) and you press **Enter**, the next paragraph is a different style, the **Normal** style.

Figure 2.17 | **Inserting lines with different styles, based on existing paragraphs.**

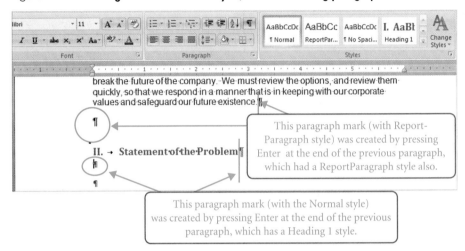

The other issue is that both styles are *based* on the **Normal** style. That means any change made to the **Normal** style that is not contradicted by formatting in the named style will be inherited by the **ReportParagraph** and **Heading 1** styles.

If, for example, you change the **Normal** style so that it has 3-D borders, every style based on **Normal** would also have 3-D borders, as shown in Figure 2.18. If you look at the styles in the **Styles** group, you can see that they all have borders because the **Normal** style was changed to have a paragraph border. If you change the line spacing, however, it would change the **Heading 1** style (because it does not specify a line spacing) but not the **ReportParagraph**. On the other hand, if you change the **Indent**, the change would affect **ReportParagraph** but not **Heading 1** because **Heading 1** specifies the indent and **ReportParagraph** does not. Changing the font wouldn't affect either because both **ReportParagraph** and **Heading 1** specify a font.

Figure 2.18 | **Modifying the Normal style, the change cascades to all styles based on Normal.**

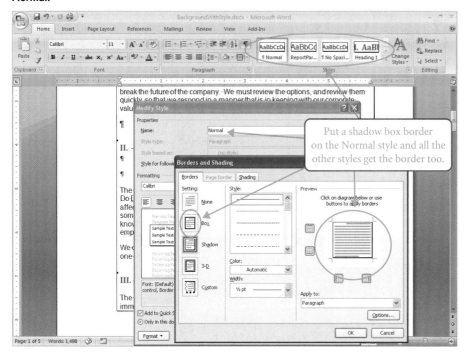

Under normal circumstances, the cascading effect is a great way to save time. To make a change in the entire document just change the base style. However, if you don't know what the base style is, or which styles are based on it, you can also do a lot of damage with one change.

COMMON MISTAKES | Reverting Formatting

You should always know what the following style will be before you press **Enter** to create a new paragraph.

Has this ever happened to you? You type in a paragraph. Then you press **Enter** to type another paragraph, but for some reason the second paragraph is indented five spaces. You move the indent section of the ruler and type your text of the next paragraph, press **Enter**, and the five spaces return.

In this case, the **Normal** style has an indent of about five spaces, but the first paragraph you typed had an applied style that didn't have an indent. However, the following style was **Normal** again, so when you pressed **Enter**, the formatting of the following paragraph reset to an indent.

If you don't want an indent, modify the **Normal** style so that it does not indent. Alternatively, you can modify the style of the first paragraph so that it follows with the same style instead of reverting to **Normal**.

Some styles are at the *paragraph level*, so whether you select the whole paragraph or just one word within the paragraph, the style would apply to the entire paragraph. Some styles are at the *text level*, not the paragraph level. You can apply text styles to just some of the text within a paragraph and not the whole paragraph.

>> *Quick Reference*

Style Bases and Follow-Ups

1. To see the base and following styles, right click on the button of the style you wish to see from the **Styles** group of the **Home** tab.
2. Choose **Modify**.

If you show the **Styles** window (which you can see by clicking on the **Show Styles Box** icon in the **Styles** group of the **Home** tab), you can see that each style has either a ¶ or an **a** or both to the right of the style name (see Figure 2.19). If there is just a ¶, the style has only paragraph-level formatting. If there is just an a, the style has only text-level formatting. But if both are shown, the style has both text-level *and* paragraph-level formatting.

Figure 2.19 | **Show Styles Box**

Storing the style definition in the paragraph mark can make combining paragraphs of different styles confusing. If your cursor is at the beginning of the second paragraph and you want to combine it with the first paragraph, you would expect that pressing **Backspace** would delete the previous paragraph mark and change the style of both paragraphs to that of the *second* paragraph. In previous versions of Word, deleting the paragraph mark would always mean the style of the second paragraph dominates. But alas, in Word 2007 the style of the *first* paragraph dominates *but only if there is text in the first paragraph*. If the first paragraph mark is *empty* and you delete the empty mark, the style of the *second* paragraph dominates.

If you copy and paste text that has text-level formatting, it will retain that text-level formatting, even when pasted into a paragraph with a style, as long as the target paragraph style does not also contain text-level formatting that will contradict the original format. To further confuse the issue, if the text-level formatting was applied manually, it will retain that format when copied *even if there is a contradictory text style in the target paragraph*. The final confusing factor is that some formatting is "either-or." It's either *on* or it's *off*, like underline or bold. Sometimes when you copy manually bolded text into a style that already has bold text formatting, it will toggle *off* the bold. You can get around all these problems by clearing the format from any text or paragraph that you want to copy prior to copying it. After you paste it where you want it, if it hasn't automatically taken the correct style, you can reapply whatever style you wish.

COMMON MISTAKES | Deleting Paragraph Marks Changes Styles

If you want to keep the style of the second paragraph, first change the style of the first paragraph to match the second and then delete the paragraph mark.

One common frustration in Word is that it is difficult to combine two paragraphs into one and keep the style of the *second* paragraph. Unless the first paragraph has no text in it, when you delete the paragraph marker, Word applies the style of the *deleted* paragraph mark to the *next* paragraph.

Modifying a Style

After you create all the styles in your document, you can modify their formatting after the fact. Changing a style automatically changes the formatting of any text where the style has been applied (as long as no manual formatting changes contradict the style format modification).

There are two ways to change the format of a style. The first way is the easier of the two:

- Make the modification to the format on one of the paragraphs with the style you want to change already applied.
- Click on the **Styles** icon in the **Styles** group of the **Home** tab and find the style you wish to modify in the list.
- Right click on the style and choose **Update *Stylename* to Match Selection**, where *Stylename* is the name of the style you are modifying.

Figure 2.20 shows the same food manufacturer report you were working on previously. To modify the formatting of the style using this first method, you do the following:

- Change the font size of one of the paragraphs with **ReportParagraph** style from 14 to 12 points.
- Right click on the **ReportParagraph** style icon and choose **Update ReportParagraph to Match Selection**.

The size of all the characters in the entire report that have the **ReportParagraph** style applied will change.

Figure 2.20 | **Update Style To Match Selection**

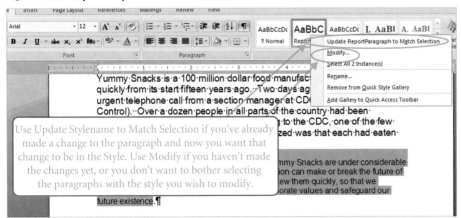

You can also see in Figure 2.20 the command to modify the style directly. In this case, you don't need to make sure the text is selected, nor do you need to worry about manually making the change first. Instead, do the following:

- Right click on the style you wish to change and click **Modify** from the list.
- Make your changes in the **Modify Style** dialog box, as shown in Figure 2.21.

Figure 2.21 | **Modify Style—Changing Font Size**

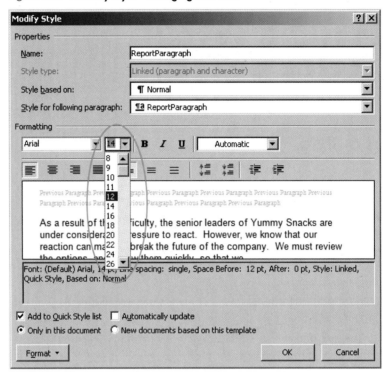

In the **Modify Styles** dialog box, you can choose any of the buttons to change any of the formatting, or you can click on the **Format** button at the bottom left to open the **Font**, **Paragraph**, **Tabs**, **Border**, or **Numbering** dialog boxes.

If you want to change the **Normal** style or many of the other built-in styles, you must use the **Modify** method to change the format. The **Update** *Stylename* **to Match Selection** choice doesn't appear for some built-in styles.

>> **Quick Reference**

Modify a Style

1. Make the formatting change you wish.
2. Right click on the **Stylename** icon in the **Styles** group of the **Home** tab.
3. Choose **Update Stylename to Match Selection**.
4. Alternatively, choose **Modify** and make the changes using the buttons or dialog boxes.

COMMON MISTAKES | **Forgetting to Update Styles**

Always update your styles as soon as you make any changes to them.
It is common to make a small formatting change to a style manually and then forget to update the style. Forgetting to update styles is frequently the cause of a format not matching the style it is supposed to or the paragraph or text not updating when the style is changed.

>> Paragraph and Text Formatting

The purpose of this workshop is to demonstrate the use of paragraph and text styles presented in this section of the chapter as well as a common business-writing procedure: turning an outline into headings to guide the writing of a report. You will see these tasks demonstrated in the following three videos: **Multilevel Outline Styles**, **Create a Style**, and **Apply and Modify Styles**. After completing each section of tasks, watch the related video. Remember to try the tasks on your own first before watching the video.

Open the file named ib_w02_backgroundoutline2 to work on for the following tasks:

1. **Multilevel Outline Styles (Video: Multi-level Outline Styles)**
   a. Select all the text in the file.
   b. Click on the **Multilevel List** icon in the **Paragraph** group of the **Home** tab.
   c. Click the choice that has *I Heading 1, A Heading 2, 1. Heading 3*.
   d. Notice the change to the outline.

2. **Create a Style (Video: Create a Style)**
   a. At the end of the first line (*Background*), press **Enter** to make a new line.
   b. Type in the following text:

      `Yummy Snacks is a 100 million dollar food manufacturer who has grown quickly from its start fifteen years ago. Two days ago, we received an urgent telephone call from a section manager at CDC (Center for Disease Control and Prevention). Over a dozen people in all parts of the country had been hospitalized with the Salmonellosis. According to the CDC, one of the few items that linked almost all of those hospitalized was that each had eaten our Zippy Do Da Cakes.`

   c. Select the text you typed in preparation for the next section.
   d. Change the font to Arial.
   e. Change the font size to 14 point.
   f. Change the line spacing to 1 (single-spaced).
   g. Add space before the paragraph.
   h. Change the paragraph setting so that the paragraph will stay together and prevent it from splitting across a page break.
   i. With the paragraph formatted and still selected, create a new style called **ReportParagraph**.

3. **Apply and Modify Styles (Video: Apply and Modify Styles)**
   a. Type the next paragraph after the first one:

      `As a result of this difficulty, the senior leaders of Yummy Snacks are under considerable pressure to react. However, we know that our reaction can make or break the future of the company. We must review the`

options, and review them quickly, so that we respond
in a manner that is in keeping with our corporate
values and safeguard our future existence.

b. Apply the style **ReportParagraph** to the second paragraph so that it matches the formatting of the first.

c. Change the font of the paragraphs to 12 points and update the **ReportParagraph** style.

d. Modify the **Heading 1** style so that the **ReportParagraph** style follows it instead of the **Normal** style.

e. Save the document and call it **ib_w02_backgroundoutline2v1.**

>> Formatting Letters

Word processing is part of just about every business, and every businessperson must be able to use a word processor like Word. But why learn all about styles? There are two main reasons:

- Your documents will be more consistently formatted and therefore look more professional.
- Editing documents will be much easier and will save much time.

Additionally, you may receive documents with styles and will need to know how to maintain the styles created by the original author. If your boss or colleague who understands styles sends you a document, and you apply manual formatting to the text on top of the styles, your boss or colleague will not be happy with you.

Exercise

The purpose of this exercise is to create a standard format for the letters that will be used by everyone in the same department at a large insurance company. Because the public relations department will also be revising the format in a few weeks, you are charged with creating a standard format using styles that may be used now and then updating the styles and format to correspond to the new guidelines in a few weeks.

Most people in the department are not extremely comfortable using Word. As a result, the letter format you create needs to be easy to use and should look like a letter with the appropriate formatting in place if you expect them to use it. If you set up styles for your formatting, later you can change it more easily.

Start by looking at one of the typical letters sent out by the office and make notes on the letter about what changes you would like to make. When you are done, the letter format should look like the one in Figure 2.22.

Figure 2.22 | **Insurance Letter**

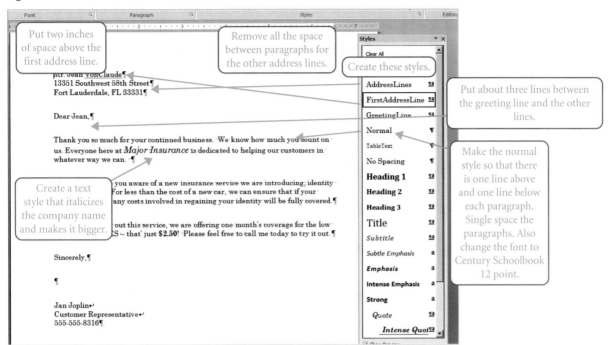

Open the file named ib_w02_insuranceletter.

1. Modify the letter so that it looks similar to the letter in Figure 2.22.

2. Create the styles as specified:

    a. Use the **FirstAddressLine** style with two inches of space above the first address line.

    b. Use the **AddressLines** style with no space above or below.

    c. Use the **Greeting** style with three spaces above.

    d. Create a text style for the words *Major Insurance* so that they always appear bigger than the other fonts and in italics.

    e. Change the **Normal** style so that there are about two lines in between the paragraphs, although the paragraphs themselves are single-spaced.

    f. Change the font for all the text to Century Schoolbook, 12 points, by changing the **Normal** style to that font.

3. Save the letter and call it **ib_wo2_insuranceletterv1**.

≫ What's Wrong with This Document?

Problem

You are the owner of a small day spa. Your office assistant has spent the past few hours grumbling because a Word document she is working on won't do what she wants it to do. You finally get tired of listening and tell her to send the document to you so that you can figure out what's wrong with it and fix it.

She e-mails you the document along with the following complaints:

1. I keep changing the **Heading 1** style to 24 points. The Color heading changes, but the Service Options heading stays the same.

2. I can't get the third leader line to appear. I keep looking at the **ServiceLine** style, and the leader line is there, but it doesn't appear for Color.

3. I want to create a style called **ColorLine**, but each time I select one of the lines and try to create the style, the entire line is bolded. I want only the first word bolded. What am I doing wrong?

Exercise

The file your assistant sends you is named ib_w02_salonoptions. What's wrong with this document? Consider the following:

1. What manual changes were made to the format after the styles were created?
2. Look at the tab settings for the different services. Is there a difference between the ones that have a leader line and the one that doesn't?
3. Why does the style your assistant created apply to the whole paragraph instead of just the text?

Write a short answer for each of these questions and then apply the style formatting techniques you have learned to fix all her complaints. Save the file as **ib_w02_salonoptionsv1**.

>> Page Formatting

Unlike letters, brochures, or other short documents, reports generally have additional requirements like headers and footers, page numbers, and a cover page. In a short document, the reader can easily "glance through" the document and find everything. With a longer document, the reader can't quickly glance through it to find whatever he or she is looking for. As the author, you must make it easy for the reader to find everything and to understand exactly where the document came from, what page he or she is currently on, when it was written, and where to get it again if needed.

It is also important for the first impression of your document to be a positive, professional one. Commonly understood but rarely verbalized "rules" subconsciously impress upon the reader, before he or she reads a single word, the level of professionalism the document conveys.

The first section showed you how to format the text and paragraphs. This section demonstrates how to format the page, including creating a cover page; adjusting the margins; and adding headers, footers, and page numbers.

Page Margins

In the previous section, you learned how to modify the space around the text and paragraphs, change the indents of the paragraphs, and change the amount of space before and after paragraphs. However, in some situations, you might need to modify the *margin* of an entire document. For example, what if you want the document to have a 1.25-inch margin around the entire page? Or what if you need to print on legal-size paper (8½" x 14") or some other size paper?

Some business documents traditionally have large margins, such as letters and memos. A letter might have 1½- to 2-inch margins on each side, more if a logo appears in the header at the top. Longer reports and document-like instructional manuals and policy guides may have slightly narrower margins, perhaps only 1 inch on each side. Brochure and flyers, especially folding documents, will need much narrower margins, probably ½ inch on each side.

The *Page Layout* tab contains page margin choices. As Figure 2.23 shows, you can see many choices just by clicking on the **Margins** icon. But if you want another choice, such as 1.5-inch margins on the top and left and 1-inch margins on the bottom and right, you need to choose *Custom Margins*. Documents may require a custom margin to match the company standard, to adjust the page length of the document, or to avoid a *widow* or *orphan*. A widow is a single line at the end of a paragraph that splits off to the next page, and an orphan is a single word that splits off to the next line.

Making a document margin just .016 point narrower or wider can have a great impact on the number of pages without impacting the visual look of the document.

Notice that on the **Page Layout** tab of the Ribbon you can change the page orientation from *Portrait* to *Landscape*.

Figure 2.23 | **Page Margins and Orientation**

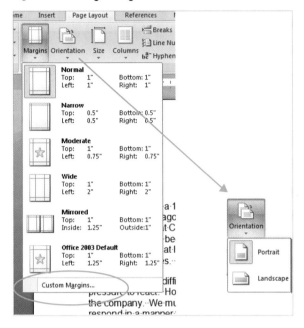

When you click on **Custom Margins**, the **Page Setup** dialog box will appear, and you can type in whatever numbers you wish, as shown in Figure 2.24.

Figure 2.24 | **Changing the Page Margins**

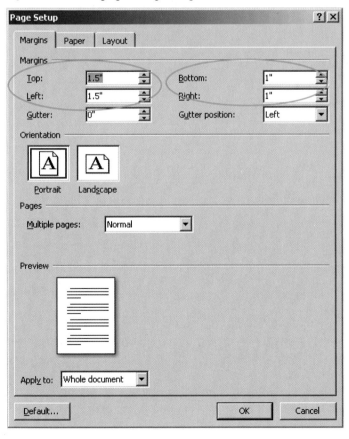

>> **Quick Reference**

Change Margins

1. Click the **Page Layout** tab on the Ribbon.
2. Click **Margins** in the **Page Setup** group.
3. Choose **Custom Margins** and enter the number of inches for the top, bottom, left, and right margins on the **Margin** tab of the **Page Setup** dialog box.

>> **Quick Reference**

Change Page Orientation

1. Click the **Page Layout** tab.
2. Click **Orientation**.
3. Click **Portrait** or **Landscape**.

Inserting Page Numbers

You will also want to add page numbers to your report. Page numbers can be found on the **Insert** tab.

If you look at Figure 2.25, you will find *Page Numbers* in the **Header & Footer** group. When you click on it, you will see many choices. The same choices also appear in the **Header & Footer Tools** tab, as shown in Figure 2.26. If you want the page numbers to appear at the bottom of the page, choose **Bottom of Page** and then choose a format, such as **Rounded Rectangle 2** shown in the figure.

Figure 2.25 | **Insert Page Numbers**

Figure 2.26 | **Choosing location for Page Numbers**

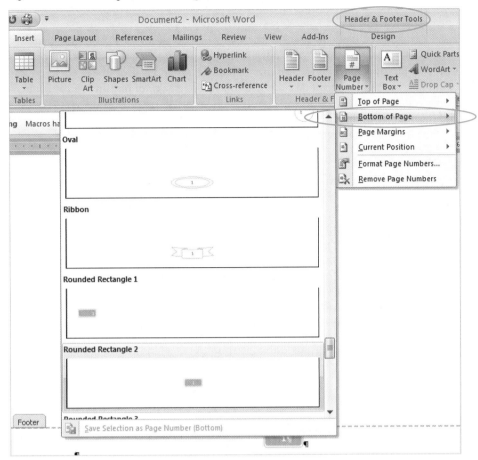

Headers and Footers

When they are used in a document, ***headers*** appear at the top of each page, and ***footers*** appear at the bottom of each page. In all business documents, it is helpful to have the name of the document on every page, as well as the author name, the date the document was created or saved, and the path and filename of the document. (A ***path*** is the location of the document, such as *c:\My Documents\Chap 2 Exercises* that precedes the document name.) Typing them on every page, every time, would be a lot of work—not to mention futile because if you edit the document, it will repaginate in different places. With headers and footers, you can type them in just once, and they will automatically repeat throughout the entire document.

Even better, Word has ***fields*** that will allow you to automate many different types of information about the document:

- Path and filename
- Save date
- Print date
- Original creation date
- Name of the person who last saved the document
- Original author name
- Document title
- Company of the author

If you use these fields, you won't have to edit any of that information if you open the document from a different place or at a different time. They will automatically update.

Putting the path and filename in the footer of a document is an especially helpful business practice. Months or years later, when you pick up the paper document, you won't have to remember where you stored it; the location is at the bottom of the page. You might not think so right away, but getting into the habit of putting the path and filename in your footer will save you much trouble and frustration as the years go on and the number of documents you need to track increases exponentially.

To type in the footer, do the following:

- Go to the **Insert** tab and choose the **Header & Footer** group.
- Click the **Footer** icon. Bypass all the footer options in the gallery and choose **Edit Footer**.
- Figure 2.27 shows the result if you choose the **Edit Footer** choices. Your cursor will jump to an area at the bottom of the page.

Figure 2.27 | **Insert Footers**

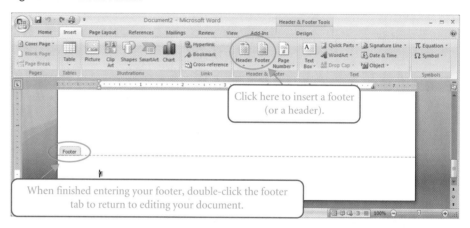

You can type text into a footer. Whatever you type will appear at the bottom of each page. You can also add the special fields discussed previously to the footer.

A filename and path can get very long, so choose a very small font, such as 6 point (which you will have to type in because it is not normally a font size choice). It's also nice to place a line (paragraph border) between the footer and the text of the page for a professional-looking touch.

Changing the **Footer** style can be a bit difficult because Word considers the footer a "hidden built-in style." If you try to create a style named **Footer**, you get an error message, as shown in Figure 2.28. You have two choices: use a different style name for the footer style or unhide the **Footer** style and make the modification there.

Figure 2.28 | **Built-In Style Error Message**

To see all the styles—those that you created, those that are unhidden and built in, and those that are built in but still hidden—you must click on the **Manage Styles** button at the bottom of the **Show Styles** box, as shown in Figure 2.29.

Figure 2.29 | **Manage Styles Button**

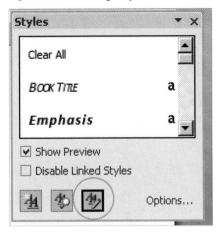

In Figure 2.30, note the list of hundreds of styles, many of which say *(Hide until used)* afterward. Also, note that you can tell if they are paragraph-level styles or text-level styles by the ¶ or a in front of each style.

Figure 2.30 | **Show and Modify Hidden Styles**

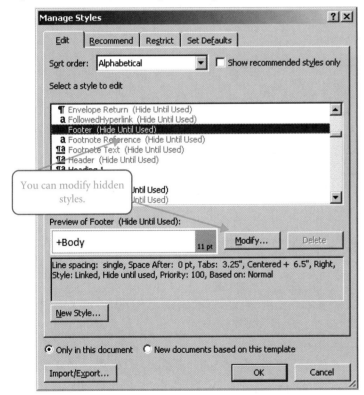

Now that you can see all the styles, you can modify them as follows:

- On the **Edit** tab, click on the **Footer (Hide Until Used)** style and then click **Modify**.
- Change the font to 8-point italic using the icon on the **Modify Style** dialog box.
- Click **Format** and then **Border**.
- Place a paragraph border at the top by clicking the top of the box in the preview diagram, as shown in Figure 2.31. (Make sure the **Apply to** box says **Paragraph**.)

Figure 2.31 | **Footer Top Border on Paragraph**

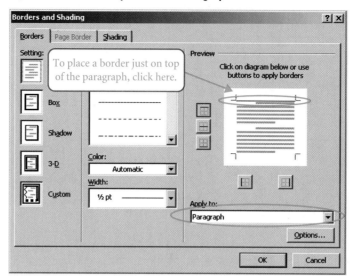

- From the **Modify Style** dialog box, click **Format** and then **Tabs**. Put a **right align** tab at the end of the line (at 6 inches).
- On the **Recommend** tab, with the **Footer (Hide Until Used)** style selected, click on the **Show** button, as shown in Figure 2.32. Now the **Footer** style will appear in the list.

Figure 2.32 | **Unhide Footer**

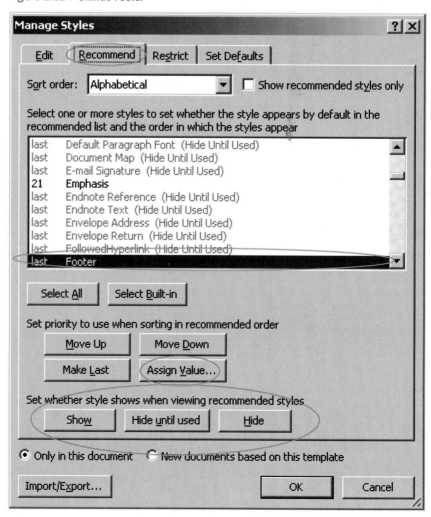

You could also, at this time, change *where* the style appears in the list. Currently, it will appear last, but you can assign a numeric value (which determines the order based on the numeric values assigned to the other unhidden styles) or simply move it up in the list.

COMMON MISTAKES | **Trying to Re-create a Hidden Style**

You should review all the hidden styles in the *Manage Styles* box and show any of those you might want to use on a regular basis. As already noted, trying to re-create a hidden built-in style is a mistake because Microsoft named its built-in styles with common names such as **Bullet**, **Heading 1**, **Header**, **Footer**, **Title**, and **Outline**. To avoid this problem, modify the format of the styles you wish to use so that they look the way you want them to look and unhide them so that you can use them.

Inserting Fields into the Footer

After you've set the style you want for the footer, you can insert the fields into the footer that will place the path and filename, the save date, and the name of the author who saved the file, as shown in the example.

Word considers fields to be *Quick Parts*, so go to the **Quick Parts** icon on the **Insert** tab. A **Quick Part** is Microsoft's name for automated text entry, automated dates, automated fields, and document properties such as author or title. If you click on the list box to the right of **Quick Parts**, you will see various options. **Property** lists a few of the more commonly used fields, but you can see *all* the fields by clicking on the **Field** choice (as shown in Figure 2.33), which opens the **Field** dialog box (as shown in Figure 2.34).

Figure 2.33 | **Quick Parts**

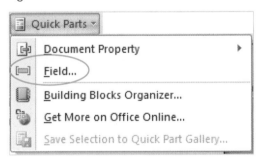

>> **Quick Reference**

Unhiding and Modifying the Footer Style

1. Click the **Home** tab.
2. Click the **Show Styles** button at the lower-left corner of the **Styles** group.
3. Click the **Manage Styles** button.
4. Click the **Recommendations** tab.
5. Choose the style you wish to unhide.
6. Click the **Show** button.

Figure 2.34 | **Field Dialog Box, Document Information Fields**

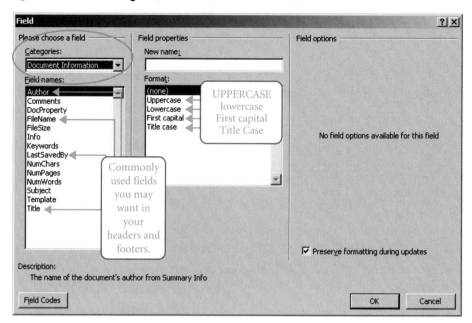

Choose the **Document Information** category, and you will see many of the fields you will be using, including *Title*, *Author*, *LastSavedBy*, and **Filename**. The **Title** and **Author** fields are taken from the **Document Properties** (shown in Figure 2.35). The **LastSavedBy** field is set by whatever or whomever is in the User field of the Word installation that is saving the file (always the author the first time a file is saved). If you send the document to someone else, and that person makes a change and saves it, the **Author** field will have your name in it and the **LastSavedBy** will have the other person's name in it. (Both of these, of course, are assuming that you are actually using a personal copy of Word. If you are using a copy of Word that someone else installed, whoever installed it set the author name.)

Figure 2.35 | **Document Properties**

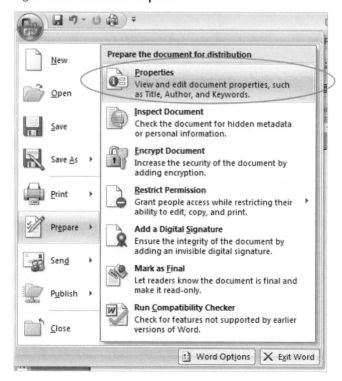

COMMON MISTAKES | Using a Regular Document as a Template

Always remember to check the **Author** and **Company** fields of any document you are working on. One of the reasons it is a mistake to use a document that someone else started as a template is that the author information in the document shows where you got the document. Nothing is more unprofessional than for someone to pull up the properties of a document you supposedly wrote and see someone else's name and company in the **Author** and **Company** fields.

If you still want to use a document someone else started as a template, at least go into the file properties and edit the **Author** and **Company** fields so that they reflect you and your company.

Now that you understand where to get the automated fields, you can set up a footer using them as follows:

- Make sure your cursor is at the beginning of the **Footer** line (by choosing **Insert, Header & Footer, Footer,** and then **Edit Footer**).
- Choose **Quick Parts** and then **Field.**
- Choose **Document Information** and then **Filename** from the **Field** dialog box, as shown in Figure 2.34.
- Choose *First capital,* as shown in Figure 2.36.
- Click on **Add path to filename** under the **Field options** section.
- Click **OK** to save your changes and go back to the document footer.

Figure 2.36 | **Path and Filename Fields**

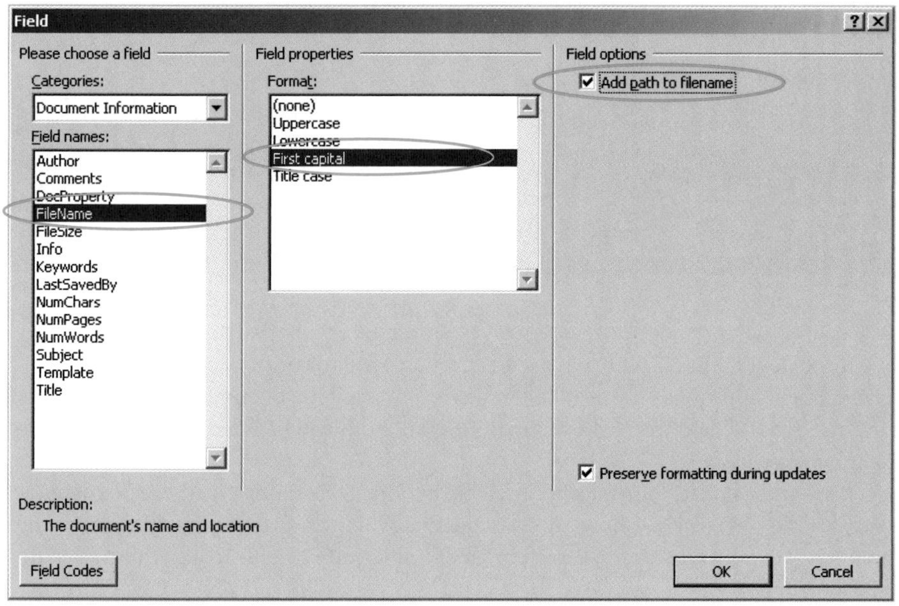

In this example, the right side of the footer will also include the date the document was saved and the name of the person who last saved the document. To add this information, follow these steps:

- Press the **Tab** key so that your cursor jumps to the **Right Align** tab set up in the footer style definition at the end of the line.
- Type the words **Last saved by** and leave a space at the end.
- Choose **Quick Parts** and then **Field.**

- Choose **Document Information** and then **LastSavedBy** from the **Field** dialog box, as shown in Figure 2.34.
- Click **OK** to return to the footer.
- Type the word **on** and leave a space at the end.
- Choose **Quick Parts** and then **Field.**
- Choose **Date and Time** and then **SaveDate** from the **Field** dialog box, as shown in Figure 2.37.
- Choose a Month Day, Year format such as (**January 1, 2008**) from the **Date Format** list of the **Field Properties** section.
- Click **OK** to return to the footer.
- Press **Enter** to go to the next line and type **Confidential. Not to be released.**
- Double click the **Footer** tab to return to the document.

Figure 2.37 | **Field Dialog Box, Date and Time**

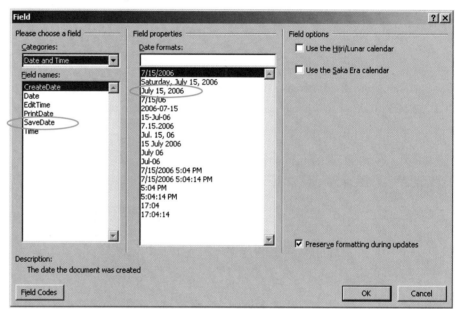

If the document hasn't been saved yet, when you look at the save date on the screen, it will appear as XXX 0, 0000. Additionally, until the document is actually saved, the **LastSavedBy** field won't show anything at all. Both will be filled in the first time the document is saved.

Inserting a header is similar to inserting a footer. The report for the food manufacturer dealing with a crisis shows an example that will include the same elements as the footer created previously and, therefore, does not require a field. To add this footer, do the following:

- From the **Insert** tab, click on **Header** in the **Header & Footer** group and then **Edit Header**.
- From the **Home** tab, click on the **Align Text Right** icon.
- Change the font size to 10 points and click the **Italics** icon.
- Add a bottom border using the **Border** icon.
- Type the words you wish to appear on the top right of every page. Figure 2.38 shows the the Header tab.
- Double-click the **Header** tab to return to the document.

Figure 2.38 | **Insert Header**

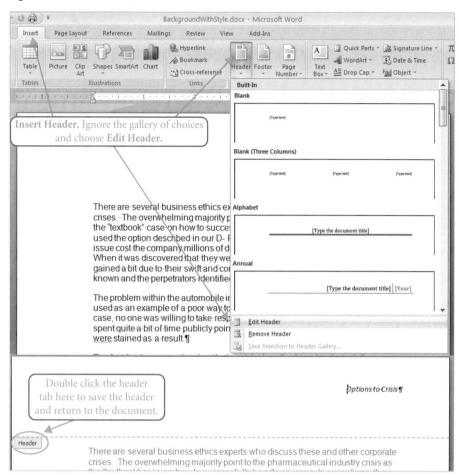

> Insert Header. Ignore the gallery of choices and choose **Edit Header**.

> Double click the header tab here to save the header and return to the document.

There are several business ethics experts who discuss these and other corporate crises. The overwhelming majority point to the pharmaceutical industry crisis as

Creating a Cover Page

A cover page elicits an immediate "this is a professional document" reaction from a reader. It typically includes the name of the document, the date it was written, and the author contact information. You can make a simple cover page by typing whatever you want on the first page of a document and pressing **Ctrl+Enter** to create a forced page break, as shown in Figure 2.39. Note that you can *see* the page break only if you have turned on the **Show Paragraph Marks** option (found on the **Home** tab of the Ribbon).

>> *Quick Reference*

Insert a Header

1. Click the **Insert** tab, **Header & Footer** group, and then the **Header** icon.
2. Choose a **Header** style or choose **Edit Header**.
3. Type the text to appear at the top of each page.
4. Double click the **Header** tab to return to the document.

>> *Quick Reference*

Insert a Footer

1. Click the **Insert** tab, **Header & Footer** group, and then the **Footer** icon.
2. Choose a **Footer** style or choose **Edit Footer**.
3. Type the text to appear at the bottom of each page.
4. Double click the **Footer** tab to return to the document.

>> *Quick Reference*

Insert a Quick Parts Field

1. Click the **Insert** tab, **Header & Footer** group, and then the **Quick Parts** icon.
2. Choose **Field** and then choose the **Category** of the field you wish to insert.
3. Click the field and any options you wish.
4. Click **OK**.

Figure 2.39 | **Cover Page Using Manual Page Break**

You can create a nice effect for the words on the cover page in a variety of ways. For example, here are three different ways to accomplish a large bordered box in the middle of the Text box, Table definition, and Paragraph Borders.

- To create a text box, click the **Insert** tab, choose the **Text Box** group, and the choose **Draw Text Box**. Then drag the mouse to create the box in the center of the page.
- To create a table definition, choose the **Page Layout** tab on the Ribbon, click on the **Margin** icon, and then choose **Center Vertical Alignment**.
- Choose the **Paragraph** group on the **Home** tab; then choose the **Outside Borders** icon with 144 points of space before and 144 points after (giving you 2 inches above and below the text).

Although you can use any of these choices, the last one, **Outside Borders**, is the easiest to implement and will have the least impact on the document. The trouble with text boxes in Word is that they often jump around unexpectedly or won't stay where you put them (unless you understand graphic placement). The problem with centering the vertical alignment is that it will cause every page in the document to center (unless you know how to set up **sections**). So the best choice is **Outside Borders**.

In Figure 2.39, the cover page for the food manufacturer report uses the last option. In this example, the font was increased to a 36-point size and the color changed. Additionally, the space was adjusted. To create the cover page, follow these steps:

- Make sure that **Show Paragraph Marks** is on (see Figure 2.40).
- Place your cursor in front of the text you wish to "push down" to the next page.
- Press **Ctrl+Enter**.
- Use the **Left Arrow** key to move your cursor to the left of the paragraph mark. Press **Enter** to make an extra line.
- Choose the **Home** tab, where all the text formatting is found.
- Click **Arial Black** in the **Font** icon list in the **Font** group.
- Click the number list to the right of the **Font** icon and type in or choose 36.
- Click the list on the **Borders** icon in the **Paragraph** group and choose **Outside Borders**.
- Click on the **Center** alignment icon in the **Paragraph** group.
- Click on the **Paragraph** dialog box and type the number **144** into the **Space Before** and **Space After**.

FIGURE 2.40 | **Paragraph Mark On and Off**

At this point in the food manufacturing report example, the header and footer still appear on the first page, now a cover sheet, which looks unprofessional. However, Word enables you to suppress the header and the footer, making it appear on all the pages except the first page. To suppress the header or the footer, do the following:

1. Click on the **Page Setup** dialog box launcher from the **Page Setup** group of the **Page Layout** tab on the Ribbon.
2. On the **Layout** tab, click **Different First Page** under the **Header and Footer** area, as shown on Figure 2.41.

Figure 2.41 | **Different First Page for Headers and Footers**

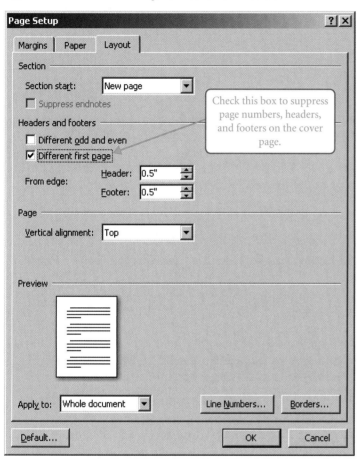

When you return to the document, the headers and footers are no longer on the first page but remain on the rest of the pages.

COMMON MISTAKES | Separate Document for Cover Page

The cover page should not be created in a separate document, but as the first page of the document itself. Without an understanding of manual page breaks or sections, people often create a separate document for the cover page of a document. There are several disadvantages to doing it that way. When you try to send the document to someone else, you have to send two documents, and that person must print them both and put them together to get the full professional impressive effect (which, of course, he or she won't do). If you want to create a PDF document (a format for which there is a free reader, Acrobat Reader, available on the Internet so you can be sure everyone will be able to read the document), you need special software to combine the cover page with the rest of the document. Finally, you might get confused, later, about which document has the actual information and which one was just the cover page—not to mention that the extra document takes up more room on your hard disk.

>> *Quick Reference*

Cover Page

1. Press **Ctrl+Enter** at the beginning of the document to create a blank page.
2. Format the text on the cover page.
3. In the **Page Setup** dialog box, on the **Layout** tab, click **Different First Page** under the **Header and Footer** area.

≫ Headers and Footers

The purpose of this workshop is to demonstrate the use of headers, footers, page numbers, and cover pages as presented in this section of the chapter. You will see these tasks demonstrated in the following four videos: **Insert Page Numbers and Change Page Margins**, **Modify Footer Style and Add Footer**, **Insert Header**, and **Create Cover Page**. After completing each section of tasks, watch the related video. Remember to try the tasks on your own first before watching the video.

Open the file named ib_w02_walrusproposal and do the following tasks:

1. **Insert Page Numbers and Change the Page Margins (Video: Insert Page Numbers and Change Page Margins)**

   a. On the **Insert** tab, click the **Page Numbers** icon in the **Header & Footer** group.

   b. Choose **Bottom of Page** from the drop-down menu and then **Brackets 1** as the format.

   c. Click the **Close header and Footer** icon to return to the document.

   d. Click on the **Page Layout** tab, choose the **Margins** icon, and then choose **Custom Margins**.

   e. In the **Page Setup** dialog box, enter 1.5" in the **Top** and **Left** margins and 1" in the **Bottom** and **Right** margins.

   f. Click **OK** to close the **Page Setup** dialog box and return to the document.

2. **Modify Footer Style and Add Footer (Video: Modify Footer Style and Add Footer)**

   a. On the Home tab, click the **Styles** dialog box launcher button to show all the styles.

   b. Click the **Manage Styles** button.

   c. On the **Edit** tab, click on the **Footer** style and then click **Modify**.

   d. Change the font to 8-point italic using the buttons on the **Modify Style** dialog box.

e. Click **Format** and then **Border**.

f. Place a paragraph border at the top by clicking the top of the box in the preview diagram. Click the **OK** button.

g. From the **Modify Style** dialog box, click **Format** and then **Tabs**.

h. Put a right align tab at the end of the line (at 6 inches). Click **OK** twice.

i. On the **Recommend** tab, with the **Footer** style selected, click on **Show** button.

j. Assign the number **5** to the position in the list of the **Footer** style.

k. Click the **OK** button in the **Manage Styles** dialog box to return to the document by double clicking the **Footer** tab.

l. On the **Insert** tab, choose the **Footer** icon from the **Headers & Footers** group and then choose **Edit Footer**.

m. On the **Header & Footer tools** tab, click on **Quick Parts**.

n. Click on **Field**.

o. Choose **Document Information** and then **FileName** from the fields list.

p. Choose **First capital**.

q. Click on **Add path to filename** under the **Field options** section.

r. Click **OK** to save your changes and go back to the document footer.

s. Press the **Tab** key so that your cursor jumps to the end of the line.

t. Type the words `Last saved by`.

u. Choose the **Quick Parts** icon and then **Field** from the menu.

v. Choose **Document Information** and then **LastSavedBy** from the **Field names**: options.

w. Click **OK** to return to the footer.

x. In the footer, after the field you just inserted, type a space and the word **on**.

y. Choose **Quick Parts** and then **Field**.

z. Choose **Date and Time** and then **SaveDate** from the **Field** dialog box.

aa. Choose a Month Day, Year format (MMM dd, YYYY) from the **Date Format** list of the **Field Properties** section.

ab. Click **OK** to return to the footer.

ac. Press **Enter** to go to the next line and type in `Confidential. Not to be released`.

ad. Double click the **Footer** tab to return to the document.

ae. To review the document, click the **Office** button, **Print**, and then **Print Preview**. Look to see if the fields fill in appropriately.

af. Save the document and name it `ib_w02_walrusproposalv1`.

3. **Insert a Header (Video: Insert a Header)**

a. From the **Insert** tab, click on **Header** and then **Edit Header** from the **Header & Footer** group.

b. From the **Home** tab, click on the **Align Text Right** icon.

c. Change the font size to 10 points Italic.

d. Add a bottom border using the **Border** icon.

e. Type `Walrus Associates Proposal`.

f. Double click the **Header** tab to return to the document.

g. To review the document, click the **Office** button, **Print**, and then **Print Preview**.

h. Save the document and name it `ib_w02_walrusproposalv2`.

4. Create a Cover Page (Video: Create a Cover Page)

a. Make sure your **Show Paragraph Marks** is on so that a forced page break will be visible in the document.

b. Place your cursor in front of the heading "Current Recommendations."

c. Press **Ctrl+Enter** to "push down" the content to the next page.

d. Place the cursor to the left of the paragraph mark on the line containing the text "Proposal." Press **Enter** to make an extra line.

e. Select the line containing the text "Proposal." Click **Arial Black** in the **Font** icon list in the **Font** group of the **Home** tab.

f. Click the **Font size** list to the right of the **Font** icon and type in or choose **36**.

g. Click the **Borders** icon list on the **Paragraph** group and choose **Outside Borders**.

h. Click on the **Center alignment** icon on the **Paragraph** group.

i. Click on the **Paragraph** dialog box launcher. On the **Indents and Spacing** tab, type the number **144** into the **Space Before** and **Space After** boxes.

j. Click on the **Page Layout** tab. Click the **Page Setup** dialog box launcher. Click **OK** to close the **Paragraph** dialog box and return to the document.

k. On the **Layout** tab of the **Page Setup** dialog box, click **Different First Page** under the **Headers and Footers** section. Click **OK**.

l. To review the document, click the **Office** button, **Print**, and then **Print Preview**.

m. Save the document and name it **ib_w02_walrusproposalv3**.

›› Creating a Decision Recommendation Report

One of the most important skills for a business executive is the ability to gather data, analyze a situation, identify the options, discern the advantages and disadvantages of each option, and make recommendations to others so that they are guided to make the right decision. Critical to this process is presenting the problem, possible options, and final recommendation in a professional-looking document that will be evaluated by decision makers. Before meeting this objective, most business documents go through several rounds of revisions. For example, coworkers often review each other's work before the documents reach their intended audience. Additionally, sharing a draft with an immediate supervisor before distributing it more widely is always a good idea. Knowing key Word formatting skills, such as how to use styles effectively, will make your task of creating multiple revisions easier. The result will also be a professional-looking document that will impress the reader.

Exercise

This purpose of this exercise is to format a report document so that it meets normal business requirements, such as including headers, footers, and page numbers. Open the document named ib_w02_optionstocrisis. Your goal will be to prepare a professional-looking report with effectively formatted styles that you could send to the senior management team at a snack food manufacturer.

1. Apply appropriate formatting changes to headings, titles, and other text following conservative design rules.

   a. Ensure adequate whitespace in margins.

   b. Ensure a large readable font for the text.

    c. Ensure adequate whitespace between sections.

    d. Ensure that all lists have numbers or bullets.

2. Insert page numbers, headers, footers, and a cover page.

3. In the footer, use fields to enter the following information:

    a. The filename, including the path

    b. The date the report was last printed

    c. The original author of the report

    d. The number of words in the entire report

4. Make sure the header and footer do not print on the cover page.

5. Save the document and name it **ib_w02_optionstocrisisv1**.

>> What's Wrong with This Document?

Problem

You are about to hire a senior-level employee for a small startup corporation selling Live Video Customer Service technology. The secretary working on the employment agreement, however, has sent you an email (see Figure 2.42) describing problems he's having with it. He has tried to fix it but has been unable to. He asks you to figure out what's wrong with it and explain the problem to him so that he can get it out today.

Figure 2.42 | **Email about Employment Agreement**

The file the secretary sent you is named ib_w02_mkemploymentagree. What's wrong with this document? Consider the following points:

1. Why does the second page start so low on the page? (Hint: Make sure you can see invisible codes.)

2. What happened to the page numbers?

3. What happened to the footers?

4. How can you get the word *Confidential*, the save date, the name of the person who last saved, and the name and location of the file to automatically appear at the bottom of each page?

5. Why is Mary's address deformed?

6. How can you get the exhibit to start on a new page?

7. What happened to the lines on the signature page?

Write a short answer to each of these questions and then fix all the problems; make sure that the date, the name of the last person to save the document, as well as the name and location of the file all update automatically. Save the document as **ib_w02_mkemploymentagreev1**.

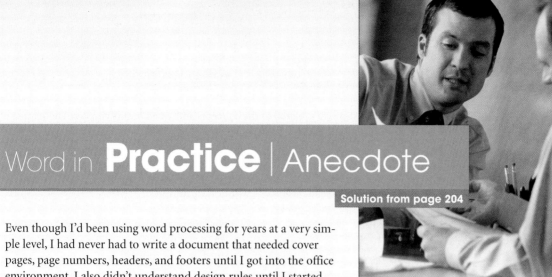

Word in **Practice** | Anecdote

Solution from page 204

Even though I'd been using word processing for years at a very simple level, I had never had to write a document that needed cover pages, page numbers, headers, and footers until I got into the office environment. I also didn't understand design rules until I started reading documents that broke the rules. Once I figured out how to follow good design rules and add professional touches to my documents, my managers noticed my work more often. The time I spent to figure out how to make my documents look impressive and professional was well worth the effort.

The big benefit came, however, because I could edit my documents quickly. Many of my coworkers would get frustrated trying to edit a document they had written before—sometimes so much that they would just start all over again and retype the whole thing. They had a difficult time diagnosing and fixing formatting problems. My managers expected multiple revisions and expected those revisions to be done very quickly. So in addition to looking more professional, my documents were often revised much more quickly as well, giving me more opportunities to work with senior-level managers in the company.

Assignment

Open the document named ib_w02_prodalldecreport. Modify this file so that it appears professional and follows good design rules. The terms defined in the first section should be boldfaced, but make sure that if you wanted to, you could change the formatting to italics for all the terms quickly and easily. Make sure you can find the file again easily. Also, make sure you know what date the file was last saved.

In addition, make sure your name appears automatically on every page as the author. Then make sure the page number, headers, and footers do not appear on the cover page.

Questions for Discussion

1. Do you think that it really makes a difference to the reader if you include headers, footers, and page numbers in a long document?

2. For which kinds of documents would these features be really important? For which ones wouldn't it make any difference (i.e., headers, footers, and page numbers are not necessary)?

3. Have you ever had problems editing a document you had already written? What kinds of problems did you encounter?

The following questions are related to the concepts addressed in this chapter. There are three types of questions: Short Answer, True or False, and Fill in the Blank. If your answer to a True or False question is False, write a short explanation as to why you think the statement is not true.

1. True or False: You can't use Word without learning to use styles.

2. True or False: There is never a problem in mixing manual format changes and styles.

3. The style of text that doesn't have a "named" style is called _____.

4. The name of the style usually used for the first-level heading in a document is called _____.

5. True or False: It is not possible to convert text that has been formatted with one style into a different style.

6. You can tell which style the current text has by looking at the _____ group on the _____ tab. The current style will have a _____ around it.

7. True or False: Word will preview selected text in a style when your mouse hovers over the style.

8. If you've already made formatting changes to text that you now want to name as a style, choose _____ from the **Style**s group.

9. True or False: A paragraph with a style will always be followed by a paragraph with the same style when you press **Enter** at the end of it.

10. True or False: The best way to get extra space between paragraphs is to press **Enter** twice.

11. If you want a heading to always stay with the first paragraph of the information below it, choose _____ from the _____ dialog box on the _____ tab.

12. True or False: A font pitch is just another word for font points.

13. True or False: It is important to save our trees, so you should usually use small fonts and tight margins.

14. True or False: Using all caps is a good way to emphasize your point.

15. The little "edges" on letters of fonts like Times New Roman and New Century Schoolbook are called _____.

16. When a font doesn't have little edges, it is called a _____ font.

17. True or False: Studies show that it is easier to read sans-serif fonts.

18. True or False: It is never appropriate to use affectations such as all lowercase or unconventionally sized headings.

19. To see the codes that actually store the paragraph style information, you need to click on _____ on the _____ group in the _____ tab.

20. Styles save the most time when _____ a document.

21. The two different kinds of styles are _____ and _____.

22. You can tell which kind of style each one is by clicking on the _____ on the _____ tab.

23. To ensure that all the text with a certain style in a document gets the change you just made to a paragraph with that style, choose _____ from the _____ group in the _____ tab.

24. To change the **Normal** style, you much choose _____ from the _____ group in the _____ tab when **Normal** is selected.

25. To put the same information at the top of every page, click on _____ on the _____ group in the _____ tab.

26. To put page numbers on a document, click on _____ on the _____ group in the _____ tab.

27. To change margins click on the _____ on the _____ group in the _____ tab.

28. To create a cover page, press _____ at the top of a document.

29. To ensure that headers and footers and page numbers don't appear on the cover page, choose _____ from the _____ group in the _____ tab.

30. To change the size of the margins, choose _____ on the _____ group in the _____ tab.

31. When you want the paper "sideways" (i.e., 11" x 8½"), choose _____ on the page orientation.

32. To unhide a built-in style, choose the _____ icon from the _____ dialog box on the _____ tab.

Skills Exam

The following exam is designed to test your ability to recognize and execute the Word skills presented in this chapter. Read each question carefully and answer the questions in the order they are listed. You should be able to complete this exam in 60 minutes or less.

1. Open the document named ib_w02_skillsexam.

2. Create a style for the text called **Paratext**. Apply it to all text that is not a heading. (Hint: If you haven't done any other styles, you can apply it to the whole document and then just change the other text as appropriate.)

3. Use the **Heading 1** and **Heading 2** styles. Make them Arial Bold 16 and 14 point, respectively.

4. Create two different styles for the lists. Call the first one **FirstBullet** and the second one **SecondBullet**. Apply as appropriate.

5. Insert page numbers, headers, footers, and a cover page.

6. Modify the header and footer style so that it has a border (bottom border for header and top border for footer).

7. In the footer, use fields to enter the following information:

   a. The filename, including the path

   b. The date the report was last saved

   c. The original author of the report

   d. The number of words in the entire report

8. Make sure the header and footer do not print on the cover page.

9. Save the file as **ib_w02_skillsexamv1.**

Challenge Questions

The following questions are designed to test your ability to apply the Word skills you have learned to complete a business objective. Use your knowledge of Word as well as your creativity to answer these questions or complete these tasks. For most questions, there are several possible ways to complete the objective.

1. What are the advantages and benefits of using styles? What are the disadvantages?

2. What are the advantages and benefits of page numbers, headers, and footers in a report? What are the disadvantages?

3. Think about the last paper or research report that you did. Did you create a cover page? Did you add page numbers? Headers? Footers? Open the file and add these professional touches.

4. Open the file named ib_w02_bylaws. How can you make this document look much more professional? Make the changes and save it as **ib_w02_bylawsv1**.

>> Chapter 3

Word Document Enhancements

Chapter Goals

You've already learned how to make a document look professional by using styles and adding page numbers, headers, footers, and a cover page. These touches make the difference between giving the reader a good impression or poor impression. In this chapter, you will learn how to use time-saving and powerful features such as find and replace. You will also learn how and when to enhance your document with tables, as well as learn the difference between a table of contents and a table. Finally, you will learn to solve long-document issues such as putting different headers and footers on the odd and even pages, restarting the page numbering on the third or fifth page, and making sure that the content always starts on the odd page. These book-like formatting touches will enable you to stand out in the crowd of amateurish word processing with high-quality documents that look professionally published.

>> Word | Skill Sets

Word in **Practice** | Anecdote

My Role as an Enterprise Network Management Consultant

After building my own technology consulting firm, I sold my business to a Systems Integrator, which is a company that sells networking hardware and software to large companies. I became president of its Enterprise Network Management Education division, which provided consulting and training to large companies about how to keep their networks safe and running. Until then, most of my documents were relatively short. Now, however, I was faced with writing proposals and reports up to 200 pages long, and they had to look highly professional, like a book. For example, many of my documents required a cover page, separate headers and footers for odd and even pages, Roman numerals for the table of contents page, and page 1 that actually started on page 5. Such complex page numbering in my early days of word processing would leave me highly frustrated. I usually just gave up and looked around for a typewriter to type the page numbers at the bottom after I had printed the pages. Today, it's difficult to even *find* a typewriter, and handwritten page numbers look unprofessional (although better than no page numbers at all). So I had no choice but to delve deeply into how Word handles complex headers, footers, and page numbering.

Another feature of Word with which I became very familiar were Word tables. We often presented tables of choices and tables of parts and quotes in our proposals and reports

Furthermore, I found that Find and Replace was essential for fixing up the formatting when copying and pasting text from other locations, especially when someone else provided the information from a mainframe download.

>> Continued on page 308

Most business writing is enhanced by tables. *Tables* present information that is related both horizontally and vertically. Tables are very useful in presenting lists of information, comparing information, and clarifying relationships. The purpose of the table should always be to *clarify* the information you are trying to convey, so every column and every row within a table must have a heading identifying *what* is in the column or row.

For example, if you were an Inventory Manager responsible for recommending products to be removed from the product line, you might find yourself writing a memo on items in inventory that were moving very slowly. The inventory list would probably contain the item number, the item name, color, unit of sale, and price. This information would be much easier for the reader to understand if you presented it in a table instead of in a paragraph. (Of course, if you have more than a few dozen items, it would be better stored in a spreadsheet. If you have more than a few hundred, it would be better stored in a database. In both cases, you wouldn't be typing the items into Word. Importing ranges from spreadsheets and importing queries from databases are covered in another chapter.)

Another example; if you were a Director of Human Resources you might need to list all employees and the percent in which they achieved their goals as well as their salary and comments from their supervisors. This information would be best presented in a table format.

Both of these examples include considerable discussion and explanation around the information in the tables, but each demonstrates a different way to use a table. Sometimes, the text summarizes the information in the table, and sometimes the table summarizes information in the text. In the employee review memo, the table summarizes information that is described in more detail in the narrative text. The employee review memo, for example, undoubtedly includes a discussion of each employee, the characteristics of the employee, and perhaps a recommendation for promotion or a raise. The text describes the detail; the table summarizes. In the inventory example, on the other hand, it probably doesn't make sense to discuss each and every item in the narrative. The table is presenting the detail information while the narrative summarizes the recommendations.

In your own business writing, you want to review your documents to see if there are any opportunities to clarify information with a table. You should review the document to see whether there is any information that is not currently discussed in detail, but might improve the document if more detailed information were provided in a table. You can also look to see whether there is any information that should be reiterated in a summary table. For example, if you are writing a consulting report or a document meant to be used in a decision (such as the food manufacturing crisis report example used in a previous chapter), you might decide that a summary table of the different options would be helpful to the reader.

Inserting Tables

Before you actually create a table, you must decide what kind of information you will be putting into it and how big the table needs to be. The food manufacturing report used in Figure 3.1 shows how a table will improve the report by summarizing the different option information in a column and row format.

Once you've identified the number of rows and columns you want to insert, choose the **Insert** tab, click the **Table** icon, and highlight the number of cells that you need in the table, as shown in Figure 3.1.

Figure 3.1 | Insert Table

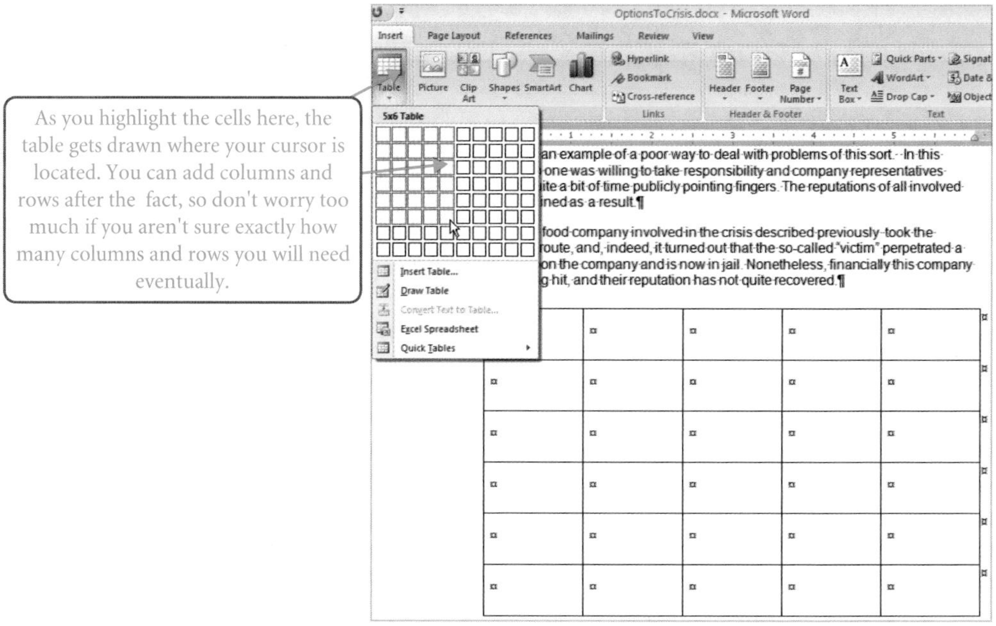

As you highlight the cells here, the table gets drawn where your cursor is located. You can add columns and rows after the fact, so don't worry too much if you aren't sure exactly how many columns and rows you will need eventually.

COMMON MISTAKES | Forgetting the Header Row or First Column

When counting the number of cells in a table, people often forget to include the header row and the first column. For example, if the information in your table has three rows and four columns, you need four rows (one for the header) and five columns (one for the category names).

Changing Column Widths

Once the table exists, you can make all sorts of changes to it either before or after you type the text into it. You can change the width of any column in the table by moving the column width tool on the ruler at the top as seen in the food manufacturer's report shown in Figure 3.2. Note that these markers appear only when the cursor is some-where in the table. You should not have anything selected if you want to change the column width of the entire column. If you want to change the width of a single cell, select the cell first, and only the cell will be affected by the column width change.

Although the vertical cells in a table are called *columns*, they are *not* synonymous with the **Columns** on the **Insert** tab. *Columns* on the **Insert** tab is a special formatting definition inside a section. Columns cannot vary in size from row to row, whereas the columns in a table can vary in size from row to row. Columns on the **Insert** tab are more appropriate for lists or information that must "continue on" either at the top of the next column or onto the same column of the next page. Although columns are useful in desktop publishing, in the business world, you more often use *tables* to present and clarify your information.

FIGURE 3.2 | **Changing Column Widths**

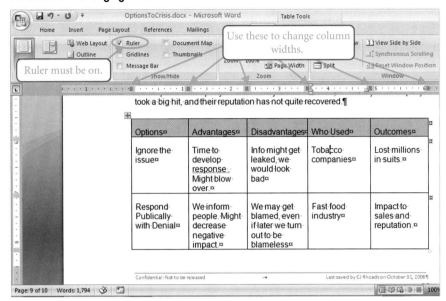

COMMON MISTAKES | **Selecting the Indent Tool Instead of the Column Width Tool**

Move only the column width tool (not the indent tool) when changing the column width. The indent tool (which looks like two triangles above a tiny box) of the current column is right next to the column width tool (which looks like a tiny grid). When the cursor is located in a column, they are very close together, so it is often hard to select just the column tool. To avoid the problem, place your cursor in a *different* column when changing a column width. In other words, change the width of the second column while your cursor is sitting in a cell in the first column.

Selecting Components of a Table

You shouldn't select a cell when changing column widths, but there are times when you do have to select the row or column before you right-click to go into the *table options menu.* This menu appears with different choices depending upon what type of table object is selected. For example, if you were putting together a budget for a nonprofit report and realized after you created the table that you needed another row to put in a forgotten item, you would need to insert a blank row. The easiest way to select the *row* (as seen in Figure 3.3) is to hover the mouse to the left of the *margin* and click when the outline arrow appears. On the other hand, to select a *cell* (as seen in Figure 3.4), you hover the mouse at the lower-left corner of the cell until the solid arrow appears. To select the *paragraph* within a cell (see Figure 3.5) or to select the text within a cell (Figure 3.6), drag over the paragraph or text *without* highlighting the area *around* the rest of the cell. These four different selections all provide different option menus and do different things. You need to know the difference to get the menu you want when you right-click. For example, notice that in the figures, the word "Micellaneous" is misspelled. If you only select the text and right-click the mouse button there, you will get the **Spelling and Grammar** options instead of the **Table** options menu.

>> *Quick Reference*

Change Column Widths

1. Click somewhere in the table. (Do not select text or cells).

2. Make sure your Ruler is **On** by looking to see that **Ruler** is checked in the **View** tab.

3. Drag the column width tool to the desired width.

Figure 3.3 | **Selecting a Row in a Table**

Dues·&·Subscriptions¤	·$38·¤¤
Internet¤	·$10·¤¤
Micellaneous¤	·$447·¤¤
Program·Expenses¤	·$3,842·¤¤

Figure 3.4 | **Selecting a Cell in a Table**

Dues·&·Subscriptions¤	·$38·¤¤
Internet¤	·$10·¤¤
Micellaneous¤	·$447·¤¤

Figure 3.5 | **Selecting a Paragraph in a Table**

Dues·&·Subscriptions¤	·$38·¤
Internet¶ ¤	·$10·¤
Micellaneous¤	·$447·¤

Figure 3.6 | **Selecting Text in a Table**

Dues·&·Subscriptions¤	·$38·¤¤
Internet¤	·$10·¤¤
Micellaneous¤	·$447·¤¤

If you were a manager for a nonprofit agency working on the budget in which a column of numbers align to the left, you might want to change the alignment of the text in the column from the left to the right so that the numbers line up better. To do this, you would select the entire column. Hover your mouse above the top of the column until you see a solid black arrow pointing down, as shown in Figure 3.7. Then click to select the entire column. You can then apply alignments, shading, border, or formatting changes to the entire column at once.

Figure 3.7 | **Selecting Entire Column**

Dues·&·Subscriptions¤	·$38·¤
Internet¤	·$10·¤
Micellaneous¤	·$447·¤
Program·Expenses¤	·$3,842·¤

>> **Quick Reference**

Selecting Table Components

1. To select a row, move your mouse out into the left margin and drag down next to the row (or rows).

2. To select a cell, hover at the lower-left corner of the cell until the arrow becomes solid pointing toward the cell and then click.

3. To select a column, hover at the top of the column until the arrow becomes solid pointing down. Click.

COMMON MISTAKES | Selecting Before Changing Column Width

If you want to change a column width, you can't have anything selected. If you have a single cell selected, the width of the column will change *for that cell only*.

Unless you want to change the width of a single cell, always make sure that your cursor is blinking and nothing is selected when moving the column width tools on the ruler.

Inserting or Deleting Rows or Columns

Once you know how to select columns and rows, it is easy to delete existing columns or rows.

- To delete, select the column or row and press the **Delete** key.

Additionally, you might need to insert a new row or column. Going back to the budget example, note that it lacks a heading row and thus requires a new row for this information. To insert a new row:

- Select a row and right-click to bring up the table options menu, as shown in the budget table example in Figure 3.8.
- Select **Insert** and then **Insert Rows Above** or **Insert** and then **Insert Rows Below**.

To insert a new column:

- Select a column.
- Choose **Insert, Insert Columns to the Right** or **Insert, Insert Columns to the Left**.

You can even insert a single cell; you just have to choose whether or not to push the other cells down or over.

Figure 3.8 | **Inserting Rows into a Table**

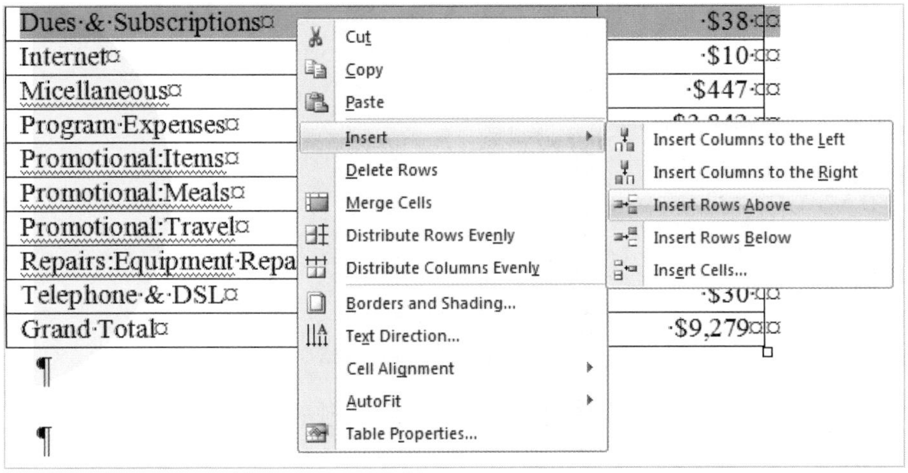

COMMON MISTAKES | Moving the Mouse Before Opening the Menu

You have to right-click within the selection to affect the row, column, or cell selected. The option menu affects only the *current* location of your cursor.

You might select a row or a column and right-click to bring up the menu—expecting it to change the selected row or column. However, sometimes your formatting choice affects a different row or column than you expected. Why? Because it is a common mistake to right-click elsewhere in the table instead of within the selection. By right-clicking somewhere else, the current location of the cursor moved *from the selection* to the *place that you clicked*.

>> **Quick Reference**

Inserting a Row into a Table

1. Click in or select a row of a table.
2. Right-click at the same spot and select **Insert**.
3. Click **Insert Rows Above** (or **Below**).

>> **Quick Reference**

Inserting a Column into a Table

1. Click in or select a column of a table.
2. Right-click at the same spot and select **Insert**.
3. Click **Insert Columns to the Left** (or **Right**).

Splitting and Merging Cells

Tables do not need to have the exact same number of rows in each column or the exact same number of columns in each row. You can split any of the cells into two, and you can merge any number of cells into one. If you look at the budget table example, notice that it might be nice to have just one large cell with the word *Promotional* in, and separate cells for *Items, Meals,* and *Travel.*

To split a cell, right-click on the cell to bring up the table option menu and choose *Split Cell,* as shown in Figure 3.9. Then you choose the number of columns or rows that you want. You can split only one cell at a time.

Figure 3.9 | **Splitting Cells**

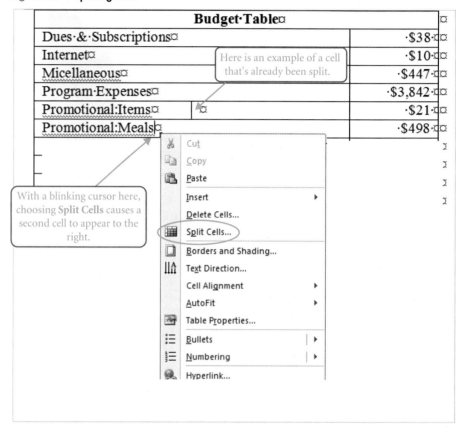

>> *Quick Reference*

Split Cells

1. Click within the cell you want to split.
2. Right-click in the cell to get the **table option** menu.
3. Choose **Split Cells** and choose two columns.

To merge cells is the opposite of splitting them. Select two or more cells and choose **Merge Cells** from the **table option menu** shown in Figure 3.10. To center align the text within a cell, right-click on the cell to bring up the **table option menu** shown in Figure 3.10. Choose **Cell Alignment** and choose the middle choice, which centers the text both vertically and horizontally.

Figure 3.11 shows the results of three cells in the Budget Table that have been merged and center-aligned.

Figure 3.10 | **Table Option Menu with Merge Cells and Cell Alignment**

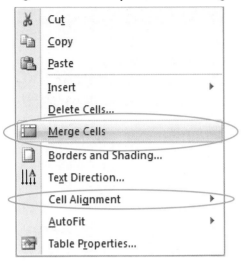

- ✂ Cu**t**
- 📋 **C**opy
- 📋 **P**aste
- **I**nsert ▶
- Delete Cells...
- 🔲 Merge Cells
- 🔲 **B**orders and Shading...
- ‖ Te**x**t Direction...
- Cell Align**m**ent ▶
- Auto**F**it ▶
- 🔳 Table P**r**operties...

Figure 3.11 | **Cells Merged and Center-Aligned**

Budget·Table¤			¤
Dues·&·Subscriptions¤			·$38·¤¤
Internet¤			·$10·¤¤
Micellaneous¤			·$447·¤¤
Program·Expenses¤			·$3,842·¤¤
Promotional¤	Items¤		·$21·¤¤
	Meals¤		·$498·¤¤
	Travel¤		·$4,368·¤¤
Repairs:Equipment·Repairs¤			·$26·¤¤
Telephone·&·DSL¤			·$30·¤¤
Grand·Total¤			·$9,279¤¤

Three cells have been merged, and the text is aligned both vertically and horizontally.

COMMON MISTAKES | Merging Cells and Trying to Select Columns

Once you have merged cells in a table, you can no longer select the columns individually with this method. To change column widths on a table with merged cells, go into **Table Properties** and select the **Column** tab.

Modifying Borders and Shading on a Table

Borders and Shading refers to the lines around the cells of a table or the color of the background of each cell in the table. Borders and shading can make clearer the difference between a header row and a regular row. Putting borders around a table can make the individual rows or columns more defined. Taking the borders away from the table might enable it to integrate more easily into the text. **Borders and Shading** options are found by right-clicking anywhere on the table to get the table options menu, as shown in Figure 3.12.

>> **Quick Reference**

Merge Cells

1. Select the cells to be merged.
2. Right-click and choose **Merge Cells**.

>> **Quick Reference**

Align Text Center

1. Select the cells to be aligned.
2. Right-click and choose **Cell Alignment**.
3. Select the middle choice.

Figure 3.12 | **Table Options Menu**

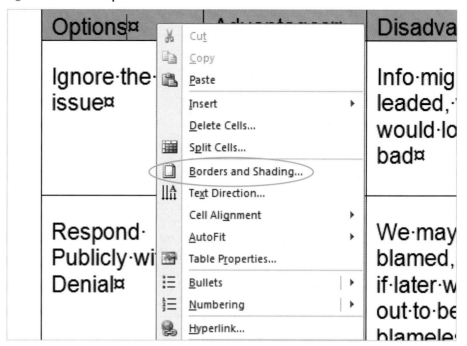

The first row of a table often has a color shading to help the reader identify the header row more easily. For example, suppose that you want to more clearly delineate the header row in the food manufacturing report table (as seen in Figure 3.13). You can do the following:

- Select the entire row. Right-click to bring up the table options menu.
- Click **Borders and Shading**.
- Click the **Shading** tab.
- Click the **Fill** options.

You can then select a color from the theme or from the standard color list. You can also select a pattern from the **Style** option. If you select a Patterns style, you can also choose a color for the pattern in the **Color** options.

Notice that you are making this shading change to just the selected cells. If you change the **Apply to** choice to **Table** instead of **Cell**, the changes you make apply to the entire table instead of just the selected row.

Figure 3.13 | **Shading a Cell in a Table**

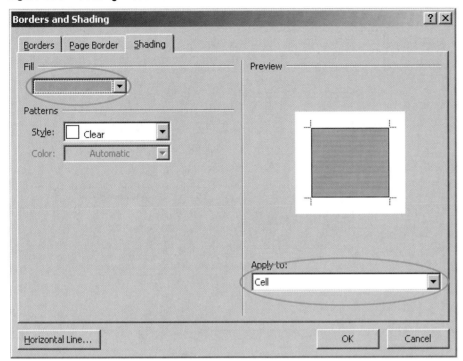

If you want to place a large thick border around the first row and get rid of the borders around the other rows, do this:

- Select the whole table and right-click to bring up the **table option menu**.
- Click **Borders and Shading.** Click the **Borders** tab.
- Click the **None** Setting.

You needed to get rid of all the borders before applying the borders just to the first row. Next you select the first row and apply a thick border:

- Select the first row and right-click on it. Click **Borders and Shading.**
- Click the **Borders** tab.
- Change the Width to 3 pt.
- Click the **Box** Setting.

The order here is important. Look carefully at the **Borders** tab on the **Border and Shading** dialog box in Figure 3.14. If you change the width in the middle section after you've chosen the **Box** in the **Setting** area on the left, the cell borders change *as long as you haven't clicked on the Preview diagram.* If, however, you have clicked on the diagram (say, for example, because you want to change the bottom line to a thinner line), you have to change the width and *then* click on the line in the **Preview** diagram. From that point forward, you can change the width, but it won't have any effect on the cell until you actually click one of the edges in the **Preview** diagram or click on the **Setting** again to reset all the lines.

Figure 3.14 | **Apply Cell Borders in a Table**

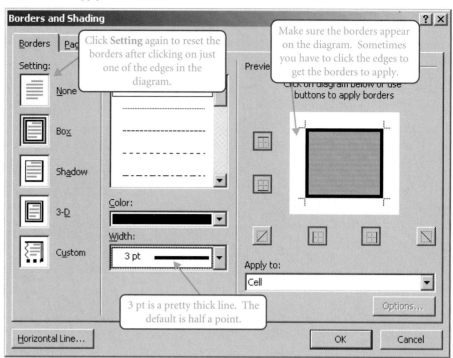

COMMON MISTAKES | Clicking the Border Width, but not Clicking the Settings or Lines

Always check to be sure the desired width has applied to the border before clicking **OK.**

Often people click **OK** right after they've changed the width without checking to see whether the change was actually made. Because under some circumstances simply clicking on the width applies the change and in other circumstances it doesn't, the new width doesn't always apply. It's especially frustrating when you go back to the dialog box and it shows the proper width, but when you return to the table, the border is still not there!

Be sure to look at the **Preview** diagram to ensure that the border has been applied. If it doesn't appear there, click on the **Setting** or the lines in the **Preview** diagram to which you want the border applied before clicking on **OK**.

Repeating Table Headers

One of the advantages of using a table in Word is the ability to use a *repeating header row*, which allows the first row to repeat at the top of the next page if the table gets split. If the table takes up multiple pages, each page will include a repeat of the first row. You might have noticed that in the food manufacturer report, the summary table split across two pages. When they get to the second page, readers might not know what the columns are for.

Setting the header row to repeat is done within the **Row** tab within the *Table Properties* dialog box (see Figure 3.15), which enables all sorts of formatting and configuration changes on the table.

- First, select the row (or rows) that you would want to be your header row.
- Right-click in the selection and click **Table Properties** in the table options menu.
- Click the **Row** tab.
- Check **Repeat as header row at top of each page.**
- Uncheck **Allow row to break across pages.**

>> **Quick Reference**

Apply Borders

1. Select the table and right-click on it. Click **Borders and Shading**.
2. Click the **Borders** tab.
3. Change the **Width** to the desired thickness.
4. Click the **Box** in the **Setting** area and return to the document.

Figure 3.15 | **Table Properties Dialog Box**

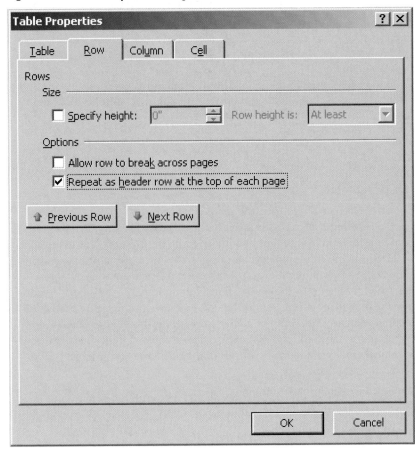

You can see the effect in Figure 3.16. The table extends beyond the first page, so the header row appears again at the top of the next page as the table continues.

Figure 3.16 | **Example of Table Header Repeating**

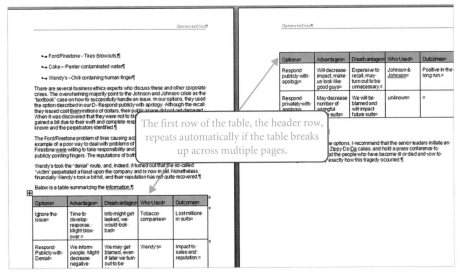

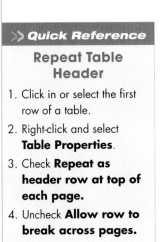

Converting Text to Table

Sometimes you are faced with information that *should* be in a table, but, for whatever reason, is not. Often this is information that's been copied and pasted from somewhere else, or text that was typed in with tabs by someone who didn't know how to set up a table. For example, if you were a manager and asked the office assistant to type up a list of names and addresses, you might expect that he would type them up in a table—columns and rows that not only look professional but increase the flexibility regarding how you use the information. But suppose he doesn't know how to create a table. He might put commas or tabs between the name, address, city, state, and postal code instead of setting up a table. As long as there is only one tab or comma between each column of information, you can easily convert that information into a table.

To convert text to table:

- Select all the text you want to convert.
- Click the **Insert** tab and the **Table** icon.
- Select **Convert Text to table**.

You see the dialog box shown in Figure 3.17. The next step is to identify how many columns you need by entering the number in the **Table Size** section. Then you identify the column *delimiter* in the **Separate Text at** area. A delimiter is a symbol, letter, or code such as a tab, paragraph marker, colon, comma, pipe, or any other symbol or mark that appears before and after the contents of each column. Commas and tabs are the most common delimiters, and files using them as delimiters are often called *Comma separated value* or *csv* files, or *tab delimited text* files.

Figure 3.17 | **Convert Text to Table Dialog Box**

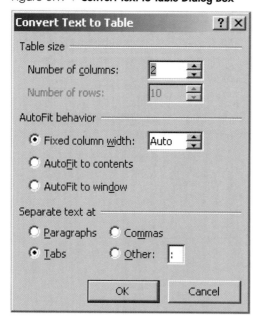

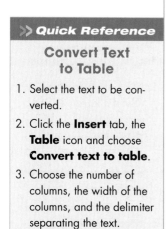

≫ Inserting Tables

VIDEO WORKSHOP

The purpose of this workshop is to demonstrate the use of tables as presented in this section of the chapter as well as a common-business writing procedure: providing a table of options for senior leaders to review when making a decision. You will see the tasks in this workshop demonstrated in the following three videos: **Creating Tables, Converting Text to Tables**, and **Formatting and Editing Tables**. Remember to try the tasks on your own first before watching the video.

1. Creating Tables (Video: Creating Tables)

  a. Open the file named ib_w03_optionstocrisis.

  b. Go to the end of the last paragraph before the "Recommendation" heading (that is, after the words *has not quite recovered.*)

  c. Type in the text **Below is a table summarizing the information**. Press **Enter** to go to the next line.

  d. Click on the **Insert** tab and then the **Table** icon to create a new table.

  e. Drag down six rows and across five columns. When you let go of the mouse, a table will be created at the current cursor location.

  f. Highlight the cells in the top row.

  g. Choose the **Shading** icon from the **Table Styles** group on the **Table Tools - Design** tab

  h. Choose the third gray shade.

  i. Type in the following headings. Use the **Tab** key to move from column to column.

     i. In the upper-left shaded cell, type **Options**.

     ii. In the second column, top shaded cell, type **Advantages**.

     iii. In the third column, top shaded cell, type **Disadvantages**.

     iv. In the fourth column, top shaded cell, type **Who Else Used**.

     v. In the fifth column, top shaded cell, type **Outcome**.

j. Type in the following options. Use the down arrow to move from row to row.

   i. In the first row, first column, type **Ignore The Issue**.
   ii. In the second row, first column, type **Respond Publicly with Denial**.
   iii. In the third row, first column, type **Respond Privately with Denial**.
   iv. In the fourth row, first column, type **Respond Publicly With Apology**.
   v. In the fifth row, first column, type **Respond Privately With Apology**.

k. Finish filling out the columns and rows with the rest of the information as shown in the following table.

Options	Advantages	Disadvantages	Who Used	Outcomes
Ignore the issue	Time to develop response; might blow over	Info might get leaked and we would look bad.	Tobacco companies	Lost millions in suits
Respond publicly with denial	Inform people; might decrease negative impact	We might get blamed, even if later we turn out to be blameless.	Fast food companies	Impact on sales and reputation
Respond privately with denial	Get our denials on record	Might increase wrongful death suits.	Automobile manufacturers	Reputation and sales impact
Respond publicly with apology	Decreases impact; makes us look like good guys	Expensive to recall; may turn out to be unnecessary	Pharmaceutical companies	Positive in the long run
Respond privately with apology	May decrease number of wrongful death suits	We will be blamed and will affect future suits	Unknown	

l. Review the table.

m. Click in the shaded row at the top of the table.

n. Right-click and choose **Table Properties** from the menu.

o. Click the **Row** tab in the **Table Properties** dialog box.

p. Uncheck **Allow row to break across pages**.

q. Check **Repeat as header row at the top of each page**.

r. Click the **OK** button to close the **Table Properties** dialog box and return to the document.

s. Click the **Two Pages** icon in the **Zoom** group of the **View** tab so that the shaded header row now appears at the top of the table on page 5 and at the top of page (in the middle of the table) on page 6.

t. Save the document as **ib_w03_optionstocrisisv1**.

2. Converting Text to Table (Video: Converting Text to Table)

   a. Open the file named ib_w03_budgetmemo.

   b. Select the text starting with **Dues and Subscriptions** and ending with **$9729**.

   c. On the **Insert** tab, click on the options button below the **Table** icon.

   d. Click on **Convert Text to Table**.

      i. **Number of Columns**: should be set to 2.

      ii. **Fixed Column Width** should be **Auto**.

      iii. Separate text at: **Tabs** and click **OK**.

   e. Save the document as **ib_w03_budgetmemov1**.

3. Formatting and Editing Tables (Video: Formatting and Editing Tables)

   a. Open the file named ib_w03_budgetmemov1.

   b. Select the second column (with all the dollar values).

   c. On the **Home** tab, click on the **Align Text Right** icon.

   d. Select the first row (the one that says **Dues and Subscriptions $38**).

   e. Right-click on the selection, and choose **Insert**, **Insert Rows Above** from the table options menu.

   f. Select the first row (it is empty).

   g. Right-click and choose **Merge Cells**.

   h. Place your cursor into the cell. On the **Home** tab, click the **Center Align** icon and type in **Budget Table**.

   i. Select the cell that says **Promotional:Items**.

   j. Right-click until you get the table option menu. (If you keep getting the spelling and grammar option menu, you have the text, and not the cell, selected.)

   k. Select **Split Cell**. Choose **2** columns.

   l. Click anywhere into the cell below (the one that says **Promotional: Meals**).

   m. Click on the **Repeat** icon in the **Quick Access** toolbar.

   n. Click anywhere into the cell below (the one that says **Promotional: Travel**).

   o. Click on the **Repeat** icon in the **Quick Access Toolbar**.

   p. Highlight the word **Items** and drag it over to the empty cell next to it. (The easiest way to highlight is to double-click on the word).

   q. Highlight the word **Meals** and drag it over to the empty cell next to it.

   r. Highlight the word **Travel** and drag it over to the empty cell next to it.

   s. Select the three cells with the word **Promotional:** in them.

   t. Right-click and choose **Merge Cells** from the menu.

   u. Delete two of the three **Promotionals**. Right-click and choose **Cell Alignment**, **Align Center** from the list. (**Align Center** is the middle one.)

   v. Save the document as **ib_w03_budgetmemov2**.

>> Creating a Consulting Proposal

Business report writers must learn *when* to *summarize* information in a table. Summarizing information effectively is critical for successful business documents. When faced with a lengthy report, business managers often look for the key points in tables and figures before reading an entire document. Business report writers must also learn *when* to present *more detail* in a table. Learning both uses for tables is a matter of experience, but you can start with two questions:

"Would summarizing these choices in a table make them easier to understand?"

"Is there any information that might be necessary or helpful for the reader to have that doesn't lend itself to description in the text?"

Knowing how and when to present information in tables using the skills covered in this section will make your business writing more effective.

Exercise

The purpose of this exercise is to review a document and identify what information might need to be added in the form of a table. Open the document named ib_w03_consultingprop. There are several places where this document would be enhanced by adding tables. Figure out where those places are, and insert an appropriate table where necessary. Can you think of a way to clarify the differences between the options that would make it easier on the reader to understand? Here are some additional places in the document you might want to look (not all of them will be appropriate for a table):

1. The list of recommendations on the first page.

2. Under the "Advice Only Option."

3. Under the "Advice Plus Network Option."

4. Under the "Advice Plus Security/Backup/Restore Option."

5. The quotes under the "What Our Clients Say" section.

6. The pricing list under the "Authorization to Begin" section.

After you have inserted the appropriate tables, save this document as **ib_w03_consultingpropv1**.

>> What's Wrong with This Document?

Problem

You are a Product Line manager in a supply company that provides products and services to salons and beauty shops. There is some confusion about some of the new color names for one particular brand of hair color, so you plan to send a memo to the Inventory Manager so that she can inform all of the people using the online inventory of the difference between the colors. You have dictated the memo to one of the junior assistants to type up. A few hours later, the assistant comes to your office and shows you what he has done so far. He is having trouble with the document, and has the following complaints:

1. The **Description** isn't wide enough. All the words wrap, and they shouldn't.

2. There is a blank spot to the left of the **Color** cell that doesn't belong.

3. I want to center the word **Color** over the text in the cells below.

4. I need another column to the right of the **Description** column for the added cost of two of the colors.

Exercise

Open the document named ib_w03_newitemsmemo. Help the assistant figure out how to fix the document so that it looks professional enough to send to the Inventory Manager. Things for you to consider:

1. Can you make a column wider? How?
2. How do you eliminate cells that don't belong?
3. How can you center a heading over multiple cells below?
4. Can you add another column to a table that's already been defined? How?

Make the changes to the file to fix the problems identified by the assistant. Save the file and name it **ib_w03_newitemsmemov1**.

>> The Power of Find and Replace   `Skill Set`

Find and Replace is a powerful combination used in a variety of ways in business documents. In addition to simply locating information, however, the most common use for Find and Replace is to reformat information so that it can be edited more quickly or placed into a table. In this section, you will use Find and Replace in a simple way and learn about its many options. Then you will progress to the much more powerful Find and Replace of invisible codes to save yourself much time when converting text to tables and doing mass editing of documents.

Finding Text

Most people are familiar with how to find information in a Word document. On the **Home** tab, at the far right end under the **Editing** group, is the **Find** icon (see Figure 3.18). For example, in the food manufacturing crisis report, if one of your reviewers came back with the suggestion to change the word "apology" to "sorrow," you could locate each incident of the word *apology* in the report to see whether changing it to *sorrow* would make sense:

- Click on **Find** on the **Editing** group.
- Type the word **apology** into the **Find what:** dialog box.
- Click the **Find All** button and choose to look in **Main document**.

Notice that *apology* has been selected throughout the document. At this point, you could go back into the document by clicking the **Close** button and then click on a formatting change or press **Delete** and it will affect all the selections at one time. Of course, if you go back to the document and click anywhere it would *click off* the selection, and the *apology* words would no longer be selected.

Figure 3.18 | **Find and Replace on the Home Tab**

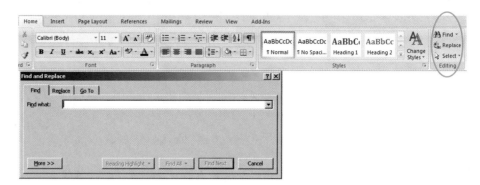

Because your objective was to simply review all the times apology was used, closing the find box at this point wouldn't help. You would want the selections to stay "marked" somehow so that you could review the entire document with all the instances of *apology* highlighted. To do that, you would select the ***Reading Highlight*** choice, as shown in Figure 3.19.

Reading Highlight does more than simply select the words; it also highlights them. This highlighting persists when you return to the document, even if you select something unrelated. However, the yellow background color automatically turns off when you print (hence the *reading* highlight).

Figure 3.19 | **Find and Reading Highlight with More Choices**

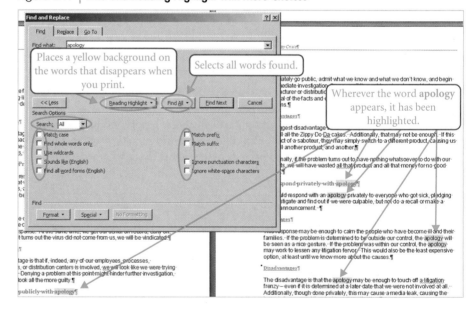

Replacing Text

In addition to finding text, you can also replace what you find with anything that you type in. In the next example, a consultant is modifying a previously written proposal for a different client. Every occasion of Walrus Associates would be replaced with Johnson Materials, Inc. (as shown in Figure 3.20).

Figure 3.20 | **Find and Replace**

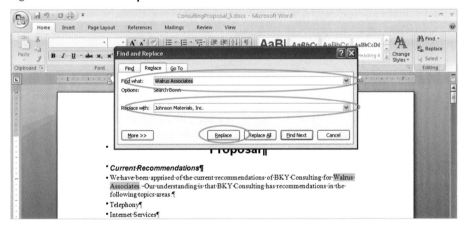

In another example, if you decide that you don't want to use the word *advantage*, but instead prefer the friendlier term *benefit,* you could replace every occasion of *advantage* with *benefit.* The replacement capitalization will match the original (unless you specifically checked **Match Capitalization**, discussed in the next section). In other words, normally the word *advantage* would be replaced with *benefit* and *Advantage* would be replaced with *Benefit*. However, if you have checked **Match Capitalization**, if you search for *advantage* to be replaced by *Benefit*, Word will replace *advantage* with *Benefit* and won't find *Advantage* at all.

You can replace just one occurrence at a time by clicking **Replace** or all the recurrences by clicking **Replace All**. Be very careful with **Replace All**; you want to be sure Word is replacing the right thing.

COMMON MISTAKES | Using Replace All Without Looking

Always do a dozen or so **Find Next** and **Replace** before committing to **Replace All** for the remaining replacements. What would have happened if you used **Replace All** to replace all occurrences of the word "I" with "we" without setting on **Match Case** and **Find whole words only**? Every single "I" in every single word would be replaced, Iweke thwes (like this). Furthermore, after a certain point, Word cannot undo all the replaces, especially if you've saved the document. In that case, there is no way to get the document back to the way it was without manually going in and changing it. (You can't search for every "we" and change it to "I" because a legitimate "we" would also change, which would be just as much trouble.) The answer is to be very careful when using **Replace All**.

>> **Quick Reference**

Replace

1. On the **Home** tab, click the **Replace** icon on the **Editing** group.
2. Type in the word or words you want to find.
3. Type in the word or words you want to replace the found word.
   - To replace just one, click **Replace**.
   - To replace them all, click **Replace All**.

>> **Quick Reference**

More on Find

1. On the **Find** dialog box, click **More>>**.
   - To limit to whole words, check the **Find whole words only** box.
   - To match capitalization, check **Match case**.
   - To use ? and * as wild-characters, check **Use Wildcards**.
   - To similar sounding words, check **Sounds like**.
   - To find singular and plural as well as different verb tenses, check **Find all word forms**.
   - To find words that start with the letters, check **Match prefix**.
   - To find words that end with the letters, check **Match suffix**.

More on Find

If you click the **More>>** button (refer to Figure 3.18), you can also see you can have many more options for your searches, as seen in Figure 3.19.

- *Match case* matches the capitalization that you enter in the **Find what:** box. If you type in **Apology**, it won't find *apology*.
- *Find whole words only* does not find the word or letters *within* a word. If you try to find *you*, it does not find *your*.
- *Use wildcards* enables you to replace one or more letters with special characters known as wildcards (*?* for a single letter and * for multiple letters).
  If you use *?*, the letter represented by *?* will be highlighted. If you use *, it will find any number of characters, but it will not highlight or select them unless you have actual text on both sides of the wildcard. Then it will highlight or select all the text between the two letters, including spaces. For example, if you search for *y*u*, *you* will get highlighted, but so will *any one for united*.
- *Sounds like* finds words with similar sounds. If you type in **il**, you will also find *ill, el,* and *all*.
- *Find all word forms* finds all the tenses of a verb, and both the singular and plural of a noun. If you type in **swim**, it also finds *swam* and *swum*. If you type in **knife**, it also finds *knives*. If you type in **lie**, it also finds *lying* and *lay*.
- To find a word that begins with the letters, check **Match prefix**.
- To find a word that ends with the letters, check **Match suffix**.
- You can also instruct **Find** to **Ignore punctuation characters**, which finds *it's* and *its* when you just type in **its**.
- If you use **Ignore white-space characters** and search for *you*, both *you* and *by our own* are found.

Let's say, for example, that your supervisor has given you the feedback that you use the word *I* too much in your report. You realize that you can search for the word *I* and replace all incidences with the word *you*. But when you search for *I*, you get 513 occurrences! You realize that the **Find** dialog box is finding every *i* in the document, even within a word, instead of just finding the complete word *I*. You can deal with that in two ways: either you can *Match Case*, which finds *I* (as well as *MIGHT*), or you can **Find whole words only**, which does not find *MIGHT*, but does find *i*. Or you can check both and only find *I*.

Finding and Replacing Invisible Codes

Finding and replacing text is often very helpful, but it is even more useful to be able to find and replace spaces, styles, and invisible codes.

What do you do, for example, if someone (who didn't know about paragraph spacing) hit the **Enter** key and put an extra paragraph mark in between each paragraph, and you copy and paste those paragraphs into a document in which you have already set the paragraph spacing? You would get three spaces between each paragraph; in other words—much too much space.

One way around that problem is to find every situation in which there are two paragraph markers together and replace it with a single paragraph marker. Of course, you can't hit the **Enter** key to put the paragraph marker into the **Find** dialog box because pressing **Enter** closes the box.

That's why Word has another set of choices. If you look at the bottom of the **More>>** button, you see another button called **Special**. Click on that **Special** button, and you will see the options for entering invisible codes into the **Find and Replace** boxes (as seen in Figure 3.21).

Figure 3.21 | **Special Codes for Invisible Characters**

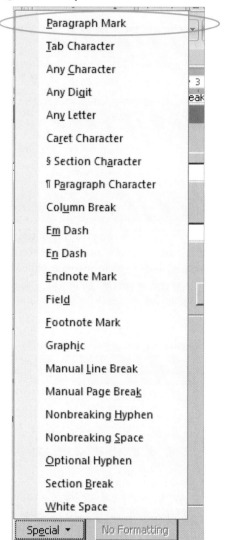

If you click on *Paragraph Mark* twice in the **Find** box and **Paragraph Mark** once in the **Replace** box, you can replace every two paragraph marks with a single paragraph mark, eliminating the multiple spacing problem. Figure 3.22 shows the ^p code, which is the code for the **Paragraph Mark**, as it appears in the **Find and Replace** dialog box. (If you already know the code, you can just type it in instead of using the **Special** button.)

Figure 3.22 | **Replacing Invisible Codes—Paragraph Marks**

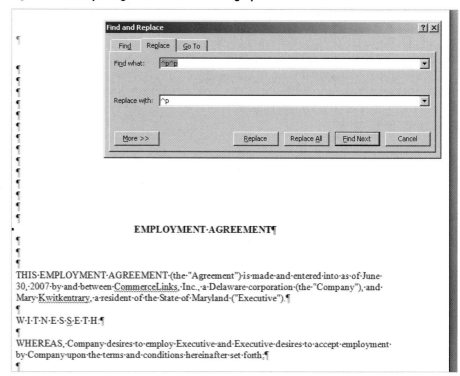

Another useful way to replace a paragraph mark is to either merge or break up lines of text, which is commonly needed when converting information that has been downloaded from a mainframe computer or web page. For example, if you download a list that puts each word onto a different line, you can replace paragraph marks with a comma or space to put them all on the same line, as shown in Figure 3.23.

Figure 3.23 | **Combining Words on Same Line with Replace**

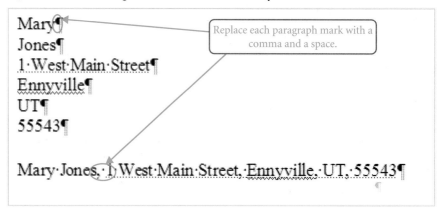

To combine all the words from different lines onto the same line, you would replace every paragraph mark (^p) with a comma and a space (,).

Another common use of **Search and Replace** is to convert double spaces into single spaces. Many people were taught to type by pressing two spaces after each period. Desktop publishing systems of today, however, expect to find just one space after each period. A single space allows the system to manage the size of the spacing after the periods. However, it is difficult to retrain people who know how to type, so having double spaces in the article is a common problem. If you were to write an article for a company newsletter or annual report, (and you were taught to type with two spaces after every sentence) you could replace all the double spaces with single spaces by going through this process after you've written the document, just before sending it to the publisher. Of course, this is a little different from the previous **Find and Replace** because you *can* just type in two spaces in the find and one space in the replace; you just can't see the fact that you've typed it in. Notice that in Figure 3.24 you can't see anything in the boxes, but something just replaced 47 occurrences. In this case, it was replacing two spaces with a single space.

Figure 3.24 | **Replacing Two Spaces with One Space**

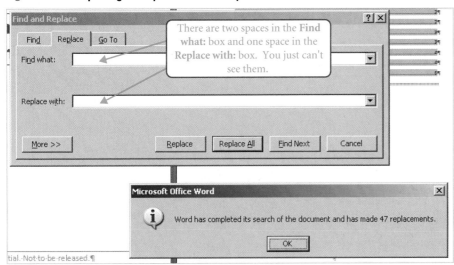

COMMON MISTAKES | Finding and Replacing Only Once

Whenever you are replacing two occurrences of the same thing with one occurrence, you have to do a **Replace All** multiple times to get all the occurrences replaced. Here's why: Imagine that you are replacing every $$ with just $. The first few pages of the document are peppered with $$$ and $$$$ and $$$ and $$$$. The first time through, the first $$$ is found, and the first two $$ are replaced with one $. Because the resulting character was just replaced, it is now *behind* the cursor. Looking forward, Word only finds a single $, so it goes on to the next set $$$$. Every occurrence of three $$$ or four $$$$ is replaced with two $$. So you have to run the **Replace All** repeatedly until you find only 1 or 0 to replace. Occasionally, you cannot get rid of the final 1 because it may be in a place where that code must exist (like the last paragraph mark in the document), so Word automatically re-enters it after it is replaced.

>> *Quick Reference*

Find and Replace Invisible Codes

1. On the **Home** tab, click the **Replace** icon on the **Editing** group.

2. Click **More>>** and then **Special** and choose the code you want to find or replace.

   • To replace just one, click **Replace**.

   • To replace them all, click **Replace All**.

You can also exchange one style for another. For example, if you had used the style **No Spacing** for certain text in a document, and later you decided that you should have used the **Heading 2** style, you could replace each occurrence of **No Spacing** style with **Heading 2** style. Figure 3.25 shows how the dialog box would look.

- Place your cursor in the **Find what** box.
- Click **Format** button and then **Style** from the menu.
- Find the style you want replaced in the list of styles. Click **OK**.
- Place your cursor in the **Replace with** box.
- Click **Format** button and then **Style** from the menu.
- Find the style you want to replace the original style. Click **OK**.

It is very important to ensure that *nothing* is in the **Find what:** and **Replace with:** boxes when you are replacing styles, not even a space. If anything is in them, the actual words will get replaced. You don't want to change the words; you only want to change the style.

Figure 3.25 | **Replacing Style with Style**

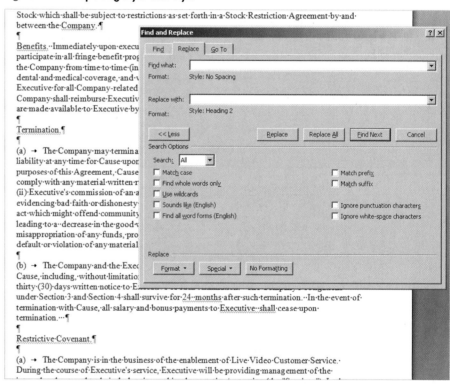

>> Quick Reference

Find and Replace Styles

1. On the **Home** tab, click the **Replace** icon on the **Editing** group.
2. Click **More>>** and then **Format** and then **Styles**.
3. In the **Find what:** text box, choose the style you want to find.
4. In the **Replace with:** text box, choose the style you want to replace it with.
   - To replace just one, click **Replace**.
   - To replace them all, click **Replace All**.

COMMON MISTAKES | Putting a Space After a Word in the Find what: or Replace with: Box

It is common to accidentally press the space bar at the end of typing something into the **Find what:** or the **Replace with:** boxes, but it could cause problems. The space is treated just like any other character, and the **Find** feature would not find the word if it did not have a space exactly where you put the space in the **Find what:** box. The problem is even worse if the errant space is typed into the **Replace with:** box because then you would be entering an extra space into each occurrence of the replacement.

>> The Power of Find and Replace

The purpose of this workshop is to demonstrate the use of Find and Replace as presented in this section of the chapter as well as a common-business editing procedure: modifying a document by replacing certain information and styles throughout, as well as eliminating double paragraph marks. You will see these tasks demonstrated in the following four videos: **Finding Text to See Context**, **Finding and Replacing**, **More Find Options**, and **Finding Special Characters**. After completing each section of tasks, watch the related video. Remember to try the tasks on your own first before watching the video.

1. **Finding Text to See Context (Video: Finding Text to See Context)**
   a. Open the file named ib_w03_optionstocrisis.
   b. Click **View** and then **Two Pages** to view page 3 and 4. Click on **Home** and then **Find** on the **Editing** group.
   c. Type in the word `apology` into the **Find what:** dialog box.
   d. Click the **Reading Highlight** button and choose **Highlight All**.
   e. Click **Reading Highlight** and **Clear Highlighting**. Then **Close** the box.
   f. Close the file (no need to save).

2. **Finding and Replacing (Video: Finding and Replacing)**
   a. Open the file named ib_w03_consultingprop.
   b. Click on **Home** and then **Replace** on the **Editing** group.
   c. Type in `Walrus Associates` for the **Find what:** box.
   d. Type in `Johnson Materials, Inc.` for the **Replace with:** box. Look at the first occurrence. Does it make sense to replace?
   e. Click on **Find Next**.
   f. Click **Replace**. Find the next two. Replace them both.
   g. Click **Replace All**.
   h. Click the Find tab. Click the More button. Check **Match case.** Type `Advice` in the **Find what:** box and click **Reading Highlight** and choose Highlight All. Notice the number of times *Advice* is found (six items).
   i. Click **Reading Highlight** and then **Clear Highlighting** to clear the highlighting.
   j. Uncheck **Match case**. Leave `Advice` in the **Find what:** box and click **Reading Highlight** and choose Highlight All. Notice how many get highlighted (eight items). Click **Reading Highlight** and then **Clear Highlighting**.
   k. Check **Match case**. Check **Find whole words only**. Type `Advantage` in the **Find what:** box and click **Reading Highlight** and choose Highlight All. Notice how many get highlighted (no items). Uncheck **Match case** and highlight again. Notice how many get highlighted (two items). Click **Reading Highlight** and then **Clear Highlighting**.

l. Check **Find whole words only** and **Match case**. Type **The** in the **Find what:** box and click **Reading Highlight** and choose Highlight All. Notice the number of times *The* is highlighted (16 items). Click **Reading Highlight** and then **Clear Highlighting**.

m. Uncheck both **Match case** and **Find whole words only** and leave *The* in the **Find what:** box. Click **Reading Highlight** and choose Highlight All again. Notice the number of times *the* is found (193 items). Click **Reading Highlight** and then **Clear Highlighting**.

n. Check **Use wildcards**.

   i. Search for **o*r**. Notice that *our* will get highlighted, but so will *of the current* (732 items). Click **Reading Highlight** and then **Clear Highlighting**.

   ii. Search for **o?r**. Notice that *our* will get highlighted, but so will *to reassess* (43 items). Click **Reading Highlight** and then **Clear Highlighting**.

   iii. Uncheck **Use wildcards**.

o. Save the proposal and name it **ib_w03_consultingpropv2**.

3. **More Find Options (Video: More Find Options)**

a. Open up the document named ib_w03_morememo.

b. Click on **Home, Find**, and then **More>>**.

c. In each case, use the **Reading Highlight** to see how many occurrences are found, looking at the document to see what has been highlighted. Then click **Reading Highlight** and then **Clear Highlighting** before going onto the next **Find what:**.

   i. With **Sounds like** unchecked, search for **il** (eight items).

   ii. With **Sounds like** checked, search for **il** (12 items).

   iii. With **Find all word forms** unchecked, search for **knife** (two items).

   iv. With **Find all word forms** checked, search for **knife** (three items).

   v. With **Find all word forms** unchecked, search for **swim** (two items).

     • What would you do to avoid finding *swimmed*?

   vi. With **Find all word forms** checked, search for **swim**. Note that it will also find *swam* and *swum*, but not *swimmed* (three items).

   vii. With **Find all word forms** unchecked, search for **lie**. Note that it will also find *lies* and *lied* (eight items).

     • What could you do to avoid finding both the type of lie that means "to rest" and the type of lie that means "to tell an untruth?"

   viii. With **Find all word forms** checked, search for **lie**. Notice that it will also find *lying* and *lay*, but not *lays* or *laid*, which are both forms of lay (to set an object down), but not lie (to rest or recline) (15 items).

   ix. With **Find all word forms** checked, search for **lay**. Notice that it will also find *lying* and *lay*, but not *lays* or *laid*, which are both forms of lay (to set an object down), but not lie (to rest or recline) (18 items).

     • Why did all the forms of *lie* get found when you were searching for *lay*?

x. Search for **er**, with **Match prefix** unchecked (24 items).

xi. Search for **er**, with **Match prefix** checked (eight items).

xii. Search for **re**, with **Match suffix** unchecked (15 items).

xiii. Search for **re**, with **Match suffix** checked (eight items).

xiv. Search for **its**, with **Ignore punctuation characters** unchecked (five items).

xv. Search for **its**, with **Ignore punctuation characters** checked (seven items).

xvi. Search for **plea**, with **Ignore white-space characters** unchecked (one item).

xvii. Search for **plea**, with **Ignore white-space characters** checked (four items).

   d. Save as document **ib_w03_morememov1**.

4. Finding Special Characters (Video: Finding Special Characters)

a. Open up the document named ib_w03_mkemployagree.

b. Click on **Home**, **Find**, and then **More>>Special**. In each case, use **Find Next** and **Replace** to see a few of the occurrences being replaced before using **Replace All** to replace all the rest.

c. Find all the double paragraph marks (¶ ¶, or ^p^p) and replace with a single paragraph mark. (¶ or ^p).

   i. With your cursor in the **Find what:** box, Click **Special** and then choose **Paragraph Mark** from the list. Click **Special** (again) and then choose **Paragraph Mark** from the list (again).

   ii. With your cursor in the **Replace with:** box, Click **Special** and then choose **Paragraph Mark** from the list.

   iii. Click **Replace**. Click **Replace**. Click **Replace**. Click **Replace**. Click **Replace All**.

d. Find all the double spaces and replace with a single space.

   i. With your cursor in the **Find what:** box, press the space bar twice.

   ii. With your cursor in the **Replace with:** box, Press the space bar once.

   iii. Click **Replace**. Click **Replace**. Click **Replace**. Click **Replace**. Click **Replace All**.

e. Find all the occurrences of the **Book Title** style and change them to **Title.** Change styles of text (not changing format of styles, but replacing one style with another).

   i. With your cursor in the **Find what:** box, click **Format**, choose **Style** from the list, and then choose **Book Title** style.

   ii. With your cursor in the **Replace with:** box, click **Format**, choose **Style** from the list, and then choose **Title** style.

   iii. Click **Replace**. Click **Replace**. Click **Replace**. Click **Replace**. Click **Replace All**.

f. Save the document and name it **ib_w03_mkemployagreev1**.

>> Creating a Comparison Table from a Download

Analyzing an industry is a critical exercise when developing business strategies. Understanding the products and features of all competing companies within an industry is important when making strategic decisions. The outcome of this analysis could support decisions such as entering a market, exiting a market, or making an acquisition. The find and replace techniques covered in this section are valuable for presenting industry comparison charts, but they can also be used with any type of information conversion from one format to another.

One of the most common tasks in business is to take information from one source, such as a mainframe computer download, and format it so that it can be presented in another source, such as a Word table. To accomplish this task, you need to be able to figure out how to get the information into the necessary format. This is one of the most powerful uses for Find and Replace, and can save you many hours of retyping information or manually editing hundreds of lines of text.

Exercise

The purpose of this exercise is to analyze the format of information provided to you and figure out what you must do (using Find and Replace) to be able to convert it to a table format. In this example, you would like the information in a table so that you can review all the companies in the video conferencing industry along with their products and services.

Open up the document ib_w03_videoconsultcomptable. This document contains the information on the different companies, products, and industries that you downloaded from the mainframe computer. You need to put it into a comparison table that looks like the following.

Choice	Quality of Service	Videoconferencing	Integration to Back End	Integration to Web Offering	Customer Relationship Management
HTEL		X			
PurePic		X			
VCFX	X (ATM solution)	X			
CNVO		X			
Ceabel					X
Cena				X	
Lanta			X		X
Validy			X		X
GatewayV		X		X	X
Comcosmo				X	
Linknets	X	X	X	X	X

1. Review what the information looks like now.

2. You can see that there is a pipe (|) and five spaces at the end of each item, and each item is on a line by itself with a paragraph marker at the end. How can you use Find and Replace to get five items on each line?

3. How can you get the information into a format that will allow you to convert text to table?

4. See if you can figure out how to go from what the document looks like now to what the table looks like *without manually retyping anything*.

Write a short answer to each of these questions and then follow the steps necessary to make the table. Save the document as **ib_w03_videoconsultcomptablev1**.

>> What's Wrong with This Document?

Problem

You are a program manager for a nonprofit organization developing programs for kids. Your boss hands you a written document that is a description of a program for children that teaches leadership skills using Taijiquan, a Chinese martial art. She wrote the original document, but she is having trouble with some of the revisions that need to be made after the last Board of Directors meeting. She wants you to fix it, and she shares with you the following items:

1. The board has reviewed the document and wants to change the name of the program to *Pacem In Vita*, which is Latin for *Peace in Life*. (The name *Peace Sensing* is in use by another organization.)

2. Sometimes the present tense was used and sometimes the past tense was used. Could you please check the tenses used throughout the document and make sure they are consistent?

3. There are inconsistencies in the heading formats. Could you please make sure headings are used consistently throughout the document? *How Do We Get Started?*, *What Happens After the Initial Pilot Program?*, and *Peace Sensing: Background* should all have the same format as *Resources Available*.

4. *Introduction*, *Combining Needs for Synergy*, and *Analysis of Research* should all have the same format as *Genesis*.

5. We will be sending this document to the printing company for publication when you are finished revising it. Could you make sure that everything is formatted the way the printer needs it formatted?

Exercise

Open the document named ib_w03_leadprgm. Use **Find and Replace** to make all the changes that your boss has asked of you. Keep the following in mind:

1. *Peace Sensing* needs to be changed throughout the document.
2. *How Do We Get Started?*, *What Happens After the Initial Pilot Program?*, and *Peace Sensing: Background* are all **Heading 6**, whereas *Resources Available* is **Heading 2**.

3. *Introduction, Combining Needs for Synergy,* and *Analysis of Research* are all **Heading 7**, whereas *Genesis* is **Heading 3**.
4. You have worked with the printing company before, and its software requires that only a single space be placed after every period. You notice that there is a double space after each sentence.
5. How can you make sure every form of the verb "is" are all present tense—not "was" or "were"?

Write a short description of what you can do about each one of these problems. Then make the revisions in the document and save it with the name **ib_w03_leadprgmv1**.

<table>
<tr><td>**Skill Set**</td><td>**>> Complex Headers, Footers, and Page Numbers (Sections)**</td></tr>
</table>

Some shorter business documents require only a simple cover page, header, and footer to appear professional. You learned simple headers, footers, page numbers, and cover pages earlier in another chapter.

Longer business documents such as consulting proposals and reports need more complex formatting. Any business document of more than 10 or so pages would benefit from the addition of a cover page and a table of contents. Longer documents look more professional with different headers and footers on the odd and even pages (just like a book). Furthermore, it is a highly professional touch to make the page numbers restart at 1 after the title page and table of contents page.

This portion introduces you to *section breaks* and demonstrates how they will help you achieve booklike formatting with odd and even headers.

Review Headers, Footers, and Fields

To review simple headers and footers and inserting fields into the headers and footers:

- To insert a footer, on the **Insert** tab, in the **Header & Footer** group, click the **Footer** icon. Bypass all the footer options in the gallery and choose **Edit Footer**.

- To insert a header, on the **Insert** tab, in the **Header & Footer** group, click the **Header** icon. Bypass all the header options in the gallery and choose **Edit Header**.

- To insert a field in the headers and footers, on the **Insert** tab, in the **Header & Footer** group, click the **Quick Parts** icon, click **Field** from the menu, and then choose the appropriate field:

    FileName: the path and filename

    SaveDate: the save date

    PrintDate: the print date

CreateDate: the original create date

LastSavedBy: the name of the person who last saved the document

Author: the original author name

Title: the document title

Company: the company of the author

You inserted headers, footers, and fields in an earlier chapter without learning about section breaks because you used the same header and footer throughout the entire document (except maybe on the first page). But now you need to go to the next level of headers and footers and page numbering for longer business documents.

Inserting a Section Break

A section break is a way of breaking up a single document so that it includes multiple page margins, page orientations, headers, footers, and page numbers. For example, if you were writing a marketing report and wanted the third page to say *Page 1* on the bottom (because the first page is the title page, and the second page is the table of contents page), you would have to insert a section break. If you were writing a proposal and wanted one page to be landscape (so that you can fit a wide graph on the page), you would need to insert a section break.

Adding section breaks to attain various margins, page orientations, headers, footers, and page numbers is a highly professional touch that will impress your superiors and coworkers.

Just as Word handles paragraph and style formatting by hiding them in the invisible code at the end of a paragraph, Word handles things such as page orientation, page numbering, headers, footers, and margins by storing them in the invisible *Section Code* marker at the end of the document. If you want different page orientations, margins, page numbers, headers, or footers in different parts of the document, you must create a second *Section Break Code* so that there is another place to store that information. This allows you to modify the formatting elements within each section, without affecting the other sections in the document.

To store section formatting elements, you must insert a section break code at the *end* of the pages you want as a separate section. The section breaks can be found in the **Page Layout** tab of the Ribbon, as seen in Figure 3.26.

Figure 3.26 | **Page Layout Section Breaks**

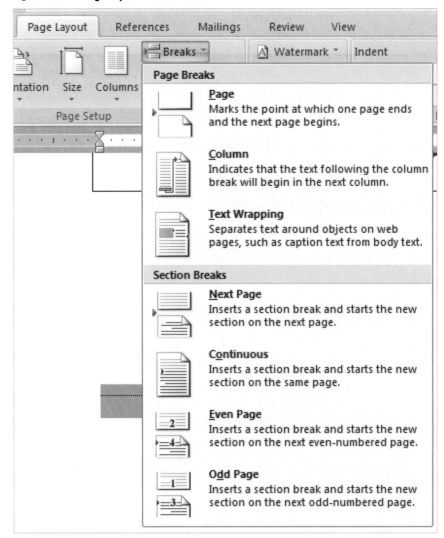

COMMON MISTAKES | Not Recognizing a New Section

Keep your paragraph marks and other codes unhidden and in view while working with a document so that you can tell where each section begins and ends.

Word has a bad habit of creating new sections without informing you. Any time you create columns or change the page orientations, Word will create a new section. If your cursor happens to be in that section when you try to set up headers and footers, you might end up creating headers and footers for just one page or in an area smaller than a page (in which case, you might not see them at all).

You may want to switch your **View** over to **Draft** mode when working with **Section Breaks** so that you can see the section breaks right next to each other, as shown in Figure 3.27. To change to **Draft** mode, choose the **View** tab and then click the **Draft** icon.

Figure 3.27 | **Draft Mode to See Section Breaks**

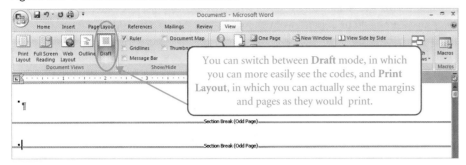

Before you insert a section break, first make sure there are no manual page breaks. A manual page break is inserted with **Ctrl+Enter**, and it appears on the screen (when **Show Paragraph Marks** is set to **On**) as a dotted line with the words *Page Break* in the center. If there is a manual page break, you might get two blank pages in a row when you insert the **Section Break** code.

COMMON MISTAKES | Combining End of Page and Section Breaks

In general, you should avoid manual page breaks entirely. Use **Keep With Next** to ensure that section headings stay with their sections (a common misuse of page breaks) and use **Section Breaks** to start a new page where required because you often also want to change the page numbering or headers and footers.

It is a common mistake (especially when you aren't looking at the invisible codes) to have both a page break and a section break combine and make extra pages you can't seem to eliminate. Here's why: The first page break starts a new page, whether appropriate or not. It doesn't care what comes next or what came before. The section break, on the other hand, has some relative intelligence built in. The section break wants the next section to start on an odd page. That means that if the previous section break ends on an odd page, the section break will add a blank page (the even page) to force the next section to start on an odd page. If there is already a manual page break code on page 2 (which creates page 3), the section break on page 3 creates page 4 (which is even). So the section break also creates page 5 so the next section can start on an odd page. If you do not see your codes, you would get three blank pages and would not understand why.

Once you have chosen to insert a section break, you must determine whether you want the *next* section to start on the next page, the next odd page, or simply be continuous. Choose **Next Page** if you want the new section to start on a new page, but it doesn't matter if the next page is odd or even.

Choose **Odd Page** if the next page will be a table of contents or the beginning of a new chapter that you always want to start on an odd page. The **Odd Page** section break is often used when you have chapters or sections of a book or report and you want each one to start on the right side for the reader because readers are not generally expecting chapters to start on the even page. Although setting a section to start on an odd page would make no difference if you are printing on one side of the page, printouts are often *copied* two-sided to save paper. It looks more professional to set up long reports for two-sided copying even when *printing* on just one-sided paper. (You never know who will be copying your report.)

If you choose **Continuous**, you cannot set separate page orientations (landscape or portrait) or start new page numbering. The only time you want **Continuous** is to set up columns in the middle of a page. For almost all other section break situations, you would choose **Next Page** or **Next Odd Page**.

COMMON MISTAKES | **Confusing Cover Page and Different First Page**

A cover page is the first page of a *document*, but the first page is the first page of any *section*. Many people confuse the two, thinking that they are making a cover page when they set **Different First Page** in a section. Although it is normal to set the headers and footers to **Different First Page** when you have a cover page, you still have to create the cover page by inserting a section break or a page break.

COMMON MISTAKES | **Conflicting Sections on Same Page**

The easiest way to avoid problems is to always start a new section on a new page. When the section is *continuous* (which means that it doesn't start on a new page), knowing which configuration will appear on the screen will be confusing. If your cursor is above the section break, the header and footer will be configured as that current section, but if you move your cursor below the section break *on the same page*, the configuration will follow *that* section. If the configurations contradict each other (for example, the first section break has a **Different First Page** and the second section break has a **Same First Page**), the **First Page Header** will appear or disappear depending on whether you are above or below the section break.

>> Quick Reference

Insert Section Breaks

1. On the **Page Layout** tab, click **Breaks** on the **Page Setup** group.
2. Choose whether you want a **Continuous, New Page, Odd page, or Even page** section break.
   - **New page** if you need to change page margins, page orientation, headers, footers or page numbers
   - **Odd page** if you want a new section to start on the right side of a two-sided booklet
   - **Continuous** if the new section should not start a new page (often used for columns within a page)

Understanding Sections and Headers/Footers

Including headers and footers in business documents looks very professional and will help you locate the document later, especially if the headers and footers contain the date, author, path and filename (as shown in the footer in Figure 3.28).

Figure 3.28 | **Footer with Fields**

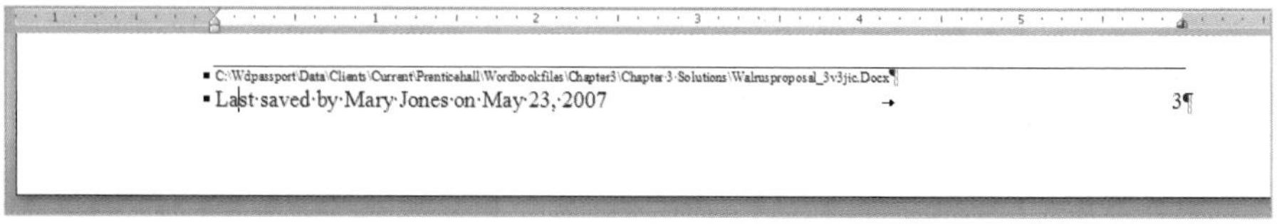

Many business documents, such as reports, proposals, manuals, and policy guides, can get very long and usually include multiple sections. To place headers and footers appropriately in such long documents, you need to understand more about how each header and footer is defined for *each* section.

Within each section of a document, you will have several different options based upon the header and footer configuration. The simplest configuration has one header and one footer for each section, as demonstrated in Figure 3.29. Each header and each footer can either be **Linked To Previous**, as shown between Section 1 and Section 2 in the diagram, or *not Linked to Previous*, as shown between Section 2 and Section 3 in the diagram. If you want all the headers in the document to be the same, you link them all. If you want them to be different, you unlink them.

If you enter text or fields or make changes in any header that is linked to any other, they will both change as if they are one header. The same goes for the footer. Make a change in a footer; any linked footers would also change. To put something *different* in the header or the footer, first you must *unlink* it from the previous header or footer, as well as *unlink* it from the next header and footer. In the diagram in Figure 3.29, the first two sections are linked, but the last one is not, so whatever is typed into that section won't affect the first two.

Figure 3.29 | **Multiple Sections with Headers and Footers**

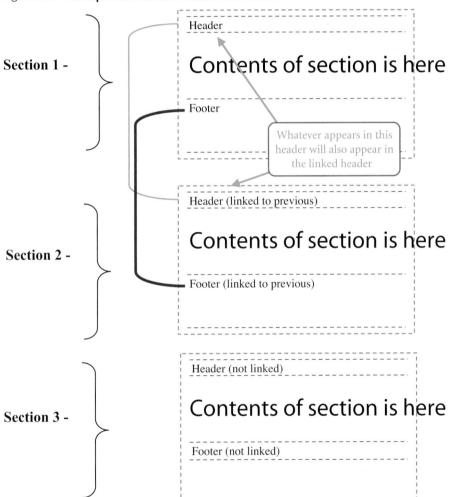

The simple configuration is just the beginning; it gets more complicated with more advanced configurations. The simple configuration can do only one header and one footer within each section. As you learned in an earlier section when you created a cover page for a consulting proposal, there are times when you want a different header and footer for the first page, such as for the cover page. To do that, you set a *Different First Page* on the section. Now there are four options: *First Page Header, First Page Footer, Header, and Footer*—or any combination thereof. To envision how this section break configuration works along with the *first page header, first page footer, header,* and *footer,* review the diagram in Figure 3.30.

Figure 3.30 | **Headers and Footers with Different First Page option**

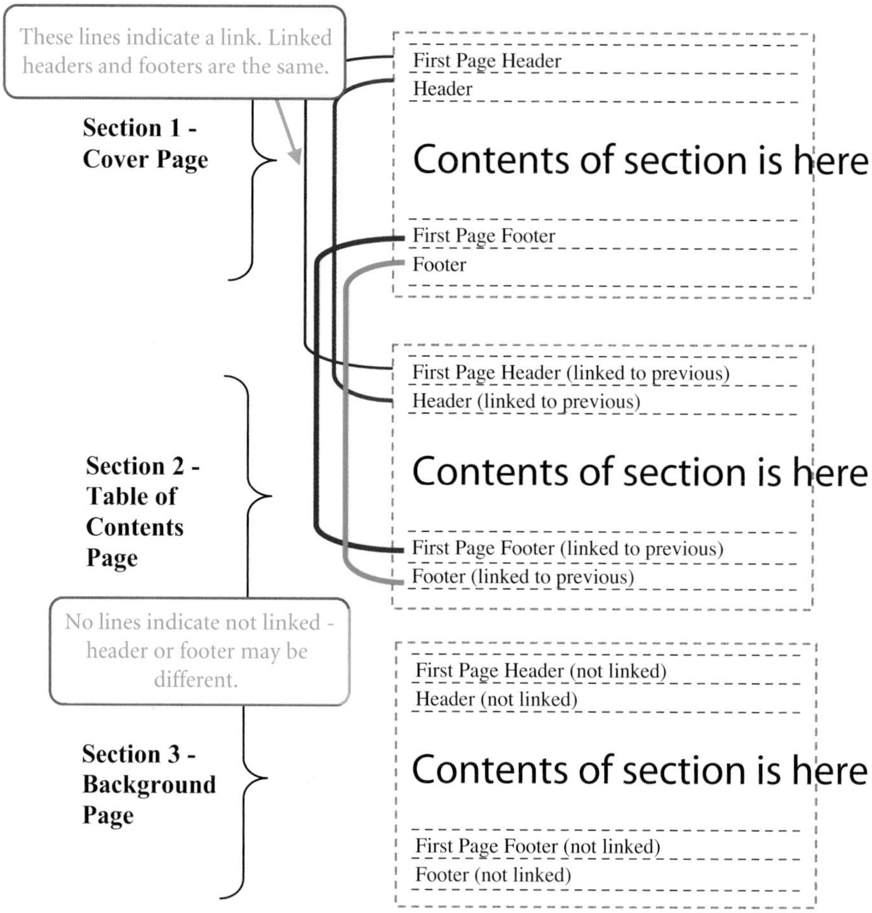

These lines indicate a link. Linked headers and footers are the same.

Section 1 - Cover Page

First Page Header
Header

Contents of section is here

First Page Footer
Footer

Section 2 - Table of Contents Page

First Page Header (linked to previous)
Header (linked to previous)

Contents of section is here

First Page Footer (linked to previous)
Footer (linked to previous)

No lines indicate not linked - header or footer may be different.

Section 3 - Background Page

First Page Header (not linked)
Header (not linked)

Contents of section is here

First Page Footer (not linked)
Footer (not linked)

- The first page header of Section 1 is linked to the first page header of section 2, so the content will be the same.
- The first page header of Section 3 is different and unlinked, so the content will be different.
- The header of Section 1 is linked to the header of section 2, so the content will be the same.
- The header of Section 3 is different and unlinked, so the content will be different.
- The footer of Section 1 is linked to the footer of Section 2, so the content will be the same.
- The Footer of section 3 is different and unlinked, so the content will be different.

Each section can have a different first page for both headers and the footers. Additionally, each one of those headers and footers can be linked (and therefore the same as the previous header or footer) or unlinked (and therefore different from the previous header or footer). As you learned in an earlier chapter, the **Page Setup** dialog box is used to check **Different first page** so that the first page of a section can have a different header, footer, and page number. You can see the **Page Setup** dialog box in Figure 3.31.

Figure 3.31 | **Page Setup Dialog Box**

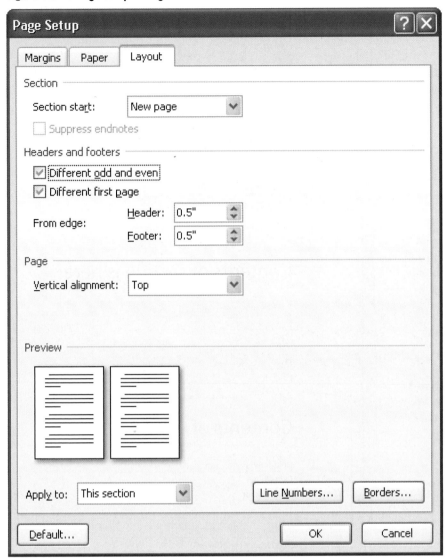

For very long reports and books, you would want to put a different header on the left side of the page than on the right side of the page. Open up any commercially published book. You will notice that the header at the top right is probably not the same as the header on the top left. Ditto for the footers. Usually the chapter name is in one and the book name is in another. Usually the page numbers on the odd page are on the right, closest to the margin, while the page numbers on the even page are on the left, closest to the margin.

To accomplish this highly professional touch for policy manuals, instructional guides, program descriptions, business plans, proposals, or any other long documents, click on **Different odd and even** in the **Page Setup** dialog box. When you have both **Different odd and even** and **Different first page** checked, the configuration can get very complicated. You would have six different linked sets of headers and footers for each section, as demonstrated in Figure 3.32.

You can have any combination of all six of these headers and footers linked or unlinked, showing or not showing. For example, if you had **Different first page** set on for the second section, but not the first, the second section **First Page Header** links to a **First Page Header** in Section 1 *that you can't see!* It does exist; you just can't see it. All six options exist all the time, even if you can't see them.

Figure 3.32 | **Headers and Footers with Different First Page Option and Different Odd and Even**

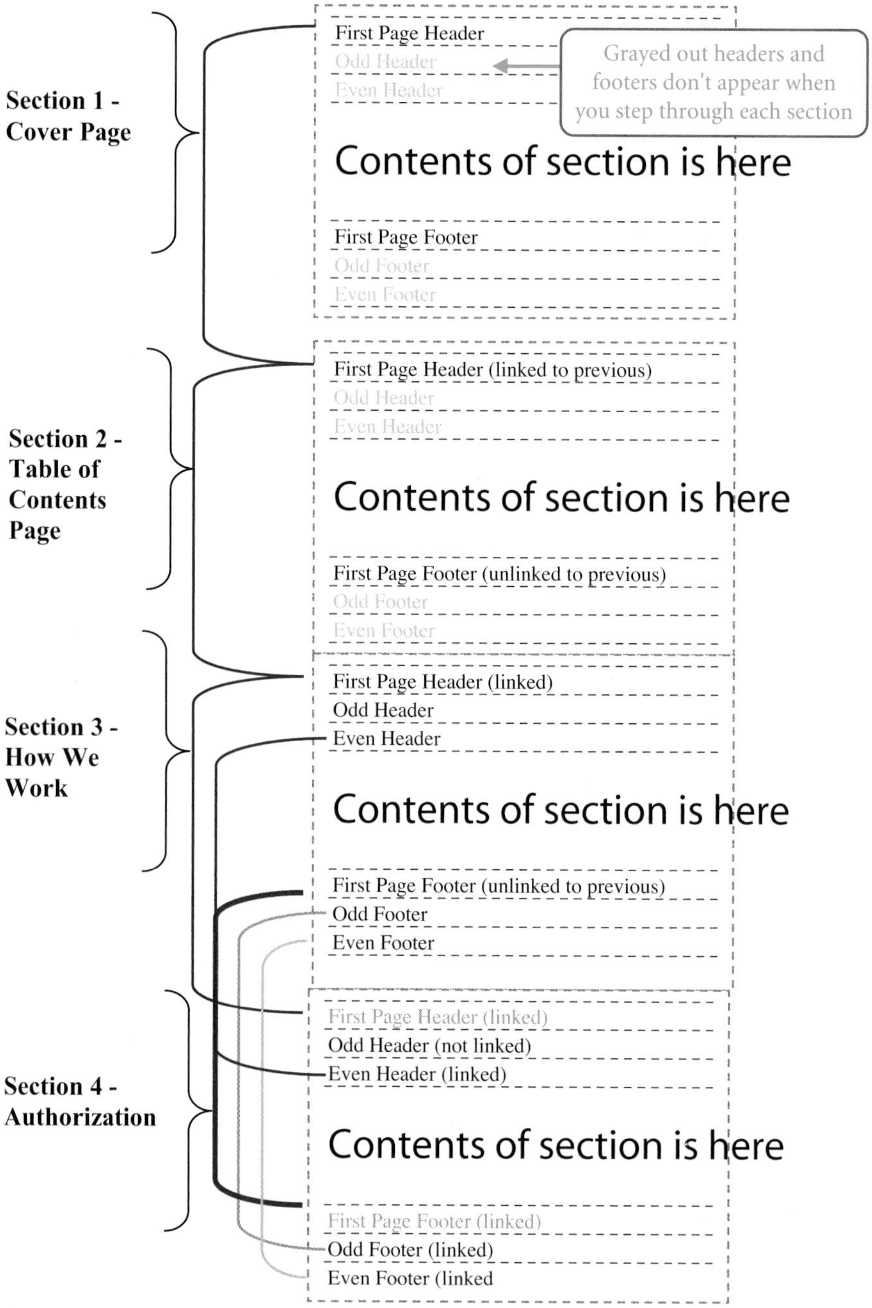

Section 1 - Cover Page

First Page Header
Odd Header
Even Header

Grayed out headers and footers don't appear when you step through each section

Contents of section is here

First Page Footer
Odd Footer
Even Footer

Section 2 - Table of Contents Page

First Page Header (linked to previous)
Odd Header
Even Header

Contents of section is here

First Page Footer (unlinked to previous)
Odd Footer
Even Footer

Section 3 - How We Work

First Page Header (linked)
Odd Header
Even Header

Contents of section is here

First Page Footer (unlinked to previous)
Odd Footer
Even Footer

Section 4 - Authorization

First Page Header (linked)
Odd Header (not linked)
Even Header (linked)

Contents of section is here

First Page Footer (linked)
Odd Footer (linked)
Even Footer (linked

Figure 3.33 pulls all this information together by depicting the results of the most common section and header/footer combination using a long consulting proposal as an example. In general, a long proposal would have a cover page, a table of contents page, and perhaps two content sections. The proposal would meet the following specifications:

- No headers or footers on the cover page
- No header, but a footer that shows a Roman numeral i for the page number on the table of contents page
- No header on the first page of the content section (Section 3), but a footer with the filename and path
- An odd header and footer as well as an even header and footer on both content sections (Sections 3 and 4)

Figure 3.33 | **Complex Headers and Footers—Results**

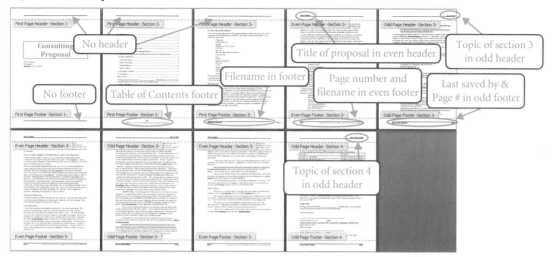

- Both footers of Section 3 and 4 to be the same
- The even header to be the same
- The odd header to include the section topic
- The first page on the second content section (Section 4) cannot be seen

Although you probably can't read the actual information in each of the pages shown in Figure 3.33, you can see the tab that appears below each header and above each footer with the type of header or footer (first page, even, or odd) and to which section number the header or footer belongs. You can also see that there is a page number in the footer on the right on the odd pages, on the left on the even pages, and in the center of the table of contents page. You will also notice that the odd header of Sections 3 and 4 are different from each other (unlinked), whereas the even header of Sections 3 and 4 are the same (linked). There is no first page header section for Section 4.

Figure 3.32 shows the order of the header and footer sections as they would be viewed if you were to start at the first one and choose **Next Section** from the **Header and Footer Tools** tab for the consulting proposal in Figure 3.33. The following combinations appear:

- The First Page Header of Section 1, 2, and 3 is linked and empty.
- The Odd and Even Headers and Footers of Sections 1 and 2 don't appear because there is only one page for each of those sections.
- The First Page Header and Footer of Section 4 don't appear because **Different First Page** is unchecked.
- The Odd Header of Section 4 is different and unlinked from the Odd Header of Section 3.
- The Odd Footer of Section 4 is linked to the Odd Footer of Section 3.
- The Even Header of Section 3 is different and unlinked.

If you click the **Header & Footer Tools** tab, the Header & Footer Tools appear in the Ribbon. Also, when you are in **Edit Header** or **Edit Footer** (from the **Header** or **Footer** icon on the **Insert** tab of the Ribbon), you can see which header or footer you are currently editing because the type (First Page, Odd, or Even) and section number appears in the blue tab, as can be seen in Figure 3.34.

- You can see whether the current header (or footer) is linked to the previous header (or footer) by looking for the **Same as Previous** notification tab on the right side of the header or footer (as can be seen in Figure 3.34).
- You can also see whether the section is set for **Different First Page** or **Different Odd & Even Pages**.

- To go to the next header or footer (in the order they are shown in Figure 3.33), you can click **Next Section**.
- To go to the previous header or footer, click **Previous Section**.
- To go to the header from the footer, click **Go to Header**. To go to the footer from the header, click **Go To Footer**.

COMMON MISTAKES | Changing the Header or Footer without First Unlinking to Previous

If you intend to have different headers and footers for each section, you have to remember to *unlink* them first. The most common mistake is to type in a header or a footer that you expected would be for *just* the current section, but forget to *unlink* the following header or footer. The header or footer you enter replaces all the linked headers and footers. Word has set the **Linked to Previous** as the default so that you need to type in only one header or footer (and ignore all the complexity), but that works only if you want the same header and footer for an entire document.

Figure 3.34 | **First Page Header and Link to Previous**

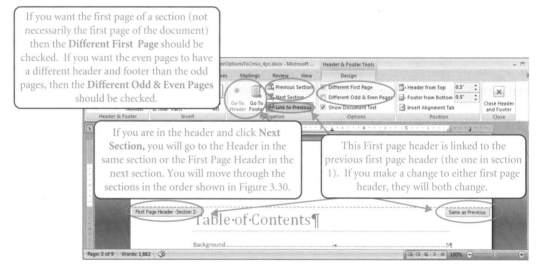

If you want the first page of a section (not necessarily the first page of the document) then the **Different First Page** should be checked. If you want the even pages to have a different header and footer than the odd pages, then the **Different Odd & Even Pages** should be checked.

If you are in the header and click **Next Section**, you will go to the Header in the same section or the First Page Header in the next section. You will move through the sections in the order shown in Figure 3.30.

This First page header is linked to the previous first page header (the one in section 1). If you make a change to either first page header, they will both change.

>> **Quick Reference**

Unlink Headers and Footers

1. On the **Insert** tab, click **Headers** or **Footers**. Choose **Edit Headers** or **Edit Footers.**

2. Click **Next Section** to go to the next header or footer.

3. Click the **Link to Previous** icon in the **Header & Footers Tools** in the Ribbon to unselect it.

Integrating Page Numbers into Header or Footer

Page numbering in Word can be difficult at times. To insert page numbers into headers and footers, it is best to use the **Current Position** on the **Page Number** icon rather than choosing from the gallery of options. There is also a shortcut alternative, **Alt+Shift+p**, which will insert the page number wherever the cursor is.

COMMON MISTAKES | Choosing from the Page Number Gallery

Use the **Current Position** on the **Page Number** icon or use the shortcut (**Alt+Shift+p**) to insert page numbers rather than choosing from the gallery of options. The problem with all of the choices in the gallery on the **Page Number** icon is that all of them may overlap your header and footer words (which would hide some of your words). You can use them without too many problems if you do not have headers or footers, but if you do have headers and footers, they will create problems.

The **Current Position** on the **Page Number** icon (as well as the shortcut **Alt+Shift+p**) inserts a field called {page} which will allow you to set the location of the page number using page margins, indents or tabs. Additionally, the page number formatting will match the rest of the footer because you can place the number in a paragraph of the **Footer** or **Header** style. If you were inserting page numbers into the footer in the table of contents page of a consulting proposal, for example, you would:

- First, put your cursor in the table of contents pages.
- Click **Insert**, **Footer**, and then **Edit Footer**.
- Click **Link To Previous** so that it is *Off* (the icon is raised and the **Same As Previous** notification tab does not appear).

You don't want to affect the footer in Section 1 (and you are currently in the footer in Section 2).

- Switch to the **Home** tab and click the **Center Alignment** icon on the **Paragraph** group.

Now you are ready to insert the page number field into the footer where your cursor is located, in the center at the bottom of the page.

- Switch to the **Headers and Footer** toolbar and click the **Page Number** icon.
- Click on **Current Position** (as shown in Figure 3.35).
- Choose **Plain Number**, as shown in Figure 3.36.

    Page Number Format dialog box shown in Figure 3.37.

Figure 3.35 | **Insert Page Number**

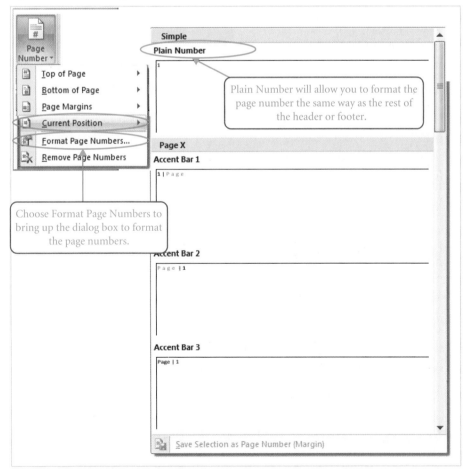

Figure 3.36 | **Page Number Dialog Box**

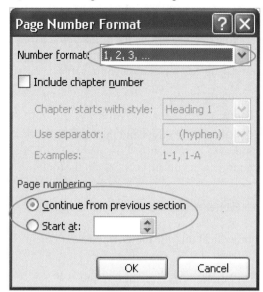

Figure 3.37 | **Formatting a Page Number for Table of Contents**

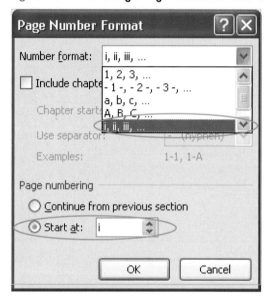

>> *Quick Reference*

Insert Page Numbers in Document with Footers

1. Open up the footer and place your cursor where you want the page number to appear.

2. On the **Header and Footer** toolbar.
   - Click the **Page Number** icon.
   - Click on **Current Position**.
   - Choose **Plain Number**.

3. Choose **Format Page Numbers** to restart at a different number or to change the format.

To change the page number at the bottom of the table of contents page to *i* (Roman numeral 1 instead of 3), do the following:

- Click the **Page Number** icon on the **Header and Footer** group on the **Insert** tab of the Ruler and choose **Format Page Numbers**.
- The **Page Number Format** dialog box will appear.
- Change the number format from 1, 2, 3 .... to i, ii, iii .... and change the **Start at** to **i**.

Inserting Table of Contents Field

Every document or report that is longer than a dozen or so pages should have a table of contents at the very beginning. Managers, colleagues, supervisors (or anyone reading the document) will appreciate knowing where to find different topics quickly instead of wading through the entire report.

You can manually type in the headings and the page numbers, of course, but why do all that work when you can get Word to do it for you? Additionally, as you edit your document, the pages on which each heading starts may change, which means you would have to constantly *manually* check the pages and update the table of contents.

To insert a table of contents, you first need to use the built-in styles **Heading 1**, **Heading 2**, **Heading 3**. Building an automatic table of contents from built-in styles is very easy. It's also possible to build a table of contents from *any* style you create, but it's easiest with the **Heading** styles already built into Word.

To add a table of contents, first you place your cursor where you want the table of contents to appear (just below the table of contents title, but above the section break, so be sure to have **Show Paragraph Marks** *On*). The following steps are demonstrated in Figure 3.38.

- Click the **Reference** tab.
- Click the **Table of Contents** icon in the **Table of Contents** group.
- Choose **Insert Table of Contents Field** (do not choose from the list of options).

Figure 3.38 | **Insert Table of Contents**

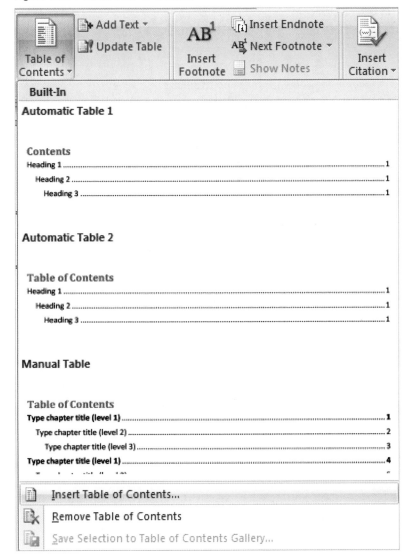

Once you've chosen to insert the **Table of Contents Field**, you need to choose how many *levels* of heading you want included, whether or not you want page numbers, and the format of those page numbers. You can make all these choices from the **Table of Contents** dialog box, as shown in Figure 3.39. You should note that if you will be printing the report, and not posting it on the Web or sending it to people on e-mail, it's a good idea to uncheck **Use hyperlinks instead of page numbers**. Even though the page numbers always appear when you print, they will not appear onscreen, which is disconcerting for a reader.

Consider the amount of detail and length of your document before choosing the levels. A document from 5 to 15 pages long (such as a proposal, a report, an instructional manual, or a policy guide) could probably get by on 2 or 3 levels, whereas a book might need 5 or 6 levels. A general rule of thumb is that if there are many items on the same page, go up to a smaller number of levels. If there are more than five or six pages between headings, go down to a larger number of levels.

Figure 3.39 | **Table of Contents Dialog Box**

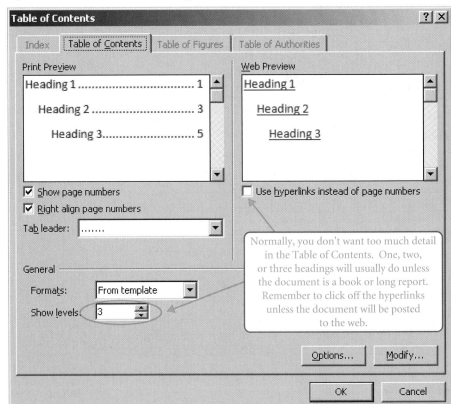

The result of adding a table of contents to a consulting proposal is illustrated in Figure 3.40.

Figure 3.40 | **Results of Table of Contents Field**

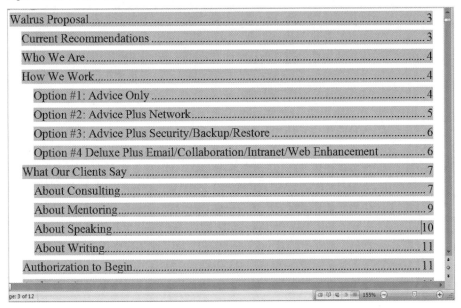

ge: 3 of 12   155%

While a table of contents looks like many lines of information, the only thing that is actually *there* is a single *Table of Contents field code* that looks like this:

{ TOC \o "1-3" \u}

You can see this code by right-clicking anywhere within the table of contents and choosing **Toggle Field Codes** from the list, as shown in Figure 3.41. As its name suggests, this is a toggle switch; you click it once to turn it *On*, and you click it again to turn it *Off*. Click it a few times, and you will see the TOC field switch between the full table of contents and the single short field code.

Figure 3.41 | **Toggle Field Codes**

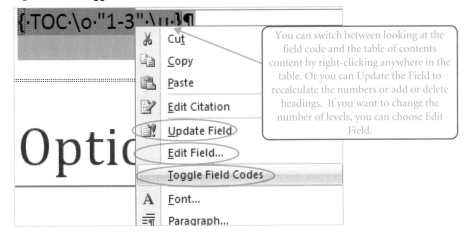

You can switch between looking at the field code and the table of contents content by right-clicking anywhere in the table. Or you can Update the Field to recalculate the numbers or add or delete headings. If you want to change the number of levels, you can choose Edit Field.

Table of Contents—Updating and Styles

Word automatically applies styles to each line of the table of contents. For example, Heading 1 items get style TOC1, Heading 2 items get TOC2, Heading 3 items get TOC3, and so on. If you modify the styles TOC1, TOC2, and TOC3, you can modify the formatting of the individual lines within the table of contents.

In the decision report for the food manufacturer in crisis, you might decide that you want to change the way the third level of the Table of Contents looks—perhaps by italicizing it or changing the location of the page numbers. In Figure 3.42, you can see that the TOC3 is the style for the third level. To change the format you would do the following:

* Select one of the lines within the table of contents that is at the third level.
* Right-click on the **TOC Style** icon in the **Style** group on the **Home** tab and click **Modify** on the **Style** option menu.
* Make changes to the font, the paragraph, or the tab formats using the dialog box that appears.

What you should *not* do is make any changes to the information *within* the table of contents because any changes you make will get wiped out when the table of content gets updated. If you see problems and errors, *fix the problem at the source within the document*, not at the table of contents. For example, if a phrase appears in the Table of Contents that does not belong, do not delete it there, change the style of that phrase within the document so that it no longer has a Heading style.

Figure 3.42 | **Showing Style of each Table of Contents Line**

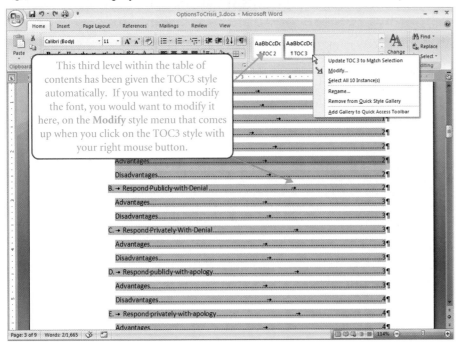

To update the table of contents:

- Right-click on the field and choose **Update Field** (refer to Figure 3.41).
- A choice appears to **Update page numbers only** or **Update entire table**, as shown in the dialog box in Figure 3.43.

Normally, you want the second choice: **Update entire table.** The only time you wouldn't want to update the entire table is when the document is extremely long and you haven't made any changes to the headings. In long documents it might take five minutes or more to do a table of contents update. If you haven't made changes to the headings, there won't be any changes reflected anyway, so you might as well save time and only update the page numbers.

Figure 3.43 | **Update Table of Contents Dialog Box**

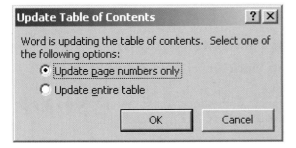

To change the levels shown in the table of contents or the leader lines, you can edit the table by choosing **Edit Field** from the options menu (previously seen in Figure 3.41). The field list will appear, so that you can click on the **Table of Contents** icon, and the **Table of Contents** dialog box will allow you to make any changes you desire.

VIDEO WORKSHOP

>> Complex Headers, Footers, Page Numbering, and Table of Contents

The purpose of this workshop is to demonstrate the Word document enhancement techniques you will need for longer business documents, which include creating complex headers and footers, page numbering, and a table of contents. You will see these tasks demonstrated in the following five videos: **Insert New Sections**, **Inserting Footers**, **Inserting Odd and Even Footers**, **Insert Odd and Even Headers**, and **Table of Contents**. Open the file named ib_w03_walrusproposal before starting this workshop. After completing each section of tasks, watch the related video. Remember to try the tasks on your own first before watching the video.

1. **Insert New Sections (Video: Insert New Sections)**

   a. If your **Show Paragraph Marks** is not on, click the **Show** icon on the **Paragraph** group.
   b. Scroll down from the beginning of the document to see the **Page Break** code (after the BTR Associates address ending in Tentville, PA 19555-0564).
   c. Put your cursor just in front of the page break and press the **Delete** key.
   d. Click on the **Page Layout** tab and choose **Break** from the **Page Setup** group.
   e. Click on the **Odd Page** group.
   f. Scroll back up, put your cursor just in front of the section break, and press the **Enter** key.

   You are only pressing **Enter** so that you can see the full section break (odd page).

g. Add another section break that starts on an odd page. You want both the table of contents *and* the start of the report to start on odd pages.

    i. Click on the **Page Layout** tab and choose **Break** from the **Page Setup** group.

    ii. Click on the **Odd Page** group.

h. Add titles to the top of the page for both new sections.

    i. Place your cursor after the first section break but before the second section break.

    ii. Press **Enter** to give yourself a new line and then **Left arrow** to move back to that empty line. On the **Home** tab, on the **Style** group, change to the **Title** style.

    iii. Type the words `Table of Contents`.

    iv. Place your cursor on the empty line before the words *Walrus Proposal* on the following page.

    v. Change to the **Title** style on the **Style** group of the **Home** tab.

    vi. Type the words `Consulting Options`.

i. Set up different first page headers and footers.

    i. On the **Page Layout** tab, click on the **Page Setup** dialog box.

    ii. On the **Layout** tab of the **Page Setup** dialog box, check the **Different First Page** option so that it is set on. Click **OK**.

j. Save the document and name it `ib_w03_walrusproposalv1`.

2. Inserting Footers (Video: Inserting Footers)

a. Place your cursor somewhere in the title box on the first page (where it says *Consulting Proposal*).

b. Click on the **Insert** tab, in the **Headers and Footers** group, click **Footer** and then **Edit Footer**.

c. Click on the **Home** tab, and in the **Font** group, click the **Font Size** icon and change to **18** point, click the **Font Color** icon and change to **Red**, and click the **Bold** icon. In the **Paragraph** group, click the **Center** icon to center the cursor.

d. Type the words `Confidential. Not to be released`.

e. Click on the **Header and Footer Tools** toolbar (which appears at the top next to the document name in the title bar).

f. Click on the **Next Section** icon on the **Navigation** group.

g. Click the **Close Header and Footer** icon in the **Close** group.

h. Put your cursor in the page with the *Table of Contents* title. Click on the **Insert** tab, in the **Headers and Footers** group, click **Footer** and then **Edit Footer**.

i. Click the **Link to Previous** icon so that it is unselected. Delete the current text.

    You don't want to delete the footer you just created on the cover page, just the footer on the Table of Contents page.

j. Switch to the **Home** tab and click the **Center** icon.

k. Type the words `Table of Contents Page. Confidential Data`.

l. Press **Enter** to go to the next line. The text should still be aligned in the center.

m. Click the **Header and Footer Tools** tab.

n. On the **Header & Footer** group, click the **Page Number** icon and choose **Current Position** from the menu. Click **Plain Number**.

o. On the **Header & Footer** group, click the **Page Number** icon and choose **Format Page Numbers** from the menu.

p. Change the **Number format** option to **i,ii,iii. . .** Enter the letter **i** in the **Start at** box. Click **OK**.

q. Click the **Close Header and Footer** icon.

r. Save the document and name it `ib_w03_walrusproposalv2`.

3. **Inserting Odd and Even Footers (Video: Inserting Odd and Even Footers)**

a. Put your cursor in the first page of the report (page four of the document, with the *Consulting Options* title and *Walrus Proposal* heading).

b. Click on the **Insert** tab; in the **Headers and Footers** group, click **Footer** and then **Edit Footer**.

c. Click the **Link to Previous** icon so that it is **unchecked** *(Off)*. *You must do this before the next two.*

You don't want what you type to change the footers you just created on the previous pages.

d. Check the **Different Odd & Even Pages** so that it is *On*. Scroll down so that you can see the odd and even headers and footers in the rest of the document. Notice that the odd footer is the same as the table of contents footer.

e. Uncheck the **Different First Page** so that it is unselected *Off*.

f. Highlight the text in the footer **Table of Contents Page, Confidential Data** *but not the paragraph mark at the end of the line* and press the **Delete** key.

g. On the **Header and Footer Tools** tab, on the **Insert** group, click the **Quick Parts** icon and choose **Field** from the menu.

h. Change the **Category** to **Document Information**. Choose **FileName**. Click on the **Field Property Format** of **Title Case**. In the **Field Option** area, click **Add path to filename**. Click **OK**.

i. Select the entire filename and pathname that you just inserted. (It will be two lines and will show grey as soon as you select just part of it. Make sure you have selected the whole thing—both lines.)

j. On the **Home** tab, on the **Font** group, click the list box next to the **Font Size** icon. Type in the number **6** and press **Enter**. (Hint: 6 won't appear in the list, but you can type it in. Don't forget to press **Enter** after you type the number.) On the **Paragraph** group, click the **Align Text Left** icon.

k. With the entire file and pathname still selected, on the **Home** tab, in the **Clipboard** group, click the **Copy** icon.

l. On the **Header and Footer Tools** tab, in the **Navigation** group, click on **Next Section**.

m. Click the **Link to Previous** icon so that it is **unselected** *(Off)*. *You must do this before the next two.*

n. On the **Home** tab, select the **Paste** icon on the **Clipboard** group. Highlight the path and filename again. On the **Paragraph** group, click the **Align Text Right** icon.

o. On the **Header and Footer Tools** tab, in the **Navigation** group, select the **Previous Section** icon.

p. Highlight the page number at the center bottom of the page. On the **Paragraph** group, click the **Align Text Right** icon.

q. With the page number still selected, on the **Home** tab in the **Clipboard** group, click the **Copy** icon.

r. On the **Header and Footer Tools** tab, in the **Navigation** group, click on **Next Section**.

s. Click at the beginning of the empty line at the bottom of the footer. On the **Home** tab in the **Clipboard** group, click the **Paste** icon and choose **Paste**. Highlight the page number again. On the **Paragraph** group, click the **Align Text Left** icon.

t. Delete the extra paragraph mark below the page number.

u. On the **Header and Footer Tools** tab, in the **Navigation** group, select the **Previous Section** icon.

v. Click on the **Page Number** icon and choose **Format Page Numbers**.

w. Type in 1 in the **Start at** box.

x. Save the document and name it ib_w03_walrusproposalv3.

4. **Insert Odd and Even Headers (Insert Odd and Even Headers)**

a. On the **Insert** tab, in the **Header and Footer** group, click the **Header** icon and choose **Edit Header** from the menu.

b. Using the **Go to Header**, **Go to Footer**, **Previous Section**, and **Next Section** icon on the **Header and Footer Tools** tab, navigate through all the headers and footers from the beginning of the document to the end of the document.

c. Go to the **Odd Page Header Section 3**. Click the **Link to Previous** icon so that it is **unselected (off)**. *You must do this before the next two.*

d. Type in Walrus Proposal. On the **Home** tab, in the **Paragraph** Group, click the **Align Text Right** icon.

e. Highlight the words *Walrus Proposal*. On the **Clipboard** group, click the **Copy** icon.

f. On the **Header and Footer Tools** tab, click **Next Section** to go to the **Even Page Header**.

g. Click the **Link to Previous** icon so that it is **unselected (off)**. *You must do this before the next two.*

h. On the **Home** tab, on the **Clipboard** group, click on the **Paste** icon and choose **Paste** from the menu to paste the **Walrus Proposal** from the Clipboard.

i. On the **Home** tab, in the **Paragraph** group, click the **Align Text Left** icon to change the alignment from Right to **Left**. Delete the extra paragraph mark underneath the word.

j. On the **Header and Footer Tools** tab, click the **Close Header and Footer** icon.

k. Go to the **View** tab. Select the **Two Pages** icon from the **Zoom** group.

l. Review all the headers and footers and page numbers.

m. Save the document and name it ib_w03_walrusproposalv4.

5. **Table of Contents (Video: Table of Contents)**

a. Place your cursor just below the **Table of Contents** title, but above the section break (be sure to have your **Show Paragraph Marks** *On*).

b. Click the **References** tab.

c. Click the **Table of Contents** icon in the **Table of Contents** group.

d. Choose **Insert Table of Contents Field**. (Do not choose from the Gallery.)

e. Change the **Show Levels** to **3**.

f. Uncheck the **Use hyperlinks instead of page numbers**. Click **OK.**

g. Look at the table that has been generated.

h. Right-click on the table and choose **Toggle Field Codes** from the menu.

i. Look at the TOC field code that is shown.

j. Right-click on the TOC field code and choose **Toggle Field Codes** from the menu.

k. On the **Home** tab, on the **Styles** group, click on the **Styles** button to **Show Styles Window**. Scroll to the bottom of the **Styles** list to see the **TOC** styles. Click into each of the lines and look at the Style in the **Style** group.

l. Place your cursor anywhere in the table of contents.

m. Right-click on the table and choose **Edit Field** from the menu.

n. Click on the **Table of Contents** icon that appears in the **Field Dialog** box.

o. Change the **Show Levels** to **2** instead of 3. (Just for purposes of the exercise, say **Cancel** when asked if you want to replace the current table of contents. Normally you would say **OK**.)

p. Review the table of contents. Note that it has not changed.

q. Click your cursor into the Heading *Option 3 Advice plus Security/Backup/Restore*. Click on the **Heading 3** in the **Styles** list box.

r. Click your cursor in the table of contents again. Right-click on the table and choose **Update Field** from the menu.

s. Choose **Update Page Numbers Only**.

t. Look at the table of contents. Note that it still has not changed. Why not?

u. Right-click on the table and choose **Update Field** from the menu.

v. Choose **Update entire table**. Notice that the table of contents has changed, and option 3 is now lined up with the other options.

w. Save the document and name it **ib_w03_walrusproposalv5**.

≫ Formatting Program Description Documents

Long documents are a way of life in the business world. Even when presentations and executive summaries are short, the details must exist and usually must be written out, in detail, in a long document.

One role you may find yourself in is writing up the description of a program and trying to convince other groups and people to either invest money or time in the program. Such a document would likely be long enough to benefit from the professional formatting of a cover page, a table of contents, headers, and footers.

Exercise

This exercise demonstrates how adding Word enhancements, such as headers, footers, and a table of contents, can dramatically improve the appearance of a document. The goal of this exercise is to revise a program description document to make it look more professional for presentation to an audience of school board members or a community organization that runs programs for kids. You are the manager responsible for presenting the new program, *Pacem In Vita*, to a local nonprofit organization in the hopes that they would include it in their summer programs.

To begin, open the file named ib_w03_paceminvita.

1. Add a cover page. Make sure that the table of contents page that comes next always appears on the right side of the booklet.

2. Add a page for the table of contents that will always be followed by the content starting on the right side of the booklet.

   a. Change the heading on the first page of the report from *What Benefits Would We See?* to **Benefits Seen**.

   b. How would you see the change you made in the table of contents?

3. Add a different header and footer for each of the three sections.

   a. In the first section, remove all the headers and footers on the first page.

   b. In the second section first page, put an italicized Roman numeral page number at the bottom center along with the original author's name underneath.

   c. In the third section, make the first page the same as the rest of the pages.

   d. In the third section, make the odd header say the name of the organization **Just for Kids** in the top-right corner.

   e. In the third section, make the odd footer say the name of the last person who saved the document, when it was saved in the bottom-right corner, and the page number in the bottom-left corner.

   f. In the third section, make the even header say the name of the program *Pacem In Vita* in the top-left corner.

   g. In the third section, make the odd footer say the name of the name of the file, including the path, in the bottom-left corner and the page number in the bottom-right corner.

4. Save the document as **ib_w03_paceminvitav1**.

>> What's Wrong with This Document?

Problem

It's not enough to know how to use all these features for the first time for a document. You also need to be able to diagnose and fix problems that inevitably crop up.

You are a consultant who has been asked by another consulting firm to work on a proposal for one of its clients. In preparation, you have sent the consulting proposal to a partner consulting firm for review before sending it on to the client. A new intern decided to try and get fancy with the file by adding page numbers, headers, footers, a table of contents, and a cover page. Unfortunately, the new intern knew enough to try to use these features, but not enough to change them when they didn't work out. You receive this e-mail (shown in Figure 3.44) from the intern with the document attached.

Figure 3.44 | **Email from Intern At BKY Consulting**

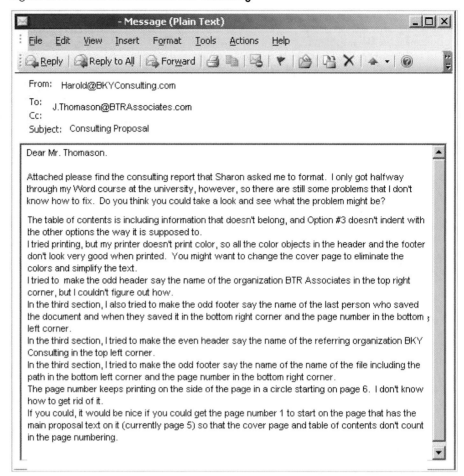

Exercise

The file the intern sent you is named ib_w03_bkyconsulting. Are you comfortable sending this document to the client, a multimillion dollar manufacturer of electrical parts? Consider the following:

1. You know that the client also does not have a color printer.
2. You want to make a very good impression on the client. You'd like to come across as simple but effective.
3. You are unhappy that the intern wasn't able to put in all of the features he described (as follows) because you think that would be a good idea:
   a. Ensuring the table of contents is correct and up to date.

   b. Ensuring that all the color objects in the header and the footer and cover page look good when printed in black and white. Simplify them.

   c. Putting the name of the organization **BTR Associates** in the top-right corner.

   d. Putting the name of the last person who saved the document and when they saved it in the bottom-right corner of the right side of the two-sided page

e. Putting the page number in the bottom-left corner of the right side of the two-sided page.

f. Putting the name of the referring organization, BKY Consulting, in the top-left corner of the left side of a two-sided page.

g. Putting the name of the file, including the path, in the bottom-left corner of the left side of a two-sided page.

h. Putting the page number in the bottom-right corner of the left side of a two-sided page.

i. Getting rid of the page number that keeps printing on the side of the page in a circle starting on page 6.

j. Setting the page number 1 to start on the page that has the main proposal text on it (currently page 5).

One hint: often it is easier to simply to *remove* the existing sections, headers, footers, and page numbers and re-enter them than it is to try and individually edit to fix each one.

Fix the proposal and save the document as **ib_w03_bkyconsultingv1**.

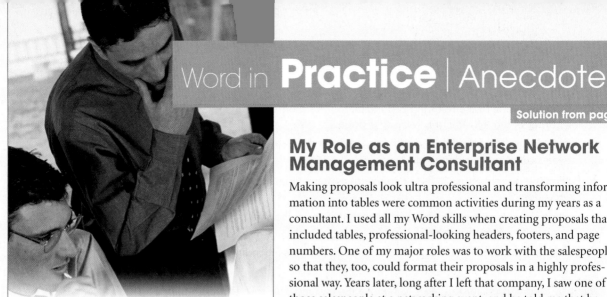

Solution from page 252

My Role as an Enterprise Network Management Consultant

Making proposals look ultra professional and transforming information into tables were common activities during my years as a consultant. I used all my Word skills when creating proposals that included tables, professional-looking headers, footers, and page numbers. One of my major roles was to work with the salespeople so that they, too, could format their proposals in a highly professional way. Years later, long after I left that company, I saw one of those salespeople at a networking event, and he told me that he still uses the same documents we had set up years earlier for all his proposals. He felt it made a major difference in his ability to be perceived as highly credible, although he was younger than many of his peers. Headers, footers, table of contents, and page numbers really made a difference.

Assignment

Open up the file named ib_w03_workreqproj. What can you do to make this document appear highly professional? Some questions you might ask yourself include the following:

1. How would this proposal strike you if you were the CEO of the bank to whom it was being presented?

2. Do you think the tables add anything to the document? Should anything else be placed in a table?

3. Do you think it really makes a difference if you set up odd and even headers?

Make the changes you feel appropriate and save the document as **ib_w03_workreqprojv1**.

Questions for Discussion

1. Is it always necessary to put headers, footers, and proper page numbering on every business document? Why or why not?

2. Review a few books and magazines in the business industry in which you want to work. What are the headers and footers like? What about the page numbering?

3. Why should you use fields instead of typing in the author's name, the date, and the file location?

4. Do you think it really makes a difference if you use a cover page and a table of contents? What are the advantages and disadvantages?

5. As a student, do you think that more professional-looking reports get better grades from teachers? Should they?

6. If you had to choose, which do you think would be better: a professional-looking report with okay information, or a report that doesn't look professional but actually has better information? Are there different situations in which one would be better than the other?

The following questions are related to the concepts addressed in this chapter. There are three types of questions: Short Answer, True or False, and Fill in the Blank. If your answer to a True or False question is False, write a short explanation as to why you think the statement is not true.

1. True or False: A table of contents is a table.

2. True or False: The word *column* has two meanings; both as the vertical cells in a table and as a section that wraps text multiple times within columns on a page.

3. The commands to place a table in the text are _____ tab _____ icon.

4. True or False: Tables always have the same number of columns in each row and the same number of rows in each column.

5. To change the column width, you should move the column width tool on the _____.

6. True or False: You should select the information in one of the cells before changing the column width.

7. To select a column, you hover at the _____ of the column until you see a _____.

8. To select a row, you hover at the _____ of the row until you see a _____.

9. To get the cell option menu, you must select the _____, not the text or paragraph within a cell.

10. True or False: New columns always insert to the right.

11. To shade a row or column, select the row or column and right-click on the selection and choose the _____ choice from the table option menu.

12. To make the header row repeat across pages, select the header row, right-click, and choose _____ menu, _____ tab, and check the _____.

13. A tab, comma, space, or any other character can be used as a _____ to convert text to tables, but there must be the same number in each row.

14. An easy way to see all the occurrences of a phrase in a document is to click _____ on the **Home** tab, type in the phrase, and click _____.

15. True or False: Highlights automatically clear when you search the next time.

16. If you want to find both *hello* and *Hello*, you would make sure that Match case is _____.

17. The _____ option will find *fly, flew, flying, flies,* and *flown.*

18. The two wildcard symbols are _____ and _____.

19. True or False: You cannot find invisible codes.

20. To change the page margins for just a part of a document, you must insert a _____.

21. True or False: Sections always begin on the very next page.

22. Section breaks can be found on the _____ tab.

23. True or False: You should hide the paragraph marker and other formatting codes when working on a document so that your screen is free from clutter.

24. To more easily see section breaks, it is often good to View_____ mode.

25. If linked to the previous, the First Page Footer of the second section is linked to the _____ of the first section.

26. To eliminate the header and footer on the first page but have it appear on all the other pages, go into the _____ tab and choose _____ while in the section.

27. To be able to change the footer in the document without affecting the footer in the previous or next section, you have to go to the _____ and choose _____.

28. True or False: The Page Number icon always provides a page number already integrated into the existing header or footer.

29. To add a page number integrated into the footer, choose the _____ icon and then the _____ from the menu, the _____ option.

30. To insert a Table of Contents, it is easiest if you've already used the Styles _____, _____, and _____.

31. True or False: You should choose a level for the table of contents that reflects about 50 pages in-between headings.

32. The **Table of Contents** icon is on the _____ tab.

33. True or False: It usually makes sense to use hyperlinks instead of page numbers.

34. To update a table of contents, right-click on it and choose _____ from the option menu.

35. To see the underlying code for the table of contents, right-click on it and choose _____ from the option menu.

36. The level of table of content items are due to their _____.

37. Changes made to the information within a **Table of Contents** field _____ when the table of contents is updated.

38. True or False: When you update a table of contents, the whole table always gets updated, not just the numbers.

39. The style of the individual lines within the table of contents always starts with _____.

≫ Skills Exam

The following exam is designed to test your ability to recognize and execute the Word skills presented in this chapter. Read each task carefully and follow the directions in the order they are listed. You should be able to complete this exam in 60 minutes or less.

You are the manager at a nonprofit organization, Healthy Eating Org, and have been asked to take the documentation for a new project and prepare it for publication.

1. Open the document named ib_w03_skillsexam.
2. Make sure there is only one space after each period instead of two spaces.
3. Add a cover page. The next page will be on the right side of the booklet.
4. Add a page for the table of contents that will always be followed by the content starting on the right side of the booklet.
5. Insert a table of contents. Don't use hyperlinks, and show 3 levels.
6. Add a heading on the first page of the report under **Backup Procedures.** The new heading should have a **Heading 3 Style** and should say *Frequency*.
7. Ensure that the table of contents will reflect the new headings.
8. Add a different header and footer for each of the three sections.
   a. In the first section, remove all the headers and footers on the first page.
   b. In the second section's first page, put an italicized Roman numeral page number at the top left along with the original author's name at the bottom center.
   c. In the third section, make the first page the same as the rest of the pages.
   d. In the third section, make the right side page of the booklet say the name of the organization **Healthy Eating Org** in the bottom-right corner.
   e. In the third section, make the left-side page of the booklet say the name of the last person who saved the document and when they saved it in the bottom-right corner and the page number in the bottom-left corner.
   f. Restart the page numbers at 1 on the first page of the third section.
   g. In the third section, make the left-side page of the booklet say the name of the program **School Health Education** in the top-left corner.
   h. In the third section, make the right side page of the booklet say the name of the file including the path in the bottom left corner and the page number in the bottom right corner. Make sure they update automatically.
9. On both tables, add a header with a thick black border and make it repeat if the table breaks across a page.
10. In the first table, put **Table** in the first column and **Description** in the second column.
11. In the second table, put **Lookup Table** in the first column and **Description** in the second column.
12. In the second table, make the first column wide enough so that none of the column text wraps.
13. In the second table, add another row at the bottom that isn't broken up into cells—just one solid row. Shade this row with blue.
14. Find every occurrence of the word *quarterly* and replace it with the word **monthly**.
15. Change every occurrence of text with the *color* red to the *color* blue.
16. Find every occurrence of the *word* **red** and replace it with the *word* **blue**.
17. Save the document as **ib_w03_skillsexamv1**.

≫ Challenge Questions

The following questions are designed to test your ability to apply the Word skills you have learned to complete a business objective. Use your knowledge of Word as well as your creativity to answer these questions or complete these tasks. For most questions, there are several possible ways to complete the objective.

1. What are the advantages and benefits of adding a cover page and table of contents to a report? What are the disadvantages?

2. Open up the file ib_w03_insuranceletter. What's wrong with this document? Fix the problem and put **Page x of y** at the top of every subsequent page in the letter where x is the current page number and y is the number of pages in the letter. Save the document as **InsuranceLetter_3v1**.

3. Open up the file named ib_w03_disasterrecovery. Find nine things wrong with it. Fix the problems and resave it as **ib_w03_disasterrecoveryv1**.

4. Find a copy of your current resume or vita. Ignore the advice about keeping it to one page and expand it to include everything that you can think of that would be a "plus" to someone considering you for a job. Add a table that would make sense and would be impressive to potential employers. Modify the formatting to make it look more professional.

Chapter 4

Word Sharing Objects and Adding References

Chapter Goals

Previous chapters covered the basics in working with Word and creating professional-looking business documents. You learned how to create an outline, investigate a topic, and create headings from an outline. You also learned how to create and use styles, add a cover page, add page numbers, add headers and footers and data tables. You also learned how to edit a document with find and replace—not just for text, but for codes and styles as well. So far, however, all of our documents focused on the words themselves, not on other applications that might integrate with Word.

In this chapter, you will learn how to integrate other programs (such as PowerPoint, Excel, and Access) and pictures and graphics into your Word documents. As a manager, for example, you might need to place an Excel chart into a progress report. As a realtor, you might need to place a picture of the house into a fact sheet. As an investor, you might need to copy information from a presentation into a summary document. There is no end to the number of times you will need to integrate graphics, pictures, charts, and slides into your Word documents.

Finally, you will learn how to identify sources by adding footnotes and endnotes to documents. Any time you cite a source in business documents, you will be expected to identify the source of the information. Additionally, there will be many times when you need to add commentary or other related (but not major) ideas to your writing that would be best presented in a footnote or endnote.

>> Word | Skill Sets

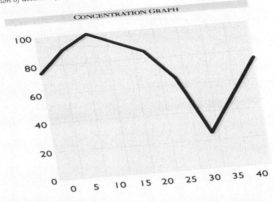

SLOREM IPSUM & SALVE PUELLAE

Subject intro 04. This is dummy text. It is intended to be read but have no meaning. As a simulation of actual copy, using ordinary words with

GRAPH HEADING

Text 06. This is intended to be read but have no meaning. As a simulation of actual copy, using ordinary words with normal letter frequencies, it cannot deceive the eye or brain. Dummy settings which use other languages or even gibberish to approximate text have

Text indented 06.2. Inherent disadvantages that distract attention towards themselves. Paragraphs may be long or short. This is dummy text. It is intended to be read but have no meaning. As a simulation of actual copy, using ordinary words with normal letter frequencies.

CONCENTRATION GRAPH

100
80
60
40
20
0

0 5 10 15 20 25 30 35 40

PIE CHART

PIE CHART HEADING

Text 06. This is intended to be read but have no meaning. As a simulation of actual copy, using ordinary words with normal letter frequencies, it cannot deceive the eye or brain. Dummy settings which use other languages or even gibberish to approximate text have

Text indented 06.2. Inherent disadvantages that distract attention towards themselves. Paragraphs may be long or short. This is dummy text. It is intended to be read but have no meaning. As a simulation of actual copy, using ordinary words with normal letter frequencies.

Word in **Practice** | Anecdote

My Role as Chief Technology Officer of an E-Commerce Software Developer

One of the most interesting jobs I ever had was when I was recruited by the board of an e-commerce software developer to serve as Chief Technology Officer. Unlike the staid conservative financial firms where I previously worked, this startup was more progressive, and this firm encouraged using pictures and graphics in their proposals and internal documentation. Because I didn't understand graphic formats at first, I would send people documents, and they would complain that they couldn't open them or they were too big for their e-mail boxes. (Many e-mail boxes back then had a 2 MB limit on attached files.)

Because we were an e-commerce firm, I would often download photos and pictures from the websites of prospective clients and put them in my proposals. Unfortunately, sometimes people would complain that when they printed the document, the pictures looked terrible. I would pull the document up on my screen, and the picture would look fine, so it took me awhile to figure out why the print version was so terrible.

Additionally, I discovered that it was important for people to know where I got my information, so I got in the habit of keeping track of the sources that were used in my proposals and consulting reports. I usually put an appendix at the end of my reports that identified the references I used for any research or findings. (As you can imagine, I was a little disappointed to find out that my days of using references and footnotes did not end with my days in school, but was glad to know how to do it!)

>> Continued on page 358

During the 1920s, a publisher named Fred Barnard was trying to sell more advertising in his trade journal, *The Printer's Ink*. To do so, he made up a saying: "*One picture is worth ten thousand words*" (often misquoted as *a picture is worth a thousand words*). When you are creating reports and presentations, you can more strongly influence the reader by including visual representation of the information you are trying to convey.

How you visually present the information depends upon what you are trying to convey. As noted in a previous chapter, comparison information is often presented in a table. However, sometimes that data doesn't come from what you type in, but instead from a database program such as Access or a spreadsheet program such as Excel. Additionally, numerical data is often best presented in column, line, or pie chart for easier comprehension.

If the purpose of the graphic is to elicit an emotion or convey a feeling, a picture or photograph might be the best choice. Nothing conveys happiness as well as a photo of a laughing child, which is perhaps the perfect choice when putting together an advertisement for a new children's toy. The picture of an angry father can speak volumes about an injustice or tragedy—a good choice for a letter soliciting donations for a lobbying group. In this section, you will investigate various ways to insert pictures, photos, query results, slides, and charts from other programs into Word documents.

About Graphics

The term *graphic* includes line art, cartoon drawings, pictures, and photographs. Although graphics can originate from different sources or media, once digitized, they are understood through only a few commonly used program formats. Pictures are often used in business to connect more closely to the reader, to encourage them to buy something or get involved with something, for example. Pictures are also used to clarify and explain. A home inspector report with actual pictures of the leaking basement or sagging foundation is much more effective than a simple text description.

You can digitize a graphic by creating it with a computer program or digital device (such as a camera), or by scanning it with a scanner to transform it into digital media. You may have noticed that when you receive pictures attached to an e-mail, they are saved as different types of files. For example, some pictures may appear with the file extension .jpg, whereas others have a .tif extension. Unlike words that are relatively easy to store digitally and take up very little space, graphics are difficult to store digitally and take up relatively large amounts of space. The more complex the graphic, the more difficult the storage and the larger the space needs. For example, a color drawing takes up more space than a black-and-white line drawing, and a photograph takes up more space than a color drawing. Over the years, various *compression* formats have developed to minimize the amount of space necessary to store graphics. Common graphic formats are the following:

- *GIF* (Graphic Interchange Format). One of the first graphic formats, used most commonly for color drawings that allow *transparency*, or the ability to see something under a certain area of the drawing. GIF files may also be animated—showing several pictures in the same spot in succession, giving the perception of movement.

- *BMP* (Bitmapped). A format developed by Microsoft for Windows graphics that doesn't normally include compression algorithms, so the files are extremely large.

- *JPEG* (Joint Photographic Experts Group). A format developed specifically for photographs that enables you to choose the amount of compression. More compression means lower quality, but for screen applications such as the web, lower quality is not necessarily a problem.

- *PNG* (Portable Network Graphics). Developed specifically for web applications, but not yet supported in all graphics programs.

- **TIFF** (Tag Interchange File Format). A format developed by Adobe that stores all the source information of a bitmap but can be compressed (though is still a very large file).

Of course, every graphics program (such as Photoshop, Corel Draw, PaintShop, and Illustrator) has its own proprietary format as well. Some of those proprietary formats can be understood by other programs. Word can import more than two dozen different graphic formats. However, for transferring data from program to program, using one of these exchange formats is recommended.

Converting from one format to the other usually necessitates the loss of some information, lowering the quality of the graphic (known as **lossy** in digital media parlance). A **lossless** format means a format that doesn't lose much information when compressed. The formats are shown in order of lossiness (and not coincidentally, the reverse order by size of file) in Figure 4.1.

Figure 4.1 | **Lossiness and File Size of Graphic Formats**

Format	Lossy/File Size	Usually Used for
BMP	Lossless; largest files	Images in Access, Microsoft Paint
TIFF	Lossless; large files	Transferring between programs when there is a need for high-quality graphics
GIF	Lossy; large files for photos, smaller files for drawings	Web graphics, pictures that require transparency, and animation
JPEG	Lossy; file size is user-determined based on compression	Web graphics, photographs
PNG	Lossy; small files	Web graphics

Many graphics programs allow you to choose the amount of compression when you save a file with a JPEG format. Figure 4.2 shows a high **resolution** photo (1600 **pixels per inch**, the measure of picture resolution on a screen) that takes 4 MB to store. A higher-resolution photo looks better than a lower-resolution photo—up to a certain point. The perceived quality of a graphic is a combination of the media in which it is presented (that is, print or screen) and the ability of the human eye to discern fine lines and shadings. A higher-quality photo does not **pixelate.** (To pixilate means that you can visually see individual pixels—an indication of poor quality.)

If the photo shown in Figure 4.2 were loaded on a web page, it would take 15 minutes to see the photo at dial-up speeds. Figure 4.3 shows a highly compressed low-resolution version of that photo, which would only take 43 seconds to download on a dial-up connection (4 seconds at broadband speeds). Research shows that most people will wait only eight seconds for a web page to download. Web designers think very carefully, therefore, before using photos. They would almost never use high-resolution photos.

Figure 4.2 | **Uncompressed JPEG Photo—4,277 Kilobyte File**

Figure 4.3 | **Low-Quality JPEG Photo(96 ppi) at 70% Compression — 14 Kilobyte File**

Show consideration for your reader when using graphics and photos in your Word documents that will be shared electronically. A Word document with a large uncompressed photo may take five or six minutes to open. Include photos only when necessary to convey the information you want conveyed, and optimize the size and compression to minimize the open time for a document.

A document intended to be read on screen or on a web page (and not printed) does not require a resolution higher than 96 pixels per inch because a computer screen can't show higher resolution. Lower resolution also saves significantly on download time. The amount of time that low-resolution photos add to the opening of a Word document would be negligible. But if the reader tried to *print* the photo, the quality would be terrible because there isn't enough information for the printer about the colors of each dot in a photo stored at 96 pixels per inch. Ink jet printers these days normally print at 600 or 1200 **dots per inch** (a measure of picture resolution on a printer). A printer needs an image of at least 200 *pixels per inch* to print correctly at 1200 *dots per inch*.

COMMON MISTAKES | Downloading and Inserting Graphics from the Web

Always keep in mind the purpose of a graphic and whether it will be shown on the screen (lower pixels per inch) or printed (higher pixels per inch). You can always lower a resolution from high quality to low quality. *You cannot raise resolution from low quality to high quality.*

You normally can't download pictures from the Web and use them for documents meant for printing. Most photos and graphics on the Web are low resolution (96 pixels per inch) to speed up the web page opening. It is simple to download a picture or photo you see on the Web. You just right-click on it and choose **Save Target As** (for Internet Explorer) or **Save Image As** (for Firefox) and choose a location to save the file on your hard drive. Because of the simplicity, you might be tempted to download a graphic or photo instead of obtaining the file from the original source. That might be a mistake, especially if you want to print the graphic. You will need a photo stored with at least 200 pixels per inch for a 1200 dots per inch printer to ensure a high resolution.

Inserting a Photo

A photo can greatly enhance the emotional impact of your words on a reader. A company newsletter describing a picnic isn't nearly as effective as a picture of the boss with barbeque sauce covering his face. A picture of a delectable ice cream cone is apt to sell more scoops than a simple "ice cream" listing.

To insert a photograph, first you must know where the photograph is stored. If the photograph is on a digital camera or a memory card or memory stick, you must transfer the photograph to a hard drive, flash drive, or floppy disk to access the file. After you know where the photo is stored, you can insert it into your document. Keep in mind that the document size will increase dramatically when you insert a large photograph.

For example, in a report to upper-level management that talks about the impact of a flood or a hurricane, including a photograph of a data center under water might provide the dramatic touch that would enable the senior leaders to feel the personal emotional impact of the tragedy that might ensue if they don't provide a budget for disaster recovery.

To add a photograph to the report, do the following:

- Place your cursor within the text where you would like the picture to appear.
- Click the **Insert** Ribbon, and choose **Picture** from the **Illustration** group.
- Choose the folder that contains the picture you wish to insert.
- If you can't see the pictures, click the View Options button (as seen in Figure 4.4) and choose **Thumbnails**. A thumbnail is a smaller representation of a picture.
- Select the picture you wish to insert and choose **Insert**.

Figure 4.4 | **Inserting a Picture Dialog Box**

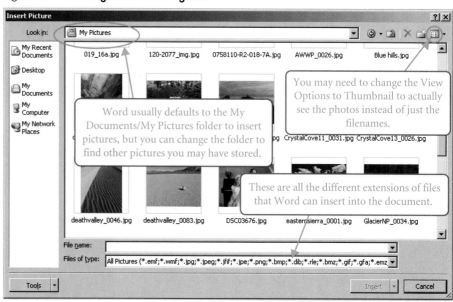

>> **Quick Reference**

Inserting a Picture

1. Place your cursor where you want the picture to appear.
2. Click the **Insert** tab.
3. Click the **Picture** icon from the **Illustration** group.
4. Change the folder to the location of the picture.
5. Select the file that contains the picture.
6. Click **Insert**.

COMMON MISTAKES | **Cursor in the Middle of a Paragraph when Inserting Graphic**

You need to watch where your cursor is when you insert a graphic. If you are not watching, the graphic will get inserted in the middle of a paragraph or word, and it will be difficult to identify exactly where the anchor ended up. If at all possible, you should create a paragraph specifically for the graphic by pressing **Enter** at the end of a paragraph to create a new one. Then you can be sure to which paragraph the graphic is attached.

Inserting a Caption

Pictures, tables, and graphics should have a *caption* when inserted into a document. A caption is a description of what is depicted by the graphic. You want your reader to understand clearly why the graphic was included. In the following example (shown in Figure 4.5), the program description for a nonprofit organization includes a photograph of one of its pilot programs. If you don't include a caption in the document, the Board member reading the document might not recognize the picture as one of the activities from the program. To add a caption to this photo, do the following:

- Select the photo. You will know that the picture has been selected because of the *handles* that appear around it (as seen in Figure 4.5).
- Right-click on the picture and choose **Insert Caption** in the **Picture Options** menu.

Figure 4.5 | **Adding a Caption for a Graphic**

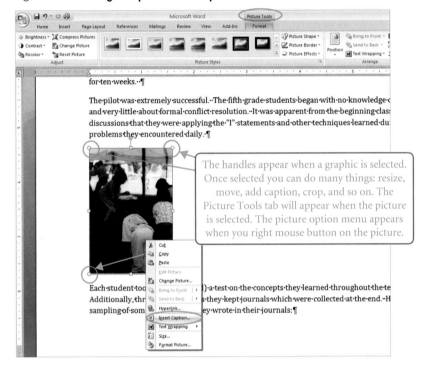

- Type the caption in the **Caption** text box within the **Caption** dialog box, as shown in Figure 4.6.
- Choose if you want the caption to appear above or below the picture.

FIGURE 4.6 | **Inserting Caption Dialog Box**

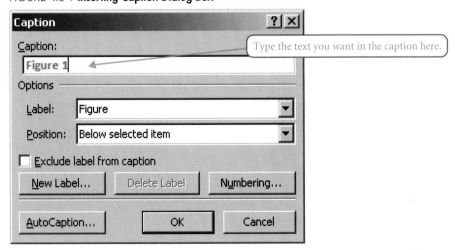

Word automatically applies the **Caption** style to the text that you enter. Whenever you insert a graphic into a business document, you refer to the graphic within the text by number. To refer to the figure within the text, it is better to use a ***cross-reference*** to the figure number instead of typing in the number directly. That way, if you insert another graphic before it, Word will automatically adjust the numbering for you. Of course, this matters only if you have more than one figure in a document.

To refer to a figure by caption, do the following:

- Place your cursor in the text where you want the figure label and number to appear (see Figure 4.7).

- Click the **References** tab and then click the **Cross-reference** icon from the **Captions** group.

- Change the **Reference type** to **Figure**, so that you can see the figure caption you already inserted.

- Change the **Insert reference to:** to **Only label and number**. The caption text is too long to insert the whole thing into the paragraph, but you want more than just the page number.

- Uncheck the **Insert as hyperlink** option because there will be no reason for someone to be reading this document on the screen and then going to the picture (because it will be right there in the same paragraph).

- In the **For which** caption list, select the caption for which you wish the figure label and number to appear. Click **Insert**.

Figure 4.7 | **Inserting a Cross-Reference to a Figure**

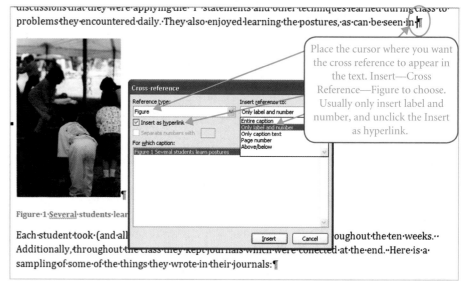

About Picture Size and Placement

Both the location and size of a picture subtly inform the reader about its importance to the document's main topic. In general, the larger the graphic, and the more white space around it, the more important it is to the main topic of the document. If you don't want the graphic to appear overly important, putting it to the side and wrapping text around it will deemphasize it, making it clear that it is ***parenthetical*** (that is, not the main topic but related to the main topic). Less-important or parenthetical graphics should be smaller with less white space around them.

Resizing a Graphic

As noted in Figure 4.5, you can also resize a graphic to better fit into the document. Returning to the program description from the previous example, once you see the picture in the document, you might decide that it is too big and takes up the entire space from the left margin to the right margin. This placement might give the impression that the picture is central to the ideas presented in the program description, which would be misleading. You want to provide a smaller picture. To make a picture smaller, do the following:

- Select the picture.
- Click the **Picture Tools** tab that appears.
- Click the down option on the **Height** button or the **Width** button until the picture is smaller, as seen in Figure 4.8.

Figure 4.8 | **Resizing a Picture Using Height and Width Buttons**

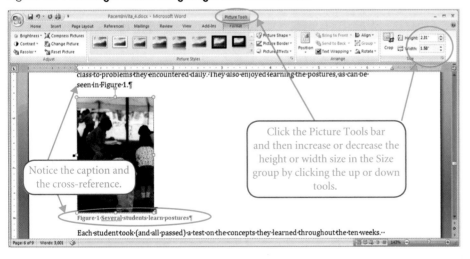

Notice the caption and the cross-reference.

Click the Picture Tools bar and then increase or decrease the height or width size in the Size group by clicking the up or down tools.

You may want to actually *see* the picture as it resizes so that you can better judge how it fits into the space. There is another way to resize a picture that allows you to view it as it is resizing. Figure 4.9 depicts another resizing method that shows a faint outline of the picture as you resize it. To use this method, do the following:

- Select the picture.
- With one hand, hold down the **Ctrl+Shift** key.
- With your other hand, click the left mouse button on one of the corner handles and drag toward the center of the picture.

If you don't hold down the **Ctrl+Shift** key, you might drag the vertical size differently from the horizontal size, which would distort the picture. The **Ctrl+Shift** combination is called the **constraint key** because it constrains the resizing to keep the vertical and horizontal axis in proportion.

Figure 4.9 | **Resizing a Picture Using Handles**

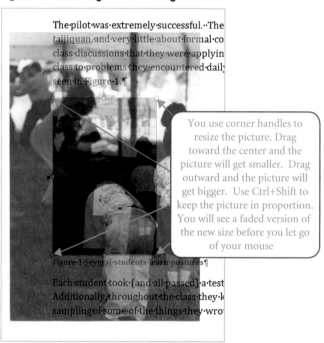

> You use corner handles to resize the picture. Drag toward the center and the picture will get smaller. Drag outward and the picture will get bigger. Use Ctrl+Shift to keep the picture in proportion. You will see a faded version of the new size before you let go of your mouse

COMMON MISTAKES | Grabbing the Wrong Handle or Failing to Use the Constraint Key

To keep pictures in proportion when resizing, use the height and width buttons on the **Picture Tools** tab. Or, if you choose to resize the picture by dragging a handle, always grab a corner handle and use the **Ctrl+Shift** constraint key. If you grab one of the handles on the sides of the graphic instead of the handle in the corner, or if you grab the corner but don't watch carefully and don't use the constraint key, the picture would "squish" and distort. If that happens, click the **Undo** icon on the Quick Access Toolbar and try to resize again using the constraint key.

Cropping a Graphic

There are times when you don't want the whole picture to resize, but you do want less of the picture to appear. From a communication perspective, you want only the most relevant details to be included to ensure that the graphic conveys the message you want it to convey. In the nonprofit program, for example, the children taking part in the activity are the important part, not the room around them. To *crop* a picture is to "chop off" the sides so that only the necessary portion remains.

- Select the graphic you wish to crop.
- From the **Picture Tools** tab, click the **Crop** icon in the **Size** group.
- Short thick lines will appear around the picture, as shown in Figure 4.10.
- Grab and drag one of the short thick lines toward the center of the graphic to the point where you wish to crop. Click anywhere in the text of the document to turn the Crop feature off.

Figure 4.10 | **Cropping a Graphic**

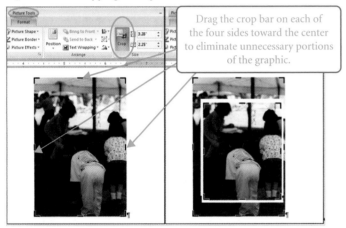

Drag the crop bar on each of the four sides toward the center to eliminate unnecessary portions of the graphic.

The result will be just the smaller portion of the graphic, as shown in Figure 4.11.

FIGURE 4.11 | **Result of Picture Cropping**

COMMON MISTAKES | Resizing Instead of Cropping

Consider carefully if it would be better to resize or crop. You often want a picture to be smaller to fit the space, so you resize it because it seems quicker than cropping. However, because a cropped picture emphasizes the important details, it will more clearly convey your information without taking up more space and will not lose the detail as it might if you resize it.

>> **Quick Reference**

Cropping a Graphic

1. Select the graphic you wish to crop.
2. On the **Picture Tools** tab, click **Crop**.
3. Click and drag one or more of the crop bars toward the center of the graphic to the desired cropping.

Compressing Pictures When Saving

As noted earlier, it is considerate to your reader (especially when e-mailing a Word document with graphics to be read on the screen) to use low-quality resolution for the graphics. If you didn't create the graphic or don't have a graphics program to save the picture as a JPEG or other compressible format, you can use the picture compression tool built into Word.

To compress some or all of the pictures within a document, do the following:

- Choose **Save As** from the menu on the **Office Button**.
- Click on **Tools** button in the lower-left corner of the **Save As** window.
- Choose **Compress Pictures. . .** from the menu, as shown in Figure 4.12.
- Click **Options**, as seen in Figure 4.13.
- Choose the appropriate options, as shown in the **Compression Settings** dialog box in Figure 4.14.
- Check **Automatically perform basic compression on save** in the **Compression Options** area.
- Check **Delete cropped areas of pictures** in the **Compression Options** area.
- If the intention is to print, select **Print** in the **Target Output** area.
- If the intention is to read on the screen, select **Screen** in the **Target Output** area.
- If you plan to send the document as an attachment or as an HTML format through email, choose **E-mail** in the **Target Output** area.
- Click **OK**.
- When you are returned to the **Compress Pictures** dialog box, choose **OK**.

If you have any pictures selected, you can apply the compressions to only those, or uncheck **Apply to selected pictures only** to apply compression to all pictures.

Figure 4.12 | **Tools Menu on the Save As Dialog Box**

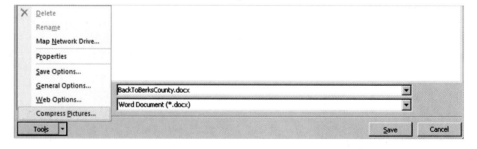

Figure 4.13 | **Compress Pictures Dialog Box**

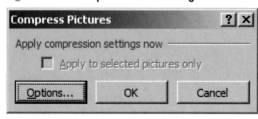

Figure 4.14 | **Compression Settings Dialog Box**

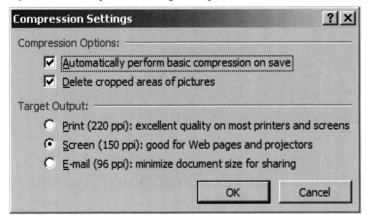

Keep in mind that the amount of compression is specific to the format of the picture, and the compressed version doesn't change the file size until the file is saved. You can check the file sizes by looking in Windows Explorer. You can see an example of various file sizes for a press release photo in Figure 4.15. You may have to click **View** and then **Refresh**, and change the **View** button to **Detail** to see the updated file sizes. The size of a Word document after being compressed can be significantly smaller.

Figure 4.15 | **Relative File Sizes of Picture Compression**

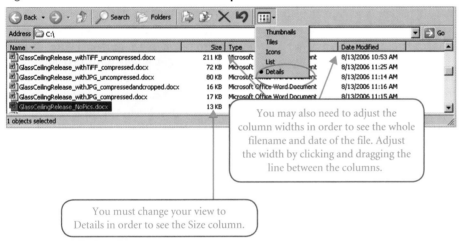

COMMON MISTAKES | Forgetting to Check on a Document's Use Before Choosing Graphics/Compression Settings

When choosing graphic compression or resolutions, it is always best to ask target readers if they will be reading the document on the screen or on paper. Alternatively, you can control the use of the document by printing it out yourself and sending it on paper instead of e-mailing it.

Moving a Graphic and Text Wrapping Choices

There are two different ways to move a graphic within a document. ***Drag and drop*** is more useful when you are moving the graphic from one place to another place that is close by, perhaps even within inches of the original placement. Additionally, you will use drag and drop more often when you want text to wrap around the graphic.

The second option for moving a graphic is ***cut and paste***, which is more useful when you are moving a picture from one part of the document to another that is relatively far away (you can't see it on the same screen without scrolling). For example, if you were a hospital administrator proposing a new type of hospital room —where family members can stay with ill patients perhaps—then you might initially place a picture of a sick patient and a family member at the beginning of a document, only to realize later that you'd rather have it at the end.

There are some underlying issues to moving graphics. To understand some of the issues that surround graphic placement, you *first* need to understand the options for ***wrapping text*** around the picture. Figure 4.16 illustrates the various choices for wrapping text around a figure or for preventing text from wrapping around a figure.

The two most common choices for text wrapping are **In Line With Text** and **Tight**. The **In Line With Text** is actually equivalent to a "none" choice; it prevents text from wrapping around the graphic. Instead, the picture becomes like a special symbol stored *within* a paragraph. The picture takes on the characteristics of the *style* of the paragraph, such as alignment and spacing between paragraphs. **In Line With Text** should be used when you want the picture location to be controlled more easily. To prevent text from wrapping around a graphic, do the following:

- Select the picture.
- Right–click on the picture to bring up the **Picture Options** menu.
- Click **Text Wrapping.**
- Click **In Line With Text**.

Tight will wrap the text around the right or left side of the picture—wherever there happens to be room (although you can specify the text to go to the right or the left). The picture "loses" its capability to be placed *within* a paragraph, and instead becomes a box that *floats* over the text with an ***anchor*** somewhere on the page (not necessarily near the graphic). The anchor marks the spot that serves as the reference point for the location of the graphic. You can see the anchor when the graphic is selected. The position of the graphic can be anywhere on any page, either relative to the location of the anchor or absolute to the margins or edges of the page. This makes it much more difficult to control the placement of the graphic. It makes it especially difficult to move the graphic. To wrap text around a picture, do the following:

- Select the picture.
- Right-click on the picture to bring up the **Picture Options** menu.
- Click **Text Wrapping**.
- Click **Tight** if you want the text to wrap around the picture.

Figure 4.16 | **Text Wrapping Options**

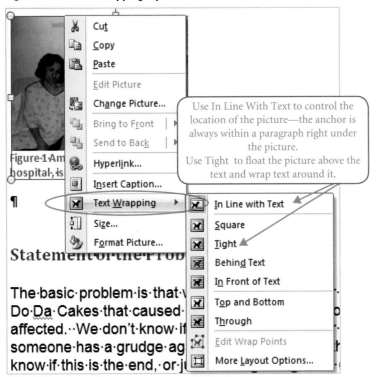

It helps to understand the text wrapping options to move a graphic because of the way Word deals with placement of a graphic that has been moved. Going back to the hospital administrator example, imagine that you have placed a picture (and its accompanying anchor) in the first paragraph of a page. The picture might appear three inches to the right and one inch below the anchor, as shown in Figure 4.17. You can see that the text is wrapping around the picture. However, if you try to move this picture to the bottom of the next page, Word will try to place the picture there, but will run into a problem because there isn't enough room at the bottom *below the anchor* in which to place the picture. So it jumps to the next page unexpectedly. If you move it back where you want it, it will jump again. This is known as a ***jumping graphic***, and it can be rather annoying. The picture won't *stay* where you put it because there isn't enough room *relative to the anchor* to place the picture where you want it. To see what the current placement for a graphic is, do the following:

- Select the picture.
- Right-click **Text Wrapping** and **More Layout Options**.
- Click the **Picture Position** tab, as seen in Figure 4.17.

Note that if the **Text Wrapping** tab selection was **In line with text**, all the picture position options are greyed-out and are not applicable because there is no anchor. The picture is placed within the paragraph just like text.

Figure 4.17 | **Picture Anchor and Position**

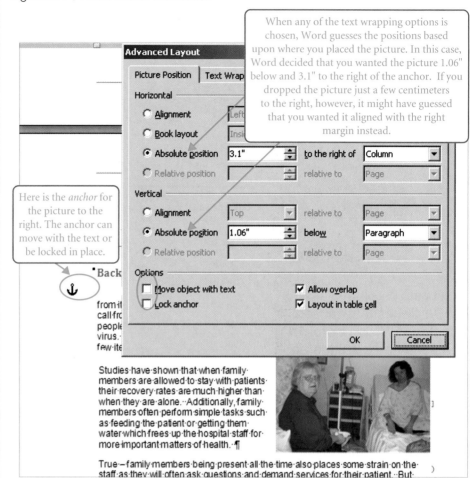

When any of the text wrapping options is chosen, Word guesses the positions based upon where you placed the picture. In this case, Word decided that you wanted the picture 1.06" below and 3.1" to the right of the anchor. If you dropped the picture just a few centimeters to the right, however, it might have guessed that you wanted it aligned with the right margin instead.

Here is the *anchor* for the picture to the right. The anchor can move with the text or be locked in place.

>> **Quick Reference**

Selecting a Text Wrapping Option

1. Select the picture.
2. Right-click.
3. Click **Text Wrapping**.
4. Click **In Line With Text** to prevent text wrapping.
5. Click **Tight** if you want the text to wrap around the picture.

>> **Quick Reference**

Viewing Picture Position

1. Select the picture.
2. Right-click.
3. Choose **Text Wrapping**.
4. Click **More Layout Options**.
5. Choose the **Picture Position** tab.

COMMON MISTAKES | Editing a Document with Graphics

Make sure you know the location settings of all your graphics. *Jumping graphics* does not only happen when you move a graphic. It is also a common problem when editing a document with many pictures or graphics. Whenever you add text or delete text, Word repaginates, which may move the picture anchors to a different page (especially if **Move with text** is checked in the **Picture Position** tab in the **Advanced Layout** dialog box). When the anchor moves, the picture might end up in a location in which it doesn't fit. You could try to uncheck **Move with text**, but if you edit and the text moves, the graphic stays at the previous location instead of with the relevant information.

COMMON MISTAKES | Trying to Wrap Text with Keep Lines Together Format

Make sure the text you are wrapping around a graphic does not have the **Keep lines together** option checked. Normally, when you choose **Tight** to wrap text around the graphic, the paragraph flows around the picture immediately. Occasionally, however, you will find that the text doesn't wrap; instead it leaves a big gap and moves above or below the picture. If that happens, change the paragraph formatting by right-clicking on the paragraph, choosing **Paragraph** from the option menu, clicking **Line and Page Breaks** tab, and unchecking the **Keep lines together** option.

Moving a Graphic with Cut and Paste

Now that you understand how the text wrapping options interact with the movement of a graphic, you are ready to learn the two different ways of moving a graphic. Suppose you are the hospital administrator placing a picture in your document about a new type of hospital room. You initially paste the picture near the summary, not really being sure where it goes. However, this placement might give the impression that the picture is central to the ideas presented in the description, which would be misleading. You might want to place the picture in a less-important position because it is just parenthetical, for the effect of reminding the hospital senior leaders that your hospital deals with real people. Your best option, then, would be to move it from where you originally placed it to another part of the document, to a section where it seems to fit with the topic being discussed.

If the place where you want the picture to move is some distance away from the original location (that is, somewhere off the immediate screen), the easiest way to move the picture is with **Cut and Paste.** Both commands can be found on the **Home** Ribbon in the **Clipboard** group, as seen in Figure 4.18.

- Make sure the text wrapping option is **In Line With Text**.
- Select the picture, the paragraph marker after the picture, and the caption (if there is one), as well as the paragraph marker at the end of the caption. You select all of these by hovering your mouse in the left margin until it changes from an I-bar to a mouse pointer, and then drag down from the top to the bottom.
- On the **Home** Ribbon, click the **Cut** icon from the **Clipboard** group.
- Scroll to the location where you want the picture to be placed.
- Place your cursor by clicking the mouse in the exact location you want the graphic to appear. If you want the picture above a paragraph, click just to the left of the first word of the paragraph. Do not click in the middle of the paragraph unless you want to split it into two paragraphs.
- On the **Home** Ribbon, click the **Paste** icon from the **Clipboard** group.

To avoid problems with jumping graphics, it is best to choose **In Line With Text** to place and move pictures. With **In Line With Text**, the actual location of the picture is not separated from its anchor. Furthermore, if you move the paragraph marker along with the picture, you can be sure of the alignment and formatting of the picture even after it is moved. If you only moved the picture, and you moved it from a paragraph that was left-aligned to a paragraph that was right-aligned, the picture would move from the left to the right. Also, if you moved the picture from a paragraph with **Space Before** to a paragraph with **Space After**, you would get extra space after the picture before the next paragraph and lose the space on top of the picture. Once the picture is moved to the location you want it to be, you can switch back to **Tight** to allow the text to wrap around the picture.

Figure 4.18 | **Clipboard Group—Cut and Paste**

Moving a Graphic with Drag and Drop

If you wish to move the graphic to a relatively close location (that is, it can be seen on the same screen), drag and drop is the easiest way to move it. Again, it is easiest to avoid jumping graphics by preventing text wrapping until the graphic is close to the final location. To move the picture using drag and drop:

- Make sure the text wrapping option is **In Line With Text**.
- Select the picture, the paragraph marker after the picture, the caption, and the paragraph marker at the end of the caption. You select all of these by hovering your mouse in the left margin until it changes from an I-bar to a mouse pointer.
- Drag down from the top of the picture to the bottom of the caption in order to select it all.
- Click and hold over the *text* part of the caption and drag it to the new location. (You can't drag from the picture portion because the text will deselect, and only the picture will move.)
- You will see the mouse pointer change to point in the other direction, with a little dotted-line box underneath (as shown in Figure 4.19). You will also see a faint dotted line that represents the new location.
- When the faint dotted line is where you want it to be, let go of the mouse button.

You can also copy the picture and caption instead of moving it by holding down the **Ctrl** key before you let go of the mouse button.

Figure 4.19 | **Moving Picture by Dragging**

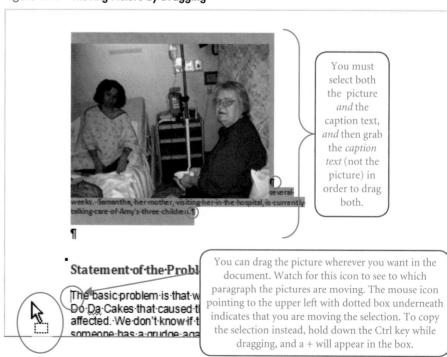

If you get near any of the margins of the document while you are dragging the picture, you will see why drag and drop is not a good choice when the target location is located somewhere off the screen. When you get to the edge of the screen, Word begins to travel swiftly in the direction of your mouse—usually too quickly to be able to stop in exactly the location you wish. If the target location is off the screen, use the cut and paste method to move the picture.

Once you've moved a graphic and its caption near the location where you want it, you can reset the text wrapping back to **Tight**. Then use drag and drop to more specifically place the picture and the caption where you want them so that the text can wrap around them.

COMMON MISTAKES | Letting Go of the Mouse Button Too Soon

You can move the picture up, down, left, right, and back again. As long as you don't let go of the mouse button, you can keep on moving. Sometimes people move "too far" (especially when they get to the edge of the screen), but instead of calmly moving back to the location they want, they instinctively let go of the mouse. This moves the picture to the wrong place.

If you accidentally move beyond the place where you wish to place the picture, don't let go of the mouse. Simply keep moving back to where you want the picture placed. If you do accidentally let go, undo it by using the **Undo** icon on the **Quick Access** toolbar and start again.

Using a Text Box

You may have noticed in magazine articles that sometimes the publisher takes a key phrase from the text and presents it again in a larger a box in one of the columns. This "pullout phrase" is one use for a text box. It grabs the readers' attention and gives them a sense of what they will find if they read the article. The font in the text box is usually larger or bolder than in the main text. If you were a marketing manager, you might use this method to write a brochure on a new product. If you were a product manager, you might format a technical white paper by pulling out a quote from one of your customers who uses the product.

Another common use for a text box is for parenthetical information: a sentence or paragraph that is related to the main topic, but not central. The font in these text boxes is more likely to be smaller than the main text. If you were a realtor, you might put the information about fair practices on home selling in a parenthetical text box.

A third use for text boxes is for when you want to wrap the text around both a picture and its caption. In the hospital administrator proposal, for example, you might want the caption to be immediately under the picture. Furthermore, you want the text to wrap around both the picture and the caption. For that you need a text box. To create a text box from text already in the document, do the following:

- Select the text you wish placed in the box.
- On the **Insert** Ribbon, click **Text Box** from the **Text** group.
- Click **Draw Text Box**.

>> **Quick Reference**

Moving a Picture with Drag and Drop

1. Select the picture and caption.
2. Click on the text portion and drag the mouse to the location to where you wish the picture to appear.
3. Let go of the mouse button.

Figure 4.20 | **Inserting a Text Box**

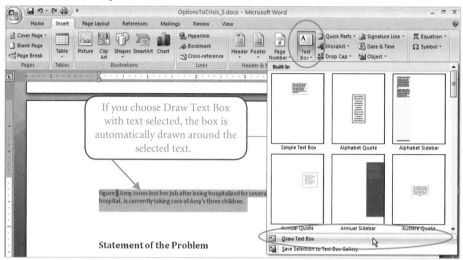

Note the example caption for the picture used in the hospital administrator example shown in Figure 4.21.

Figure 4.21 | **Selecting a Text Box to Resize or Move**

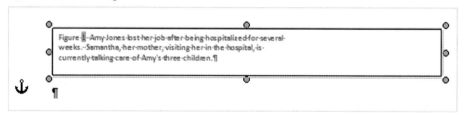

If you want to make any modifications to the text box, make sure that the *text box* is selected, not the *text inside* the text box. If you can see a blinking cursor, or if the text inside the box is highlighted, you've selected the text inside the box, not the box itself. If you select the text box and change the font, all the text within the box will change. If you select just some of the text (or have a blinking cursor indicating placement within the text), changing the font affects only your selection. Similarly, if you select the text box to cut and paste, the entire box will get cut and pasted, but if you have text within the box selected, just the selected text will get cut and pasted.

Once you've selected the text box, you can do many things. Many of these options were covered in the discussion of graphics, but with a text box it takes an extra step to display the same dialog boxes. To change the text wrapping option around the text box so you can move the box more easily, do the following:

- Right-click on the text box to bring up the text box option menu.
- Click **Format Text Box**. (If **Format Text Box** is not on the options menu, you have text selected instead of the whole text box. Reselect and try again.)
- Click **Layout** tab.
- Click **In line with text**.
- Click **OK** in the **Format Text Box** dialog box.
- Drag and drop the text box to the desired location or cut and paste it to the desired location.

When dragging, remember to drag on one of the *straight lines* around the edges with the move tool. If you click in the center of the text box, you will switch from having the text box selected to having the text selected. If you drag from a handle, you will resize the box with the resize tool instead of moving the box.

To change whether or not there is a line around the box, do the following:

- Right-click on the text box to bring up the text box option menu.
- Click **Format Text Box**.
- Click the **Colors and Lines** tab.
- In the Lines section of the dialog box, select a color in the **Color** option to display a line. (You can also indicate whether the line should be dashed, the style, and the weight of the border.) If you don't want a visible line, make sure the color selected is **No Color**.

To resize the box, do the following:

- Right-click on the text box to bring up the text box option menu.
- Click and drag on one of the handles around the text box.
- Drag a handle on the right or left edge to make the box shorter or longer in width.
- Drag a handle on the top or bottom edge to make the box taller or shorter in length.
- Drag a handle on the corner to make smaller or larger both width and height.

To change the text wrapping option so the text will wrap around it, do the following:

- Right-click on the text box to bring up the text box option menu.
- Right-click on the box to bring up the text box option menu.
- Click **Format Text Box**.
- Click the **Layout** tab.
- Select the **Tight** wrapping style.
- Click the **Advanced** button.
- Click the **Picture Position** tab.
- Change the vertical or horizontal position until the text box appears where you want it in the document.

Once you put the text into a text box, you need to move it separately from the picture itself because you can't select a text box and a graphic at the same time.

COMMON MISTAKES | Selecting the Text and not the Text Box

It is best to click on one of the straight lines around the box instead of inside the box when selecting a text box. As noted, it is easy to mistakenly select the text within a text box instead of the text box object itself. You can tell if this has happened because when you right-click to get the text box option menu, **Format Text Box** is not on the menu. If this happens, just click off (click somewhere on the page away from the text), reselect, and try again.

>> *Quick Reference*

Inserting a Text Box Around Existing Text

1. Select the text you wish placed in the box.
2. On the **Insert** Ribbon, click **Text Box** from the **Text** group.
3. Click **Draw Text Box**.

≫ Pictures and Graphics

The purpose of this workshop is to demonstrate how to deal with graphics and pictures in your Word documents. You will see these skills demonstrated in the following four videos: **Inserting Pictures**, **Enhancing Picture Placement**, **Wrapping Text and Cropping**, and **Compressing Pictures**. After completing each section of tasks, watch the related video shown in parentheses. Open the file named ib_w04_backtoberkscounty before starting this workshop. Remember to try the tasks on your own first before watching the video.

1. Insert a Photograph (Video: Inserting Pictures)

a. Place the insertion point at the end of the first paragraph on the second page, which ends with "for I know where I am."

b. Press **Enter** to create a new paragraph.

c. On the **Insert** tab, click **Picture**.

d. In the **Insert Picture** dialog box, click the JPEG file named ib_w04_berkscounty and then click the **Insert** button.

e. Save the document.

2. Resize a Photograph. (Video: Inserting Pictures continued)

a. Click on the picture you just inserted to select it.

b. Hold down the **Ctrl+Shift** keys.

c. Click and drag a handle toward the center of the picture until the picture is about one-inch wide.

3. Add a Caption to the Picture (Video: Inserting Pictures continued)

a. Click on the picture to select it.

b. Right-click on the picture and select the **Insert Caption** option.

c. In the **Caption** text box, type in **Reading—the heart of Berks County** and click **OK**.

d. If the caption appears above the picture, move it to be below the picture by selecting the caption and then dragging it to a new location.

4. Move the Picture and Caption (Video: Inserting Pictures continued)

a. Make sure the text wrapping choice for the picture is **In Line With Text**. This is done by right-clicking on the picture and clicking **Text wrapping**. If the **In Line With Text** option is not selected, click on **In Line With Text**.

b. Select the picture and the caption under it (remember to position your mouse in the left margin and drag from the top down).

c. Click on **Cut** from the **Clipboard** group on the **Home** tab.

d. Scroll to the beginning of the document and click your cursor to the left of the paragraph that starts with "Take the local paper".

e. Click on **Paste** from the **Clipboard** group on the **Home** tab.

f. Save the document as **ib_w04_backtoberkscountyv1**.

5. **Put the Caption in a Text Box (Video: Enhancing Picture Placement).**

   a. Open the file named ib_w04_backtoberkscountyv1.

   b. Select the text in the caption by dragging over it with the mouse.

   c. On the **Insert** tab, in the **Text** group, click the **Font Box** icon.

   d. Click on the **Draw Text Box** option to place the caption in a text box.

6. **Make the Font of the Text Box Smaller (Video: Enhancing Picture Placement continued)**

   a. Select the text in the caption by dragging over it with the mouse.

   b. On the **Home** tab, in the **Font** group, select the number in the **Font size** icon.

   c. Press the **Delete** key to delete the current number and type **7**.

   d. Press **Enter** to apply the font size.

7. **Make the Text Box Smaller (Video: Enhancing Picture Placement continued)**

   a. Select the text box by clicking on one of the lines around the text box.

   b. Drag the handle on the right side of the box toward the center to make the text box the same size as the picture (about one-inch wide).

8. **Remove the Line Around the Text box (Video: Enhancing Picture Placement continued)**

   a. Select the text box by clicking on one of the lines around the text box.

   b. Right-click on the text box and click on **Format Text Box**.

   c. On the **Colors and Lines** tab, in the Line section, change the Color choice to No Color. Click **OK**.

   d. Save the document as **ib_w04_backtoberkscountyv2**.

9. **Change the Text Wrapping Around the Picture and the Text Box (Video: Wrapping Text and Cropping)**

   a. Open the file named ib_w04_backtoberkscountyv2.

   b. Click on the picture to select it. Right-click on the picture and click **Text wrapping** and then **Tight**.

   c. Click on the caption under the picture.

   d. Right-click on the outline around the text box, click **Format Text Box**, click **Layout**, and then **Tight**.

10. **Crop the Picture (Video: Wrapping Text and Cropping continued)**

    a. Click on the picture to select it.

    b. On the **Picture Tools—Format** tab, click **Crop**.

    c. Grab each crop bar in turn and shave off about 1/4-inch from each side of the picture. Click anywhere in the text of the document to turn the Crop feature off.

11. **Move the Picture and Caption to the Right Side of the Page (Video: Wrapping Text and Cropping continued)**

    a. Click on the picture to select it.

    b. Drag the picture over to the right until it is just under the paragraph that ends "great community Berks County was until after I left."

c. Click on the caption.

d. Drag the caption over to the right until it is just under the picture.

e. Select both the paragraph that starts "The truth was. . . " and the paragraph that starts "Take the local paper". Right-click the mouse button while pointing at the selection and click **Paragraph** in the menu.

f. In the **Paragraph** dialog box, click the **Lines and Page Breaks** tab and uncheck **Keep lines together**.

g. Click **OK**.

h. Save the document as **ib_w04_backtoberkscountyv3**.

12. **Save the Document and Compress the Pictures (Video: Compressing Pictures)**

a. Open the file named ib_w04_backtoberkscountyv3.

b. From the **Office Button**, click **Save As**.

c. Click **Tools, Compress Pictures**, and then **Options**.

i. Make sure there is a check mark next to **Automatically perform basic compression on save** on the **Compression Options** section.

ii. Make sure there is a check mark next to **Delete cropped areas of pictures** on the **Compression Options** section.

iii. Select **Print** on the **Target Output** section. Choose **OK** to return to the **Compress Pictures** dialog box.

d. Click **OK** to perform the compression.

e. Type the name **ib_w04_backtoberkscountyv4** in the **File name** text box and save the document.

» Consultants Workshop Press Release

One common business use for inserting pictures in documents is the "head shot" that accompanies biographies, press releases, and other marketing materials advertising a workshop, conference, or other event. The issues to consider when sending out a document with a picture apply to all documents with embedded pictures and press releases. Will the reader be printing the picture or just viewing it on the screen? Will the document will be sent through e-mail, or printed first and then sent through the postal mail to the recipient? Understanding these issues (and how the size of the graphic is affected by the answers) is critical to the effectiveness of the document as a whole.

Exercise

The purpose of this exercise is to attach a press release to an e-mail that will be sent to local newspapers. Open the file named ib_w04_glassceilingpressrelease and complete the following tasks:

1. Insert the picture from the file named ib_w04_maryellenharve between the first and second paragraphs. Add a text caption underneath the picture with the consultant's name: **Maryellen Harve**.

2. Create a text box for the caption. Place the picture and the caption just to the right of the second paragraph, (the one that starts "Previous to founding MAH Associates").

3. Wrap the text around the picture so that the head shot is integrated directly into the description of the workshop. This provides a highly professional touch.

4. Save the document as **ib_w04_glassceilingpressreleasev1**, but make sure that the size does not exceed 30 kilobytes so that it can be sent easily through e-mail and posted on the website without taking a long time to download.

>> What's Wrong with This Document?

PROBLEM & EXERCISE

Problem

One of the project managers working for you in your technology consulting firm is writing a new procedure for testing the disaster recovery plan. His document includes a form that project participants will cut out and send back to him. The project also has a graphic illustration of the network in the appendix at the end. He is struggling with both the form and the graphic and sends you the following message asking for help:

"I can't seem to fix the Data Recovery Test Plan document that I've been working on. I want the form to be at the bottom of the page at the end of the text section of the document, but after the *Your participation is appreciated* paragraph. Every time I place it there, it jumps to the top of the next page! I also can't figure out why my table is being covered up by the network illustration that I added. I've tried to move it several times, but it just covers up whatever is underneath it."

You assure him that you can help and ask him to send you the document.

Exercise

The file the project manager sends you is named ib_w04_disasterrecoverytestplan. Open the file and review the problems he described in his message. What's wrong with this document? Consider the following:

On the last page, why is the network illustration covering up a table and some text?
On the second page, why has the form jumped down to the next page?

How can you fix it? Write a short description of what is causing the problem in each case. Then, fix the document and name it **ib_W04_disasterrecoverytestplanv1**.

>> Inserting Slides, Spreadsheets, Charts, and Query Results

Skill Set

In addition to pictures and graphics, you may also need to copy and paste elements from other Microsoft applications into your business documents. For example, a marketing manager might include a portion of an Excel spreadsheet to enhance a status report. A sales manager might want to put results of the last few quarters into a "State of the Company" memo. A retail store clerk might want to make a flyer out of a slide presentation that came from the corporate leaders. Performing these tasks can be difficult. In this section, you will investigate the options and optimum ways for copying PowerPoint slides, Excel spreadsheets and charts, and Access query results into Word documents.

Inserting a PowerPoint Slide

PowerPoint is a simple-to-use presentation program with basic drawing capabilities that is frequently used in business presentations. A common business task is to write a document based upon a PowerPoint presentation, or copy and paste a graphic or logo found in a PowerPoint presentation into a Word document.

How you handle the transfer depends upon what, exactly, you want from the PowerPoint presentation. The most well-known and common method for getting information from PowerPoint to Word is to copy and paste, as shown in Figure 4.22.

- Open the PowerPoint presentation that contains the item you wish to copy.
- Select the object you wish to copy.
- Click the **Copy** icon on the **Home** tab.
- Open the Word document to which you wish to paste the object.
- Click the cursor where you want the object to paste.
- Click **Paste** from the **Home** tab.

This method works fine when you want to copy a single object that is currently in PowerPoint into a Word document. If you were an entrepreneur trying to attract investors to your company, for example, you might be working on a script for an upcoming meeting with some good prospects, but you need the logo displayed at the top of the Word document to show up (as if it were letterhead). You might not have a separate file with the logo in it, but you remember that your partner had copied the logo into the investor presentation, where you can get it. Getting the logo would involve simply copying and pasting the logo from the PowerPoint presentation into the header of the script, as shown in Figure 4.22.

Problems may arise, however, when you try to paste anything more complex, such as multiple objects or the entire slide. Word has many options for pasting. Word bases the current option on a combination of the type of object you are pasting and the option chosen the last time you pasted in that installation of Word. The options used before may not necessarily be appropriate for the current object, so you should always choose **Paste Special** and choose an option instead of just choosing **Paste**.

Figure 4.22 | **Copying and Pasting from PowerPoint to Word**

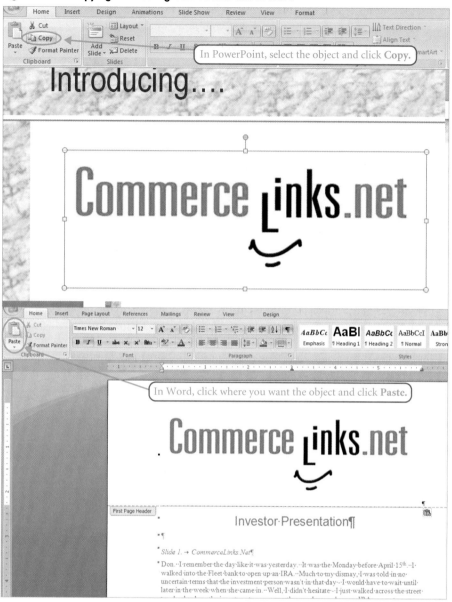

Going back to the script document example, imagine that you are the entrepreneur creating the Word document and want to add little pictures of each slide next to the script to make it easier for you and your partner to learn the script and know what is coming next. To insert those slides, you need to know how to paste the entire slide, background and all. Figure 4.23 shows the different pasting options. Characteristics of the first seven paste options are:

- **Microsoft Graphic Object** does not fit itself to page margins; does not fill in background
- **JPEG** does not fit itself to page margins; does fill in black background
- **PNG** does not fit itself to page margins; does not fill in black background
- **GIF** does not fit itself to page margins; does fill in black background and comes in with a border
- **Picture Enhanced Metafile** does fit itself to page margins; does not fill in black background
- **Bitmapped** does fit itself to page margins; does fill in black background
- **Windows Enhanced Metafile** does not fit itself to page; does fill in black background

Figure 4.23 | **Different Options for Pasting from PowerPoint**

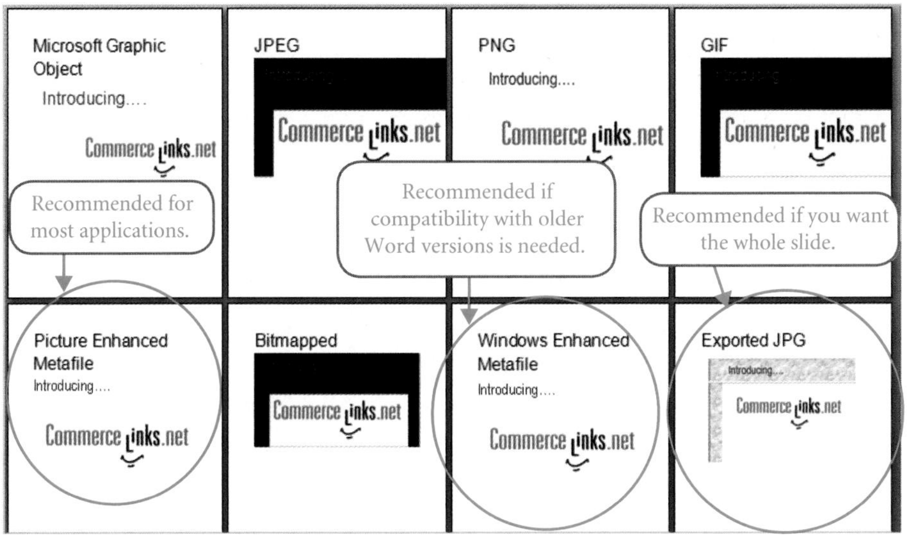

For most applications and uses, Picture Enhanced Metafile is the best format to choose because the graphic will not get distorted if resized. Picture Enhanced Metafile is a 32-bit newer version of Windows Enhanced Metafile, which is a 16-bit version. The "32-bit version" means that the Picture Enhanced can store more information than the Windows Enhanced; it also means that some older programs can't handle the additional information, so if you require compatibility with older versions, choose Windows Enhanced Metafile.

However, even knowing these options may not be enough. In this example, you are trying to get a small image of each slide at the top of each section of the script. Note that none of the first seven options actually *looks like* the slide itself: each option copied the objects on the slide, but not the background or master graphics that also appear when viewing the slide in PowerPoint. If you want the slide to look just like the screen in PowerPoint, you need to **export** the slide and choose the **JPEG** format.

To get the whole slide, including master objects and backgrounds, do the following:

- Open PowerPoint and navigate to the slide that you wish to export, as shown in Figure 4.24.
- From the **Office Button**, click on **Save As**.
- In the **File name** text box, type in a new filename: **FirstSlide_4v1**.
- In the **Save as type** option list, click on **JPEG File Interchange Format (*.jpg)**.
- **Save** the slide in the new format. On the **Export Slides** dialog box shown in Figure 4.25, choose **Current Slide Only**.
- Open up Word and navigate to the place where you wish the slide to appear (such as above the slide heading, as shown in Figure 4.26).
- On the **Insert** tab, click **Picture**. Navigate to the folder that contains the file you just saved and double-click on the file.

Keep in mind that this is a normal graphic, as discussed earlier in the chapter. Issues of resizing, text wrapping, and placement all apply.

Figure 4.24 | **Saving PowerPoint Slide as a JPEG**

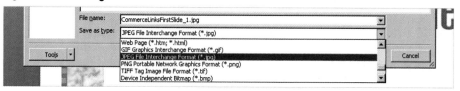

Figure 4.25 | **Export Slides Dialog Box**

Figure 4.26 | **Inserting a PowerPoint Slide as a JPG**

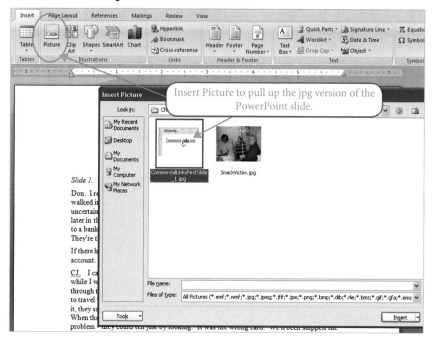

COMMON MISTAKES | Forgetting to Rename an Exported Slide

When exporting slides from PowerPoint, remember to give a different name to the exported slide. You want to keep the original PowerPoint file and not overwrite it. When using Save As to export, if you don't put a new filename into the **File Name** box, there's a chance that PowerPoint will save over your original presentation *with the graphic of just the one slide.* You would then lose the original file (not a good thing).

>> *Quick Reference*

Inserting PowerPoint Slide into Word

1. In PowerPoint, with the slide you wish to copy displayed, choose **Save As** from the **Office Menu Button**.

2. Change the file type to JPEG and rename the file.

3. Create one file with **Current Slide Only** or create multiple files with **Every Slide**.

4. In Word, place the insertion point where you want the slide to appear.

5. On the **Insert** tab, click **Picture** and navigate to the folder that contains the file you just exported from PowerPoint.

Inserting an Excel Chart

One of the most common business tasks is to paste an Excel chart into a Word document. A technical support manager might want to illustrate the number of work orders that have been fulfilled in a line chart. A sales professional might want use a column chart to show how solid her sales have been for the past three years. A car manufacturer might want to show a pie chart that categorizes the source of defects. A broker might want to demonstrate with a hi-lo chart the historical stock price for a stock he's trying to sell.

Pasting an Excel chart into a document is similar to copying and pasting the logo from PowerPoint. However, unless you choose the correct option through **Paste Special,** the chart may unexpectedly change once you paste it into your document. This is because the default paste option for an Excel object is **Microsoft Graphic Object**. A **Microsoft Graphic Object** retains more inherent detail and gives you the option to link to the original file (so that you can double-click on the object and it will bring up the original program for you to edit the object).

The problem with the **Microsoft Graphic Object** is that it *also* retains its original formatting, but because it is in a new environment, it generally doesn't *look* very good. Word tries to "rearrange" the objects when you resize them, instead of just making them proportionately bigger or smaller.

The next example is an Excel chart showing the net income of a light bulb manufacturing company over the first five years of the decade. The Finance Manager has pasted it into a division progress report for the senior leaders of the holding company. If you choose the Microsoft Graphic Object, the objects within the chart will rearrange when you try to resize it, as shown in the top half of Figure 4.27. The bottom half shows the chart resized after being pasted with **Picture (Enhanced Metafile)** format.

Figure 4.27 | **Resizing Microsoft Object and Picture Enhanced Metafile**

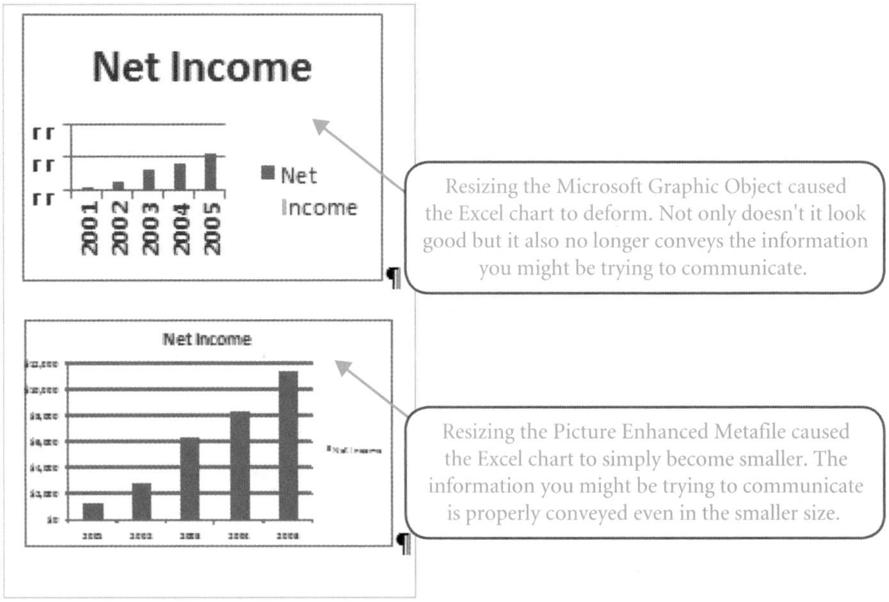

Therefore, when you paste an Excel chart, choose **Picture (Enhanced Metafile)**, as shown in the dialog box in Figure 4.28. The **Picture (Enhanced Metafile)** pastes a "snapshot" of the object, as it appeared in the original program, but without any of the individual object formatting. A **Picture (Enhanced Metafile)** resizes without changing individual objects, which means that the whole chart will get proportionately larger or smaller (which is usually preferable).

Figure 4.28 | **Paste Special Dialog Box**

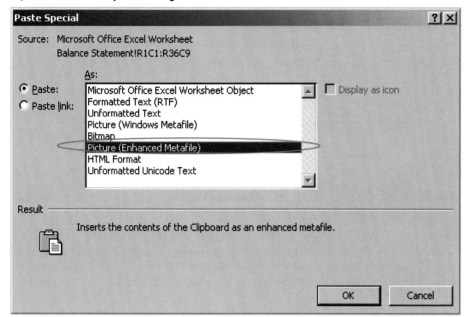

Figure 4.29 shows another example of a chart from Excel being pasted into an already existing Word document. In this case, a sporting goods industry consultant is copying a column chart into a business research paper to demonstrate the trends of the industry. After copying the chart from an Excel file, you would place the cursor in your Word document where you want the chart to appear. Then click the **Paste** list box to open the **Paste Special** dialog box and select the **Picture (Enhanced Metafile)** option.

Figure 4.29 | **Paste Chart from Excel**

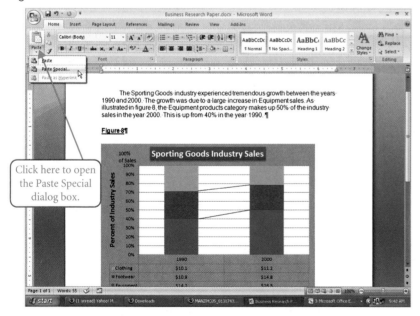

>> *Quick Reference*

Inserting an Excel Chart into Word

1. Activate a chart in an Excel file and click the **Copy** icon on the **Home** tab.

2. Open a Word file and place the cursor where the chart should appear.

3. Click the **Home** tab in the Ribbon.

4. Click the down arrow below the **Paste** icon.

5. Select the **Paste Special** option to open the **Paste Special** dialog box.

6. Select the **Picture (Enhanced Metafile)** option and click the **OK** button in the **Paste Special** dialog box.

7. Adjust the size of the chart by clicking and dragging the sizing handles as needed.

Inserting an Excel Spreadsheet

Another common business task is to describe and explain an Excel spreadsheet within a Word document. A financial manager may want to embed a balance sheet into an annual report. A mortgage broker may want to embed a comparison of three different mortgage alternatives. A nonprofit organization might want to put the budget and actual comparisons in a quarterly newsletter. An entrepreneur might want to put different what-if scenarios into the business plan. A customer service manager might want to put the call report results into the monthly progress update. There is no end to the examples because Excel and Word are used so often together in business.

Charts and graphs are often easier to understand at a glance than columns of numbers, so they are used more often. However, sometimes the numbers themselves are necessary to communicate your point. Going back to the investor script example from Figure 4.30, you might decide that you need to include the asset numbers of the balance sheet in the script in case the investors ask questions. To accomplish this, do the following:

- Open the Excel file and select the cells you want to be copied into the Word document.
- Click **Copy** on the **Home** tab.
- Open the Word document and place your insertion point where you want the spreadsheet to appear.
- On the **Home** tab, click the list box below the **Paste** icon and select the **Paste Special** option. Choose **Picture (Enhanced Metafile)** and click **OK**.

Figure 4.30 | **Paste Excel Range into Word**

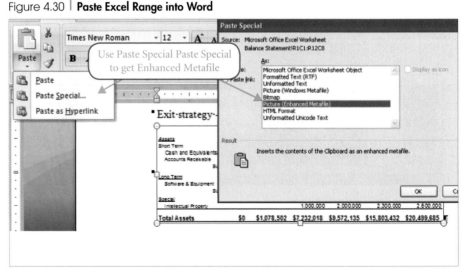

Inserting the Results of an Access Query

Similar to copying and explaining spreadsheet data, another common business task is to describe and explain the results of an Access query in a Word document. Access is a database program, noted for its capability to store larger amounts of data than Excel, as well as a more effective and efficient way to manage that data. Because an Access database might have hundreds of thousands or even millions of records, you can't copy the whole thing into Word. Instead, you can create a set of conditions for the records to meet to be listed. For example, a sales manager might want to see just the total sales for each quarter instead of each individual invoice. Or the purchasing manager might want to see the orders placed on a certain date. A realtor might want to see just the houses listed for more than $500,000. A *query* stores the condition you use to determine which information from the database will be displayed. You can see the results of the query by *running* it. Note that you cannot copy the *query* from Access itself; you can copy only the *results* of the query.

Unfortunately, you don't normally get a **Picture (Enhanced Metafile)** option when you copy the results of an Access query because the information gets transferred as text, not graphics. As you can see in Figure 4.31, there are only four choices:

- *HTML*: The formatting language used by most web pages.
- *Formatted Text (RTF)*: Developed by IBM in the early days of word processing to store both text and simple formatting.
- *Unformatted Text:* Text with no formatting at all. Bold, underline, italic—anything that formats the numbers, letters, or paragraphs will be gone.
- *Unformatted Unicode Text:* Same as Unformatted Text, but a smaller character set designed to be internationally compatible.

For example, suppose that you are a consultant working on explaining the relationship between the advertising budget and the sales of different regions of an electronic parts manufacturer. You might want to copy the quarterly sales into your report. You can see from the examples in Figure 4.31 that there are problems with each of the methods of pasting the data copied from Access. One of the biggest problems is that the query was designed to show the results of these sales without the decimal points, as shown in the actual query results displayed in Figure 4.32. None of the paste choices keeps that formatting option. In general, none of the paste special options works very well if you want to quickly show the results of a query as it is displayed on the screen in Access. Furthermore, each paste option requires significant rework and formatting after it has been pasted into Word.

Figure 4.31 | **Paste Special Options for Access Query Results**

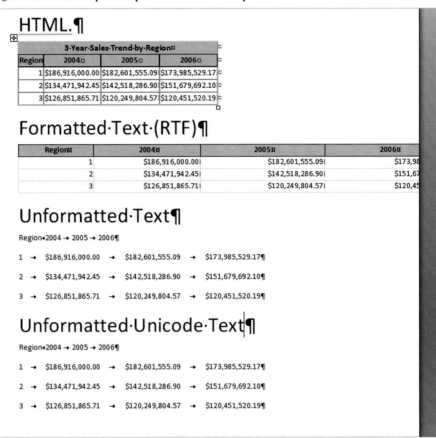

Inserting a Picture of an Access Query into a Word Document

1. In Access, run the query and arrange the window so that it shows just the query results you want to copy.
2. Press **Alt+PrintScreen**.
3. Open a Word file and place the cursor where the query results should appear.
4. Click the **Home** tab in the Ribbon.
5. Click the list box below the **Paste** icon.
6. Select the **Paste Special** option to open the **Paste Special** dialog box.
7. Select the **Picture (Enhanced Metafile)** or **Device Independent Bitmap** option and click the **OK** button.

Figure 4.32 | **Picture of Access Query Results**

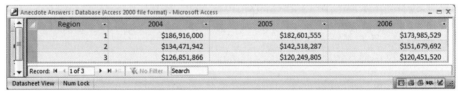

Another option is to return to Access and take a "picture" of the query on the screen. Almost all computers have a *PrintScreen* key. When used in combination with **Alt** or **Ctrl**, you can use the **PrintScreen** (sometime abbreviated as **Prt Scrn**) key to take a "snapshot" of the screen and copy it into the Clipboard and then paste it into Word as a graphic. Going back to the consultant helping the electronics manufacturer, the historical sales by region should be shown without decimal places, so that is how you want it to appear in the Word document you are writing. Do the following:

- Launch Access and navigate to the query that you wish to copy, as shown in Figure 4.32.
- Rearrange the window so that the only information you see are the results of the query. Remove or narrow the pane with the list of queries on the left side of the screen.
- Press **Alt+PrintScreen** to copy the window into the Clipboard. (If you had pressed **Ctrl+PrintScreen,** everything that is on the screen, including all the windows or desktop, would be copied into the Clipboard. **Alt** just copies the active window or dialog box.)

- Open the Word document and place your insertion point where you would like to see the picture of the query.
- From the **Home** tab, click **Paste Special** and choose **Picture (Enhanced Metafile)** or **Device Independent Bitmap** if the first choice is not available.
- Crop and resize as necessary.

COMMON MISTAKES | **Copying Too Much From Access**

Before pasting the results of your Access query, shorten the columns and make sure that only relevant data is being copied. You want to copy less than three-fourths of the screen width.

Just like spreadsheets, query results often have too many columns of information to copy into a word processing document.

≫ Inserting Slides, Spreadsheets, Charts, and Query Results

VIDEO WORKSHOP

The purpose of this workshop is to demonstrate how to copy selections from other Microsoft applications into your Word documents. You will see these tasks demonstrated in the following three videos: **Copying from PowerPoint**, **Copying from Excel**, and **Copying from Access**. After completing each section of tasks, watch the related video. Remember to try the tasks on your own first before watching the video.

1. **Copying from PowerPoint (Video: Copying from PowerPoint)**
   a. Open the Word document named ib_w04_investorpresentationwords.
   b. Launch PowerPoint and open ib_w04_investorpresentation.
   c. On the first slide, select the **Commercelinks** logo.
   d. Copy the logo into the Clipboard.
   e. Return to the Word document and edit the header by doing the following:
      i. Paste the logo into the center of the header.
      ii. Resize it to make it much smaller.
   f. On the **Header & Footer Tools—Design** tab, click the **Close Header and Footer** icon to return to the main Word document.
   g. Return to PowerPoint.
   h. While viewing the first slide, click the **Office Button** and choose **Save As**.
   i. In the **File name** text box, type the new filename `FirstSlide_4`.
   j. In the **Save as type** option list, click on **JPEG File Interchange Format (*.jpg)**. Click the **Save** button.
   k. On the **Export Slides** dialog box, choose **Current Slide Only** to save only the first slide in the new format.
   l. Return to Word and place the insertion point at the beginning of the paragraph just below the first heading (*Slide 1. CommerceLinks.Net*).
   m. On the **Insert** tab, click **Picture**. Navigate to the folder that contains the file you just saved and double-click on the file.

n. Resize the picture to approximately one inch by one inch. Change the wrapping style so that the text wraps around the picture.

o. Save the Word file and name it **ib_w04_investorpresentationwordsv1**, then close the file.

2. Copying from Excel (Video: Copying from Excel)

a. Launch Excel and open ib_w04_financials.

b. Go to the Summary Worksheet and select the chart at the bottom of the data.

c. Copy the chart into the Clipboard.

d. Return to Word and open the document named **ib_w04_investorpresentationwordsv1.**

e. Place your cursor at the end of the **Slide 6 Funding Opportunity** paragraph, which ends with *acquisition in 3 to 5 years*. Press **Enter** to create a new paragraph.

f. Choose the **Paste** list box from the **Home** tab and click on **Paste Special**. Choose **Picture (Enhanced Metafile)**. Click **OK** to paste the chart into the Word document.

g. Use the sizing handles to resize the chart to about half its original size.

h. Return to the Excel spreadsheet named ib_w04_financials.

i. Go to the Balance Statement Worksheet and select the range from A1 to H36.

j. Copy the range into the Clipboard.

k. Return to Word and place your cursor just below the paragraph in the **Slide 7 Summary** section that ends with *as we walk down this path together*. Press **Enter** to create a new paragraph.

l. Choose the **Paste** list box from the **Home** tab and click on **Paste Special.** Choose **Picture (Enhanced Metafile)**.

m. Resize the spreadsheet graphic and make it slightly smaller (about 4/5th the size).

n. Save the Word file and name it **ib_w04_investorpresentationwordsv2**, then close the file.

3. Copying from Access. (Video: Copying from Access)

a. Open the Word file named ib_w04_corporatesalesmeeting.

b. Launch Access and open the file ib_w04_electronicsmanufacturersales.

c. Double-click on the query **3 Year Sales Trend By Region**.

d. Double-click the window title of the query results to maximize the window.

e. Make each of the columns slightly narrower. Do this by placing the mouse pointer between the columns in the heading row. When the pointer becomes a cross with a double headed arrow, click and drag the column boundary to the desired width.

f. Click on the **Close** button of the **Shutter bar,** which is to the right of the panel title and looks like two arrows pointing to the left.

g. Press **Alt+PrintScreen** to make a screen shot of the query results.

h. Return to the Word document and place your cursor just below the paragraph in the **Review Regional Sales** section that ends with *The numbers are as follows:*.

i. Choose the **Paste** list box from the **Home** tab and click on **Paste Special**. Then choose **Device Independent Bitmap**. Click **OK** to insert the graphic of the Access query into the Word document.

j. Using the sizing handles, resize the spreadsheet graphic to about 4/5th of its original size.

k. Save the Word file and name it `ib_w04_corporatesalesmeetingv1`, then close the file.

>> INTEGRATING INFORMATION FROM A VARIETY OF SOURCES TO PERSUADE

It is common practice for business executives to create PowerPoint presentations, Excel spreadsheets, and Access queries, and then require a written Word document that contains more detailed information and explanations. These tasks are also common among nonprofit organizations, especially among board members or people who want to implement new programs. This exercise is designed to help you figure out the best option for presenting information that is copied from other programs into Word so that your documents can clearly and concisely communicate exactly what you need them to, regardless of the source of the information.

Exercise

The purpose of this exercise is to prepare a comprehensive document in Word for the board of directors of a nonprofit organization that is based on information from several different sources: a budget from an Excel spreadsheet, a list of contacts in an Access query, and a slide from a PowerPoint presentation. Open up the file named ib_w04_peacesensing in Word and then complete the following tasks:

1. Insert a Logo from PowerPoint into a header in Word.

(It's very common to obtain a logo out of an existing presentation instead of trying to find the original graphic.)

a. Open the ib_w04_peacesensingpresentation file in PowerPoint.

b. Click the **View** tab in the Ribbon and click the **Slide Master** icon.

c. Select the logo at the top of the slide and click the right mouse button while pointing at it and click **Copy** on the object option menu.

d. Click the **Close** button in the Ribbon.

e. Return to the ib_w04_peacesensing file in Word.

f. Click the **Insert** tab in the Ribbon, click the **Header** icon, and choose **Edit Header**.

g. Delete the phrase *{Insert Logo from PeaceSensingPresentation Here}*.

h. Paste the logo and center it.

i. Close the header.

j. Save the Word document as `ib_w04_peacesensingv1`.

2. Insert a slide from PowerPoint into a Word document.

a. Return to the ib_w04_peacesensingpresentation in PowerPoint.

b. Click the **Slide Sorter** icon and find the **Project Plan Progress** slide. (It is the 8th slide).

c. Select the **Project Plan Progress** slide and choose **Save As** from the **Office Button** menu.

d. Change the **File Name** to `ProjectPlanSlide`. Change the type of file to **JPEG File Interchange Format (*.jpg)**.

e. Save the slide in the new format. On the **Export Slides** dialog box, choose **Current Slide Only**.

f. Return to the ib_w04_peacesensingv1 file in Word. Find the phrase *{insert project plan from PeaceSensePresentation slide here}*.

g. Delete the phrase and replace it with the **ProjectPlanSlide**.

h. Return to the ib_w04_peacesensingpresentation in PowerPoint.

i. Navigate to the 9th slide, titled **Successful Pilot Programs**.

j. Select the quote that starts with *I have really thought about this. . . .* Copy it.

k. Return to the ib_w04_peacesensing file in Word. Find the phrase *{insert 2 quote boxes from PeaceSensePresentation slide here}*.

l. Delete the phrase and replace it with the quote you just copied.

m. Return to the ib_w04_peacesensingpresentation file in PowerPoint.

n. Select the quote by Eudora Linde. Copy it.

o. Return to the ib_w04_peacesensing file in Word. Paste the second quote. Ensure that the quotes can both be seen and stand out within the text.

p. Save the Word document as **ib_w04_peacesensingv2**.

q. Return to and close the PowerPoint presentation.

3. Insert a range from Excel into Word.

(Getting original numbers from Excel and pasting them into a Word document so that you can explain or discuss them is a very common process in business.)

a. Open the ib_w04_peacesensingfinances in Excel.

b. Click the **Sample Budget** worksheet tab.

c. Select the range A2:B13, and choose **Copy** from the **Home** tab.

d. Return to the ib_w04_peacesensingv2 file in Word.

e. Find the phrase *{insert budget from PeaceSensingFinances spreadsheet here}*.

f. Delete the phrase

g. Click the **Paste** list box from the **Home** tab, choose **Paste Special** and select **Picture (Enhanced Metafile)**.

h. Resize and reposition as necessary.

i. Save the Word document as **ib_w04_peacesensingv3**.

4. Insert a chart from Excel into Word. It is even more common in business to create a graph or chart in Excel and copy it into Word to explain or discuss it.

a. Return to the ib_w04_peacesensingfinances in Excel.

b. Click the **Number Of Kids Helped** worksheet tab.

c. Select the chart and choose **Copy** from the **Home** tab.

d. Return to the ib_w04_peacesensingv3 file in Word.

e. Find the phrase *{insert the chart showing number of children helped in an ongoing program from PeaceSensingFinances here}*.

f. Delete the phrase.

g. Click the **Paste** list box from the **Home** tab, choose **Paste Special** and select **Picture (Enhanced Metafile)**.

h. Add a caption identifying the chart as a projection of the number of kids helped based upon the number of starting pilots. Resize and reposition as necessary.

i. Save the Word document as **ib_w04_peacesensingv4**.

j. Close the Excel spreadsheet.

5. Insert a query result from Access into Word. Databases like Access hold corporate data that is often explained or discussed in Word documents, so being able to copy and paste information from a database query is an important business skill.

   a. Open the ib_w04_peacesensingdb file in Access. (If you get a message asking if you want to block unsafe expressions, say **No**. If you get a message telling you there may be security issues, open the file anyway.)

   b. Double-click the **PeaceSensingContacts** query under the **Enthusiast** table.

   c. If the Access window is maximized, click the **Restore Down** button at the top-left corner of the window.

   d. Click the **Shutter Bar Close** button to get rid of the table list. Rearrange the window so that you only see the query results.

   e. Press the **Alt+Printscreen** keys.

   f. Return to the ib_w04_peacesensingv4 file in Word.

   g. Find the phrase *{insert Access Query PeaceSensingContacts here}*.

   h. Delete the phrase.

   i. Click the **Paste** list box from the **Home** tab, choose **Paste Special** and select **Device Independent Bitmap**.

   j. Crop the picture as necessary to eliminate the window borders and just show the names and contact information.

   k. Save the Word document as **ib_w04_peacesensingv5**.

   l. Close the Access database.

>> What's Wrong with This Document?

PROBLEM & EXERCISE

Problem

You are a consultant working on a process improvement proposal for a major local bank. A colleague has been working on another project for the bank, so the two of you have gotten together to propose another project to follow when the current project is over. You have gathered some statistics over the past year that are applicable to the project you are proposing for them and you shared them with your colleague who pasted the information from the Excel spreadsheet (range A3:F10 and the two charts) into Word.

Your colleague has been working on the proposal for days, and you call him up one day to see what the holdup is.

"I'm having problems," he tells you. "I can't seem to get the information from Excel to look good once I've copied it into Word. I don't understand why it looks so good in Excel, but when I copy the range into Word, it looks terrible! The charts look fine until you try to make them smaller so that they can fit on the same page with the range. Then they either distort, or the chart disappears entirely. Could you please take a look and figure out what's the deal?"

Exercise

Your colleague sent you a Word document named ib_w04_proposalforworkrequest. The Excel spreadsheet he is trying to copy is found in ib_w04_workrequeststats. Open both files and arrange them so you see them side by side. What's your opinion of the proposal your colleague has been working on? Would you be comfortable giving the proposal in its current state to the bank decision-makers? Consider the following:

1. What happened when the range was copied?

2. What would you do to enhance the look of the information?

3. What happens if you double-click on the charts?

4. What happens when you try to resize the charts?

5. What would help you to resize the chart information?

Write a short answer to each question. Then fix the problems with the proposal and save it as **ib_w04_proposalforworkrequestv1**. (Hint: often it is better to delete everything that has been done and redo it correctly instead of modifying what has already been done.)

Skill Set

>> Footnotes and Endnotes

As a student, you must provide "sources" for the information you use to write research papers. You are expected to infuse into your paper the knowledge and facts found elsewhere (without copying them word for word) by paraphrasing what other people say or write. You are then expected to take the information one step further and add original thoughts or unique perspectives. At the end of the paper, you provide a list of references that list where you got the information you wrote about in the paper. You've probably written papers in school and followed this process many times.

You may think that this process is unique to academia, but it is not. In the world of business, there are only a few careers (such as researcher, consultant, or domain authority) that require formal research papers, but almost every businessperson must learn new information from a variety of sources. It always adds significantly to your credibility to give references for your sources for reports, decision-making documents—even letters when you quote someone else. Although most of the time references can be documented right in the text, other times the number or complexity of the sources would detract from the message. At those times, using *footnotes* (if there are only a few) or *endnotes* (if there are many) to document the sources is preferable. A footnote is displayed at the bottom of the page. An endnote is displayed at the end of the section, chapter, or document. In addition to references, you can also use footnotes and endnotes to make statements on something parenthetical to the topic.

Adding an Endnote

When there are more than one or two items that require references or statements that are parenthetical to the text, it makes more sense to put them all at the end of the chapter or document. This is especially true if any of the items are very long, and would require a lot of space at the bottom of the page if entered as footnotes on each page.

The following example considers a book proposal about *Information Technology* intended for several publishers who might be interested in publishing it. Although the proposal mentions a book in one of the paragraphs, it does not include its reference, author, publisher, and year of publication, which would enable the reader to track down the book if necessary. You will go through the steps of adding that reference as an endnote, as shown in Figure 4.33.

- Place your cursor at the spot where you want the endnote number to appear.
- On the **References** tab, click **Insert Endnote**.
- A superscript number will be inserted at the end of the document, and your cursor will jump immediately after this number (in sequence to the other endnotes already entered).

- Type the text you wish to appear: **You Can't Teach a Kid To Ride a Bike At A Seminar, Sandler, D.H., Bay Head Publishing, New York,1995.**

If the reference is a book, you would write the title of the book, the author with the last name first, the publisher, the city of the publisher, and the year the book was published,

Figure 4.33 | **Inserting a Reference as an Endnote**

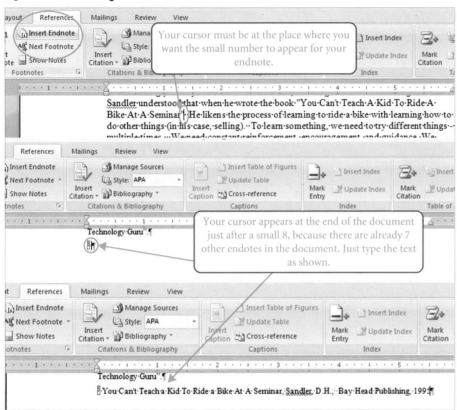

To delete an endnote, you do not delete the text at the end. Instead, you find the associated number within the text and delete the little number. Deleting the endnote *number* automatically deletes all the text within the endnote.

COMMON MISTAKES │ Accidentally Deleting the Endnote

Don't delete the number associated with an endnote unless you want to delete the text of the endnote. It is common when editing to delete a word or a phrase, but if there was an endnote attached to the word or phrase and you delete, you will also delete the entire endnote. If you want to delete all the text around an endnote, but want to safeguard the endnote itself, cut and paste the endnote number to a different part of your text.

Adding a Footnote

When there are only a few items that require references or statements that are parenthetical to the text and they are relatively short, it makes more sense to put them on each page in a footnote. As mentioned earlier, it always increases your credibility to include the references for your information, and footnotes are a good way of doing that.

Additionally, footnotes can enhance communication because they can enable you to provide remarks and side notes without breaking the reader's concentration and/or drawing too much attention to them (as a sidebar box would do).

The next example involves a document developed for the board of directors of a nonprofit organization. Although the document mentions the fact that teachers must qualify for the program, it does not specify what those qualifications are. To avoid breaking up the list that mentions this information, you choose to put the qualifications in a footnote, as shown in Figure 4.34.

- Place your insertion point at the end of the word where you wish the associated footnote number to appear.
- On the **References** tab in the **Footnotes** group, click **Insert Footnote**.
- The cursor will move to the end of the page after the separator bar, as shown in Figure 4.35.

Figure 4.34 | **Insert a Footnote**

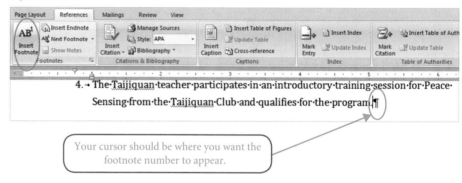

Figure 4.35 | **Type in the Footnote Text**

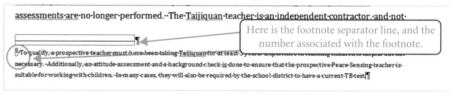

>> **Quick Reference**

Inserting an Endnote

1. Place your insertion point in the location you would like the endnote number to appear.

2. On the **References** tab, click **Insert Endnote**.

3. Type in the text of the endnote.

>> **Quick Reference**

Inserting a Footnote

1. Place your cursor at the spot where you would like the footnote number to appear.

2. On the **References** tab, click **Insert Footnote**.

3. Type in the text of the footnote.

Converting Endnotes to Footnotes and Vise Versa

The choice between using footnotes or endnotes depends upon the custom of your organization, the requirements of the reader, and the number and length of footnotes and endnotes. There are times when you start out one way, and realize that you need to switch to the other. There is an easy way to convert all your footnotes to endnotes or all your endnotes to footnotes. This example is shown in the book proposal document shown in Figure 4.38.

- Click on the dialog box launcher at the bottom corner of the **Footnotes** group on the **Reference** tab.
- Click on the **Convert** icon.
- Choose to **Convert all endnotes to footnotes**.
- Click **OK**.

If there were footnotes already in the document, you would have a choice between **Convert all footnotes to endnotes, Convert all endnotes to footnotes,** or **Swap all**

endnotes and footnotes. If you look through the document, you will notice that each of the former endnotes now appears on the page where the linking number appears.

Figuer 4.36 | **Converting Endnotes to Footnotes**

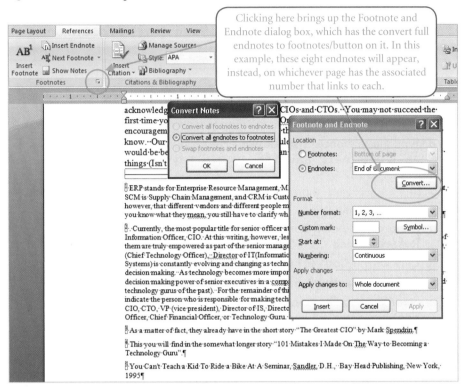

Clicking here brings up the Footnote and Endnote dialog box, which has the convert full endnotes to footnotes/button on it. In this example, these eight endnotes will appear, instead, on whichever page has the associated number that links to each.

>> Footnotes and Endnotes

The purpose of this workshop is to demonstrate how to insert footnotes and endnotes. You will see these tasks demonstrated in the following two videos: **Footnoting** and **Switching Between Footnotes and Endnotes**. After completing each section of tasks, watch the related video. Remember to try the tasks on your own first before watching the video.

1. Footnoting (Video: Footnoting)

a. Open up the document ib_w04_peacesensing.

b. At the bottom of page 2, at the end of the fourth item, place your cursor after the words *and qualifies for the program.*

c. Click **Insert Footnote** on the **References** tab in the **Footnotes** group.

d. Type in the footnote text: `To qualify, a prospective teacher must have been taking Taijiquan for at least 3 years. Experience in teaching children is helpful but not necessary. Additionally, an attitude assessment and a background check is done to ensure that the prospective Peace Sensing teacher is suitable for working` with children. In many cases, they will also be required by the school district to have a current TB test.

   e. Scroll back to the main text and save the document as **ib_w04_peacesensingv6** and close the Word document.

2. Switching Between Footnotes and Endnotes (Video: Switching Between Footnotes and Endnotes)

   a. Open up the document ib_w04_bookproposal.

   b. Place your cursor on the third page near the bottom, just after the words *You Can't Teach a Kid To Ride a Bike At A Seminar*.

   c. On the **References** tab, in the **Footnotes** group, click **Insert Endnote**.

   d. Type the reference: **You Can't Teach a Kid To Ride a Bike At A Seminar, Sandler, D.H., Bay Head Publishing, New York,1995.**

   e. Scroll back to the main document and save it as **ib_w04_bookproposalv1**.

   f. Click on the dialog box launcher for the **Footnotes** group on the **Reference** tab.

   g. Click on the **Convert** button.

   h. Choose to **Convert all endnotes to footnotes**, then click **OK**.

   i. Scroll back to the main document and save it as **ib_w04_bookproposalv2**, then close the document.

≫ Making a Case for a Recommendation

When working with any decision-makers, this question is often asked: Where did you get this information? You will appear knowledgeable and organized if you include references to anything that anyone might ask that question about in all your documents. This next exercise is designed to help you figure out where you might need such information and to insert appropriate footnotes into the document.

Exercise

The goal of this exercise it to use the skills you have learned in this section on supporting information with references to present a series of recommendations to the senior management team of a technology services company. You are a consultant who has been working with a university development office, and you are proposing a new program. Open the document named ib_w04_sourcesexecedproposal. Review your notes from each source found in the ib_w04_sourcesexecedproposal document and complete the following tasks:

   1. Convert the table to text in preparation for copying into footnotes. It will be easier to copy and paste the references for the next step if they are not in a table.

      a. Select the table.

      b. Click the **Table Tools** tab, and choose the **Layout** tab.

      c. In the **Data** group, choose the **Convert to Text** icon.

      d. Choose paragraph marks to separate the text.

   2. Open up the document ib_w04_execedproposal.

      a. Review the entire document, looking for locations where one of the decision makers reviewing the proposal might ask the question "Where did you get that?"

b. In each one of those locations, create a footnote for a source that appears to match the statement. You will find at least six places.

3. Save the document as **ib_w04_execedproposalv1**.

>> What's Wrong with This Document?

Problem

You have a coworker who is writing a series of articles about using technology projects in various industries to be submitted to a local paper to publicize the consulting business. The coworker knows that you are knowledgeable in Word, so one day he e-mails you for help. He writes: "I am having trouble with the attached document. There are a couple of things that are wrong, and I was hoping that you could help me with them." He goes on to list two things:

1. There are too many footnotes, and the editor tells me that putting them on each page is causing a problem with the layout.
2. A blank line keeps appearing between the first footnote and the footnote section. Plus, the first footnote keeps showing up with a 2 instead of a 1.

Exercise

The document attached to the email is ib_w04_techrulesarticle which you open and read. What can you do to help your coworker solve these dilemmas? Consider the following:

a. Is there a way to get the footnotes off the bottom of the page without losing the information and without retyping?

b. Why is there a blank line above the first footnote? And why does the first footnote keep using the wrong number?

c. Which footnote/endnote numbering type is being used? Is that the expected numbering type?

Write a short answer for each of the questions and fix the document so that your coworker will be happy. Save the document as **ib_w04_ techrulesarticlev1**.

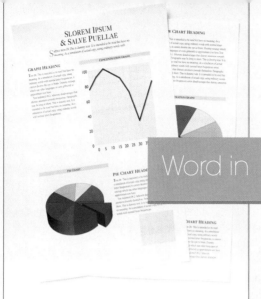

I found that graphics and pictures within business documents can be used very effectively—especially in proposals and decision documents. Furthermore, I found footnotes to be an excellent way for me to share opinions and side information in a way that didn't break up the main point I was trying to make in each paragraph. In this exercise, I share with you an early draft of description of a new product I wrote for the Board of Directors when I was working with them to decide on our next course of action.

Assignment

Open up the document ib_w04_newproductdescription. Review the placement of graphics, footnotes, headers, footers, and formatting, then consider the following points:

1. What can be done to improve this document?

2. Would a cover page be appropriate? Can you put the title in a box on the cover page?

3. Would a table of contents help the reader? Add one.

4. What kinds of graphics were included in this document? Why do you think they were included? Do the graphics need captions? Are they placed where they should be? Move them.

5. What kinds of headers and footers would work best for this document? Make sure that you could find this document again even if it is resaved and renamed. Also make sure you know who last saved it and when. Make sure anyone reading any page of the document knows that it is confidential.

6. Make sure there are page numbers and that the content starts on page one, whereas the cover page has no page number and the table of contents has page *i* at the bottom.

7. Do you think the choice of footnotes instead of endnotes was a good one for this document? Why or why not? Convert the footnotes to endnotes.

8. What other ways do you think that this document could be improved? Find at least two more improvements to apply.

9. Save the improved version as **ib_w04_newproductdescriptionv1**.

Questions for Discussion

1. Have you ever had problems with jumping graphics? How did you deal with it? How will you deal with it now?

2. What kinds of spreadsheet graphs have you seen in business documents? What kinds of tables of numbers or ranges from Excel have you seen? Can you think of five examples of when you might need to use information from Excel in Word?

3. What are the advantages of leaving the source information in Excel, Access, or PowerPoint instead of just putting the information into Word documents? What are the disadvantages?

>> Review Questions

The following questions are related to the concepts addressed in this chapter. There are three types of questions: Short Answer, True or False, and Fill in the Blank. If your answer to a True or False question is False, write a short explanation as to why you think the statement is not true.

1. A general word that refers to line art, cartoons, drawings, pictures, and photographs is _____.

2. Which type of graphic format would you use if you needed transparency?

3. Which type of graphic format would you use if you needed to vary the encryptions percentage of a picture for different purposes?

4. Which type of graphic format would you use if you needed the highest quality but wanted to be able to compress the file?

5. When a picture loses detail information because of an encryption format, you call it _____.

6. True or False: It is a good thing when a picture pixelates.

7. True or False: You should use the highest resolution possible on your web page.

8. True or False: You can increase the resolution of a picture you downloaded from the web to increase its quality.

9. A small picture that represents a larger, higher resolution picture is called a(n) _____.

10. A title or description of a graphic in a document is known as a(n) _____.

11. To resize a graphic, you click and drag the _____ to the desired size.

12. To keep a graphic proportional while you resize it, use the _____keys.

13. When you want to refer to a figure or picture, it is best to use a(n) _____ instead of typing the figure or picture number.

14. True or False: The size and location of a graphic within a document indicates its relationship to the main topic of the document.

15. True or False: If something is parenthetical, it is critical to the main idea of a document.

16. To cut off the top of a picture, you would use the _____ icon from the _____ tab.

17. If you plan to send a document through e-mail and have pictures in it, it's a good idea to _____ when you save it.

18. True or False: A resolution of 24 ppi is plenty for printing high-quality photos.

19. The most common text wrapping choice for enabling the paragraph to flow around a picture is _____.

20. To have the most control over the position of a picture, the best text wrapping choice is _____.

21. To put a paragraph in a box in the middle of a page and have the rest of the text flow around it, you would draw a(n) _____.

22. True or False: To move a text box, you drag and drop the corner handle.

23. To include a PowerPoint slide exactly as it looks on the screen of the presentation, export the slide and use the _____ tab of the Ribbon and the _____ icon from the _____ group to get it into Word.

24. For most Excel ranges and charts, the best paste special option to use when copying is _____.

25. To "take a picture" of the entire computer screen and paste it into Word, use the keys _____.

26. To "take a picture" of the current window on the screen and paste it into Word, use the keys _____.

27. True or False: Identifying sources of information within your business documents adds credibility to your ideas.

28. Parenthetical remarks or references placed at the bottom of the page are called _____, whereas parenthetical remarks or references placed at the end of the document are called _____.

29. True or False: To delete a footnote, go into the footnote and delete the text.

The following exam is designed to test your ability to recognize and execute the Word skills presented in this chapter. Read each task carefully and follow the directions in the order they are listed. You should be able to complete this exam in 60 minutes or less.

1. Open the file ib_w04_skillsexam.

2. Under the Discussion heading, insert the photo ib_w04_hospitalpic picture.

3. Create a caption under the photo that says *Amy Jones and her mother, Margaret Jones.*

4. Make the photo smaller.

5. Crop the photo just above the people's heads.

6. Save the file as **ib_w04_skillsexamv1**.

7. Move the photo to the heading *Statement of the Problem.*

8. Wrap the text around the photo and caption.

9. Save the file as **ib_w04_skillsexamv2**.

10. Open the Excel file ib_w04_infectionrate.

11. Copy the graph to under the heading *About Infection.*

12. Place a caption under the graph.

13. Make the graph smaller.

14. Make the text wrap around the graph and caption.

15. Place a sentence in the text that refers to the graph.

16. Make sure that if you added another graph, the reference would automatically change.

17. Add a footnote to the sentence in the text you just added, identifying the source of the graph.

18. Save the file as **ib_w04_skillsexamv3**.

19. Open the PowerPoint file ib_w04_newinitiatives.

20. Copy the company logo found on the first slide to the cover page of the Word file.

21. On the last page of the Word file, insert the last slide of the ib_w04_newinitiatives file *just as it looks on the screen.*

22. Save the file as **ib_w04_skillsexamv4**.

The following questions are designed to test your ability to apply the Word skills you have learned to complete a business objective. Use your knowledge of Word as well as your creativity to answer these questions or complete these tasks. For most questions, there are several possible ways to complete the objective.

1. What sort of information is stored in spreadsheets? Databases? PowerPoint slides? Why don't we store that type of information in a Word document?

2. If you were the president of a Fortune 1000 organization and you had to prepare a presentation for a stockholders' meeting, what kinds of information would you expect to put in the handout? Create the handout for the meeting and identify in which program (Excel, Access, or PowerPoint) the information would be normally found. The handout should look professional and should include a description of the past quarter income, expense, and stock price as well as an estimate of each of them for next quarter. You might also want to include information about a new enterprise-wide computer system being implemented, including the budget and expected savings.

3. Some graphic designers are adamant that files should be stored as TIFF. Others expect to see JPG, and others want to see BPM. Can you figure out why each graphic designer is partial to their graphic format?

   In Word, open the file ib_w04_peacesensing and place a picture of the first slide from ib_w04_peacesensingpresentation at the top of the first page with the text wrapped around it. Add a caption. Change the format of the heading styles so that they are all underlined and a serif font. Save the file and name it **ib_w04_peacesensingv7**.

4. In Word, open the file ib_w04_peacesensingv7. Open the Excel spreadsheet ib_w04_peacesensingfinances. Copy the assumptions from the **Curriculum Developers** tab to an appropriate place within the Word document. Add a cover page, as well as a table of contents and more appropriate headers and footers to the Word document. Save the file and name it **ib_w04_peacesensingv8**.

>> Chapter 1

Introduction

Chapter Goals

Few software programs have elevated the importance of desktop computers for business managers as much as Microsoft Excel. Similar to the way they use e-mail, business managers use Excel every day to accomplish their daily routines and objectives. This chapter provides a general overview of Excel and the reasons it is such a vital tool for business managers. The rest of the chapters in this text will illustrate how Excel is used to complete business objectives in fields that include, but are not limited to, marketing, transportation, finance, manufacturing, and accounting. It is important to note the basic terminology covered in this chapter because it will be referenced throughout the text.

>> Excel Skill Sets

Excel in Practice | Anecdote

Excel in Business

Over the course of my career, I have experienced how information systems have changed the ways in which business professionals manage data and make decisions. I am often amazed when I think back to the beginning of my career and remember the analytical projects I used to do on paper. Doing these same projects on paper today would be unthinkable. Excel played a significant role in this transformation. In fact, the ways in which I used Excel throughout my career seemed to grow every year. I initially used Excel once in a while to project the monthly sales of my department. However, it was not long before I was using Excel every day to complete objectives such as managing inventory, tracking orders, communicating production plans, or developing sales strategies.

Throughout this text I will be using this anecdote section to share my professional experiences and explain how I use Excel to make decisions, analyze data, or communicate information in business. I have used Excel to complete business objectives in industries such as fashion, grocery, food, toys, finance, and technology. At the beginning of each chapter, I will share an experience describing how I used Excel to manage or complete a specific business objective. At the end of each chapter, you will have an opportunity to use Excel to complete a similar business objective. These are all real business objectives and situations that actually happened in my career, and you may be faced with these same objectives at some point in your own career.

>> Continued on page 377

≫ What Is Excel?

The focus of this text will be to illustrate how you can use Excel to complete a variety of business objectives. However, it is important to understand why Excel was created and the need it fulfills for business managers. In addition, you will need a basic understanding of the ways commands and features are accessed and activated. This section provides a fundamental definition of Excel and illustrates its basic functionality.

Why Are We Here?

In its most basic form, Excel is an electronic version of a paper *spreadsheet*. The primary use of any spreadsheet is to record numeric and text *data* for the purposes of making calculations, analyzing results, or tracking and storing information. As mentioned in the anecdote, before the use of electronic spreadsheets such as Excel, spreadsheets were created by hand on paper. Figure 1.1 shows an example of a paper spreadsheet. Notice that it consists of numbered columns and rows. Each digit of a number is written in a separate rectangle on the spreadsheet. An Excel spreadsheet has a similar purpose and design.

Figure 1.1 | **Example of Paper Spreadsheet**

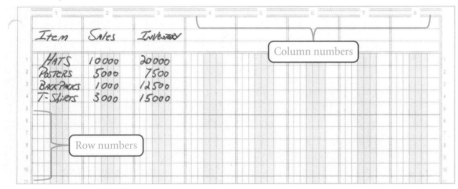

Figure 1.2 shows an example of a sales analysis project for 100 items sold in a small retail store. Because this project was done on a paper spreadsheet, the sales results for all 100 items are written by hand. In addition, a cumulative total is added in the second column to show the total after adding the sales results for each item. As a result, 100 calculations were performed using a calculator and added to the spreadsheet by hand. Just think how long it would take to write 100 numbers and make 100 calculations for this simple project.

Figure 1.2 | **Sales Project Done on Paper Spreadsheet**

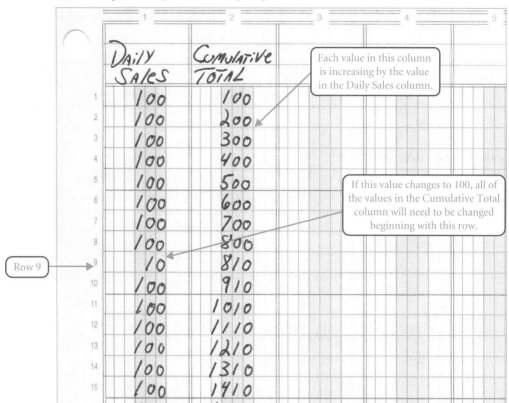

Now, let's assume you completed the spreadsheet shown in Figure 1.2 and noticed that the sales result in row 9 should be 100 instead of 10. After you erase this mistake and write the correct entry, you will have to recalculate all the values in the Cumulative Total column beginning with row 9. This means you will have to erase, recalculate, and rewrite 92 numbers. However, if you did this same project in Excel, the Cumulative Total column would automatically be adjusted after you typed the correct value into row 9. In fact, an Excel spreadsheet could be created such that if any of the numbers in your project are changed, all computations will automatically produce new outputs in a fraction of a second. This is what makes Excel extremely valuable for making business decisions and sets it apart from a paper spreadsheet.

Figure 1.3 shows how the project in Figure 1.2 appears in Excel. Notice that the column and row configuration are similar to the paper spreadsheet. However, letters are used to label each column instead of numbers.

Figure 1.3 | **Example of Project in an Excel Spreadsheet**

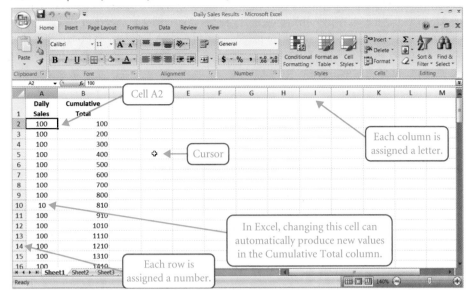

Another similarity between Figures 1.2 and 1.3 is that both spreadsheets are filled with small rectangles. In Excel, these rectangles are known as *cells*, which is the intersection of a row and column. Data is typed into these cells as opposed to being handwritten, as shown in Figure 1.2. Each cell has a specific address called the *cell location*, which is the column letter followed by the row number. In Figure 1.3, cell location A2 is activated. This is called cell *A2* because it is in column A and row 2.

Cell locations play a critical role when calculating data in Excel. If you were conducting mathematical computations using a calculator, you would enter numbers and mathematical operators to produce a result. With Excel, you will usually use cell locations, such as A2, instead of numbers when conducting the same mathematical computations. If the number in cell A2 is changed, Excel will automatically produce a new output. This is called *cell referencing*, and it is this concept that gives Excel its power. You will learn more details about mathematical computations in Chapter 3.

A Decision-Making Tool

Business managers are often required to make numerous decisions in uncertain environments. These decisions can range from buying a publicly traded stock to calculating how many pairs of jeans to buy for a clothing store. In making these decisions, a business manager might ask questions such as "What if the stock market declines after buying a particular stock?" or "What if I don't buy enough jeans to satisfy the sales potential of a store?" These questions form the basis of *what-if scenarios*. Business managers use what-if scenarios to understand how potential outcomes will impact the decisions they make. For example, a business manager who is buying a publicly traded stock might calculate how much he stands to lose if the stock declines 5%, 10%, or 20%. On the other hand, he could also calculate how much he could gain if the stock increases 5%, 10%, or 20%. Calculating these declines and increases equates to a total of six possible scenarios or outcomes to consider before making this decision. This manager could use Excel to calculate the results of each scenario by simply changing one number.

Most business executives would agree that information is power. Excel can be used to produce and evaluate far more information over a shorter period of time compared to paper spreadsheets. This fulfills a critical need for business managers to make informed decisions, which is usually a prerequisite for completing most business objectives. A variety of these objectives will be examined throughout this text as commands and applications are reviewed in each chapter.

An Overview of Excel

When you first launch the Excel application, you will see a blank spreadsheet or worksheet, as shown in Figure 1.4. The term *worksheet* is used to describe one page of an Excel file or workbook. The term *workbook* refers to the entire Excel file that contains a collection of worksheets. You can switch from one worksheet to another by clicking the tabs at the bottom of the screen. Each worksheet has a capacity of over 1 million rows and over 16,000 columns.

Figure 1.4 | **Blank Excel Worksheet**

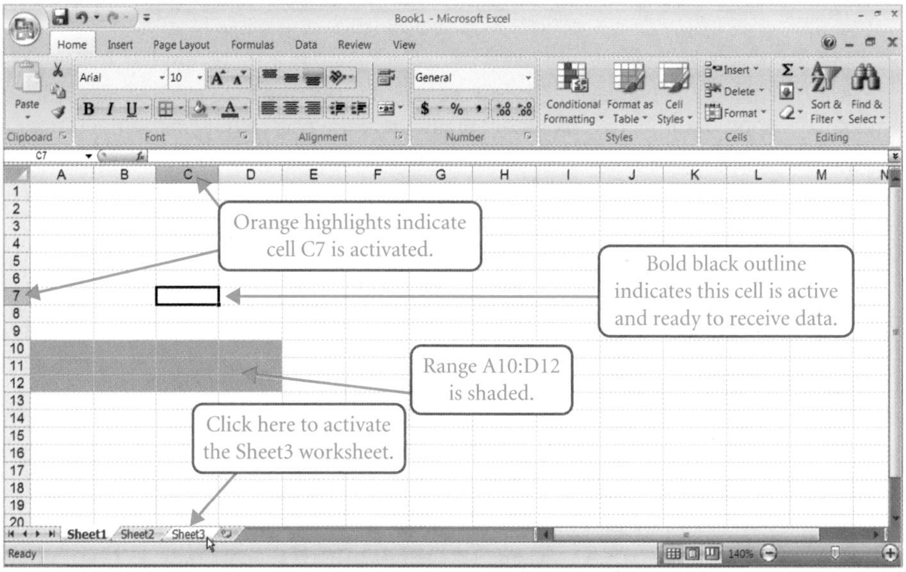

As shown in Figure 1.4, the highlighted column letter and row number indicate which cell is currently active. Notice that column letter C and row number 7 are highlighted in orange, indicating that cell C7 is active and ready to receive data. The cell is also outlined with a bold black line, which also indicates it is active. To activate other cells, use the arrow keys on your keyboard to move the black outline or move the cursor with the mouse and left click on a cell. You also can use your mouse to activate several cells or a range of cells at one time by left clicking and dragging. The term *range* refers to a group of cells on a worksheet and is noted by any two cell locations separated by a colon. For example, Figure 1.4 shows the range A10:D12 highlighted.

Ribbon, Tabs, and Icons

Excel commands and features are contained in the area at the top of the screen called the *Ribbon*. As shown in Figure 1.5, the Ribbon consists of several *icons* arranged in related groups that are used to activate any Excel command. For example, the **Number** group of icons is used to format any numbers that are typed into the cells of a worksheet. If you are familiar with Microsoft Word, you already know how to use many of these icons. For example, Excel icons such as **Save**, **Copy**, **Paste**, and **Bold** are identical to Word's icons.

Along the top of the Ribbon are several *tabs*. Each tab opens a separate page of the Ribbon that contains a different set of icons. Additional tabs will automatically be added to the Ribbon if you are working with special objects such as charts or text boxes. You will learn how to use the commands in each tab of the Ribbon throughout this text. The following is a brief description for each of the tabs shown in Figure 1.5:

- **Home**: Contains fundamental commands that are most frequently used when working in Excel. Commonly used icons such as **Copy** and **Paste** as well as formatting icons such as **Bold** and **Italics** are found in this tab.
- **Insert**: Contains commands used when inserting objects such as charts, circles, or arrows onto a worksheet.
- **Page Layout**: Provides access to commands used to prepare a worksheet for printing.
- **Formulas**: Provides access to mathematical functions and formula auditing tools.
- **Data**: Provides access to sorting commands. In addition, this tab contains features used to import data from external sources such as Microsoft Access.
- **Review**: Provides access to commands such as Spell Check and Track Changes.
- **View**: Contains commands used for adjusting the visual appearance of your Excel screen. For example, this tab contains the **Zoom** icon, which is identical to the **Zoom** icon in Microsoft Word.

Figure 1.5 shows icons that are contained in the **Home** tab of the Ribbon. Notice that when the cursor is placed over the **Copy** icon, a description of the command appears on the worksheet.

Figure 1.5 | **The Home Tab of the Ribbon**

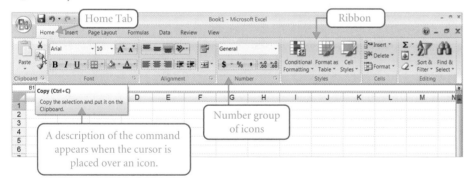

In addition to using the Ribbon, you can also access Excel commands through the *Quick Access Toolbar*. The **Quick Access Toolbar** contains a few commonly used icons such as **Save** and **Undo**. As you can see in Figure 1.6, you can add additional icons by clicking the down arrow on the right side of the toolbar and selecting one of the commands listed in the menu or by clicking the **More Commands** option.

Figure 1.6 | **The Quick Access Toolbar**

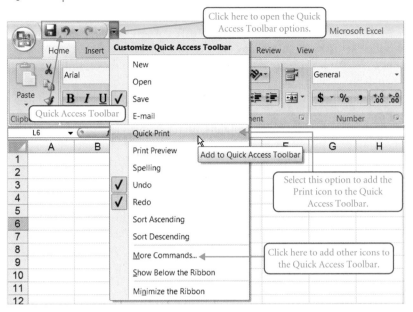

The File Menu

If you have worked with previous versions of Microsoft Excel, such as Microsoft Excel 2003, you may have noticed that something was missing when you first looked at Figure 1.3. There are no drop-down menus. The drop-down menus have been replaced with the Ribbon system, which provides faster access to the commands you need. However, one drop-down menu does exist in this version of Excel: The **File** menu. The file menu is opened by clicking the **Office Button** as shown in figure 1.7. Use the **File** menu for executing tasks such as opening existing Excel workbooks, creating new workbooks, or printing worksheets. Figure 1.7 shows the commands that are available in the **File** menu.

Figure 1.7 | **Commands in the File Menu**

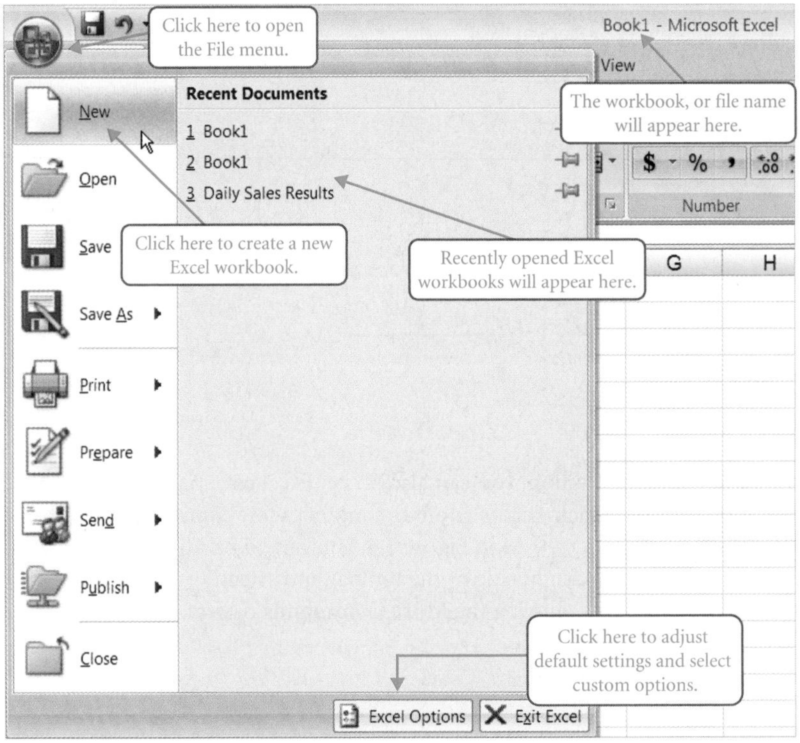

Excel 97-2003 File Format

It is important to note that the **Save As** command is found in the **File** menu. If you are working with people who are using older versions of Microsoft Excel, you will need to save your workbooks in the Excel 97–2003 format. Someone who is using Microsoft Office 2003 will not be able to open workbooks saved in the 2007 format. You save files in this format as follows:

- Open an existing Excel workbook or create a new one (see Figure 1.7).
- Click the **Office Button**.
- Click the arrow pointing to the right next to the **Save As** option.
- Select the **Excel 97-2003 Workbook** option on the right side of the **File** menu (see Figure 1.8).

Figure 1.8 shows an Excel workbook that has been saved in the Excel 97–2003 format. Notice at the top of the Excel screen the words [**Compatibility Mode**] appear next to the workbook name. This naming convention indicates that the workbook is compatible with older versions of Excel. In addition, notice that the **Convert** option appears in the **File** menu list of options. Select this option to convert a workbook saved in an older version of Excel to the 2007 version.

Figure 1.8 | **Saving a Workbook in Excel 97–2003 Format**

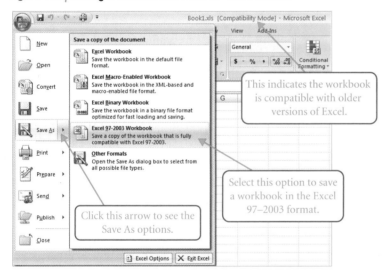

Right Click and Control Keys

If you have experience using older versions of Excel, you may be accustomed to accessing commands by right clicking or using Control keys. Both options are available in the 2007 version of Excel.

Right clicking provides you with the option of accessing a variety of commands without having to go to the Ribbon. As previously mentioned, older versions of Excel utilized a system of drop-down menus to access various Excel commands. Depending on the command you needed, you may have clicked through several drop-down menus

Quick Reference

Saving in Excel 97-2003 File Format

1. Open an existing Excel workbook or create a new one.
2. Click the **Office Button**.
3. Click the arrow to the right of the **Save As** option.
4. Click the **Excel 97-2003 Workbook** option on the right side of the **File** menu.
5. Select a location and type a file name in the **Save As** dialog box.

to complete a task. However, the Ribbon system in the 2007 version of Excel considerably reduces the amount of clicking you need to do before activating a command. Therefore, you may or may not find right clicking useful. Figure 1.9 shows the Excel commands and icons that appear after the right mouse button is clicked on a worksheet. These options will change when you are working with other objects on a worksheet such as charts or text boxes.

Figure 1.9 | **Options When Right Clicking**

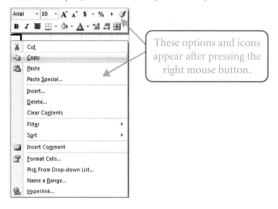

As mentioned, the other option for accessing Excel commands is through Control keys. In the earliest version of Microsoft Office, using Control keys was the primary method for accessing commands. That is, you activated a command by holding down the **Ctrl** key on your keyboard and pressing a letter or character. You can still use this system in Microsoft Office 2007. For several icons in the Ribbon, there is a corresponding **Ctrl** key combination. In fact, notice that the description for the **Copy** icon in Figure 1.5 shows that this command can also be activated by holding down the **Ctrl** key and pressing the letter C.

Settings and Status Bar

You have the ability to customize the settings and *Status Bar* of the Excel screen. For example, when you first open Excel, all data typed into a worksheet will have a Calibri font style with an 11-point font size. However, you can change this to whatever font style and font size you wish. The following explains how to change these settings:

- Click the **Office Button**.
- Click the **Excel Options** button at the bottom of the menu (see Figure 1.7). This will open the **Excel Options** dialog box.
- Click the **Popular** option on the left side of the **Excel Options** dialog box.
- Click the down arrow next to the **Use this font** option. This option can be found under the section heading **When creating new workbooks**.
- Select a new font style.
- Click the **OK** button at the bottom of the dialog box. For some settings, you may have to close and reopen Excel for any change to take place.

Figure 1.10 shows the options in the **Popular** section of the **Excel Options** dialog box. Notice that there are several other options you can adjust to customize the settings of your Excel screen such as the font size and your user name.

Figure 1.10 | **Excel Options Dialog Box**

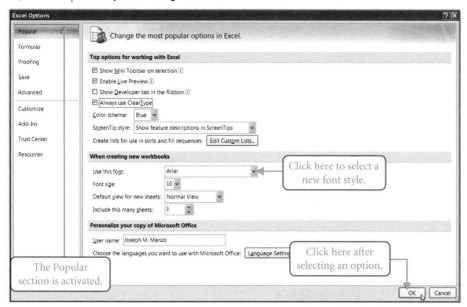

You can also customize the appearance of the Status bar at the bottom of the Excel screen. The Status bar in Figure 1.11 contains shortcuts for switching between various views as well as the Zoom Slider. To change what is displayed on the Status bar, place the cursor anywhere in the Status bar and right click. This will open the list of options shown in Figure 1.11.

Figure 1.11 | **Status Bar Options List**

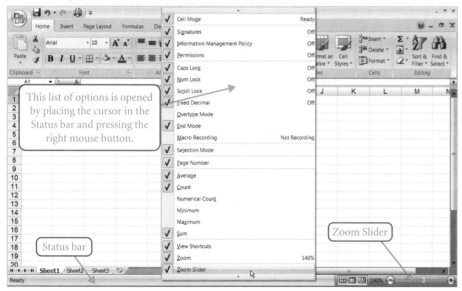

> **Quick Reference**

**Changing the Font
Setting for New
Workbooks**

1. Open a blank Excel
   workbook.
2. Click the **Office Button**.
3. Click the **Excel Options**
   button.
4. Click the **Popular** section
   on the left side of the
   Excel Options dialog
   box.
5. Select a font style and size
   in the **When creating
   new workbooks** sec-
   tion of the **Excel Options**
   dialog box.
6. Click the **OK** button at the
   bottom of the dialog box.

Excel Help

The last area that will be covered in this introduction to Excel is the **Help** window. The **Help** window is a reference tool that you can use to research various Excel commands. To open the **Help** window, click the **Help** icon, as shown in Figure 1.12. Then type a question or topic in the input box of the **Help** window and press the **Enter** key or click the **Search** button. You will then see a list of links that contain topics related to what you typed into the input box. Click a link to see instructions and information related to your topic.

Figure 1.12 | **The Help Window**

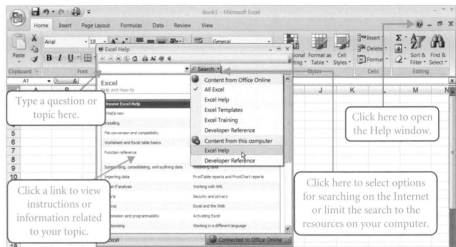

>> Introduction to Excel

This workshop is the first of several that will be presented in this text. These workshops serve two purposes. The first is to give you an opportunity to practice the skills illustrated in each section of every chapter. The second is to watch the author demonstrate these skills. Many people have an easier time learning software skills after they see techniques and commands demonstrated. You can watch a video demonstration of each workshop by opening the related video file. Each workshop will usually require you to open an Excel file so that you can complete the tasks listed. However, there is no Excel file required for this workshop.

The purpose of this workshop is to open a blank Excel workbook and examine a few of the basic features that were described in this chapter. Try completing each task and then watch the video named **Introduction**.

1. **Open Excel (Video: Introduction)**

   a. Launch the Excel application.

   b. Use the up and down arrows to activate cell C7.

   c. Use the mouse to activate cell E3.

   d. Highlight the range B5:G10.

   e. Click each tab of the Ribbon and view the icons that are showing in each tab.

   f. Click the **Office Button** and save your workbook in Excel 97–2003 format. Save the workbook to any location on your computer and use any file name you wish.

   g. Activate **Sheet2** by clicking the worksheet tab.

   h. Use the Zoom Slider to increase the zoom to 140%.

   i. Open the **Help** window.

   j. Change the Search Option in the **Help** window to
      `Excel Help - Content from this computer`.

   k. Close the **Help** window.

   l. Close your workbook and then close Excel.

>> An Introduction to Cell Referencing

This exercise is the first of several that are presented in each section of this text. The purpose of these exercises is to show how Excel skills are applied to typical business situations. These exercises will also illustrate how to use Excel's cell referencing capabilities to construct multiple scenarios or outcomes depending on the business objective. In addition to the exercise format that is presented here, you will also see an exercise that asks you to fix a spreadsheet that has errors. This exercise will come under the heading "What's Wrong with This Spreadsheet?"

Exercise

Cell referencing is Excel's most critical feature because it allows you to produce many mathematical outputs by changing just one or many inputs. The purpose of this exercise is to provide an introduction to Excel by looking at how cell referencing is used in the sales project example from the beginning of the chapter. You will need to open the file named ib_e01_dailysalesresults before completing the tasks in this exercise.

1. Activate cell A10. The number in this cell should be 10. Notice that the number in cell B10 is 810. This number is the result of a formula that takes the number in cell A10 and adds it to the value in cell B9. Each number in column B is calculated by similar formulas. Creating formulas in Excel will be covered in Chapter 3.

2. After activating cell A10, type the number **100**.

3. Press the **Enter** key. The number in cell B10 should change to 900, and every cell below B10 should also change. This is an example of how cell referencing is able to change many outputs by changing just one input.

4. Save and close your file.

Few tools changed my job performance and decision-making abilities like Excel. With Excel, I was able to evaluate large amounts of information in a fraction of the time it took using a calculator and paper spreadsheet. I was not only more productive, but also more confident about the recommendations and decisions I made. Although the amount of time I spent ensuring that my results were accurate remained the same, once I started using Excel, there was no way I could ever consider going back to paper.

Questions for Discussion

1. Could a company gain a competitive advantage in its respective industry by having access to more information over its competitors? Why?

2. Does having more information automatically result in better business decisions?

3. The author mentioned that the amount of time ensuring the accuracy of results remained the same. Why wouldn't Excel automatically increase the accuracy of analytical projects?

4. The author mentions that after he started using electronic spreadsheets he could never consider going back to paper. Why do you think this is so?

This section features questions that will help you review the key concepts and skills that were presented in the chapter. There will always be a mix of Fill in the Blank, True or False, or Short Answer questions. For the True or False questions, if you think an answer is false, provide a short explanation as to why you think the phrase or comment is false.

1. Multiple outcomes or potential results are also known as_____.

2. What methods can you use to activate a cell?

3. True or False: An Excel file is made up of multiple workbooks.

4. A _____ is two cell locations separated by a colon.

5. Excel's capability to automatically produce new mathematical outputs when one or more inputs are changed is possible because of _____.

6. Commands used to prepare a worksheet for printing can be found in the _____ tab of the Ribbon.

7. True or False: The **Quick Access Toolbar** can contain only four icons, and it must always appear at the top of the Ribbon.

8. You must click the_____ to activate various worksheets in a workbook.

9. Explain how you would open an existing workbook that is saved on your computer.

10. What could you do if you need to send an Excel workbook to someone who is using the 2003 version of Excel?

The Skills Exam section will also be included at the end of each chapter and is used to test your knowledge of executing various skills presented in the text. As mentioned, the primary mission of this book is to explain and demonstrate how Excel is used to complete objectives in the field of business. However, knowing how to execute key skills that are required to operate Excel is also important. This section will present several skill-based questions that you will have to apply to an Excel workbook. Because this is an introductory chapter, the Skills Exams will begin at the end of Chapter 2.

This section will follow the Skills Exam section and feature questions that require you to apply the skills you have learned to complete typical business objectives. There is usually no right or wrong method for completing the objectives presented in this section. However, the results you obtain must be accurate. This section might also include questions that ask you to identify how Excel or spreadsheets play a role in the success of a business or in the decision-making process of a business.

1. Identify three specific electronic devices or computer software programs that have changed the way you do things to such an extent that you cannot imagine living life without them? Explain the needs these devices or programs satisfy and the benefits they provide.

>> Chapter 2

Excel Basics

Chapter Goals

Chapter 1 provided an overview of Excel and its benefits. This chapter covers the following basic Excel skills you need to begin creating an Excel spreadsheet: data entry, copy and paste, formatting, editing, and printing. It also features two common types of spreadsheets used in business: Financial Plans and Merchandise Sales Reports. It is important to note that business terms such as Gross Sales, Cost of Goods Sold, Gross Profit, and Unit Sales will be mentioned but not explained in detail. These terms are commonly used in the business world and will be covered in depth in your core business courses.

>> Excel | Skill Sets

Excel in **Practice** | Anecdote

The Role of a Production Planning Manager

You may think that in business, information is processed and communicated electronically. This is the 21st century, after all. Imagine my surprise when not all that long ago I started working as a production planning manager for a large apparel manufacturing company that produced thousands of garments every year. My role was to manage all of the production plans sent to our offices in China—a seemingly straightforward task, except for the fact that the production plans were handwritten on 17" x 14" paper spreadsheets, reduced in a copy machine, and mailed overnight to China. Each garment had a separate production plan that documented every detail: buttons, color, fabric, labels, zippers, and packaging. And guess what happened if a designer decided to use corduroy instead of denim at the last minute? Out came the correction fluid, followed by a trip to the mailroom for another costly overnight delivery. Communicating information in this cumbersome way was simply part of the company's culture, which I inherited. However, after gallons of correction fluid (and lots of noxious fumes), I decided there had to be a better way to track and communicate this information.

>> Continued on page 428

The different ways Excel spreadsheets are used in business are too numerous to count. However, using spreadsheets to track the sales results of retail merchandise or to create a financial plan are probably the most common. With regards to tracking and planning financial data, business managers typically use spreadsheets to evaluate whether a company is achieving its financial goals in a current year or to plan its financial goals for future years. This section illustrates how you can use Excel's data management skills to begin constructing these spreadsheets. In fact, data management skills such as entering data, adjusting the widths of columns and rows, copying and pasting, and sorting are typically needed in the early stages of developing any spreadsheet.

Data Entry

Data entry is the most basic and fundamental Excel skill. The term *data* refers to any numbers or text items that will be analyzed or displayed on a spreadsheet. In a financial plan, the text items usually typed into an Excel worksheet include a title and the financial category labels, such as Gross Sales, Net Sales, Cost of Goods Sold, and so on. To type a title into a worksheet, do the following:

- Open a blank workbook.
- Activate cell A1 by left clicking it with the mouse, or use the keyboard arrow key to move the black outline to cell A1. The black outline indicates an active cell.
- Type the words Financial Plan.
- Enter the title into cell A1 by performing one of the following actions:
  - Press the **Enter** key.
  - Press one of the arrow keys.
  - Left click another cell location.

Figure 2.1 shows the title entered into cell A1 as well as the financial category labels entered into cells A3 through A7.

Figure 2.1 | **Building a Worksheet for Financial Planning**

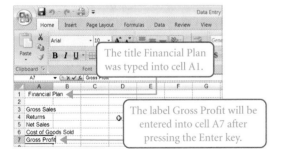

> The title Financial Plan was typed into cell A1.

> The label Gross Profit will be entered into cell A7 after pressing the Enter key.

COMMON MISTAKES | Data Entry

The most common data entry mistake is forgetting to press the **Enter** key after typing an entry. *Data will not be entered into a cell unless you press the **Enter** or arrow keys.* Other data entry mistakes typically occur from typing the wrong number or transposing numbers. For example, the number 253 could be *transposed* as 235. Always proofread your spreadsheet for any data entry errors.

When you are entering numeric data, it is good practice to omit any symbols, such as commas. Future chapters will address the use of formulas and functions when you are developing an Excel spreadsheet. Typing commas to separate thousands (for example, 10,000) for numbers used in functions will prevent the function from working or produce erroneous results. The next section of this chapter reviews how to add symbols, such as commas, dollar signs, percent signs, and so on, to numbers typed into a worksheet.

Auto Fill

Commonly used in data entry tasks, **Auto Fill** automatically completes a set of data points that are in sequential order, such as numbers, years, months, or days of the week. With regards to the Financial Plan worksheet shown in Figure 2.1, the years 2008 through 2012 will be entered in cells B2 through F2. You can use the **Auto Fill** feature to complete this sequence of years by typing only the first two years in cells B2 and C2. The following points explain how this is accomplished.

- Type the year 2008 in cell B2 and 2009 in cell C2. Two sequential data points must be entered into two adjacent cells to use **Auto Fill**. For example, when completing a series of numbers in 100 unit increments, enter the number 100 into one cell and 200 in another. For creating a daily schedule, enter the word Monday in one cell and Tuesday in another.

- Highlight cells B2 and C2. To use the **Auto Fill** feature, you must have highlighted two cells containing sequential data.

- Place the cursor over the **Auto Fill Handle**. The **Auto Fill Handle** is the black square in the lower-right corner of a highlighted range.

- When you place the cursor over the **Auto Fill Handle**, it will change from a white plus sign to a black plus sign. When this occurs, left click and drag across to the right until the years increase to 2012 (see Figures 2.2 and 2.3).

COMMON MISTAKES | Auto Fill

Remember that to complete a sequence of data using the **Auto Fill** feature, you must highlight two or more adjacent cell locations. If you click and drag the **Auto Fill Handle** when only one cell is activated, you will duplicate the contents of this one cell to other cells without completing any sequence.

Figure 2.2 | **Typing Years into the Financial Plan Worksheet**

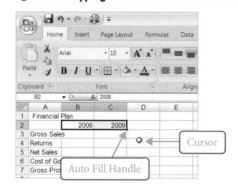

>> **Quick Reference**

Auto Fill

1. Enter sequential data into at least 2 adjacent cell locations.

2. Highlight all cell locations containing sequential data.

3. Drag the cursor over the **Auto Fill Handle**.

4. When the cursor changes from a white to a black plus sign, click and drag across or down to continue the sequence of data.

Figure 2.3 | **Using Auto Fill to Complete the Sequence of Years**

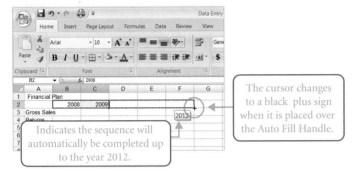

Adjusting Columns and Rows

When entering data into a spreadsheet, you may need to adjust the *column width* or *row height,* depending on the size of your entry. Entries too wide for a particular cell location may extend into one or more columns or appear truncated. For example, notice in Figure 2.1 that the Cost of Goods Sold entry in cell A6 extends into column B. However, when a number is typed into cell B6, the Cost of Goods Sold entry appears truncated, as shown in Figure 2.4.

Figure 2.4 | **Entries Too Long for a Cell Location Appear Truncated**

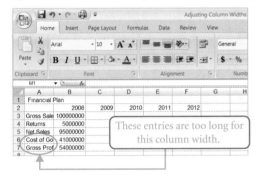

To prevent the entries shown in Figure 2.4 from being truncated, you will need to expand the width of column A. To accomplish this, do the following:

- Place the cursor between two columns.

- When the cursor changes from a white plus sign to a double black arrow, left click and drag to increase or decrease the column width (see Figure 2.5).

- Alternatively, when the cursor changes from a white plus sign to a double black arrow, double click with the left mouse button, and the column will automatically expand to fit the longest entry that has been typed. This method is especially helpful when you're working with large spreadsheets where you cannot see the largest entry on your screen.

Figure 2.5 | **Using the Cursor to Adjust Column Width**

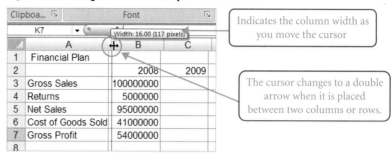

Indicates the column width as you move the cursor

The cursor changes to a double arrow when it is placed between two columns or rows.

COMMON MISTAKES | Columns Too Narrow for Numbers

When entering numbers into a worksheet that is too long for the width of a column, you may see the symbols shown in Figures 2.6 and 2.7.

People often think these symbols are errors. However, they simply mean the column is too narrow to fit the number entered into the cell. Excel will not truncate numbers if a column is too narrow because you could be misled into thinking the number is a smaller value than reality. Therefore, increase the width of a column to remove scientific notation or "######" signs.

Figure 2.6 | **Scientific Notation When Number Is Too Wide for Column**

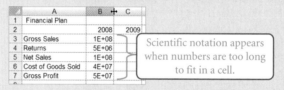

Scientific notation appears when numbers are too long to fit in a cell.

Figure 2.7 | **"#####" Signs When Number Is Too Wide for Column**

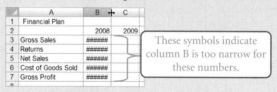

These symbols indicate column B is too narrow for these numbers.

Similar to adjusting the width of a column, you may need to adjust the height of a row to show that cell's content. However, you can also use row height to highlight important information on a worksheet. For example, with regards to our example of a Financial Plan, the Gross Profit is an important financial result that can be highlighted by increasing the height of a row. The method for adjusting the height of rows is almost identical to adjusting the width of columns:

- Place the cursor between two rows.

- When the cursor changes from a white plus sign to a double black arrow, left click and drag up or down to increase or decrease the height of a row.

- Alternatively, when the cursor changes from a white plus sign to a double black arrow, double click with the left mouse button, and the row will automatically expand to fit the largest entry.

Figure 2.8 shows the Financial Plan worksheet with an expanded row 7. Notice that all of the numbers as well as the words *Gross Profit* automatically stay at the bottom of the cells when the row height is increased. This creates space between the Cost of Goods Sold numbers and the Gross Profit numbers, which makes it easier for a business manager to evaluate the Gross Profit results of this plan. Adjusting the vertical position of data within a cell is covered in more detail in the next section.

Figure 2.8 | **Using the Cursor to Increase Row Height**

	A	B	C	D	E	F
1	Financial Plan					
2		2008	2009	2010	2011	2012
3	Gross Sales	100000000	110000000	120000000	140000000	160000000
4	Returns	5000000	5500000	6000000		
5	Net Sales	95000000	104500000	114000000	13...	
6	Cost of Goods Sold	41000000	45100000	49200000	57400000	65600000
7	Gross Profit	54000000	59400000	64800000	75600000	86400000
8						

The increased height of this row accents the Gross Profit results.

Height: 20.25 (27 pixels)

Click and drag up or down to adjust the row height.

An alternative way of changing the width of columns or the height of rows is to use the **Format** icon in the **Home** tab of the Ribbon (see Figure 2.9). Clicking the **Format** icon will open the following options.

- **Row Height:** Use to set a specific height for a row or group of rows. You must highlight at least one cell location in every row you intend to change *before* selecting this option. After you select this option, a dialog box will appear, asking you to enter a specific height number (the higher the number, the greater the height).
- **Auto Fit Row Height:** This option is identical to double clicking the cursor when it is placed between two rows. The height of rows containing cell locations that have been highlighted will automatically adjust to fit any data entries.
- **Column Width:** Use to set a specific column width. You must highlight at least one cell in every column you intend to change before selecting this option. After you select this option, a dialog box will appear, asking you to enter a specific width number (the higher the number, the wider the column).
- *Auto Fit Column Width:* This option automatically changes the width of a column to fit the width of the longest entered data. You must highlight at least one cell in each column to apply this option.
- **Default Width:** Use to set a specific width for every column in a spreadsheet. Since every column is being formatted, you don't need to highlight any cells to apply this option.

Figure 2.9 | **Using the Ribbon to Change Column Width and Row Height**

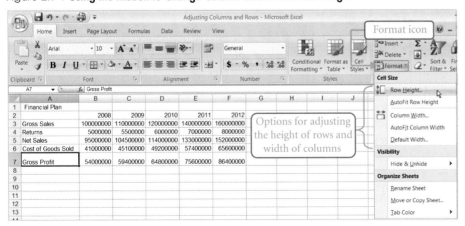

> **Quick Reference**

Adjusting Column Widths

1. Place the cursor between 2 columns.
2. Click and drag to desired width or double click to automatically set to the widest data point.

Or

1. Highlight at least one cell in the columns you want to change.
2. Click the **Home** tab of the Ribbon.
3. Click the **Format** icon.
4. Select **Column Width**.
5. Enter a desired width number in the **Column Width** dialog box.
6. Click the **OK** button.

> **Quick Reference**

Adjusting Row Heights

1. Place the cursor between 2 rows.
2. Click and drag to desired height or double click to automatically set to the largest data point.

Or

1. Highlight at least one cell in the rows you want to change.
2. Click the **Home** tab of the Ribbon.
3. Click the **Format** icon.
4. Select **Row Height**.
5. Enter a desired height number in the **Row Height** dialog box.
6. Click the **OK** button.

Hiding Columns and Rows

In some situations you may want to hide a column or row in a worksheet. Hiding certain columns or rows might make a worksheet easier to read, depending on its use. For example, if someone was interested only in using the Financial Plan worksheet (see Figure 2.8) to compare the years 2008 and 2012, columns containing data for the years 2009 through 2011 can be hidden from view. The following points explain how to hide these columns:

- Highlight the range C1:E1. At least one cell in each column you wish to hide must be highlighted. It does not matter which row number is highlighted.
- Click the **Home** tab of the Ribbon.
- Click the **Format** icon.
- Click the **Hide & Unhide** option. This will open a submenu of options showing items that you can hide or unhide.
- Select the **Hide Columns** option.

Figure 2.10 shows the Financial Plan worksheet with columns C, D, and E hidden from view. Notice that the column letters at the top of the worksheet grid are out of sequence.

Figure 2.10 | **Hiding Columns**

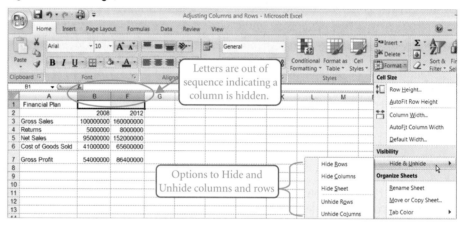

COMMON MISTAKES | Checking for Hidden Columns and Rows

Always check for hidden columns and rows when you're working with an Excel file that was created by someone else. People often spend time re-creating or adding data to a worksheet because it appears to be missing when in fact it is contained in a hidden column or row. Remember that the column letters at the top of a worksheet or row numbers along the left side of a worksheet will be out of sequence if a column or row is hidden.

Hiding columns is a valuable feature because you do not have to move or delete data from a worksheet you may need in the future. With regards to the Financial Plan worksheet in Figure 2.10, you can always unhide columns C through E when needed, which is accomplished as follows:

- Highlight a cell on the left and right of the hidden column. Notice in Figure 2.10, cell locations B1 and F1 are highlighted. The reason is that both cell locations border the columns that are hidden.
- Click the **Home** tab of the Ribbon.
- Click the **Format** icon.
- Click the **Hide & Unhide** option.
- Select **Unhide Columns**.

Copy and Paste

The *Copy* and *Paste* commands are perhaps the most convenient and commonly used Excel commands. This section demonstrates these commands using both a Merchandise Sales Report and the Financial Plan worksheet (created in Figures 2.1 through 2.10).

The purpose of the Merchandise Sales Report in this example is to show the sales results for products sold in an apparel retail store. The first few items in the report are from the Tops category. Here, we will use the **Copy** and **Paste** commands instead of typing the word "Tops" several times in the Category column:

- Activate cell A2 (see Figure 2.11). Before copying data, you must activate the cell or range of cells you need duplicated. In this example, the word *Tops* in cell A2 must be duplicated 4 times.
- Click the **Home** tab of the Ribbon.
- Click the **Copy** icon (see Figure 2.11).
- Highlight the range A3:A6. After clicking the **Copy** icon, highlight the cell, or range of cells, where the data needs to be duplicated.
- Click the **Paste** icon (see Figure 2.12). After you click the **Paste** icon, the word "Tops" will appear in cells A3 through A6.

Figure 2.11 | **Copying Data on the Merchandise Sales Report**

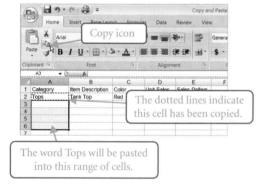

Figure 2.12 | **Pasting Data**

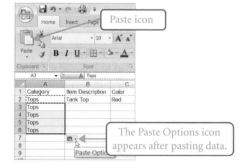

It is important to note that the **Paste** icon pastes all data and formats from the cell that was copied. However, you can choose various pasting options by clicking the smaller **Paste Options** icon, which appears on your worksheet each time you click the

Paste icon. These options are also referred to as **Paste Special** options and will be covered in the next chapter.

Data can also be duplicated using the **Auto Fill Handle**. As previously mentioned, **Auto Fill** is usually used to complete a sequence of data when two cells are highlighted. However, if you click and drag on the **Auto Fill Handle** when only one cell location is activated, the contents of that cell will be duplicated to other cell locations (see Figure 2.13).

Figure 2.13 | **Using Auto Fill to Duplicate Data**

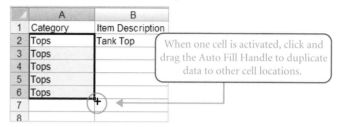

Another common use of the **Copy** and **Paste** commands is to create duplicate copies of an entire worksheet. Business managers can use this technique to create different scenarios for sales plans or business strategies. For example, a sales manager might need to develop three different scenarios showing the potential sales results for a region of retail stores. A financial planning manager might want to show a base case, worst case, or best case scenario for a company's profit plan. In these situations, a base worksheet is created and then copied and pasted into several blank worksheets. Once the worksheet is duplicated, the data can be changed to reflect the various scenarios for a particular business situation.

The following example explains how you use the **Copy** and **Paste** commands to create different versions for the example of the Financial Plan:

- Highlight the entire worksheet by clicking the box in the upper-left corner of Sheet1 (see Figure 2.14).

Figure 2.14 | **Copying an Entire Worksheet**

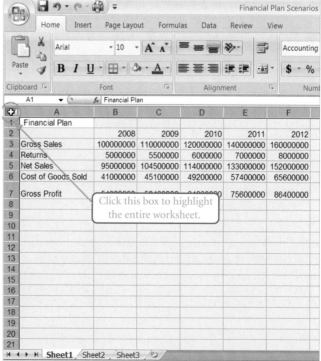

- Click the **Home** tab of the Ribbon.
- Click the **Copy** icon to copy the entire contents of the worksheet.
- Click the Sheet2 worksheet tab and activate cell A1. When pasting the contents of an entire worksheet, you must activate cell A1; otherwise, Excel will produce an error message.
- Click the **Paste** icon (see Figure 2.15).

Figure 2.15 | **Pasting an Entire Worksheet**

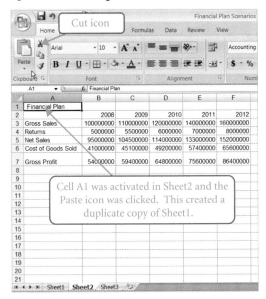

In some cases you may want to remove contents from one area of a worksheet and paste it to another. For these situations you can use the Cut command, which is activated by clicking the scissors icon in the **Home** tab of the Ribbon. After clicking the **Cut** icon, activate a cell or range of cells where the data should be replaced and click the **Paste** icon.

Sorting Data (Single Level)

After you construct a spreadsheet, you may need to sort the data. *Sorting* is one of the most critical Excel commands because it can rearrange data in a specific sequence or rank that enables business managers to assess information efficiently and make key decisions. For example, retail managers use sorting to rank merchandise based on sales results. This allows them to identify top-selling items that should be reordered as well as low-selling items that should be discontinued. Finance managers may rank a list of public companies with the highest shareholder return. This could help them identify stocks that should either be purchased or sold. Sorting data in Excel can be broken down into two broad categories: single level and multiple level. This segment will focus on single-level sorting, and the following segment will focus on multiple-level sorting.

Figure 2.16 shows the completed Merchandise Sales worksheet originally started in Figure 2.11. As previously mentioned, a retail manager might sort the items in this worksheet based on the Unit Sales column. If the manager wanted to identify the best-selling items, this data could be sorted so items with the highest unit sales appear at the top of the worksheet (*descending order*). If the manager wanted to identify the lowest-selling items, this data could be sorted so items with the lowest unit sales appear at the top of the worksheet (*ascending order*). These sorting options are considered single level because one column of data is used as the basis for ranking the items. The following explains how you sort the worksheet in Figure 2.16 in descending order:

- Activate any cell location that contains a number in column D. Since the goal is to sort this worksheet in descending order based on data in the Unit Sales column,

Quick Reference

Copy and Paste

1. Highlight a cell or range of cells to be copied.
2. Click the **Copy** icon in the Ribbon.
3. Highlight a cell or range of cells where copied data should appear.
4. Click the **Paste** icon in the Ribbon.

one cell in this column must be activated. Note that the cell you activate cannot be blank; otherwise, you will get an error message.

- Click the **Data** tab at the top of the Ribbon.
- Click the **Z to A** icon in the **Sort & Filter** group of the Ribbon (see Figure 2.17). After you click this icon, the Unit Sales column as well as all adjacent columns will be sorted in descending order. It is important to note that only adjacent columns are sorted when you use either the **Z to A** or **A to Z** icons (see Common Mistakes for this section).

Figure 2.16 | **Merchandise Sales Report Before Sorting**

	A	B	C	D	E	F
1	Category	Item Description	Color	Unit Sales	Sales Dollars	
2	Tops	Sweater	Brown	3500	119000	
3	Tops	Sweater	Grey	8500	289000	
4	Tops	T-Shirts	Black	10000	115000	
5	Tops	Tank Top	Pink	2500	21250	
6	Tops	T-Shirts	Blue	8500	97750	
7	Tops	T-Shirts	Yellow	4500	51750	
8	Bottoms	Shorts	Brown	8500	161500	
9	Tops	Tank Top	White	6500	55250	
10	Shoes	Boots	Brown	750	45000	
11	Bottoms	Shorts	Tan	12500	237500	
12	Tops	Tank Top	Red	1500	12750	
13	Bottoms	Shorts	White	9500	180500	
14	Bottoms	Shorts	Blue	5500	104500	
15	Shoes	Sandals	Black	3000	66000	
16	Shoes	Boots	Black	1600	96000	
17	Shoes	Sandals	Green	850	18700	
18	Tops	Sweater	Red	1500	51000	
19	Shoes	Sandals	Grey	1200	26400	

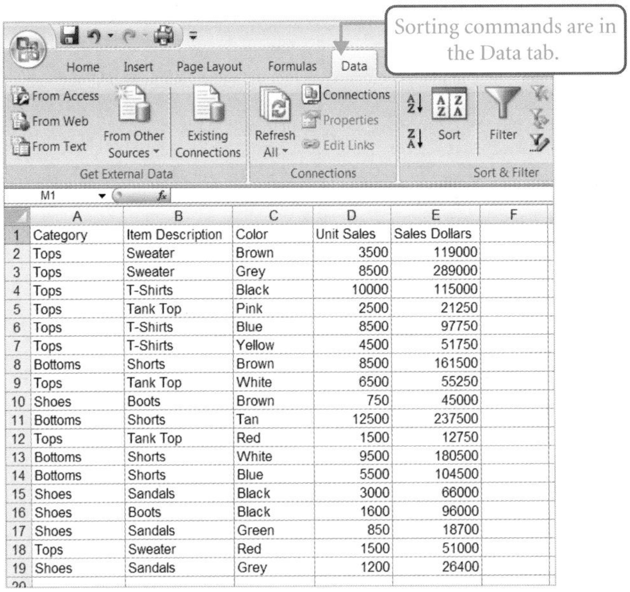

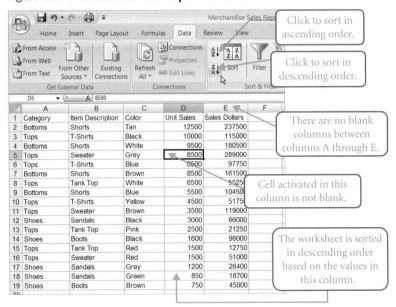

Figure 2.17 shows the Merchandise Sales Report after the items are sorted in descending order based on the Unit Sales column. The manager of this business can quickly glance at the top of this report and see that the Tan Shorts and the Black T-Shirts are the two highest-selling items based on unit sales.

> **Quick Reference**
>
> **Sorting Data (Single Level)**
>
> 1. Activate a cell in the column you wish to use as the basis for sorting your data. The cell you activate must not be blank.
> 2. Make sure there are no blank columns separating data you wish to sort and the column containing the cell you activated in step 1.
> 3. Click the **Data** tab at the top of the Ribbon.
> 4. Click the **Z to A** (descending order) or **A to Z** (ascending order) icon in the **Sort & Filter** section of the Ribbon.

Figure 2.17 | **Merchandise Sales Report Sorted Based on the Unit Sales Column**

	A	B	C	D	E	F
1	Category	Item Description	Color	Unit Sales	Sales Dollars	
2	Bottoms	Shorts	Tan	12500	237500	
3	Tops	T-Shirts	Black	10000	115000	
4	Bottoms	Shorts	White	9500	180500	
5	Tops	Sweater	Grey	8500	289000	
6	Tops	T-Shirts	Blue	8500	97750	
7	Bottoms	Shorts	Brown	8500	161500	
8	Tops	Tank Top	White	6500	5525	
9	Bottoms	Shorts	Blue	5500	10450	
10	Tops	T-Shirts	Yellow	4500	5175	
11	Tops	Sweater	Brown	3500	119000	
12	Shoes	Sandals	Black	3000	66000	
13	Tops	Tank Top	Pink	2500	21250	
14	Shoes	Boots	Black	1600	96000	
15	Tops	Tank Top	Red	1500	12750	
16	Tops	Sweater	Red	1500	51000	
17	Shoes	Sandals	Grey	1200	26400	
18	Shoes	Sandals	Green	850	18700	
19	Shoes	Boots	Brown	750	45000	

Figure 2.18 | **Example of a Sorting Error When Using the Ascending Icon**

	A	B	C	D	E	F
1	Category	Item Description	Color	Unit Sales		Sales Dollars
2	Shoes	Boots	Brown	750		237500
3	Shoes	Sandals	Green	850		115000
4	Shoes	Sandals	Grey	1200		180500
5	Tops	Tank Top	Red	1500		289000
6	Tops	Sweater	Red	1500		97750
7	Shoes	Boots	Black	1600		161500

This column is not sorted and does not align with the data on this worksheet.

Sorting Data (Multiple Levels)

The focus of the preceding segment was single-level sorting. This segment will focus on multiple-level sorting. Use multiple-level sorting when duplicate values appear in the column that is used to sort the data in a worksheet. For example, notice in Figure 2.17 that 8500 units were sold for the Grey Sweater, Blue T-Shirt, and Brown Shorts. With multiple-level sorting, all items that sold 8500 units can be sorted by the values in the Sales Dollars column. This could help a manager prioritize the ordering of these items based on the number of sales dollars they generate for the business. The following explains how to accomplish this sort:

- Highlight the range A1:E19. Notice that this range includes the column headings in row 1. Also, when you are sorting data, it is important to note that all columns related to a single row of data must be highlighted. Leaving a column out of the highlighted range could distort the data, making it unusable.

- Click the **Data** tab on the Ribbon.

- Click the **Sort** icon in the Ribbon. This will open the **Sort** dialog box.

- Click the **Options** button and check to see that the **Sort top to bottom** option is selected. You can sort data from left to right in rows or top to bottom in columns. However, you will need to select the **Sort top to bottom** option when working with a list of items such as this example.

- Click the **OK** button in the **Sort Options** dialog box.

- Make sure a green check appears in the box next to the **My data has headers** option in the upper-right side of the **Sort** dialog box. Since column headings were included in the highlighted range before you opened the **Sort** dialog box, you must check this option.

- Click the drop-down arrow of the option box below the **Column** heading and select the Unit Sales column.

- Click the drop-down arrow of the option box below the **Sort On** heading and select the Values option. This drop-down box also contains options that allow you to sort data based on the font color or cell color in a column.

- Click the drop-down arrow of the option box below the **Order** heading and select **Largest to Smallest**. This box also contains an option called **Custom List**. This option is helpful when you need to sort data by months of the year or days of the week.

- Click the **Add** button in the upper-left corner of the **Sort** window. This will add another set of option boxes to create a second sort level. You can add as many sort levels as needed.
- Make the following settings in the second sort level:
  - Column: **Sales Dollars**
  - Sort On: **Values**
  - Order: **Largest to Smallest**
- Click the **OK** button at the bottom of the **Sort** dialog box.

Figure 2.19 shows the final settings entered into the **Sort** dialog box. The data in a worksheet will be sorted in the order of the levels listed. Therefore, the Merchandise Sales Report will be sorted by the values in the Unit Sales column first. If duplicate values appear in the Unit Sales column, the data will be sorted by the values in the Sales Dollars column. You can change the order in which the sort levels are listed by clicking a level and then clicking one of the arrow buttons at the top of the **Sort** dialog box.

Figure 2.19 | **Settings in the Sort Dialog Box for the Merchandise Sales Report**

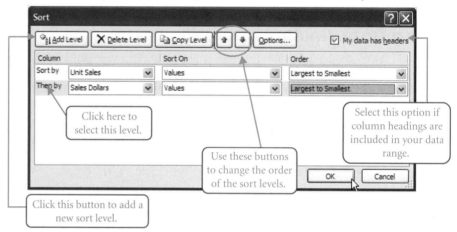

Figure 2.20 shows the final results of sorting the Merchandise Sales Report by the Unit Sales column and then by the Sales Dollars column. Notice that three items which sold 8500 units are now sorted in descending order based on the values in the Sales Dollars column.

COMMON MISTAKES | Missing Column Headings in the Sort Dialog Box

The column headings in your worksheet should appear in the drop-down box below the **Column** heading in the **Sort** dialog box. If you do not see the column heading names in these drop-down boxes, check to make sure you included them when you highlighted the range of cells to be sorted. If the column headings are included in your highlighted range but still do not appear in the drop-down boxes, check to see that the **My data has headers** option is selected in the upper-right corner of the **Sort** dialog box.

Figure 2.20 | **Merchandise Sales Report Sorted Based on Unit Sales and Sales Dollars**

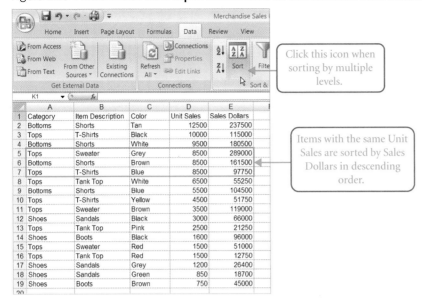

	A	B	C	D	E
1	Category	Item Description	Color	Unit Sales	Sales Dollars
2	Bottoms	Shorts	Tan	12500	237500
3	Tops	T-Shirts	Black	10000	115000
4	Bottoms	Shorts	White	9500	180500
5	Tops	Sweater	Grey	8500	289000
6	Bottoms	Shorts	Brown	8500	161500
7	Tops	T-Shirts	Blue	8500	97750
8	Tops	Tank Top	White	6500	55250
9	Bottoms	Shorts	Blue	5500	104500
10	Tops	T-Shirts	Yellow	4500	51750
11	Tops	Sweater	Brown	3500	119000
12	Shoes	Sandals	Black	3000	66000
13	Tops	Tank Top	Pink	2500	21250
14	Shoes	Boots	Black	1600	96000
15	Tops	Sweater	Red	1500	51000
16	Tops	Tank Top	Red	1500	12750
17	Shoes	Sandals	Grey	1200	26400
18	Shoes	Sandals	Green	850	18700
19	Shoes	Boots	Brown	750	45000

Click this icon when sorting by multiple levels.

Items with the same Unit Sales are sorted by Sales Dollars in descending order.

COMMON MISTAKES | Multiple-Level Sorting

When you are defining multiple levels to sort the data in a worksheet, it is important to highlight all data that is to be sorted first. *Any data that is not highlighted will not be sorted.* For example, if you forget to highlight a column that is related to your dataset, Excel will sort the highlighted columns creating an alignment problem with the column that was not highlighted. This will distort your data, and it may not be possible to correct this error. This problem is similar to the Common Mistake illustrated for the **Z to A** and **A to Z** icons in the previous segment.

>>Data Management Skills

The purpose of this workshop is to demonstrate the data management skills presented in this section of the chapter. We will be creating a spreadsheet that tracks the sales results of a product line that could be sold at a university bookstore. I will be demonstrating the tasks in this workshop in the following four videos: **Data Entry**, **Adjusting Rows and Columns**, **Copy and Paste**, and **Sorting Data**. After completing each section of tasks, watch the related video in parentheses. Remember to try the tasks on your own first before watching the video.

VIDEO WORKSHOP

1. Open and Save a Workbook (Video: Data Entry)

a. Open a blank Excel workbook.

b. Save the workbook as **ib_e02_videoworkshop**.

c. Remember where you save this file. You will need this file to complete the three remaining video workshops in this chapter.

2. Data Entry (Video: Data Entry continued)

a. Activate Sheet1 by clicking the worksheet tab.

b. Type the following data into the cell locations listed:

Cell A1: **University Bookstore Sales Report**
Cell A2: **Season**
Cell A3: **Fall**
Cell A4: **Spring**
Cell A5: **Spring**
Cell A6: **Fall**
Cell A7: **Spring**
Cell A8: **Fall**
Cell A9: **Spring**
Cell A10: **Fall**
Cell A11: **Fall**
Cell A12: **Spring**
Cell B2: **Item Description**
Cell B3: **Sweatshirt**
Cell B4: **T-Shirts**
Cell B5: **Baseballs**
Cell B6: **Scarves**
Cell B7: **Sunglasses**
Cell B8: **Sweaters**
Cell B9: **Sandals**
Cell B10: **Blankets**
Cell B11: **Footballs**
Cell B12: **Sunscreen**
Cell D2: **Unit Sales**
Cell D3: **5000**
Cell D4: **8500**
Cell D5: **1200**
Cell D6: **2200**
Cell D7: **1800**
Cell D8: **3200**
Cell D9: **2200**
Cell D10: **900**
Cell D11: **500**
Cell D12: **1800**
Cell E2: **Average Price**
Cell E3: **49.99**
Cell E4: **18.99**
Cell E5: **12.99**
Cell E6: **9.99**
Cell E7: **22.99**
Cell E8: **69.99**
Cell E9: **29.99**
Cell E10: **32.99**
Cell E11: **59.99**
Cell E12: **5.99**
Cell F2: **Sales Dollars**
Cell F3: **249950**
Cell F4: **161415**
Cell F5: **15588**
Cell F6: **21978**
Cell F7: **41382**
Cell F8: **223968**
Cell F9: **65978**

Cell F10: **29691**
Cell F11: **29995**
Cell F12: **10782**

   c. In cell C2, type **Item Number**.

   d. In cell C3, type the number **70500**.

   e. In cell C4, type the number **70501**.

   f. Use **Auto Fill** to extend the series to cell C12. The number in Cell 12 should be 70509.

3. Adjusting Rows and Columns (Video: Adjusting Rows and Columns)

   a. Expand the height of row 1 to 27 points.

   b. Expand the height of row 2 to 31.5 points.

   c. Expand the width of column B to 12 points.

4. Copy and Paste (Video: Copy and Paste)

   a. Select all contents in Sheet1 by clicking the square in the upper-left corner next to column A.

   b. Click the **Copy** icon in the **Home** tab of the Ribbon to copy Sheet1.

   c. Activate Sheet2 by clicking the worksheet tab.

   d. Activate cell A1.

   e. Click the **Paste** icon in the **Home** tab of the Ribbon to paste Sheet1 into Sheet2.

   f. Activate Sheet3.

   g. Activate cell A1.

   h. Paste Sheet1 into Sheet3 by using the **Paste** icon.

5. Sort (Video: Sorting Data)

   a. Sort the data in Sheet1 as follows:

      i. Season: **A to Z**
      ii. Sales Dollars: **Largest to Smallest**

   b. Sort the data in Sheet2 as follows:

      i. Unit Sales: **Largest to Smallest**
      ii. Sales Dollars: **Largest to Smallest**

   c. Sort the data in Sheet3 as follows:

      i. Average Price: **Smallest to Largest**
      ii. Item Description: **A to Z**

6. Save (Video: Sorting Data continued)

   a. Save and close your workbook. Remember where you save this file as you will need it to do the next video workshop on formatting skills.

>> Creating Merchandise Sales Reports

Knowing the skills covered in this section is essential for creating spreadsheets in Excel. For example, if you don't know how to adjust the width of columns, you may not be able to see the data that was entered onto a spreadsheet. Or, if you don't know how to use the copy and paste commands, you would always have to retype data when you wanted to create an identical or similar spreadsheet. Finally, knowing how to use a basic skill such as sorting can be critical in making business decisions.

Exercise

The purpose of this exercise is to create Merchandise Sales Reports for three different business managers. Each business manager will need a different arrangement of the merchandise report based on the decisions they are required to make. As a result, the spreadsheets you will create in this exercise will highlight information that is most important to the reader. Open the file named ib_e02_merchandise performancereport and complete the following tasks:

1. Copy the data in Sheet1 and paste it into Sheet2 and Sheet3.

2. Use Sheet1 to create a sales report for a buyer. The buyer will need to evaluate the sales performance of merchandise within each category. Sort the data in Sheet1 based on the columns listed below to show the buyer what item is generating the most sales dollars within each category:

   a. Category: Ascending order

   b. Total Sales Dollars: Descending order

3. Use Sheet2 to create a report for an inventory manager. An inventory manager will typically focus on the unit inventory and weeks of supply for each item. This information will be used to decide which orders to rush into the warehouse and which orders to postpone. Sort the data based on the columns listed below:

   a. Weeks of Supply: Ascending order

   b. Inventory Units: Descending order

4. Since the inventory manager is focusing only on the Weeks of Supply and Inventory Units column, hide the Units Sales, Price, and Total Sales Dollar columns.

5. Use Sheet3 to create a report for a pricing manager. The pricing manager will need to manage how items are priced and determine how many price tickets should be printed for each price point. Sort Sheet3 based on the columns listed below:

   a. Price: Ascending order

   b. Color: Ascending order

6. Since the pricing manager is focusing on the price for each item, hide the Unit Sales, Total Sales Dollars, Inventory Units, and Weeks of Supply columns.

7. Which item generates the most dollars for each category?

8. How many $19 price tickets will the pricing manager need to print?

>> What's Wrong with This Spreadsheet?

Problem

You are approached by a coworker who is having some difficulty with an Excel project. He sends you an Excel file with two spreadsheets in it. Sheet1 is the original spreadsheet that was given to him by an assistant buyer. Sheet2 is the spreadsheet he has been working on and is causing him trouble. The following is a list of problems the coworker has sent to you:

1. I don't know why these "####" errors appear on the spreadsheet. I was only entering numbers for the sales report, and these "####" errors keep popping up.

2. The data in Sheet1 was given to me by an assistant buyer. She told me that this worksheet would include the cost for each item. I don't see it! She keeps insisting the cost information is in there; however, I have a feeling I am going to have to enter this data myself.

3. I copied the data in Sheet1, pasted it into Sheet2, and sorted it by Sales Dollars. I had no problem sorting it except I did not see the name of each column in the Column drop-down boxes. I read somewhere that you should see the column names in those boxes, but I just saw Column A, Column B, and so on. I showed the report to one of the buyers in my department, and she said the department numbers don't seem to match the department name. I wonder if the assistant buyer did something wrong?

Exercise

The file this coworker sent you is named ib_e02_salesreporthelp. What's wrong with this spreadsheet? Consider the following points:

1. What would cause the "####" signs to appear on a spreadsheet? Is this really an error? How can this be fixed?

2. In point 2 of the Problem, the cost information is indeed in the spreadsheet. How can you tell if data exists on a spreadsheet if it cannot be seen?

3. Assume that the data in Sheet1 is accurate. What can you do to check the accuracy of the data your coworker sorted in Sheet2? Why is the coworker not seeing the column names in the Column drop-down boxes?

Write a short answer for each of these questions and fix the data in Sheet2. If a problem cannot be fixed, explain why.

> Formatting

The previous section demonstrated how you can use Excel to construct a Financial Plan and a Merchandise Sales Report. This section will demonstrate how Excel's *formatting* commands can enhance the visual appearance of these spreadsheets. Excel's formatting features can transform the appearance of a basic spreadsheet into a professional-looking document. However, formatting also serves a more functional purpose in that it guides the reader's attention to the most critical information. This allows a business manager to scan a spreadsheet efficiently and identify the most important information required to make key decisions.

Excel's primary formatting features are found in the **Font**, **Alignment**, and **Number** groups of the **Home** tab in the Ribbon (shown in Figure 2.21). This section

Figure 2.21 | **Formatting Features Are Found in the Home Tab of the Ribbon**

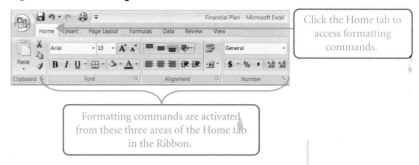

will illustrate the formatting commands that are available in each of these three groups and demonstrate how you apply them to the Financial Plan or Merchandise Sales Report spreadsheets, which were introduced previously in this chapter.

Data Formats

Commands you use to format the appearance of data are found in the Font group, as shown in Figure 2.22. Frequently used icons in this Group are the **Font Size, Font Color, Bold, Italic,** and **Underline**.

Figure 2.22 | **Format Icons in the Font Group**

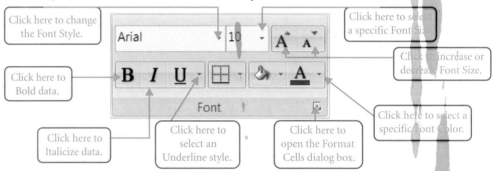

The icons highlighted in Figure 2.22 are valuable when you're making data stand out on a worksheet. For example, you can use them to enlarge the title of a worksheet, bold a critical row of data, or enhance the appearance of column headings. Formatting column headings can be particularly important because it separates the heading from the actual data, making it easier for the reader to locate specific types of data. The following points explain how to format the column headings for the Merchandise Sales Report shown in Figure 2.20:

- Highlight the range A1:E1. Before using any of the formatting icons in the Home tab of the Ribbon, you must first highlight a cell or range of cells that will be formatted.
- Click the **Home** tab of the Ribbon.
- Click the **Bold** icon.
- Click the **Italic** icon.
- Click the down arrow next to the **Font Color** icon and click the Dark Red square. When using icons such as the **Font Color, Font Size,** or **Font Style,** you will see the data in your highlighted range change as you move the cursor over the various options. This allows you to preview what your data will look like when it is formatted before making a choice (see Figure 2.23).

Figure 2.23 shows the Merchandise Sales Report with the column headings formatted. This simple enhancement makes it easy for the reader to separate the column headings from the actual data and identify what each column of data represents.

Figure 2.23 | **Formatted Column Headings for the Merchandise Sales Report**

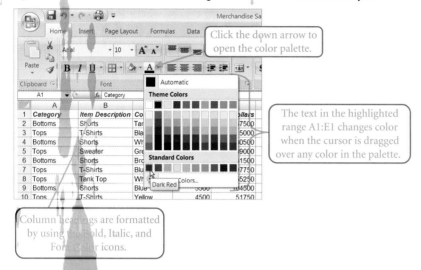

Click the down arrow to open the color palette.

The text in the highlighted range A1:E1 changes color when the cursor is dragged over any color in the palette.

Column headings are formatted by using the Bold, Italic, and Font Color icons.

The **icons** shown in Figure 2.22 should satisfy almost all of your data format needs. However, you can find additional formatting options by opening the **Format Cells** dialog box. The **Format Cells** dialog box contains almost every available formatting option in Excel. You can open it by clicking the button in the lower-right corner of the **Font**, **Alignment**, and **Number** groups in the **Home** tab of the Ribbon (see Figure 2.22). Figure 2.24 shows the **Format Cells** dialog box and highlights options where an icon is not available in the Ribbon.

Figure 2.24 | **The Format Cells Dialog Box**

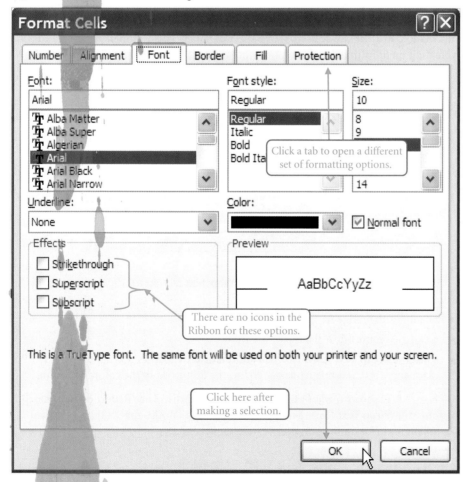

Click a tab to open a different set of formatting options.

There are no icons in the Ribbon for these options.

Click here after making a selection.

>> **Quick Reference**

Formatting Data

1. Highlight a range of cells to be formatted.
2. Click the **Home** tab of the Ribbon.
3. Click one of the icons in the **Font** group of the Ribbon or open the **Format Cells** dialog box by clicking the button in the lower-right corner of the **Font** group.
4. If using the **Format Cells** dialog box, click the **OK** button after making a selection.

Data Alignment

After applying data formatting techniques to a worksheet, you may need to adjust the *alignment* of data in a cell. For example, you may need to use the **Horizontal Alignment** icons to center or right justify data in a cell. If you are setting up accounting statements, you will need to use the **Indent** icons for certain financial headings. Figure 2.25 highlights the icons available in the **Alignment** group in the **Home** tab of the Ribbon.

Figure 2.25 | **Alignment Icons**

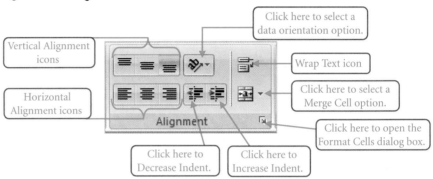

The *Wrap Text* icon is a commonly used feature because it will automatically expand the row height and create a second line to fit long entries. This reduces the need to expand the width of columns, which decreases the amount of information that can be seen on one screen or one page. For example, in Figure 2.26, the font size of the column headings in the Merchandise Sales Report was increased. These headings are now too large to fit in the space allocated for each column. You could resolve this problem by expanding the width of each column; however, doing so may reduce the amount of information a reader can see across one sheet of paper. This will make reading and evaluating the information on a report more difficult for a business manager who is trying to obtain information as efficiently as possible to make key decisions.

Figure 2.26 | **Column Headings Are Truncated When Font Size Is Increased**

	A	B	C	D	E	F
1	*Category*	*Item Descrip*	*Color*	*Unit Sale*	*Sales Dollars*	
2	Bottoms	Shorts	Tan	12500	237500	
3	Tops	T-Shirts	Black	10000	115000	
4	Bottoms	Shorts	White	9500	180500	

These column headings are truncated when the font size is increased.

The following explains how to use the **Wrap Text** feature to correct the column headings in the range A1:E1 in Figure 2.26:

- Highlight the range A1:E1.
- Click the **Home** tab at the top of the Ribbon.
- Click the **Wrap Text** icon. This will automatically expand the height of row 1 and place any word that was truncated below the first word in the column heading.

Figure 2.27 shows the appearance of the Merchandise Sales Report column headings after the **Wrap Text** feature is applied. In addition, notice that both the *Vertical Alignment* and *Horizontal Alignment* were set to center.

Figure 2.27 | **Columns Headings with Wrap Text Applied**

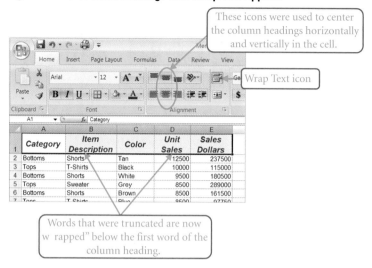

Another common feature used in the **Alignment** area is the **Merge & Center** icon. *Merge & Center* allows you to create one big cell out of several smaller cells and is commonly used to center a title at the top of a spreadsheet. For example, Figure 2.28 shows the Financial Plan spreadsheet. The **Merge & Center** icon will be used to center the title in cell A1 over the center of the worksheet. The following points explain how you accomplish this:

- Highlight the range A1:F1 (see Figure 2.28). When you are using the **Merge & Center** icon, cell locations within a highlighted range will be transformed into one cell.
- Click the **Home** tab of the Ribbon.
- Click the down arrow next to the **Merge & Center** icon and select the **Merge & Center** option. This will transform the cells in the range A1:F1 into one cell and horizontally center any data in the range. You could also use the **Merge Cells** option to just combine cells without centering the data.

Figure 2.28 | **Merge Cell Options**

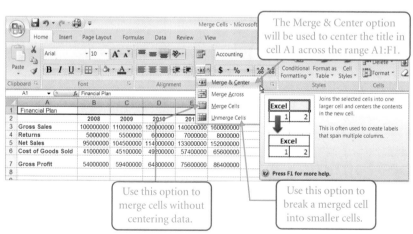

> **Quick Reference**

Horizontal and Vertical Alignment

1. Highlight a range of cells to be formatted.
2. Click the **Home** tab of the Ribbon.
3. Click one of the **Vertical Alignment** icons to place data on the top, center, or bottom of a cell.
4. Click one of the **Horizontal Alignment** icons to left justify, center, or right justify data in a cell.

> **Quick Reference**

Wrap Text

1. Highlight a range of cells to be formatted.
2. Click the **Home** tab of the Ribbon.
3. Click the **Wrap Text** icon.

Figure 2.29 shows the results of using the **Merge & Center** option to format the title of the Financial Plan. Notice that the font size was increased to 14 points, with bold and italic formats added.

Figure 2.29 | **Formatted Title in the Financial Plan Worksheet**

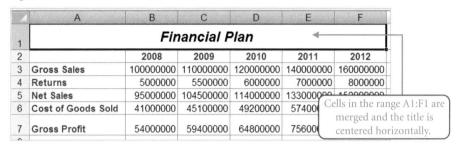

	A	B	C	D	E	F
1	*Financial Plan*					
2		2008	2009	2010	2011	2012
3	Gross Sales	100000000	110000000	120000000	140000000	160000000
4	Returns	5000000	5500000	6000000	7000000	8000000
5	Net Sales	95000000	104500000	114000000	133000000	150000000
6	Cost of Goods Sold	41000000	45100000	49200000	57400000	
7	Gross Profit	54000000	59400000	64800000	75600000	

Cells in the range A1:F1 are merged and the title is centered horizontally.

As mentioned in the previous section, in some situations you may need to access additional formatting features through the **Format Cells** dialog box. The **Format Cells** dialog box will be opened to the **Alignment** tab when you click the button in the lower-right corner of the **Alignment** section of the Ribbon (see Figure 2.25). Figure 2.30 highlights a few useful features such as the indent and *orientation* settings. These options provide you with more detail when making specific indent settings or orienting data on a specific angle within a cell.

Figure 2.30 | **Alignment Tab of the Format Cells Dialog Box**

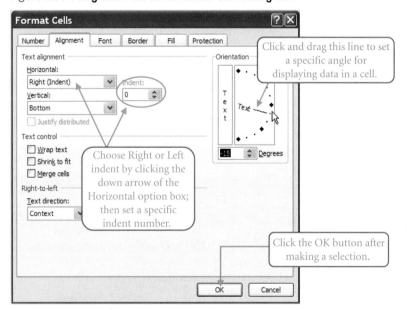

Click and drag this line to set a specific angle for displaying data in a cell.

Choose Right or Left indent by clicking the down arrow of the Horizontal option box; then set a specific indent number.

Click the OK button after making a selection.

>> **Quick Reference**

Merge Cells

1. Highlight a range of cells to be merged.
2. Click the **Home** tab of the Ribbon.
3. Click the down arrow of the **Merge & Center** icon and select an option.

Number Formats

Commands used to format the appearance of numbers are found in the **Number** group, as shown in Figure 2.31. These options allow you to format numeric data such as currency, percentages, dates, or fractions.

Figure 2.31 | **Icons for Number Formats**

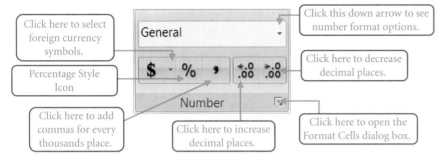

Click here to select foreign currency symbols.

Percentage Style Icon

Click here to add commas for every thousands place.

Click here to increase decimal places.

Click this down arrow to see number format options.

Click here to decrease decimal places.

Click here to open the Format Cells dialog box.

Figure 2.32 shows the options that are available when clicking the down arrow of the **Number Format** icon.

Figure 2.32 | **Number Format Icons Drop-Down Box**

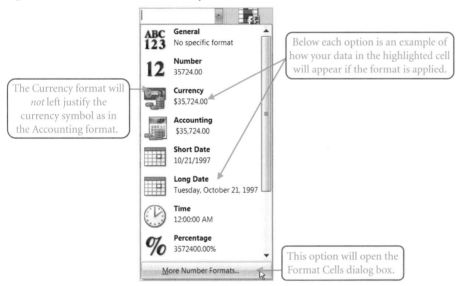

The Currency format will *not* left justify the currency symbol as in the Accounting format.

Below each option is an example of how your data in the highlighted cell will appear if the format is applied.

This option will open the Format Cells dialog box.

The following steps explain how you apply the Accounting format to the numbers in the Financial Plan worksheet. The Accounting format will left justify the currency symbol, add a comma for every thousands place, add two decimal places, and place negative numbers in parentheses.

- Highlight the range B3:F7. As with other formatting commands, you must highlight a range of cells first before selecting a number format.
- Click the **Home** tab on the Ribbon.
- Click the **Accounting Number Format** icon. If you are working with foreign currency, you can select a different currency symbol such as Euros or English Pounds by clicking the down arrow of this icon.
- Click the **Decrease Decimal** icon twice. As with most financial plans, carrying financial projections to two decimal places is not necessary. Therefore, you remove the decimal places by clicking the **Decrease Decimal** icon twice.

> **Quick Reference**

Accounting Format

1. Highlight a range of cells to be formatted.
2. Click the **Home** tab of the Ribbon.
3. Click the **Accounting Number Format** icon $\boxed{\$ \cdot}$. Click the down arrow next to this icon to change the currency symbol.
4. Click the **Increase** or **Decrease Decimal** icons and as needed.

Figure 2.33 | **Accounting Format Applied to the Financial Plan Worksheet**

	A	B	C	D	E	F
1				*Financial Plan*		
2		2008	2009	2010	2011	2012
3	Gross Sales	$ 100,000,000	$ 110,000,000	$ 120,000,000	$ 140,000,000	$ 160,000,000
4	Returns	$ 5,000,000	$ 5,500,000	$ 6,000,000	$ 7,000,000	$ 8,000,000
5	Net Sales	$ 95,000,000	$ 104,500,000	$ 114,000,000	$ 133,000,000	$ 152,000,000
6	Cost of Goods Sold	$ 41,000,000	$ 45,100,000	$ 49,200,000	$ 57,400,000	$ 65,600,000
7	Gross Profit	$ 54,000,000	$ 59,400,000	$ 64,800,000	$ 75,600,000	$ 86,400,000

> The Accounting format will left justify the dollar sign.

As you can see in Figure 2.32, you can open the **Format Cells** dialog box by selecting the **More Number Formats** option in the **Number Format** drop-down box. When you are applying number formats, the **Format Cells** dialog box provides several options that are not available in the Ribbon. For example, when applying the Currency format, you can choose an option that converts negative numbers to a red font color. This color is most helpful when you need to bring the reader's attention to negative results that are critical, such as Gross Profit or Net Income. The **Format Cells** dialog box also provides more options for formatting dates compared to the **Number Format** icon. These options are highlighted in Figure 2.34.

Figure 2.34 | **Number Tab of the Format Cells Dialog Box**

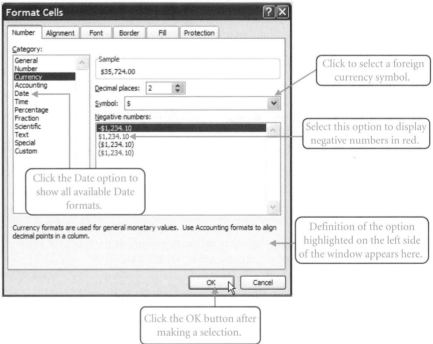

> Click to select a foreign currency symbol.

> Select this option to display negative numbers in red.

> Click the Date option to show all available Date formats.

> Definition of the option highlighted on the left side of the window appears here.

> Click the OK button after making a selection.

>> **Quick Reference**

Formatting Numbers

1. Highlight a range of cells containing numbers to be formatted.

2. Click the **Home** tab of the Ribbon.

3. Click one of the icons in the **Number** group of the Ribbon or open the **Format Cells** dialog box by clicking the button in the lower-right corner of the **Number** group.

4. If using the **Format Cells** dialog box, click the **OK** button after making a selection.

COMMON MISTAKES | Using the Currency Format

When selecting the Currency format from the **Format Cells** dialog box, check the **Symbol** setting. Occasionally, this box may be set to **none**. Also, if you are working on an accounting assignment and would like to left justify the dollar signs, use the Accounting format. Dollar signs will be placed in front of the value and will not align when using the Currency format.

Borders (Line Formats)

Use the *Border* command to place lines on an Excel worksheet. As previously mentioned, a key purpose for enhancing the appearance of a worksheet is to make it easy for a reader to find and analyze needed information. Adding lines to a worksheet advances this purpose because it helps the reader keep track of data associated with each row and also helps distinguish labels from data.

The **Borders** icon is found in the **Font** group in the **Home tab** of the Ribbon. Figure 2.35 illustrates the options that are available when you click the down arrow of the **Borders** icon. You add borders to a worksheet by first highlighting a range of cells and then selecting one of the line styles and placement options shown in the figure.

Figure 2.35 | **Line and Placement Options in the Borders Icon**

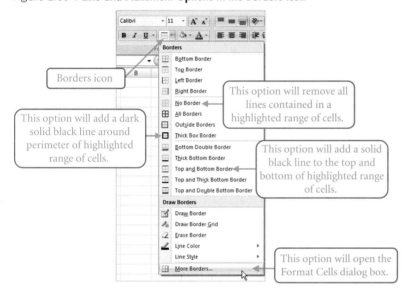

As illustrated in Figure 2.35, the **Borders** icon provides several options for adding lines to a worksheet. However, you may find these options limiting. For example, the options in the **Borders** icon will only provide black lines and contain only a few line styles. As a result, you may need to use the **Format Cells** dialog box when adding lines to a worksheet. The following steps explain how you use both the **Borders** icon and the **Format Cells** dialog box to add lines to the Merchandise Sales Report:

- Highlight the range A1:E19.
- Click the **Home** tab of the Ribbon.
- Click the down arrow in the **Borders** icon.
- Select the **Thick Box Border** option. A dark black line will appear around the perimeter of the highlighted range.
- Highlight the range A2:E19.
- Click the down arrow in the **Borders** icon and select the **More Borders** option. This will open the **Format Cells** dialog box to the **Border** tab. You can also click the button in the lower-right corner of the **Font** section in the Ribbon and click the **Border** tab when the **Format Cells** dialog box opens.
- Click the down arrow of the **Color** box and select the black square.
- Click the regular solid line style on the left side of the dialog box.
- Click the **Inside** icon at the upper-right side of the dialog box. You will see vertical and horizontal lines appear in the locator box. This option of placing lines only on

the inside of a range of cells and not the perimeter is not available in the **Borders** icon. This is why the **Format Cells** dialog box is needed in this case.

- Click the down arrow of the **Color** box and select the Dark Red square in the lower-left corner of the color palette.
- Click the dark solid line style on the left side of the dialog box.
- Click the top of the locator box on the right side of the dialog box. This will place a dark solid red line at the top of the highlighted range. Different line colors are not available in the **Borders** icon options. Therefore, you must use the **Format Cells** dialog box in these situations.

Figure 2.36 shows the final settings that were made in the **Border** tab of the **Format Cells** dialog box. Notice the red line that appears at the top of the locator box. This indicates that the line will be placed at the top of the highlighted range cells. If the middle of the locator box were selected, a red line would appear between every row in the middle of the highlighted range.

Figure 2.36 | **The Border Tab of the Format Cells Dialog Box**

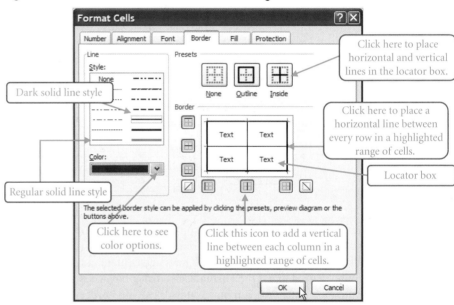

COMMON MISTAKES | Borders

Forgetting to select the color and line styles first are the most common mistakes people make when using the **Format Cells** dialog box to add borders to a worksheet. You must select the line color and style first before selecting a placement in the locator box.

Figure 2.37 shows the results of adding lines to the Merchandise Sales Report. The lines make it easier to read all the data pertaining to each row and also help to separate each column. Notice that the numbers in columns D and E are formatted.

Figure 2.37 | **Results of Adding Lines to the Merchandise Sales Report**

	A	B	C	D	E
1	Category	Item Description	Color	Unit Sales	Sales Dollars
2	Bottoms	Shorts	Tan	12,500	$237,500
3	Tops	T-Shirts	Black	10,000	$1
4	Bottoms	Shorts	White	9,500	$18
5	Tops	Sweater	Grey	8,500	$28
6	Bottoms	Shorts	Brown	8,500	$161,500
7	Tops	T-Shirts	Blue	8,500	$97,750
8	Tops	Tank Top	White	6,500	$55,250
9	Bottoms	Shorts	Blue	5,500	$104,500
10	Tops	T-Shirts	Yellow	4,500	$51,750
11	Tops	Sweater	Brown	3,500	$119,000
12	Shoes	Sandals	Black	3,000	$66,000
13	Tops	Tank Top	Pink	2,500	$21,250
14	Shoes	Boots	Black	1,600	$96,000
15	Tops	Sweater	Red	1,500	$51,000
16	Tops	Tank Top	Red	1,500	$12,750
17	Shoes	Sandals	Grey	1,200	$26,4
18	Shoes	Sandals	Green	850	$18,7
19	Shoes	Boots	Brown	750	$45,0

Vertical lines were added to the range A1:E1 using the Format Cells dialog box.

Numbers in these columns are formatted.

Cell Color (Fill Color)

Changing the color of the cells in a worksheet is another formatting technique that makes titles and column headings stand out. You change the cell colors in a worksheet by using the **Fill Color** icon shown in Figure 2.38.

Figure 2.38 | **Fill Color Icon**

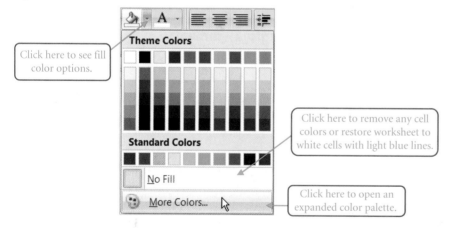

Click here to see fill color options.

Theme Colors

Standard Colors

No Fill

More Colors...

Click here to remove any cell colors or restore worksheet to white cells with light blue lines.

Click here to open an expanded color palette.

The following explains how you change the cell colors in the Financial Plan worksheet to make the title stand out:

- Highlight the range A1:F1.
- Click the **Home** tab of the Ribbon.
- Click the down arrow in the **Fill Color** icon.
- Click the Dark Blue box at the bottom of the color palette. You will notice the highlighted range changes as you move the cursor over the color palette. This allows you to see how your worksheet will appear before making a selection.
- Click the down arrow in the **Font Color** icon and select the white square. Since a dark cell color is being used, changing the color of the text to white will make the text stand out.

Figure 2.39 shows the results of the Financial Plan worksheet with cell colors added. In addition to the title, cells in the range B2:F2 and A3:A7 were changed to orange.

>> **Quick Reference**

Cell Color

1. Highlight range of cells to be colored.
2. Click the **Home** tab of the Ribbon.
3. Click the down arrow of the **Fill Color** icon.
4. Select a color from the palette.

Figure 2.39 | **Results of Adding Cell Color to the Financial Plan**

	A	B	C	D	E	F
1				*Financial Plan*		
2		2008	2009	2010	2011	2012
3	Gross Sales	$ 100,000,000	$ 110,000,000	$ 120,000,000	$ 140,000,000	$ 160,000,000
4	Returns	$ 5,000,000	$ 5,500,000	$ 6,000,000	$ 7,000,000	$ 8,000,000
5	Net Sales	$ 95,000,000	$ 104,500,000	$ 114,000,000	$ 133,000,000	$ 152,000,000
6	Cost of Goods Sold	$ 41,000,000	$ 45,100,000	$ 49,200,000	$ 57,400,000	$ 65,600,000
7	Gross Profit	$ 54,000,000	$ 59,400,000	$ 64,800,000	$ 75,600,000	$ 86,400,000
8						

VIDEO WORKSHOP

>> Formatting

The purpose of this workshop is to demonstrate the formatting skills presented in this section of the chapter. We will continue to build the spreadsheet that was started in the Data Management Video Workshop. I will be demonstrating the tasks in this workshop in the following four videos: **Data Alignment**, **Number and Font Formats**, **Cell Color**, and **Borders**. After completing each section of tasks, watch the related video in parentheses. Remember to try the tasks on your own first before watching the video.

1. **Open File**
   a. Open the file named ib_e02_videoworkshop, which you completed for the Data Management Video Workshop previously in this chapter.

2. **Data Alignment (Video: Data Alignment)**
   a. Activate Sheet1 by clicking the worksheet tab.
   b. Highlight the range A1:F1.
   c. Merge the cells in the highlighted range without centering the text using the **Merge & Center** icon in the Ribbon.
   d. Set the horizontal and vertical alignment for the highlighted range to center.
   e. Highlight the range A2:F2.
   f. Wrap the text in the highlighted range by clicking the **Wrap Text** icon in the Ribbon. Then set the horizontal and vertical alignment to center.

3. **Adjusting Columns and Rows (Video: Data Alignment continued)**
   a. Change the width of column D to 7 points.
   b. Change the width of column F to 12 points.
   c. Change the height of row 8 to 23 points. Use the **Height** option in the **Format** icon, which is in the **Home** tab of the Ribbon.
   d. Repeat steps a and b for Sheet2 and Sheet3.

4. **Numbers and Fonts (Video: Number and Font Formats)**
   a. Activate Sheet1.
   b. For cell A1, make the following font settings: Type: Garamond; Style: Bold and Italic; Size: 14 points.
   c. Bold the text in the range A2:F3 and A8:F8
   d. Format the range D3:D12 with commas and 0 decimal places.
   e. Format the range E3:E12 to U.S. currency and 2 decimal places.

f. Format the range F3:F12 to U.S. currency and 0 decimal places.

g. Repeat steps d, e, and f for Sheet2 and Sheet3.

5. Cell Color (Fill Color) (Video: Cell Color)

a. Activate Sheet1.

b. For cell A1, change the cell color to brown and change the text color to white.

c. Change the cell color to yellow for the range A2:F2.

d. Change the text color to blue for the range A3:F3 and A8:F8.

6. Borders (Video: Borders)

a. Highlight the range A1:F12 and add a thick bold black line around the perimeter of the range. Use the **Format Cells** dialog box to add this border.

b. Highlight the range A1:F2 and add a horizontal bold black line in the middle and bottom of the range. Use the **Format Cells** dialog box to add these borders.

c. Highlight the range A2:F2 and add a vertical regular black line to the middle of the range. Use the **Format Cells** dialog box to add this border.

d. Highlight the range A3:F12 and add horizontal and vertical regular black lines to the middle of the range. Use the **Format Cells** dialog box to add these borders.

e. Highlight the range A7:F7 and add a red double line to the bottom of the range. Use the **Format Cells** dialog box to add this border.

f. Save and close your file. Remember where you saved this file because it will be used in the Editing Video Workshop.

>> Creating a Store Performance Report

EXERCISE

Why Do I Need This?

Formatting techniques are used to direct the reader to the most critical information on a spreadsheet and are often the difference between a mediocre and professional spreadsheet. It is important for you to be aware of the formatting commands available in Excel and how they can be applied to create an effective spreadsheet.

Exercise

Open the file named ib_e02_storeperformancereport. You will see a worksheet without any formatting techniques applied. Your goal will be to format this spreadsheet for the distribution manager of a retail store chain. Follow the directions and remember to save your work periodically.

1. Copy Sheet1 and paste it into Sheet2.

2. Make the title of the report stand out so that it can be easily distinguished from other reports this manager will be evaluating. Highlight the range A1:N1 in Sheet2 and apply the following formats:

   a. Merge the cells.

   b. Set the horizontal and vertical alignment to center.

   c. Change the font size to 14, the font style to bold, and change the font color to white.

   d. Change the cell color to green.

3. Your next task is to fix the column headings of the report. You will notice that in some instances you cannot see the entire column heading because it is too long to fit in a cell. Adjust the headings as follows:

    a. Highlight the range I2:N2. Merge the cells, set the horizontal alignment to center, and then bold and italicize the text.

    b. Highlight the range A3:N3. Instead of increasing the width of these columns to show the column headings, format the cells to wrap text, set the horizontal alignment to center, bold the text, and change the color of the cells to yellow.

    c. Since this spreadsheet has several columns, keep the width as narrow as possible. Make the following column width adjustments:

        i.   Column A: **7.5**

        ii. Column B: **12**

        iii. Column C: **6**

        iv. Column E: **10**

        v. Column H: **10**

        vi. Column J: **9**

4. Format the numbers on the spreadsheet as follows:

    a. D4:E28: Number format with commas, 0 decimal places.

    b. F4:G28: U.S. Currency format, 0 decimal places. You may need to readjust the column widths.

    c. H4:H28: Number format with 0 decimal places.

    d. I4:N28: U.S. Currency format, 0 decimal places. You may need to readjust the column widths.

5. The information the distribution manager is most concerned about is the estimated annual truck deliveries. The distribution manager will need this information to calculate the shipping costs by store and for the entire retail chain. To make this column of data stand out, add the following format settings to the range H4:H28:

    a. Set the horizontal alignment to center.

    b. Bold and italicize the text.

    c. Italicize the text in cell H3.

    d. Change the color of the text in the range H3:H28 to dark blue.

6. The distribution manager will use the right side of this spreadsheet as a reference to get an idea of how the volume of deliveries might change from month to month. This section needs to be visually separated form the rest of the worksheet. Change the cell color to light green for the range I4:N28.

7. The last step in this formatting exercise is to add lines to the spreadsheet. Without lines, it will be very difficult to follow the data for each store across the spreadsheet. Add the following lines to the spreadsheet:

    a. Add regular black lines to the inside of the range A3:N28. Every cell in this range should have a regular black outline.

    b. Add a heavy dark bold line around the perimeter of the range A3:N28.

    c. Add a regular bold line around the perimeter of the range A3:N3.

    d. Add a regular bold line to the bottom of cell A1.

    e. Add a bold line to the left of range I2:I28.

8. Sort the worksheet based on the Estimated Annual Truck Deliveries column in descending order.

9. Compare Sheet1 and Sheet2. What formatting techniques make the biggest impact?

10. What stores are expected to receive 37 annual truck deliveries, and what is the size of these stores in square feet?

11. What information was necessary before adding format techniques to this spreadsheet?

12. Save and close your file.

>> What's Wrong with This Spreadsheet?

Problem

You are approached by a coworker who works in the price change division of a jewelry store. The company is having a sale and reducing the prices on several pieces of jewelry. Your coworker was asked to prepare a spreadsheet that lists all the items that will be included in the sale, the original price, and the new reduced price. She attaches an Excel file in an e-mail and asks for your help. Her e-mail includes the following points:

1. I set up a spreadsheet that shows all the sale items for this weekend. I listed each item with the current price, and I am trying to add a column to show the new reduced price. For some reason, no matter what I type into this column, nothing appears. Try it! I entered the first price which is $90. But nothing shows up in the cell. When I activate the cell (D3), I can see it says $90 in the formula bar, but I can't see it in the cell. I can't understand why this is happening. I didn't do anything but type in the price. Oh wait. . . I did try something. I tried to change the color of the cells by clicking on one of those icons at the top, but it didn't work. That still doesn't explain why nothing shows up in the cell.

2. The other problem I am having is with the border around the worksheet. I am simply trying to add a bold outline around the worksheet. I opened the Format Cells dialog box to the Border tab and clicked on all four sides of the locator box on the left. Then I clicked the dark bold line on the right and clicked the OK button. However, the regular thin line keeps appearing instead of the bold line. I must have clicked that bold line a hundred times, but I keep getting this stupid thin black line. At this point, I am beginning to think there is something seriously wrong with my computer! However, I heard you were really good with this stuff. Can you help?

Exercise

Open the file named ib_e02_pricechangeproblems. What's wrong with this spreadsheet? Consider the following points:

1. Try typing a number in any of the cells in the range D3:D12. Why can't you see the number?

2. Why is this coworker having trouble getting the bold line to appear on the worksheet? Follow the steps she explained in point 2 carefully. Is this right?

Write a short answer for each of these points and fix the spreadsheet for this coworker.

After creating a spreadsheet, you may need to make edits. Editing a spreadsheet may involve changing the data in a cell location, adding a new column of data, or deleting an existing column of data. The editing commands covered in this section can be found in the **Home** tab of the Ribbon. As in previous sections, we will again use the Financial Plan and Merchandise Sales Report spreadsheets to demonstrate the editing commands.

Editing Data in a Cell

After typing data into a cell location, you can change it by using the *formula bar* or by double clicking the cell. The formula bar, as shown in Figure 2.40, will always show the contents of an active cell. To change the data in an active cell, click the formula bar, type any adjustments, and press the **Enter** key. Figure 2.40 shows how the word "Description" was added to cell A1 using the formula bar. This edit can also be accomplished by double clicking cell A1.

Figure 2.40 | **Editing Data Using the Formula Bar**

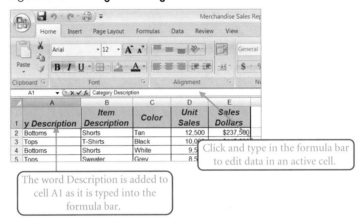

The word Description is added to cell A1 as it is typed into the formula bar.

Click and type in the formula bar to edit data in an active cell.

COMMON MISTAKES | Editing Data

Even though you are editing data, as opposed to entering data, you must still press the **Enter** key after completing your edits. Edits will not be finalized unless you press the **Enter** key, or you left click another cell. If you are using the formula bar to edit data in a cell, you can enter the change by clicking the check mark that appears on the left of the formula bar.

Moving Data

You can move data in Excel by clicking and dragging the edge of an active cell or a range of cells. Move the cursor to the edge of the active cell or range cells. When the cursor changes from a white plus sign to crossed arrows, click and drag the data to a new location on a spreadsheet (see Figure 2.41).

Figure 2.41 | **Moving Data**

	A	B	C	D	E
1	**Category**	**Item Description**	**Color**	**Unit Sales**	**Sales Dollars**
2	Bottoms	Shorts	Tan	12,500	$237,500
3	Tops	T-Shirts	Black	10,000	$115,000
4	Bottoms	Shorts	White	9,500	$180,500
5	Tops	Sweater	Grey	8,500	$289,000
6	Bottoms	Shorts	Brown	8,500	$161,500
7	Tops	T-Shirts	Blue	8,500	$97,750
8	Tops	Tank Top	White	6,500	$55,250
9	Bottoms	Shorts	Blue	5,500	$104,500
10	Tops	T-Shirts	Yellow	4,500	$51,750
11	Tops	Sweater	Brown	3,500	$119,000
12	Shoes	Sandals	Black	3,000	$66,0
13	Tops	Tank Top	Pink	2,500	$21,2
14	Shoes	Boots	Black	1,600	$96,0
15	Tops	Sweater	Red	1,500	$51,0
16	Tops	Tank Top	Red	1,500	$12,7
17	Shoes	Sandals	Grey	1,200	$26,400
18	Shoes	Sandals	Green	850	$18,700
19	Shoes	Boots	Brown	750	$45,000

This range of cells can be moved by clicking and dragging to a new location when the cursor changes to crossed arrows.

Deleting Columns and Rows

A common Excel editing feature is deleting columns and rows, which is especially help-ful when you are using a subset of data from a larger spreadsheet. For example, you may have received a large dataset from a classmate or coworker and want to reduce the spreadsheet to only the data you need. Or, you may need to remove rows of data that are no longer relevant to the purpose of a spreadsheet. The command to delete columns and rows is found in the **Cells** group of the **Home** tab in the Ribbon, as shown in Figure 2.42.

Figure 2.42 | **Icons in the Cells Group of the Ribbon**

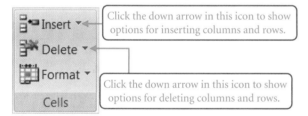

Click the down arrow in this icon to show options for inserting columns and rows.

Click the down arrow in this icon to show options for deleting columns and rows.

The following steps explain how you delete a row from the Merchandise Sales Report. This example assumes that the Green Sandals are being returned to the manu-facturer and will no longer be sold in the store. Therefore, this row is being deleted from the sales report.

- Activate any cell in row 18. Since the Green Sandals are in row 18, you can activate any cell in this row to delete the entire row.
- Click the **Home** tab in the Ribbon.
- Click the drop-down arrow in the **Delete** icon in the **Cells** group.
- Select the **Delete Sheet Rows** option. This will remove row 18 and shift the data in row 19 up to row 18.

Figure 2.43 illustrates how row 18 is deleted from the Merchandise Sales Report. Note that the steps for deleting a column are identical to deleting a row; however, you need to activate one cell in the column that is being deleted. For example, notice that cell F18 in Figure 2.43 is activated. When the **Delete Sheet Rows** option is selected from the **Delete** icon, this row will be deleted. However, if the **Delete Sheet Columns** option is selected, *column* F will be deleted.

>> **Quick Reference**

Deleting Columns or Rows

1. Activate one cell in the row or column you want to delete.
2. Click the **Home** tab in the Ribbon.
3. Click the down arrow in the **Delete** icon in the **Cells** group.
4. Select the **Delete Sheet Columns** or **Delete Sheet Rows** options.

Figure 2.43 | **Deleting a Row from the Merchandise Sales Report**

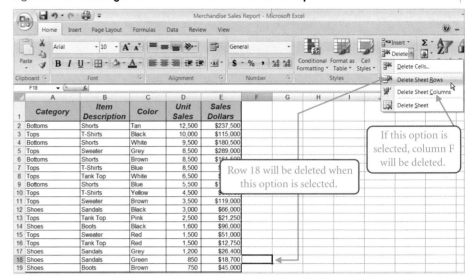

COMMON MISTAKES | Deleting Columns and Rows

You cannot delete a column or row by highlighting cells and pressing the **Delete** key. When you delete a column, the remaining columns should shift to the left. When you delete a row, the remaining rows should shift up.

Deleting Worksheets

Included in the **Delete** icon in the **Cells** group of the Ribbon is an option for deleting entire worksheets from a workbook. The reasons you may need to delete an entire worksheet are similar to the reasons explained for deleting columns and rows. The following steps explain how you delete a worksheet from a workbook:

- Activate a worksheet that will be deleted by clicking the worksheet tab.
- Click the **Home** tab of the Ribbon.
- Click the down arrow in the **Delete** icon in the **Cells** group.
- Select the **Delete Sheet** option (see Figure 2.44). When the **Delete Sheet** option is selected, a warning box will appear if there is data in the worksheet you are trying to delete.
- Click the **Delete** button on the warning box to delete the active worksheet (see Figure 2.45).

>> **Quick Reference**

Deleting Worksheets

1. Activate the worksheet you want to delete by clicking the worksheet tab.
2. Click the **Home** tab of the Ribbon.
3. Click the down arrow in the **Delete** icon in the **Cells** group.
4. Click the **Delete Sheet** option.
5. Check the worksheet carefully to make sure it is okay to delete.
6. Click the **Delete** button at the bottom of the warning box.

Figure 2.44 | **Deleting Worksheets**

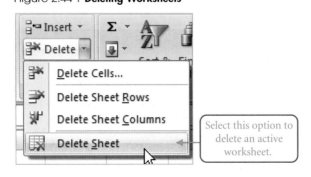

Figure 2.45 | **Warning Message When Deleting Worksheets**

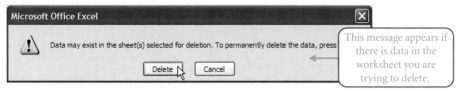

COMMON MISTAKES | **Deleting Worksheets**

You cannot use the **Undo** icon after a worksheet is deleted. Therefore, check the worksheet carefully before clicking the **Delete** button on the warning box shown in Figure 2.45. There is no way to retrieve a worksheet after it is deleted.

Inserting Columns and Rows

Another common Excel editing feature is inserting columns and rows. Often, you may need to add additional rows or columns of data to your own or other people's spreadsheets. For example, a noticeable omission in the Merchandise Sales Report (see Figure 2.43) is a title. If the report is without a title, it is impossible to know if the data in the Unit Sales column represents a week of sales, annual sales, or monthly sales. Therefore, a new row above the first row must be inserted for a title.

Similar to deleting columns and rows, the icon for inserting columns and rows also resides in the **Cells** group in the **Home** tab of the Ribbon (see Figure 2.42). The following steps explain how you add a row to the Merchandise Sales Report for the purpose of adding a title:

- Activate cell A1. Rows are always inserted above an active cell or range of cells. In this example, a row needs to be added above the first row in the worksheet. Therefore, cell A1 is activated.
- Click the **Home** tab in the Ribbon.
- Click the down arrow in the **Insert** icon in the **Cells** group.
- Click the **Insert Sheet Rows** option. After you select this option, a blank row will appear above row 1.

Figure 2.46 illustrates a row being inserted in the Merchandise Sales Report worksheet. Note the steps for inserting a column are identical to inserting a row; however, a column will always be inserted to the left of an active cell after you select the **Insert Sheet Columns** option from the **Insert** icon.

Figure 2.46 | **Inserting a Row in the Merchandise Sales Report**

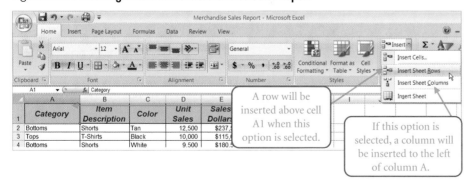

Figure 2.47 shows the results of adding a title to the Merchandise Sales Report. This figure reflects formatting enhancements that were added to make the title stand out. A reader can now see that the sales data shown in this worksheet are for the month of June.

Figure 2.47 | **Title Added to the Merchandise Sales Report**

	A	B	C	D	E
1			Sales for the Month of June		
2	Category Description	Item Description	Color	Unit Sales	Sales Dollars
3	Bottoms	Shorts	Tan	12,500	$237,500
4	Tops	T-Shirts	Black	10,000	$115,000
5	Bottoms	Shorts	White	9,500	$180,500
6	Tops	Sweater	Grey	8,500	$289,000
7	Bottoms	Shorts	Brown	8,500	$161,500
8	Tops	T-Shirts	Blue	8,500	$97,750

Inserting, Moving, and Renaming Worksheet Tabs

As mentioned earlier in this chapter, business managers will often create multiple versions or scenarios of a plan by copying an existing worksheet and pasting it into other worksheets in a workbook. This scenario was illustrated in Figure 2.14 for the Financial Plan spreadsheet. As a result, you may need to add additional worksheets to a workbook, arrange the order of those worksheets, and rename each worksheet tab. The following points explain how to accomplish each of these tasks:

- Click the **Insert Worksheet** tab at the bottom of a worksheet to add additional worksheets to a workbook (see Figure 2.48).
- Click and drag a worksheet tab to adjust the order it appears among the other worksheet tabs (see Figure 2.49).
- Double click a worksheet tab and type a new name. Press the **Enter** key after you type a desired name into the worksheet tab (see Figure 2.50).

Figure 2.48 | **Inserting New Worksheets**

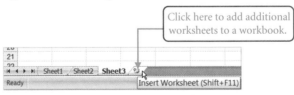

Click here to add additional worksheets to a workbook.

Sheet1 Sheet2 **Sheet3**

Insert Worksheet (Shift+F11)

Ready

Figure 2.49 | **Moving Worksheets**

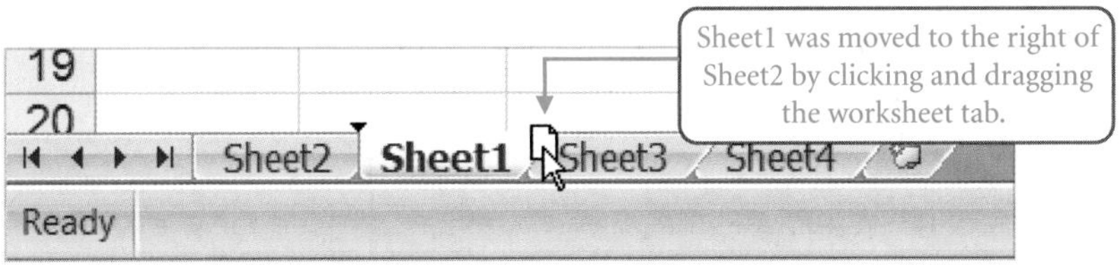

Sheet1 was moved to the right of Sheet2 by clicking and dragging the worksheet tab.

| 19 | |
| 20 | |

Sheet2 **Sheet1** Sheet3 Sheet4

Ready

>> Quick Reference

Insert Columns or Rows

1. Activate a cell depending on where a blank column or row should be inserted. Rows are inserted above an active cell; columns are inserted to the left of an active cell.

2. Click the **Home** tab.

3. Click the down arrow in the **Insert** icon in the **Cells** group of the Ribbon.

4. Select **Insert Sheet Rows** or **Insert Sheet Columns**.

Figure 2.50 | **Renaming Worksheets**

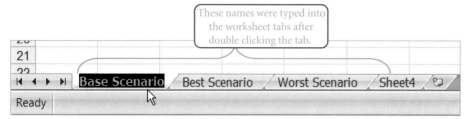

These names were typed into the worksheet tabs after double clicking the tab.

You can also rename worksheets by placing the cursor over a worksheet tab and clicking the right mouse button. This will open the set of worksheet commands shown in Figure 2.51. These commands are also contained in the **Format** icon in the **Cells** section of the Ribbon. The benefit of using this method is that it provides other options such as changing the color of the worksheet tab.

Figure 2.51 | **Changing the Worksheet Tab Color**

These commands appear by placing the cursor over a worksheet tab and clicking the right mouse button.

Click here to change the color of the worksheet tab.

COMMON MISTAKES | Naming Worksheet Tabs

Excel will not let you use the same name for multiple worksheet tabs. Each tab must have a unique name. If you are getting a duplicate worksheet name error but do not see another worksheet with the same name, check to see whether any worksheets are hidden by selecting the **Unhide Sheet** option in the **Hide & Unhide** submenu of the **Format** icon.

>> *Quick Reference*

Inserting Worksheets

1. Click the **Insert Worksheet** tab at the bottom of the Excel screen.

>> *Quick Reference*

Moving Worksheets

1. Click and drag the worksheet tab.

>> *Quick Reference*

Renaming a Worksheet Tab

1. Double click the worksheet tab you wish to rename.
2. Type the new name.
3. Press the **Enter** key.

>> *Quick Reference*

Worksheet Tab Color

1. Click the worksheet tab where the color is to be changed.
2. Place the cursor over the worksheet tab.
3. Right click.
4. Select **Tab Color**.
5. Select a color from the color palette.

>> Editing

The purpose of this workshop is to demonstrate the editing skills presented in this section of the chapter. We will continue to work on the spreadsheet that was used in the Formatting Video Workshop. I will be demonstrating the tasks in this workshop in the following four videos: **Editing Data**, **Inserting and Deleting Columns and Rows**, **Moving Data**, and **Renaming Worksheet Tabs**. After completing each section of tasks, watch the related video in parentheses. Remember to try the tasks on your own first before watching the video.

1. Open File

a. Open the file named ib_e02_videoworkshop, which you completed for the Formatting Video Workshop.

2. Editing Data (Video: Editing Data)

a. Activate cell A1 in Sheet1.
b. Click in the formula bar and type the word **Merchandise** in front of the word *Sales*. Then press the **Enter** key. In Sheet1, double click cell F2.
c. Add the word **Total** in front of the word *Sales* and press the **Enter** key.
d. Copy the range A1:F2 in Sheet1 and paste into cell A1 of Sheet2.
e. Copy the range A1:F2 in Sheet1 and paste into cell A1 of Sheet3.

3. Inserting and Deleting Columns and Rows (Video: Inserting and Deleting Columns and Rows)

a. Insert a row above row 1 in all three worksheets.
b. Delete row 1 in Sheet1.
c. For Sheet2 in cell A1, type **Arranged for Distribution Center**.
d. For Sheet3 in cell A1, type **Arranged for Merchandisers**.
e. For Sheet3, insert a column between columns A and B.

4. Moving Data and Adjusting Formats (Video: Moving Data)

a. In Sheet3, move the range D3:D13 to column B beginning in cell B3.
b. Move the range G3:G13 to column D beginning in cell D3.
c. Adjust the width of column D to 12 points.
d. Delete column G.
e. For cell D3, convert the bold line on the right side of the cell to a regular line.
f. Highlight the range A2:F13 and add a heavy bold line on the left, right, and bottom of the range.
g. Highlight the range A4:F13 and add regular horizontal and vertical lines inside the range.
h. Activate Sheet2.
i. Highlight the range A4:F13 and add a heavy bold line to the left, right, and bottom of the range and add regular horizontal and vertical lines inside the range.

5. Worksheet Tabs (Video: Renaming Worksheet Tabs)

   a. Change the tab name for Sheet1 to **Standard**.

   b. Change the tab name for Sheet2 to **DC Format**.

   c. Change the tab name for Sheet3 to **Merchant Format**.

   d. Save and close the file. Remember where this file is saved because you will use it in the next Video Workshop on Printing.

>> Editing Store Sales Reports

In business, you will always need to adjust and format spreadsheets based on your reader's requirements. The editing skills covered in this section provide you with more tools to accomplish this task. Business managers are often very demanding when it comes to seeing information and reports that address their needs. This often results in your creating several spreadsheets that are different in appearance but display the same or similar data.

Exercise

Open the spreadsheet named ib_e02_monthlystoresalesreport. The goal of this exercise will be to edit this report for the manager of store 6214. We will assume that the primary concern of this manager is the change in sales year to date this year over last year. In addition, the manager would like to compare how his store is performing against other stores in his district. Make the following adjustments to create this report:

1. Copy the spreadsheet in the **Original Data** tab and paste it into Sheet2.

2. In Sheet2, sort the data based on the values in the District column in ascending order and the values in the Change in Sales to Date column in descending order.

3. Since this store manager wants to focus only on his store and the other stores in his district, delete any rows pertaining to districts 1 and 3.

4. Since the primary concern of this manager is the sales information for his store and other stores in his district, delete the following columns:

   a. Current Inventory Value

   b. Inventory pr Sqr Foot

   c. Total Deliveries

   d. Week 1

   e. Week 2

   f. Week 3

   g. Week 4

5. To place the Change in Sales to Date column next to the Size in Sqr Feet column, first insert a column between column C and D. Then move the Change in Sales to Date column next to the Size in Sqr Feet column.

6. Unmerge the range A1:G1 by clicking the **Merge & Center** and **Center Cells** icons and merge the cells in the range A1:F1.

7. Add a heavy bold border around the range A1:F13 and remove the line at the top of cell G1.

8. Change the name of the worksheet tab for Sheet2 to **Store Manager Report**.

9. Hide the Original Data worksheet.

10. Delete Sheet3.

11. How is store 6214 performing relative to other stores in this district?

12. What stores are experiencing a decrease in sales compared to last year?

13. Overall, how does the district appear to be performing? Are most stores seeing an increase in sales over last year, decrease, no change?

14. Save and close your file.

PROBLEM & EXERCISE

>> What's Wrong with This Spreadsheet?

Problem

You are the manager of an audio electronics store and have a meeting scheduled with your district manager. You have asked your assistant to make some changes to the annual Merchandise Sales Report since your conversation with the district manager will be focused on the change in sales this year verses last year. You have given your assistant the following instructions:

1. Copy the spreadsheet in the Original Report tab and paste it into Sheet2.

2. Rename the tab for Sheet2 as **Sales Change**.

3. Delete the following columns: Receipt Date, Next Order Date, and Inventory.

4. Sort the spreadsheet by the Sales Change column in descending order.

Your assistant completes everything except he keeps getting an error when trying to rename the tab for Sheet2 to Sales Change. He explains that everything else you requested has been done.

Exercise

Open the file named ib_e02_audiobreakdown and look at what the assistant completed on Sheet2. Are you comfortable presenting this spreadsheet to your district manager? Consider the following questions:

1. Did the assistant delete the columns you asked for? If not, what did he do? How could you fix this?

2. Why is your assistant getting an error when he tries to rename the tab for Sheet2 to Sales Change?

3. Do you have any other concerns with this spreadsheet?

Write a short answer to each of the following questions. Correct any problems you see on the spreadsheet. If you cannot correct a problem explain why.

After completing formatting and editing adjustments to a worksheet, you may want to print a hard copy or bring several copies to a business meeting. This section covers the features and commands used for printing Excel worksheets.

Page Setup

Before printing a worksheet, you will need to apply settings that manage how a document will appear when it is printed. These settings can be found in the **Page Layout** tab of the Ribbon. Commands related to printing a worksheet are found in the **Page Setup**, **Scale to Fit**, and **Sheet Options** groups, as shown in Figure 2.52.

Figure 2.52 | **Commands Used to Prepare a Worksheet for Printing**

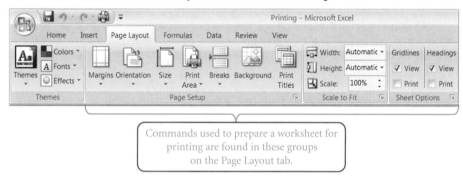

The commands needed to prepare a worksheet for printing will vary from project to project. If you are printing a small worksheet for your own reference, you may be able to print without using any of the commands shown in Figure 2.52. However, most worksheets will require some type of preparation. The following commands from the **Page Layout** tab are commonly used:

- *Margins*: Click this icon to select one of three preset margin settings for a document. The **Custom Margins** option will open the **Page Setup** dialog box. Here, you can make your own settings for the margins of a document. The **Page Setup** dialog box is covered later in this section.

- **Orientation**: Click this icon to select either a *Portrait* or *Landscape* orientation for a document.

- **Size**: Click this icon to select from a list of different paper sizes. The **More Paper Sizes** option will open the **Page Setup** dialog box.

- *Print Area*: Use this icon if you wish to print only a portion of a worksheet. Highlight the range of cells you wish to print, click this icon, and select the **Set Print Area** option.

- *Print Titles*: This feature duplicates the column headings or row headings of a worksheet on each page that is printed. Clicking this icon opens the **Page Setup** dialog box, which is covered later in this section.

- **Width**: This icon allows you to determine how many pages are used to print the width of a worksheet. If you wish to print all the data contained in a worksheet on one piece of paper, you would set both the **Width** and **Height** icons to 1 page. The **More** option in this icon will open the **Page Setup** dialog box.

- **Height**: This icon is similar to the **Width** icon, but it allows you to determine how many pages are used to print the length of a worksheet.

- *Scale*: Click this icon to manually reduce or enlarge the printed appearance of a worksheet.
- **Gridlines**: Click the box next to the **Print** option if you wish to print the *gridlines* that appear on the worksheet. Gridlines that appear on a worksheet when the Fill Color is set to No Fill will not appear in print unless this option is selected.
- **Headings**: Click the box next to the **Print** option if you wish to print the column letters and row numbers.

Similar to Excel's formatting commands, several of the features used to prepare a worksheet for printing are not available through the icons in the Ribbon. For these features, you will need to use the **Page Setup** dialog box. The descriptions of the icons in Figure 2.52 provided earlier indicate how you can open the **Page Setup** dialog box. In addition, you can open the **Page Setup** dialog box by clicking any of the buttons in the lower-right corner of the **Page Setup**, **Scale to Fit**, and **Sheet Options groups** sections of the Ribbon.

Figure 2.53 shows the **Page** tab of the **Page Setup** dialog box. The **Page Setup** dialog box will open to the **Page** tab when you click the button in the lower-right corner of the **Page Setup** section or select the **More Paper Sizes** option in the **Size** icon. Options in this tab include the printed orientation of a worksheet (Portrait or Landscape), the number of pages used to print the worksheet, and the paper size.

Figure 2.53 | **Page Tab of the Page Setup Dialog Box**

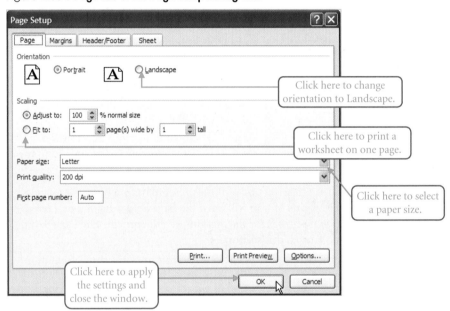

Figure 2.54 shows the **Margins** tab of the **Page Setup** dialog box. This tab allows you to make specific settings for the printed margins of a worksheet.

Figure 2.54 | **Margins Tab of the Page Setup Dialog Box**

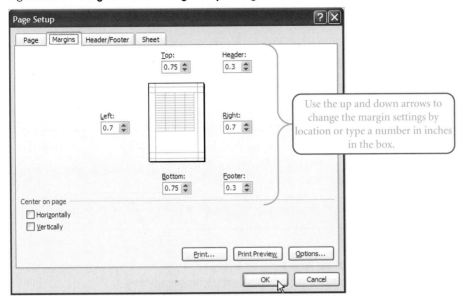

Figure 2.55 shows the **Header/Footer** tab of the **Page Setup** dialog box. This tab provides preset header and footer options that you can use to display items such as the page number, file name, or worksheet tab name at the top or bottom of a printed document. In addition, you can create your own header of footer by clicking either the **Custom Header** or **Custom Footer** buttons. Figure 2.56 shows the **Custom Header** dialog box, which opens after you click the **Custom Header** button. This is one of two options for creating custom *headers* and *footers*. The second option is to type a header or footer directly on the worksheet when the workbook is in **Page Layout** view.

Figure 2.57 shows the **Sheet** tab of the **Page Setup** dialog box. Options in this tab allow you to set a specific print range, designate columns or rows to be printed on each page, or show gridlines in the printed output.

Figure 2.55 | **Header/Footer Tab of the Page Setup Dialog Box**

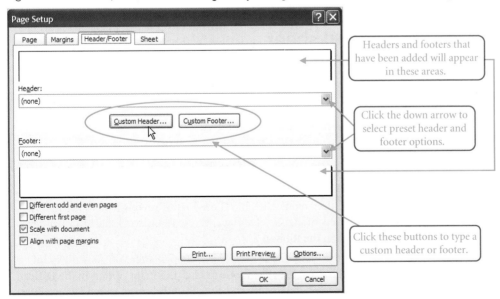

Figure 2.56 | **The Custom Header Dialog Box**

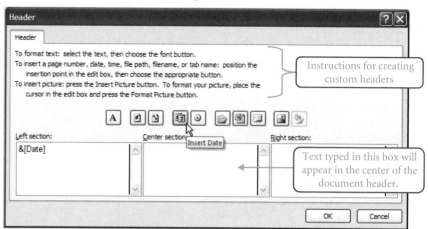

Instructions for creating custom headers

Text typed in this box will appear in the center of the document header.

Figure 2.57 | **Sheet Tab of the Page Setup Dialog Box**

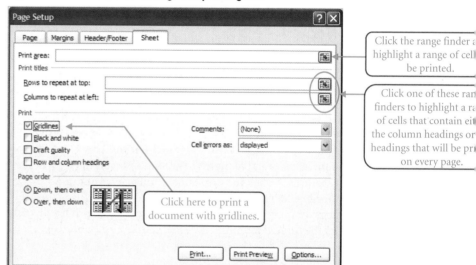

Click the range finder a highlight a range of cell be printed.

Click one of these ran finders to highlight a ra of cells that contain eit the column headings or headings that will be pr on every page.

Click here to print a document with gridlines.

>> **Quick Reference**

Printing Worksheets

1. Activate a worksheet to be printed.

2. Click the **Page Layout** tab of the Ribbon.

3. Make any necessary Page Setup adjustments by using the icons in the Ribbon or by opening the **Page Setup** dialog box.

4. Click the **Office Button**.

5. Click the side arrow next to the **Print** option and select **Print Preview** to view the document.

6. Click the **Print** icon in the **Print Preview** mode Ribbon.

7. Make any necessary settings in the **Print** dialog box.

8. Click the **OK** button in the **Print** dialog box.

Printing a Worksheet

When you have finished setting any **Page Setup** options for a worksheet, you should *preview* the worksheet in **Print Preview** mode before printing. Viewing a worksheet before printing will reveal any additional changes that need to be made and could save you wasted paper if the document is distorted from setting an option improperly. The following points explain how you accomplish this:

- Click the **Office Button** in the upper-left corner of the Excel screen.
- Place the cursor over the side arrow of the **Print** option.
- Select the **Print Preview** option from the submenu.
- After reviewing the document, click the **Close Print Preview** icon in the Ribbon to exit the **Print Preview** mode. Or, if you want to send the worksheet to a printer, click the **Print** icon in the Ribbon.

Figure 2.58 shows the **Print** dialog box. This will open after you click the **Print** icon in the Ribbon of the **Print Preview** mode or click the **Print** option in the **Office Button**. Make any necessary adjustments and click the **OK** button to send your worksheet to a printer.

Figure 2.58 | **The Print Dialog Box**

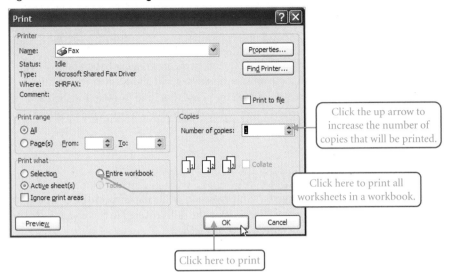

Click the up arrow to increase the number of copies that will be printed.

Click here to print all worksheets in a workbook.

Click here to print

>> Printing

The purpose of this workshop is to demonstrate the printing features and commands reviewed in this section. We will be printing the spreadsheet that was completed in the Editing Video Workshop. I will be demonstrating the tasks in this workshop in the video named **Printing**. Remember to try the tasks on your own first before watching the video.

1. Open the File

a. Open the file named, ib_e02_videoworkshop, which you completed for the Editing Video Workshop.

2. Page Setup (Video: Printing)

a. Make the following Page Setup adjustments for the Standard worksheet:
   i.   Set the orientation to Landscape.
   ii. Set the scaling to fit on 1 page wide by 1 page tall.
   iii. Increase the left and right margins to 1 inch.
   iv. Add a header with the date left justified and the following title in the center: **Standard Report Format**. Format this title to a 12-point font and italicize.
   v.   Click the drop-down arrow to show the list of preset footers. Select the option that shows the file name of your Excel workbook and the page number.

b. Make the same Page Setup adjustments for the DC Format worksheet and add the following title in the header: **Unit Volume Performance Report**.

c. Make the same Page Setup adjustments for the Merchant Format worksheet and add the following title in the header: **Sales Revenue by Item**.

3. Print (Video: Printing)

a. Preview each spreadsheet before printing.

b. Print the three spreadsheets in this workbook.

c. Save and close your file.

Solution from page 382

I was using electronic spreadsheets on a regular basis, and it seemed that the most basic skills would allow us to get rid of the paper spreadsheets and the correction fluid forever. If we had all our production data produced electronically, we could eliminate all paper and mailing charges.

Assignment

The following is a similar version of the paper spreadsheet used for our production plans. Using the skills covered in this chapter, create the same spreadsheet in Excel.

Production Spreadsheet							
Plan Number:	S143W	Season:	Fall 07		Division:	Men's Sportswear	
Style Number:	K44435		Description:		3 Button Rugby Long Sleeve Knit		
Packaging code:	PB			Button Style Code:	SRB.W7		
Production Details							
			Size				
Color	S	M	L	XL	XXL	Dozens	Ship Date
Solid Blue	10%	25%	30%	25%	10%	5.000	7/15/07
Solid Ivory	10%	25%	30%	25%	10%	2.500	7/15/07
Solid Green	10%	25%	30%	25%	10%	5.000	7/15/07
Navy / Ivory Stripe	10%	25%	30%	25%	10%	5.000	8/30/07
Green / Gold Stripe	10%	25%	30%	25%	10%	2.500	8/30/07
Green / Ivory Stripe	10%	25%	30%	25%	10%	2.500	8/30/07

Questions for Discussion

1. What other benefits, beyond those described in the anecdote, can you think of by converting the paper production plans into Excel spreadsheets?

2. What are some of the things that could go wrong with this project?

3. Identify solutions that could prevent any potential problems from occurring.

The following questions are related to the concepts addressed in this chapter. There are three types of questions: Short Answer, True or False, and Fill in the Blank. If your answer to a True or False question is False, write a short explanation as to why you think the statement is not true.

1. The following number was entered exactly as shown into a cell: 2,000. Is there anything wrong with this entry?

2. Besides pressing the **Enter** key, what else can you do to ensure data is entered into a cell?

3. What could typically go wrong with data entry tasks?

4. The following months were entered into two consecutive cells: January, June. Can **Auto Fill** be used to complete the rest of the months of the year? Why or why not?

5. What causes these symbols to appear in a cell: ####?

6. When using the **Format** icon to increase the height or width of a row or column, you must _____ in either the row or column you are adjusting.

7. The row numbers on the left side of a spreadsheet read 1,2,4,5,6,8,9,11. What does this mean?

8. What icon in the Ribbon can you use to hide a column?

9. In what Ribbon tab will you find the **Sort** command?

10. When you are using the **Sort** command, any column that is _____ will not be sorted.

11. True or False: Column headings should never be highlighted when sorting data.

12. True or False: If a column letter is missing at the top of a spreadsheet, it means that the column was deleted.

13. To center data over several cells, you would use the _____ command.

14. True or False: Selecting the **Currency** option when formatting numbers will always add a $ in front of the number.

15. True or False: There is no special accounting format for projects that require dollar signs and decimals to align.

16. True or False: Numbers and text entries will always be truncated if they are too large to fit into a cell. This is why you need the wrap text command.

17. You must select a _____ first when using the **Border** tab of the **Format Cells** dialog box.

18. The difference between a mediocre and professional-looking spreadsheet is often the result of _____ techniques.

19. List two options for changing data that has already been entered into a cell.

20. The cursor must change from a _____ sign to _____ before data can be dragged to a new location on a spreadsheet.

21. True or False: When you delete a column, the data disappears and an empty column remains.

22. Columns are inserted to the _____ of an active cell, and rows are inserted _____ an active cell.

23. Which icon in the Ribbon can you use to change the color of a worksheet tab?

24. True or False: To change the name of a worksheet tab, you can simply double click on the tab and type the new name.

25. How can you find out if there are any hidden spreadsheets in a workbook?

26. How can you change the order in which worksheet tabs are displayed in a workbook?

27. True or False: You cannot print all the spreadsheets in a workbook at one time. You have to activate each spreadsheet and print them one at a time.

28. True or False: Grid lines, besides the ones you may have added to a spreadsheet, will always appear on paper when a worksheet is printed.

29. How can you get column headings or row headings to print on every page when printing long or wide spreadsheets?

The following exam is designed to test your ability to recognize and execute the Excel skills presented in this chapter. Read each question carefully and answer the questions in the order they are listed. You should be able to complete this exam in 60 minutes or less.

1. Open the ib_e02_skillsexam.

2. Copy the worksheet named "Original" and paste it into Sheet2.

3. For Sheet2, insert 2 rows above row 1.

4. Enter the title **Cost Analysis Report** in cell A1.

5. Merge the cells in the range A1:H1. Then color the cells Blue, change the color of the text to white, change the font size to 16, bold and italicize the text, and set both the horizontal and vertical alignment to center.

6. Increase the height of row 1 to 25 points.

7. For the range A3:H3, wrap the text, color the cells light yellow, bold the text, and set the horizontal alignment to center.

8. Adjust the column widths as follows:

    a. Column B: **11.5**

    b. Column C: **8**

    c. Column D: **8**

    d. Column E: **11**

    e. Column F: **9.5**

    f. Column G: **13**

    g. Column H: **14**

9. In Sheet2, use Auto Fill to add 18 more cost components to the list in column A. There should be a total of 20 cost components beginning in cell A4 and ending in cell A23.

10. Copy the range B4:B23 and paste it into column G beginning with cell G4.

11. Enter data into the following cells: H4: 5000, H5: 2500, H6: 8500, H7: -2000, H8: 3100, H9: 10000, H10: 1000, H11: -5000, H12: 4050, H13: 2925, H14: -150, H15: 1800, H16: -200, H17: 3800, H18: 5500, H19: -3000, H20: 250, H21: 16500, H22: 2000, H23: 35000.

12. Delete row 2.

13. Add a heavy bold border around the perimeter of the range A1:H24.

14. Add horizontal and vertical regular solid black lines to the range A1:H22.

15. Add a bold black line to the bottom of the range A2:H2.

16. Add a bold black line to the bottom of cells D22 and F22.

17. Bold and italicize the text in cells A24, D24, and F24.

18. Format the following ranges to a number with commas and 0 decimal places: B3:B22, E3:E22, and G3:G22.

19. Format the range C3:C22 to U.S. currency 2 decimal places.

20. Format the range D3:D22 and F3:F22 to U.S. currency 0 decimal places.

21. Format cells D24 and F24 to U.S. currency 2 decimal places.

22. Format the range H3:H22 as a number with commas, 0 decimal places, and show any negative numbers in parentheses and in red.

23. Eliminate any #### errors that may have appeared on the spreadsheet.

24. Rename the tab for Sheet2 to **All Cost Data**.

25. Make a copy of the All Cost Data spreadsheet and paste it into Sheet3.

26. Rename the tab for Sheet3 as **Total Cost Analysis**.

27. Add two new worksheets to the workbook. Paste a copy of the All Cost Data spreadsheet into these two worksheets.

28. Change the tab name for one of the two new worksheets to **Inventory Cost Analysis**. Change the tab name of the remaining worksheet to **Purchasing Analysis**.

29. Arrange the worksheet tabs in the following order and change the color of each tab as indicated:

    a. Original: Blue

    b. All Cost Data: Green

    c. Total Cost Analysis: Red

    d. Inventory Cost Analysis: Yellow

    e. Purchasing Analysis: Purple

30. Make the following adjustments to the Total Cost Analysis worksheet:

    a. Delete the following columns: Current Inventory Units, Inventory Cost, Future Consumption, and Current Inventory Less Future Consumption.

    b. Sort the spreadsheet based on the Total Cost column in descending order and for any duplicate entries sort by the Unit Cost column in descending order. Note: The Totals row (row 24) must remain at the bottom of the spreadsheet.

    c. Add a heavy bold line to the right side of the range D1:D24.

    d. Change the text in cell A1 to read **Total Cost Analysis**.

31. Make the following adjustment to the Inventory Cost Analysis spreadsheet:

    a. Delete the following columns: Total Cost, Future Consumption, and Current Inventory Less Future Consumption.

    b. Sort the spreadsheet based on the Inventory Cost column in descending order and for any duplicate entries sort by the Current Inventory Units column in ascending order. Note: The Totals row (row 24) must remain at the bottom of the spreadsheet.

    c. Add a heavy bold line to the right side of the range E1:E24.

    d. Change the text in cell A1 to read **Inventory Cost Analysis**.

32. Make the following adjustments to the Purchasing Analysis spreadsheet:

    a. Delete the following columns: Current Inventory Units, Unit Cost, Total Cost, and Inventory Cost.

    b. Sort the spreadsheet based on the Current Inventory Less Future Consumption column in ascending order and for any duplicate entries sort by the Item column in ascending order. Note: The Totals row (row 24) must remain at the bottom of the spreadsheet.

    c. Add a dark bold line to the right side of the range D1:D24.

    d. Change the text in cell A1 to read **Purchasing Analysis**.

33. What two components have both the highest Total cost and the highest Inventory cost?

34. If this company has a standard of not going below 1000 units when considering current inventory less future consumption, what components would have to be purchased?

35. Make the following adjustments so each worksheet will print as follows:

    a. Landscape

    b. Fits onto one page

    c. 1 inch margin for top, bottom, left, and right

    d. The date on the left side of the header and the worksheet name in center of the header

    e. The page number in the right side of the footer

    f. Print grid lines

36. Save and close your file.

The following questions are designed to test your ability to apply the Excel skills you have learned to complete a business objective. Use your knowledge of Excel as well as your creativity to answer these questions. For most questions, there are several possible ways to complete the objective.

1. What information will you need before starting an Excel project?

2. You are evaluating a long-term project for building several retail stores. The project will start on March 20 of this year and will take 35 months before the stores will be open for business. The months of January through April are very slow business periods. Historical sales suggest that it is best to open stores in May or August. Given the start date and the 35-month duration, are the stores opening at a good time? Using the skills in this chapter, how can you use Excel to help answer this question?

3. Open the file named ib_e02_purchasingmanagerdata. This file needs to be formatted and adjusted for the purchasing manager of a sports equipment store who is responsible for assessing the current unit inventory for each item and the weeks of supply for each item. From this information, the manager will determine which items need to be purchased or which items should be returned to the manufacturer. The purchasing manager will make this decision based on the weeks of supply data. Any item with a weeks of supply less than 4 will be purchased. Any item with a weeks of supply greater than 20 will be returned to the manufacturer. Use the skills covered in this chapter to format the spreadsheet based on the needs of this purchasing manager.

4. Open the file named ib_e02_furniturefiasco. How many mistakes can you find in this spreadsheet? Make a copy of the spreadsheet and correct as many mistakes as you can. If you cannot correct a mistake, explain why.

5. Open the file named ib_e02_merchandisedataforpresentation. Look at this spreadsheet carefully. Would you be comfortable presenting this information for a class project or to the executive managers of a company? Why or why not?

Chapter 3

Calculating Data

Formulas and Functions

Chapter Goals

This chapter introduces the calculating power of Excel through two main objectives. The first is to present the fundamental techniques of creating formulas and functions, which are the primary tools used to calculate data. The second is to show how cell referencing is used within formulas and functions to maximize the dynamic abilities of Excel. In other words, formulas and functions will automatically produce new outputs when the data in one or more cell locations is changed. In business, these dynamic abilities are critical when evaluating what-if scenarios. Chapter 2 introduced the concept of what-if scenarios by demonstrating how to create multiple versions of a worksheet within a workbook. This chapter develops this concept even further by demonstrating how to perform common business calculations and analyses using formulas and functions.

>> **Excel** | Skill Sets

Excel in **Practice** | Anecdote

My Role as a Merchandise Analyst

If asked, could you predict how well printed skirts will sell this summer or say with certainty whether hip huggers are going out of style? Posing such what-if scenarios was my livelihood when I worked as a merchandise analyst for a women's fashion retail company where I projected the sales and profit for my department. Our goal each season was to sell all the clothes in the casual sportswear line with nothing left over. For example, every year we might purchase 25,000 pairs of shorts, which sold from the end of March to the end of July. If shorts still hung from the racks by the end of July, we were stuck with inventory, costing the department thousands of dollars in profit. To make matters worse, no one wanted last season's shorts, so reselling a previous season's inventory rarely worked.

Using a paper spreadsheet, I evaluated the sales of every item in my department, trying to determine what was hot and what was in danger of hitting the markdown table. While markdowns often increased the sales of an item, they also decreased our profits. Fortunately, sales in my department were booming, so I found myself working until midnight almost every day, recalculating sales and inventory data on my spreadsheets. While being part of a fast-growing business was a great experience, I had to find a better way of managing the sales and profit of my department; otherwise, I would burn out from exhaustion.

>> Continued on page 482

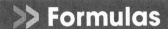
The most basic method of calculating mathematical outputs in Excel is through formulas. In fact, several numeric values shown in the financial plan created in Chapter 2 (see Figure 2.39) can be created using formulas. For example, the Net Sales values in row 5 can be produced with a formula that subtracts the Returns in row 4 from the Gross Sales in row 3. The formula does the work of calculating the Net Sales values as opposed to your typing these values into each cell manually, which increases the risk of data-entry errors. As a result, formulas not only reduce the risk of data-entry errors by producing values electronically, but they also provide the ability to evaluate what-if scenarios. This section will highlight the analytical benefits of formulas and demonstrate the construction of several formulas typically used in business.

Basic Formulas

For the purposes of this text, **basic formulas** are defined as any equations that consist of two variables separated by a **mathematical operator** such as + (addition), - (subtraction), etc. Business managers use a variety of basic formulas to calculate key metrics such as Gross Profit, Net Sales, or Inventory Turn. The types of formulas used by business managers depend on their areas of responsibility. Typical basic formulas used in business include

- **Gross Profit**: Net Sales − Cost of Goods Sold
- **Net Sales**: Gross Sales − Returns
- **Average Price**: Sales Dollars ÷ Unit Sales
- **Inventory Turn:** Net Sales ÷ Average Inventory Value
- **Sales Dollars**: Price × Sales Units

It is important to note that the math operators you see on a calculator are not always the same in Excel. For example, the "×" symbol on a calculator is usually used for the multiplication operation. However, in Excel you would use the asterisk (*) for multiplication. Figure 3.1 shows a list of symbols used for constructing formulas in Excel.

Figure 3.1 | **Mathematical Operator Symbols Used in Excel**

Symbol	Operation
+	Addition
−	Subtraction
/	Division
*	Multiplication
^	Power/Exponent

As previously mentioned, you can use a basic formula to calculate the Net Sales for the Financial Plan created in Chapter 2. This formula is added to the worksheet as follows:

- Activate cell B5. This cell represents the Net Sales for the year 2008 (see Figure 3.2).
- Type an equal sign. An equal sign signifies that Excel will be calculating data instead of displaying what is typed into a cell.
- Type the cell location B3. As illustrated earlier, the formula for Net Sales is Gross Sales – Returns. Since cell B3 contains the Gross Sales for 2008, this cell is added to the formula first. You can also add this cell to the formula by clicking the cell location after typing the equal sign.
- Type a subtraction sign.

- Type cell location B4. The value in cell B4 represents the Returns for the year 2008. Since this cell location comes after the subtraction sign, it will be subtracted from the value that is contained in cell B3.
- Press the **Enter** key.

Figure 3.2 shows the setup of the formula calculating Net Sales in the Financial Plan worksheet. It is important to note that this formula is composed of *cell references*. As a result, any value typed into cell B4 will be subtracted from any value typed into cell B3. If the value in either cell B3 or B4 is changed, the output of the formula will also change.

Figure 3.2 | **Basic Formula Calculating Net Sales**

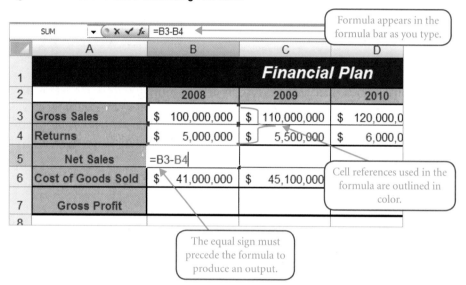

Figure 3.3 shows the result of the Net Sales formula in cell B5. Notice that when B5 is activated, you can see the formula =B3 – B4 in the formula bar. This indicates that the value $95,000,000 is a formula output and that the number itself has not been entered into the cell. Excel is calculating this output because an equal sign precedes the formula. If the equal sign was omitted, you would see B3-B4 displayed in the cell.

Figure 3.3 | **Results of the Net Sales Formula**

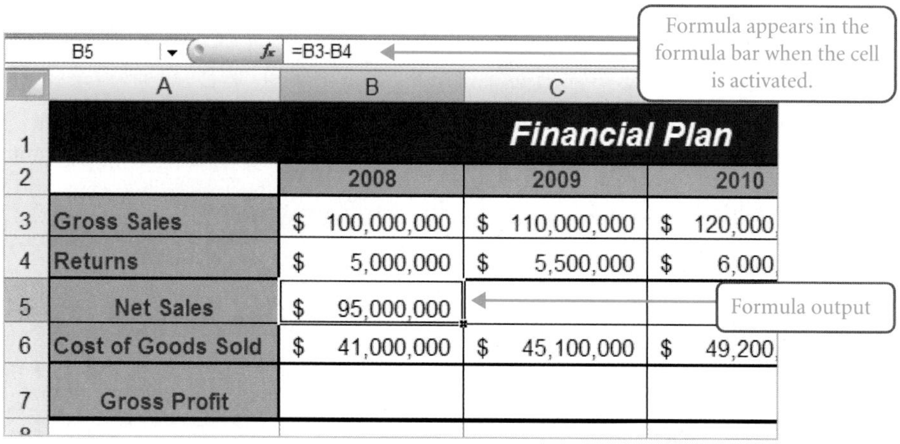

COMMON MISTAKES | Formulas

When doing calculations in Excel, never use a calculator and type the result into a spreadsheet. Typing computed results into a spreadsheet completely eliminates Excel's cell referencing capabilities. Formulas created with cell references will automatically recalculate outputs when data is changed in any of the referenced cell locations. In addition, creating formulas with cell references provides a record of how outputs are being calculated.

As previously mentioned, the formula shown in Figure 3.2 utilizes cell references. If the values in cells B3 or B4 are changed, the formula will produce a new output. Therefore, what will happen to Net Sales if returns are $10 million higher than planned for the year 2008? Type 15000000 in cell B4, and the formula automatically calculates a new value, as shown in Figure 3.4.

Figure 3.4 | **Changing the Returns Value in Cell B4 Produces a New Value for Net Sales**

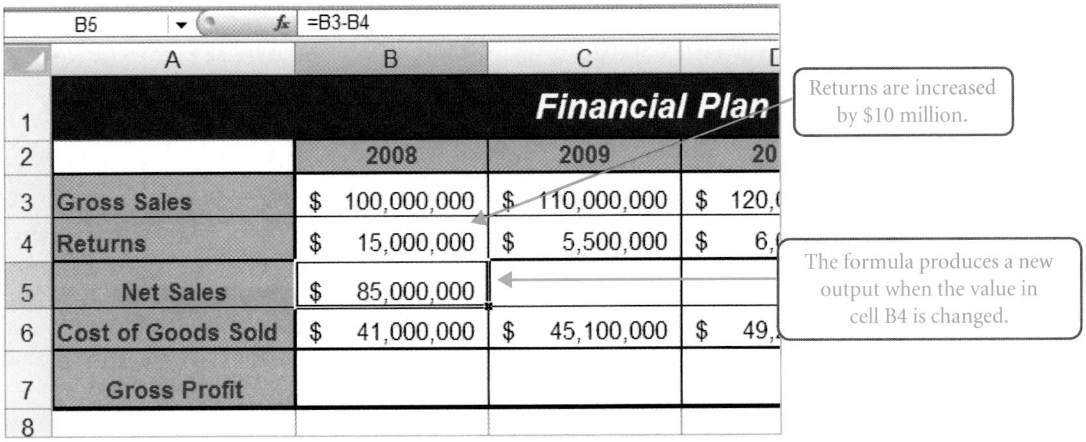

Figures 3.5 and 3.6 show the setup and result of a basic formula calculating the Gross Profit in the Financial Plan worksheet. Notice that this formula references cell B5, which contains the formula for Net Sales. Therefore, if the output of the Net Sales formula is changed, the output of the Gross Profit formula will also change.

Figure 3.5 | **Basic Formula Calculating Gross Profit**

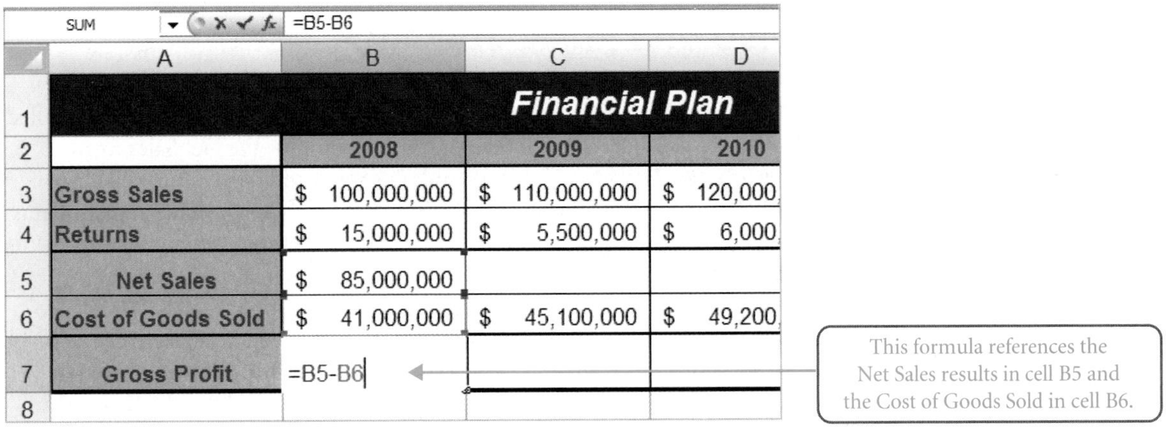

Figure 3.6 | **Results of the Gross Profit Formula**

	A	B	C	D
	B7	fx =B5-B6		
1			Financial Plan	
2		2008	2009	2010
3	Gross Sales	$ 100,000,000	$ 110,000,000	$ 120,000,0(
4	Returns	$ 15,000,000	$ 5,500,000	$ 6,000,0(
5	Net Sales	$ 85,000,000		
6	Cost of Goods Sold	$ 41,000,000	$ 45,100,000	$ 49,200,0(
7	Gross Profit	$ 44,000,000		Gross Profit formula output
8				

As mentioned, the formula calculating Gross Profit in the Financial Plan worksheet is referencing cell B5, which contains the formula for Net Sales. As a result, what will happen to the Gross Profit if the Returns value in cell B4 is reduced by $10 million? Type the value 5000000 in cell B4, and both the formula for Net Sales in cell B5 and the formula for Gross Profit in cell B7 produce new outputs, as shown in Figure 3.7.

Figure 3.7 | **Net Sales and Gross Profit Increase When Returns Decrease**

	A	B	C	D
	B7	fx =B5-B6		
1			Financial Plan	
2		2008	2009	The output for Net Sales and Gross Profit automatically increases when Returns are decreased to $5 million.
3	Gross Sales	$ 100,000,000	$ 110,000,	
4	Returns	$ 5,000,000	$ 5,500,	
5	Net Sales	$ 95,000,000		
6	Cost of Goods Sold	$ 41,000,000	$ 45,100,000	$ 49,20(
7	Gross Profit	$ 54,000,000		
8				

>> **Quick Reference**

Basic Formulas

1. Activate the cell where formula output should appear.
2. Type an equal sign.
3. Type or click a cell location that contains a value that will be used to compute the formula output.
4. Type a math operator (see Figure 3.1).
5. Type or click a second cell location that contains a value that will be used to compute the formula output.
6. Press the **Enter** key.

Copying and Pasting Formulas (Relative Reference and Paste Special)

After constructing a formula in Excel, you can copy and paste it to other locations on a worksheet. When you paste a formula to a new location, Excel utilizes a process called *relative referencing* to adjust any cell references. For example, the Net Sales formula shown in Figure 3.2 is =B3 – B4. If this formula is copied and pasted into cell C5 (one cell to the right), the formula will automatically adjust to =C3 – C4. This adjustment is the result of relative referencing. Relative referencing is a very convenient feature because, without it, you would have to retype every formula in a worksheet even though it may be performing the same mathematical function.

The following example further demonstrates the convenience of relative references. Figure 3.8 shows a merchandise sales worksheet similar to the one created in Chapter 2 (see Figure 2.37). In this case, a basic formula is created in cell D2 to calculate the average price for the item in row 2. Notice that the forward slash symbol is used for division.

Figure 3.8 | **Average Price Formula**

	A	B	C	D
	SUM	▾ ● × ✓ ƒx	=B2/C2	
1	Item	Sales Dollars	Unit Sales	Average Price
2	T-Shirts	$ 150,000	12,000	=B2/C2
3	Notebooks	$ 85,000	32,500	
4	Sweatshirts	$ 225,000	5,000	
5	Hats	$ 125,000	8,200	
6	Scarves	$ 9,000	750	
7	Sweaters	$ 120,000	2,500	
8	Diploma Frames	$ 187,500	1,500	

Forward slash is used for division.

Figure 3.9 shows the results of copying and pasting the formula in cell D2 to cells D3 through D5. Notice that the formula in cell D5 reads =B5/C5, which accurately calculates the average price for the Hats in row 5. However, the formula that was typed into cell D2, as shown in Figure 3.8, was =B2/C2. Relative referencing increased the row numbers of the cell references by 3 because the formula was pasted 3 rows below its original location. Without relative referencing, this formula would calculate the average price of the T-Shirts in row 2 for every item in the worksheet.

Figure 3.9 | **Relative Referencing Adjusts Cell References in the Average Price Formula**

	A	B	C	D
	SUM	▾ ● × ✓ ƒx	=B5/C5	
1	Item	Sales Dollars	Unit Sales	Average Price
2	T-Shirts	$ 150,000	12,000	$12.50
3	Notebooks	$ 85,000	32,500	$2.62
4	Sweatshirts	$ 225,000	5,000	$45.00
5	Hats	$ 125,000	8,200	=B5/C5
6	Scarves	$ 9,000	750	
7	Sweaters	$ 120,000	2,500	
8	Diploma Frames	$ 187,500	1,500	

Row numbers in the cell references increase by 3 because the formula is pasted 3 rows below the original location.

While relative references provide a convenient way to copy and paste formulas, in some situations you may need to paste only the value of a formula and not the formula itself. For example, Figure 3.10 shows a worksheet used to calculate the sales plans for six retail stores. Column D contains basic formulas to add the Planned Growth values to the Last Year Sales values for each store.

Figure 3.10 | **Retail Store Sales Plans**

	A	B	C	D
	SUM	▾ ● × ✓ ƒx	=B2+C2	
1	Store Number	Last Year Sales	Planned Growth	Total Sales Plan
2	1	$5,750,000	$125,000	=B2+C2
3	2	$4,250,000	$400,000	$4,650,000
4	3	$6,500,000	$250,000	$6,750,000
5	4	$3,250,000	$750,000	$4,000,000
6	5	$5,250,000	$500,000	$5,750,000
7	6	$2,750,000	$1,000,000	$3,750,000
8				

This formula is calculating the Total Sales Plan by adding the Last Year Sales values to the Planned Growth values.

Figure 3.11 shows a new worksheet that will be used by a manager to monitor the Actual Sales for each store to see if the store is achieving its Total Sales Plan. Therefore, the Total Sales Plan numbers calculated in Figure 3.10 need to be pasted into this new worksheet.

Figure 3.11 | **Plan versus Actual Sales Worksheet**

	A	B	C	D
	B2	f_x		
1	Store Number	Total Sales Plan	Actual Sales	Difference
2	1			
3	2			
4	3			
5	4			
6	5			
7	6			
8				

The values from the formulas created in column D from Figure 3.10 will be placed in this column.

As mentioned, the Total Sales Plan numbers calculated in Figure 3.10 need to be pasted into the Plan versus Actual Sales worksheet in Figure 3.11. However, using the **Copy** and **Paste** icons in this situation will paste the formula that is used to calculate the Total Sales Plan values, not the result. To paste only the result of this formula, you will need to use a command called **Paste Values.** You accomplish this by doing the following:

- Highlight the range D2:D7 in the worksheet shown in Figure 3.10. This is the range of cells that contain the formulas which calculate the Total Sales Plan values.
- Click the **Copy** icon.
- Activate cell B2 in the worksheet shown in Figure 3.11.
- Click the down arrow below the **Paste** icon to open a list of paste options (see Figure 3.12). The paste options list allows you to access a few commonly used commands from the *Paste Special* dialog box.

Figure 3.12 | **Paste Options List**

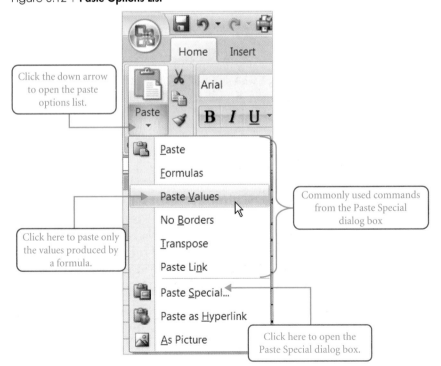

Click the down arrow to open the paste options list.

Click here to paste only the values produced by a formula.

Commonly used commands from the Paste Special dialog box

Click here to open the Paste Special dialog box.

- Select the **Paste Values** option from the paste options list. This will paste only the values created by the Total Sales Plan formulas and not the formulas themselves (see Figure 3.13).

Figure 3.13 shows the results of pasting the values of the Total Sales Plan formulas from Figure 3.10. When cell B2 is activated, the formula bar shows that the content of the cell is a number. In addition, notice the **Paste Options** icon, which appears on the worksheet after selecting a paste command. You can use this icon to select a different paste option if the one you originally selected does not provide desirable results.

Figure 3.13 | **Pasting Formulas as Values**

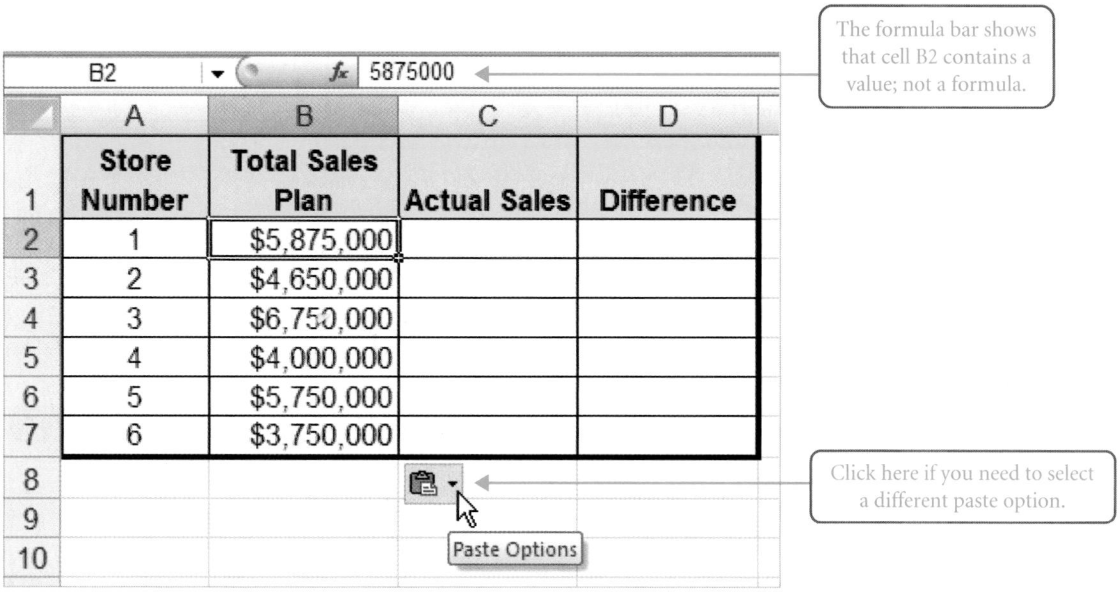

The formula bar shows that cell B2 contains a value; not a formula.

	Store Number	Total Sales Plan	Actual Sales	Difference
1				
2	1	$5,875,000		
3	2	$4,650,000		
4	3	$6,750,000		
5	4	$4,000,000		
6	5	$5,750,000		
7	6	$3,750,000		

Click here if you need to select a different paste option.

Paste Options

The paste options list contains a few commonly used commands from the **Paste Special** dialog box shown in Figure 3.14. To open the **Paste Special** dialog box and view all the available commands, click the **Paste Special** option, as shown in Figure 3.12. The following are a few key options:

- **Formats**: This option allows you to paste only the formats from a range of cells that has been copied. As a result, you can paste a specific arrangement of borders, number formats, or cell colors from one area of a worksheet to another.
- **All except borders**: This option appears as **No Borders** in the paste options list. Use it in situations in which you need to paste all content and formats from a range of copied cells except for the borders.
- **Formulas**: Use this option when you want to paste only the formulas from a range of copied cells without any of the format settings.
- **Transpose**: This option, found at the bottom of the **Paste Special** dialog box, can be used in situations in which a range of cells copied in a column needs to be transposed to a row or vice versa. Figure 3.15 illustrates an example of this option.

Figure 3.14 | **Paste Special Dialog Box**

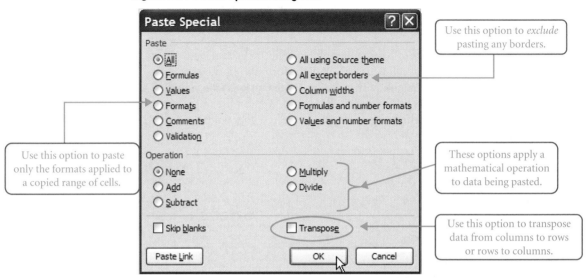

Use this option to *exclude* pasting any borders.

Use this option to paste only the formats applied to a copied range of cells.

These options apply a mathematical operation to data being pasted.

Use this option to transpose data from columns to rows or rows to columns.

Figure 3.15 | **Transpose Option in the Paste Special Dialog Box**

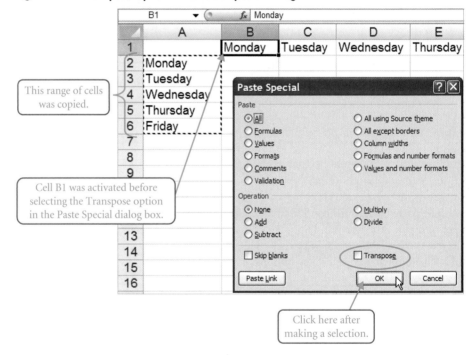

This range of cells was copied.

Cell B1 was activated before selecting the Transpose option in the Paste Special dialog box.

Click here after making a selection.

Complex Formulas

For the purposes of this text, ***complex formulas*** are defined as any equations that consist of more than two variables and require two or more mathematical operators. As previously illustrated, basic formulas are used to conduct several key calculations in business. However, business computations often require the use of formulas that consist of more than two variables. For example, you may need to add several components together to calculate the cost of a product. Or, you may need to estimate daily sales from weekly sales to calculate an annual inventory turn. These situations require more than two variables and may also require the use of constants or numeric values. In addition, parentheses may be necessary to change the standard order of mathematical operations.

Since a complex formula contains at least two or more mathematical operations, it is important to note the order in which Excel will execute each mathematical operation when calculating an output. Figure 3.16 lists the order in which Excel executes mathematical operations in a formula that does not contain parentheses. Note that the symbols shown in this figure were previously defined in Figure 3.1.

Figure 3.16 | Order of Math Operations

Symbol	Operation Order
^	First: Excel executes all exponential calculations.
* or /	Second: Excel executes multiplication and division after exponents. If both symbols are used in a formula, they are executed in order from left to right.
+ or -	Third: Excel executes addition and subtraction after multiplication and division. If both symbols are used in a formula, they are executed in order from left to right.

The complexity of formulas created in Excel is virtually limitless. As mentioned, when you are creating complex formulas involving several cell locations with several mathematical operators, Excel calculates the order of each operation as shown in Figure 3.16. However, in many situations you will need to change the order that each math operation is executed by adding parentheses. Math operations enclosed in parentheses are always executed first and override the order of operations shown in Figure 3.16. When several parentheses are used in a formula, Excel executes math operations by starting with the innermost parentheses and ends with the outermost parentheses.

Figure 3.17 illustrates an example in which parentheses are required in a complex formula. This worksheet shows an item from a merchandise worksheet similar to the example shown in Figure 3.9. The purpose of the formula in cell D2 is to estimate the inventory days on hand, which is calculated by dividing the inventory units by the number of units sold per day. However, notice that the sales results shown in column B are for last week. Therefore, assuming this store sells merchandise 7 days a week, the unit sales must first be divided by 7, and then the inventory units must be divided by this result to calculate the inventory days on hand.

Figure 3.17 | Calculating Inventory Days on Hand

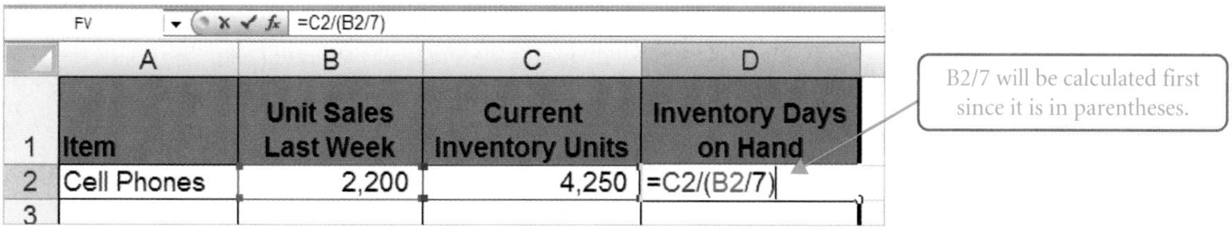

B2/7 will be calculated first since it is in parentheses.

Figure 3.18 shows the results of the Inventory Days on Hand formula, which is 13.52. Thus, if no additional inventory is received, this company will sell out of cell phones in approximately two weeks. Retail buyers often use this type of calculation to determine when products should be reordered from suppliers.

Figure 3.18 | Results of Calculating Days on Hand Inventory

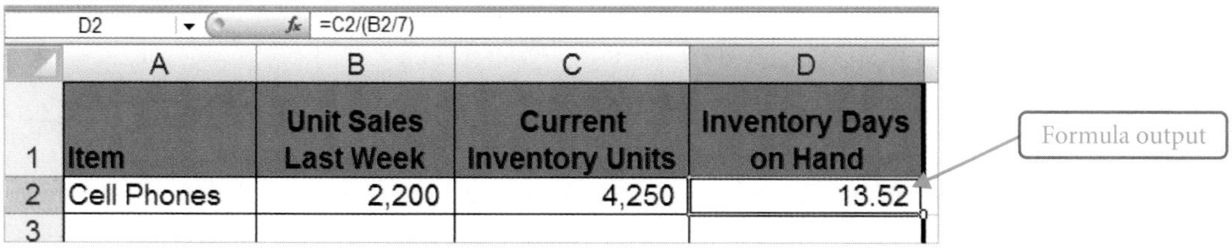

Formula output

Figure 3.19 illustrates the importance of using parentheses when creating the Inventory Days on Hand formula from Figure 3.17. Notice that no parentheses are used in this formula (see formula bar). As a result, Excel will execute each division operation in the order it appears in the formula from left to right. Therefore, Excel will first divide B2 into C2, and this result will be divided by 7. This produces an erroneous result of .28.

Figure 3.19 | **Invalid Result When Removing Parentheses**

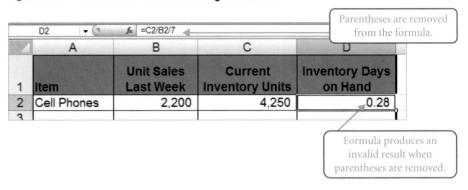

Parentheses are removed from the formula.

Formula produces an invalid result when parentheses are removed.

COMMON MISTAKES | Using Numeric Values in Formulas

Be careful when using numeric values in formulas, as shown in Figure 3.17. You should use numeric values when dealing with constant values that do not change, such as days of the week, months of the year, minutes in an hour, and so on. Do not type numeric values that exist in cell locations into a formula. Typing the numeric value instead of using the cell reference eliminates the ability to recalculate an output when data is changed in the referenced cell or cells. Whenever possible, always use cell references when creating formulas.

Figure 3.20 illustrates a second example requiring the use of parentheses to control the order of mathematical operations. The manager of a transportation company might use this worksheet to determine how much a customer should be charged for delivering merchandise to a warehouse or retail store. The method used by a transportation company to calculate a customer's price may vary depending on the company and the merchandise that is being delivered. This example assumes that a customer will be charged the company's total cost per mile plus a 25% markup for profit. The formula shown in cell F2 is calculating the price for a 750-mile trip.

Figure 3.20 | **Calculating the Price of a Merchandise Delivery**

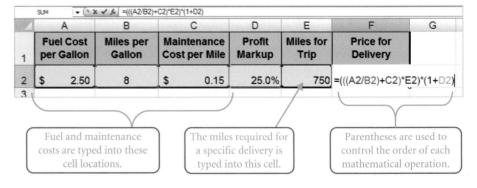

Fuel and maintenance costs are typed into these cell locations.

The miles required for a specific delivery is typed into this cell.

Parentheses are used to control the order of each mathematical operation.

As previously mentioned, when several parentheses are used in a formula as shown in Figure 3.20, Excel will execute the math operation in the innermost parentheses first and continue toward the outermost parentheses. The order of each calculation for this example is as follows:

1. `(A2 / B2)`: This is the innermost set of parentheses, which is why this operation is being calculated first. This part of the formula is calculating the fuel cost per mile by dividing the Fuel Cost per Gallon in cell A2 by the Miles per Gallon in cell B2.

2. `((A2 / B2) + C2)`: After the fuel cost per mile is calculated, the Maintenance Cost per Mile is added. At this point, Excel has calculated one number that represents the fuel and maintenance cost per mile.

3. `(((A2 / B2) + C2) * E2)`: After Excel has calculated one number representing the transportation manager's cost per mile, it is multiplied by the number of miles typed into cell E2. The customer for this particular example has a delivery that requires a distance of 750 miles. At this point, Excel has calculated the total cost for a 750-mile trip.

4. `(((A2 / B2) + C2) * E2) * (1 + D2)`: This is the complete formula shown in Figure 3.20. The last operation to be performed is multiplying the cost of the trip by the markup. As previously mentioned, it is assumed that this company establishes a price based on a 25% profit markup. Excel will first add 1 to the markup percent typed into cell D2 because this operation is in its own set of parentheses. Then, this result is multiplied by the total cost of the trip established in step 3. Since .25 is typed into cell D2, the total cost of this trip will be increased by 1.25 or 25%.

COMMON MISTAKES │ Unequal Number of Parentheses

When constructing formulas, remember that each opening parenthesis must always have a closing parenthesis. This mistake occurs mostly in situations in which you are creating a formula that contains multiple sets of parentheses. If you have an unequal number of parentheses, the Formula Error dialog box will appear, as shown in Figure 3.21. The good news is that Excel will offer to fix the error for you if you click the **Yes** button.

Figure 3.21 │ **Formula Error Dialog Box for Unequal Parentheses**

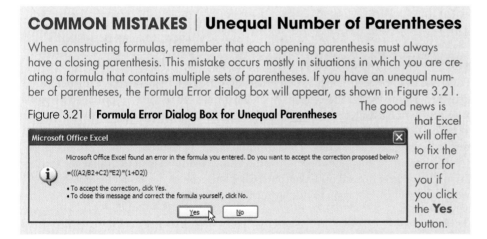

Figure 3.22 shows the final result of the formula calculating the price of a 750-mile trip. Because cell references were used in the construction of this formula, a new output can be calculated when any of the values in the yellow cells is changed. In fact, the cells in the range A2:E2 were intentionally colored yellow to indicate that these values can and should be changed when calculating a price for a new customer.

Figure 3.22 │ **Results of Calculating the Price of a Merchandise Delivery**

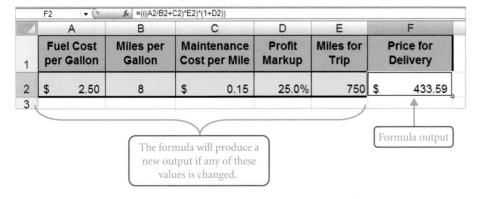

Because cell references are used in the formula shown in Figure 3.20, Excel calculates a new output when any of the values are changed in the range A2:E2. In fact, a transportation manager will most likely be changing these values on a daily basis. For example, the price of fuel might change, a new customer may request a price for a trip that is only 250 miles, or the company may need to lower its profit targets because of increased competition. How much will the company charge for the 750-mile trip shown in Figure 3.22 if the price of fuel increases to 2.75, and the profit markup is reduced to 20%? The answer is shown in Figure 3.23.

Figure 3.23 | **Formula Calculates a New Output When Data is Changed**

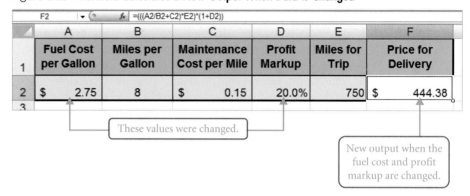

Auditing Formulas

Formulas will not be visible on a spreadsheet unless a cell that contains a formula is activated. However, a group of icons in the **Formulas** tab of the Ribbon called *Formula Auditing* contains features that can be used for viewing and checking all formulas in a worksheet. This feature is most helpful when you are proofreading formulas for accuracy or tracing the cell references of a formula that may be producing an erroneous result. Figure 3.24 illustrates how to use the **Show Formulas** icon to display the formulas in a worksheet instead of the outputs. Click this icon to display all formulas in a worksheet and click it again to display formula outputs.

Figure 3.24 | **Show Formulas Instead of Outputs on a Worksheet**

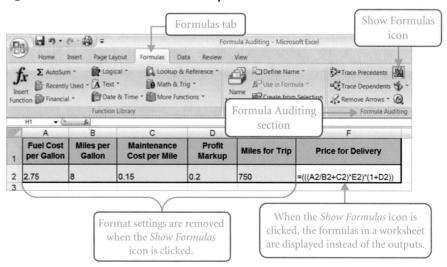

>> *Quick Reference*

Complex Formulas

1. Activate the cell where formula output should appear.

2. Type an equal sign.

3. Type or click cell locations or type numeric values if necessary.

4. Use parentheses and math operators where necessary.

5. Check that each opening parenthesis has a closing parenthesis.

6. Press the **Enter** key.

Another helpful proofreading option in the **Formula Auditing** section is the **Trace Precedents** icon. This feature will trace all cell references that are used in a formula. Activate a cell location that contains a formula and click the **Trace Precedents** icon. A blue arrow will appear on the worksheet indicating which cell locations are used in a formula, as shown in Figure 3.25. To remove the blue arrow, click the **Remove Arrows** icon, or click the down arrow next to this icon and select **Remove Precedent Arrows**.

Figure 3.25 | **Trace Precedents Arrow**

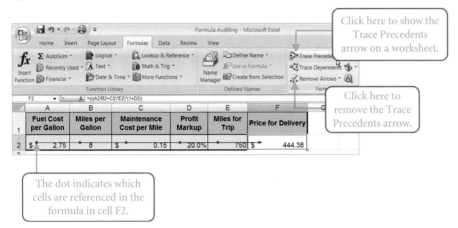

The dot indicates which cells are referenced in the formula in cell F2.

Click here to show the Trace Precedents arrow on a worksheet.

Click here to remove the Trace Precedents arrow.

Use the **Trace Dependents** icon when you need to see where a particular cell is referenced in a formula. This capability is helpful if a cell has been improperly referenced in several formulas and you need to identify which formulas need to be edited. Activate a cell location and click the **Trace Dependents** icon. A blue arrow will point to the cell location that contains a formula where the cell is referenced, as shown in Figure 3.26. To remove the arrow, click the **Remove Arrows** icon, or click the down arrow next to this icon and select **Remove Dependent Arrows**.

Figure 3.26 | **Trace Dependents Arrow**

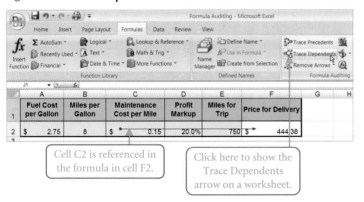

Cell C2 is referenced in the formula in cell F2.

Click here to show the Trace Dependents arrow on a worksheet.

> **Quick Reference**

Show Formulas

1. Click the **Formulas** tab of the Ribbon.
2. Click the **Show Formulas** icon.
3. Click the **Show Formulas** icon again to display the formula outputs.

> **Quick Reference**

Trace Precedents

1. Activate a cell location that contains a formula.
2. Click the **Formulas** tab on the Ribbon.
3. Click the **Trace Precedents** icon.
4. Use the **Remove Arrows** icon to remove the **Trace Precedents** arrow.

> **Quick Reference**

Trace Dependents

1. Activate a cell location that is referenced in a formula on a worksheet.
2. Click the **Formulas** tab on the Ribbon.
3. Click the **Trace Dependents** icon.
4. Use the **Remove Arrows** icon to remove the **Trace Dependents** arrow.

>> Formulas

The purpose of this workshop is to demonstrate the use of basic and complex formulas presented in this section of the chapter. We will be using formulas to develop sales projections for items sold in a retail clothing store. I will be demonstrating the tasks in this workshop in the **Formulas** and **Paste Special** videos. After completing each section of tasks, watch the related video shown in parentheses. Open the file named ib_e03_salesprojections before starting this workshop. Remember to try the tasks on your own first before watching the video.

1. Data Entry (Video: Formulas)

a. Type the following data into the Sheet1 worksheet for the cell locations listed:

   Cell C3: **10**
   Cell C4: **-15**
   Cell C5: **-50**
   Cell C6: **20**
   Cell C7: **0**

b. Type the formula **=B3+(B3*C3)** into cell D3 to calculate the Plan Unit Sales This Year.

c. Copy the formula in cell D3 and paste it into cells D4:D7.

d. Type the formula **=F3*D3** into cell G3 to calculate the Plan Sales Dollars for the first item.

e. Copy the formula in cell G3 and paste it into cells G4:G7.

f. Type the formula **=(G3-(D3*E3))/G3** into cell H3 to calculate the profit as a percent of sales for the first item.

g. Copy the formula in H3 and paste it into cells H4:H7.

h. Type the formula **=H3*G3** into cell I3 to calculate the estimated profit dollars for the first item.

i. Copy the formula in cell I3 and paste it into cells I4:I7.

j. Type the formula **=I3 + I4 + I5 + I6 + I7** in cell I9 to add up the plan profit dollars for all items.

2. Creating a New Scenario (Video: Formulas)

a. Rename the Sheet1 worksheet tab to **Profit Scenario 1**.

b. Insert a new worksheet.

c. Change the name of this new worksheet tab to **Profit Scenario 2**.

d. Copy the entire Profit Scenario 1 worksheet.

e. Activate cell A1 in the Profit Scenario 2 worksheet and click the **Paste** icon.

f. In the Profit Scenario 2 worksheet, type the following values in the cell locations listed:

C4: **0**

C5: **0**

3. Paste Special (Video: Paste Special)

a. Copy the range D3:D7 in the Profit Scenario 2 spreadsheet.

b. Activate cell C3 in the Sales Report spreadsheet.

c. Click the down arrow below the **Paste** icon and select the **Paste Values** option.

d. Click the **Paste Options** icon, which appears in cell D8 after completing step c.

e. Select the **Values and Number Formatting** option.

f. Save and close your workbook.

≫ Startup Costs for a New Business

Have you ever thought about starting your own business? One of the most significant challenges in starting a new business is determining how much sales are needed to pay for startup costs. Startup costs usually involve purchases such as machines, office equipment, or permanent marketing materials such as signs. In addition, certain statistics will either be fixed or inflexible. For example, the market price that customers are willing to pay for certain products and services may be fairly rigid. In these cases, raising the price of your product or service to cover startup costs will usually result in a losing proposition.

Exercise

The purpose of this exercise is to use Excel to determine how much sales are required to pay the startup costs of a landscaping business. Open the file named ib_e03_landscapingstartup and complete each of the following tasks:

1. Type the number **25** in cell B3 and change the color of the cell to yellow. You change the cell color to yellow to indicate where values need to be typed into the worksheet. The number 25 is simply a place holder for the number of customers this business might service in a year. This number will be adjusted in later steps of the exercise.

2. Indent the range A9:A11 by clicking the **Increase Indent** icon twice. Indenting will make the spreadsheet easier to read and is a common practice on most accounting and financial documents.

3. Indent cell A16 twice and then indent the range A21:A23 twice.

4. Type a formula in cell C12 that adds the values in cells C9, C10, and C11. This type of calculation is typically done with a function, which will be covered in the next section of this chapter. For now, use a formula to add these three values. This amount represents the total startup costs for this business. The primary focus of this business will be lawn care. Therefore, this exercise assumes that a lawnmower, trimmer, and blower are necessary startup purchases.

5. Type a formula that calculates the total cost of supplies in cell C16. The formula should multiply the value in cell B16 by the value in cell B3. This exercise assumes that supplies will cost $10 for every customer serviced. Costs such as fuel, garbage bags, and oil are usually consumed on every job. Therefore, the purpose of the formula is to multiply the cost per customer by the total number of customers planned for the business.

6. Type a formula in cell C18 that adds the value in cell C12 and C16. The output of this formula represents the total costs of the business.

7. Type a formula in cell B23 that calculates the Average Sales Revenue per Customer, which is Price per Acre multiplied by the Average Number of Acres per Lawn. This exercise assumes that the customer is willing to pay only $30 to service 1 acre of land. In addition, this case assumes that the average amount of land a customer will own in neighborhoods you service is 1.5 acres.

8. Type a formula in cell C25 that multiplies the Average Sales Revenue per Customer by the Number of Customers Serviced This Year.

9. Type a formula in cell B5 that takes the Total Sales in cell C25 and subtracts the Total Costs in cell C18. This is the Net Profit of the business. Is this business making any money if it services only 25 customers per year?

10. Change the value in cell B3 to **100**. Will this business be profitable if 100 customers are serviced per year?

11. How many customers must be serviced for the Net Profit to be approximately 0? How many customers for the profit to be approximately $5,000?

12. What if the price customers were willing to pay per acre dropped to $25, but the average number of acres per lawn increased to 1.75? How many customers will it take to achieve approximately $5,000 in Net Profit?

13. Save and close your file.

PROBLEM & EXERCISE

>> What's Wrong with This Spreadsheet?

Problem

You are directing a division of a major department store company. Your division is made up of four departments. At the beginning of each year, the directors from every division meet with the president of the company to discuss sales and profit targets. A colleague in another division gave you a spreadsheet with an assurance that it included all necessary formulas and that the only thing you had to do was enter numbers in the yellow cells that relate to your sales and profit targets.

Exercise

The spreadsheet that was given to you is named ib_e03_departmentstoreplanning meeting. Open this file and examine the Sheet1 worksheet carefully. Would you be comfortable using this worksheet to plan the sales and profit targets for your division? Consider the following:

1. Look at the totals in cells B8, C8, and F8. Do the numbers add up?

2. Give the spreadsheet a test drive by changing the value in cell D4 to `.10`. The sales results in column C are calculated by multiplying the Sales Last Year in column B by the Sales Growth percentages in column D. Do you see a new sales plan number in cell C4 that makes sense?

3. Change the value in cell B4 to `8000000`. Do you see a new sales plan number in cell C4 when the value in cell B4 was changed?

4. The Profit Dollars in column F are calculated by multiplying the Profit Percent values in column E by the Sales values in column C. Change the value in cell E4 to `.20`. Does this change produce a new profit dollar value in cell F4?

5. Look at the totals in cells B8, C8, and F8. Do the numbers still add up?

6. What could you use to see and check all the formulas in this worksheet? What clues would tell you that something might be wrong with a formula?

What's wrong with this spreadsheet? Write a short answer for each of the points listed in the preceding problem. Then, fix any errors, adjust, or add formulas that you believe would make this spreadsheet more reliable.

>> Basic Functions

As previously mentioned, the two primary tools for conducting mathematical computations in Excel are formulas and functions. **Functions** are slightly different from formulas in that you do not have to define mathematical operators to produce an output. The mathematical operations are predefined depending on the function that is used. For example, the **AVERAGE** function can be used to calculate the average for a range of ten cells in a worksheet. Functions can produce exactly the same output as formulas. However, when a mathematical output requires the use of many cell locations, it is easier and faster to add a function to a worksheet as opposed to a formula. This section will review the use of basic statistical functions and illustrate why it is more efficient to use them for certain calculations instead of formulas.

Basic Statistical Functions

Using basic statistical methods to analyze data is a common practice in business. For example, a business manager may sum the sales results for a group of stores in a district, calculate the average trips per week for a fleet of trucks, or evaluate the most common number of items purchased when customers visit a store. In Excel, basic statistical functions can provide a convenient way to accomplish these computations, as opposed to using formulas. For example, the Merchandise Sales Report worksheet introduced in Chapter 2 (see Figure 3.28) contains sales information for 18 items. If you wanted to calculate the sum of the Unit Sales for all items in column D, you could add all 18 cell

Basic Functions | Excel   453

locations from D2 to D19 individually to a formula. Or, you could just add the range D2:D19 to the **SUM** function to produce the same result.

All Excel functions can be created using the following method:

- Type an equal sign. Similar to formulas, all functions begin with an equal sign in a cell location. The equal sign signifies that Excel will be performing some type of computation instead of displaying what is typed in a cell.

- Type the function name. After you type the first letter of a function, a list of possible function names beginning with the letter you typed will appear (see Figure 3.27). This feature is especially helpful if you forgot how to spell a particular function name. After you find the name of the function you would like to use, you can double click the name from the list or continue typing the function name manually.

- Type an open parenthesis. If you double click a function name from the function list as shown in Figure 3.27, Excel will insert the open parenthesis for you automatically.

- Type a cell range or define arguments. The information you type after the open parenthesis will depend on the type of function you are using. For the basic statistical functions covered in this section, you will need to type a cell range (two cell locations separated by a colon) after the open parenthesis. You can also type specific cell locations separated by commas if you are applying the function to cells that are not contained in a continuous range (for example, B2,H5,D10). Note that functions containing arguments are covered in the next section.

- Type a close parenthesis and press the **Enter** key. After you press the **Enter** key, the function output will be displayed in the cell.

As mentioned, when you begin typing the name of a function, a list of possible function names beginning with the first letter you typed will appear on the worksheet. For example, Figure 3.27 shows the function list after typing an equal sign and the letter S. In addition, if you click a function name one time, a definition of the function will appear.

Figure 3.27 | **The Function List**

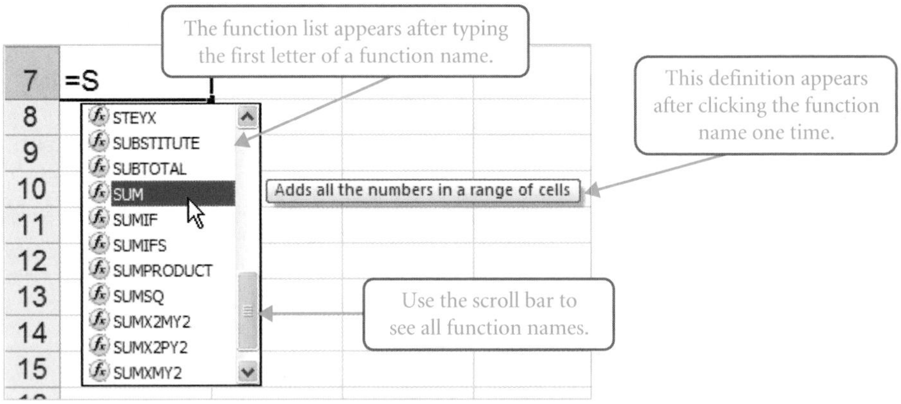

Figures 3.28 and 3.29 show the setup and results of adding a **SUM** function to the Merchandise Sales Report worksheet, which was constructed in Chapter 2. Here, the **SUM** function was added to calculate the total number of units sold for all items in the worksheet. As mentioned, it is more convenient to use the **SUM** function in this situation because a total is being computed from 18 cell locations. The following explains how to add this function to the worksheet:

- Activate cell D20. This is the last cell at the bottom of the Unit Sales column.
- Type an equal sign.
- Type the function name SUM. You can also double click the word **SUM** from the function list.
- Type an open parenthesis. If you double clicked the function name from the function list, the open parenthesis will already be added.

- Type the range D2:D19. You can also add this range to the function by clicking and dragging over cells D2 through D19.
- Type a close parenthesis.
- Press the **Enter** key.

Figure 3.28 | **Adding the SUM Function to the Merchandise Sales Report**

	A	B	C	D	E
	Category Description	**Item Description**	**Color**	**Unit Sales**	**Sales Dollars**
2	Bottoms	Shorts	Tan	12,500	$237,500
3	Tops	T-Shirts	Black	10,000	$115,000
4	Bottoms	Shorts	White	9,500	$180,500
5	Tops	Sweater	Grey	8,500	$289,000
6	Bottoms	Shorts	Brown	8,500	$161,500
7	Tops	T-Shirts	Blue	8,500	$97,750
8	Tops	Tank Top	White	6,500	$55,250
9	Bottoms	Shorts	Blue	5,500	$104,500
10	Tops	T-Shirts	Yellow	4,500	$51,750
11	Tops	Sweater	Brown	3,500	$119,000
12	Shoes	Sandals	Black	3,000	$66,000
13	Tops	Tank Top	Pink	2,500	$21,250
14	Shoes	Boots	Black	1,600	$96,000
15	Tops	Sweater	Red	1,500	$51,000
16	Tops	Tank Top	Red	1,500	$12,750
17	Shoes	Sandals	Grey	1,200	$26,400
18	Shoes	Sandals	Green	850	$18,700
19	Shoes	Boots	Brown	750	$45,000
20	**Total**			=SUM(D2:D19)	

Formula bar: =SUM(D2:D19)

The function appears in the formula bar when cell D20 is activated.

This range can be added to the function by clicking and dragging over cells D2 through D19 after typing =SUM(.

Figure 3.29 | **Results of the SUM Function in the Merchandise Sales Report**

	A	B	C	D	E
	Category Description	**Item Description**	**Color**	**Unit Sales**	**Sales Dollars**
2	Bottoms	Shorts	Tan	12,500	$237,500
3	Tops	T-Shirts	Black	10,000	$115,000
4	Bottoms	Shorts	White	9,500	$180,500
5	Tops	Sweater	Grey	8,500	$289,000
6	Bottoms	Shorts	Brown	8,500	$161,500
7	Tops	T-Shirts	Blue	8,500	$97,750
8	Tops	Tank Top	White	6,500	$55,250
9	Bottoms	Shorts	Blue	5,500	$104,500
10	Tops	T-Shirts	Yellow	4,500	$51,750
11	Tops	Sweater	Brown	3,500	$119,000
12	Shoes	Sandals	Black	3,000	$66,000
13	Tops	Tank Top	Pink	2,500	$21,250
14	Shoes	Boots	Black	1,600	$96,000
15	Tops	Sweater	Red	1,500	$51,000
16	Tops	Tank Top	Red	1,500	$12,750
17	Shoes	Sandals	Grey	1,200	$26,400
18	Shoes	Sandals	Green	850	$18,700
19	Shoes	Boots	Brown	750	$45,000
20	**Total**			90,400	

Output produced by the SUM function.

The example in Figure 3.30 illustrates the **AVERAGE** function. This worksheet contains the sales and profit results for six stores in a district of a retail company. The **AVERAGE** function is used to calculate the average sales results that are achieved for each store in the district. Notice that the range in the **AVERAGE** function includes cell C7, which does not contain a numeric value. Statistical functions will ignore cells that are blank or do not contain numeric data. Therefore, the **AVERAGE** function will ignore this cell until a numeric value is typed into it.

Figure 3.30 | **The AVERAGE Function**

	A	B	C	D
				=AVERAGE(C2:C7)
1	**District**	**Store Number**	**Annual Sales**	**Net Profit**
2	5	505	$ 3,007,782	$
3	5	522	$ 5,738,273	$
4	5	560	$ 7,144,261	$
5	5	575	$ 3,058,901	$
6	5	580	$ 5,646,718	$ 656,467
7	5	590	New Store	N/A
8		**Averages**	=AVERAGE(C2:C7)	

The AVERAGE function will ignore this cell because it does not contain a numeric value.

Relative referencing (explained previously in the "Formulas" section) also applies to functions. Figure 3.31 shows the **AVERAGE** function after it was pasted into cell D8, which is one cell to the right of the cell location shown in Figure 3.30. Notice that the column letters of the range in the function changed from C to D. This function will show the average of the Net Profit results in column D and will ignore cell D7 because it does not contain a numeric value.

FIGURE 3.31 | **Relative Referencing Adjusts the Range in the AVERAGE Function**

	A	B	C	D	E
				=AVERAGE(D2:D7)	
1	**District**	**Store Number**	**Annual Sales**	**Net Profit**	
2	5	505	$ 3,007,782	$ 320,311	
3	5	522	$ 5,738,273	$ 716,445	
4	5	560	$ 7,144,261	$ (142,885)	
5	5	575	$ 3,058,901	$ 467,068	
6	5	580	$ 5,646,718	$ 656,467	
7	5	590	New Store	N/A	
8		**Averages**	$ 4,919,187	=AVERAGE(D2:D7)	

The column letters in this range automatically adjusted when the function was pasted into cell D8 from C8.

Figure 3.32 shows how the **AVERAGE** function produces a new output when numeric data is typed into C7 and D7. As mentioned, these cells were previously ignored by the function because they did not contain numeric values. However, because of cell referencing, the functions automatically produce a new output when numeric values are typed into these cells.

Figure 3.32 | The AVERAGE Function Produces a New Output When Data Is Changed

	A	B	C	D
1	District	Store Number	Annual Sales	Net Profit
2	5	505	$ 3,007,782	$ 320,311
3	5	522	$ 5,738,273	$ 716,445
4	5	560	$ 7,144,261	$ (142,885)
5	5	575	$ 3,058,901	$ 467,068
6	5	580	$ 5,646,718	$ 656,467
7	5	590	$ 8,534,000	$ 775,640
8		Averages	$ 5,521,656	$ 465,508

Values are typed into cells C7 and D7.

This output changed when a value was typed into cell C7.

COMMON MISTAKES | Cell Ranges versus Specific Cells in Functions

Be careful when using a range of cells versus selected cells in basic statistical functions. If you want to apply a statistical function to a group of consecutive cells, you must use a range. A range is any two cells separated by a colon, NOT a comma. For example, the **SUM** function shown in Figure 3.33 will add only cells A2 and A6, providing an output of 3000. The reason is that a *comma* is separating the two cell locations. For this **SUM** function to add all of the values in cells A2 through A6, the range **A2:A6** must be typed between the parentheses of the function. Therefore, always check the outputs of all functions used in a worksheet. If you were expecting the **SUM** function to add all the values in column A in Figure 3.33 and saw an output of 3000, you would know something is wrong because one of the values in this column is 5000 (cell A4).

Figure 3.33 | SUM Function Adding Values in Only Two Cell Locations

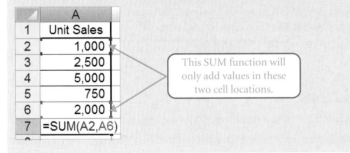

	A
1	Unit Sales
2	1,000
3	2,500
4	5,000
5	750
6	2,000
7	=SUM(A2,A6)

This SUM function will only add values in these two cell locations.

The **SUM** function and the **AVERAGE** function were used to demonstrate basic statistical functions in this section. However, this usage just scratches the surface of the 300+ functions in Excel. Figure 3.34 shows other commonly used statistical functions. The details of what these functions do and how they are applied in business situations will likely be covered in your business statistics or economics courses.

>> Quick Reference

Basic Functions

1. Activate a cell where the output of the function should appear.
2. Type an equal sign.
3. Type the name of the function or double click a function name from the function list.
4. Type an open parenthesis if you typed the function name manually.
5. Type a range or click and drag a range of cells (if you are using specific cells not in a continuous range, type or click each cell and separate with a comma).
6. Type a closing parenthesis.
7. Press the **Enter** key.

Figure 3.34 | **Table of Common Statistical Functions**

Function Name	Purpose
SUM	Calculates the total for numeric values in a range of cells or selected cells.
AVERAGE	Calculates the average for a series of numeric values.
MEDIAN	Returns the value that is in the middle of a *sorted* numeric series (the range of cells used with this function must be sorted in order for the function to produce an accurate result).
MODE	Identifies the value that occurs the most in a numeric series.
STDEV	Calculates the standard deviation for a range of cells.
VAR	Calculates the variance for a range of cells.
MIN	Returns the lowest value in a numeric series.
MAX	Returns the highest value in a numeric series.
COUNT	Counts the number of cells that contain a numeric value.
COUNTA	Counts the number of cells that contain either a numeric value or text value.
PRODUCT	Calculates the product of the values contained in a range of cells or selected cells.
SQRT	Returns the square root of a number.
ABS	Returns the absolute value of a number.

AutoSum

The **AutoSum** icon in the **Formulas** tab of the Ribbon provides quick access to a few basic statistical functions covered in this section. The following explains how to use the **AutoSum** icon to add the **AVERAGE** function to a worksheet:

- Activate a cell location where the output of the function should appear. This cell location should be below or to the right of a range of cells that will be used in the function.
- Click the **Formulas** tab.
- Click the down arrow next to the **AutoSum** icon (see Figure 3.35).
- Select the **AVERAGE** option. This selection will add the **AVERAGE** function to the worksheet and automatically select a range of cells immediately above the activated cell location (see Figure 3.36).
- Press the **Enter** key.

Figure 3.35 | **Options in the AutoSum Icon**

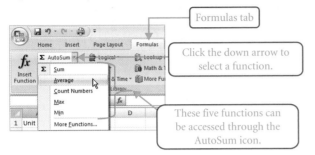

Figure 3.36 | **The Range Is Added to the AVERAGE Function Automatically**

When creating a function with the AutoSum icon, this range is automatically defined.

	A	B	C
1	Unit Sales		
2	1,000		
3	2,500		
4	5,000		
5	750		
6	2,000		
7	=AVERAGE(A2:A6)		

SUM — =AVERAGE(A2:A6)

Absolute References (Turning Off Relative References)

As previously mentioned, because of relative referencing, Excel will automatically adjust the cell references used in formulas and functions when they are pasted into new cell locations. However, certain circumstances may require you to turn off this relative reference feature. In other words, you may need to paste a formula or function to a new cell location but do not want Excel to adjust the cell references. In these situations you will need to apply an *absolute reference* or a *mixed reference* to the cell references in a formula.

To place an absolute reference on a cell location, type a dollar sign in front of the column letter and row number. Placing the dollar sign here prevents relative referencing from adjusting the cell location when the formula is pasted to a new cell location. You can also create mixed references which is when a dollar sign is typed in front of the column letter *or* the row number. For example, if a dollar sign is typed only in front of the row number, the row number becomes an absolute reference, but the column letter remains a relative reference. If this cell was referenced in a formula, the column letter will change, but the row number will not when the formula is pasted into a new cell location. The following are examples of absolute and mixed references.

- $C$10: This is an absolute reference. This cell reference will not change when it is pasted to another cell location on a worksheet.
- C$10: This is a mixed reference. The row number will not change when this cell is pasted to a new location on a worksheet.
- $C10: This is another example of a mixed reference. The column letter will not change when this cell is pasted to a new location on a worksheet.

The example in Figure 3.37 illustrates when an absolute reference is used in a business situation. This worksheet shows a list of annual expenses for a hypothetical company. A **SUM** function was created in cell B8 to total the Cost Values for all expense items in column B. The goal for this example is to create a formula in column C that divides the Cost Value for each expense item by the total in cell B8. This will show what percentage each item contributes to the total expenses for the business.

Figure 3.37 | **Annual Expense Information for a Hypothetical Business**

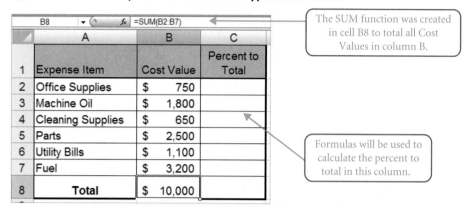

Figure 3.38 shows the formula that was created in cell C2 to compute the Percent to Total for Office Supplies. The result shows that Office Supplies makes up 7.5% of the total annual expenses for this business. This formula will be copied and pasted to cells C3 through C7 to calculate the Percent to Total for the rest of the Expense Items in column A.

Figure 3.38 | **Formula Used to Compute the Percent to Total**

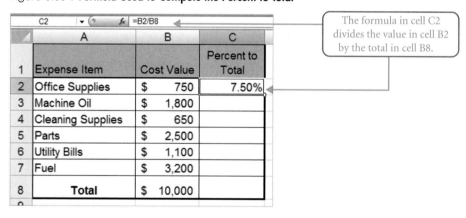

Figure 3.39 shows that a divide by zero error (#DIV/0!) occurs when the formula created in cell C2 is pasted into cells C3 through C7. This error occurred because relative referencing is adjusting the cell that is being divided into the Cost Value for each Expense item.

Figure 3.39 | **Divide by Zero Error**

	A	B	C
			Percent to
1	Expense Item	Cost Value	Total
2	Office Supplies	$ 750	7.50%
3	Machine Oil	$ 1,800	#DIV/0!
4	Cleaning Supplies	$ 650	#DIV/0!
5	Parts	$ 2,500	#DIV/0!
6	Utility Bills	$ 1,100	#DIV/0!
7	Fuel	$ 3,200	#DIV/0!
8	**Total**	$ 10,000	

Divide by zero error symbols

Figure 3.40 shows why the divide by zero error occurred in Figure 3.39. The goal of the formula created in cell C2 is to divide the Cost Value for the Office Supplies expense by the total annual expenses for the business. Therefore, the value in cell B2 is divided by the total in cell B8. However, notice how relative referencing adjusted the cell references in this formula when it was pasted into cell C3. The value in cell B3 is being divided by the value in cell B9. Since there is nothing in cell B9, the divide by zero error appears. Therefore, we need to prevent relative referencing from changing cell B8 when it is copied from cell C2 to other cell locations in the column. This is done by adding an absolute reference to cell B8 in the formula that was created in cell C2 (see Figure 3.38).

Figure 3.40 | **How Relative Referencing Causes the Divide by Zero Error**

SUM =B3/B9

	A	B	C
			Percent to
1	Expense Item	Cost Value	Total
2	Office Supplies	$ 750	7.50%
3	Machine Oil	$ 1,800	=B3/B9
4	Cleaning Supplies	$ 650	#DIV/0!
5	Parts	$ 2,500	#DIV/0!
6	Utility Bills	$ 1,100	#DIV/0!
7	Fuel	$ 3,200	#DIV/0!
8	**Total**	$ 10,000	
9			

Because of *relative* referencing, the second part of this formula is being divided by an empty cell.

As mentioned, to prevent relative referencing from adjusting cell B8 in the formula shown in Figure 3.38, we must use an absolute reference. This is accomplished by typing a dollar sign in front of the column letter and row number of cell B8, as shown in Figure 3.41.

Figure 3.41 | **Adding an Absolute Reference to Cell B8**

SUM =B2/$B$8

	A	B	C
			Percent to
1	Expense Item	Cost Value	Total
2	Office Supplies	$ 750	=B2/$B$8
3	Machine Oil	$ 1,800	
4	Cleaning Supplies	$ 650	
5	Parts	$ 2,500	
6	Utility Bills	$ 1,100	
7	Fuel	$ 3,200	
8	**Total**	$ 10,000	

Absolute reference is added to cell B8 with a dollar sign ($) in front of the column letter and row number.

Figure 3.42 shows the results of pasting the formula in Figure 3.41 to cell locations C3 through C7. As shown in the figure, there are no divide by zero errors. The reason is that cell B8 did not change when it was pasted to other cell locations in column C. Now all the Cost Values in column B are being divided by the total in cell B8.

Figure 3.42 | **Results of Pasting a Formula with an Absolute Reference**

	A	B	C
	SUM ▾ ✗ ✓ ƒx =B4/$B$8		
1	Expense Item	Cost Value	Percent to Total
2	Office Supplies	$ 750	7.50%
3	Machine Oil	$ 1,800	18.00%
4	Cleaning Supplies	$ 650	=B4/$B$8
5	Parts	$ 2,500	25.00%
6	Utility Bills	$ 1,100	11.00%
7	Fuel	$ 3,200	32.00%
8	Total	$ 10,000	

Cell B8 does not change when the formula is pasted to a new cell location.

VIDEO WORKSHOP

>> Statistical Functions

The purpose of this workshop is to demonstrate the use of statistical functions when conducting mathematical computations. We will be using statistical functions to summarize transaction data for a typical retail business. I will be demonstrating the tasks in this workshop in the **Statistical Functions** video. Open the file named ib_e03_retailtransactions before starting the following tasks:

1. **Statistical Functions (Video: Statistical Functions)**

   a. Type the **COUNT** function in cell G3 to count all the Transaction Numbers in the range A3:A50.

   b. Type a **SUM** function in cell G4 to add up the Amount Paid in the range C3:C50.

   c. Type an **AVERAGE** function in cell G5 to calculate the average Number of Items in the range B3:B50.

   d. Type an **AVERAGE** function in cell G6 to calculate the average of the range C3:C50.

   e. Calculate the average price per item purchased by using a **SUM** function to add up the values in the range C3:C50 and divide it by another **SUM** function adding up the values in the range B3:B50. The entry should be as follows: =Sum(C3:C50)/Sum(B3:B50).

   f. Type a **MAX** function in cell G8 to show the highest amount paid in the range C3:C50.

   g. Type a **MIN** function in cell G9 to show the lowest amount paid in the range C3:C50.

   h. Type a **MODE** function in cell G10 to calculate the most frequent number of items purchased in the range B3:B50.

   i. Save and close your file.

≫ Absolute References

The purpose of this workshop is to demonstrate how and why absolute references are used in business situations. We will be using an absolute reference to calculate the percent to total for items on a merchandise sales spreadsheet. I will be demonstrating the tasks in this workshop in the **Absolute Reference** video. Open the file named ib_e03_ merchandisesales before starting the following tasks:

1. **Functions (Video: Absolute Reference)**

   a. Create a **SUM** function in cell E12 to add up the profit dollars in column E.

2. **Formulas (Video: Absolute Reference)**

   a. Type a formula in cell F3 that divides the profit dollars in cell E3 by the total profit dollars in cell E12.

   b. Format the output of the formula in cell F3 to a percentage with 2 decimal places.

3. **Absolute References (Video: Absolute Reference)**

   a. Edit the formula in cell F3 by placing an absolute reference on cell E12.

   b. Copy cell F3 and paste it into cells F4:F11.

   c. Save and close your file.

≫ Evaluating a Transportation Business

Summarizing data plays a critical role in making business decisions. The amount of data businesses store and analyze can be massive, especially in large corporations. Most business managers face the constant challenge of quickly summarizing large sets of data to assess business results. Knowing how to summarize data using the statistics functions covered in this section will enable you to quickly summarize and assess large sets of data relating to almost any business situation.

Exercise

The purpose of this exercise is to use statistical functions to evaluate the performance of a transportation company. Open the file named ib_e03_transportation performance and complete the following tasks:

1. Using the **COUNT** function in cell C3, calculate the number of trips in the range A13:A52.

2. Use the **AVERAGE** function in cell G3 to calculate the average miles per trip in the range C13:C52.

3. Find the highest miles driven for a single trip in the range C13:C52 by using the **MAX** function in cell C4.

4. Find the lowest miles driven for a single trip in the range C13:C52 by using the **MIN** function in cell G4.

5. Using the **MODE** function in cell C6, determine which trailer size was used the most from the range B13:B52.

6. Calculate the average capacity per trip by typing an **AVERAGE** function in cell G6. The capacity for each trip is in the range D13:D52.

7. Use the **MAX** function in cell C7 to determine the highest capacity for a single trip in the range D13:D52.

8. Use the **MIN** function in cell G7 to determine the lowest capacity for a single trip in the range D13:D52.

9. Type the value **2.50** in cell G9 and **.25** in cell G10.

10. Calculate the total fuel cost in cell C9 by using a **SUM** function to add up all the fuel consumed in the range E13:E52 and multiplying it by the fuel cost in cell G9.

11. Calculate the dollars billed in cell C10 by using a **SUM** function to add up all the miles driven in the range C13:C52 and multiplying it by the current charge per mile in cell G10.

12. Compare the output of the formulas you created in cells C9 and C10. Is this company making enough money to cover its fuel cost?

13. If fuel prices are increased to $3.05 per gallon, how much will this company have to increase its charge per mile to cover the cost of fuel plus make approximately $1,000 in profit?

14. This company has a goal of maintaining an average capacity per trip of 90%. Is this company achieving its goal?

15. What could this company do to get closer to its capacity target of 90%? How else could you analyze the Trip Detail statistics in the range A12:E52 to answer this question? HINT: What size trailers are reaching the highest capacity levels on a consistent basis?

16. Save and close your file.

PROBLEM & EXERCISE

≫ What's Wrong with This Spreadsheet?

Problem

Your classmate is having trouble with a project and has come to you for help. He is using Excel for an industry analysis project that is due for one of his business classes. He completed the spreadsheet but explains that for some reason a lot of the numbers do not look right. He e-mails the Excel file to you with the following explanation:

1. I am trying to calculate the market share for each company on the spreadsheet, which is nothing more than a percent to total. I used an absolute reference on one of the cell locations in the formula (you know, that dollar sign thing), but I still keep getting this error.

2. I'm wondering if my market share error in column C has something to do with the **SUM** function I used in cell B8. It worked fine, but before I e-mailed the file to you, I noticed that the number looked a little low.

3. The other thing that looks weird is the average I calculated in cell B9. The result is $43,750,000, but every company is below this number except for Company A. I used the **AVERAGE** function, so it must be right. I don't know; it just seems weird.

4. Finally, I used the **COUNT** function in cell C11 to count the number of companies in the spreadsheet, but it keeps giving me a result of 0. At this point I am wondering if this file got corrupted somehow. Can you take a look at this and let me know if I should just make another spreadsheet on a different computer?

Exercise

The file this classmate has sent to you is named ib_e03_industryanalysistrouble. Open the file and review each of the concerns listed in the Problem section. Is it the computer that's causing these problems? What's wrong with this spreadsheet? Write a short answer explaining what mistakes were made for each of the points your classmate listed. Then, correct any errors you find.

>> Financial Functions

The statistical functions demonstrated in the previous section were constructed by typing a range of cells or specific cell locations separated by commas between parentheses. However, other functions may require the definition of several inputs or *arguments* to produce an output. The purpose and number of arguments will vary depending on the function. This section reviews two such functions: Future Value and Payment. Both are related to the financial aspects of business with regard to evaluating investments and loans. This section will demonstrate how these functions are constructed and highlight how they can be used for making both professional and personal business decisions.

The Future Value Function

The *Future Value*, or *FV* function, is used to calculate the value of investments over a specific period of time. To better understand how the **Future Value** function calculates the value of an investment, it is helpful to review an example relating to the time value of money.

Figure 3.43 illustrates the principles of the time value of money by showing how a bank account grows over three years. This example assumes that a bank is very generous and offers an interest rate of 8% for a traditional savings account. In reality, the interest rate that is usually offered for a traditional savings account is much less. The first row of the table, labeled Year 1, shows that an account is opened with $10. Assuming the interest rate does not change, the value of the account after one year will be $10.80 as shown in the End Balance column. The reason is that $.80 was paid in interest (see the Interest Earned column). The second row, labeled Year 2, assumes that another $10 is deposited into the account as shown in the Deposit column. Notice that the Interest Earned column increases from $.80 in Year 1 to $1.66 in Year 2. The value of the account at the end of Year 2 is $22.46, as shown in the End Balance column. At the end of the third year, the ending balance of the account is $35.06. However, if you add the values in the Deposits column, only $30 was added to this account. The additional money is the total amount of interest paid over the three-year period, which is $5.06. This is the sum of the values in the Interest Paid column.

Figure 3.43 **Time Value of Money Example**

	Begin Balance	Deposit	Interest Rate	Interest Paid	End Balance
Year 1	0	$10.00	8% × $10.00	$ .80	$10.80
Year 2	$10.80	$10.00	8% × $20.80	$1.66	$22.46
Year 3	$22.46	$10.00	8% × $32.46	$2.60	$35.06

The Future Value function will be used to calculate this result.

The **Future Value** function can be used to calculate the End Balance value, which is circled in Figure 3.43. You add the function to a worksheet by typing an equal sign (=), the function name FV, and an open parenthesis. You can also double click the function name FV from the function list after typing the equal sign and the letter F. To complete the function, you will need to define at least three of the five arguments shown in Figure 3.44. The arguments will appear in a hint box after you type an open parenthesis or double click the function name from the function list. The following is a definition for each of these arguments:

- **rate**: The interest rate applied to an investment.
- **nper**: The number of periods an investment is added to an account or the amount of time an investment is being measured. This argument must correspond to the interest rate entered in the **rate** argument. For example, if an annual interest rate is entered in the **rate** argument, the **nper** argument must be the number of years. If a monthly interest rate is entered in the **rate** argument, the **nper** argument must be the number of months. If a daily interest rate is used in the **rate** argument, the **nper** argument must be the number of days.
- **pmt**: The value of the payments that are added to an account. This argument is used when money is being added to an account over a period of time (such as $100 per month or $2,000 per year). The period of time will be the value that is entered in the **nper** argument. A negative sign must be placed in front of values or cell locations used to define this argument.
- **[pv]: *Present Value***: The argument used when a one-time investment is made to an account. It can be used with or without the **pmt** argument. You must place a negative sign in front of values or cell locations used to define this argument.
- **[type]**: The argument used to define when payments are made to an account; it can either be a 1 or 0. If this argument is not defined, Excel will assume the value is 0.
  - 1: Used for payments made at the beginning of a period (i.e., at the beginning of a month, year, etc.).
  - 0: Used for payments made at the end of a period.

Figure 3.44 | **Arguments of the Future Value Function**

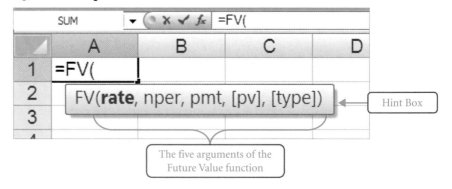

The five arguments of the Future Value function

Hint Box

As mentioned, the **Future Value** function can be used to calculate the End Balance value circled in Figure 3.43. The following illustrates how each argument of the function would be defined based on the Time Value of Money Example (Figure 3.43). Remember, you must use a comma to separate each value that is used to define the arguments of the function.

- **rate**: `.08` This represents the annual interest rate shown in the Interest Rate column in Figure 3.43. When you are entering numbers into this function, it is best *not* to use any symbols except for decimal points. This is why the 8% interest rate is typed into the function as .08. If you are not sure how to convert a percentage to a decimal, simply divide the percent by 100 (i.e., `8 ÷ 100 = .08`).

- **nper**: `3` The Time Value of Money Example in Figure 3.43 shows that $10 is deposited into a bank account every year for three years. Therefore, the number 3 (representing 3 years) is entered for this argument. It is important to note that since an annual interest rate was entered in the **rate** argument, the time period entered for this argument must be in years.

- **pmt**: `-10` Since $10 is being deposited into a bank account over a three-year period, the number -10 is entered for this argument. *You must put a negative sign in front of any number or cell location used for this argument.*

- **[pv]**: This argument is used to evaluate a one-time lump sum investment. However, this example assumes that deposits are being made to the account annually. Therefore, this argument will be skipped by adding a comma with no spaces.

- **[type]**: For this example, we will assume that the $10 is being deposited into the account at the beginning of each year. Therefore, a value of 1 is entered for this argument.

Figure 3.45 shows how the arguments of the **Future Value** function are defined based on the Time Value of Money Example in Figure 3.43. Notice that each argument is separated with a comma. In addition, since the **[pv]** argument was skipped, a comma was typed with no spaces.

Figure 3.45 | **Setup of the Future Value Function Based on the Time Value of Money Example**

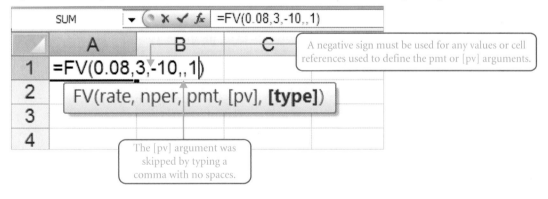

Figure 3.46 shows the results of the **Future Value** function after the **Enter** key was pressed. Notice that this output is identical to the End Balance number in Year 3 from the Time Value of Money Example in Figure 3.43.

Figure 3.46 | **Results of the Future Value Function**

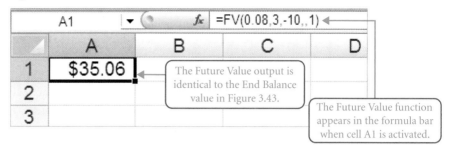

The Future Value output is identical to the End Balance value in Figure 3.43.

The Future Value function appears in the formula bar when cell A1 is activated.

COMMON MISTAKES | Separate Arguments with Commas

You must type a comma after each argument of the **Future Value** function. If you are skipping an argument, as in Figure 3.45, type a comma with no spaces. If you are skipping both the **[pv]** and **[type]** arguments, you can type a closing parenthesis after the **pmt** argument. This is the reason these arguments are displayed in brackets [ ]. The function will produce an output if these arguments are not defined. Note that Excel assumes payments are made at the *end* of the year if the **[type]** argument is skipped.

As previously mentioned, the **Future Value** function can also evaluate an investment made in one lump sum. This would require the [**pv**] argument to be defined instead of the **pmt** argument. When using the [**pv**] argument, you must use a negative sign for all values or cell locations as in the **pmt** argument. Figure 3.47 shows how the arguments of the **Future Value** function are defined if $30 is deposited into a bank account at the beginning of Year 1 as opposed to making $10 deposits over a three-year period as shown in the Time Value of Money Example in Figure 3.43. It is assumed that the annual interest rate is 8% and that it will not change over the three-year period.

Figure 3.47 | **Setup of the Future Value Function for a One-Time Investment**

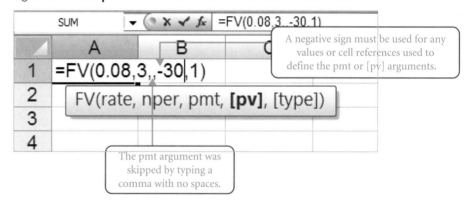

A negative sign must be used for any values or cell references used to define the pmt or [pv] arguments.

The pmt argument was skipped by typing a comma with no spaces.

Figure 3.48 shows the output of the **Future Value** function which was set up in Figure 3.47. Notice that this output is higher than the output shown in Figure 3.46. The reason is that more interest is being paid into the account since $30 is deposited into the bank account on day 1 as opposed to being deposited over three years.

A1	▾	f_x =FV(0.08,3,,-30,1)

	A	B	C
1	$37.79		
2			

Figure 3.49 shows another example of the **Future Value** function. In this example, the information from the Time Value of Money Example (Figure 3.43) has been typed into a worksheet. Notice that the arguments of the function are defined using cell references (see the formula bar). As a result, the **Future Value** function will calculate a new output when any of the values are changed in the range B2:B5. Also, you will see that the output of the function is identical to the output shown in Figure 3.46. The reason is that the values that are typed into the cell references used to define the arguments of the function are identical to the values that were used to set up the **Future Value** function in Figure 3.45.

Figure 3.49 | **Future Value Function Using Cell References Instead of Numeric Values**

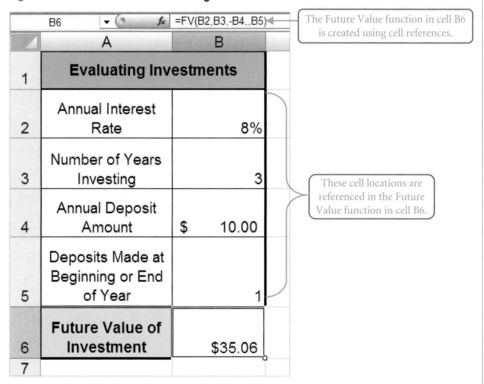

B6	▾	f_x =FV(B2,B3,-B4,,B5)

> The Future Value function in cell B6 is created using cell references.

	A	B
1	**Evaluating Investments**	
2	Annual Interest Rate	8%
3	Number of Years Investing	3
4	Annual Deposit Amount	$ 10.00
5	Deposits Made at Beginning or End of Year	1
6	**Future Value of Investment**	$35.06
7		

> These cell locations are referenced in the Future Value function in cell B6.

The benefit of using cell references to define the arguments of the **Future Value** function is that it allows you to conduct what-if scenarios with investments you may be evaluating professionally or personally. For example, what if you increased the Annual Deposit Amount in Figure 3.49 from $10 to $12, and what if you invested this money over a four-year period instead of a three-year period? Figure 3.50 shows how the output of the **Future Value** function changes when these values are changed in the worksheet.

Figure 3.50 | **Values in Cells Referenced by the Future Value Function Are Changed**

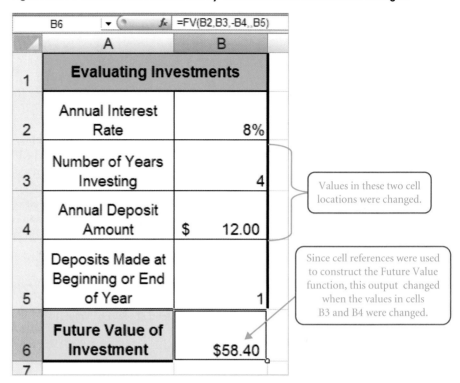

Values in these two cell locations were changed.

Since cell references were used to construct the Future Value function, this output changed when the values in cells B3 and B4 were changed.

The Payment Function

A close relative of the **Future Value** function is the *Payment* or *PMT* function. The **PMT** function is most helpful when calculating the payments of a loan. For example, if you were buying a home and had to borrow $225,000, how much would your monthly payment be if a bank charged 6% interest over a 30-year period? The **PMT** function can be used to answer this question.

Similar to the **Future Value** function, at least three of five arguments must be defined for the **Payment** function to produce an output. Figure 3.51 shows the five arguments of the **Payment** function, which are very similar to the arguments of the **Future Value** function. The following defines each of these arguments:

- **rate**: The interest charged by a lender.
- **nper**: The number of payments or, as in the **Future Value** function, a period of time (i.e., years, months, weeks, etc.).
- **pv**: Present Value; the argument used to define the amount of money being borrowed or the principal of the loan. As in the **Future Value** function, *you must use a negative sign for any values or cell references used for this argument.*
- **[fv]**: Future Value; the argument used when part of a loan is paid off with periodic payments and the balance of the loan is paid off in one lump sum at a future point

in time. This argument is especially helpful when evaluating the lease payments of a car. However, if a loan is structured such that there is no lump sum payoff at a future point in time, you can skip this argument by adding a comma with no spaces.

- **[type]**: A value that determines if payments are made at the beginning or end of a period and can either be a 1 or 0. If this argument is not defined, Excel will assume the value is 0.

  - 1: Used for payments made at the beginning of a period (i.e., at the beginning of a month, year, etc.).

  - 0: Used for payments made at the end of a period.

Figure 3.51 | **Arguments of the Payment Function**

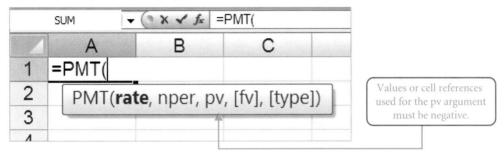

Figure 3.52 shows a worksheet that contains loan information for the purchase of a $250,000 home. The **Payment** function will be used in cell B6 to calculate the monthly mortgage payments for this loan. This example assumes that the bank will charge an interest rate of 6.5%, which is shown in cell B2. In addition, the repayment period for the loan is 30 years, as shown in cell B3. The amount of money that will be borrowed from the bank is $225,000. This example assumes a down payment of $25,000. Therefore, the remaining balance to pay for the house is $225,000, which is shown in cell B4. Finally, the number 1 is shown in cell B5, indicating that payments will be made at the beginning of each month.

FIGURE 3.52 | **Using the Payment Function to Determine the Monthly Payments of a Loan**

	A	B
1	**Monthly Mortgage Payments**	
2	Annual Interest Rate	6.5%
3	Number of Years to Pay Loan	30
4	Amount Borrowed (Principal)	$ 225,000
5	Payments made at Beginning or End of Month	1
6	**Monthly Payments**	
7		

The Payment function will be added here to calculate the monthly mortgage payments for this loan.

As mentioned, the **Payment** function will be constructed in cell B6 of Figure 3.52 to determine the monthly mortgage payments for this loan. The following explains the setup of this function:

- Activate cell B6.
- Type an equal sign, the function name PMT, and an open parenthesis. This will open the hint box showing the arguments of the function (see Figure 3.51).
- Define the arguments of the **Payment** function as follows:
  - **rate**: B2/12 The formula B2/12 is used to define the **rate** argument of the function. The goal of this example is to calculate the monthly payments of the loan. However, cell B2 contains an annual interest rate. Therefore, this annual interest rate must be converted to a monthly interest rate so the payments can be expressed in terms of months instead of years.
  - **nper**: B3 * 12 The formula B3 * 12 is used to define the **nper** argument. Since the goal of this exercise is to calculate the monthly payments, the repayment period of the loan must be defined in terms of months. Therefore, the number of years in cell B3 is multiplied by 12.
  - **pv**: -B4 The present value argument is defined using cell B4 which contains the principal of the loan. However, a negative sign must precede any value or cell reference used for this argument.
  - **[fv]**: , The future value argument will be skipped in this example. Therefore, a comma is typed with no spaces.
  - **[type]**: B5 Cell B5 contains a value that indicates if payments are made at the beginning or end of the month. Therefore, it is referenced for this argument of the function.
- Type a closing parenthesis.
- Press the **Enter** key.

Figure 3.53 shows the results of the **Payment** function. Cell B6 is activated so you can see the setup of the function in the formula bar. Notice how formulas were used to define the **rate** and **nper** arguments. Similar to the **Future Value** function, the **rate**,

Figure 3.53 | **Results of the Payment Function**

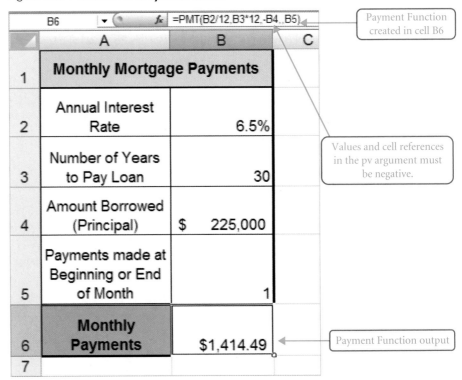

nper, and **[pv]** arguments of the **Payment** function must be expressed in equivalent terms. The formulas in the **rate** and **nper** arguments are converting the interest rate and repayment period to months. The results in this figure show that the monthly mortgage payment for this loan is $1,414.49.

COMMON MISTAKES | Negative Output for the FV or PMT Functions

If the output of a **Future Value** function or **Payment** function is negative, check the **pmt** and **[pv]** arguments of the **Future Value** function or the **pv** argument of the **Payment** function. Values and cell references used to define these arguments must be negative. If the negative sign is omitted for these arguments, the function will produce a negative number.

It is important to note that the **Payment** function constructed in Figure 3.53 uses cell references to define each of the arguments. As a result, if the values in cells B2 through B5 are changed, the function will produce a new output. Therefore, what if you decided that the loan payments shown in Figure 3.53 are too expensive for your budget? You can lower the principal in cell B4 and lower the interest rate in cell B2. Lowering these values will decrease the monthly mortgage payments. Figure 3.54 shows the results of the **Payment** function if the value in cell B4 is lowered to $205,000 and the interest rate in cell B2 is lowered to 6%.

FIGURE 3.54 | **New Output When Data Is Changed**

	B6		f_x	=PMT(B2/12,B3*12,-B4,,B5)	
	A		B		C
1	**Monthly Mortgage Payments**				
2	Annual Interest Rate		6.0%		*The values in these cells were changed.*
3	Number of Years to Pay Loan		30		
4	Amount Borrowed (Principal)	$	205,000		
5	Payments made at Beginning or End of Month		1		*New output when data is changed in cells B2 and B4.*
6	**Monthly Payments**		$1,222.96		
7					

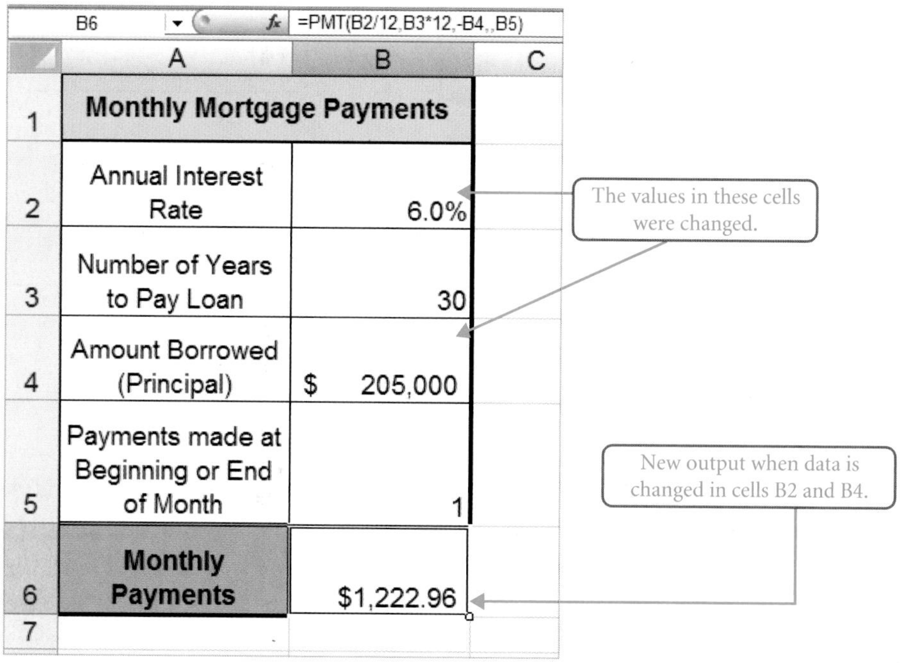

As previously mentioned, you can also use the **Payment** function to calculate the lease payments of a car. Leasing cars is often used as an alternative to buying. When leasing a car, a person pays only the value of the car that is used during a set period of time. The car dealer usually charges an interest rate for allowing the buyer to pay off the lease over several years.

The worksheet in Figure 3.55 contains data that will be used to calculate the monthly lease payments for a $23,000 car. The interest rate charged on the lease is 5% as shown in cell B2, and the car will be leased over a four-year period, as shown in cell B3. The residual value, or the future value, of the car is assumed to be $9,500 in four years (see cell B5). Therefore, if the car is worth $9,500 in four years, and the price of the car is $23,000, then the value of the car used during the four-year lease period is $13,500 ($23,000 - $9,500). The **Payment** function will automatically calculate this difference, factor in the interest rate, and determine the monthly payments.

Figure 3.55 | **Data Used to Calculate the Lease Payments of a Car**

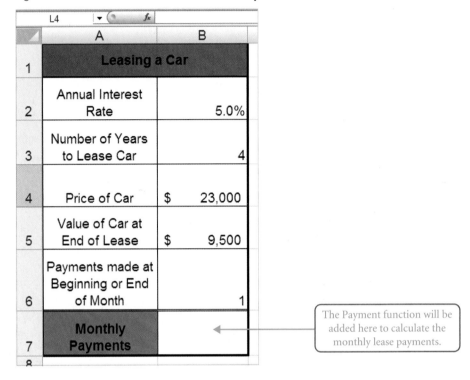

The Payment function will be added here to calculate the monthly lease payments.

The following explains how the **Payment** function is constructed in cell B7 in the worksheet shown in Figure 3.55 to calculate the lease payments of the car:

- Activate cell B7.
- Type an equal sign, the function name PMT, and an open parenthesis.
- Define the arguments of the **Payment** function as follows:
  - **rate**: `B2/12` This formula converts the annual interest rate to a monthly interest rate.
  - **nper**: `B3*12` This formula converts the number of years to lease the car to months. As a result, both the **rate** and **nper** arguments are expressed in terms of months.
  - **pv**: `-B4` The present value argument is defined using cell B4, which contains the price of the car. This cell reference is preceded by a negative sign.
  - **[fv]**: `B5` The future value argument is defined by referencing cell B5, which contains the value of the car at the end of the lease.
  - **[type]**: `B6` Cell B6 contains a value indicating if payments are made at the beginning or end of the month.
- Type a closing parenthesis.
- Press the **Enter** key. The results of the function are shown in Figure 3.56.

>> Quick Reference

Payment Function

1. Activate a cell where output should appear.

2. Type an equal sign.

3. Type the function name PMT or double click **PMT** from the function list.

4. Type an open parenthesis (if you double clicked the function from the function list, this will already be added).

5. Define the following arguments:

   rate: Interest rate

   nper: Number of payments or period of time

   pv: Present value

   [fv]: Future value

   [type]: When payments are made (1 = beginning of year, 0 = end of year)

6. Close the parenthesis.

7. Press the **Enter** key.

Figure 3.56 | **Results Showing the Monthly Lease Payments**

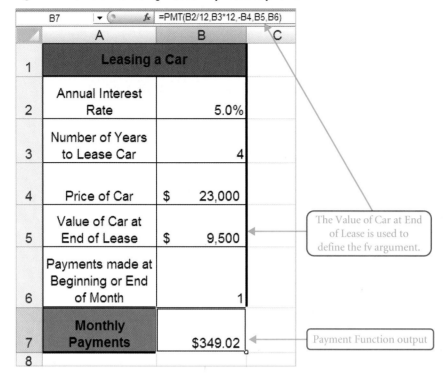

| B7 | ▼ | f_x | =PMT(B2/12,B3*12,-B4,B5,B6) |

	A	B	C
1	Leasing a Car		
2	Annual Interest Rate	5.0%	
3	Number of Years to Lease Car	4	
4	Price of Car	$ 23,000	
5	Value of Car at End of Lease	$ 9,500	
6	Payments made at Beginning or End of Month	1	
7	Monthly Payments	$349.02	
8			

The Value of Car at End of Lease is used to define the fv argument.

Payment Function output

The Function Library

The Function Library is a resource that can be used to research and build any of the functions available in Excel. As shown in Figure 3.57, the Function Library is a group in the **Formulas** tab of the Ribbon. The icons in Function Library categorize all the functions in Excel by topic. For example, to see a list of all financial functions, click the **Financial** icon.

FIGURE 3.57 | **The Function Library**

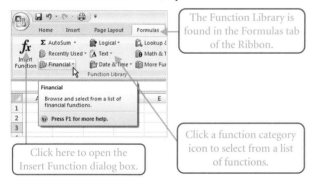

The Function Library is found in the Formulas tab of the Ribbon.

Click a function category icon to select from a list of functions.

Click here to open the Insert Function dialog box.

Use the Function Library to research detailed information regarding the purpose and arguments for all Excel functions. In addition, the Function Library can serve as an alternative way of building functions. After activating a cell location, select a function from one of the category icons in the Function Library. This will open the **Function Arguments** dialog box, which provides input boxes for each argument as well as a link to get detailed help in building the function. Figure 3.58 shows the **Function Arguments** dialog box for the **Future Value** function.

>> **Quick Reference**

Insert Function

1. Activate a cell where the output of a function should appear.
2. Click the **Formulas** tab in the Ribbon.
3. Select a function from one of the function category icons in the Function Library or click the **Insert Function** icon.
4. If using the **Insert Function** icon, select a function from the **Insert Function** dialog box and click the **OK** button.
5. Use the input boxes or range finders to define the arguments of the function in the **Function Arguments** dialog box.
6. Click **Help on this function** to see an expanded definition and instructions for building the function.
7. Click the **OK** button at the bottom of the **Function Arguments** dialog box.

Figure 3.58 | **The Function Arguments Dialog Box for the Future Value Function**

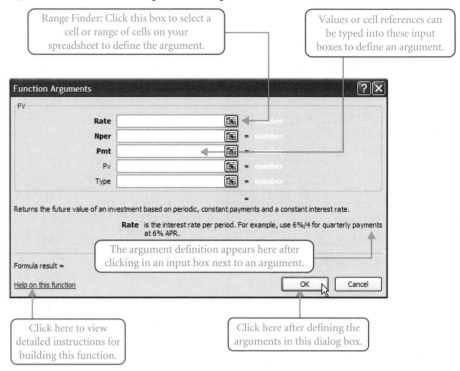

Range Finder: Click this box to select a cell or range of cells on your spreadsheet to define the argument.

Values or cell references can be typed into these input boxes to define an argument.

The argument definition appears here after clicking in an input box next to an argument.

Click here to view detailed instructions for building this function.

Click here after defining the arguments in this dialog box.

Excel functions can also be researched and built from the **Insert Function** icon. After activating a cell location where the output of the function should appear, click the **Insert Function** icon. This will open the **Insert Function** dialog box, as shown in Figure 3.59. Select a function from the middle of the dialog box and click the **OK** button. This will open the **Function Argument**s dialog box, as shown in Figure 3.58. Note that you can also open the **Insert Function** dialog box by clicking the **fx** symbol next to the formula bar.

Figure 3.59 | **The Insert Function Dialog Box**

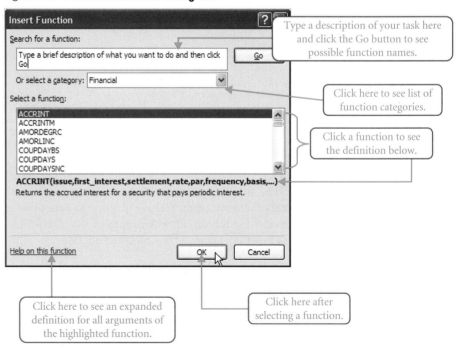

Type a description of your task here and click the Go button to see possible function names.

Click here to see list of function categories.

Click a function to see the definition below.

Click here to see an expanded definition for all arguments of the highlighted function.

Click here after selecting a function.

>> Future Value Function

The purpose of this workshop is to review the use and construction of the **Future Value** function. I will be demonstrating the tasks in this workshop in the **Future Value Function** video. Open the file named ib_e03_thetimevalueofmoney before starting the following tasks.

1. Data Entry (Video: Future Value Function)

a. Activate the Periodic Investment worksheet.

b. Type the following values into the cell locations listed:
   Cell B2: **.08**
   Cell B3: **3**
   Cell B4: **10**
   Cell B5: **1**

c. Format cell B2 to a percent with 1 decimal place and then format cell B4 to U.S. currency with 2 decimal places.

2. Calculating the Future Value of a Periodic Investment (Video: Future Value Function)

a. Type an equal sign in cell B6, followed by the function name **FV** and an open parenthesis.

b. Click cell B2 and type a comma.

c. Click cell B3 and type a comma.

d. Type a negative sign.

e. Click cell B4 and type a comma.

f. Type another comma.

g. Click cell B5 and type a closing parenthesis.

h. Press the **Enter** key.

3. Calculating the Future Value of a One-Time Investment (Video: Future Value Function)

a. Activate the One Time Investment worksheet.

b. Type an equal sign in cell B6, followed by the function name **FV** and an open parenthesis.

c. Click cell B2 and type a comma.

d. Click cell B3 and type a comma.

e. Type another comma.

f. Type a negative sign.

g. Click cell B4 and type a comma.

h. Click cell B5 and type a closing parenthesis.

i. Press the **Enter** key.

j. Save and close your file.

>> Payment Function

This purpose of this workshop is to demonstrate how the **Payment** function is used to determine the mortgage payments for buying a home and the lease payments for a car. I will be demonstrating the tasks in this workshop on the video named **Payment Function**. Open the file named ib_e03_buyingahomeleasingacar before starting this workshop:

1. **Data Entry (Video: Payment Function)**
   a. Activate the Buying a Home worksheet.
   b. Type the following values into the cell locations listed:
      Cell B2: **.065**
      Cell B3: **30**
      Cell B4: **225000**
      Cell B5: **1**
   c. Format cell B2 to a percent with 1 decimal places and then format cell B4 to U.S. currency with 0 decimal places.

2. **Calculating the Monthly Payments for a Loan (Video: Payment Function)**
   a. Type an equal sign in cell B6, followed by the function name **PMT** and an open parenthesis.
   b. Click cell B2, type a forward slash (for division), type the number **12**, and type a comma.
   c. Click cell B3, type an asterisk (for multiplication), type the number **12**, and type a comma.
   d. Type a negative sign.
   e. Click cell B4 and type a comma.
   f. Type another comma.
   g. Click cell B5 and type a closing parenthesis.
   h. Press the **Enter** key.

3. **Data Entry (Video: Payment Function)**
   a. Activate the Leasing a Car worksheet.
   b. Type the following values into the cell locations listed:
      Cell B2: **.05**
      Cell B3: **4**
      Cell B4: **23000**
      Cell B5: **9500**
      Cell B6: **1**
   c. Format cell B2 to a percent with 1 decimal place and then format cells B4 and B5 to U.S. currency with 0 decimal places.

4. **Calculating the Lease Payment of a Car (Video: Payment Function)**
   a. Type an equal sign in cell B7, followed by the function name **PMT** and an open parenthesis.

b. Click cell B2, type a forward slash (for division), type the number **12**, and type a comma.

c. Click cell B3, type an asterisk (for multiplication), type the number **12**, and type a comma.

d. Type a negative sign.

e. Click cell B4 and type a comma.

f. Click cell B5 and type a comma.

g. Click cell B6 and type a closing parenthesis.

h. Press the **Enter** key.

i. Save and close your file.

>> The Function Library

The purpose of this workshop is to demonstrate the Function Library. I will be demonstrating the tasks in this workshop on the video named **Function Library**. Open the file named ib_e03_propertyvalue before starting this workshop:

1. Selecting a Function (Video: Function Library)

a. Activate cell D5 in the Commercial Property worksheet.

b. Click the **Formulas** tab on the Ribbon.

c. Click the **Financial** icon in the Function Library.

d. Click the **FV** function.

e. Click **Help on this function** in the lower left of the **Function Arguments** dialog box.

f. Close the help window by clicking the X in the upper-right corner.

2. Defining Arguments for the Future Value Function (Video: Function Library)

a. Click the range finder (box with the red arrow) to the right of the Rate argument.

b. Click cell D2 on the worksheet and press the **Enter** key.

c. Click the range finder next to the **nper** argument.

d. Click cell D3 on the worksheet and press the **Enter** key.

e. Type a negative sign in the box next to the **pv** argument.

f. Click the range finder next to the **pv** argument.

g. Click cell D4 on the worksheet and press the **Enter** key.

h. Type the number 1 in the box next to the Type argument.

i. Click the **OK** button at the bottom of the window.

j. Save and close your file.

⟫ Financial Planning for Retirement

A potential career goal for a person studying finance might be to work as a financial planner. One of the responsibilities a financial planner might have is to help people plan for retirement. This involves estimating how many years a person will work before they retire and how much money they can contribute to a retirement account. The financial planner's job is to evaluate various scenarios to see how clients can maximize the growth of a retirement account so they can live comfortably when they stop working. In this situation, the **Future Value** function can become a critical tool.

Exercise

Whether you have aspirations of being a financial planner or not, retirement is something everyone will eventually face. The purpose of this exercise is to construct a spreadsheet for a person who is planning to open a retirement account. Your job is to evaluate what interest rate and amount of contribution this person needs to achieve to make the account grow to $2 million. In addition, this person is age 25 and, for now, would like to plan on retiring at age 65. To do the tasks listed here, you will need to open the file named ib_e03_retirementplanning.

1. Type the value **.04** in cell B6 and type the word **Low** in cell C6. In this scenario, the money for this person's retirement will be invested in a conservative fashion. Therefore, the risk of losing money is low, but the potential growth is also low.

2. Type the value **.08** in cell B7 and the word **Medium** in cell C7. In this scenario, the risk is increased to Medium, but the potential return is increased to 8%.

3. For the final scenario, type the value **.15** in cell B8 and the word **High** in cell C8. In this scenario, both the risk and the potential return are high.

4. Type the number **40** in cell E2. Since this person is now 25 and is planning to retire at 65, she will be working and making contributions to her retirement account for 40 years.

5. Type the number **75** in cell E3. This person was thinking of putting $75 a month into this account but is not sure if this will get her to the goal of $2 million.

6. Calculate the future value of the conservative scenario. Use the **Future Value** function in cell D6 and define each argument of the function as follows:

    a. Use cell B6 to define the rate. This represents the Annual Potential Growth of the retirement investments.

    b. Use cell E2 to define the **nper** argument. Add an absolute reference to this cell reference. This function will be pasted into cells D7 and D8 to calculate the future value for the other two scenarios. Therefore, an absolute reference is used for cell E2 to prevent it from changing when the function is pasted.

    c. Type the formula **-E3 * 12** for the **pmt** argument and add an absolute reference to cell E3. This formula is used to convert the monthly payments to annual payments since both the **rate** and **nper** arguments are annual numbers. The absolute reference is used on cell E3 for the same reason explained in letter b.

    d. Type a closing parenthesis and press the **Enter** key. This person will not be making any lump sum investments to this account, and deposits will be made at the end of the month. Therefore, it is not necessary to define the **[pv]** or **[type]** arguments.

7. Copy the function created in cell D6 and use the **Paste Special** command to paste only the function into cells D7 and D8.

8. Given the current contribution of $75 per month, will this person reach her target through any of the scenarios?

9. How much money will she have to deposit in her account per month (approximately) to reach $2 million taking the Aggressive investment scenario?

10. How much money will she have to deposit in her account per month (approximately) to reach $2 million taking the Conservative investment scenario?

11. Save and close your file.

>> What's Wrong with This Spreadsheet?

Problem

You are the director of a real estate investment firm. An intern has just completed a project for you evaluating a potential investment. You are about to present the results to the president of the firm showing the potential return on property near a growing U.S. city. A recent assessment has shown that similar commercial properties in this area have been increasing in value 15% every six months. You will propose that the firm buy 10 acres of land at a total price of $1,750,000. You will recommend that the land be held for three years and then sold to developers.

You have asked the intern to

1. Evaluate the future value of the investment in three years given the 15% growth rate stated in the problem. The property will be purchased in one lump sum investment at the beginning of the first year.

2. Calculate the monthly payments of this loan considering the following: The company may opt to finance the price of the property through a bank instead of paying for the land in cash. A bank has offered a 15-year loan at a 3.5% interest rate if the company makes a $500,000 down payment. Payments will be made at the end of the month.

Open the file the intern has completed, named ib_e03_realestateresults. Look at the file carefully. Are you comfortable presenting these numbers to the president of the company? Consider the following:

1. Look at the results calculated on the spreadsheet. Do they make sense? What estimates can you quickly do to see if the results are in the "ballpark."

2. Were the arguments in the **PMT** and **FV** functions properly defined?

3. Are the statistics of the investment properly considered in the analysis?

Exercise

Write a short answer for each of the points in the Problem section. Then, make any adjustments or corrections that will improve the reliability of the spreadsheet.

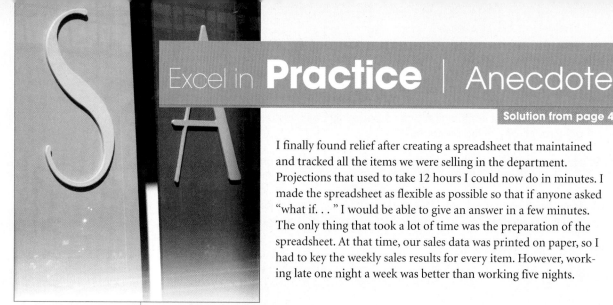

Solution from page 436

I finally found relief after creating a spreadsheet that maintained and tracked all the items we were selling in the department. Projections that used to take 12 hours I could now do in minutes. I made the spreadsheet as flexible as possible so that if anyone asked "what if. . . " I would be able to give an answer in a few minutes. The only thing that took a lot of time was the preparation of the spreadsheet. At that time, our sales data was printed on paper, so I had to key the weekly sales results for every item. However, working late one night a week was better than working five nights.

Assignment

Open the file named ib_e03_casualappareldepartment. This file includes data for several items that are typically sold in a women's specialty retail store. Create a flexible spreadsheet that will evaluate the sales performance of each item and project the sales and profit for the department. You will have to add formulas, functions, and formatting to this spreadsheet. Following are formulas and information that will help in completing this assignment:

1. Current Weeks of Supply = Current Inventory Units ÷ Last Week Unit Sales

2. New Price = Current Price – (Markdown Percent x Current Price)

3. Projected Sales Dollars = Sales Dollars YTD + (Current Inventory x New Price)

4. Total Cost = Total Units Purchased x Item Cost

5. Projected Profit = Projected Sales Dollars – Total Cost

6. The price of any product that has a Current Weeks of Supply greater than 8 should be reduced through a markdown.

7. When the price of an item is reduced, unit sales for next week will generally increase as follows: a 50% price reduction will double sales; a 25% price reduction will increase unit sales by 50%; a 10% price reduction will increase sales by 25%.

8. If the price of an item is not reduced, assume unit sales remain constant.

9. Come up with a plan that reduces the overall weeks of supply for the department to 8.5, while maintaining at least 34% profit (Projected Profit ÷ Projected Sales Dollars).

Questions for Discussion

1. When creating spreadsheets for business, why is it important to make them as flexible as possible?

2. What are some of the things that could go wrong with the spreadsheet solution described in the case?

3. Besides saving time, what other benefits could the spreadsheet solution described in the anecdote bring to the business?

The following questions are related to the concepts addressed in this chapter. There are three types of questions: Short Answer, True or False, and Fill in the Blank. If your answer to a True or False question is False, write a short explanation as to why you think the statement is not true.

1. The _____ is used when creating formulas in Excel that require multiplication.

2. Hold the Shift key and press the number _____ key when using exponents or raising a number to a certain power when creating formulas in Excel.

3. Explain why you should never do computations on a calculator and type the result into an Excel spreadsheet.

4. True or False: In cell referencing, the cell locations in a formula automatically change when you paste them to a new location.

5. When should you use numbers in Excel formulas?

6. True or False: You cannot use both numbers and cell locations in an Excel formula.

7. The_____ _____ command can be used to paste the value of a formula instead of the formula itself.

8. Why would you need to use parentheses in a formula?

9. True or False: Even if a formula contains only two cell references and one mathematical operator, you must still use parentheses.

10. In the following formula, what will be calculated second?
    `=((A4+B8)/C10)+A9+E6`.

11. True or False: This is a formula that will add the values in ten cell locations:
    `=SUM(A2:A10)`.

12. All functions start with an _____, an _____, and a _____.

13. What function could you use to count the names of people listed on a spreadsheet?

14. How would you type an **AVERAGE** function in a spreadsheet if you wanted to take the average of five cells in column C starting with cell location C1?

15. True or False: The following function will find the minimum value in cell locations B3 through and including B15: `=MIN(B3,B15)`.

16. A _____ _____ is used to apply an absolute reference to a cell location.

17. True or False: You cannot add two functions together like a formula; for example, `=SUM(C3:C10)+SUM(A4:A9)`.

18. True or False: Cell referencing will work with formulas but not with functions. Therefore, you must always retype functions and cannot copy and paste them to new cell locations.

19. True or False: If the following cell reference is used in a formula, the row number will change, but the column letter will remain the same when the formula is pasted to a new location: `C$10`.

20. What is the purpose of the **pmt** argument in the **Future Value** function?

21. What is the purpose of the **fv** argument in the **Payment** Function?

22. If you use the **Future Value** function to evaluate the growth of an investment over a 16-month period at a growth rate of 12% per year, what number would you enter in the **rate** argument?

23. When you use the **Future Value** function, you use the _____ argument if you are making a one-time lump sum investment.

24. True or False: You cannot define both the **pmt** argument and the **pv** argument of the **Future Value** function. You must define one or the other; otherwise, Excel will give you an error message.

25. True or False: The following **Payment** function will return the monthly payments of a loan that charges a 6% annual interest rate over ten years with a principal of $25,000 and a down payment of $5,000. The payments will be made at the beginning of each month. `=PMT(.06,10,-25000,5000,1)`.

26. What should you do if you are skipping an argument in either the **PMT** or **FV** function?

27. What does Excel assume if you skip the **type** argument of either the **PMT** or **FV** function?

28. You must use a negative sign for numbers or cell locations entered for the _____ argument and the _____ argument when using the **Future Value** function.

29. True or False: You must always use a negative sign for both the **fv** and **pv** arguments of the **Payment** function.

30. What tab in the Ribbon would you click to find the Function Library?

Skills Exam

The following exam is designed to test your ability to recognize and execute the Excel skills presented in this chapter. Read each question carefully and answer the questions in the order they are listed. You should be able to complete this exam in 60 minutes or less.

1. Open the file named ib_e03_skillsexam.

2. Type a **SUM** function in cell B9 that adds the values in cells B3 through B8. Correct any #### signs if necessary.

3. Copy the **SUM** function in cell B9 and paste it into cell C9. Correct any #### signs if necessary.

4. Type a formula in cell D3 to calculate the growth rate. Your formula should subtract the Value Last Year in cell B3 from the Present Value in cell C3 and divide that result by the Value Last Year in cell B3: `(Present Value - Value Last Year) ÷ Value Last Year`.

5. Format the result in cell D3 to a percentage with 1 decimal place.

6. Copy cell D3 and paste it into cells D4:D9.

7. Type an **AVERAGE** function in cell B10 that calculates the average of cells B3 through B8.

8. Copy cell B10 and paste it into C10.

9. Calculate the average growth rate in cell D10 using the **SUM** and **COUNT** functions. Follow this example: `((Sum of Present Value C3:C8 ÷ Count of Present Value C3:C8)-(Sum of Value Last Year B3:B8 ÷ Count of Value Last Year B3:B8))/(Sum of Value Last Year B3:B8 ÷ Count of Value Last Year B3:B8)`.

10. Format the result in cell D10 to a percentage with 1 decimal place. The result in D10 should match the value in cell D9.

11. Type a formula in cell E3 that divides the present value in cell C3 by the total of the present values in cell C9. Place an absolute reference on cell C9.

12. Format the result in cell E3 to a percent with 2 decimals. Then, copy cell E3 and paste it to cells E4 through E8.

13. Use the **Payment** function in cell D14 to calculate the monthly mortgage payments. Your function should use cell A14 for the rate, B14 for the periods, and C14 for the present value. Assume that payments are made at the end of the month.

14. Use the **Payment** function in cell E18 to calculate the monthly lease payments. Your function should use cell A18 for the rate, B18 for the periods, C18 for the present value, and D18 for the future value. Assume payments made at the end of the month.

15. Use the **Future Value** function in cell E21 to calculate the future value of all the investments in two years. Your function should use cell D9 for the rate and the number 2 for the periods. The total present value for all investments in cell C9 should be treated as a one-time lump sum investment. Assume that this investment is made at the beginning of the year. Format the result to U.S. currency with 0 decimal places. Correct any #### signs if necessary.

16. Type a formula in cell E22 that subtracts the total present value of all investments in cell C9 from the future value of all investments in cell E21.

17. Type a formula in cell E23 that multiplies the monthly mortgage payments in cell D14 by 24. Format the result to U.S. currency with 0 decimal places.

18. Type a formula in cell E24 that multiplies the monthly lease payments in cell E18 by 24. Format the result to U.S. currency with 0 decimal places.

19. Type a formula in cell E25 that subtracts the result of adding cells E23 and E24 from cell E22. Format the result to U.S. currency with 0 decimal places. Fix any #### signs if necessary.

20. Sort the range A2:E8 in ascending order based on the values in the Present Value column.

21. Save and close your file.

Challenge Questions

The following questions are designed to test your ability to apply the Excel skills you have learned to complete a business objective. Use your knowledge of Excel as well as your creativity to answer these questions. For most questions, there are several possible ways to complete the objective.

1. *Without* using the **Future Value** function, create a worksheet that determines the value of an investment if a person deposits $1,500 into a mutual fund at the beginning of every year for 20 years. Assume that the mutual fund achieves a 6% annual growth rate every year. Your worksheet should show the value of this investment at the end of every year for 20 years. In addition, your worksheet should be flexible to show what the value of the account would be at different deposit amounts or annual growth rates. For example, be able to show the value of the account in 20 years if a person decides to deposit only $1,200 per year but achieves an annual growth rate of 7%. Then, show the value of the account if a person deposits $1,000 per year but achieves an annual growth rate of 8%.

2. Complete question 1 again using the **Future Value** function. However, your worksheet should show only one number indicating the value of the investment in 20 years. Remember to keep your worksheet flexible so a new output will be produced if the annual deposit amount or annual growth rate values are changed.

3. A person asks you for help on an investment she is thinking of making. She wants to invest $5,000 into a medium-term bond that earns 4.5% interest per year. In addition, she wants to add $100 at the beginning of every month into the account. She wants to know what the value of her investment will be after five years. Create a worksheet showing her the value of this investment.

4. If you were going to lease a car, but could afford to pay only *$175 a month*, what would be the maximum price you could pay for a car? Assume the lease will run for four years, the annual interest rate is 3%, and that the car will retain 40% of its value after four years. Create a worksheet that shows the maximum price of the car you can lease.

5. You have an opportunity to invest in residential property that will cost $325,000. A real estate survey has shown that the value of property in this town has been increasing at a rate of 25% per year. However, you will have to take out a loan to be able to purchase the property. You can secure a 30-year loan at an annual interest rate of 6.5%. You will also be making a down payment of $75,000. Your plan is to sell this property after three years. After selling the property, you will pay off the loan. Create a spreadsheet that will calculate how much money you will make on this investment.

>> Chapter 4

Evaluating Data

Chapter Goals

Business managers are responsible for making numerous decisions every day based on various measures and statistics. For example, a retail buyer may decide to place orders, cancel future orders, issue returns, or do nothing depending on the ratio of current sales to current inventory. A finance manager may decide to sell, buy, or hold a particular stock based on a client's unrealized gain or loss. The challenge for these business managers is usually not the decision itself, but rather the volume of decisions they are required to make. For example, a retail buyer might be responsible for purchasing thousands of items. A finance manager might be managing portfolios for hundreds of clients. This chapter will review how business managers use Excel's logical and lookup functions to evaluate large volumes of data and produce decision outputs. As you will soon discover, logical and lookup functions can dramatically increase a business manager's decision-making power through Excel.

>> Excel | Skill Sets

Excel in **Practice** | Anecdote

Managing Retail Store Expansion

Location is everything, especially in the retail industry. I learned this quickly while working on a consulting project for a major retail corporation. One of our biggest challenges was deciding where the company should build new stores as part of a growth strategy plan. Constructing a new store costs several million dollars and requires significant sales revenue to justify the investment. To support our recommendations, my team analyzed enormous amounts of data to determine the best locations for potential new stores. Our analysis began with a spreadsheet containing over 20,000 United States ZIP codes and associated population, population growth, number of households, household income, population by gender, and, most important, competitors. We finally limited the number of potential locations to 400 ZIP codes and set a meeting with the company's president to discuss our findings. However, at 7:00 PM the night before our meeting, my partner and I made a startling discovery. The real estate analyst who originally sent us the data did not include the state or city names in his file. We had no idea what state or city belonged to each ZIP code. To make matters worse, not only had the real estate analyst gone home for the day, but he was going to be on vacation for the next week. Needless to say, we were not thrilled with the idea of looking up 400 ZIP codes and manually typing the state and city names into our spreadsheet.

≫ Continued on page 525

Logical Functions (The IF Function)

Chapter 3 demonstrated how functions are used to conduct statistical and financial calculations in business. However, functions can also be used to evaluate data and provide an output based on the results of a test. These are known as *logical functions.* The most commonly used logical function in Excel is the IF function. The IF function can produce an output that you define based on the results of a *logical test.* As with all logical functions, the results of a logical test will either be true or false. This section will demonstrate how business managers use IF functions to evaluate and highlight key statistics that require their attention for the purposes of making decisions.

IF Function

The IF function is used to evaluate data and provide an output based on the results of a logical test. Business managers often use the IF function to highlight key statistics related to their area of responsibility. For example, the inventory control manager of a candy company might be required to maintain at least 10,000 pounds of each ingredient used to produce a line of chocolate bars. Maintaining a specific inventory target is a common practice for companies that continually use the same components to produce a product, such as a candy manufacturer. Figure 4.1 shows a worksheet that contains ingredients that might be used to produce chocolate bars. An inventory control manager could use the IF function in the Status column (column C) to identify items in which the inventory in column B is less than 10,000 pounds.

Figure 4.1 | **Inventory Data for Chocolate Bar Production**

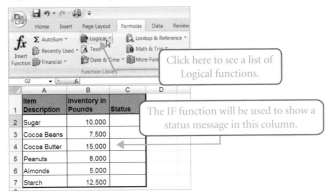

To use the **IF** function, you will need to define three arguments, as shown in Figure 4.2. The definition for each of these arguments is as follows:

- **logical_test:** Used for evaluating the data in a cell location based on a test that you define. The results of this test will be either true or false. A basic logical test usually starts with a cell reference followed by a comparison operator (see Figure 4.3 for a list of comparison operators used in logical tests). The second part of the test can be a multitude of possibilities. For example, you may need to compare the value in a cell to a number, another cell location, a formula, a function, or a word. If you are using words, or text data, you must put them in quotation marks. Examples of logical tests are

- B9 > 25
- H7 < D12
- L8 = "Car"
- D17 < (A9 - 12) * 10

- **[value_if_true]**: Used for defining the output of the **IF** function if the results of the logical test are true. This argument can be defined with a cell reference, formula, function, number, or words. As in the **logical_test** argument, if you are going to use words, you must put them in quotation marks.

- **[value_if_false]**: Used to define the output of the function if the results of the logical test are false. The options for defining this argument are identical to the **[value_if_true]** argument.

Figure 4.2 | **Arguments of the IF Function**

These arguments appear after you type an equal sign, the function name IF, and an open parenthesis.

	A	B	C	D	E	F	G
1	Item Description	Inventory in Pounds	Status				
2	Sugar	10,000	=IF(				
3	Cocoa Beans	7,500	IF(**logical_test**, [value_if_true], [value_if_false])				
4	Cocoa Butter	15,000					

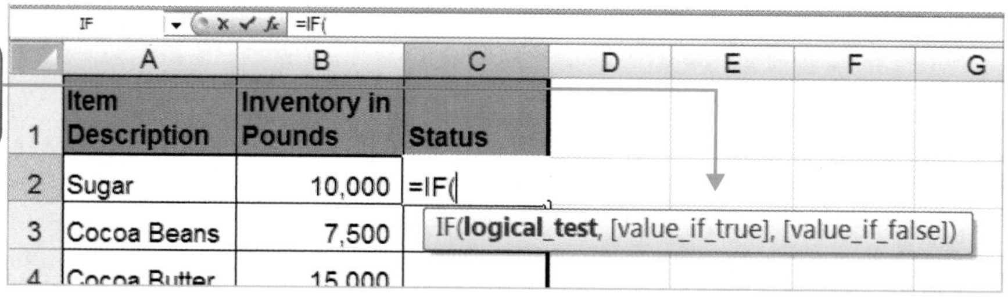

Figure 4.3 | **Comparison Operators Used in Logical Tests**

Symbol	Definition
=	Equal To
>	Greater Than
<	Less Than
<>	Not Equal To
>=	Greater Than or Equal To
<=	Less Than or Equal To

An inventory control manager could use the **IF** function in the worksheet shown in Figure 4.1 to identify items in which the inventory is less than 10,000 pounds. The following points explain how you add this to the worksheet:

- Activate cell C2.
- Type an equal sign, the function name IF, and an open parenthesis.
- Type B2<10000 to define the **logical_test** argument. This will test if the value in cell B2 is less than 10000. As noted previously, this example assumes that the inventory control manager is maintaining at least 10,000 pounds of inventory for each item. Type a comma after this argument.
- Type "LOW INV" to define the **[value_if_true]** argument. If the value in cell B2 is less than 10000, the message LOW INV will be displayed in cell C2. Notice that since this is a text message, it is put in quotation marks. Type a comma after this argument.

- Type "OK" to define the [**value_if_false**] argument. If the value in cell B2 is not less than 10000, the message OK will be displayed in cell C2. Again, notice that since this a text message, it is enclosed in quotation marks.
- Type a closing parenthesis and press the **Enter** key.
- Copy cell C2, which now contains the completed **IF** function, and paste it to cells C3 through C7. Since the cell reference B2 was used in the **logical_test** argument, it will automatically adjust to the appropriate row number because of relative referencing.

Figure 4.4 shows the arguments of the **IF** function that were typed into cell C2 of the worksheet shown in Figure 4.1. Notice that the text messages used to define the [**value_if_true**] and [**value_if_false**] arguments are enclosed in quotation marks. Also, notice that no commas were used in the value 10000 in the **logical_test** argument.

Figure 4.4 | **Setup of the IF Function to Evaluate Inventory Values in Column B**

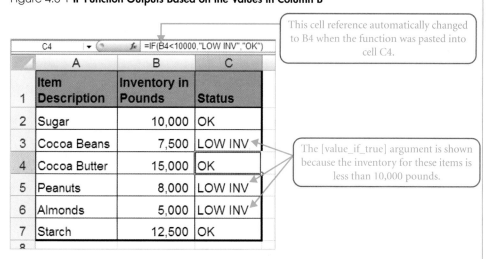

Figure 4.5 shows the output of the **IF** functions in the range C2:C7. By glancing at the worksheet, the inventory control manager can easily see that three items—Cocoa Beans, Peanuts, and Almonds—are below the target of 10,000 pounds.

Figure 4.5 | **IF Function Outputs Based on the Values in Column B**

Figure 4.6 shows another way the **IF** function can be used to help an inventory control manager maintain a target of at least 10,000 pounds for each item shown in Figure 4.1. In this example, the **IF** function is used to calculate how much inventory needs to be purchased if an item is below the 10,000 pound target. As a result, notice that a formula is used to define the [**value_if_true**] argument. Each argument of the function is defined as follows:

- **logical_test:** `B2 < 10000` This is the same test that was used for the example shown in Figure 4.4.

- [value_if_true]: `10000 - B2` If the value in cell B2 is less than 10000, the function will calculate how many pounds need to be purchased to reach the 10,000 pound target.
- [value_if_false]: `0` If the value in cell B2 is at or above 10000, the function will display a value of 0, indicating there is no need to purchase additional inventory.

Figure 4.6 | **Using the IF Function to Calculate Order Quantities**

> If the logical_test is true, the function will display the results of this formula.

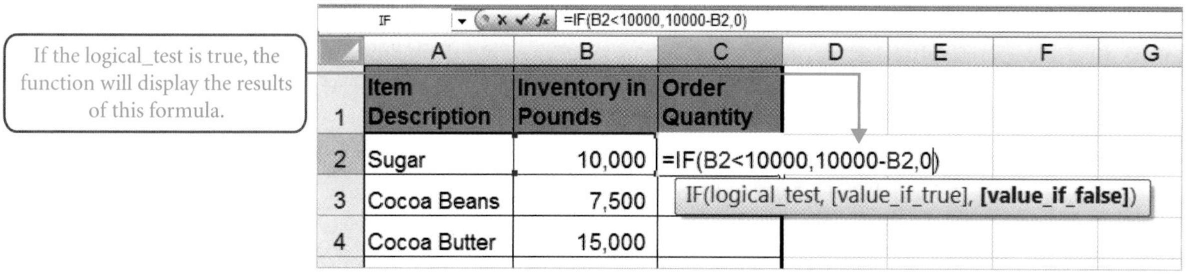

Figure 4.7 shows the output of the IF function created in Figure 4.6. Similar to the example shown in Figure 4.5, this function was created in cell C2 and then copied to cells C3 through C7. In addition, the worksheet was sorted in descending order based on the order quantities produced by the IF function. As a result, the IF function not only identifies items that need to be ordered, but automatically calculates how much inventory needs to be purchased by item.

Figure 4.7 | **Results of Using the IF Function to Calculate Order Quantities**

> The worksheet is sorted based on the outputs of the IF function in this column.

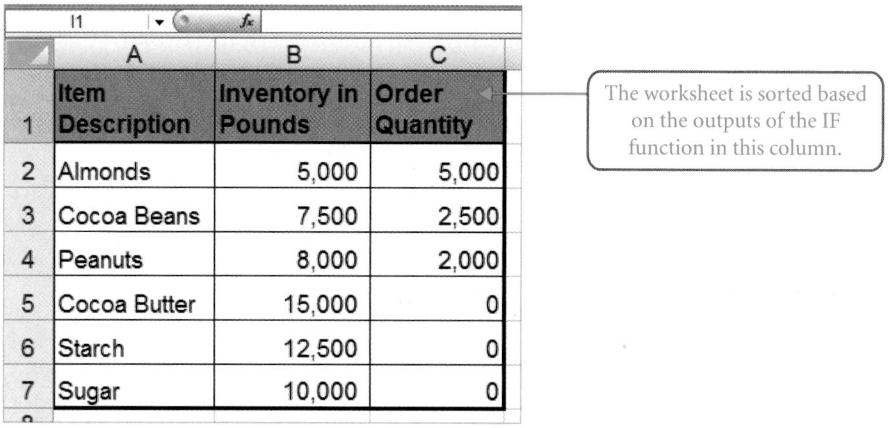

COMMON MISTAKES | Defining Arguments of the IF Function

People often make the mistake of using commas in values typed into the **logical_test** argument of the **IF** function. For example:

`=IF(C2 < 10,000,"Low","High")`

Excel will read the logical test for this function as C2 < 10, not C2 < 10000. The reason is that a comma signals the end of one argument and the start of another. For this example, Excel will display a warning stating too many arguments were entered because it assumes you are trying to define four arguments instead of three.

Nested IF Functions

By itself, the IF function provides the entry of one logical test and one output (value if true or value if false). However, a business project may require the function to display one of many possible outputs. For example, the items shown in Figure 4.1 may require a status rating based on five potential options: Very Low, Low, Good, High, or Very High. To produce one output from these five possibilities, you would need to create an IF function with four logical tests. You can accomplish this by using a nested IF function.

A nested IF function will be used to evaluate the inventory data shown in Figure 4.8, which contains revised data from Figure 4.1. For this example, we will assume the target inventory remains at 10,000 pounds. However, if the inventory level is too high for any item, it may spoil. On the other hand, if the inventory is significantly below 10,000 pounds, the company may fall short of its production goals. This example will use a nested IF function to display one of the following four outputs:

- Less than 5,000 pounds: Display the message "Prod Risk."
- Greater than 5,000 pounds but less than 10,000 pounds: Display the message "Low."
- Greater than 14,000 pounds: Display the message "Spoil Risk."
- Between 10,000 and 14,000 pounds: Display the message "OK."

Figure 4.8 | **Revised Inventory Data for Chocolate Bar Production**

	A	B	C
1	Item Description	Inventory in Pounds	Status
2	Sugar	10,000	
3	Cocoa Beans	7,500	
4	Cocoa Butter	22,000	
5	Peanuts	5,200	
6	Almonds	1,200	
7	Starch	12,500	

> A nested IF function will be created in column C to categorize each inventory value in column B as Prod Risk, Low, Spoil Risk, or OK.

The following points explain how to create a nested IF function in cell C2 of Figure 4.8 to display one of four outputs:

- Activate cell C2.
- Type an equal sign, the function name IF, and an open parenthesis.
- Type B2<5000 to define the **logical_test** argument. This will be the first of three logical tests that will be created in this function. Type a comma after this argument.
- Type "Prod Risk" to define the [**value_if_true**] argument. If the first logical test is true, the function will display this message. Type a comma after this argument.
- Type the function name IF followed by an open parenthesis to define the [**value_if_false**] argument. If the logical test is false, you will need to conduct a second logical test. You do this by starting a second IF function.
- Type B2 < 10000 to define the **logical_test** argument of the second IF function. If the first logical test, which is B2 < 5000, is false, then this logical test will evaluate if the value in cell B2 is less than 10000. Note that if the first logical test failed, and this logical test is true, then you can conclude that the value in cell B2 is greater

than 5,000 pounds but less than 10,000 pounds. Type a comma after this argument.

- Type "Low" to define the [value_if_true] argument of the second IF function. As previously mentioned, if the inventory quantity is greater than 5,000 pounds but less than 10,000 pounds, the status message should read "Low." Type a comma after this argument.

- Type the function name **IF** followed by an open parenthesis to define the [value_if_false] argument of the second IF function. As previously mentioned, to show one of four potential outputs, you will need to conduct three logical tests. To conduct a third logical test, you start a third **IF** function.

- Type B2 > 14000 to define the **logical_test** argument of the third **IF** function. If the previous two logical tests are false, then you can conclude that the value in cell B2 is greater than or equal to 10,000. Therefore, the third and final logical test will evaluate if the value in B2 is greater than 14,000 pounds. As mentioned, if any item has an inventory greater than 14,000 pounds, it will be at risk of spoiling. Type a comma after this argument.

- Type "Spoil Risk" to define the [value_if_true] argument of the third **IF** function. Type a comma after this argument.

- Type "OK" to define the [value_if_false] argument of the third **IF** function. If all logical tests are false, then you can conclude that the value in cell B2 is between 10,000 and 14,000 pounds.

- Type three closing parentheses. It is important to note that a closing parenthesis is required for every **IF** function you started. In this example, you started a total of three **IF** functions for the purpose of conducting three logical tests. Therefore, you must type three closing parentheses at the end of the function.

- Press the **Enter** key.

- Copy the cell C2, which now contains the nested **IF** function, and paste it into cells C3 through C7.

Figure 4.9 shows the setup of the nested IF function that was created in cell C2. In this example, a new IF function is started in the [value_if_false] argument for the purpose of conducting multiple logical tests. However, both the [value_if_true] and [value_if_false] arguments could be used to add multiple logical tests.

Figure 4.9 | **Setup of the Nested IF Function**

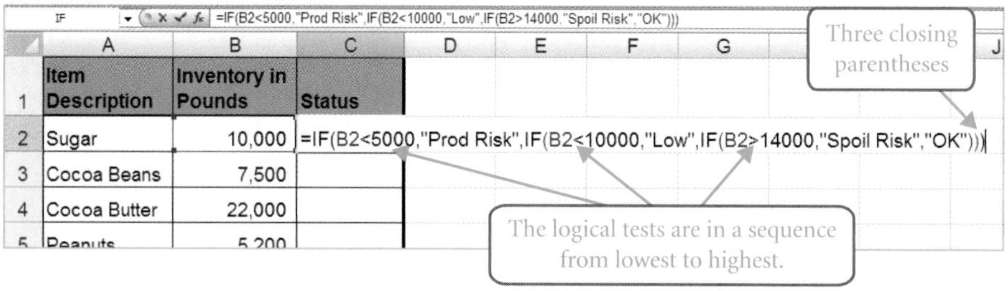

Figure 4.10 shows the outputs of the nested **IF** functions in column C. The inventory control manager can use this information to decide which items need to be purchased or which items may need to be monitored and tested for spoilage. In this case, the manager can easily see that purchasing additional inventory for Almonds is critical to support the production goals of the business. On the other hand, the Cocoa Butter needs to be monitored for possible spoilage. The inventory control manager might also inform the production manager to use containers of Cocoa Butter with the oldest receipt date first to reduce potential waste.

Figure 4.10 | **Outputs Produced by the Nested IF Function**

	A	B	C
1	Item Description	Inventory in Pounds	Status
2	Sugar	10,000	OK
3	Cocoa Beans	7,500	Low
4	Cocoa Butter	22,000	Spoil Risk
5	Peanuts	5,200	Low
6	Almonds	1,200	Prod Risk
7	Starch	12,500	OK

This nested IF function displays one of four potential outputs for each item.

COMMON MISTAKES | Nested IF Functions

You *cannot* enter a logical test directly into the **[value_if_false]** or **[value_if_true]** argument without typing the function name IF followed by an open parenthesis. For example, the following nested **IF** function will not work:

```
=IF(B2 < 5000,"Very Low",B2 < 10000,"Low","OK")
```

The logical test B2 < 10000 was entered directly into the **[value_if_false]** argument. This will produce an error stating too many arguments were defined. The following is the corrected version of this example:

```
=IF(B2 < 5000,"Very Low",IF(B2 < 10000,"Low","OK"))
```

It is important to note that Excel will execute the logical tests of a nested IF function from left to right. Therefore, the sequence of each logical test shown in Figure 4.9 makes the nested IF function work. Notice that each logical test is in a sequence that tests for the lowest possible value in cell B2 to the largest possible value. For example, the first logical test looks for the lowest possible values (B2 < 5000). The second test looks for any values below 10,000 (B2 < 10000), and the third test looks for the highest values (B2 > 14000). What would happen if the first logical test in this example was B2 < 10000 instead of B2 < 5000? It would be impossible to test if B2 contains a value less than 5000 because these values would immediately test true for B2 < 10000. Therefore, you must carefully plan the sequence of each logical test in a nested IF function so that a value cannot test true for two tests.

COMMON MISTAKES | Logical Test Sequence in a Nested IF Function

Excel will execute the logical tests in a nested **IF** function from left to right. If you are using the **[value_if_false]** argument only to add additional logical tests to a nested **IF** function, the function will immediately end when the results of a logical test are true. Therefore, you must check the sequence of each logical test to make sure a value cannot test true for two tests. The following points can help you create a valid logical test sequence:

1. Identify the lowest and highest values you are testing in your worksheet. The logical tests should be sequenced to look for the lowest values to highest values, or highest values to lowest values. This will prevent a value from testing true for two logical tests.

2. Talk through each logical test in sequence for a few data points on your spreadsheet and write down the result. In addition, try to consider various hypothetical data points that would trigger a true output for each test.

>> **Quick Reference**

IF Functions and Nested IF Functions

1. Activate a cell where the output of the function should appear.

2. Type an equal sign, the function name **IF**, and an open parenthesis.

3. Create a test for the **logical_test** argument.

4. Define an output for the **[value_if_true]** argument (text outputs must be in quotation marks).

5. Define an output for the **[value_if_false]** argument or enter another **IF** function by typing the function name **IF** and an open parenthesis.

6. Type a closing parenthesis. If creating a nested **IF** function, type a closing parenthesis for each **IF** function that you started.

7. Press the **Enter** key.

>> IF Functions

The purpose of this workshop is to demonstrate the use of the **IF** and nested **IF** functions. I will be demonstrating the tasks in this workshop in the **IF Functions** and **Nested IF Functions** videos. After completing each section of tasks, watch the related video shown in parentheses. Open the file named ib_e04_markdownanalysis. Remember to try the tasks on your own first before watching the videos.

1. Basic IF Function (Video: IF Functions)

a. Activate cell G3.

b. Type an equal sign, the function name **IF**, and an open parenthesis.

c. Define the **logical_test** argument by typing **B3 = C3** and then type a comma.

d. Define the **[value_if_true]** argument by typing the word **"Regular"**. Be sure to include the quotation marks. Then type a comma.

e. Define the **[value_if_false]** argument by typing the word **"Markdown"**.

f. Type a closing parenthesis and press the **Enter** key.

g. Copy cell G3 and paste it into cells G4:G7 using the **Paste Formulas** option.

2. Nested IF Function (Video: Nested IF Functions)

a. Activate cell H3.

b. Type an equal sign, the function name **IF**, and an open parenthesis.

c. Define the **logical_test** argument by typing **F3 <= 8** and then type a comma.

d. Define the **[value_if_true]** argument by typing the number **0** and then type a comma.

e. Define the **[value_if_false]** argument by starting a second **IF** function. Type the function name **IF** followed by an open parenthesis.

f. Define the **logical_test** argument of the second **IF** function by typing **F3 <= 12** and then type a comma.

g. Define the **[value_if_true]** argument of the second **IF** function by typing the number **.15** and then type a comma.

h. Define the **[value_if_false]** argument of the second **IF** function by adding a third **IF** function. Type the function name **IF** followed by an open parenthesis.

i. Define the **logical_test** argument of the third **IF** function by typing **F3 <= 16** and then type a comma.

j. Define the **[value_if_true]** argument of the third **IF** function by typing the number **.25** and then type a comma.

k. Define the **[value_if_false]** argument of the third **IF** function by typing the number **.50**.

l. Finish the function by typing three closing parentheses and then press the **Enter** key.

m. Copy cell H3 and paste it to cells H4:H7 using the **Paste Formulas** option.

n. Save and close your file.

>> Price Management

Price management is a common exercise for any business. As consumer demand changes, business managers must manage the price of their products and services to be able to maintain a company's sales goals and market share. Price management is especially critical for companies that need to sell large amounts of inventory. However, there are many questions to consider before changing the price of a product. For example, will sales increase for a given item if a price is decreased? If so, how much will sales increase? If the price of an item is decreased, its profitability will usually decrease. Therefore, how much can a price decrease before the company starts losing money on the item? A flexible spreadsheet that can evaluate product sales, inventory, and pricing is an extremely valuable tool in answering these questions.

EXERCISE

Why Do I Need This?

Exercise

This exercise demonstrates how **IF** functions can dramatically increase the calculating flexibility of Excel. Your goal is to build a price management tool that will not only calculate price changes, but enable a pricing manager to override these calculations if needed. To begin this exercise, open the Excel file named ib_e04_pricemanagementreport.

1. Enter a **SUM** function in cell D8 that adds the values in the range D3:D7.

2. Copy the **SUM** function in cell D8 and paste it into cells E8 and F8.

3. Type a formula in cell G3 that divides the Current Unit Inventory (cell F3) by the Sales Units LW (cell D3). Then copy the formula and paste it into cells G4:G8. This formula calculates the current weeks of supply, which will give the pricing manager an idea of how much the current inventory supply will last if sales remain constant.

4. Type a nested **IF** function in cell H3 that will calculate the suggested markdown. This type of calculation could be used by a company that sets target weeks of supply for the items it sells. If the weeks of supply get too high, the company may reduce, or mark down, the price to increase sales. Use the following criteria when creating the function. Also, make sure each logical test is entered into the function in the order listed here:

   a. If the Current Weeks of Supply <= 8, the suggested markdown should be 0.

   b. If the Current Weeks of Supply <= 14, the suggested markdown should be .15.

   c. If the Current Weeks of Supply <= 18, the suggested markdown should be .25.

   d. If the Current Weeks of Supply is greater than 18 (or not less than or equal to 18), the markdown should be .40.

5. Copy and paste the nested **IF** function in cell H3 to cells H4:H7.

6. Type a nested **IF** function into cell I3 to calculate the New Price. The goal of this worksheet is to allow the price change manager to override this calculation by entering a new price into one of the cells in column J. This **IF** function will see whether the price entered into column J is greater than 0. If it is, that number will become the new price. If the value in column J is less than or equal to 0, the nested **IF** function will calculate the new price based on the suggested markdown. The logical tests and outputs for this nested **IF** function are as follows. Be sure to enter each logical test in the sequence listed.

   a. If J3 > 0, the output of the function should be the value in cell J3. If J3 is greater than 0, the pricing manager has manually set a new price for this item.

b. If H3 = 0, the output of the function should be cell C3. If H3 is 0, then there is no suggested markdown. The output of the function should be whatever the current price is in cell C3.

c. If both logical tests (J3 > 0 and H3 = 0) are false, then the function should calculate the new price using the formula C3 - (C3 * H3).

7. Copy the function in cell I3 and paste it to cells I4:I7.

8. Type a regular **IF** statement in cell K3 to calculate the markdown in dollars. If the New Price (cell I3) is equal to the Current Price (cell C3), then the markdown dollars are 0 because the price did not change. Otherwise, calculate the markdown dollars using the formula (C3 - I3) * F3.

9. Copy the function in cell K3 and paste it to cells K4:K7. Then enter a **SUM** function in cell K8 to add the markdown dollars in this column.

10. Type the formula **(D3 - E3) / E3** in cell L3 to calculate the change in sales. Copy this formula and paste it into cells L4:L8.

11. Even though the weeks of supply for T-shirts is below 8, the directors of the company are concerned that a major competitor will be having a T-shirt sale this weekend. Override the new price by typing **7.99** in cell J3.

12. Even though the weeks of supply for denim shirts is slightly higher than 8, sales are up compared to last year. Maintain the current price by typing **24.99** in cell J6.

13. The company did not want to go over 150,000 markdown dollars (cell K8). Is it achieving this goal? Override the price for the Polo and Twill shirts so the company does not go over its target.

14. Save and close your file.

PROBLEM & EXERCISE

>> What's Wrong with This Spreadsheet?

Problem

You just started a new job as a raw materials buyer for a manufacturing company. One of the analysts in your division has prepared a spreadsheet analyzing the firm's current inventory position. The goal of the spreadsheet is to help you decide which items need to be purchased because inventory is too low, or which items should be canceled or returned because inventory is too high. Your boss left a copy of the company's inventory policy on your desk. The inventory guidelines are as follows:

1. Weeks of Supply <= 4: Orders must be rushed in because the company may be at risk of losing production.

2. Weeks of Supply < 8: It's time to place new orders to keep up with the production schedule.

3. Weeks of Supply >10: Try to get suppliers to postpone the delivery date to keep inventory from accumulating too high.

4. Weeks of Supply > 15: Place a hold on all current and new orders. At this level the inventory is getting too high and will be at risk of spoiling.

5. Weeks of Supply > 20: Consumer demand must be declining for the product that uses this item for production. Return item to the supplier if possible.

6. The inventory status is normal for any item that does not fit into these categories.

The analyst e-mails the spreadsheet containing the inventory analysis to you. He states the following in his e-mail: "Sorry I could not discuss this with you in person. I have an Excel training seminar all morning. In any event, the inventory status for the department is in good shape. By looking at the Suggested Action column, you will see that a few items need to be purchased, and there are a few items for which we might need to push back the delivery date. Thankfully, there are no major things like rush orders or returns! I will stop by when I am finished with the training seminar."

Exercise

The spreadsheet this analyst sent to you is named ib_e04_inventorystatus. Are you comfortable making decisions based on the Suggested Action column? Consider the following:

1. Do the suggested actions make sense given the inventory guidelines listed in the Problem section?

2. How is the data for the Suggested Action column being calculated?

3. Follow the calculation method used for the Suggested Action column for a few data points in the Weeks of Supply column. Does the method make sense?

4. What else could you do to make this spreadsheet easier to read?

What's wrong with this spreadsheet? Write a short answer for each of the points listed and fix any errors you see on the spreadsheet that the analyst sent to you.

⟫ Logical Functions (AND OR)   Skill Set

The previous section identified how **IF** functions are used to evaluate data and produce various outputs based on a logical test. This section introduces two other logical functions that are also used to evaluate data based on logical tests. They are the **AND** and **OR** functions. These functions can be used independently but are often used in the logical test argument of an **IF** function. This section will first review how the **AND** and **OR** functions are used independently and then will demonstrate how they are used with the **IF** function to dramatically increase Excel's analytical capabilities.

AND Function

In many situations, business managers must decide if a group of conditions apply to a specific aspect of their business. This is especially relevant for companies that make specialized products for a specific target customer. For example, Figure 4.11 shows customer demographic data from a company that is seeking to sell a new product to people who are female, have children, and are less than 45 years old. The marketing manager of this firm would probably find it challenging to identify these people from a list of 100,000 potential customers. However, the **AND** function can automatically evaluate and highlight customers that meet all of the characteristics targeted by this product.

Figure 4.11 | **Customer Data**

	A	B	C	D	E	F
1	Customer Detail Information					
2	Name	State of Residence	Gender	Age	Children	Target Customer
3	Customer 1	CA	F	22	No	
4	Customer 2	MO	M	44	Yes	
5	Customer 3	TX	F	65	Yes	
6	Customer 4	NJ	M	73	No	
7	Customer 5	FLA	M	29	Yes	
8	Customer 6	PA	F	26	Yes	
9	Customer 7	GA	F	34	No	
10	Customer 8	NH	F	54	Yes	
11	Customer 9	NY	M	36	No	
12	Customer 10	CO	F	41	Yes	
13	Customer 11	NJ	M	30	Yes	
14	Customer 12	NM	F	24	No	
15	Customer 13	NY	F	28	Yes	
16	Customer 14	VA	M	44	No	
17	Customer 15	PA	M	52	Yes	

The AND function will be used in this column to identify the target customers.

This worksheet continues down to row 22.

The **AND** function evaluates data using the same logical test that was explained in the **IF** function section. However, with this function, you can enter up to 30 logical tests. Based on the results of all logical tests entered, the **AND** function will produce one of two possible outputs. If all logical tests are true, the function will display the word TRUE. If the results of any logical test are false, the function will display the word FALSE. The following points explain how to use the **AND** function to evaluate the customer data in Figure 4.11 to highlight any customers who are female, have children, and are younger than 45:

- Activate cell F3, which is the first cell location in the Target Customer column. Remember, the **AND** function will display either the word TRUE or FALSE based on the results of the logical tests. Therefore, the **AND** function will identify target customers by displaying the word TRUE.

- Type an equal sign, the function name AND, and an open parenthesis.

- Type C3 ="F" to define the first logical test. Since being female is one of the characteristics of the target customer, the first logical test will evaluate if the gender of the customer is female. Notice that since the logical test uses text data, it is placed in quotation marks. Just as in the logical test in the **IF** function, any words or text data must be placed in quotation marks. Type a comma after this argument.

- Type D3 < 45 to define the second logical test. This will evaluate if the age of the customer is less than 45. Type a comma after this argument.

- Type E3 ="Yes" to define the third logical test. This will evaluate if the customer has children. Similar to the first logical test, since text data is being used, it is enclosed in quotation marks.

- Type a closing parenthesis and press the **Enter** key.

- Copy the completed **AND** function in cell F3 and paste it into cells F4 through F22. Since cell references were used in each of the three logical tests, they will automatically adjust through relative referencing when the formula is pasted to the rest of the cells in this column.

>> **Quick Reference**

AND Function

1. Activate a cell location where the output of the function should appear.

2. Type an equal sign, the function name AND, and an open parenthesis.

3. Create at least one but no more than 30 logical tests. Separate each logical test with a comma. *All* tests must be true to produce a TRUE output.

4. Type a closing parenthesis.

5. Press the **Enter** key.

- Sort the worksheet based on the **AND** function outputs in the Target Customer column in descending order. This will place any customers showing a TRUE output in the Target Customer column at the top of the worksheet.

Figure 4.12 shows the setup of the **AND** function that will be used to identify target customers. Notice that each argument of the function is a complete logical test utilizing the comparison operators shown in Figure 4.3.

Figure 4.12 | **Setup of the AND Function**

	A	B	C	D	E	F
	AND		=AND(C3="F",D3<45,E3="Yes")			
1		Customer Detail Information				
2	Name	State of Residence	Gender	Age	Children	Target Customer
3	Customer 1	CA	F	22	No	=AND(C3="F",D3<45,E3="Yes")
4	Customer 2	MO	M	44	Yes	AND(logical1, [logical2], **[logical3]**, [logical4], ...)
5	Customer 3	TX	F	65	Yes	
6	Customer 4	NJ	M	73	No	

Each argument of this function is a complete logical test.

Figure 4.13 shows the results of the **AND** function. The word TRUE is displayed in the Target Customer column for any customer that meets all three logical tests that were typed into the function. The word FALSE is displayed if the results are false for any of the three logical tests. Notice how all target customers are grouped together in the first rows of the worksheet. The marketing manager using this worksheet can easily identify the target customers since the data is sorted based on the results of the **AND** function.

Figure 4.13 | **Results of the AND Function**

	A	B	C	D	E	F
	F10		=AND(C10="F",D10<45,E10="Yes")			
1		Customer Detail Information				
2	Name	State of Residence	Gender	Age	Children	Target Customer
3	Customer 6	PA	F	26	Yes	TRUE
4	Customer 10	CO	F	41	Yes	TRUE
5	Customer 13	NY	F	28	Yes	TRUE
6	Customer 16	MD	F	20	Yes	TRUE
7	Customer 18	PA	F	39	Yes	TRUE
8	Customer 1	CA	F	22	No	FALSE
9	Customer 2	MO	M	44	Yes	FALSE
10	Customer 3	TX	F	65	Yes	FALSE
11	Customer 4	NJ	M	73	No	FALSE
12	Customer 5	FLA	M	29	Yes	FALSE
13	Customer 7	GA	F	34	No	FALSE
14	Customer 8	NH	F	54	Yes	FALSE
15	Customer 9	NY	M	36	No	FALSE

Because of sorting, all TRUE outputs are grouped at the top of the worksheet.

The AND function produces a FALSE output here because one of the three logical tests is false (see formula bar).

COMMON MISTAKES | Outputs for the AND Function

You cannot define the output for the **AND** function. People often try to define the output for the **AND** function similar to the **[value_if_true]** or **[value_if_false]** arguments of the **IF** function. The only arguments you can define for the **AND** function are logical tests. The only output that will be produced by the **AND** function is the word TRUE or FALSE. This is also true for the **OR** function, which is covered in the next section.

OR Function

A close relative of the **AND** function is the **OR** function. The arguments of both functions are defined by logical tests. However, if *any* logical test is true, the **OR** function will display the word TRUE. The function displays the word FALSE if *all* logical tests are false. The **OR** function is used to evaluate data where the existence of just one criterion is required to trigger a decision or action. For example, a company may have a limited number of states where it can sell and distribute products. The **OR** function can be used to identify if a customer lives in one of the states within the company's territory. This information can then be used to distribute marketing information or promotional material relating to the company's product line.

The following demonstrates a variation for identifying target customers in Figure 4.11. In this example, a target customer is any person who lives in any of these three states: New York, Pennsylvania, or New Jersey. You use the **OR** function in this situation to produce a TRUE output if a person lives in *any* one of these three states. You add this function to the worksheet as follows:

- Activate cell F3.
- Type an equal sign, the function name OR, and an open parenthesis.
- Type B3="NJ" to define the first logical test. This will evaluate if the person lives in the state of New Jersey. Notice that quotation marks are placed around NJ because it is text data. Type a comma after this argument.
- Type B3="NY" to define the second logical test. This will evaluate if the customer lives in the state of New York. Type a comma after this argument.
- Type B3 ="PA" to define the third logical test. This will evaluate if the customer lives in the state of Pennsylvania.
- Type a closing parenthesis and press the **Enter** key.
- Copy the completed **OR** function in cell F3 and paste it into cells F4 through F22.

Figure 4.14 shows the setup of the **OR** function that is being used to evaluate if a customer lives in one of three states. Notice that each argument of the **OR** function, similar to the **AND** function, is a complete logical function.

Figure 4.14 | **Setup of the OR Function**

	A	B	C	D	E	F
1			Customer Detail Information			
2	Name	State of Residence	Gender	Age	Children	Target Customer
3	Customer 1	CA	F	22	No	=OR(B3="NJ", B3="NY",B3="PA")
4	Customer 2	MO	M	44	Yes	
5	Customer 3	TX	F	65	Yes	
6	Customer 4	NJ	M	73	No	

This function will display the word TRUE if any of these logical tests is true.

COMMON MISTAKES | Arguments of the OR and AND Functions

You must type complete logical tests when defining the arguments of both the **AND** and **OR** functions. People often try to enter multiple results separated by commas to test multiple values for one cell location as shown in the following example. This **OR** function will produce a TRUE output regardless of what value is contained in cell D10:

```
=OR(D10 = 14,25,33,55)
```

The following example illustrates how you should create the **OR** function if you are evaluating if *one* of four values (14, 25, 33, 55) is contained in cell D10.

```
=OR(D10 = 14,D10 = 25,D10 = 33,D10 = 55)
```

Figure 4.15 shows the results of the **OR** function. Similar to the output of the **AND** function in Figure 4.13, this worksheet was also sorted based on the function outputs in the Target Customer column. Notice that if NY or NJ or PA is shown in the State of Residence column for a customer, the output of the **OR** function is TRUE. A marketing manager can use this information to initiate a direct mail marketing campaign to the target customers identified in this worksheet.

Figure 4.15 | **Results of the OR Function**

	A	B	C	D	E	F
	F6	▾	*fx*	=OR(B6="NJ", B6="NY",B6="PA")		
1			Customer Detail Information			
2	Name	State of Residence	Gender	Age	Children	Target Customer
3	Customer 4	NJ	M	73	No	TRUE
4	Customer 6	PA	F	26	Yes	TRUE
5	Customer 9	NY	M	36	No	TRUE
6	Customer 11	NJ	M	30	Yes	TRUE
7	Customer 13	NY	F	28	Yes	TRUE
8	Customer 15	PA	M	52	Yes	TRUE
9	Customer 18	PA	F	39	Yes	TRUE
10	Customer 20	NJ	M	41	Yes	TRUE
11	Customer 1	CA	F	22	No	FALSE
12	Customer 2	MO	M	44	Yes	FALSE
13	Customer 3	TX	F	65	Yes	FALSE
14	Customer 5	FLA	M	29	Yes	FALSE
15	Customer 7	GA	F	34	No	FALSE
16	Customer 8	NH	F	54	Yes	FALSE

The function produces a TRUE output in these cells because at least one of the three logical tests is true (see formula bar).

This worksheet continues down to row 22.

Combining AND, OR, and IF Functions

The **OR** and **AND** functions can produce only one of two outputs: the word TRUE or the word FALSE. However, you can use these functions with the **IF** function to produce any output that is required for your project. This technique will be demonstrated using the worksheet shown in Figure 4.16, which contains customer buying data from a hypothetical retail company. Retailers typically offer a variety of reward promotions or discounts based on the buying history of their customers. For example, you may have signed up for a frequent shopper card at your favorite store or agreed to have a company contact you regarding future promotions when you purchased something online. These activities are usually indicative of a company that is running some type of customer loyalty program. A marketing manager will use the data collected from these programs to develop various discounts and promotional programs depending on a customer's buying history. The technique of combining the **AND**, **OR**, and **IF** functions can be used to tell the marketing manager what promotions should be sent to each customer.

The following points explain how you combine the **AND** and **IF** functions to show which promotion each customer should receive in Figure 4.16. This example assumes that a customer could receive one of two discount coupons. The first is a 50% off coupon for customers who have been purchasing products from the company for more than one year and have not made a purchase in the last 12 months. All other customers will receive a regular 10% off promotional coupon.

Figure 4.16 | **Customer Rewards Program**

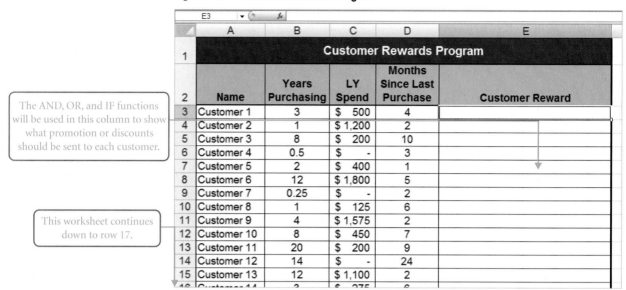

The AND, OR, and IF functions will be used in this column to show what promotion or discounts should be sent to each customer.

This worksheet continues down to row 17.

Name	Years Purchasing	LY Spend	Months Since Last Purchase	Customer Reward
Customer 1	3	$ 500	4	
Customer 2	1	$ 1,200	2	
Customer 3	8	$ 200	10	
Customer 4	0.5	$ -	3	
Customer 5	2	$ 400	1	
Customer 6	12	$ 1,800	5	
Customer 7	0.25	$ -	2	
Customer 8	1	$ 125	6	
Customer 9	4	$ 1,575	2	
Customer 10	8	$ 450	7	
Customer 11	20	$ 200	9	
Customer 12	14	$ -	24	
Customer 13	12	$ 1,100	2	
Customer 14	3	$ 275	6	

- Activate cell E3, which is the first cell location in the Customer Reward column.
- Type an equal sign, the function name IF, and an open parenthesis.
- Type the function name AND followed by an open parenthesis. The **AND** function will be used in defining the **logical_test** argument of the IF function.
- Type B3>1 to define the first logical test of the **AND** function. This test will evaluate if the value in the Years Purchasing column is greater than 1. Type a comma after defining this argument.
- Type D3>=12 to define the second logical test of the **AND** function. This test will evaluate if the value in the Months Since Last Purchase column is greater than or equal to 12.
- Type a closing parenthesis to complete the **AND** function.
- Type =TRUE followed by a comma to complete the **logical_test** argument of the **IF** function. The logical test of the **IF** function will now evaluate if the output of the **AND** function is TRUE. Notice that quotation marks are *not* placed on the word TRUE. The reason is that the word TRUE is an output of the **AND** function and not a text message or word that has been typed into a cell.
- Type "Please Come Back 50% Off" to define the [**value_if_true**] argument of the **IF** function. If the logical test of the **IF** function is true, then the output of the **AND** function is true. This indicates a person has been buying products from the company for more than one year *and* has not made a purchase in 12 or more months. Therefore, this message tells the marketing manager to send this customer a 50% off coupon. Type a comma after this argument.
- Type "Customer Appreciation 10% Off" to define the [**value_if_false**] argument of the **IF** function. Any customer that does not qualify for the 50% off coupon will be sent a 10% off coupon.
- Type a closing parenthesis and press the **Enter** key to complete the function.
- Copy the function in cell E3 and paste it into cells E4 through E17.
- Sort the worksheet based on the Customer Reward column in descending order.

Figure 4.17 shows the setup of the functions. Notice that the **AND** function defines the left side of the logical test. Also, note that the messages defining the value_if_true and value_if_false arguments are placed in quotation marks.

Figure 4.17 | **Setup for Combining the IF and AND Functions**

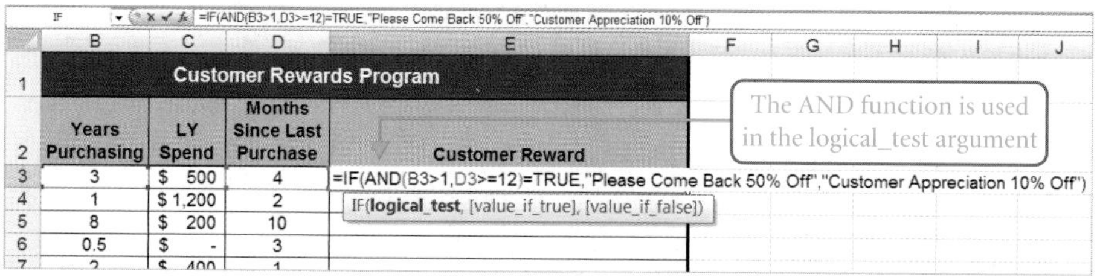

Figure 4.18 shows the results of combing the **IF** function and **AND** function to determine the type of discount coupon that should be sent to each customer. Since the spreadsheet was sorted, the marketing manager can easily see that the first two customers listed on the worksheet should be sent the 50% off coupon.

Figure 4.18 | **Results of Combining the IF and AND Functions**

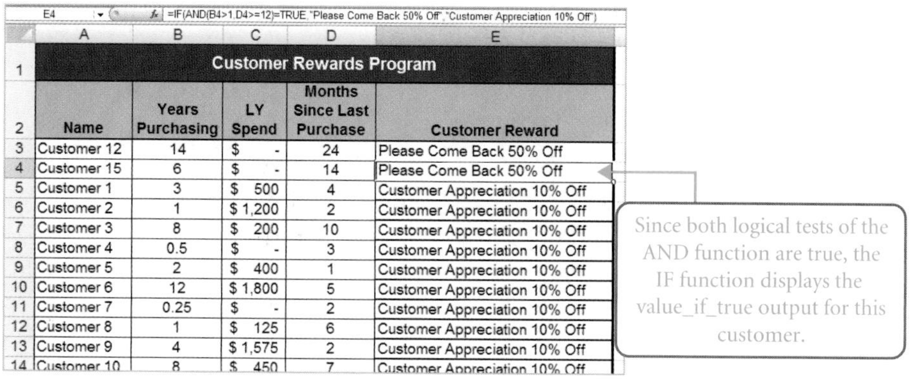

Figure 4.19 shows the setup of combining the **IF** and **OR** functions. This example assumes that the marketing manager will send a 25% off discount coupon to customers who have either been making purchases for more than two years or have spent more than $1,000 in the past year. Since customers will qualify for this coupon if they satisfy either criteria, the **OR** function will be used in defining the logical test of the **IF** function. The following points explain how you create this function using the worksheet shown in Figure 4.16:

- Activate cell E3.
- Type an equal sign, the function name IF, and an open parenthesis.
- Type the function name OR followed by an open parenthesis.
- Type B3>2 to define the first logical test of the **OR** function. This test will evaluate if the value in the Years Purchasing column is greater than 2. Type a comma after defining this argument.
- Type C3>1000 to define the second logical test of the **OR** function. This test will evaluate if the value in the LY Spend column is greater than 1000.
- Type a closing parenthesis to complete the **OR** function.
- Type =TRUE followed by a comma to complete the **logical_test** argument of the **IF** function. The logical test of the IF function is now evaluating if the output of the **OR** function is TRUE. Notice that quotation marks are *not* placed on the word TRUE.
- Type "Thanks for being loyal 25% Off" to define the [**value_if_true**] argument of the **IF** function. If the logical test of the **IF** function is true, then the output of the **OR** function is true. This indicates a person has been purchasing products from the company for more than two years *or* has spent more than $1,000 in the past year. Type a comma after defining this argument.
- Type "Customer Appreciation 10% Off" to define the [**value_if_false**] argument. Any customer who does not satisfy either criteria specified in the **OR** function will be sent a 10% off coupon.

- Type a closing parenthesis and press the **Enter** key to complete the function.
- Copy the completed function in cell E3 and paste it to cells E4 through E17.
- Sort the worksheet based on the Customer Reward column in descending order.

Figure 4.19 | **Combining the IF and OR Functions**

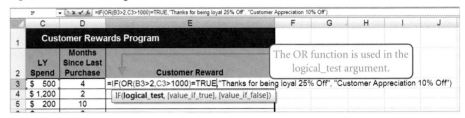

Figure 4.20 shows the results of combining the **IF** and **OR** functions. Similar to the results shown in Figure 4.18, the marketing manager can easily see which discount coupon goes to each customer because the worksheet was sorted based on the output in the Customer Reward column.

Figure 4.20 | **Results of Combining the IF and OR Functions**

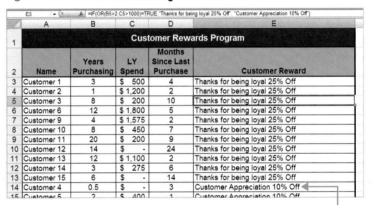

Both logical tests in the OR function were false for this customer.

COMMON MISTAKES | Combining the AND, OR, and IF Functions

You cannot use the word **AND** or the word **OR** to combine multiple logical tests in an **IF** function. For example, the following **IF** function will produce an error:

```
=IF(B3 > 2 AND C3 > 500 AND D3 > 12,"Free Gift","Discount
Coupon")
```

Based on the preceding example, if you wanted to show the words *Free Gift* in a cell if the value in cell B3 is greater than 2 *and* the value in C3 is greater than 500 *and* the value in D3 is greater than 12, then you need to use the **AND** function. The corrected **IF** function is as follows.

```
=IF(AND(B3 > 2,C3 > 500,D3 > 12) = TRUE, "Free Gift",
"Discount Coupon")
```

Notice that the **AND** *function* is used in the **logical_test** argument of the **IF** function. If the **AND** function produces a TRUE output, the words *Free Gift* will appear in the cell. If the **AND** function produces a FALSE output, the function will show the words *Discount Coupon* in the cell.

≫ AND and OR Functions

The purpose of this workshop is to demonstrate the use of the **AND** and **OR** functions. We will be using these functions to construct a merchandise allocation plan. I will be demonstrating the tasks in this workshop in the following three videos: **AND Function**; **OR Function**; and **Combining AND, OR, and IF Functions**. After completing each section of tasks, watch the related video shown in parentheses. Open the file named ib_e04_merchandiseallocations. Remember to try these tasks on your own first before watching the video.

1. The AND Function (Video: AND Function)

a. Activate cell G3 in Sheet1.

b. Type an equal sign, the function name **AND**, and an open parenthesis.

c. Type **B3 = "Yes"** to define the first logical test and then type a comma.

d. Type **F3 = "Yes"** to define a second logical test.

e. Type a closing parenthesis and then press the **Enter** key.

f. Copy cell G3 and paste it into cells G4:G13.

2. The OR Function (Video: OR Function)

a. Activate cell H3.

b. Type an equal sign, the function name **OR**, and an open parenthesis.

c. Type **C3 = "Yes"** to define the first logical test and then type a comma.

d. Type **D3 = "Yes"** to define a second logical test and then type a comma.

e. Type **E3 >= 5000000** to define a third logical test.

f. Type a closing parenthesis and press the **Enter** key.

g. Copy cell H3 and paste it into cells H4:H13.

3. OR, AND, and Nested IF Function (Video: Combining AND, OR, and IF Functions)

a. Activate cell I3.

b. Type an equal sign, the function name **IF**, and an open parenthesis.

c. Define the **logical_test** argument by typing the function name **AND** followed by an open parenthesis.

d. Type the following logical tests for the **AND** function:

```
B3 = "Yes"
F3 = "Yes"
```

e. Type a closing parenthesis to complete the **AND** function.

f. Type an equal sign followed by the word **FALSE** and then type a comma to complete the **logical_test** argument of the **IF** function.

g. Define the **[value_if_true]** argument by typing a **0** followed by a comma.

h. Define the **[value_if_false]** argument by starting a new **IF** function. Type the function name **IF** followed by an open parenthesis.

i. Define the **logical_test** argument of the second **IF** function by typing the function name **OR** followed by an open parenthesis.

j. Enter the following logical tests for the **OR** function:

```
C3 = "Yes"
D3 = "Yes"
E3 >= 5000000
```

k. Type a closing parenthesis to complete the **OR** function.

l. Type an equal sign followed by the word **TRUE** and then type a comma to complete the **logical_test** argument of the second **IF** function.

m. Define the **[value_if_true]** argument of the second **IF** function by typing the number **1** followed by a comma.

n. Define the **[value_if_false]** argument of the second **IF** function by typing **0**. Then complete the function by typing two closing parentheses and press the **Enter** key.

o. Copy cell I3 and paste it into cell I4:I13.

p. Save and close your file.

≫Managing Product Shipments

When it comes to managing the process of shipping merchandise from a distribution center to a retail store, transportation managers often find themselves stuck between a rock and a hard place. On one hand they are under a lot of pressure to keep shipping costs as low as possible. To do this, transportation managers will try to maximize either the cubic capacity or weight capacity of every truck that leaves the distribution center. On the other hand, they need to ship products as frequently as possible so all stores have every item in stock all the time. As a result, if they wait too long to maximize the capacity of a truck, a store may run out of certain products, which could decrease sales.

Exercise

The goal of this exercise is to evaluate the shipping status for a fleet of trucks servicing a chain of retail stores. You will use the **AND**, **OR**, and **IF** functions to determine which trucks should ship and which trucks should be held at the distribution center. You will need to open the file named ib_e04_transportationstatus before completing the following tasks:

1. A truck must have fuel and not require any maintenance before it can be released to ship products. Use the **AND** function in cell J3 to determine if the first truck can be cleared for shipping. The function should show the word TRUE if cell H3 in the Fuel column is Yes and cell I3 in the Maintenance Required column is No.

2. Copy the **AND** function in cell J3 and paste it into cells J4:J20.

3. Use the **OR** function in cell K3 to determine if the first truck achieved the company capacity goal. The capacity goal is achieved when either the Current Cube (cell F3) or the Current Weight (cell G3) is greater than or equal to 90% of capacity. The logical tests to evaluate the current weight and cubic capacity are as follows:

   a. Current Cubic Capacity: `F3 >= D3 * .90`

   b. Current Weight Capacity: `G3 >= E3 * .90`

4. Copy the **OR** function in cell K3 and paste it to cells K4:K20.

5. Enter a nested **IF** function in cell L3 to determine if a truck should be held or shipped. The following logical tests should be used in this function in the order listed.

   a. If the output of the **AND** function in cell J3 is FALSE, then the output of this **IF** function should be the word *HOLD*. If the truck does not have fuel or requires maintenance, the transportation manager cannot allow it to leave the distribution center.

   b. If the output of the **OR** function in cell K3 is TRUE, then the output of this function should be SHIP.

   c. If the output of the **OR** function in cell K3 is FALSE and the value in cell C3 (Days Since Last Delivery) is greater than or equal to 3, the function should display the word *SHIP*. As mentioned, in order for the transportation manager to control shipping costs, the capacity of each truck must be maximized before shipping. However, a store needs to receive frequent deliveries to prevent merchandise from going out of stock. Therefore, even if a truck has not reached its capacity goal, it must be shipped.

   d. If all logical tests in this function fail, you can assume that a truck has not reached its capacity goal and it has been less than three days since the store received a delivery. Therefore, the output should be HOLD.

6. Copy the function in cell L3 and paste it to cells L4:L20.

7. Sort the spreadsheet based on the Ship or Hold column (column L) in ascending order and then based on the Fuel & Maintenance Ready column (column J) in ascending order.

8. How many trucks are being held?

9. How many trucks are being held only because of fuel and maintenance issues?

10. How many trucks had to be shipped without reaching their capacity goals?

11. Save and close your file.

>> What's Wrong with This Spreadsheet?

Problem

Your friend is working on a project for her finance class. She is having trouble putting together a spreadsheet in Excel and asks for your help. She attaches an Excel workbook to an e-mail and includes the following message:

Hi, I pulled together some data for a project I have to do for my finance class. I am trying to complete the Status column and the Investment Opportunity column. I thought these would be easy calculations; however, as you can see, something is going radically wrong here! Please help.

1. *For the Status column I'm trying to show the words Market Leader if the market share is greater than 20% or the sales growth is greater than 10%. I figured the **OR** function would be perfect for this, but as you can see, I keep getting errors.*

2. *For the Investment Opportunity column, I am just trying to identify public companies that have a 5-year sales growth rate greater than 10%. I am trying to use the **AND** function for this one, but as you can see, this is not working either.*

Exercise

The workbook your friend e-mailed to you is named ib_e04_companyanalysis. Take a look at the functions in the Status column and the Investment Opportunity column. What's wrong with this spreadsheet? Consider the following points:

1. Based on the criteria explained in your friend's e-mail, is she using the right functions to accomplish her goals?

2. Are the arguments for each function properly defined?

Write a short answer for each of the preceding points and fix the spreadsheet based on the facts stated from the message in the Problem section.

Skill Set　　**>> Lookup Functions**

The previous sections in this chapter addressed how logical functions are used to evaluate the data in a worksheet. This section will review functions that can be used for assembling data in a worksheet. The data required for business projects rarely comes in one neat convenient spreadsheet. In many instances, you will have to pull data from several sources or pick specific points from larger datasets. The anecdote at the beginning of this chapter is an excellent example of having to pull pieces of information from one data source and insert them into a worksheet. Theses tasks can be accomplished through *Lookup functions.* Lookup functions are valuable assets when you are assembling data from several sources. The two lookup functions covered in this section are **VLookup** and **HLookup**.

VLookup Function

VLookup is a lookup function used mostly to display data from one worksheet or workbook into another. For example, you may have a worksheet filled with ZIP codes and need to insert the city and state, similar to the anecdote at the beginning of the chapter. Or, you may have a list of product codes and need to insert the product description. You can use the **VLookup** function to look for specific data values in a second worksheet or workbook and display the needed values in your primary worksheet.

The data in Figure 4.21 shows product sales and inventory data for a hypothetical retail store. The Sales Data worksheet contains several product numbers along with sales and inventory data. Notice that the Product Description column is blank. Therefore, we do not know which products are associated with each product number. However, the Product Data worksheet contains a list of the same product codes found on the Sales Data worksheet along with a variety of descriptive information.

Figure 4.21 | **Sales and Inventory Data by Product**

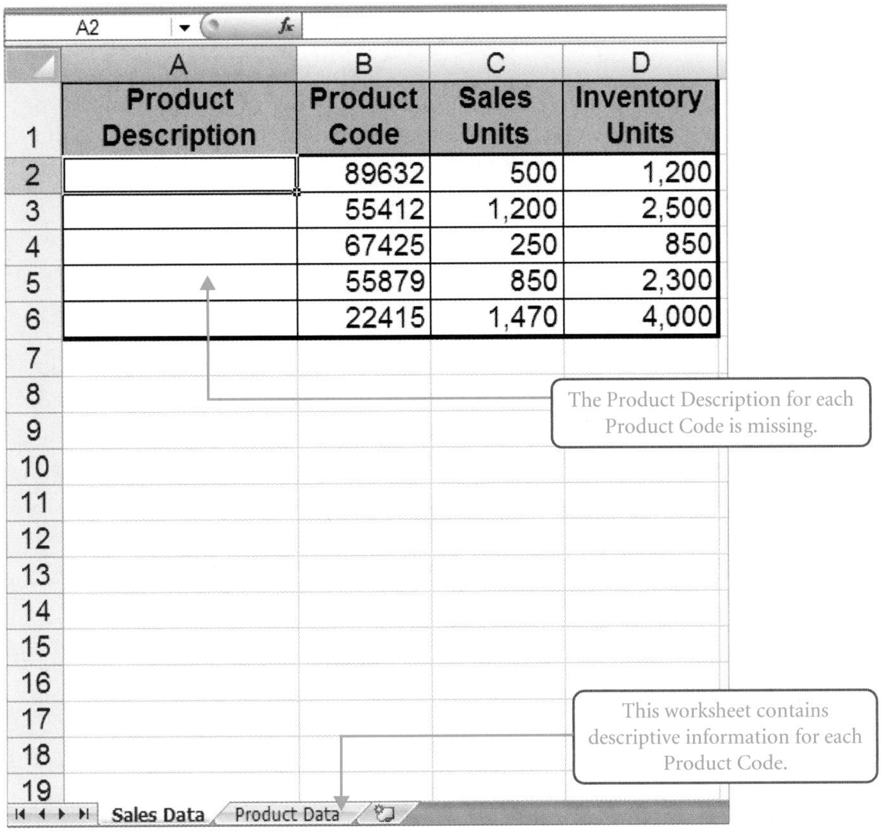

	A	B	C	D
1	Product Description	Product Code	Sales Units	Inventory Units
2		89632	500	1,200
3		55412	1,200	2,500
4		67425	250	850
5		55879	850	2,300
6		22415	1,470	4,000

Figure 4.22 shows the data contained in both worksheets from Figure 4.21 side by side. The goal of this example is to show how you can use the **VLookup** function to match the product codes in the Sales Data worksheet with the product codes in the Product Data worksheet. When a match is found, the function will show the Product Description from column C of the Product Data worksheet in column A of the Sales Data worksheet. There are two main reasons why you would want to accomplish this task using the **VLookup** function instead of typing these descriptions manually into the worksheet. The first is accuracy. As mentioned in Chapter 2, data entry errors are very common when information is manually typed into a worksheet. Using the **VLookup** function to bring data from one worksheet into another prevents data entry errors. The second reason is time. The data in Figure 4.22 represents a simplified example so it is easier for you to learn this function. However, imagine if you were faced with the situation that was described in the anecdote. It would probably take you a few hours to accurately type the state and city names for 400 ZIP codes into a worksheet. With the **VLookup** function, this task would take just a few minutes.

Figure 4.22 | **Sales Data and Product Data Worksheets Side by Side**

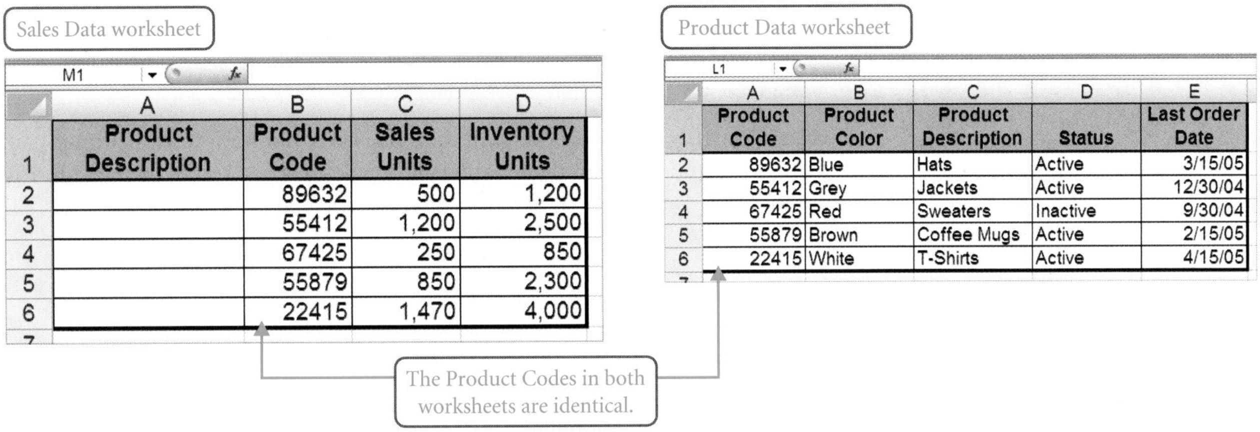

	A	B	C	D
1	Product Description	Product Code	Sales Units	Inventory Units
2		89632	500	1,200
3		55412	1,200	2,500
4		67425	250	850
5		55879	850	2,300
6		22415	1,470	4,000

	A	B	C	D	E
1	Product Code	Product Color	Product Description	Status	Last Order Date
2	89632	Blue	Hats	Active	3/15/05
3	55412	Grey	Jackets	Active	12/30/04
4	67425	Red	Sweaters	Inactive	9/30/04
5	55879	Brown	Coffee Mugs	Active	2/15/05
6	22415	White	T-Shirts	Active	4/15/05

As shown in Figure 4.23, the **VLookup** function contains four arguments that must be defined in order to display data from one worksheet or workbook into another. Each of these arguments is defined as follows:

- **lookup_value:** The common data point that exists in two different worksheets or in two parts of the same worksheet. Based on the data shown in Figure 4.22, the lookup value would be defined using cell locations in the Product Code column because these values exists in both the Sales Data and Product Data worksheets.

- **table_array:** The range of cells where both the lookup value and the data that will be used for the output of the function exist. *The first column of this range must contain the lookup value.* The function will look vertically (hence the name **Vlookup**) down the first column of this range to find the lookup value. Based on the data in Figure 4.22, the table array would be the range A2:E6 in the Product Data worksheet. This range starts with cell A2 because column A contains the product codes that would be used to define the **lookup_value** argument.

- **col_index_num:** The column number, counting from left to right beginning with the first column in the table array range, which contains the data you wish to display as the output of the function. As mentioned, the function will look vertically down the first column of the table array range to find the lookup value. When the lookup value is found, the function will use the column index number to count the number of columns from left to right to find the data you wish to display. When determining the column index number, you must consider the first column in the table array range as 1. Based on the data shown in Figure 4.22, the column index number would be 3, because the Product Description column in the Product Data worksheet is the third column in the range A2:E6.

- **[range_lookup]:** This argument guides the function to look for values that are either a close match or an approximate match to the lookup value. In most situations you will want the function to look for an exact match to the lookup value. However, you might want to look for close matches in situations such as survey scores. For example, a survey score of 90 to 100 might be given a description of "Excellent." The actual value on your primary worksheet might be the number 97. However, the worksheet containing the description of each score might have only the number 90. In this situation, setting the **range_lookup** argument to find an approximate match would be necessary. This argument is defined with one of two possible options:

  - **True:** Type the word True (no quotation marks) if you want the function to look for approximate matches to the lookup value. You must consider the following if you are using this option:

    - The range of cells used to define the **table_array** range *must be sorted in ascending order*; otherwise, the function may produce erroneous results.

    - The function will look for the next highest value that is *less than* the lookup value. For example, if the table array range contains the number 90, and the lookup value is 97, the function will match to the number 90. If the number 90 was the lowest value in the table array range, and the lookup value was 89, the function will produce an error. There reason is that there is no number in the table array range that is less than 89.

  - **False:** Type the word False (no quotation marks) if you want the function to look for exact matches to the lookup value. *It is important to note that if you do not define the [range_lookup] argument, the function will assume the True option.*

Figure 4.23 | **Arguments of the VLookup Function**

	A	B	C	D	E	F
	VLOOKUP ▾ ✕ ✔ fx =VLOOKUP(					
1	Product Description	Product Code	Sales Units	Inventory Units		
2	=VLOOKUP(	89632	500	1,200		
3	VLOOKUP(**lookup_value**, table_array, col_index_num, [range_lookup])					
4		67425	250	850		

As mentioned, the **VLookup** function will be used to complete the Product Description column in the Sales Data worksheet shown in Figure 4.22. The following explains how you accomplish this:

- Activate cell A2 in the Sales Data worksheet shown in Figure 4.22.
- Type an equal sign, the function name VLOOKUP, and an open parenthesis.
- Type cell B2 to define the **lookup_value** argument. Cell B2 contains the product code for the first item in the Sales Data worksheet.
- Type a comma.
- Click the Product Data worksheet tab (see Figure 4.24).

Figure 4.24 | **Click the Product Data Worksheet Tab to Define the Table Array Range**

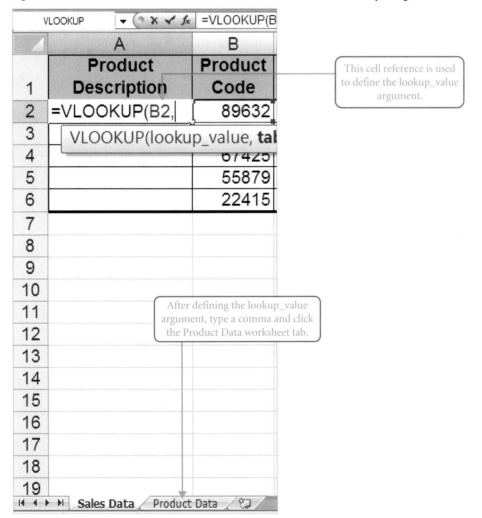

This cell reference is used to define the lookup_value argument.

After defining the lookup_value argument, type a comma and click the Product Data worksheet tab.

- Highlight the range A2:E6 in the Product Data worksheet to define the **table_array** argument. You may notice in the formula bar that this range is preceded by the worksheet name enclosed in apostrophes followed by an exclamation point. The reason is that the function is being created in the Sales Data worksheet but is referencing a range in the Product Data worksheet. This is known as a *link* and will be covered in Chapter 6 (see Figure 4.25).
- Type a comma after defining the **table_array** argument.

Figure 4.25 | **Defining the Table Array Range in the Product Data Worksheet**

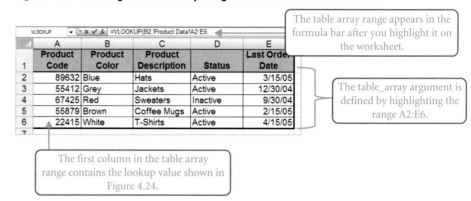

- Type the number 3 to define the **col_index_num** argument. The Product Description is the third column in the table array range. It is important to note that since the Product Data worksheet was activated to define the **table_array** argument, you will remain in this worksheet until you press the **Enter** key. Therefore, you will have to look in the formula bar to see the arguments of the function being defined (see Figure 4.26).
- Type a comma after defining the **col_index_num** argument.

Figure 4.26 | **Defining the Column Index Number**

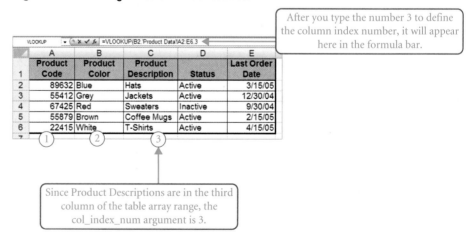

- Type the word False (no quotation marks) to define the [**range_lookup**] argument. You enter False into this argument so the function will look for an exact match for the lookup value. Remember to look in the formula bar to see this argument being defined as you type.
- Complete the function by typing a closing parenthesis and press the **Enter** key. After you press the **Enter** key, you will return to the Sales Data worksheet.
- Double click cell A2 in the Sales Data worksheet and add an absolute reference to both cell locations in the range used to define the **table_array** argument. You do

this so the range does not change from relative referencing when the function is pasted to the rest of the cell locations in column A. Remember that you add an absolute reference by typing a dollar sign in front of the column letter and row number of the cell reference.

- Copy the completed **VLookup** function in cell A2 and paste it into cells A3 through A6.

Figure 4.27 shows the final setup and results of the **VLookup** function. The function displays the word *Hats* in cell A2 of the Product Description column. The reason is that it found Product Code 89632 in the first column of the table array range, which is A2:E6 in the Product Data worksheet, and pulled the word *Hats* in the third column of this range (see Figure 4.26). In addition, notice that an absolute reference is placed on the range used to define the **table_array** argument.

Figure 4.27 | **Final Setup and Results of the VLookup Function**

A2 =VLOOKUP(B2,'Product Data'!$A$2:$E$6,3,FALSE)

	A	B	C	D	E
1	Product Description	Product Code	Sales Units	Inventory Units	
2	Hats	89632	500	1,200	
3	Jackets	55412	1,200	2,500	
4	Sweaters	67425	250	850	
5	Coffee Mugs	55879	850	2,300	
6	T-Shirts	22415	1,470	4,000	
7					

An absolute reference is placed on this range defining the table_array argument.

The VLookup function displays the product descriptions relating to all the product codes in column B.

COMMON MISTAKES | VLookup

The following mistakes are often made when using the **VLookup** function:

1. After defining the range for the **table_array** argument, immediately type a comma. People often click the original worksheet tab before typing a comma after defining the range for the **table_array** argument. This will distort the **table_array** argument and prevent the function from working.
2. Before pasting the **VLookup** function to other cells, do not forget to add an absolute reference on the table array range. The **#N/A** error codes in the worksheet shown in Figure 4.28 happened because the table array range was added without an absolute reference.

Figure 4.28 | **#N/A Errors After Pasting the VLookup Function**

K15

	A	B	C	D
1	Product Description	Product Code	Sales Units	Inventory Units
2	Hats	89632	500	1,200
3	Jackets	55412	1,200	2,500
4	#N/A	67425	250	850
5	#N/A	55879	850	2,300
6	T-Shirts	22415	1,470	4,000

3. When defining the column index number **(col_index_num)**, count the first column in table array range as 1. You will get an output that is one column to the left of what is intended if you forget to count the first column.

Quick Reference

VLookup

1. Activate the cell where the output should appear.
2. Type an equal sign, the function name VLookup, and an open parenthesis.
3. Define the following arguments:
   a) **lookup_value**: Cell location that contains the value to be searched and matched in a second worksheet.
   b) **table_array**: Range in a second worksheet or workbook that contains both the lookup value and data for the output of the function (first column in the range *must* contain the lookup value).
   c) **col_index_num**: Number of columns in the table array range counting from left to right that contains data for the output of the function (count the first column as 1).
   d) **range_lookup**: Type the word False to find an exact match to the lookup value. This argument will assume True and look for an approximate match for the lookup value if this argument is not defined.
4. Type a closing parenthesis and press the **Enter** key.
5. Use an absolute reference ($) on the range used to define the **table_array** argument if pasting the function to other cells.

HLookup Function

The previous section demonstrated how you use the **VLookup** function to search for a lookup value vertically down the first column of a range of cells. However, your data might be organized such that you have to look across a row instead of down a column to search for a lookup value. In these situations you will need to use an *HLookup* function. The **HLookup** function is identical to the **VLookup** function; however, it looks horizontally across the first row of a range of cells to find a lookup value instead of vertically down a column. For example, Figure 4.29 contains a workbook that a strategic planning manager might use to compare financial statistics between his company and other competitors in the industry. There are two worksheets in this workbook: Comparison and Competitor Data. The Competitor Data worksheet contains the financial statistics that need to be displayed in column C of the Comparison worksheet. However, the competitor names, as shown in cell C2 in the Comparison worksheet, are listed across row 2 in the Competitor Data worksheet. Therefore, the **HLookup** function would be needed to display the competitor data in Column C of the Comparison worksheet.

Figure 4.29 | **Data for Competitor Analysis**

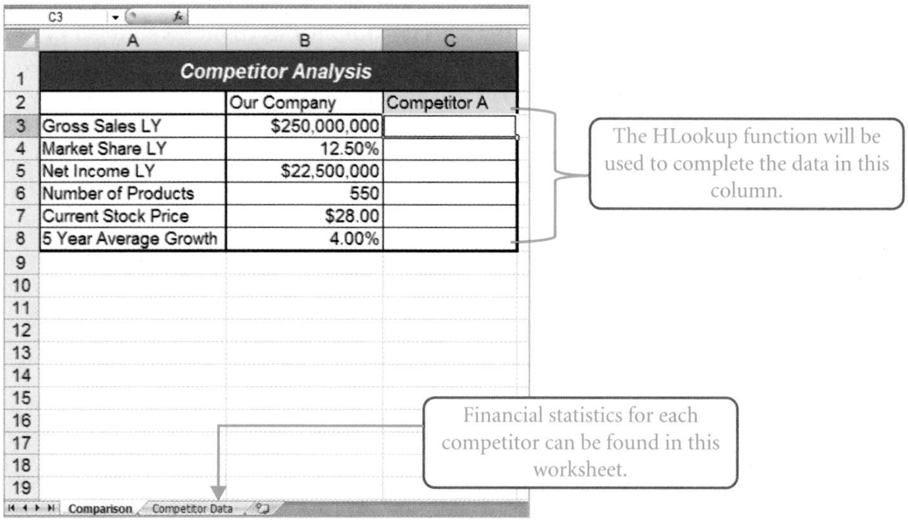

Figure 4.30 shows the two worksheets from Figure 4.29 side by side. Notice that the competitor names are listed across row 2, and the financial statistics relating to each competitor are listed in the column below each competitor's name. The **HLookup** function will be used to look for the competitor name typed into cell C2 of the Comparison worksheet in row 2 of the Competitor Data worksheet. When a match is found, the function will show the relevant financial statistic in the Comparison worksheet.

Figure 4.30 | **Comparison and Competitor Data Worksheets**

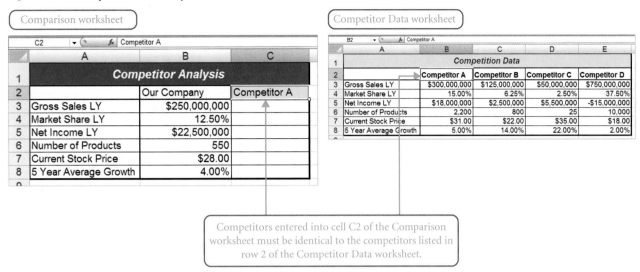

The arguments of the **HLookup** function are identical to the **VLookup** function with the exception of the **col_index_num** argument. Since the **HLookup** function looks horizontally across a row, it uses a row index number to count the number of rows from top to bottom in the range used to define the **table_array** argument. Similar to the column index number, the first row in the table array range must be counted as 1.

As mentioned, the **HLookup** function will be used to show the competitor information in column C of Figure 4.30. Here is how you accomplish this:

- Activate cell C3 in the Comparison worksheet. The **HLookup** function will be used to show the Gross Sales LY for the competitor typed into cell C2.

- Type an equal sign, the function name HLOOKUP, and an open parenthesis.

- Type cell C2 to define the **lookup_value** argument. The function will look for the competitor name that is typed into cell C2 of the Comparison worksheet.

- Type a comma.

- Click the Competitor Data worksheet tab.

- Highlight the range B2:B8 on the Competitor Data worksheet to define the **table_array** argument. When you are defining the **table_array** argument for the **HLookup** function, the first *row* in this range must contain the values used to define the **lookup_value** argument. This is similar to the **VLookup** function where the first *column* of the table array must contain the lookup values. The **HLookup** function will search horizontally (hence the name **HLookup**) across the first row in the range used to define the **table_array** range to find the lookup value.

- Type a comma.

- Type the number 2 to define the **row_index_num** argument. As previously mentioned, the purpose of this **HLookup** function is to show the Gross Sales LY for the competitor name typed into cell C2 of the Comparison worksheet. In the Competitor Data worksheet, the Gross Sales LY is in the second row of the range that was used to define the **table_array** argument (B2:E8). Remember to count the first row in the table array range as 1.

- Type a comma.

- Type the word False (no quotation marks) to define the [**range_lookup**] argument. For this example, you must search for an exact match to the lookup value. The rules applying to the **range_lookup** argument for the **HLookup** function are identical to the **VLookup** function. However, if you are using the **True** option for this function, the range used to define the **table_array** argument must be sorted in ascending order from left to right based on the values in the first row of the range.

- Type a closing parenthesis and press the **Enter** key to complete the function. This will bring you back to the Comparison worksheet.
- Double click cell C3 in the Comparison worksheet, which contains the complete **HLookup** function. Place an absolute reference on the cell reference used to define the **lookup_value** argument and the range used to define the **table_array** argument. The competitor name will always be entered into cell C2; therefore, this reference cannot change when the function is pasted to a new location. In addition, the range used to define the **table_array** argument must not change when the function is pasted to a new location. Therefore, you place an absolute reference on the range defining this argument. Press the **Enter** key after completing these adjustments.

Figure 4.31 shows the setup of the completed **HLookup** function in the Comparison worksheet. Notice that absolute references are used in the **lookup_value** and **table_array** arguments.

Figure 4.31 | **Setup for the HLookup Function in the Comparison Worksheet**

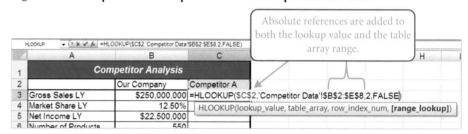

Figure 4.32 shows the output of the **HLookup** function. The function found Competitor A in the first row of the table array range in the Competitor Data worksheet, moved down two rows (counting the first row as 1), and displayed the value in this cell location. Following this path, you will find that two rows down from Competitor A (cell B2) in the Competitor Data worksheet is the number $300,000,000. Therefore, this number becomes the output of the function in cell C3 of the Comparison worksheet.

Figure 4.32 | **Results of the HLookup Function in the Comparison Worksheet**

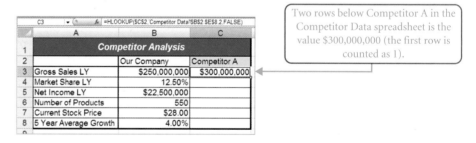

To complete the rest of the cell locations in column C of the Comparison spreadsheet, you cannot copy and paste the **HLookup** function without making additional adjustments. The reason is that each statistic in column C will require a different row index number. For example, cell location C5 in the Comparison worksheet is the Net Income LY statistic. This is four rows down from the first row in the table array range in the Competitor Data worksheet. The following points explain how to paste and adjust the **HLookup** function to complete cells C4 through C8 in Figure 4.32.

- Copy cell C3 in the Comparison worksheet, which contains the completed **HLookup** function.

- Highlight the range C4:C8 and select the **Formulas paste** option from the **Paste** icon.
- Double click cell C4, change the **row_index_num** to 3, and press the **Enter** key.
- Double click cell C5, change the **row_index_num** to 4, and press the **Enter** key.
- Double click cell C6, change the **row_index_num** to 5, and press the **Enter** key.
- Double click cell C7, change the **row_index_num** to 6, and press the **Enter** key.
- Double click cell C8, change the **row_index_num** to 7, and press the **Enter** key.

When the spreadsheet is complete, you can change the competitor name in cell C2 of the Comparison worksheet, and the data for column C will automatically change to reflect the financial statistics of the new competitor. Figure 4.33 shows a completed spreadsheet with the competitor changed to Competitor D.

Figure 4.33 | **Final Outputs of the HLookup Function**

	A	B	C
C5	*fx* =HLOOKUP($C$2,'Competitor Data'!$B$2:$E$8,4,FALSE)		
1	Competitor Analysis		
2		Our Company	Competitor D
3	Gross Sales LY	$250,000,000	$750,000,000
4	Market Share LY	12.50%	37.50%
5	Net Income LY	$22,500,000	-$15,000,000
6	Number of Products	550	10,000
7	Current Stock Price	$28.00	$18.00
8	5 Year Average Growth	4.00%	2.00%

The row index number for each of these cells was adjusted to pull the proper financial statistic from the Competitor Data spreadsheet.

COMMON MISTAKES | Error Codes for HLookup and VLookup

The following two error codes are common when using either the **VLookup** or **HLookup** functions.

#N/A: The Not Available error signifies that the function cannot find the lookup value in the table array range. Typical reasons this error occurs include

1. The first column of the table array range does not contain the lookup value. Check the range in the **table_array** argument and make sure the first column of the range contains the lookup value.

2. The lookup value does not exist at all in the second spreadsheet. Check the spreadsheet you are using for the table array range and make sure the lookup value is there.

3. The table array range or the lookup value was changed when the function was pasted to a new cell location. If you are copying and pasting the function, check both the **lookup_value** and **table_array** arguments. In most cases, you will need to use an absolute reference for these arguments to prevent cell references from changing when the function is pasted to a new location.

#REF!: The Reference error occurs because either the column index number or row index number is too high given the range that was used to define the **table_array** argument. For example, if the table array range contains four rows for an **HLookup** function and the row index number is 8, the Reference error will appear.

>> The VLookup Function

The purpose of this workshop is to demonstrate the use of the **VLookup** function. We will be reviewing the same example that was presented earlier in this section. I will be demonstrating the tasks in this workshop in the video named **VLookup Function**. Watch this video after completing the tasks in this workshop. Open the file named ib_e04_vlookuppractice before starting the following tasks:

1. **Defining the VLookup Arguments (Video: VLookup Function)**
   a. Activate cell A2 on the Sales Data worksheet.
   b. Type an equal sign, the function name **VLOOKUP**, and an open parenthesis.
   c. Type **B2** or click on cell location B2 to define the **lookup_value** argument.
   d. Type a comma.
   e. Click the **Product Data** worksheet tab.
   f. Highlight the range A2:E6 to define the **table_array** argument.
   g. Type a comma.
   h. Counting column A as number 1, count the number of columns to go from column A to column C. Column C should be the third column, which is the Product Description column.
   i. Type the number **3** to define the **col_index_num** argument.
   j. Type a comma.
   k. Type the word **False** with no quotation marks.
   l. Type a closing parenthesis and press the **Enter** key.

2. **Absolute Reference (Video: VLookup Function)**
   a. Double click cell A2 on the Sales Data worksheet.
   b. Add an absolute reference to the range A2:E6 in the **table_array** argument.
   c. Press the **Enter** key.

3. **Copy and Paste Formulas (Video: VLookup Function)**
   a. Copy cell A2 on the Sales Data worksheet.
   b. Highlight the range A3:A6.
   c. Click the **Home** tab of the Ribbon.
   d. Click the down arrow on the **Paste** icon.
   e. Select the **Formulas** option.
   f. Save and close your file.

>> The HLookup Function

The purpose of this workshop is to demonstrate the use of the **HLookup** function. We will be reviewing the same example that was presented earlier in this section. I will be demonstrating the tasks in this workshop in the video named **HLookup Function**. Watch this video after completing the tasks in this workshop. Open the file named ib_e04_hlookuppractice before starting the following tasks:

VIDEO WORKSHOP

1. **Defining the HLookup Arguments (Video: HLookup Function)**

   a. Activate cell C3 on the Comparison worksheet.

   b. Type an equal sign, the function name **HLOOKUP**, and an open parenthesis.

   c. Type **C2** or click cell location C2 to define the **lookup_value** argument.

   d. Type a comma.

   e. Click the **Competitor Data** worksheet tab.

   f. Highlight the range B2:E8 to define the **table_array** argument.

   g. Type a comma.

   h. Counting row 2 as number 1, count the number of rows to go from row 2 to row 3. This should be the second row, which is Gross Sales LY.

   i. Type the number **2** to define the **row_index_num** argument.

   j. Type a comma.

   k. Type the word **False** with no quotation marks.

   l. Type a closing parenthesis and press the **Enter** key.

2. **Absolute Reference (Video: HLookup Function)**

   a. Double click cell C3 on the Comparison worksheet.

   b. Add an absolute reference to cell location C2 in the **lookup_value** argument. Then add an absolute reference to the range B2:E8 in the **table_array** argument.

   c. Press the **Enter** key.

3. **Copy and Paste Formulas (Video: HLookup Function)**

   a. Copy cell C3 on the Comparison worksheet.

   b. Highlight the range C4:C8.

   c. Click the **Home** tab of the Ribbon.

   d. Click the down arrow on the **Paste** icon.

   e. Select the **Formulas** option.

4. **Editing the Row Index Numbers (Video: HLookup Function)**

   a. Double click cell C4 on the Comparison worksheet.

   b. Change the row index number from 2 to **3** and press the **Enter** key.

   c. Repeat step **b** for each cell in the range C5:C8 increasing the row index number from 2 to **4**, then 2 to **5**, then 2 to **6**, and 2 to **7** for the last cell.

5. Evaluate the Competition (Video: HLookup Function)

    a. Change the competitor in cell C2 on the Comparison worksheet to read **Competitor D**.

    b. Change the competitor again to **Competitor B**.

    c. Save and close your file.

>> Personal Investment Strategies

A professional financial planner will develop investment strategies for people based on their risk preference. That is, some people prefer to make low risk investments, whereas others will take on higher risk strategies with the hopes of higher returns. The lookup functions covered in this chapter can provide significant value to a financial planner who is managing investments for several clients.

Exercise

The purpose of this exercise is to develop a spreadsheet for a financial planner who is deciding how to invest money for several clients. Open the file named ib_e04_investmentstrategies before starting this exercise.

1. Use a **VLookup** function in cell C3 of the Investment Plan worksheet to find the Risk Preference of the customer showing in cell C2. You can find the data in the Customers worksheet. Define the arguments of the function as follows:

    a. lookup_value: Cell location C2. The function will look for the customer name that is typed into this cell in the Customers worksheet.

    b. table_array: The range A2:C11 in the Customers worksheet. Once the **lookup_value** argument is defined, you can click the Customers worksheet tab and highlight this range.

    c. col_index_num: The number 3. The reason is that the Risk Preference column is the third column in the range defined for the **table_array** argument.

    d. range_lookup: The word **False**.

2. Use a **VLookup** function in cell C4 of the Investment Plan worksheet to find the number of dollars being invested for the customer name showing in cell C2. Each argument will be defined identically to the **VLookup** function that was created in number 1. However, the **col_index_num** argument should be 2 instead of 3.

3. Use the **HLookup** function in cell C7 of the Investment Plan worksheet to calculate the customer's proposed investment for Bonds. Use the function to find the investment percentage for Bonds in the Risk Levels worksheet based on the customer's risk preference showing in cell C3 on the Investment Plan worksheet. The arguments of this function should be defined as follows:

    a. lookup_value: Cell location C3. The function will look for the risk preference that appears in cell C3 of the Investment Plan worksheet in the Risk Levels worksheet.

    b. table_array: The range B2:D5 in the Risk Levels worksheet. Once the **lookup_value** argument is defined, you can click the Risk Levels worksheet and then highlight this range.

c. **row_index_num**: The number 2. The reason is that the percentage for the Bonds category is in the second row of the range defined for the **table_array** argument.

d. **range_lookup**: The word **False**.

4. Edit the **HLookup** function you created in step 3 by typing an asterisk after the function and cell location C4. This will multiply the Dollars Investing in cell C4 of the Investment Plan worksheet by the percentage for Bonds in the Risk Levels worksheet.

5. Use the **HLookup** function in cell D8 of the Investment Plan worksheet to calculate the customer's investment plan for Mutual Funds. This function will be identical to the function created in steps 3 and 4. However, the row index number should be 3 instead of 2.

6. Use the **HLookup** function in cell D9 of the Investment Plan worksheet to calculate the customer's investment plan for Stocks. This function will be identical to the function created in steps 3 and 4. However, the row index number should be 4 instead of 2.

7. Change the customer name in cell C2 of the Investment Plan worksheet to Customer 2. Is this customer investing more money or less money compared to Customer 1?

8. How much money is Customer 8 planning to invest in Stocks?

9. On the Risk Levels worksheet, change the Moderate investment strategy to 30% Bonds, 30% Mutual Funds, and 40% Stocks.

10. How did the change you made to the Risk Levels worksheet in number 9 change the investment strategy for Customer 8?

11. Save and close your file.

>> What's Wrong with This Spreadsheet?

Problem

In one of your business classes, you are working on a project that involves researching historical data for Company D. You must compare the current stock price of Company D with other firms in the industry. One of your teammates volunteers to compile everyone's research and create a spreadsheet. He explains that by simply typing the year into a cell, you will be able to use the spreadsheet to pull the historical data for Company D. In addition, he explains that by typing a ticker symbol into another cell, you can compare Company D's current stock price with other firms in the industry. Impressed with his plan, the team agrees to let him build the spreadsheet to complete the analysis required for the project.

Exercise

The spreadsheet your teammate created is named ib_e04_groupproject. Look at the data in this spreadsheet. Would you be comfortable submitting this file to your professor for your team grade? Consider the following points.

1. Look at the data on the Company D Analysis worksheet. Does the data appear to make sense?

Lookup Functions | **Excel** 523

2. Test-drive the spreadsheet. Your teammate explained that the Year in cell C3 and the Stock Symbol in cell C9 can be changed. In addition, you will see the values that are available to enter on the right of these cell locations. When you change the Year and Stock Symbol, does the data still make sense?

3. What method is your teammate using to show the data in cells C4:C6 and C10:C11? Do these methods appear to be entered correctly?

4. How many worksheets does this workbook contain? What will you need to do to check the accuracy of the data appearing in the Company D Analysis worksheet?

What's wrong with this spreadsheet? Write a short answer to each of the questions listed here. Then fix any errors you discover in the Company D Analysis worksheet.

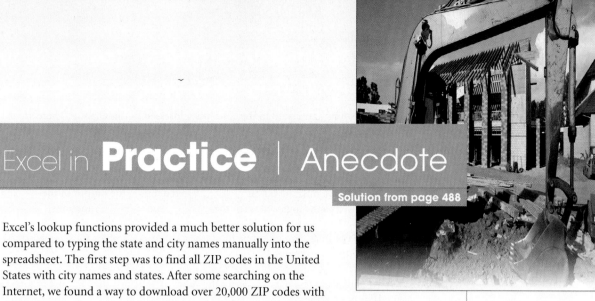

Excel's lookup functions provided a much better solution for us compared to typing the state and city names manually into the spreadsheet. The first step was to find all ZIP codes in the United States with city names and states. After some searching on the Internet, we found a way to download over 20,000 ZIP codes with state and town names included. Once we had this data in a separate worksheet, our problem was essentially solved. A few seconds later we had the states and city names in our worksheet for every ZIP code.

Assignment

1. Open the file named ib_e04_newstorestrategy. This is a small subset of data similar to what was described in the anecdote.

2. Use this data to create a spreadsheet that will evaluate potential locations for new stores. You will need to add formulas, functions, and formats.

3. Your spreadsheet should include the following:

   a. Add the city and state for each ZIP code listed on the Potential Locations worksheet. You can find a master list of several ZIP codes, states, and cities on the Zip Codes worksheet.

   b. Add a column that shows if a ZIP code has a high population of children and a low number of competitors. High child population is anything greater than or equal to 30% of children population over total population. Low competitors is if a ZIP code has less than or equal to two competitors.

   c. Add a column that shows what ZIP codes would qualify as being potential locations for a new store. A potential location is any ZIP code that has high children and low competition, or an average household income greater than $50,000. However, a ZIP code cannot be considered for a new store if it has more than five competitors.

4. Show ZIP codes that qualify as potential locations for new stores on a separate worksheet. Assume this will be presented to the president of the company. Create a way to summarize this data on another worksheet so you can start off the presentation with highlights of your analysis.

Questions for Discussion

1. Why is it important to know alternative ways of calculating and manipulating data?

2. The anecdote mentioned that ZIP codes were downloaded from the Internet. What other sources are available on the Internet that could be used for the project described in the anecdote (i.e., population statistics, household income, number of household)?

Review Questions

The following questions are related to the concepts addressed in this chapter. There are three types of questions: Short Answer, True or False, and Fill in the Blank. If your answer to a True or False question is False, write a short explanation as to why you think the statement is not true.

1. Words or text data must be put in _____ when defining the output of the _____ function as well as the logical tests of the _____ and _____ functions.

2. Explain why commas should not be used when entering numbers for the logical test argument of the IF function.

3. When you are using text data for either the **value_if_true** or **value_if_false** arguments of the IF function, the comma separating the arguments goes _____ the quotation marks.

4. What are the differences and similarities between financial functions and logical functions?

5. True or False: A spreadsheet cannot be sorted based on the output of an IF function.

6. True or False: The sequence of the logical tests in a nested IF function does not matter because the function will always evaluate all logical tests.

7. True or False: When you are creating a nested IF function, you can add logical tests without typing the function name IF and an open parenthesis.

8. Explain what you can do to make sure the logical tests of a nested IF function are in the appropriate sequence.

9. True or False: A nested IF function will not work if the logical tests are in the wrong sequence. An error code will appear telling you that something is wrong with the function.

10. What are the arguments of the AND function?

11. Briefly explain how the AND function works.

12. True or False: You do not need to use quotation marks when using text data with either an OR or AND function.

13. If only one of five logical tests in an OR function is False, the function will display the word _____.

14. True or False: This function will test whether D7 is equal to the value in either C7, A7, or H7: =OR(D7 = C7,A7,H7).

15. What would you do to try to fix an #N/A error when using either the **VLookup** or **HLookup** functions?

16. What does the #REF! error mean?

17. When you are defining the column index number of the **VLookup** function, it is important to always count the first column as number _____.

18. Before pasting either a **VLookup** or an **HLookup** function, always check to see whether _____ are needed.

19. The range of cells used to define the table array of either a **VLookup** or an **HLookup** function must contain both the _____ and the _____ that is needed for the output.

20. True or False: You cannot use a **VLookup** function or an **HLookup** function to calculate data.

21. True or False: Lookup functions cannot be combined with logical functions.

22. True or False: When defining the **table_array** argument of either the **VLookup** or **HLookup** functions, you can just click another worksheet tab and highlight the range of cells needed.

23. True or False: Excel will always assume you need to find an exact match for the lookup value when using either a **VLookup** or an **HLookup** function.

24. What is the Range lookup argument used for in the either the **VLookup** or **HLookup** functions?

The following exam is designed to test your ability to recognize and execute the Excel skills presented in this chapter. Read each question carefully and answer the questions in the order they are listed. You should be able to complete this exam in 60 minutes or less.

1. Open the ib_e04_skillsexam file. All of the tasks listed in this exam should be executed in the Portfolio worksheet.

2. Use the **HLookup** function in cell C4 to display the minimum cash requirement. The function should look for the Risk Level code showing in cell C3 on the Portfolio worksheet in row 3 of the Investment Strategy worksheet. The minimum cash requirements are listed for each risk level in row 8.

3. Enter a formula in cell C6 that subtracts the minimum cash requirement in cell C4 from the current cash value in cell C5.

4. Use an **IF** function in cell A6 to determine if there is a shortage or surplus of cash. The function should display the message *Cash Surplus* if the value in cell C6 is greater than or equal to 0. Otherwise, the function should display the message *Cash Shortage*.

5. Enter a formula in cell E9 that calculates the value of the original investment. The formula should multiply the Shares Owned by the Purchase Price. Copy and paste this formula to cells E10:E15.

6. Use a **VLookup** function to calculate the Current Investment Value in cell F9. The function should look for the symbol in cell A9 of the Portfolio worksheet in column A of the Current Prices worksheet and determine what Current Price relates to that symbol. The result of the **VLookup** function should be multiplied by the Shares Owned in cell D9.

7. Copy the function in cell F9 and paste it into cells F10:F15.

8. Use an **IF** function to calculate the Dividend Value in cell H9. The function should check to see if cell G9 is greater than 0. If it is, then multiply cell G9 by D9. Otherwise, display the number 0.

9. Determine the Strategy in cell I9 by entering a nested **IF** function. The function should display the following outputs based on the criteria listed.

   If the dividend in cell G9 is greater than 0 *and* the Current Investment in cell F9 is greater than or equal to the Original Investment in cell E9, display the word *HOLD*.

   If the Current Investment in cell F9 is less than the Original Investment in cell E9 *or* the Current Investment is less than the Original Investment multiplied by 1.035, then display the word *SELL*.

   Otherwise, display the word *HOLD*.

10. Copy the function in cell I9 and paste it to cells I10:I15.

11. Enter a **SUM** function in cell D17 to add the values in the range D9:D15.

12. Copy the **SUM** function in cell D17 and paste it to cells E17 and F17.

13. Use the **Future Value** function in cell E23 to calculate the Target value of the portfolio in 20 years. This function should use cell C20 as the rate of return, C21 as the target payments to be made every year for the next 20 years, and F17 as the one-time lump sum payment. The function should calculate payments being made at the beginning of the period. Correct any ### signs if they appear.

14. Use your judgment in adding any formatting features that will enhance the visual appearance and readability of the spreadsheet.

15. Save and close your file.

The following questions are designed to test your ability to apply the Excel skills you have learned to complete a business objective. Use your knowledge of Excel as well as your creativity to answer these questions. For most questions, there are several possible ways to complete the objective.

1. Open the spreadsheet named ib_e04_frequentshopper. Use a nested **IF** function to complete the Customer Reward column. The output and criteria of the function are listed below.

   - **Welcome & Thanks 30% Off:** This reward is given to customers who spent $0 last year and the number of years purchasing is less than one.
   - **Please Come Back 50% Off:** This reward is given to customers who have been purchasing from the store for more than one year but have not made a purchase in the past 12 months.
   - **Thanks for Being Loyal 25% Off:** This reward is given to customers who have been making purchases for more than two years or spent more than $1,000 last year.
   - **Customer Appreciation 10% Off:** This reward is given to any customer who does not meet the criteria of the other three rewards.

2. Open the spreadsheet named ib_e04_competitoranalysis. This is the same spreadsheet that was used for the video workshop. Edit this spreadsheet so that the **HLookup** function can be created in cell C3 and then copied and pasted to cells C4:C8. Your revised spreadsheet should have the same appearance as the original. Hint: Cell locations should be used for every argument of the function except for the range lookup.

3. Open the file named ib_e04_investmentstrategy. This file was used for the exercise in the **VLookup** function section. How would you modify this file such that the financial planner can override any of the proposed investments in cells C7:C9?

>> Chapter 5

Presenting Information with Charts

Chapter Goals

Presenting data and information is a common and often critical routine for most business managers. So far, this text has demonstrated how you can use Excel as a flexible analytical tool to accomplish a variety of business objectives. Although Excel worksheets are useful for tracking, reporting, calculating, and analyzing data, they are typically ineffective for presenting business data and information to an audience. As a result, most business managers rely on charts when preparing and delivering presentations. This chapter illustrates a variety of charts available in Excel and demonstrates how business managers use them to study and communicate key information and trends.

>> Excel | Skill Sets

Excel in **Practice** | Anecdote

My Role as a Consultant

You may *think* that, after you've completed hours of intense research and analysis related to a project, the hard work is over. However, in reality, how you present your findings is just as critical as the quality of the information you present. I learned this lesson quickly when I first began working as a consultant. My primary responsibility was to analyze the performance of a client's business and compare it with other companies within that industry. My results then served as a basis for developing rec-ommendations on ways my clients could improve or grow their business. Although I had piles of written documents to support my findings, my main forum for sharing this information was in front of an audience of business owners or head managers at meetings called progress reviews. These people had busy schedules and little time. The pressure to deliver an accurate, appropriate, and efficient presentation was always an intense challenge.

>> Continued on page 583

This section will illustrate one of two methods for creating charts in Excel. If you are working with data that is arranged in adjacent columns or rows, you can use Excel to automatically assign values to the X- and Y-axes of a chart. In these situations, you can simply highlight a range of cells before selecting the chart you wish to create. This section will use this method to illustrate four basic charts commonly used by business managers: column charts, stacked column charts, line charts, and pie charts.

Column Charts (Data Comparisons)

The *column chart* is the most common chart type used to present business data and is most useful when making comparisons. For example, it can compare the earnings of companies within an industry, sales projections for a new business, or the sales growth of product categories. The column chart can compare data at a specific point in time or show how this comparison changes over a period of time. Figure 5.1 shows four years' worth of data for a hypothetical car manufacturer. The example demonstrates the construction of a column chart that compares the sales for each automobile class in the year 2006. Then a second column chart will show how the sales for each auto class changes over a four-year period.

Figure 5.1 | **Automobile Sales Data**

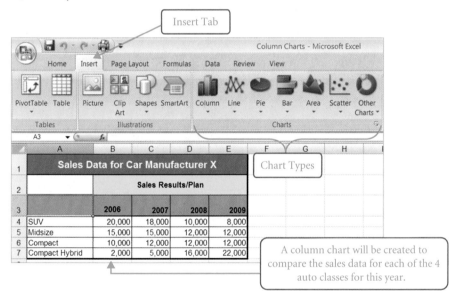

Creating a chart in Excel typically involves the following five steps:

- *Identify the data that will be used to define the X- and Y-axes values.* This section will demonstrate examples in which the data used to define the X- and Y-axes are in a contiguous range. Therefore, you can highlight a range of cells before selecting a chart type.

- *Select a chart type.* Figure 5.1 shows the chart types available in the **Insert** tab on the Ribbon.

- *Select a chart format.* For each chart type, Excel provides a variety of format options. These options establish the arrangement of data and visual appearance of a chart.

- *Specify a location.* When a chart is initially created, it will be embedded in the worksheet that is currently activated. You can then move the chart to another worksheet or create a new worksheet that is dedicated for the chart, which is known as a *chart sheet*.

- *Add or adjust the chart and axis titles.* A chart will not contain proper titles for the X- and Y-axes when it is initially created. You must add or adjust them after creating the chart.

This example creates a column chart to compare the 2006 sales by automobile class from Figure 5.1. The following points explain how to create this chart:

- Highlight the range A3:B7 on the worksheet shown in Figure 5.1. The data in this range will define the values for the X- and Y-axes of the chart.

- Click the **Insert** tab on the Ribbon.

- Select a chart type by clicking the **Column** icon on the Ribbon (see Figure 5.2).

- Select a chart format by clicking the **Clustered Column** option under the **2-D Column** heading (see Figure 5.2). After you select this option, the column chart will appear in the worksheet that is currently active.

Figure 5.2 shows the selections that were made to create a two-dimensional column chart. Excel provides a variety of format options for creating a column chart. Some options give the chart a three-dimensional appearance, and others change the shape of the columns to cylinders, cones, or pyramids. In addition, selecting an option called **All Chart Types** at the bottom of the format list opens the **Create Chart** dialog box, which provides access to every chart type and format available in Excel. Use this as an alternative method for selecting a chart type and format. After you select the chart format from either the list shown in Figure 5.2 or the dialog box shown in Figure 5.3, the chart will appear in the worksheet that is currently active.

Figure 5.2 | **Selecting a Chart Type and Format**

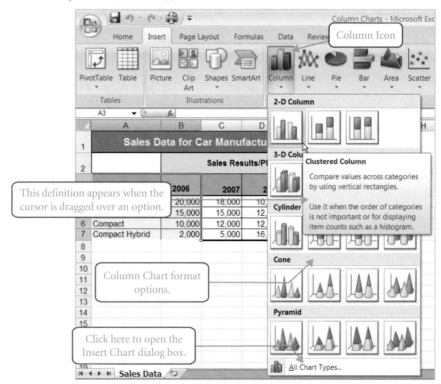

Figure 5.3 | **Create Chart Dialog Box**

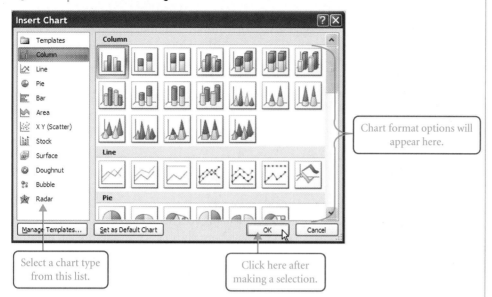

Select a chart type from this list.

Chart format options will appear here.

Click here after making a selection.

Figure 5.4 shows the column chart created to display the sales of each automobile class from Figure 5.1. This is known as an *embedded chart* because it appears within a worksheet that could also contain other data. After embedding the chart in a worksheet, you can move it on that worksheet by clicking and dragging the chart frame. You then can adjust the size of the chart by clicking and dragging on any of the dotted areas on the frame, which are also known as *sizing handles*. Notice that a new set of tabs

Figure 5.4 | **Embedded Column Chart**

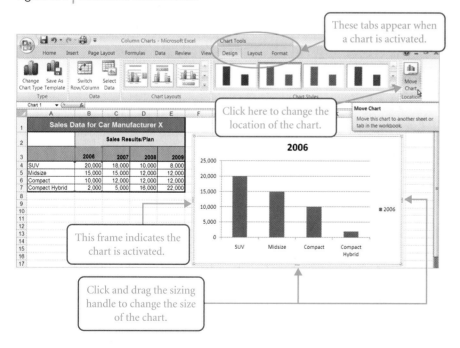

These tabs appear when a chart is activated.

Click here to change the location of the chart.

This frame indicates the chart is activated.

Click and drag the sizing handle to change the size of the chart.

called *Chart Tools* has been added to the Ribbon. The commands contained in this new set of tabs will be used to complete this chart.

After creating charts, you can adjust them as necessary by using the **Chart Tools** tabs that are added to the right side of the Ribbon. The following steps explain how to change the location, change the chart title, and add the X- and Y-axes titles:

- Activate the chart by clicking it. A chart is activated when a frame appears around its perimeter, as shown in Figure 5.4.
- Click the **Move Chart** icon in the **Design** tab of the **Chart Tools** set of tabs on the Ribbon (see Figure 5.4). This will open the **Move Chart** dialog box.
- Click the **New Sheet** option in the **Move Chart** dialog box and type the name **Auto Sales 2006** in the box next to this option (see Figure 5.5). Then click the **OK** button at the bottom of the dialog box. This will place the chart in a dedicated worksheet called a chart sheet with the tab name Auto Sales 2006.
- Activate the chart title at the top of the chart by clicking it once. Then click a second time at the beginning of the title to place the cursor in front of the first number of the year 2006 (see Figure 5.6). This will allow you to change or type a new chart title. For this example, the title is changed to Unit Sales by Auto Class 2006.
- Click the **Layout** tab in the **Chart Tools** set of tabs on the Ribbon and click the **Axis Titles** icon. Then place the cursor over the **Primary Horizontal Axis Title** option. This will open a set of options for placing a title along the X-axis.
- Select the **Title Below Axis** option. This will place a box at the bottom of the *X-axis* that can be used for typing a title.
- Type **Auto Class** in the X-axis title box. The method for adding or adjusting the title in this box is identical to the method described for adjusting the chart title.
- Click the **Axis Titles** icon again, but this time, place the cursor over the **Primary Vertical Axis Title** option. This will show a list of options for placing a title along the Y-axis.
- Select the **Rotated Title** option. This will place a box along the left side of the *Y-axis* that can be used for typing a title.
- Type **Sales in Units** in the Y-axis title box. The method for adding or adjusting the title in this box is identical to the method described for the chart title.

Figure 5.5 | **Move Chart Dialog Box**

Figure 5.6 shows the adjustment that was made to the chart title. Notice the dots that appear on each corner of the chart title box. They indicate that the title box is activated. Also, notice that the cursor was placed in front of the year 2006 by clicking a second time. This method is also used for adjusting the X- and Y-axes titles.

Figure 5.6 | **Adjusting the Title of a Chart**

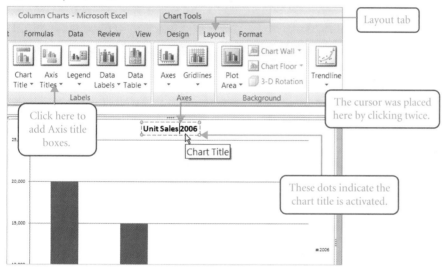

Figure 5.7 shows the completed column chart using the automobile sales data from Figure 5.1. The reader of this chart can immediately see that SUVs generated the most unit sales compared to the other three auto classes in the year 2006. Notice that the bars appear on the chart in order from tallest to shortest. The reason is that the values in column B of Figure 5.1 are sorted in descending order.

Figure 5.7 | **Final Column Chart for the Car Manufacturer Sales Data**

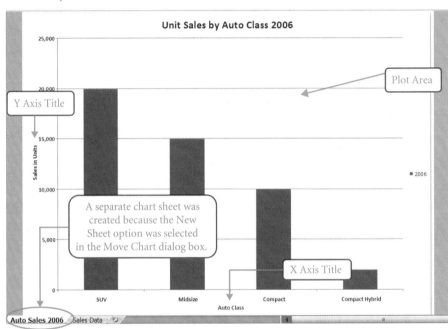

Figure 5.8 shows the second chart created using the worksheet shown in Figure 5.1. The purpose of this chart is to show how the sales comparison of each auto class changes over time. The method used to create this chart is identical to the first column chart shown in Figure 5.4. However, the range A3:E7 was highlighted before creating the chart. This range includes all the values for each auto class for the years 2006 through 2009. Notice how Excel automatically adjusted the X-axis and the *chart legend*. Instead of placing each auto class on the X-axis (see Figure 5.7), Excel shows each year. As a result, each bar on the chart represents a different auto class. The legend shows which color corresponds to the appropriate auto class. In addition, an alternate chart style was selected from the **Design** tab on the Ribbon to enhance the colors of each bar in the chart. The next section covers some additional formatting features that can be used to enhance the appearance of a chart.

Figure 5.8 | **Second Column Chart Showing a Four-Year Sales Comparison**

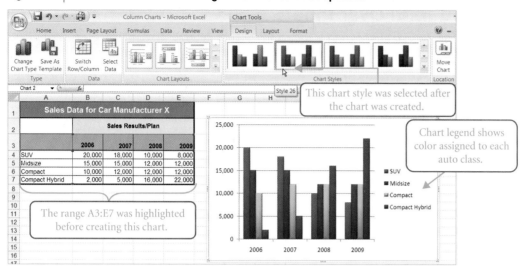

Figure 5.9 shows the final version of the second column chart. The method used to place this chart in a separate worksheet, or chart sheet, along with the addition of axis titles, is identical to that used for the first column chart shown in Figure 5.7. The chart title was added by selecting **Centered Overlay Title** from the **Chart Title** icon in the **Layout** tab of the **Chart Tools** section on the Ribbon. This places the title over the *plot area* of the chart. The reader of this chart can quickly see a shift in the projected sales of the car manufacturer's product line. In the year 2006, the SUV class dominates the other three auto classes in unit sales. However, by the year 2009 the Compact Hybrid is expected to become the dominant class in unit sales. The chart also shows a small decrease in the Midsize line of cars, while the Compact line of cars remains mostly consistent over the four-year period. A business manager can use this chart to visually show how the product sales of the company are expected to change over time.

Figure 5.9 | **Final Column Chart Showing Four-Year Automobile Sales Comparison**

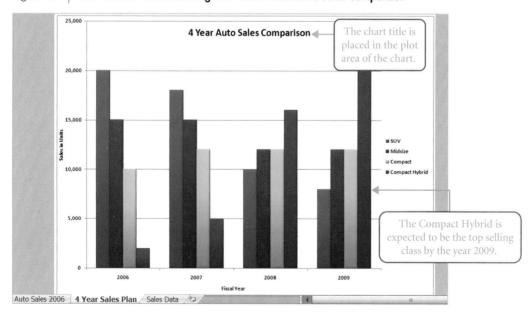

Stacked Column Charts (Percent to Total Over Time)

The *stacked column chart* is similar to a regular column chart in that it uses vertical bars to display data. However, the stacked column chart shows the proportion or percentage each category contributes to a total. For example, a stacked column chart can be used to show the percentage each division contributes to the overall sales of a large corporation, the percentage each product category represents to the total sales of an industry, or the market share percent by company for an industry. In each of these cases, the stacked column chart can also show how these percent to totals change over time. Figure 5.10 shows hypothetical data for the Sporting Goods Industry for the years 1990 and 2000. The 100% Stacked Column format option is selected to show the percentage each product category represents to the total sales of the Sporting Goods industry between the years 1990 and 2000. Looking at the data in Figure 5.10, you will notice that sales have increased for each product category. However, this chart will show how the *rate* of sales growth for each product category has changed over time.

Figure 5.10 | **Hypothetical Sales Data for the Sporting Goods Industry**

The following points explain how a 100% Stacked Column Chart is created using the data from Figure 5.10:

- Highlight the range A2:C5 in the worksheet shown in Figure 5.10.
- Click the **Insert** tab on the Ribbon.
- Click the **Column** chart type icon.
- Click the **100% Stacked Column** format option, as shown in Figure 5.10.

Figure 5.11 shows the initial result of the column chart, which was created using the data in Figure 5.10. Notice that each bar shows the percentage each year represents for each product category. However, the goal of this chart is to compare the sales percent of each product category for each year. This requires that the year is shown on the X-axis as opposed to the product category. Therefore, you need to click the **Switch Row/Column** icon in the **Design** tab of the **Chart Tools** area on the Ribbon. This places the years that are currently displayed in the legend on the X-axis and places the product categories that are shown on the X-axis in the legend.

The following steps explain additional options used to complete the column chart that was started in Figure 5.11:

- Click the **Layout** tab of the **Chart Tools** section on the Ribbon.
- Click the **Data Table** icon (see Figure 5.12) and select the **Show Data Table with Legend Keys** option. This will place a table at the bottom of the chart showing the

Figure 5.11 | **Initial Result of the 100% Stacked Column Chart**

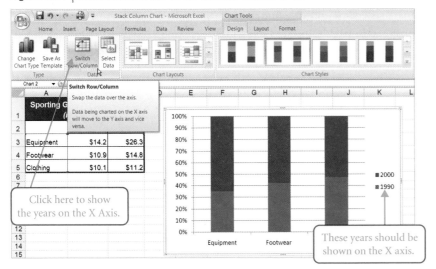

dollar values for each product category. In addition, the legend showing which color corresponds to each product category will be included in the table.

- Click the **Legend** icon.
- Select the **None** option. This will remove the legend that is shown on the right side of the chart in Figure 5.11. As shown in Figure 5.12, the data table that was added to the bottom of the chart shows which color corresponds to each product category. Therefore, the legend on the right side of the chart is not needed.

Figure 5.12 shows the final 100% Stacked Column chart. By looking at the Y-axis, you can see how the percentage each product represents to the total sales of the industry changes from 1990 to the year 2000. Notice that the "Equipment" category represents 40% of the industry's sales in 1990 and grows to 50% in the year 2000. The "Footwear" category is approximately the same at 30% in 1990 and 2000. However, the "Clothing" category declines from approximately 30% of the industry's sales in 1990 to 20% in 2000. Product and/or marketing managers typically conduct this type of analysis to identify what areas of an industry present the best opportunities for growth.

Figure 5.12 | **Final 100% Stacked Column Chart**

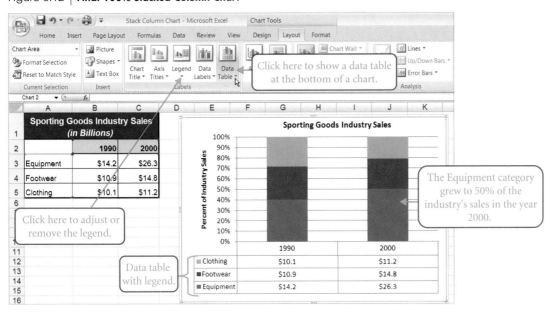

Line Charts (Trends Over Time)

Business managers commonly use ***line charts*** in a number of situations. For example, they effectively show data trends over a period of time, such as changes in stocks or stock market averages. Line charts are also great tools to compare trends. For example, the 12-month trend of a stock can be compared to the 12-month trend of an index like the Dow Jones Industrial Average. Figure 5.13 shows data for the Dow Jones Industrial Average for the year 2004. A line chart will be used to show the adjusted closing price for each month.

Figure 5.13 | **2004 Adjusted Average Close of the Dow Jones**

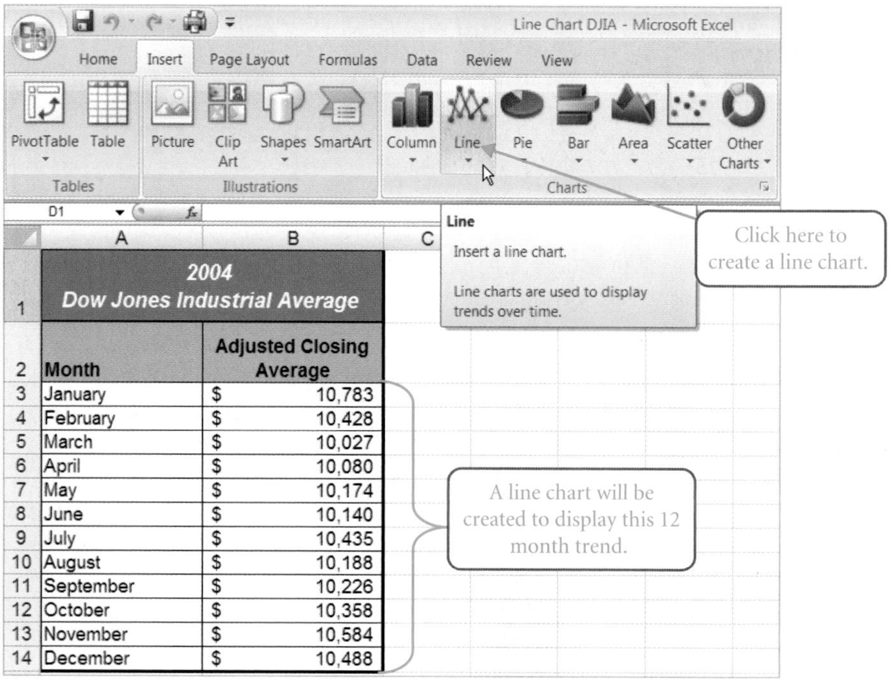

	A	B
1	2004 Dow Jones Industrial Average	
2	Month	Adjusted Closing Average
3	January	$ 10,783
4	February	$ 10,428
5	March	$ 10,027
6	April	$ 10,080
7	May	$ 10,174
8	June	$ 10,140
9	July	$ 10,435
10	August	$ 10,188
11	September	$ 10,226
12	October	$ 10,358
13	November	$ 10,584
14	December	$ 10,488

The following points explain how to create a line chart using the data in Figure 5.13:

- Highlight the range A2:B14. Then click the **Insert** tab on the Ribbon.
- Click the **Line** icon and select the **Line with Markers** format option. This will display a line on the chart with a diamond-shaped marker indicating each specific value from column B in Figure 5.13.
- Click the **Move Chart** icon to open the **Move Chart** dialog box.
- Select the **New sheet** option in the **Move Chart** dialog box and type **`DJIA 2004`** in the box used for the tab name. Then click the **OK** button.
- Click the **Layout** tab in the **Chart Tools** set of tabs on the Ribbon.
- Click the **Legend** icon and then select the **None** option. Because there is only one line of data on this chart, the legend is not needed.

Figure 5.14 shows the completed line chart, which displays the trend of the Dow Jones Industrial Average in 2004. The title for this chart was adjusted and a title for the Y-axis was added. The reader of this line chart can immediately see how the Dow Jones Industrial Average trended during the year 2004. The chart clearly shows a significant drop in the beginning of the year from January to March. With the exception of a spike in the month of July, there is a gradual increase for the remainder of the year. However, the chart shows that the Dow Jones ended the year a few hundred points lower than the beginning.

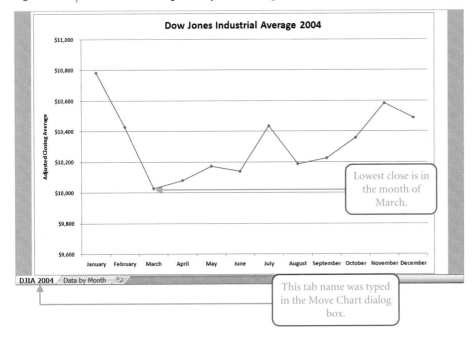

Pie Charts (Percent to Total)

The *pie chart* is the last chart demonstrated in this section. Similar to the stacked column chart, the pie chart shows a percent to total comparison for various data categories. However, unlike the stacked column chart, the pie chart is not effective in showing a percent to total change over time. It is mostly used to show how several components make up a total for one specific point in time. For example, a business manager might use a pie chart to show the percentage each asset category contributes to the total startup costs for a business. Examples of asset categories are Land, Machines, Office Supplies, Automobiles, and so on. An example of this data is shown in Figure 5.15.

Figure 5.15 | **Startup Costs for a Business**

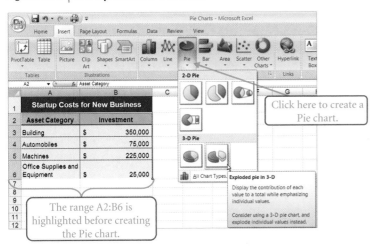

The following points explain how to create a pie chart to visually show the percentage each asset category in column A in Figure 5.15 represents to the total startup costs of the business:

- Highlight the range A2:B6 in the worksheet shown in Figure 5.15. Then click the **Insert** tab on the Ribbon.

- Click the **Pie** icon and then click the **Exploded pie in 3-D** format option, as shown in Figure 5.15. This will produce a three-dimensional view of the pie chart and slightly separate each section from the center of the chart. This view will enhance the visual display showing the amount each investment represents to the total.

- Click the chart title and change the title to Startup Costs.

Figure 5.16 shows the initial setup of the pie chart. Notice that a legend appears on the right side of the chart. Pie charts typically show the category name next to each wedge of the pie chart. A legend could be used in cases in which several categories are displayed in a pie chart. However, adding too many categories to a pie chart can make it difficult or impossible to see any relationships to the total. A pie chart is typically used to show a maximum of 10 to 12 categories.

Figure 5.16 | **Initial Setup of the Pie Chart**

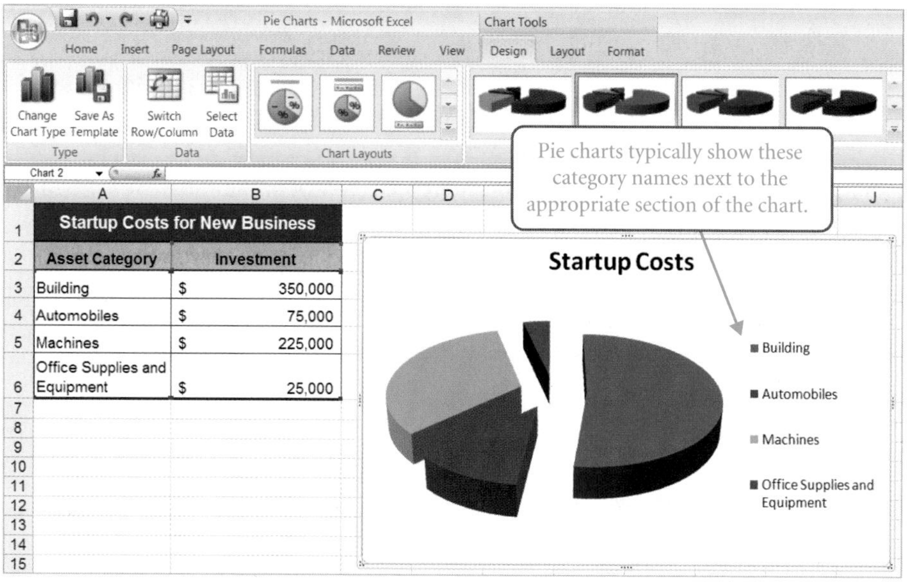

COMMON MISTAKES | Too Many Categories for a Pie Chart

The most common mistake people make when creating pie charts is trying to add too many categories. A pie chart can typically show a maximum of 10 to 12 categories. As the number of categories added to a pie chart exceeds 12, it becomes increasingly difficult to determine what each category represents to the total. If you need to create a chart with more than 12 categories, consider using a column chart or create subgroups that represent multiple categories.

The following points explain how to show each Asset Category shown in the legend of Figure 5.16 next to each section of the pie chart:

- Click the **Layout** tab in the **Chart Tools** set of tabs on the Ribbon.

- Click the **Legend** icon and select the **None** option. Because the category name will be placed next to each section of the chart, the legend is not needed.

- Click the **Data Labels** icon and select the **More Data Label Options** (see Figure 5.17). This will open the **Format Data Labels** dialog box.

- In the **Format Data Labels** dialog box, click the box next to the **Value** option to remove the green check. Then click the box next to the **Category name** option to add a green check (see Figure 5.18).

- Click the **Outside End** option and then click the **Close** button at the bottom of the **Format Data Labels** dialog box. This will add the category labels next to each section of the pie chart. You can adjust the position of these labels by clicking and dragging.

Figures 5.17 and 5.18 show how to open the **Format Data Labels** dialog box. Notice the settings in the **Format Data Labels** dialog box in Figure 5.18.

Figure 5.17 | **Opening the Format Data Labels Dialog Box**

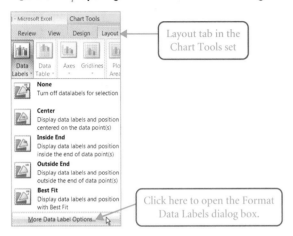

Figure 5.18 | **Settings in the Format Data Labels Dialog Box**

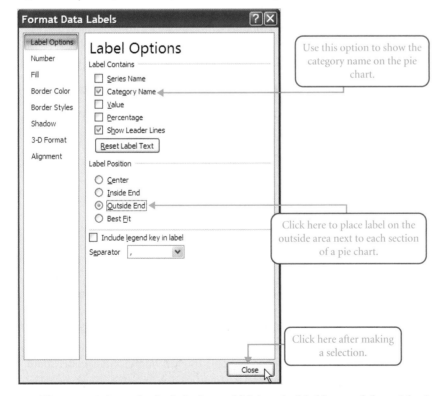

>> **Quick Reference**

Creating Charts

1. Highlight a range of cells that contain values that will be used to define the X- and Y-axes of the chart.
2. Click the **Insert** tab on the Ribbon.
3. Click one of the **Chart Type** icons in the **Charts** group on the Ribbon.
4. Select a chart format option based on the needs of your project and the desired visual appearance.
5. Click the **Switch Row/Column** icon (in the **Design** tab) if the data on the X- and Y-axes needs to be reversed.
6. Click the **Move Chart** icon (in the **Design** tab) to move the chart to another existing worksheet or place the chart in a separate chart sheet.
7. Click the **Layout** tab in the **Chart Tools** section on the Ribbon and click the **Chart Title** and/or **Axis Titles** icons to add or adjust boxes for the chart title or axis titles.
8. After adding a title box to the chart, click it twice to type a new title or description.

Figures 5.19 shows the final pie chart, which is embedded in a worksheet. A business manager can use this chart to demonstrate that most of the startup costs for this business will be dedicated to the Building and Machines asset categories. Notice how each section of the pie chart is separated or pulled away from the center. This makes it easier to see the proportion each section represents to the total. The reader of this chart can easily see that the cost of the Building represents a little over 50% of the total startup costs for this business.

Figure 5.19 | **Final Pie Chart**

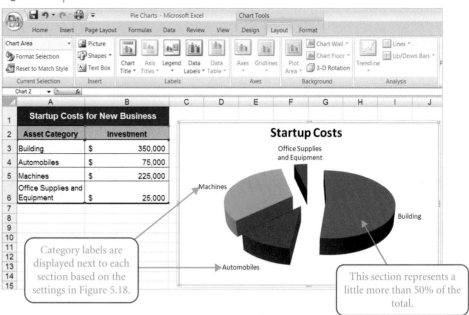

Category labels are displayed next to each section based on the settings in Figure 5.18.

This section represents a little more than 50% of the total.

>> Creating Charts

The purpose of this workshop is to demonstrate how charts are created in Excel. I will be demonstrating the tasks in this workshop in the following four videos: **Column Charts**, **Stacked Column Charts**, **Line Charts**, and **Pie Charts**. Each video name appears at the beginning of each section of tasks. Open the file named ib_e05_chartsforbusiness before starting this workshop. Try completing the tasks on your own and then watch the video.

1. Column Charts (Video: Column Charts)

a. Activate the worksheet named Auto Sales Data.

b. Highlight the range A3:E7 and then click the **Insert** tab on the Ribbon.

c. Click the **Column** icon and select the two-dimensional **Clustered Column** format option.

d. Select **Style 34** from the **Chart Style** options found in the **Design** tab.

e. Use the **Move Chart** icon in the **Design** tab on the Ribbon to the move the column chart to its own chart sheet. The tab name of this chart sheet should be **4 Year Sales Plan**.

f. Click the **Chart Title** icon in the **Layout** tab on the Ribbon to add a title box to the chart. Select the **Above Chart** option.

g. Click the chart title box and change the title to **4 Year Auto Sales Comparison**.

h. Using the **Axis Titles** icon, add a title box to the X- and Y-axes. For the Y-, or vertical, axis, select the **Rotated Title** option.

   i. Click the X-axis title box twice and change the title to `Fiscal Year`.

   j. Click the Y-axis title box twice and change the title to `Sales in Units`.

2. Stacked Column Charts (Video: Stacked Column Charts)

   a. Activate the worksheet named Industry Sales.

   b. Highlight the range A2:C5 and then click the **Insert** tab on the Ribbon.

   c. Click the **Column** icon and select the **100% Stacked Column** format option.

   d. Click the **Switch Row/Column** icon in the **Design** tab on the Ribbon to show the years on the X-axis instead of the product categories.

   e. Select **Style 10** from the **Chart Style** options found in the **Design** tab.

   f. Remove the legend on the chart by clicking the **Legend** icon in the **Layout** tab on the Ribbon and select the **None** option.

   g. Move the chart so the upper-left corner is in cell E2 by clicking and dragging the frame.

   h. Place a data table at the bottom of the chart by clicking the **Data Table** icon and selecting the **Show Data Table with Legend Keys** option.

   i. Increase the size of the chart by clicking and dragging the bottom sizing handle to the bottom of row 20. Then click and drag the right sizing handle to the right side of column N.

   j. Add a chart title `Sporting Goods Industry Sales`. Use the **Above Chart** option in the **Chart Title** icon.

   k. Add a title to the Y-axis `Percent of Industry Sales`. Use the **Rotated Title** option from the **Axis Title** icon.

3. Line Charts (Video: Line Charts)

   a. Activate the worksheet named Dow Jones Data.

   b. Highlight the range A2:B14 and click the **Insert** tab on the Ribbon.

   c. Click the **Line** icon and select the **Line with Markers** format option.

   d. Use the **Move Chart** icon in the **Design** tab on the Ribbon to move the line chart to its own chart sheet. The tab name of this chart sheet should be `DJIA 2004`.

   e. Use the **Legend** icon in the **Layout** tab to remove the legend.

   f. Change the chart title to `Dow Jones Industrial Average 2004`.

   g. Add a Y-axis title `Adjusted Closing Average`.

4. Pie Charts (Video: Pie Charts)

   a. Activate the worksheet named Startup Cost.

   b. Highlight the range A2:B6 and click the **Insert** tab on the Ribbon.

   c. Click the **Pie** icon and select the **Exploded pie in 3-D** format option.

   d. Select the **Style 26** chart style.

   e. Remove the legend.

   f. Change the title of the chart to `Startup Costs`.

   g. Open the **Format Data Labels** dialog box. Select the **More Data Label Options** in the **Data Labels** icon in the **Layout** tab on the Ribbon.

h. In the **Format Data Labels** dialog box, click the **Value** option to remove the green check. Then click the **Category Name** option to add a green check. Then click the **Outside End** option and click the **Close** button.

i. Save and close your file.

>> Analyzing Industry Statistics

Analyzing an industry is a critical exercise when developing business strategies. Understanding whether an industry is growing or declining and identifying the top-performing companies are critical when making strategic decisions. The outcome of this analysis could support decisions such as entering a market, exiting a market, or making an acquisition. The chart techniques covered in this section are valuable for presenting industry statistics, but they can also be used as analytical tools.

Exercise

The purpose of this exercise is to construct two charts for the purpose of analyzing and presenting statistics that have been collected for a hypothetical industry. To begin the exercise, open the file named ib_e05_industryx.

1. Activate the worksheet named Sales Growth.

2. Highlight the range A3:H7 and create a line chart. Use a chart format that shows markers at each data point. The purpose of this chart is to show the seven-year sales trend for each of the companies listed in the Sales Growth worksheet. Notice that the averages located in row 7 are included in the highlighted range. This will enable the reader of the chart to compare the growth trends for each company with the overall average of the industry.

3. Select a chart style that assigns a different color for each of the lines on the chart. Select a style that keeps the plot area white or light grey.

4. Move the line chart to a separate chart sheet. The tab name for this chart sheet should be **Industry Sales by Company**.

5. Move the legend to the bottom of the chart.

6. Add the title **Industry X Sales Analysis** to the chart. The title should appear above the chart.

7. Add a title **Change in Sales** to the Y-axis. Use the **Vertical Title** option.

8. What company is showing a sales growth trend from the year 2000 to 2006 that is most similar the overall average of the industry?

9. Activate the worksheet named Competitors.

10. Highlight the range A2:B6 and create a pie chart. Use a chart format that will show each section of the chart separated from the center and have a three-dimensional appearance. The purpose of this chart is to show the total net sales for all the companies in Industry X. When placed in a pie chart, this data will show how much market share or percentage of sales each company

obtained in the industry last year. This chart will show if the industry is dominated by a few companies or if the sales are divided among several small firms.

11. Select a chart style that assigns a different color for each section of the pie chart. Select a style that keeps the plot area white or light grey.

12. Change the title of the chart to **LY Market Share**.

13. Remove the chart legend.

14. Add data labels outside each section in the chart. The data labels should show both the category name and the value. As a result, the chart should show the company name as well as the total net sales.

15. Which company has the highest market share in the industry?

16. Does the company with the highest market share also have the highest sales growth rate relative to the industry average?

17. Which company—A, B, or C—has the lowest market share?

18. Reports in this industry claim Company A is "stealing" market share away from Company C. Does this claim make sense when looking at the line chart you created? Why?

19. Save and close your file.

>> What's Wrong with This Spreadsheet?

PROBLEM & EXERCISE

Problem

You are a business analyst working in the product development division of a large products manufacturing company. Your boss, the director of product development, is preparing for a meeting with the president of the company to explain potential sales opportunities based on three years' worth of historical sales data. He is having difficulty creating a chart that visually displays the sales trends for five product categories and asks for your help. He explains his goal for this chart as follows:

1. I am trying to create a basic column chart that shows how the product sales mix of the company has changed over the past three years. Our sales are increasing every year; however, the sales of some product categories have increased dramatically, whereas others have actually declined. Therefore, I am trying to create a chart that shows the three years at the bottom of the chart with bars representing the sales for each of the five product categories. However, the column chart I created shows the exact opposite configuration. I was wondering if I should re-create my data so the column headings in row 2 show the product categories instead of the years.

2. If possible, I would like to show the bars for the year 2004 in order, starting with the tallest bar down to the shortest. I know the height of the bars will change for the following two years; however, it is so much easier to see these trends when the bars for the first year are in order.

3. Is there any way to create this chart without having all the bars green? It would be nice if each bar is a different color. Someone told me that there is a **Design** tab on the Ribbon that would allow me to select a new color scheme. However, I must have a different version of Excel because I don't see this tab.

The chart your boss created is in the Excel file named ib_e05_productmixpresentation. Open the file and consider the following points:

1. Your boss mentioned that he might have to re-create the data in his worksheet to display the years on the bottom of the chart. Is this necessary?
2. In the second point, your boss mentioned that he would like to change the order in which the bars are displayed for the year 2004. Is this possible? How?
3. With regards to the third point, why is your boss not seeing the **Design** tab?
4. Is anything missing from the chart your boss attempted to create in this file?
5. Read the first point carefully. Your boss mentioned that he would like to create a basic column chart. Would you recommend that your boss use another chart in this situation? Why?

Write a short answer for each of the points listed here. Then fix the chart based on the points your boss mentioned and add anything you think is missing. In addition, create an alternate version of this chart that might improve your boss's presentation to the president.

Skill Set	>> **Formatting Charts**

The previous section demonstrated how charts are created and used in a variety of business situations. However, formatting can significantly enhance the appearance of these charts. In Chapter 2, you saw how appropriate formatting can often make the difference between a mediocre and professional-looking spreadsheet. The same rule applies to charts. Formatting can direct the reader to the most critical data points on a chart and bring the appearance of charts to a professional level. This section will demonstrate various formatting techniques using the charts created in the previous section.

Titles and Legends

After creating a chart, you might need to make formatting adjustments to the legend and titles. For example, you may have noticed that the axis titles as well as the legend in the column chart shown in Figure 5.9 are hard to read because the font size is so small. Formatting adjustments can solve this problem.

There are many ways to apply formatting commands to any area of a chart. The best method to use ultimately depends on your preference and needs. The following points demonstrate these methods using the chart title from Figure 5.9:

- Activate the chart title and select one of the formatting icons on the **Home** tab on the Ribbon. When an area on the chart is activated, you can click the **Home** tab and use any of the formatting icons such as **Font Size**, **Bold**, **Italics**, and so on.
- Activate the chart title and right click on it. Right clicking will provide access to the formatting icons in the **Home** tab on the Ribbon as well as other commands. The benefit of using this method is that you can access icons on the **Home** tab while another tab on the Ribbon is active (see Figure 5.20).
- Activate the chart title and use the commands in the **Format** tab in the **Chart Tools** area on the Ribbon (see Figure 5.21).
- Activate the chart title and open the **Format Chart Title** dialog box (see Figure 5.22). A formatting dialog box can be opened for every area of a chart. For example, there is a **Format Plot Area** dialog box, **Format Axis** dialog box, **Format Legend** dialog box, and so on. You can open these format dialog boxes by clicking

the **Format Selection** icon in the **Format** tab after activating the area of the chart you wish to format (see Figure 5.21). The benefit of this method is that it provides access to more detailed formatting controls in addition to the commands found in the **Format** tab.

Figure 5.20 through 5.22 illustrate the various methods for accessing and implementing formatting commands for charts. As previously mentioned, the method you choose depends on your preference and project needs.

Figure 5.20 | **Right-Click Method to Access Formatting Commands**

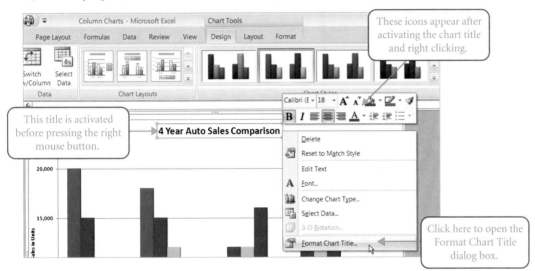

Figure 5.21 | **Chart Formatting Commands in the Format Tab**

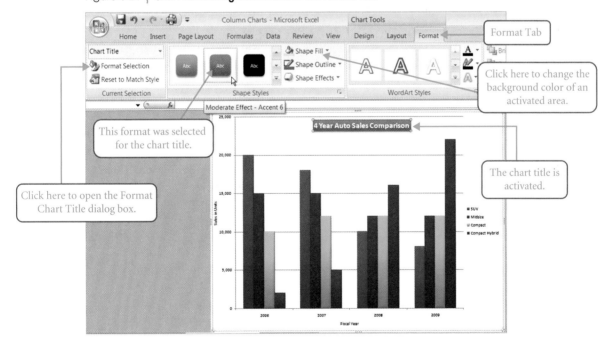

Figure 5.22 | **Format Chart Title Dialog Box**

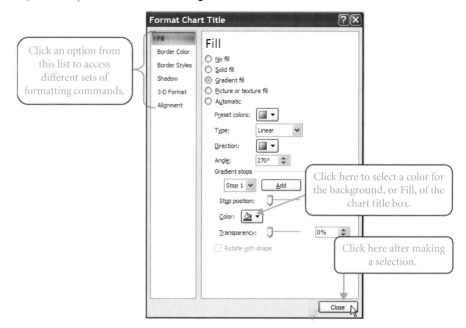

Figure 5.24 shows the results of the final formatting applied to the legend and titles on the column chart from Figure 5.9. The formatting changes made include the following:

- **Chart Title:** In addition to applying the style that was shown in Figure 5.21, the font size was increased to 20 points and italicized. The title was also repositioned above the chart by selecting the **Above Chart** option in the **Chart Title** icon of the **Layout** tab.

- **X- and Y-Axes Titles:** The font size was increased to 14 points. This was done by selecting the axis title box and clicking the right mouse button, as shown in Figure 5.20. The font size was then adjusted to 14 points.

- **Legend:** Several formatting adjustments were applied to the legend:

  - Using the right-click method, the font size was increased to 16 points, and the bold and italics formats were added.

  - A black line was added around the perimeter of the legend. This was done by opening the **Format Legend** dialog box, clicking the Border Color category on the left side of the dialog box, selecting the **Solid Line** option, and selecting the color black from the color palette (see Figure 5.23).

  - The size of the legend was changed by clicking and dragging the sizing handles that appear when it is activated. Words will automatically wrap to a second line when the width of the legend is decreased. For example, notice the Compact Hybrid category in Figure 5.24.

  - The legend was moved by clicking and dragging after it was activated.

Figure 5.23 | **Format Legend Dialog Box**

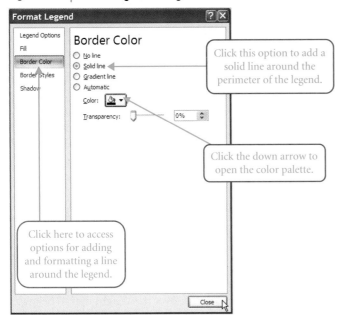

Figure 5.24 | **Formatting Changes Applied to the Legend and Titles**

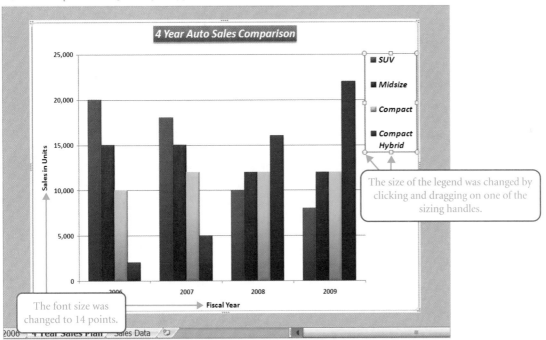

Plot Area and Data Series

The plot area is an area of a chart that frequently requires formatting adjustments. The color of the plot area can make a significant difference in the appearance of the data that is being displayed. The color or background you choose for the plot area will depend on the colors and type of chart you are constructing. This section will illustrate how the plot area of the column chart in Figure 5.24 is formatted. In addition, this segment will also illustrate how you can apply formatting adjustments to the data series of a chart.

After activating the plot area of a chart, you usually format it using the **Shape Fill** and **Shape Outline** icons in the **Format** tab or by opening the **Format Plot Area** dialog box. The following steps explain how to format the plot area for the column chart in Figure 5.24 using the icons in the **Format** tab:

- Activate the plot area by clicking inside the X-and Y-axes but not on one of the grid lines.
- Click the **Format** tab.
- Click the **Shape Fill** icon and select the color light grey (darker 15%) from the palette. This will change the color of the plot area to light grey.
- Click the **Shape Outline** icon and place the cursor over the **Weight** option below the color palette (see Figure 5.25). Then select the **1 ½ pt** option. This will place a black outline around the perimeter of the plot area.

Figure 5.25 | **Adding a Black Outline around the Perimeter of the Plot Area**

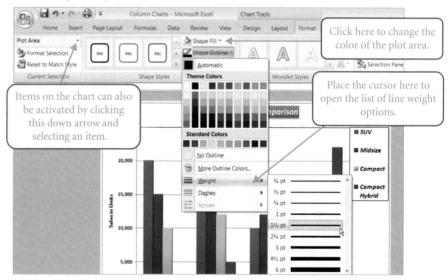

Figure 5.26 shows the results of the final formatting adjustments made to the plot area of the column chart. In addition, space was created on the bottom, left, and right sides of the plot area by clicking and dragging on the sizing handles, which appear when the plot area is activated. Notice how the axis labels and values appear more prominent when the color of the plot area is changed to light grey. This makes it easy for the reader to see the magnitude of the bars in the plot area.

Figure 5.26 | **Formatted Plot Area**

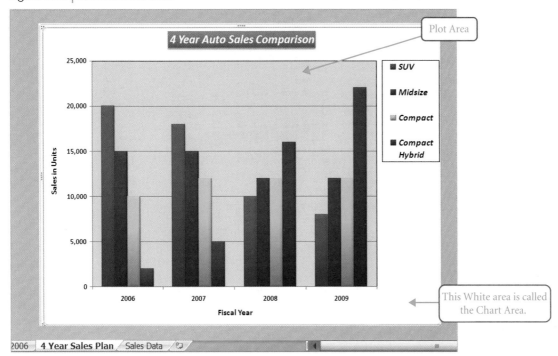

As previously mentioned, you can also format the data series displayed on a chart. A *data series* refers to the image that appears on the chart that is representing a category of values. For example, the blue bars in the column chart shown in Figure 5.26 represent the SUV data series. On a line chart, markers could be used to represent a data series. For this formatting example, the color of the bars representing the Compact and Compact Hybrid categories will be changed. You may recall that the color of these bars was determined by selecting one of the chart styles in the **Design** tab when the chart was initially created (see Figure 5.8). However, what if you wanted the bars for the Compact Hybrid category to be green because this car is environmentally friendly? You can change this color to green by applying formatting techniques to the data series.

The method used to format the data series of a chart is similar to formatting the plot area. When one element of a data series is clicked one time, images related to the data series will be activated. For example, when one of the bars representing the Compact Hybrid category is clicked, all the Compact Hybrid bars will be activated. If one of the bars representing the Compact Hybrid category is clicked a second time, that specific bar, or *series point*, will be activated. This gives you the option of formatting all the bars or images related to a data series or just one. After activating a data series or series point, you can use the **Shape Fill** and **Shape Outline** icons in the **Format** tab to change the color and the line around its perimeter. The following points explain how to format both the Compact and Compact Hybrid data series:

- Click one of the green bars representing the Compact car category on the column chart shown in Figure 5.26. This will activate all the green bars on the chart.

- Click the **Format** tab and then click the **Shape Fill** icon. Select the color yellow at the bottom of the palette (see Figure 5.27). You should see the color of the bars change as you drag the cursor over a color in the palette. In addition, the **Shape Fill** icon also contains an option called **Picture**. This option enables you to import a digital picture you have saved on your computer into the area that is activated on the chart.

- Click one of the purple bars representing the Compact Hybrid car category on the column chart. This will activate all the purple bars on the chart.

- Click the **Format** tab and then click the **Shape Fill** icon. Select the color light green at the bottom of the palette.

>> Quick Reference

Formatting the Plot Area

1. Activate the plot area by clicking it once.

2. Click the **Format** tab in the **Chart Tools** set of tabs.

3. Click the **Shape Fill** icon and select a color from the palette to change the plot area color.

4. Click the **Shape Outline** icon and select a color from the palette, one of the **Weight** options, or one of the **Dashes** options.

Figure 5.27 | **Using the Shape Fill Icon to Format a Data Series**

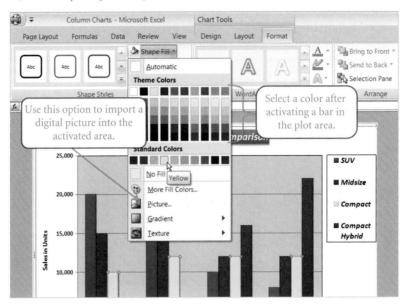

Figure 5.28 shows the final changes made to the Compact and Compact Hybrid data series. Notice that the legend adjusts automatically after the color of the data series is changed. Remember that you can access other formatting features by opening the **Format Data Series** dialog box using the **Format Selection** icon. For example, you can adjust the size of the gap between each set of bars. This capability is helpful when you want to show more or less space between each category on the X-axis of a column chart.

Figure 5.28 | **Completed Formatting Adjustments to the Data Series**

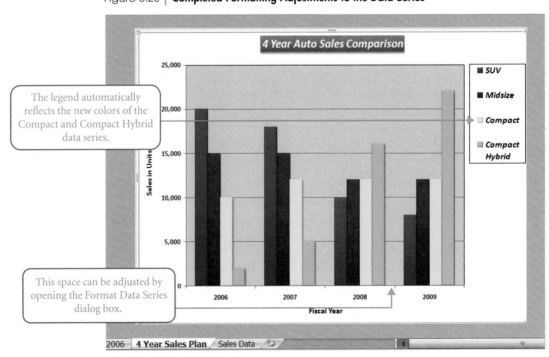

X- and Y-Axes Labels

The last areas that will be formatted on the column chart shown in Figure 5.28 are the X- and Y-axes. Similar to the Axis titles, the values or labels along the X- and Y-axes frequently require formatting so they are easy to see and read.

As with other chart formatting features, you can change the appearance of either the X- or Y-axis by clicking it once and using the icons in the **Home** and **Format** tabs. However, you can access other important features such as controlling the scale of an axis, tick marks, position of the axis labels, or grid lines through the **Format Axis** dialog box. You open it by clicking the axis one time and selecting the **Format Selection** icon in the **Format** tab. Figure 5.29 shows the **Format Axis** dialog box for the Y-axis of the column chart in Figure 5.28.

Figure 5.29 | **Format Axis Dialog Box**

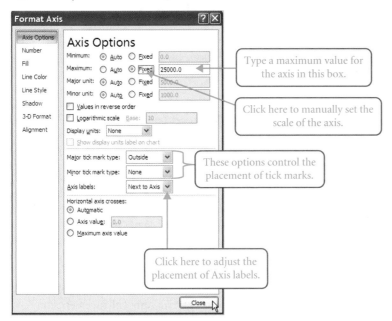

Figure 5.30 shows the final column chart that was started in Figure 5.9. The font size for the sales values and years along the X- and Y-axes was increased to 14 points. Notice how formatting features were used to make all the key elements of the chart easier to see and read such as the titles, legend, and bars.

Figure 5.30 | **Final Automobile Sales Chart with the X- and Y-Axes Formatted**

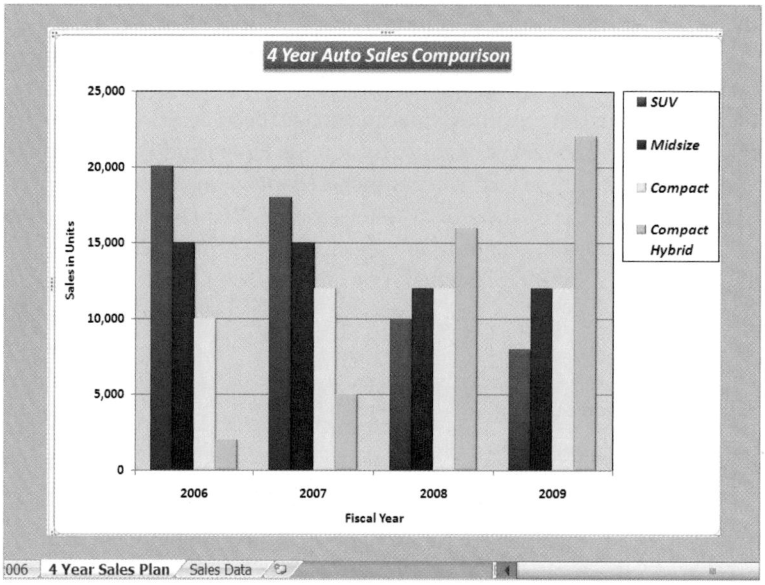

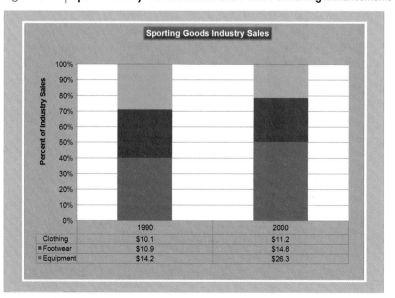

Adding Annotations and Objects

Depending on your project, you may need to add annotations, callouts, or other shapes to a chart. These items can be especially helpful in guiding the attention of an audience during a presentation or for adding additional information that helps the reader identify key facts and trends. The next example demonstrates these formatting features using the 100% Stacked Column chart originally created in Figure 5.12.

As shown in Figure 5.31, the Sporting Goods Industry chart (previously shown in Figure 5.12) includes several formatting features, and it was moved to its own chart sheet. Two formatting enhancements are typically added to stacked column charts such as the one shown in this Figure 5.31. The first shows the total value for all the stacks in each bar. Because the Y-axis shows only the percent to total, it is difficult to see the total sales that were generated in the industry. The second formatting enhancement connects the top of each stack with a line. This feature will make it easier for the reader to see how the percent to total changes over time for each stack in the bar.

>> **Quick Reference**

**Formatting X- and
Y-Axes Labels**

1. Activate the X- or Y-axis by clicking once anywhere along the axis.

2. Select any of the format icons in the **Home** tab on the Ribbon and/or the icons in the **Format** tab of the **Chart Tools** area on the Ribbon.

3. To access more detailed formatting controls such the axis scale, tick marks, or label position, click the **Format Selection** icon in the **Format** tab to open the **Format Axis** dialog box.

Figure 5.31 | **Sports Industry 100% Stacked Chart with Formatting Enhancements**

The following steps explain how to add annotations to the chart in Figure 5.31 to show the total industry sales at the top of each bar:

- Activate the chart.
- Click the **Layout** tab in the **Chart Tools** section on the Ribbon.
- Click the **Text Box** icon. Then click and drag a rectangle box over the top of the Y-axis, as shown in Figure 5.32. This text box can be used for typing annotations or information onto the chart.
- Place the cursor over one of the sizing handles of the text box and click the right mouse button. This will open a menu of options used for adding and formatting the data or message typed into the text box (see Figure 5.33). Select the **Edit Text** option and type **100% of Sales =**. This tells the reader that sales figures showing at the top of each bar represent the total sales results for the industry. Additional text boxes will be added to show these sales figures on the chart.
- Highlight the message you typed into the text box and click the right mouse button. Use the formatting icons as shown in Figure 5.33 to change the font size to 12 and then bold and italicize the text.
- Click and drag the right sizing handle to the right so the message does not wrap to two lines.

Figure 5.32 | **Adding a Text Box to a Chart**

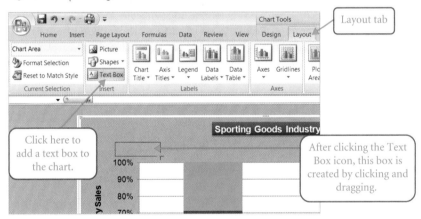

Figure 5.33 | **Right-Click Options for a Text Box**

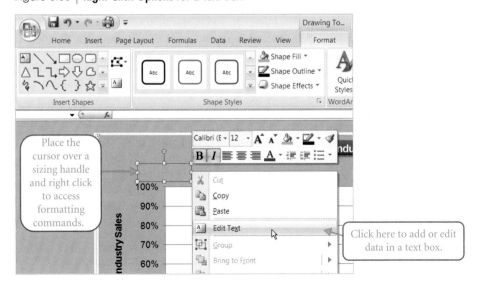

Figure 5.34 shows the completed text box. Notice that after the text box is added to the chart, a **Format** tab is added to the Ribbon under the heading **Drawing Tools**. The commands in this tab are used for applying formatting features to any added object that is activated on a chart or worksheet. Similar to the **Chart Tools Format** tab, the benefit of using icons in this tab is that you can see how a particular formatting command appears before selecting it.

Figure 5.34 | **Completed Text Box**

As mentioned earlier, the second formatting enhancement usually applied to a 100% Stacked Column chart is a line connecting the top of each stacked section of the bar. Besides text boxes, other objects can also be added to a chart, such as lines, arrows, circles, callout boxes, and so on. You can access these objects in the **Layout** tab of the **Chart Tools** section on the Ribbon. The following points explain how to add a line to the 100% Stacked Column chart in Figure 5.31:

- Activate the chart.
- Click the **Layout** tab in the **Chart Tools** section on the Ribbon.
- Click the **Shapes** icon. This will open a list of objects that can be added to the chart (see Figure 5.35).
- Click the **Line** option from the shapes list. Then move the cursor to the top of the blue stack of the bar for 1990 and click and drag over to the top of the blue stack for the year 2000 (see Figure 5.36).
- Click the **Shape Outline** icon in the **Format** tab of the **Drawing Tools** section on the Ribbon. The line must be activated to see the **Drawing Tools** section on the Ribbon. Select black from the palette; then click the icon again and select the **1 ½ pt** weight option.

Figure 5.35 | **Options for Adding Shapes to a Chart**

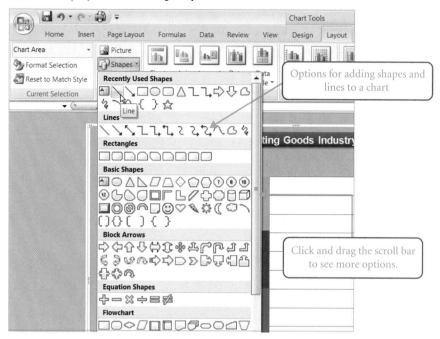

Figure 5.36 shows the line that was added to the 100% Stacked Column chart. Notice that because the line is moving in an upward direction, the reader can easily see that the percent to total sales for Equipment increased from 1990 to 2000.

Figure 5.36 | **Adding a Line to a 100% Stacked Column Chart**

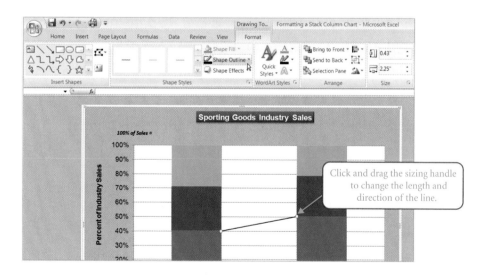

Figure 5.37 shows the final 100% Stacked Column chart showing the sales trend for the Sporting Goods Industry. Notice that text boxes were added to the top of each bar showing the total industry sales for the year. In addition, a second line was added connecting the "Footwear" category between the 1990 and 2000 bars.

>> *Quick Reference*

Adding Annotations and Objects

1. Activate the chart.
2. Click the **Layout** tab of the **Chart Tools** area on the Ribbon.
3. Click the **Text Box** icon to add an annotation or the **Shapes** icon to add an object. If adding an object, select an option after clicking the **Shapes** icon.
4. Click and drag on the chart to place and set the desired size of the text box or object.
5. Format the text box or object by activating it and right clicking, or using the icons in the **Format** tab of the **Drawing Tools** area on the Ribbon.

Figure 5.37 | **Final 100% Stacked Column with Lines and Annotations Added**

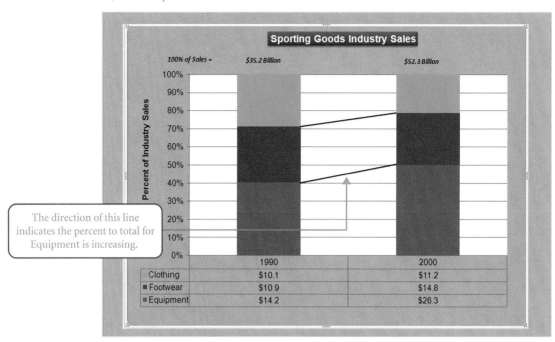

The direction of this line indicates the percent to total for Equipment is increasing.

>> Formatting Charts

The purpose of this workshop is to review the techniques used to format the appearance of charts. I will be demonstrating the tasks in this workshop in the **Formatting Charts** and **Adding Annotations and Objects to Charts** videos. Open the file named ib_e05_formattingcharts before starting the following tasks. Try completing these tasks on your own and then watch both videos.

1. **Formatting Titles and Legends (Video: Formatting Charts)**
   a. Activate the worksheet named Column Chart.
   b. Activate the chart title by clicking it once.
   c. Click the **Format** tab in the **Chart Tools** section on the Ribbon. Then select the "Intense Effect-Accent 6" **Shape Styles** icon. This option has an orange background with white letters. You will have to click the scroll down arrow to find this option.
   d. Using the right-click method, change the font size of the chart title to 20 points and italicize the text.
   e. Activate the Legend. Using either the right-click method or the format icons in the **Home** tab on the Ribbon, increase the font size to 14 points; then bold and italicize the text.
   f. Click the **Shape Outline** icon in the **Format** tab on the Ribbon. Place the cursor over the **Weight** option and select the **1 pt** line weight. Then click the **Shape Outline** icon again and select the color black.
   g. Click the top edge of the legend and move it up so the top of the legend is aligned with the 35,000 grid line. Make sure you do not click and drag on a sizing handle to move the legend.

h. Click the X-axis title and increase the font size to 14 points.

i. Click the Y-axis title and increase the font size to 14 points.

2. **Formatting the Plot Area and Data Series (Video: Formatting Charts)**

   a. Activate the plot area of the column chart.

   b. Click the **Format** tab on the Ribbon.

   c. Click the **Shape Fill** icon and select the white color in the upper-left side of the palette.

   d. Click the **Shape Outline** icon, place the cursor over the **Weight** option, and click the **1 ½ pt** line weight. Then click the **Shape Outline** icon again and select the color black.

   e. Activate the Compact data series by clicking one of the green bars.

   f. Click the **Shape Fill** icon in the **Format** tab and select the color yellow.

   g. Activate the Compact Hybrid data series by clicking one of the purple bars.

   h. Click the **Shape Fill** icon in the **Format** tab and select the color light green.

3. **Formatting the X- and Y-Axes Labels (Video: Formatting Charts)**

   a. Click any of the years on the X-axis.

   b. Change the font size to 12 points.

   c. Click any sales value on the Y-axis.

   d. Change the font size to 12 points.

4. **Annotations and Objects (Video: Adding Annotations and Objects to Charts)**

   a. Activate the worksheet named Stacked Column Chart.

   b. Activate the chart.

   c. Click the **Layout** tab and then click the **Text Box** icon.

   d. Click and drag the shape of a rectangle above the Y-axis.

   e. Place the cursor over one of the sizing handles on the text box and click the right mouse button. Then select the **Edit Text** option.

   f. Type the description **100% of Sales =**. Then highlight this description, right click, and change the font size to 12. Then bold and italicize the text.

   g. Click anywhere in the chart area to deactivate the text box.

   h. Click the **Layout** tab and then click the **Text Box** icon to add a second text box.

   i. Click and drag the shape of a rectangle above the 1990 bar.

   j. Place the cursor over one of the sizing handles on the text box and click the right mouse button. Then select the **Edit Text** option.

   k. Type the description **$35.2 Billion**. Then highlight this description, right click, and change the font size to 12. Then bold and italicize the text.

   l. Click anywhere in the chart area to deactivate the text box.

   m. Click the **Layout** tab and then click the **Text Box** icon.

   n. Click and drag the shape of a rectangle above the year 2000 bar.

   o. Place the cursor over one of the sizing handles on the text box and click the right mouse button. Then select the **Edit Text** option.

p. Type the description **$52.3 Billion**. Then highlight this description, right click, and change the font size to 12. Then bold and italicize the text.

q. Click anywhere in the chart area to deactivate the text box.

r. Click the **Layout** tab and then click the **Shapes** icon.

s. Click the first **Line** option in the Lines category of shapes.

t. Place the cursor at the top right of the blue stack of the 1990 bar. Then click and drag to the top left of the blue stack in the year 2000 bar.

u. Click the **Shape Outline** icon and select the color black. Then click the **Shape Outline** icon again and select the **1 ½ pt** line weight.

v. Click anywhere in the chart area to deactivate the line.

w. Click the **Layout** tab and then click the **Shapes** icon. Select the first **Line** option in the Lines category of shapes.

x. Place the cursor at the top right of the red stack of the 1990 bar. Then click and drag to the top left of the red stack in the year 2000 bar.

y. Click the **Shape Outline** icon and select the color black. Then click the **Shape Outline** icon again and select the **1 ½ pt** line weight.

z. Click anywhere in the chart area to deactivate the line.

aa. Save and close the file.

<table>
<tr><td>**EXERCISE**
Why Do I Need This?</td></tr>
</table>

» Charting Stocks versus the Dow Jones Industrial Average

Formatting enhancements are often needed when a chart is initially created. In fields such as consulting, adding formatting enhancements to charts can be a critical component to running a successful client meeting. In addition, the formatting enhancements made to a chart are often a sign of a consulting firm's professionalism and attention to detail.

Exercise

The purpose of this exercise is to enhance the appearance of a chart that has been created for a business presentation. The purpose of the chart is to compare the change in a company's stock price to the change in the adjusted closing average of the Dow Jones Industrial Average. Open the file named ib_e05_stockpricecomparison. The following tasks will require you to add several formatting features to this chart:

1. Add the title **Change in Market Value by Month** to the chart. Add the following formatting enhancements:

   a. Font size should be 18 points, bold, and italic.

   b. Add a white fill by selecting the color white from the **Shape Fill** icon.

   c. Add a black line around the title with a 1-point weight.

   d. Add a shadow. You do this by clicking the **Shape Effects** icon, placing the cursor over the **Shadow** option, and selecting the **Offset Diagonal Bottom Right** option, which is the first option in the Outer set of options.

2. Add the title **Change in Value Year to Date** for the Y-axis. Apply the same formatting features that are listed in number 1 except make the font size 14 points instead of 18. Move the title to the left to create space between the title and the percentages along the Y-axis.

3. Format the Legend by applying the same formatting features listed in step 1. Then adjust the size of the legend so all the text is visible and move it so it is centered at the bottom of the chart.

4. Activate the Chart Area and change the color to light green by clicking the **Shape Fill** icon. Then click the **Shape Fill** icon again and place the cursor over the **Gradient** option. Select the **From Corner** option. This is the fourth option in the first row of the Dark Variations set of gradients.

5. Format the percentages along the Y-axis to a 12-point font size and change the color to white. Because this side of the chart is dark green, a white font will make the percentages easier to read.

6. Format the months along the X-axis to a 12-point font size.

7. Add a 2 ¼ point black line around the perimeter of the plot area.

8. Activate the "DJIA" data series. Change the color of the line to dark red and increase the weight of the line to 2 ¼ points. You can apply both formatting features by using the **Shape Outline** icon. This will make it easier to see the Dow Jones Industrial Average trend against the white background of the plot area.

9. Activate the "Our Company" data series. Change the color of the line to dark blue and increase the weight of the line to 2 ¼ points. This will make it easier to see the trend of the stock price for the managers of this company.

10. Add a text box named **Fed Rate Increase in March** to the plot area of the chart. Notice that the DJIA trend drops significantly from February to March. This text box will tell the reader that this was a key factor contributing to the decline in the market. Therefore, place this text box by the month of March at the 2% grid line and apply the following formats:
    a. The text should have a font size of 12 points, bold, and italic.
    b. The fill color should be orange.
    c. The perimeter should have a black line with a 1-point weight.
    d. Adjust the size of the text box so all the text is visible.

11. Add a second text box named **Earnings Decrease Announced in Sept** to the plot area of the chart. Notice that the trend for the company's stock drops significantly from September to December. This text box will explain why this decline occurred. Therefore, place this text box by the month of September at the 6% grid line and apply the same formats listed in step 10.

12. Save and close your file.

>> What's Wrong with This Spreadsheet?

Problem

You just finished creating a chart for a strategy meeting and have asked one of the interns in the department to make a few formatting enhancements to help highlight the product trends. After several hours, the intern comes to you in a panic asking for help. He explains that he tried to make several of the formatting enhancements you requested but is afraid he may have ruined the chart. He admits he was rushing to get this job done and thinks the entire chart will have to be deleted and re-created. The intern mentions the following points in his discussion with you:

1. I'm not sure what happened, but one of the bars seems to have disappeared. I was trying to change the color of the bars for the Casual Knits category to purple. I though this might look better. However, the bar for 2007 has mysteriously disappeared.

2. The other thing that happened was a bunch of the bars got cut off. I was using the dialog box to format the Y-axis, and then the phone rang. I went to pick up the phone and dropped it on my keyboard. I looked at the screen and a bunch of the bars were cut off.

3. Finally, I added the data labels to each bar like you asked, but they look terrible. A lot of the numbers are running into each other, and you really can't see them that well.

Exercise

The chart the intern was working on is named ib_e05_chartchaos. Open this file and look at the Product Chart. Consider the following points:

1. Did the Casual Knits bar in the year 2007 really disappear? Can an individual bar be formatted on a column chart?
2. Why are some of the bars cut off at the top of the chart? Look at the worksheet named Sales Data. What is the highest unit sales value? Compare this to the highest sales value along the Y-axis. How could the values or scale for the Y-axis change?
3. In the years 2007 and 2008, several data labels merged together. Can an individual data label be formatted or moved?

What's wrong with this chart? Write a short answer for each of the points listed here. Then fix the formatting problems for the Product Chart. In addition, add any other formatting enhancements that you think will make the chart easier to read.

≫ Advanced Chart Options

This section will illustrate techniques that utilize Excel's dynamic capabilities. As long as you use cell locations to define the source data, a chart will adjust itself automatically when the source data changes. Therefore, charts are useful for visually studying data trends when certain inputs are changed. This capability is helpful in economic fields that study changes in consumer demand or market supplies. This section will also illustrate how charts are created when data is not contained in adjacent columns and rows. Finally, this section will close with an illustration on how you can paste Excel charts into Word documents when writing reports or PowerPoint slides for presentations.

Defining the X- and Y-Axes Manually

Throughout this chapter so far, all the examples and exercises have utilized the method in which Excel automatically assigns values and labels to the X- and Y-axes. This method is used when the data you are displaying on a chart exists in a contiguous range of cells. However, in business, you will frequently be working with data that is not in a continuous range. For example, look at the column chart displayed in Figure 5.38. The purpose of this chart is to show the sales values in column C for each item listed in column A. However, notice that column B contains descriptive information that is not related to the sales of each item. When the range A2:C8 is highlighted to create the column chart, the data in column B distorts the labels along the X-axis.

Figure 5.38 | **Distorted Column Chart**

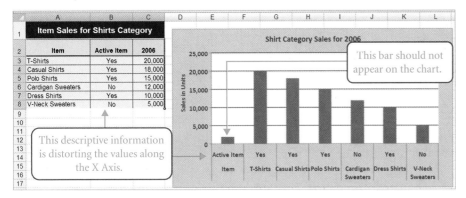

To create a basic column chart using the data in Figure 5.38, you will manually define the labels shown on the X-axis and the values shown on the Y-axis. As a result, instead of highlighting a range of cells and selecting a chart type in the **Insert** tab, you will activate a blank cell. This will produce a blank chart where the data series, as well as the values and labels assigned to the X- and Y-axes, can be defined manually. You accomplish this method as follows:

- Activate any blank cell that is at least two columns to the right or two rows below the data shown in Figure 5.38. You must leave at least one blank column or one blank row between the activated cell and the data on your worksheet. For this example, cell F2 is activated.

- Click the **Insert** tab, click the **Column** icon, and select the **Clustered Column** chart format. This will add a blank column chart to the worksheet, as shown in Figure 5.39.

- In the **Design** tab of the **Chart Tools** section on the Ribbon, click the **Select Data** icon. This will open the **Select Data Source** dialog box, as shown in Figure 5.40.

Figure 5.39 shows the appearance of a blank column chart and the **Select Data** icon, which is used to open the **Select Data Source** dialog box shown in Figure 5.40. Using the **Select Data Source** dialog box, you can define data series and the values and labels that are assigned to the X- and Y-axes. For a column chart, you use the left side of the **Select Data Source** dialog box to add data series or bars to the chart, which also adds values to the Y-axes and creates the legend. On the right side of the **Select Data Source** dialog box, you can define the range of cells that will be used to display the labels along the X-, or horizontal, axis.

Figure 5.39 | **Inserting a Blank Column Chart**

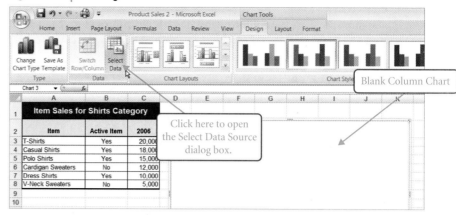

Figure 5.40 | **Select Data Source Dialog Box**

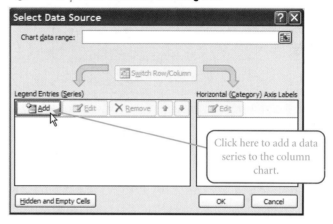

To complete the blank chart shown in Figure 5.39, you must define the data series and the labels for the X-, or horizontal, axis. You accomplish this as follows:

- Click the **Add** button on the left side of the **Select Data Source** dialog box under the **Legend Entries (Series)** heading. This will open the **Edit Series** dialog box (see Figure 5.41). For a column chart, a data series represents the bars that appear in the plot area of the chart. Therefore, the settings in the **Edit Series** dialog box will define how the bars are classified in the legend and assign values to the Y-, or vertical, axis.

- Click the range finder next to the **Series name** input box, highlight cell C2, and press the **Enter** key. This will add one data series to the column chart with the name "2006" in the legend.

- Click the range finder next to the **Series values** input box, highlight the range C3:C8, and press the **Enter** key. This will define the values for the 2006 data series. It is important to note that a bar will appear on the chart for every cell in the range C3:C8. As a result, six bars will appear on the column chart—one for each item in column A of the worksheet.

- Click the **OK** button at the bottom of the **Edit Series** dialog box after defining the Series values.

- Click the **Edit** button on the right side of the **Edit Data Source** dialog box. This will open the **Axis Labels** dialog box (see Figure 5.42).

- Click the range finder next to the **Axis Label Range** input box, highlight the range A3:A8, and press the **Enter** key. As previously mentioned, six bars will be added to the chart for each item in column A. Therefore, the X-, or horizontal, axis labels are defined using the descriptions in the range A3:A8.

- Click the **OK** button on the **Axis Labels** dialog box and then click the **OK** button on the **Select Data Source** dialog box.

Figure 5.41 shows the settings in the **Edit Series** dialog box. Notice that the description in the cell location used to define the Series name appears in the legend. Figure 5.42 shows the **Axis Labels** dialog box. The descriptions in the range of cells that appear in the input box will appear on the X-axis.

Figure 5.41 | **Edit Series Dialog Box**

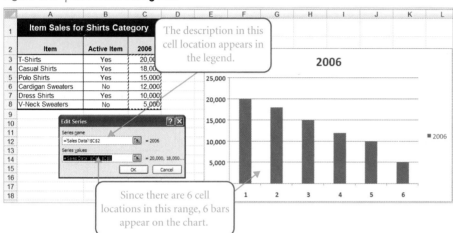

COMMON MISTAKES | Defining a Series Name

When using the **Edit Series** dialog box to add a data series to a chart, be sure to use only one cell location for the **Series name** input box. Highlighting a range of cells for this input box will distort your chart. You can also define the Series name by typing a description; however, you must place your description in quotation marks.

Figure 5.42 | **Axis Labels Dialog Box**

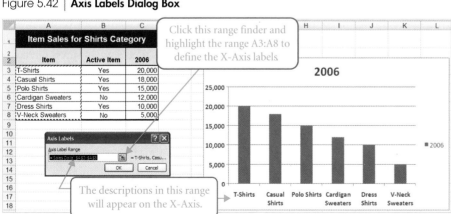

Figure 5.43 shows the final settings in the **Select Data Source** dialog box. Figure 5.44 shows the final column chart that was created by manually defining the data series, and the values and labels along the X- and Y-axes. In addition, several formatting enhancements were added to the chart. Notice that the legend was removed because the chart represents only one year's worth of data. If this chart displayed several years' worth of data, such as the chart shown in Figure 5.30, a data series would be added for each item in column A, and the years would be used as labels for the X-axis. This would require you to click the **Add** button in Figure 5.43 six times and set the **Edit Series** dialog box for each of the six items in column A in Figure 5.44.

>> *Quick Reference*

Manually Defining a Column Chart

1. Activate a blank cell on a worksheet. A blank column or a blank row must appear between the data on a worksheet and the blank cell that is activated.

2. Select a chart type from the **Insert** tab on the Ribbon.

3. Select a chart format.

4. With the blank chart activated, click the **Select Data** icon in the **Design** tab on the Ribbon.

5. Click the **Add** button on the left side of the **Select Data Source** dialog box to add a data series.

6. Define the Series name in the **Edit Series** dialog box with one cell location or type a name in quotation marks.

7. Define the Series values with a range of cells.

8. Click the **OK** button to close the **Edit Series** dialog box.

9. Repeat steps 5–8 to add additional data series if needed.

10. Click the **Edit** button on the right side of the **Select Data Source** dialog box.

11. Use a range of cells to define the Axis Label Range. The descriptions in this cell range will be used for the X-axis labels.

12. Click the **OK** button on the **Axis Labels** dialog box.

13. Click the **OK** button on the **Select Data Source** dialog box.

Figure 5.43 | **Final Settings in the Select Data Source Dialog Box**

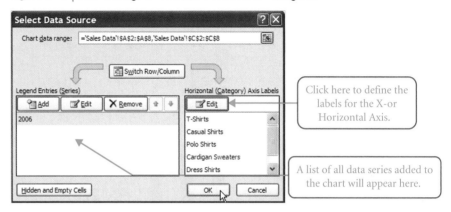

Figure 5.44 | **Final Column Chart Including Format Enhancements**

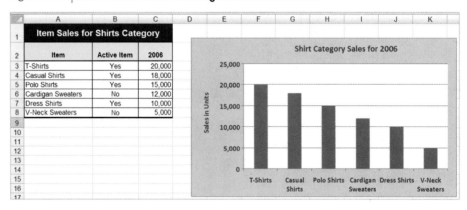

The Scatter Plot Chart

Throughout this text you have seen the benefits of Excel's cell referencing capabilities through the use of formulas and functions to complete various business objectives. Cell referencing can also play a valuable role when using charts to analyze business or economic data. That is, if the values change in the cells used to define the data series, X-axis, or Y-axis of a chart, this change will automatically be reflected in the appearance of the chart. For example, the worksheet shown in Figure 5.45 contains hypothetical price and demand data for four beverages: Coffee, Tea, Decaf Coffee, and Herbal Tea. Notice the value called the "Price Change Driver" in cell D15. This cell location is used in formulas that calculate a change in price for each week for each beverage. Therefore, if the value in D15 is changed to 5%, the price of all beverages will increase by 5% every week for each of the 10 weeks listed on the worksheet (see Figure 5.46). If the value is changed to –5%, the price for each beverage will decrease 5% every week for the 10 weeks listed on the worksheet. As the price changes for each beverage in columns B through E, another set of formulas calculates the sales demand in columns F through I. As a result, when this data is used to create a chart, if the value is changed in cell D15, all the values in the worksheet will change, which will automatically be reflected in the appearance of the chart.

Figure 5.45 | **Beverage Demand Data Worksheet**

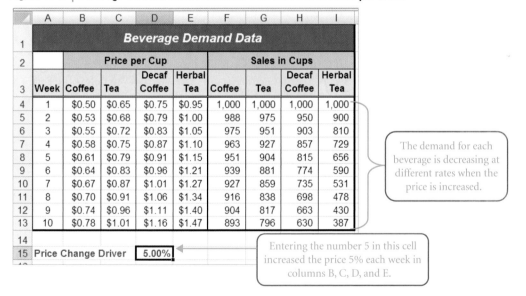

	A	B	C	D	E	F	G	H	I
1				Beverage Demand Data					
2			Price per Cup				Sales in Cups		
3	Week	Coffee	Tea	Decaf Coffee	Herbal Tea	Coffee	Tea	Decaf Coffee	Herbal Tea
4	1	$0.50	$0.65	$0.75	$0.95	1,000	1,000	1,000	1,000
5	2	$0.50	$0.65	$0.75	$0.95	1,000	1,000	1,000	1,000
6	3	$0.50	$0.65	$0.75	$0.95	1,000	1,000	1,000	1,000
7	4	$0.50	$0.65	$0.75	$0.95	1,000	1,000	1,000	1,000
8	5	$0.50	$0.65	$0.75	$0.95	1,000	1,000	1,000	1,000
9	6	$0.50	$0.65	$0.75	$0.95	1,000	1,000	1,000	1,000
10	7	$0.50	$0.65	$0.75	$0.95	1,000	1,000	1,000	1,000
11	8	$0.50	$0.65	$0.75	$0.95	1,000	1,000	1,000	1,000
12	9	$0.50	$0.65	$0.75	$0.95	1,000	1,000	1,000	1,000
13	10	$0.50	$0.65	$0.75	$0.95	1,000	1,000	1,000	1,000
14									
15	Price Change Driver		0.00%						

Hypothetical data shows 1,000 cups sold at the current price for each beverage.

Values entered in this cell will change the Price and Sales data.

Figure 5.46 | **Beverage Demand Data Worksheet with 5% Price Increase per Week**

	A	B	C	D	E	F	G	H	I
1				Beverage Demand Data					
2			Price per Cup				Sales in Cups		
3	Week	Coffee	Tea	Decaf Coffee	Herbal Tea	Coffee	Tea	Decaf Coffee	Herbal Tea
4	1	$0.50	$0.65	$0.75	$0.95	1,000	1,000	1,000	1,000
5	2	$0.53	$0.68	$0.79	$1.00	988	975	950	900
6	3	$0.55	$0.72	$0.83	$1.05	975	951	903	810
7	4	$0.58	$0.75	$0.87	$1.10	963	927	857	729
8	5	$0.61	$0.79	$0.91	$1.15	951	904	815	656
9	6	$0.64	$0.83	$0.96	$1.21	939	881	774	590
10	7	$0.67	$0.87	$1.01	$1.27	927	859	735	531
11	8	$0.70	$0.91	$1.06	$1.34	916	838	698	478
12	9	$0.74	$0.96	$1.11	$1.40	904	817	663	430
13	10	$0.78	$1.01	$1.16	$1.47	893	796	630	387
14									
15	Price Change Driver		5.00%						

The demand for each beverage is decreasing at different rates when the price is increased.

Entering the number 5 in this cell increased the price 5% each week in columns B, C, D, and E.

Looking at Figure 5.46, you can see that the formulas calculating the Sales in Cups for each beverage are based on fundamental economic principles. That is, as the Price per Cup for each beverage increases in columns B through E, the Sales in Cups, or quantity demanded, decrease in columns F through I. However, a key question that most business managers try to answer is how much will demand increase or decrease when the price of a product is changed? To help answer this question, the next example constructs a scatter plot chart using the data from Figure 5.45. A scatter plot chart will place a marker for each beverage in the plot area based on its price and quantity demanded. Therefore, for each data series, or each beverage, the value for both the Y-axis and X-axis must be defined. This example is different from the charts that were demonstrated in the first two sections of this chapter; in those examples, values were assigned only to the Y-axis and labels were assigned to the X-axis (i.e., months, product category). Furthermore, the values for the X- and Y-axes in Figure 5.45 are not in a continuous range. Therefore, you must use the method of manually defining the data series, X-axis and Y-axis, that was demonstrated in the preceding section. The following points explain how this is accomplished:

- Activate cell K5, which is a blank cell. This will create a blank chart on the worksheet.
- Click the **Scatter** icon in the **Insert** tab on the Ribbon.
- Select the **Scatter with Straight Lines and Markers** format option. This will create a chart that has the visual appearance of a line chart with markers.
- Click the **Select Data** icon in the **Design** tab to open the **Select Data Source** dialog box.
- Click the **Add** button in the **Select Data Source** dialog box to add the first data series, which is Coffee. Notice that when the **Edit Series** dialog box opens, it has input boxes for both the X-axis and Y-axis values (see Figure 5.47).
- Click the range finder next to **Series name**, highlight cell B3, and press the **Enter** key. Cell B3 contains the word *Coffee*, which will appear in the legend to describe this data series.
- Click the range finder next to **Series X values**, highlight the range F4:F13, and press the **Enter** key. As mentioned, the goal of this chart is to show the quantity demanded, or Sales in Cups on the X-axis and the Price per Cup on the Y-axis. The range F4:F13 contains the quantity demanded for Coffee.
- Click the range finder next to **Series Y values**, highlight the range B4:B13, and press the **Enter** key. This range contains the price of Coffee for each of the 10 weeks listed in column B.
- Click the **OK** button to close the **Edit Series** dialog box. Then click the **Add** button in the **Select Data Source** dialog box to add the next data series, which is "Tea."
- Add the "Tea, Decaf Coffee, and Herbal Tea" data series using the same method described for Coffee. For each data series, use "Sales in Cups" to define the Series X values and Price per Cup to define the Series Y values.
- Click the **OK** button at the bottom of the **Select Data Source** dialog box to complete the chart.

Figure 5.47 shows the completed **Edit Series** dialog box for the Coffee data series. Notice that it has input boxes for defining both the X- and Y-axes values. In addition, as you define a data series, you will see a sample of the values appear on the right side of the **Edit Series** dialog box as well as on the chart itself.

Figure 5.47 | Edit Series Dialog Box for Scatter Plot Chart

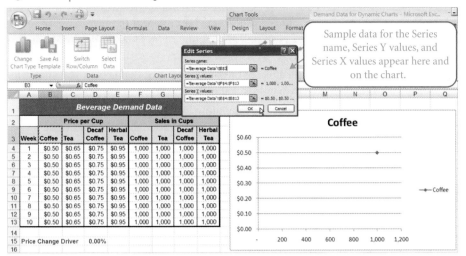

Figure 5.48 shows the completed **Select Data Source** dialog box after adding and defining each data series as shown in Figure 5.47. The name of each data series is listed on the left side of the **Select Data Source** dialog box. Notice that a unique marker is displayed for each data series, or beverage, in the plot area of the chart.

Figure 5.48 | Final Settings in the Edit Data Source Dialog Box

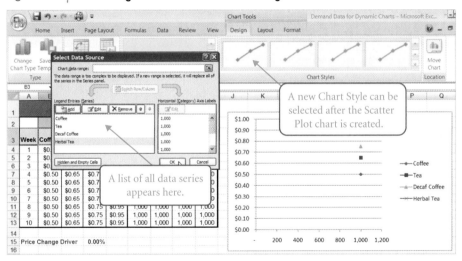

To complete the chart in Figure 5.48, several formatting techniques are applied such as adding titles, adjusting font sizes, and changing the color of the chart area. However, the most important formatting adjustment is fixing the scale of both the X- and Y-axes. The goal of this example is to show how the appearance of the chart changes when the formulas in the worksheet produce new outputs. Seeing how the data series changes, or moves, on the chart will provide insights as to how significant the Sales per Cup will change when the price is changed. However, the scale of the X- and Y-axes will constantly readjust when the data is changed, making it impossible to accurately read any data movements. Therefore, the scale of the X- and Y-axes must be fixed. You accomplish this as follows:

- Activate the Y-axis.

- Click the **Format** tab and then click the **Format Selection** icon. This will open the **Format Axis** dialog box, which was originally shown in Figure 5.29.

- In the **Axis Options** section, click the **Fixed** option next to the **Minimum** setting and type the number **.40** in the input box to the right. This will fix the **Minimum** value on the Y-axis at .40. Then click the **Fixed** option next to the **Maximum** setting and type the number **1.80** in the box to the right. This will fix the **Maximum** value of the Y-axis at 1.80.

- Click the **Close** button at the bottom of the **Format Axis** dialog box. Then activate the X-axis and open the **Format Axis** dialog box again.

- Use the same method for fixing the **Maximum** and **Minimum** values for the X-axis. The **Maximum** value should be set to 1,100 and the **Minimum** value should be set to 200.

Figure 5.49 shows the final scatter plot chart with all formatting enhancements added.

Figure 5.49 | **Final Scatter Plot Chart**

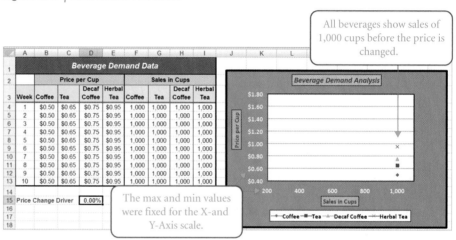

Figures 5.50, 5.51, and 5.52 illustrate how the data series representing each of the four beverages moves on the chart when cell D15 is set to 1, 3, and 5%. After examining each of these three figures, a business manager would be able to see how significant the change in sales is as the price is increased. For example, notice in Figure 5.50 that the line for Herbal Tea extends farthest to the left compared to the other beverages when the price is increased by 1% per week for 10 weeks. This suggests that the quantity demanded for Herbal Tea is very sensitive to increases in price, assuming this data represents industrywide changes in price and quantity demanded. Conversely, the line for Coffee does not move nearly as far to the left because sales per cup are not significantly declining when the price is increased.

Figure 5.50 | **Sales in Cups When Price Is Increased 1%**

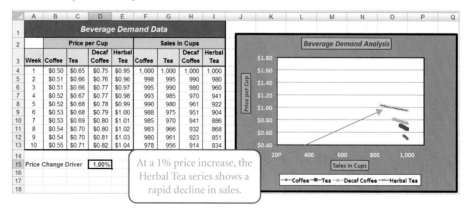

Figure 5.51 | Sales in Cups When Price Is Increased 3%

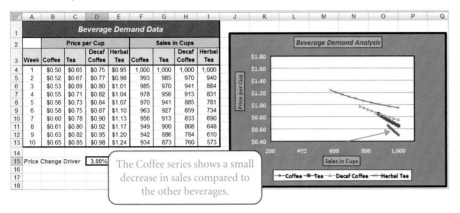

Figure 5.52 | Sales in Cups When Price Is Increased 5%

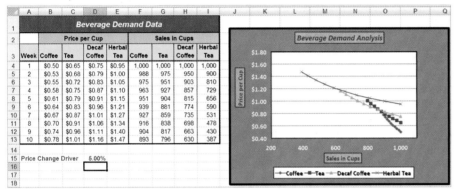

Pasting Charts into PowerPoint and Word

Excel charts are frequently added to PowerPoint slides or Word documents for business presentations and reports. This section will demonstrate how you can copy and paste Excel charts into either a PowerPoint slide or Word document.

Figure 5.53 shows a PowerPoint slide that could be used by a business manager who is presenting the results of the column chart shown in Figure 5.30. The following steps explain how to copy and paste this chart into this slide:

- Open both the PowerPoint file and the Excel file containing the column chart.
- Activate the Excel file by clicking it in the taskbar at the bottom of the screen (see Figure 5.54).
- Activate the column chart and click the **Copy** icon.
- Activate the PowerPoint file by clicking it in the taskbar at the bottom of the screen.
- Select the **Paste Special** option in the **Paste** icon in **Home** tab on the Ribbon in the PowerPoint file. This will open the **Paste Special** dialog box.
- Select the **Picture (Enhanced Metafile)** option in the **Paste Special** dialog box and click the **OK** button. The chart will appear in the slide.
- Use the sizing handles on the chart to change the size of the chart and click and drag the chart to reposition on the slide if necessary.

>> **Quick Reference**

Scatter Plot Charts

1. Activate a blank cell on a worksheet. A blank column or a blank row must appear between the data on a worksheet and the blank cell that is activated.
2. Click the **Scatter** icon in the **Insert** tab on the Ribbon.
3. Select a chart format.
4. With the blank chart activated, click the **Select Data** icon in the **Design** tab on the Ribbon.
5. Click the **Add** button on the left side of the **Select Data Source** dialog box to add a data series.
6. Define the Series name in the **Edit Series** dialog box with one cell location or type a name in quotation marks.
7. Define the X Series values with a range of cells.
8. Define the Y Series values with a range of cells.
9. Click the **OK** button to close the **Edit Series** dialog box.
10. Repeat steps 5–9 to add additional data series if needed.
11. Click the **OK** button on the **Select Data Source** dialog box.

Figure 5.53 | **View of a PowerPoint Slide**

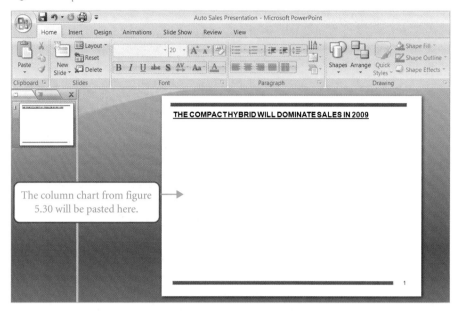

Figure 5.54 shows the **Paste Special** dialog box that is opened by clicking the down arrow of the **Paste** icon and selecting **Paste Special**. The chart will appear in the slide after you select the **Picture (Enhanced Metafile)** option and click the **OK** button.

Figure 5.54 | **Paste Special Dialog Box for Pasting a Chart**

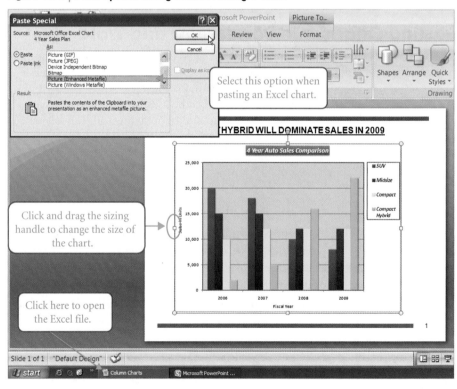

Figure 5.55 shows the final PowerPoint slide with the Excel chart. Notice that the chart was repositioned on the slide to make room for the triangle and text box.

Figure 5.55 | **Final PowerPoint Slide**

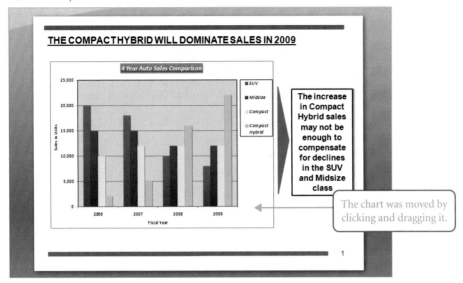

Figure 5.56 shows an example of pasting the 100% Stacked Column chart shown in Figure 5.37 into a Word document. This business research paper example demonstrates the trends in the Sporting Goods industry. The method for pasting this chart into the Word document is identical to the method illustrated for pasting a chart into a PowerPoint slide. After copying the chart in an Excel file, place the cursor in your Word document where you want the chart to appear. Then open the **Paste Special** dialog box and select the **Picture (Enhanced Metafile)** option.

Figure 5.56 | **Excel Chart Pasted into a Word Document**

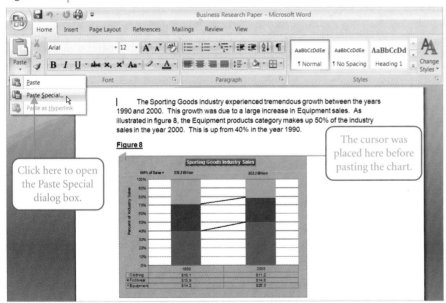

>> **Quick Reference**

Pasting Charts into PowerPoint and Word

1. Activate a chart in an Excel file and click the **Copy** icon.

2. Open a PowerPoint file to a slide where the chart should appear. For a Word document, place the cursor where the chart should appear.

3. Click the **Home** tab in the Ribbon.

4. Click the down arrow below the **Paste** icon.

5. Select the **Paste Special** option to open the **Paste Special** dialog box.

6. Select the **Picture (Enhanced Metafile)** option and click the **OK** button in the **Paste Special** dialog box.

7. Adjust the size of the chart by clicking and dragging the sizing handles as needed.

≫Scatter Plot Charts

The purpose of this workshop is to review the construction of scatter plot charts. I will be demonstrating the tasks in this workshop on the video named **Scatter Plot Charts**. You will need to open the file named ib_e05_beveragedemandanalysis before starting this workshop. Try completing the following tasks on your own and then watch the video.

1. **Creating a Scatter Plot Chart (Video: Scatter Plot Charts)**

   a. Activate cell L1 on the worksheet named Beverage Data.

   b. Click the **Scatter** icon in the **Insert** tab on the Ribbon. Then select the **Scatter with Straight Lines and Markers** format option.

   c. Click and drag the frame of the blank chart so the upper-left corner is in cell J1.

   d. Click the **Select Data** icon in the **Design** tab on the Ribbon.

   e. Click the **Add** button to add the "Coffee" data series to the chart. Use the range finder to define the following components of the **Edit Series** dialog box:
      i. **Series name**: B3
      ii. **Series X Values**: F4:F13
      iii. **Series Y Values**: B4:B13

   f. Click the **OK** button to go back to the **Select Data Source** dialog box.

   g. Click the **Add** button to add the "Tea" data series to the chart. Use the range finder to define the following components of the **Edit Series** dialog box:
      i. **Series name**: C3
      ii. **Series X Values**: G4:G13
      iii. **Series Y Values**: C4:C13

   h. Click the **OK** button to go back to the **Select Data Source** dialog box.

   i. Click the **Add** button to add the "Decaf Coffee" data series to the chart. Use the range finder to define the following components of the **Edit Series** dialog box:
      i. **Series name**: D3
      ii. **Series X Values**: H4:H13
      iii. **Series Y Values**: D4:D13

   j. Click the **OK** button to go back to the **Select Data Source** dialog box.

   k. Click the **Add** button to add the "Herbal Tea" data series to the chart. Use the range finder to define the following components of the **Edit Series** dialog box:
      i. **Series name**: E3
      ii. **Series X Values**: I4:I13
      iii. **Series Y Values**: E4:E13

   l. Click the **OK** button at the bottom of the **Edit Series** dialog box and then click the **OK** button at the bottom of the **Select Data Source** dialog box.

   m. Select the **Style 18 Chart Styles** icon in the **Design** tab on the Ribbon.

   n. Click the **Legend** icon in the **Layout** tab and select the **Show Legend at Bottom** option.

o. Add the chart title **Beverage Demand Analysis**. Use the **Above chart** option.

p. Add the title **Price per Cup** to the Y-axis.

q. Add the title **Sales in Cups** to the X-axis.

2. Formatting (Video: Scatter Plot Charts)

a. Center the title over the middle of the chart and then center the legend at the bottom of the chart.

b. Format the chart title with a 12-point font, bold, italics, orange background, and black outline with a 1-point weight.

c. Format the legend with a 10-point font, bold, white background, and black outline with a 1-point weight.

d. Create space between the left side of the plot area and the Y-axis title. Decrease the plot area to the right and move the Y-axis title to the left.

e. Make the same formatting enhancements to the X- and Y-axes titles as the chart title, except keep the font size at 10 points.

f. Change the color of the chart area to green.

g. Change the color of the Y-axis and X-axis values to white.

3. Fixing the Scale for the X- and Y-Axes (Video: Scatter Plot Charts)

a. Click anywhere on the Y-axis and click the **Format Selection** icon in the **Format** tab on the Ribbon.

b. Set the **Minimum** and **Maximum** options to **Fixed**. Then type the following values in the input box next to each option:
   i. **Minimum**: .40
   ii. **Maximum**: 1.80

c. Click the **Close** button at the bottom of the **Format Axis** dialog box.

d. Click anywhere on the X-axis and click the **Format Selection** icon in the **Format** tab on the Ribbon.

e. Set the **Minimum** and **Maximum** options to **Fixed**. Then type the following values in the input box next to each option:
   i. **Minimum**: 200
   ii. **Maximum**: 1100

f. Click the **Close** button at the bottom of the **Format Axis** dialog box.

g. Change the value in cell D15 to **1**. Then change it to **3**.

h. Save and close your file.

>> Pasting Charts into Word

VIDEO WORKSHOP

The purpose of this workshop is to demonstrate the method of pasting Excel charts into a Word document. I will be demonstrating the tasks in this workshop in the video named **Pasting Charts into Word**. You will need to open the Word file named ib_e05_businessplanpaper and the Excel file named ib_e05_costschart before starting this workshop. Try completing the following tasks on your own and then watch the video.

1. Inserting Charts into Word Documents (Video: Pasting Charts into Word)

a. Activate the Excel file named ib_e05_costschart.

b. Activate the pie chart named Startup Costs and copy it.

c. Activate the Word document named ib_e05_businessplanpaper and place the cursor below the **Figure 2** heading along the left margin.

d. Open the **Paste Special** dialog box by clicking the down arrow below the **Paste** icon.

e. Select the **Picture (Enhanced Metafile)** option in the **Paste Special** dialog box and click the **OK** button.

f. Select the chart and reduce the height of the pie chart to 2.5 inches using the **Height** icon in the **Format** tab on the Ribbon. This will automatically reduce the width to 4.06 inches.

g. Save and close your file.

>> Analyzing Supply and Demand

Studying changes in supply and demand is a common area of research for professional economists and business analysts. Changes in supply and demand can impact decisions such as product pricing, entry into new markets, exiting existing markets, increasing product lines, or decreasing product lines. Having the ability to visually display these trends can not only serve as a powerful presentation tool, but can also serve as a powerful analytical tool.

Exercise

The purpose of this exercise is to create a supply and demand chart using a scatter plot chart. In addition, this exercise will demonstrate how a change in price impacts the quantity supplied and the quantity demanded for a hypothetical industry. Your goal will be to change the price to identify where the demand and supply lines intersect, which is also known as *reaching equilibrium*. This data can be found in the file named ib_e05_supplyanddemand. Open this file before working on the following tasks:

1. Type the number **10** into cell C15. Note the price in cell B12 by typing it into a blank cell on the worksheet or jot it down on a piece of paper. You will need to know this number later in the exercise.

2. Type the number **−10** into cell C15. Note the quantity value in cell D12 by typing it into another blank cell on the worksheet or jot it down on a piece of paper. You will need to know this number later in the exercise.

3. Type the number **0** into cell C15. Then activate a blank cell for the purposes of creating a blank chart.

4. Create a blank **Scatter** chart using the **Scatter with Straight Lines and Markers** format option. After creating the blank chart, move it so the upper-left corner is in cell E1.

5. Open the **Select Data Source** dialog box and add the Supply data series to the chart. The settings in the **Edit Series** dialog box should be as follows:

   a. **Series name**: Cell C2, which contains the word *Supply*.

   b. **Series X values**: The range C3:C12, which contains the quantity supplied values.

   c. **Series Y values**: The range B3:B12, which contains the price.

6. Add the Demand data series to the chart using the following details in the **Edit Series** dialog box:

   a. **Series name**: Cell D2, which contains the word *Demand*.

   b. **Series X values**: The range D3:D12, which contains the quantity demand values.

   c. **Series Y values**: The range B3:B12, which contains the price.

7. Change the **Chart Style** of the chart to **Style 34**. This will change the color of the Demand data series to red and the Supply data series to blue.

8. Add the following titles to the chart:

   a. **Chart Title**: Supply and Demand for Product A

   b. **X-Axis Title**: Quantity

   c. **Y-Axis Title**: Price

9. Change the font size of the chart title to 14 points and change the font size of the X- and Y-axes titles to 12 points. Then move the Y-axis title to the left to create space between the title and Y-axis values.

10. Fix the scale of the Y-axis using the **Format Axis** dialog box. Use the number you identified in step 1 rounded *up* to the nearest dollar to set the **Maximum** value for the axis. Set the **Minimum** value of the axis to **0**.

11. Fix the scale of the X-axis using the **Format Axis** dialog box. Use the number you identified in step 2 to set the **Maximum** value for the axis. Set the **Minimum** value to **0**.

12. Type the number **3**, then **5**, and then **10** into cell C15. At what price (approximately) does the demand line intersect the supply line?

13. Enter the number **0**, then **-3**, then **-5**, and then **-10** into cell C15. Can the quantity supplied satisfy the quantity demanded at these prices?

14. Save and close your file.

≫ What's Wrong with This Spreadsheet?

Problem

A coworker in your department is trying to create a chart for a strategy presentation being held tomorrow morning. She is having difficulty creating a column chart based on the sales results contained in an Excel file and has come to you for help. Her goal is to show the change in Net Sales from the year 2006 to 2007 for each company in her worksheet. Her conversation with you includes the following points:

1. I am trying to create a basic column chart that shows the Net Sales values along the Y-axis and the name of each company on the X-axis. Because I have two years' worth of data, I thought I would use the legend to show what bar pertains to what year.

2. A friend of mine showed me this trick in which you just highlight everything on the worksheet; click that chart icon in the Ribbon, and bingo, the chart appears. I did the same exact thing as my friend, but my chart is horrible!

3. The other thing I noticed is the Public Company indicator (Column B) keeps popping up in the chart. I just want the sales data in a simple column chart. However, I guess this is more complicated than I thought!

PROBLEM & EXERCISE

Exercise

The chart your coworker tried to create is on the file named ib_e05_charttrouble. Open this file and take a look at the Chart1 chart sheet. Consider the following points:

1. What method is your coworker using to create the chart? Will this enable her to achieve her goals?
2. Why is the Public Company indicator (column B) appearing in the chart?
3. Your coworker is trying to create a column chart. Is that apparent in the chart that was attempted on the file?
4. Your coworker wants the year to be in the legend of the chart. How can this be accomplished?

What's wrong with this chart? Write a short answer to each of the points listed here. Then create a second chart in the ib_e05_charttrouble Excel file based on the requirements stated here. Apply any formatting features that you think will make the chart easier to read. The chart you create should appear in its own chart sheet.

Solution from page 532

Excel in **Practice** | Anecdote

Using charts is the key to conducting an effective progress review meeting. A well-constructed chart can explain trends, relationships, and results in a very short period time. Therefore, I converted the data calculated and evaluated in numerous Excel files to a few charts, pasted them into PowerPoint slides, and presented them at progress review meetings. Constructing charts this way not only increased the efficiency of the meetings, but also demonstrated a professional standard that my clients often appreciated.

Assignment

1. The file named ib_e05_clientresearchdata contains data for a meeting with the executives of a major corporation.

2. Create a chart that will best display the sales trend by region in the Regional Sales worksheet. This chart should demonstrate how the overall sales of the company have shifted between the regions.

3. Use any annotations, objects, and formatting techniques to highlight changes in the company's sales by region. Note that the total sales for the company by year are in row 8 of the worksheet. Your chart must show these total sales results.

4. Create a PowerPoint slide with the title **Region 4 Provides Future Growth**. Display the chart you created in this slide. This PowerPoint slide as well as the chart should have a professional appearance.

Questions for Discussion

1. Why are charts better to use in presentations as opposed to worksheets?

2. Is it possible to have too much formatting on a chart?

3. What do you need to know to create an effective chart?

The following questions are related to the concepts addressed in this chapter. There are three types of questions: Short Answer, True or False, and Fill in the Blank. If your answer to a True or False question is False, write a short explanation as to why you think the statement is not true.

1. Excel charts are usually used for displaying and analyzing _____ data.

2. How are charts used in business?

3. The _____ tab on the Ribbon is used for creating charts.

4. True or False: You must *always* highlight data on a worksheet before creating a chart.

5. What three tabs are added to the Ribbon after you create a chart?

6. After you create a chart, if the data you wanted on the X-axis appears on the Y-axis, you can use the _____ icon in the _____ tab on the Ribbon.

7. Explain when you would use a 100% Stacked Column chart instead of a pie chart.

8. What is the purpose of adding lines to a 100% Stacked Column chart?

9. A _____ chart is commonly used to display trends over time, such as stock prices or market indices.

10. A data table can be added to the bottom of a chart using the _____ icon in the _____ tab on the Ribbon.

11. Specific data values can be added to a chart by using the _____ icon in the _____ tab on the Ribbon.

12. True or False: The formatting icons in the **Home** tab cannot be used when formatting an area of a chart.

13. True or False: The data values or data table added to a chart cannot be formatted.

14. Explain when you would need to use the **Format Axis** dialog box when formatting either the X- or Y-axis.

15. How would you change the color of one individual bar on a column chart?

16. The _____ icon in the _____ tab is used for adding annotations to a chart.

17. Lines and arrows can be added to a chart by clicking the _____ icon in the _____ tab on the Ribbon.

18. True or False: A **Format** dialog box can be opened for any area of the chart by activating that area, right clicking, and selecting the appropriate command.

19. Explain why you would want to manually define the data series, X-axis values, and Y-axis values for a chart.

20. True or False: For a column chart, both the X and Y series values can be defined for each data series added to the chart.

21. True or False: Once a chart is created, it will never change even if the data used to create it changes.

22. What chart would you need to use if you wanted to define X-axis and Y-axis values for each data series.

23. For you to see data moving on a chart, it is best to use the _____ of the X- and Y-axes.

24. What option in the **Paste Special** dialog box should you use when pasting charts into a Word or PowerPoint file?

25. True or False: When you are pasting a chart into a Word file, the chart will always appear in the upper-left corner of the page that is currently visible on the screen.

The following exam is designed to test your ability to recognize and execute the Excel skills presented in this chapter. Read each question carefully and answer the questions in the order they are listed. You should be able to complete this exam in 60 minutes or less.

1. Open the ib_e05_skillsexam.

2. For the Global Sales worksheet, create a 100% Stacked Column chart that can be used to evaluate the sales growth of this company by country/region. The chart should include the following details:

   a. The X-axis should display the years in the range B3:E3.

   b. The Legend should display the name of the country or region from column A.

   c. The chart title above the chart should be **Global Net Sales**.

   d. The title for the Y-axis should be **Percent of Total Net Sales**.

   e. Data labels showing the sales value for each country should appear on the inside end of the bars.

   f. The chart should appear in its own chart sheet with the tab name **Global Sales Chart**.

3. Change the font size for the percentages along the Y-axis to 12 points.

4. Change the font size for the years along the X-axis to 14 points.

5. Make the following format adjustments to the Y-axis title:

   a. Add a black outline with a 1-point weight.

   b. Change the background color to blue.

   c. Change the font size to 12 and change the text color to white.

6. Make the following format adjustments to the chart title:

   a. Add a black outline with a 1-point weight.

   b. Change the background color to blue.

   c. Change the font size to 18 and change the text color to white.

7. Decrease the height of the plot area so there is approximately ½ inch of space between the top of the plot area and the chart title.

8. Make the following format adjustments to the chart legend:

   a. Add a black outline with a 1-point weight.

   b. Change the font size to 16 and bold the text.

   c. Move the legend next to the plot area.

   d. Increase the height of the legend so it is the same height as the plot area.

9. Change the color of the Europe data series to red, the Canada data series to orange, and the Asia Pacific data series to light green.

10. For all the data labels on the bars of the chart, increase the font size to 12 points.

11. Add the following annotation to the chart: **Dollars in U.S. Billions**. This annotation should appear in the upper-left corner of the chart area. Change the font size to 10 points and add italics.

12. Add the following annotation to the chart: **100% Net Sales =**. This annotation should appear next to the left border of the chart area above the Y-axis. The font size should be 10 points, bold, and italic.

13. Add an annotation to the top of each bar of the chart showing the total Net Sales for each year. The total sales for each year can be found in row 8 of the Global Sales worksheet. A dollar sign should appear in front of each number, and the font should be 12 points, bold, and italic. Make sure the number is completely visible.

14. Connect the top of each bar for the USA data series with a *black* line. Do the same for the Europe and Canada data series. Use a 1-point weight for all lines.

15. Create a line chart based on the data in the Income Summary worksheet. The chart should include the following details:

    a. The X-axis should display the years in the range B2:J2.

    b. The Legend should display the name of the income categories in column A.

    c. The chart title shouldbe **Income Summary**.

    d. The title for the Y-axis should be **Percent Change at Year End**.

    e. The legend should appear at the bottom of the chart.

    f. The chart should appear in its own chart sheet with the tab name **Income Summary Chart**.

    g. The Style of the chart should be set to the **Style 2** option.

16. Change the font size of the percentages and years on the Y- and X-axes to 12 points.

17. Make the following format adjustments to the chart legend:

    a. Add a black outline with a 1-point weight.

    b. Change the font size to 12 points and bold the text.

    c. Move the legend so that it is centered under the plot area.

18. Change the line weight for each data series to 2¼ points. Do not change the colors.

19. Fix the scale of the Y-axis as follows:

    a. Minimum: -**.08**

    b. Maximum: **.16**

    c. Major Unit: **04**

20. Open the Word document named ib_e05_internationalsalesreport.

21. Paste the **Global Sales Chart** from the Excel file into this Word document. The chart must appear below the words *Figure 1* in bold text. Leave one space between the chart and this heading.

22. Save and close both the Word file and the Excel file.

≫ Challenge Questions

The following questions are designed to test your ability to apply the Excel skills you have learned to complete a business objective. Use your knowledge of Excel as well as your creativity to answer these questions. For most questions, there are several possible ways to complete the objective.

1. If you are presenting data for an international company, what chart would you use to show the percent of sales generated by country for one year? Assume this company is operating in five countries. Create a spreadsheet showing one year of sales data for an international company by country. You can make up the countries and the sales numbers. Create a chart to present this data.

2. Pick two public companies and research the historical closing price of the stock for every month last year. In addition, research the historical adjusted closing price of the Dow Jones Industrial Average for every month last year. Record your data onto an Excel worksheet and create an appropriate chart to present this information. Your chart should have a professional appearance and should clearly highlight any significant trends displayed.

3. What chart would you use to show a two-year divisional sales trend of a corporation? The divisions of the corporation could be three different retail store chains such as clothing stores, jewelry stores, and sports equipment. Another example can be a corporation that sells different brands of candy such as a chocolate brand, a marshmallow brand, and a hard candy brand. Research the financial statement of a public company that operates several divisions such as these. Find and record two years' worth of sales data for each division on an Excel worksheet. Then create an appropriate chart to present this data and place it in a PowerPoint slide. Your chart, as well as the PowerPoint slide, should have a professional appearance.

4. The following formula is used to calculate the quantity supplied for a given market:

$Q = P \times 27 - 5$, where Q = quantity supplied and P = price

Create a spreadsheet with three columns of data. The first column should be labeled **Data Points** and should contain a list of numbers from 1 to 10. The second column should be labeled **Price**. The first value in the Price column should be **$3**. The third column should be **Quantity**. Use the supply formula shown here to calculate the data in this column. Create a formula for the remainder of the values in the Price column so that you can control how much the price increases for each of the remaining nine data points. You should be able to enter a percentage into another cell on the spreadsheet and have the Price column calculate a price each week based on the value you enter. A positive number will increase the price for every data point; a negative number will decrease the price for every data point. After constructing the spreadsheet, create an appropriate chart that can be used to study the data as the price is changed.

Chapter 6

Applying Core Competency Skills

Financial Planning and Accounting

Chapter Goals

The purpose of this chapter is to show how the skills covered in this text can be applied to two common business practices. The first is financial planning. Business managers often use Excel to develop financial strategies for improving the performance and growth of existing businesses or for starting new ones. The second is constructing a full set of financial accounting statements. Excel is a great tool for building basic accounting spreadsheets, especially when you are working on assignments for accounting courses. You can accomplish both of these critical business exercises in Excel utilizing the core competency skills you have learned in previous chapters of this text. This chapter begins by demonstrating the technique of linking data between worksheets or workbooks. Worksheets are often linked when spreadsheets for financial planning or accounting are constructed, which is why they are covered in the first section of this chapter.

>> Excel | Skill Sets

Excel in **Practice** | Anecdote

My Role as a Strategic Planning Manager

When I worked as a strategic planning manager, I was responsible for developing business plans that demonstrated the financial potential of new businesses ideas and corporate initiatives. These plans were constructed from several assumptions related to almost every aspect of the business. Assumptions could include the cost of shipping goods, expected growth in sales, change in the cost of goods sold, the number of full-time employees, the wage per employee, and so on. The decision to invest in a new business or initiative depended on the result of a net present value analysis, which showed whether an investment could provide an adequate return. I would then present the completed business plans with net present value results to the directing officers of the company, which often included both the CEO and CFO. One of the biggest challenges in preparing for these meetings was to show different scenarios regarding the potential performance of a business idea. For example, the executives would often ask questions such as "What if the business requires more employees? What if the cost of construction goes over budget? What if sales come in lower than planned?" A negative change in any of these assumptions could reduce or eliminate any potential profits. Therefore, I had to construct and present several different plans showing a worst, best, and target case scenario. Constructing so many plans and being prepared to answer any question from the directing officers appeared to be in impossible task at first.

>> Continued on page 639

Linking data between multiple worksheets or workbooks is a common technique used in financial planning and financial accounting spreadsheets. This section will demonstrate how you can use the technique of linking data to construct a sales and gross profit plan for a division of a hypothetical manufacturing company. This plan will be very similar to the one introduced in Chapter 2 (see Figure 2.39). Linking data is also commonly used with the **SUMIF** function, which will also be introduced in this section.

Linking Worksheets and Workbooks

Chapter 4 demonstrated the concept of cell referencing when working with formulas and functions on a specific worksheet. However, you can also use cell referencing to link data between two worksheets or workbooks. This is also referred to as a *3-D reference* and was first introduced in Chapter 4 in the VLookup section. You may recall that to define the **table_array** argument of the **VLookup** function you highlighted a range of cells in a second worksheet. This is essentially how data is linked from one worksheet to another. Linking data is especially valuable when constructing financial plans because business managers are typically required to show various scenarios when planning the financial goals for their area of responsibility. Since linking data uses cell references, the business manager can change values in key cell locations to produce new outputs for the formulas and functions used to create the plan.

This example demonstrates the technique of linking data by creating a sales and gross profit plan for a division in a hypothetical manufacturing company (Division B). Large companies will typically require the managing director of each division to create a comprehensive financial plan which outlines all expenses, sales, and profits that will be generated by their product line or service. For example, a large electronics manufacturer might consist of four divisions: Personal Computers, Cameras, Corporate Services, and Copy Machines. The directors for each of these divisions would be required to develop and present a financial plan to the executive officers of the company. This demonstration will focus on the sales and gross profit portion of these financial plans. Figures 6.1 through 6.3 show the data that will be used for this example. The worksheet shown in Figure 6.3 is the blank financial plan that will be completed by creating links to the worksheets shown Figure 6.1 and 6.2.

Figure 6.1 | **Financial Results LY Workbook: Results for 2006 Worksheet**

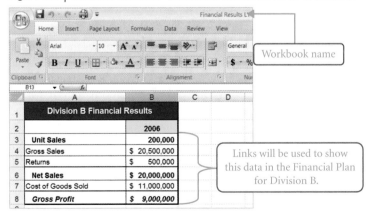

Figure 6.2 | **Division B Financial Plan Workbook: Plan Assumptions Worksheet**

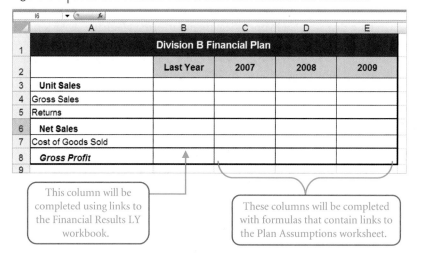

	A	B	C	D	E
1	**Division B Financial Plan Assumptions**				
2		**2007**	**2008**	**2009**	
3	Returns (Percent of Gross Sales)	2.00%	2.00%	2.00%	
4	Gross Sales Change (Percent)	10.00%	5.00%	5.00%	
5	Average Price per Item	$100.00	$102.50	$102.50	
6	Cost of Goods Sold (Percent of Gross Sales)	55.00%	55.00%	55.00%	

This data will be referenced in the formulas used to create the Financial Plan for Division B.

The Financial Plan for Division B is in this worksheet.

Plan Assumptions / Financial Plan

Figure 6.3 | **Division B Financial Plan Workbook: Financial Plan Worksheet**

	A	B	C	D	E
1	**Division B Financial Plan**				
2		**Last Year**	**2007**	**2008**	**2009**
3	**Unit Sales**				
4	Gross Sales				
5	Returns				
6	**Net Sales**				
7	Cost of Goods Sold				
8	**Gross Profit**				
9					

This column will be completed using links to the Financial Results LY workbook.

These columns will be completed with formulas that contain links to the Plan Assumptions worksheet.

As mentioned, Figure 6.3 shows the blank Financial Plan for Division B. Creating a link to the Financial Results LY workbook shown in Figure 6.1 completes the Last Year column in this worksheet. Once the link is created, if the data is changed in the Financial Results LY workbook, those changes will be reflected in the Division B Financial Plan workbook. Adjustments to last year data are rare but can happen in situations in which a company moves a product line from one division to another. The following points explain how to create this link:

- Open the Division B Financial Plan workbook and then open the Financial Results LY workbook.

- Type an equal sign in cell B3 of the Financial Plan worksheet (see Figure 6.3). This cell represents the Unit Sales for Division B last year.

- Activate the Financial Results LY workbook by clicking the workbook name in the task bar (see Figure 6.4).

- Activate cell B3 in the Results for 2006 worksheet in the Financial Results LY workbook.
- Press the **Enter** key.

Figures 6.4 and 6.5 show the setup and results of creating a link between the Division B Financial Plan and Financial Results LY workbooks. Notice in Figure 6.5 that the workbook and worksheet name precede the cell location that was used to create the link in cell B3 to show the Unit Sales for Last Year.

Figure 6.4 | **Creating a Link in the Financial Plan Worksheet**

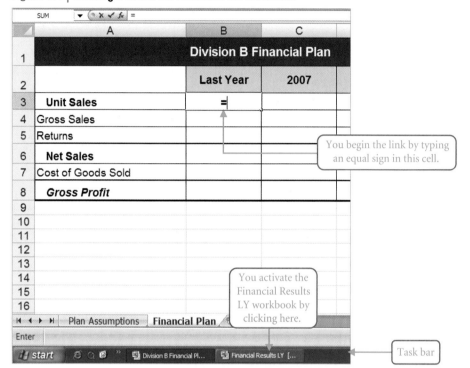

Figure 6.5 | **Results of Creating a Link in the Financial Plan Worksheet**

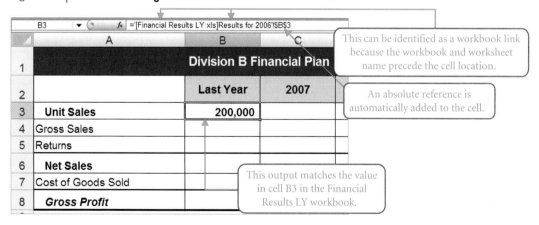

Copying the link that was created in cell B3 and pasting it to cells B4 through B8 completes the Last Year column in Figure 6.5. This example can use relative referencing to adjust the link because the financial items listed in the Financial Plan worksheet in Figure 6.5 are in the same sequence as the financial items listed in the Financial Results LY workbook in Figure 6.1. However, notice that the cell reference in the link shown in the formula bar of Figure 6.5 contains an absolute reference that must be removed before copying and pasting the link. You accomplish this by doing the following:

- Edit cell B3 in the Financial Plan worksheet to remove the absolute reference on cell B3 in the link.

- Copy cell B3 in the Financial Plan worksheet and then highlight the range B4:B8.

- Select the **Formulas** option from the **Paste** icon in the Ribbon. Using the **Formulas** option will paste the link without changing any of the formats in the worksheet.

Figure 6.6 shows the completed Last Year column in the Financial Plan worksheet. Notice that the absolute reference was removed from the link (see formula bar).

Figure 6.6 | **Completed Last Year Column in the Financial Plan Worksheet**

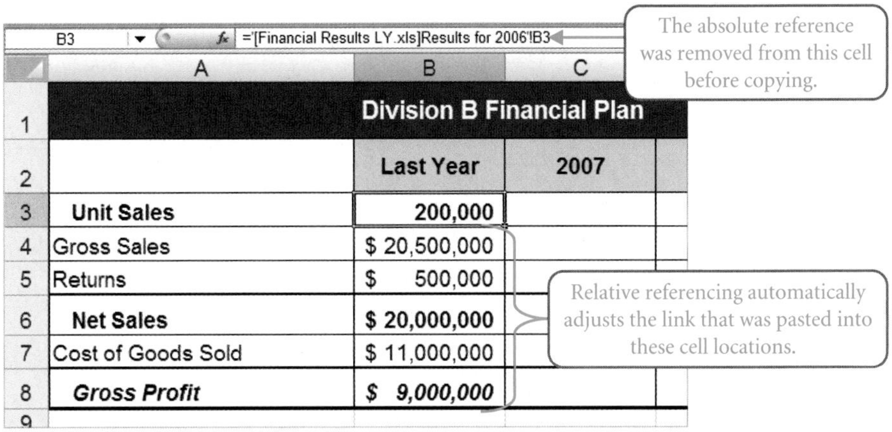

COMMON MISTAKES | Copying and Pasting Workbook Links

Excel will automatically place an absolute reference on cell references used to link data between two workbooks. Therefore, you must remove the absolute reference after creating the link if you intend to use relative referencing to automatically adjust the link when it is pasted to a new location on the worksheet.

The remaining columns in the Financial Plan worksheet will be completed using formulas that contain links to the Plan Assumptions worksheet in Figure 6.2. When developing a financial plan, business managers must make key assumptions about their business based on research and trends that are occurring in their industry and the overall economy. You will learn more about these techniques in your business courses. For example, a business manager might assume that the gross sales for his division will increase 10% next year based on current growth trends in the industry. The Plan Assumptions worksheet contains these types of assumptions and will be used to calculate data for the Financial Plan worksheet. The following points explain how data for the year 2007 (column C) is calculated in the Financial Plan worksheet:

- Activate cell C4 in the Financial Plan worksheet. Skip the Unit Sales formula for now because the Net Sales has not been calculated. That said, skipping this formula is not a requirement. You could still type the formula for Unit Sales, and a result will be produced once the Net Sales is calculated.

- Type an equal sign and the beginning of the formula B4 + B4*.

- Activate the Plan Assumptions worksheet and then activate cell B4, which contains the percent change for Gross Sales. This will place a link in the formula that will reference the value in cell B4 in the Plan Assumptions worksheet. The formula will take the Gross Sales for Last Year (cell B4) in the Financial Plan worksheet and add to it the Gross Sales from Last Year multiplied by the percent change in Gross Sales on the Plan Assumptions worksheet (this formula was covered in the Formulas workshop in Chapter 3).

- Press the **Enter** key.

Figure 6.7 shows the result of the formula calculating the Gross Sales for 2007. Notice in the formula bar that the worksheet name Plan Assumptions is enclosed in apostrophes and is followed by an exclamation point. This indicates that the formula will use the value in cell B4 in the Plan Assumptions worksheet. The first two cell references in the formula, which are also B4, are from the Financial Plan worksheet. Since these cell references are not preceded by a worksheet name, they relate to the current worksheet that contains this formula.

Figure 6.7 | **Calculating Gross Sales for 2007 in the Financial Plan Worksheet**

C4   =B4+B4*'Plan Assumptions'!B4

This cell can be identified as a link because it is preceded by the worksheet name Plan Assumptions.

	A	B	C
1		Division B Finar	
2		**Last Year**	
3	**Unit Sales**	200,000	
4	Gross Sales	$ 20,500,000	$ 22,550,000
5	Returns	$ 500,000	
6	**Net Sales**	$ 20,000,000	
7	Cost of Goods Sold	$ 11,000,000	
8	**Gross Profit**	$ 9,000,000	

This output will change if the value in cell B4 in the Plan Assumptions worksheet is changed.

The following steps explain how to create formulas to complete the data for 2007 in the Financial Plan worksheet:

- Activate cell C5. This cell will contain the planned Returns for 2007.
- Type an equal sign and the beginning of the formula C4 *.
- Activate the Plan Assumptions worksheet and then activate cell B3. This formula will multiply the Gross Sales, which was calculated in cell C4 of the Financial Plan worksheet, by the percentage in cell B3 of the Plan Assumptions worksheet.
- Press the **Enter** key.
- Activate cell C6.
- Type an equal sign, type the formula C4-C5, and then press the **Enter** key. This formula will calculate the Net Sales by subtracting the Returns from the Gross Sales (this formula was covered in the first section of Chapter 3).
- Activate cell C3. Since the Net Sales are calculated, you can now calculate the Unit Sales.
- Type an equal sign and the beginning of the formula C6 / (cell C6 divided by).
- Activate the Plan Assumptions worksheet and activate cell B5. This formula will take the Average Price per Item and divide it into the Net Sales to calculate the planned Unit Sales for the division.
- Press the **Enter** key.
- Activate cell C7.
- Type an equal sign and the beginning of the formula C4 *.
- Activate the Plan Assumptions worksheet and then activate cell B6. This formula will calculate the Cost of Goods Sold by multiplying the percentage in cell B6 of

>> **Quick Reference**

Linking Data between Worksheets

1. Activate a cell location where the data or output of a formula or functions should appear.
2. Type an equal sign, or type an equal sign and the beginning of a formula or function.
3. Click a **Worksheet** tab that contains the data you wish to display in the first worksheet or use in a formula or function.
4. Activate a cell location that contains the data you wish to display or use in a formula or function.
5. Press the **Enter** key, or complete the formula or function and then press the **Enter** key.

the Plan Assumptions worksheet by the Gross Sales in cell C4 of the Financial Plan worksheet.

- Press the **Enter** key.
- Activate cell C8.
- Type an equal sign, type the formula `C6-C7`, and then press the **Enter** key. This formula will calculate the Gross Profit by subtracting the Cost of Goods Sold from the Net Sales (this formula was also covered in the first section of Chapter 3).
- Copy the range C3:C8. Then highlight cells D3 and E3 and select the **Formulas** option from the **Paste** icon. This will paste the formulas created for the year 2007 into the years 2008 and 2009 to complete the Financial Plan worksheet. Relative referencing will automatically adjust the cell references for the links and formulas to make the appropriate calculations for the years 2008 and 2009.

Figure 6.8 shows the completed Financial Plan worksheet. As previously mentioned, this represents part of a financial plan that the directing manager of a division in a large company would typically create. In addition, the formats and items included in a financial plan will vary depending on the business that is being managed.

Figure 6.8 | **Completed Financial Plan Worksheet**

This formula was originally created in cell C4 but was adjusted through relative referencing.

E4	f_x =D4+D4*'Plan Assumptions'!D4			
	A	B	C	D	E
1		Division B Financial Plan			
2		Last Year	2007	2008	2009
3	Unit Sales	200,000	220,990	226,380	237,699
4	Gross Sales	$ 20,500,000	$ 22,550,000	$ 23,677,500	$ 24,861,375
5	Returns	$ 500,000	$ 451,000	$ 473,550	$ 497,228
6	Net Sales	$ 20,000,000	$ 22,099,000	$ 23,203,950	$ 24,364,148
7	Cost of Goods Sold	$ 11,000,000	$ 12,402,500	$ 13,022,625	$ 13,673,756
8	Gross Profit	$ 9,000,000	$ 9,696,500	$ 10,181,325	$ 10,690,391

>> **Quick Reference**

Linking Data between Workbooks

1. Open two workbooks.

2. Activate a cell location in the workbook where the data or output of a formula or functions should appear.

3. Type an equal sign, or type an equal sign and the beginning of a formula or function.

4. Click the name of the second workbook in the task bar.

5. Click a **Worksheet** tab that contains the data you wish to display or use in a formula or function.

6. Activate a cell location that contains the data you wish to display or use in a formula or function.

7. Press the **Enter** key, or complete the formula or function and then press the **Enter** key.

Business managers will most likely be required to present their financial plans to the executive officers of the company. During this presentation, the business manager might be asked questions such as "What if our sales only increase 5% in 2007?" or "What if our cost of goods sold increases to 60%?" Simply typing new assumptions into the Plan Assumptions worksheet in Figure 6.2 easily answers these questions. Because of cell referencing, the outputs of the financial plan shown in Figure 6.8 will automatically change when the data in the Plan Assumptions worksheet is changed.

Updating Workbook Links

When an Excel file contains workbook links, a *Security Alert* prompt will appear just below the Ribbon of the Excel screen, as shown in Figure 6.9, when the file is opened. The purpose of this prompt is to inform you that data is being linked to an external workbook and to give you the option of updating these links. Workbook links must be updated to show any changes that might have occurred in the external workbook. You can use two methods for updating workbook links. The first is to click the **Options** button in the Security Alert prompt, as shown in Figure 6.9. After you click this button, a dialog box will open giving you the option to automatically update all workbook links. To update any workbook links, you click the *Enable this content* option and click the **OK** button in the dialog box. Once the workbook links are updated, or *refreshed*, any changes that might have occurred in the external workbook will appear in the current workbook.

Figure 6.9 | **Updating Workbook Links Using the Security Alert Prompt**

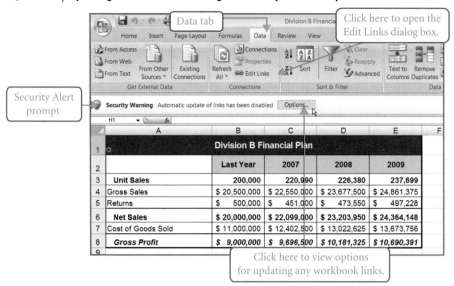

The second method for updating workbook links is through the **Edit Links** dialog box. You can open the **Edit Links** dialog box by clicking the **Edit Links** icon in the **Data** tab of the Ribbon (see Figure 6.9). As shown in Figure 6.10, this dialog box allows you to select and manually update any workbook links that are in your Excel file. In addition, it provides options for checking a selected workbook link to see if it needs to be updated, changing the source file for a selected workbook link, or breaking a workbook link.

Figure 6.10 | **Edit Links Dialog Box**

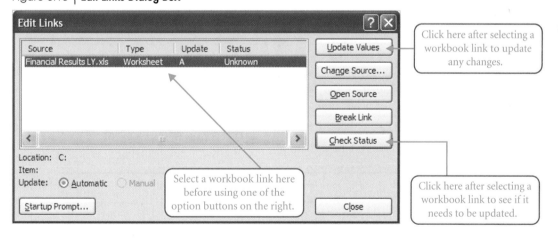

SUMIF Function

The **SUMIF** function allows you to add specific values in a worksheet based on the results of a logical test. In business, this function is often used to summarize financial or statistical data. For example, Figure 6.11 shows a worksheet that contains gross sales projections for the departments of a hypothetical electronics retail company. Notice that several departments are assigned to each division. The **SUMIF** function will be used to total the gross sales projections for each division in the Sales Summary worksheet.

Figure 6.11 | Gross Sales Projections by Division/Department

	A	B	C	D	E	F
1	Gross Sales Projections by Division / Department					
2	Division	Department	2007	2008	2009	3 Year Total
3	Electronics	PDA	$2,100,000	$2,750,000	$3,750,000	$8,600,000
4	Electronics	Video	$1,750,000	$2,500,000	$3,250,000	$7,500,000
5	Computers	Laptop	$1,500,000	$2,100,000	$2,850,000	$6,450,000
6	Electronics	Home Audio	$1,500,000	$1,750,000	$2,250,000	$5,500,000
7	Appliances	Kitchen	$1,450,000	$1,880,000	$2,005,000	$5,335,000
8	Computers	Desktop	$1,750,000	$1,500,000	$1,500,000	$4,750,000
9	Furniture	Family Room	$1,230,000	$1,500,000	$1,700,000	$4,430,000
10	Computers	Video Game	$1,230,000	$1,260,000	$1,300,000	$3,790,000
11	Computers	Accessories	$750,000	$900,000	$1,100,000	$2,750,000
12	Appliances	Laundry	$650,000	$700,000	$700,000	$2,050,000
13	Furniture	Office	$250,000	$300,000	$300,000	$850,000
14	Furniture	Bedroom	$125,000	$200,000	$225,000	$550,000

The gross sales for each division will be summarized in this worksheet.

Sales Detail / Sales Summary

Figure 6.12 shows the worksheet that will be used to summarize the gross sales projections for each division. Since this is a different worksheet, a link will be used in the **SUMIF** function to reference the data in the Sales Detail worksheet shown in Figure 6.11. Using links in the **SUMIF** function is a common technique, especially when you are creating summary reports such as the one shown in Figure 6.12. The **SUMIF** function will be used to search for the division listed in column A from the Sales Summary worksheet in the Sales Detail worksheet and calculate a total for each division for each year.

> **Quick Reference**

Updating Workbook Links

1. Click the **Options** button in the Security Alert prompt.
2. Select the **Enable this content** option in the **Security Options** dialog box and click the **OK** button.

Or

1. Click the **Data** tab of the Ribbon.
2. Click the **Edit Links** icon.
3. Select the workbook link you wish to update from the **Edit Links** dialog box.
4. Click the **Update Values** button on the right side of the **Edit Links** dialog box.
5. Click the **Close** button at the bottom of the **Edit Links** dialog box.

Figure 6.12 | Sales Summary Worksheet

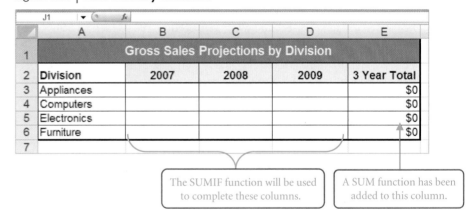

	A	B	C	D	E
1	Gross Sales Projections by Division				
2	Division	2007	2008	2009	3 Year Total
3	Appliances				$0
4	Computers				$0
5	Electronics				$0
6	Furniture				$0

The SUMIF function will be used to complete these columns.

A SUM function has been added to this column.

As shown in Figure 6.13, the **SUMIF** function contains three arguments. Each of these arguments is defined as follows:

- **range**: The range of cells that will be evaluated by the logical test or data used to define the **criteria** argument. In some cases, this argument may be identical to the range of data that is being summed.

- **criteria**: The logical test or data that will be used to determine which values are summed. This is similar to the **logical_test** argument of the **IF** function. However, this argument can be defined by a particular value, cell location, text, and so on, without entering a complete logical test.

- **[sum_range]**: The range of cells that contain data that will be summed if the data in the **criteria** argument is found in the **range** argument. This argument is needed only if the range of cells used for the **range** argument does not contain the values that need to be summed. Otherwise, it can be omitted.

Figure 6.13 | **Arguments of the SUMIF Function**

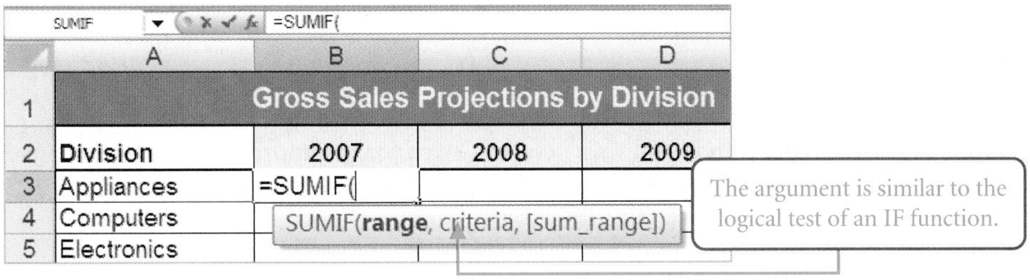

As mentioned, the Sales Summary worksheet in Figure 6.12 summarizes by division the gross sales projections by department (from Figure 6.11). The following steps explains how you accomplish this:

- Activate cell B3 in the Sales Summary worksheet. This cell will show the gross sales projections for the Appliances division for the year 2007.
- Type an equal sign, the function name SUMIF, and an open parenthesis.
- Define the **range** argument by clicking the Sales Detail worksheet and highlighting the range A3:A14. This will create a link to the Sales Detail worksheet. Type a comma after defining this argument.
- Type the cell location A3 to define the **criteria** argument. The function will search for the division name in cell A3 in the Sales Summary worksheet by looking in the range A3:A14 in the Sales Detail worksheet. Note that you will still be in the Sales Detail worksheet when you define this argument; therefore, you must type cell A3 instead of clicking it. Type a comma after defining this argument.
- Define the **[sum_range]** argument by highlighting the range C3:C14 in the Sales Detail worksheet, which contains the gross sales projections for the year 2007. You will still be in the Sales Detail worksheet, so you can simply click and drag over this range. This will create a second link in the function. When a match is found in the **criteria** argument, the function will add whatever value is in the same row in the range of cells used to define this argument.
- Type a closing parenthesis and press the **Enter** key. This will bring you back to the Sales Summary worksheet.

Figure 6.14 shows the results of the **SUMIF** function. The function found the word *Appliances* in column A of the Sales Detail worksheet and summed whatever value is in the same row in the range C3:C14, which contains the gross sales projections for 2007. Notice the links that are created in the **range** and **[sum_range]** arguments.

Figure 6.14 | **Results of the SUMIF Function**

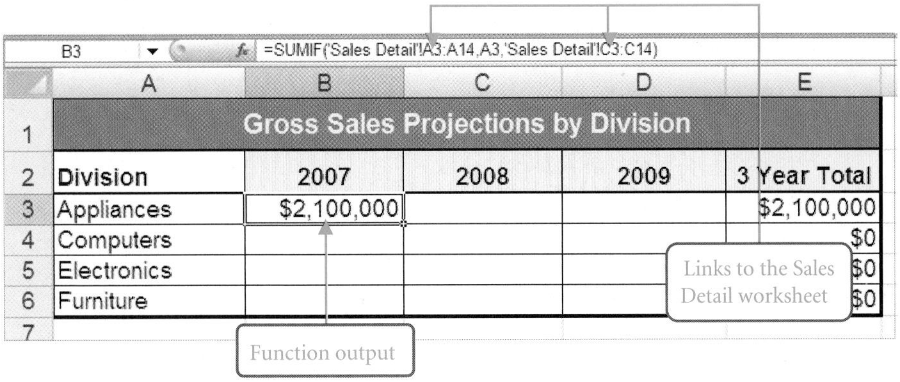

You can copy and paste the **SUMIF** function to calculate the gross sales projections for the rest of the divisions and years in Figure 6.14. However, you would need to add absolute references to the function to prevent relative referencing from making unwanted adjustments to the cell locations in each argument. You accomplish this as follows:

- Double click cell B3 in the Sales Summary worksheet to edit the function, or activate cell B3 and click in the formula bar.
- Place an absolute reference on the link used to define the **range** argument. Type a dollar sign in front of both the column letters and row numbers of the range A3:A14. The function will always need to search for the appropriate division name in column A of the Sales Detail worksheet. Therefore, this range cannot be adjusted by relative referencing when it is pasted to other cell locations on the worksheet.
- Type a dollar sign *only* in front of the column letter of cell A3 in the **criteria** argument. This argument requires a mixed reference because a different division is in each row in column A of the Sales Summary worksheet (see Figure 6.14). Therefore, it is important for relative referencing to adjust the row number when the function is pasted to a new location. However, the column letter must not change.
- Type a dollar sign *only* in front of the two row numbers in the link used to define the [**sum_range**] argument. This argument also requires a mixed reference because each year of sales projections is in a different column in the Sales Detail worksheet. Therefore, it is important for relative referencing to adjust the column letters when the function is pasted to columns C and D of the Sales Summary worksheet. However, the row numbers must not change. Press the **Enter** key after making this adjustment.
- Copy cell B3 and paste it down to cells B4 through B6. Then copy the range B3:B6 and paste it into the range C3:C6 and D3:D6.

Figure 6.15 shows the completed Sales Summary worksheet. Notice the mixed references that were placed on the **criteria** and [**sum_range**] arguments.

Figure 6.15 | **Completed Sales Summary Worksheet**

Mixed references are used in these two arguments.

B3 f_x =SUMIF('Sales Detail'!$A$3:$A$14,$A3,'Sales Detail'!C$3:C$14)

	A	B	C	D	E
1	Gross Sales Projections by Division				
2	Division	2007	2008	2009	3 Year Total
3	Appliances	$2,100,000	$2,580,000	$2,705,000	$7,385,000
4	Computers	$5,230,000	$5,760,000	$6,750,000	$17,740,000
5	Electronics	$5,350,000	$7,000,000	$9,250,000	$21,600,000
6	Furniture	$1,605,000	$2,000,000	$2,225,000	$5,830,000
7					

≫ Linking Data

The purpose of this workshop is to review the techniques of linking data between workbooks and worksheets. I will be demonstrating the tasks in this workshop on the **Workbook Links** and **Worksheet Links** videos. After completing each section of tasks, watch the related video shown in parentheses. You will need to open the following two Excel files before starting this workshop: ib_e06_financialplan and ib_e06_lastyeardata. Both are identical to the example demonstrated earlier in this section. You must open both files before completing the tasks in this workshop.

VIDEO WORKSHOP

1. **Linking Data between Two Workbooks (Video: Workbook Links)**
   a. Activate the Financial Plan workbook.
   b. Activate cell B3 in the Plan worksheet and type an equal sign.
   c. Activate the Last Year Data workbook, activate cell B3, and press the **Enter** key.
   d. Edit the workbook link that was created in cell B3 in the Plan worksheet to remove the absolute reference.
   e. Copy the workbook link in cell B3 of the Plan worksheet and paste it into cells B4 through B8 using the **Formulas** option in the **Paste** icon.
   f. Activate the Last Year Data workbook and close it.

2. **Linking Data between Two Worksheets (Video: Worksheet Links)**
   a. In cell C4 of the Plan worksheet, type the beginning of the formula =B4 + B4 *.
   b. Activate cell B4 in the Plan Assumptions worksheet and press the **Enter** key.
   c. In cell C5 of the Plan worksheet, type the beginning of the formula =C4*.
   d. Activate cell B3 in the Plan Assumptions worksheet and press the **Enter** key.
   e. Type the formula =C4-C5 in cell C6 of the Plan worksheet.
   f. In cell C3 of the Plan worksheet, type the beginning of the formula =C6/.
   g. Activate cell B5 in the Plan Assumptions worksheet and press the **Enter** key.

h. In cell C7 of the Plan worksheet, type the beginning of the formula `=C4 *`.

i. Activate cell B6 in the Plan Assumptions worksheet and press the **Enter** key.

j. Type the formula `=C6 - C7` into cell C8 of the Plan worksheet.

k. Copy the range C3:C8 in the Plan worksheet. Using the **Paste Formulas** option, paste this range into cells D3 through D8 and cells E3 through E8.

l. Save and close your file.

>> SUMIF Function

The purpose of this workshop is to demonstrate the **SUMIF** function. I will be demonstrating the tasks in this workshop in the video named **SUMIF Function**. Open the file named ib_e06_divisionsalessummary and then complete the tasks in this workshop.

SUMIF (Video: SUMIF Function)

a. Activate cell B3 in the Sales Summary worksheet.

b. Type an equal sign, the function name **SUMIF**, and an open parenthesis.

c. Activate the Sales Detail worksheet and highlight the range A3:A14. Then type a comma.

d. Type the cell location A3 and then type a comma.

e. Highlight the range C3:C14 in the Sales Detail worksheet, type a closing parenthesis, and press the **Enter** key.

f. Add the following absolute and mixed references to the **SUMIF** function in cell B3 in the Sales Summary worksheet:

   i. Add an absolute reference to the worksheet link used to define the **range** argument. You will need to add four dollar signs to the range A3:A14 in this argument.

   ii. Add an absolute reference to the column letter only in the **criteria** argument (cell A3). The row number should remain a relative reference.

   iii. Add an absolute reference to the row numbers only in the worksheet link used to define the **[sum_range]** argument. You will need to add two dollar signs to the range C3:C14. The column letters for this range should remain a relative reference.

g. Copy cell B3 and paste it to cells B4:B6. Then copy the range B3:B6 and paste it into the range C3:D6.

h. Type a **SUM** function in cell E3 in the Sales Summary worksheet that totals the values in the range B3:D3. Then copy and paste this function into the range E4:E6.

i. Save and close your file.

>> Store Construction Plans

This section demonstrated how linking data can be used to develop a financial plan for the division of a corporation. However, linking data can also be useful when planning other aspects of business such as the construction of stores, the distribution of merchandise, or the capacity of a distribution center. These exercises involve separate components or assumptions that have to be planned and then utilized to calculate a final output.

Exercise

The goal of this exercise is to develop a store construction plan for a hypothetical retail company. You will use the technique of linking data to calculate the construction cost of each store and also to produce a summary report. The summary report will use the **SUMIF** function to show how much total retail space is constructed or planned by state. To begin this exercise, open the file named ib_e06_storeconstruction.

1. Calculate the Construction Cost in cell G3 on the Construction Plan worksheet. You calculate this cost by multiplying the "Size (square feet)" column in the Construction Plan worksheet by the "Cost per Square Foot" column in the Cost by State worksheet. You will need to create this formula using the **VLookup** function to find the cost per square foot for each state listed in column C of the Construction Plan worksheet in column B of the Cost by State worksheet. The arguments of the **VLookup** function should be defined as followed:

   a. **lookup_value**: C3

   b. **table_array**: The range A2:B12 in the Cost by State worksheet

   c. **col_index_num:** 2

   d. **[range_lookup]**: False

2. Add an absolute reference to the range used to define the **table_array** argument of the VLookup portion of the formula you created in number 1. Then copy the formula and paste it into cells G4 through G25.

3. Type a formula into cell H3 in the Construction Plan worksheet that calculates the Total Cost to Open. Your formula should add the Construction Cost calculated in number 1 to the Inventory Value. Copy your formula and paste it into cells H4 through H25.

4. Create a link in cell A3 of the Store Summary worksheet to cell A2 in the Cost by State worksheet. Then copy this link and paste it into cells A4 through A12.

5. Type a **SUMIF** function in cell B3 of the Store Summary worksheet to calculate the total square feet of store space in the state of Massachusetts. The arguments of the function should be defined as follows:

   a. **range**: C3:C30 in the Construction Plan worksheet

   b. **criteria**: A3

   c. **[sum_range]**: E3:E30 in the Construction Plan worksheet

6. Add an absolute value to the link used to define the **range** and **[sum_range]** arguments of the **SUMIF** function created in step 5. Then copy the function and paste it into cells B4 through B12.

7. Type a **SUMIF** function in cell E33 of the Construction Plan worksheet. The purpose of this function is to add the total square footage of retail space that

exists for each size category of store. The definitions for each argument are listed here. Notice that only two of the three arguments are listed because the range that is used to define the **range** argument contains the values that are being summed.

    a. range = `E3:E30`

    b. criteria = `D33`

8. Place an absolute reference on the range E3:E30 in the **SUMIF** function that you created in step 7. Then copy the function and paste it into cells E34 through E36.

9. Which size category has the highest square footage of retail space for this company?

10. You may have noticed that the range used to define the **range** argument of the **SUMIF** function created in step 7 included blank cells. This is so the summary report will automatically include new stores when they are added. For example, type **VA** in cell A10 in the Cost by State worksheet and add a Cost per Square Foot of **32** in cell B10.

11. In row 26 of the Construction Plan spreadsheet, type open date: **3/23/2008**; store number: **2801**; state: **VA**; city: **Reston**; size: **15000**; and inventory value: **3700500**.

12. Copy cells G25 and H25 in the Construction Plan worksheet and paste them into cells G26 and H26.

13. Which size category has the highest total square footage?

14. Look at the Store Summary worksheet. Is Virginia (VA) added to the list? Sort this worksheet based on the values in the Total Space (sqr feet) column in descending order. Which state has the highest square footage of retail space?

15. Save and close your file.

>> What's Wrong with This Spreadsheet?

Problem

You are managing a department in a large public corporation. Each year the company holds a planning meeting to determine what sales targets will be announced to the stockholders. You receive an e-mail from a coworker who created an Excel spreadsheet to help you plan the sales of your department. He explains how the spreadsheet works as follows:

1. The spreadsheet shows two years of history (2005 and 2006) and three years of projections. The history is linked to another workbook named Sales History, which is attached to this e-mail. You do not have to enter any history data for your sales plan. The history workbooks for each department are maintained by the accounting department. As a result, if they make any adjustments to the results of your department (mostly returns), the changes will automatically show up on the Department Sales Plan workbook I attached to this e-mail.

2. The only things you have to enter in the Department Sales Plan workbook are the Growth of Gross Sales, percent of Returns, and the Average Price. These

items are in the Assumptions worksheet. When you change any of the numbers on this worksheet, it will automatically update the Sales Plan.

3. The Sales Plan worksheet contains all the plan data for the department. Just print this worksheet and bring it to the meeting. It's that easy!

Exercise

Your coworker e-mailed you the Sales History and Department Sales Plan workbooks. Open the file named ib_e06_departmentsalesplan. Would you be comfortable printing the Sales Plan worksheet and presenting this data at the sales meeting? Consider the following points:

1. Do the numbers appear to make sense? For example, the formula to calculate Net Sales is `Gross Sales – Returns`. The Unit sales are calculated by dividing the Net Sales by the Average Price entered onto the Assumptions worksheet.

2. Give the spreadsheet a test drive. The coworker explained that changing the data in the Assumptions worksheet will produce new outputs on the Sales Plan worksheet. Change the data in the Assumptions worksheet one item at a time and check the Sales Plan worksheet. For example, change the Growth of Gross Sales percentages and check the Gross Sales results on the Sales Plan worksheet.

3. Does the historical data for 2005 and 2006 look suspicious?

4. Do the Net Sales results still make sense?

Write a short answer for each of the points listed here. Then fix any errors you find in the Department Sales Plan workbook.

>> Financial Planning   Skill Set

The previous section demonstrated how the sales and gross profit portion of a financial plan is constructed in Excel using the technique of linking data. This section will provide an illustrative review of how you can use the core competency skills in this text to construct a comprehensive financial plan for starting a new business. A total of three worksheets will be used to construct this plan, as opposed to the two worksheets that were used in the previous section: Financial Assumptions, Financial Data, and Cash Analysis. In addition, this section introduces the **NPV** function, which you use to compute the net present value of an investment. It is important to note that this section will mention and work with several terms and rules that apply to the disciplines of finance, but they will not be explained in detail. You will receive more detailed instruction regarding these concepts in your financial accounting courses and reference material.

Financial Assumptions

Figures 6.16 and 6.17 show the first component that will be demonstrated for the comprehensive financial plan: the Financial Assumptions worksheet. The purpose of this worksheet is identical to the Plan Assumptions worksheet that was shown in Figure 6.2.

All of the assumptions related to the financial plan will be entered into this worksheet. In addition, this will be the only worksheet in the plan that is used for any data entry needs. The other two worksheets, Financial Data and Cash Analysis, will be constructed using formulas and functions. A business manager would use the Financial Assumptions worksheet to enter all critical decisions required to develop the comprehensive financial plan such as startup investments, first-year sales estimates, sales growth rates, cost of goods sold, and so on.

The Financial Assumptions worksheet, shown in Figures 6.16 and 6.17, is designed to enter plan data for five financial categories. The number and types of categories that are used to create a financial plan will change depending on the business and purpose of the plan. As previously mentioned, this financial plan will be used for starting a new business. In addition, this example will assume that the business will be manufacturing a product that will be sold to retail stores. Therefore, items such as Cost of Goods Sold and Inventory are included on the Financial Assumptions spreadsheet. If you were planning a service business, these items would not be included in the design of the plan. The following five categories are used for the design of this plan:

- Startup Investments
- Sales Information
- Cost and Expense Information
- Asset Information
- Liability Information

Figure 6.16 | **Financial Assumptions Worksheet (Rows 1 — 25)**

SUM function in this cell: =SUM(B4:B7)

Descriptions state the type of data required for yellow cells.

Formulas in this row multiply Number of Employees by Average Annual Salary with Benefits.

This Financial Plan consists of three worksheets.

	A	B	C	D
1	**Financial Assumptions**			
2	**Startup Investments**			
3	**Total Initial Investment**	$ 400,000		
4	Amount Funded by Loans	$ 325,000	Interest Rate	6.50%
5	Amount Invested by Owner 1	$ 25,000		
6	Amount Invested by Owner 2	$ 25,000		
7	Amount Invested by Owner 3	$ 25,000		
8	**Sales Information**	Year 1	Year 2	Year 3
9	Inflation		2.00%	2.00%
10	First Year Gross Sales Estimate (Dollars)	$ 175,000		
11	Gross Sales Growth (Percent)		150.00%	90.00%
12	Price Charged to Retailers	$ 22.00	$ 22.00	$ 22.00
13	Returns (Percent of Gross Sales)	3.50%	2.00%	1.75%
14	**Cost & Expense Information**	Year 1	Year 2	Year 3
15	Cost of Goods Sold (Percent of Gross Sales)	48.00%	46.00%	44.00%
16	Average Life of Assets (Years Depreciating)	10	10	10
17	Employee Salary and Benefits	$ 90,000	$ 140,000	$ 200,000
18	Number of Employees	3	4	5
19	Average Annual Salary with Benefits	$ 30,000	$ 35,000	$ 40,000
20	Shipping Expense (as a percent of Sales)	1.50%	1.50%	1.50%
21	Annual Rent	$ 15,000	$ 16,000	$ 17,000
22	Utilities (Dollars)	$ 5,000	$ 6,500	$ 10,000
23	Advertising Expense (Dollars)	$ 25,000	$ 40,000	$ 60,000
24	Office Expenses	$ 4,000	$ 6,000	$ 10,000
25	Taxes (percent)	38.00%	38.00%	38.00%

Financial Assumptions / Financial Data / Cash Analysis

Figure 6.17 | **Financial Assumptions Worksheet (Rows 26 – 39)**

	A	B	C	D
1	**Financial Assumptions**			
26	*Asset Information*	Year 1	Year 2	Year 3
27	Accounts Receivable (Turn)	12	12	12
28	Inventory (Turn)	5	5	6
29	Other Assets	$ 75,000	$ 75,000	$ 75,000
30	*Property*	$ -	$ -	$ -
31	*Equipment*	$ 75,000	$ 75,000	$ 75,000
32	*Liability Information*	Year 1	Year 2	Year 3
33	Accounts Payable (Cost of Goods Sold Turn)	6	6	6
34				
35	NOTES:			
36	Loan has a 15 year repayment period from National Good Bank.			
37	Loan Payments are made annually at the beginning of the year.			
38				
39				

Row 1 remains at the top of the worksheet when the Freeze Panes command is activated.

SUM functions in this row calculate the total Property and Equipment.

The following list highlights how a few of the core competency skills were used in the construction of the Financial Assumptions worksheet in Figures 6.16 and 6.17:

- **Formatting (Chapter 2):** Besides the obvious use of formatting techniques such as borders, alignment, number formats, and so on, the use of cell color (also known as fill color) is used as a way of communicating how to use this worksheet. For example, the yellow cells indicate that a business manager must enter key financial data. The white cells indicate labels or calculations that should not be changed. The color grey identifies unused cells.

- **Formulas (Chapter 3):** Basic formulas are used to calculate the cost of Employee Salary and Benefits in row 17. The formula multiplies the Number of Employees entered in row 18 by the Average Annual Salary with Benefits in row 19 for each year. If your project requires, you could add another worksheet to this workbook that is dedicated to calculating the employee costs for this business. The results of that worksheet would then be linked into the Financial Assumptions worksheet.

- **Functions (Chapter 3):** Two **SUM** functions are used in this worksheet. The first is in cell B3, which calculates the total investments planned to start the business in the range B4:B7. Similar to the way you calculate employee costs, you could add another worksheet to this workbook that is dedicated for creating a more detailed plan of how investments are being obtained. This worksheet can include various types of loans and other investment arrangements. The results of this worksheet can then be linked into the Financial Assumptions worksheet. The second **SUM** function is used in row 29 to total the Other Assets in rows 30 and 31.

Freeze Panes

You may have noticed in Figure 6.17 that the first row number showing on the left side of the figure is 1, but the second number is 26. Although it appears as if rows 2 through 25 are hidden, this is not the case. Since the Financial Assumptions spreadsheet is very long, a feature called **Freeze Panes** was used to prevent row 1 from moving off the screen when scrolling down the worksheet. Commonly used when working with long or wide worksheets, this feature allows you lock a specific row and column when

>> *Quick Reference*

Freeze Panes

1. Activate a cell that is below the row and to the right of the column you wish to lock in place when scrolling (except cell A1).
2. Click the **View** tab in the Ribbon.
3. Click the **Freeze Panes** icon.
4. Select the **Freeze Panes** option (select the **Unfreeze Panes** option to remove any locked rows and columns).
5. Use the **Freeze Top Row** or **Freeze First Column** options to lock the first column or row.

scrolling up and down or left and right. The following steps explain how to apply **Freeze Panes** to the Financial Assumptions worksheet in Figure 6.17:

- Click the **View** tab of the Ribbon.
- Click the **Freeze Panes** icon.
- Select the **Freeze Top Row** option. Select the **Unfreeze Panes** option to remove any locked columns and rows on the worksheet.

Financial Data

Figures 6.18 and 6.19 show the next component of the comprehensive financial plan: the Financial Data worksheet. The purpose of this worksheet is to show the financial results of the plan based on the data that is entered into Financial Assumptions spreadsheet. Most of the data shown in this worksheet is produced by formulas and functions that are linked to the Financial Assumptions worksheet. A business manager will most likely focus on the Net Income in row 14 to see if the data that was entered in the Financial Assumptions worksheet results in a profit. Notice that in year 1, the Net Income shows a loss of ($75,038), a small loss of ($1,432) in year 2, and a profit in year 3 of $87,365. This trend is typical for new businesses.

Figure 6.18 | **Financial Data Worksheet Rows 1 – 15**

Changes made to the data in the Financial Assumptions worksheet will produce new outputs in this worksheet.

The Net Income trend shown in this row is typical for new businesses.

	A	B	C	D
1	Financial Data for Business Strategy			
2	Sales and Income	Year 1	Year 2	Year 3
3	Unit Sales	7,676	19,878	38,623
4	Gross Sales	$ 175,000	$ 446,250	$ 864,833
5	Returns	$ 6,125	$ 8,925	$ 15,135
6	Net Sales	$ 168,875	$ 437,325	$ 849,698
7	Cost of Goods Sold	$ 84,000	$ 205,275	$ 380,526
8	Gross Profit	$ 84,875	$ 232,050	$ 469,172
9	Depreciation	$ 7,500	$ 7,500	$ 7,500
10	Selling, General & Admin. Expenses	$ 141,625	$ 215,194	$ 309,972
11	Interest	$ 10,788	$ 10,788	$ 10,788
12	Income Before Taxes	$ (75,038)	$ (1,432)	$ 140,911
13	Taxes	$ -	$ -	$ 53,546
14	Net Income	$ (75,038)	$ (1,432)	$ 87,365
15	Percent of Net Sales	-44.4%	-0.3%	10.3%

Figure 6.19 | **Financial Data Worksheet Rows 16 – 23**

The Freeze Panes command is locking this row at the top of the worksheet.

This row contains links to the Cash Analysis worksheet.

	A	B	C	D
1	Financial Data for Business Strategy			
16	Assets	Year 1	Year 2	Year 3
17	Cash	$ 189,423	$ 106,394	$ 108,242
18	Accounts Receivable	$ 14,583	$ 37,188	$ 72,069
19	Inventory	$ 35,000	$ 89,250	$ 144,139
20	Other Assets	$ 75,000	$ 75,000	$ 75,000
21	Total Assets	$ 314,007	$ 307,832	$ 399,450
22	Liabilities	Year 1	Year 2	Year 3
23	Accounts Payable	$ 14,000	$ 34,213	$ 63,421

As previously mentioned, the numbers shown on the Financial Data worksheet (Figures 6.18 and 6.19) are produced by formulas and functions, most of which contain links to the Financial Assumptions worksheet. With the exception of linking data, which was covered previously in this chapter, the core competency skills that were applied to this worksheet were covered in Chapters 2 through 4. The appearance of the worksheet is a result of the formatting and data management techniques covered in Chapter 2. The formulas and the **Payment** function were covered in Chapter 3, and the **IF** function was covered in Chapter 4. The following lists each formula or function that was created for Year 1. These formulas and functions are copied and pasted to produce the results for Year 2 and Year 3 unless otherwise noted:

- **Unit Sales:** `B6/'Financial Assumptions'!B12` This formula takes the Net Sales value calculated in cell B6 of the Financial Data worksheet and divides it by the Price Charged to Retailers in cell B12 of the Financial Assumptions worksheet.

- **Gross Sales Year 1:** `'Financial Assumptions'!B10` Since this is a new business, the first year of sales is typed into cell B10 of the Financial Assumptions worksheet. Therefore, the Gross Sales for Year 1 on the Financial Data worksheet is simply a link to cell B10 on the Financial Assumptions worksheet.

- **Gross Sales Year 2 and 3:** `(B4 + B4*'Financial Assumptions'!C11)*` `(1 + 'Financial Assumptions'!C9)` The first part of this formula is identical to the one used in Figure 6.7 in the previous section, which calculates the Gross Sales based on a percentage change. However, in this example an adjustment is made for inflation. The percentage change in inflation, which is entered into cell C9 in the Financial Assumptions worksheet, is added to 1 and then multiplied by the result of calculating the Gross Sales. This formula is copied and pasted into to cell D4 to calculate the Gross Sales for Year 3.

- **Returns:** `B4*'Financial Assumptions'!B13` The returns are calculated by multiplying the percentage entered into cell B13 on the Financial Assumptions worksheet by the Gross Sales calculated in cell B4.

- **Net Sales:** `B4 - B5` This basic formula takes the Gross Sales calculated in cell B4 and subtracts the Returns calculated in cell B5.

- **Cost of Goods Sold:** `B4*'Financial Assumptions'!B15` The Cost of Goods Sold percentage in the Financial Assumptions worksheet is multiplied by the Gross Sales in cell B4.

- **Gross Profit:** `B6-B7` This basic formula subtracts the Cost of Goods Sold from the Net Sales.

- **Depreciation:** `'Financial Assumptions'!B29/'Financial` `Assumptions'!B16` This formula takes a straight-line depreciation method approach (depreciation methods will be covered in your accounting courses). The Other Assets calculated in cell B29 in the Financial Assumptions worksheet is simply divided by the number of years entered into cell B16 of the Financial Assumptions worksheet.

- **Selling, General & Admin. Expenses:** `'Financial Assumptions'!B17+` `('Financial Assumptions'!B20*B4)+SUM('Financial` `Assumptions'!B21:B24)` The first part of this formula is simply a link to the total Employee Salary and Benefits cost in cell B17 in the Financial Assumptions worksheet. This is added to the Shipping Expenses, which are calculated by multiplying the percentage in cell B20 of the Financial Assumptions worksheet by the Gross Sales in cell B4. This result is then added to the summation of all expenses in the range B21:B24 in the Financial Assumptions worksheet.

- **Interest:** `PMT('Financial Assumptions'!D4,15,-'Financial` `Assumptions'!B4)-('Financial Assumptions'!B4/15)` This formula estimates the interest expense paid on a loan entered into cell B4 in the Financial Assumptions worksheet. The annual payments calculated by the **PMT** function include the principal *and interest* of the loan. When the principal divided by the number of periods is subtracted from this result, what is left is an estimate of the interest that is paid each year. Years 2 and 3 for the interest expense simply reference the output of this formula in cell B11.

- **Income Before Taxes:** `B8 - SUM(B9:B11)` The **SUM** function adds the expenses in the range B9:B11 and subtracts it from the Gross Profit calculated in cell B8.

- **Taxes:** `IF(B12 > 0,B12 * 'Financial Assumptions'!B25,0)` An **IF** function is used to calculate the projected tax expense. This function checks to see if the Income Before Taxes, which is calculated in cell B12, is greater than zero. If the Income Before Taxes is greater than 0, it is multiplied by the tax percentage entered into cell B25 in the Financial Assumptions worksheet. If the Income Before Taxes is not greater than 0, the tax expense is assumed to be 0. This is a rather simple approach to projecting tax expenses. Depending on your project, you may be required to apply other tax accounting methodologies.

- **Net Income:** `B12 - B13` The Net Income is calculated by taking the Income Before Taxes and subtracting any taxes calculated in cell B13.

- **Percent of Net Sales:** `B14 / B6` This formula calculates Net Income as a percentage of Net Sales.

- **Cash:** `'Cash Analysis'!B11` This is a link to cell B11 in the Cash Analysis worksheet. The methods of data calculation in the Cash Analysis worksheet will be covered in the next section.

- **Accounts Receivable:** `B4 / 'Financial Assumptions'!B27` This formula estimates the accounts receivable by dividing the Accounts Receivable Turn in cell B27 in the Financial Assumptions worksheet into the Gross Sales in cell B4.

- **Inventory:** `B4 / 'Financial Assumptions'!B28` This formula divides the Inventory Turn in cell B28 in the Financial Assumptions worksheet into the Gross Sales in cell B4.

- **Other Assets:** `'Financial Assumptions'!B29` This is simply a link to cell B29 in the Financial Assumptions worksheet.

- **Account Payable:** `B7 / 'Financial Assumptions'!B33` The accounts payable is calculated by dividing the Accounts Payable Turn in cell B33 in the Financial Assumptions worksheet into the Cost of Goods Sold calculated in cell B7.

Cash Analysis (The NPV Function)

The third and final component of the comprehensive financial plan is the Cash Analysis worksheet, which is shown in Figure 6.20. The purpose of this worksheet is to show how much cash is used or accumulated as a result of the assumptions entered into the Financial Assumptions worksheet. Similar to the Financial Data worksheet, the Cash Analysis worksheet is created entirely of formulas and functions. In fact, most of the formulas and functions created in the Cash Analysis worksheet are linked to the Financial Data worksheet. Therefore, when the outputs of the formulas and functions change in the Financial Data worksheet, the outputs of the Cash Analysis worksheet will also change. The results of the Cash Analysis worksheet enable you to conduct a net present value analysis, which is a method used to determine the value of an investment or business. This will be calculated through the **NPV** function, which is covered in this section.

FIGURE 6.20 | Cash Analysis Worksheet

	A	B	C	D
1		Cash Analysis		
2		Year 1	Year 2	Year 3
3	Beginning Cash	$ 400,000	$ 189,423	$ 106,394
4	Net Income	$ (75,038)	$ (1,432)	$ 87,365
5	Depreciation	$ 7,500	$ 7,500	$ 7,500
6	Change in Inventory	$ (35,000)	$ (54,250)	$ (54,889)
7	Change in Accounts Receivable	$ (14,583)	$ (22,604)	$ (34,882)
8	Change in Accounts Payable	$ 14,000	$ 20,213	$ 29,209
9	Capital Expenditures	$ (75,000)	$ -	$ -
10	Repayment of Debt	$ (32,455)	$ (32,455)	$ (32,455)
11	Ending Cash	$ 189,423	$ 106,394	$ 108,242
12				
13				
14	Net Present Value of Plan for Three Years	$ (36,363)		
15				
16	Net Present Value Assuming Ending Cash in Year 3 is Sustained 3 More Years	$ 186,477		

The data in this area of the worksheet is produced by formulas and functions that contain links to the Financial Data worksheet.

The NPV function has been entered into these two cells.

With the exception of linking data and the **NPV** function, the skills used to create the Cash Analysis worksheet in Figure 6.20 were covered in Chapters 2 and 3. The appearance of the worksheet is a result of the formatting and data management techniques covered in Chapter 2. The formulas and **Payment** function were covered in Chapter 3. The following is a list of the formulas and functions that were created for Year 2. In several cases, a different calculation method is required for Year 1 and is noted accordingly:

- **Beginning Cash**: `B11` The Beginning Cash for Year 2 references the Ending Cash from Year 1. The Beginning Cash for Year 1 is a link to cell B3 in the Financial Assumptions worksheet, which contains the Total Initial Investment to start the business.

- **Net Income**: `'Financial Data'!C14` The Net Income is a link to the Financial Data worksheet.

- **Depreciation**: `'Financial Data'!C9` This is also a link to the Financial Data worksheet.

- **Change in Inventory**: `'Financial Data'!B19 - 'Financial Data'!C19` This formula takes the inventory value in Year 2 from the Financial Data worksheet and subtracts it from the inventory value in Year 1. As inventory increases from one year to the next, the formula produces a negative number, which shows that more cash is absorbed from the business. For Year 1 the inventory value in cell B18 in the Financial Data worksheet is subtracted from 0. As a result, the entire inventory required to start the business in Year 1 absorbs cash from the business.

- **Change in Accounts Receivable**: `'Financial Data'!B18 - 'Financial Data'!C18` Similar to the Change in Inventory calculation, the Change in Accounts Receivable is calculated by subtracting the Accounts Receivable value in Year 2 in the Financial Data worksheet from Year 1. Year 1 is calculated by subtracting the Accounts Receivable value from 0.

- **Change in Accounts Payable**: `'Financial Data'!C23 - 'Financial Data'!B23` This formula subtracts the Accounts Payable value in Year 1 from Year 2 in the Financial Data worksheet. This calculation is the opposite of the calculations used for Change in Inventory and Change in Accounts Receivable because, as Accounts Payable increases, cash is added to the business. The value for

Year 1 is a link to the Accounts Payable value in Year 1 on the Financial Data worksheet.

- **Capital Expenditures**: `'Financial Data'!B20 - 'Financial Data'!C20` This formula subtracts the Other Assets value in Year 2 from Year 1 in the Financial Data worksheet. If the value of Other Assets increases in Year 2 over Year 1, a negative number will be produced, indicating cash was used. The value for Year 1 subtracts the Other Assets value in cell B20 in the Financial Data worksheet from 0.

- **Repayment of Debt**: `PMT('Financial Assumptions'!D4,15,-'Financial Assumptions'!B4,,1) * -1` The **Payment** function calculates the annual payments of the loan based on the details listed in the Financial Assumptions worksheet. The result of the function is multiplied by –1 because it reduces the cash available to the business.

- **Ending Cash**: `C3 + SUM(C4:C10)` The Ending Cash is calculated by adding all of the items that add or reduce the cash of the business and adding that number to the beginning cash value.

The final calculation shown on the Cash Analysis worksheet in Figure 6.20 is the net present value of the comprehensive financial plan. This value is calculated using the **NPV** function. Details regarding the concepts of a net present value analysis will be covered in your finance courses. However, the following definitions for the arguments of the **NPV** function will provide a few insights as to what a net present value analysis can tell a business manager:

- **rate**: This is the interest rate or cost of borrowing money for the business. The goal of the **NPV** function is to calculate the present value of cash that is generated by a business in the future. It might be best to think of this concept as the **Future Value** function in reverse. That is, the **Future Value** function calculates how much money will be worth in the future when interest is added to a principal value over a period of time. The **NPV** function takes cash that is expected to be generated in the future and calculates how much that money is worth today. A new business is often considered a worthy investment if the NPV is a positive number.

- **value1**: This is the initial investment required to start, rebuild, or enhance a business. A negative sign must be used when entering values or cell locations for this argument.

- [**value(n)**]: Each value entered into the function after the **value1** argument is the cash flow that is expected for the year. Therefore, if you are using the **NPV** function to calculate the net present value for a ten-year financial plan, you will have ten cash values after you input the initial investment for the **value1** argument.

The arguments for the **NPV** function entered into cell C14 in the Cash Analysis worksheet are defined as follows:

- **rate**: `'Financial Assumptions'!D4` This is the interest rate from the loan details on the Financial Assumptions spreadsheet. This rate is used as the cost of borrowing money for this business.

- **value1**: `'Financial Assumptions'!B3` This is the principal of the loan from the Financial Assumptions worksheet. Notice that a negative sign is placed in front of this link.

- [**value2**]: `B11` This is the Ending Cash value in Year 1 on the Cash Analysis worksheet.

- [**value3**]: `C11` This is the Ending Cash value in Year 2 on the Cash Analysis worksheet.

- [**value4**]: `D11` This is the Ending Cash value in Year 3 on the Cash Analysis worksheet.

The Cash Analysis worksheet also shows a second **NPV** function that was entered into cell C16. The purpose of this function is to show the net present value of the comprehensive financial plan if the Ending Cash in Year 3 were produced for another three years. As a result, the cell reference D11 is simply repeated for the [**value5**] through [**value7**] arguments. Notice that the output of the **NPV** function in cell C14 is negative. This suggests that the financial plan for this new business does not generate a substantial return if it were in operation only for three years. However, the second **NPV** function in cell C16 shows a substantial return if the business operates for six years and continues to generate the same Ending Cash in Year 3 for an additional three years.

One of the key benefits of setting up a comprehensive financial plan through the methods described in this section is that the outputs in the Financial Data worksheet and Cash Analysis worksheet will automatically change when you change the inputs in the Financial Assumptions worksheet. This feature allows you to evaluate multiple scenarios to determine what would happen to the profitability or net present value of the business when certain assumptions are changed. The importance of this concept was demonstrated in a variety of situations throughout this text. It is this process of evaluating several scenarios that helps business managers make key financial decisions, such as how much money can be spent on advertising, how many people should be hired, or how much equipment should be purchased. There is no way to say for certain what will happen in business. However, business managers will use Excel to construct plans similar to what was described in this section to determine what is possible with respect to various business initiatives and ultimately decide which initiatives to execute and which initiatives to drop.

>> NPV Function

The purpose of this workshop is to demonstrate how the **NPV** function is used to evaluate an investment. I will be demonstrating the tasks in this workshop in the video named **NPV Function**. Open the file named ib_e06_investmentvalue and complete the tasks in this workshop.

1. NPV Function (Video: NPV Function)

  a. Activate cell E8 on the NPV Analysis worksheet.
  b. Type an equal sign, the function name **NPV**, and an open parenthesis.
  c. Click cell D3 to define the rate segment and type a comma.
  d. Type a negative sign and click cell D2. Then type a comma.
  e. Click cell A6 and type a comma.
  f. Click cell B6 and type a comma.
  g. Click cell C6 and type a comma.
  h. Click cell D6 and type a comma.
  i. Click cell E6 and type a closing parenthesis.
  j. Press the **Enter** key.
  k. Change the value in cell D2 to **975000**.
  l. Save and close your file.

>> Financial Plans

The purpose of this workshop is to construct the comprehensive financial plan that was presented in this section. I will be demonstrating the tasks in this workshop in the following three videos: **Financial Assumptions**, **Financial Data**, and **Cash Analysis**. These video names appear at the beginning of each section of tasks. Open the file named ib_e06_newbusinessfinancialplan. Complete each section of tasks and then watch the related video.

1. **Financial Assumptions (Video: Financial Assumptions)**

    a. Activate the Financial Assumptions worksheet.

    b. Type a **SUM** function in cell B3 that adds the values in the range B4:B7.

    c. Type the formula `B18 * B19` in cell B17.

    d. Copy the formula in cell B17 and paste it into cells C17 and D17 using the **Formulas** option.

    e. Type a **SUM** function in cell B29 that adds the values in the range B30:B31.

    f. Copy the **SUM** function in cell B29 and paste it into cells C29 and D29 using the **Formulas** option.

    g. Type the following text in cell A38: **Target Scenario for New Business**.

    h. Bold and italicize the text in cell A38 and change the text color to red.

2. **Financial Data (Video: Financial Data)**

    a. Activate the Financial Data worksheet.

    b. Type a link in cell B4 that displays the Gross Sales value in cell B10 in the Financial Assumptions worksheet.

    c. Type a formula in cell C4 that calculates the Gross Sales for Year 2. Your formula should add to the Gross Sales value in cell B4 the result of multiplying the Gross Sales value in cell B4 by the Gross Sales Growth in cell C11 in the Financial Assumptions worksheet.

    d. Edit the formula that was created in cell C4 to account for inflation. Place parentheses around the formula and then multiply it by the result of adding 1 to the inflation percentage in cell C9 of the Financial Assumptions worksheet.

    e. Copy the formula in cell C4 and paste it into cell D4 using the **Formulas** option.

    f. Type a formula in cell B5 that calculates the Returns for Year 1. Your formula should multiply the Gross Sales value in cell B4 by the Returns percent in cell B13 in the Financial Assumptions worksheet.

    g. Copy the formula in cell B5 and paste it into cell C5 and D5 using the **Formulas** option.

    h. Type a formula in cell B6 that calculates the Net Sales. Your formula should subtract the Returns from the Gross Sales. Then copy this formula and paste it into cells C6 and D6 using the **Formulas** option.

    i. Type a formula in cell B3 that calculates the Unit Sales. Your formula should divide the Net Sales value in cell B6 by the Price Charged to Retailers in cell B12 in the Financial Assumptions worksheet.

j. Copy the formula in cell B3 and paste it into cells C3 and D3 using the **Formulas** option.

k. Type a formula in cell B7 that calculates the Cost of Goods Sold for Year 1. Your formula should multiply the Gross Sales value in cell B4 by the percentage in cell B15 in the Financial Assumptions worksheet.

l. Copy the formula in cell B7 and paste it into cells C7 and D7 using the **Formulas** option.

m. Type a formula in cell B8 that calculates the Gross Profit. Your formula should subtract the Cost of Goods Sold value in cell B7 from the Net Sales value in cell B6. Then copy this formula and paste it into cells C8 and D8 using the **Formulas** option.

n. Type a formula in cell B9 that calculates the Depreciation for Year 1. Your formula should divide the Other Assets value in cell B29 in the Financial Assumptions worksheet by the Average Life of Assets in cell B16, which is also in the Financial Assumptions worksheet.

o. Copy the formula in cell B9 and paste it into cells C9 and D9 using the **Formulas** option.

p. Type a formula in cell B10 that calculates the Selling, General & Admin. Expenses for Year 1. Your formula should add the Employee Salary and Benefits, the Shipping Expense, and all expenses in the range B21:B24 from the Financial Assumptions worksheet. Note that the Shipping Expense is calculated by multiplying the percentage in cell B20 in the Financial Assumptions worksheet by the Gross Sales value in cell B4 in the Financial Data worksheet.

q. Copy the formula in cell B10 and paste it into cells C10 and D10 using the **Formulas** option.

r. Type a formula in cell B11 that estimates the Interest Expense for Year 1. Your formula should first calculate the payments on the loan value in cell B4 in the Financial Assumptions worksheet using the **Payment** function. Use the Interest Rate in cell D4 of the Financial Assumptions worksheet to define the rate argument, use the number **15** to define the **nper** argument, and assume that payments are made at the beginning of the period. Then subtract from the output of this **Payment** function the result of dividing the loan value in cell B4 in the Financial Assumptions worksheet by 15.

s. Type the cell reference **B11** in cells C11 and D11 to display the output of the formula showing the Interest Expense in Year 1.

t. Type a formula in cell B12 to calculate the Income Before Taxes in Year 1. Your formula should subtract the sum of the expenses in the range B9:B11 from the Gross Profit value in cell B8. Then copy this formula and paste it into cells C12 and D12 using the **Formulas** option.

u. Type an **IF** function in cell B13 to calculate the Taxes for Year 1. If the Income Before Taxes is greater than 0, the function should multiply the Tax percent in cell B25 in the Financial Assumptions worksheet by the Income Before Taxes value in cell B12. Otherwise, the function should display a value of 0.

v. Copy the **IF** function in cell B13 and paste it into cells C13 and D13 using the **Formulas** option.

w. Type a formula in cell B14 to calculate the Net Income for Year 1. Your formula should subtract the Taxes value in cell B13 from the Income Before Taxes in cell B12. Then copy this formula and paste it into cells C14 and D14 using the **Formulas** option.

x. Type a formula in cell B15 to calculate the Percent of Net Sales for Year 1. Your formula should divide the Net Income value in cell B14 by the Net

Sales value in cell B6. Then copy this formula and paste it into cells C15 and D15 using the **Formulas** option.

y. Show the value of the Cash Assets in cell B17 by creating a link to cell B11 in the Cash Analysis worksheet. Then copy this link and paste it into cells C17 and D17 using the **Formulas** option.

z. Type a formula in cell B18 to calculate the Accounts Receivable for Year 1. Your formula should divide the Gross Sales value in cell B4 by the Accounts Receivable Turn in cell B27 in the Financial Assumptions worksheet.

aa. Copy the formula in cell B18 and paste it into cells C18 and D18 using the **Formulas** option.

bb. Type a formula in cell B19 to calculate the Inventory value for Year 1. Your formula should divide the Gross Sales in cell B4 by the Inventory Turn value in cell B28 in the Financial Assumptions worksheet.

cc. Copy the formula in cell B19 and paste it into cells C19 and D19 using the **Formulas** option.

dd. In cell B20, create a link to cell B29 in the Financial Assumptions worksheet. Then copy this link and paste it into cells C20 and D20 using the **Formulas** option.

ee. Type a **SUM** function in cell B21 that totals the values in the range B17:B20. Then copy the function and paste it into cells C21 and D21 using the **Formulas** option.

ff. Type a formula in cell B23 to calculate the Accounts Payable for Year 1. Your formula should divide the Cost of Goods Sold value in cell B7 by the Accounts Payable value in cell B33 in the Financial Assumptions worksheet.

gg. Copy the formula in cell B23 and paste it into cells C23 and D23 using the **Formulas** option.

3. **Cash Analysis (Video: Cash Analysis)**

a. Activate the Cash Analysis worksheet.

b. Create a link in cell B3 in the Cash Analysis worksheet that shows the value in cell B3 in the Financial Assumptions worksheet.

c. Type the cell reference **B11** in cell C3 to show the Ending Cash for Year 1. Then copy this cell reference and paste it into cell D3 using the **Formulas** option.

d. Create a link in cell B4 that shows the Net Income value in cell B14 in the Financial Data worksheet. Then copy this link and paste it into cells C4 and D4 using the **Formulas** option.

e. Create a link in cell B5 that shows the Depreciation value in cell B9 in the Financial Data worksheet. Then copy this link and paste it into cells C5 and D5 using the **Formulas** option.

f. Type a formula in cell B6 that calculates the Change in Inventory for Year 1. Your formula should subtract the value in cell B19 in the Financial Data worksheet from 0.

g. Type a formula in cell C6 that calculates the Change in Inventory for Year 2. Your formula should subtract the value in cell C19 in the Financial Data worksheet from the value in cell B19 in the Financial Data worksheet.

h. Copy the formula in cell C6 and paste it into cell D6 using the **Formulas** option.

i. Type a formula in cell B7 that calculates the Change in Accounts Receivable for Year 1. Your formula should subtract the value in cell B18 in the Financial Data worksheet from 0.

j. Type a formula in cell C7 that calculates the Change in Accounts Receivable for Year 2. Your formula should subtract the value in cell C18 in the Financial Data worksheet from the value in cell B18 in the Financial Data worksheet.

k. Copy the formula in cell C7 and paste it into cell D7 using the **Formulas** option.

l. Create a link in cell B8 that displays the value in cell B23 in the Financial Data worksheet.

m. Type a formula in cell C8 that calculates the Change in Accounts Payable for Year 2. Your formula should subtract the value in cell B23 in the Financial Data worksheet from the value in cell C23 in the Financial Data worksheet.

n. Copy the formula in cell C8 and paste it into cell D8 using the **Formulas** option.

o. Type a formula in cell B9 that calculates the Capital Expenditures for Year 1. Your formula should subtract the value in cell B20 in the Financial Data worksheet from 0.

p. Type a formula in cell C9 that calculates the Capital Expenditures for Year 2. Your formula should subtract the value in cell C20 in the Financial Data worksheet from the value in cell B20 in the Financial Data worksheet.

q. Copy the formula in cell C9 and paste it into cell D9 using the **Formulas** option.

r. Use the **Payment** function in cell B10 to calculate the Repayment of Debt in Year 1. Use the Interest Rate in cell D4 of the Financial Assumptions worksheet to define the **rate** argument, use the number **15** to define the **nper** argument, use the value in cell B4 in the Financial Assumptions worksheet to define the **pv** argument, and assume that payments are made at the beginning of the period. Multiply this function by −1 to show a negative number in cell B10.

s. Type the cell reference **B10** in cell C10 and D10.

t. Type a formula in cell B11 that adds the sum of the range B4:B10 to the value in cell B3. Then copy this formula and paste it into cells C11 and D11 using the **Formulas** option.

u. Type an **NPV** function into cell C14 to determine the net present value of the plan. Use the value in cell D4 in the Financial Assumptions worksheet to define the **rate** argument, the value in cell B3 in the Financial Assumptions worksheet to define the **[value1]** argument, and the Ending Cash values in the Cash Analysis worksheet to define the **[value2]**, **[value3]**, and **[value4]** arguments.

v. Save and close your file.

>> Evaluating Business Initiatives Using Net Present Value

EXERCISE

Why Do I Need This?

Business managers frequently evaluate how various financial assumptions change the profitability and cash flow of a business. This information is vital before making critical investment or operational decisions. These decisions include areas such as acquiring new businesses, starting new businesses, or improving existing businesses. In addition, many businesses evaluate the quality of an investment through a net present value analysis.

Exercise

The purpose of this exercise is to evaluate a decision to invest money in a new computer system that is expected to increase the productivity of a division within a major corporation. You will use a net present value analysis to evaluate the investment and its expected return. Open the file named ib_e06_systemimprovements.

1. Examine the formulas used to produce the data in the Revised Plan worksheet. What will happen if any value in the yellow cells of the Assumptions worksheet is changed?

2. Type a formula in cell B3 on the Change in Plan worksheet that subtracts cell B3 in the Current Plan worksheet from cell B3 in the Revised Plan worksheet. This will calculate the change in Gross Sales from the current to the revised plan. Copy this formula and paste it into the cells C3 through E3.

3. Type a formula in cell B4 in the Change in Plan worksheet to calculate the change in Returns by subtracting cell B4 in the Current Plan from cell B4 in the Revised Plan. Copy this formula and paste it into cells C4 through E4. What impact is the new system expected to have on returns?

4. Type a formula in cell B5 in the Change in Plan worksheet that shows the Change in Returns as a percent of Gross Sales. Your formula should subtract cell B5 in the Current Plan worksheet from cell B5 in the Revised Plan worksheet. Copy this formula and paste it into cells C5 through E5.

5. Copy the range B3:E3 and paste it into the range B6:E15. This will show the difference between the Current Plan and Revised Plan for each financial item listed in column A. You will want to use the Formulas option when pasting to maintain the formatting of the worksheet.

6. Type a **SUM** function in cell G3 on the Change in Plan worksheet that totals the values in the range B3:E3. What is the total increase in sales over four years the new system is expected to generate for the business?

7. Copy the **SUM** function in cell G3 and paste it in to cells G4, G6, G7, G9, and the range G11:G14. How much additional Net Income is the new system expected to generate for the business over a four-year period? Compare this number to the Total Initial Investment value in cell B2 in the Assumptions worksheet. Does this system seem be a good investment?

8. As previously mentioned, many business managers measure the quality of an investment based on the results of a net present value analysis. This will tell the business manager if the profits generated from an investment make sense given the time value of money. Therefore, type an **NPV** function in cell C18 on the Change in Plan worksheet. Define each argument of the function as follows:

   a. **Rate**: Cell B3 in the Assumptions worksheet. This is the division's cost to borrow money to pay for the initial cost of the new computer system.

   b. **value1**: Cell B2 in the Assumptions worksheet. This is the investment that is required to purchase and install the system.

   c. **[value2]**: The range B14:E14 in the Change in Plan worksheet. We will assume that the entire increase in Net Income will be incremental, or extra, cash added to the business as a result of the computer system.

9. Assume that this company has a policy that states all investments must prove that a minimum net present value of $5,000 is achievable over a four-year period. Should the manager of this division buy the computer system? Why?

10. In the Assumptions spreadsheet, change the values in the range B7:E7 to **15%**. This will assume that Gross Sales will increase 15% over the current

financial plan of the division. What is the total increase in Gross Sales (cell G3 in the Change in Plan worksheet) after making this change? Is the NPV of this investment positive or negative after making this change? Is it at least $5,000?

11. Change the Gross Sales percent values in the range B7:E7 on the Assumptions worksheet back to **10%**. Then change the values in the range B8:E8 to **2%**. This assumes that the new system will decrease the amount of Returns as a Percent of Gross Sales by 2% instead of 1%. Check the NPV on the Change in Plan worksheet. Is it positive or negative? Is it positive by at least $5,000?

12. Go back to the Assumptions worksheet and change the Gross Sales percent values in the range B7:E7 to **5%**. This assumes that the new system will increase Gross Sales over the current plan by only 5%. However, it will still assume that Returns as a Percent of Gross Sales will be reduced by 2%. Check the NPV of the investment. Is it positive or negative? Is it at least $5,000?

13. What does your assessment of step 12 tell you about the value of business initiatives that increase quality or reduce costs versus increasing sales?

14. Save and close your file.

>> What's Wrong with This Spreadsheet?

Problem

You are the CEO of a corporation. Your directors of Strategic Planning are presenting the results of a financial plan for starting a new business. This business will operate as a separate division and will add a new brand of merchandise to the current portfolio of the corporation. You have set the following NPV standard for evaluating investments made by the company:

1. For new businesses, the NPV must be positive by at least $10,000 considering three years of cash flow.

2. For existing businesses, the NPV must be positive by at least $5,000 considering four years of cash flow.

With these standards in mind, the directors of Strategic Planning are very excited to present this new business idea. They explain that a $2,500,000 investment will be required to start the business. In addition, the results of the plan show that the NPV is positive and well over $100,000. They explain that this business will generate Net Sales of over $3.3 million over a three-year period and will produce over $2 million in gross profit over the same time period. However, the directors point out that the business will lose a considerable amount of money in the first year and show that the Net Income is negative by over $600,000 in Year 1. That said, they also show that the Net Income makes a dramatic improvement in Year 2 and that the company is expected to show a profit in Year 3.

You look carefully at the spreadsheets the team has printed out for you, and they appear to be well constructed. As you glance at the numbers, they all appear to make sense. You congratulate the Strategic Planning team for a job well done and tell them that you would like to look at the plan one more time before approving the $2,500,000 investment. In addition, you ask the team to e-mail you the Excel file that was used to produce the spreadsheets in the meeting.

The Excel file that the Strategic Planning department e-mailed to you is named ib_e06_agreatbusinessidea. Would you let the team spend the $2,500,000? Consider the following points:

1. Look at the numbers in the Financial Data worksheet. This information was presented to you at the meeting. Do the numbers make sense?

2. The formulas in the Financial Data worksheet are based on the numbers entered on the Assumptions worksheet. Do the outputs on the Financial Data worksheet change when the assumptions are changed?

3. Is the NPV really positive and over $100,000?

What's wrong with this spreadsheet? Write a short answer for each of the points listed here and explain why you would or would not approve this investment? Then fix any errors you find in the workbook.

Skill Set ▷▷ **Financial Accounting**

The previous section illustrated how you can use the core competency skills in this text to construct a comprehensive financial plan. This section will provide an illustrative review of how you can use the core competency skills to construct spreadsheets used for financial accounting. Business professionals will typically use specialized software for managing the accounting needs of their business. However, for business students, Excel can be a very convenient and valuable tool for completing assignments typically required in accounting courses. As a result, several financial accounting concepts and rules will be mentioned but not explained in detail. You will receive more detailed instruction regarding these concepts in your financial accounting courses and reference material.

T-Accounts

Many financial accounting courses include assignments related to T-accounts. T-accounts are often considered a teaching tool when you are learning how certain transactions are treated according to the rules of accounting. Figure 6.21 shows an example of a blank T-account that was created in Excel. The layout of the T-account utilizes formatting techniques that were covered in Chapter 2. You use the **Borders** command to create the "T," and cells at the top of the T-account are merged so the name of the account can be centered over the "T."

Figure 6.21 | **Blank T-Account**

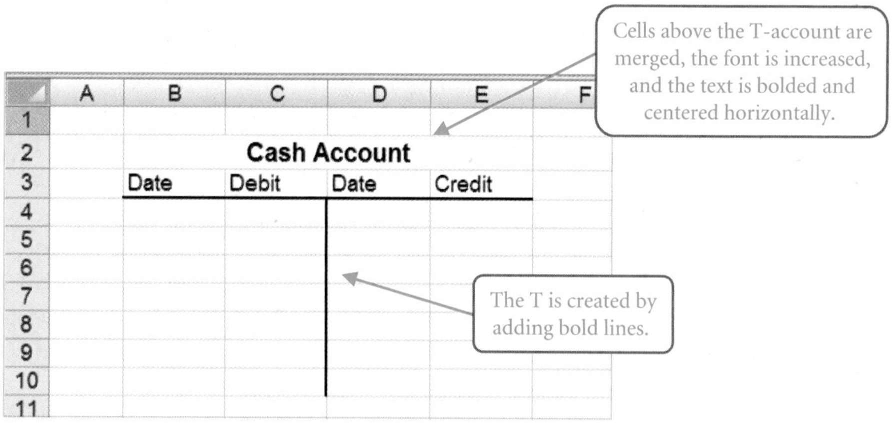

Cells above the T-account are merged, the font is increased, and the text is bolded and centered horizontally.

The T is created by adding bold lines.

Figure 6.22 shows the T-account with dates and numbers entered into the debits and credits columns. A standard rule in accounting is that debits are always shown on the left and credits are always shown on the right. The **SUM** function is used at the bottom of the T-account to total the Debit and Credit columns.

Figure 6.22 | **T-Account with Dates and Dollar Entries**

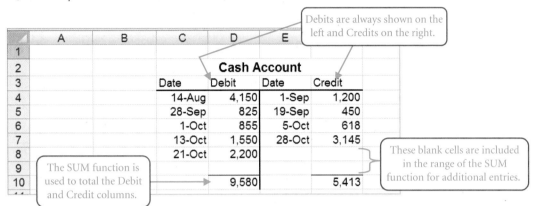

Figure 6.23 shows a completed T-account which includes a formula that calculates the balance of the Cash Account (see cell B10). It is important to remember that the formula for calculating the balance of an account will change depending on the account. For example, Cash is an asset account, which means debits will increase the account and credits will decrease the account. For liability accounts, debits decrease the account and credits increase the account. These rules will be covered in your accounting courses.

Figure 6.23 | **Completed T-Account with Formula Calculating the Balance**

	B10	▾	fx =D10-F10				
	A	B	C	D	E	F	
2				Cash Account			
3			Date	Debit	Date	Credit	
4			14-Aug	4,150	1-Sep	1,200	
5	For asset accounts, the balance is calculated by subtracting the total credits from the total debits.		28-Sep	825	19-Sep	450	
6			1-Oct	855	5-Oct	618	
7			13-Oct	1,550	28-Oct	3,145	
8			21-Oct	2,200			
9							
10	Balance	4,167		9,580		5,413	

A big benefit of doing T-accounts in Excel is that you can easily copy and paste them for other accounts. If you were assigned to do a T-account for another asset account, such as Accounts Receivables, you could copy the Cash Account, paste it to another location, delete the dates and numbers, and enter new dates and numbers. As shown in Figure 6.24, the **SUM** function totaling the debits and credits and the formula calculating the balance of the account produce new outputs when new data is entered. However, you must be careful when pasting a T-account from one account class to another. *The formula calculating the balance for an asset account will be different for a Liability account.* Therefore, if you are creating a Liability T-account from an asset account, you must delete the formula and re-create it to properly account for debits and credits.

Figure 6.24 | **Creating a New T-Account Using the Copy and Paste Commands**

	A	B	C	D	E	F
				Cash Account		
2						
3			Date	Debit	Date	Credit
4			14-Aug	4,150	1-Sep	1,200
5			28-Sep	825	19-Sep	450
6			1-Oct	855	5-Oct	618
7			13-Oct	1,550	28-Oct	3,145
8			21-Oct	2,200		
9						
10	Balance	4,167		9,580		5,413
11						
12				**Accounts Receivable**		
13			Date	Debit	Date	Credit
14			30-Jun	5,000	1-Aug	2,500
15			15-Aug	3,450	1-Sep	2,500
16					1-Oct	625
17					4-Nov	640
18						
19						
20	Balance	2,185		8,450		6,265

B20 =D20-F20

Since Cash and Accounts Receivable are both asset accounts, the formula calculating the balance remains the same.

The SUM functions produce new outputs when new data is entered for this account.

COMMON MISTAKES | T-Accounts

The most common mistake made when creating T-accounts in Excel is copying old T-accounts into different account classes. When you copy an old T-account to create a new one, *always check the formula that is calculating the balance of the account.* You may need to adjust the formula to properly account for debits and credits in order to calculate an accurate balance.

Journals

Creating a journal is another common exercise that is required in accounting courses. A journal is used to keep track of all transactions that occur in a business and consists of the transaction date, the account description, and a monetary entry in either a Debit or Credit column. Formatting skills covered in Chapter 2 are used to create the appearance of the journal, similar to T-accounts. Figure 6.25 shows an example of a journal with several entries. Notice that each entry consists of at least two accounts (at least one debit and one credit), debit entries are listed before credit entries, and accounts with credit entries are indented (also see Figure 2.25, which shows the indent icons).

Figure 6.26 shows the Accounting journal with the **SUM** function added to total the Debit and Credit columns. The amount of debits entered in a journal must equal the amount of credits. If the outputs of the two **SUM** functions are not identical, then there was most likely an error with one of the entries in the journal.

Figure 6.25 | **Accounting Journal**

	A	B	C	D	E
1		JOURNAL			*Accounts with a credit entry along with the transaction description are indented.*
2	Date	Description	Post. Ref.	Debit	Credit
3	10-Nov	Supplies	14	$ 1,350.00	
4	10-Nov	Accounts Payable	21		$ 1,350.00
5		*Purchased supplies on account*			
6					
7	18-Nov	Cash	11	$ 7,500.00	
8	18-Nov	Fees Earned	41		$ 7,500.00
9		*Received fees from customers*			
10					
11	30-Nov	Wages Expense	51	$ 2,125.00	
12	30-Nov	Rent Expense	52	$ 800.00	
13	30-Nov	Utilities Expense	54	$ 450.00	
14	30-Nov	Miscellaneous Expense	59	$ 275.00	
15	30-Nov	Cash	11		$ 3,650.00
16		*Paid Expenses*			
17					
18	30-Nov	Accounts Payable	21	$ 950.00	
19	30-Nov	Cash	11		$ 950.00
20		*Paid creditors on account*			

The Accounting number format is used for the dollar values in these columns.

Figure 6.26 | **The SUM Function Is Used to Total the Debit and Credit Entries**

D22   *fx* =SUM(D3:D18)

	A	B	C	D	E
1		JOURNAL			*The Freeze Panes command was used to lock these two rows.*
2	Date	Description	Post. Ref.	Debit	Credit
9		*Received fees from customers*			
10					
11	30-Nov	Wages Expense	51	$ 2,125.00	
12	30-Nov	Rent Expense	52	$ 800.00	
13	30-Nov	Utilities Expense	54	$ 450.00	
14	30-Nov	Miscellaneous Expense	59	$ 275.00	
15	30-Nov	Cash	11		$ 3,650.00
16		*Paid Expenses*			
17					
18	30-Nov	Accounts Payable	21	$ 950.00	
19	30-Nov	Cash	11		$ 950.00
20		*Paid creditors on account*			
21					
22				$ 13,450.00	$ 13,450.00

SUM functions are used to total all debit and credit entries.

Ledgers

This section will illustrate how you use Excel to create an Accounting Ledger. A ledger is used to record all transactions for one specific account such as Cash, Accounts Payable, Inventory, and so on. Figure 6.27 shows an example of a blank ledger for the Cash account. As in the previous examples, formatting techniques from Chapter 2 were used to create the appearance of this ledger.

Figure 6.27 | **Blank Ledger for the Cash Account**

	A	B	C	D	E	F	G
1	ACCOUNT			*Cash*		ACCOUNT NO.	*11*
2							Balance
3	Date	Item	Post Ref	Debit	Credit	Debit	Credit
4							
5							
6							

Transactions for this account will be listed here.

To complete the ledger shown in Figure 6.27, entries for the Cash Account are taken directly from the journal as shown in Figure 6.28. As demonstrated in the Data Management section of Chapter 2, a copy of the journal is pasted into a new worksheet (see Figure 2.14) and then sorted by the Description and Date columns in ascending order (see Figure 2.19). After the data is sorted, the Cash Account entries can be copied and pasted into the ledger. This eliminates the need to manually type the data into the ledger, which opens the possibility for data entry errors.

Figure 6.28 | **Journal Entries Sorted for Pasting Data into the Ledger**

These cash entries are grouped together after sorting the worksheet.

	A	B	C	D	E
1		JOURNAL			
2	Date	Description	Post. Ref.	Debit	Credit
3	10-Nov	Accounts Payable	21		$ 1,350.00
4	30-Nov	Accounts Payable	21	$ 950.00	
5	18-Nov	Cash	11	$ 7,500.00	
6	30-Nov	Cash	11		$ 3,650.00
7	30-Nov	Cash	11		$ 950.00
8	18-Nov	Fees Earned	41		$ 7,500.00
9	30-Nov	Miscellaneous Expense	59	$ 275.00	
10		*Paid creditiors on account*			

Figure 6.29 shows the entries that were pasted into the Cash account ledger from the journal in Figure 6.28. The next step will be to calculate the balance for the account. As previously mentioned, since Cash is an asset account, debits will increase the account and credits will decrease the account. Therefore, an **IF** function will be used to determine if the balance of the account should be increased or decreased based on the entry.

Figure 6.29 | **Cash Account Ledger with Entries Added**

	A	B	C	D	E	F	G
1	ACCOUNT			*Cash*		ACCOUNT NO.	*11*
2							Balance
3	Date	Item	Post Ref	Debit	Credit	Debit	Credit
4	1-Nov	Balance				$ -	
5	18-Nov		1	$ 7,500.00			
6	30-Nov		2		$ 3,650.00		
7	30-Nov		2		$ 950.00		
8							

The first entry reflects a beginning balance of 0.

An IF function will be created in this cell to calculate the balance.

The **IF** function is used to calculate the balance of the Cash ledger shown in Figure 6.29. The technique of using the **IF** function when making calculations was introduced in Chapter 4 (see Figure 4.6). The function will be created in cell F5 under the Debit column because asset accounts have a normal debit balance. Your accounting course will provide instruction on what the normal balance is for each type of account. The arguments of this **IF** function are defined as follows:

- **logical_test**: `D5 > 0` The logical test of the **IF** function will be used to determine if there is a value entered in the Debit column.

- **[value_if_true]**: `F4 + D5` If the logical test is true, it can be assumed that there is no entry in the Credit column. An entry *cannot* have a value in both the Debit and Credit columns. As a result, if the logical test is true, then this is a debit entry, which increases the balance of an asset account. Therefore, the value in cell D5 is added to the prior balance of the account, which is in cell F4.

- **[value_if_false]**: `F4 - E5` If the logical test is false, then it is assumed that there is a value in the Credit column. For asset accounts, credits decrease the balance. Therefore, the value in cell E5 is subtracted from cell F4, which is the prior balance of the account.

After the **IF** function is created in cell F5, it can be copied and pasted to the rest of the rows in the ledger. Figure 6.30 shows the completed ledger for the Cash account with the balance being calculated by the **IF** function.

Figure 6.30 | **Complete Ledger for the Cash Account**

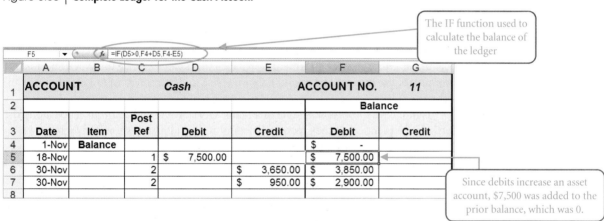

Trial Balance and Work Sheets

This section will illustrate two key components of the financial accounting system. The first is a Trial Balance. A Trial Balance is a list showing the current balance of all accounts for a particular business. The second is an accounting Work Sheet. Work Sheets are used to make any necessary adjustments and finalize the balance of all accounts for a business.

As previously mentioned, each account type has either a normal debit or credit balance. The purpose of the Trial Balance is to assess whether the total for all accounts that carry a debit balance are equal to the total for all accounts that carry a credit balance. Figure 6.31 shows an example of a completed Trial Balance. If a ledger was created in Excel for each account listed in column A, the balance can either be pasted, or preferably linked, into the Trial Balance. A **SUM** function is used to add both columns of the Trial Balance in row 20 to see whether they are equal. The double underline at the bottom of each result signifies that the accounts are balanced, meaning the sum of all debit balances is equal to the sum of all credit balances. You can access the double underline through the **Underline** icon (see Figure 2.22).

Figure 6.31 | **Example of a Completed Trial Balance**

	A	B	C
1	**Company A**		
2	**Trial Balance**		
3	**December 31, 2006**		
4	Cash	$ 3,000.00	
5	Accounts Receivable	$ 2,500.00	
6	Supplies	$ 2,000.00	
7	Prepaid Insurance	$ 2,500.00	
8	Land	$ 20,000.00	
9	Office Equipment	$ 2,000.00	
10	Accounts Payable		$ 1,000.00
11	Unearned Rent		$ 500.00
12	Owner A, Capital		$ 25,000.00
13	Owner A, Drawing	$ 4,000.00	
14	Fees Earned		$ 18,000.00
15	Wages Expense	$ 4,500.00	
16	Rent Expense	$ 1,500.00	
17	Utilities Expense	$ 1,000.00	
18	Supplies Expense	$ 1,000.00	
19	Miscellaneous Expense	$ 500.00	
20		$ 44,500.00	$ 44,500.00
21			

The balance for each account can be pasted or linked to the ledger.

SUM functions are used to total the debit and credit columns.

An accounting Work Sheet is used to make adjusting entries to the Trial Balance of each account and calculate a new balance if necessary. Not all accounts will have an adjusting entry; therefore, the calculated balance on the worksheet may be identical to the trial balance. In addition, the Work Sheet is used to identify the balance of each account as either income statement or balance sheet values. Once the Work Sheet is completed, the Income Statement, Balance Sheet, and Statement of Owners Equity can be created.

Figure 6.32 shows an example of a blank Work Sheet. The accounts listed along the left side are identical to the accounts listed in the Trial Balance shown in Figure 6.31; however, additional accounts can be added to the Work Sheet if necessary. The balance

Figure 6.32 | **Blank Accounting Work Sheet**

	A	B	C	D	E	F	G	H	I	J	K
1					Company A						
2					Work Sheet						
3					For Year End December 31, 2006						
4		Trial Balance		Adjustments		Adjusted Trial Balance		Income Statement		Balance Sheet	
5	Account Title	Dr	Cr	Dr	Cr	Dr	Cr	Dr	Cr	Dr	Cr
6	Cash										
7	Accounts Receivable										
8	Supplies										
9	Prepaid Insurance										
10	Land										
11	Office Equipment										
12	Accounts Payable										
13	Unearned Rent										
14	Owner A, Capital										
15	Owner A, Drawing										
16	Fees Earned										
17	Wages Expense										
18	Rent Expense										
19	Utilities Expense										
20	Supplies Expense										
21	Miscellaneous Expense										
22											
23											
24											
25											
26											
27											

The abbreviation for Debit is Dr and for Credit is Cr.

The Trial Balance is in this worksheet.

The accounts in this column are identical to the Trial Balance.

H ◄ ► H | Trial Balance | **Work Sheet**

for each account in the first two columns of the Work Sheet should be identical to the Trial Balance. The next set of columns is for adding any necessary adjustments. Columns F and G are used for calculating a new balance for each account to include any adjusting entries. The Income Statement and Balance Sheet columns are for categorizing the adjusted balance for each account in its respective financial statement. Therefore, the balance for each account used to construct an income statement will be shown in the Income Statement columns, and the balance for each account used to construct a balance sheet will be shown in the Balance Sheet columns.

As previously mentioned, the balance that appears in the first two columns of the Work Sheet must match the Trial Balance. Therefore, links are created in the Work Sheet to show the debit and credit values under the Trial Balance heading. If the order of the accounts in the Work Sheet is identical to the Trial Balance, the first link can be copied and pasted for the other accounts. Linking data in this situation ensures that the balance for each account in the Trial Balance matches the Work Sheet. If any changes are made to the Trial Balance, it will automatically be reflected in the Work Sheet. Figure 6.33 shows the links that were created in the Work Sheet.

Figure 6.33 | **Work Sheet with Links to the Trial Balance**

	B6	▼	f_x =Trial Balance!B4			
	A	B	C	D	E	
1					Company A	
2					Work Sheet	
3					For Year End December	
						A
4		Trial Balance		Adjustments		
5	Account Title	Dr	Cr	Dr	Cr	
6	Cash	3,000				
7	Accounts Receivable	2,500				
8	Supplies	2,000				
9	Prepaid Insurance	2,500				
10	Land	20,000				
11	Office Equipment	2,000				
12	Accounts Payable		1,000			
13	Unearned Rent		500			
14	Owner A, Capital		25,000			
15	Owner A, Drawing	4,000				
16	Fees Earned		18,000			
17	Wages Expense	4,500				
18	Rent Expense	1,500				

This value is linked to cell B4 in the Trial Balance worksheet.

The values in these columns are produced by links to the Trial Balance worksheet.

The next set of columns in the Work Sheet is used for adding any adjusting entries for each account. Once the adjustments are added into the Work Sheet, an adjusted balance is calculated. Similar to calculating the balance on a ledger, the **IF** function will be used to calculate the adjusted balance on the Work Sheet by determining if the adjustments in columns D and E should be added or subtracted from the balance in the Trial Balance columns (columns B and C). To do this, you must first determine how debits and credits change the balance of an account. For the accounts on this Work Sheet, *debits will increase the balance of an account except for* Accounts Payable; Unearned Rent; Owner A, Capital; and Fees earned. For these accounts, the formula in the **IF** function must be adjusted so that any value in the Debit column is subtracted from the trial balance. Figure 6.34 shows an example of two **IF** functions that are used to calculate the Adjusted Trial Balance columns in the Work Sheet.

Figure 6.34 | Using the IF Function to Calculate the Adjusted Trial Balance in the Work Sheet

Account	Trial Balance Cell Location	Adjusting Entry Cell Locations	Account Type	IF Function
Cash	B6	Debits = D6 Credits = E6	**Asset:** Debits increase the balance.	=IF(D6 > 0,B6 + D6,B6 - E6)
Accounts Payable	C12	Debits = D12 Credits = E12	**Liability:** Debits decrease the balance.	=IF(D12 > 0,C12 - D12,C12 + E12)

Figure 6.35 shows the Work Sheet with adjusting entries added to columns D and E and the adjusted trial balance calculated by **IF** functions in columns F and G. In addition, **SUM** functions were added to row 22 to show the total debits and credits for each set of columns. Notice that the debits match the credits for each set of columns.

Figure 6.35 | Work Sheet with Adjustments and Adjusted Trial Balance Added

The IF function calculating the balance of this account is =IF(D12 > 0, C12 - D12,C12 + E 12).

The IF function calculating the balance of this account is =IF(D6 > 0,B6 + D6,B6 - E6).

SUM functions are used to add the total debits and credits for each set of columns.

The last columns to be completed on the Work Sheet are the Income Statement and Balance Sheet columns. These columns are used to classify the adjusted trial balances as either income statement or balance sheet accounts. This is accomplished by referencing the appropriate cell location in the Debit or Credit column of either the Income Statement or Balance Sheet headings. Your accounting course will provide details on which accounts are income statement or balance sheet accounts.

Figure 6.36 shows how each account in the Work Sheet is classified with respect to the Income Statement or Balance Sheet columns. For the first account, which is Cash, the cell reference =F6 is used to display the Adjusted Trial Balance in the Debit column under the Balance Sheet heading. As a result, any changes to the Adjusted Trial Balance for each account will be reflected in either the Income Statement or Balance Sheet columns.

COMMON MISTAKES | Accounting Work Sheets

Make sure cell references are typed into the appropriate Debit or Credit column for the Income Statement or Balance Sheet columns of the Work Sheet. If an account shows a debit balance in the Adjusted Trial Balance column, then it must also have a debit balance in either the Income Statement or Balance Sheet columns. The same is true for accounts that have credit balances.

Figure 6.36 | **Work Sheet with Income Statement and Balance Sheet Columns Completed**

	Trial Balance		Adjustments		Adjusted Trial Balance		Income Statement		Balance Sheet	
Account Title	Dr	Cr	Dr	Cr	Dr	Cr	Dr	Cr	Dr	Cr
Cash	3,000			500	2,500				2,500	
Accounts Receivable	2,500		500		3,000				3,000	
Supplies	2,000			500	1,500				1,500	
Prepaid Insurance	2,500				2,500				2,500	
Land	20,000				20,000				20,000	
Office Equipment	2,000		500		2,500				2,500	
Accounts Payable		1,000	250			750				750
Unearned Rent		500				500				500
Owner A, Capital		25,000				25,000				25,000
Owner A, Drawing	4,000				4,000				4,000	
Fees Earned		18,000		500		18,500		18,500		
Wages Expense	4,500				4,500		4,500			
Rent Expense	1,500				1,500		1,500			
Utilities Expense	1,000				1,000		1,000			
Supplies Expense	1,000		250		1,250		1,250			
Miscellaneous Expense	500				500		500			
	44,500	44,500	1,500	1,500	44,750	44,750	8,750	18,500	36,000	26,250

(Company A — Work Sheet — For Year End December 31, 2006)

The cell reference =F6 is entered here.

SUM functions are used to total the debit and credit columns.

The final step in completing the Work Sheet is entering a formula to calculate the Net Income. You may have noticed in Figure 6.36 that the total debits and credits for the Income Statement and Balance Sheet columns do not match. This is why a double under-line was not added to these results. For the Debit and Credit columns to match, the Net Income must be calculated and added to the Debit column of the Income Statement and to the Credit column of the Balance Sheet. This is done using basic formulas. For the Income Statement column, you calculate the Net Income by subtracting the total debits from the total credits. For the Balance Sheet column, you subtract the total credits from the total debits. You enter this formula in the Debit column for the Income Statement and in the Credit column for the Balance Sheet. When the net income is added to the total debits in the Income Statement column, the total debits will match the total credits. When the net income is added to the total credits of the Balance Sheet column, the total credits will match the total debits. The final Work Sheet is shown in Figure 6.37.

Figure 6.37 | **Final Work Sheet**

	Trial Balance		Adjustments		Adjusted Trial Balance		Income Statement		Balance Sheet	
Account Title	Dr	Cr	Dr	Cr	Dr	Cr	Dr	Cr	Dr	Cr
Cash	3,000			500	2,500				2,500	
Accounts Receivable	2,500		500		3,000				3,000	
Supplies	2,000			500	1,500				1,500	
Prepaid Insurance	2,500				2,500				2,500	
Land	20,000				20,000				20,000	
Office Equipment	2,000		500		2,500				2,500	
Accounts Payable		1,000	250			750				750
Unearned Rent		500				500				500
Owner A, Capital		25,000				25,000				25,000
Owner A, Drawing	4,000				4,000				4,000	
Fees Earned		18,000		500		18,500		18,500		
Wages Expense	4,500				4,500		4,500			
Rent Expense	1,500				1,500		1,500			
Utilities Expense	1,000				1,000		1,000			
Supplies Expense	1,000		250		1,250		1,250			
Miscellaneous Expense	500				500		500			
	44,500	44,500	1,500	1,500	44,750	44,750	8,750	18,500	36,000	26,250
							9,750			9,750
							18,500	18,500	36,000	36,000

(Company A — Work Sheet — For Year End December 31, 2006)

The formula entered into this cell is =I22 - H22.

This is the output of a formula adding cells H22 and H23.

The formula entered into this cell is =J22 - K22.

Statements

Once the Work Sheet is completed, you can create a set of financial statements. The data used to create these statements will be linked to the Work Sheet. As a result, when the data is changed in the Work Sheet, it will adjust the outputs of the financial statements. Three statements will be created from the Work Sheet shown in Figure 6.37: an Income Statement, a Balance Sheet, and a Statement of Owners Equity.

The purpose of an Income Statement is to report the profitability of a business by showing all sales and expenses incurred by a company. Figure 6.38 shows an example of a blank Income Statement. The first item listed in column A (cell A4) is Fees earned, which is typically used to represent the sales of a service business. The items listed in the range A7:A11 represent various expenses for this service business. The total expenses in row 12 will be subtracted from the Fees earned to calculate the Net Income.

Figure 6.38 | **Blank Income Statement**

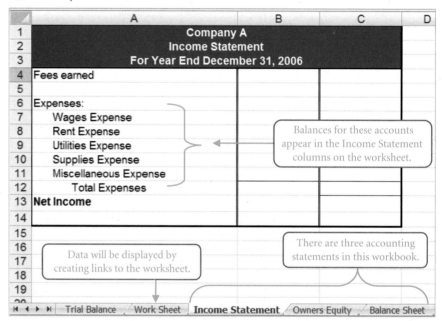

Figure 6.39 shows the completed Income Statement. The value for the Fees earned is the result of a link to cell I16 in the Work Sheet shown in Figure 6.37. Links are also created for each expense account listed in column A. A **SUM** function is used in cell C12 to calculate a total for all expenses. Then a formula is entered in cell C13 to calculate the Net Income; this formula subtracts the Total Expenses from the Fees earned.

Figure 6.39 | **Complete Income Statement**

The formula bar shows that this cell contains a link to cell I16 in the worksheet.

A SUM function is entered in this cell totaling the values of the expenses in the range B7:B11.

The formula in this cell subtracts cell C12 from C4.

	A	B	C
		C4	▼	fx	='Work Sheet'!I16
1	Company A		
2	Income Statement		
3	For Year End December 31, 2006		
4	Fees earned		$ 18,500.00
5			
6	Expenses:		
7	Wages Expense	$ 4,500.00	
8	Rent Expense	$ 1,500.00	
9	Utilities Expense	$ 1,000.00	
10	Supplies Expense	$ 1,250.00	
11	Miscellaneous Expense	$ 500.00	
12	Total Expenses		$ 8,750.00
13	Net Income		$ 9,750.00
14			

In your accounting classes, you will learn that the assets of a company are entitled to either owners or creditors. The Statement of Owners Equity presents the value of a company's assets that is entitled to the owners. Figure 6.40 shows a blank Statement of Owners Equity.

Figure 6.40 | **Blank Statement of Owners Equity**

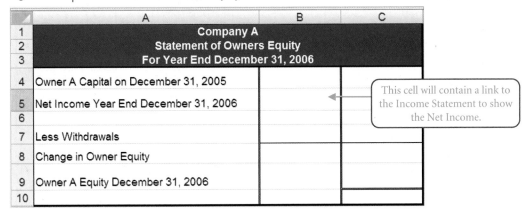

Figure 6.41 shows a completed Statement of Owners Equity. The value for the first item—Owner A Capital on December 31, 2005—is the result of link to cell K14 on the Work Sheet in Figure 6.37. This is the Owners Equity balance in the Balance Sheet column. The Withdrawals value in row 7 is linked to the Owner A Drawing account balance in cell J15 of the Work Sheet. The Net Income value in row 5 is linked to the Net Income that was calculated in cell C13 on the Income Statement in Figure 6.39. The Change in Owner Equity is calculated with a formula that subtracts the Withdrawals in row 7 from the Net Income in row 5. The Owners Equity for this period is calculated using a formula in cell C9 that adds the Change in Owner Equity in cell C8 from Owner's Capital in cell C4.

Figure 6.41 | **Completed Statement of Owners Equity**

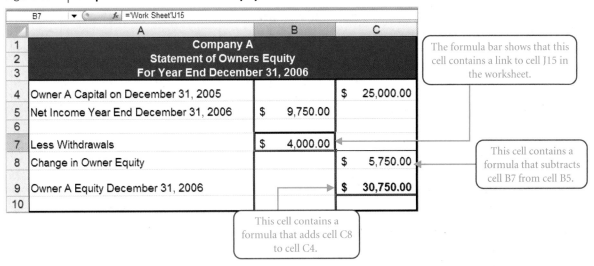

Figure 6.42 shows an example of a blank Balance Sheet. The Balance Sheet contains current account balance information for all Asset accounts, Liability accounts, and Owners Equity. The Balance Sheet follows the accounting equation `Assets = Liabilities + Owners Equity`. Details regarding this equation will be covered in your accounting courses. However, a cursory knowledge of this equation is required when constructing a Balance Sheet. The data used for the Balance Sheet will come from links to the worksheet in Figure 6.37 and the Statement of Owners Equity in Figure 6.41.

Figure 6.42 | **Blank Balance Sheet**

	A	B	C	D	E	F
1			Company A			
2			Balance Sheet			
3			December 31, 2006			
4	Assets			Liabilities		
5	Current assets:			Current liabilities:		
6	Cash			Accounts payable		
7	Accounts receivable			Unearned Rent		
8	Supplies			Total liabilities		
9	Prepaid insurance					
10	Total current assets					
11	Property, Plant, & Equipment (net of Accumulated Depreciation):					
12	Land					
13	Office equipment			Owners Equity		
14	Total PP&E			Owner A, Capital		
15						
16	Total assets			Total Liabilities and OE		
17						

Figure 6.43 shows a completed Balance Sheet. With the exception of the Owner A Capital, links for all accounts on the Balance Sheet can be found in the Balance Sheet column on the Work Sheet in Figure 6.37. The links for each account are created in columns B and E in Figure 6.43. The **SUM** function is used in column C to total each category of accounts such as Current assets and Property, Plant, & Equipment. At the bottom of the Balance Sheet, formulas are used to add the Total assets and the Total Liabilities and OE. The results of these formulas will match if the Balance Sheet, Work Sheet, Income Statement, and Statement of Owners Equity were properly constructed.

Figure 6.43 | **Completed Balance Sheet**

	A	B	C	D	E	F
1			Company A			
2			Balance Sheet			
3			December 31, 2006			
4	Assets			Liabilities		
5	Current assets:			Current liabilities:		
6	Cash	$ 2,500.00		Accounts payable	$ 750.00	
7	Accounts receivable	$ 3,000.00		Unearned Rent	$ 500.00	
8	Supplies	$ 1,500.00		Total liabilities		$ 1,250.00
9	Prepaid insurance	$ 2,500.00				
10	Total current assets		$ 9,500.00			
11	Property, Plant, & Equipment (net of Accumulated Depreciation):					
12	Land	$ 20,000.00				
13	Office equipment	$ 2,500.00		Owners Equity		
14	Total PP&E		$ 22,500.00	Owner A, Capital		$ 30,750.00
15						
16	Total assets		$ 32,000.00	Total Liabilities and OE		$ 32,000.00
17						

VIDEO WORKSHOP

>> Financial Accounting

The purpose of this workshop is to demonstrate how to use Excel to construct the financial accounting spreadsheets and statements illustrated in this section. I will be demonstrating the tasks in this workshop in the following seven videos: **T-Accounts**, **Journals**, **Ledgers**, **Trial Balance and Work Sheet**, **Income Statement**, **Owners Equity**, and **Balance Sheet**. The name of the video appears at the beginning of each section. At the beginning of each section, you will be instructed to open the Excel file that is required to complete the tasks. Complete each section and then watch the related video.

1. T-Accounts (Video: T-Accounts)

a. Open the file named ib_e06_t-accounts.

b. Type a **SUM** function in cell D12 that sums the values in the range D5:D11.

c. Type a **SUM** function in cell F12 that sums the values in the range F5:F11.

d. Type a formula in cell B12 that subtracts cell F12 from D12.

e. Bold and italicize cell B12.

f. Copy the range A3:F12 and paste it after activating cell A15.

g. Type `Accounts Receivable` in cell C15.

h. Delete the contents in the range C17:D21 and E17:F20.

i. Type the data listed for the following cell locations:
   i. C17: `June 30`
   ii. C18: `August 15`
   iii. D17: `5000`
   iv. D18: `3000`
   v. E17: `August 1`
   vi. F17: `2500`

j. Copy the range A15:F24 and paste it after activating cell H3.

k. Delete the contents in J5:K6, L5:M5, and cell I12.

l. Type `Accounts Payable` in cell J3.

m. Type the data listed for the following cell locations:
   i. L5: `June 1`
   ii. L6: `June 30`
   iii. M5: `3000`
   iv. M6: `3000`
   v. J5: `August 1`
   vi. K5: `1000`

n. Type a formula into cell I2 that subtracts cell K12 from M12.

o. Save and close your file.

2. Journals (Video: Journals)

a. Open the file named ib_e06_journals.

b. Type the date `November 30` in cells A18 and A19.

c. Type the data listed for the following cell locations:
   i. B18: `Accounts Payable`
   ii. C18: `21`
   iii. D18: `950`
   iv. B19: `Cash`
   v. C19: `11`
   vi. E19: `950`
   vii. B20: `Paid creditors on account`

d. Indent cell B19 once and cell B20 twice. Then italicize the text in cell B20.

e. Type a **SUM** function into cell D22 that totals the values in the range D3:D20.

f. Copy the **SUM** function in cell D22 and paste it into cell E22 using the **Formulas** option.

g. Save and close your file.

3. Ledgers (Video: Ledgers)

a. Open the file named ib_e06_ledger.

b. Type the word **Cash** in cell C1 in the Ledger worksheet.

c. Add a new worksheet to the workbook.

d. Copy the Journal worksheet and paste it into the new worksheet.

e. Sort the Journal pasted in the new worksheet by the Description and Date column in ascending order.

f. Copy cells A5:A7 in the copy of the Journal. Activate cell A5 on the Ledger worksheet and paste.

g. Copy cells D5:E7 on the copy of the Journal. Activate cell D5 on the Ledger worksheet and paste.

h. Type an **IF** function into cell F5 of the Ledger worksheet that tests whether the value in cell D5 is greater than 0. If the test is true, then have the function add the value in cell D5 to the value in cell F4. If the test is false, have the function subtract the value in cell E5 from the value in cell F4.

i. Copy cell F5 in the Ledger worksheet and paste it to cells F6 through F8.

j. Type the date **October 1** into cell A8 and the number 100 into cell E8. Then format cell E8 with the Accounting number format.

k. Save and close your file.

4. Trial Balance and Work Sheet (Video: Trial Balance and Work Sheet)

a. Open the file named ib_e06_trialbalanceandworksheet.

b. Type a **SUM** function into cell B20 in the Trial Balance worksheet that totals the values in the range B4:B19. Then copy this function and paste it into cell C20 using the **Formulas** option.

c. Add a double underline to cells B20 and C20.

d. Activate the Work Sheet worksheet.

e. Create a link in cell B6 that shows the value in cell B4 in the Trial Balance worksheet.

f. Copy cell B6 and paste it into the range B7:C21 using the **Formulas** option. Then delete any links in the range B7:C21 that display a value of 0.

g. Type a **SUM** function in cell B22 that totals the values in the range B6:B21. Then copy this function and paste it into the range C22:E22.

h. Add a double underline to cells B22:E22.

i. Type an **IF** function into cell F6. If the value in cell D6 is greater than 0, the function should add the value in cell B6 to the value in cell D6. Otherwise, the function should subtract the value in cell E6 from the value in cell B6.

j. Copy the **IF** function in cell F6 and paste it into the range F7:F11, cell F15, and cells F17:F21.

k. Type an **IF** function into cell G12. If the value in cell D12 is greater than 0, the function should subtract the value in cell D12 from the value in cell C12. Otherwise, the function should add the value in cell C12 to the value in cell E12.

l. Copy cell G12 and paste it into G13, G14, and G16.

m. Type the cell reference **=F6** into cell J6.

n. Copy cell J6 and paste into the range J7:J11 and J15.

o. Type the cell reference **=G12** into cell K12.

p. Copy cell K12 and paste it into cells K13 and K14.

q. Type the cell reference **=G16** into cell I16.

r. Type the cell reference **=F17** into cell H17. Then copy cell H17 and paste it into the range H18:H21.

s. Type a **SUM** function into cell F22 that totals the values in the range F6:F21.

t. Copy the **SUM** function in cell F22 and paste it into cells G22:K22.

u. Add a double accounting underline to cells F22 and G22.

v. Type a formula in cell H23 that subtracts H22 from I22.

w. Type a formula in cell K23 that subtracts K22 from J22.

x. Type a formula in cell H24 that adds cells H22 and H23. Then copy this formula and paste it into cell K24.

y. Type the cell reference **=I22** into cell I24. Then copy this cell reference and paste it into cell J24.

z. Add a double underline to the range H24:K24.

aa. Save and close your file.

5. Income Statement (Video: Income Statement)

a. Open the file named ib_e06_accountingstatements. Use this file for sections 5–7.

b. Activate the Income Statement worksheet.

c. Create a link in cell C4 that displays the value in cell I16 in the Work Sheet worksheet.

d. Create a link in cell B7 that displays the value in cell H17 in the Work Sheet worksheet. Then copy this link and paste it into the range B8:B11.

e. Type a **SUM** function in cell C12 that totals the values in the range B7:B11.

f. Type a formula in cell C13 that subtracts the value in cell C12 from the value in cell C4.

6. Owners Equity (Video: Owners Equity)

a. Activate the Owners Equity worksheet.

b. Create a link in cell C4 that displays the value in cell K14 in the Work Sheet worksheet.

c. Create a link in cell B5 that displays the value in cell C13 in the Income Statement worksheet.

d. Create a link in cell B7 that displays the value in cell J15 in the Work Sheet worksheet.

e. Type a formula in cell C8 that subtracts the value in cell B7 from the value in cell B5.

f. Type a formula in cell C9 that adds cells C4 and C8.

7. Balance Sheet (Video: Balance Sheet)

a. Activate the Balance Sheet worksheet.

b. Create a link in cell B6 that displays the value in cell J6 in the Work Sheet worksheet. Then copy this link and paste it into the range B7:B9.

c. Type a **SUM** function into cell C10 that totals the values in the range B6:B9.

d. Create a link in cell B12 that displays the value in cell J10 in the Work Sheet worksheet. Then copy this link and paste it into cell B13.

e. Type a **SUM** function into cell C14 that totals the values in the range B12:B13.

f. Type a formula into cell C16 that adds the value in cell C10 to the value in cell C14.

g. Create a link in cell E6 that displays the value in cell K12 in the Work Sheet worksheet. Then copy this link and paste it into cell E7.

h. Type a **SUM** function into cell F8 that totals the values in the range E6:E7.

i. Create a link in cell F14 that displays the value in cell C9 in the Owners Equity worksheet.

j. Type a formula in cell F16 that adds the value in cell F8 to the value in cell F14.

k. Add double underlines to cells C16 and F16.

l. Save and close your file.

>> Analyzing Adjusting Entries and Net Income

The benefits of Excel's cell referencing features are very apparent in the construction of financial accounting spreadsheets and statements. A change in the value of just one account can impact every accounting statement. As a result, this section demonstrated how to use linking techniques so that when the value of one account changes in the Trial Balance, or when adjustments are made on the Work Sheet, every statement will automatically calculate new outputs. Imagine doing these spreadsheets with paper and pencil! A change in one account would require you to erase, recalculate, and rewrite the outcome of every statement.

Exercise

The purpose of this exercise is to show how to use cell referencing and linking techniques to analyze how adjustments to certain accounts impact the Net Income of a company. As a result, this exercise will focus on the construction of an accounting Work Sheet and the adjustment of various accounts. Open the file named ib_e06_accountinganalysis before starting this exercise.

1. Type an **IF** function in cell F6 of the Work Sheet to calculate the Adjusted Trial Balance of the Cash account. The arguments of the **IF** function should be defined as follows:

   a. logical_test: D6 > 0

   b. [value_if_true]: B6 + D6

   c. [value_if_false]: B6 – E6

2. The **IF** function you created in number 1 will add any debits in the Adjustment column to the Trial Balance for Cash (cell B6). If there are any credits in the Adjustment column, it will subtract them from the balance. This is because Cash is an Asset account and debits increase the value of the account and credits decrease the value of the account. Every account on the Work Sheet follows this rule except for Accounts Payable, Unearned Rent, Owner A Capital, and Fees earned. Therefore, copy cell F6 and paste it into the range F7:F11, cell F15, and the range F17:F21.

3. Type an **IF** function in cell G12 to calculate the Adjusted Trial Balance of the Accounts Payable account. The segments of the function should be defined as follows:

   a. **[logical_test]**: D12 > 0

   b. **[value_if_true]**: C12 – D12

   c. **[value_if_false]**: C12 + E12

4. Copy the **IF** function in cell G12 and paste it into cells G13, G14, and G16.

5. Create a **SUM** function in cell F22 that sums the values in the range F6:F21. Copy the function and paste it to cell G22. Add a double underline to cells F22 and G22.

6. Type a cell reference in cell J6 to show the Adjusted Trial balance for the Cash account in cell F6. Copy this cell reference and paste it into the range J7:J11 and into cell J15. These are all Balance Sheet accounts that carry a normal debit balance.

7. The Accounts Payable account is also a Balance Sheet account; however, it carries a normal credit balance. Therefore, type a cell reference into cell K12 that displays the value in cell G12. Copy this link to cells K13 and K14.

8. Fees earned is an Income Statement account, which carries a normal credit balance. Type a cell reference into cell I16 that shows the value in cell G16. The rest of the accounts on the Work Sheet from Wages Expense down to Selling Expense are also Income Statement accounts. Type a cell reference into cell H17 that shows the value in cell F17. Then copy this cell reference and paste it into the range H18:H21.

9. Create a **SUM** function in cell H22 that adds the values in the range H6:H21. Copy this function and paste it into the range I22:K22.

10. Calculate the Net Income in cell H23 using a formula that subtracts cell H22 from cell I22. Create another formula in cell K23 that subtracts cell K22 from J22.

11. Type a formula in cell H24 that adds cells H22 and H23. Copy this formula and paste it into cell K24.

12. Type a cell reference into cell I24 that displays the value in cell I22. Then type a cell reference into cell J24 that displays the value in cell J22. Add a double underline to the range H24:K24.

13. Assume that a customer was not satisfied with the service this company provided and demanded a refund. Type a **5000** debit adjustment for Fees earned in cell D16 and a **5000** credit to Accounts Receivable in cell E7. What was the change in Net Income?

14. Assume this company was issued a rent rebate from the landlord. Type a **3000** credit adjustment to Rent Expense in cell E18 and a **3000** debit adjustment to Cash in cell D6. What happened to the Net Income?

15. The CEO of this company promised its shareholders that it would achieve a target of $78,000 in Net Income. As you can see, this company is falling significantly short of this goal. An unethical accountant proposes an idea of reclassifying $50,000 in sales training expenses as Other Assets. Activate the Trial Balance worksheet and reduce the balance of selling expenses in cell B19 to **120000**. Then increase the balance of Other Assets in cell B7 to **52000**. Check to make sure the values in cell B20 and C20 match. What happened to the Net Income in cells H23 and K23 on the Work Sheet?

16. Save and close your file.

>> What's Wrong with This Spreadsheet?

Problem

You and two other classmates are working on a group project for a Financial Accounting class. The assignment includes a Trial Balance, T-accounts, and Ledgers. Your professor mentions the following list of key accounting rules for each of the three requirements of the project:

1. Trial Balance: The sum of the debits must equal the sum of the credits.

2. T-accounts and Ledgers: For Asset accounts (i.e., Cash and Accounts Receivable), the balance is calculated by subtracting total credits from total debits. For Liability accounts (i.e., Accounts Payable), the balance is calculated by subtracting the sum of all debits from the sum of all credits.

Exercise

One of your teammates says that this project will be easy and offers to do the assignment for the team in Excel. She completes the project and e-mails a completed file to each team member to review before printing and handing in at class the next day. The file your teammate e-mailed is named ib_e06_accountingproject. Would you be comfortable printing each worksheet and handing them in for a grade? Consider the following points:

1. Compare the requirements listed in the Problems section to the data in each worksheet. Does the data in this file comply with these rules?

2. Your teammate thought this assignment would be easy to do in Excel. Why?

What's wrong with this spreadsheet? Write a short answer for each of the points listed here. Then correct any mistakes you find in the workbook.

Using Excel to prepare and manage business plans made my job so much easier and fun. In fact, when presenting business plans at executive meetings, I would bring my laptop to the meeting, pull up my business plan workbook, and type changes in my assumptions spreadsheet to answer any questions the directing officers asked. However, I had to make sure that all possible assumptions that were related to the business I was presenting were included in the spreadsheet. As a result, the details of every business plan I constructed were different, but the techniques I used to construct them in Excel were always the same.

Assignment

1. Open the file named ib_e06_financialprojectionsfornewbusiness.

2. This file includes a worksheet showing five years' worth of financial assumptions for a new business. Construct a financial data and a cash analysis worksheet showing the five-year financial performance of this new business based on the assumptions included in this file.

3. The format of the financial data and cash analysis worksheets should be modeled after the example that was illustrated in the Financial Planning section of this chapter. This section also includes extensive details on how each financial statistic was calculated for each worksheet.

4. Adjust the assumptions in this file such that the NPV of this business achieves at least a positive $10,000 result.

Questions for Discussion

1. This anecdote mentions that researching the assumptions for a business plan was one of the key factors for creating a successful business plan. What else is required to build a successful and accurate business plan?

2. How would you present a business plan to a group of executive officers? What Excel techniques can you use to build an effective and dynamic presentation?

The following questions are related to the concepts addressed in this chapter. There are three types of questions: Short Answer, True or False, and Fill in the Blank. If your answer to a True or False question is False, write a short explanation as to why you think the statement is not true.

1. Cell referencing can be used to _____ data between worksheets or workbooks.

2. Explain how a link is created between two workbooks.

3. Data can be identified as a link to a workbook because the _____ and _____ names precede the cell location.

4. True or False: Data linked to another workbook will always be automatically updated.

5. True or False: Excel will automatically add an absolute value to any cell location that is linked to another workbook.

6. Explain how you can check the Status of data that is linked to other workbooks.

7. The three arguments of the **SUMIF** function are _____, _____, and _____.

8. What range of cells will be added in the following **SUMIF** function:
   `=SUMIF(A3:A6,D18,C3:C10)`

9. True or False: You must always complete all three arguments of the **SUMIF** function.

10. True or False: Creating ledgers in Excel is easy because after you create the first ledger, you can simply copy and paste it to another worksheet, delete all the entries and dates, enter new dates and entries, and the formulas and functions will automatically calculate a new output.

11. Why should you minimize the need to enter data manually into a worksheet when constructing financial plans?

12. What function can be used to calculate the balance on either a ledger or Work Sheet?

13. Explain the value in using links between the Trial Balance, Work Sheet, and Accounting Statements.

14. The _____ command in the _____ tab of the Ribbon is used to lock specific rows and columns when scrolling a worksheet.

15. What is the **value1** argument used for in the **NPV** function?

16. Why is it important to add a Notes section to the Assumptions worksheet of a financial plan?

17. True or False: The data-linking techniques used to construct financial plans do not work well with other business planning exercises.

18. True or False: An **NPV** function will always give you a positive number if you forget to add a negative sign in front of the **value1** argument.

Skills Exam

The following exam is designed to test your ability to recognize and execute the Excel skills presented in this chapter. Read each question carefully and answer the questions in the order they are listed. You should be able to complete this exam in 60 minutes or less.

1. Open the ib_e06_skillsexam.

2. Calculate the construction cost for restaurant 11, which is cell D3 in the Restaurant Detail worksheet. Use a formula that multiplies the size of the restaurant in cell C3 by the cost listed for its appropriate state in the Cost by State worksheet. Use the **VLookup** function to find the cost for the appropriate state for restaurant 11 in the Cost by State worksheet and multiply it by the restaurant size in the Restaurant Detail Worksheet.

3. Copy the formula you created in cell D3 of the Restaurant Detail worksheet and paste it into the range D4:D12 using the **Formulas** option. Be sure to add absolute references where needed.

4. Use **SUMIF** functions to calculate the Total Profit per Square Foot for MD, which is cell F16 of the Restaurant Detail worksheet. This will require two **SUMIF** functions. The first **SUMIF** function will look for the state entered in cell E16 in the range B3:B12 and sum the corresponding values in the range F3:F12. This should be divided by a second **SUMIF** function that will look for the state entered in cell E16 in the range B3:B12 and sum the corresponding values in the range C3:C12.

5. Copy the formula created in cell F16 and paste it into cells F17 and F18 using the Formulas option. Add absolute references where needed.

6. Type a **SUM** function in cell B3 of the Assumptions worksheet that adds the values in the range D3:D12 in the Restaurant Detail worksheet.

7. Type a **SUM** function in cell B2 of the Sales and Profit Plan worksheet that adds the values in the range E3:E12 in the Restaurant Detail worksheet.

8. Type a formula in cell C2 of the Sales and Profit Plan worksheet that uses the percentage in cell B8 in the Assumptions worksheet to calculate the projected sales for Year 1. Copy this formula and paste it to cells D2 and E2.

9. Type a **SUM** function into cell B3 of the Sales and Profit Plan worksheet that adds the values in the range F3:F12 in the Restaurant Detail worksheet.

10. Type a formula into cell B4 of the Sales and Profit Plan worksheet that divides the value in cell B3 by the value in cell B2.

11. Create a formula into cell C3 that multiplies the sales value in cell C2 by the value in cell B4. Place an absolute reference on cell B4 in this formula. Then copy the formula and paste it into cells D3 and E3.

12. Copy cell B4 and paste it into the range C4:E4.

13. Type a formula into cell C5 of the Sales and Profit Plan worksheet that multiplies cell C2 by cell B9 in the Assumptions worksheet. Copy the formula and paste it into the range D5:E5.

14. Type a formula in cell B7 of the Sales and Profit Plan worksheet that subtracts the sum of the range B5:B6 from the value in cell B3.

15. Copy cell B7 and paste it into the range C7:E7.

16. Type an **IF** function into cell C8 of the Sales and Profit Plan worksheet that evaluates whether cell C7 is greater than 0. If it is, then multiply cell C7 by the value in cell B10 on the Assumptions worksheet. If the value in cell C7 is not greater than 0, then show 0. Copy this function and paste it into cells D8 and E8.

17. Type a formula into cell B9 of the Sales and Profit Plan worksheet that subtracts the value in cell B8 from the value in cell B7. Copy this formula and paste it into the range C9:E9.

18. Calculate the loan payments in cell B11 on the Sales and Profit Plan worksheet using the **PMT** function. You should use Cell B4 in the Assumptions worksheet for the rate, cell B5 in the Assumptions worksheet for the periods, and cell B3 for the principal of the loan. Assume that these loan payments are made annually at the beginning of each year.

19. For cells C11, D11, and E11 on the Sales and Profit plan worksheet, type a cell reference that shows the value in cell B11.

20. Type a formula into cell B13 that subtracts the value in cell B11 from the value in cell B9.

21. Type a formula into cell C13 that adds the value in cell B13 to the result of subtracting the value in cell C11 from cell C9.

22. Copy the formula in cell C13 and paste it into cells D13 and E13.

23. Type an **NPV** function in cell E16. The rate of the function should be cell B4 in the Assumptions worksheet, the initial investment value should be cell B3 in the Assumptions worksheet, the cash flow values should be the range B13:E13 in the Sales and Profit Plan worksheet.

24. Add any appropriate formats to the values in the Sales and Profit Plan worksheet. In addition, add formatting features that you think will enhance the appearance of the spreadsheet and make it easier to read.

25. Save and close your file.

Challenge Questions

1. Open the file named ib_e06_companye. This is a completed Trial Balance. Use this Trial Balance to construct a worksheet and set of three financial statements (Income Statement, Statement of Owners Equity, and Balance Sheet). Model the worksheet and statements from the example that was illustrated in the Financial Accounting section of this chapter. After completing the Work Sheet, note the net income. Then add the following adjustments to the Work Sheet and note how the net income changes.

   a. **Fees earned**: Debit $500,000

   b. **Accounts Receivable**: Credit $500,000

   c. **Accounts Payable**: Debit $25,000

   d. **Office Equipment**: Credit $25,000

2. You are considering the purchase of a company that was offered to you at a price of $1,200,000. Your cost to borrow money to buy this firm, or the interest rate charged by a bank, will be 6.0%. Would you buy this company? Develop a spreadsheet to analyze this offer and explain why you would or would not buy this company from a purely five-year financial point of view. What other considerations might you make beyond this financial perspective when considering the purchase of a company? The company has been generating the following cash flows for the past five years:

   a. Year 1 = $150,000

   b. Year 2 = $175,000

   c. Year 3 = $250,000

   d. Year 4 = $350,000

   e. Year 5 = $550,000

3. This chapter illustrated that the balance of a ledger can be calculated using an **IF** function. In addition, you learned that there should never be a number entered for both a debit and credit for a single entry in a ledger. How would you calculate the balance of a ledger and show an error message if a person makes a mistake and enters both a debit and credit for a single entry on the ledger. Create a hypothetical ledger in Excel and type your solution in the balance column.

4. Get a financial statement from any public company. In an Excel spreadsheet, type the financial statistics for the current reporting year and the prior reporting year from the firm's Income Statement. Then create a second spreadsheet with assumptions estimating how you think this company will perform over the next three years. For example, do you think Gross Sales will increase 5% per year over the next three years, do you think the company will maintain its current cost of goods sold percentage of gross sales, and so on? Then create a third spreadsheet showing your projected financial statistics for each item on the firm's income statement.

Chapter 1

Introduction

Chapter Goals

The amount of data that is stored and analyzed today in most corporations is enormous. Business managers use this data to produce valuable information regarding trends within their business, industry, and the overall economy. They then use this information every day to make decisions and complete business objectives. Microsoft Access is a tool that is frequently used by business managers to retrieve data that is stored in a company's database system. The purpose of this chapter is to define Microsoft Access and database systems, as well as to provide an overall view of the organization and features of this textbook.

Before proceeding to the next section, it is important to note that this book assumes that you have a basic understanding of Microsoft Excel 2007. If you have had no previous instruction or experience with Excel, it is recommended that you review Chapters 1 and 2 of *Microsoft Office Excel 2007 In Business, Core.* It is helpful if you also know Chapters 3 and 4 of this text, but it is not required.

>> **Access** | Skill Sets

Access in **Practice** | Anecdote

Access in Business

Over the course of my career, database systems have drastically changed how business managers analyze data and make decisions. I am often amazed when I recall the beginning of my career and remember doing analytical projects in which historical data was kept on paper in four-inch ring binders. Researching the same data today using paper would be unthinkable. Tools such as Microsoft Access played a major role in transforming how I obtained and analyzed the data required to make key business decisions. These decisions ranged from determining which items to ship to stores to what stocks to purchase for an investment portfolio.

Throughout this text I will be using the "Anecdote" sections to share my professional experiences and explain how I used Access to make decisions, research data, or produce valuable information while working for a variety of companies. I have used Access to complete business objectives in industries such as fashion, grocery, food, toys, finance, and technology. At the beginning of each chapter, I will share an experience of how I used Access to manage or complete a specific business objective. At the end of each chapter, you will have an opportunity to use Access to complete a similar business objective. These are all real business objectives and situations that actually happened in my career, and you might face these same objectives at some point in your own career.

>> Continued on page 658

What Is Access?

Most business professionals would agree that information is power. Today, the vast amount of information about businesses (and its easy accessibility) has had a profound impact on how companies operate and compete for market share. This information can include anything from changes in the stock price of publicly traded companies to consumer spending trends by product category in foreign countries. The availability of this information has forced companies to collect and manage enormous amounts of **data** to make the best decisions possible. The type of data a company collects depends on its business. For example, a retail company might collect the number of units sold for each product by store, whereas a manufacturing company might collect the number of customers calling into its call center.

Data by itself does not automatically produce **information**. This is why many business managers use Access, a versatile database tool that can transform data into actionable information. The purpose of this text is to demonstrate how Access is used in a variety of business situations. The following segments in this chapter provide an introduction to Access and define the nature of databases.

Databases

Access is a tool that is used to create databases or work with existing database systems. A **database** can contain one or many **tables** of data. Tables, which are covered in Chapter 2, are similar to Excel spreadsheets, but they have a much larger capacity than spreadsheets for storing data. In some cases, a database table might contain billions of rows of data, whereas an Excel spreadsheet is limited to approximately one million rows. Many business managers use Access to connect to tables that are contained on a central **Relational Database Management System (RDBMS)**. These systems are usually developed and maintained by a company's Information Systems (IS) or Information Technology (IT) departments.

Corporations' RDBMSs typically contain several tables of data that are related to a specific aspect of business. One way to understand relational databases is to think of the organization of a university. A university might be broken up into different colleges, depending on the focus of study. For example, there might be a college for the performing arts, a business college, an engineering college, and a liberal arts college. In an RDBMS, the colleges would make up different and distinct databases. Within each college there are several majors. For example, if you are enrolled in the business school, you might major in accounting, finance, marketing, or business information systems. In an RDBMS, each major would represent a table of data. After you declare a major, you have classes to attend, text books to buy, papers to write, and so on. In an RDBMS, the requirements for your major would be the data that is contained in each table.

Figure 1.1 shows a diagram of an RDBMS that contains three distinct databases.

Figure 1.1 | **Diagram of a Relational Database Management System**

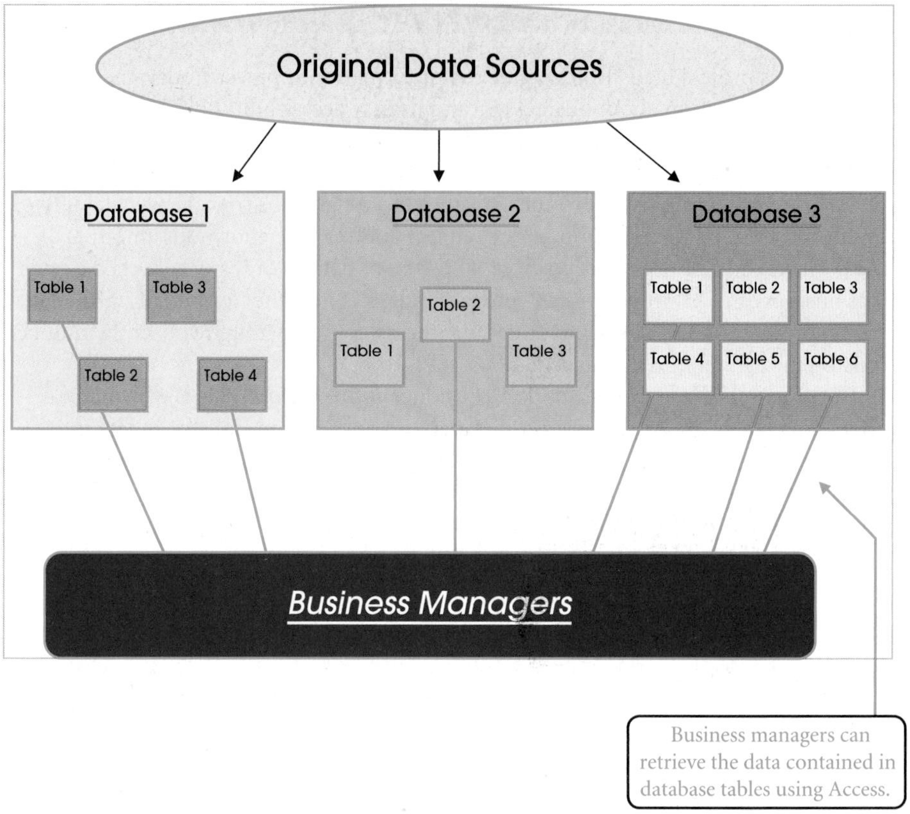

When looking at the diagram from top to bottom, you will notice that data is loaded into the database from original sources of data. The original data source varies, depending on the needs of a business. For example, one of the data sources used by retail companies is the cash register. When your purchase is scanned by a cashier, the cash register stores data such as the item you purchased, the price you paid, the date your purchase was made, the cashier's ID number, and so on. At the end of the day, every register in every store of the company will transmit all its data to one of the tables in the RDBMS (transmitting times and process varies by company). Business managers can then use Access to retrieve the data that has been transmitted to the database table to evaluate the sales performance of products that were sold.

Business Decisions and Databases

Databases play a critical role in the business decisions that are made every day. For many business managers, the decision process starts by reviewing some type of report that was created using data from the tables of a database. The purpose of these reports is to transform data into information that can be used as a basis for making decisions. For example, let's assume you are the investment director for a large financial firm. Your responsibility is to decide which stocks should be purchased or sold to maximize the profitability of your department's investment portfolio. To make these buy or sell decisions, you first want to know if the portfolio is currently making or losing money. Then, you might want to know whether the overall value of the portfolio has been increasing or decreasing over the past six weeks. Finally, you might want to review the number of stocks for which the price has been declining over the past six weeks and the number of stocks for which the price has been increasing over the past six weeks. Based on this information, you can start the process of deciding whether you need to buy or sell stocks in your investment portfolio. All this information can be produced from five simple data components: stock symbols, dates, purchase price, shares purchased, and current price. How can these five data components be transformed into all that information? The answer is Access.

The use of databases has grown rapidly in most companies because tools like Access can produce so much information that can lead to real profits. For example, have you ever signed up for a frequent shopper card or a preferred customer card in your favorite store? This strategy is very common in grocery stores: customers present their frequent shopper cards when they buy groceries and then usually receive some type of discount at the cash register. The grocery company then stores a record of all items they purchased in its database system. The next time the customers go to the grocery store, they might receive coupons for items they usually purchase, or promotional offers for products they usually buy might be mailed directly to their homes. This activity is usually the result of a business manager's decision about where to mail promotions for items that will increase the sales and profitability of the company. Access can be used to produce this information from the grocer's database.

COMMON MISTAKES | Garbage In, Garbage Out

Like any software program, Access is not automatically accurate and does not guarantee perfect results. The accuracy of the information produced by Access depends greatly on how it is used. Throughout this text, I will be using this reference box to point out mistakes that people who use Access in business situations commonly make. It is important that you read these sections carefully when they appear in a chapter. Many of the difficulties people have when using Access are a result of the points I raise in these "Common Mistakes" boxes. The benefit for you is that you can recognize mistakes if they do happen, or (better yet) you can avoid making these mistakes altogether.

Creating a New Access Database

Now that you have an overview of the type of information Access can produce, let's take a look at a blank Access database. When you first launch the Access application, you see the screen shown in Figure 1.2. The right side of this screen is used for opening existing Access databases that you might save on your computer or network. The center area of the screen provides online links to research information about Access or to download templates for specific types of databases that you might create. Click the **Blank Database** button, as shown in the figure, to create a new Access database.

Figure 1.2 | **Creating a New Database After Launching Access**

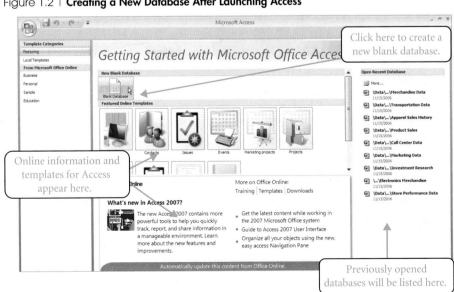

Figure 1.3 shows how to assign a file name to a new blank database. After clicking the **Blank Database** button shown in Figure 1.2, you can assign a file name and location on the right side of the screen. Type the file name of the database in the box under the **File Name** heading. Then click the **Folder** icon to assign a location for the new database on your computer or network. A new Access database is opened after you click the **Create** button shown at the bottom of Figure 1.3.

Figure 1.3 | **Assigning a File Name and Location for a New Database**

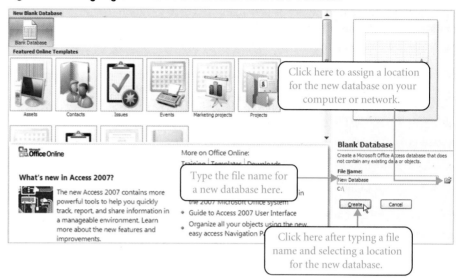

Figure 1.4 shows the appearance of a new blank database after clicking the **Create** button in Figure 1.3. When a new Access database is initially opened, a blank table appears, as shown in this figure. If you do not plan on using this blank table, you can remove it by clicking the **X** in the upper-right corner. Similar to Excel, the Ribbon appears at the top of the Access screen. Many of the commands contained in each tab of the Ribbon will be covered in this text.

Figure 1.4 | **A Blank Access Database**

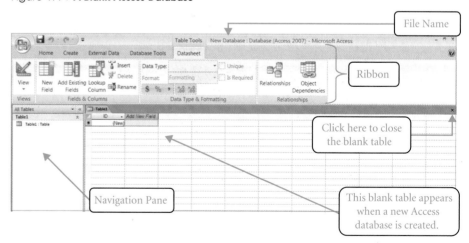

Navigation Pane and Access Objects

The components of an Access database are known as *Objects*. Examples of Access Objects include Tables, Queries, and Reports. You can open Objects contained in an Access database through the **Navigation Pane**, which is identified in Figure 1.4. There are several options that change the way Access Objects are displayed in the **Navigation Pane**. Figure 1.5 shows how these options are accessed. Selecting the **Object Type** and **All Access Objects** options, as shown in Figure 1.6, displays a list of Access Objects by type in the **Navigation Pane**. For example, it lists any Tables contained in the database, then lists all Queries, then lists all Reports, and so on.

Figure 1.5 | **Options for Displaying Objects in the Navigation Pane**

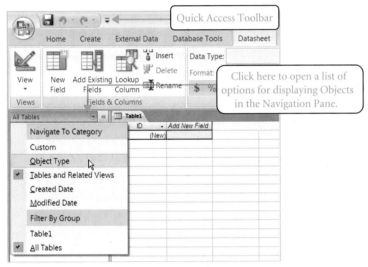

Figure 1.6 | **Navigation Pane Settings for Showing All Access Objects by Type**

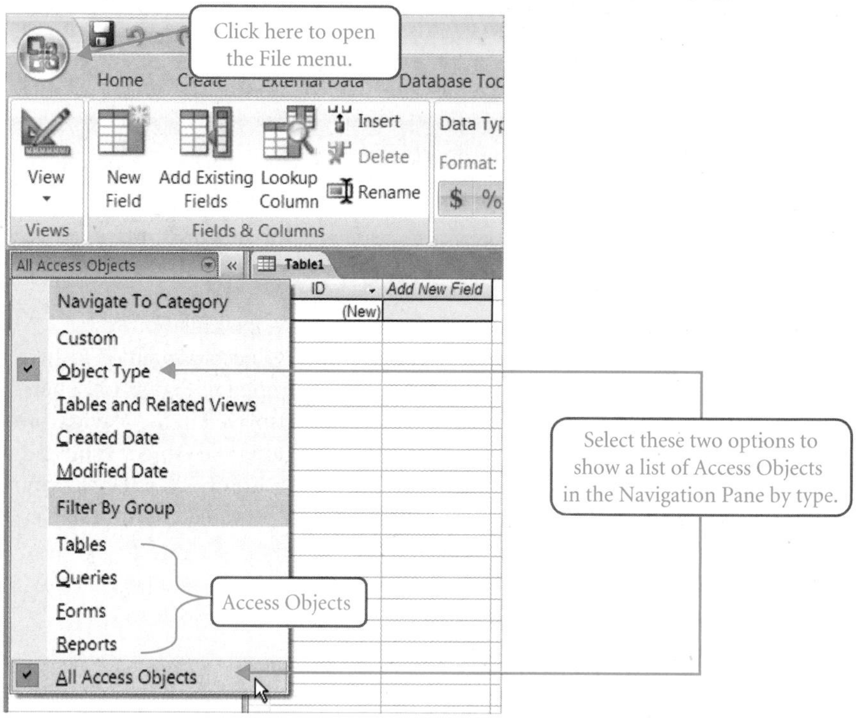

The **Navigation Pane** displays all the Objects that are contained in an Access database. This text focuses on three Access Objects that are commonly used by business managers: Tables, Queries, and Reports. The following list defines these three Objects (as well as the other Access Objects shown in Figure 1.6).

- **Tables:** Used for creating tables of data or linking to tables that are stored and maintained in an external RDBMS. Business managers working in large companies usually use this Object for linking to tables that are maintained by their firms' IT departments.

- **Queries:** Used for extracting data from the tables that are created or linked into an Access database. Especially in large corporations, business managers rarely use all the data that is contained in a table. Therefore, they use this Object to select only the data that is needed from the tables to satisfy the needs of a business objective.

- **Reports:** Used for taking data that is contained in either Tables or Queries and putting it in the form of a report. Business managers use Reports to create the final document containing information used to make decisions.

- **Forms:** Used for creating templates for entering or viewing data in tables.

- **Macros:** Used for automating groups of Access commands or tasks.

- **Modules:** Used for creating fully automated applications with VBA (Visual Basic for Applications).

File Formats and Other Access Settings

Similar to Excel, Access provides the ability to create databases using file formats that are compatible with older versions of Microsoft Office. This is especially important if you are sharing an Access database with fellow coworkers or classmates who are using an older version of Office, such as Office 2003. If you create an Access database using the 2007 file format, a person running Office 2003 cannot open it. However, you can convert an Access database created using the 2007 file format to an older file format through the

Office Button. The following explains how a 2007 file format is converted to a format that is compatible with Office 2002 (also called Office XP) or Office 2003:

- Open an existing Access database or create a new one.
- Click the **Office Button** (refer to Figure 1.6) This will open the **File** menu.
- Click the arrow next to the **Save As** option.
- Select the **Access 2002-2003 Database** option on the right side of the **File** menu.
- This will convert the database to a file format that can be opened by someone using Office 2002 or 2003. Note that if you have an Object open, such as a Table or Query, a prompt appears, notifying you that these objects must be closed before the database can be converted.
- Type a new file name and select a location on your computer or network in the **Save As** dialog box. Then click the **Save** button at the bottom of the dialog box.

Figure 1.7 shows the options in the **File** menu. The options on the right side of the menu appear after clicking the arrow next to the **Save As** option. Notice the various file format options that can be used to convert an existing database.

Figure 1.7 | **Converting the File Format of an Access Database**

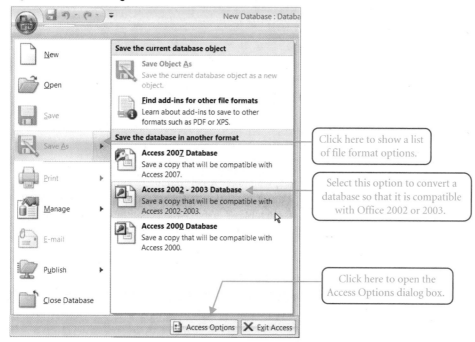

Figure 1.8 shows the top of the Access database after it is converted to a new file format. The file format reads Access 2002-2003 instead of Access 2007.

Figure 1.8 | **Database Showing 2002-2003 File Format**

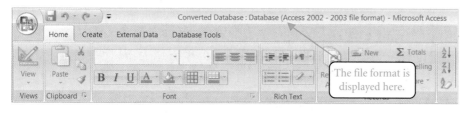

As demonstrated, you can change the file type of an existing Access database by using the **Save As** option in the **File** menu. However, if you are working with people who are using an older version of Office on a regular basis, you might want to create all new databases using the 2002-2003 file format by clicking the **Access Options** button at the bottom of the **File** menu (refer to Figure 1.7).

Figure 1.9 shows the **Access Options** dialog box, which opens after clicking the **Access Options** button at the bottom of the **File** menu. The **Default file format** option in the **Popular** category of the dialog box sets the file format of all new databases that are created.

Figure 1.9 | **Popular Category of the Access Options Dialog Box**

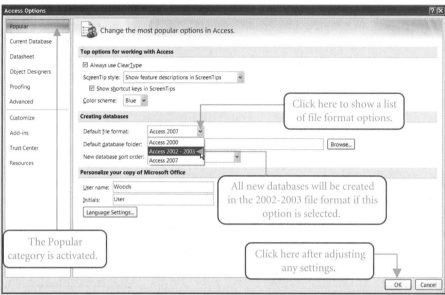

Similar to the **Excel Options** dialog box, the **Access Options** dialog box enables you to adjust the settings that are applied when new Access databases and Objects are created. Figure 1.10 shows the options that are available in the Datasheet category. These settings are applied when data is displayed in a table or query. Notice that the default Font has been set to Arial and the font size is set to 10 (originally Calibri font with size of 11).

Figure 1.10 | **Datasheet Category of the Access Options Dialog Box**

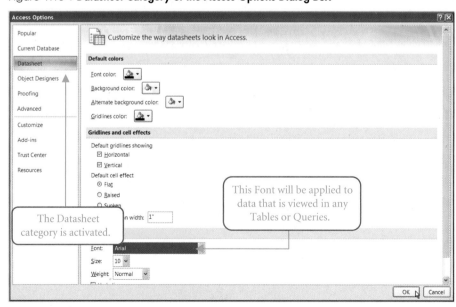

>> *Quick Reference*

Changing the Default File Format for New Databases

1. Open a new or existing Access database.
2. Click the **Office Button**.
3. Click the **Access Options** button at the bottom of the **File** menu.
4. Click the **Popular** category on the left side of the **Access Options** dialog box.
5. Click the down arrow of the **Default file format** option and select a format option.
6. Click the **OK** button at the bottom of the **Access Options** dialog box.

Access Help

The **Help** window, which is the last area covered in this Access introduction, is a reference tool that you can use to research various Access commands. To open it, click the **Help** icon, as shown in Figure 1.11. Then type a question or topic in the input box of the **Help** window and press the **Enter** key or click the **Search** button. You then see a list of links that contain topics related to what you typed into the input box. Click a link to see instructions and information related to your topic.

Figure 1.11 | **Help Window**

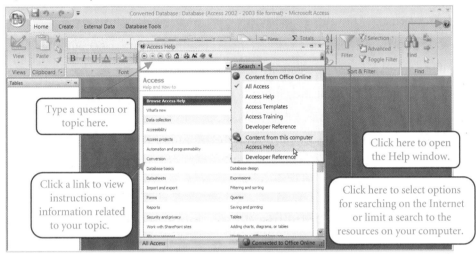

Using versus Creating Databases

Before moving on to the next chapter, it is important to understand how you will be using Access in this text. You can use Access to build a complete database of tables or to retrieve data from tables contained in an existing database. Most business managers use Access to work with tables contained in an existing RDBMS that is maintained by their companies' IT departments. It would be very time-consuming and counterproductive to the goals of a company if business managers were required to build and maintain their own database tables. This is why they use Access to retrieve data from external RDBMSs maintained by a dedicated group of technology managers.

The primary focus of this text is to show how Access is used with external database systems. However, most of the Access databases that are created for this text contain static tables. That is to say, although one of the main goals of an RDBMS is to continually update or add to the data contained in a table, the tables contained in the databases provided with this text do not change. The purpose of the databases provided with this text is to simulate how data might appear in a variety of business situations and fields. When you begin using Access in a professional environment, you will most likely be using tables that are connected to an RDBMS that provides routine updates.

VIDEO WORKSHOP

>> Introduction to Access

This is the first of several workshops that will be presented in this text. These workshops serve two purposes: to give you an opportunity to practice the skills illustrated in each section of every chapter and to watch me, the author, demonstrate these skills. Many people have an easier time learning software skills after they see techniques and commands demonstrated. Therefore, you can watch a video demonstration of each workshop by opening the related video file that is provided with this text. Although the workshops usually require you to open an Access database to complete the tasks listed, there is no Access database required for this workshop. The purpose of this workshop is to create a blank Access database and become familiar with the layout of the software. Try completing each of the tasks listed as follows and then watch the video named **Introduction**.

1. **Creating a New Database (Video: Introduction)**
   a. Launch Access.
   b. Click the **Blank Database** button.
   c. Click in the **File Name** input box on the right side of your screen and delete the file name that appears in the box.
   d. Type the file name **New Database** in the **File Name** input box.
   e. Click the **Folder** icon next to the **File Name** input box. Select a location on your computer or network. Then click the **OK** button at the bottom of the **File New Database** dialog box.
   f. Click the **Create** button below the **File Name** input box.
   g. Click the X in the upper-right corner of the blank table to close it.

2. **Change the Font Setting for Datasheets (Video: Introduction)**
   a. Click the **Office Button** menu icon above the Ribbon.
   b. Click the **Access Options** button at the bottom of the **File** menu.
   c. Click the **Datasheet** category on the left side of the **Access Options** dialog box.
   d. Click the down arrow next to the **Font** drop-down box in the Default font section.
   e. Select the **Arial** font option.
   f. Click the **OK** button at the bottom of the **Access Options** dialog box.
   g. Close the database by clicking the X in the upper right corner of your screen.

>> How Companies Use Databases

This is one of the two types of exercises that are presented after each section in every chapter of the text. The purpose of these exercises is to show how Access is used to complete a hypothetical business objective or make a business decision. The data that is used for these exercises is very similar to what might be found in a variety of business fields. However, because this chapter deals with a general overview of Access and database systems in general, there is no database required for this exercise.

Exercise

The purpose of this exercise is to identify ways in which database systems are utilized in business today. Research various media sources such as newspapers, magazines, on-line journals, or the Internet to find a current article relating to the use of database systems. Write a short summary of the firm's business and how it is using database systems to make key business decisions.

EXERCISE

Why Do I Need This?

>> What's Wrong with This Database?

Problem

This is the second type of exercise that is presented at the end of each section of every chapter. The purpose of these exercises is to practice fixing problems that might arise when working with Access databases. Furthermore, when you begin using Access in a professional environment it is likely that you will be using an Access database that someone else created. These exercises help you develop the skill of evaluating the validity and accuracy of databases that might be given to you from other people. Although these exercises usually require you to open and evaluate an Access database that is provided with the text, there is no database required for this particular exercise.

Exercise

You are working as an analyst in a large company. One of your coworkers is having trouble with Access and asks for your help. He explains that he is trying to open two Access databases on his desktop. However, every time he tries to open the second database, the first closes. He asks if you know some trick for preventing the first database from closing when the second one is opened.

Is there anything wrong with this database? Explain why your coworker is having trouble opening a second Access database?

PROBLEM & EXERCISE

Throughout my career, not only did databases become more important to the decisions I had to make, but my ability to use and master
database software such as Access increased my value as an employee
for the companies I worked for.

Assignment

This section of the text contains two parts. The first part is an assignment in which you
construct a database to solve a similar business problem or make a similar business
decision to those explained in the anecdote. The second part presents broad business
issues mentioned in the anecdote that are related to managing businesses or making
business decisions. Because skills for developing an Access database are not addressed in
this chapter, there is no assignment.

Questions for Discussion

1. Businesses are always relying on data to make decisions. Do you think companies that
   have the most data will be guaranteed success? Why?

2. What key decisions do business managers have to make in the following types of
   companies: investment firm, grocery store, and food manufacturer?

3. How can databases help business managers improve the decisions you identified in
   question 2?

This section features questions that help you review the key concepts and skills that presented in the chapter. There are three types of questions: Short Answer, True or False, and Fill in the Blank. If your answer to a True or False question is False, write a short explanation as to why you think the statement is not true.

1. True or False: Similar to Excel, if you are comparing tables of data that exist in two different Access databases, you can open both databases using the Open command.

2. What do the letters RDBMS stand for?

3. What is the difference between information and data?

4. True or False: One of the reasons why so many businesses use Access is because it is always accurate.

5. In a database, the actual data is stored in _____.

6. To change the default file format of an Access database when it is created, you must click the _____ _____ button in the _____ menu.

7. True or False: After a database is created in a specific file format, it cannot be changed to an alternate file format.

8. Which three Objects of an Access database are most commonly used by business managers?

9. The _____ Object of an Access database is used for selecting specific sets of data from a table.

10. Why would a business manager in a large corporation prefer to use tables that are maintained on the firm's external RDBMS instead of using Access to create his own tables?

>> Skills Exam

This section, also included at the end of each chapter, is used to test your knowledge of executing various skills presented in the text. As mentioned, the primary mission of this book is to explain and demonstrate how Access is used by business managers to complete business objectives or make business decisions. However, knowing how to execute key skills that are required to operate Access is also important. This section presents several skill-based questions that you have to apply to an Access database that is provided with this text. The first question of this section asks you to either create an Access database or open an existing Access database. Because skills for constructing an Access database have not yet been covered, there is no Skills Exam for this chapter.

This section, which follows the Skills Exam section, features questions that require you to apply the skills you have learned to complete typical business objectives. There is usually no right or wrong method for completing the objectives presented in this section. However, the results you obtain must be accurate. This section might also include questions that ask you to identify how databases play a role in the success of a business or the decision-making process of a business.

1. Identify two companies that demonstrate the importance of databases in their decision-making process. Compare and contrast the similarities and differences between the two companies. Use media resources such as journals, magazines, newspapers, or Internet sites to do your research.

>> Chapter 2

The Database Table

Chapter Goals

Understanding the design and contents of tables is critical for mastering the use of any database system. The primary Access functions and commands are designed so that you can build, manage, and extract data from tables. This chapter will focus on how to construct Access tables by covering skills, such as defining data types and entering data into Access tables. In addition, it will explain how to create tables through linking or downloading data. Most business managers use this technique to create tables as opposed to entering data into a table. However, learning the process of setting data types and entering data is a good way to achieve a deeper understanding of database tables.

>> **Access** Skill Sets

Access in Practice | Anecdote

Merchandise Planning in the Fashion Industry

My first experience in working with database systems such as Access occurred when I was a merchandise planning manager in the women's fashion industry. The company I worked for manufactured and sold women's clothes in retail stores across the country. The company sold a variety of products such as formal and casual clothes, shoes, jewelry, and fragrances. My role was to develop the merchandise sales plans for the casual clothing department. The purpose of these plans was to analyze how much our department needed to sell for each item purchased to achieve our sales and profit goals. To estimate the sales units for each item, we evaluated emerging fashion trends as well as historical sales results by item. At the time I held this position, historical data was stored on Excel spreadsheets. At the end of each year, I would enter and store the sales results for each item in an Excel file. Because each year of historical data was stored in a different Excel file, analyzing a few years of data at once was often cumbersome and difficult. In fact, I usually spent most of my time gathering and preparing data for analysis. I was certain that, if I could spend more time analyzing the results of the business, I could increase the accuracy of the plans for the department.

>> Continued on page 714

>> Creating Tables

Tables are the primary component of any database system. Data used to evaluate the performance of a business is extracted from tables, analyzed, and used for developing reports. This section will illustrate the fundamental skills required for creating and editing tables in Access. These skills include defining data types, entering data, and setting the data sequence or index.

Creating a New Table

This section demonstrates the construction of an Access table using the data shown in Figure 2.1. This figure shows data that has been collected by the manager of a hypothetical university bookstore. This manager can keep track of the daily sales results for every item sold in the store on a database table, which is typically done in most retail companies. Over time, this information will provide the manager with more analytical options for evaluating the performance trends of the items sold in the bookstore and might improve future purchasing and marketing decisions.

Figure 2.1 | **Sales Data from a Hypothetical University Bookstore**

Sales Date	Category Number	Category Description	Daily Unit Sales	Daily Sales Dollars
10/5/2006	16	T-Shirts	30	540
10/5/2006	25	Sweatshirts	17	748
10/5/2006	36	Hats	22	264
10/5/2006	55	Supplies	64	576
10/5/2006	96	Gift Items	12	408
10/6/2006	16	T-Shirts	40	880
10/6/2006	25	Sweatshirts	22	836
10/6/2006	36	Hats	10	160
10/6/2006	55	Supplies	52	728
10/6/2006	96	Gift Items	26	832
10/7/2006	16	T-Shirts	44	968
10/7/2006	25	Sweatshirts	33	1254
10/7/2006	36	Hats	12	192
10/7/2006	55	Supplies	43	602
10/7/2006	96	Gift Items	18	576

As mentioned in Chapter 1, a blank table will automatically appear when a new Access database is created. However, to add additional tables to a new or existing database, click the **Table** icon or the **Table Design** icon in the **Create** tab on the Ribbon, as shown in Figure 2.2.

Figure 2.2 | **Options for Creating a New Table**

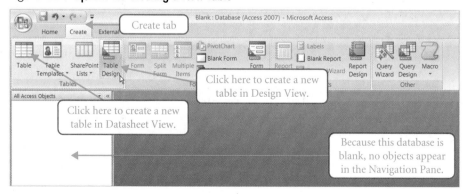

Clicking the **Table** icon, as shown in Figure 2.2, will open a blank Access table in *Datasheet View*. This view allows you to type directly into an empty table in a manner similar to entering data into an Excel spreadsheet. Figure 2.3 shows an example of a blank table in **Datasheet View**. Notice that the first column or *field* in the table is labeled ID. This label is automatically added when you use the **Table** icon and is used for assigning a unique value to each row or *record* in the table. In addition, notice that the name Table1 appears in the **Navigation Pane**. When you click the **Save** icon after creating the table, you will be prompted to assign a new name, which will replace the Table1 name in the **Navigation Pane** under the **Tables** object. Finally, you will see the **Datasheet** tab added to the Ribbon when working with a table in **Datasheet View**.

Figure 2.3 | **Blank Table in Datasheet View**

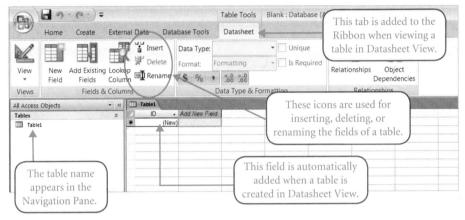

The second option for creating a new table in Access is to click the **Table Design** icon (see Figure 2.2). When you're entering data manually, this is usually the preferred option for creating a new table because it gives you the most control for defining the data types for each field in a table. This approach also provides a way of adding descriptions for each field. The next segment illustrates this approach in more detail.

Figure 2.4 shows an example of a blank table in *Design View*. Notice that the **Design** tab is added to the Ribbon when you open a table in **Design View**. In addition, notice the options that are available when the down arrow under the **View** icon is clicked. This feature is mostly used to switch a table to the **Datasheet View** that was illustrated in Figure 2.3. When a table is in **Datasheet View**, you can select the **Design View** option from the **View** icon to switch back to **Design View**. To create an Access table for the data shown in Figure 2.1, you will use a combination of both the **Design View** and **Datasheet View commands**.

Figure 2.4 | **Design View of a Blank Table**

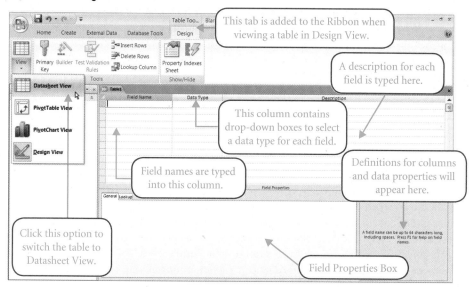

Field Names, Data Types, and Field Properties

To begin creating an Access table for the data shown in Figure 2.1, you will assign field names to each column of data. Field names are similar to the descriptions that you might type into the first cell of a column in an Excel spreadsheet. However, a field in Access is considered one complete set of data rather than a list of values in a column. The following points explain how to add the field names to a table when it is initially created in the **Design View**:

- Create a new database and close the table that is automatically started when the database is created. You do this by clicking the X in the upper-right corner of the table.

- Click the **Create** tab on the Ribbon.

- Click the **Table Design** icon. This will open a blank table in **Design View**, as shown in Figure 2.4.

- Type the words Sales Date in the first row of the Field Name column. When the table opens in **Design View**, the cursor will already be placed in the first row of the Field Name column so you can begin typing.

- Press the **Down Arrow** key on your keyboard. This will enter the first field name into the table and set the cursor in the second row of the Field Name column.

- Type the following field names into the table and press the **Down Arrow** key after each one: Sales Date, Category Number, Category Description, Daily Unit Sales, Daily Sales Dollars.

Figure 2.5 shows the **Design View** of the table after the field names have been typed. Notice in the column next to each field name is the word *Text*. This is the current *data type* setting for each field, which will be adjusted next.

>> **Quick Reference**

Creating a New Table

1. Click the **Create** tab on the Ribbon.

2. Click either the **Table** icon or the **Table Design** icon.

Figure 2.5 | **Entering Field Names in the Design View of a New Table**

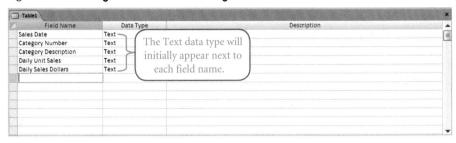

After you type the field names into the **Design View** of a table, you must then select the data type for each field. A data type serves three purposes. First, it defines what kind of data can be entered into a field, such as numbers, dates, and text. Second, it controls the amount of data or the storage capacity for each cell in a field. For example, a field might use a *Text* data type for descriptions that are up to 100 characters long. Therefore, text data consisting of 1 to 100 characters can be typed into each cell of this field. The third purpose of data types is to ensure data consistency among all cells of a field. Unlike in an Excel spreadsheet, the columns or fields of an Access table act as one unit of data. For example, formulas in Excel use individual cell locations to compute results. However, you *cannot* apply mathematical calculations to an individual cell of an Access table. In Access, formulas apply mathematical computations to an entire field of data. Therefore, you will be using field names when creating formulas in Access, and the mathematical operations of that formula will be applied to every data value contained in each cell of the field. Therefore, you would not want to have a field that contained some cells with text data and some cells with numeric data because that would create errors when the field is used in a mathematical formula. Figure 2.6 provides a list of common data types, their purpose, and storage capacity.

Figure 2.6 | **Common Data Types Used in Business**

Data Type	Purpose	Storage Capacity
Memo	Used for messages or long descriptions. Entries for this data type can be a combination of both words and numbers. Numbers entered for this data type *cannot* be used in calculations.	Up to 65,535 characters.
Text	Used for descriptive information such as the name of items, categories, customer names, etc. This can also be used for numbers that will not be used in calculations such as phone numbers or ZIP codes.	Up to 255 characters.
Date/Time	Used for date and time data. The date format can be changed in the Field Properties box.	For dates up to the year 9999.
Currency	Used for monetary data. Entries for this data type can be used in mathematical formulas.	For monetary values up to 999 trillion.
Number	Used for any number that is required or might be required for mathematical computations.	The data size that can be used for this type will vary depending on the option selected in the Field Size property.

The storage capacity and format for each data type can be adjusted in the **Field Properties** box at the bottom of a table when it is in **Design View**. For example, when assigning the **Text** data type to a field, you can set the maximum number of characters that can be entered into each cell in the **Field Properties** box. If you are using the **Currency** data type, you can use the field properties to set the monetary symbol (dollars or euros) and the decimal places. The following explains how to set the data type and field properties for the Sales Date field shown in Figure 2.5:

- Click in the Data Type column next to the Sales Date field name. A drop-down arrow will appear next to the word *Text* when you click in this column (see Figure 2.7).
- Click the drop-down arrow to open the list of data type options.
- Select the **Date/Time** data type option because the Sales Date field will contain only dates.
- Click in the Format row of the **Field Properties** box.
- Click the drop-down arrow that appears after clicking in this row and select the **Short Date** format option.

Figure 2.7 shows the data type setting and the field property setting for the Sales Date field. Note that the Short Date shown in the Format row of the **Field Properties** box was selected by clicking the down arrow that appears on the right side of the row after clicking in it.

Figure 2.7 | **Data Type and Field Property Setting for the Sales Date Field**

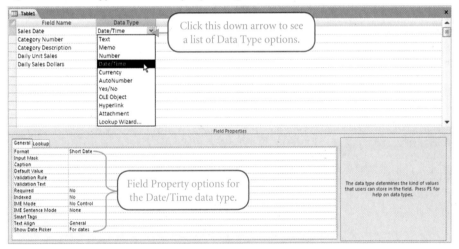

It is important to note that the properties listed along the left side of the **Field Properties** box, as shown in Figure 2.7, will change depending on the data type that is selected. For example, if the **Text** or **Number** data type option is selected, the *Field Size* property will be listed in the first row of the **Field Properties** box. As you can see in Figure 2.6, you can define up to 255 characters for a **Text** data type. With regards to the **Number** data type, the **Field Size** property is used for defining the type of number that will be entered into a field. The **Field Size** property options for the **Number** data type are listed in the Figure 2.8.

Figure 2.8 | **Common Number Field Size Options Used in Business**

Number Field Size	Purpose	Storage Capacity
Integer	Used for smaller numbers that do not require a decimal point. Decimals cannot be used for this option.	Numbers that fall in the range –32,768 to 32,767. Total storage capacity of 2 bytes.
Long Integer	Used for larger numbers that do not require a decimal point. Decimals cannot be used for this option.	Numbers that fall in the range –2,147,483,648 to 2,147,483,647. Total storage capacity of 4 bytes.
Single	Used for smaller numbers that require a decimal.	38 digits for values greater than 1. 45 digits for values less than 1. Total memory capacity of 4 bytes.
Double	Used for larger numbers that require a decimal.	308 digits for values greater than 1. 324 digits for values less than 1. Total memory capacity of 8 bytes.

Figure 2.9 shows the data type and **Field Size** setting that was used for the Category Number field. Notice that the Field Size is set to **Integer**. The reason is that the Category Number will always be a two-digit number. Therefore, the **Integer Field Size** option is adequate for the purposes of this field.

Figure 2.9 | **Data Type and Field Size for the Category Number Field**

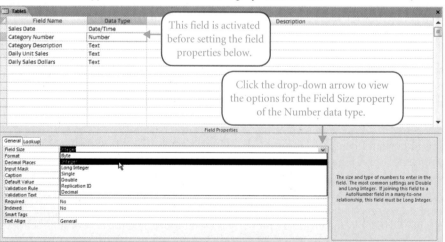

COMMON MISTAKES | Data Types and Field Properties

It is important to choose a data type and field size that closely match your data. Choosing a data type and field size that are too large for your data will waste the memory resources of your computer. Choosing a data type and field size that are too small for your data will prevent certain entries from being added to your table.

The following is a recap of the data type and field property settings that were used for each field name shown in Figure 2.5:

- **Sales Date**: The **Date/Time** data type was used and the **Short Date** option was selected from the **Format** properties (see Figure 2.7).
- **Category Number**: The **Number** data type was used and the **Integer** option was selected from the **Field Size** properties. Because the category number will not be more than two digits, the **Integer Field Size** is adequate (see Figure 2.9).
- **Category Description**: The **Text** data type was used and the **Field Size** property was set to 20 characters. Because no description is more than 20 characters, this limit is adequate for the field.
- **Daily Unit Sales**: The **Number** data type was used and the **Long Integer** option was selected from the **Field Size** properties. This field cannot contain any numbers with decimal points because you cannot sell a fraction of an item (it's all or nothing). Therefore, the **Long Integer Field Size** option is appropriate for this field.
- **Daily Sales Dollars**: The **Currency** data type was used and the **Decimal Places** property was set to 0.

Figure 2.10 shows the final field names, data types, and field property settings for the table that was started in Figure 2.5. Notice that a description was entered in the third column for each field name. This description will appear in the status bar of the screen when any cell in the field is activated. It is important to note that this table was constructed in a vertical method. In other words, all the field names were entered into the table, then the data type and ***field properties*** were defined, and then the descriptions were added. However, you could also work horizontally, meaning the data type, field properties, and descriptions can be added after each field name is typed into the table.

Figure 2.10 | **Final Settings in the Design View of the University Bookstore Sales Table**

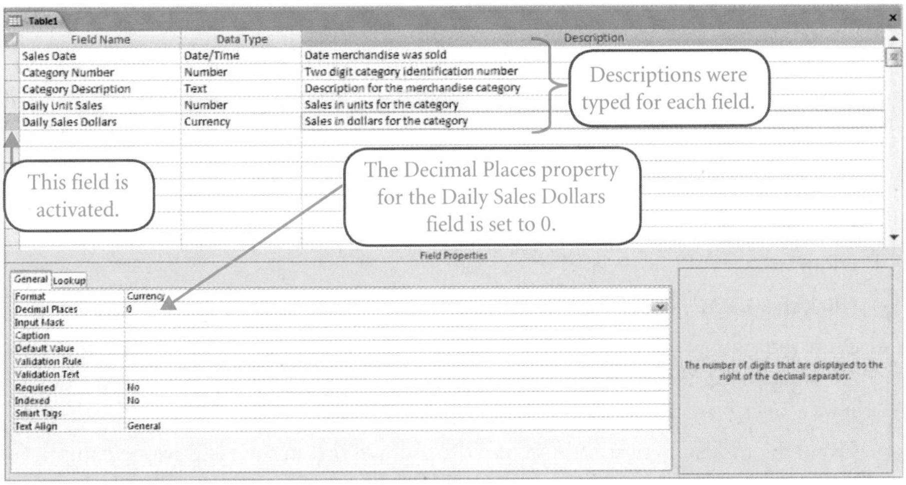

Indexing and Primary Keys

After defining the field names and data types, you will need to define the index and primary key of a new table. The ***index*** is used to determine how data is organized or sequenced in a table. Remember, one of the primary functions of Access is to search and extract data from large tables. Indexing a table makes this process more efficient. For example, a telephone book is indexed by a person's last name, which makes it easy to find a phone number. Just think how long it would take you to find a person's phone number if the numbers in a phone book were listed in random order. The purpose of indexing a table follows the same principle and is especially critical for large tables of data. If you are building small tables in Access, indexing is not very critical. However, if

Quick Reference

Field Names, Data Types, and Field Properties

1. Create a new table in **Design View** or open an existing table in **Design View**.
2. Type field names in the Field Name column.
3. Click in the Data Type column next to the appropriate field name.
4. Click the down arrow and select a data type from the list of options.
5. Click next to one of the field properties in the **Field Properties** box.
6. Click the down arrow next to the appropriate field property and select an option or type the field property setting.
7. Type a description for the field in the Description column.

you plan on, or currently are, working for a company that manages a large database, you will likely need to know how the tables in that database are indexed before extracting any data.

When you're setting the index for a table, it is important to determine which fields are likely to be used to search for data. This will depend on the type of data that is being entered or downloaded into the table. For example, a table with personal financial information will likely be searched by a person's last name or account number. In this case the index might involve both the last name and account number. An index can be established with up to, but no more than, ten fields. The table shown in Figure 2.10 will be indexed by the following fields:

1. **Sales Date:** This field will be used to establish the primary sequence of the data entered into the table. It is very common to search by date when evaluating the sales performance of a business. For example, the manager of the university bookstore might be holding promotions or sales events on certain dates. Therefore, the sales results for each item will need to be analyzed for a specific date to see whether the promotion was successful.

2. **Category Number:** This is the second field that will be used to organize the data in this table. As a result, the data will be sequenced by date and category number, which will allow sales data to be extracted for a specific category on a specific date. For example, if the store manager was running a promotion on T-shirts, this category can be extracted for specific data or dates to analyze the sales results.

The preferred method for setting the index of a table is to use the **Indexes** icon in the **Design** tab on the Ribbon. This method allows you to establish an index using multiple fields and also provides the option of indexing the table in either ascending or descending order. The following points explain how to index the table in Figure 2.10 based on the Sales Date and Category Number fields:

- Click the **Design** tab on the Ribbon. Note that the table must be in **Design View** to see this tab.
- Click the **Indexes** icon. This will open the **Indexes** dialog box.
- In the first column of the **Indexes** dialog box, type any name that describes the index. The field names used to establish the index are typically used for the index name. For this example, the index name is Date/Cat Number. However, any naming convention will work.
- Press the right arrow key to activate the first drop-down box in the Field Name column.
- Click the down arrow of the drop-down box and select the Sales Date field name.
- Press the right arrow key to activate the first drop-down box of the Sort Order column and select **Descending**. This will sort the data in the table based on the dates in the Sales Date field from the most recent date to the oldest date.
- Using the mouse, activate the second drop-down box in the Field Name column and select the Category Number field. This field should automatically be set to Ascending in the Sort Order column.
- Click the X in the upper-right corner of the Indexes dialog box to complete the index of the table and close the dialog box.

Figure 2.11 shows the final settings in the **Indexes** dialog box that was used to establish the index for the table shown in Figure 2.10.

Figure 2.11 | **Indexes Dialog Box**

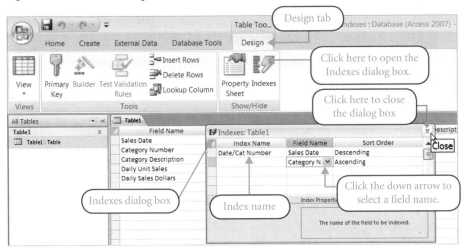

COMMON MISTAKES | Indexing

Many people confuse the indexing command with the sorting command. Sorting will change the *appearance* of data sequenced in a table. Indexing refers to the way data is stored in a table. Therefore, you *cannot* change the sequence of data as it appears in a table through indexing. This is done through the sorting command.

As previously mentioned, the next area that will be defined for the table shown in Figure 2.10 is the *primary key*. The primary key is set on the field or fields that make each record in the table unique. For example, if a bank manager was creating a table of customers and account numbers, the account number would be the primary key of the table because two customers *cannot* have the same account number. However, it is possible for the bank to have two customers with identical names. The main benefit of assigning a primary key is that it prevents any duplicate records from being entered into a designated field. This would be essential in the case of the banking manager because every customer must have a unique account number. In addition, a table cannot be saved if a record is created and the primary key field is left blank. As a result, the primary key ensures the integrity of the data that is entered into an Access table. This is also referred to as *entity integrity*, and it forces critical information to be entered into a table. In the case of the banking manager, if an account number is not entered into the table for each customer, it would be impossible to maintain accurate balance information.

Many of the database tables used in business environments frequently require several fields to identify a unique record. For the University Bookstore sales data shown in Figure 2.1, a unique record is defined by a combination of the Sales Date and Category Number fields. The reason is that each category number can be listed only one time for each date. Imagine if you looked at an Access table containing the sales results for the bookstore and saw category number 25 listed twice for 10/30/2006. As shown in Figure 2.12, one record for category 25 shows that the Unit Sales is 10 and the Dollar Sales is $557. In another record the Unit Sales is 10 but the Dollar Sales is $575. Which record is correct? Should you add both records? There is really no way of determining the sales for category 25 in this case. However, if a primary key is assigned to both the Sales Date and Category Number fields, Access would prevent the table from being saved with two records containing the same date and category numbers.

>> **Quick Reference**

Defining Indexes

1. Open a table in **Design View**.
2. Click the **Design** tab on the Ribbon.
3. Click the **Indexes** icon to open the **Indexes** dialog box.
4. Type an index name in the far left column of the **Indexes** dialog box.
5. Select a field from the **Field Name** drop-down box.
6. Select **Ascending** or **Descending** in the Sort Order column.
7. Click the X in the upper-right corner to finish the index and close the **Indexes** dialog box.

Figure 2.12 | **Bookstore Sales Table without a Primary Key**

Bookstore Table with Error				
Sales Date ·	Category Number ·	Category Description ·	Daily Unit Sales ·	Daily Sales Dollars ·
	25	Sweatshirts	10	$557
	25	Sweatshirts	10	$575
	36	Hats	22	$264
10/30/2006	55	Supplies	64	$576
10/30/2006	96	Gift Items	12	$408
*	0		0	$0

Category 25 is mistakenly listed twice.

Assigning a primary key to both fields will ensure only one category number is entered for each sales date.

The following explains how to define the primary key for the table in Figure 2.10:

- Place the cursor in the box next to the Sales Date field.
- Left click when the cursor changes to a black arrow pointing to the right and drag down to the Category Number field. This will place a bold orange outline around both fields. If you need to highlight fields that are not in consecutive order, hold the **Ctrl** key and click the desired fields.
- Click the **Design** tab on the Ribbon.
- Click the **Primary Key** icon. A small key will appear to the left of both the Sales Date and Category Number fields. This key indicates that both fields make up the primary key of the table.
- Click the **Save** icon in the **Quick Access** toolbar. Then type the name University Bookstore Daily Sales in the **Save As** dialog box and click the **OK** button.

Figure 2.13 shows the primary key defined for the University Bookstore Daily Sales table, which was started in Figure 2.10. Notice that the cursor changes to a black arrow pointing to the right when it is placed in the box to the left of the Field Name column.

Figure 2.13 | **Defining the Primary Key with Multiple Fields**

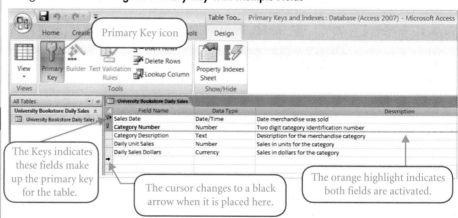

>> **Quick Reference**

Defining Primary Keys

1. Open a table in **Design View**.
2. Activate a field by clicking the box to the left of the field name, or click and drag to highlight several fields.
3. Click the **Design** tab on the Ribbon.
4. Click the **Primary Key** icon.

Entering and Formatting Data

After defining the field names, data types, field properties, indexes, and primary keys, you can enter data into a new table. After saving the table, you enter data by switching to the **Datasheet View**, as illustrated in Figure 2.3. Typing data into an Access table is similar to typing data into an Excel spreadsheet. Simply activate a cell by clicking it once and begin typing. After entering data into a cell, you can press the **Enter** key, the

Tab key, or the **Arrow** keys to advance to another cell on the table. Symbols such as dollar signs will automatically be added based on the field properties that were entered in the **Design View** of the table (see Figure 2.10).

Figure 2.14 shows the University Bookstore Daily Sales table, which now includes sales for 10/5/2006 and 10/6/2006 from Figure 2.1. Notice the calendar icon that appears when a cell is activated in the Sales Date field. You use this feature to select a date from a calendar instead of typing it into the cell. Access produces this option because the data type setting for this field was set to **Date/Time**.

Figure 2.14 | **Data Typed into the University Bookstore Daily Sales Table**

Sales Date	Category Number	Category Description	Daily Unit Sales	Daily Sales Dollar	Add New Field
10/5/2006	16	T-Shirts	30	$540	
10/5/2006	25	Sweatshirts	17	$748	
10/5/2006	36	Hats	22	$264	
10/5/2006	55	Supplies	64	$576	
10/5/2006	96	Gift Items	12	$408	
10/6/2006	16	T-Shirts	40	$880	
10/6/2006	25	Sweatshirts	22	$836	
10/6/2006	36	Hats	10	$160	
10/6/2006	55	Supplies	52	$728	
10/6/2006	96	Gift Items	26	$832	

Click here to select a date from the calendar.

Because of the field property settings, numbers typed into this field will automatically be formatted to currency with 0 decimal places.

The description typed in the Design View for the activated field appears here.

Number of records in this table

Record: 11 of 11   No Filter   Search

Date merchandise was sold

COMMON MISTAKES | Data Type and Data Entry

You must enter data that is compatible with the data type and field property settings of a field. An error message will appear if the data entered into a field is not compatible with the data type assigned to that field. Figure 2.15 shows an example of a text description that was typed into the Category Number field. Notice that the message states the data type for this field is a **Number**. The options listed allow you to enter a new value or convert the data type of the column to text. Check the design and purpose of your table carefully before selecting the convert data type option. This could create compatibility problems with your table.

Figure 2.15 | **Incompatible Data Error Message**

10/6/2006	25	Sweatshirts	22	$836
10/6/2006	36	Hats	10	$160
10/6/2006	55	Supplies	52	$728
10/6	Gift Items	Gift Items	26	$832

The value you entered does not match the Number data type in this column.

Enter new value.

Convert the data in this column to the Text data type.

Help with data types and formats.

You can format the appearance of the data entered into a table with the icons found in the **Home** tab on the Ribbon, as shown in Figure 2.16. The formatting icons in this tab on the Ribbon are identical to those in other Microsoft applications such as Excel. However, the formatting icons that are selected will be applied to the entire Access table. For example, if you change the font size to 12 points, this change will be applied to all the data in the table. You cannot change the format of an individual cell or field of an Access table.

Figure 2.16 | **Format Icons in the Home Tab on the Ribbon**

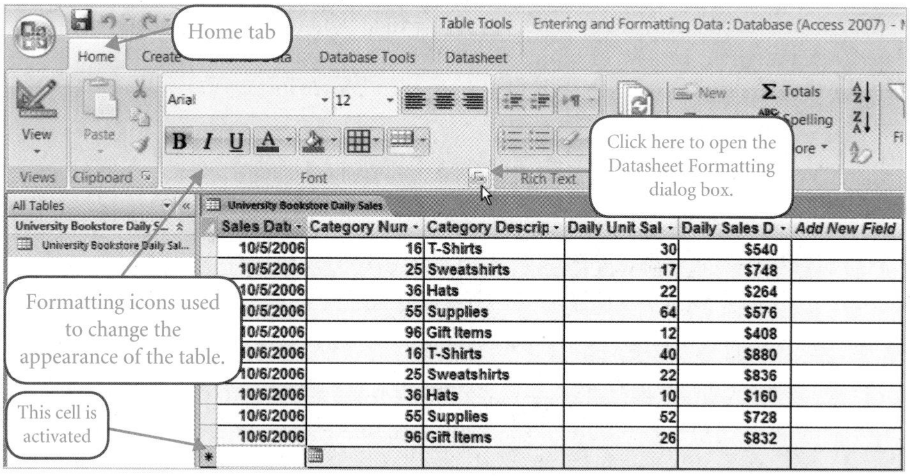

To access additional formatting features for a table, open the **Datasheet Formatting** dialog box, as shown in Figure 2.17. This dialog box provides options for changing the cell color and grid lines of a table. You can also apply effects such as giving cells the appearance of being raised on the table. You open this dialog box by clicking the button in the lower-right side of the **Font** group of icons.

Figure 2.17 | **The Datasheet Formatting Dialog Box**

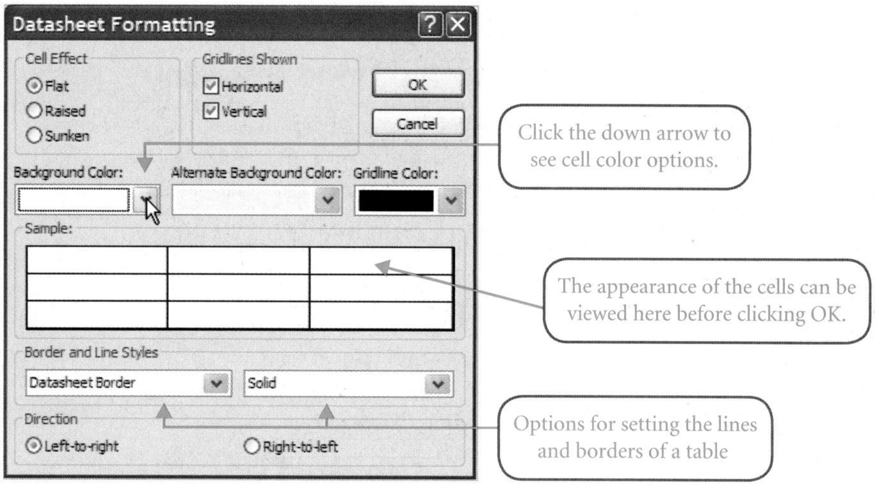

>> **Quick Reference**

Data Entry

1. Open a table in **Datasheet View**.

2. Activate a cell and type the appropriate text or numeric value. Make sure the data you are typing is compatible with the data type assigned to the field.

3. Use the **Enter**, **Arrow**, or **Tab** keys to enter the data and move to the next cell.

>> **Quick Reference**

Formatting a Table

1. Open a table in **Datasheet View**.

2. Click the **Home** tab on the Ribbon.

3. Select any of the formatting icons. Note that formats will be applied to the entire table.

Adjusting and Hiding Columns and Rows

As data is being entered into an Access table, you may need to adjust the width or height of columns and rows. Adjusting columns and rows in Access is identical to adjusting columns and rows in Excel. As in Figure 2.18, place the cursor between two fields, and when the cursor changes to double arrows, click and drag to the desired width. Apply the same method for adjusting the height of rows.

Figure 2.18 | **Adjusting Columns and Rows**

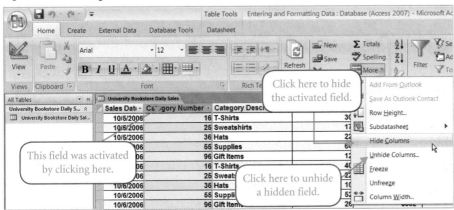

Sales Date	Category Number	Category Descrip	Daily Un
10/5/2006	16	T-Shirts	
10/5/2006	25	Sweatshirts	
10/5/2006	36	Hats	
10/5/2006	55	Supplies	
10/5/2006	96	Gift Items	

Click and drag to adjust the column width.

Similar to Excel, Access provides the option for hiding columns. Hiding columns can help reduce the amount of data displayed on a table, which can make it easier to analyze data contained in a few targeted fields. To hide a column, activate a field on the table, click the **More** icon in the **Home** tab on the Ribbon, and select the **Hide Columns** option. Figure 2.19 shows the options available in the **More** icon.

Figure 2.19 | **Hiding Columns**

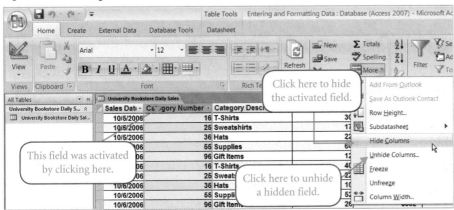

Click here to hide the activated field.

This field was activated by clicking here.

Click here to unhide a hidden field.

Copying and Pasting Data

Similar to Excel, data can be copied and pasted in Access tables. In fact, you can copy data from an Excel spreadsheet and paste it into an Access table. Pasting data from existing sources such as Excel spreadsheets decreases both the time needed to enter data into a table as well as the potential for data entry errors. The following points explain how to copy data from an Excel spreadsheet and paste it into the University Bookstore Daily sales table from Figure 2.16:

- Copy several rows of data from an Excel spreadsheet using the **Copy** icon in the **Home** tab on the Ribbon in the Excel application.
- Activate the next available record in the University Bookstore Daily Sales table. To do this, click the asterisk to the left of the first empty record on the table (see Figure 2.20).
- Click the **Paste** icon in the **Home** tab on the Ribbon in the Access application.
- A message will be displayed asking whether you want to add records to the table. Click **Yes** to complete pasting the data into the table.

>> **Quick Reference**

Adjusting Column Widths and Row Heights

1. Open a table in **Datasheet View**.
2. Place the cursor between two fields or two records.
3. Click and drag when the cursor changes to double arrows.

>> **Quick Reference**

Hiding Columns

1. Open a table in **Datasheet View**.
2. Activate a field by clicking the field name.
3. Click the **Home** tab on the Ribbon.
4. Click the **More** icon.
5. Select the **Hide Columns** option.

Figure 2.20 | **Copying and Pasting Data from Excel**

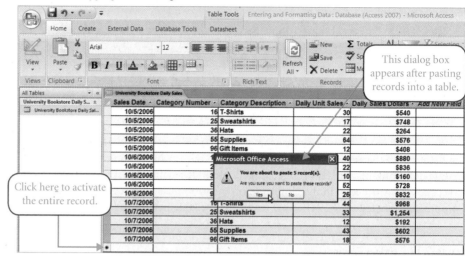

COMMON MISTAKES | Pasting Data from Excel

If you are pasting data from an Excel spreadsheet into an Access table, make sure the sequence of the columns in the Excel spreadsheet is identical to the sequence of the fields in the Access table. If they are not in the same sequence, you could be pasting the wrong type of data into one of the Access fields, which could result in an error.

Sorting and Filtering Data

After entering data into an Access table, you can analyze it by using the **Sort** and **Filter** icons. The purpose of sorting the data in a table is to make initial assessments on the performance of a business or to assess the accuracy of the data. The sorting techniques for an Access table do not provide significant analytical power because only one field or column can be used to set the sequence. This is different from the sorting options in Excel, where multiple columns can be used to establish a tiered sorting sequence. Techniques for tiered sorting in Access will be covered in Chapters 3 and 5.

To sort the data in an Access table, activate a field and click one of the two sort icons in the **Home** tab on the Ribbon. Figure 2.21 shows the University Bookstore

Quick Reference

Copying and Pasting Data

1. Copy data from an existing Access table or from an Excel spreadsheet.
2. Open a table in **Datasheet View**.
3. Activate a blank record by clicking the asterisk to the left of the first blank cell.
4. Click the **Home** tab on the Ribbon.
5. Click the **Paste** icon.
6. Click the **Yes** button at the bottom of the Paste Records message.

Figure 2.21 | **Sorting the University Bookstore Daily Sales Table**

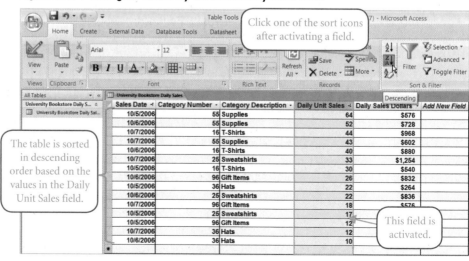

Daily Sales table sorted based on the values in the Daily Unit Sales field in descending order. This sort order makes it easy to identify the category that generated the most unit sales for the dates included in the table.

Data filters are used to temporarily remove records from a table based on a defined set of parameters. In business, these filters are often used to conduct an initial analysis for a specific category, item, date, and so on. For example, the manager using the University Bookstore Daily Sales table from Figure 2.21 may want to focus on the data in the table pertaining only to category 25. You can easily apply filters to a table by

Figure 2.22 | **Opening the Filter Options for the Category Number Field**

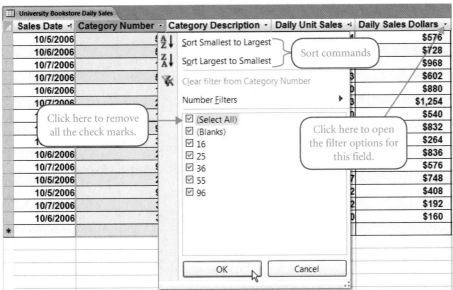

clicking the arrow next to the field name. Figure 2.22 shows the options that appear when clicking the filter next to Category Number field name. Notice that this also gives you access to the sort commands.

As mentioned, a manager can use the filter options shown in Figure 2.22 to focus on data that pertains only to category 25. This is accomplished as follows:

- Click the box next to the (**Select All**) option to remove the check marks next to all the category numbers.
- Click the box next to the number 25. A check mark will appear in this box.
- Click the **OK** button.

Figure 2.23 shows the results of setting a filter on the Category Number field for the University Bookstore Daily Sales table. Notice that the Filtered indicator is highlighted at the bottom of the table. This indicates that the table contains other records that are not visible because a filter has been applied. To remove the filter, click the **Toggle Filter** icon in the **Home** tab on the Ribbon.

Figure 2.23 | **Table with Filter Applied to the Category Number Field**

![Screenshot of Microsoft Access showing a table with a filter applied to the Category Number field. The ribbon shows Home, Create, External Data, Database Tools, and Datasheet tabs. A callout points to "Click here to remove the filter." The table displays University Bookstore Daily Sales with columns Sales Date, Category Number, Category Description, Daily Unit Sales, and Daily Sales Dollars. Three rows show dates 10/7/2006, 10/6/2006, 10/5/2006 all with Category Number 25 Sweatshirts. Callouts indicate "This symbol indicates a filter has been applied to this field." and "This indicates that a filter is applied to this table."]

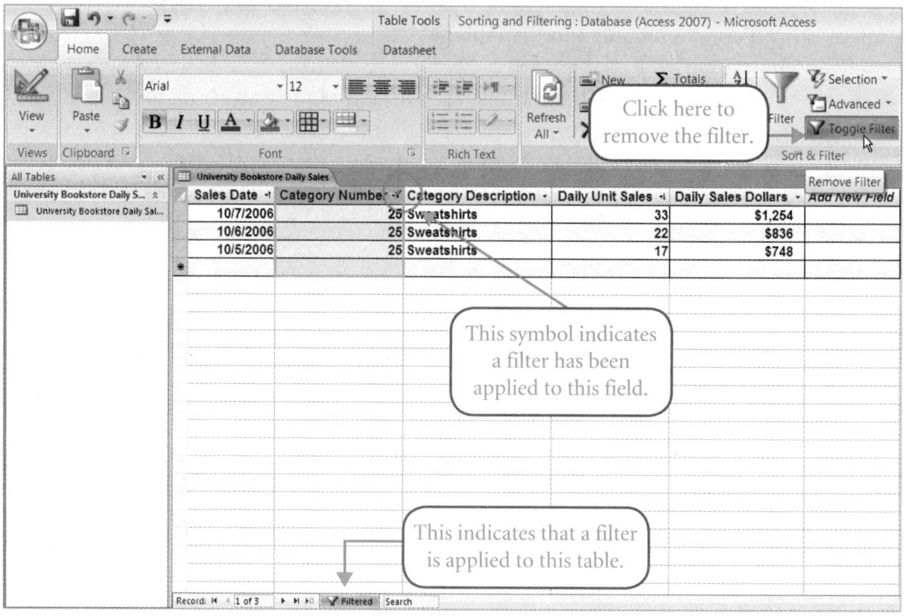

You also can use filters to target a range of values based on a condition. For example, the University Bookstore manager might want to see all items that generated sales greater than $700. This is known as a custom filter and is accomplished as follows:

- Click the filter arrow next to the Daily Sales Dollars field.
- Place the cursor over the **Number Filters** option and then select the **Greater Than** option (see Figure 2.24). After you select the **Greater Than** option, the **Custom Filter** dialog box will open. Here, you can type a specific value that will be filtered from the table based on the **Greater Than** condition.
- Type the number 700 in the **Custom Filter** dialog box and click the **OK** button (see Figure 2.25). After you click the **OK** button, the table will show only those items that generated $700 or more in daily sales.
- Click the filter arrow next to the Daily Sales Dollars field again and select the **Sort Largest to Smallest** option. This will sort the filtered results in descending order based on the Daily Sales Dollars field.

Figure 2.24 | **Selecting a Custom Filter for Numbers**

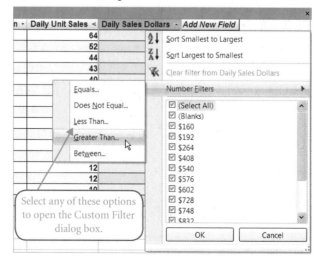

Figure 2.25 | **The Custom Filter Dialog Box**

> Type a number here to set the filter.

COMMON MISTAKES | Check for Filters

Always check for filters before analyzing the data in a table. If a table has been filtered, the word *Filtered* will be highlighted at the bottom of the table next to the
record counter.

Figure 2.26 shows the custom filter that was applied to the Daily Sales Dollars
field. Notice that the table shows only items for which the Daily Sales Dollars are
greater than $700. As in the previous example, to remove the filter, click the **Toggle
Filter** icon.

Figure 2.26 | **Results of Applying a Customer Filter to the Daily Sales Dollars Field**

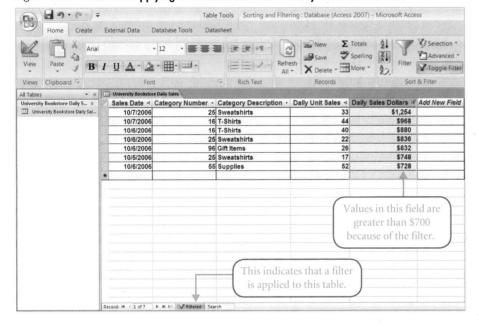

> Values in this field are greater than $700 because of the filter.

> This indicates that a filter is applied to this table.

>> **Quick Reference**

Filter

1. Open a table in **Datasheet View**.

2. Click the down arrow next to the field name that contains the value you wish to filter.

3. Click the **(Select All)** option to remove all check marks.

4. Click next to the value or values that you wish to show in the table.

5. Click the **OK** button.

6. Click the **Toggle Filter** icon in the **Home** tab on the Ribbon to remove the filter.

>> Creating an Access Table

The purpose of this workshop is to review the methods for creating an Access table. I will be demonstrating the tasks in this workshop in the following six videos: **Designing a Table**, **Indexing**, **Primary Keys**, **Data Entry & Formats**, **Copy & Paste**, and **Sorting & Filtering**. The title of the video is placed next to each section of tasks. Try to complete the tasks in each section and then watch the video. Even if you are confident that you completed a section correctly, you should still watch the video. I will be explaining the rationale and reasoning for each set of tasks to help you get a better understanding of Access.

1. **Field Names, Data Types, and Field Properties (Video: Designing a Table)**
   a. Create a new Access database and name it **ib_a02_storesalesdata**.
   b. Close the table that is automatically created when the new database is created.
   c. Click the **Table Design** icon in the **Create** tab on the Ribbon.
   d. Type the following field names in the Field Name column:
      i. **Sales Date**
      ii. **Store Number**
      iii. **Location**
      iv. **Total Sales**
   e. Set the following data types for each field:
      i. Sales Date: **Date/Time**
      ii. Store Number: **Number**
      iii. Location: **Text**
      iv. Total Sales: **Currency**
   f. Adjust the field properties for each field as follows:
      i. Sales Date: Set the Format to **Short Date**.
      ii. Store Number: Set the Field Size to **Integer**, the Format to **General Number**, and the Decimal Places to **0**.
      iii. Location: Set the Field Size to **30 characters**.
      iv. Total Sales: Set the Decimal Places to **0**.
   g. Type the following descriptions for each field in the Description column:
      i. Sales Date: **Transaction date for gross sales**
      ii. Store Number: **Number assigned to each store**
      iii. Location: **City location for each store**
      iv. Total Sales: **Total gross sales at the close of business for the Sales Date**

2. **Setting the Index (Video: Indexing)**
   a. Click the **Indexes** icon in the **Design** tab on the Ribbon.
   b. Type **Date/Store Number** in the first column for the Index Name.

c. In the first cell of the Field Name column, use the drop-down box to select the Sales Date field. In the second cell, use the drop-down box to select the Store Number field.

d. In the Sort Order column, set the Sales Date field to **Descending**.

e. Click the X in the upper-right corner to close the **Indexes** dialog box.

3. Setting the Primary Key (Video: Primary Keys)

a. Click the box to the left of the Sales Date field and drag down to the Store Number field. Both rows should be highlighted.

b. Click the **Primary Key** icon in the **Design** tab on the Ribbon.

c. Click the **Save** icon in the **Quick Access** toolbar. Type the table name **Daily Store Sales** in the **Save As** dialog box and then click the **OK** button.

d. Close the table named Daily Store Sales by clicking the X in the upper-right corner of the table.

4. Entering and Formatting Data (Video: Data Entry & Formats)

a. Set the organization of the **Navigation Pane** to **Object Type**.

b. Open the table named Daily Store Sales by double clicking it in the **Navigation Pane** under the Tables object heading. The table should open in **Datasheet View**.

c. Increase the column width for any field that is not completely visible.

d. Type the following records into the table. Note that for entries in the Sales Date field, you can select a date by clicking the **Calendar** icon.

Date	Store Number	Location	Total Sales
10/1/2006	5304	New York	116500
10/1/2006	5306	Miami	90000
10/1/2006	5308	San Francisco	72000
10/1/2006	5310	Boston	122000
10/1/2006	5312	Chicago	50000

e. Select 14 from the **Font Size** icon in the **Home** tab on the Ribbon.

f. Click the **Bold** icon in the **Home** tab on the Ribbon.

g. Increase the width of any column in the table where the field name or data is not completely visible.

h. Save the table and close it by clicking the X in the upper-right corner.

5. Copying and Pasting (Video: Copy & Paste)

a. Open the Excel file named ib_a02_dailysalesdata.

b. Highlight the range A2:D31 in the Sheet1 worksheet and click the **Copy** icon in the **Home** tab on the Ribbon.

c. Activate the database named ib_a02_storesalesdata by clicking it in the task bar at the bottom of your screen.

d. Open the table named Daily Store Sales in **Datasheet View**.

e. Activate the empty record at the bottom of the table by clicking the asterisk at the left of the record.

f. Click the **Paste** icon in the **Home** tab on the Ribbon. Then click the **Yes** button when the "paste records" warning appears.

g. Save and close the table.

6. Sorting and Filtering Data (Video: Sorting & Filtering)

a. Open the table named Daily Store Sales in **Datasheet View**.

b. Activate any cell in the Total Sales field.

c. Click the **Descending sort** icon in the **Home** tab on the Ribbon.

d. Click the down arrow next to the Location field name.

e. Click the **(Select All)** option to remove the check marks next to all locations.

f. Click the box next to the Chicago location and click the **OK** button.

g. Click the **Toggle Filter** icon in the **Home** tab on the Ribbon.

h. Save and close the table.

i. Close the database named ib_a02_storesalesdata by clicking the X in the upper-right corner. Then close the Excel workbook.

j. *Remember where this database is saved.* This database will be used in the next video workshop in this chapter.

>> Collecting Customer Data for Marketing Promotions

Did you ever wonder how companies know what promotions or discount offers to send their customers? For example, did you ever get a coupon for something you usually buy when you paid for groceries? Or, have you ever received a discount offer in the mail after making a big purchase at your favorite clothing store? For most businesses, these promotions are managed through database systems. Businesses collect customer information through loyalty or frequent shopper programs. When the customer fills out an application for a loyalty card, the company will enter the customer's personal information into a table on a database. The company will then track the purchasing activity for each customer and send promotions and discounts accordingly.

Exercise

The purpose of this exercise is to create an Access table that might be used by the marketing manager for a retail company. The data that will be added to this table is found in the Excel file named ib_a02_customerloyalty. Open this file and minimize it before completing the following tasks.

1. Create a new Access database with the name **ib_a02_customerloyaltydb**.

2. Open a new table in **Design View**.

3. Type the following field names:

   Customer ID Number

   Customer Name

   State of Residence

   Gender

   Age

   Years Since Customer

   LY Spend

   Value of Last Purchase

4. Set the following data types for each field:

   Customer ID Number: **Text**

   Customer Name: **Text**

State of Residence:	**Text**
Gender:	**Text**
Age:	**Number**
Years Since Customer:	**Number**
LY Spend:	**Currency**
Value of Last Purchase:	**Currency**

5. Adjust the field properties for each field as follows:

Customer ID Number:	Field Size set to 6 characters
Customer Name:	Field Size set to 50 characters
State of Residence:	Field Size set to 2 characters
Gender:	Field Size set to 1 character
Age:	Field Size set to **Integer**
Years Since Customer:	Field Size set to **Integer**
LY Spend:	Decimal Places set to 2
Value of Last Purchase:	Decimal Places set to 2

6. Enter the following descriptions for each field:

Customer ID Number:	**Unique customer ID number**
Customer Name:	**Name of customer**
State of Residence:	**State abbreviation**
Gender:	**Gender of customer (F=Female M=Male)**
Age:	**Customer age at beginning of year**
Years Since Customer:	**Number of years since loyalty application was submitted**
LY Spend:	**Total dollar value of purchases last year**
Value of Last Purchase:	**Dollars spent on most recent purchase**

7. Define the index of this table using the Gender field in ascending order and the Age field in descending order. The name of the index should be **Gender/Age**. The index is being placed on these fields because marketing managers rarely search a customer table by customer name. If they are working for a company that sells merchandise for men and women, they may pull data based on gender. Or, if certain merchandise appeals to certain age groups, they may pull a group of customers by age.

8. Set the primary key on the Customer ID Number field. This table must assign a unique ID number for each customer. Therefore, setting the primary key on the Customer ID Number field will prevent the same ID number from being entered for two different customers.

9. Save the table and type the name **Customer Data** in the **Save As** dialog box.

10. Switch the table to **Datasheet View** and expand the column widths so all field names are visible.

11. Activate the Excel file named ib_a02_customerloyalty and copy the range A2:H41.

12. Activate the first record in the table named Customer Data and click the **Paste** icon. Click **Yes** to confirm that you want to paste the records.

13. Sort the table in descending order based on the LY Spend field. What is the highest amount of money spent last year by a customer? In what states do the top five customers with the highest LY Spend value live? What is the age range of these customers?

14. Sort the table in descending order by the Value of Last Purchase field. Are the customers with the five highest amounts in the Value of Last Purchase field the same as the top five customers with the highest amounts in the LY Spend field?

15. Filter the data in this table to show only female customers living in the state of New York. How many female customers are in New York? Which customer would you send a discount coupon to? Why?

16. Remove the filter.

17. Use a filter to determine the number of customers living in the state of California. Which customer from California spent the most money last year? How much was spent?

18. Which customer from California spent the least money last year? How much was spent?

19. Remove the filter.

20. Save and close the table named Customer Data.

21. Close the database named ib_a02_customerloyaltydb and the Excel workbook.

<table>
<tr><td>PROBLEM &
EXERCISE</td></tr>
</table>

>> What's Wrong with This Database?

Problem

You are directing a division of a medium-size clothing retail company. Every Monday you, along with other directors, meet with the CEO of the company to discuss the previous week's sales results. For this meeting, you will be discussing the sales results of week 15. You are most concerned with the results of category 20, Casual Sport Shirts. The company was running a promotion last week, and your division was expected to sell a total of 1,200 shirts for this category. Each week an analyst in your division receives a hard copy of the sales results by category and enters the numbers into an Access table. A recently hired analyst e-mailed the results of week 15 to you and mentioned that there was a slight problem entering the results for category 20. He explained that he was able to fix the problem and attached the database to the e-mail. As you look at the numbers listed in the e-mail, you notice that the unit sales for category 20 are 1,732.

Exercise

The database the analyst e-mailed to you is named ib_a02_divisionsalesdata. The table containing the sales results for the division is named Division Sales by Category. Open the table and look at the results for week 15. Would you be comfortable telling the CEO that the division exceeded its 1,200 unit sales target for category 20? Consider the following points:

1. Look at the sales results for category 20 for all weeks in this table. Is there anything unique about the results for week 15? What technique could help you focus only on category 20?

2. Why did the analyst state in the e-mail that the sales results for category 20 were 1,732 units for week 15?

3. Can you go to the meeting and tell the CEO that the sales for category 20 in week 15 are 1,732 units? Why?

4. The analyst mentioned that he had to fix a "problem" with the table to be able to enter the results for category 20. What do you think he did?

What's wrong with this database? Write a short answer for each of the points listed here. Can you fix this database? If not, explain why. What would you do to prevent this problem from occurring in the future?

>> Editing Tables

Skill Set

After creating an Access table, you might need to make adjustments to the table design or the data contained in a particular record or field. These adjustments might also be done to tables that you did not create. In these situations you will need to use a variety of editing commands and techniques that are covered in this section.

Changing Data Types and Field Properties

In some situations, you may have to change the data type or field properties after entering data into an Access table. The most common reason for making these edits is an unexpected change in the type of data entered into the field of a table. For example, the field properties might be set to **Integer** for the Units Sold field of a merchandise table. Units of merchandise are usually sold in whole units. However, a product could have two parts, and it is possible to buy only part of the product. In this case, you might have to record a sale of .5 units. This would require the field properties to be changed from **Integer** to **Double** because you cannot use decimals in a field with an **Integer** property. Another common example is changing the **Text** data type to **Memo**. The **Text** data type can store a maximum of 255 characters in a field. However, if certain descriptions exceed this limit, the data type must be changed to **Memo**, which can hold over 65,000 characters.

To demonstrate the method of changing data types and field properties, you will make two adjustments to the University Bookstore Daily Sales table shown in Figure 2.21. The data type for the Category Number field will be changed from the **Number** data type to the **Text** data type. Even though this field contains two-digit numbers representing a specific category, the numbers will not be used in any mathematical calculations. This is similar to a ZIP code, which is also a number that is not used in mathematical calculations. A second adjustment to this table will be made to the Daily Unit Sales field. The Field Size will be changed to **Double** and the Decimal Places will be changed to 1. As mentioned, this adjustment is typical if a company sells multiple components to a product. The following points explain how to make these adjustments:

- Highlight the University Bookstore Daily Sales table in the **Navigation Pane** by clicking it once.
- Click the right mouse button and select **Design View** from the list of options. Right clicking is an alternative way to access commands (see Figure 2.27). This will open the table in **Design View**.

Figure 2.27 | **Right-Click Options for an Access Table**

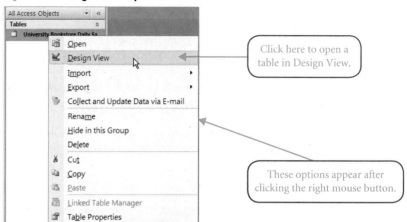

Click here to open a table in Design View.

These options appear after clicking the right mouse button.

- Click in the Data Type column next to the Category Number field. Then click the down arrow and select the **Text** data type.
- While the data type for the Category Number field is still highlighted, change the Field Size in the **Field Properties** box to 2. Since the category numbers in this example are two-digit numbers, the Field Size is set to 2 characters.
- Click in the Data Type column next to the Daily Unit Sales field.
- Select the **Double** option for the Field Size in the **Field Properties** box. This will allow decimal places to be shown for the number entered into the Daily Unit Sales field.
- Change the Decimal Places in the **Field Properties** box to 1. Note that when you're changing the format or decimal points for a field, the *Property Update Options* icon will appear (see Figure 2.28). You use this icon to update the format of this field in other reports, queries, or forms, a process known as *propagating field properties.*
- Save the table and check the results by switching to **Datasheet View.**

Figure 2.27 shows the right-click options after selecting the University Bookstore Daily Sales table.

Figure 2.28 shows the final data type and field property adjustments that were made to the University Bookstore Daily Sales. Notice the **Property Update Options** icon that appears when changing the Decimal Places for the Daily Unit Sales field.

Figure 2.28 | **Editing Data Types and Field Properties in Design View**

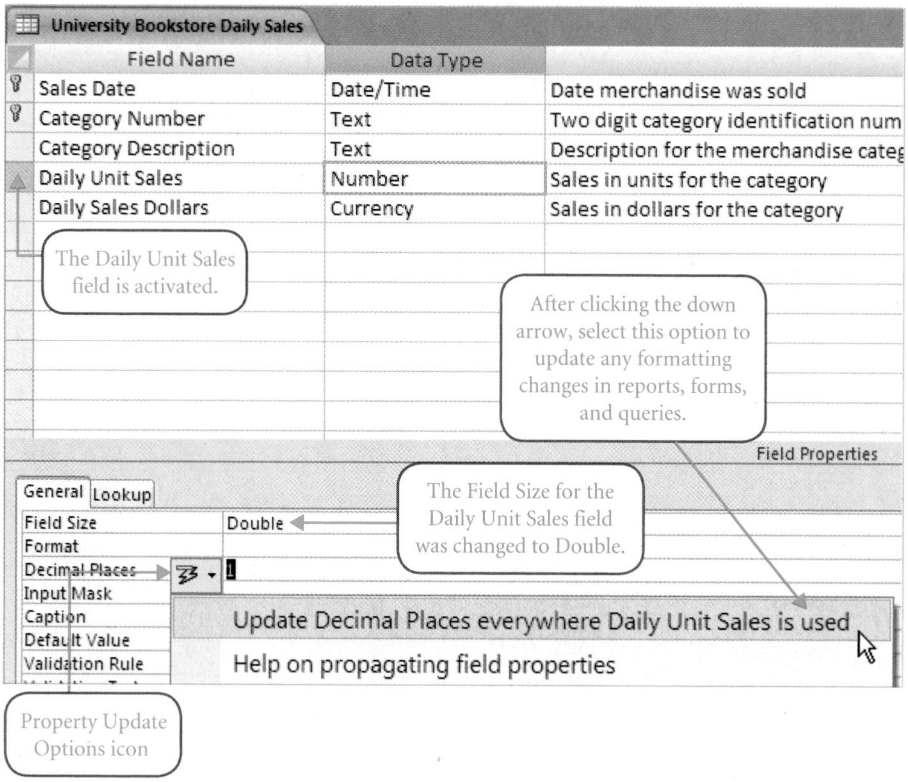

Field Name	Data Type	
Sales Date	Date/Time	Date merchandise was sold
Category Number	Text	Two digit category identification num
Category Description	Text	Description for the merchandise categ
Daily Unit Sales	Number	Sales in units for the category
Daily Sales Dollars	Currency	Sales in dollars for the category

The Daily Unit Sales field is activated.

After clicking the down arrow, select this option to update any formatting changes in reports, forms, and queries.

Field Properties

General | Lookup

Field Size	Double
Format	
Decimal Places	
Input Mask	
Caption	
Default Value	
Validation Rule	

The Field Size for the Daily Unit Sales field was changed to Double.

Update Decimal Places everywhere Daily Unit Sales is used

Help on propagating field properties

Property Update Options icon

COMMON MISTAKES | Editing Field Properties

Remember to activate the row containing a field name first before updating the field size or format. Clicking the field name, data type, or description will activate a row. If a row containing a field name and data type is not activated, the **Field Properties** box will be blank.

Changing the Sequence of Fields

After designing tables, you might need to change the sequence of field names. Field names listed from top to bottom in the **Design View** will appear in the same order from left to right in **Datasheet View**. You have the option of changing the sequence of fields in either the **Design View** or **Datasheet View**. To change the sequence of fields in the **Datasheet View**, activate the field by clicking the field name and then click and drag to the desired sequence. To change the sequence of fields in **Design View**, activate an entire row by clicking the box to the left of the field name and then click and drag to the desired sequence. Figures 2.29 and 2.30 illustrate how the position of the Daily Unit Sales field is changed in both **Design View** and **Datasheet View**.

Figure 2.29 | **Changing the Sequence of Fields in Design View**

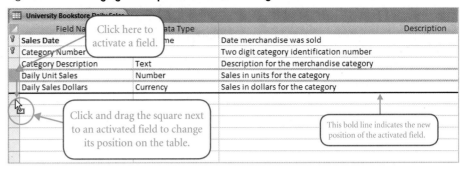

Figure 2.30 | **Changing the Sequence of Fields in Datasheet View**

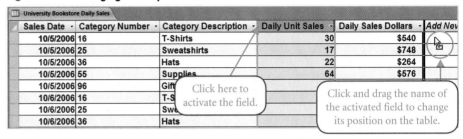

Editing Data and Field Names

In some cases you may need to adjust or edit the data entered into a table. Ideally, tables used in an Access database will be linked to a source that, when changed, will automatically update the data in your table. However, for smaller tables, editing certain data values manually might be easier. To make any data edits, open a table in **Datasheet View** (see Figure 2.31) or double click the table name from the **Navigation Pane**. Then activate a cell and type any necessary edits.

Figure 2.31 | **Editing Data in Datasheet View**

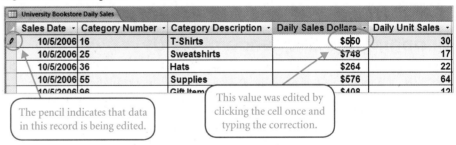

>> **Quick Reference**

Editing Data Types and Field Properties

1. Open a table in **Design View**.

2. Activate the field that requires editing.

3. Select a new data type if necessary.

4. Make any adjustments to the field properties while the field name or data type for a field is activated.

You may also need to edit or change the name of a field. There are two ways to change a field name. The first is to open a table in **Design View** and edit or retype a new field name. The second method is to double click the field name in **Datasheet View** (see Figure 2.32). After double clicking the field name, you will be able to make edits or retype the name. To complete any edits, press the **Enter** key or click another cell in the table.

Figure 2.32 | **Changing a Field Name in Datasheet View**

University Bookstore Daily Sales				
Sales Date ⌄	Category Number ⌄	Category Description ⌄	Total Sales Dollars	Daily Unit Sales ⌄
10/5/2006	16	T-Shirts	$650	30
10/5/2006	25	Sweatshirts	$748	17
10/5/2006	36	Hats	$264	22

This field name was edited by double clicking it.

Inserting Fields

After designing a table, you may need to add an additional field at a future point in time. For example, in the University Bookstore Daily Sales table shown in Figure 2.32, the manager might want to add a field showing the ending inventory for each category. There are two methods that can be used for adding this field. The first is to add the field in the **Design View** of the table, which is accomplished as follows:

- Open the University Bookstore Daily Sales table in **Design View**.
- Type the field name Ending Inventory Units in the Field Name column of the empty row at the bottom of the table (see Figure 2.33).
- Set the data type to **Number**.
- Set the Field Size to **Long Integer**, the Format to **Standard**, and the Decimal Places to 0 in the **Field Properties** box.
- Type the description Inventory on hand at the close of business for the Sales Date in the Description column.
- Activate the field by clicking the box next to the field name.
- Click and drag the field so it appears above the Total Sales Dollars field.
- Save the table.
- Switch to **Datasheet View** and enter data for the new field.

Figure 2.33 shows the results of adding the Ending Inventory Units field to the University Bookstore Daily Sales table. Notice that the field is activated so that it can be dragged above the Sales Dollars field.

Figure 2.33 | **Inserting a New Field in Design View**

University Bookstore Daily Sales		
Field Name	Data Type	Description
Sales Date	Date/Time	Date merchandise was sold
Category Number	Text	Two digit category identification number
Category Description	Text	Description for the merchandise category
Daily Unit Sales	Number	Sales in units for the category
Total Sales Dollars	Currency	Sales in dollars for the category
Ending Inventory Units	Number	Inventory on hand at the close of business for the Sales Date

This field was added to the table.

Click and drag here to change the position of the field.

Field Properties

General	Lookup
Field Size	Long Integer
Format	Standard
Decimal Places	0
Input Mask	
Caption	
Default Value	

Field properties set for the Ending Inventory Units field.

The second method for adding the Ending Inventory Units field to the University Bookstore Daily Sales table is through the **Datasheet View** of the table. A blank field will appear whenever you open a table in **Datasheet View**, as shown in Figure 2.34. Double click the Add New Field placeholder and type the new name of the field. Then activate the new field and use the **Data Type** and **Format** icons in the **Datasheet** tab on the Ribbon to set the **Data Type** and **Field Properties** for the new field.

Figure 2.34 | **Inserting a New Field in Datasheet View**

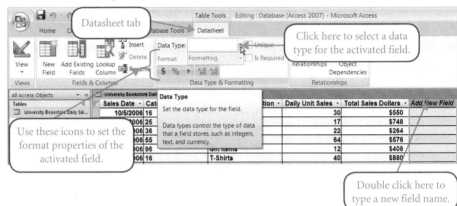

Deleting Fields and Records

In some cases you may need to delete a field or record from a table. Fields can be deleted when a table is in **Datasheet** or **Design View**. The following points explain how to delete a field when a table is in **Datasheet View**:

- Activate a field by clicking the field name or activate one cell in the field you wish to delete.
- Click the **Delete** icon in the **Datasheet** tab on the Ribbon.
- Click the **Yes** button in the warning box (see Figure 2.35).

>> **Quick Reference**

Inserting a Field

1. Open a table in **Design View**.

2. Type a new field name, select a data type, and adjust the field properties.

3. Click and drag the field to the desired sequence in the list of field names.

OR

1. Open a table in **Datasheet View**.

2. Double click the Add New Field placeholder to type a new field name.

3. Use the **Data Type** and **Format** icons in the **Datasheet** tab to select a data type and format for the new field.

Figure 2.35 | **Deleting a Field When a Table Is in Datasheet View**

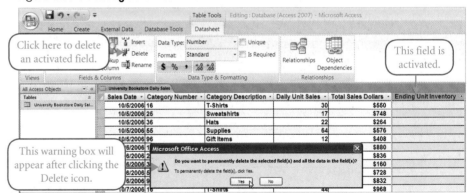

The following points explain how to delete a field when a table is in **Design View**:

- Activate a field by clicking the box to the left of the field name.
- Click the **Delete Rows** icon in the **Design** tab on the Ribbon (see Figure 2.36).

Figure 2.36 | **Deleting a Field When a Table Is in Design View**

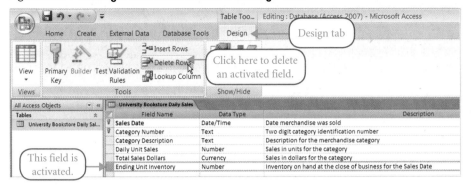

For deleting records, activate a record or several records when a table is in **Datasheet View** and press the **Delete** key on your keyboard. You can also click the **Delete** icon in the **Home** tab on the Ribbon (see Figure 2.37). Similar to deleting fields, a warning box will appear, asking whether you are sure you want to delete the records. It is very important to remember that there is no **Undo** function for undeleting fields and records. *After you click the Yes button on the warning box, the record or field will be permanently deleted.*

FIGURE 2.37 | **Deleting Records**

Sales Date	Category Number	Category Description	Daily Unit Sales	Total Sales Dollars	Add New Field
10/5/2006	16	T-Shirts	30	$550	
10/5/2006	25	Sweatshirts	17	$748	
10/5/2006	36	Hats	22	$264	
10/5/2006	55	Supplies	64	$576	
10/5/2006	96	Gift Items	12	$408	
10/6/2006	16	T-Shirts	40	$880	
10/6/2006	25	Sweatshirts	22	$836	
10/6/2006	36	Hats	10	$160	

These three records are activated.

Click here to delete the activated records.

COMMON MISTAKES | No Undo for Deleted Fields and Records

Check any field or record carefully before clicking the **Yes** button on the delete warning box. After you delete a field or record, it will be permanently deleted, and you cannot use the **Undo** icon to bring it back.

>> **Quick Reference**

Deleting Fields

1. Open a table in **Datasheet View**.
2. Activate a field by clicking the field name or activate one cell in the field to be deleted.
3. Click the **Delete** icon in the **Datasheet** tab on the Ribbon.

>> **Quick Reference**

Deleting Records

1. Open a table in **Datasheet View**.
2. Activate the record(s) to be deleted by clicking and dragging in the box to the left of the record(s).
3. Press the **Delete** key on your keyboard or click the **Delete** icon in the **Home** tab on the Ribbon.

>> Editing a Table

The purpose of this workshop is to demonstrate the editing techniques covered in this section. To complete this workshop, you will need to open the database named ib_a02_storesalesdata that you created in the previous workshop. I will be demonstrating the techniques in this workshop in the video named **Editing**. Try completing each of the following tasks first and then watch the video.

1. Editing Data Types and Field Properties (Video: Editing)

a. Open the table named Daily Store Sales in **Design View**.
b. Change the data type for the Store Number field to **Text**. Then change the Field Size to 10 characters.
c. Change the data type for the Total Sales field to **Number**.
d. Change the Field Size to **Double**.
e. Check that the Format is set to **Currency** and the Decimals are set to 0.
f. Save the table.

2. Editing Data and Field Names (Video: Editing)

a. Switch the table from **Design View** to **Datasheet View**.
b. Activate the cell containing the Total Sales for New York on 10/1/2006.
c. Delete the value in the cell, which should be 116500, and type **125000**.
d. Double click the field name Total Sales and type the word **Dollars** after the word *Sales*.
e. Select another cell on the table. Then increase the width of the Total Sales Dollar field so the field name is visible.

3. Inserting Fields (Video: Editing)

a. Switch the table from **Datasheet View** to **Design View**.
b. Type the field name **Ending Inventory** below Total Sales Dollars.
c. Set the data type to **Currency** and change the Decimal Places to 0.
d. Type the following in the Description column for Ending Inventory: **Retail value of inventory at close of business**.
e. Save the table.

4. Changing the Sequence of Fields (Video: Editing)

a. Activate the Ending Inventory field.
b. Click and drag the Ending Inventory field above the Total Sales Dollars field.
c. Save the table.

5. Adding Data (Video: Editing)

a. Switch the table to **Datasheet View**.
b. Change the width of the Ending Inventory column to 20.
c. Minimize the Access database and open the Excel file named ib_a02_dailystoresalesandinventorydata.

d. Highlight only the range D2:D36 on the Excel spreadsheet and click the **Copy** icon.

e. Minimize Excel and go back to the Access database with the table named Daily Store Sales open in **Datasheet View**.

f. Activate the Ending Inventory field by clicking the field name.

g. Click the **Paste** icon in the **Home** tab on the Ribbon and then click the **OK** button on the "paste records" warning box.

6. **Deleting Records and Fields (Video: Editing)**

a. Activate the last five records of the table. This should be all records that contain the date 10/7/2006.

b. Press the **Delete** key.

c. Click **Yes** on the "delete records" warning box.

d. Activate the Location field by clicking the field name.

e. Click the **Delete** icon in the **Datasheet** tab on the Ribbon.

f. Click the **Yes** button on the warning box.

g. Save and close the table.

7. **Changing the Name of a Table (Video: Editing)**

a. Right click the table named Daily Store Sales in the **Navigation Pane**.

b. Select the **Rename** option.

c. Change the name of the table to `Daily Store Sales and Inventory` and press the **Enter** key.

d. Save and close the table.

>> Managing Transportation Data

The amount and type of data collected by businesses frequently change. Additional data can be added to an existing Access table as long as the data is compatible with the data types and field properties of the table. However, if the type of data changes or additional areas of the business are being measured, you will have to edit the table. In some cases, you may also need to make adjustments to data that has already been added to a table. The editing skills covered in this section are vital in handling all these data management issues.

Exercise

The purpose of this exercise is to use the editing skills covered in this section to make adjustments to an Access table used to manage a fleet of trucks. Open the Access database named ib_a02_transportationdata. Then open the table named Trailer Information in **Datasheet View**.

1. Examine the data in this table. You will notice that the numbers in the Trailer Number field are all five digits.

2. Switch the table to **Design View** and change the Field Size in the **Field Properties** box for the Trailer Number field to 6. New trailers that require six digits will be added to the table. When business managers change the number of digits on key elements such as item numbers, store numbers, or trailer numbers, this type of edit to the tables in the company's database is usually required.

3. Change the Field Size in the **Field Properties** box for the Status field to 13. A new status called **Temp Inactive** will be added to the table. This will require an increase to the size properties of this field.

4. Change the data type for the Length field to **Number**. Then set the Field Size to **Integer**. Even though the Length field contains numbers, it was considered a descriptive trait when this table was designed. Therefore, the data type for this field was set to **Text**. However, this data type will prevent the use of these numbers in calculations. The data in this field could be valuable for calculating the cubic capacity of the trailer. As a result, this field will be converted to a **Number** data type.

5. Trailers that are inactive will be deleted from the table. It will be easier to see what trailer numbers are inactive if the Status field is moved to the second field of the table. Therefore, change the sequence so the Status field appears before the Length field.

6. Save the table and switch to **Datasheet View**.

7. Change the status of trailer 64222 to **Temp Inactive**.

8. Delete any record from the table that shows an **Inactive** status in the Status field. A total of three records should be deleted from the table.

9. Add the following three records to the table.

Trailer Number	Status	Length	Years in Service
64922	Active	22	1
641022	Active	22	1
74748	Active	48	1

10. Save and close the table.

PROBLEM & EXERCISE

» What's Wrong with This Database?

Problem

You are working in the buying office of an apparel manufacturing company. You are approached by a coworker who is having considerable difficulty adding data and making edits to an Access table. You agree to help and ask her to send you the database. She attaches the database to an e-mail, which includes the following information:

1. Thank you so much for helping me with this! The table I am trying to edit is named Item Detail. It is a really basic table with only four columns. I need to add the following item to the table: Item Number: 4794013, Category Number: 75, Description: Cotton Sweater. For some reason I can enter the item number only up to 479401. I keep pressing the **3** key, but nothing happens. I think something may be wrong with my keyboard.

2. For item 377899, I need to change the description to Red and White Whale Print with Stripes. However, I can type Red and White Whale, and for some reason it will not let me type the rest of the description.

Exercise

The database your coworker sent you is named ib_a02_editingdilemma. What's wrong with this database? Explain why your coworker is having so much difficulty adding data to this table. Then, make the necessary adjustment to the Item Detail table and add the data that is stated in points 1 and 2 above.

The purpose of creating tables through manual data entry is to gain a deeper understanding of how data is structured and organized in an Access table. However, business managers rarely create database tables through data entry. In most corporate environments, database tables are created and maintained by the firm's Information Technology (IT) or Management Information Systems (MIS) departments. Business managers will use these tables by either importing or linking them into an Access database. This section will cover the methods used for importing and linking tables as well as printing commands.

Importing Data

You can create a table in Access by importing data from such sources as Excel spreadsheets, other Access databases, text files, or proprietary database systems. You do this by using the **Import** group of icons found on the **External Data** tab on the Ribbon (see Figure 2.38). The benefit of using these import icons is that it eliminates the need to enter data directly into the **Datasheet View** of a table, and it allows you to utilize data that already exists in other programs or databases. This section will illustrate how to import data from three sources: an Access database, an Excel spreadsheet, and a Text file.

Figure 2.38 | **Import Group on the External Data Tab**

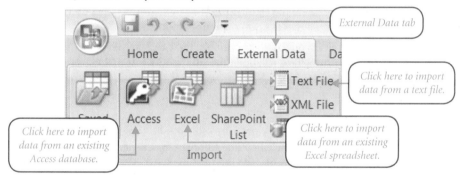

The process of creating Access tables using the **Import** icons shown in Figure 2.38 will differ slightly depending on the data source. This example will explain how to create an Access table by importing data from another Access database. The following points demonstrate how to import the University Bookstore Daily Sales table shown in Figure 2.37 into a blank Access database:

- Click the **External Data** tab on the Ribbon.
- Click the **Access** icon in the **Import** group of icons (see Figure 2.38). This will open the **Get External Data** dialog box (see Figure 2.39).

Figure 2.39 | **Get External Data Dialog Box for an Access Data Source**

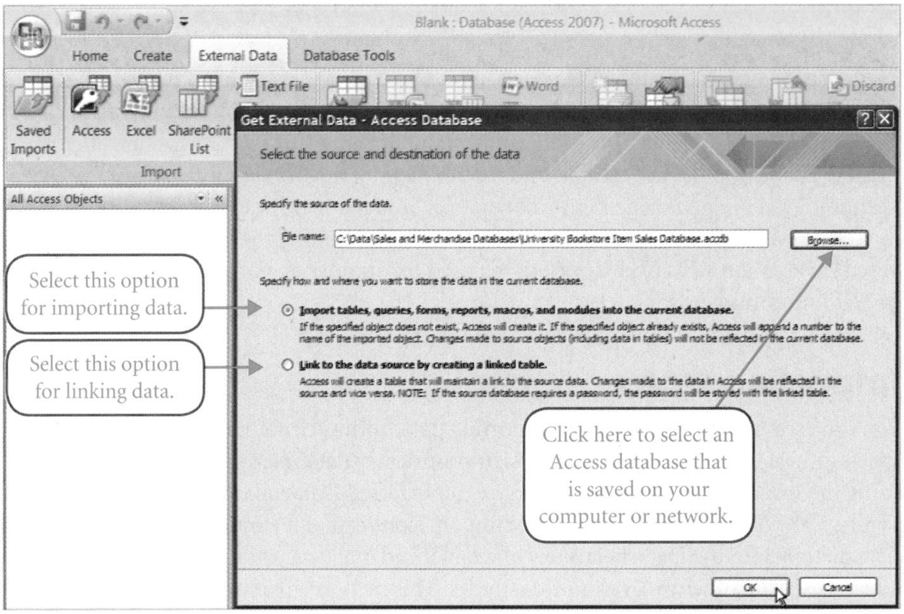

- Click the **Browse** button on the right side of the **Get External Data** dialog box to select an Access database that is saved on your computer or network.

- Select the **Import tables, queries. . .** option on the **Get External Data** dialog box and click the **OK** button. This will open the **Import Objects** dialog box. Note that a third option will appear in the **Get External Data** dialog box if you are importing data into a database that already contains tables. This option allows you to append or import data into an existing table.

- Select the University Bookstore Daily Sales table on the **Tables** tab of the **Import Objects** dialog box (see Figure 2.40). The **Import Objects** dialog box contains several tabs for importing other objects contained in an Access database, such as queries, reports, and so on.

- Click the **OK** button on the right side of the **Import Objects** dialog box to import the University Bookstore Daily Sales table into the blank Access database.

- Click the **Close** button at the bottom of the **Save Import Steps** dialog box (see Figure 2.41). This technique is used in situations in which you need to import data from the same source on a routine basis. For this example, the University Bookstore Daily Sales table will be imported into this Access database only one time. Therefore, you can close the **Save Import Steps** dialog box without saving these import steps.

Figure 2.40 shows the **Import Objects** dialog box. Notice that several tabs run across the top of the box. They enable you to select any object that is contained in the Access database designated in the **Get External Data** dialog box. Click a tab to see what objects are available for importing.

Figure 2.40 | **Import Objects Dialog Box**

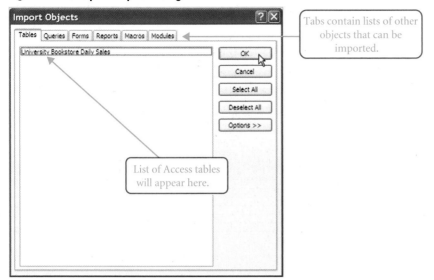

Figure 2.41 shows the **Save Import Steps** dialog box. You use it when you need to import the same data from the same source on a routine basis. Select the **Save Import Steps** option and click the **Close** button. This will open another dialog box that you use to assign a name to the import steps; you then can retrieve them by clicking the **Saved Imports** icon in the **External Data** tab on the Ribbon.

Figure 2.41 | **Save Import Steps Dialog Box**

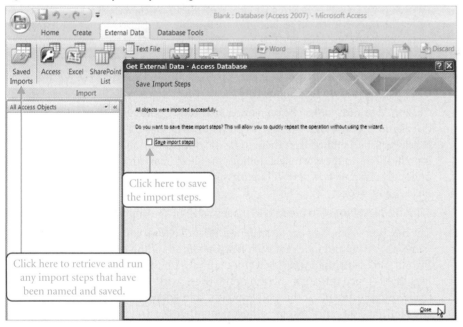

Figure 2.42 shows the result of importing the University Bookstore Daily Sales table into the blank Access database. The table was opened by double clicking the name in the **Navigation Pane**. It is important to note that after a table is imported into an Access database, it will not change. That is, if the data is changed or additional data is added to the University Bookstore Daily Sales table in the source database, it will need to be imported again into the blank Access database. This is the reason you might want to save the import steps. If you know you will need to import this table on a regular

basis, you can save the import steps and then activate the import process by clicking the **Saved Imports** icon in the **External Data** tab on the Ribbon.

Figure 2.42 | **Results of Importing the University Bookstore Daily Sales Table**

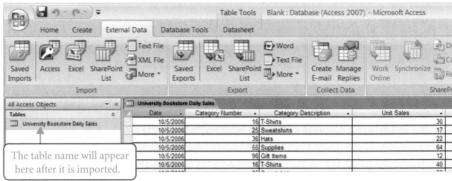

The table name will appear here after it is imported.

Data can also be imported from an Excel spreadsheet into an Access database. This example assumes that the data for the University Bookstore Daily Sales table shown in Figure 2.42 is contained in an Excel spreadsheet. The following points explain how to import this data into a blank Access database and place it into a new table:

- Click the **External Data** tab on the Ribbon.
- Click the **Excel** icon in the **Import** group of icons. Be careful not to click the **Excel** icon in the **Export** group (see Figure 2.38).
- Click the **Browse** button on the right side of the **Get External Data** dialog box to select an Excel workbook that is saved on your computer or network.
- Select the **Import the source data into a new table. . .** option on the **Get External Data** dialog box and click the **OK** button (see Figure 2.43). This will open the **Import Spreadsheet Wizard**.
- Select a worksheet from the list at the top of the **Import Spreadsheet Wizard** and click the **Next** button (see Figure 2.44).
- Click the box next to the option named **First Row Contains Column Headings** (see Figure 2.45). Access will take whatever descriptions are in the first row of the Excel worksheet and convert them to field names in the table. If there are no column headings in the worksheet, remove the check mark in the box next to this option by clicking it. Access will then assign generic field names such as Field 1, Field 2, and so on.
- Click the **Next** button to proceed to the next step of the **Import Spreadsheet Wizard**.
- The next step of the **Import Spreadsheet Wizard** allows you to adjust the field name, data type, and index for each field or column of the Excel worksheet (see Figure 2.46). Note that Access will automatically adjust the data type based on the data that is typed into each column of the Excel worksheet. You do not have to make any adjustments at this point and can simply skip this step by clicking the **Next** button. You can also make adjustments after the data is imported into the Access database by opening the table in **Design View**.
- The next step of the **Import Spreadsheet Wizard** is for defining the primary key. It is best to select the **No Primary Key** option and click the **Next** button (see Figure 2.47). The reason is that you can set the primary key on only one field through this wizard. After the table is imported, you can open it in **Design View** mode and select a combination of fields for the primary key.
- The final step of the **Import Spreadsheet Wizard** is for adjusting the name of the table that will be added to the Access database. Access will automatically use the Excel worksheet tab label as the name of the table that will be added to the database.

However, you can change that name in this step of the **Import Spreadsheet Wizard**. For this example, the Excel workbook name will suffice (see Figure 2.48).

- Click the **Finish** button at the bottom of the last step of the **Import Spreadsheet Wizard**. This will open the **Save Import Steps** dialog box shown in Figure 2.41. You don't need to save the import steps for this example, so click the **Close** button at the bottom. This will add a new table to the database containing the data from the Excel worksheet. The name of the table will appear in the **Navigation Pane**, as shown in Figure 2.42.

Figure 2.43 | **Get External Data Dialog Box for an Excel Data Source**

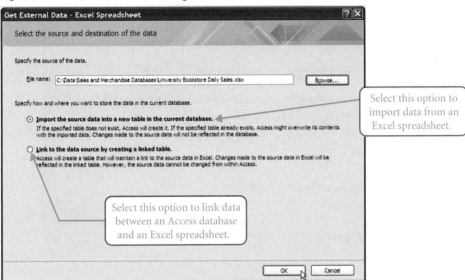

Figure 2.44 through 2.48 show each step of the **Import Spreadsheet Wizard**. This wizard will appear when you are importing or linking to data in an Excel spreadsheet.

Figure 2.44 | **Import Spreadsheet Wizard: Step 1**

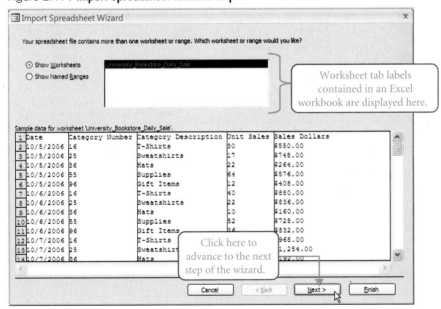

Figure 2.45 | **Import Spreadsheet Wizard: Step 2**

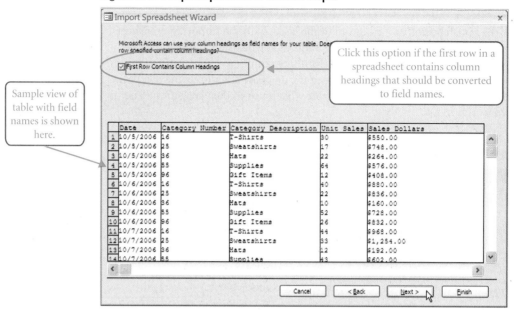

Figure 2.46 | **Import Spreadsheet Wizard: Step 3**

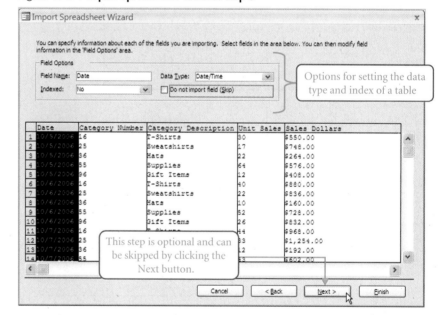

Figure 2.47 | **Import Spreadsheet Wizard: Step 4**

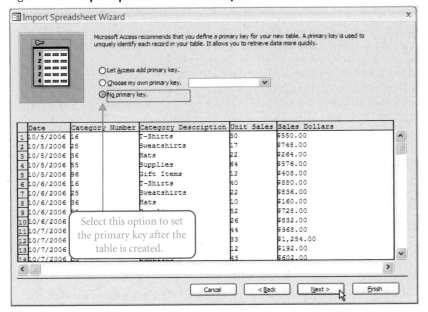

Figure 2.48 | **Import Spreadsheet Wizard: Step 5**

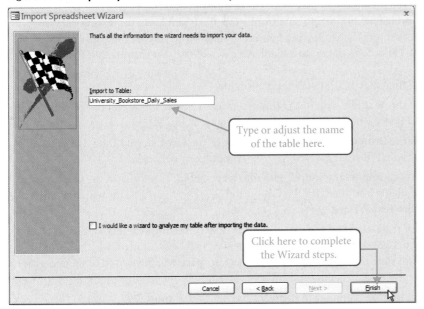

Text files are the final source that will be used to demonstrate the process of importing data into Access. In business, an IT specialist will probably send you any data you require in the form of a text file. The reason is that most systems can usually read and produce data in text file formats, thus allowing data to be transferred between different systems. Text files used in business typically end in .txt or .csv file extensions.

The process of importing data from a text file is similar to importing data from Excel spreadsheets. The following points explain how to import the University Bookstore Daily Sales data into a blank Access database if it is contained in a text file:

- Click the **External Data** tab on the Ribbon.

- Click the **Text File** icon in the **Import** group of icons. Be careful not to click the **Text File** icon in the **Export** group (see Figure 2.38).

- Click the **Browse** button on the right side of the **Get External Data** dialog box to select a text file that is saved on your computer or network.

- Select the **Import the source data into a new table. . .** option on the **Get External Data** dialog box and click the **OK** button (see Figure 2.49). This will open the **Import Text Wizard**.

- Check the **Delimited** options in the first step of the **Import Text Wizard** (see Figure 2.50). Most text files used in business will be Delimited, which means a symbol such as a comma, semicolon, tab, or space will be used to designate where a column of data begins and ends.

- Select the **Tab** delimiter in the second step of the **Import Text Wizard**. Then check the **First Row Contains Field Names** option (see Figure 2.51). This file uses a tab to designate the beginning and end of a column. In addition, the first row of the text file contains descriptions that should be used for the field names. Finally, select the quotation marks in the **Text Qualifier** drop-down box. The quotation marks in the text file designate data that is text such as the category descriptions.

- Click the **Next** button to advance to the next step of the **Import Text Wizard**.

- Click the **Next** button to skip the next step of the **Import Text Wizard**. The next step of the **Import Text Wizard** is identical to **Import Spreadsheet Wizard** shown in Figure 2.46.

- Select the **No Primary Key** option in the next step of the **Import Text Wizard** and click the **Next** button. This step is identical to the **Import Spreadsheet Wizard** shown in Figure 2.47.

- Type a name for the table and click the **Finish** button in the last step of the **Import Text Wizard**. Then click the **Close** button at the bottom of the **Save Import Steps** dialog box to import the data in the text file into a new table in the blank Access database.

Figure 2.49 | **Get External Data Dialog Box for a Text File**

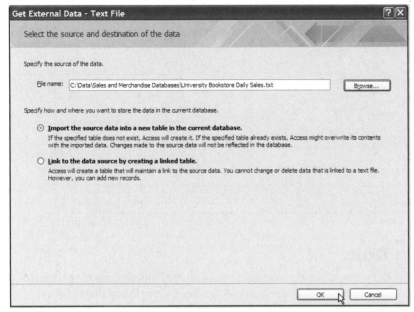

Figure 2.50 and 2.51 show the first two steps of the **Import Text Wizard**. Steps 3 through 5 are identical to the Import Spreadsheet Wizard, shown in Figures 2.46, 2.47, and 2.48.

Figure 2.50 | **Import Text Wizard: Step 1**

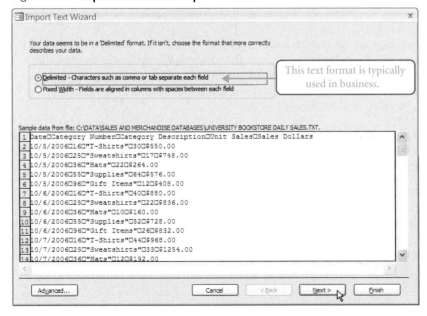

Figure 2.51 | Import Text Wizard: Step 2

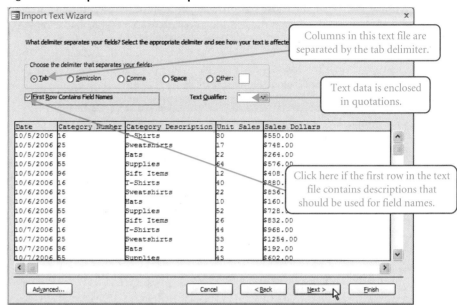

Figure 2.51 | Import Text Wizard: Step 2

Linking Data

The process of creating tables through linking is almost identical to creating tables by importing data. In fact, you may have noticed the **Get External Data** dialog boxes, shown in Figure 2.39, 2.43, and 2.49, include an option that allows you to link to a data source as opposed to importing it. The difference is that when an Access table is linked to a data source, any changes in the data source will automatically be reflected in the Access table. This method is used frequently in business environments because business data usually changes on a daily and, in some cases, on a minute-by-minute basis. As a result, creating tables through links ensures that you are always working with the most current data. It is important to note that when a table is linked, data from the source will always overwrite any changes that are made to the table. The transfer of data is only one way, which means you cannot update the data in a linked source from an Access table.

The data sources most commonly used for the link option are other Access tables and Excel spreadsheets. However, you can also create a table by linking to a text file. Similar to using the import option, creating a link to another Access table is slightly different from creating a link to an Excel spreadsheet. The following points explain the process for linking to another Access table:

- Click the **External Data** tab on the Ribbon.
- Click the **Access** icon in the **Import** group of icons (see Figure 2.38). This will open the **Get External Data** dialog box (see Figure 2.39).
- Click the **Browse** button on the right side of the **Get External Data** dialog box to select an Access database that is saved on your computer or network.
- Select the **Link to the data source. . .** option on the **Get External Data** dialog box and click the **OK** button (see Figure 2.39). This will open the **Link Tables** dialog box.
- Select a table from the **Link Tables** dialog box and click the **OK** button (see Figure 2.52). Notice that only one tab appears at the top of this dialog box. The reason is that the only object in an Access database that can be linked to another Access database is a table. After you click the **OK** button in the **Link Tables** dialog box, the link to the access table will be created.

Figure 2.52 | **Link Tables Dialog Box**

Figure 2.53 shows the final result of creating a link in a blank Access database. Notice the arrow that appears next to the table symbol. This indicates that the table is linked to a table in another Access database.

Figure 2.53 | **Appearance of a Linked Table**

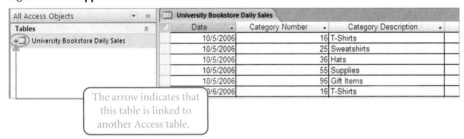

COMMON MISTAKES | Linking Excel Spreadsheets and Access Tables

Two common mistakes are usually made when linking to either Excel spreadsheets or Access tables:

- The name and location of the Excel file or Access database file used to create a link must remain the same. When a link is created, Access stores the name and location of the file to retrieve data. However, if the file name or location is changed, Access will not be able to find the source, which will create an error message.
- Once a link is created, the order and number of columns cannot be changed in the Excel spreadsheet or Access file. Changing the order or number of columns in an Excel file after it is used to create a link will create errors in the Access table. If the columns need to be modified, delete the link and re-create it after modifications to the source file are completed.

As mentioned, Access tables can also be created by linking to an Excel spreadsheet. As a result, when any changes are made to the worksheet in an Excel workbook, that change will be reflected in the table in an Access database. The following points explain how to create tables by linking to an Excel spreadsheet:

- Click the **External Data** tab on the Ribbon.
- Click the **Excel** icon in the **Import** group of icons (see Figure 2.38). This will open the **Get External Data** dialog box (see Figure 2.43).
- Click the **Browse** button on the right side of the **Get External Data** dialog box to select an Excel workbook that is saved on your computer or network.
- Select the **Link to the data source. . .** option on the **Get External Data** dialog box and click the **OK** button. This will open the **Link Spreadsheet Wizard**, which is identical to the **Import Spreadsheet Wizard** shown in Figure 2.44.
- Select a worksheet from the list shown in the first step of the **Link Spreadsheet Wizard** and click the **Next** button.
- Select **First Row Contains Column Headings** in the second step of the **Link Spreadsheet Wizard** if the first row of the Excel worksheet contains descriptions that should be used as field names. This step is identical to the **Import Spreadsheet Wizard** shown in Figure 2.45.
- The third and final step of the **Link Spreadsheet Wizard** is identical to the **Import Spreadsheet Wizard** shown in Figure 2.48. Make any adjustments to the table name if necessary and click the **Finish** button. Then click the **OK** button in the confirm link message box.

Figure 2.54 shows the final result of linking an Excel spreadsheet in an Access database. Notice the arrow and Excel symbol that precede the table name in the **Navigation Pane**. They indicate that the table is linked to an Excel spreadsheet.

Figure 2.54 | Table Linked to an Excel Spreadsheet

The Excel icon with an arrow indicates that this table is linked to an Excel spreadsheet.

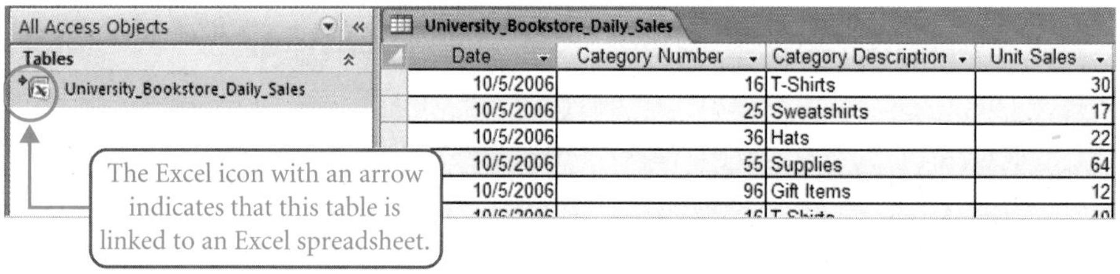

COMMON MISTAKES | Linking Excel Spreadsheets

When you are linking to an Excel file, the data entered in each column of a spreadsheet must be consistent. As mentioned earlier, when an Excel spreadsheet is *imported* with numbers and text data in the same column, Access will define the field as a **Text** data type. However, when you use the link option, inconsistencies in the data typed into a column will create errors in the Access table. For example, entering N/A in a column that has mostly numeric data will create errors in the table.

Printing Tables

The commands for printing tables can be found in the **File** drop-down menu, as shown in Figure 2.55. To change the Page Layout settings, click the arrow next to the **Print** option and select **Print Preview** on the right side of the menu.

Linking Data

1. Open a blank or existing Access database.
2. Click the **External Data** tab on the Ribbon.
3. Click one of the icons in the **Import** group based on the format of the source data (i.e., if linking data in an Excel workbook, click the **Excel** icon).
4. Click the **Browse** button in the **Get External Data** dialog box to select a file or database saved on your computer or network.
5. Select the **Link** option in the **Get External Data** dialog box.
6. Click the **OK** button at the bottom of the **Get External Data** dialog box.
7. Follow the steps of the wizard if linking to data in an Excel or text file, or select a table from the **Link Tables** dialog box if linking to an Access table.

Figure 2.55 | **Print Command in the File Drop-Down Menu**

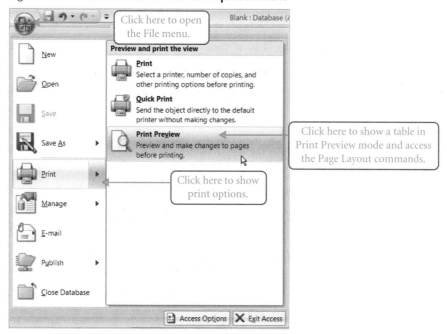

Figure 2.56 shows the University Bookstore Daily Sales table in **Print Preview** mode. Use the icons in the **Page Layout** group to make any printing adjustments such as the margin size or orientation. After making the Page Layout adjustments, click the **Print** icon to send the table to a printer.

Figure 2.56 | **Page Layout and Print Preview Commands**

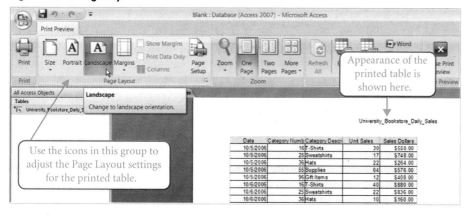

Quick Reference

Printing Tables

1. Open a table in **Datasheet** view.
2. Click the **File** icon.
3. Click the arrow next to the **Print** option.
4. Click the **Print Preview** option on the right side of the menu.
5. Use the icons in the **Page Layout** group on the Ribbon to make any necessary adjustments.
6. Click the **Print** icon on the Ribbon.

VIDEO WORKSHOP

≫ Linking and Importing Tables

The purpose of this workshop is to demonstrate the importing and linking methods for creating tables in an Access database. I will be demonstrating the techniques in this workshop in the videos named **Importing Data** and **Linking Data**. The title of the video related to each section of tasks appears in parentheses next to the heading. Try completing each of the following tasks first and then watch the video.

1. Importing an Access Table (Video: Importing Data)

    a. Create a new Access database and name it **ib_a02_importingdata**.

    b. Close the table that is created when the database is opened.

    c. Click the **Access** icon from the **Import** group in the **External Data** tab on the Ribbon.

    d. Click the **Browse** button in the **Get External Data** dialog box and double click the database named ib_a02_storeinformationdata.

    e. Check to see that the **Import tables, queries. . .** option is selected in the **Get External Data** dialog box and click the **OK** button.

    f. Click the **Tables** tab at the top of the **Import Objects** dialog box and then click the Store Location Information table.

    g. Click the **OK** button in the **Import Objects** dialog box and then click the **Close** button at the bottom of the **Save Import Steps** dialog box.

2. Importing an Excel Spreadsheet (Video: Importing Data)

    a. Click the **Excel** icon from the **Import** group in the **External Data** tab on the Ribbon.

    b. Click the **Browse** button in the **Get External Data** dialog box and double click the Excel file named ib_a02_salesbylocation.

    c. Check to see that the **Import the source data. . .** option is selected in the **Get External Data** dialog box and click the **OK** button.

    d. Check to see that the Sheet1 worksheet is highlighted in the first step of the **Import Spreadsheet Wizard** and click the **Next** button.

    e. Check to see that a check mark appears in the box next to the **First Row Contains Column Headings** option in the next step of the wizard. If not, click the box once.

    f. Click the **Next** button.

    g. Skip the next step of the **Import Spreadsheet Wizard** by clicking the **Next** button.

    h. Select the **No Primary Key** option in the next step of the wizard and click the **Next** button.

    i. Name the table **Sales by Location** in the last step of the **Import Spreadsheet Wizard** and click the **Finish** button.

    j. Click the **Close** button at the bottom of the **Save Import Steps** dialog box.

    k. Open the table you just created in **Datasheet View** by double clicking it.

    l. Adjust the column widths of the table to fit the data and field names.

    m. Switch the table to **Design View** by clicking the **View** icon in the **Home** tab on the Ribbon.

n. Highlight the Sales Date and Store Number fields and click the **Primary Key** icon.

o. Change the decimal places in the Total Sales fields to 0.

p. Save the table and switch to **Datasheet View**.

q. Close the table and then the database.

3. **Linking to an Excel Spreadsheet (Video: Linking Data)**

a. Create a new Access database and name it **ib_a02_linkingtables**.

b. Close the table that is created when the database is opened.

c. Click the **Excel** icon from the Import group in the **External Data** tab on the Ribbon.

d. Click the **Browse** button in the **Get External Data** dialog box and double click the Excel file named ib_a02_salesbystorebyday.

e. Select the **Link to data source...** option in the **Get External Data** dialog box and click the **OK** button.

f. Make sure there is a check in the box next to the **First Row Contains Column Headings** option in the first step of the Link Spreadsheet Wizard and click the **Next** button.

g. Name the table **Sales by Store by Day** in the next step of the **Link Spreadsheet Wizard** and click the **Finish** button.

h. Open the table you just created in **Datasheet View** by double clicking it. Adjust the width of the columns to fit the data and field names.

i. Save the table and close it. Then minimize Access.

j. Open Excel and then open the file named ib_a02_salesbystorebyday.

k. Enter the following data into the spreadsheet beginning in cell A37. The column headings are listed. Make sure you enter the data in the proper column.

Date	Store Number	Location	Ending Inventory	Total Sales
10/1/2006	5314	Philadelphia	9000000	100000
10/2/2006	5314	Philadelphia	8900000	100000
10/3/2006	5314	Philadelphia	8800000	100000
10/4/2006	5314	Philadelphia	8700000	100000
10/5/2006	5314	Philadelphia	8600000	100000
10/6/2006	5314	Philadelphia	8500000	100000
10/7/2006	5314	Philadelphia	8400000	100000

l. Save the Excel workbook and then close Excel.

m. Maximize Access and open the table named Sales by Store by Day in **Datasheet View**.

n. Activate the Sales Date field. Then hold down the **Shift** key and activate the Store Number field.

o. Click the **Ascending sort** icon (A-Z) in the **Home** tab on the Ribbon. Do you see store number 5314 / Philadelphia?

p. Save and close the table.

q. Close the Access database.

≫ Marketing Strategies

One of the biggest challenges facing most companies is the sharing of information on a timely basis. Big companies are usually composed of several divisions that are sometimes located in different buildings or even locations. However, the information and decisions made in one division can have a significant impact on the operations of another. For example, the marketing division will usually develop promotion and advertising strategies based on the products purchased in the merchandising division. Imagine if the marketing division developed and executed an elaborate advertising strategy for a product that the merchandising division canceled. Unfortunately, these things happen in business. However, the technique of creating Access tables by linking to an external data source is a common practice business managers use to share critical information between divisions and prevent costly mishaps.

Exercise

The purpose of this exercise is to use the linking techniques demonstrated in this section to create a table that might be used by the marketing division of an audio/electronics company. The table will be linked to an Excel spreadsheet that is updated by the merchandising division. The Excel spreadsheet that will be used for this exercise is named ib_a02_merchandiseplans.

1. Create a new database and name it **ib_a02_merchandisedata.** Close the blank table that appears when the database opens.

2. Create a new table by creating a link to the Excel file named ib_a02_merchandiseplans.

3. Select the Current Data worksheet in the first step of the **Link Spreadsheet Wizard**.

4. The first row of the Excel spreadsheet contains column headings. Therefore, make sure the **First Row Contains Column Headings** option is checked in the second step of the **Link Spreadsheet Wizard**.

5. Name the table **Current Merchandise Plan Data** in the last step of the **Link Spreadsheet Wizard**.

6. Open the table you just created in **Datasheet View**. Adjust the width of the columns to fit the field names and the data.

7. Sort the table in descending order based on the Projected Sales Units by Month field. This sort order will make it easy to see what items are projected to sell the highest number of units. Marketing strategies for items that are expected to sell large quantities are usually critical.

8. Based on the monthly projected sales, which three items will need critical marketing support? How many units are being purchased for each of these items? What is the price for each of these items?

9. Save and close the table. Then minimize the database.

10. Open the Excel file used to create the link for the table named Current Merchandise Plan Data. Copy the range A2:E21 in the Sheet2 worksheet. Activate cell A2 in the Current Data worksheet and click the **Paste** icon.

11. Save and then close the Excel workbook.

12. Maximize the Access database and open the table named Current Merchandise Plan Data.

13. Evaluate the top three items based on the projected monthly sales again. Were there any changes? Based on your answer to question 8, what changes will you need to make to your marketing strategy and why?

14. Save and close the table; then close the database.

≫ What's Wrong with This Database?

Problem

Your coworker has created an Access database to help communicate any changes in the merchandise plans to the marketing division. He explains that the database was working great when he first set it up. However, recently the folks in the marketing division complained that they keep getting errors when they try to open the two tables in the database. He asks for your help and explains the following in an e-mail:

1. Thank you very much for taking a look at this for me! The following error is happening when the guys in marketing try to open the Delivery Date table. This is a link to an Excel spreadsheet that we update in the merchandising division. Basically, the system will not let them open the table, and they keep getting this error:

Microsoft Office Access

⚠ The Microsoft Office Access database engine could not find the object 'Sheet1$'. Make sure the object exists and that you spell its name and the path name correctly.

[OK] [Help]

2. The other problem is with the Merchandise Plan table. This is also linked to an Excel spreadsheet that we update in the merchandising division. At the beginning of this week, these strange errors started appearing in the Price and Projected Sales Units by Month fields:

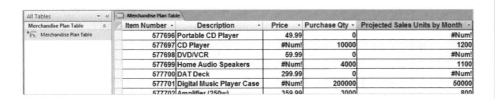

Item Number	Description	Price	Purchase Qty	Projected Sales Units by Month
577696	Portable CD Player	49.99	0	#Num!
577697	CD Player	#Num!	10000	1200
577698	DVD/VCR	59.99	0	#Num!
577699	Home Audio Speakers	#Num!	4000	1100
577700	DAT Deck	299.99	0	#Num!
577701	Digital Music Player Case	#Num!	200000	50000
577702	Amplifier (250w)	359.99	3000	800

Exercise

Look at the two error examples your coworker sent to you. What's wrong with this database? Consider the following points.

1. What would prevent a linked table from being opened? Look at the error message from point 1 in the Problem section carefully. What does this mean?

2. Why are the #Num! errors appearing in the Current Merchandise Plans table in point 2. The Excel spreadsheet that is linked to this table is named ib_a02_marketingmayhem.

Write a short answer for each of these points and explain how your coworker can fix this database.

My role as a merchandise planner changed dramatically when the company started using database systems such as Access. Data that used to take me a few days to put together, I could now get in a few minutes. I now had more time to analyze the trends of the business, which was a big step in creating better merchandise plans.

Assignment

1. Open a new Access database and create a table by linking to the Excel file named ib_a02_historicalsalesresults.

2. After creating the table, open it in **Datasheet View** and use the sort and filter features to answer questions 3 through 6.

3. The table contains six years' worth of data. What are the top three items based on unit sales in a single year? What year were these sales achieved?

4. A buyer mentions that pink jeans are coming back into style. He explains that the last time the company sold pink jeans, they were really successful. He suggests buying 10,000 pairs. Do you agree?

5. Is the sales trend for tan twill pants increasing or decreasing?

Questions for Discussion

1. The anecdote mentioned that gathering and manipulating data took a significant amount of time before Access was used. Why do you think this is so?

2. Besides increasing the speed of gathering data, what other benefits do you think the database brought to the role of the merchandise planner?

3. The anecdote mentions that analyzing trends was a big step in creating better merchandise plans. Why?

The following questions are related to the concepts addressed in this chapter. There are three types of questions: Short Answer, True or False, and Fill in the Blank. If your answer to a True or False question is False, write a short explanation as to why you think the statement is not true.

1. Explain the purpose of data types.

2. If a **Text** data type has a field size setting of 6, how many digits of a number can you type into that field?

3. True or False: The number 65750 can be entered into a field that has a **Number** data type and a field size set to **Integer**.

4. True of False: Numeric values can be typed into a field that is defined with a **Text** data type. However, words or letters cannot be typed into a field that is defined with a **Number** data type.

5. Which data type has the highest storage capacity for words?

6. Explain the purpose of *entity integrity*?

7. If the primary key is set on one field in a table, then there can be no _____ values entered into that field.

8. Before setting the primary key for a table, you must determine what _____ make each record_____.

9. True or False: Indexing is used to sort the data in a table when it is viewed in **Datasheet View**.

10. Indexing makes _____ for data more efficient.

11. True or False: Numbers can be formatted in an Access table by activating a cell or field and selecting one of the formatting icons in the Home tab of the Ribbon.

12. What do you need to check before pasting data from an Excel spreadsheet into an Access table?

13. What option could you use to temporarily remove records from an Access table?

14. The _____ _____ _____ will appear when changing the format or decimal places of a field.

15. True or False: To change the sequence of a field, simply click and drag on the field name when a table is in **Datasheet View**.

16. True or False: Fields can be inserted in either the **Design View** or **Datasheet View** of an Access table.

17. How do you delete a field from an Access table when it is in **Datasheet View**?

18. How do you delete records from an Access table?

19. True or False: If you delete a row or field from an Access table, you can simply click the **Undo** icon to bring them back even after you have clicked **Yes** on the delete warning box.

20. When creating an Access table by importing data from an Excel spreadsheet, you must check to make sure the field names are valid. What is a valid field name?

21. True or False: After a table is created through linking, Access will always keep track of the source file even if it is moved to another location on your computer.

22. How will Access define the data type if you are importing a column of data from an Excel spreadsheet that is mixed with words and numbers?

The following exam is designed to test your ability to recognize and execute the Access skills presented in this chapter. Read each question carefully and answer the questions in the order they are listed. You should be able to complete this exam in 60 minutes or less.

1. Open the Excel file named ib_a02_productioncostdetail. Minimize this file because it will be used later in the exam.

2. Create a new database and name it **ib_a02_skillsexam.**

3. Create a new table with the following field names:

    Manufacture Date

    Product Line Number

    Raw Material Number

    Raw Material Description

    Estimated Inventory

    Units Consumed

    Cost per Unit

4. Set the following data types for each field:

Manufacture Date: Date/Time

Product Line Number: Number

Raw Material Number: Text

Raw Material Description: Text

Estimated Inventory: Number

Units Consumed: Number

Cost per Unit: Currency

5. Make the following adjustments to the field properties for each field:

Manufacture Date: Format = Short Date

Product Line Number: Field Size = Integer

Raw Material Number: Field Size = 5

Raw Material Description: Field Size = 35

Estimated Inventory: Field Size = Double

Units Consumed: Field Size = Long Integer

Cost per Unit: Decimal Places = 2

6. Set the index for the table as follows:

Index Name = Date/Product Line

Field 1 = Manufacture Date – Descending order

Field 2 = Product Line Number – Ascending order

7. Set the primary key for the table on the Manufacture Date, Product Line Number, and Raw Material Number fields.

8. Save the table and name it **Production Cost Data**.

9. Copy the range A2:G19 in the Excel file named ib_a02_productioncostdetail. Paste this data into the Access table named Production Cost Data.

10. Format the data in the table so the font size is 14 points and the color is blue.

11. Adjust the column widths to fit all data and field names.

12. Sort the data in the table based on the Units Consumed field in descending order.

13. Change the sequence of the fields so the Cost per Unit field is just to the right of the Raw Materials Description field and the Units Consumed field is just to the right of the Cost per Unit field.

14. Delete the Estimated Inventory field.

15. Save and close the table.

16. Create a second table in the database by *importing* the Excel file named ib_a02_regionsalesdata. Select the **No Primary Key** option in the next-to-last window of the **Import Spreadsheet Wizard**. Give the following name to the table: **Imported Region Sales Data**

17. After importing the table, set the primary key on the Week and Region fields. Then save and close the table.

18. Create a third table in the database by linking to the Excel file named ib_a02_regionsalesdata. This is the same Excel file that was used in step 17. Call this table **Linked Region Sales Data**.

19. Save and close any open tables.

20. Close the Excel Workbook and your Access database.

The following questions are designed to test your ability to apply the Access skills you have learned to complete a business objective. Use your knowledge of Access as well as your creativity to answer these questions. For most questions, there are several possible ways to complete the objective.

1. What is the primary key(s) for the following table?

Sales and Inventory

Year	Week	Store	Category	Item Number	Price	Unit Sales	Unit Inventory
2005	1	5302	25	678501	$29.99	200	2,500
2005	1	5302	25	678502	$18.99	112	1,500
2005	1	5302	25	678503	$9.99	75	1,500
2005	1	5304	25	678501	$29.99	360	4,800
2005	1	5304	25	678502	$18.99	355	4,700
2005	1	5304	25	678503	$9.99	190	1,200
2005	1	5306	25	678501	$30.99	275	3,200
2005	1	5306	25	678502	$19.99	55	1,000
2005	1	5306	25	678503	$10.99	450	4,500

2. How could you add data from a spreadsheet to an existing table in a database without using the copy and paste commands?

3. What are the pros and cons of linking or importing Excel data to create an Access table? Both provide certain benefits as well as potential shortcomings. What factors should you consider when deciding which method to use?

4. Create a database that contains a table of names and contact information for at least five people (real or fictional). For each person you must have at least one phone number and one e-mail address. Your table must have at least four fields. Design this table and enter the information. Remember to assign a primary key or keys and set an index for the table.

>> Chapter 3

Selecting and Summarizing Data from Tables

Chapter Goals

The preceding chapter covered various techniques for creating tables. This chapter will cover techniques for selecting data that is contained in a table. In business you will rarely, if ever, use an entire table of data to evaluate the performance of a company or analyze trends. Generally, you will select subsets of data from a table for the purposes of analyzing data, adding computations, or developing reports. These tasks are accomplished through queries. To create a query that accurately selects and calculates data, you must thoroughly understand how a table is organized, as well as the definitions of the fields contained in it. Therefore, this chapter begins with data evaluation techniques and then illustrates both fundamental and advanced techniques for using queries.

>> **Access** Skill Sets

Access in **Practice** | Anecdote

Databases in Practice

One of the biggest challenges I experienced when I was managing a consulting project for a food manufacturing company was getting data to measure the past performance of the business. The goal of this project was to determine how the company could improve the sales results of the firm's marketing strategies. The company spent millions of dollars every year in marketing promotions, such as sponsoring prizes at sporting events, sending direct mail coupons, and advertising on radio. However, the company's sales had not grown significantly for the past several years. Therefore, our first task was to analyze the sales performance of the business over the past three years and compare it to the amount of money spent on marketing promotions. However, the company did not have historical performance statistics stored on one central database system. Instead, the company maintained three regional offices in the United States, and each region maintained its own sales and marketing data. Therefore, our challenge was to get data in a consistent format from three different locations in the United States so the business could be analyzed. This presented a major roadblock for the project because we could not develop an effective recommendation on how the company could increase its sales without analyzing the past performance of the business.

>> Continued on page 774

>> Know Your Data

When using Access, most business managers will link to tables contained in external database systems known as *data warehouses* or *data marts*. These systems contain data relating to a specific business area, such as marketing, logistics, or sales and inventory, for example. A business manager will typically use the tables found in a data warehouse or data mart to analyze the historical results of a business and then produce reports. However, knowing the purpose and organization of the data contained in these tables is critical to produce accurate and valid results. This section will demonstrate techniques for evaluating the data contained in tables that might be found in a data warehouse or data mart. These techniques will then become particularly important in the next section, which explains the process of selecting data from tables through queries.

Getting Started

If you are using Access in a business environment, you will most likely be working with tables that you did not design or create. This is especially true if you have aspirations of being a consultant who works with several different companies. Before using a table for any analytical project, you must identify the following key pieces of information:

- The purpose of the table
- The definition or description of each field contained in the table
- The index of the table
- The field or fields that make up the primary key of the table

It is important to identify the purpose of any table you plan to use. Ideally, the table's name should indicate its purpose and the type of data it contains. For example, a table named 2005 Total Sales by Item probably contains the 2005 sales results for each item sold by a particular company. However, a table name may not always be as descriptive as this example. You may see a table serving exactly the same purpose named SbI05. In this case you would need to reference a *data dictionary* or speak with an information systems specialist within the company to find out the contents of the table. A data dictionary is a document that is usually maintained by a company's information systems division and contains a list of tables that are designed and maintained for the firm's business managers. Some companies may refer to this document as a *data catalog*, which is identical to a data dictionary. A well-constructed data dictionary will provide the purpose of each table, the definition of each field, the index for the table, and the primary key.

Before using a table, you will need to know the definition of each field. Similar to the table name, the field name may or may not be helpful in describing the data it contains. However, knowing exactly what the data represents in each field is critical for constructing valid and accurate analytical projects in Access. This information is also contained in the firm's data dictionary.

Another key piece of information to obtain before using a table is the index. As mentioned in Chapter 2, the index is the order in which data is stored in a table. For the enormous tables of data typically found in large corporations, you will not be able to extract data efficiently unless you know the index of each table. The next section on queries provides more information on how to use indexes.

The last critical piece of information you will need is the primary key. This element is most critical when you're adding or summarizing the data contained in a field. As previously mentioned, the primary key is the field or group of fields that make each record in a table unique. It is common to work with tables where the data in a field or group of fields is repeated for several records. Identifying the primary key in these tables is critical for conducting any mathematical computations. Examples of how the primary key is used to evaluate the data contained in a table are presented next.

COMMON MISTAKES | Table Purpose and Field Definitions

Some of the most fluent Access users make mistakes because they do not understand the definition of a field or the purpose of a table. If you are using tables of data that you did not create, it is critical to find accurate information regarding the purpose of the data and the definitions of each field. For businesses, you can find this information through a data dictionary or data catalog, by speaking with an information systems expert, or by speaking with the person who designed or maintains the table.

Single Field Primary Key Tables

Most tables in business fall into either a single field or multiple field primary key design. Figure 3.1 shows an example of a single field primary key design. Notice that every value in the Item Number field is unique. As a result, this one field is the primary key of the table.

Figure 3.1 | **Table with Single Field Primary Key**

Item Number	Item Description	Sales Units	Sales Dollars
12343	Coffee Mugs	64	$320.00
23575	Sweatshirts	365	$19,710.00
32567	Scarves	34	$374.00
44567	Back Packs	28	$2,184.00
53765	Notebooks	255	$1,211.25
55786	Short Sleeve T-Shirts	285	$3,277.50
57563	Baseball Hats	64	$896.00
65788	Long Sleeve T-Shirts	365	$10,220.00
77955	Printer Paper	55	$426.25
87966	Jackets	285	$18,240.00
99246	Pencils	75	$243.75

Table Name — Sales by Item Last Week

The Sales Dollars can be summed to calculate the total sales for last week.

This field is the primary key because every value is unique.

Because the table in Figure 3.1 has only one field that makes every record unique, there is no risk of adding the same value multiple times when conducting mathematical computations. For example, if you assume that the 11 items contained in this table are the only items sold in this company, you can sum all the data in either the Sales Units or Sales Dollars fields to calculate the total sales for the company.

Figure 3.2 shows another table with a single field primary key design. This example contains the current balance of bank accounts for a small bank. Similar to the Sales by Item Last Week table shown in Figure 3.1, one field in this table, the Account Number field, makes every record unique. As a result, statistical summaries such as sum or average can be applied to the Deposits, Withdrawals, or Current Balance fields to calculate overall statistics for the bank.

Figure 3.2 | **Account Balance Report for a Small Bank**

Account Number	Customer Name	Deposits YTD	Withdrawals YTD	Current Balance
4568907	Customer 1	$8,000.00	$8,750.00	$750.00
4568908	Customer 2	$16,000.00	$17,500.00	$1,334.00
4568909	Customer 3	$12,000.00	$10,000.00	$3,232.00
4568910	Customer 4	$18,400.00	$15,000.00	$4,750.00
4568911	Customer 5	$24,000.00	$26,250.00	$211,296.00
4568912	Customer 6	$18,400.00	$15,000.00	$4,750.00
4568913	Customer 7	$12,000.00	$10,000.00	$3,232.00
4568914	Customer 8	$1,600.00	$1,750.00	$765,293.00
4568915	Customer 9	$22,400.00	$24,500.00	$10,245.00
4568916	Customer 10	$8,000.00	$8,750.00	$5,567.00
4568917	Customer 11	$16,000.00	$17,500.00	$24,289.00
4568918	Customer 12	$25,600.00	$28,000.00	$80,724.00
4568919	Customer 13	$6,400.00	$7,000.00	$1,078.00
4568920	Customer 14	$6,000.00	$5,500.00	$734.00

> This field is the primary key because every value is unique.

> The data in these fields can be summed to calculate total statistics for the bank.

Multiple Field Primary Key Tables

When you are using tables with a single field primary key design, there is little risk of making errors when applying mathematical functions. However, this is not the case when the primary key of a table is made up of several fields. A table that requires multiple fields to define the primary key will usually contain data that is repeated over several records. When you are applying mathematical functions, you run the risk of using the same value several times in your calculations which will produce erroneous results. Therefore, it is critical to identify the primary key and the field the primary key relates to or describes before using the data in mathematical computations.

Figure 3.3 shows a table that requires multiple fields to define the primary key. The purpose of this table is to show how many units were sold for each item in category 20. The table shows data for two weeks. There is a total of three items in category 20: Sweatshirts, Short Sleeve T-Shirts, and Long Sleeve T-Shirts.

Figure 3.3 | **Table with Multiple Field Primary Key**

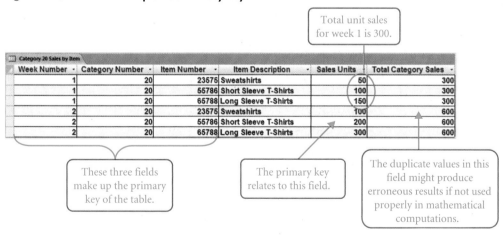

> Total unit sales for week 1 is 300.

Week Number	Category Number	Item Number	Item Description	Sales Units	Total Category Sales
1	20	23575	Sweatshirts	50	300
1	20	55786	Short Sleeve T-Shirts	100	300
1	20	65788	Long Sleeve T-Shirts	150	300
2	20	23575	Sweatshirts	100	600
2	20	55786	Short Sleeve T-Shirts	200	600
2	20	65788	Long Sleeve T-Shirts	300	600

> These three fields make up the primary key of the table.

> The primary key relates to this field.

> The duplicate values in this field might produce erroneous results if not used properly in mathematical computations.

Look at the table in Figure 3.3 carefully. Notice that values are duplicated in almost every field. This duplication immediately indicates that multiple fields are required to define the primary key. The primary key will relate to or describe a specific field or group of fields in a table. For example, the primary key for the table in Figure 3.3 is the combination of the Week Number, Category Number, and Item Number fields, and it is related to the Sales Units field. For any given week there can be only one sales result for each item in category 20. However, the primary key is not related to the Total Category Sales field. This field contains the total sales for category 20 each week. Because there are three items in category 20, the data values in this field are duplicated three times. This arrangement of data is common in business. Fields such as the Total Category Sales field are usually added to tables to calculate the percentage each item contributes to the total. For this table, the data in the Total Category Sales field can be divided into the Sales Units field to determine what percentage each item represents to the total sales of the category.

Because the primary key in the Category 20 Sales by Item table shown in Figure 3.3 relates to the Sales Units field, aggregate mathematical functions can be used to summarize the data in this field. For example, notice that the Week Number field contains only two weeks' worth of data (week numbers 1 and 2). If you wanted to calculate the total unit sales for both weeks 1 and 2, you could sum all the values in the Sales Units field. Or, you could calculate the sales for each week individually. For example, the sales for just week 1 are 300. It is important to note that these computations are possible because each value in the Sales Units field is unique and there is no risk of adding duplicate values. However, you could not sum the values in the Total Category Sales field. Summing the values in this field would give you a sales result of 900 for week 1, when, in fact, only 300 units were sold. This is why it is critical to know the definitions of every field in a table before using the data.

Another key mistake that is made in tables with multiple field primary keys is counting the occurrence of data points within a field. For example, a project might require you to count the number of items in the table. However, notice that the item numbers keep repeating each week. Counting the items listed in the Item Number field will show a result of 6 instead of 3.

Figure 3.4 shows another table that contains a multiple field primary key design. This table contains financial asset data by customer for a wealth management firm. The Portfolio Number field represents a customer's account number. The Stock Symbol and Current Value fields show what stocks each customer is currently holding in his portfolio. The Total Portfolio Value field contains the current value of the customer's account.

Figure 3.4 | **Customer Information for a Wealth Management Firm**

Portfolio Number	Stock Symbol	Current Value	Total Portfolio Value
678444	SS1	$2,000.00	$6,000.00
678444	SS2	$2,000.00	$6,000.00
678444	SS3	$2,000.00	$6,000.00
678555	SS1	$1,000.00	$4,000.00
678555	SS2	$1,000.00	$4,000.00
678555	SS3	$1,000.00	$4,000.00
678555	SS4	$1,000.00	$4,000.00

These two fields make up the primary key of the table.

The primary key relates to this field.

Similar to the fields in Figure 3.3, each field in the Current Portfolio Value Detail table in Figure 3.4 contains duplicate values, indicating multiple fields are required to define the primary key. The primary key for this table is the combination of the Portfolio Number and Stock Symbol fields. The primary key is related to the Current Value field, and by definition, every value in this field is unique even though the values are *coincidentally* the same. The data in this entire field can be summed to calculate the total value of assets managed by this company, or the values can be summed within each Portfolio Number to determine the current value of a customer's account. For example, Portfolio Number 678444 consists of three stocks: SS1, SS2, and SS3. By coincidence, the current value for each stock is $2,000. The value of this portfolio can be calculated by summing the data in the Current Value field for each of the three stocks, to equal $6,000.

It is important to note that the primary key for the table in Figure 3.4 does not relate to the Total Portfolio Value field. Notice the total value of portfolio 678444 is $6,000, which was calculated by summing the current value of the three stocks in the portfolio. However, the value of $6,000 is listed three times in the Total Portfolio Value field, or once for each stock in the portfolio. If you summed the values in this field to calculate the value of the portfolio, the result would be $18,000, when, in fact, the value of the portfolio is $6,000. Therefore, this field can be used to determine what percentage each stock represents to the total portfolio value but *cannot* be summed to calculate the total value of the portfolio.

COMMON MISTAKES | Using Fields with Duplicate Values

People often produce erroneous results with Access by applying mathematical calculations to a field that contains duplicate values. Access will *not* give you a warning when you have used duplicate values in a mathematical summary or calculation. Therefore, it is difficult to know if you have made a mistake when using data from a table to produce mathematical outputs. The following points can help you avoid producing incorrect results when conducting mathematical calculations with database tables:

- Identify the fields that make up the primary key of the table.
- Identify the fields the primary key relates to. Fields that are related to a primary key by definition cannot have any duplicate values. Therefore, there is no risk in producing erroneous results when conducting mathematical calculations with the data in these fields.
- Check to see whether the results of your calculations make sense. Check previously published reports or cross-reference your results with another data source.
- Always try to get detailed information on the tables you are using. Check with a firm's information systems department to see whether it maintains a data dictionary for the database tables that are created and maintained for business managers.

>> Evaluating Tables

The purpose of this workshop is to practice the techniques for evaluating the data contained in a database table that were covered in this section. I will explain each of the tasks in this workshop in the video named **Know Your Data**. Try to complete each of the following tasks and then watch the video.

1. **Analyzing a Single Field Primary Key Table (Video: Know Your Data)**
   a. Open the Excel file named ib_a03_datadictionaryforbanktables.
   b. Activate the Table Definitions worksheet and find the definition of the Account Balance table.

    c. How many fields make up the primary key of this table?

    d. Identify the index for the Account Balance table. Are the index and primary key fields identical?

    e. Activate the Field Definitions worksheet and read the definitions for each of the fields in the Account Balance table.

    f. Open the Access database named ib_a03_bankdata. Then open the Account Balance table in **Datasheet View**.

    g. Look at the data in each of the fields of this table. Do any fields contain consecutive duplicate values?

    h. Calculate the total deposits for the bank by adding each value in the Deposits YTD field.

    i. Calculate the total current balance for the bank by adding all the values in the Current Balance field.

    j. Check the Primary Key and Index setting by going into the **Design View** of the Account Balance table.

    k. Close the Account Balance table.

2. Analyzing a Multifield Primary Key Table (Video: Know Your Data)

    a. Find the definition for the Financial Portfolio Detail table in the Excel file named ib_a03_datadictionaryforbanktables.

    b. How many fields make up the primary key of this table?

    c. Identify the index of the table. Are the index and primary key fields identical?

    d. Activate the Field Definitions worksheet and read the definitions for each of the fields in the Financial Portfolio Detail table.

    e. Open the Financial Portfolio Detail table in **Datasheet View** from the Access database named ib_a03_bankdata.

    f. Look at the data in each of the fields of this table. Do any fields contain consecutive duplicate values?

    g. Count the number of stock symbols assigned to portfolio number 678400.

    h. Add the values in the Current Value field for portfolio 678400.

    i. Add the values in the Total Portfolio Value field for portfolio 678400.

    j. Divide your answer for step h into your answer for step i. The result should equal the number of stock symbols you counted in step g.

    k. Divide the current value of stock symbol SS17 for portfolio number 678440 by the value in the Total Portfolio Value field.

    l. Look at the data in the Current Value field for portfolio number 678444. Does this field contain consecutive duplicate values? What field does the primary key relate to in this table?

    m. Add the values in the Current Value field for portfolio 678444.

    n. Close the Financial Portfolio Detail table, the Access database named ib_a03_bankdata, and the Excel file.

EXERCISE

Why Do I Need This?

>> Analyzing a Call Center Database

The use of databases has drastically increased the amount of information available for business managers in today's companies. Having access to a vast amount of information can improve the quality of the decisions business managers are required to make. These decisions can range from how much product to buy based on historical sales to whether stocks are likely to provide a significant return based on the current trends of an industry. To use the data contained in the tables of a database, a business manager must know all relevant details regarding the organization of the table and the field definitions. Using a data dictionary is one method of communicating this type of information. Without having detailed knowledge of the data contained in a table, a manager can easily misinterpret the results of an analytical project, which can lead to poor decisions.

Exercise

The purpose of this exercise is to analyze a table that might be used in the call center of a company that sells computer software. The database named ib_a03_callcenterdata contains this table. One table in this database is named Call Center Activity. The data dictionary for this table is located in an Excel file named ib_a03_callcenterdatadictionary. Open both the database and Excel file before completing the following tasks:

1. Review the information contained in the file named ib_a03_callcenterdatadictionary. You will need this information to answer the remaining questions in this exercise.

2. Open the Call Center Daily Activity table in **Datasheet View** from the database named ib_a03_callcenterdata.

3. List the fields in the table that contain consecutive duplicate values.

4. How many calls did customer service rep 416788 receive on 10/21/2006? How many unique customers did this customer service rep help on 10/21/2006?

5. What field can you use to sum the total retail value of all the products sold by customer service rep 416788 on 10/21/2006? Calculate this value.

6. Given the primary key of this table, is it possible for two records to have the same customer service rep number and customer ID number on the same day? Why?

7. How many calls did customer service rep 416788 receive on 10/22/2006? How many unique customers did this customer service rep help on 10/22/2006?

8. What field can you use to *sum* the total minutes spent on the phone by customer service rep 446827?

9. What fields could you use to show what percentage each call represents to the total minutes of the call center for each day?

10. How can you determine the number of calls received by the call center for both 10/21/2006 and 10/22/2006?

11. How can you use the Sales Dollars field to check the values in the Tot Day Sales field?

12. Can you calculate the total sales of the call center for both 10/21/2006 and 10/22/2006 by adding all the values in the Sales Dollars field? Why?

13. If you added all the values in the Call Minutes field for 10/21/2006, would the total equal the sum of all the values in the Tot Day Minutes field for 10/21/2006? Why?

14. Would you be able to calculate the total daily sales for this software company by adding the values in the Tot Day Sales field? Why?

15. Close the Access database and Excel file.

>> What's Wrong with This Database?

Problem

You are a team director working for a consulting firm. Your team was recently assigned to a company that owns and operates a large chain of retail stores. The team's first task is to evaluate the sales and profit performance of the company's business over the past five years. An analyst on your team was given a password to access the company's database. He uses Access to link to one of the tables in the database and produces a report showing the firm's annual sales by merchandise category over the past five years. He brings the report to a team meeting and explains that one of the most significant trends that occurred over the past five years is the growth of digital audio. He shows the team that the digital audio category used to be 4.3% of the company's business but is now the number one category, representing 26.4% of the company's sales. In addition, he also explains that the team does not have to burden any of the analysts employed by the company because he can extract and evaluate any data needed from the firm's database using Access.

Exercise

The analyst on your team created the Excel file named ib_a03_categorysalestrends. The analyst created this spreadsheet from a table contained in the Access database named ib_a03_retailcompanyadata. The table he used in this database is named Cat Sales History. Would you be comfortable using the data in this Excel spreadsheet in a presentation to the executives of the company? Why or why not? Consider the following points:

1. Look at the data in the Cat Sales History table. Does it look like the analyst used the data in the table properly to construct accurate results on the Excel spreadsheet?

2. Did the analyst follow a reliable process for using the data in the Cat Sales History table?

3. What questions, if any, would you ask this analyst before presenting the data in the Excel spreadsheet to the managers of this company?

Write a short answer for each of the points listed here. Then explain why you would or would not use the information prepared by the analyst in a presentation to the executives of the company.

>> Fundamental Query Techniques (The Select Query)

When you have a complete understanding of the organization and field definitions in a table, you can extract data and apply mathematical computations. The tool used to extract, manipulate, and calculate data from a table is called a *query*. The term *query* is synonymous with the word *question* and is often referred to as a tool that asks a table "questions." The table "answers" these questions by returning data based on specific criteria that you define. This section will focus on using the *select query*, which is the most fundamental type of query in Access. This section will also explain techniques such as creating new queries, defining criteria, formatting data, editing existing queries, and exporting data to Excel.

Creating a New Query

Similar to the way you create a new table, you can create a new query by using an icon in the **Create** tab on the Ribbon. Figure 3.5 shows an Access database containing one table named Customer Purchases Year to Date. You can add a query to this database by clicking the **Query Design** icon on the right side of the Ribbon. This will open a new query in **Design View**.

Figure 3.5 | **Adding a New Query to a Database**

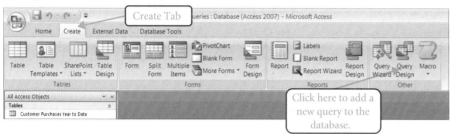

The **Query Design** icon shown in Figure 3.5 provides the most flexibility when you are designing and setting the parameters of a new query. The second icon, which is the **Query Wizard**, provides step-by-step windows for creating various types of queries. However, this option may or may not offer the flexibility to produce the results you need. When you understand how to create queries using the **Query Design** icon, you will be able to assess the wizard options to see whether they suit your needs.

After you click the **Query Design** icon, the **Show Table** dialog box will open, as shown in Figure 3.6. Here, you can add tables to the **Design View** of a new query. The **Show Table** dialog box also contains a **Queries** tab, which provides a list of queries that have been previously created in your database. Queries that select data from existing queries are called *nested queries*; they will be covered in the next section of this chapter. Also, notice in Figure 3.6 that the **Design** tab is added to the Ribbon. The commands in this tab will appear after you add a new query to a database or open a query in **Design View**. This chapter covers several icons in this tab.

Figure 3.6 | **The Show Table Dialog Box**

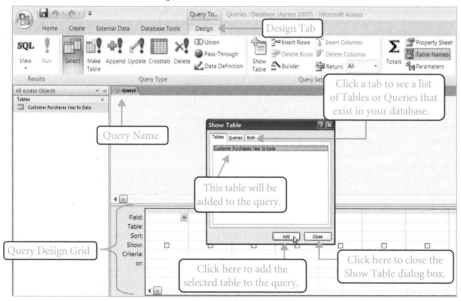

Figure 3.7 shows a select query opened in **Design View**. A select query is one of several types of queries available in Access and is primarily used for selecting and adding computations to the data contained in a table. The **Design View** for the select query is separated into two parts. The top part shows the table that was selected from the **Show Table** dialog box as well as the field names it contains. The lower part is used for setting parameters such as the criteria used to extract data from the table. This section of the query is referred to as the design grid.

Figure 3.7 shows the Customer Purchases Year to Date table added to the select query. This table contains data that might be used by the marketing division of a retail

Figure 3.7 | **Design View of a Select Query**

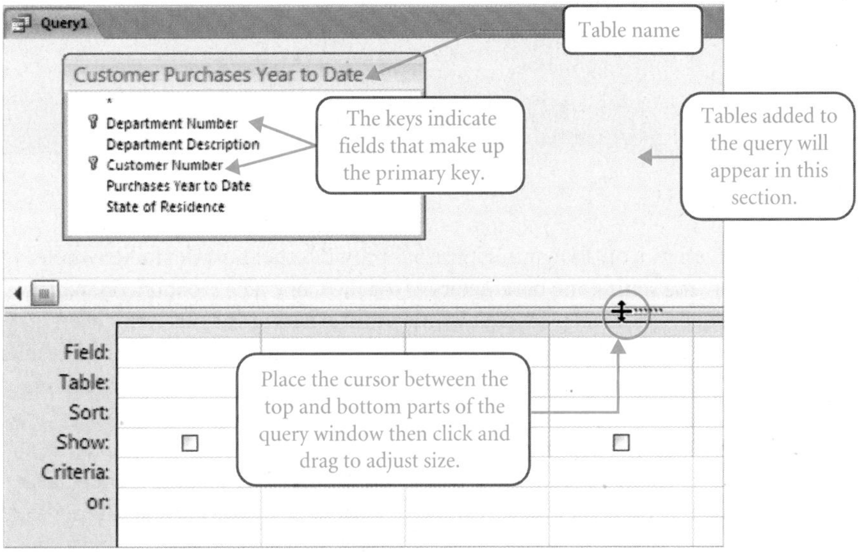

department store. In this section we will construct queries to select and analyze data from this table. The data selected could be used by a marketing manager to execute various promotional strategies. Figure 3.8 shows the first several rows of data from this table.

Figure 3.8 | **Customer Purchases Year to Date Table**

A query can be used to select all records where a purchase was made in the Children's Apparel department.

Department Number	Department Description	Customer Number	Purchases Year to Date	State of Residence
20	Women's Apparel	832001	629	CA
40	Electronics	832091	229	NY
20	Women's Apparel	832199	1210	MD
30	Men's Apparel	832199	376	MD
50	Jewelry	832986	575	CA
20	Women's Apparel	832986	1532	CA
40	Electronics	832992	8932	NY
20	Women's Apparel	833209	91	MD
10	Children's Apparel	833209	170	MD
50	Jewelry	833400	820	NY

As mentioned previously, you must completely understand the data contained in a table before using it in a query. You will need to know the following critical points before selecting data from the Customer Purchases Year to Date table shown in Figure 3.8:

- **Table Purpose:** The purpose of this table is to track purchases made by customers who have a customer loyalty card. These customers signed up for the company's loyalty rewards program and agreed to have their purchases tracked to receive targeted discount promotions. The table keeps track of how much money each customer spends by department when she presents her loyalty card at the time of purchase.

- **Department Number Field:** The department number from which the customer made a purchase.

- **Department Description Field:** A description of the department number.
- **Customer Number Field:** The number assigned to the customer upon submission of the application for the loyalty rewards program.
- **Purchases Year to Date Field:** The total money spent by each customer by department since the first day of the current fiscal year. The data in this field is updated once a week. These values are current as of the close of business last Sunday.
- **State of Residence Field:** The state entered on the customer loyalty application.
- **Index:** The table is indexed based on the Department Number and State of Residence fields.
- **Primary Key:** The primary key is composed of the Department Number and Customer Number fields. The primary key is related to the Purchases Year to Data field.

Adding Fields and Adjusting Columns

Data will be selected from a table based on the fields that are added in the **Design View** of a select query. The fields you select will depend on the needs of your project. For example, the goal of this section is to create a query that determines which customers spent the most money in the Children's Apparel department. This information could be used to identify the most valuable customers for the Children's Apparel product line. Marketing managers can then use this information to offer these customers promotional discounts or solicit their feedback through marketing surveys. As a result, you will be adding all fields in the Customer Purchases Year to Date table to the query because each field contains information that could be valuable or used by a marketing manager.

There are two methods for adding fields to a select query. The first is to click the field name in a table and drag it to the first row of a column in the design grid (see Figure 3.9). The second method is to click in the first row of any column in the design grid and click the drop-down arrow. Then you select a field from the drop-down list.

Figure 3.9 shows the method of dragging a field from the Customer Purchases Year to Date table into the design grid of the select query.

Figure 3.9 | **Click-and-Drag Method for Adding Fields**

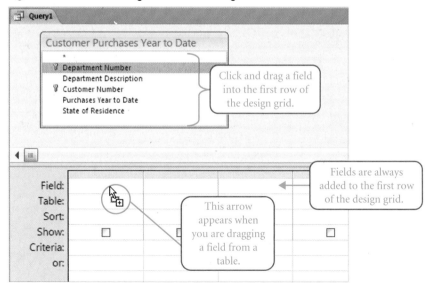

>> *Quick Reference*

Creating a New Query

1. Click the **Create** tab on the Ribbon.
2. Click the **Query Design** icon.
3. Select a table from the **Show Table** dialog box.
4. Click the **Add** button in the **Show Table** dialog box.
5. Click the **Close** button in the **Show Table** dialog box.
6. Research the data contained in the table that is selected for the query.

Figure 3.10 shows how a field can be added to a select query by clicking the drop-down arrow in the Field row of the design grid.

Figure 3.10 | **Drop-Down Arrow Method for Adding Fields**

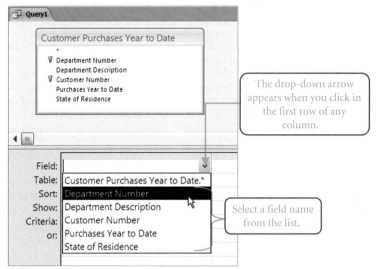

Figure 3.11 shows the fields that were added from the Customer Purchases Year to Date table to the design grid of the select query. As fields are added to the query, you will most likely need to adjust the width of the columns to see the entire field name. To do this, place the cursor between two fields and drag to the desired width when the cursor changes to a double arrow.

Figure 3.11 | **Fields Added to the Select Query**

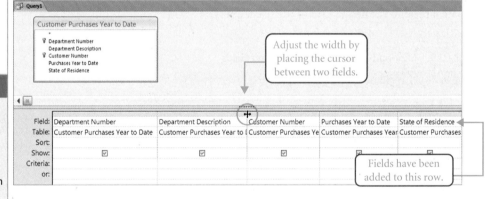

>> **Quick Reference**

Adding Fields to a Query

1. Add a table or group of tables to a query.
2. Click and drag a field from the table to the first row of the design grid of the query.

OR

1. Click in the first row of any column in the design grid of a query.
2. Click the drop-down arrow.
3. Select a field from the list.
4. Click in the second row to select a table if multiple tables are used in the query.

Query Name and Properties

Periodically saving a query as you construct it is a good practice. The first time you save a query, the **Save As** dialog box, which is used to enter a name for the query, will appear, as shown in Figure 3.12. The query name should be related to the expected output or data that will be selected from a table. As previously mentioned, the purpose of the query in this example is selecting from the Customer Purchases Year to Date table those customers who made a purchase in the Children's Apparel department. Therefore, the query is named Customers Buying Children's Apparel, as shown in Figure 3.12. After you type its name, the query will be listed in the **Navigation Pane**.

Figure 3.12 | **Naming a Query**

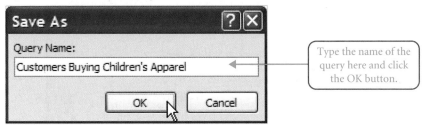

Type the name of the query here and click the OK button.

After a query is added to a database, you can change the query name through the following actions:

- Right click the query name in the **Navigation Pane**. This will open a menu of options.
- Click **Rename** from the menu.
- Type a new name for the query and press the **Enter** key.

Figure 3.13 shows the contextual menu options when renaming a query. Notice that the query name appears in the **Navigation Pane** after the query is saved.

Figure 3.13 | **Contextual Menu Options for a Query**

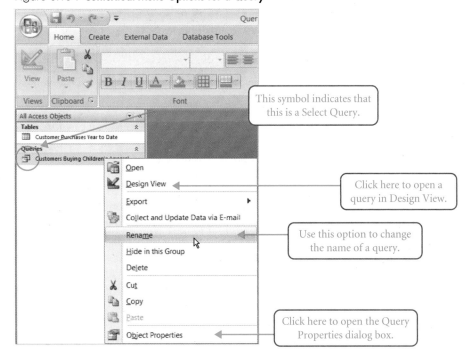

This symbol indicates that this is a Select Query.

Click here to open a query in Design View.

Use this option to change the name of a query.

Click here to open the Query Properties dialog box.

As mentioned, the query name should provide some indication of the type of data it will produce. However, you can also add more descriptive information to the query through the **Query Properties** dialog box. To open the **Query Properties** dialog box, right click the query name in the **Navigation Pane** and select the **Object Properties** option from the menu (see Figure 3.13). It is good practice to enter a description in this dialog box explaining why the query was created and its intended purpose. Adding a description is especially critical if you are sharing a database with several people. Figure 3.14 shows the description that was added to the **Query Properties** dialog box for the Customers Buying Children's Apparel query.

Figure 3.14 | **The Query Properties Dialog Box**

COMMON MISTAKES │ Adding a Description to the Query Properties Box

The Description area of the **Query Properties** dialog box has a 255-character limit. Therefore, if you are unable to finish typing a description, you most likely exceeded this 255-character limit.

Defining Basic Criteria (OR AND)

After the field names have been added to the **Design View** of a query, you can add criteria that will be used to select data from a table. Depending on your project, you type specific values into the Criteria row of a field or fields in the design grid of a select query. For example, the purpose of the query shown in Figure 3.11 is to select from the Customer Purchases Year to Date table those customers who purchased merchandise in the Children's Apparel department, which is department 10. As a result, you type the number 10 under the Department Number field in the Criteria row, as shown in Figure 3.15.

>> **Quick Reference**

Renaming a Query

1. Right click a query name in the **Navigation Pane.**
2. Select the **Rename** option from the menu.
3. Type a new name.
4. Press the **Enter** key.

>> **Quick Reference**

Adding a Query Description

1. Right click a query name in the **Navigation Pane**.
2. Select the **Object Properties** option.
3. Type a description that is no more than 255 characters in the **Description** box.
4. Click the **OK** button.

Figure 3.15 | **Adding Criteria to a Select Query**

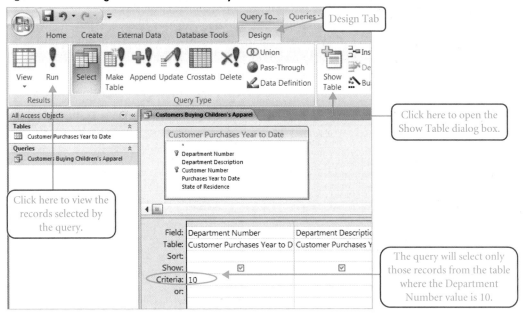

As shown in Figure 3.15, the number 10 was typed into the Criteria row under the Department Number field. As a result, the query will select records from the Customer Purchases Year to Date table only where the Department Number is equal to 10, which is Children's Apparel. However, to enter this criterion, you first have to determine that the number 10 relates to the Children's Apparel department. It may seem that using the Department Description field to set the criteria of this query would be easier because it saves the trouble of having to find the right department number. However, the criterion is entered in the Department Number field because this is one of the indexes of the table. When you're entering criteria for a query, it is good practice to use a field that makes up the index of the table, especially if the table contains thousands of records. Not using an index field to set the criteria of a query is like searching for a person's name in a phone book using a phone number. You literally have to look at every number in the book until you get a match. Therefore, it is important to check which fields make up the index of a table before adding any criteria.

COMMON MISTAKES | **Entering Criteria for a Query**

One of the most common mistakes made in business environments when creating queries is forgetting to enter criteria for the index fields. Entering criteria in these fields is especially critical when you're using large tables of data. The bigger the table, the longer it will take to find and select records if criteria are not defined for the index field. In fact, many corporate systems will place a limit on the amount of time a query can search and select records from a table. Therefore, if your query seems to be taking an unusually long time to select records or if no records are returned, check to make sure criteria are entered for the index fields.

After entering criteria, you can run the query by clicking the **Run** icon in the **Design** tab on the Ribbon (see Figure 3.15). Remember that the **Design** tab will appear only when a query is opened in **Design View**. After you click the **Run** icon, the query will select records from the table and display them in **Datasheet View**. The data retrieved by a query is referred to as a *record set*. The record set of a query is a temporary display of the records that were selected from the table. After the query is closed, you will have to run it again to view the records selected from a table. You can do this by either double clicking the query name in the **Navigation Pane**, opening the query in **Design View** and clicking the **Run** icon, or opening the query in **Datasheet View**. Figure 3.16 shows the record set of the Customers Buying Children's Apparel query. Because the number 10 was entered in the criteria row of the Department Number field, only records containing the number 10 in this field are selected.

Figure 3.16 | **Record Set from the Customers Buying Children's Apparel Query**

Department Number	Department Description	Customer Number	Purchases Year to Date	State of Residence
10	Children's Apparel	833209	170	MD
10	Children's Apparel	834698	235	PA
10	Children's Apparel	836125	90	CA
10	Children's Apparel	837653	90	PA
10	Children's Apparel	837965	46	NY
10	Children's Apparel	838100	39	MD
10	Children's Apparel	838906	129	PA
10	Children's Apparel	839145	646	NY
10	Children's Apparel	839178	589	PA

Only records containing the number 10 in the Department Number field have been selected.

Click and drag to expand column width.

COMMON MISTAKES | Do Not Delete Records from a Select Query

Do not delete records in the record set of a select query. Many people make the mistake of thinking that deleting records from the **Datasheet View** of a query will change only the record set of the query. However, any records deleted from the record set of a query will also be deleted from the table. After the records are deleted and you click the **OK** button on the delete warning box, there is no way to get them back. They will be permanently deleted from the query *and the table.*

The Customers Buying Children's Apparel query required only one criterion to be entered in one field. However, several criteria can be entered for any particular field. For example, suppose you wanted to expand the marketing strategy for this example and identify customers who made purchases in either the Children's Apparel department, the Women's Apparel department, or the Jewelry department. This would require the numbers 10, 20, and 50 to be entered in the criteria rows of the Department Number field.

Figure 3.17 shows how multiple department numbers are added to the criteria row of the Department Number field in a new select query. Notice that these additional department numbers are typed vertically in each row in the Department Number field. This query will now select from the Customer Purchases Year to Date table the records that contain the department number 10 or 20 or 50. These department numbers could have also been typed into the Criteria row as follows: 10 Or 20 Or 50.

Figure 3.17 | **Adding Multiple Criteria to a Field**

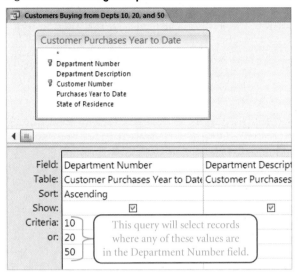

Figure 3.18 shows a portion of the record set from the new select query that was created in Figure 3.17. Notice that the only numbers showing in the Department Number field are 10, 20, and 50.

Figure 3.18 | **Record Set with Criteria 10, 20, and 50 Entered in the Department Number Field**

Query name

Department Number	Department Description	Customer Number	Purchases Year to Date	State of Residence
10	Children's Apparel	837965	46	NY
10	Children's Apparel	837653	90	PA
20	Women's Apparel	837653	560	PA
50	Jewelry	839105	379	MD
20	Women's Apparel	836057	859	NY
50	Jewelry	836057	149	NY
10	Children's Apparel	836125	90	CA
50	Jewelry	837155	329	MD

Only records containing department numbers 10, 20, or 50 are selected.

So far, criteria have been entered in only one field of a select query. However, if your project required, you could enter criteria into multiple fields. For example, suppose your marketing strategy was to target promotions for any customers buying merchandise from either the Jewelry department or the Electronics department in the state of Pennsylvania. To select these records, you will enter the numbers 40 and 50 in the criteria rows for the Department Number field and "PA" in the criteria rows for the State of Residence field.

Figure 3.19 shows how criteria are entered into the Department Number and State of Residence fields for a new select query. Notice that "PA" is entered twice under the State of Residence field because Access will read the criteria entered into a query one row at a time. For example, Access will read the first row of criteria as department number 40 *and* state of residence PA. Therefore, any record that contains the number 40 in the Department Number field *and* PA in the State of Residence field will be selected. Access will then read the next row of criteria. In addition to the records selected for the first row of criteria, Access will also select any records that contain 50 in the Department Number field *and* PA in the State of Residence field.

Figure 3.19 | **Adding Criteria to Multiple Fields**

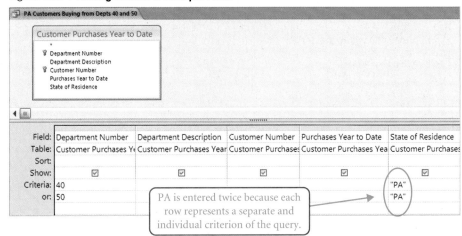

Another point to notice in Figure 3.19 is that the criteria for the State of Residence field are put in quotation marks. The reason is that the data type in this field is set to **Text**. When you are entering criteria for a text field, it is good practice to use quotation marks. However, if you forget, Access will add the quotation marks for you.

COMMON MISTAKES | Entering Criteria for Multiple Fields

People frequently make the mistake of entering multiple values in the Criteria row for one field but forget to enter the same number of values in another field. For example, Figure 3.20 shows two different numbers entered into the Criteria row for the Department Number field, but only one entry was made in the State of Residence field.

Figure 3.20 | **Query with Uneven Criteria**

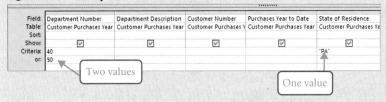

Based on the criteria entered into the query shown in Figure 3.20, Access will select records as follows:

1 Any records that contain the number 40 in the Department Number field *and* PA in the State of Residence field

2 In addition to the records selected in point 1, any record that contains the value 50 in the Department Number field

Figure 3.21 shows a portion of the record set from the query shown in Figure 3.20. Notice that for department 40, only the state of PA appears in the record set. However, several different states appear for department number 50. The reason is that "PA" was *not* entered in the criteria row under the State of Residence field where the value of 50 was entered under the Department Number field.

Figure 3.21 | **Record Set of Query with Uneven Criteria**

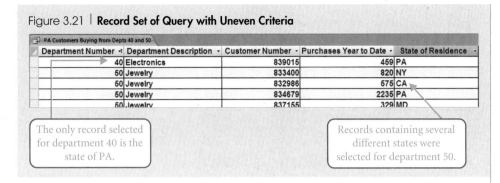

Department Number	Department Description	Customer Number	Purchases Year to Date	State of Residence
40	Electronics	839015	459	PA
50	Jewelry	833400	820	NY
50	Jewelry	832986	575	CA
50	Jewelry	834679	2235	PA
50	Jewelry	837155	329	MD

The only record selected for department 40 is the state of PA.

Records containing several different states were selected for department 50.

Figure 3.22 shows the record set of the select query shown in Figure 3.19. The records selected for this query contain departments 40 and 50 only for the state of Pennsylvania, which is a total of two records. When you interpret the results of this query, your first impression might be that only one customer in the state of Pennsylvania made a purchase from the Electronics department and another customer made a purchase from the Jewelry department. However, there could be many reasons why the table shows only two records. In the beginning of this section, details were provided regarding the purpose of the Customer Purchases Year to Date table and the field definitions it contains. The purpose of the table is to store purchase information of customers who are members of the loyalty program and who present their loyalty card at the time of purchase. Therefore, it is possible that more than two customers in Pennsylvania are making purchases in the Electronics and Jewelry departments. However, these customers may not have joined the loyalty program, or they are not presenting their loyalty card at the time of purchase. Therefore, interpreting the results of a query further underscores the importance of knowing the details of the data contained in a table from which records are being selected.

Figure 3.22 | **Records Selected with Criteria Entered into Multiple Fields**

Department Number	Department Description	Customer Number	Purchases Year to Date	State of Residence
40	Electronics	839015	459	PA
50	Jewelry	834679	2235	PA

The query selected only records containing the state of PA for departments 40 and 50.

COMMON MISTAKES | Confusing AND and OR Criteria

People frequently confuse logical operators such as AND and OR. It is important to note that if you use AND to separate the values entered into the Criteria row of a select query, the cell within the field of the table must contain both values. For example, if you wanted to select records that have a department number of either 40 or 50 from the table shown in Figure 3.23, you would enter **40 OR 50** in the Criteria row of the Department Number field. If you entered **40 AND 50** in the Criteria row, Access would look for records where a cell in the Department Number field contains both values 40 and 50. As you can see from Figure 3.23, each cell in the Department Number field contains only one value. Therefore, your query will not return any records. Generally, it is very rare to enter criteria for a field where the values are separated by the word AND. If you create a query that does not select any records, check any criteria that was entered where the values are separated by the word AND instead of OR.

Figure 3.23 | **Customer Purchases Year to Date**

Department Number ▾	Department Description ▾	Customer Number ◄	Purchases Year to Date ▾	State of Residence ▾
20	Women's Apparel	832001	629	CA
40	Electronics	832091	229	NY
20	Women's Apparel	832199	1210	MD
30	Men's Apparel	832199	376	MD
50	Jewelry	832986	575	CA
20	Women's Apparel	832986	1532	CA
40	Electronics	832992	8932	NY

Formatting and Sorting Data

Formatting and sorting can significantly enhance your ability to read and analyze the records selected by a query. For example, you might want to format the Purchases Year to Date field from the query in Figure 3.19 to a Currency format. The following steps explain how to accomplish this:

- Open a query in **Design View.** You can do this by right clicking a query name in the **Navigation Pane** and selecting **Design View** from the list of options in the menu (see Figure 3.13).

- Click any row under the field you wish to format. For this example, a row under the Purchases Year to Date field is clicked.

- Click the **Design** tab on the Ribbon.

- Click the **Property Sheet** icon on the right side of the Ribbon. This will open the **Property Sheet** window pane on the right side of the screen, as shown in Figure 3.24.

- Click the Description row to type descriptive information about the field. Then click in the Format row to select a number format and click in the Decimal Places row to set the number of decimal places.

- Click the X in the upper-right corner of the **Property Sheet** window pane to apply the format settings and close the window.

Figure 3.24 shows the **Property Sheet** window and the settings that were made for the Purchases Year to Date field.

Figure 3.24 | **Formatting a Field (Property Sheet Window)**

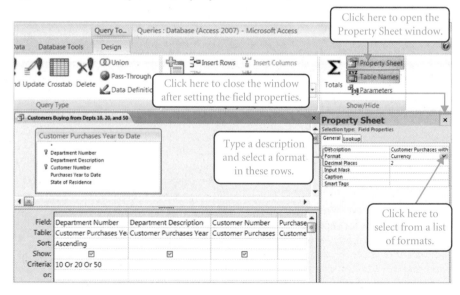

>> **Quick Reference**

Adding Criteria to a Query

1. Click the criteria row of a field.

2. Enter a value or expression using comparison operators.

3. Enter criteria for other fields if necessary.

4. Check your criteria by reading each criteria row one at a time.

To sort fields, you click in the Sort row of a field when a query is in **Design View.** Clicking the Sort row causes a drop-down arrow to appear; from this list, you can select either the **Ascending** or **Descending** option. If you are sorting multiple fields in a tiered sequence, Access will sort records by the first field on the far left side of the design grid and continue reading from left to right any fields where the sort option was selected. For example, Figure 3.25 shows a query that will be sorted by the Department Number field in ascending order, the Purchases Year to Date field in descending order, and the State of Residence field in ascending order. Access will sort the record set of the query based on the data in the Department Number field first because it is the first field on the far left of the design grid. Access will then sort the data within each department number based on the Purchases Year to Date field in descending order. This data will show which customers spent the most money in each department. The last field that will be sorted is the State of Residence because it is the last field in the design grid. If two customers spent an identical amount of money in any given department, the records will be sorted by the state of residence in ascending or alphabetical order.

Figure 3.25 | **Sorting the Records of a Query**

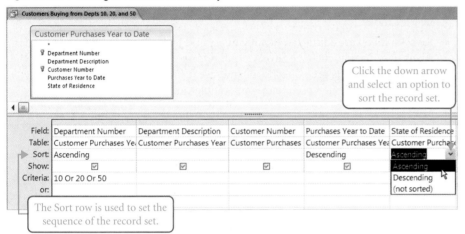

Figure 3.26 shows a portion of the record set for the select query that was shown in Figure 3.25. The values in the Purchases Year to Date field are formatted to Currency with two decimal places because of the settings that were made in the **Property Sheet** window. Also, notice how the data is sorted in this record set. A business manager can quickly see which customers spent the most money year to date within each department.

Figure 3.26 | **Record Set of a Query with Formatting and Sorting Options Applied**

Department Number	Department Description	Customer Number	Purchases Year to Date	State of Residence
10	Children's Apparel	839145	$646.00	NY
10	Children's Apparel	839178	$589.00	PA
10	Children's Apparel	834698	$235.00	PA
10	Children's Apparel	833209	$170.00	MD
10	Children's Apparel	838906	$129.00	PA
10	Children's Apparel	836125	$90.00	CA
10	Children's Apparel	837653	$90.00	PA
10	Children's Apparel	837965	$46.00	NY
10	Children's Apparel	838100	$39.00	MD
20	Women's Apparel	832986	$1,532.00	CA
20	Women's Apparel	836899	$1,258.00	NY
20	Women's Apparel	832199	$1,210.00	MD
20	Women's Apparel	837800	$870.00	NY

Both customers spent $90; records are sorted based on their state of residence.

Customers spending the most money appear at the top of each department because the sort row for this field was set to Descending.

>> **Quick Reference**

Formatting Query Fields

1. Click any row in the design grid of the field you need to format.
2. Click the **Design** tab on the Ribbon.
3. Click the **Property Sheet** icon.
4. Type descriptive information in the first row of the **Property Sheet** window.
5. Make any necessary formatting adjustments in the **Property Sheet** window.
6. Click the X in the upper-right corner of the **Property Sheet** window to apply the format settings and close the window.

>> **Quick Reference**

Sorting Query Record Sets

1. Click the Sort row of the field that will be used to sort the record set of the query.
2. Click the drop-down arrow and select either **Ascending** or **Descending**.

Editing Queries

After you create a query and save it to a database, you can make edits to change components such as the fields of the query, the criteria, or the sort sequence. To edit a query, right click the query name in the **Navigation Pane** and click the **Design View** option (see Figure 3.13). This will open the query in **Design View**. The following are a few commonly used editing commands:

- **Inserting a Column:** Activate a field and click the **Insert Columns** icon in the **Design** tab on the Ribbon. Columns will be inserted to the left of the field that is activated.

- **Deleting a Column:** Activate a field and click the **Delete Columns** icon in the **Design** tab on the Ribbon, or press the **Delete** key on your keyboard.

- **Changing the Sequence of Columns:** Activate a field and then click and drag to a new location.

- **Save As:** If you are editing an existing query and wish to save the final edits under a new query name, click the **Save As** option from the **File** menu. This will keep the original query in its pre-edited form and save the new query under a new name. This technique is often used to create multiple variations of the same query.

Figure 3.27 shows an example of inserting a column into the design grid of a select query.

Figure 3.27 | **Inserting a Blank Column**

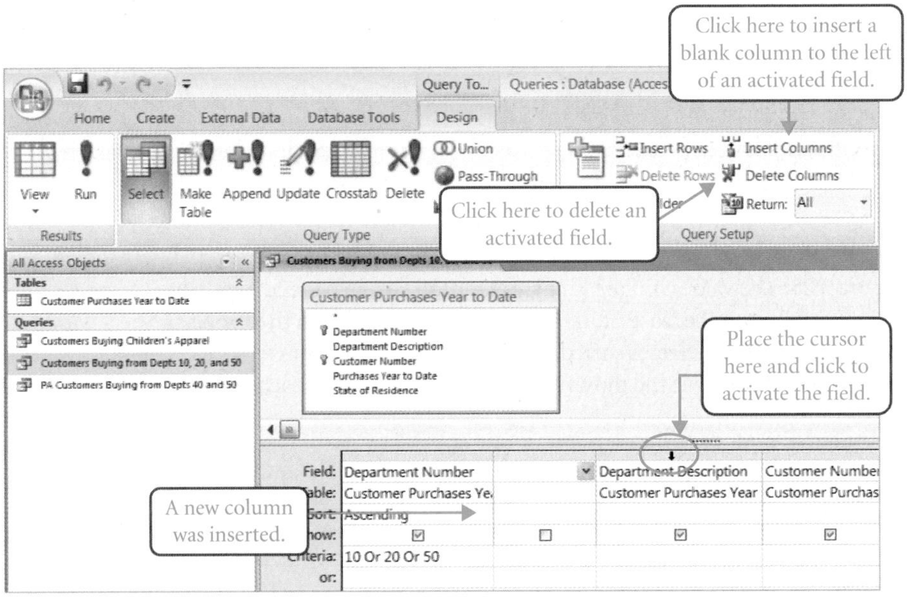

Figure 3.28 shows the **Save As** dialog box, which opens when you select the **Save As** option from the **File** menu when a query is open in **Design View**. Notice that the **As** section of the dialog box is set to **Query** so that the existing query will be saved as a new query with a new name.

Figure 3.28 | **The Save As Dialog Box**

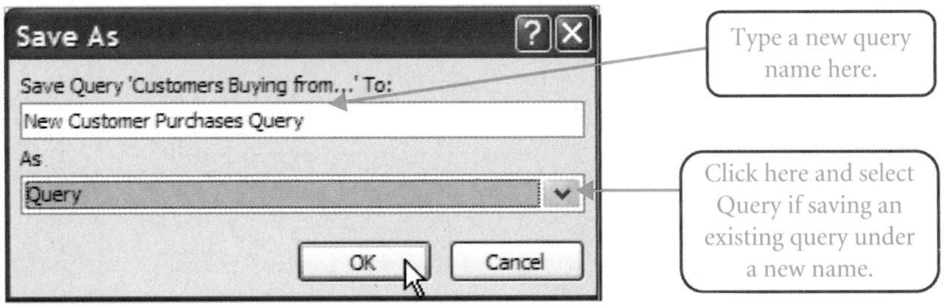

Exporting Queries to Excel

Access gives you the option of converting or exporting the results of a query to an Excel spreadsheet. After the record set of the query is converted to an Excel spreadsheet, additional calculations or formats can be applied using any of the techniques and commands available in Excel. The following points explain how to export the select query in Figure 3.25 to Excel:

- Click the query name in the **Navigation Pane** or open the query in either **Design View** or **Datasheet View**.
- Click the **External Data** tab on the Ribbon.
- Click the **Excel** icon in the **Export** group of icons (see Figure 3.29). This will open the **Export Excel Spreadsheet** dialog box.
- Click the **Browse** button on the **Export Excel Spreadsheet** dialog box to select a location on your computer or network and assign a name for the Excel workbook that will be created.
- Select the **Excel Workbook** option from the **File format** drop-down box. Note that if you intend to share the Excel workbook that will be created from this export command, you may want to select the **Excel 97-Excel 2003 Workbook** option. This will enable you to share the workbook with people who have older versions of Microsoft Office.
- If you wish to keep the format settings that were applied to the query, select the **Export data with formatting and layout** option in the center of the **Export Excel Spreadsheet** dialog box. For this example, this option will not be selected because Excel provides more formatting flexibility. Therefore, formatting techniques will be applied after the data is exported to an Excel workbook.
- Click the **OK** button at the bottom of the **Export Excel Spreadsheet** dialog box. This will convert the record set of the query into an Excel workbook that will be saved in the location specified after clicking the **Browse** button.
- Click the **Close** button in the **Save Export Steps** dialog box. This technique is used in cases in which the same query will be exported to Excel on a routine basis. If you click the **Save export steps** option, you can assign a name to this export routine, which can then be executed again by clicking the **Saved Exports** icon in the **External Data** tab on the Ribbon.

Figure 3.29 shows the **Excel** icon in the **External Data** tab on the Ribbon. In this example, the query in the Navigation Pane was selected before clicking the **Excel** icon. However, you can also open a query in either **Design View** or **Datasheet View** before exporting it to Excel.

Figure 3.29 | **Exporting the Record Set of a Query to Excel**

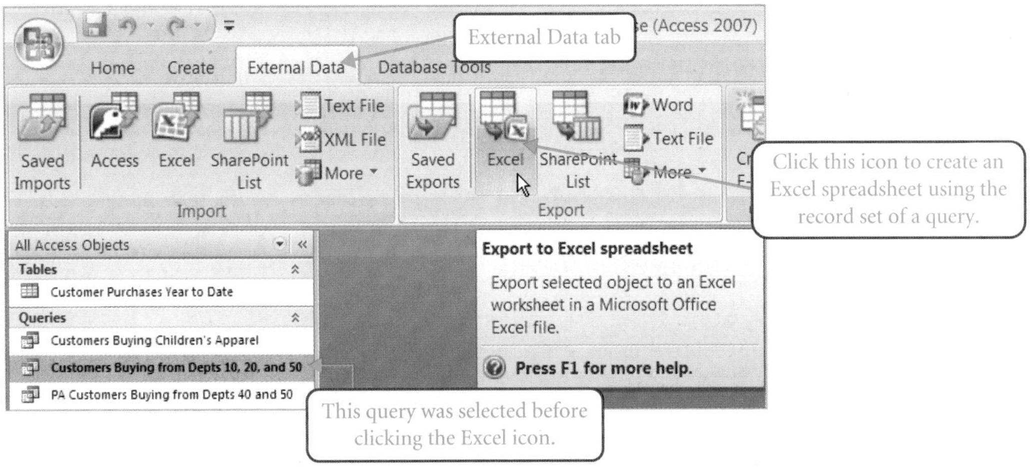

Figure 3.30 shows the **Export Excel Spreadsheet** dialog box. Notice that Access will automatically use the name of the query to assign a name to the Excel workbook that will be created from this export command.

Figure 3.30 | **Export Excel Spreadsheet Dialog Box**

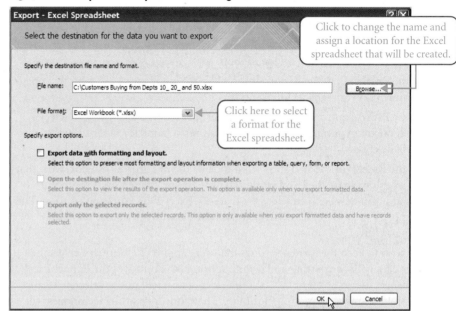

Exporting the results of a query into an Excel spreadsheet is a common practice for business managers. For example, after they have exported data from a query to an Excel spreadsheet, business managers might use this information to construct additional calculations or use the file for a report or presentation. Figure 3.31 shows a portion of the Excel spreadsheet that was created as a result of exporting the Customers Buying from Depts 10, 20, and 50 select query. Notice that several Excel formatting commands were used to improve the appearance of the data. In addition, notice that the data is still sorted based on the settings that were made in Figure 3.25.

Figure 3.31 | **Excel Spreadsheet Created by Exporting a Select Query**

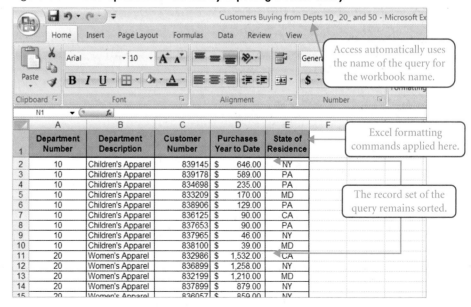

>> **Quick Reference**

Exporting Queries to Excel

1. Select a query from the **Navigation Pane**.
2. Click the **External Data** tab on the Ribbon.
3. Click the **Excel** icon in the **Export** group of icons.
4. Click the **Browse** button in the **Export Excel Spreadsheet** dialog box to select a location on your computer or network and change the file name if necessary.
5. Select the appropriate file format in the **Export Excel Spreadsheet** dialog box.
6. Click the **OK** button.
7. Click the **Close** button in the **Save Export Steps** dialog box or save the export steps if you plan to export the same query on a regular basis.

>> Basic Queries

VIDEO WORKSHOP

The purpose of this workshop is to review techniques used to create basic queries in Access. I will be demonstrating the following tasks on the video named **Basic Queries** (except for step 6). I will be demonstrating the tasks listed for step 6 on the video named **Exporting Queries to Excel**. Open the Access database named ib_a03_marketingdata. Try to complete each of the following tasks listed and then watch the videos.

1. **Creating a New Query (Video: Basic Queries)**

   a. Create a new select query by clicking the **Query Design** icon in the **Create** tab on the Ribbon.

   b. Select the Customer Loyalty Purchases table in the **Show Table** dialog box and click the **Add** button. After adding the table to the query, click the **Close** button.

   c. Expand the width and height of the Customer Loyalty Purchases table in the select query so the table name and field names are visible.

2. **Adding Fields (Video: Basic Queries)**

   a. Click the Department Number field in the Customer Loyalty Purchases table and drag it to the first column, first row of the design grid.

   b. Add each of the remaining fields in the Customer Purchases Loyalty table to the design grid of the query.

   c. Adjust the width of each column in the design grid so the field names are visible. Place the cursor between two columns and click and drag when the cursor changes to a double arrow.

3. **Adding Criteria (Video: Basic Queries)**

   a. Type the number **30** in the Criteria row under the Department Number field. Then type the number **40** in the row directly below the number 30.

   b. Type the state **"NY"** in the Criteria row under the State of Residence field. Then type the state **"NY"** again in the row directly below the first Criteria row. The abbreviation "NY" should appear twice in two criteria rows under the State of Residence field.

4. **Formatting and Sorting (Video: Basic Queries)**

   a. Click in any row under the Purchases Year to Date field.

   b. Click the **Property Sheet** icon in the **Design** tab on the Ribbon.

   c. Set the format to Currency and the Decimal Places to 0. Then close the **Property Sheet** window by clicking the X in the upper-right corner.

   d. Set the Sort row in the Department Number field to **Ascending**. Set the Sort row in the Purchases Year to Date field to **Descending**.

   e. Run the query by clicking the **Run** icon in the **Design** tab on the Ribbon.

5. **Saving and Naming (Video: Basic Queries)**

   a. Click the **Save** icon in the **Quick Access** toolbar and type **Department 30 and 40 NY** in the **Save As** dialog box.

b. Click **OK** in the **Save As** dialog box and close the query.

c. Close the query by clicking the X in the upper-right corner of the query.

6. **Exporting to Excel (Video: Exporting Queries to Excel)**

a. Select the Department 30 and 40 select query in the **Navigation Pane**.

b. Click the **External Data** tab in the Ribbon and then click the **Excel** icon in the **Export** group of icons.

c. Click the **Browse** button in the **Export Excel Spreadsheet** dialog box.

d. Select any location on your computer or network and change the name of the file to **ib_a03_purchasedataforny**. Then click the **Save** button.

e. Click the **OK** button at the bottom of the **Export Excel Spreadsheet** dialog box.

f. Click the **Close** button in the **Save Export Steps** window of the **Export Excel Spreadsheet** dialog box.

g. Open the Excel workbook that was created and check the results.

h. Close the Excel workbook and then close the Access database.

EXERCISE

Why Do I Need This?

>> Analyzing Transportation Data

Databases can provide significant value to business managers because they are capable of storing enormous amounts of data for almost any aspect of a company's operations. By themselves, tables can provide some value if they contain a relatively small and focused set of data. However, database tables typically found in large corporations can contain hundreds of thousands of records. Therefore, you will need to use a query to select only the data you need or is relevant to your project. Queries are an essential tool to make effective use of the data contained in database tables found in most corporations.

Exercise

The purpose of this exercise is to create basic queries that will be used to select data from a table. The table that will be used in this exercise contains data that might be used in the transportation department of a merchandise company. Open the Access database named ib_a03_shipping before completing each of the following tasks:

1. Open the Trailer Status Detail table and examine the data. What is the primary key of the table? Close this table.

2. Open a new select query in **Design View**. Add the Trailer Status Detail table.

3. Make any necessary adjustments to the size of the Trailer Status Detail table so the table name and field names are visible.

4. Add the Trailer Number, Length, Current Weight, Maintenance Required, and Capacity Status fields to the query. Adjust the width of each column as necessary so the field names are visible in the design grid area of the query.

5. Enter the number **53** in the Criteria row of the Length field and type **"Ship"** in the Criteria row of the Capacity Status field. The Length field contains the length of the trucks that are being managed by this company. The Capacity Status field contains one of two possible values: **Ship** or **Hold**. The criteria entered for this query will show a transportation manager any 53 foot trailers that have achieved their capacity targets and are ready to ship.

6. Set the Sort row for the Trailer Number field to **Ascending**. This will sequence the record set of the query based on the values in the Trailer Number field.

7. Format the values in the Current Weight field to a Standard number format with commas and 0 decimal places. You will need to open the **Property Sheet** window to make this formatting adjustment.

8. Run the query and examine the data in the record set of the query. Do any of the trailers require maintenance?

9. Save the query and name it `Ship Status 53 Foot`. Then close the query.

10. Export the Ship Status 53 Foot query to an Excel spreadsheet. Save the export to any location on your computer. Use the query name as the name of the Excel file.

11. Create a new select query in **Design View**. Add the Trailer Status Detail table.

12. Add the Trailer Number, Length, Cubic Capacity, Current Cube, Maintenance Required, and Capacity Status fields to the query. Adjust the width of each column as necessary so the field names are visible.

13. Enter the numbers **48** and **22** in two Criteria rows under the Length field. Enter **"Ship"** in two Criteria rows under the Capacity Status field. This query will show a similar record set as the first query but for trailers that are 48 and 22 feet in length.

14. Set the Sort row to **Ascending** for the Length field and **Descending** for the Cubic Capacity field. This will create a tiered sorting sequence for the query record set based on the Length field. Records with identical length values will be sorted based on the values in the Cubic Capacity field.

15. Format the values in the Current Cube field to a standard number with commas and 0 decimal places.

16. Run the query and examine the data in the record set of the query. Do any of the trailers require maintenance?

17. Switch the query back to **Design View**.

18. Enter **"No"** in two criteria rows under the Maintenance Required field.

19. Run the query. Then save the query and name it `Ship Status for 48 and 22 Feet`.

20. Close the query and then the database.

>> What's Wrong with This Database?

Problem

You are working as a merchandise analyst for an apparel retail firm. A coworker in your division is having trouble using Access to select data from one of the tables in a database and approaches you for help. You agree to help your coworker and ask him to send you an e-mail explaining his needs. He sends you the following message:

Thanks so much for helping me out with this! I thought this would be simple, but for some reason I can't get anything to work. A friend of mine sent me this database that he used for a prior analysis. It contains one table and two queries. The following explains what I am trying to accomplish and where I am getting stuck:

1. *The first thing I tried to do was modify the query named Sales for Prior 3 Weeks. The query was originally designed to select weeks 15, 14, and 13 from the table. I need to look at these same three weeks' worth of data but only for category 50. Therefore, I entered 50 in the Criteria row of the Category Number field. However, this worked only for week 15. All the other weeks are still showing all the other categories. Why is this not working for weeks 14 and 13?*

2. *When I was having trouble showing sales for only category 50, I thought I would export the query to Excel and modify the results manually. However, when I clicked the Excel icon in the External Data tab on the Ribbon, I only see options in the dialog box for importing data. Do you have to buy the exporting option separately?*

3. *The last thing I tried to do was create a new query. I needed to look at the sales of category 30 for weeks 1 and 2. I typed 1 AND 2 in the Criteria row of the Week Number field and typed 30 in the Category Number field. However, I get no records returned when I try to run the query. I thought for some reason weeks 1 and 2 were removed from the table, but my friend insists they are there. I saved this query under the name Weeks 1 and 2 Category 30.*

Exercise

The Access database your coworker mentions in his e-mail is named ib_a03_apparelsalesdata. Open the database and look at the queries your coworker refers to in his
e-mail. Consider the following points:

- Look at the criteria that were entered in the Sales for Prior 3 Weeks query. Why does week 15 show only category 50 but weeks 14 and 13 show all categories?

- Why is your coworker not finding the **Export** option in the dialog box?

- Look carefully at the entry in the Criteria row for the Week Number field in the query named Weeks 1 and 2 Category 30. Run the query. Why are no records returned for this query?

What's wrong with this database? Write a short answer for each of the points stated here. Then fix any errors that were made in the Sales for Prior 3 Weeks and Weeks 1 and 2 Category 30 queries. Also, after fixing the Sales for Prior 3 Weeks query, export the results to an Excel spreadsheet.

Skill Set	>> **Advanced Queries**

Business managers are constantly challenged with summarizing the overall performance of their business. For example, a business manager may need to report the total sales of a division, show what products are selling faster than others, or identify which companies have the highest sales growth within an industry. Access queries can accomplish these types of analytical projects. This section will demonstrate advanced query techniques that provide managers with the ability to summarize and analyze business data.

Grouping Data

The first query technique that will be demonstrated in this section is the grouping of data. Grouping data is most valuable when using a table that contains fields with duplicate values. For example, the table shown in Figure 3.32 contains data that might be found in a typical retail company. Notice that several fields contain data that is duplicated over several records such as the Week, Region, and District fields. By looking at the first few records of this table, you can determine if the table contains data only for Week 1 or if other weeks are included. You would have to scroll through every record to identify each unique week, region, or district that is included in the table. However, with the grouping technique, you can create a query to show each unique value that is contained in fields that contain several duplicate values.

Figure 3.32 | **Store Sales by Week Table**

Week	Region	District	Store Number	Store Sales	Store Ending Inventory	Total District Sales	Total Region Sales
1	5	15	5010	$115,385	$1,661,544	$341,355	$1,021,372
1	5	15	5012	$105,770	$1,692,320	$341,355	$1,021,372
1	5	15	5014	$120,200	$1,346,240	$341,355	$1,021,372
1	5	25	5020	$93,500	$1,645,600	$329,050	$1,021,372
1	5	25	5022	$129,750	$1,453,200	$329,050	$1,021,372
1	5	25	5024	$105,800	$1,523,520	$329,050	$1,021,372
1	5	35	5030	$62,500	$1,200,000	$350,967	$1,021,372
1	5	35	5032	$91,350	$1,607,760	$350,967	$1,021,372
1	5	35	5034	$96,155	$1,692,328	$350,967	$1,021,372
1	5	35	5036	$100,962	$1,453,853	$350,967	$1,021,372
1	7	17	7010	$139,425	$1,338,480	$452,900	$887,475

You would have to scroll through every record to see how many unique weeks are included in the table.

Several duplicate values appear in these fields.

As with any query, before demonstrating the grouping technique, you must identify key information for the Store Sales by Week table. This table will be used throughout this section to demonstrate other advanced query techniques. Therefore, the following information will be referenced frequently:

- **Table Purpose:** The purpose of this table is to track the sales revenue achieved by each store in the company for each week of the year. A new week of sales results is added to the table at the close of business every Sunday. In addition to listing each store, the table shows the region and district number.
- **Week Field:** The week number of the current year.
- **Region Field:** The region number of the store. The company manages stores in two regions in the United States. Region number 5 is the East and number 7 is the West.
- **District Field:** The district number of the store. Each region is divided into several districts.
- **Store Number Field:** The number assigned to a store.
- **Store Sales Field:** Sales in U.S. dollars achieved by the store each week. Sales are accumulated at the open of business on Monday through the close of business on Sunday.
- **Store Ending Inventory Field:** The dollar value of the inventory booked to the store at the close of business on Sunday for each week.
- **Total District Sales Field:** The total sales achieved for the district each week. The intended purpose of this field is to calculate the percent of sales each store contributes to the sales of the district.
- **Total Region Sales Field:** The total sales achieved by the region each week. The intended purpose of this field is to calculate the percent of sales each district or store contributes to the overall sales of the region.
- **Index:** The table is indexed by the Week, Region, District, and Store Number fields.
- **Primary Key:** The primary key consists of the Week, Region, District, and Store Number fields. The primary key is related to the Store Sales and Store Ending Inventory fields.

Since key information has been defined for the Store Sales by Week table, we can begin constructing a query. As mentioned, the grouping technique can be used to show what week numbers are contained in the Store Sales by Week table. A select query will be constructed to demonstrate this technique through the following points:

- Create a new select query in **Design View** and add the Store Sales by Week table.
- Add the Week field to the query.
- Click the **Totals** icon in the **Design** tab on the Ribbon. This will add a new row to the design grid of the query called Total.
- Click in the Total row for the Week field and click the drop-down arrow. This will open a list of options. Select **Group By** from the list. Note that when you first add the Total row to the query, this option may already be selected.

Figure 3.33 shows how the **Group By** setting is applied in the Total row of the Week field. Notice that several options appear when the down arrow in the Total row is clicked for a field. These options will be reviewed later in this section.

Figure 3.33 | **Query Setup for Grouping the Data in the Week Field**

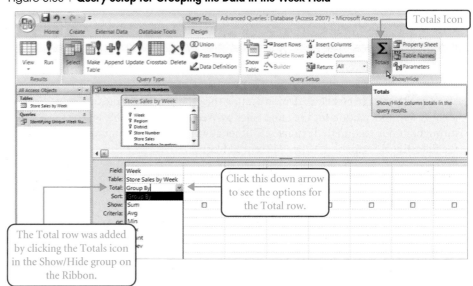

Figure 3.34 shows the record set of the query that was designed in Figure 3.33. Because of the **Group By** setting in the Total row, the record set of this query shows only the unique week numbers that are contained in the Week field of the Store Sales by Week table. Notice that this table contains data for week numbers 1 through 4.

Figure 3.34 | **Record Set Showing the Results of Setting the Group by Option for the Week Field**

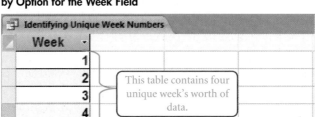

Another valuable use of the **Group By** option when using the Store Sales by Week table is to show the districts assigned to each region. Because both the region number and district numbers are duplicated for each store listed in the table, it is difficult to see which districts are assigned to each region (see Figure 3.32). The **Group By** option can be used to eliminate all duplicate records in the District field. When the Region field is added to the design grid of the query, the record set will show which districts belong to each of the two regions in the table. Figure 3.35 illustrates the setup of this new select query. Notice that the **Group By** option is set in the Total row for each field.

Figure 3.35 | **Setup of Districts by Region Query**

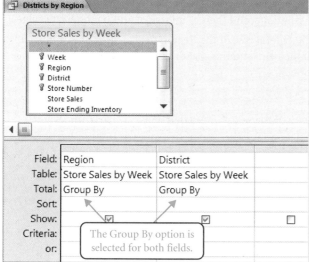

Figure 3.36 shows the record set of the query that was designed in Figure 3.35. Notice that even though the **Group By** option was used for the Region field, duplicate values are still shown in the record set. The reason is that several districts are assigned to each region. However, each value in the District field is unique.

Figure 3.36 | **Results of the Districts by Region Query**

Region	District
5	15
5	25
5	35
7	17
7	27

The Group By option eliminated all duplicate values in the District field.

>> *Quick Reference*

Grouping Data

1. Open a select query in **Design View**.
2. Click the **Design** tab on the Ribbon.
3. Click the **Totals** icon to add the Total row to the design grid of the query.
4. Click in the Total row for a field that contains duplicate values to be grouped.
5. Click the down arrow and select the **Group By** option. Note that this option will already be selected when the Total row is initially added to the query.
6. Run the query.

Mathematical Summaries (Aggregate Functions)

As previously mentioned, when clicking the down arrow in the Totals row of a field, you will see several other options in addition to the **Group By** option, such as **Sum**, **Avg**, **Count**, and so on (see Figure 3.33). These options are known as *aggregate functions* and are used for conducting mathematical summaries of the data contained in a field. For example, the director of Region 5 might want to see the total sales of the region for each of the four weeks in the Store Sales by Week table. The **Sum** option in the **Totals** drop-down list can be used to sum the Store Sales field for this region. This will provide a sales summary for the director so the sales trend of the region for the four weeks can be evaluated. The following points illustrate how to construct this query:

- Create a new select query.
- Add the Store Sales by Week table.
- Add the Week, Region, and Store Sales fields to the query.
- Add the Total row to the query by clicking the **Totals** icon in the **Design** tab on the Ribbon.
- Select the **Group By** option in the Total row for the Week and Region fields.
- Select the **Sum** option in the Total row for the Store Sales field. These values can be summed because the primary key of the table is related to this field. As a result, every record in this field is unique, and there is no risk of adding duplicate values.
- Enter the number 5 in the criteria row of the Region field. This is one of the fields used to index the data in the field, and the goal of this query is to summarize the sales results only for region 5.
- Click the **Run** icon.

Figure 3.37 shows the setup of the select query that will summarize the Sales Results for Region 5. Notice that because the goal of this query is to sum the Store Sales field for an entire region, the District and Store Number fields are not added to the design grid. If the District field were added to the query, the Store Sales field would be summed by district.

Figure 3.37 | **Setup of Region 5 Sales by Week**

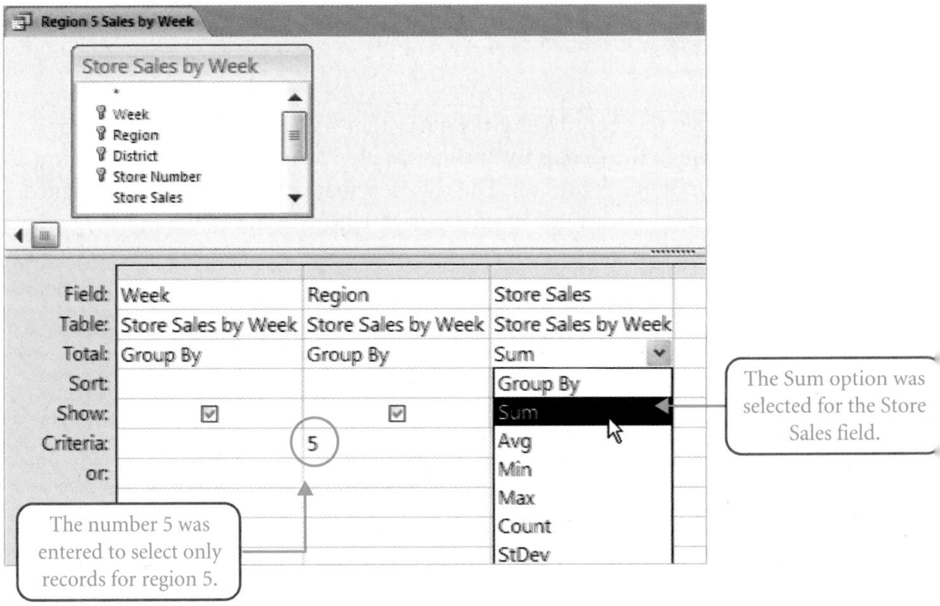

Figure 3.38 shows the record set of the query that was constructed in Figure 3.37. The director of region 5 can use this data to see that sales have been declining from week 1 to week 3 with a slight increase in week 4. Notice that the Store Sales field was automatically renamed to SumOfStore Sales. This indicates that these values in the record set are the result of summing data from the table. Finally, it is important to note that this query was *not* created by summing the values in the Total Region Sales field. This field contains duplicate values and using the **Sum** option would show a much higher sales result than the actual sales of the region.

Figure 3.38 | **Results of Summing the Store Sales Field by Region**

Week	Region	SumOfStore Sales
1	5	$1,021,372.00
2	5	$998,790.61
3	5	$990,017.71
4	5	$993,913.85

The field is automatically renamed because this data is being summed.

COMMON MISTAKES | Summing Fields with Duplicate Values

Before using any aggregate function on a field, check for duplicate values. The first section of this chapter explained the importance of knowing the data contained in a table before executing any queries. This is especially critical when you're applying aggregate functions to a field. Generally, aggregate functions are applied to a field that is related to the primary key of the table. The primary key ensures that all the data entered for a particular field is unique.

Figure 3.39 illustrates another query where aggregate functions are utilized. This example assumes that the director for region 5 needs to calculate the average sales and average ending inventory per week. This information will show if the average inventory value per store is following the same trend as sales. As a result, notice that the **Avg** function is selected in the Total row for the Store Sales and Store Ending Inventory fields. In addition, note that the primary key of the table is related to both of these fields. Therefore, there is no risk of including duplicate values when calculating these averages.

Figure 3.39 | **Region 5 Average Sales and Inventory per Store**

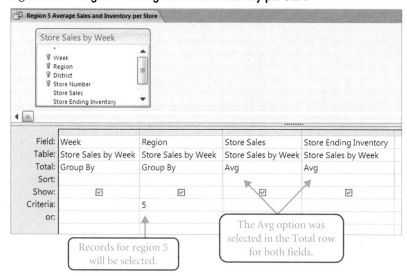

Region 5 Average Sales and Inventory per Store

Store Sales by Week
- Week
- Region
- District
- Store Number
- Store Sales
- Store Ending Inventory

Field:	Week	Region	Store Sales	Store Ending Inventory
Table:	Store Sales by Week	Store Sales by Week	Store Sales by Week	Store Sales by Week
Total:	Group By	Group By	Avg	Avg
Sort:				
Show:	☑	☑	☑	☑
Criteria:		5		
or:				

Records for region 5 will be selected.

The Avg option was selected in the Total row for both fields.

Figure 3.40 shows the record set of the query that was created in Figure 3.39. The director of this region may be particularly interested in the fact that the average ending inventory per store is declining each of the four weeks. This information might suggest that a key product or products that were driving sales for the stores in the region are out of stock. This might explain the decrease in sales from week 1 to week 4.

Figure 3.40 | **Results of Averaging the Store Sales and Store Ending Inventory Fields**

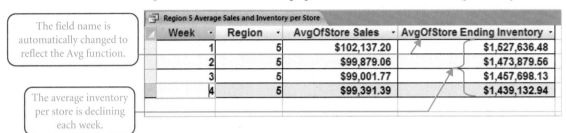

The field name is automatically changed to reflect the Avg function.

The average inventory per store is declining each week.

Notice that the record set of the queries shown in Figure 3.38 and 3.40 are sorted. However, no sort criteria were specified for any of the fields in these queries. The reason is that Access automatically sorts the record set when the **Group By** or any aggregate function is selected for a field. The records are sorted based on the index of the table. Finally, this section illustrated the **Sum** and **Avg** aggregate functions. However, several other aggregate functions are available. Figure 3.41 provides definitions for these aggregate functions.

FIGURE 3.41 | **Aggregate Functions in the Drop-Down List of the Total Row**

Option	Definition
Sum	Sums all numeric values in a field. Values will be summed for each group if a query contains a field(s) with grouped data.
Avg	Calculates the average of all values in a field. The average will be calculated for each group if a query contains a field(s) with grouped data.
Min	Returns the lowest value in a field. The lowest value will be returned for each group if a query contains a field(s) with grouped data. This option can also be used with text data and will return the entry that begins with a letter closest to the letter *A*.
Max	Returns the highest value in a field. The highest value will be returned for each group if a query contains a field(s) with grouped data. This option can also be used with text data and will return the entry that begins with a letter closest to the letter *Z*.
Count	Counts the number of values or entries in a field. The number of entries or values will be counted for each group if a query contains a field(s) with grouped data.

(continued)

Option	Definition
StDev	Calculates the statistical standard deviation of the numeric values contained in a field. The standard deviation will be calculated for each group if a query contains a field(s) with grouped data.
Var	Calculates the statistical variance of the numeric values contained in a field. The variance will be calculated for each group if a query contains a field(s) with grouped data.
First	Returns the first value or entry in a field. This is based on the index of the table. If your query contains a field(s) with grouped data, the first value in the field will be returned with respect to the index of the table.
Last	Identical to the First option except the last value or entry in a field will be returned.

Nested Queries

So far, all the queries demonstrated in this chapter used a table. However, you may recall that the **Show Table** dialog box also contains a tab for queries (see Figure 3.6). This tab is for creating nested queries, which are used for selecting the records or applying calculations to the record set of another query. They are most helpful for isolating data from a table through one query and then performing calculations or functions through another. For example, a nested query will be used to calculate the number of stores per district using the Store Sales by Week table. A nested query is required here because the stores are duplicated for every week of the year. Therefore, one query will be used to create a list of all stores per district. Then a second query will be used to count the stores within each district.

The following steps explain how to set up the first query, or base query, which will be used in this nested query example. The goal of this base query is to create a list of stores for each district in the Store Sales by Week table.

- Open a select query in **Design View**.
- Add the Store Sales by Week table.
- Add the Region, District, and Store Number fields.
- Add the Total row to the design grid by clicking the **Totals** icon in the **Design** tab on the Ribbon. Each field should automatically be set to **Group By** when the Total row is added.
- Save and name the query Store List by District.

> ## >> Quick Reference
>
> ## Using Aggregate Function
>
> 1. Open a select query in **Design View**.
> 2. Click the **Design** tab on the Ribbon.
> 3. Click the **Totals** icon to add the Total row to the design grid of the query.
> 4. Identify any fields that contain duplicate values. Applying an aggregate function to a field with duplicate values could produce erroneous results.
> 5. Choose an aggregate function by clicking the down arrow in the Total row under the appropriate field.
> 6. Run the query.

Figure 3.42 shows the setup of the base query that will be used in this nested query example. Notice that this query is grouping the duplicate values in the Region, District, and Store Number fields.

Figure 3.42 | **Design View of the Store List by District Query**

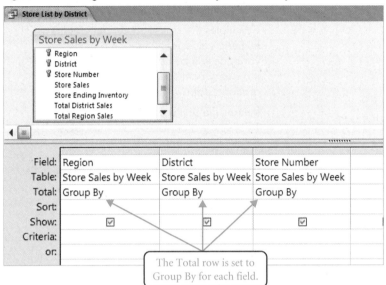

Figure 3.43 shows the results of the Store List by District query, which was created in Figure 3.42. There are 18 records for this query. The reason for this number of records is that there is a total of 18 stores among all districts in both regions. It is important to note that if the **Group By** option was not used for all the fields in this query, the results shown in Figure 3.43 would be repeated for each of the four weeks in the table even though the Week field was not added to the query.

Figure 3.43 | **Results of Grouping the Region, District, and Store Number Fields**

Region	District	Store Number
5	15	5010
5	15	5012
5	15	5014
5	25	5020
5	25	5022
5	25	5024
5	35	5030
5	35	5032
5	35	5034
5	35	5036
7	17	7010
7	17	7012
7	17	7014
7	27	7020
7	27	7022
7	27	7024
7	27	7026
7	27	7028

There are no duplicate values in the Store Number field.

There is a total of 18 records in this record set, which indicates there are 18 stores in the table.

Record: 1 of 18   No Filter   Search

To complete this example of a nested query, you will construct a second query to count the number of stores for each district using the record set of the Store List by District query in Figure 3.43. As a result, you will add this query to the **Design View** of a new select query. The following points explain how to accomplish this:

- Open a new select query in **Design View**.
- Click the **Queries** tab in the **Show Table** dialog box and select the Store List by District query.
- Add the Region, District, and Store Number fields to the query.
- Click the **Totals** icon in the **Design** tab on the Ribbon to add the Total row to the design grid of the query.
- Select the **Group By** option in the Total row for the Region and District fields.
- Select the **Count** option in the Total row for the Store Number field. You can add an aggregate function to this field because every value in the record set of the Store List by District query is unique for this field (see Figure 3.43).
- Save and name the query **Store Count by District**.
- Run the query.

Figure 3.44 shows the setup of the nested query. Notice that the Store List by District query is added to this new select query.

Figure 3.44 | **Setup of a Nested Query**

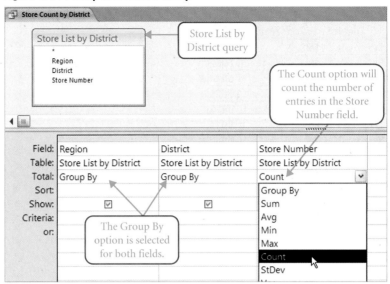

Figure 3.45 shows the record set of the nested query that was created in Figure 3.44. The **Count** function in the Total row of the Store Number field shows the number of stores assigned to each district.

Figure 3.45 | **Results of the Nested Query**

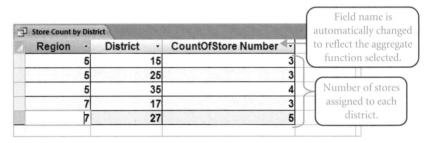

It is important to note that the most critical step in creating the nested query shown in Figure 3.44 is grouping the Store Number field in the base query, which is the Store List by District query in Figure 3.42. The grouping function removed the duplicate values in the Store Number field, which enabled the stores to be accurately counted for each district.

Figure 3.46 illustrates why a nested query is necessary to produce an accurate count of stores for each district. The setup of this query is identical to the Store Count by District query in Figure 3.44. However, the **Count** aggregate function is applied directly to the Store Number field from the Store Sales by Week table. Therefore, the query in this figure is not a nested query because data is being selected directly from a table.

Figure 3.46 | Setup of a Flawed Query to Count the Stores per District

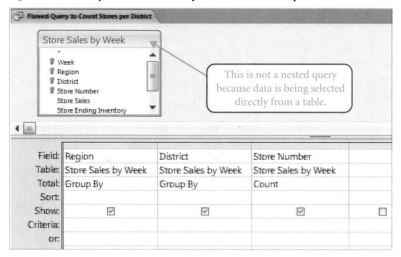

Figure 3.47 shows the record set of the query that was created in Figure 3.46. Notice that the number of stores per district is much higher than the results shown in Figure 3.45. In fact, the number of stores shown for each district is increased by a multiple of 4. For example, the number of stores shown for district 15 is 12 instead of 3. The reason is that there are four weeks' worth of data in the Store Sales by Week table (see Figure 3.34). As a result, the query created in Figure 3.46 counts each store four times.

Figure 3.47 | Results of the Flawed Query to Count the Stores per District

Region	District	CountOfStore Number
5	15	12
5	25	12
5	35	16
7	17	12
7	27	20

This query produced an inaccurate count of stores per district.

Advanced Criteria

The queries demonstrated in this chapter were constructed to select data based on a value that was entered into the criteria row of a particular field. If the field contains the value in the criteria row, the record is selected from a table, or query in the case of a nested query. However, you can use several comparison operators in Access to expand the types of criteria used to select records. For example, a business manager might want to select records from the Store Sales by Week table where the store sales are between 100,000 and 150,000. This would require the use of the BETWEEN and AND comparison operators. Figure 3.48 provides a list and definition of frequently used comparison operators in Access.

>> Quick Reference

Nested Queries
1. Click the **Create** tab on the Ribbon.
2. Click the **Query Design** icon.
3. Click the **Queries** tab on the **Show Table** dialog box.
4. Select a query and click the **Add** button in the **Show Table** dialog box.
5. Click the **Close** button in the **Show Table** dialog box.
6. Research the construction and record set of the query that is selected to identify any fields that contain duplicate values.

FIGURE 3.48 | **Frequently Used Comparison Operators**

Comparison Operator	Definition
>	Greater than. The query will select records greater than the value entered in the criteria row.
<	Less than. The query will select records less than the value entered in the criteria row.
>=	Greater than or equal to. The query will select records greater than or equal to the value entered in the criteria row.
<=	Less than or equal to. The query will select records less than or equal to the value entered in the criteria row.
<>	Not equal to. The query will select records that are not equal to the value entered in the criteria row.
Not	Provides similar results as the <> symbol. This symbol is also used to select records that are Not Null or Not Between.
Between	Enables you to select records that fall between two values entered in the criteria row of query. This operator is used with the And operator. For example, Between 2 And 10 will select records that contain any values between 2 and 10 including the values 2 and 10.
Or	Enables you to select records that contain *any* of the values entered in the criteria row of a query.
And	Is commonly used with the Between operator. In some cases this operator can be used when a cell in a field contains *all* the values entered in the criteria row of a query.

Figure 3.49 shows the setup of a select query that is designed to select records from the Store Sales by Week table where the values in the Store Sales field are between $100,000 and $150,000 for week 1. Notice how the criteria are typed under the Store Sales field. In addition, notice that the query will be sorted based on the values in the Store Sales field in descending order. A business manager could use this type of query to identify stores that are achieving a specific threshold of sales. This data can then be used to determine what types of products the store should be selling.

Figure 3.49 | Setup of High Volume Stores Week 1 Query

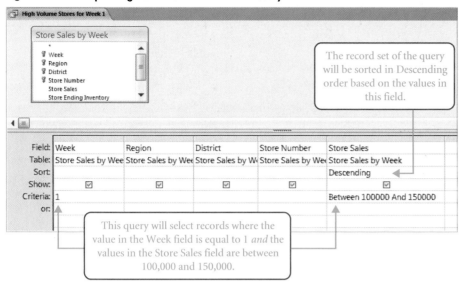

Figure 3.50 shows the record set of the query that was created in Figure 3.49. Notice that every record is from week 1 and all stores show sales between $100,000 and $150,000. In addition, the records are sorted in descending order based on the values in the Store Sales field. This sort order allows an executive to immediately identify which store achieved the highest sales volume in week 1 within a sales threshold of $100,000 to $150,000.

Figure 3.50 | Results of the High Volume Stores Week 1 Query

High Volume Stores for Week 1

Week	Region	District	Store Number	Store Sales
1	7	17	7014	$145,200
1	7	17	7010	$139,425
1	5	25	5022	$129,750
1	5	15	5014	$120,200
1	7	27	7020	$120,150
1	5	15	5010	$115,385
1	7	27	7022	$110,575
1	5	25	5024	$105,800
1	5	15	5012	$105,770
1	5	35	5036	$100,962

The values in this field are all between 100,000 and 150,000.

Figure 3.51 shows the setup of a second select query using a combination of several different criteria options. The purpose of this query is to identify stores that achieved sales between $100,000 and $150,000 and have an ending inventory of less than $1,200,000 for week 4. This type of analysis might provide a business manager with an indication of high-volume stores that are in danger of running low on inventory. Low levels of inventory could significantly jeopardize the sales potential of a store.

Figure 3.51 | **Setup of High Volume Stores and Inventory Week 4 Query**

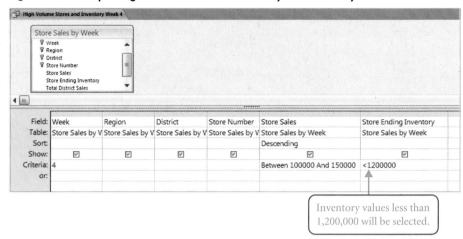

Inventory values less than 1,200,000 will be selected.

COMMON MISTAKES | No Commas When Typing Numbers in the Criteria Row of a Query

Do not use any commas when typing numbers into the criteria row of a query. People often make the mistake of using commas to separate each thousands place for numbers that are typed into the Criteria row for a query. However, this will result in an error message when you try to run the query. Figure 3.51 shows the proper way of typing numbers into the Criteria row of a query. Notice that no commas appear in the numbers typed in the Criteria row for the Store Sales or Store Ending Inventory fields.

Figure 3.52 shows the record set of the query that was constructed in Figure 3.51. Two records in the Store Sales by Week table match the criteria entered into the **Design View** of the query. Notice that the values in the Store Ending Inventory field are *less than* $1,200,000. If the <= operator were used, the query would select values that were less than or equal to $1,200,000.

Figure 3.52 | **Results of the High Volume Stores and Inventory Week 4 Query**

Inventory values are less than 1,200,000.

Week	Region	District	Store Number	Store Sales	Store Ending Inventory
4	7	27	7020	$134,989	$1,187,899
4	7	17	7010	$101,591	$1,056,543

In some cases you may need to select records from a table or query based on the values in a particular field but not want to show that field in the record set of the query. For example, the manager of region 7 may want to analyze the sales for each store in his region. However, he may not need to see the data for the Region field because this will simply show the number 7 repeated for each row. In this situation the number 7 can be typed into the Criteria row for the Region field, and one of two options can be used to remove the field from the record set of the query. The first option is to click the box with the check mark in the Show row of the design grid. You click the box once to remove check mark. The second is to select the Where option from the drop-down list in the Total row. Selecting the Where option will automatically remove the check mark in the Show row. This is illustrated in Figure 3.53.

Figure 3.53 | Setup of the Region 7 Store Sales Query

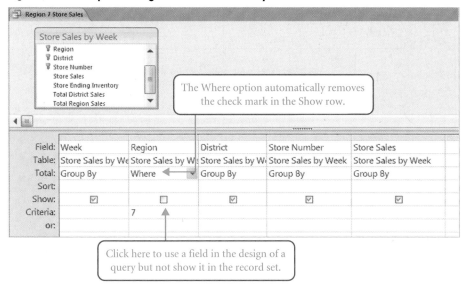

The Where option automatically removes the check mark in the Show row.

Click here to use a field in the design of a query but not show it in the record set.

Figure 3.54 shows the record set of the query that was created in Figure 3.53. The stores and districts are from region 7; however, the Region field is not shown in the record set of the query.

Figuer 3.54 | Results of the Region 7 Store Sales Query

Week	District	Store Number	Store Sales
1	17	7014	$145,200
1	27	7020	$120,150
1	27	7022	$110,575
1	27	7024	$48,075
1	27	7026	$62,500
1	27	7028	$93,275
2	17	7010	$122,694
2	17	7012	$166,592
2	17	7014	$171,336
2	27	7020	$126,158
2	27	7022	$108,364
2	27	7024	$58,652
2	27	7026	$69,375
2	27	7028	$90,477
3	17	7010	$110,425

All stores are from region 7, but the Region field does not appear in the record set.

Crosstab Queries

All the queries demonstrated to this point in the chapter have been select queries. However, Access contains several different types of queries that perform different actions depending on your needs. This section will demonstrate the crosstab query. The crosstab query is a valuable tool for evaluating the trends of a business over a period of time by placing data into a two-dimensional grid. For example, Figure 3.55 shows a sketch illustrating how you might use the crosstab query to analyze the total sales by week for each region in the Store Sales by Week table.

Figure 3.55 | **Sketch of Two-Dimensional Grid for Analyzing Region Sales by Week**

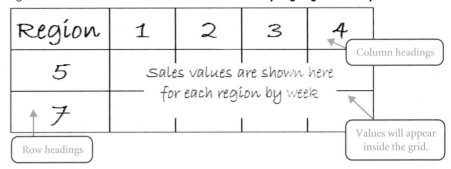

Planning the desired output of a crosstab query is highly recommended. When you have a clear idea of how the final output of the query should appear, defining each of the required settings is fairly simple. The following points explain how to construct a crosstab query to duplicate the sketch in Figure 3.55:

- Open a select query in **Design View**.
- Add the Store Sales by Week table.
- Click the **Crosstab** icon in the **Design** tab on the Ribbon. This will convert the select query to a crosstab query.
- Add the Week, Region, and Store Sales fields to the query.
- In the Total row, set the Week and Region field to **Group By** and set the Store Sales field to **Sum**.
- Click in the **Crosstab** row for the Week field. Then click the down arrow and select the **Column Heading** option. This will show the week numbers across the top of the grid, as illustrated in Figure 3.55.
- Click in the **Crosstab** row for the Region field. Then click the down arrow and select the **Row Heading** option. This will show the region numbers along the left side of the grid.
- Click in the Crosstab row for the Store Sales field. Then click the down arrow and select the **Value** option. This will use the values in the Store Sales field to fill in the grid for each week and region.
- Save and name the query Sales Grid by Week and Region.
- Run the query. Note that you may have to increase the column widths when viewing the results of the query to remove any ##### signs.

Figure 3.56 illustrates the setup of this crosstab query. After you convert a select query to a crosstab query, the Total row is automatically added to the design grid. The reason is that all fields used in a crosstab query must be grouped or summarized through an aggregate function. In addition, you will also see a Crosstab row. This row contains options for using the data in a field as a **Row Heading, Column Heading,** or **Value.**

Figure 3.56 | **Constructing a Crosstab Query**

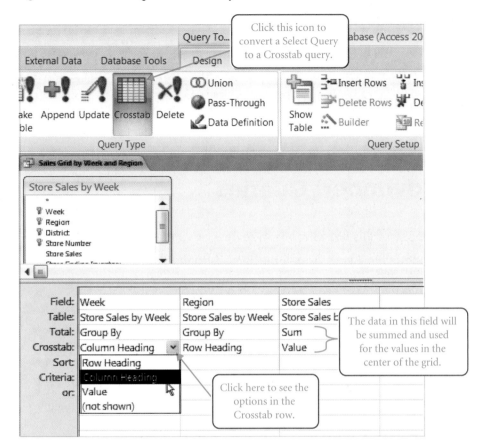

COMMON MISTAKES | Aggregate Functions in Crosstab Queries

You must use an aggregate function such as **Sum**, **Avg**, or **Count** for a field where the Crosstab row is set to **Value**. Figure 3.57 shows the error message that will appear if the Crosstab row for a field is set to **Value** and there is no aggregate function set in the Total row.

Figure 3.57 | **Error Message When Aggregate Function Is Not Used**

Figure 3.58 shows the record set of the crosstab query that was created in Figure 3.56. The business manager reading the results of this query can easily see that the overall sales trend for region 5 is declining from weeks 1 through 3 with a slight increase in week 4. Conversely, the overall sales trend for region 7 is increasing every week. Notice that the appearance of the query is identical to the sketch illustrated in Figure 3.55.

>> **Quick Reference**

Crosstab Queries

1. Open a select query in **Design View**.

2. Add any required tables or queries.

3. Convert to a crosstab query by clicking the **Crosstab** icon in the **Design** tab on the Ribbon.

4. Add any required fields.

5. Set the Total row to **Group By** for fields that will be used for either **Row Headings** or **Column Headings**.

6. Select an aggregate function in the Total row for fields where the Crosstab row is set to **Value**.

7. Identify a field as a **Row Heading**, **Column Heading**, or **Value** in the Crosstab row.

8. Run the query.

Figure 3.58 | **Results of the Sales Grid by Week and Region Crosstab Query**

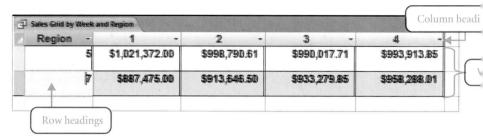

Region	1	2	3	4
5	$1,021,372.00	$998,790.61	$990,017.71	$993,913.85
7	$887,475.00	$913,646.50	$933,279.85	$958,288.01

Row headings

Column headi...

≫ Advanced Queries

The purpose of this workshop is to review advanced techniques used to create queries in Access. I will be demonstrating the following tasks in the following four videos: **Grouping Data and Mathematical Summaries**, **Nested Queries**, **Advanced Criteria**, and **Crosstab Queries**. Open the Access database named ib_a03_storesalesdata. Information regarding the purpose of the table contained in the database as well as the field definitions is listed at the beginning of this section of the chapter. Try to complete each of the following tasks and then watch the videos.

1. **Grouping Data and Mathematical Summaries (Video: Grouping Data and Mathematical Summaries)**

   a. Create a new select query by clicking the **Query Design** icon in the **Create** tab on the Ribbon and add the Store Sales and Inventory table.

   b. Add the Week and Store Sales fields to the query. Adjust the width of the columns in the Design Grid so the field names are visible.

   c. Add the Total row by clicking the **Totals** icon in the **Design** tab on the Ribbon.

   d. Check that the Total row for the Week field is set to **Group By**. Set the Total row for the Store Sales field to Sum.

   e. Run the query by clicking the red exclamation point icon.

   f. Bold the values and increase the font size of the values in the record set to 12 points. Then adjust the columns in the record set so all values and field names are visible.

   g. Save the query and type the name `Total Company Sales by Week` in the **Save As** dialog box. Then close the query.

   h. Create a second select query by clicking the **Query Design** icon in the **Create** tab on the Ribbon and add the Store Sales and Inventory table.

   i. Add the Week, Store Number, Store Sales, and Store Ending Inventory fields to the query. Adjust the column widths in the design grid so the field names are visible.

   j. Add the Total row by clicking the **Totals** icon in the **Design** tab on the Ribbon.

   k. Make the following settings in the Total row for each field:
      i. Week: Count

ii. Store Number: Group By

iii. Store Sales: Sum

iv. Store Ending Inventory: Avg

l. Format the Store Sales and Store Ending Inventory fields to Currency, 0 Decimal Places. You will need to open the **Property Sheet** window by clicking the **Property Sheet** icon in the **Design** tab on the Ribbon.

m. Run the query.

n. Bold the values and increase the font size of the values in the record set to 12 points. Then adjust the columns in the record set so all values and field names are visible.

o. Save the query and type the name `Total Sales and Avg Inventory by Store` in the **Save As** dialog box. Then close the query.

2. **Nested Queries (Video: Nested Queries)**

a. Create a new select query by clicking the **Query Design** icon in the **Create** tab on the Ribbon and add the Store Sales and Inventory table.

b. Add the Week, Region, and Total Region fields to the query. Adjust the width of the columns in the design grid so the field names are visible.

c. Add the Total row by clicking the **Totals** icon.

d. Run the query. Then save the query and type the name `Region Sales by Week` in the **Save As** dialog box.

e. Close the query.

f. Create a new select query by clicking the **Query Design** icon in the **Create** tab on the Ribbon.

g. Click the **Queries** tab in the **Show Table** dialog box and add the Region Sales by Week query, which was saved in step d.

h. Add the Week and Total Region Sales fields to the query.

i. Add the Total row to the design grid of the query.

j. Set the Total row for the Total Region Sales field to **Sum**. The Total row for the Week field should be set to **Group By**.

k. Run the query.

l. Bold the values and increase the font size of the values in the record set to 12 points. Then adjust the columns in the record set so all values and field names are visible.

m. Save the query and type the name `Total Company Sales by Week Method 2` in the **Save As** dialog box.

n. Close the query.

3. **Advanced Criteria (Video: Advanced Criteria)**

a. Create a new select query by clicking the **Query Design** icon in the **Create** tab on the Ribbon and add the Store Sales and Inventory table.

b. Add the Week, Region, District, Store Number, Store Sales, and Store Ending Inventory fields to the query. Adjust the width of the columns in the design grid so the field names are visible.

c. Enter the number **5** to the Criteria row of the Region field.

d. Enter **<>35** in the Criteria row of the District field.

e. Enter **Not Between 90000 And 110000** in the Criteria row of the Store Sales field.

f. Run the query.

g. Bold the values and increase the font size of the values in the record set to 12 points. Then adjust the columns in the record set so all values and field names are visible.

h. Convert the query to **Design View** by clicking the **View** icon in the **Home** tab on the Ribbon.

i. Delete the criteria in the Store Sales field and replace it with the following: `<=90000 Or >= 110000`.

j. Convert the query to **Datasheet View** by clicking the **View** icon in the **Home** tab on the Ribbon.

k. Save the query and type the name `Region 5 High and Low Volume Stores` in the **Save As** dialog box. Then close the query.

4. Crosstab Queries (Video: Crosstab Queries)

a. Create a new select query by clicking the **Query Design** icon in the **Create** tab on the Ribbon and add the Store Sales and Inventory table.

b. Convert the select query to a crosstab query by clicking the **Crosstab** icon in the **Design** tab on the Ribbon.

c. Add the Week, Region, and Store Sales fields to the query. Adjust the width of the columns in the design grid so the field names are visible.

d. Set the Crosstab row for the Week field to **Column Heading**.

e. Set the Crosstab row for the Region field to **Row Heading**.

f. Set the Crosstab row for the Store Sales field to **Value**.

g. Set the Total row of the Store Sales field to **Sum**.

h. Run the query.

i. Bold the values and increase the font size of the values in the record set to 12 points. Then adjust the columns in the record set so all values and field names are visible.

j. Save the query and type `Region Sales by Week Grid` in the **Save As** dialog box.

k. Close the query and then close the database.

>> Analyzing Merchandise Sales Trends

Business managers are constantly analyzing both the current and past performance of their business to identify key areas of improvement and growth. Through the use of a database, business managers can identify key trends by evaluating performance statistics over long periods of time. For example, evaluating the historical sales of certain product categories might identify long-term trends or cycles indicating when people buy more or less of certain products. This information can help business managers decide how many products to produce, how many people to hire, or how many stores to open. The type of data you analyze for a business will change depending on your level of responsibility. For example, the president of a company will likely analyze less detail regarding the performance of a company compared to a department manager. The benefit of using a tool like Access is that it can summarize data and provide various levels of detail depending on the needs of the reader.

Exercise

The purpose of this exercise is to use the advanced query skills introduced in this section to evaluate the performance of a business using various levels of detail. The tasks in this exercise will require the use of the database named ib_a03_apparelsaleshistory. Detailed information regarding the table contained in this database can be found in the Excel file named ib_a03_apparelsaleshistorydatadictionary. Open the Access database and the Excel file before completing the following tasks.

1. Review the file named ib_a03_apparelsaleshistorydatadictionary to identify key facts such as the primary key, index, field definitions, and so on.

2. Create a select query and add the Annual Unit Sales by Item table. This query will be used to provide details for a specific item sold by the company. This information could be used by a planning manager who decides how many units of a certain item to produce.

3. Add the Year, Category Number, Category Description, Item Number, Color, and Unit Sales fields to the query.

4. Enter criteria into the design grid of the query so records are selected from the table where the Category Number is equal to 80 and the Item Number is equal to 678510.

5. Run the query. Explain the unit sales trend for this item.

6. Save the query and name it **Pink Shorts Sales Trend**. Then close the query.

7. Create a new select query and add the Annual Unit Sales by Item table. This query will be designed for a merchandise director who will be evaluating the number of top-selling items for the company over the past six years.

8. Add the Year, Item Number, and Unit Sales fields to the query.

9. Set the Total row for the Item Number field to **Count**. The Total row for the Year field should remain set to **Group By**.

10. The goal of this query is to show how many items the company sold each year where sales were greater than or equal to 4000. Therefore, enter this criterion for the Unit Sales field. Then set the Total row of the Unit Sales field to **Where**. This will select any record where 4000 units or more were sold for an item, but the Unit Sales field will not be seen in the record set.

11. Run the query. In which year did the company have the highest number of items where at least 4000 units or more were sold? Which year or years have the least number of items where at least 4000 units were sold?

12. Save the query and name it Number of Top Selling Items by Year. Then close the query.

13. Create a new select query and add the Annual Unit Sales by Item table. This query will be designed for a merchandising director. The purpose of this query is to show how many items were produced for each category over the past six years.

14. Add the Category Number, Category Description, and Item Number fields to the query.

15. Set the Total row for each field to **Group By**. This will show each unique item number that has been sold for each category.

16. Run the query. Each number in the Item Number field should be unique (i.e., no duplicate values).

17. Save and name the query **Unique Item List by Category**. Then close the query.

18. Create a new select query and add the Unique Item List by Category query.

19. Add the Category Number, Category Description, and Item Number fields to the query.

20. Set the Total row for the Item Number field to **Count**. The Total row for the Category Number and Category Description fields should remain set to **Group By**.

21. Run the query. How many unique items were produced for the Twill Pants category? How many unique items were produced for the Twill Shorts category?

22. Save the query and name it **Item Count by Category**. Then close the query.

23. Create a new select query and add the Annual Unit Sales by Item table. This query will be designed for a merchandising vice president who needs to evaluate the overall sales trend of the company by category. This will be accomplished through the use of a crosstab query. The goal is to show the years running across the top of the grid as column headings and the category descriptions along the side of the grid as row headings. The unit sales will be summed for each year by category.

24. Convert the select query to a crosstab query.

25. Add the Year, Category Description, and Unit Sales fields to the query.

26. Set the Total row for the Unit Sales field to **Sum**.

27. Set the Crosstab row for the Year field to **Column Heading**.

28. Set the Crosstab row for the Category Description field to **Row Heading**.

29. Set the Crosstab row for the Unit Sales field to **Value**.

30. Run the query. Which category shows a sales increase each year? Which category showed the strongest sales growth from the year 2003 to 2005? Which category had the largest decrease in unit sales from 2000 to 2006?

31. Save the query and name it **6 Year Sales Trend by Category**.

32. Close the query and then close the database and the Excel workbook.

>> What's Wrong with This Database?

Problem

You are the director of a marketing division in a large corporation. You are about to attend a weekly meeting to present the sales results of a strategy that was executed in the New York region to the CEO of the company. The goal of the strategy was to boost the sales of category 40 to $500,000 last week. A new analyst in the division creates an Access query to retrieve sales data for category 40 from the company database. She sends the results to you in the following e-mail.

Sorry to report bad news on my first assignment. I ran the numbers, and we fell significantly short of our sales target for category 40. The system shows total sales last week of $116,755. I was very surprised to see this considering the discounts and all the radio advertisements we ran in the NY area. I used to work for a company that had a marketing campaign similar to this one. We had plenty of customers, but not enough inventory to satisfy the demand we generated. If you want, I can do some digging to check the inventory levels in the NY stores last week.

Exercise

The database the analyst used is named ib_a03_productsales. The query the analyst created is named Category 40 Sales LW. In addition, detailed information for the table used in this query can be found in the Excel file named ib_a03_productsalesdatadictionary. Would you be confident presenting the results of the query in this database at the meeting? Consider the following:

1. Evaluate the design of the Category 40 Sales LW query. Explain how the total sales for category 40 are being calculated?
2. Based on the design of the Category 40 Sales LW query, are the total sales accurately calculated for category 40?
3. What other information will you need to evaluate in assessing the integrity of the results produced by this query?

What's wrong with this database? Write a short answer for each of the points here. Then explain why you would or would not be comfortable using the results in this database in your weekly meeting with the CEO.

To get the data we needed for the project, we asked each regional director to provide the total sales dollars and marketing spend dollars for their region in an Excel spreadsheet. After we received an Excel file for each region, we were able to use Access to combine the data and analyze the sales and marketing trends for the entire company. This information enabled us to produce powerful recommendations that changed the way the company developed its future marketing strategies. In addition, as a result of our project, the executive officers of the company started thinking about changing the way they managed key performance data for the business to increase accessibility and accuracy.

Assignment

1. The Excel files that were received from each regional director are named as follows: ib_a03_salesmarketingforregion1, ib_a03_salesmarketingforregion2, and ib_a03_salesmarketingforregion3. Create a new table in an Access database by importing the spreadsheets into one table. Name the table **Company Sales and Marketing Data**.

2. Set a primary key for the Company Sales and Marketing Data table. Explain why you chose a certain field or fields to define the primary key.

3. Create a query that shows the total sales of the company for each year and the total dollars spent on marketing activities. Briefly describe the sales and marketing dollar trends for the years 2004 to 2006. Does the money spent on marketing activities appear to be providing a significant sales benefit for the company? Export the results of this query to an Excel spreadsheet.

4. Create a query that shows the sales trend for each region for all three years. Explain the sales trend for each region.

5. Create three queries that show the sales and dollars spent on marketing activities for each region for three years. Does any region appear to be getting a sales benefit from the money spent on marketing activities? Why? Is it safe to assume that sales will increase if the money spent on marketing activities increases? Why?

6. Evaluate the sales and marketing dollars for region 1 in the third quarter for each of the three years. Does this region appear to be executing an effective marketing strategy? Why?

Questions for Discussion

1. What are the benefits of analyzing the past performance of a business?

2. The anecdote mentions that at the completion of the consulting project the firm's executives started thinking about improving the way data was managed in the company. What improvements do you think they should make and why? Hint: What disadvantages does a company face by maintaining data in three different locations?

The following questions are related to the concepts addressed in this chapter. There are three types of questions: Short Answer, True or False, and Fill in the Blank. If your answer to a True or False question is False, write a short explanation as to why you think the statement is not true.

1. What information will you need if you plan to use a table in an Access database that you did not create?

2. True or False: If you mistakenly apply an aggregate function to a field that contains duplicate values, Access will give you a warning stating that your query may produce erroneous results.

3. Before applying an aggregate function to a field, you must know the _____ of the table.

4. True or False: When creating a new select query, you have only the option of adding tables.

5. Explain where and how you can enter a short description explaining the purpose of a query.

6. If you wanted a query to select all records for the years 2005 and 2006 from a table, both years separated by the word _____ would be typed into the _____ row of the Year field.

7. Look at the design grid from the following select query and explain how the query will select records from the table.

Field:	Year	Category Number	Unit Sales
Table:	Annual Unit Sales by Item	Annual Unit Sales by Item	Annual Unit Sales by Item
Sort:			
Show:	☑	☑	☑
Criteria:	2004	50	
or:	2005		
	2006		

8. True or False: When entering criteria for a field that contains text data, you should enclose the entry or entries within quotation marks. However, if you forget, Access will add quotation marks for you automatically.

9. When you're setting the sort row to **Ascending** or **Descending** for multiple fields, how does Access determine which field to use first, then second, then third, and so on, when sorting the record set?

10. Explain how you can apply a number format such as **Currency** to a field used in a select query.

11. The _____ option in the _____ row is used to show only unique values that are contained in a field in the record set of a select query.

12. True or False: The Total row will always appear in the design grid of a select query.

13. Before applying an aggregate function to a field, you should check to see if the field contains _____ _____.

14. What is the purpose of the **Count** aggregate function?

15. True of False: The following two criteria will provide identical results: Between 1 And 3 and >1 And <3.

16. What symbol is used when specifying not equal to in the criteria row of query?

17. True or False: The following two criteria will provide identical results: Not Between 3 And 6 and <3 And >6.

18. When creating a Crosstab query, if the Crosstab row is set to _____ the values in a field will be displayed across the top of the record set and if the Crosstab row is set to _____ the values in a field be displayed on the left side of the record set.

19. If the Crosstab row is set to **Value** for a particular field, then the Total row for that field cannot be set to _____.

20. True or False: When creating a crosstab query, you must add the Total row by clicking the **Totals** icon.

>> Skills Exam

The following exam is designed to test your ability to recognize and execute the Access skills presented in this chapter. Read each question carefully and answer the questions in the order they are listed. You should be able to complete this exam in 60 minutes or less.

1. Open the Access database named ib_a03_skillsexam. Then open the Excel file named ib_a03_skillsexamdatadictionary. Both files will be used in this exam.

2. What is the primary key of the table FP/MD Annual Cat Sales? What field is the primary key related to?

3. Can you add the values in the Cat Year field to calculate the total sales of the company for each year? Why?

4. Create a select query using the FP/MD Annual Cat Sales table. Complete the following for this query:

   a. Add the Year, Cat, Description, FP/MD, and Sales fields to the design grid.

   b. Enter criteria into the design grid so the query selects records for the years 2002, 2004, and 2006 for category 20. Only category 20 should appear in the record set of this query.

   c. Sort the record set of the query based on the values in the FP/MD field in ascending order and the Sales field in descending order.

   d. Format the values in the Sales field to Currency with 0 decimal places.

   e. Run the query. Then save the query and name it **Cat 20 Sales**.

   f. Close the query.

5. Type the following description into the **Properties** dialog box for the Cat 20 Sales query: **Shows the full price and markdown sales for category 20 for the years 2002, 2004, and 2006**.

6. Export the results of the Cat 20 Sales query to an Excel spreadsheet. Name the Excel file ib_a03_category203yearsalestrend. Export the data so that any format settings made in the query are included in the Excel spreadsheet.

7. Create a select query that shows what years are included in the FP/MD Annual Cat Sales table. Complete the following for this query:

   a. Add the Year field.

   b. Set the Total row for the Year field to **Group By**.

   c. Run the query. Then save the query and name it **Years in Cat Sales Table**.

   d. Close the query.

8. Create a select query that shows the total full price and markdown sales by category for all years included in the FP/MD Annual Cat Sales table. Complete the following for this query:

   a. Add the Cat, Description, FP/MD, and Sales fields to the query.

   b. Set the Total row for the Sales field to **Sum**. All other fields should be set to **Group By**.

   c. Format the values in the Sales field to **Currency** with 0 decimal places.

   d. Sort the record set of the query based on the values in the FP/MD field in ascending order and the Sales field in descending order.

   e. Run the query. Then save the query and name it **Total 5 Year Sales by Cat**.

   f. Close the query.

9. Create nested select queries that will count the total number of categories sold by the company each year. Complete the following for these queries:

a. Create a new select query and add the FP/MD Annual Cat Sales table.

b. Add the Year and Cat fields to the query and set the Total row to **Group By** for both fields.

c. Run the query. Then save the query and name it **Years and Unique Cat Numbers**.

d. Close the query.

e. Create a new select query. Add the Years and Unique Cat Numbers query.

f. Add the Year and Cat fields to the query.

g. Set the Total row for the Cat field to **Count**.

h. Run the query. Then save the query and name it **Number of Categories per Year**.

i. Close the query.

10. Create a new select query using the FP/MD Annual Cat Sales table and add the Year, Cat, Description, FP/MD, and Sales fields to the query. This query should select records based on the following criteria:

a. Years 2002 or 2006.

b. Values in the Sales field *not* between 20000000 and 50000000.

c. Category numbers *not* equal to 30.

d. Values in the FP/MD field equal to 2.

e. Run the query. Then save the query and name it **High and Low MD Sales for 2002 and 2006**.

f. Close the query.

11. Create a crosstab query using the FP/MD Annual Cat Sales table. Complete the following for this query:

a. Add the Year, FP/MD, and Sales fields to the query.

b. The values in the Year field should be the column headings.

c. The values in the FP/MD field should be the row headings.

d. The values in the Sales field should be summed.

e. The Sales field will be used for the values in the record set of the crosstab query.

f. Format the values in the Sales field to Currency with 0 decimal places.

g. Run the query. Then save the query and name it **Company Sales by Year FP and MD**.

h. Expand the width of the columns in the record set so all values are visible.

i. Close the query.

12. Close the database and the Excel file.

The following questions are designed to test your ability to apply the Access skills you have learned to complete a business objective. Use your knowledge of Access as well as your creativity to answer these questions. For most questions, there are several possible ways to complete the objective.

1. Open the database named ib_a03_challengea. Create a select query using the Store Sales by Week table that will check the values in the Total District Sales field by summing the Store Sales field for each *district*. Your query should show data for each week included in the table. For each record, the value in the Store Sales field should be equal to the value in the Total District Sales field.

2. Using the database named ib_a03_challengea, create a query using the Store Sales by Week table that will show both the average inventory per store for region 5 and the total inventory for region 5 for each of the four weeks in the Store Sales by Week Table.

3. Open the database named ib_a03_challengeb. Using the Annual Unit Sales by Item table, calculate the average number of items sold for each category where unit sales are greater than 0 and show on average how many units were sold for each item. Your final result must show one record for each category that takes into account all six years' worth of data. For example, if you were presenting this data, you want to be able to say that over the past six years, the company sold an average of X number of items for each category, and on average the number of units sold for each item is Y. Hint: You will need to use nested queries to get this result.

4. Using the database named ib_a03_challengeb, create a crosstab query that will show the total unit sales by category for each year using the Category Total Unit Sales field. The values in the Year field should be used as column headings and the values in the Category Number field should be used as row headings.

Chapter 4

Applying Calculations to Data

Chapter Goals

As mentioned in the Introduction, Access is a tool business managers use to analyze and evaluate data relating to their business. Formulas and functions play a critical role in this analytical process. If constructed properly, Access formulas and functions can be as dynamic as Excel formulas and functions. That is to say, as data changes in a table used in a query, the mathematical outputs of the formulas and functions will automatically change. The purpose of this chapter is to demonstrate the fundamental techniques for creating formulas and functions in Select Queries. In addition, this chapter will review typical formulas and functions used in business. It is important to note that formulas and functions are created and executed through Access queries. Therefore, you need a complete understanding of the material covered in Chapter 3 before beginning this chapter.

>> **Access** Skill Sets

Access in Practice | Anecdote

My Role as an Information Systems Advisor

Have you ever gone to a store and noticed that the sales staff was very persistent in trying to sell you a particular product? This might have been because the company was running a sales contest. When I worked for several retail corporations, sales contests were used to motivate the sales staff to sell certain products that were very profitable or had high inventory levels. The prizes awarded to the winning team ranged from a free dinner to a trip to Hawaii. As a result, people were usually very motivated to win the contest. However, creating a system to judge the contest fairly was not easy. In fact, this was one of my first assignments when I worked in the information systems division of a major retail corporation. I was asked to analyze the sales results by store over a set period of time using the company's database system. I initially believed that this would be an easy project. I figured I would use Access to select records from the Item Sales by Store by Week table, sum the sales for the contest period and then sort the records in descending order. The store that sold the highest number of units would win the contest. However, determining the winner fairly proved much more difficult. For example, some of the stores had certain advantages because of their location and customer demographics such as income and population density. Therefore, I needed to come up with a way of judging the performance of almost 1000 stores that took these advantages into consideration when awarding a winner.

» Continued on page 831

Formulas

Skill Set

This section will cover the fundamental techniques of creating formulas in Access. The purpose of a formula is to calculate a mathematical result using numeric data that is contained in a field within a table or query. For example, the formula `Gross Sales - Returns` is used to calculate `Net Sales`. In Access, this formula would be entered into the design grid of a query using the Gross Sales and Returns fields, which might be contained in an existing table or query. Other formulas that are commonly used by business managers are as follows:

- **Net Sales** = Gross Sales - Returns
- **Average Price** = Sales Dollars ÷ Sales Units
- **Gross Profit** = Net Sales − Cost of Goods Sold
- **Inventory Turn** = Net Sales ÷ Average Inventory Value
- **Sales Dollars** = Price × Sales Units

Custom Fields

Formulas and functions are created in Access by adding a new field to the design grid of a query. These are ***custom fields*** that you create in the query and are *not* included in a table. A custom field can show a specific data value that you type into the first row of the query design grid such as a constant (number), a word, a date, or a letter. These fields can also show the result of a formula or function. When a custom field contains the results of a formula or function it is referred to as a ***calculated field***. This segment will explain how to create a custom field for the purposes of displaying a number in the record set of a query. The next segment will explain how to create a calculated field which contains the result of a formula.

Figure 4.1 shows a table that might be found in a data mart maintained by an electronics retail company. Notice that fields such as Unit Sales and Sales Dollars end with the letters LW, which stands for Last Week. This is because the table will always show the sales and inventory results for each item as of last week. The design of this table is common in retail firms because it provides business managers with easy access to the sales results of the most current week of the year. This table will be used through out this section to construct various Select Queries for the purpose of demonstrating custom fields and formulas.

Figure 4.1 | **Electronics Merchandise Sales Data Table**

Electronics Merchandise Sales Data

Cat Number	Cat Description	Item Number	Item Description	Price	Status	Unit Sales LW	Sales Dollars LW	Current Inventory Units	Category Sales Dollars LW
10	Digital Music Players	10243	10 GB Digital Player	$159.99	0	225	$11,999	850	$171,991
10	Digital Music Players	10344	40 GB Digital Player	$199.99	1	775	$154,992	6,000	$171,991
10	Digital Music Players	10655	80 GB Digital Player	$249.99	1	20	$5,000	195	$171,991
20	Video Games	22054	Game 4	$69.99	1	150	$10,499	3,500	$70,737
20	Video Games	22333	Game 2	$49.99	0	15	$750	150	$70,737
20	Video Games	22765	Game 3	$39.99	0	550	$21,995	2,100	$70,737
20	Video Games	22888	Game 5	$59.99	1	245	$14,698	2,500	$70,737
20	Video Games	22980	Game 1	$59.99	1	380	$22,796	3,000	$70,737
30	Video Game System	33245	System 2	$229.99	1	85	$19,549	550	$54,048
30	Video Game System	33989	System 1	$299.99	1	450	$34,499	3,200	$54,048
40	Home Video	44332	Multi Disc DVD	$259.90	1	54	$14,035	500	$87,479
40	Home Video	44339	DVD/VCR	$129.99	1	525	$68,245	2,250	$87,479
40	Home Video	44556	DVD Player	$159.99	1	10	$1,600	105	$87,479
40	Home Video	44977	VCR	$89.99	0	40	$3,600	1,350	$87,479

As mentioned in Chapter 3, before creating a query it is important to review key information regarding the table that you will use. Key points and definitions for the Electronics Merchandise Sales Data table shown in Figure 4.1 include:

- **Table Purpose**: To track the weekly sales results of merchandise sold by the company. The table contains sales data in both units and dollars for every item sold.
- ***Primary Key***: The Item Number field is the primary key. An item can only appear once in this table.
- ***Index***: The table is indexed by the Cat Number and Item Number fields

- **Cat Number Field**: The category number assigned to the item.
- **Cat Description Field**: Description pertaining to the Cat Number.
- **Item Number Field:** The number used to identify an item.
- **Item Description Field**: The description of the item.
- **Price Field**: The original retail price of the item.
- **Status Field**: Shows if an item is active or not active (Active = 1, Not Active = 0). A company will no longer sell an item with a status of 0 once the inventory is sold.
- **Unit Sales LW Field**: The number of units sold for an item at the close of business last week. Data included in this field include sales that occurred when stores opened for business Monday morning to the close of business Sunday night.
- **Sales Dollars LW Field**: The total dollar value of sales generated for the item at the close of business last week.
- **Current Inventory Units Field**: The total number of inventory units as of the close business last week.
- **Category Sales Dollars LW**: The total sales dollars generated for all items within the category. The purpose of this field is to calculate the percent of sales each item represents to the total category. This field contains duplicate values and should not be summed to calculate total company sales.

Now that we have an understanding of the purpose and field definitions of the Electronics Merchandise Sales Data table in Figure 4.1, we can begin constructing queries. The purpose of the first query is to show a target weeks of supply value in the record set of a Select Query. This will require the use of a custom field which will be used to show the number 8 for every record in the query record set. A business manager can use this field in a formula to determine the difference between the actual weeks of supply for an item and the target weeks of supply. This query is initially created as follows:

- Click the **Query Design** icon in the **Create** tab of the Ribbon. Then, add the Electronics Merchandise Sales Data table and close the **Show Table** dialog box.
- Add the Item Number, Item Description, Unit Sales LW, and Current Inventory Units fields to the design grid of the query.
- Save the query and name it Item Inventory Analysis.

Figure 4.2 shows the initial construction of the Item Inventory Analysis query. A custom field will be added to this query so business mangers can see the target weeks of supply for each item, which for this example will be the number 8.

Figure 4.2 | **Item Inventory Analysis Query**

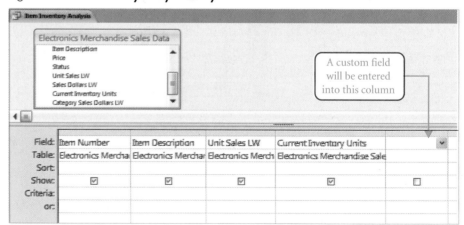

COMMON MISTAKES | Creating Custom Fields

Do not forget to type a colon after the field name of a custom field. The following error will appear if you try to add a custom field without typing a colon after the field name

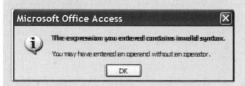

Figure 4.3 illustrates how the custom field was typed into the design grid of the Item Inventory Analysis query. Notice that the field name "Target Weeks of Supply" precedes the colon. The number 8 will appear in every row of the query record set because it is typed after the colon of the custom field name. A custom field can be identified if the field name precedes a colon or if there is no table name in the Table row of the design grid.

Figure 4.3 | **Custom Field Added to a Select Query**

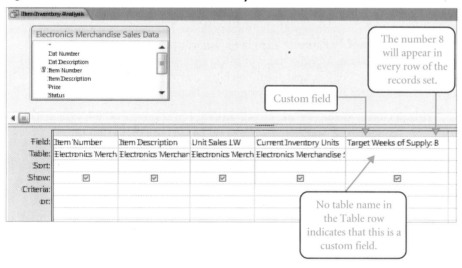

Figure 4.4 shows the record set of the Select Query that is shown in Figure 4.3. Notice that the number 8 appears in every row of the Target Weeks of Supply field.

Figure 4.4 | **Record Set of the Item Inventory Analysis Query**

Item Number	Item Description	Unit Sales LW	Current Inventory Units	Target Weeks of Supply
10243	10 GB Digital Player	225	850	8
10344	40 GB Digital Player	775	6,000	8
10655	80 GB Digital Player	20	195	8
22054	Game 4	150	3,500	8
22333	Game 2	15	150	8
22765	Game 3	550	2,100	8
22888	Game 5	245	2,500	8
22980	Game 1	380	3,000	8
33245	System 2	85	550	8
33989	System 1	450	3,200	8
44332	Multi Disc DVD	54	500	8
44339	DVD/VCR	525	2,250	8
44556	DVD Player	10	105	8
44922	VCR	40	1,350	8

The number 8 appears in every row since it was typed after the colon of this custom field.

Calculated Fields

Calculated fields display the result of a formula or function. When a formula is entered after the colon of a new field name, the result of the mathematical calculation will be displayed in the record set of a query. For example, the weeks of supply formula will be entered into the Item Inventory Analysis query shown in Figure 4.3. The result of this formula will be displayed for each item in the record set.

A basic formula in Access consists of a field name, a mathematical operator, and another field name. For example, the following is the weeks of supply formula that will be added to the Item Inventory Analysis query in Figure 4.3:

```
[Electronic Merchandise Sales Data]![Current Inventory Units]
    / [Electronic Merchandise Sales Data]![Unit Sales LW]
```

This formula will take the Current Inventory Units and divide it by the Unit Sales LW for each item in the query record set. Notice that each field name is preceded by the table name in brackets followed by an exclamation point. The exclamation point distinguishes table names from field names. Anything typed before the exclamation point is considered a table name. You will use table names when adding field names to a formula because it is possible for a query to contain multiple tables with identical field names (adding multiple tables to a query is covered in Chapter 6). The brackets in this formula indicate to Access that a mathematical calculation must be performed. This is similar to typing an equal sign into a cell location before entering a formula in an Excel spreadsheet.

Similar to Excel, mathematical operator symbols used on a calculator are slightly different compared to Access. Figure 4.5 shows a table of mathematical operator symbols and definitions. These symbols are identical to the ones used in formulas for Excel.

Figure 4.5 | **Access Mathematical Operators**

Symbol	Definition
+	**Addition**
–	**Subtraction**
/	**Division**
*	**Multiplication**
^	**Power / Exponent**

The following explains how a formula is added to the Item Inventory Analysis query in Figure 4.3 to calculate the weeks of supply for each item in the query record set:

- Click the first row of an empty column in the design grid of the query.
- Type the field name Weeks of Supply and then type a colon.
- Type an open bracket, the table name Electronic Merchandise Sales Data, and then a close bracket.
- Type an exclamation point.
- Type an open bracket, the field name Current Inventory Units, and then a close bracket.
- Type a back slash for division.
- Type an open bracket, the table name Electronic Merchandise Sales Data and a close bracket.
- Type an exclamation point.
- Type an open bracket, the field name Unit Sales LW, and a close bracket.
- Save and run the query.

Figure 4.6 shows the appearance of the formula calculating the weeks of supply in the Item Inventory Analysis query. Notice that the table and field names are enclosed in brackets. This indicates that Access will be displaying the result of a mathematical calculation in each record of the query record set.

Figure 4.6 | **Weeks of Supply Formula**

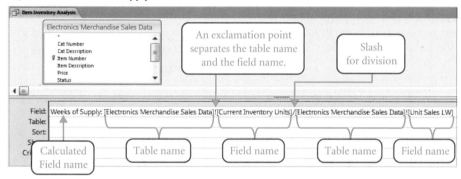

Figure 4.7 shows the results of the Item Inventory Analysis query. Notice the Weeks of Supply field is dividing the Units Sales LW field into the Current Inventory Units field for each record in the query record set. The results of the Weeks of Supply field can be compared to the Target Weeks of Supply field to see which items are above or below the target. Finally, notice that the values in the Weeks of Supply field are formatted to one decimal place. This was done through the Property Sheet window, which was covered in Chapter 3.

Figure 4.7 | **Results of the Item Inventory Analysis Query**

Item Number	Item Description	Unit Sales LW	Current Inventory Units	Target Weeks of Supply	Weeks of Supply
10243	10 GB Digital Player	225	850	8	3.8
10344	40 GB Digital Player	775	6,000	8	7.7
10655	80 GB Digital Player	20	195	8	9.8
22054	Game 4	150	3,500	8	23.3
22333	Game 2	15	150	8	10.0
22765	Game 3	550	2,100	8	3.8
22888	Game 5	245	2,500	8	10.2
22980	Game 1	380	3,000	8	7.9
33246	System 2	85	550	8	6.5
33989	System 1	450	3,200	8	7.1
44332	Multi Disc DVD	54	500	8	9.3
44339	DVD/VCR	525	2,250	8	4.3
44556	DVD Player	10	105	8	10.5
44922	VCR	40	1,350	8	33.8

Results of the Weeks of Supply formula

It is important to note that when creating formulas in Access, mathematical operations are applied to an entire field of data. This is different from creating formulas in Excel where you apply mathematical operations to specific cell locations. In Access, you *cannot* apply a mathematical formula to specific cells in the record set of a query. Chapter 2 briefly mentioned this concept when explaining the importance of assigning data types to a field. The benefits of using fields in Access formulas is that when data is changed in the field of a table, the formula will automatically produce a new output after running the query or opening it in **Datasheet View**. This is similar to using cell locations in Excel formulas. As a result, when creating formulas in Access, it is good practice to use field names whenever possible. You can also use constants or numbers when creating formulas in Access. However, this should be limited to numbers that will not change such as minutes in an hour, weeks in a year, etc.

COMMON MISTAKES | Using Numeric Values in Access Formulas

Be careful when using numeric values in Access formulas. Numeric values should be used when dealing with numbers such as days of the week, months of the year, minutes in an hour, etc. These are constant values that do not change. *Do not* type numeric values that exist in a field into a formula. Typing numeric values into a formula instead of using field names will eliminate the ability to recalculate an output when data is changed or added to a table.

So far, we demonstrated how to add a basic formula to an Access query. However, complex formulas containing several fields and several mathematical operators can also be added to a query. One of the most important tasks in creating complex queries is determining the order in which mathematical operations are executed. Similar to Excel, you control the order of operations through the use of parentheses. Access will execute mathematical computations that are placed in parenthesis first. If several parentheses are used, Access will execute the mathematical computation in the inner most parentheses first. If no parentheses are used, Access will execute computations depending on the mathematical operators that are used in the formula as shown in Figure 4.8.

FIGURE 4.8 | **Order of Operations**

Order	Symbol	Definition
1	^	**Power / Exponent**
2	* or /	**Multiplication or Division**
3	+ or -	**Addition or Subtraction**

The next example demonstrates the use of parentheses in Access formulas by adding the Days of Supply formula to the Item Inventory Analysis query. The Days of Supply formula is similar to the Weeks of Supply formula however it estimates how many days of inventory are available for each item instead of weeks. Since the Electronics Merchandise Sales Data table contains sales for one week, a formula must be created to estimate how many units are sold each day. We will assume that the items presented in the Electronics Merchandise Sales Data table are sold 7 days a week at approximately the same rate each day. Therefore, to calculate an estimate as to how many units are sold for each item every day, the Unit Sales LW field will be divided by 7. Then, the Current Inventory Units will be divided by this result. The following explains how this formula is added to the Item Inventory Analysis query.

- Click in the first row of the empty column in the design grid of the query.
- Click the right mouse button. This will display a menu of options as shown in Figure 4.9
- Select the **Zoom** option from the menu. This will open the **Zoom** window which is a helpful tool when creating complex formulas. It provides a larger window so you can see each of the fields being added to the formula.

Figures 4.9 and 4.10 illustrate how the **Zoom** window is opened from the menu options that appear when right clicking in the first row of the query design grid.

Figure 4.9 | **Right Click Menu Options**

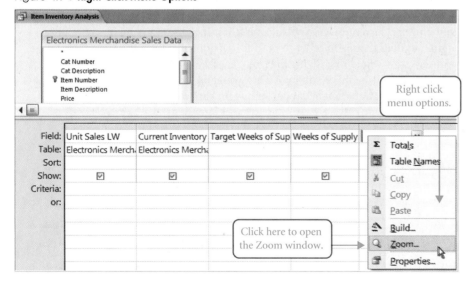

Figure 4.10 | **The Zoom Window**

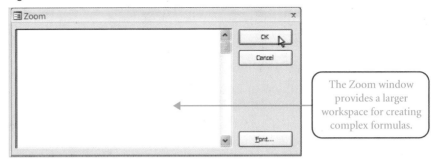

The Zoom window provides a larger workspace for creating complex formulas.

- Once the Zoom window opens type the field name Days of Supply followed by a colon.
- Type the following to use the Current Inventory Units field in the formula:`[Electronics Merchandise Sales Data]![Current Inventory Units]`
- Type a slash for division.
- Type an open parenthesis.
- Type the following to use the Unit Sales LW field in the formula: `[Electronics Merchandise Sales Data]![Unit Sales LW]`
- Type a slash for division.
- Type the number 7. This will divide the values in the Unit Sales LW field by 7 which will serve as an estimate for how many units were sold each day of the week.
- Type a closing parenthesis.
- Click the OK button in the upper right corner of the Zoom window.
- Run the query.

Figure 4.11shows how the Days of Supply formula appears in the Zoom window. Notice that the second part of the formula, `[Electronics Merchandise Sales Data]![Unit Sales LW]/7,` is enclosed in parentheses. As a result, Access will first divide the values in the Unit Sales LW field by 7, and then divide this result into the Current Inventory Units field. It is important to note the parentheses are required in this formula in order to produce accurate results. If the parentheses were omitted, Access would first divide the Unit Sales LW into the Current Inventory Units field, and then divide this result by 7. This would produce an erroneous number that was much less than the actual days of supply for each item.

Figure 4.11 | **Days of Supply Formula Entered in the Zoom Window**

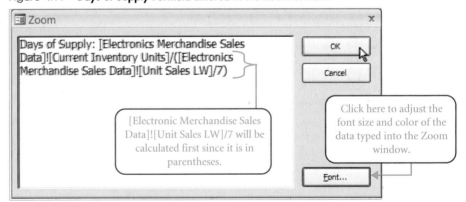

Days of Supply: [Electronics Merchandise Sales Data]![Current Inventory Units]/([Electronics Merchandise Sales Data]![Unit Sales LW]/7)

[Electronic Merchandise Sales Data]![Unit Sales LW]/7 will be calculated first since it is in parentheses.

Click here to adjust the font size and color of the data typed into the Zoom window.

Figure 4.12 shows the formula in the design grid of the Item Inventory Analysis query after clicking the **OK** button in the **Zoom** window. The width of the column in the design grid would have to be increased significantly to see the entire formula. This is why the **Zoom** window is a more effective tool for creating this formula.

Figure 4.12 | **Days of Supply Formula in the Design Grid of the Item Inventory Analysis Query**

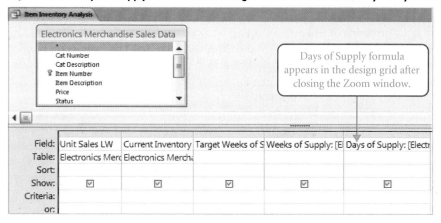

Figure 4.13 shows the record set of the Item Inventory Analysis query shown in Figure 4.12. The results of the Days of Supply formula provide business managers with additional detail regarding the inventory supply of each item. This information can help managers make decisions such as when to order more units of a particular item, or which orders to rush out to the stores in order to prevent out of stock situations.

Figure 4.13 | **Record Set of the Inventory Analysis Query with the Days of Supply**

Item Number	Item Description	Unit Sales LW	Current Inventory Units	Target Weeks of Su	Weeks of Supply	Days of Supply
10243	10 GB Digital Player	225	850	8	3.8	26.4
10344	40 GB Digital Player	775	6,000	8	7.7	54.2
10655	80 GB Digital Player	20	195	8	9.8	68.3
22054	Game 4	150	3,500	8	23.3	163.3
22333	Game 2	15	150	8	10.0	70.0
22765	Game 3	550	2,100	8	3.8	26.7
22888	Game 5	245	2,500	8	10.2	71.4
22980	Game 1	380	3,000	8	7.9	55.3
33245	System 2	85	550	8	6.5	45.3
33989	System 1	450	3,200	8	7.1	49.8
44332	Multi Disc DVD	54	500	8	9.3	64.8
44339	DVD/VCR	525	2,250	8	4.3	30.0
44556	DVD Player	10	105	8	10.5	73.5
44922	VCR	40	1,350	8	33.8	236.3

Results of the Days of Supply formula

COMMON MISTAKES | Check the Spelling of Table and Field Names

When typing formulas into the query design grid or **Zoom** window, be sure to check the spelling of any table names and field names. If a table or field name is spelled incorrectly, the dialog box shown in Figure 4.14 will appear. This indicates that

Figure 4.14 | **Enter Parameter Value Dialog Box**

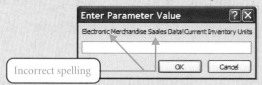

Incorrect spelling

Access can not find a field or table that was enclosed in brackets and will ask the user to enter a value. This is a valid technique if you want the user to define the value for a specific variable in the formula. However, in this case the dialog box appears because the table name Electronics Merchandise Sales Data is misspelled.

>> **Quick Reference**

Creating Formulas (Calculated Fields)

1. Click the first row of an empty column in the design grid of a Select Query.
2. Type the name of the Calculated Field followed by a colon.
3. Add fields to the formula by using the following syntax: `[Table Name]![Field Name]`.
4. Type the desired mathematical operator.
5. Add another field using the syntax in number 3.
6. If using several fields and operators, use parentheses to control the order in which computations are executed.

>> **Quick Reference**

Opening the Zoom Window

1. Click the first row of any column in the design grid of a Select Query.
2. Right click to open a menu of options.
3. Select **Zoom** from the menu.
4. If the **Zoom** window is opened when clicking in a column that contains a field or formula, the contents of the column will be displayed in the window.

The Expression Builder

The previous segment demonstrated how to type formulas directly into the design grid of a query. This is one of two options available for creating formulas in Access. You can also create formulas using a tool called the **_Expression Builder_**. The Expression Builder allows you to create a formula in the design grid of a query using a point and click method. A key benefit of using this method is that it eliminates the risk of spelling errors when adding fields to a formula.

The next example demonstrates the Expression Builder through a new query created using the Electronics Merchandise Sales Data table shown in Figure 4.1. The purpose of this query is to show the percent of sales dollars each item represents to its total category sales. For example, if an item generated $500 in sales and it is part of a category where the total sales are $1,000, then the item represents 50% of the total category sales. A business manager can use the results of this formula to identify items that generate the majority of sales dollars for each category in an assortment of merchandise. This information can then be used to identify key trends within a merchandise category, prioritize merchandise orders issued to suppliers, or expedite shipments being delivered to stores. The following explains the initial setup of this query.

- Open a new Select Query by clicking the **Query Design** icon in the **Create** tab of the Ribbon.
- Add the Electronics Merchandise Sales Data table and close the **Show Table** dialog box.
- Add the Cat Number, Cat Description, Item Number, Item Description, Sales Dollars LW, and Category Sales Dollars LW fields to the design grid of the query.
- Save the query and enter the name Item Sales Dollars Analysis.

Figure 4.15 shows the initial set up of the Items Sales Dollars Analysis query. A formula will be added to this query using the Expression Builder.

Figure 4.15 | **Initial Setup of the Item Sales Dollars Analysis Query**

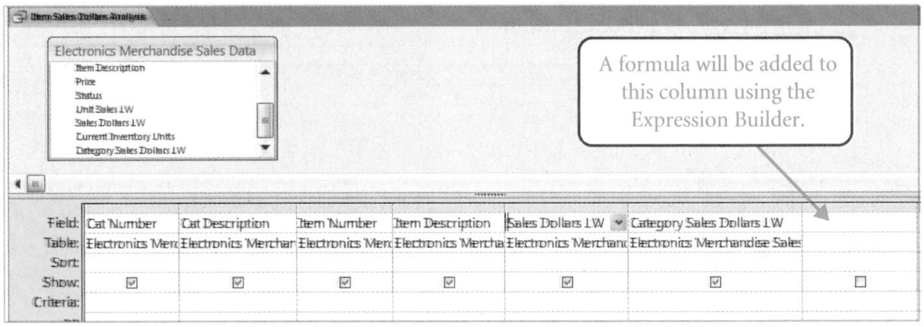

The following explains how the Expression Builder is used to create a formula that calculates the percent of sales each item represents to its category:

- Click in the first row of an empty column in the query design grid.
- Click the **Builder** icon in the **Design** tab of the Ribbon. This will open the Expression Builder dialog box as shown in Figure 4.16.
- Click in the upper window of the Expression Builder, type the field name Sales Percent of Category, and then type a colon (see Figure 4.16).

Figure 4.16 | **The Expression Builder Dialog Box**

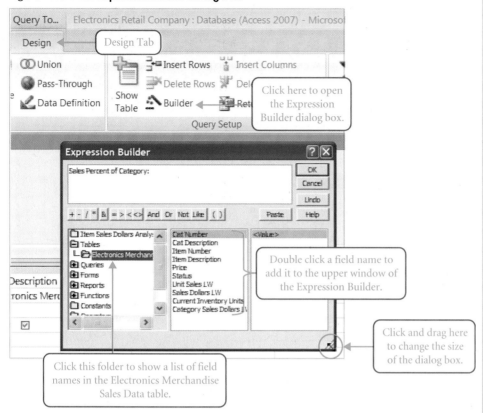

- Double-click the Tables folder on the left side of the **Expression Builder** dialog box to display the Electronics Merchandise Sales Data folder as shown in Figure 4.16.

- Click the Electronics Merchandise Sales Data folder to display a list of fields contained in the table.

- Double-click the field Sales Dollars LW in the center of the **Expression Builder** dialog box. This will add the field to the upper window of the Expression Builder.

- Click the slash button under the upper window of the **Expression Builder** dialog box.

- Double-click the Category Sales Dollars LW field in the center window of the **Expression Builder** dialog box. This will add the field to the upper window after the slash.

- Click the **OK** button to add the completed formula to the design grid of the query.

Figure 4.17 shows the completed formula entered into the **Expression Builder** dialog box. Notice that the Expression Builder automatically adds the brackets and exclamation point when a field is added to a formula by double-clicking it in the center window. This is a much faster method for adding fields to a formula, and as previously mentioned, eliminates the risk of misspelling a table or field name.

Figure 4.17 | **Completed Formula in the Expression Builder Dialog Box**

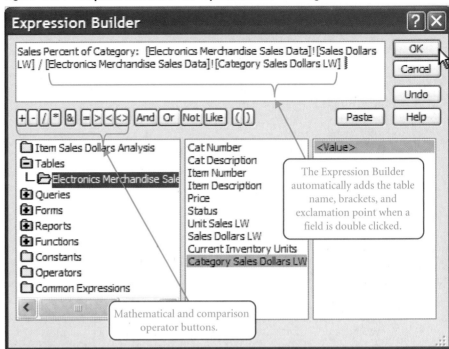

Figure 4.18 shows the completed formula in the design grid of the query. The formula is added to the design grid after clicking the **OK** button in the upper right corner of the **Expression Builder** dialog box.

Figure 4.18 | **Item Sales Dollars Analysis Query with Sales Percent of Category Formula**

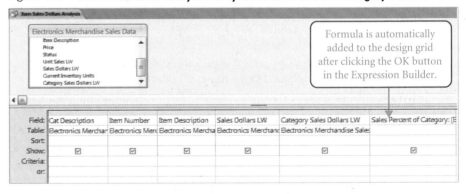

Figure 4.19 shows the record set of the Item Sales Dollars Analysis query. The Sales Percent of Category field shows the results of the formula that was created using the **Expression Builder**. Notice that the results were formatted to a percentage. In addition, notice that the record set was sorted based on the Cat Number field in ascending order and the Sales Percent of Category field in descending order. This will show the items that generate the highest percentage of sales for each category first. Notice that the 40 GB Digital Player generates 90% of the sales for category 10.

Figure 4.19 | **Record set of the Item Sales Dollars Analysis Query**

Cat Number	Cat Description	Item Number	Item Description	Sales Dollars LW	Category Sales Dollars LW	Sales Percent of Category
10	Digital Music Player	10344	40 GB Digital Player	$154,992	$171,991	90.12%
10	Digital Music Player	10243	10 GB Digital Player	$11,999	$171,991	6.98%
10	Digital Music Player	10655	80 GB Digital Player	$5,000	$171,991	2.91%
20	Video Games	22980	Game 1	$22,796	$70,737	32.23%
20	Video Games	22765	Game 3	$21,995	$70,737	31.09%
20	Video Games	22888	Game 5	$14,698	$70,737	20.78%
20	Video Games	22054	Game 4	$10,499	$70,737	14.84%
20	Video Games	22333	Game 2	$750	$70,737	1.06%
30	Video Game System	33988	System 1	$34,499	$54,048	63.83%
30	Video Game System	33245	System 2	$19,549	$54,048	36.17%
40	Home Video	44339	DVD/VCR	$68,245	$87,479	78.01%
40	Home Video	44332	Multi Disc DVD	$14,035	$87,479	16.04%
40	Home Video	44922	VCR	$3,600	$87,479	4.11%
40	Home Video	44556	DVD Player	$1,600	$87,479	1.83%

> The 40 GB Digital Player generates 90.12% of Category 10 sales.

COMMON MISTAKES | The <Expr> Symbol in the Expression Builder

When using the Expression Builder, the symbol **<Expr>** may appear when creating a formula as shown in Figure 4.20. This is automatically generated by Access and serves as a place holder for entering field names or requirements of a formula. In the example shown in Figure 4.20, the **<Expr>** serves as a place holder to enter the field name for the formula being created. However, even if a field name is entered into the Expression Builder, the **<Expr>** symbol may still appear after the formula is created. Therefore, you must *click the symbol once and delete it*. If the **<Expr>** is not deleted, an error message will appear when you to run the query or click in another column in the query design grid.

Figure 4.20 | **<Expr> Symbol in the Expression Builder**

> Delete this symbol from the Expression Builder before clicking the OK button.

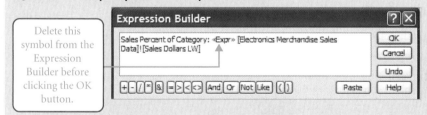

The following error message will appear if the **<Expr>** symbols are not removed from the upper window of the Expression Builder.

>> **Quick Reference**

Opening the Expression Builder

1. Click the first row of any column in the design grid of query.
2. Click the **Design** tab in the Ribbon.
3. Click the **Builder** icon.

>> Formulas

The purpose of this workshop is to review the techniques of adding custom and calculated fields to a query. I will be demonstrating the tasks in this workshop in the following three videos: **Custom Fields**, **Calculated Fields**, and **Expression Builder**. Open the Access database named ib_a04_electronicsmerchandise. Try to complete each of the tasks below before watching the videos.

1. **Custom Fields (Video: Custom Fields)**

    a. Create a new Select Query and add the Sales Data table.

    b. Add the following fields to the design grid of the query:
       i. Item Number
       ii. Item Description
       iii. Unit Sales LW
       iv. Current Inventory Units

    b. Save the query and name it **Inventory Analysis**.

    c. Click in the first row in the empty column next to the Current Inventory Units field. Then, type **Target WOS** followed by a colon.

    d. Type the number **8** after the colon of the Target WOS field.

    e. Save and run the query.

    f. Change the query back to Design View.

2. **Calculated Fields (Video: Calculated Fields)**

    a. Click in the first row of the blank column next to the Target WOS field.

    b. Type the field name **Weeks of Supply** followed by a colon.

    c. Right click next to the Weeks of Supply field name created in b. and select **Zoom** from the list of options.

    d. Click to the right of the colon after the Weeks of Supply field name in the **Zoom** window.

    e. Type the following after the colon of the Weeks of Supply field name: **[Sales Data]![Current Inventory Units]**

    f. Type a slash, and then type the following: **[Sales Data]![Unit Sales LW]**

    g. Click the **OK** button on the **Zoom** window.

    h. Run the query.

    i. Switch the query back to **Design View**.

    j. Open the **Property Sheet** window and format the Weeks of Supply field to a Fixed number format with 1 decimal place. Then, close the **Property Sheet** window.

    k. Save and then run the query.

    l. Switch the query back to **Design View.**

3. **Using the Expression Builder (Video: Expression Builder)**

    a. Click the first row of the empty column next to the Weeks of Supply field.

    b. Type the field name **Days of Supply** followed by a colon.

c. Open the **Expression Builder** by clicking the **Builder** icon in the **Design** tab of the Ribbon.

d. Double-click the Tables folder, and then click the Sales Data folder.

e. Double-click the Current Inventory Units field name in the lower center window of the Expression Builder.

f. Click the **slash** button on the Expression Builder, and then click the **Open Parenthesis** button.

g. Double-click the Units Sales LW field name, and then click the slash button.

h. Type the number **7**, and then click the **Close Parenthesis** button.

i. Click the **<<Expr>>** symbol, which appears directly after the colon of the Days of Supply field and press the **Delete** key on your keyboard.

j. Click the **OK** button on the **Expression Builder**.

k. Run the query.

l. Switch the query back to **Design View**.

m. Open the **Property Sheet** window and format the Days of Supply field to a Fixed number format with 1 decimal place. Then, close the Property Sheet window.

n. Save and then run the query.

o. Close the query and then close the database.

>> Stock Analysis

EXERCISE
Why Do I Need This?

People who make investments in the stock market often rely on research that is published by financial analysts. One of the goals of this research is to identify opportunities in the stock market that might provide investors with significant returns. In fact, investors are often willing to pay a financial analyst or a finance firm hundreds of dollars for a subscription to financial research reports. These research reports are valuable because the amount of data a financial analyst or finance firm collects and stores is far greater than what casual investors can accumulate on their own. This data usually includes several years of financial statistics for public companies and the industries in which they operate. Database tools such as Access play a critical role in the collection and analysis of the data that is used to produce these financial research reports.

Exercise

The purpose of this exercise is to analyze data from a table that might be used by a financial analyst. This exercise will require you to construct calculated fields with formulas that are frequently used by financial analysts to evaluate the stock performance of public companies. You will need to open the Access database named ib_a04_investmentresearch before completing the tasks below.

1. Open the Stock Data query in **Design View**.

2. The first calculated field that will be added to the Stock Data query is the Market Cap. The purpose of this field is to calculate the total value of the money that is invested in each company. The market cap is calculated by multiplying the Current Price field by the Average Outstanding Shares field. Use the following guidelines to create this calculated field.

   a. The location of this calculated field should be in the empty column next to the Current Price field in the design grid of the Stock Data query.

   b. The field name should be **Market Cap**.

c. Enter a formula that multiplies the Current Price field by the Average Outstanding Shares field. You can use the Expression Builder or type this formula directly into the design grid of the query.

3. Format the results of the Market Cap field to Currency with zero decimal places.

4. The next calculated field that will be added to the design grid of the Stock Data query is Earnings per Share. The Earnings per Share is calculated by dividing the outstanding shares into a company's net income. This gives a financial analyst an indication of a company's ability to generate profits. Use the following guidelines to create this calculated field.

   a. The location of this calculated field should be in the empty column next to the Market Cap field in the design grid of the Stock Data query.

   b. The field name should be `EPS`.

   c. The formula should divide the Average Shares Outstanding field into the Net Income Last Year field.

5. Format the results of the EPS field to Currency with 2 decimal places.

6. The next calculated field that will be added to the design grid of the Stock Data query is the Price to Earnings ratio or P/E ratio. The P/E ratio is calculated by dividing the Earnings per Share for a company into its current stock price. This indicates how much additional money investors are willing to pay for one share of a company's stock compared to the amount of net income earned for one share. For example, a P/E ratio of 10 means the price for one share of a company's stock is 10 times greater than the amount of net income the company generates for each share. A high P/E ratio might indicate that investors expect the earnings of a company to increase in the future. Use the following guidelines to create this calculated field.

   a. The location of this calculated field should be in the empty column next to the EPS field in the design grid of the Stock Data query.

   b. The field name should be `PE Ratio`.

   c. The formula should divide the EPS field into the Current Price field. You can use the **Expression Builder** or type this formula directly into the design grid of the query. Note that the EPS field is a calculated field that you created in number 4. You will need to save the query in order to see this field when you double-click the Queries/Stock Data folder in the Expression Builder.

7. Format the results of the PE Ratio field to a Standard format with 2 decimal places.

8. The last calculated field that will be added to the design grid of the Stock Data query is the Compound Annual Growth Rate, or CAGR. The CAGR of each company's stock price is calculated by dividing the current stock price by the stock price 3 years ago. This result will be raised to a power which is the result of dividing 1 by the number of years of growth being measure which is 3. The total result of the formula is then subtracted from the number 1. The CAGR calculation is frequently used by analysts to determine how much a stock has grown over two points in time. Generally, a stock with a high CAGR provides a significant return to investors. Use the following guidelines to create this calculated field.

   a. The location of this calculated field should be in the empty column next to the PE Ratio field in the design grid of the Stock Data query.

   b. The field name should be `Stock Price CAGR.`

c. The formula for this field is as follows: ((Current Price/Price Three Years Ago)^(1/3))−1

d. Note that the power symbol is added to the formula by holding the **Shift** key down and pressing the number **6** on your keyboard.

9. Format the results of the Stock Price CAGR field to a Percentage.

10. Save and run the query.

11. What stock has the highest CAGR? Does this stock also have the highest EPS?

12. What is the CAGR of the stock with the highest Market Cap?

13. What stock has the lowest CAGR? Does this stock also have the lowest EPS?

14. How many stocks have an EPS greater than $3.00?

15. Save and close the query. Then, close the database.

>> What's Wrong with This Database?

PROBLEM & EXERCISE

Problem

You are working in the merchandise division of an electronics retail company. A coworker in your division is having trouble with Access and sends you an e-mail asking for help. She explains that she is having trouble with calculated fields and provides the following details in her e-mail.

The first query I tried to create is called Unit Profit. I tried to add a calculated field to this query that subtracts the Cost field from the Price field. However, when I run the query I keep getting this strange message saying I need to enter a parameter value. I have no idea what this means, so I keep clicking the cancel button. But then I can't get the query to run.

I created a second query called Total Profit Dollars Last Week. I added a field to this query called Profit Dollars. The purpose of this field is to multiply the Unit Sales LW by the unit profit for each item, which is simply the Price field minus the Cost field. Since I could not get this formula to work when I typed it into the design grid of the Unit Profit query, I figured I would try out the Expression Builder. The good news is that I am not getting the Enter Parameter thing. However, all the numbers in this field are negative. How could this be? We make a profit on every item we sell.

Exercise

The database your coworker attached to her e-mail to you is named ib_a04_calculationchaos. Evaluate the two queries and the calculated fields that were attempted by your coworker. Consider the following points.

1. Why would the **Enter Parameter** dialog box open when you try to run a query?

2. In the second point of the coworker's e-mail, she mentioned that she tried to type the formula for the calculated field in the Unit Profit query. What mistake might happen when formulas are typed into the design grid of the query?

3. Look at the formula that was created in the Profit Dollars field in the Total Profit Dollars Last Week query. Explain how this formula is calculating an output. Is this what your coworker intended?

What's wrong with this database? Write a short answer for each of the points listed above. Then fix the calculated fields in both the Unit Profit and Total Profit Dollars Last Week fields in the ib_a04_calculationchaos database.

>> IIF Function

This section will demonstrate the **IIF** function in Access. The **IIF** function provides business managers with powerful methods for analyzing enormous amounts of data. Just think, if a company sells thousands of products, or services millions of customers, how do business managers know if an item is about to run out of inventory or if a customer's subscription for a service is about to expire? The **IIF** function allows business managers to apply tests to a field of data in a table or query to identify key trends or needs within their business. Instead of analyzing thousands or millions of records individually, business managers can use the **IIF** function to determine which records they need to evaluate.

Basic IIF Function

The **IIF** function in Access is almost identical to the **IF** function in Excel. The **IIF** function stands for Immediate IF, which is why there is an extra "I" in front of the word IF. Similar to the **IF** function in Excel, the **IIF** function contains three arguments. The name of each argument in the **IIF** function is different compared to Excel's **IF** function, however, the functionality is identical. The following explains each of these three arguments.

- **expr:** This argument is used for entering a logical test into the **IIF** function and is identical to the logical_test argument of Excel's **IF** function. This argument is used for evaluating the data in a field based on a test that you define. A logical test usually starts with a field name and then a comparison operator (i.e., =, >,<). The second part of the test can be a multitude of possibilities. For example, you may need to compare the values in a field to a number, another field, a formula, or a word. If you are using words or text data in any argument of the **IIF** function, you must put them in quotations. The following are examples of logical tests:
  - Units Sales LW > 100
  - Item Description = "Game 1"
  - Weeks of Supply > Target Weeks of Supply
  - Price > Sales Dollars LW / Units Sales LW

- **truepart:** This argument is used for defining the output of the function if the results of the logical test are true. This argument can be defined with a field name, formula, number, or words. As in the **expr** argument, if you are going to use words, you must put them in quotes.

- **falsepart:** This argument is used for defining the output of the function if the results of the logical test are false. The options for defining this argument are identical to the **truepart** argument.

This example demonstrates the **IIF** function by adding a field to the Item Inventory Analysis query shown in Figure 4.21 to evaluate the Days of Supply field. If you recall, the Days of Supply is a calculated field that was added to the query to determine how much inventory is available for each item in terms of days (see Figure 4.12). An **IIF** function will be created to determine what items need to be reordered. In creating this function, we will assume it takes 60 days for the electronics company to receive merchandise after an order is submitted to a supplier. As a result, any item showing a value less than or equal to 60 days in the Days of Supply field must be reordered.

Figure 4.21 | Item Inventory Analysis Query with Days of Supply Field

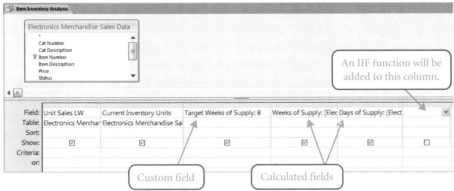

The **IIF** function can be used to create a calculated field by typing it directly into an empty column in the design grid of a query. Unlike Excel, when you start typing a function in Access, you *will not* see a hint box showing each of the function arguments. However, you can see the arguments of a function if you use the **Expression Builder**. The following explains how the **IIF** function is added to the Item Inventory Analysis query in Figure 4.21 using the **Expression Builder**.

- Type the field name Reorder Status followed by a colon into the empty column next to the Days of Supply field (see Figure 4.21).
- Open the **Expression Builder** dialog box by clicking the **Builder** icon in the **Design** tab of the Ribbon.
- Double click the **Functions** folder in the lower left window of the **Expression Builder** dialog box. Then, click the **Built-In Functions** folder which is in the **Functions** folder (see Figure 4.22). This will add several function categories to the lower center window of the Expression Builder dialog box.
- Click the <**All**> option in the lower center window of the **Expression Builder** dialog box to show all Access functions in alphabetical order in the lower right window. Double-click the **IIF** function in the lower right window to add it to the upper window of the **Expression Builder**.

Figure 4.22 shows the appearance of the **IIF** function when it is double-clicked in the lower right window of the Expression Builder dialog box. Notice that placeholders appear for each argument of the **IIF** function in the upper window of the **Expression Builder**.

Figure 4.22 | **Using the Expression Builder to Create an IIF Function**

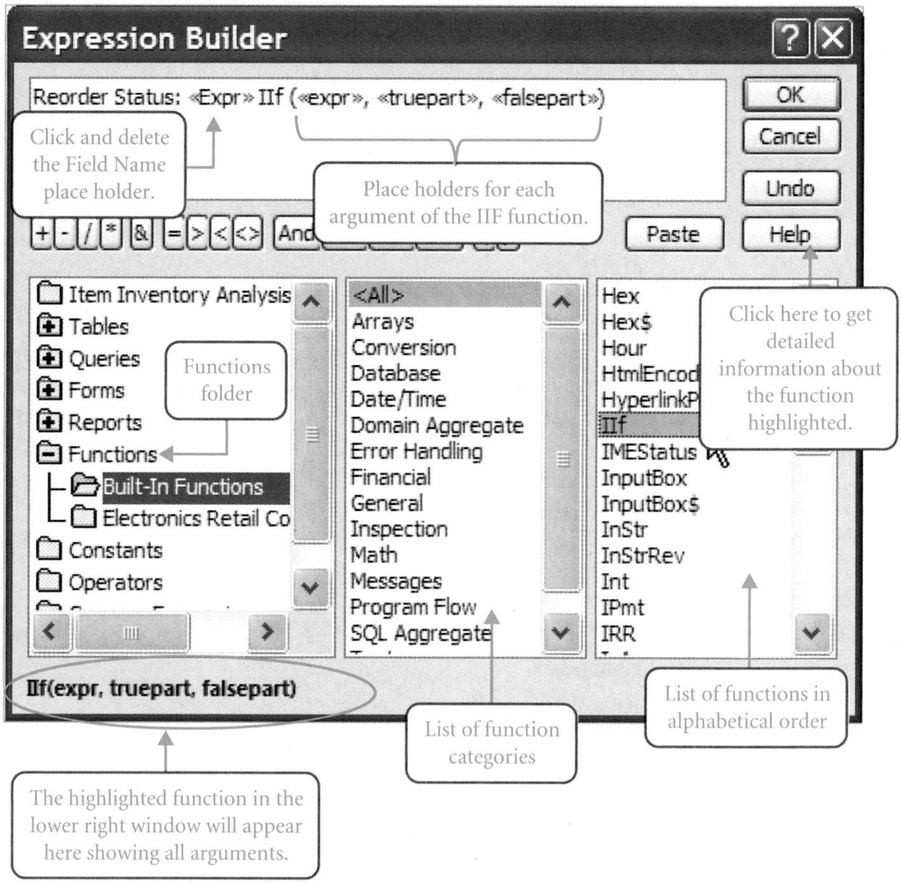

The following explains how the **IIF** function is completed for the Item Inventory Analysis query shown in Figure 4.21using the Expression Builder.

- Delete the field name place holder, which is the <<**Expr**>> symbol that precedes the **IIF** function. When a function is added to the upper window of the **Expression Builder**, the <<**Expr**>> place holder for the field name will automatically be added in front of the function name. If you typed the field name in the design grid of the query before opening the Expression Builder, you must click and delete this place holder.

- When the **IIF** function appears in the upper window of the Expression Builder, you will see place holders for each argument. The following explains how to define the **expr** argument which is the logical test of the function.

    - Click the <<**expr**>> argument place holder.
    - Double-click the **Queries** folder in the lower left window of the **Expression Builder**.
    - Click the **Item Inventory Analysis** query which is in the **Queries** folder. This will show a list of all field names contained in the Item Inventory Analysis query in the lower center window of the **Expression Builder**. If you are creating a new query, you must save the query first before any fields appear in the **Expression Builder**.
    - Double-click the Days of Supply field name in the lower center window of the **Expression Builder**. This will add the field to the upper window of the **Expression Builder** in the **expr** argument. Note that you will not see a table name preceding this field because it is a calculated field within the query.
    - Type the less than sign followed by the equal sign and the number 60. The purpose of this function is to identify any items where the Days of Supply is less

than or equal to 60. You could also use the operator buttons in the Expression Builder to add the less than and equal signs to the logical test. However, Access will add an <<**expr**>> place holder for each symbol that is added. Therefore, you must remember to delete these placeholders if you do not use them.

- Define the **truepart** argument by clicking the <<**truepart**>> placeholder and type the word "Reorder". Remember, when using words in the **IIF** function, you must put them in quotations. The function will display the word Reorder for an item if the Days of Supply field is equal to or less than 60.

- Define the **falsepart** argument by clicking the <<**falsepart**>> placeholder and type the word "OK". If the Days of Supply field is not equal to or less than 60, we can assume the inventory is adequate.

- Check to make sure each argument is separated by commas. When using the **Expression Builder**, Access will automatically add commas for each argument. However, it is good practice to check that no commas were accidentally deleted.

Figure 4.23 shows the completed **IIF** function in the **Expression Builder**. Once each argument of the **IIF** function is completed, click the **OK** button to add the function to the design grid of the query.

Figure 4.23 | **Completed IIF function in the Expression Builder**

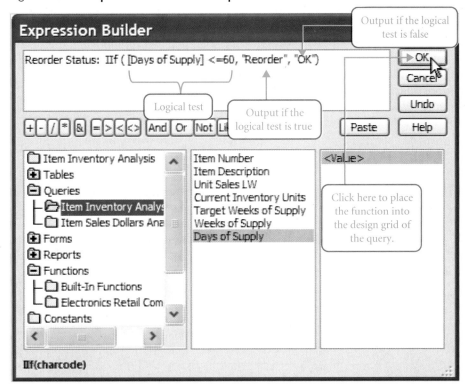

Figure 4.24 shows the record set of the Item Inventory Analysis query. The Reorder Status field shows the output of the **IIF** function. A business manger can use this field to identify which items need to be reordered.

Figure 4.24 | **Record Set of the Item Inventory Analysis Query with The IIF Function**

Item Numb ~	Item Description ~	Unit Sales LY ~	Current Inventory Unit ~	Target Weeks of Su ~	Weeks of Suppl ~	Days of Suppl ~	Reorder Status ~
10243	10 GB Digital Player	225	850	8	3.8	26.4	Reorder
10344	40 GB Digital Player	775	6,000	8	7.7	54.2	Reorder
10655	80 GB Digital Player	20	195	8	9.8	68.3	OK
22054	Game 4	150	3,500	8	23.3	163.3	OK
22333	Game 2	15	150	8	10.0	70.0	OK
22765	Game 3	550	2,100	8	3.8	26.7	Reorder
22888	Game 5	245	2,500	8	10.2	71.4	OK
22980	Game 1	380	3,000	8	7.9	55.3	Reorder
33245	System 2	85	550	8	6.5	45.3	Reorder
33989	System 1	450	3,200	8	7.1	49.8	Reorder
44332	Multi Disc DVD	54	600	8	9.3	64.8	OK
44339	DVD/VCR	525	2,250	8	4.3	30.0	Reorder
44556	DVD Player	10	105	8	10.5	73.5	OK
44922	VCR	40	1,350	8	33.8	236.3	OK

Output from the IIF function

The number of records shown in Figure 4.24 is relatively small compared to the thousands of records that are typically selected by business managers in large corporate environments. In these situations, a business manager could isolate only those records that show the word Reorder in the Reorder Status field. However, a nested query must be created in order to enter criteria for this field. This is because the output of the Reorder Status field depends on the results of another calculated field, which is the Days of Supply field. Therefore, a new query must be created with the Item Inventory Analysis query added. Then, the Reorder Status field can be added to the new query and criteria can be entered for the field.

Figure 4.25 shows a new nested query named Item Reorder List. The Item Inventory Analysis query is added to this new query and the Item Number, Item Description, Current Inventory Units, Days of Supply, and Reorder Status fields have been added to the design grid. Notice that the word Reorder is entered into the Criteria row for the Reorder Status field.

Figure 4.25 | **Criteria Added to the Reorder Status Field in a Nested Query**

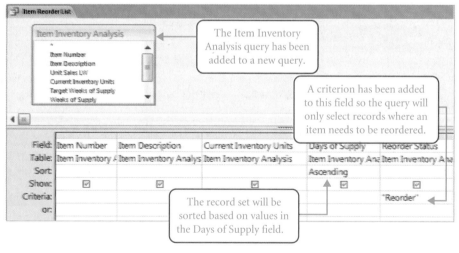

The Item Inventory Analysis query has been added to a new query.

A criterion has been added to this field so the query will only select records where an item needs to be reordered.

The record set will be sorted based on values in the Days of Supply field.

Figure 4.26 shows the record set of the Item Reorder List query shown in Figure 4.25. Notice that all records show the word Reorder in the Reorder Status field. Instead of looking at thousands of rows of data to determine which items to order, Access does all of the work for the business manager by showing only those items that need to be ordered. In addition, notice that the record set is sorted based on the values in the Days of Supply field in ascending order. As a result, a business manager can prioritize items that need to be ordered first.

Figure 4.26 | **Results of the Item Reorder List Query**

Item Number ⁃	Item Description ⁃	Current Inventory Units ⁃	Days of Supply ⁃	Reorder Status ⁃
10243	10 GB Digital Player	850	26.4	Reorder
22765	Game 3	2,100	26.7	Reorder
44339	DVD/VCR	2,250	30.0	Reorder
33245	System 2	550	45.3	Reorder
33989	System 1	3,200	49.8	Reorder
10344	40 GB Digital Player	6,000	54.2	Reorder
22980	Game 1	3,000	55.3	Reorder

Only records where the output of the Reorder Status field is Reorder are selected.

COMMON MISTAKES | Adding Criteria to a Calculated Field

You cannot enter criteria for a calculated field that relies on the result of another calculated field in the same query. If you create a calculated field that uses another calculated field in the same query, you will need to create a nested query in order to add criteria to these fields.

Nested IIF Functions

The previous segment demonstrated the use of a basic **IIF** function which contained one logical test and two potential outputs (**truepart** or **falsepart**). This segment will demonstrate how several logical tests and potential outputs are added through a nested IIF function. The construction of a nested **IIF** function in Access is identical to the construction of a nested **IF** function in Excel.

The Item Inventory Analysis query shown in Figure 4.21 will be used to demonstrate the nested **IIF** function. The purpose of this nested **IIF** function will be to compare the Target Weeks of Supply field with the Weeks of Supply field. The **IIF** function will be used to suggest price reductions or markdowns if the Weeks of Supply is greater than the Target Weeks of Supply. The suggested markdowns will be based on the following scenarios:

- If the Weeks of Supply minus the Target Weeks of Supply is less than 1 week, then the price will not be changed.
- If the Weeks of Supply is greater than the Target Weeks of Supply by 1 week but less than or equal to 5 weeks, the suggested markdown will be 25% off the current price.
- If the Weeks of Supply is greater than the Target Weeks of Supply by 5 weeks but less than or equal to 8 weeks, the suggested markdown will be 35% off the current price.
- If the Weeks of Supply is greater than the Target Weeks of Supply by more than 8 weeks, the suggested markdown will be 50% off the current price.

Figure 4.27 shows the design grid of the Item Inventory Analysis query. A nested **IIF** function will be used to create a calculated field called Suggested Markdown. This field will be entered in the blank column next to the Weeks of Supply field. Note that this blank column was added by clicking the first row of the Days of Supply field and clicking the **Insert Column** icon in the **Design** tab of the Ribbon.

Figure 4.27 | **Adding a Nested IIF Function to the Item Inventory Analysis Query**

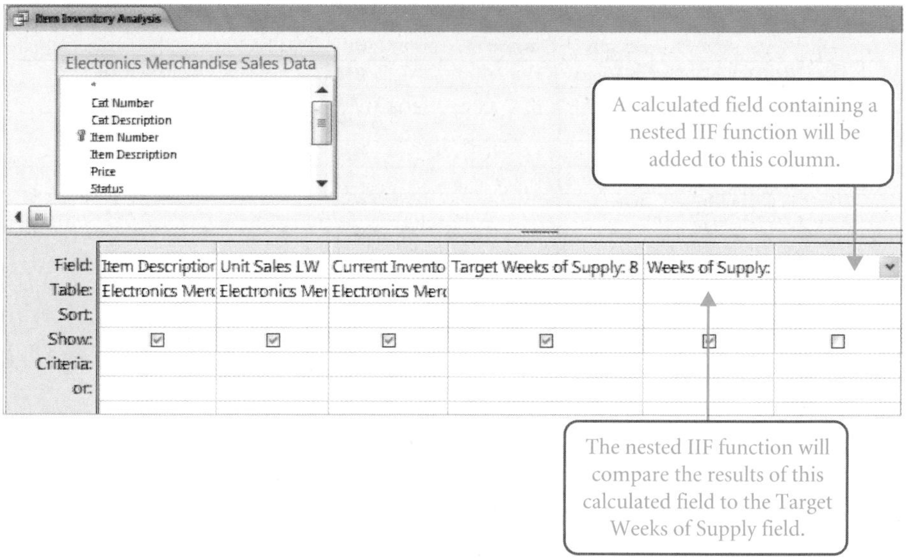

Similar to Excel, a nested **IIF** function in Access is created by adding a new **IIF** function to the **falsepart** argument. In this example, the nested **IIF** function will be used to assist a business manager in making price decisions for each item in the Electronics Merchandise Sales Data table. The following explains how this function is added to the Item Inventory Analysis query.

- Type the name Suggested Markdown followed by a colon in the empty column next to the Weeks of Supply field.
- Open the **Expression Builder** dialog box by clicking the **Builder** icon in the **Design** tab of the Ribbon. Then, click to the right of the field name Suggested Markdown in the upper window of the **Expression Builder** dialog box.
- Double-click the **Functions** folder in the lower left window of the **Expression Builder** dialog box. Then, click the **Built-In Functions** folder.
- Click the <**All**> option in the lower center window of the **Expression Builder** dialog box.
- Double-click the **IIF** function in the lower right window of the **Expression Builder** dialog box.
- Remove the <<**Expr**>> symbol preceding the IIF function by clicking it once and pressing the **Delete** key on your keyboard.

Figure 4.28 shows the initial setup of the nested **IIF** function in the Expression Builder dialog box. There will be a total of three logical tests added to this nested **IIF** function. Each logical test will be comprised of a formula which subtracts the Target Weeks of Supply field from the Weeks of Supply field. The results of this formula will determine what markdown value is displayed in the field.

Figure 4.28 | **Initial Setup of the Nested IIF Function**

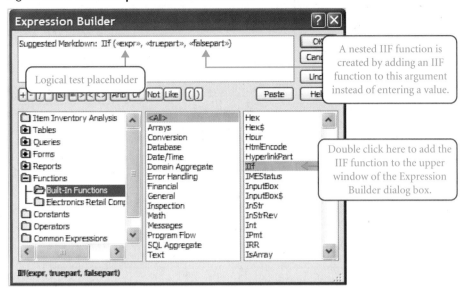

The following explains the setup of the first logical test for the nested IIf function:

- Click the <<**expr**>> argument placeholder for the logical test in the **IIF** function and double-click the **Queries** folder in the lower left window of the **Expression Builder** dialog box.

- Click the **Item Inventory Analysis** subfolder in the **Queries** folder. Then, double-click the Weeks of Supply field in the lower center window of the **Expression Builder** dialog box.

- Type a minus sign, and then double-click the Target Weeks of Supply field in the lower center window of the **Expression Builder** dialog box.

- Type a greater than sign and the number 8. This completes the first logical test which is comprised of a formula that subtracts the Target Weeks of Supply field from the Weeks of Supply field. The function will evaluate if the result of this formula is greater than 8.

- Click the <<**truepart**>> place holder and type the number .50. If the result of subtracting the Target Weeks of Supply from the Weeks of Supply field is greater than 8, then the function will display .50 or 50% in the Suggested Markdown field. This will indicate that the price of an item should be reduced by 50%.

- Click the <<**falsepart**>> place holder, and then click the **Built in Functions** folder in the lower left window of the Expression Builder dialog box.

- Double-click the IIF function in the lower right window of the Expression Builder dialog box. This will add a new IIF function to the **falsepart** argument of the first **IIF** function.

Figure 4.29 shows the partial construction of the nested **IIF** function. Notice the formula in the logical test argument of the function. If the result of this formula is greater than 8 for an item in the record set of the query, then the value of .50 will be displayed in the Suggested Markdown field for that item.

Figure 4.29 | **Partial Construction of a Nested IIF Function**

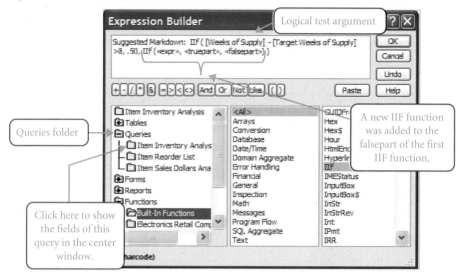

The following explains how the rest of the nested **IIF** function is completed:

- Click the <<**expr**>> placeholder in the second **IIF** function that was added to the **falsepart** argument of the first **IIF** function (see Figure 4.29).

- Click the **Item Inventory Analysis** query in the **Queries** folder of the Expression Builder dialog box (see Figure 4.29).

- Double-click the Weeks of Supply field, type a minus sign, and then double-click the Target Weeks of Supply field.

- Type a greater than sign, and then the number 5. This completes a second logical test which evaluates if the result of subtracting the Target Weeks of Supply field from the Weeks of Supply field is greater than 5.

- Click the <<**truepart**>> argument placeholder for the second **IIF** function and type the number .35. If the logical test is true, the function will display the number .35 or 35% in the Suggested Markdown field.

- Click the <<**falsepart**>> argument place holder of the second **IIF** function, and then click the **Built in Functions** folder.

- Double-click the **IIF** function in the lower right window of the **Expression Builder** dialog box. This will add a new **IIF** function to the falsepart argument of the second **IIF** function.

- Click the <<**expr**>> argument placeholder of the third **IIF** function.

- Click the **Item Inventory Analysis** query in the **Queries** folder in the **Expression Builder** dialog box.

- Double-click the Weeks of Supply field, type a minus sign, and then double-click the Target Weeks of Supply field.

- Type a greater than sign, and then the number 1. This completes the third and final logical test which evaluates if the result of subtracting the Target Weeks of Supply field from the Weeks of Supply field is greater than 1.

- Click the <<**truepart**>> argument placeholder and type the number .25. If this logical test is true, the function will display the number .25 or 25% in the Suggested Markdown field.

- Click the <<**falsepart**>> placeholder and type the number 0. If all three logical tests are false, then the difference between the target weeks of supply and the actual weeks of supply is less than one week. Therefore, the price will not be reduced.

Figure 4.30 shows the final nested **IIF** function in the **Expression Builder**. Notice that three **IIF** functions are used to create three different logical tests.

Figure 4.30 | **Completed Nested IIF Function**

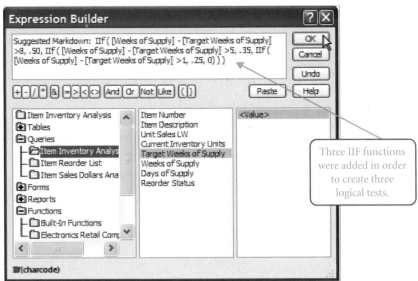

Three IIF functions were added in order to create three logical tests.

Figure 4.31 shows the results of the nested **IIF** function in the record set of the Item Inventory Analysis query. The Property Sheet window for the Suggested Markdown field was set to Percent, which is why the decimals that were entered into the **truepart** arguments of the **IIF** functions are being displayed as a percentage. Notice that the 80 GB Digital Player is showing 25% in the Suggested Markdown field. This is because the difference between the Weeks of Supply field (9.8) and the Target Weeks of Supply (8) is 1.8. If the difference between the Weeks of Supply field and the Target Weeks of Supply field is greater than 1, (but not greater than 5 or 8), a 25% markdown will be suggested.

Figure 4.31 | **Record Set of the Item Inventory Analysis Query with Suggested Markdown Field**

Item Number ▾	Item Description ▾	Unit Sales LW ▾	Current Inventory Unit: ▾	Target Weeks of Su ▾	Weeks of Supply ▾	Suggested Markdown ▾
10243	10 GB Digital Player	225	850	8	3.8	0.00%
10344	40 GB Digital Player	775	6,000	8	7.7	0.00%
10655	80 GB Digital Player	20	195	8	9.8	25.00%
22054	Game 4	150	3,500	8	23.3	50.00%
22333	Game 2	15	150	8	10.0	25.00%
22765	Game 3	550	2,100	8	3.8	0.00%
22888	Game 5	245	2,500	8	10.2	25.00%
22980	Game 1	380	3,000	8	7.9	0.00%
33245	System 2	85	550	8	6.5	0.00%
33989	System 1	450	3,200	8	7.1	0.00%
44332	Multi Disc DVD	54	500	8	9.3	25.00%
44339	DVD/VCR	525	2,250	8	4.3	0.00%
44556	DVD Player	10	105	8	10.5	25.00%
44922	VCR	40	1,360	8	33.8	50.00%

Results of the nested IIF function.

It is important to note that what makes the nested **IIF** function shown in Figure 4.30 work is the order in which the logical tests were entered into function. A nested **IIF** function will provide a result as soon as it finds a logical test that is true. Therefore, the order in which the logical tests are entered into the function can have a significant impact on the results that are produced. For example, if the first logical test and **truepart** output were defined as **Weeks of Supply** − **Target Weeks of Supply > 1, .25**, then the function would not be able to identify if the difference between the Weeks of

Supply field and Target Weeks of Supply field is greater than 5 or 8. If the difference between the Weeks of Supply and Target Weeks of Supply is greater than 8, then it is also greater than 1. As a result, the nested **IIF** function in Figure 4.29 was designed so the first logical test checks if the difference between the two fields is greater than 8, then 5, then 1. This allows the function to differentiate between varieties of results and assign values entered in the **truepart** argument accordingly.

As mentioned earlier in this chapter, one of the key benefits of creating formulas and functions in Access is that when data is changed in any of the fields used in a query, the outputs of the formulas and functions will automatically change. For example, the Target Weeks of Supply field was used in the logical tests of the nested **IIF** function shown in Figure 4.30. Suppose this electronics company wanted to mark down merchandise to increase the unit sales of each item based on a 4 weeks of supply target instead of 8? The number 8, which was typed after the colon of the Target Weeks of Supply field, can be changed to a 4 and the output of the Suggested Markdown field will automatically adjust to this new target.

Figure 4.32 shows the number changed in the Target Weeks of Supply field to 4. Figure 4.33 shows the record set of the Item Inventory Analysis query after this change is made. Notice that a 35% markdown is now suggested for some items in the Suggested Markdown field. This is a change from the record set shown in Figure 4.31where only 25% and 50% markdowns are suggested.

Figure 4.32 | **Changing the Target Weeks of Supply to 4**

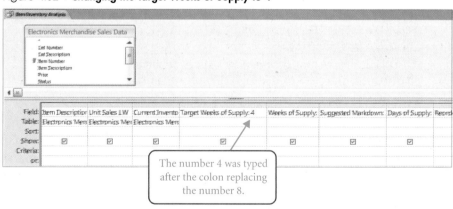

The number 4 was typed after the colon replacing the number 8.

Item Number	Item Description	Unit Sales LW	Current Inventory Units	Target Weeks of Su	Weeks of Supply	Suggested Markdown
10243	10 GB Digital Player	225	850	4	3.8	0.00%
10344	40 GB Digital Player	775	6,000	4	7.7	25.00%
10655	80 GB Digital Player	20	195	4	9.8	35.00%
22054	Game 4	150	3,500	4	23.3	50.00%
22333	Game 2	15	150	4	10.0	35.00%
22765	Game 3	550	2,100	4	3.8	0.00%
22888	Game 5	245	2,500	4	10.2	35.00%
22980	Game 1	380	3,000	4	7.9	25.00%
33245	System 2	85	550	4	6.5	25.00%
33989	System 1	450	3,200	4	7.1	25.00%
44332	Multi Disc DVD	54	500	4	9.3	35.00%
44339	DVD/VCR	525	2,250	4	4.3	0.00%
44556	DVD Player	10	105	4	10.5	35.00%
44922	VCR	40	1,350	4	33.8	50.00%

Results of the nested IIF function automatically change when a new value is entered for the Target Weeks of Supply field.

>> IIF Functions

VIDEO WORKSHOP

The purpose of this workshop is to demonstrate both the regular and nested IIF function. I will be demonstrating the tasks in this workshop in the **IIF Function** and **Nested IIF Function** videos. You will need to open the Access database named ib_a04_electronicsmerchandise, which was used for the first workshop in this chapter. You must complete the first workshop on Formulas before continuing with this workshop. Complete each of the tasks in this workshop, then watch the video.

1. **Basic IIF Function (IIF Function Video)**

   a. Open the Inventory Analysis query in **Design View**. This query was completed in the Formulas workshop in the first section of this chapter.

   b. Click the first row of the empty column next to the Days of Supply field.

   c. Type the field name **Reorder Indicator** followed by a colon.

   d. Open the **Expression Builder**.

   e. Double-click the **Functions** folder, and then click the Built in Functions folder.

   f. Double-click the **IIF** function in the lower right window of the **Expression Builder**.

   g. Click the **<<expr>>** placeholder for the logical argument in the **IIF** function.

   h. Double-click the Queries folder, and then click the Inventory Analysis folder.

   i. Double-click the Days of Supply field name, and type a less than sign.

   j. Type the number **60**.

   k. Click the **<<truepart>>** argument placeholder. Then, type the word **Reorder**.

   l. Click the **<<falsepart>>** argument placeholder. Then, type the word **OK**.

   m. Click the **<<Expr>>** symbol in front of the IIF function and press the **Delete** key on your keyboard.

   n. Click the **OK** button on the **Expression Builder**.

   o. Save and run the query.

   p. Switch the query back to **Design View.**

2. Nested IIF Function (Video: Nested IIF Function)

   a. Click the first row in the empty column next to the Reorder Indicator field and type the field name `Suggested Markdown` followed by a colon.

   b. Open the **Expression Builder**.

   c. Double-click the Functions folder, and then click the Built in Functions folder. Then, locate and double-click the **IIF** function.

   d. Click the **<<expr>>** logical test placeholder, and double-click the Queries folder. Then, click the Inventory Analysis folder.

   e. Double-click the Weeks of Supply field, type a minus sign, and then double-click the Target WOS field.

   f. Type the greater than sign (>) followed by the number **8**.

   g. Click the **<<truepart>>** placeholder and type the number **.50**.

   h. Click the **<<falsepart>>** placeholder and add a new **IIF** function.

   i. Click the **<<expr>>** argument placeholder for the **IIF** function that was added in h., and click the Inventory Analysis folder.

   j. Double-click the Weeks of Supply field, type a minus sign, and then double-click the Target WOS field.

   k. Type the greater than sign (>) followed by the number **5**.

   l. Click the **<<truepart>>** argument placeholder and type the number **.35**.

   m. Click the **<<falsepart>>** argument placeholder and add a new IIF function.

   n. Click the **<<expr>>** argument placeholder for the **IIF** function that was added in m., and click the Inventory Analysis folder.

   o. Double-click the Weeks of Supply field, type a minus sign, and then double-click the Target WOS field. Then, type a greater than sign followed by the number **1**.

   p. Click the **<<truepart>>** argument placeholder and type the number **.25**.

   q. Click the **<<falsepart>>** argument placeholder and type the number **0**.

   r. Click the **<<Expr>>** symbol in front of the IIF function and press the **Delete** key on your keyboard.

   s. Click the **OK** button on the **Expression Builder**.

   t. Press the **Enter** key on your keyboard, and then click in any row under the Suggested Markdown field.

   u. Open the Property Sheet window for the Suggested Markdown field and set the format to Percent. Then, close the Property Sheet window.

   v. Save and run the query.

   w. Convert the query back to **Design View** and change the value for the Target WOS field to **4**.

   x. Save and run the query.

   y. Close the query and then the database.

>> Developing a Promotion Strategy

Most business managers would agree that listening to and communicating with their customers is critical to running a successful business. Businesses execute several strategies in order to get feedback from potential or existing customers, including focus groups, surveys, or frequent shopper cards. A business will implement different strategies depending on the needs and type of business they operate. However, the fundamental goal of these programs is to obtain information from customers on a regular basis. This information is often stored in large database tables, which require tools such as Access to select and analyze data. The results of these analyses help businesses make decisions such as what promotions to send to a customer, what products to develop, or what products to drop.

Exercise

The purpose of this exercise is to use Access to evaluate the data contained in a table that might be used by a marketing manager. This exercise will utilize the **IIF** function to determine what types of promotions to send to various customers based on the data contained in the table. Open the Access database named ib_a04_marketingdata before completing the following tasks.

1. Open the query Customer Promotions in **Design View**.

2. The purpose of the first calculated field will be to identify new customers. New customers are identified if the Years Purchasing field contains a value of zero. Use the following details as a guide for creating this calculated field.

    a. The location of this calculated field should be in the empty column next to the Months Since Last Purchase field in the design grid of the Customer Promotions query.

    b. Type the field name **New Customer** followed by a colon.

    c. Enter an **IIF** function by defining each argument as follows:

        i. **expr (logical test):** If the value in the Years Purchasing field = 0

        ii. **truepart:** Enter the word "True".

        iii. **falsepart:** Enter the word "False".

3. Save and run the query. All new customers should be identified if the word True appears in the New Customer field. Marketing managers can use this information to send these customers discount offers or other promotions to encourage repeat business.

4. The next calculated field will be used to identify what promotions should go to each customer based on their level of spending last year. A nested **IIF** function will be required to create this calculated field. The information provided by this function can help marketing managers identify their most valuable customers and provide them with promotional offers that encourage their continued business. Use the following details as a guide for creating this calculated field.

    a. The location of this calculated field should be in the empty column next to the New Customer field in the design grid of the Customer Promotions query.

    b. Type the field name **Promotion Offer** followed by a colon.

    c. Enter a nested **IIF** function that produces the following outputs.

        i. If the value in the LY Spend field is greater than or equal to $1,000, then the output of the function should be **"50% off any selected item"**.

ii. Else, if the value in the LY Spend field is greater than or equal to $400, then the output of the function should be "**25% off any selected item**".

iii. If both conditions of the IIF function are false, the output of the function should be "**10% off your next purchase**".

5. Save and run the query. The Promotion Offer field should state which promotion should be sent to each customer based on their total spend for last year.

6. Make adjustments to the Customer Promotions query to show only the new customers that are identified by the New Customer field. Use the Save As command to save your adjustments under the query name New Customers. What promotional offer will these customers receive?

7. Without entering any criteria under the Promotion Offer field, make adjustments to the Customer Promotions query to show only customers that will receive a 50% Off discount on any selected item. How many customers will receive this promotion? Use the **Save As** command to save your adjustments under the name 50% Off Customers.

8. Without entering any criteria under the Promotion Offer field, make adjustments to the Customer Promotions query to show only customers that will receive a 25% Off discount on any selected item. How many customers will receive this promotion? Use the **Save As** command to save your adjustments under the name 25% Off Customers.

9. Close all queries and then close the database

PROBLEM & EXERCISE

>> What's Wrong with This Database?

Problem

You are the director of the planning division for a product manufacturing company. You have asked one of your analysts to evaluate the inventory levels for each raw material component required to manufacture your company's line of products. You ask him to calculate order quantities for each raw material component based on the following criteria:

- Do not order any item where the weeks of supply is greater than 12.

- Any item where the weeks of supply is less than or equal to 12 but greater than 10, submit an order for 2 weeks worth of units. This would be the units consumed last week multiplied by 2.

- Any item where the weeks of supply is less than or equal to 10 but greater than 6, submit an order for 3 weeks worth of units. This would be the units consumed last week multiplied by 3.

- Any item where the weeks of supply is less than or equal to 6 but greater than 3, submit an order for 4 weeks worth of units. This would be the units consumed last week multiplied by 4.

- For any item below 3 weeks of supply, submit an order for 6 weeks worth of units.

Exercise

The analyst in your division created a query and added a calculated field using a nested **IIF** function to determine how much quantity should be submitted for each raw material component. The Access database containing the query the analyst created is named ib_a04_rawmaterialinventory. The query the analyst created is called Component Order Quantities. Open and examine this query. Would you be comfortable using this data to submit orders to your suppliers? Consider the following.

1. Look at the values in the Order Quantity field and compare them to the weeks of supply listed for each component. Do the order quantities seem to be in line with the criteria listed above?

2. Look at the **IIF** function created for the Order Quantity field. Explain how this function is evaluating data and providing an output for the Order Quantity field.

What's wrong with this database? Write a short answer explaining why you would or would not use the data in the Component Order Quantities query. Then fix the calculated field to produce outputs based on the criteria listed at the beginning of this exercise.

>> Financial Functions Skill Set

Similar to Excel, Access contains a variety of financial functions. You can use these functions when making financial calculations such as the mortgage payment of house, the lease payments of car, or the future value of an investment. This section will address two financial functions that are commonly used in business. The first is the **Future Value** function which is used to calculate the growth of an investment given a constant interest rate. The second is the **Payment** function which used to calculate either mortgage payments or lease payments.

Future Value

Business managers use the **Future Value**, or **FV** function to evaluate the return on investments that provide a constant interest rate over a specific period of time. To better understand how this function is calculating the value of an investment, it is best to review an example relating to the time value of money.

The time value of money pertains to the growth of an investment over a certain period of time. The amount of growth depends on how much money is invested, and the interest or growth rate that is applied. For example, Figure 4.34 shows the growth of a hypothetical bank account over a three year period. This example assumes the bank is very generous and offers an interest rate of 10% on account balances. In reality, the interest that is usually offered for a traditional bank account is much less. The first row of the table, labeled Year 1, shows that an account is opened with a $500 deposit. Assuming the interest rate does not change, the value of the account after one year will be $550 as shown in the End Balance column. This is because $50 was paid in interest. The second row of the table, labeled Year 2, shows that another $500 is deposited into the account. Notice that the Interest Paid column increases from $50 in Year 1, to $105 in Year 2. As the account grows the amount of interest paid increases as illustrated in the Interest Paid column. At the end of the third year, the table shows that the value of the account grows to $1,820.50. This is the number the **Future Value** function would produce if it were used to calculate the value of this account over a three year period.

Figure 4.34 | Time Value of Money Example

	Begin Balance	Deposit	Interest Rate	Interest Paid	End Balance
Year 1	0	$500	10% x $500	$ 50	$550
Year 2	$550	$500	10% x $1,050	$105	$1,155
Year 3	$1,155	$500	10% x $1,655	$165.50	$1,820.50

The Future Value function calculates this result.

This next example demonstrates the **Future Value** function using the database table shown in Figure 4.35. This table is similar to what might be found in a data mart for a banking or finance company. This example assumes that a bank is offering its customers an opportunity to invest in an annuity that pays a 5.7% interest rate. An annuity allows customers to make investments over a set period time while earning a fixed or variable interest rate. For this example, we will assume that customers are making *annual_*investments into an annuity over a period of 3, 5 or 10 years. The bank will automatically deduct a specified sum of money from the customer's account at the end of each year and invest it into the annuity. The **Future Value** function will be used to calculate the value of each customer's investment at the end of the specified period. The following provides a brief definition for each of the fields in this table along with the index and primary key.

- **Index and Primary Key**: The table is indexed based on the values in the Account Number field. This field is also the primary key of the table.

- **Customer Name Field**: Contains the name of the customer.

- **Account Number Field**: Contains the customer's account number.

- **Annual Investment Field**: A dollar amount specified by the customer, which will be automatically deducted from the account and invested into the annuity. Investments are made at the end of each year.

- **Number of Years Investing Field**: Number of years specified by the customer for the investment period. The value of the annuity will be transferred to the customer's account at the conclusion of this time period.

- **Annual Interest Rate Field**: The interest earned by the annuity.

Figure 4.35 | Investment Table from a Hypothetical Bank

Annuity Investments

Customer Name	Account Number	Annual Investment	Number of Years Investing	Annual Interest Rate
Tom T.	801734	$420	10	5.75%
Bernice B.	807684	$6,400	5	5.75%
Ed D.	810859	$14,400	3	5.75%
Bill B.	819994	$9,000	10	5.75%
Gloria A.	834957	$3,900	5	5.75%
Hale C.	836939	$576	3	5.75%
Tyler T.	838954	$900	5	5.75%
Gary E.	841195	$1,620	3	5.75%
Mary J.	845082	$2,640	5	5.75%
Alice K.	853302	$6,540	10	5.75%
Anthony G.	881409	$3,900	3	5.75%
Sanntino H.	884700	$1,800	5	5.75%
Olivia I.	888020	$360	10	5.75%
Carlotta K.	892213	$300	10	5.75%
Robert F.	899934	$960	5	5.75%

This field shows the amount of money each customer will invest at the end of each year.

The **Future Value** function will be used to calculate the value of each customer's investment at the end of the specified time in the Number of Years Investing field in the Annuity Investment table (Figure 4.35). This will be done by adding a calculated field to the Select Query shown in Figure 4.36. As seen in the figure, all five fields from the Annuity Investments table are added to the design grid of the query.

Figure 4.36 | **Design of the Investment Value Select Query**

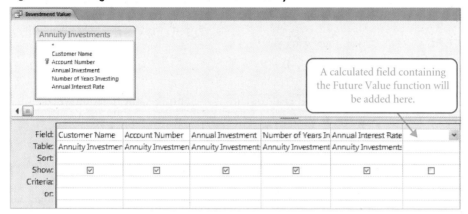

There are five arguments in the **Future Value** function. These arguments are almost identical to the arguments of the **Future Value** function that is used in Excel. The following lists and defines each argument of the function when it is used in Access:

- **rate**: The interest rate earned from an investment.
- **nper**: The number of periods money is invested into an account or the amount of time an investment is measured. This argument must correspond to the interest rate entered in the rate argument. For example, if an annual interest rate is entered in the rate argument, the **nper** must be the number of years. If a monthly interest rate is entered in the rate argument, the nper must be the number of months. If a daily interest rate is used in the rate argument, the **nper** must be the number of days.
- **pmt**: The amount of money or payments that are added to an investment. This argument is used if money is being invested periodically such as once a month, once a year, etc. The function will use the value in the nper argument to determine the number of payments that are added to an investment. All fields or values in this argument must be preceded by a negative sign.
- **pv**: Present Value. This argument is used when a one time investment is made to an account. It can be used with or without the pmt argument. Any fields or values entered for this argument must be preceded by a negative sign.
- **due**: This argument is used to define when money is invested into an account. Money is invested at the beginning or end of a period (i.e. end of the month or beginning of the month). If this argument is not defined, Access will assume the value is 0.
  - 1: Used for payments made at the beginning of a period (i.e., at the beginning of a month, year, etc.).
  - 0: Used for payments made at the end of a period.

COMMON MISTAKES | RATE, NPER, and PMT Arguments

Always check that the **rate, nper**, and **pmt** arguments of the **Future Value** function are expressed in equal terms. For example, investments might be made on a monthly basis, but the interest or return rate quoted by a bank or financial institution might be expressed on an annual basis. In this case, you would have to define the **rate** argument by dividing the annual interest rate by 12 if the number of months is used to define the **nper** argument and the monthly investment value is used to define the **pmt** argument. The key is to make sure the **rate, nper,** and **pmt** arguments are always defined using equivalent terms

As mentioned, a calculated field containing the **Future Value** function will be added to the Investment Value query shown in Figure 4.36. The following explains how this field is created using the **Expression Builder.**

- Click the first row of the empty column next to the Annual Interest Rate field (see Figure 4.36). Then, type the field name Value of Annuity followed by a colon.
- Open the **Expression Builder** by clicking the **Builder** icon in the **Design** tab of the Ribbon.
- Double-click the **Functions** folder, and then click the **Built in Functions** folder.
- Click the word **Financial** in lower center window of the **Expression Builder** dialog box. This will show a list of all financial functions in the lower right window of the Expression Builder dialog box as shown in Figure 4.37.
- Double-click **FV** in the lower right window of the **Expression Builder** dialog box. This will add the Future Value function to the upper window of the **Expression Builder.**

Figure 4.37 shows the Future Value function in the **Expression Builder** dialog box before defining each argument in the function. Notice that there are placeholders for each argument of the function.

Figure 4.37 | **Creating the FV Function in the Expression Builder**

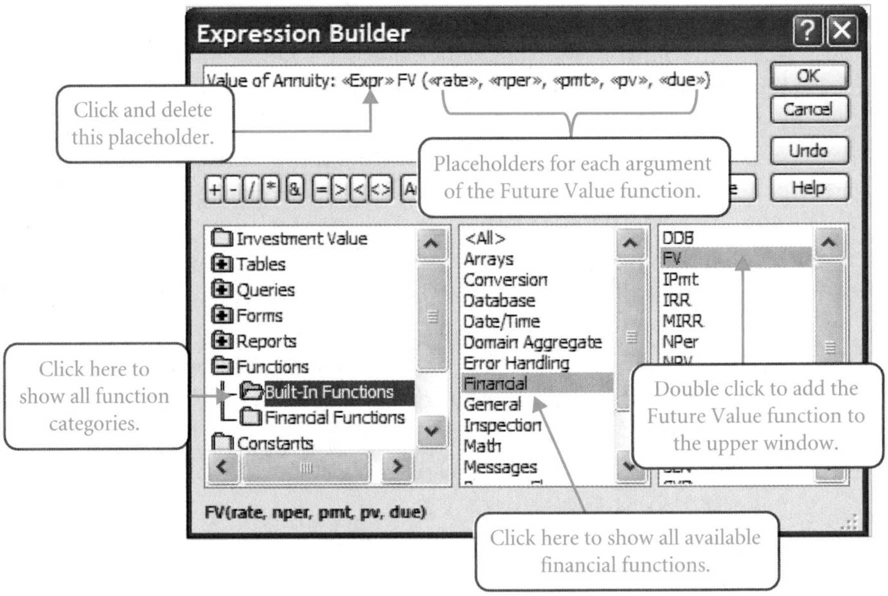

The following explains the completion of the Future Value function which was started in Figure 4.37.

- Click the <<**Expr**>> symbol that appears to the left of the **Future Value** function and press the **Delete** key.
- Click the <<**rate**>> argument placeholder.
- Double-click the **Tables** folder, and then click the **Annuity Investments** folder. This will show a list of fields for this table in the lower center window of the **Expression Builder** dialog box.
- Double-click the Annual Interest Rate field.
- Click the <<**nper**>> argument placeholder, and then double-click the Number of Years Investing field.
- Click the <<**pmt**>> argument placeholder and type a negative sign. Any values or fields added to this argument must be preceded by a negative sign. Then, double-click the Annual Investment field.
- Click the <<**pv**>> argument placeholder and press the **Delete** key. Then, click the <<**due**>> placeholder and press the **Delete** key. Since there are no lump sum investments being made at one time, there is no need to define the **pv** argument. Also, the **Future Value** function will assume that payments will be made at the end of a period if the **due** argument is not defined.
- Delete any commas and spaces that come after the **pmt** argument.
- Click the OK button in the **Expression Builder** dialog box.

Figure 4.38 shows the completed **Future Value** function in the **Expression Builder** dialog box. Notice that each argument of the function is defined using fields that contain data expressed in years. Once the **OK** button is clicked, the function will appear in the design grid of the Investment Value query (see Figure 4.36).

Figure 4.38 | **Completed Future Value Function in the Expression Builder**

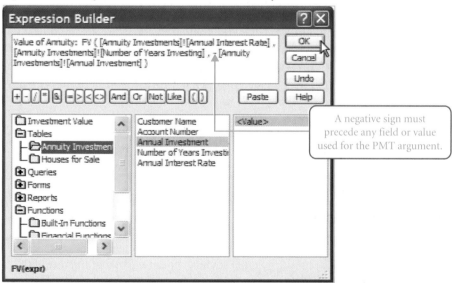

Figure 4.39 shows the record set of the Investment Value query. The Value of Annuity field shows the results of the Future Value function for each customer. For the first customer, Tom T., the result of the function shows that his annuity will grow to $5,471 by investing $420 every year for 10 years at an interest rate of 5.75%. In addition, since fields were used to define each argument of the function, when data within the field is changed, or data is added to the Investment Value table, the function will automatically produce a new output after running the query.

Figure 4.39 | **Record Set of the Investment Value Query**

Customer Name	Account Number	Annual Investment	Number of Years Investing	Annual Interest Rate	Value of Annuity
Tom T.	801734	$420	10	5.75%	$5,471
Bernice B.	807684	$5,400	5	5.75%	$30,289
Ed D.	810659	$14,400	3	5.75%	$45,732
Bill B.	819994	$9,000	10	5.75%	$117,244
Gloria A.	834957	$3,900	5	5.75%	$21,875
Hale C.	836939	$576	3	5.75%	$1,829
Tyler T.	838954	$900	5	5.75%	$5,048
Gary E.	841195	$1,620	3	5.75%	$5,145
Mary J.	845082	$2,640	5	5.75%	$14,808
Alice K.	853302	$6,540	10	5.75%	$85,197
Anthony G.	881409	$3,900	3	5.75%	$12,386
Sanntino H.	884700	$1,800	5	5.75%	$10,096
Olivia L.	888020	$360	10	5.75%	$4,690
Carlotta K.	892213	$300	10	5.75%	$3,908
Robert F.	899934	$960			$5,385

Calculated field showing the results of the Future Value function

Payment Function

A close relative of the **Future Value** function is the **Payment** or **Pmt** function. A common use of the payment function is to calculate the mortgage payments for a house or the lease payments of a car. The **Payment** function contains arguments that are similar to the **Future Value** function. These arguments are defined as follows:

- **rate:** The interest charged by the lender.
- **nper:** The number of payments, or, as in the **Future Value** function, a period of time (i.e., years, months, weeks, etc.)
- **pv:** Present Value; this is used to define the amount of money being borrowed or the principal of a loan. As in the Future Value function, *you must use a negative sign for any values or fields used to define this argument.*
- **fv:** Future Value; this is used when part of a loan is paid off with periodic payments, and the balance of the loan is paid off in one lump sum at a future point in time. This argument is especially helpful when evaluating the monthly lease payments of a car. When calculating the lease payments of a car, use this argument to enter the residual value, which is the value of the car at the end of the lease. *Do not add a negative sign in front of fields or values used for this field .*
- **due:** The value of this argument determines if payments are made at the beginning or end of period and can either be a 1 or 0. If this argument is not defined, Access will assume the value is 0.
  - 1: Used for payments made at the beginning of a period (i.e., at the beginning of a month, year, etc.)
  - 0: Used for payments made at the end of a period.

The **Payment** function will be used to calculate the mortgage payments of the homes listed in the table shown in Figure 4.40. The function will calculate the monthly payment a buyer might expect given the price of the house, the average down payment, the mortgage terms and interest rate. The actual mortgage payment a buyer will have to make upon purchasing the house could be different depending on the structure of the loan. For example, a buyer might choose to make more or less of a down payment compared to what is listed in this table. A change in the down payment could decrease or increase the buyer's actual mortgage payments. However, real estate agents often use this type of data to provide buyers with an estimate of what the mortgage payments might be so they can determine if the price of the house is within their financial budget.

>> **Quick Reference**

Future Value Function

1. Click in the first row of an empty column in the design grid of a query.

2. Type a name for the calculated field followed by a colon.

3. Click the **Builder** icon in the **Design** tab to open the **Expression Builder**.

4. Double-click the **Functions** folder.

5. Click the **Built in Functions** folder.

6. Click the **Financial** category in the lower center window.

7. Double-click the **FV** option in the lower right window.

8. Define each of the following arguments with numbers or field names:

   a. **rate:** Interest Rate
   b. **nper:** Number of Payments or Period of Time
   c. **pmt:** Amount of money invested or paid
   d. **pv:** Present Value
   e. **due:** When payments are made (1=begin year, 0=end of year)

9. Click the **OK** button.

Figure 4.40 | **Houses for Sale Table**

Listing	Price	Average Down Payment	Loan Amount	Term	Rate
House 1	$175,000	$35,000	$140,000	30	6.50%
House 10	$340,000	$68,000	$272,000	30	6.50%
House 11	$580,000	$116,000	$464,000	30	6.50%
House 12	$420,000	$84,000	$336,000	30	6.50%
House 13	$765,000	$153,000	$612,000	30	6.50%
House 14	$675,000	$135,000	$540,000	30	6.50%
House 15	$450,000	$90,000	$360,000	30	6.50%
House 2	$220,000	$44,000	$176,000	30	6.50%
House 3	$205,000	$41,000	$164,000	30	6.50%
House 4	$457,000	$91,400	$365,600	30	6.50%
House 5	$875,000	$175,000	$700,000	30	6.50%
House 6	$1,023,500	$204,700	$818,800	30	6.50%
House 7	$425,000	$85,000	$340,000	30	6.50%
House 8	$228,000	$45,600	$182,400	30	6.50%
House 9	$285,000	$57,000	$228,000	30	6.50%

> The Pmt function will use these three fields to calculate the estimated mortgage payments for each home.

The following is a list of key points and definitions regarding the Houses for Sale table shown in Figure 4.40.

- **Index and Primary Key:** The table is indexed based on the values in the Listing field. This field is also the primary key of the table.

- **Listing Field:** This field contains generic names for each house available for sale. If this were an actual real estate table, this field would contain the addresses for each house.

- **Price Field:** This field contains the price each owner is asking for their house.

- **Average Down Payment Field:** Contains an estimated down payment for each house, which is 20% of the value in the Price field. The actual mortgage payment could increase or decrease if a prospective buyer chooses to put more or less money down on the purchase of the home.

- **Loan Amount Field:** This field shows the amount of money a prospective buyer would borrow from a bank after subtracting the down payment from the price of the house. These values are also referred to as the loan principal.

- **Term Field:** Shows the amount of time in years a buyer would have to pay back a loan for the house. For the purposes of this table, it is assumed that all buyers will payback loans to the bank over 30 years. However, the actual monthly payments of mortgage could increase if the buyer chooses to pay back a loan over a shorter period of time.

- **Rate Field:** This field contains an estimated interested rate that might be charged by a bank for a loan. The actual monthly payments of a mortgage could increase or decrease depending on the actual interest rate charged by a bank. For the purposes of this table, 6.5% is used to provide prospective buyers with a monthly payment estimate.

This example uses the **Payment** function to calculate the estimated monthly mortgage payments for each of the homes listed in the Houses for Sale table (Figure 4.40). This will be done by adding a calculated field to the Select Query shown in Figure 4.41. Notice that all six fields from the Houses for Sale table are added to the design grid of the query.

Figure 4.41 | **Design of the Estimated Mortgage Payments Select Query**

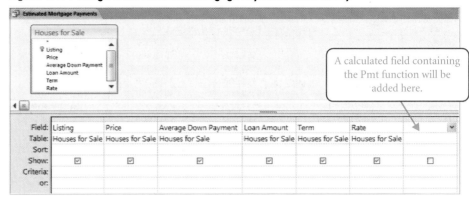

The following explains how the **Pmt** function is constructed in a calculated field that is added to the Estimated Mortgage Payments query:

- Click in the first row of the empty column next to the Rate field (see Figure 4.41). Then, type the field name Monthly Payments followed by a colon.
- Open the Expression Builder by clicking the **Builder** icon in the **Design** tab of the Ribbon.
- Double-click the **Functions** folder, and then click the **Built in Functions** folder.
- Click the word **Financial** in the lower center window of the **Expression Builder** dialog box to show a list of all financial functions in the lower right window.
- Double-click the **Pmt** function in the lower right window to add the **Payment** function to the upper window of the Expression Builder (see Figure 4.42).

Figure 4.42 shows the **Paymen**t function in the **Expression Builder** dialog box before defining each argument. Similar to the **Future Value** function, notice that there are placeholders for each argument of the function.

Figure 4.42 | **Creating the Pmt Function in the Expression Builder**

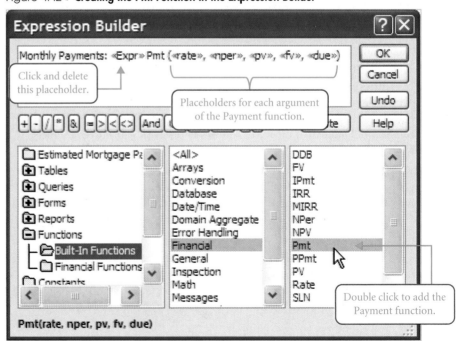

The following explains the remaining requirements for completing the **Payment** function:

- Click the <<**Expr**>> symbol to the left of the **Pmt** function and press the **Delete** key.
- Click the <<**rate**>> argument place holder.
- Double-click the **Tables** folder, and then click the *Houses for Sale* folder. This will show all fields in the Houses for Sale table in the lower center window of the **Expression Builder** dialog box.
- Double-click the Rate field. Then, type a slash followed by the number 12. The goal of this function is to calculate the *monthly* mortgage payments. However, the Rate field contains an annual interest rate. Therefore, this annual interest rate is converted to a monthly interest rate by dividing it by 12.
- Click the <<**nper**>> argument placeholder and double-click the Term the field. Then, click an asterisk followed by the number 12. Similar to the interest rate, the term, or amount of time to repay the loan, is in years. This must be converted to months as well in order to calculate a monthly payment for the loan. Therefore, the value in the Term field will be multiplied by 12 to convert it to the number of months.
- Click the <<**pv**>> argument placeholder and type a negative sign. Remember, any fields or values entered into this argument of the function must be preceded by a negative sign.
- Double-click the Loan Amount field. This will add the principal of the loan to the function.
- Delete all place holders and commas after the **pv** argument. This example will assume that no portion of the loan will be paid in a lump sum payment. Therefore, it is not necessary to define the **fv** argument. This example also assumes that the mortgage payments will be made at the end of the month. Access automatically assumes this if the **due** argument is not defined.
- Click the **OK** button in the **Expression Builder**.

Figure 4.43 shows the completed **Pmt** function in the **Expression Builder**. Notice that formulas were used in the **rate** and **nper** arguments to convert the interest rate and repayment period to months.

Figure 4.43 | Completed Payment Function in the Expression Builder

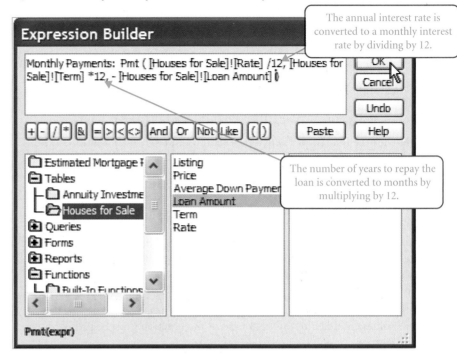

The annual interest rate is converted to a monthly interest rate by dividing by 12.

The number of years to repay the loan is converted to months by multiplying by 12.

Quick Reference

Payment Function

1. Click in the first row of an empty column in the design grid of a query.
2. Type a name for the calculated field followed by a colon.
3. Click the **Builder** icon in the **Design** tab of the Ribbon to open the **Expression Builder**.
4. Double-click the **Functions** folder.
5. Click the **Built in Functions** folder.
6. Click the **Financial** category in the lower center window.
7. Double-click the **Pmt** function in the lower right window.
8. Define each of the following arguments with numbers or field names:
   a. **rate** = Interest Rate
   b. **nper** = Number of Payments or Period of Time
   c. **pv** = Present Value
   d. **fv** = Future Value
   e. **due** = When payments are made (1=begin year, 0=end of year)
9. Click the **OK** button.

Figure 4.44 show the record set of the Estimated Mortgage Payments query that was started in Figure 4.41. The **Pmt** function is calculating the monthly mortgage payment for each house in the Monthly Payments field. It is important to remember that in order to calculate the monthly payment the annual interest rate had to be converted to a monthly interest rate by dividing by 12 and the years to repay the loan had to be converted to months by multiplying by 12.

Figure 4.44 | Record Set of the Estimated Mortgage Payments Query

Listing	Price	Average Down Payment	Loan Amount	Term	Rate	Monthly Payments
House 1	$175,000	$35,000	$140,000	30	6.50%	$885
House 10	$340,000	$68,000	$272,000	30	6.50%	$1,719
House 11	$580,000	$116,000	$464,000	30	6.50%	$2,933
House 12	$420,000	$84,000	$336,000	30	6.50%	$2,124
House 13	$765,000	$153,000	$612,000	30	6.50%	$3,868
House 14	$675,000	$135,000	$540,000	30	6.50%	$3,413
House 15	$450,000	$90,000	$360,000	30	6.50%	$2,275
House 2	$220,000	$44,000	$176,000	30	6.50%	$1,112
House 3	$205,000	$41,000	$164,000	30	6.50%	$1,037
House 4	$457,000	$91,400	$365,600	30	6.50%	$2,311
House 5	$875,000	$175,000	$700,000	30	6.50%	$4,424
House 6	$1,023,500	$204,700	$818,800	30	6.50%	$5,175
House 7	$425,000	$85,000	$340,000	30	6.50%	$2,149
House 8	$228,000	$45,600	$182,400	30	6.50%	$1,153
House 9	$285,000	$57,000	$228,000	30	6.50%	$1,441

Results of the Payment function

Help with Functions

This chapter demonstrated how the **Expression Builder** serves as a convenient tool for creating calculated fields in Access. However, the **Expression Builder** can also serve as an information resource if you have difficulty recreating the functions in this chapter or creating other functions available in Access. The following explains how additional information can be researched for any function in Access:

- Click the first row of any blank column in the design grid of a query and open the Expression Builder by clicking the **Builder** icon in the **Design** tab of the Ribbon.
- Double-click the **Functions** folder, and then click the **Built in Functions** folder.
- Click a function category or select <**All**> in the center lower window.
- Click any function in the lower right window which you are seeking information.
- Click the **Help** button on the right side of the **Expression Builder** as shown in Figure 4.45. This will open a window providing details regarding the use and setup of the function.

Figure 4.45 | **Using the Expression Builder to Research Functions**

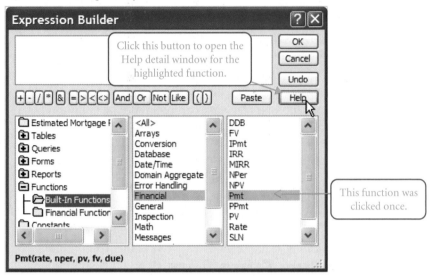

Figure 4.46 shows the help information window that opens after clicking the **Help** button shown in Figure 4.45. The help window in this Figure provides detailed information for the **Pmt** function. Other functions can be researched by clicking the function name one time and then clicking the **Help** button in the **Expression Builder** dialog box.

Figure 4.46 | **Help Details for the Pmt Function**

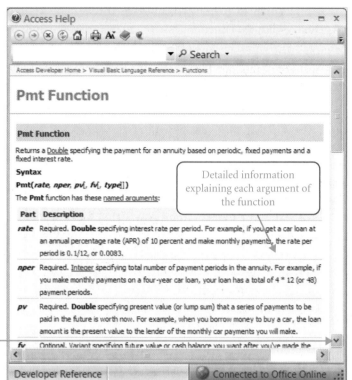

>> Future Value Function

The purpose of this workshop is to review the **Future Value** function. I will be demonstrating the tasks in this workshop on the video named **Future Value**. You will need to open the Access database named ib_a04_ financialdata. Completed each of the tasks first, and then watch the video.

1. **Create the Query (Video: Future Value)**
   a. Create a new Select Query and add the Annuity Data table.
   b. Add all fields in the Annuity Data table to the design grid of the query.
   c. Save the query and name it Investment Value.
   d. Click the first row in the empty column next to the Annual Interest Rate field. Then, type the field name **Investment Future Value** followed by a colon.

2. **Add the Future Value Function (Video: Future Value)**
   a. Open the **Expression Builder** by clicking the **Builder** icon in the **Design** tab of the Ribbon.
   b. Double-click the Functions folder, and then click the Built in Functions folder.
   c. Click the Financial category in the lower center window of the **Expression Builder**.
   d. Double-click the **FV** function in the lower right window of the **Expression Builder**.

e. Click the **<<rate>>** argument placeholder of the **FV** function in the upper window of the **Expression Builder**.

f. Double-click the Tables folder, and then click the Annuity Data folder.

g. Double-click the Annual Interest Rate field.

h. Click the **<<nper>>** argument placeholder of the FV function in the upper window of the Expression Builder, and then double-click the Number of Years Investing field.

i. Click the **<<pmt>>** argument placeholder of the FV function, and type a minus sign. Then, double-click the Annual Investment field.

j. Delete the **<<pv>>** and **<<due>>** argument placeholders along with any remaining commas.

k. Click the **<<Expr>>** symbol to the left of the **FV** function and press the **Delete** key.

l. Click the **OK** button on the **Expression Builder**, and then press the **Enter** key.

m. Open the **Property Sheet** window for the Investment Future Value field and set the format to Currency.

n. Save the query then run it.

o. Close the query and then the database.

>> Payment Function

The purpose of this workshop is to review the Payment function. I will be demonstrating the tasks in this workshop on the video named **Payment Function**. You will need to open the Access database named ib_a04_realestatedata. Completed each of the tasks first, and then watch the video.

1. **Create the Query (Video: Payment Function)**

   a. Create a new Select Query and add the add the Houses for Sale table.

   b. Add all fields in the Houses for Sale table to the design grid of the query.

   c. Save the query and name it Mortgage Estimates.

   d. Click the first row in the empty column next to the Rate field. Then, type the field name **Monthly Payments** followed by a colon.

2. **Add the Payment Function (Video: Payment Function)**

   a. Open the **Expression Builder** by clicking the **Builder** icon in the **Design** tab of the Ribbon.

   b. Double-click the Functions folder, and then click the Built in Functions folder.

   c. Click the Financial category in the lower center window of the **Expression Builder**.

   d. Double-click the **Pmt** function in the lower right window.

   e. Click the **<<rate>>** argument placeholder of the **Pmt** function in the upper window of the **Expression Builder**.

   f. Double-click the Tables folder, and then click the Houses for Sale folder.

   g. Double-click the Rate field. Then, type a slash followed by the number **12**.

h. Click the **<<nper>>** argument placeholder of the **Pmt** function in the upper window of the **Expression Builder**, and then double-click the Term field. Then, type an asterisk followed by the number **12**.

i. Click the **<<pv>>** argument placeholder in the **Pmt** function and type a minus sign. Then, double-click the Loan Amount field.

j. Delete the **<<fv>>** and **<<due>>** argument placeholders along with any remaining commas.

k. Click the **<<Expr>>** symbol to the left of the **Pmt** function and press the **Delete** key.

l. Click the **OK** button on the **Expression Builder**, and then press the **Enter** key.

m. Open the **Property Sheet** window for the Monthly Payment field and set the format to Currency.

n. Save the query and then run it.

o. Close the query and the database.

<table>
<tr><td>**EXERCISE**

Why Do I Need This?</td></tr>
</table>

>> Assessing the Value of Real Estate

Most financial advisors agree that investing in real estate is usually a good financial decision. However, people do not always attain the same amount of profit or return on their investment when they sell their property. Several factors influence how much money a person will make when property is sold such as location, interest rates, fees, and maintenance requirements. A real estate advisor can use a tool such as Access to help potential buyers determine the potential return for investing in certain properties.

Exercise

The purpose of this exercise is to use the financial functions covered in this section to evaluate the investment return potential of several properties available for sale. Open the Access database named ib_a04_realestateopportunities before completing the following tasks.

1. Open the query named Investment Potential in **Design View**.

2. The first calculated field that will be added to the Investment Potential query is the Future Property Value. The purpose of this field is to calculate the future value of each property in the Available Properties table. Use the following guidelines to create this calculated field.

   a. The location of this calculated field should be in the empty column next to the Estimated Annual. Increase in Property Value field in the design grid of the Investment Potential query.

   b. The field name should be **Estimated Property Value in 5 Years**.

   c. Create a Future Value function for this field defining each of the arguments as follows:

      i. **rate:** Use the Estimated Annual Increase in Property Value field to define this argument.

      ii. **nper:** The number 5 since the goal is to calculate the future value of the property in 5 years.

      iii. **pmt:** This argument will not be used. Therefore, define this argument with the number zero.

    iv. **pv:** Use the Price field to define this argument. Do not forget to use a negative sign.

    v. **due:** Define this argument with the number 1.

3. Save and then run the query. The Estimated Property Value in 5 Years should show how much each property will be worth in 5 years.

4. Format the values in the Estimated Property Value in 5 Years field to Currency format with 0 decimal places.

5. The purpose of the next calculated field is to estimate the annual mortgage payment for each property. This will require the use of the Payment function. Use the following guidelines:

    a. The location of this calculated field should be in the empty column next to the Estimated Property Value in 5 Years field in the design grid of the Investment Potential query.

    b. The field name should be **Annual Loan Payment**.

    c. Create a Pmt function for this field and define the arguments as follows:

        i. **rate:** Enter the number **.06**. This assumes that an investor would be able to get a loan from a bank to purchase the property at a 6 percent interest rate.

        ii. **nper:** Enter the number **30**. This assumes that a bank will issue a loan that must be repaid over 30 years.

        iii. **pv:** Enter a formula in this argument that multiplies the values in the Price field by .80. This assumes that an investor will be able to pay 20% of the price for each property in cash. The balance will be borrowed from the bank. Don't forget to add a negative sign for this argument.

        iv. **fv:** Delete this argument. This argument is not required because we are assuming no part of the loan will be paid in one lump sum.

        v. **due:** Delete this argument. We will assume payments for the loan will be made at the end of the year so this argument is not necessary. After deleting this argument, make sure there is no comma after the **pv** argument.

6. Save and then run the query. The Annual Loan Payment should be calculated for each property.

7. Format the values in the Annual Loan Payment field to Currency with 2 decimal places.

8. The purpose of the next calculated field is to *estimate* the amount of interest paid annually for the loan calculated in number 5. Calculating the interest cost in dollars is necessary for calculating the total investment return on the property. Use the following guidelines to create this calculated field.

    a. The location of this calculated field should be in the empty column next to the Annual Loan Payment field in the design grid of the Investment Potential query.

    b. The field name should be `Annual Interest Dollars`.

    c. To estimate the amount of interest paid each year on the loan, the loan amount, or principal, will be divided by 30. This value will then be subtracted from the Annual Loan Payment field. The Annual Loan Payment field contains the annual payment for both the principal and the interest charge. Therefore, by subtracting the principal of the loan divided by 30 we arrive at an estimate of how much interest is being paid each year. The formula is as follows: Annual Loan Payment $-$ ((Price $\times$.80)/30)

9. Save and then run the query.

10. Format the values in the Annual Interest Dollars field to Currency with 0 decimal places.

11. Create a calculated field called Investment Return that shows how much money can be potentially gained for each property in 5 years. You must first calculate the dollar value of the increase in property value by subtracting the Price field from the Estimated Property Value in 5 Years field. Then, you must subtract from this number the cost of owning the property. The cost of owning the property includes the Purchasing Fees, Estimated Annual Maintenance Costs, and the Annual Interest Dollars fields. These fields contain annual values, so you will need to multiply these values by 5 to calculate the costs that will be paid over 5 years.

12. If you had the money, which property would you purchase?

13. Save the query.

14. Close the query and the database.

PROBLEM & EXERCISE

>> What's Wrong with This Database?

PROBLEM

You are directing the real estate division of an investment firm. Your division is responsible for purchasing real estate that has the greatest potential for increasing in value. You have been asked by the president of the company to make a presentation discussing investments that could potentially yield big returns for the firm. As a result, you ask one of the analysts on your staff to help analyze available properties for sale contained in a database table. The results of this analysis will be used to develop your presentation to the president of the company. You ask the analyst to do the following:

- Calculate the future value of each property 3 years from today. The quarterly growth field shows how much the value of the property will increase each quarter of the year.

- Calculate the annual loan payments for each property. Assume the company will pay for 35% of the property in cash. The remaining cost of the property will be borrowed from a bank. Assume the company can negotiate a rate of 4.25% with the bank and that the loan will be paid off over 15 years.

Exercise

The database the analyst was using is named ib_a04_reinvestments. The completed analysis you requested is in the query named Real Estate Value. Would you be comfortable using the data in the record set of this query to develop a presentation to the president of the company? Consider the following points.

1. Look at the values in the Property Value in 3 Years field. Do these numbers appear to make sense? If a value of 1% is in the Quarterly Growth field, it indicates that a property will increase its value by 1% every quarter or 4% per year. Do the values in Quarterly Growth field seem to align with the values in the Property Value in 3 Years field?

2. Look at the function that was entered for the Annual Loan Payment calculated field. Based on how the arguments for this function were defined, explain how this function will calculate an output. Is this intended output for this analysis?

What's wrong with this database? Write a short answer for each of the points listed above. Then, fix any errors in the Real Estate value query.

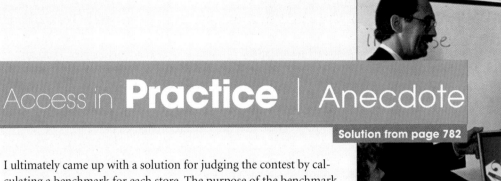

Solution from page 782

I ultimately came up with a solution for judging the contest by calculating a benchmark for each store. The purpose of the benchmark was to calculate the percent to total each store contributed to the total category sales of the company last year. For example, the item sold in the contest was part of category 85. Last year if the company sold 10,000 units in this category, and a store sold 1,000 units, then that store was given a benchmark of 10%. I then calculated the percent to total for the item sold in the contest by store. The store that had the highest increase when comparing the percent to total sales for the item versus their benchmark would win the contest.

Assignment

1. Open the Access database named ib_a04_contestdata. The database contains one table labeled Item Sales by Store by Week. The primary key of the table is comprised of the Week, Category, Item Number, and Store Number fields. The primary key relates to the Item Sales and Total Category Sales LY fields. The table contains 4 weeks of sales data for item 322455 and sales data from last year for category 20. All data values are in units.

2. Your assignment is to recreate the analysis described in the anecdote to determine which store should win the contest of selling item 322455. To do this, you will need to calculate a benchmark for each store. The benchmark should be the percent of sales each store contributed to last year's total sales for category 20. You will need to divide the total category sales for each store last year by the total company sales for category 20 last year.

3. You will then need to calculate a percent to total for the sales of item 322455. Each store's total sales for this item should be divided by the total sales of the company. The store that has the largest percent to total *increase* over the benchmark will win the contest. This is calculated by subtracting the benchmark from the item percent to total.

4. Assume that the contest runs for *all 4 weeks* of data contained in the Item Sales by Store by Week table (Hint: you will need to use nested queries for this assignment and your first query must sum and group all 4 weeks of data first).

Questions for Discussion

1. The author explains that in order to judge the results of the contest fairly a benchmark had to be created for each for each store. Why is this a better way to judge the performance of a store instead of total sales?

2. The author states that he added several calculated fields to the Access query to complete this project. Would it be easier to export the data to Excel and then do the calculations in a spreadsheet?

The following questions are related to the concepts addressed in this chapter. There are three types of questions: Short Answer, True or False, and Fill in the Blank. If your answer to a True or False question is False, write a short explanation as to why you think the statement is not true.

1. A _____ field contains the result of a formula or function.

2. True or False: Access will show an invalid syntax error if you forget to add a semi colon after the name of a calculated field.

3. Explain why it is necessary to include the table name when identifying fields in formulas or functions.

4. The following formula is from an Access query:

   [Sales Data]![Sales Dollars] / [Sales Data]![Unit Sales]

   What is the name of the table where these fields came from?

5. In the following Access formula, explain what mathematical operation will be executed first?

   [Sales Data]![Beginning Sales]/[Sales Data]![Ending Sales]^.33

6. Explain one of the benefits of using the **Zoom** window?

7. Upon running a query, Access will ask the user to input a parameter value if a table or field name is _____ incorrectly.

8. True or False: Spelling mistakes can be eliminated by using the Zoom window.

9. True or False: In Access, the three arguments of the **IF** function are the **Logical Test**, **Value if True**, and **Value if False**.

10. In order to add additional logical tests and possible outputs to an **IIF** function, a second **IIF** function can be added to the _____ argument.

11. What will be the output of the following **IIF** function if the value in the WOS field is 27?

    IIF([Data]![WOS]<6,"Reorder",IIF([Data]![WOS]>6,"Hold",IIF([Data]![WOS]
       >20,"Discontinue",IIF([Data]![WOS]>26,"Return","OK"))))

12. Based on the **IIF** function in number 11, what will be the output of the function if the value in the WOS field is 6.5?

13. True or False: You can not use an **IIF** function to assess the values in a calculated field and produce an output.

14. True or False: You can not add criteria to a calculated field if it utilizes another calculated field in the same query to produce a result.

15. The _____ function can be used to calculate the monthly payments of home mortgage or automobile lease.

16. Explain why you would use the **PV** argument of the **Future Value** function.

17. At the end of every month for 10 years you invest $200 into an annuity that generates a 12% annual return. What number would be entered into the Rate argument of the **Future Value** function in order to calculate the value of your investment in 10 years?

18. True or False: If you are buying a home that costs $200,000 and are paying 10% in cash, then the number 20000 must be entered into the FV argument of the Payment function in order to calculate your monthly payments.

19. If you are investing $2,750 into an annuity at the beginning of every year for 5 years that produces a 6.8% return on your investment, what do you need to enter into the Due argument?

20. True or False: The **Expression Builder** can provide you with detailed information on every function that is available in Access.

The following exam is designed to test your ability to recognize and execute the Access skills presented in this chapter. Read each question carefully and answer the questions in the order they are listed. You should be able to complete this exam in 60 minutes or less.

1. Open the Access database named ib_a04_skillsexam.

2. Open the Item Sales Analysis query in **Design View**.

3. Add a calculated field to the design grid of the Item Sales Analysis query that calculates the unit sales year to date. The formula for this calculated field should subtract the Current Inventory Units field from the Units Purchased field. Name this calculated field Unit Sales YTD.

4. Format the values in the Unit Sales YTD field to a Standard number. Then, save the query.

5. Add a calculated field to the design grid of the Item Sales Analysis query that calculates the percent of merchandise sold. The formula for this calculated field should divide the Units Purchased field into the Unit Sales YTD field. Name this calculated field Percent of Units Sold.

6. Format the values in the Percent of Units Sold field to a Percentage. Then, save the query.

7. Add a calculated field to the design grid of the Item Sales Analysis query that calculates the percent variance to plan. Use the following formula for this calculated field: (Actual Unit Sales This Month - Plan Unit Sales This Month) ÷ Plan Unit Sales This Month. Name this calculated field Percent Chg to Plan.

8. Format the values in the Percent Chg to Plan field to a Percentage format. Then, save the query.

9. Add a calculated field to the design grid of the Item Sales Analysis query that identifies items where the actual unit sales are below the plan unit sales. An IFF function should be used for this calculated field. If the Actual Unit Sales This Month is less than the Plan Unit Sales This Month, then the words Below Plan should be displayed in this calculated field. Otherwise, the word OK should be displayed in this calculated field. Name this calculated field Below Plan Indicator.

10. Add a calculated field to the design grid of the Item Sales Analysis query that calculates the dollar variance of the plan versus actual unit sales. Use the following formula for this calculated field: (Actual Unit Sales This Month - Plan Unit Sales This Month) * New Price. Name this calculated field Dollar Chg to Plan.

11. Format the values in the Dollar Chg to Plan field to Currency.

12. Save and then run the Item Sales Analysis query.

13. Close the Item Sales Analysis query and open the Property Investment query in Design View.

14. Add a custom field to the design grid of the Property Investment query that displays the number 150000. The name of this field should be Investment Growth Target.

15. Add a calculated field to the design grid of the Property Investment query that calculates the future value of each property in *3 years*. Use the **Future Value** function to calculate the output for this field. Use the Annual Change in Value field for the Rate argument, use the Price field for the **PV** argument, and assume that the investment is made at the beginning of the year. The name of this field should be Property Value in 3 Years.

16. Format the values in the Property Value in 3 Years field to Currency. Then, save the query.

17. Add a calculated field to the design grid of the Property Investment query that calculates the potential investment gains. The formula for this calculated field should

subtract the Price field from the Property Value in 3 Years field. The name of this field should be Investment Gains.

18. Format the values in the Investment Gains field to Currency. Then, save the query.

19. Add a calculated field to the design grid of the Property Investment query that identifies Investment Gains that meet or exceed the Investment Growth Target. Use the **IIF** function to determine the output for this field. If the value in the Investment Gains field is greater than or equal to the Investment Growth Target field then this field should display the words: Meets or Exceeds Target. Otherwise, this field should display the words: Below Target. The name of this field should be Investment Potential.

20. Add a calculated field to the design grid of the Property Investment query that calculates the *monthly* loan payments for each property. Use the Payment function to calculate the output for this field. The annual interest rate is 6.75%, the loan will be repaid over a 20 year period, the principal of the loan will be 75% of the value in the Price field, and payments will be made at the end of each month. The name of this field should be Monthly Loan Payment.

21. Format the values in the Monthly Loan Payment field to Currency. Then, save the query.

22. Run the Property Investment query.

23. Close the Property Investment query and then the database.

The following questions are designed to test your ability to apply the Access skills you have learned to complete a business objective. Use your knowledge of Access as well as your creativity to answer these questions. For most questions, there are several possible ways to complete the objective.

1. Open the ib_a04_challengea database. Add a field to the Inventory Status query that shows a different Target Weeks of Supply for each item based on the category. For category 10 the target should be 8, for category 20 the target should be 6, for category 30 the target should be 5, and for category 40 the target should be 7. Then, create a field showing the difference between the target weeks of supply and the actual weeks of supply. The actual weeks of supply is the current unit sales divided into the current unit inventory.

2. Using the ib_a04_challengea database and the fields that were added to the Inventory Status query in question 1, create a list of items that should be marked down. If an item does not need to be marked down, it should not appear in the record set of the query. An item should be marked down if the actual weeks of supply is greater than the target weeks of supply by more than two weeks.

3. Open the ib_a04_challengeb database. Add a calculated field to the Investment Value query that determines the value of each customer's investment in 10 years. Customers are making monthly payments into an investment fund which provides a fixed annual return of 5.25%. The Monthly Investment field shows how much money each customer invests at the end of each month. The Initial Investment field shows any lump sum payments that the customer invested along with the first monthly investment.

4. Open the ib_a04_challengec database. Create a query that identifies the car with the lowest lease payments. Assume the lease runs for 4 years with an annual interest rate of 4.9%. Customers will be required to make lease payments at the end of each month.

5. Using the query that was created in number 4, show the difference in monthly payments if a customer wanted to buy the car and pay off a loan over 4 years instead of leasing the car for 4 years. Assume the interest rate to buy the car is the same as leasing and that loan payments are due at the end of the month. Calculate the difference between the two monthly payments.

Chapter 5

Reports

Chapter Goals

After creating queries and adding calculated fields to analyze data from a database table, you may need to construct a report. Reports are used to organize and present data from either a table or query. In some cases, you may be able to format and print the record set of a query. However, most business reports require some type of organization and formatting depending on the content and audience. Access reports provide considerable flexibility to arrange, format, group, and calculate data. These techniques are most valuable when designing reports based on specific business objectives. Business managers usually require specific data needs to make decisions within their area of responsibility. Access provides the ability to design multiple report variations using the same data source. This chapter will illustrate how to construct reports so that you have the most flexibility and options for arranging and formatting data. The first section of this chapter will focus on the fundamental skills for creating a basic Access report. The second section illustrates advanced techniques for organizing and reporting data in groups, adding calculations, and using special formats.

>> **Access** Skill Sets

My Role as a Retail Store Analyst

Performance reports have always played a critical role in all my business experiences. These reports communicate the performance of business to all levels of management and serve as the basis for deciding when and how to take action. However, their complexity became clear to me when I worked as a retail store analyst in the regional headquarters of a large retail corporation. The headquarters managed the operations of approximately 100 retail stores that generated $1 billion in annual sales. The stores in our region were divided into several districts, and each district was assigned to a district manager who was responsible for evaluating the performance of all the stores in the territory and working with the store managers to help improve sales and profit. The district managers would frequently ask me to develop various reports to monitor the weekly performance of their stores. The challenge was that each manager needed to focus on different business components. With 12 district managers in the region, I found myself creating many different reports. The person who held the position previously had typed the data into an Excel spreadsheet and then manually created the 12 weekly performance reports. Besides being very time-consuming, with so much data entry, the risk of errors was very high.

≫ **Continued on page 897**

Reports are Access objects that are created using the data contained or produced in tables and queries. This section will demonstrate the construction of a basic Access report using the record set of a query. You may also create reports using the records contained in a table. However, tables that are typically found in most medium–to-large companies might contain millions of records. As a result, business mangers will first create a query to select only the records that are needed from a table. Then, a report is created from the data produced in the record set of the query.

Creating a New Report

Figure 5.1 shows an example of a basic Access report that was created using the record set of a query. The data used to create this report is very similar to what business managers might use in an electronics retail company. The purpose of the report is to list all active items sold by the company and the current retail price of each item. A store manager can use this report to help customers identify products and their prices.

Figure 5.1 | **Active Item Price Report**

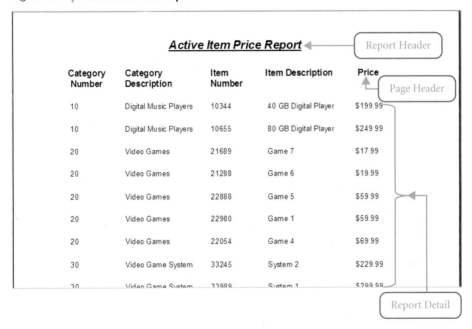

The **Reports** group in the **Create** tab of the Ribbon contains the commands for creating a new Access Report, as shown in Figure 5.2. Notice that there are options for automatically creating a simple report or creating a report using the **Report Wizard**. This chapter will illustrate the use of the *Report Design* option, which is used for creating Access reports from scratch. Reports created using the **Report** icon option or the **Report Wizard** icon usually require some adjustments after they are created. As a result, learning the **Report Design** option will provide you with the skills necessary to adjust reports created from the **Report** or **Report Wizard** options as well as creating reports from scratch. The following illustrates how the Active Item Price Report in Figure 5.1 is initially created.

- Click the **Create** tab in the Ribbon.
- Click the **Report Design** icon (see Figure 5.2). This will open a blank report in **Design View** (see Figure 5.3). In addition, three new tabs will be added to the

Ribbon under the **Report Design Tools** heading. These tabs contain commands that are used for building a report.

- Click the **Property Sheet** icon in the **Design** tab of the Ribbon. This will open the **Property Sheet** window on the right side of your screen.
- Click the **Data** tab in the **Property Sheet** window. Then click in the box next to the **Record Source** heading (see Figure 5.3). Click the down arrow on the right side of the box next to the Record Source heading and select a table or query that will be used to supply fields of data for the report. The list will show any tables and queries that have been created or linked into your database. For this example, fields from the Active Items and Price query will be used to create the report.
- After selecting a query or table in the **Property Sheet** window, close it by clicking the X in the upper-right corner of the window (see Figure 5.3).
- Click the **Add Existing Fields** icon in the **Design** tab of the Ribbon. This will open the **Field List** window on the right side of your screen (see Figure 5.4). The fields listed in this window will be from the query or table that is selected in the **Data** tab of the **Property Sheet** window.

Figure 5.2 | **Reports Group in the Create Tab of the Ribbon**

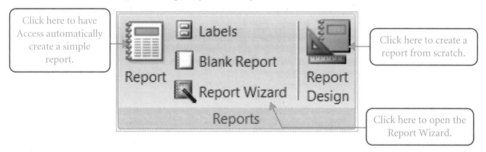

Figure 5.3 shows the appearance of a blank Access report in **Design View**. Notice the **Property Sheet** window on the right side of the screen. This was opened by clicking the **Property Sheet** icon which is in the **Design** tab of the Ribbon. In this Figure, the **Data** tab at the top of the **Property Sheet** window is activated. The box next to the **Record Source** heading shows that the Active Items and Price query will be used to supply data for the report.

Figure 5.3 | **Blank Report with Property Sheet Window Open**

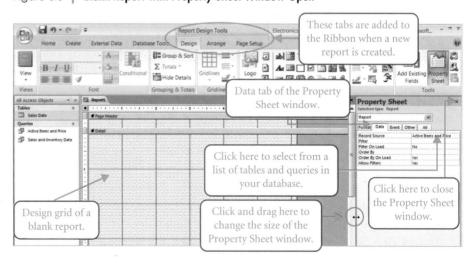

Figure 5.4 shows the **Field List** window opened next to the blank report that was shown in Figure 5.3. After selecting the Active Items and Price query in the Record Source box of the **Data** tab, the **Property Sheet** window was closed by clicking the X in the upper-right corner of the window. The **Field List** window was opened by clicking the **Add Existing Fields** icon in the **Design** tab of the Ribbon. The **Field List**, **Design Grid**, and **Controls** icons are the primary tools used to create an Access report. The following is a brief description for each of these tools.

- **Design Grid**: The design grid is used to place data and descriptive labels in specific locations on a report. There are solid vertical and horizontal lines spaced one-inch apart, which are used to help coordinate the alignment of headings and data in the report. The design grid is also broken down into sections that enable you to place labels and data in the body or headings of the report. More details are provided on each section of the design grid in later segments of this section.

- **Field List**: The Field List shows a list of fields that are available in the table or query that was selected in the **Data** tab of the **Property Sheet** window. The fields can be dragged and placed onto the design grid of the report. Any data that is contained in a field will appear in the report. In addition, when data is updated or changed in the table or query, the fields used in the design grid will automatically reflect the new data in the report.

- **Controls Group**: The **Controls** group of icons in the **Design** tab of the Ribbon contains a set of commands used for adding various features, data, and labels to the design grid of a report. The two most commonly used icons are the **Label** and **Text Box** icons, as shown in Figure 5.5. The **Labels** icon is used for adding descriptive information about the data contained in the fields that are added to the report. In business reports, this feature is typically used to create the column headings of a columnar report. The **Text Box** icon is used for displaying data or calculations on a report. A **Text Box** is usually connected to a field from a query or table, but you can also use them to produce calculated results in a report. Adding calculated results to a report is covered in the next section of this chapter.

Figure 5.4 | **Blank Report with Field List Window Open**

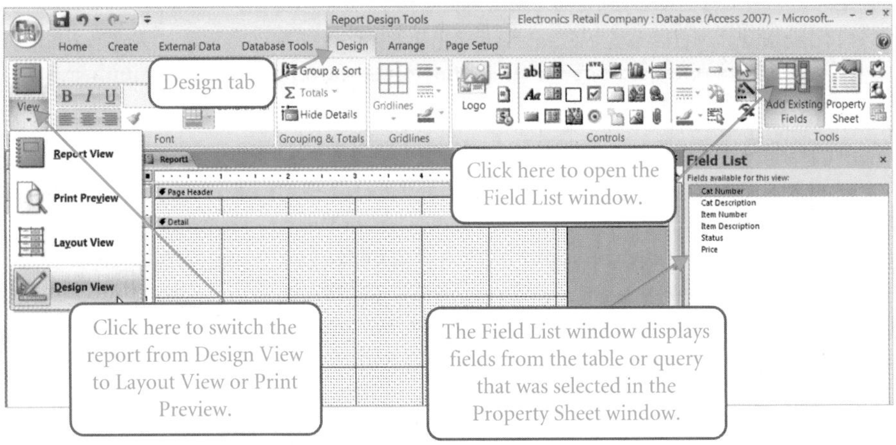

Figure 5.5 | **Controls Group of Icons**

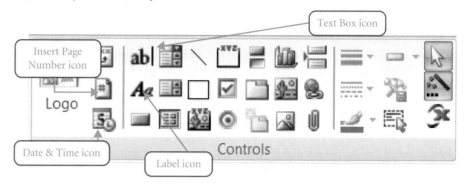

Setting the Dimensions of a Report

After creating a new Access report, you may need to adjust the margin settings. It is good practice to set the margins of the report and the width of the design grid before building a report. As previously mentioned, the purpose of the design grid is to show you the exact dimensions of where items will appear on a report. Therefore, it is important to set the width of the design grid first before adding text boxes and labels.

The left, right, top, and bottom margins of a report will usually be set to .25 inches. However, you can adjust these settings in the **Page Setup** tab of the Ribbon. The following explains how to open the **Page Setup** dialog box and adjust the margins for a new report.

- Create a new report or open an existing one in **Design View**.
- Click the **Page Setup** tab in the Ribbon.
- Click the **Page Setup** icon on the right side of the **Page Layout** group (see Figure 5.6). This will open the **Page Setup** dialog box.
- Click the **Print Options** tab at the top of the **Page Setup** dialog box (see Figure 5.7). Then, click in the box next to the area of the report where you want to change the margin. For example, if you want to change the top margin of the report, click in the box next to the word *Top*.
- Type a number that represents the number of inches for the margin. For example, if you want a one-half inch margin at the top of the report, type the number **.5** in the box next to the word *Top*.
- Click the **OK** button after entering the desired margin settings.

Figure 5.6 shows the icons available in the **Page Setup** tab of the Ribbon. The **Page Setup** tab appears only if a report is opened in **Design View** or **Layout View**. Notice that this tab provides other options for adjusting the layout of a report when it is printed on paper, such as adjusting the paper size and orientation of the report. For the Active Item Price report shown in Figure 5.1, the orientation is set to **Portrait** and the paper size is set to 8.5 × 11 inches.

>> *Quick Reference*

Creating a New Report

1. Click the **Report Design** icon in the **Create** tab of the Ribbon.

2. Click the **Property Sheet** icon in the **Design** tab of the Ribbon.

3. Click the **Data** tab at the top of the **Property Sheet** window.

4. Click the box next to the **Record Source** heading in the **Property Sheet** window.

5. Click the down arrow in the box next to the **Record Source** heading and select a query or table from the list.

6. Close the **Property Sheet** window by clicking the X in the upper-right corner of the window.

7. Click the **Add Existing Fields** icon in the **Design** tab of the Ribbon to open the **Field List** window.

Figure 5.6 | **Page Setup Tab of the Ribbon**

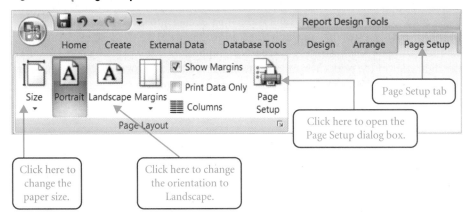

Figure 5.7 shows the **Page Setup** dialog box. Notice that the margins for the Active Item Price Report (Figure 5.1) are set to 1 inch for the Top, Bottom, Left, and Right sides. The **Page Setup** dialog box can also be used to adjust the paper size and orientation of a report by clicking the **Page** tab.

Figure 5.7 | **Page Setup Dialog Box**

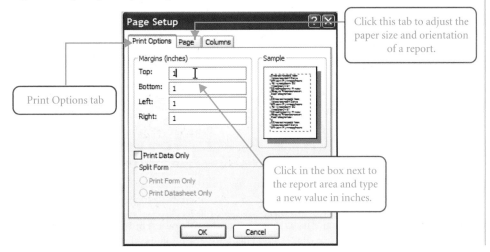

It is important to note that the paper dimensions of the Active Item Price Report are set to 8.5 × 11 inches. Therefore, because the margins are set to 1 inch on all sides, the available space in width that can be used to add data and labels is 6.5 inches (8.5−2 = 6.5). As a result, you will need to adjust the width of the design grid to 6.5 inches. Figure 5.8 illustrates how this is accomplished. After placing the cursor at the right edge of the grid, click and drag to the desired width when the cursor changes to a double arrow. Once the margins and size of the design grid are adjusted, you can begin adding data and labels to the report.

Figure 5.8 | **Adjusting the Width of the Design Grid**

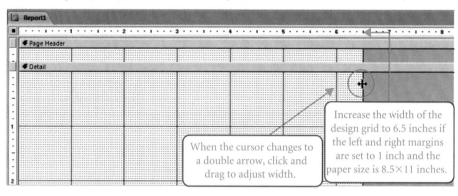

When the cursor changes to a double arrow, click and drag to adjust width.

Increase the width of the design grid to 6.5 inches if the left and right margins are set to 1 inch and the paper size is 8.5×11 inches.

COMMON MISTAKES | Setting the Width of the Design Grid

Remember to adjust the width of the design grid of a report based on the paper size and margin settings. For example, if you are using 8.5 × 11 inch paper and set one-half inch margins on both the right and left side of the report, the width of the design grid must be set to 7.5 inches.

Report Header

The Report Header is usually used for creating the title of a report. Any descriptive label or data that is added to the Report Header section will be shown at the top of the *first page* of a report when it is printed. Note that when a new report is created, the Report Header section will *not* be visible in the design grid (see Figure 5.8). Therefore, you must add the Report Header section by clicking the **Report Header/Footer** icon, which is found in the **Arrange** tab of the Ribbon, as shown in Figure 5.9.

>> *Quick Reference*

Report Margins and Orientation

1. Create a new report or open an existing report in **Design View**.
2. Click the **Page Setup** tab in the Ribbon.
3. Use the icons or open the **Page Setup** dialog box by clicking the **Page Setup** icon.
4. Click the **OK** button if making any adjustments in the **Page Setup** dialog box.

>> *Quick Reference*

Adjusting the Width of the Report Design Grid

1. Open a new or existing report in **Design View**.
2. Place the cursor at the right edge of the design grid.
3. When the cursor changes to a double arrow, click and drag to desired width.

Figure 5.9 | **Adding the Report Header and Footer**

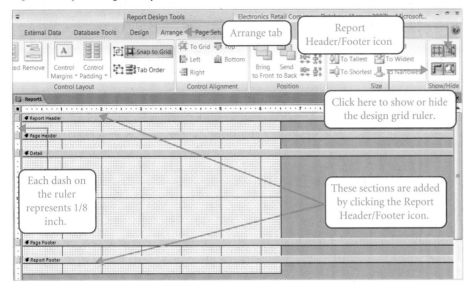

After adding the Report Header to the design grid of a report, you may need to adjust the height of the section. For example, Figure 5.9 shows that the height of the Report Header section is 1/4 inch. This is easy to see because two dashes appear on the left side ruler (each dash is 1/8 inch). The Active Item Price Report will require the height of the Report Header section to be increased to 1/2 inch. Figure 5.10 illustrates how this is accomplished. Place the cursor at the top edge of the Page Header section, and then click and drag down when the cursor changes to a double arrow.

Figure 5.10 | **Increasing the Height of a Section**

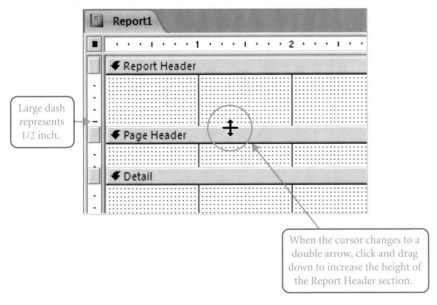

>> **Quick Reference**

Adding a Report Header and Footer

1. Create a new report or open an existing report in **Design View**.
2. Click the **Arrange** tab in the Ribbon.
3. Click the **Report Header/Footer** icon in the Show/Hide group.

Once the **Report Header** section is added to the design grid and the height is adjusted, a title can be added. Titles, descriptions, or column headings are added to a report using the **Label** icon (see Figure 5.5). The following explains how the title is created for the Active Item Price Report.

- Click the **Design** tab of the Ribbon.
- Click the **Label** icon.
- Click and drag the shape and dimensions of a square that will contain the title of the report in the Report Header section of the design grid (see Figure 5.11). After you release the left mouse button, a white box will appear in the Report Header section.
- Type the title of the report. Once the label box is created, a blinking cursor will appear at the far left side. This indicates the label box is open for typing or editing text (see Figure 5.12).
- Press the **Enter** key.

Figure 5.11 illustrates how to add a label box to the Report Header section of a report. Notice that the width and height dimensions of the label box are highlighted in the design grid ruler. This is helpful for managing the space that will be used for the title of the report.

Figure 5.11 | **Adding a Label Box to the Design Grid**

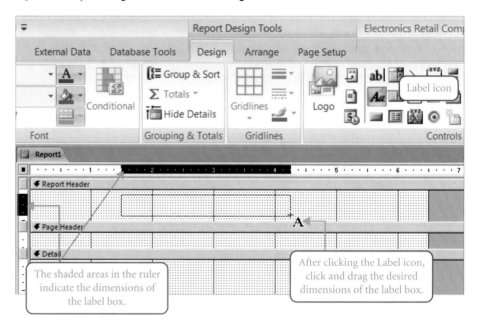

Figure 5.12 illustrates the appearance of the **Label** box after typing the title for the Active Item Price Report and pressing the **Enter** key. The dark outline that appears around the label box indicates the label box is active. You may use the boxes around the perimeter for moving or adjusting the dimensions of the label box.

Figure 5.12 | **Title Typed into the Label Box Prior to Formatting**

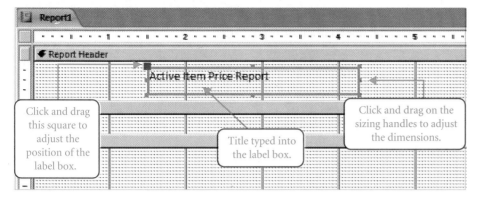

You can format text typed into a label box by using icons in the **Font** group in the **Design** tab of the Ribbon. For example, Figure 5.13 shows the formatting commands that were applied to the label box that was created in Figure 5.12. You must first activate the label box before using any formatting commands. Recall that the dark border around the label box indicates it is activated. To active a label box, click anywhere inside its border.

Figure 5.13 | **Formatting the Text Typed into a Label Box**

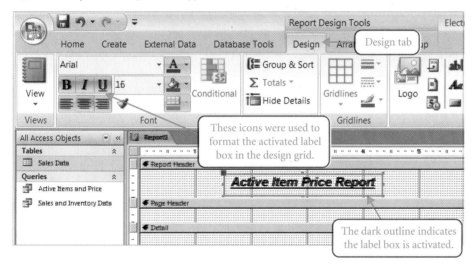

Once you have added label boxes containing titles or descriptive information, you will need to check the appearance of the report. **Print Preview** is one way to do this. The **Print Preview** command is activated from the **File** menu and was covered in Chapter 2 (see Figure 2.55). You can also switch a report to **Print Preview** by clicking the **View** icon in the **Design** tab. The benefit of using this method is that it will show the appearance of a report as if it were printed on paper. This is helpful for identifying formatting or position adjustments that might be needed for any label boxes on the report. For example, Figure 5.14 shows the appearance of the title for the Active Item Price Report, which was formatted in Figure 5.13. Notice that the title is slightly off-center and needs to be moved to the right. This can be done by clicking and dragging the label box to the right when the report is switched back to **Design View**.

Figure 5.14 | **Active Item Price Report in Print Preview**

Figure 5.15 shows the Active Item Price Report in **Layout View**, another way to view the appearance of a report. The benefit of this method is that adjustments can be made without having to switch the report back to **Design View**. For example, you can move the label box to the right by clicking and dragging it. You can also apply formatting adjustments when a report is in **Layout View**. Notice that formatting commands are found in the **Format** tab when a report is in **Layout View** as opposed to the **Design** tab when a report is in **Design View**.

Figure 5.15 | **Active Item Price Report in Layout View**

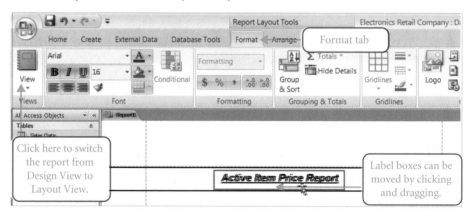

>> *Quick Reference*

Adding a Label Box

1. Open a report in **Design View**.
2. Click the **Design** tab on the Ribbon.
3. Click the **Label** icon in the **Controls** group.
4. Click and drag the dimensions of the label box on the design grid.
5. Adjust the dimensions of the label box by clicking and dragging it.

>> *Quick Reference*

Formatting a Label Box

1. Activate the label box by clicking anywhere inside the border of the box.
2. Click the **Design** tab if a report is opened in **Design View** or click the **Format** tab if a report is opened in **Layout View**.
3. Click any of the formatting icons in the **Font** group.

Page Header

Column style reports such as the Active Item Price Report shown in Figure 5.1 are typically used in business environments. This type of report organizes data in columns with descriptive headings at the top of each column. These headings are added to an Access report in the Page Header section of the design grid. Label boxes that are added to the Page Header section of the design grid will appear at the top of each page of an Access report. The following explains how the column headings are created for the Active Item Price Report.

- Change the height of the Page Header section to 1/2 inch. This is done by placing the cursor at the top of edge of the Detail section. When the cursor changes to a double arrow, click and drag down (see Figure 5.16).
- Add a label box to the far left side of the Page Header section. A label box will be added for each column of data in the Active Item Price report. Because there are a total of five columns in the report, the first column label is placed to the far left of the design grid. Add the label box by clicking the **Label** icon in the **Design** tab of the Ribbon, and then click and drag the box on the design grid.
- Type the column description *Category Number* in the label box and press the **Enter** key.

- Format the text in the label box to an Arial font size 12. In addition, bold the text and align the text on the left side of the label box. Remember that the label box must be activated to use the formatting icons. The label box is activated by clicking it once.
- Adjust the width of the label box so it is wide enough to fit the word *Category*. Then, adjust the height of the label box so the word *Number* is visible. Text that is typed into a label box will automatically wrap to a second line if it exceeds the width of the box. Adjust the width and height of the label box by clicking and dragging on one of the sizing handles (see Figure 5.12).

Figure 5.16 | **Adjusting the Height of the Page Header Section**

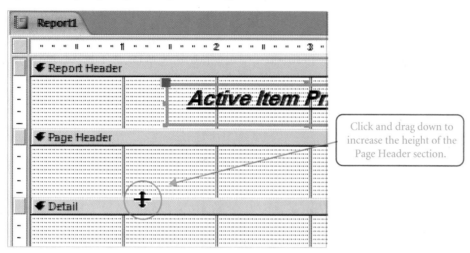

Figure 5.17 shows how the label box for the Category Number column should appear in the Page Header section of the design grid. The process used for adding this label will be repeated for each of the column headings in the Active Item Price Report.

Figure 5.17 | **Label Box Added to the Page Header Section**

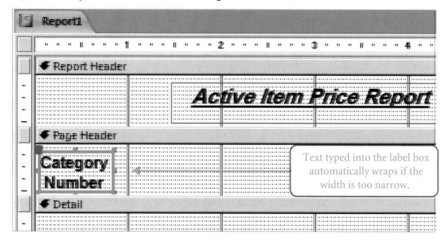

Figure 5.18 shows all five column heading labels added to the Page Header section of the design grid. The purpose of these labels is to define the data that will appear in the columns of the report. Data for the Active Item Price Report will be added to the Detail section of the design grid in the next segment.

Figure 5.18 | **5 Label Boxes are Added to the Page Header Section**

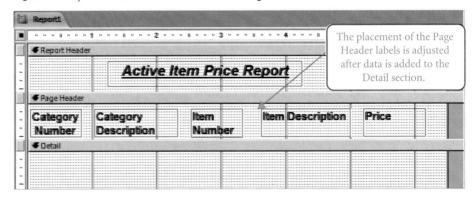

Figure 5.19 shows the appearance of the Active Item Price Report in Print Preview. Once you add data to the report, you need to adjust the placement of the column heading labels. For now, the column heading labels are evenly spaced on the report.

Figure 5.19 | **Print Preview of Active Item Price Report with Title and Column Headings**

Detail

Use the Detail section in the design grid of a report for adding, positioning, and formatting data in an Access report. The data that appears in the report will come from the query or table that is selected in the **Data** tab of the **Property Sheet** window (see Figure 5.3). With regard to the Active Item Price Report, the following shows how to use the Detail section to create the columns of data in the report. The following explains how these columns are created.

- Adjust the height of the Detail section. The height of the Detail section will dictate the space that is created between each row of data on the report. As the height of the Detail section *increases*, the amount of data that can be displayed on one page of the report *decreases*. However, you must be sure that the height of the Detail section is adequate to accommodate the font size that is used to format the data in the report. For the Active Item Price Report, the height of the Detail section should be 3/8 an inch. This is done by placing the cursor on the upper edge of the Page Footer section heading, and then clicking and dragging up when the cursor changes to a double arrow (see Figure 5.20).

Figure 5.20 | **Adjusting the Height of the Detail Section**

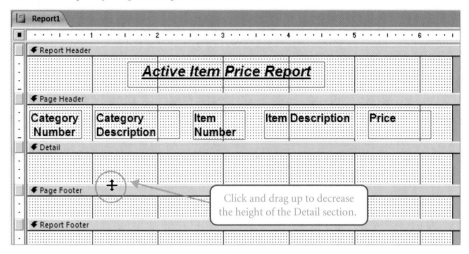

COMMON MISTAKES | Managing Line Spacing on an Access Report

People often forget that the space between lines on an Access report is managed by the height of the Detail section in the design grid. If you want to fit more lines of data on an Access report, you must decrease the height of the Detail section.

- Open the **Field List** window by clicking the **Add Existing Fields** icon in the **Design** tab of the Ribbon.
- Click and drag field names from the **Field List** window into the Detail section of the design grid. For the Active Item Price report, the first field that will be added to the Detail section is the Cat Number field because the first label that was added to the far left of the Page Header section is the Category Number label. Therefore, click the Cat Number field from the Field List window and drag it over to the left side of the Detail section on the design grid, as shown in Figure 5.21.

Figure 5.21 | **Adding Data from the Field List to the Detail Section**

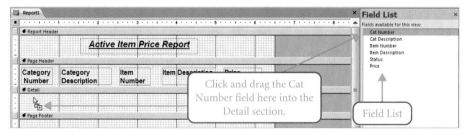

- Remove the label box from the Detail section. After you drag a field into the Detail section of the design grid, two boxes will appear: a label box and a text box. A label box will always appear when you drag fields into the design grid, and can be identified by the transparent background (you can see the dots of the design grid through the box). This is to ensure that the data being dragged into the design grid has a way of being identified. However, we already added labels to the Page Header section of the design grid. As a result, the label box for the Cat Number field can be deleted. This is illustrated in Figure 5.22. Activate the label box for the Cat Number field by clicking it once, and then press the **Delete** key on your keyboard.

Figure 5.22 | **Deleting the Label Box for the Cat Number Field**

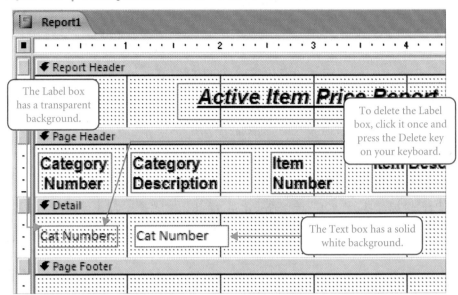

Figure 5.22 | **Deleting the Label Box for the Cat Number Field**

- Adjust the position and dimensions of the text box. The text box controls the space that will be used to show the data that is contained in the fields of a table or query. The best way to adjust the positioning and dimensions of a text box is to switch the report from **Design View** to **Layout View**, as shown in Figure 5.23. Notice that the category numbers are not aligned under the Category Number label. This can be partially adjusted by clicking and dragging the first category number to the left. However, the most important adjustment is to set the alignment to left justify. This is done by activating the text box and clicking the **Align Text Left** icon.

Figure 5.23 | **Checking the Alignment of Data in Layout View**

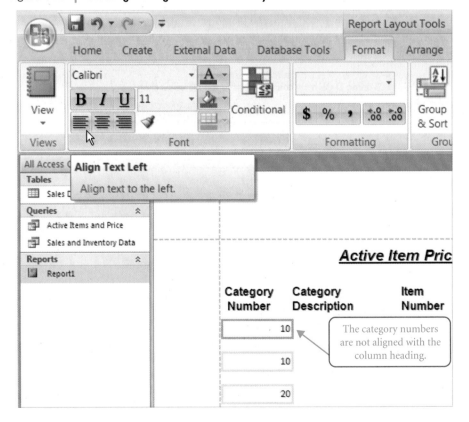

- Format the text box. It is most convenient to format text boxes while the report is in **Layout View**. This is because you will be able to see whether additional adjustments are required for the dimension or position of the text box after formatting enhancements are added. For the Active Item Price Report, the Cat Number text box will be formatted to bold, font type changed to Arial, and font size changed to 10. This is done by activating the first category number on the report and clicking the format icons in the **Format** tab, as shown in Figure 5.24.

Figure 5.24 | **Making Format Adjustments in Layout View**

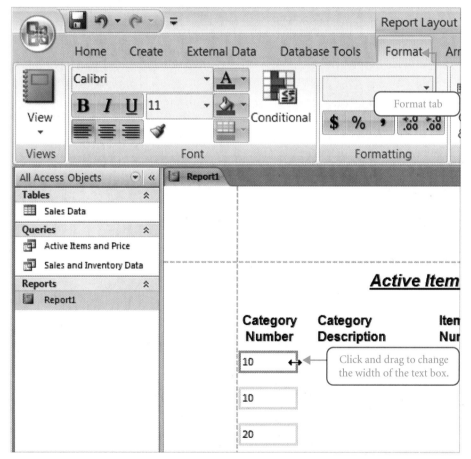

The positioning and formatting of data in an Access report is an iterative process. That is to say, as labels and data are added to the design grid of a report in **Design View**, you will need to periodically switch the report to **Layout View** to check the appearance and alignment. Any necessary adjustments to data and label position, as well as formats, should be made while the report is in **Layout View**. For example, Figure 5.25 shows the Active Items Price Report in **Layout View** after adding all the required fields to the Detail section while the report was in **Design View**. Notice that the first two items in the Category Description column appear to run into the Item Number column. Both the Item Number label in the Page Header section and the Item Number text box in the Detail section will need to be moved to the right. Also, notice that the first few items in the Item Description column are cut off. The width of the Item Description column will need to be increased.

Figure 5.25 | **Checking the Alignment of Data in Layout View**

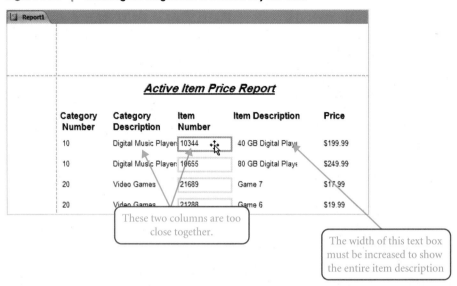

Figure 5.26 shows the adjustments that were made to the Active Item Price Report in **Layout View**. Notice that the data in each column is aligned under the column heading and all the data in each column is visible.

Figure 5.26 | **Adjustments Made to the Active Item Price Report in Layout View**

The width of this text box was increased to show the entire description.

Figure 5.27 shows the Report Header, Page Header, and Detail sections of the Active Item Price Report in **Print Preview**.

Figure 5.27 | **Print Preview of the Active Item Price Report**

Category Number	Category Description	Item Number	Item Description	Price
10	Digital Music Players	10344	40 GB Digital Player	$199.99
10	Digital Music Players	10655	80 GB Digital Player	$249.99
20	Video Games	21689	Game 7	$17.99
20	Video Games	21288	Game 6	$19.99
20	Video Games	22888	Game 5	$59.99

Page Footer

The Page Footer section of a report will show any labels or data at the bottom of each page of report. For the Active Item Price Report, the Page Footer section will be used for adding page numbers. The following explains how this is done.

- Open the report in **Design View**.
- Adjust the height of the Page Footer section to 1/4 inch. This is done by placing the cursor at the top of the Report Footer section heading and then dragging up when the cursor changes to a double arrow.
- Open the **Page Numbers** dialog box by clicking the **Insert Page Number** icon in the **Design** tab of the Ribbon (see Figure 5.5).
- Select the **Page N of M** format option in the **Page Numbers** dialog box. This will show the current page number (N) and the total number of pages on the report (M). Then, select the **Bottom of Page [Footer]** position option. This will place the page numbers in the Page Footer section of the design grid. Finally, in the Alignment section, click the drop-down arrow and select **Right**. This will place the page number text box on the right side of the Page Footer section.
- Click the **OK** button on the **Page Numbers** dialog box.

Figure 5.28 shows the final settings that were selected in the **Page Numbers** dialog box for the Active Item Price Report.

>> *Quick Reference*

Adding Data Fields to a Report

1. Open a new or existing report in **Design View**.
2. Open the Field List window by clicking the **Add Existing Fields** icon in the **Design** tab of the Ribbon.
3. Click and drag a field from the **Field List** window into one of the sections in the design grid of a report.
4. Delete the label box that is attached to the field if labels or headings have already been added to the report.
5. Check the alignment and appearance of your data and labels by switching the report to **Layout View**.
6. Make any adjustments to label or text boxes while the report is in **Layout View**.

Figure 5.28 | **Page Numbers Dialog Box**

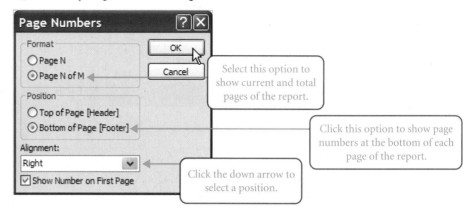

Figure 5.29 shows the design grid of the Active Item Price Report after clicking the **OK** button in the **Page Numbers** dialog box. The text box in the Pager Footer section indicates that page numbers will be displayed at the bottom-right side of each page of the report. The page numbers can be formatted by clicking the text box and selecting any of the formatting icons in the **Design** tab of the Ribbon.

Figure 5.29 | **Design Grid Showing the Page Number Text Box**

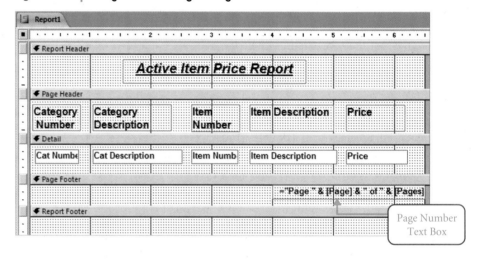

Report Footer

The last section that will be added to the Active Item Price report is the Report Footer. The Report Footer will display text from a label box or data from a text box on the last page of the report. With regard to the Active Item Price Report, this section will be used for showing who constructed the report. The following explains how this is accomplished:

- Adjust the height of the Report Footer section to 3/8 inch by placing the cursor at the bottom edge of the design grid. When the cursor changes to a double arrow, click and drag down.
- Click the **Label** icon in the **Design** tab of the Ribbon.
- Draw a label box on the far left side of the Report Footer section by clicking and dragging.
- Type the text *Created by: Joseph M. Manzo*. Then, press the **Enter** key.
- Format the label box to an Arial font, font size of 10, bold, and left alignment.
- Switch the report to **Layout View** to identify and necessary adjustments.

Figure 5.30 shows the label box that was added to the Report Footer section of the Active Item Price Report. Additional adjustments can be made to the label box when the report is switched to **Layout View**.

Figure 5.30 | **Adding a Label Box to the Report Footer Section**

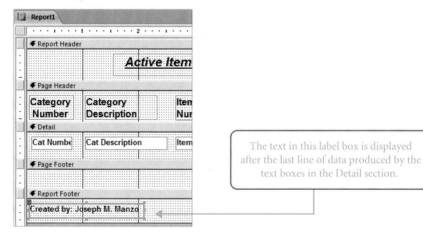

The text in this label box is displayed after the last line of data produced by the text boxes in the Detail section.

Figures 5.31 and 5.32 show the final result of the Active Item Price Report in Print Preview. The figures illustrate which section on the design grid was used for the various labels and data that displayed on the report.

Figure 5.31 | Top Half of the Active Item Price Report in Print Preview

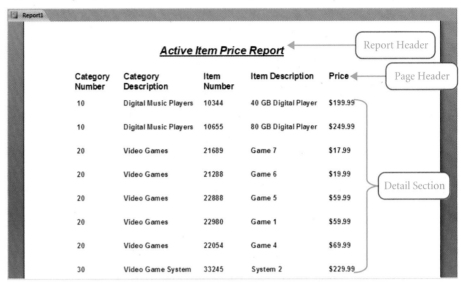

Figure 5.32 | Bottom Half of the Active Item Price Report in Print Preview

⟫ Fundamental Report Skills

The purpose of this workshop is to demonstrate the fundamental techniques of creating reports in Access. The report that you will be creating in this workshop is identical to the one demonstrated earlier in this section. I will be demonstrating the tasks in this workshop in the following six videos: **Creating a New Report**, **Report Headers**, **Page Headers**, **Report Details**, **Page Numbers**, and **Report Footers**. You will need to open the Access database named ib_a05_ electronicsmerchandisedata. Try completing the tasks in each section first before watching the related video.

1. **Creating a New Report (Video: Creating a New Report)**

   a. Create a new Access Report by clicking the **Report Design** icon in the **Create** tab of the Ribbon.

   b. Open the **Property Sheet** window by clicking the **Property Sheet** Icon in the **Design** tab of the Ribbon.

   c. Click the **Data** tab in the **Property Sheet** window and then click in the box next to the Record Source.

   d. Click the Record Source drop-down arrow and select the Active Items and Price query. Then close the **Property Sheet** window by clicking the X in the upper-right corner of the window.

   e. Open the **Page Setup** dialog box from the **Page Setup** tab of the Ribbon. Set the Top, Bottom, Right, and Left margins to one inch. Then, close the **Page Setup** dialog box.

   f. Increase the width of the design grid to 6.5 inches.

   g. Save the report and assign the name `Price Report`.

2. **Report Header Section (Video: Report Headers)**

   a. Click the **Arrange** tab of the Ribbon and then click the **Report Header/Footer** icon.

   b. Increase the height of the Report Header section to 3/8 inch.

   c. Click the **Label** icon in the **Design** tab of the Ribbon and draw a label box in the center of the Report Header section of the design grid.

   d. Type `Price List` into the label box, Then press the **Enter** key.

   e. Format the label box with the following: bold, italics, center alignment, underline, Arial font, and font size of 16 points.

   f. Switch the report to **Layout View** and make any necessary adjustments to the position or dimensions of the label box so the title is centered and visible.

   g. Switch the report back to **Design View** and save.

3. Page Header Section (Video: Page Headers)

a. Increase the height of the Page Header section to ½ inch.

b. Add five label boxes to the Page Header section beginning at the far left side. Following are the descriptions that should be typed into each box. Remember to press the **Enter** key after typing each description.

   i. Label Box 1: `Category Number`

   ii. Label Box 2: `Category Description`

   iii. Label Box 3: `Item Number`

   iv. Label Box 4: `Item Description`

   v. Label Box 5: `Price`

c. Format each of the label boxes that you created in step b to bold, Arial font, font size of 12 points, and left alignment.

d. Switch the report to **Layout View** and adjust the position and dimensions of the label boxes so all the descriptions are visible and evenly spaced across the report.

e. Switch the report back to **Design View** and save.

4. Detail Section (Video: Report Details)

a. Adjust the height of the Detail section to 3/8 of an inch.

b. Open the **Field List** window by clicking the **Add Existing Fields** icon in the **Design** tab of the Ribbon.

c. Click and drag the Cat Number field from the Field List into the Detail section of the design grid.

d. Activate the label box for the Cat Number field by clicking it once and press the **Delete** key on your keyboard.

e. Click and drag the Cat Number text box so it is in the far left side of the Detail section and is aligned under the Category Number label in the Page Header section.

f. Repeat tasks c, d, and e for the fields listed following. After deleting the label box for each field, align the text box under the appropriate label in the Page Header section.

   i. Cat Description

   ii. Item Number

   iii. Item Description

   iv. Price

g. Make the following format adjustments for each of the fields added to the Detail Section: Arial font, font size of 10 points, and left alignment.

h. Close the **Field List** window by clicking the X in the upper-right corner of the window. Then switch the report to Layout View.

i. Adjust the position and dimensions of the text boxes that were added to the Detail section so all the data is visible and aligned under the headings in the Page Header section.

j. Switch the report back to **Design View** and save.

5. Page Footer Section (Video: Page Numbers)

a. Increase the height of the Page Footer section to ¼ inch.

b. Click the **Insert Page Number** icon in the **Design Tab** of the Ribbon.

c. Select the Page N of M, Bottom of Page [Footer], and Right alignment options in the **Page Numbers** dialog box and click the **OK** button.

d. Activate the **Page Number** text box by clicking it. Then make the following format adjustments: Arial font, font size 10 points, bold, italics, and right alignment.

e. Switch the report to **Layout View** to check the appearance of the page number at the bottom of the report. Then switch the report back to **Design View** and save.

6. **Report Footer Section (Video: Report Footers)**

a. Increase the height of the Report Footer section to ¼ inch.

b. Add a label box on the left side of the Report Footer section.

c. Type the words **Created by**: followed by your name. Then press the **Enter** key.

d. Make the following format adjustments to the label box you created in step c: Arial font, font size of 10 points, bold, italics, and left alignment.

e. Switch the report to **Layout View** and make any necessary adjustments to the label box at the bottom of the report. Make sure your name is visible.

f. Examine the report in **Print Preview** mode.

g. Save and then close the report.

≫ Human Resource Status Report

Reports are used for a variety of purposes in business. A basic report that is used in most businesses is a reference list, which can be used to show the price of items sold in a store, the stock symbols of publicly traded companies, or the address and size of each store owned by a retail company. The value of creating these types of reports in Access is that any time data is changed or added to the Access database, it will automatically be reflected in the report. This provides business managers with the ability to view the most current information depending on the design and purpose of the report.

Exercise

The purpose of this exercise is to construct a reference list that could be used by a Human Resources manager. The report will list every employee in the company, along with other descriptive information such as their title and years of service with the company. A Human Resource manager can use this information to assign certain benefits to each employee such as vacation time or stock options. Open the Access database named ib_a05_employeedata and complete the following tasks.

1. Create a Select Query that selects records from the Employee Master table where the Status field is equal to W. The purpose of this report is to show the HR manager a list of employees who are currently employed by the company. The Employee Master table contains records for people who are currently Working, Resigned, Terminated, or Retired from the company. The letter W is assigned to any employee who is currently working for the company. The query should include all fields from the table and should be sorted in alphabetical order based on the employee's last name. After constructing this query, name it **Active Employees** and close it.

2. Create a new Access report using the **Active Employees** query constructed in step 1. Set the margins of the report to one inch on all sides and the orientation to portrait. Because the left and right margins are one inch, the width of the design grid should be set to 6.5 inches.

3. Add the Report Header section to the design grid. Then save the report and name it **Active Employee Report**.

4. Increase the height of the Report Header section to 3/8th of an inch. Then, add a label box in the Report Header section and type the words **Active Employee List** in the label box. The purpose of this label box is to create a title for the report.

5. Make the following format adjustments to the label box created in number 4: Arial font, font size of 14 points, bold, italics, underline, and center alignment.

6. Using the **Layout View**, check the appearance of the title to make sure it is centered at the top of the report and that all the text is visible. Then switch the report back to **Design View**.

7. Increase the height of the Page Header section to ½ inch.

8. Add six label boxes to the Page Header section. The purpose of these label boxes is to create the column headings of the report. The descriptions that should appear in each label box are listed as follows:
   a. Label Box 1 = **Last Name**
   b. Label Box 2 = **First Name**
   c. Label Box 3 = **Division**
   d. Label Box 4 = **Title**
   e. Label Box 5 = **Annual Salary**
   f. Label Box 6 = **Years of Service**

9. Make the following format adjustments to the label boxes created in number 8: Arial font, font size of 10 points, bold, and left alignment. Check the appearance of the label boxes in **Layout View** and make any necessary adjustments. Note that the width of the Years of Service label box should be reduced so the text wraps to two lines.

10. Switch the report to **Design View** and increase the height of the Detail section to 3/8 inch.

11. Add the following fields from the Active Employees query to Detail section of the report. Each field should be aligned under the appropriate label box in the Page Header section. After dragging each field into the Detail section, remove the label box that is attached to it.
   a. Last Name
   b. First Name
   c. Division
   d. Title
   e. Annual Salary
   f. Years of Service

12. Make the following format adjustments to the text boxes that were added to the Detail section in number 11: Arial font, font size of 10 points, and left alignment. Then switch the report to **Layout View** and make any necessary adjustments. The data produced by each text box should be visible and aligned under the appropriate column heading.

13. Switch the report back to **Design View** and increase the height of the Page Footer section to ¼ inch.

14. Add page numbers to the **Page Footer** section of the design grid. Select the **Page N of M** option in the **Page Numbers** dialog box and align the page number on the far right side of the **Page Footer** section at the bottom of the page.

15. Make the following format adjustments to the **Page Numbers** text box: Arial font, font size of 10 points, bold, italics, and right alignment. Then check the appearance of the page number in **Layout View**. Make any necessary adjustments to the **Page Numbers** text box.

16. Switch the report back to **Design View** and increase the height of the Report Footer section to ¼ inch.

17. Add a label box to the left side of the Report Footer section. Type the words **Created by:** and then your name in the label box. Then make the following format adjustments: Arial font, font size of 12 points, bold, italics, and left alignment.

18. Check the appearance of the Report Footer in **Layout View** and make any necessary adjustment to the label box.

19. Check the appearance of the report in **Print Preview** mode.

20. Save and close the report.

≫ What's Wrong with This Database?

Problem

PROBLEM & EXERCISE

You are working in the store construction division of a retail company. A coworker in your department is trying to construct an Access report and is having considerable difficulty. He asks for your help and explains the problems he is having in an e-mail. He listed the following points in his e-mail to you:

- I am trying to put together a basic list of all the stores we are currently operating in the company. For some reason the right margin seems unusually large. I keep checking the margins in the Page Setup dialog box and they are all set to one inch. The text and label boxes are up against the far right side of the design grid. However, there seems to be an extra inch or one and one-half inches of space on the right side of the report.

- For some reason, I can't get the data produced by the text boxes to align with the column headings I added to the Page Header section. It seems like all the boxes are aligned in the design grid, but some of the data is way off when I switch the report to Print Preview mode.

- I can't find the line spacing option to reduce the space between each row of data. There is a huge space between each row of data and I want to reduce this so I can see more stores on one sheet of paper.

- Finally, I would like to add the title "Store Detail List" to only the first page of the report. Someone told me to add a label box to the Report Header section, but I don't have a Report Header section on my design grid. Please help!

Exercise

The Access database your coworker attached to his e-mail is named ib_a05_reporthelp. Open the report named Store List. Consider the following points:

1. What would prevent you from filling the entire width of an Access report between the set margins?

2. In addition to adjusting the position of text and label boxes in the design grid, what else should be checked for data to be aligned on an Access report?

3. The coworker mentioned that he is trying to reduce the space between each row of data on the report. What adjustment needs to be made to reduce this space?

4. Is the Report Header section automatically included in a new Report?

   What's wrong with this report? Write a short answer for each of the points listed. Then, fix the Store List report based on the points listed in your coworker's email.

Skill Set **Advanced Report Techniques**

Performance reports provide critical information for almost every business. Depending on their areas of responsibility, business managers will use performance reports to evaluate information such as the overall sales of a company, the performance of stocks, or the number of invoices that have not been paid. The prior section illustrated a basic report that listed items and prices for merchandise that might be sold in a typical electronics retail store. This section uses similar data to demonstrate the construction of a Sales and Inventory Report for an electronics retail company.

Figure 5.33 shows the report that will be constructed in this section. A business manager might use this report on a weekly basis to evaluate the unit sales and inventory for each item sold in an electronics retail store by category. In addition to showing sales and inventory statistics by *item*, the report also provides a summary of sales and inventory statistics for each *category*. This will require the use of advanced report techniques such as grouping and sorting data, adding totals and calculations, and conditional formatting.

Figure 5.33 | **Sales and Inventory Report**

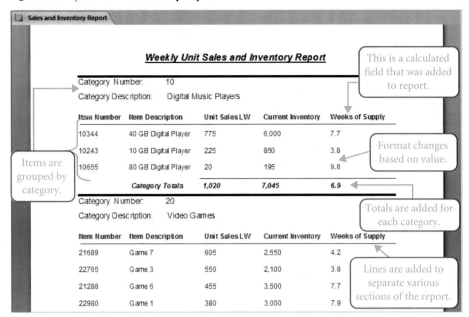

Grouping Data

A key feature of the Sales and Inventory Report shown in Figure 5.33 is that the items are grouped by category. This will enable business managers to focus on the sales results for their specific area of responsibility. This was accomplished using the *Group & Sort* command in the **Design** tab, which will be demonstrated in this segment. However, details regarding the initial construction of the report will be explained first.

Figure 5.34 shows the initial setup of the design grid for the Sales and Inventory Report shown in Figure 5.33. The following is an overview of the details that were executed in the initial setup of this report.

- The width of the design grid was expanded to 6.5 inches. The Top, Bottom, Right, and Left margins were set to 1 inch and the paper dimensions were set to 8.5 × 11 inches.

- The Report Header and Footer sections were added to the design grid.

- The Report Footer section will be used to add a summary of sales and inventory statistics for the entire report (this will be demonstrated in the Adding Totals segment). However, the Report Header will not be used. Therefore, the height of the Report Header section was reduced to zero.

- The height of the Page Header section was to set 3/8 inch, the height of the Detail section was set to 1/4 inch, the height of the Page Footer section was set to 1/4 inch, and the height of the Report Footer section was set to 1/2 inch.

- A label box containing the title of the report was added to the Page Header section. This will show the title of the report at the top of each page.

- The title was formatted to an Arial font, font size of 14 points, bold, italics, underline, and center justification.

Figure 5.34 | **Initial Design Grid Setup for the Sales and Inventory Report**

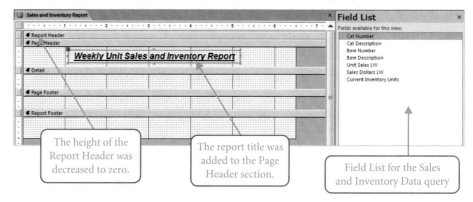

The height of the Report Header was decreased to zero.

The report title was added to the Page Header section.

Field List for the Sales and Inventory Data query

As illustrated in Figure 5.33, the items shown on the Sales and Inventory Report are grouped by category. Also notice that there are totals at the bottom of the first group of items for Category 10. This is accomplished by using the Group & Sort command, which adds a custom header and footer section to the report based on the values in the Cat Number field. In other words, a new header and footer section is added to the report for each unique category number in the Cat Number field. The following explains how the Group & Sort command is used to create the Sales and Inventory Report:

- Click the **Group & Sort** icon in the **Design** tab of the Ribbon. This will open a dialog box below the design grid of the report that is used for grouping and sorting the data in a report, as shown in Figure 5.35.

Figure 5.35 | **The Grouping Dialog Box Appears Below the Design Grid**

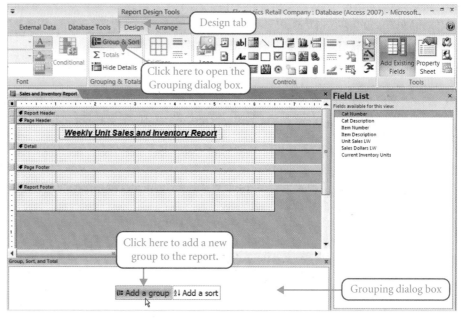

Design tab

Click here to open the Grouping dialog box.

Click here to add a new group to the report.

Grouping dialog box

- Click the **Add a Group** button in the **Grouping** dialog box. This will open a window showing a list of fields that are available in the Field List.
- Select a field from the window in the **Grouping** dialog box that will be used to create the groups in the report. For the Sales and Inventory Report, the Cat Number field is selected, as shown in Figure 5.36.

Figure 5.36 | **Selecting a Field to Establish Groups of Data**

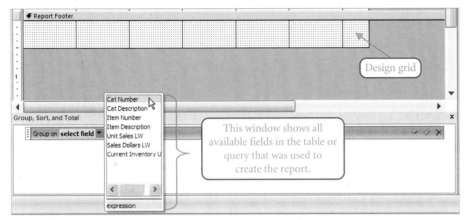

- Select a sort order for the groups that are created on your report. For this example, the **from smallest to largest** sort order is selected (see Figure 5.37). As a result, groups that are created for each unique value in the Cat Number field will appear on the report from lowest to highest.
- Click the **More** option in the **Grouping** dialog box. This will open more options for setting the groups that are created on the report (see Figure 5.37).
- Change the footer section option to **with a footer section**. This will add a footer section for each group on the report, which will be used to show totals.
- Check to make sure the **by entire value option** is selected. This will create a group for each unique value in the Cat Number field.
- Select the **keep whole group together on one page** option. This will keep all the details for a group on one page. For example, let's assume a category contains 10 merchandise items and this group begins at the bottom of a report. Instead of showing two items on one page and eight items on the next page, Access will move the entire category to the next page.
- Click the X in the upper-right corner of the **Grouping** dialog box to close it.

Figure 5.37 shows the **Grouping** dialog box after the Cat Number group is initially created. The sort order option will appear to the right of the field name that was selected to create the group. Notice in this figure that the sort option selected will display the groups on the report beginning with the smallest value to the largest value. Also, notice that the **More** option appears to the right of the sort option. This is used to show additional settings for creating the group.

Figure 5.37 | **Setting the Sort Order for Groups**

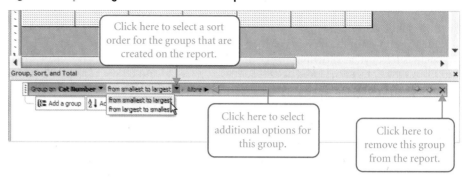

Figure 5.38 shows the final settings in the **Grouping** dialog box for the Sales and Inventory Report. Notice that the Cat Number Header and Cat Number Footer sections are added to the design grid of the report. Once the group is created, you can close the **Grouping** dialog box by clicking the X in the upper-right corner, as shown in the figure.

Figure 5.38 | **Final Settings for the Cat Number Group**

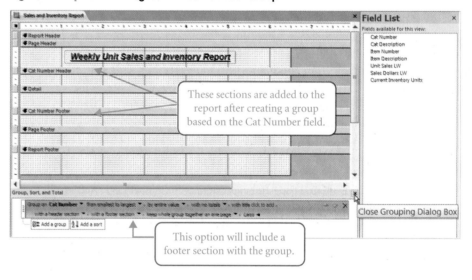

After creating the Cat Number group, you must drag the Cat Number field from the Field List into the Cat Number Header section. In addition, label boxes will be used in this section to provide column heading descriptions for the data that will be added to the Detail section. The following explains how this is accomplished:

- Increase the height of the Cat Number Header section to 1 inch.
- Click and drag the Cat Number field from the Field List into the upper-left area of the Cat Number Header section in the design grid. This will display the category number for each group of items on the report.
- Change the description in the label box to read Category Number. In the prior section, the label box that appeared with the text box when a field was dragged

into the design grid was deleted. However, in this section we will use these labels. Click the label one time to activate it. Then, place the curser at the beginning of the description and click again to modify the current description in the label box. Occasionally, the text box may overlap the label box when a field is dragged into the design grid. You can separate them by clicking and dragging the square in the upper-left corner of the text box.

- Make the following format adjustments to the label and text box: Arial font, font size of 12 points, and left alignment.
- Switch the report to **Layout View** to make any adjustments to the size and position of the label box and text box. The description Category Number and the category number should appear in the upper-left corner of the section.

Figure 5.39 shows the final position and dimensions of the label and text box in **Design View**. Adjustments to the size and position of the both the text box and the label box were made while the report was in **Layout View**.

Figure 5.39 | **Final Position and Dimension of the Label and Text Boxes**

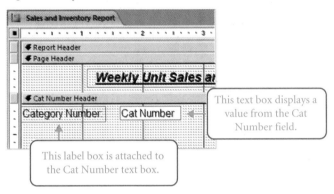

After the Cat Number field is placed and formatted in the Cat Number Header section, the Cat Description field is added. The Cat Description field is dragged from the Field List and placed directly below the Category Number label box in the Cat Number Header section. In addition, the label box for the Cat Description field is changed to Category Description. The column headings are also added to the Cat Number Header section using label boxes. Figure 5.40 and 5.41 show the final setup of the Cat Number Header section in **Design View** and **Print Preview** modes. Note that adjustments were made to both the text and label boxes by switching the report to **Layout View**.

Figure 5.40 | **Cat Number Header Section in Design View**

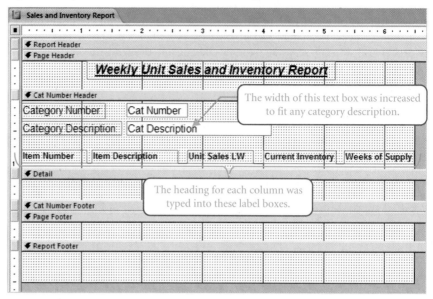

Figure 5.41 | **Completed Cat Number Header Section Shown in Print Preview Mode**

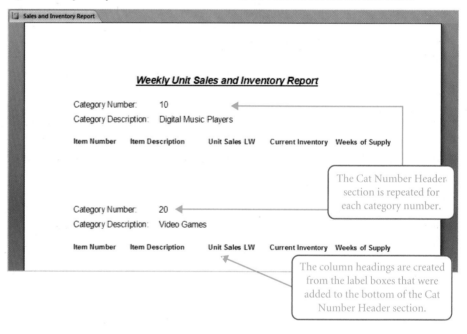

Note that when you add label boxes to a section of the design grid that contains text boxes, you will see an error icon stating that you have a label that is not associated with a control. As shown in Figure 5.42, the error icon appears when label boxes are added to the Cat Number Header section of the design grid. The purpose of the error icon is to help ensure that any text box that is added to the report has a label. However, in this report the label box and the text box will be in two different sections. Therefore, the **Ignore Error** option can be selected after clicking the error icon.

Figure 5.42 | **Label Box Error Icon**

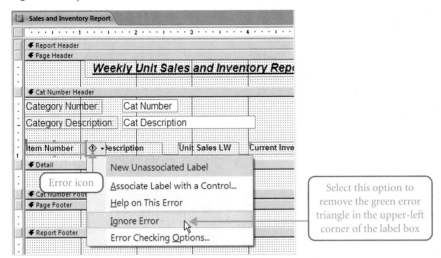

Sorting Data

The next section of the Sales and Inventory Report (see Figure 5.41) that will be constructed is the Detail section. The Detail section contains the sales and inventory data for each merchandise item. The merchandise items will be sorted based on the Unit Sales LW values. The following explains how this data is added and sorted.

- Set the height of the Detail section to 1/4 inch.
- Click and drag the Item Number, Item Description, Unit Sales LW, and Current Inventory Units fields from the Field List to the Detail section of the design grid. Each field should be placed directly below its corresponding label box in the Cat Number Header section.
- Because labels have been added to the Cat Number Header section, delete the label boxes that are attached to the text boxes when the fields are dragged into the design grid.
- Format each text box in the Detail section to an Arial font, 10 point font size, and left alignment. Then switch the report to **Layout View** to make any necessary adjustments to the position and width of each text box.

Figure 5.43 shows how the text boxes should appear in the Detail section of the design grid. These text boxes will provide the data that will appear on the report.

Figure 5.43 | **Detail Section of the Design Grid**

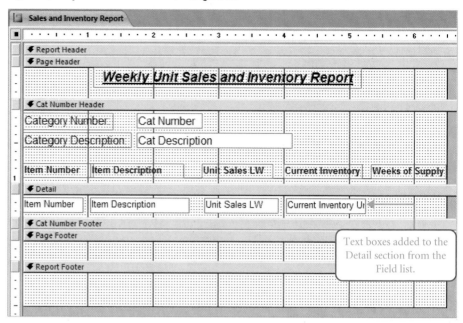

After you drag fields into the detail section of a report, you can then establish the sort sequence for the data that appears on the report. Sorting data and establishing groups of data on a report uses the same command: the Group & Sort command. The following explains how the Group & Sort command is used to sort data on the Sales and Inventory Report.

- Open the **Grouping** dialog box by clicking the **Group & Sort** icon in the **Detail** tab of the Ribbon. When the dialog box opens you will see the settings for the Cat Number group that was created in the prior segment (see Figure 5.37).

- Click the **Add a Sort** button, which is shown in Figures 5.38 and 5.35 This will open a window showing a list of fields that are available in the Field List. This is the same window that appears when creating a group (see Figure 5.36).

- Select the Unit Sales LW field from the window of available fields. This will sort the data in the Detail section of the report based on the values in the Unit Sales LW field. This will also create new levels in the **Grouping** dialog box called **Sort by**.

- Select a sort order that appears to the right of the Unit Sales LW field name. For this example, select the **from largest to smallest** option.

- Click the X in the upper-right corner of the **Grouping** dialog box to close it.

Figure 5.44 shows the final settings in the **Grouping** dialog box for sorting the data in the Sales and Inventory Report. These settings will display the items in the Detail section of the report based on the values in the Unit Sales LW field in descending order. Note that you can add another sorting tier by clicking the **Add a Sort** button. You might use this second sorting tier in cases where duplicate values in the Unit Sales LW field exist. Also, notice that the **without a header section**, **without a footer section**, and **do not keep together on one page** options are all selected. These options will automatically be selected when setting a sort sequence. If these options are changed, the **Sort by** level shown in this figure will automatically be changed to a **Group on** level.

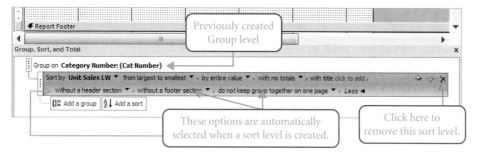

Figure 5.45 shows the Sales and Inventory Report in Print Preview. Notice that the items listed in the Detail section are listed in descending order based on the values in the Unit Sales LW column.

Figure 5.45 | **Sales and Inventory Report with Detail Section Sorted**

Weekly Unit Sales and Inventory Report

Category Number: 10
Category Description: Digital Music Players

Item Number	Item Description	Unit Sales LW	Current Inventory	Weeks of Supply
10344	40 GB Digital Player	775	6,000	
10243	10 GB Digital Player	225	850	
10655	80 GB Digital Player	20	195	

Category Number: 20
Category Description: Video Games

Item Number	Item Description	Unit Sales LW	Current Inventory	Weeks of Supply
21689	Game 7	605	2,550	
22765	Game 3	550	2,100	
21288	Game 6	455	3,500	

The items for each group are sorted based on the values in the Unit Sales LW column.

Data for this column will be produced from a calculated field.

Calculated Fields

So far, we have demonstrated how to create reports using fields from a query or typing descriptions into a label box. However, Access can also produce data through a calculated field. With regards to the Sales and Inventory Report shown in Figure 5.45, a calculated field is added to the Detail section to produce data for the Weeks of Supply column. The following explains how this is accomplished:

- Click the **Text Box** icon in the **Design** tab of the Ribbon (see Figure 5.5).
- Click and drag the shape of a box in the Detail section of the design grid under the Weeks of Supply heading in the Cat Number Header section, as shown in Figure 5.46. This will add an *unbound control* to the design grid, which is a text box that is not associated to a field in a query or table.
- Delete the label box that is added to the design grid when the text box is drawn, as shown in Figure 5.46. A label box will always appear with a text box when it is dragged onto the design grid from the Field List or manually added to the design grid using the **Text Box** icon. Because the Weeks of Supply label was already added to the Cat Number Header section, the label box that appears when the text box is drawn can be removed.

Figure 5.46 | Opening the Property Sheet Window for a Text Box

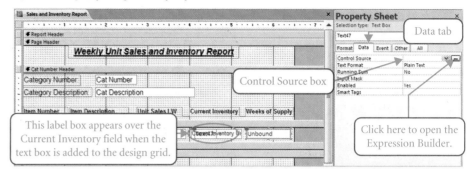

COMMON MISTAKES | Adding Calculations to a Report

Remember to use the **Text Box** icon when adding calculations to a report. People often select the **Label** icon by mistake when creating calculations. However, you cannot produce calculated results from a label box.

- Double click the text box that was added in the Detail section below the Weeks of Supply, as shown in Figure 5.46. This will open the **Property Sheet** window for this text box to the right of the design grid. The **Property Sheet** window is used to access advanced features for either text boxes or label boxes.

- Click the **Data** tab on the **Property Sheet** window.

- Click in the box next to the Control Source label. Then, open the Expression Builder by clicking the small button next to the drop-down arrow, as shown in Figure 5.46.

- Enter the weeks of supply formula into the Expression Builder. After the Expression Builder is open, you can create formulas or functions, as demonstrated in Chapter 4. The weeks of supply formula for the Sales and Inventory Report will take the Unit Sales LW field and divide it into the Current Inventory Units field. As shown in Figure 5.47, click the <**Field List**> option in the center window of the Expression Builder to see a list of fields for the query or table that is being used to create the report.

Figure 5.47 | **Expression Builder Showing the Weeks of Supply Formula**

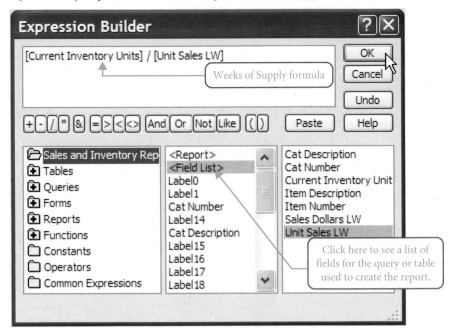

- Click the **OK** button in the Expression Builder after entering the weeks of supply formula.

- Format the text box containing the weeks of supply formula by clicking the **Format** tab of the **Property Sheet** window. Then, click in the first box next to the Format heading, and click the drop-down arrow. Select the **Fixed format** option.

- Click in the **Decimal Places** box and select the number 1. Then, in the lower area of the **Property Sheet** window, change the Font Name to Arial, the Font Size to 10 points, and the Text Align to Left (see Figure 5.48).

- Close the **Property Sheet** window by clicking the X in the upper-right corner.

- Switch the report to **Layout View** to make any necessary adjustments to the position or dimensions of the text box containing the weeks of supply formula.

Figure 5.48 shows the formatting options that were selected for the text box containing the weeks of supply formula. This text box could have also been formatted using the icons in the Font group in the **Design** tab of the Ribbon. Notice that in the text box, an equal sign was placed in front of the formula. Access does this automatically when formulas are created in the Expression Builder.

Figure 5.48 | **Formatting Options in the Properties Window**

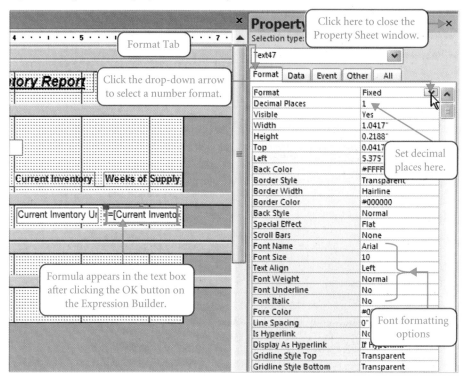

Figure 5.49 shows the Sales and Inventory Report in **Print Preview**. The report now includes a field that calculates the weeks of supply for each item on the report.

Figure 5.49 | **Sales and Inventory Report with Calculated Field in Print Preview**

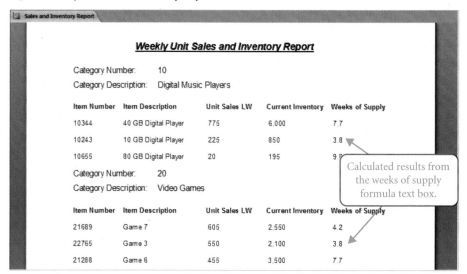

Conditional Formatting

Conditional formatting is a common feature that is used to highlight critical information on a business report. You may use it to change the appearance of data in a report depending on the value or output. With regard to the Sales and Inventory Report shown in Figure 5.49, this example shows how to use the conditional formatting feature to highlight any weeks of supply value that is greater than 9. If the weeks of supply value for any item is greater than 9, the conditional formatting feature will automatically bold the value and change the color to red. This will help a business manager to quickly identify any items that are selling at a slow rate. A business manager might use this information to decide that the price of an item should be reduced to increase sales. The following explains how this is accomplished:

- Activate the text box containing the formula for calculating the weeks of supply (see Figure 5.48).
- Click the **Conditional** icon in the **Design** tab of the Ribbon. This will open the **Conditional Formatting** dialog box.
- Check the Default Formatting settings in the top section of the **Conditional Formatting** dialog box. The formats selected in this section will be applied if the conditions set in the next section of this window are *not* met.
- Set a logical test in the Condition 1 section of the **Conditional Formatting** dialog box. As previously mentioned, the goal for using the Conditional Formatting feature in the Sales and Inventory Report is to highlight any weeks of supply value greater than 9. Therefore, the first box of the Condition 1 section should be set to **Field Value Is**. The next box should be set to **greater than**. Type the number 9 in the box next to the **greater than** setting.
- Adjust the format settings if the condition is true. Set the format of the Condition 1 section to a bold and red font. This is done by clicking the **Bold** icon and selecting Red from the **Font Color** icon.
- After setting the conditions and formats in the **Conditional Formatting** dialog box, click the **OK** button and view the report in **Print Preview** to check the results.

Figure 5.50 shows the final settings in the **Conditional Formatting** dialog box for the Sales and Inventory Report. Notice that the **Condition 1** settings will change the font to bold and text color to red if the value in the field is greater than 9.

Figure 5.50 | **Final Settings in the Conditional Formatting Dialog Box**

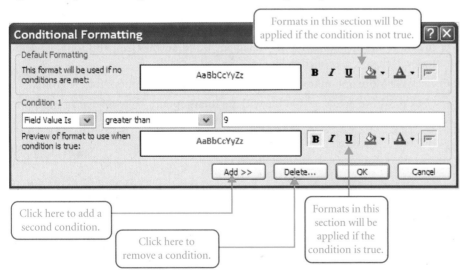

>> **Quick Reference**

Calculated Fields

1. Open an existing report in **Design View**.
2. Add a text box to the design grid.
3. Double click the text box to open the **Property Sheet** window.
4. Click the **Data** tab in the **Property Sheet** window.
5. Click the box to the right of the Control Source label.
6. Click the button to the right of the drop-down arrow in the **Control Source** box to open the Expression Builder.
7. Enter a formula or function into the Expression Builder.
8. Click the **OK** button on the Expression Builder.
9. Click the **Format** tab of the **Property Sheet** window to adjust the format of the Text Box producing the calculated results.
10. Close the **Property Sheet** window by clicking the X in the upper-right corner.

Figure 5.51 shows the Sales and Inventory Report in Print Preview. As a result of the conditional format settings in Figure 5.50 any value in the Weeks of Supply column that is greater than 9 is bolded and the text color is changed to red.

Figure 5.51 | **Sales and Inventory Report with Conditional Formats Applied**

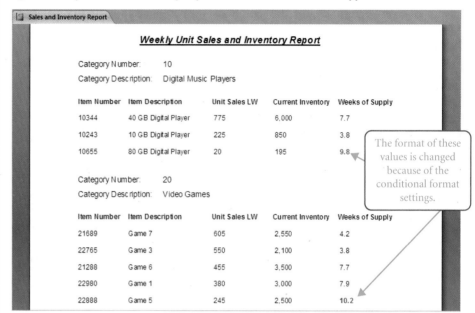

Group and Report Totals

As previously mentioned, an important feature of the Sales and Inventory Report shown in Figure 5.33 is that totals are calculated for each group of items. In addition, this report also includes a total summary of all unit sales, inventory, and weeks of supply, which is not seen in the figure. These totals are added to the report through the Grouping dialog box. In fact, you may have noticed that one of the settings in the Grouping dialog box shown in Figure 5.38 is **with no totals.** The following explains how this option is used to add totals for each category and for the entire report.

- Click the **Group & Sort** icon in the **Design** tab of the Ribbon. For the Sales and Inventory Report, the Grouping dialog box will show the **Group on** and the **Sort by** levels that were created in Figures 5.38 and 5.44.
- Click the **More** option in the **Group on** level to show all options for the group.
- Click the down arrow next to the **with no totals** option. This will open a window that is used to add totals to the report, as shown in Figure 5.52.

Figure 5.52 | **The Totals Option in the Grouping Dialog Box**

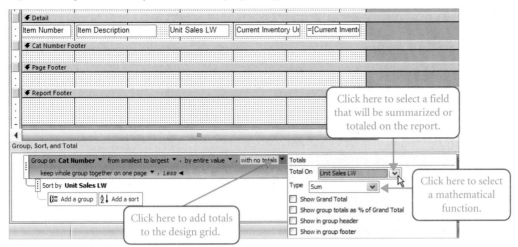

- Click the down arrow next to the **Total On** box and select the **Unit Sales LW** field.

- Click the down arrow next to the **Type** box and select the **Sum** option. There are several mathematical summaries in this drop-down box such as Average, Count Values, Standard Deviation, and so on. For the purposes of the Sales and Inventory Report, the **Sum** option is selected so the values in the Unit Sales LW field are totaled for each category and for the entire report.

- Click the box next to the **Show Grand Total** option. Once this box is clicked, a text box containing a SUM function will appear in the Report Footer section of the design grid.

- Click the box next to the **Show in group footer** option. Once this box is clicked, a text box containing a SUM function will appear in the Cat Number Footer section of the design grid.

- Click the down arrow next to the **Totals On** box and select the **Current Inventory Units** field. Once a total has been added, other fields can be selected to add additional totals to the design grid.

- Click the down arrow next to the **Type** box and select the **Sum** option.

- Click the box next to the **Show Grand Total** option. Once this box is clicked, a second text box containing a SUM function will appear in the Report Footer section of the design grid.

- Click the box next to the **Show in group footer** option. Once this box is clicked, a second text box containing a SUM function will appear in the Cat Number Footer section of the design grid.

Figure 5.53 shows the results of adding totals to the Cat Number Footer and Report Footer sections of the design grid. The Grouping dialog box can be used to add as many totals to the design grid as needed based on the available fields in the Field List.

Figure 5.53 | **Adding Totals to the Design Grid**

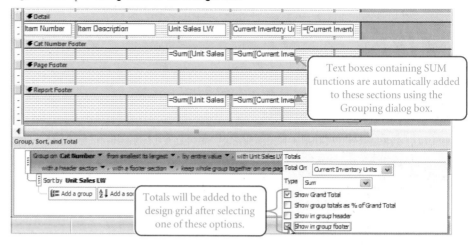

Figures 5.54 and 5.55 show the beginning and end of the Sales and Inventory Report in **Print Preview**. Notice that several formatting adjustments were applied to the totals and a label box was added to both the Cat Number Footer and Report Footer sections. Once text boxes are added to the design grid of a report, as shown in Figure 5.53, formatting adjustments can be applied using the **Property Sheet** window. In addition, the placement and size of the text boxes can be adjusted by switching the report to **Layout View**.

Figure 5.54 | **Beginning of the Sales and Inventory Report Showing Group Totals**

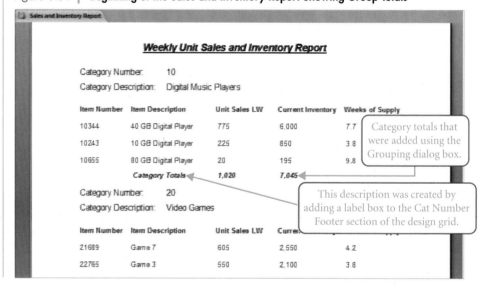

Figure 5.55 | **End of the Sales and Inventory Report Showing Report Totals**

Sales and Inventory Report				
44339	DVD/VCR	525	2,250	4.3
44332	Multi Disc DVD	54	500	9.3
44922	VCR	40	1,350	33.8
44556	DVD Player	10	105	10.5
	Category Totals	*629*	*4,205*	

Category Number: 50
Category Description: Accessories

Item Number	Item Description	Unit Sales LW	Current Inventory	Weeks of Supply
52708	Earbud Headphones	770	3,200	4.2
54670	Soft CD Case	320	1,850	5.8
58900	Basic Headphones	220	1,250	5.7
53210	CD Carry Box	84	1,200	14.3
	Category Totals	*1,394*	*7,500*	
	Grand Totals	***5,978***	***39,800***	

This label was created using a label box.

Grand totals that were added from the Grouping dialog box.

The final total that needs to be added to the Sales and Inventory Report is the weeks of supply. Because Weeks of Supply is a calculated field on the report, a formula must be created to calculate the overall weeks of supply for the category. That is to say, the weeks of supply for each category cannot be calculated by simply summing the weeks of supply for each item. To calculate the weeks of supply for the entire category, the total Units Sales LW for the category must be divided into the total Current Inventory units for the category. The following explains how this is added to the report:

- Add a text box to the Cat Number Footer section and align it under the Weeks of Supply label box in the Cat Number Header section.
- Delete the label box that is attached to the text box.
- Double click the text box to open the **Property Sheet** window.
- Click the **Data** tab in the **Property Sheet** window and open the Expression Builder.
- Type the beginning of the Sum function: **SUM(**. Click the **<Field List>** option in the center window of the Expression Builder, double click the Current Inventory Units field, type a closing parenthesis, and type a slash for division.
- After the slash, type the beginning of another Sum function: **SUM(**. Double click the Unit Sales LW field, and type a closing parenthesis.
- Click the **OK** button on the Expression Builder.
- Close the **Property Sheet** window.

Figure 5.53 shows how the formula for the total weeks of supply should appear in the Expression Builder.

Figure 5.56 | **Formula for Calculating the Total Weeks of Supply for a Category**

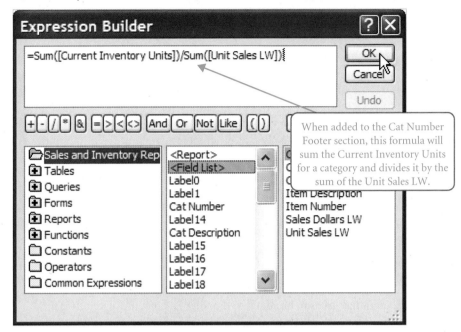

Figure 5.57 shows the completed text box in the Cat Number Footer section, which contains a formula that will calculate the total weeks of supply for the category. Notice that a similar text box appears in the Report Footer section. This is because the text box in the Cat Number Footer section was copied and pasted to the Report Footer section. Since the text box was pasted into the Report Footer section, Access will automatically use the formula to calculate the total weeks of supply for the entire report. Both text boxes and label boxes can be copied and pasted using the **Copy** and **Paste** icons in the **Home** tab of the Ribbon.

Figure 5.57 | **The Total Weeks of Supply for the Group and Report Is Calculated Using a Formula**

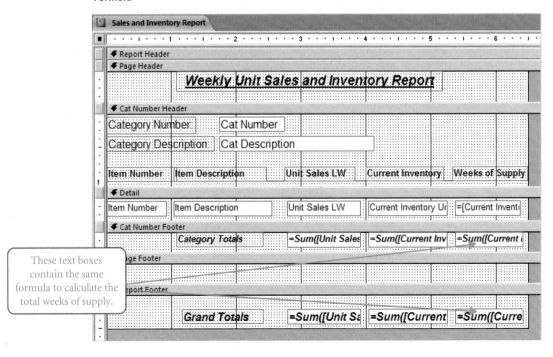

Figure 5.58 shows the end of the Sales and Inventory Report in Print Preview. Notice that formatting adjustments were applied to the weeks of supply totals. Also, notice that the total weeks of supply is not a summation of the weeks of supply values for each item.

Figure 5.58 | Sales and Inventory Report with Total Weeks of Supply

Item Number	Item Description	Unit Sales LW	Current Inventory	Weeks of Supply
44339	DVD/VCR	525	2,250	4.3
44332	Multi Disc DVD	54	500	9.3
44922	VCR	40	1,350	33.8
44556	DVD Player	10	105	10.5
	Category Totals	*629*	*4,205*	*6.7*

Category Number: 50
Category Description: Accessories

Item Number	Item Description	Unit Sales LW	Current Inventory	Weeks of Supply
52708	Earbud Headphones	770	3,200	4.2
54670	Soft CD Case	320	1,850	5.8
58900	Basic Headphones	220	1,250	5.7
53210	CD Carry Box	84	1,200	14.3
	Category Totals	*1,394*	*7,500*	*5.4*
	Grand Totals	*5,978*	*39,800*	*6.7*

The total weeks of supply formula produces different results depending on the section the text box is placed.

Lines

A subtle, yet important, formatting feature on the Sales and Inventory Report shown in Figure 5.33 is the lines. Lines are often used to separate the main sections of a report or to separate the column headings from the detail of a report. Lines make reports easier to read and help business managers focus on areas that contain the most critical information. With regards to the Sales and Inventory Report, lines are used to separate each category of merchandise, the column headings, and the bottom of each category where the totals are displayed. The following explains how lines are added to the report:

- Click the **Line** icon in the **Design** tab of the Ribbon.
- Click and drag across the top of the Cat Number Header section of the design grid.
- Click the **Line Thickness** icon in the **Design** tab of the Ribbon and select the **2 pt** option. This will place a heavy bold line at the top of each category section of the report.

Figure 5.59 shows the appearance of the line at the top of the Cat Number Header section. The line will be activated when it is initially added to the design grid. It is important to note that a line must be activated before applying any formatting enhancements such as line thickness or color. The placement of a line can be adjusted on the design grid by using the arrow keys on your keyboard if it is activated. To activate a line, click it once. To deactivate a line, click any empty space on the design grid.

>> **Quick Reference**

Group and Report Totals

1. Open an existing report in **Design View**.
2. Click the **Group & Sort** icon in the **Design** tab of the Ribbon.
3. Create a group for your report (see Grouping Data).
4. Click the **More** option for one of the Group levels in the **Grouping** dialog box.
5. Click the down arrow next to the **with no totals** option in the **Grouping** dialog box.
6. Select a field and mathematical function at the top of the totals window.
7. Select **Show Grand Total** at the bottom of the totals window when totaling data for an entire report.
8. Select **Show in group footer** at the bottom of the totals window when totaling data at the end of each group.
9. Repeat steps 6 through 8 when adding more than one total to a report.
10. Close the **Grouping** dialog box.

Figure 5.59 | **Adding a Line to the Design Grid**

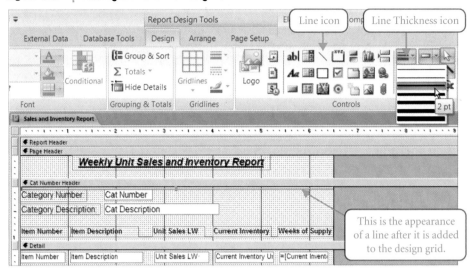

Figure 5.60 shows the appearance of the Sales and Inventory Report in Print Preview after adding additional lines to the design grid. Notice that a second line was added to the Cat Number Header section to separate the column headings and details of the report. A line was also added to the top of the Cat Number Footer section to separate the detail from the totals. Finally, two lines were added to the top of the Report Footer section to separate the Grand Totals from the rest of the report.

Figure 5.60 | **Sales and Inventory Report with Lines**

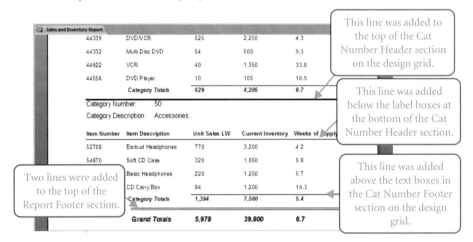

Dates

The final elements that will be added to the Sales and Inventory Report are the page numbers and the date. Both the page numbers and date will be added to the Page Footer section of the design grid. Adding page numbers was covered in the first section of this chapter (see Figure 5.28). The following explains how to add the date to a report:

- Add a text box to the left side of the Page Footer section on the design grid.
- Delete the label box.
- Double click the text box to open the **Property Sheet** window.
- Click the **Data** tab of the **Property Sheet** window and open the Expression Builder.
- Type the word Date followed by an open and close parenthesis in the upper window of the Expression Builder. Then click the **OK** button. This will produce the current date at the bottom of the Access report.
- Format the text box to an Arial font, 8 point font size, bold, italics, and left alignment.

Figure 5.61 shows the text box containing the date that was added to the Page Footer section of the design grid. An alternative method of adding the current date to an Access report is to use the **Date** icon in the **Design** tab of the Ribbon. However, this command will only add the date to the Report Header section. You will need to use this method if you wish to place the date at the bottom of the report.

Figure 5.61 | **Final Design Grid for the Sales and Inventory Report**

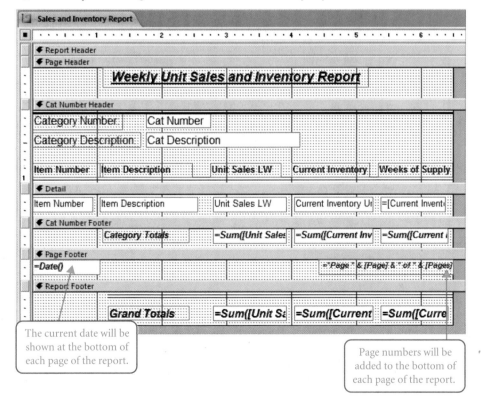

The current date will be shown at the bottom of each page of the report.

Page numbers will be added to the bottom of each page of the report.

>> **Quick Reference**

Lines

1. Open an existing report in **Design View**.
2. Click the **Line** icon in the **Design** tab of the Ribbon.
3. Click and drag in the desired section on the design grid to add a line to the report.
4. While the line is activated, click the **Line Thickness** icon in the **Design** tab of the Ribbon to change the thickness of the line.
5. Check the position and appearance of the line by switching the report to **Print Preview**.

Figures 5.62 and 5.63 show the top and bottom of the first page of the final Sales and Inventory Report. Notice that the page number and date appear at the bottom the report.

Figure 5.62 | **Final Sales and Inventory Report in Print Preview (Top of Page 1)**

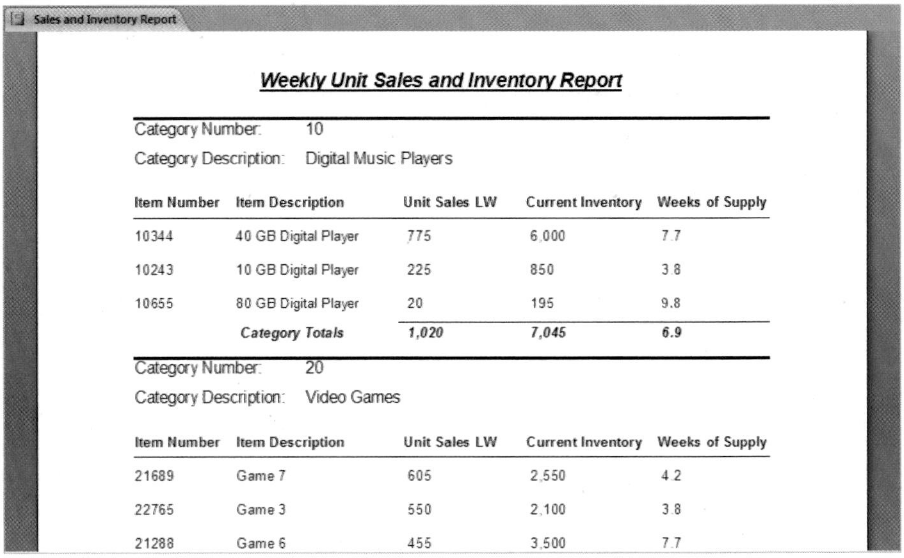

Sales and Inventory Report

Weekly Unit Sales and Inventory Report

Category Number: 10

Category Description: Digital Music Players

Item Number	Item Description	Unit Sales LW	Current Inventory	Weeks of Supply
10344	40 GB Digital Player	775	6,000	7.7
10243	10 GB Digital Player	225	850	3.8
10655	80 GB Digital Player	20	195	9.8
	Category Totals	*1,020*	*7,045*	*6.9*

Category Number: 20

Category Description: Video Games

Item Number	Item Description	Unit Sales LW	Current Inventory	Weeks of Supply
21689	Game 7	605	2,550	4.2
22765	Game 3	550	2,100	3.8
21288	Game 6	455	3,500	7.7

Figure 5.63 | **Final Sales and Inventory Report in Print Preview (Bottom of Page 1)**

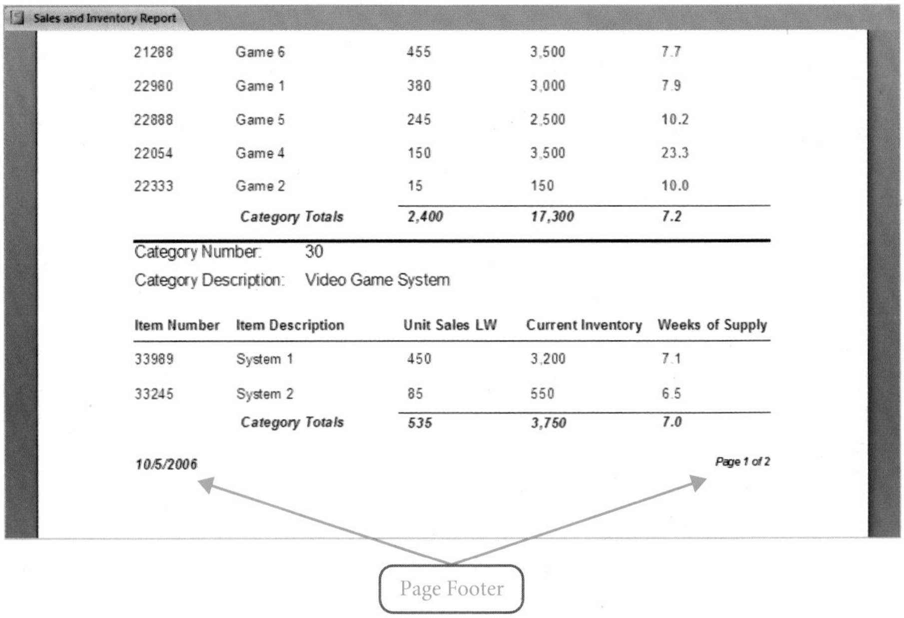

Sales and Inventory Report

21288	Game 6	455	3,500	7.7
22980	Game 1	380	3,000	7.9
22888	Game 5	245	2,500	10.2
22054	Game 4	150	3,500	23.3
22333	Game 2	15	150	10.0
	Category Totals	*2,400*	*17,300*	*7.2*

Category Number: 30

Category Description: Video Game System

Item Number	Item Description	Unit Sales LW	Current Inventory	Weeks of Supply
33989	System 1	450	3,200	7.1
33245	System 2	85	550	6.5
	Category Totals	*535*	*3,750*	*7.0*

10/5/2006 *Page 1 of 2*

> **Quick Reference**
>
> **Dates**
>
> 1. Open an existing report in **Design View**.
> 2. Add a text box in the Page Footer section of the design grid.
> 3. Open the **Property Sheet** window.
> 4. Click the Data tab of the Property Sheet window and open the Expression Builder.
> 5. Type **DATE()** in the upper window of the Expression builder.
> 6. Click the **OK** button on the Expression Builder.
> 7. Make any desired formatting adjustments.

>> Advanced Report Skills

The purpose of this workshop is to demonstrate advanced techniques and features for creating Access reports. The report that will be created in this workshop is identical to the one constructed in this section. I will be demonstrating the tasks in this workshop over the following eight videos: **Advanced Report Setup**, **Grouping Data**, **Sorting**, **Report Calculated Fields**, **Conditional Formatting**, **Group and Report Totals**, **Adding Lines to a Report**, and **Dates**. The name of the video will appear in parentheses next to the heading for each section of tasks. You will need to open the Access database named ib_a05_electronicsmerchandisedata. Try completing the tasks in each section first before watching the related video. You can complete this workshop in stages by saving and closing the report after completing a section of tasks. To resume work on the report, open it in **Design View** and continue on to the next section of tasks.

1. **Report Setup (Video: Advanced Report Setup)**
   a. Create a new Access Report by clicking the **Report Design** icon in the **Create** tab of the Ribbon.
   b. Open the **Property Sheet** window by clicking the **Property Sheet** Icon in the **Design** tab of the Ribbon.
   c. Click the Data tab in the Property Sheet window, and then click in the box next to the Record Source.
   d. Click the Record Source drop-down arrow and select the Sales and Inventory Data query. Then close the **Property Sheet** window by clicking the X in the upper-right corner of the window.
   e. Open the Page Setup dialog box from the **Page Setup** tab of the Ribbon. Set the Top, Bottom, Right, and Left margins to one inch. Then close the **Page Setup** dialog box.
   f. Increase the width of the design grid to 6.5 inches.
   g. Save the report and name it `Sales and Inventory Performance Report`.
   h. Add the Report Header and Footer sections to the design grid by clicking the Report Header/Footer icon in the **Arrange** tab of the Ribbon.
   i. Decrease the height of the Report Header section to 0. Then increase the height of the Page Header section to 3/8 inch.
   j. Add a label box to the top center of the Page Header section. Type `Sales and Inventory Performance Report` in the label box..
   k. Make the following format adjustments to the label box that was created in j.: Arial font, font size of 14 points, bold, italics, underline, and center alignment.
   l. Save the report.

2. Grouping Data (Video: Grouping Data)

a. Click the Group & Sort icon in the **Design** tab of the Ribbon.

b. Click the Add a Group button in the **Grouping** dialog box below the design grid. Then select the Cat Number field from the field window.

c. Click the **More** option to show additional group settings.

d. Click the down arrow next to the without a footer section option and select the **With a footer section** option.

e. Select the keep whole group together on one page option.

f. Click the X in the upper-right corner of the **Grouping** dialog box to close it.

g. Increase the height of the Cat Number Header section to 1 inch.

h. Open the Field List by clicking the **Add Existing Fields** icon in the **Design** tab of the ribbon.

i. Drag the Cat Number field from the field list into the upper-left corner of the Cat Number Header section.

j. Click and drag the upper-left corner of the Cat Number text box to the right to separate the text box from the label box.

k. Change the description in the Cat Number label box to Category Number.

l. Make the following format adjustments to the Cat Number label and text boxes: Arial font, 12 point font size, and left alignment.

m. Switch the report to **Layout View**. Make any necessary adjustments to the Cat Number label and text boxes. Make sure all the data is visible and that the Category Number description is in the upper-left corner of the Cat Number Header section.

n. Switch the report back to **Design View**.

o. Drag the Cat Description field from the Field List into the Cat Number Header section below the Cat Number label box. Adjust the Cat Description label box so that it is aligned below the Cat Number label box. Then, adjust the Cat Description text box so that it is aligned below the Cat Number text box.

p. Change the description in the Cat Description label box to Category Description.

q. Make the following format adjustments to the Cat Description label and text boxes: Arial font, 12 point font size, and left alignment.

r. Switch the report to **Layout View**. Make any necessary adjustments to the Cat Description label and text boxes. Make sure all of the data is visible and that the category description is aligned below the category number.

s. Switch the report back to **Design View** and save.

t. Add five label boxes to the bottom of the Cat Number Header section, beginning at the far left side. Following are the descriptions that should appear in each box. Remember to press the **Enter** key after typing each description. If the error icon appears, click it once and select the **Ignore Error** option.

   i. Label Box 1: `Item Number`

   ii. Label Box 2: `Item Description`

   iii. Label Box 3: `Unit Sales LW`

   iv. Label Box 4: `Current Inventory`

   v. Label Box 5: `Weeks of Supply`

u. Apply the following formats to the five label boxes that were created in step t: Arial font, font size of 10 points, bold, and left alignment.

v. Switch the report to **Layout View** to check the label boxes that were created in step t. Make any necessary adjustment to the position and dimensions of the label boxes so that all the descriptions are visible and are distributed evenly across the report.

w. Switch the report back to **Design View** and save.

3. Sorting Data (Video: Sorting)

a. Set the height of the Detail section to ¼ inch.

b. Drag the following fields from the Field List into the Detail section. Delete the label box attached to each text box and align each text box under the appropriate label box in the Cat Number Header section.

   i. Item Number

   ii. Item Description

   iii. Unit Sales LW

   iv. Current Inventory Units

c. Apply the following formats to the four text boxes that were added to the Detail section in step b: Arial font, font size of 10 points, and left alignment.

d. Switch the report to **Layout View** to check the text boxes that were formatted in step c. Make any necessary adjustment to the position and dimensions of the text boxes so that all the data is visible and is aligned below the headings.

e. Switch the report back to **Design View** and save.

f. Click the Group & Sort icon in the **Design** tab of the Ribbon.

g. Click the **Add a Sort** button in the **Grouping** dialog box below the design grid.

h. Select the Unit Sales LW field from the field window in the **Grouping** dialog box. Then, select the from largest to smallest sort option.

i. Click the X in the upper-right corner of the **Grouping** dialog box to close it.

j. Save the report.

4. Calculated Fields (Video: Report Calculated Fields)

a. Add a text box to the Detail section and align under the Weeks of Supply heading in the Cat Number Header section. Remove the label box that is attached to the text box.

b. Double click the text box that was added in step a to open the Property Sheet window.

c. Click the **Data** tab of the top of the **Property Sheet** window. Then, click in the box next to the Control Source label and open the Expression Builder by clicking the small button next to the drop-down arrow.

d. Enter the following weeks of supply formula in the upper window of the Expression Builder: Current Inventory Units / Unit Sales LW. Remember to click the **<Field List>** option in the lower-center window of the Expression Builder to show a list of fields in the Sales and Inventory Data query.

e. Click the **OK** button on the Expression Builder.

f. Click the Format tab at the top of the **Property Sheet** window. Make the following format selections: Fixed number format, 1 decimal place, Arial Font Name, Font Size of 10 points, and Text Align Left.

g. Close the **Property Sheet** window by clicking the X in the upper-right corner.

h. Switch the report to **Layout View** to check the text box that is calculating the weeks of supply results. Make any necessary adjustment to the position and dimensions of the text box so that the data is visible and is aligned below the Weeks of Supply heading.

i. Switch the report back to **Design View** and save.

5. Conditional Formatting (Video: Conditional Formatting)

a. Activate the text box containing the weeks of supply formula in the Detail section by clicking it once.

b. Click the **Conditional** icon in the **Design** tab of the Ribbon.

c. Select the **Field Value Is** option in the first drop-down box of the Condition 1 section of the **Conditional Formatting** dialog box.

d. Select the greater than option in the second drop-down box of the Condition 1 section of the **Conditional Formatting** dialog box.

e. Type the number **9** in the input box of the Condition 1 section of the **Conditional Formatting** dialog box.

f. Select the red font color and click the **Bold** icon in the Condition 1 section of the **Conditional Formatting** dialog box.

g. Close the **Conditional Formatting** dialog box by clicking the **OK** button. Then, switch the report to **Layout View** and check the results of the Weeks of Supply column.

h. Switch the report back to **Design View** and save.

6. Report Totals (Video: Group and Report Totals)

a. Increase the height of the Report Footer section to ½ inch. Then, increase the height of the Cat Number Footer section to ¼ inch.

b. Click the **Grouping** icon in the **Design** tab of the ribbon.

c. Click the **More** option in the Group on level in the **Grouping** dialog box below the design grid.

d. Click the down arrow next to the with no totals option in the Group on level.

e. Select the Unit Sales LW field from the Total On drop-down box. Then, select the Show Grand Total and Show in group footer options.

f. Select the Current Inventory Units field from the **Total On** drop-down box. Then, select the Show Grand Total and Show in group footer options.

g. Close the **Grouping** dialog box by clicking the X in the upper-right corner.

h. Open the **Property Sheet** window for the **Unit Sales LW totals** text box in the Cat Number Footer section. Make the following format settings: Standard number format, 0 decimal place, font size of 10 points, italics, and bold.

i. Click the Current Inventory Units totals text box in the Cat Number Footer section and make the following format settings in the Property Sheet window: Standard number format, 0 decimal place, font size of 10 points, italics, and bold.

j. Close the **Property Sheet** window.

k. Add a label box to the Cat Number Footer section and align to the left of the Unit Sales LW text box.

l. Type **Category Totals** in the label box added in step k. Apply the following formats to this label box: Arial font, font size of 10 points, italics, bold, and left alignment.

m. Switch the report to **Layout View** and make any necessary adjustments to the label and text boxes in the Cat Number Footer section. The Category Totals label should be aligned below the Item Descriptions. The totals for Unit Sales LW and Current Inventory should be aligned under their respective column headings.

n. Switch the report back to **Design View** and save.

o. Add a text box to the Cat Number Footer section and align below the Weeks of Supply heading in the Cat Number Header section. Delete the label box that is attached to this text box.

p. Double click the text box that was added in step o and click the **Data** tab in the **Property Sheet** window.

q. Click in the box next to the Control Source label and open the Expression Builder.

r. Enter the following formula in the upper window of the Expression Builder: **Sum([Current Inventory Units])/Sum([Unit Sales LW])**. Then, click the **OK** button in the Expression Builder.

s. Click the Format tab in the **Property Sheet** window and make the following format settings: Fixed number format, 1 decimal place, Arial font, font size of 10 points, italics, bold, and left alignment. Then, close the **Property Sheet** window.

t. Switch the report to **Layout View** and make any necessary adjustments to the text box calculating the weeks of supply totals. The data should be visible and aligned below the Weeks of Supply heading.

u. Switch the report back to **Design View** and save.

v. In the **Report Footer** section, click and drag the Unit Sales LW grand total text box to the bottom of the section. Do the same for the Current Inventory Units grand total text box.

w. Activate the weeks of supply totals text box in the **Cat Number Footer** section and click the **Copy** icon in the **Home** tab of the Ribbon.

x. Click anywhere in the **Report Footer** section and click the **Paste** icon in the **Home** tab of the Ribbon. Then, click and drag the text box to align under the Weeks of Supply heading at the bottom of the Report Footer section.

y. Add a label box to the **Report Footer** section and enter the description **Grand Totals** in the box. The box should be aligned below the Category Totals label box in the **Cat Number Footer** section at the bottom of the **Report Footer** section.

z. Make the following format adjustments to the label and text boxes in the **Report Footer** section: Arial Font, font size of 12 points, bold, italics, and left alignment. For the Unit Sales LW and Current Inventory Units grand total text boxes, set the number format to Standard with zero decimal places. For the Weeks of Supply grand total text box, set the number format to Fixed with 1 decimal place.

aa. Switch the report to **Layout View** and make any necessary adjustments to the label and text boxes in the Report Footer section.

ab. Switch the report back to **Design View** and save.

7. Lines (Video: Adding Lines to a Report)

a. Click the Line icon in the **Design** tab of the Ribbon.

b. Click and drag a line across the top of the **Cat Number Header** section.

c. With the line activated, click the **Line Thickness** icon in the **Design** tab of the Ribbon and select the 2 pt option.

d. Click the Line icon in the **Design** tab of the Ribbon and add a line to the bottom of the Cat Number Header section below the label boxes. The line should extend the entire length of the **Cat Number Header** section.

e. Click the **Line** icon in the **Design** tab of the Ribbon and add a line above the label and text boxes in the Cat Number Footer section. Begin drawing the line at the left edge of the Category Totals label box.

f. Click the Line icon in the **Design** tab of the Ribbon and add a line at the top of the **Report Footer** section. Begin drawing the line at the left edge of the Grand Totals label box. Add a second line below this line so there are two lines at the top of this section.

g. Save the report.

8. Adding the Date (Video: Dates)

a. Increase the height of the Page Footer section to ¼ of an inch.

b. Add a text box to the lower left side of the Page Footer section and remove the label box that is attached. Then, open the Property Sheet window for this text box.

c. Open the Expression Builder and type **DATE ( )** in the upper window.:.

d. Click the **OK** button on the Expression Builder and then format the text box to bold, italics, left justification, Arial font, and font size of 10 points.

e. Add the page number to the lower-right side of the Page Footer section. Select the **Page N of M** option in the **Page Numbers** dialog box. Then format to bold, italics, Arial font, font size of 10 points, and right alignment.

f. Switch the report to **Layout View** and make any necessary adjustments.

g. View the report in **Print Preview** mode. Then, save and close the report.

>> Industry and Company Performance Report

Most business managers would agree that performance reports are a vital resource for making business decisions. These reports not only show whether a business is achieving its goals but can also highlight critical business trends. For example, a performance report designed for a retail business manager could highlight stores that are underperforming in certain regions or states. A report could also be designed for a financial analyst to show the sales and profit performance of public companies that have been purchased as part of an investment portfolio. The report can highlight overall declines and growth within certain industries as well as specific companies.

Exercise

The purpose of this exercise is to construct a report that might be used by a financial analyst. The report will contain the net sales and income results for several companies that comprise a hypothetical investment portfolio. A financial analyst would use this report to monitor the change in net sales and income for each company as well as the overall trend for each industry. Open the Access database named ib_a05_financialstatistics before completing the tasks below.

1. Create a new Access report using the Sales and Profit by Company table in the database called ib_a05_financialstatistics. The margins of the report should be set to one inch on all sides, and the orientation should be set to portrait. Set the appropriate width of the design grid assuming the paper size is 8.5 × 11 inches.

2. Add the Report Header and Footer to the design grid. Reduce the height of the Report Header to zero.

3. Add a Group Header and Footer to the design grid based on the Industry field. Choose the **with a footer section option**, and **keep whole group together on one page** option in the **Grouping** dialog box. This will be used to group the companies into their respective industries and calculate financial statistics for each industry.

4. Save the report and name it **Financial Performance Report by Industry**.

5. Increase the height of the Page Header section to ½ inch and add a report title using a label box. The title of the report should be **Company Performance by Industry**. Apply the following formats to the title: Arial font, font size of 14 points, bold, italics, underline, and center alignment. Check the position of the label box so the title is centered on the report.

6. Increase the height of the Industry Header section to 5/8 of an inch. Add the Industry field to the upper-left corner of this section.

7. Separate the Industry field label box from the text box. There should be approximately ¼ of an inch space between the label and text boxes. Apply the following formats to both the label and text boxes: Arial font, font size of 12 points, bold, italics, and left alignment. Adjust the dimensions of both boxes so the description and data are visible.

8. Add five label boxes to the bottom of the Industry Header section starting on the far left side. The description that should appear in each label box is listed as follows. These label boxes are being used as the column headings for the data that will be added to the Detail section. Apply the following formats to these label boxes: Arial font, font size of 10 points, bold, and left alignment.

   a. Label box 1: **Company Name**
   b. Label box 2: **Net Sales LY**
   c. Label box 3: **Change in Net Sales**
   d. Label box 4: **Net Income LY**
   e. Label box 5: **Change in Net Income**

9. Decrease the width of the **Change in Net Sales** and **Change in Net Income** label boxes in the Industry Header section to approximately 5/8 inch. Increase the height of these boxes so the description wraps to two lines. Check the appearance of these label boxes and make any additional needed adjustments.

10. Adjust the height of the Detail section to 3/8 inch.

11. Add the Company Name field to the upper-left area of the Detail section and delete the label box that is attached to the text box. Then, align the text box under the **Company Name** label box in the Industry Header section.

12. Add the Net Sales LY field to the Detail section and delete the label box that is attached to the text box. Then, align the text box under the Net Sales LY label box in the Industry Header section.

13. Add the Net Income LY field to the Detail section and delete the label box that is attached to the text box. Then, align the text box under the *Net Income LY* label box in the Industry Header section.

14. Apply the following formats to the three text boxes in the Detail section: Arial font, font size of 10 points, and left alignment.

15. Draw two text boxes in the Detail section and align one box under the Change in Net Sales label box and the other under the Change in Net Income label box in the Industry Header section. Delete the label box that is attached to each text box. Formulas will be added to both text boxes to calculate the change in Net Sales and Net Income for each company.

16. Open the **Property Sheet** window for the text box in the Detail section under the Change in Net Sales label box. Use the Expression Builder to calculate the percent change in net sales from two years ago to last year. The formula is as follows: =(Net Sales LY-Net Sales 2YrAgo) / Net Sales 2YrAgo. Start this formula by adding an equal sign to the upper window of the Expression Builder.

17. Format the text box containing the change in net sales formula as follows: Percent number format, 1 decimal place, Arial font, font size of 10 points, and left alignment.

18. Open the **Property Sheet** window for the text box in the Detail section under the Change in Net Income label box. The purpose of this text box is to calculate the percent change in net income from two years ago to last year. Type the following formula into the Expression Builder for this text box: **=(Net Income LY-Net Income 2YrAgo)/Net Income 2YrAgo**. Start this formula by adding an equal sign to the upper window of the Expression Builder.

19. Format the text box containing the change in net income formula as follows: Percent number format, 1 decimal place, Arial font, font size of 10 points, and left alignment.

20. Check the appearance of the data produced by the text boxes in the Detail section. Make any necessary adjustments to the position and size of the text boxes. All the data should be visible and should be aligned under the appropriate heading.

21. Increase the height of the Industry Footer section to ⅜ inch. Then, increase the height of the Report Footer section to ½ inch.

22. Add a label box in the Industry Footer section and type the description **Industry Totals** inside the box. Format the label box as follows: Arial font, font size of 10 points, bold, italics and left alignment. Align the label box under the Company Name text box in the Detail section.

23. Add totals for the Net Sales LY field and Net Income LY field to the Industry Footer and Report Footer. In the Industry Footer section, move the text boxes to the middle of the section. In the Report Footer section, move the text boxes to the bottom of the section.

24. Format the text boxes that are calculating the totals for Net Sales LY and Net Income LY in both the Industry Footer and Report Footer sections as follows: Currency number format, 0 decimal places, Arial font, font size of 10 points, bold, italics, and left alignment. After applying the formats, check the appearance of the data and make any necessary adjustments to the position and size of the text boxes.

25. Add two text boxes to the Industry Footer section. Align one box under the Change in Net Sales label box in the Industry Header section and align the second box under the Change in Net Income label box in the Industry Header section. Delete the label box that is attached to each text box. These text boxes will be used to calculate the total change in net sales and net income for each industry.

26. Use the Expression Builder to enter the following formulas into the text boxes that were added to the Industry Footer section in number 25. Start each formula by adding an equal sign to the upper window of the Expression Builder and pay careful attention to the parentheses.

    a. **Change in Net Sales text box**:

    =(SUM([Net Sales LY])–SUM([Net Sales 2YrAgo]))/SUM([Net Sales 2YrAgo])

    b. **Change in Net Income text box**:

    =(SUM([Net Income LY])–SUM([Net Income 2YrAgo]))/SUM([Net Income 2YrAgo])

27. Format the Change in Net Sales and Change in Net Income text boxes in the Industry Footer section as follows: Percent number format, 1 decimal place, Arial font, font size of 10 points, bold, italics, and left alignment. After applying the formats, check the appearance of the data and make any necessary adjustments to the position and size of the text boxes.

28. Copy the Change in Net Sales and Change in Net Income text boxes in the Industry Footer section. Paste the text boxes into the Report Footer section. Move the text boxes so they are aligned under the appropriate heading and in line with the Report Footer totals.

29. Add a label box in the Report Footer section and type the description **Grand Totals** inside the box. Format the label box as follows: Arial font, font size of 10 points, bold, italics and left alignment. Align the label box under the Industry Totals label box in the Industry Footer section.

30. Increase the height of the Page Footer section to 1/4 inch. Then, insert page numbers in the lower-right corner of this section. Use the Page N of M format. Then format the page number as follows: Arial font, font size of 8 points, bold, italics, and right alignment.

31. Add a dark bold line (2 pt width) at the top of the Industry Header section and a regular line at the bottom of the Industry Header below the label boxes.

32. Add a regular line at the top of the Industry Footer section and two regular lines at the top of the Report Footer section.

33. Check the appearance of the report and make any adjustments to the size and position of all text boxes and label boxes.

34. View the report in **Print Preview**. Which industry is experiencing the largest Net Sales and Net Income growth? Which industry is experiencing the largest decline in Net Income?

35. Save and close the report. Then close the database.

>> What's Wrong with This Database?

Problem

You are the electronics buyer for a large department store company. Each week you review the sales of your division with your boss, who is the vice president of merchandising. For this week's meeting, your assistant shows you a new report he created in Access showing the actual sales and planned sales for each item sold in your division. He explains that this report is easier to read and is more effective in evaluating the performance of the business as opposed to the report you were previously using. He points out the following key features of the report:

- The report calculates the difference between the Actual Unit Sales LW (Last Week) and Plan Unit Sales LW for each item.
- The report groups each set of items by merchandise category. The items are sorted within each category based on the actual unit sales last week.
- Totals have been added for each merchandise category showing the total actual and planned sales.
- The last page of the report shows the total sales statistics for the entire division.

Exercise

The report your assistant created can be found in the Access database named ib_a05_buyersmeeting. Open the report named Merchandise Performance Report. Would you be comfortable using this report in your meeting with the Vice President? Consider the following:

1. Look at the overall appearance of the report. Is it easy to read?
2. Look at the sort order for the items listed within each category of the report. Are the items sorted based on the Actual Unit Sales LW field?
3. The Plan Difference and Plan vs. Actual columns are supposed to calculate the difference between the Actual Sales and Plan Sales columns. Do the results in these columns make sense?
4. Examine the Plan vs. Actual percentages that have been calculated for the Category Totals and Grand Totals. Pick any category and subtract the value in the Plan Unit Sales LW column from the value in the Actual Unit Sales LW column, and then divide this result by the value in the Plan Unit Sales LW column. Does your result match the percentage that is on the report?

What's wrong with this report? Write a short answer for each of the points listed above then make any necessary corrections to the report. With regard to point 1, add lines and make formatting adjustments to enhance the appearance of the report.

Access in **Practice** | Anecdote

Access provided me with an outstanding solution for satisfying all the performance reporting needs of the region. The biggest benefit for creating these reports in Access is that I only had to create each report one time. Each week when data was updated in the table linked to the Access database, the reports would automatically be updated. Each manager simply clicked and printed on the report they preferred to use for monitoring the stores in their district or tracking the overall performance of the region.

Assignment

The Access database named ib_a05_storeperformancedata contains a similar subset of data that was used in the regional office described in the anecdote. Your assignment is to create *two performance reports* that might be used by the regional business executives of this retail company. The following explains how each report should be constructed.

1. Open the Access database named ib_a05_storeperformancedata.
2. The table Store Sales by Region District contains sales data for several regions.
3. Create one report for the District Managers in Region 5. This report should group the stores in Region 5 by district. Provide totals for each district and the overall region.
4. Create a second report for the Region 5 Vice President. This report should show the sales performance for each district with *no store detail*, and should fit onto 1 page.
5. Each report should include the following fields:
    a. Size in SqrFt (Square Feet): Total by district for number 4.
    b. Sales LW TY (Last Week This Year)
6. Each report should include the following calculated data:
    a. **Sales per SqrFt TY LW:** Sales LW TY / Size in SqrFt
    b. **Percent Change:** (Sales LW TY – Sales LW LY) / Sales LW LY
7. Both reports should be sorted by the **Sales per SqrFt TY LW** data that you will calculate as per step 6.
8. Show any **Percent Change** value less than 0% in red with a bold font.
9. Both reports should have a professional appearance and should include title, lines, and formats that make them easy to read.

Questions for Discussion

1. Why are performance reports important for business managers? What types of decisions could business managers make using the information contained in a performance report?
2. The author explains that the risk of errors was high when performance reports were created by manually typing data into an Excel spreadsheet. Why?
3. What are the advantages of using Access to create performance reports as opposed to Excel? What are the disadvantages?

The following questions are related to the concepts addressed in this chapter. There are three types of questions: Short Answer, True or False, and Fill in the Blank. If your answer to a True or False question is False, write a short explanation as to why you think the statement is not true.

1. To create an Access report using the record set of a query, you must open the _____ _____ window and select a _____ _____ in the _____ tab.

2. What are the three primary components used in the construction of an Access report?

3. You will need to click the _____ _____ tab in the Ribbon to set the margins for a new Access report.

4. True or False: The width of the design grid will automatically expand or contract after the report margins are set.

5. What features are provided *on the design grid* that can help you position and align data on a report?

6. If a label box containing a description is added to the Report Header section, how many times and where will it appear on a report when the report is printed?

7. True or False: The Report Header section always appears at the top of the design grid when starting a new Access report.

8. The space between each row of data on an Access report is controlled by the _____ of the _____ _____ on the design grid.

9. True or False: To create the column headings of a columnar report, add text boxes to the Page Header section and type the column heading description in the box.

10. What should you check if you are having difficulty aligning the data in the Detail section of a report with the column headings that have been added in the Page Header section?

11. The following figure contains data from an Access report. What could you do to fix the appearance of the Item Numbers and Item Descriptions?

Sales and Inventory Report	
Item Number	**Item Description**
10344	40 GB Digital Player
10243	10 GB Digital Player
10655	80 GB Digital Player

12. True or False: Page numbers are automatically added to the lower-right corner of every Access report.

13. The _____ icon in the _____ tab of the Ribbon is used to add a section to the design grid for the purposes of categorizing or grouping data in an Access report.

14. Explain why a label box is always attached to a text box when a field is dragged into the design grid or a text box is drawn on the design grid.

15. True or False: You can add a formula to a label box to produce a calculated result on an Access report.

16. The following figure shows the settings in the Conditional Formatting dialog box, which was applied to the Unit Sales field of an Access report. Based on these settings, what format will be applied to the Unit Sales value if it is 49?

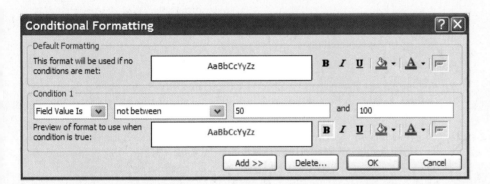

17. True or False: To draw a vertical line on an Access report, click the **Line** icon in the **Design** tab of the Ribbon and then click and drag vertically on the design grid.

18. True or False: You cannot add multiple totals to a report through the **Grouping** dialog box.

19. The _____ function is used to total the number of values or records contained in a field.

20. True or False: A text box containing a **SUM** function in the category or group section of the design grid will produce exactly the same value if it is copied and pasted into the Report Footer section of the design grid.

The following exam is designed to test your ability to recognize and execute the Access skills presented in this chapter. Read each question carefully and answer the questions in the order they are listed. You should be able to complete this exam in 60 minutes or less.

1. Open the Access database named ib_a05_skillsexam.

2. Create a new report using the Call Data table.

3. Set all margins to one inch and assume the report will printed on 8.5 × 11 inch paper. Set an appropriate width for the design grid. Then, save the report and name it **Call Center Performance**.

4. Add the Report Header and Footer sections to the report. Then, decrease the height of the Report Header section to zero.

5. Add a Group Header and Footer section to the design grid based on the Service Rep Number field. The sort order of the groups should appear in descending order. In addition, the group should always be kept together on one page.

6. Increase the height of the Page Header section to 3/8 inch and add a title for the report called **Call Center Statistics**.

7. Apply the following formats to the report title created in number 6: Arial font, font size 14 points, bold, italics, and underline. Then, make the necessary adjustments so that the title is centered on the report.

8. Increase the height of the Service Rep Number Header section to 5/8 inch.

9. Add the Service Rep Number and Service Rep Name fields to the Service Rep Number Header section of the design grid. The two fields should be aligned next to each other horizontally running across the upper area of the section.

10. Apply the following formats to the Service Rep Number and Service Rep Name fields in the Service Rep Number Header section: Arial font, font size of 12 points, and bold. Make the necessary adjustments so that all the Service Rep Numbers and Service Rep Names are visible on the report and evenly spaced across the top of the Service Rep Number Header section.

11. Add five label boxes to the lower area of the Service Rep Number Header section beginning on the far left side. Set any errors that appear to ignore. The following descriptions should appear in the label boxes:

    a. Box 1: **Date**

    b. Box 2: **Customer ID**

    c. Box 3: **Call Minutes**

    d. Box 4: **Sales Dollars**

    e. Box 5: **Call Hours**

12. Apply the following formats to the label boxes created in number 11: Arial font, font size of 10 points, bold, and left alignment. Adjust the position and dimensions of the label boxes so the descriptions are visible and are aligned in a straight horizontal line across the report.

13. Set the height of the Detail section to ¼ inch,

14. Add the following fields to the Detail section. Remove the label box that is attached to the text box and set any errors to ignore. Align the text boxes under the appropriate label box in the Service Rep Number Header section.

a. **Date**
b. **Customer ID Number**
c. **Call Minutes**
d. **Sales Dollars**

15. Apply the following formats to the text boxes added to the Detail section in number 14: Arial font, font size of 10 points, and left alignment. Adjust the position of each field so it is aligned directly below the appropriate label box in the Service Rep Number Header section.

16. Add a text box to the Detail section that calculates the Call Hours. Your formula should divide the Call Minutes field by 60. Apply the following formats to this text box: Fixed number format with two decimal places, Arial font, 10 point font size, and left alignment. Align the text box under the Call Hours label box in the Service Rep Number Header section. Remove the label box attached to the text box after adding it to the Detail section.

17. Set the height of the Service Rep Number Footer section to 3/8 inch. Then, add a label box to the lower far left side of this section. Type the description **Rep Totals** in the label box and then apply the following formats: Arial font, font size of 12 points, bold, italics, and left alignment.

18. Add a text box to the Service Rep Number Footer section that *counts* the number of Customer IDs for each service rep. Align the text box below the Customer ID label box in the Service Rep Number Header section and next to the label box created in number 17. Apply the following formats to this text box: fixed number format with 0 decimal places, Arial font, font size of 12 points, bold, italics, and left alignment.

19. Add two text boxes to the Service Rep Number Footer section that *sum* the values in the Call Minutes and Sales Dollars fields for each service rep. Align the boxes under the appropriate field. Make the same formatting adjustments as stated in step 18 except set the number format for the Sales Dollars total to Currency.

20. Add a text box to the Service Rep Number Footer section that calculates the total Call Hours. Your formula should Sum the Call Minutes field and divide it by 60. Align the text box under the appropriate field and remove the label box. Apply the same formats as stated in number 18 except set the decimal places to 1.

21. Add the same totals created in the Service Rep Number Footer section to the *Report Footer* section. The label box for this section should read Grand Totals. The formatting for these totals should be identical to the totals in the Service Rep Number Footer section. Align the totals under the appropriate label box in the Service Rep Number Header section and place the totals at the bottom of the Report Footer section.

22. Sort the data in the Detail section of the report based on the Sales Dollars field in descending order.

23. Add a dark bold line to the top of the Service Rep Number Header section and a regular line to the bottom of the section.

24. Add a regular line to the top of the Service Rep Number Footer section and two regular lines to the top of the Report Footer Section.

25. Add the page number to the lower-right side of the Page Footer section. Apply the following formats to the page number: Arial font, font size of 8, bold, italics, and right alignment.

26. Save and close the report. Then close the database.

The following questions are designed to test your ability to apply the Access skills you have learned to complete a business objective. Use your knowledge of Access as well as your creativity to answer these questions. For most questions, there are several possible ways to complete the objective.

1. Open the Access database named ib_a05_challengec. Create a basic list report with the data contained in the Store Location Information table. Your report should include the title **Store Details** at the top of the first page. Sort the data in the report by State, and sort the stores by Store Size Sqr Feet in Descending order within each State. Use both horizontal and vertical lines to separate the columns and rows of detail on the report.

2. Open the Access database named ib_a05_challenged. Using the Employee Master table, create a report that groups the employees by Status. At the end of each Status section and for the entire report, show the number of employees, the average salary, and the average years of service with the company. Create a title for the report and sort the employees in each section based on the Years of Service in descending order. Include lines and other formatting techniques to give the report a professional appearance.

3. Open the Access database named ib_a05_challengea. Create a report that shows the financial statistics for each company in the Sales and Profit by Company table grouped by Industry. Show *all* dollar figures abbreviated in terms of millions. For example, 1,000,000 would be shown simply as 1. Add a notation on the first page of the report that shows dollar figures are in terms of "Millions (000,000)". The detail of your report should include the Net Sales and Net Income for each company last year. Calculate the dollar increase or decrease in net sales and income compared to two years ago. Include lines and other formatting techniques to give the report a professional appearance.

4. Open the Access database named ib_a05_challengeb. Create a report that groups the customers in the Customer Data table by State of Residence. Then create a second group within each State of Residence by Gender. For each State of Residence there should be a Male and Female group. The detail of the report should include the customer's name, ID number, age, years since customer, and last year spend. For each State of Residence *and* Gender group show the total number of customers, the average age, the average years since customer, and the total dollars spent last year. Include vertical and horizontal lines as well as other formatting techniques to give the report a professional appearance.

>> Chapter 6

Applying Core Competency Skills

Chapter Goals

So far, the queries demonstrated in this text have used only one table. However, queries are often constructed using several tables. As mentioned in Chapter 1, companies will typically design and maintain a Relational Database Management System (RDBMS) that contains many tables of data. As a result, a business manager might need to retrieve and combine information from more than one table when constructing a query. The number of tables that are required will depend on the business manager's project and the design of the database system that is being used. This chapter begins by demonstrating how to create queries using multiple tables. It then concludes with a comprehensive Access project to illustrate how multiple tables are used in a project. This project will also review several key skills that were covered throughout this text.

>> **Access** Skill Sets

Managing a Strategic Alliance

Starting a new business within a large corporation was one of my most memorable career experiences. I had the rare opportunity of developing a strategic alliance between my employer, a children's retail company, and one of the world's largest grocery store chains. The goal of this strategic alliance was to set up a merchandise display of my company's products in one of the aisles of a grocery store. This alliance benefited both companies. The grocery chain was able to offer products other than typical groceries for their customers, which helped it compete with big discount merchandise stores and shopping clubs. My company, in turn, could sell our products in hundreds of grocery stores in addition to our own retail stores. For me, this opportunity was very exciting, but also a lot of work. Because I was running this business with only a few other people, we had to solve every problem ourselves. For example, tracking and billing the merchandise shipped to the grocery stores was one of our key challenges. Our systems were designed to ship merchandise to our own stores, but not to other businesses. Furthermore, each grocery store that received a shipment of merchandise needed a document called an Advanced Shipment Notification (ASN). The grocery receiving manager would use this document to verify that merchandise was actually received and would send a copy to the accounts payable department. After a few months of operating this business, we realized that we were not getting paid for any of the merchandise that was shipped to the grocery stores. Then, we received notification from the grocer's accounts payable department, saying it would not pay any of our bills unless we furnished a signed ASN document from the grocery receiving managers. This was big problem that we needed to solve right away!

>> Continued on page 942

When using Access for business projects, you will likely encounter several situations where you will need two or more tables when constructing queries. For example, one table might contain the following two fields: Item Number and Sales Units LW (Last Week). A second table might contain these two fields: Item Number and Item Description. If your goal is to construct a report that shows the item number, item description, and sales units for last week, you need to construct a query using both of these tables. The purpose of this section is to explain how multiple tables are added and joined together in a query.

Joining Tables

If you are creating a query with more than one table, you need to use a join. *Joins* are used to combine data from two or more tables or queries (if creating a nested query). The way in which data is selected and displayed in the record set of the query will depend on the type of join that is used. Inner and outer joins are two join types commonly used in business projects (they will be defined and explained in the next section). This segment focuses on the fundamental techniques for creating joins.

Figure 6.1 shows a few records from a table that contains item numbers and item descriptions for an apparel retailer. The purpose of this table is to show all products sold by the company and the item number that is assigned to each product. This example assumes that the same item number *cannot* be used for two different products. Therefore, the Item Number field is the primary key of the table.

Figure 6.1 | **Apparel Item Descriptions Table**

Apparel Item Descriptions	
Item Number ⌄	Item Description ⌄
23575	Sweatshirts
55786	Short Sleeve T-Shirts
65788	Jackets

> Placing the Item Descriptions into a separate table makes it easier for the company to update any changes.

Figure 6.2 shows weekly sales data for an apparel retailer. Notice that there are no descriptions to identify the item numbers listed in the table. If a business manager wanted to create a sales report that shows the description of each item along with the weekly unit sales, the tables shown in Figure 6.1 and Figure 6.2 must be used when constructing a query. To eliminate data redundancy, most retailers never include product descriptions in tables that contain sales data. When the same data is duplicated in several tables, there is a significant risk of having two tables with the same field containing different data values. This represents a breakdown in the integrity of the firm's database system and could severely weaken a business manager's confidence in the data and results produced by the system.

Figure 6.2 | **Apparel Sales by Item Table**

Week Number	Item Number	Sales Units
1	23575	50
1	55786	75
1	65788	50
2	23575	25
2	55786	50
2	65788	25
3	23575	50
3	55786	75
3	65788	50

A second table is needed to show the descriptions of these item numbers.

COMMON MISTAKES | Avoid Data Redundancy

If you are designing your own tables in an Access database, do not duplicate the same data in several tables. When data is duplicated in several tables, you are forced to update the same field or fields several times when any changes are made. This could increase the risk of errors in your database, especially if you update a field in one table and forget to update the same field in subsequent tables. Data such as the item descriptions in Figure 6.1 are usually stored in only one table because it eliminates any risk of having two different descriptions for the same item number in two different tables.

As previously mentioned, joins are required when using two or more tables in the construction of a query. Joins are created between a common field that exists in both tables. The data contained in this common field *must have the same data type and serve an identical purpose* in each table. The following explains how the tables in Figures 6.1 and 6.2 are joined in a query.

- Create a new query by clicking the **Query Design** icon in the **Create** tab of the Ribbon.
- Click the first table in the **Show Table** dialog box and then click the **Add** button. For this example, the first table that will be added to the query is the Apparel Item Descriptions table shown in Figure 6.1.
- Click the second table in the **Show Table** dialog box and then click the **Add** button. For this example, the second table that will be added to the query is the Apparel Sales by Item table shown in Figure 6.2. You can also highlight both tables by holding the Shift key and clicking each table. Then click the **Add** button to add both tables to the query.
- Click the **Close** button in the **Show Table** dialog box after the tables are added to the query.
- Identify the common field in the two tables being joined. For this example, the common field is the Item Number field, which is contained in both the Apparel Sales by Item table and the Apparel Item Descriptions table (see Figure 6.3). It is important to note that this field serves the same purpose in both tables. That is to say, the item number represents the unique code that is assigned to every item sold by the company.
- Click the Item Number field in the Apparel Item Descriptions table and drag it over to the Item Number field in the Apparel Sales by Item table. This will create a join line between the two tables, as seen in Figure 6.4.

Figure 6.3 shows the two tables that were added to a new query. Notice that the common field in both tables is the Item Number field.

Figure 6.3 | **Two Tables Added to a Query**

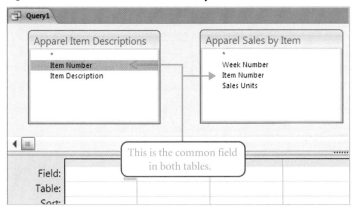

Figure 6.4 shows the appearance of the join line that was created between the Apparel Sales by Item and Apparel Item Descriptions tables. The line between these two tables will appear after clicking the Item Number field in the Apparel Item Descriptions table and dragging it over to the Item Number field in the Apparel Sales by Item table.

Figure 6.4 | **Joining Two Tables**

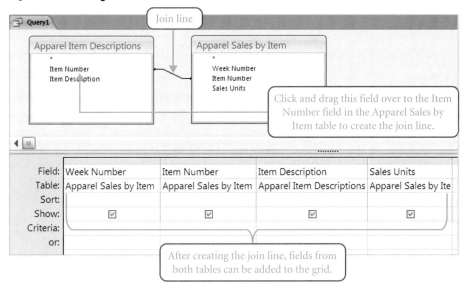

As mentioned, the join line illustrated in Figure 6.4 was created manually by clicking and dragging the Item Number field. However, if the Item Number field in the Apparel Item Descriptions table had been designated as the primary key, Access would have created the join line automatically through a feature called *AutoJoin*. This feature creates a join line when a field in one table is designated as the primary key, and a field with an identical name and data type appears in a second table. This identical field in the second table is also known as a *foreign key*. It is important to note that Access will not create a join line if the common field is designated as the primary key in both tables. A primary key and a foreign key are required for Access to automatically create a join line. The AutoJoin feature is controlled by the **Access Options** dialog box, as shown in Figure 6.5. As mentioned in Chapter 1, this dialog box is opened by clicking the **Access Options** button in the **File** menu.

Figure 6.5 | **Object Designers Options**

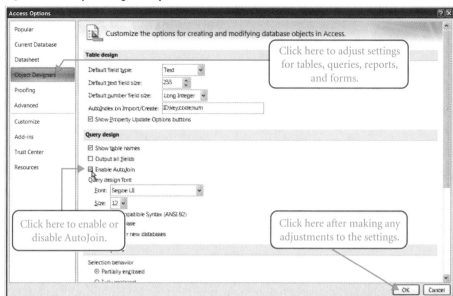

Inner Joins

As previously mentioned, the join shown in Figure 6.4 is an *Inner Join* (sometimes referred to as a Simple Join or an Equal Join). An Inner Join will display data in the record set of a query in which the values in both fields used to create the join line are identical. For example, the Inner Join used in Figure 6.4 will force the query to select records where the values in the Item Number field are identical in both the Apparel Item Descriptions and Apparel Sales by Item tables. If an Item Number is missing from either table, the entire record associated with the item number will be eliminated from the record set of the query.

Figure 6.6 shows the record set of the query illustrated in Figure 6.4. However, item number 65788, Jackets, was removed from the Apparel Item Descriptions table (see Figure 6.1). Even though item 65788 remains in the Apparel Sales by Item table (see Figure 6.3), it will not appear in the record set of the query because of the Inner Join.

Figure 6.6 | **Apparel Sales Query Record Set**

Week Number	Item Number	Item Description	Sales Units
1	23575	Sweatshirts	50
1	55786	Short Sleeve T-Shirts	75
2	23575	Sweatshirts	25
2	55786	Short Sleeve T-Shirts	50
3	23575	Sweatshirts	50
3	55786	Short Sleeve T-Shirts	75

Only two items appear for each week because the Apparel Item Descriptions table is missing item number 65788.

Because an Inner Join will select only records that have identical values in the common field used to create the join line, it can be used as a technique for limiting or selecting specific values from another table. As demonstrated in Chapter 3, specific records can be selected from a table by entering criteria into a Select Query. However, if there are several specific values that need to be selected from a large table, it may be

>> **Quick Reference**

Joining Tables (Inner Join)

1. Add two or more tables to a new query.
2. Identify a common field between two tables that contain the same data type and serve the same purpose.
3. Click the field name of the common field identified in number 2 in one table and drag it over to the common field name in the second table (it does not matter from which table you click and drag).
4. Add any necessary fields from both tables to the lower grid of the query.

>> **Quick Reference**

Enabling/Disabling AutoJoin

1. Click the **File** menu icon.
2. Click the **Access Options** button.
3. Click the Object Designers option on the left side of the **Access Options** dialog box.
4. Click the **Enable AutoJoin** option to add or remove the check mark.
5. Click the **OK** button.

more convenient to create a table of those values and join it to the larger table using an Inner Join. For example, Figure 6.7 shows a master table of more than 70 hypothetical stock symbols and closing prices for two days. If you wanted to analyze 20 specific stocks from this table, you could enter all 20 stock symbols into the criteria row of a Select Query. Or you could create a table of target stock symbols, as shown in Figure 6.8, and join it to the master table in Figure 6.7 using an Inner Join. This will force the query to select only the stock symbols from the master table that are identical to the stock symbols in the target table.

Figure 6.7 | **Master Stock Symbol and Price Table**

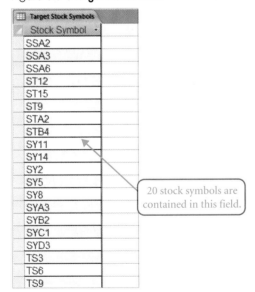

Closing Date	Stock Symbol	Closing Price
10/25/2005	STB2	$23.82
10/25/2005	STA2	$24.52
10/25/2005	STB3	$25.22
10/25/2005	STA3	$25.92
10/25/2005	STB4	$26.62
10/25/2005	STA4	$27.32
10/25/2005	ST8	$28.02
10/25/2005	ST9	$28.72
10/25/2005	ST10	$29.42
10/25/2005	ST11	$18.00
10/25/2005	ST12	$19.0
10/25/2005	ST13	$20.0
10/25/2005	ST14	$21.0
10/25/2005	ST15	$22.12
10/25/2005	TS1	$23.15
10/25/2005	TS2	$24.18
10/25/2005	TS3	$25.21

71 unique stock symbols are listed in this field.

This table contains a total of 142 records.

Figure 6.8 | **Target Stocks Table**

Stock Symbol
SSA2
SSA3
SSA6
ST12
ST15
ST9
STA2
STB4
SY11
SY14
SY2
SY5
SY8
SYA3
SYB2
SYC1
SYD3
TS3
TS6
TS9

20 stock symbols are contained in this field.

Figures 6.9 and 6.10 show the setup and record set of the query containing the Master Stock Symbols and Price table (see Figure 6.7), and the Target Stock Symbols table (see Figure 6.8). The record set illustrates how the Inner Join selects only records from the Master Stock Symbols and Price table that are identical to the Target Stock Symbols table. There are a total of 40 records in the record set because the Master Stock Symbols and Price table contains two closing dates. If stock symbols are added or removed from the Target Stock Symbols table, the query will select different records from the Master Stock Symbols and Price table based on the changes.

Figure 6.9 | **Stock Analysis Select Query**

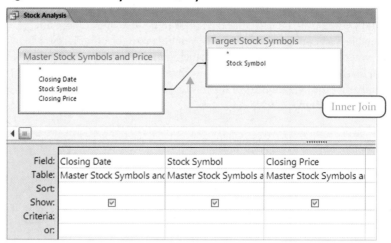

Figure 6.10 | **Stock Analysis Query Record Set**

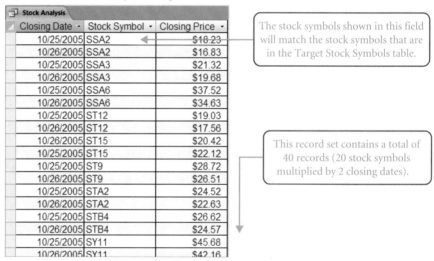

The stock symbols shown in this field will match the stock symbols that are in the Target Stock Symbols table.

This record set contains a total of 40 records (20 stock symbols multiplied by 2 closing dates).

Outer Joins

An Inner Join will automatically be created when you create a join line between two tables manually or if Access automatically creates the join line. However, there may be situations in which you might need to change an Inner Join to an Outer Join. An *Outer Join* is sometimes referred to as a Left Join, Right Join, or One Way Join. When you use an Outer Join, a query will select all records from one table and only the matching records from a second table. For example, Figure 6.6 demonstrated how item number 65788 was removed from the record set of the query because it existed in the Apparel Sales by Item table, but not the Apparel Item Descriptions table. However, the Inner Join can be changed to an Outer Join so that all records from the Apparel Sales by Item table are selected and only the matching records from the Apparel Item Descriptions table are selected. This will produce a blank or null entry in the Item Description column for item number 65788. The following explains how the Inner Join is converted to an Outer Join to produce this result.

- Create a join line between two tables in a query. For this example, a join line is created between the Item Number fields in the Apparel Sales by Item table and Apparel Item Descriptions table (see Figure 6.4).
- Double click the join line. This will open the **Join Properties** dialog box.

- Select an **Outer Join** option in the **Join Properties** dialog box. For this example, there are three join type options listed in the lower area of the **Join Properties** dialog box as illustrated in Figure 6.11. Option 1 is an Inner Join type. Options 2 and 3 are both Outer Join types. The description next to each option states the table that will be used to select all records. Option 2 is selected for this example because the goal is to select all records from the Apparel Sales by Item table and only the records that have the same Item Number value in the Apparel Item Descriptions table.

- Click the **OK** button at the bottom of the **Join Properties** dialog box.

Figure 6.11 shows the **Join Properties** dialog box. Options 2 and 3 are both Outer Join options.

Figure 6.11 | **Join Properties Dialog Box**

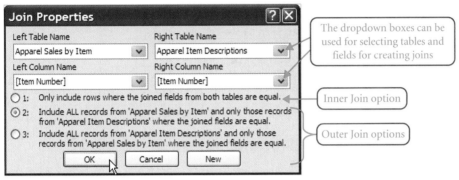

Figure 6.12 shows the set up of a query using an Outer Join. Notice that the join line between the two tables has an arrow on one side, which signifies that it is an Outer Join. In this example, all records will be selected from the Apparel Sales by Item table, and only those records that have a match in the Item Number field will be selected from the Apparel Item Descriptions table.

Figure 6.12 | **Query Setup with an Outer Join**

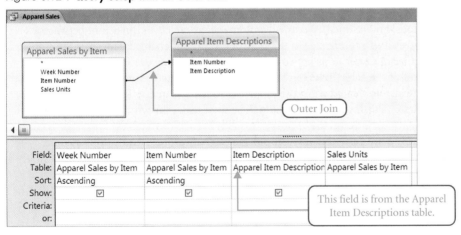

Figure 6.13 shows the record set of the query from Figure 6.12. Notice that there is a blank cell or null value next to item number 65788. Because of the setup of the Outer Join, all records were selected from the Apparel Sales by Item table, and only records containing the same values in the Item Number field from the Apparel Item Descriptions table were selected. However, because there is no record for item number 65788 in the Apparel Item Descriptions table, a null value appears in the Item Description field for this item. This method of joining tables is extremely valuable

when the data contained in one table is more critical than the data in another. In this example, all the records were selected from the Apparel Sales by Item table because this table contains the sales results of the business. It is likely that a business manager will need to see these results regardless of whether item descriptions are missing from the Apparel Item Descriptions table. As demonstrated in Figure 6.6, the Inner Join completely removes item 65788 from the record set of the query, which prevents a business manager from conducting a complete assessment of the business.

Figure 6.13 | **Record Set of a Query Using an Outer Join**

Apparel Sales

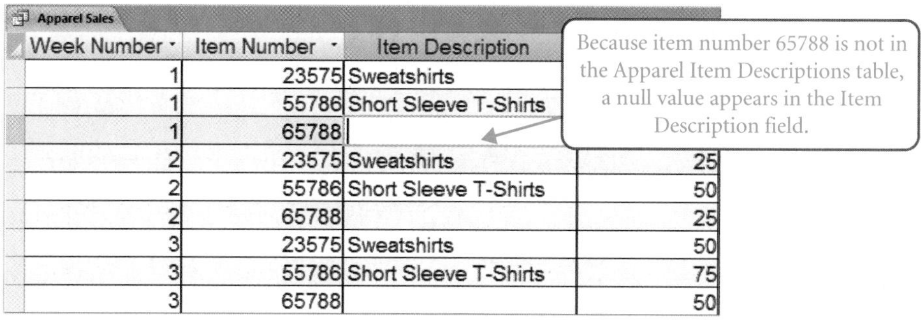

Week Number	Item Number	Item Description	
1	23575	Sweatshirts	
1	55786	Short Sleeve T-Shirts	
1	65788		
2	23575	Sweatshirts	25
2	55786	Short Sleeve T-Shirts	50
2	65788		25
3	23575	Sweatshirts	50
3	55786	Short Sleeve T-Shirts	75
3	65788		50

Because item number 65788 is not in the Apparel Item Descriptions table, a null value appears in the Item Description field.

COMMON MISTAKES | Inner Joins

The danger in using an Inner Join is that it can eliminate data from the record set of a query that might be important. This is especially common when using one table that contains sales data and another table that contains descriptive data. If you are relying on the data in one table to evaluate the performance of business and joining it to a second table that contains descriptive information, *it is a good practice to test the query using an Outer Join.* If null values appear in a field from the table containing descriptive information, data from the table containing performance statistics will be removed from the record set of the query when an Inner Join is used.

Defining Table Relationships

As previously mentioned, Access will automatically create an Inner Join between a primary key and a foreign key if the AutoJoin feature is enabled. However, you can preset Inner or Outer Joins between two tables by defining the Table Relationship properties. If the Table Relationship properties are defined, joins that you specify will automatically be created when the tables are added to a query. The benefit of defining these relationships is that it eliminates the risk of using the wrong type of join or forgetting to set joins on the appropriate fields between two tables. This is especially helpful if you are designing an Access database that will be used by other people.

The process of defining Table Relationships will be demonstrated using the four tables shown in Figure 6.14 through 6.17. Similar to the tables used to demonstrate joins, these tables might also be found in a database developed for an apparel retailer.

>> *Quick Reference*

Outer Joins

1. Create a join line between two tables.
2. Open the **Join Properties** dialog box by double clicking the join line.
3. Select option 2 or 3 in the lower area of the **Join Properties** dialog box, depending on the table in which you want to select all records.

Figure 6.14 | **Item Unit Sales by Week Table**

Week Number ▾	Category Number ▾	Item Number ▾	Unit Sales ▾
1	10	210009	162
1	10	221094	340
1	10	290089	280
1	10	290982	89
1	20	310992	129
1	20	345090	150
1	20	390087	189
1	30	901543	
1	30	955220	
1	30	992820	
1	40	519552	
1	40	554632	
1	40	571930	60
2	10	210009	183
2	10	221094	384
2	10	290089	316
2	10	290982	100
2	20	310992	146

> The primary key is made up of the Week Number, Category Number, and Item Number fields.

Figure 6.15 | **Item Descriptions Table**

Item Number ▾	Item Description ▾
210009	Grey Fleece w/ Hood
221094	White T-Shirt
290089	Black T-Shirt
290982	White Twill
310992	Brown Corduroy
345090	Denim Jeans
390087	Tan Twill
519552	Baseball Cap
554632	Black Knit
571930	Red Wool
901543	Denim
955220	Denim w/ Leather Collar
992820	Black Leather

> The primary key in this table is the Item Number field.

Figure 6.16 | **Category Descriptions Table**

> The primary key in this table is the Category Number field.

Category Number ▾	Category Description ▾
10	Tops
20	Pants
30	Jackets
40	Hats

Figure 6.17 | **Category Sales by Week Table**

Week Number ▾	Category Number ▾	Unit Sales ▾
1	10	871
1	20	468
1	30	219
1	40	270
2	10	983
2	20	529
2	30	247
2	40	305
3	10	909
3	20	489
3	30	229
3	40	282

> The primary key in this table is the Week Number and Category Number fields.

Use the **Table Relationships** window for defining the relationships between tables in an Access database. To open the window, click the **Relationships** icon in the **Database Tools** tab of the Ribbon. Then click the **Show Table** icon in the **Design** tab of the Ribbon to open the **Show Table** dialog box. The process of adding tables to the **Relationships** window is identical to adding tables to a new query. Because we are defining the relationships for all four tables illustrated in Figures 6.14 through 6.17, all four tables are added to the **Relationships** window, as shown in Figure 6.18. After you add the tables to the **Relationships** window, they can be moved and resized as if they were added to a query.

Figure 6.18 | **Relationship Window with Four Tables Added**

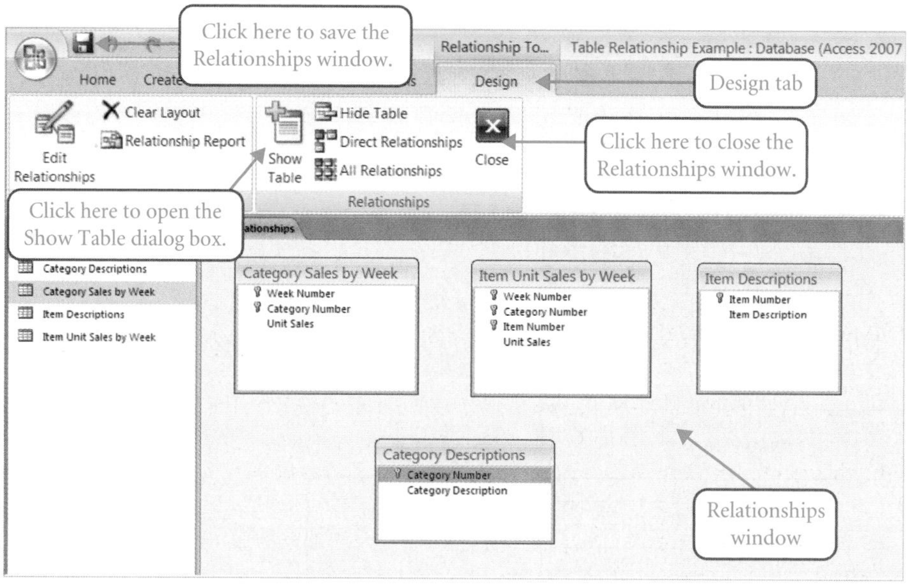

After adding tables to the **Relationships** window, you can create joins. The process for creating a join in the **Relationships** window is identical to creating joins in a query. However, after creating the join line, the **Edit Relationships** dialog box automatically opens, enabling you to set a specific join type. For example, Figure 6.19 shows the **Edit Relationships** dialog box after creating a join line between the Item Number field in the Item Descriptions and the Item Unit Sales by Week tables. The following explains each of the key features of the Edit Relationships dialog box and the settings that were used to create this join.

- **Primary and Related Tables:** The top of the **Edit Relationships** dialog box shows the two tables that are being joined. Access defines one table as the Primary or Master table and the second as the Related table. The Primary table is listed on the upper-left side of the window, and the Related table is listed on the right.

- **Relationship Type:** Access defines a table as either a Primary or Related table based on the Relationship Type. The Relationship Type will automatically be displayed at the bottom of the Edit Relationships dialog box when a join is created. Most tables will be classified as having either a One to Many or One to One relationship, which are defined as follows:

  - **One to Many:** Figure 6.19 shows a One to Many relationship between the Item Descriptions and Item Unit Sales by Week tables. These tables are classified as One to Many based on the values in the field used to create the join line, which in this case is the Item Number field. Each value in the Item Number field for the Item Descriptions table appears only one time. Therefore, this table is considered the "One" side of the One to Many relationship. Access defines any table that represents the "One" in a One to Many relationship as the Primary table. With regard to the Item Unit Sales by Week table, each value in the Item

Number field appears several times in the table. Therefore, this table represents the "Many" side of the One to Many relationship and is considered the Related table.

- **One to One:** This relationship is classified when a join is made between two tables that have identical primary keys. As a result, the values in the field used to create the join line appear only one time in both tables. Technically, in a One to One relationship both tables can be defined as Primary tables. However, Access will define the Primary table depending on where the join line originates. Therefore, the table that is clicked first when creating a join line becomes the primary table. Note that *this applies only in One to One relationships.*

- **Join Type Button:** This button opens the **Join Properties** dialog box and is identical to double clicking the join line in a query. Joins created in the **Relationship** window will initially be an Inner Join type. The **Join Type** button is used to change the Inner Join to an Outer Join if necessary. For the example shown in Figure 6.19, the Inner Join was changed to an Outer Join. The third option was selected in the **Join Properties** dialog box, which selects all records from the Item Unit Sales by Week table and only records that match the item numbers in the Item Descriptions table.

- **Enforce Referential Integrity:** This option is used to ensure that the common field, which is used to join two tables, always contains identical values. In the case of Figure 6.19, Item Numbers could not be added or changed in the Item Unit Sales by Week table without making the same additions or changes in the Item Descriptions table.

- **Cascade Update Related Fields:** Selecting this option will update any changes made in the Primary table to the Related table. For the example in Figure 6.19, any changes to the item numbers in the Item Descriptions table will automatically be changed in the Item Unit Sales by Week table.

- **Cascade Delete Related Records:** This option is similar to the Cascade Update option *but is rarely used.* When this option is enabled, any records deleted in the Primary table will also be deleted in the Related table. For example, if an item number is removed by deleting a record from the Item Descriptions table, the record containing the same item number will automatically be deleted from the Item Unit Sales by Week table. However, it is unlikely that you would want records deleted from the Item Unit Sales by Week table. Doing so would remove all historical sales records for that item.

It is important to note you will use the **Enforce Referential Integrity, Cascade Update,** and **Cascade Delete** options only if you are creating and managing your own tables. As a business professional, you will most likely be linking to tables that are created and maintained by your firm's IT department. In this case, you would not have a need for these options.

Figure 6.19 shows the final settings in the **Edit Relationships** dialog box for the Item Descriptions and Item Unit Sales by Week tables. Click the **Create** button to apply the relationship settings to these tables.

Figure 6.19 | **Edit Relationships Window**

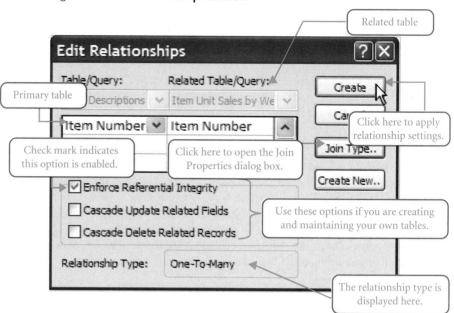

Figure 6.20 shows the join line between the Item Descriptions and Item Unit Sales by Week tables in the **Relationships** window. Notice the symbols that appear at each end of the join line. These symbols are shown because the **Enforce Referential Integrity** option was selected in the **Edit Relationships** dialog box (see Figure 6.19). The symbols indicate that there is a One to Many relationship between the two tables and that Referential Integrity will be enforced. Once the **Relationships** window is saved and closed, this join will automatically be created when these tables are added to a query.

Figure 6.20 | **Outer Join Created in the Relationships Window**

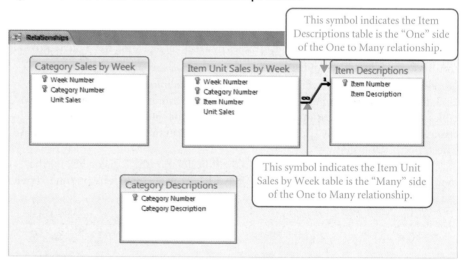

The next tables that will be joined in the **Relationships** window are the Category Sales by Week and the Item Unit Sales by Week. These tables will require two join lines because multiple fields make up the primary key in both tables, which in this case is the Week Number and Category Number fields. It is good practice to check if every field that makes up the primary key in a table can be joined to an identical field in another table. If the same primary key fields exist in both tables, they should be joined. Multiple join lines are added between two tables in the Relationships window by using the drop-down arrows under the respective table in the middle of the **Edit**

Relationships dialog box. Figure 6.21 shows the settings in the **Edit Relationships** dialog box for the Category Sales by Week and Item Unit Sales by Week tables.

Figure 6.21 | **Adding Multiple Join Lines in the Edit Relationships Window**

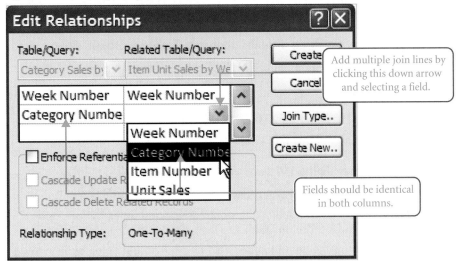

COMMON MISTAKES | Joining Tables with Multiple Primary Key Fields

It is important to check if a join line can be created for every field that makes up the primary key of a table. If a field makes up the primary key of a table *and it is not* connected to an identical field in a second table, Access could improperly combine the fields from both tables. This error will produce distorted or erroneous results in the record set of the query. Therefore, it is critical to identify the primary key of both tables before creating any join lines.

Figure 6.22 shows all the joins that were set in the **Relationships** window. Notice that the Category Descriptions table is joined to both the Category Sales by Week and the Item Unit Sales by Week tables. All the joins set in the **Relationships** window will automatically be created when these tables are added to a query. To close the **Relationships** window, click the **Close** icon in the **Design** tab of the Ribbon (see Figure 6.18).

Figure 6.22 | **Final Appearance of the Relationships Window**

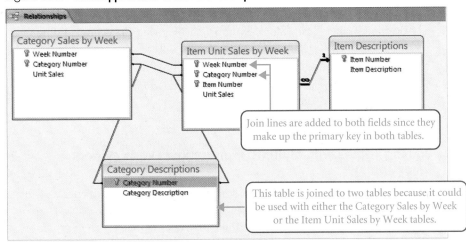

>> **Quick Reference**

Defining Table Relationships

1. Open the **Relationships** window by clicking the **Relationships** icon in the **Database Tools** tab of the Ribbon.

2. Click the **Show Table** icon in the **Design** tab of the Ribbon.

3. Add tables from the **Show Tables** dialog box to the **Relationships** window.

4. Create a join between two tables to open the **Edit Relationships** dialog box.

5. If necessary, create additional joins by clicking the drop-down arrow and selecting fields in the middle of the **Edit Relationships** dialog box.

6. Change the Join Type and enable the **Enforce Referential Integrity** options as needed.

7. Click the **Create** button.

8. Click the **Save** icon in the **Quick Access** toolbar to save the **Relationships** window.

9. Close the **Relationship** window by clicking the **Close** icon in the **Design** tab.

>> Joining Tables

The purpose of this workshop is to demonstrate techniques for joining multiple tables in a query. I will be demonstrating the skills in this workshop in the following three videos: **Joining Tables**, **Inner Joins**, and **Outer Joins**. This workshop will utilize a few different databases. Therefore, you will be instructed to open the appropriate database at the beginning of each section of tasks. Try completing each set of tasks on your own before watching the video.

1. **Creating Inner Joins (Video: Joining Tables)**
   a. Open the Access database named ib_a06_apparelretaildata.
   b. Create a new Select Query and add the Apparel Sales by Item and Apparel Item Descriptions tables to the query.
   c. Click and drag the Item Number field in the Apparel Sales by Item table over to the Item Number field in the Apparel Item Descriptions table.
   d. Add the Week Number and Item Number fields from the Apparel Sales by Item table to the query design grid.
   e. Add the Item Description field to the query design grid from the Apparel Item Descriptions table.
   f. Add the Sales Units field to the query design grid from the Apparel Sales by Item table.
   g. Sort the query by the Week Number field in ascending order.
   h. Save the query and name it **Apparel Sales with Descriptions**.
   i. Run the query and view the record set.
   j. Close the query and then the database.

2. **Using Inner Joins to Limit Data (Video: Inner Joins)**
   a. Open the Access database named ib_a06_historicalstockprices.
   b. Open the Master Stock Symbols and Price table and note the number of records. Then close the table.
   c. Open the Target Stock Symbols table and note the number of records in the table. Then close the table
   d. Create a new Select Query and add the Master Stock Symbols and Price and Target Stock Symbols tables to the query.
   e. Add the Closing Date, Stock Symbol, and Closing Price fields to the query design grid from the Master Stock Symbols and Price table.
   f. Sort the query based on the Stock Symbol field in ascending order.
   g. Run the query to view the record set. Then save the query and name it **Target Stock Data**.
   h. Close the query and then close the database.

3. **Joining Tables with Multiple Primary Key Fields (Video: Inner Joins)**
   a. Open the Access database named ib_a06_apparelcategoryanditemsales.
   b. Create a new Select Query and add the Item Descriptions, Item Unit Sales by Week, and Category Sales by Week tables.

c. Click and drag the Item Number field in the Item Descriptions table over to the Item Number field in the Item Unit Sales by Week table.

d. Click and drag the Week Number field in the Item Unit Sales by Week table over to the Week Number field in the Category Sales by Week table.

e. Click and drag the Category Number field in the Item Unit Sales by Week table over to the Category Number field in the Category Sales by Week table.

f. Add the Week Number, Category Number, and Item Number fields from the Item Unit Sales by Week table to the query design grid.

g. Add the Item Description field from the Item Descriptions table to the query design grid, and then add the Unit Sales field from the Item Unit Sales by Week table to the query design grid.

h. Add the Unit Sales field from the Category Sales by Week table to the query design grid. The Unit Sales field will now appear twice in the query design grid.

i. In the query design grid, click in front of the Unit Sales field that was added from the Category Sales by Week table. Type **Category Unit Sales**, followed by a colon, and then press the **Enter** key.

j. Sort the query based on the values in the Week Number field and Item Number field in ascending order.

k. Run the query to view the record set.

l. Save the query and name it **Item and Category Sales by Week**.

m. Close the query and then the database.

4. Creating Outer Joins (Video: Outer Joins)

a. Open the ib_a06_apparelretaildata database that was used in the first task.

b. Open the Apparel Sales by Item table and note how many unique item numbers appear in the table. Then close the table.

c. Open the Apparel Sales with Descriptions query that was created in step 1 and note how many unique item numbers appear in the record set.

d. Switch the Apparel Sales with Descriptions query to **Design View**.

e. Open the **Join Properties** dialog box by double-clicking the join line connecting the two tables in the query.

f. Click option 3 in the lower area of the Join Properties dialog box and then click the **OK** button.

g. Run the query and observe the record set. Note the item number that has a blank space in the Item Description field.

h. Save and close the query. Then close the database.

>> Table Relationships

The purpose of this workshop is to demonstrate the techniques for defining the relationships between tables. I will be demonstrating the tasks listed in this workshop on the video named **Table Relationships**. You will need to open the Access database named ib_a06_appareltablerelationships before completing the following tasks. Complete the tasks on your own first and then watch the video.

VIDEO WORKSHOP

1. Defining Table Relationships (Video: Table Relationships)

   a. Click the **Relationships** icon in the **Database Tools** tab of the Ribbon.

   b. Click the **Show Table** icon in the **Design** tab of the Ribbon.

   c. Add all tables that are listed in the **Show Tables** dialog box and then click the **Close** button.

   d. Click and drag the Item Number field in the Item Descriptions table over to the Item Number field in the Item Unit Sales by Week table.

   e. Open the **Edit Relationships** dialog box. Click the **Join Type** button on the right side of the **Edit Relationships** dialog box. Convert the join to an Outer Join by selecting the option that states, "Include ALL records from 'Item Unit Sales by Week' and only. . . ".

   f. Click the **OK** button in the **Join Properties** dialog box. This will bring you back to the **Edit Relationships** dialog box.

   g. Click the Enforce Referential Integrity option in the **Edit Relationships** dialog box and then click the **Create** button.

   h. Click and drag the Week Number field in the Category Sales by Week table over to the Week Number field in the Item Unit Sales by Week table.

   i. Open the **Edit Relationships** dialog box. Click in the box below the Week Number field in the middle of the Edit Relationships dialog box on the left side. Click the drop-down arrow and select the Category Number field.

   j. Click in the empty box to the right of the Category Number field and click the drop-down arrow. Select the Category Number field from the list.

   k. Click the **Create** button in the **Edit Relationships** dialog box.

   l. Click and drag the Category Number field in the Category Descriptions table over to the Category Number field in the Category Sales by Week table.

   m. Click the **Create** button in the **Edit Relationships** dialog box.

   n. Click the **Save** icon in the **Quick Access** toolbar.

   o. Click the **Close** icon in the **Design** tab of the Ribbon. Then, close the database.

EXERCISE

Why Do I Need This?

>> Evaluating Marketing Strategies and Sales

Marketing promotions play a critical role in supporting the sales of almost all businesses. Companies will use promotional strategies such as TV advertising, discount coupons, or direct mail fliers when launching new product lines or supporting existing ones. However, not all promotional strategies are successful. Marketing managers must measure the sales impact of various marketing campaigns to determine whether they were effective and worth the cost of executing. One way to determine the impact of marketing initiatives is to compare the sales of products or categories of products between this year and last year. Depending on the business, companies will usually execute several analytical tactics to evaluate the true value of a marketing campaign. The first step is usually checking whether the company is growing its sales compared to last year. As a result, the historical sales results stored in databases play a key role in evaluating how a business performs from one year to the next.

Exercise

The purpose of this exercise is to construct a query that could be used by a marketing analyst of a home furnishings retail company. The goal is to assess the impact of various promotion strategies that were executed during the first six months of the year. Open the Access database named *ib_a06_marketingpromotionsdata* and complete the following tasks.

1. The database contains five tables that are related to the company's sales performance and marketing promotions. The table named Category Promotions TY contains the marketing strategies that were executed for several product categories. Open this table and note the category numbers and week numbers that are listed.

2. Create a new Select Query and add all five tables contained in the database to the query. The next several tasks will address the joins that need to be created between these tables. It will be helpful to arrange the tables based on the joins that need to be created. Starting from left to right, the order of the tables should be Category Sales by Week LY, Category Sales by Week TY, and Category Promotions TY. Move the Category Descriptions table below the Category Sales by Week LY and Category Sales by Week TY tables. Move the Promotion Description table below the Category Promotions TY table.

3. Create a join between the Category Sales by Week LY and Category Sales by Week TY tables. Joining these tables will make it possible to compare sales from this year and last year. The primary key for both tables is the Week Number and Category Number fields. Therefore, two joins will be required for these tables. Click the Week Number field in the Category Sales by Week LY table and drag it over to the Week Number field in the Category Sales by Week TY table. Repeat this process for the Category Number fields.

4. Create a join between the Category Description table and Category Sales by Week LY table. Because the Category Sales by Week LY and Category Sales by Week TY tables are joined together, the Category Description table can be joined to either table. For this exercise, join the Category Description table to the Category Sales by Week LY table using the Category Number field.

5. The join line created in step 4 will be changed to an Outer Join. If for some reason the Category Description table is missing a category, the Outer Join will prevent needed sales records from being removed from the record set of the query. Therefore, double click the join line between the Category Description and Category Sales by Week LY tables to open the **Join Properties** dialog box. Click the join option at the bottom of the dialog box that states "Include ALL records from 'Category Sales by Week LY' and only. . . " and then click the **OK** button.

6. Create a join between the Category Promotions TY and the Category Sales by Week TY tables. The primary key for both tables is the Week Number and Category Number fields. Therefore, use these fields to create two join lines. You should now have join lines on the Week Number and Category Number fields between the Category Sales by Week LY, Category Sales by Week TY, and Category Promotions TY tables. Because these are all Inner Joins, only the week numbers and category numbers that you observed in step 1 will appear in the record set of the query because the Category Promotions TY table has fewer category and week numbers when compared with the Category Sales by Week TY and Category Sales by Week LY tables.

7. Create a join between the Promotion Description and Category Promotions TY tables. The primary key of the Promotion Description table is the Promotion Code field. Therefore, use this field to create the join line. Then convert the join to an Outer Join, which selects ALL records from the Category Promotions TY table.

8. Add the following fields to the query design grid:
   a. Week Number: Category Sales by Week LY table
   b. Category Number: Category Sales by Week LY table
   c. Category Description: Category Description table
   d. Promotion Code: Category Promotions TY table
   e. Promotion Description: Promotion Description table
   f. Unit Sales: Category Sales by Week LY table
   g. Units Sales: Category Sales by Week TY table

9. The query design grid should have two fields called Unit Sales. Click in front of the Unit Sales field from the Category Sales by Week LY table and type **Units Sales LY**, followed by a colon. Then, click in front of the Unit Sales field from the Category Sales by Week TY table and type **Units Sales TY**, followed by a colon. This will identify which sales values are from this year and last year.

10. Create a computed field that calculates the percent change in sales from last year to this year. The formula in this computed field should be as follows: **(Unit Sales TY − Unit Sales LY)/Unit Sales LY**. The name of the computed field should be Change in Sales. Format the results of this field to a percentage with two decimal places.

11. Sort the record set of the query based on the values calculated in the Change in Sales field in descending order.

12. Save the query and name it **Marketing Promotion Sales Analysis**.

13. Run the query and observe the record set. Which promotional strategies achieved the top three highest increases in sales?

14. The finance department of this company calculated that a marketing strategy needs to increase sales at least five percent to cover the cost of execution. Based on this requirement, which promotional strategies would you not want to execute in the future?

15. Save and close the query. Then close the database.

>> What's Wrong with This Database?

Problem

You are a senior team manager working for a large consulting firm. Your team recently started working for a client that is one of the largest frozen food manufacturers in the country. This company sells frozen foods throughout the United States and generates more than $3 billion per year in annual sales revenue. However, sales over the past five years have been stagnant. Your team's mission is to propose and develop ideas that will increase the overall sales of the company. Your team has been analyzing current and historical performance data for the past two weeks, and tomorrow you have a meeting with the CEO of the company to discuss your initial findings and potential ideas for a growth strategy.

One of the analysts on your team has been working with data from the company's database and brings a report to you showing the food company's total sales revenue for last year by region. He explains that sales in the Northeast region are considerably lower than regions in the South and Midwest. Based on this information, he suggests that the Northeast presents a significant growth opportunity for the company. In addition, he explained that before he constructed the query that produced these results, he received a copy of the firm's data guide and spoke with one of the managers in the IT department regarding the best tables to use. He assures you that the numbers are accurate and explains that the company defines the primary key for every table so that joins are created automatically when tables are added to a query. He states, "It's impossible to make a mistake with these tables."

Exercise

The Access database that the analyst on your team constructed is named ib_a06_foodsalesdata. A portion of the data guide that was used by the analyst can also be found in this folder, which is an Excel file named ib_a06_foodsalesdataguide. Would you be comfortable presenting this data to the CEO of the company at your meeting tomorrow? Consider the following:

1. Open the Access database and look at the construction and record set of the Annual Sales Results by Region query. Does the query appear to be constructed properly? Are the tables properly joined?

2. Are there any tests you could run to verify the accuracy of the data that is produced by the query?

3. Read the data guide in the Excel file. Is the analyst misinterpreting any fields or tables?

What's wrong with this database? Write a short answer for each the preceding points. Correct any problems you find with the database and explain why you would or would not be comfortable presenting a strategy to the CEO that focuses on growing sales in the Northeast.

>> Comprehensive Access Project   Skill Set

Most business executives agree that customer service is critical for maintaining a healthy business and a competitive edge. A call center is one resource that many companies use to provide services for their customers. If operated effectively, a call center can be a valuable resource for both customers and business executives. The information obtained by the associates and systems of a call center can help business executives identify faulty or defective products, new product opportunities, or product shortages. The purpose of this section is to demonstrate how the Access skills demonstrated in this text are used together to create a business performance report for the call center of a hypothetical computer manufacturing company.

Selecting Tables

As mentioned throughout this text, most business professionals use tables that are created and maintained by their company's IT department. Companies usually configure their employees' computers and assign passwords to allow them access to servers that contain one or several databases. Within each database are several related tables that business managers use to create queries and reports in Access. As a result, the goals of an Access project must be clearly defined to identify and link to the appropriate tables. The goal of the Access project that will be demonstrated in this section is to create a report for the call center of a computer manufacturing company. The following are more specific goals and requirements for the project.

- Identify defective products that are being returned by customers for the most recent available week of data. This company manufactures and sells computers directly to customers over the internet. Managers will use this report to identify defective computers being returned by customers and notify the production and quality control departments.

- Calculate the sales value of all returned products. Product returns will negatively affect the net sales results of the company. Business managers will need this information to provide accurate sales information to executives and/or shareholders of the company.

- Identify the state of residence for customers returning products. This could help the company identify the location of additional defective computers and prevent them from being sold.

- Show the difference between the most recent week of returns by a customer and the total units purchased year to date. This information is especially helpful for monitoring large business customers who might be purchasing several computers each year.

COMMON MISTAKES | Selecting the Right Tables

Obtaining or linking to the right tables is often the difference between producing information that can lead to powerful business decisions or enduring a frustrating experience that provides little value to the business. As a result, it is critical to develop a detailed list of goals and requirements at the beginning of every Access project. Your list of requirements should satisfy the answers to the following questions.

- What is the business question you are trying to answer?
- What business decisions will you need to make?
- What details are required to support the first two points?

Based on the goals and requirements listed for this project, tables can now be selected and linked into an Access database (see Figures 2.38 and 2.39 for examples of linking tables). Figures 6.23 through 6.27 show each of the tables that are linked into an Access database for this project. Preceding each figure is a description and key facts for the table.

Figure 6.23 shows the main data table for the computer company's call center. Data is usually collected on a daily basis for most call centers. However, the table in Figure 6.23 summarizes the call center data for this company by week. Businesses usually create and maintain tables that summarize data at various levels such as week, month, or year. The following are key points regarding this table:

- **Table Purpose**: To show the details of all calls made to the call center by week.
- **Primary Key**: The primary key is made up of the Week Number, Service Rep Number, Customer ID Number, and Product Number fields.
- **Fields**: The Week Number field represents the week of the company's fiscal year. For this example, the first week in January is considered week number 1. The Service Rep Number field identifies the call center associate who spoke to the customer. The Customer ID Number field is the number assigned to the customer when they called or purchased a computer at a prior point in time. The Product Number field represents the product the customer was calling about, purchasing, or returning. The Transaction Code field identifies the reason why the customer called. There are a total of five transaction codes that are defined in the Transaction Description table.

Figure 6.23 | **Call Center Activity by Week Table**

Week Number	Service Rep Number	Customer ID Number	Product Number	Transaction Code	Units Sold / Returned
2	1244	100266	86532	2	2
2	1244	100968	35900	9	0
3	1467	102679	86422	7	0
1	1467	103991	86532	2	1
3	1244	107768	86422	7	0
3	1834	108650	86320	2	1
1	1467	109123	86320	5	0
3	1467	109256	35677	2	1
3	1467	109456	86532	2	3
1	1244	117768	86422	7	0
3	1778	120004	35877	2	1
3	1244	127650	35900	1	2
3	1467	128650	86422	2	1
1	1244	133567	86532	2	1
1	1244	137650	35900	0	0

Values in this field represent units returned if the Transaction Code is 2.

Figure 6.24 shows the Purchase Activity by Customer table. The price each customer pays for the same computer could vary because of promotional offers or discounts that apply to high volume orders. To calculate the sales value of the merchandise returned, the price each customer paid for the computer will need to taken from this table. The following are other key points regarding this table:

- **Table Purpose:** To show the product, price, and quantity purchased by each customer.
- **Primary Key:** The primary key is made up of the Customer ID Number, Product Number, and Purchase Price fields. The same customer might purchase two different products or purchase the same product at two different prices. Therefore, all three fields are required to define the primary key.
- **Fields:** The Purchase Price field is the price the customer paid for the product after applying any discounts. The Units Purchased YTD field shows the total number of units the customer purchased at the price listed.

Figure 6.24 | **Purchase Activity by Customer Table**

Customer ID Number	Product Number	Purchase Price	Units Purchased YTD
108650	86320	$855	1
109256	35677	$675	2
109456	86532	$1,233	4
120004	35877	$925	1
128650	86422	$1,035	1
150903	86422	$1,150	1
190266	86532	$1,450	1
220911	86532	$1,450	1
337090	86320	$855	1
358900	35677	$574	3
603001	86532	$1,450	1
670921	86532	$1,233	4
690907	86532	$1,160	5
700921	86532	$1,160	7

This field contains the price the customer paid for the product.

Figure 6.25 shows the Customer Detail table that contains the name and state of residence for each customer. As mentioned in the requirements, the state of residence is needed on the report to identify the location of defective returns. The following are other key points regarding this table:

- **Table Purpose**: To show the name and state of residence for each customer ID number.
- **Primary Key**: The Customer ID Number field is the primary key of the table.

Figure 6.25 | **Customer Detail Table**

Customer Detail

Customer ID Number	Customer Name/Organization	State of Residence
905433	B.D. Law Associates	TX
209477	L.L. Accounting Practice	NJ
109123	Bob May	TX
330998	A & A Finance Co.	TX
133567	Natalie Blu	TX
448990	Fay Law Associates	PA
178223	Lori Hon	NY
408723	R&F Consulting	TX
137650	Hale Charles	PA
117768	Anthony Gil	CA
414456	BG Consulting	GA
159081	Bernice Bee	NC
167109	Larry Glee	NJ
187090	Bruce Lite	CA

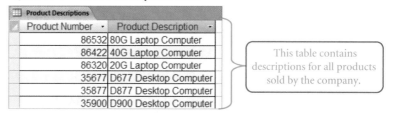

Figure 6.26 shows the Product Descriptions table. The company manufactures and sells six different computer models. This table will be needed so the name of each product can be displayed on the final report. The Product Number field is the primary key of the table.

Figure 6.26 | **Product Descriptions Table**

Product Descriptions

Product Number	Product Description
86532	80G Laptop Computer
86422	40G Laptop Computer
86320	20G Laptop Computer
35677	D677 Desktop Computer
35877	D877 Desktop Computer
35900	D900 Desktop Computer

This table contains descriptions for all products sold by the company.

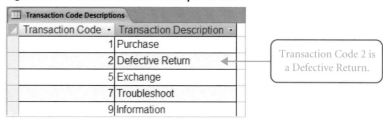

Figure 6.27 shows the final table that will be used for this project, which is the Transaction Code Descriptions table. Because the Call Center Activity by Week table shows only the transaction codes, this table will be needed to see what code is used to identify Defective Returns. The Transaction Code field is the primary key for the table.

Figure 6.27 | **Transaction Code Descriptions Table**

Transaction Code Descriptions

Transaction Code	Transaction Description
1	Purchase
2	Defective Return
5	Exchange
7	Troubleshoot
9	Information

Transaction Code 2 is a Defective Return.

Adding and Joining Tables in a Select Query

Now that tables have been selected and linked into an Access database, a query will be created to select records and produce data for a report. The query will contain all five tables illustrated in Figures 6.23 through 6.27. Depending on how a table is created, the primary key fields may or may not be defined. If the primary key is not defined for a table, and table relationships have not been established, you will have to manually create joins lines between the tables in your query (see Figure 6.4 for creating join lines manually). This project assumes that joins have to be manually created. It is critical that all records related to defective returns be selected from the Call Center Activity by Week table (see Figure 6.23). Therefore, Outer Joins are used for the following list of tables (see Figure 6.11 for creating Outer Joins):

- **Purchase Activity by Customer** table and **Call Center Activity by Week** table: Two join lines are created between the Customer ID Number and Product Number fields. These are primary key fields in both tables, which is why two join lines are needed.

- **Product Descriptions** table and **Call Center Activity by Week** table: A join line is created between the Product Number fields in these tables.

- **Customer Detail** table and **Call Center Activity by Week** table: A join line is created between the Customer ID Number fields in these two tables.

- **Transaction Code Descriptions** table and **Call Center Activity by Week** table: A join line is created between the Transaction Code fields in these two tables.

Figure 6.28 shows the five tables added to a Select Query with Outer Join lines. The Outer Joins are selecting all records from the Call Center Activity by Week table and only records with matching values in the joined fields from the other four tables. After the tables are added and joined, the query is saved and named Call Center Returns.

Figure 6.28 | **Tables Added to a Select Query and Outer Joins are Created**

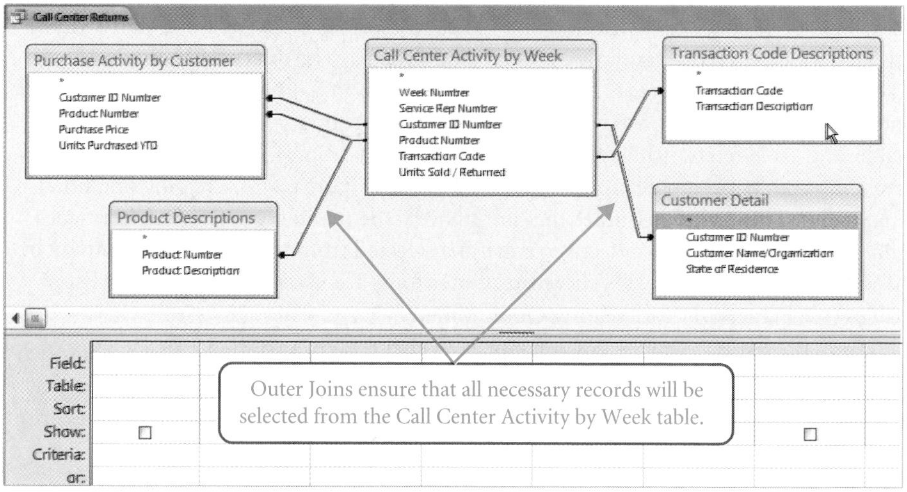

Creating a Parameter Query

The next requirement of building the query for this project is to add fields and enter the required criteria in the query design grid. The requirements for this project state that the most recent week of data is to be selected from the Call Center Activity by Week table. As a result, the value that is entered in the criteria row for the Week Number field will change depending on the time of year the query is run. Therefore, instead of typing a permanent value in the criteria row for the Week field, the user will be asked to enter a value for the Week Number field upon running the query or opening the report. This query, known as a *parameter query*, will request a value from the user that will be used in the criteria row for a particular field. The following is how the parameter query is created for this project.

- All fields required for the project are added to the query design grid (see Figure 6.29).
- The following is typed into the criteria row for the Week Number field: [Enter a Week Number from 1 to 12]. This phrase will appear on an input box upon running the query. The input box will allow the user to enter a value that will be used for the criteria row of the Week Number field. Therefore, the phrase typed in brackets is usually instructions telling the user what kind of value to enter (see Figure 6.30).

Figure 6.29 shows the final settings in the design grid of the query. Notice that 2 was entered for the criteria row of the Transaction Code field because the number 2 represents transactions that are Defective Returns. This was identified by opening the Transaction Code Descriptions table after it was linked to the database.

Figure 6.29 | **Criteria Settings for the Call Center Returns Query**

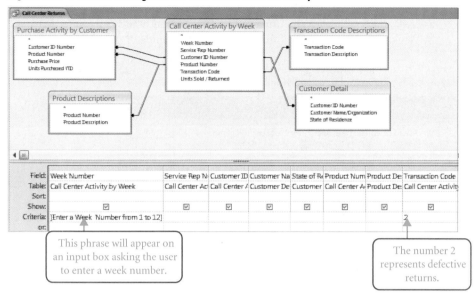

This phrase will appear on an input box asking the user to enter a week number.

The number 2 represents defective returns.

Figure 6.30 shows the input box that appears when the query is run. Notice that the description typed into the criteria row of the Week Number field in Figure 6.29 appears at the top of the input box. When a value is typed into the box and the OK button is clicked, the query will run and produce the record set.

Figure 6.30 | **Parameter Value Input Box**

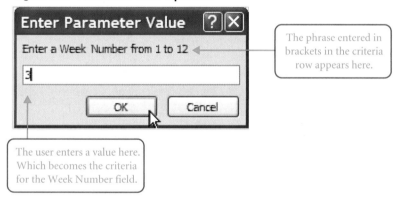

The phrase entered in brackets in the criteria row appears here.

The user enters a value here. Which becomes the criteria for the Week Number field.

Adding Calculations

So far in this project, you selected tables, added them to a Select Query, created Outer Joins, added fields to the query design grid, entered criteria to select records relating to defective returns, and created a parameter query that asks the user to enter a week number. This segment will address the creation of calculated fields. As stated in the project requirements, one of the goals is to calculate the sales value of all returned defective computers. Therefore, a calculated field called Return Sales Value will be added to the query. This field will multiply the price each customer paid by the number of units returned. The following explains how this field is created (see Chapter 4 for creating Custom and Calculated fields).

- Type the field name **Return Sales Value**, followed by a colon in an empty column in the query design grid.
- Open the Expression Builder (see Figure 4.16 for how to open the Expression Builder).

>> **Quick Reference**

Parameter Queries

1. Create a new Select Query.
2. Add fields to the query design grid.
3. Choose a field that you want the user to define when the query is run.
4. Type a phrase in brackets [ ] in the criteria row of the field that the user will define. This phrase should tell the user which type of value should be entered in the input box.
5. Run the query to check the appearance of the input box.

- Using the Tables folder on the left side of the Expression Builder, double click the Purchase Price field in the Purchase Activity by Customer table. Then type an asterisk and double click the Units Sold/Returned field in the Call Center Activity by Week table. See Figure 6.31 for the completed formula.

Figure 6.31 | **Return Sales Value Formula**

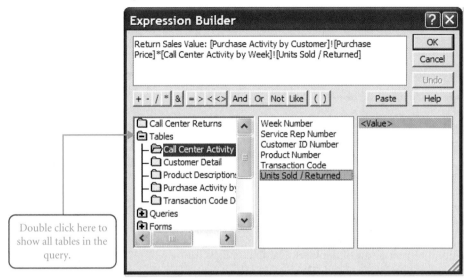

Double click here to show all tables in the query.

After completing the calculated field for the Return Sales Value, the query for the project is tested to evaluate the records and the result of the formula. The record set of the query is composed of 13 fields. Therefore, the record set is displayed in Figures 6.32 and 6.33.

Figure 6.32 | **Record Set of the Call Center Returns Query Fields 1 through 7**

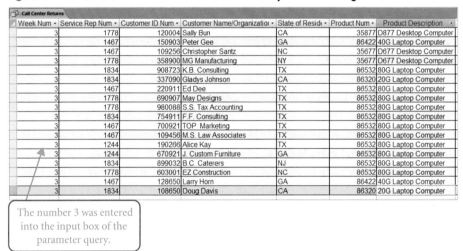

The number 3 was entered into the input box of the parameter query.

Figure 6.33 | **Record Set of the Call Center Returns Query Fields 8 through 13**

Transaction Code ▾	Transaction Description ▾	Units Purchased YTD ▾	Purchase Price ▾	Units Sold / Returned ▾	Return Sales Value ▾
2	Defective Return	1	$925	1	$925
2	Defective Return	1	$1,150	1	$1,150
2	Defective Return	2	$675	1	$675
2	Defective Return	3	$574	2	$1,148
2	Defective Return	10	$1,160	7	$8,120
2	Defective Return	1	$855	1	$855
2	Defective Return	1	$1,450	1	$1,450
2	Defective Return	5	$1,160	4	$4,640
2	Defective Return	2	$1,305	2	$2,610
2	Defective Return	6	$1,160	3	$3,480
2	Defective Return	7	$1,160	5	$5,800
2	Defective Return	4	$1,233	3	$3,698
2	Defective Return	1	$1,450	1	$1,450
2	Defective Return	4	$1,233	3	$3,698
2	Defective Return	4	$1,233	3	$3,698
2	Defective Return	1	$1,450	1	$1,450
2	Defective Return	1	$1,035	1	$1,035
2	Defective Return	1	$855	1	$855

Only records in which the Transaction Code is equal to 2 are selected.

The Return Sales Value is calculated by multiplying the values in these two fields.

COMMON MISTAKES | Checking the Record Set of a Query

It is very import to check the record set of a query even if the final goal of a project is to create a report. Mistakes that appear in an Access report often originate in the query that is supplying the data. The following is a checklist that can be used to evaluate the record set of a query.

- Evaluate whether joins are removing required data from the record set. This is especially important when Inner Joins are used. You may need to create a test query using one table to see how many records are selected before subsequent tables are added and joined.

- Look at the data in the record set to see that it matches and is in line with the criteria required for the project.

- Check the results of any calculated fields to ensure formulas and functions are producing valid results.

Constructing the Final Report

Creating the final report is the last requirement for this comprehensive project. The record set of the Call Center Returns query will supply the data for the report. The report is created by dragging fields from the Field List, adding label boxes, adding totals, and adding lines. The following is a list of techniques that was used to build each section of the completed design grid shown in Figure 6.34. The techniques explained in this list can be found in Chapter 5.

- **Report Header:** The Report Header and Report Footer sections were added to the design grid (see Figure 5.9 for an example of adding the Report Header and Footer). However, because the Report Header will not be used, the height of the section was reduced to zero.

- **Page Header:** The Page Header section is used to display the title of the report. The title is created by dragging the Week Number field from the Field List into the Page Header section. The description in the label box attached to the Week Number text box was changed to read "Call Center Product Returns for Week Number:". Therefore, this becomes the title of the report, and the week number that is entered into the parameter query will be displayed next to the title (see Figure 5.4 for opening and adding fields to the design grid from the Field List).

- **Product Number Header:** A group was created based on the Product Number field (see Figures 5.35 and 5.36 for opening and using the **Grouping** dialog box). A header and footer will be displayed on the report for each product number that appears in the record set of the Call Center Returns query. The Product Number Header section is used to display the product number and description of the items being returned. In addition, label boxes are drawn at the bottom of this section, which will serve as column headings for the data displayed for each product number (see Figure 5.40 for adding label boxes in a group header section).

- **Detail:** The Detail section is used to display the data for each product that appears on the report. For this section, fields were dragged from the Field List into the Detail section of the design grid. The label box that is attached to the field when it is dragged onto the report was removed because column headings were added to the Product Number Header section (see Figure 5.22 for deleting a label box that is attached to a field). In addition, a calculated field was added to this section to calculate the percent of total units returned. The formula divides the units returned by the units purchased year to date.

- **Product Number Footer:** This section contains text boxes with Sum functions that are producing subtotals for each product (see Figure 5.52 for adding group and report totals). In addition, a calculated field was added to determine the total percent of returns for each product. A label box was added to the far left of the section, indicating that the values represent totals for the product.

- **Page Footer:** This section contains the date and page numbers for the report. Both will be displayed at the bottom of each report page.

- **Report Footer:** This section contains text boxes with Sum functions that are producing grand totals for the entire report. In addition, a calculated field was added to determine the total percent of returns for the entire report. At the far left of the section, a label box was added, indicating that the values in this section represent the grand totals for the report.

Figure 6.34 | **Design Grid for the Project Final Report**

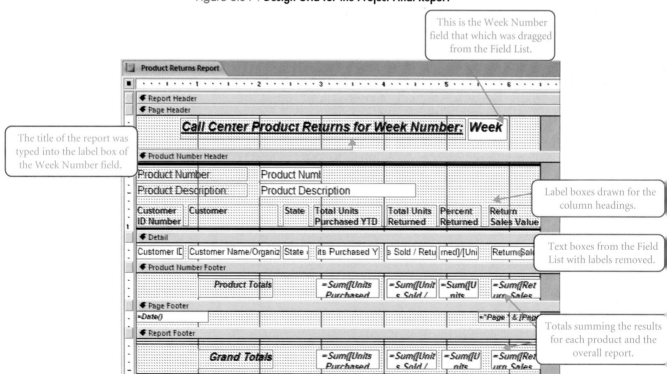

Figures 6.35 and 6.36 show the final report for this project. When the report is switched to either **Layout View** or **Print Preview**, the input box for the parameter query will open. As a result, this report can be used to monitor product returns for the current week or prior weeks of the year. For this example, week number 3 was entered into the input box for the parameter query. The details in the report satisfy the requirements stated at the beginning of this section and provide valuable information regarding computers that are being returned by customers in week 3. The following are few key observations from the report:

- Page 1 shows the details for item 86532, which is an 80 gigabyte laptop computer. This product had the highest number of returns on the report, and most of the returns are coming from the state of Texas. The business manager reading this report might contact the distribution center that ships computers to Texas and order an inspection of any remaining inventory. The company might even stop all shipments of this computer until the cause of the defect is identified and eliminated.

- The next item shown on page 1 is item 86422, which is also a laptop computer. The number of returns for this product is much lower than 86532, but both returns came from the state of Georgia. The business manager using this information will probably want to monitor this item over the next few weeks to see whether the number of returns increases from this state.

- The second page of the report shows returns from three items. The number of returns from these items is also much lower than item 86532. However, two different items were returned only from the state of California. The business manager using the information from this report will want to monitor returns to see whether there is an overall increase in products returned from this state.

- The bottom of page 2 shows the total statistics for the report. For week 3, there was almost $47,000 in returns. However, most of these returns are coming from item 86532. This data will help the business managers of this company prioritize efforts to focus on item 86532, which will have the greatest impact on reducing product returns if the problem can be identified and corrected.

Figure 6.35 | **Final Report Page 1**

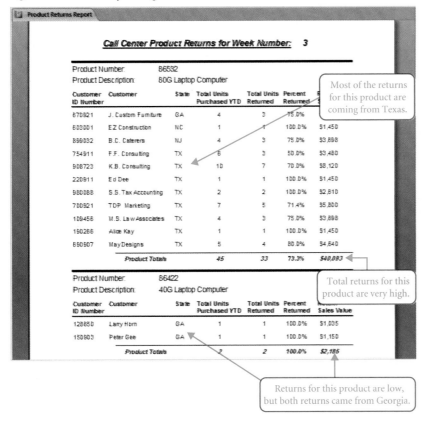

Figure 6.36 | **Final Report Page 2**

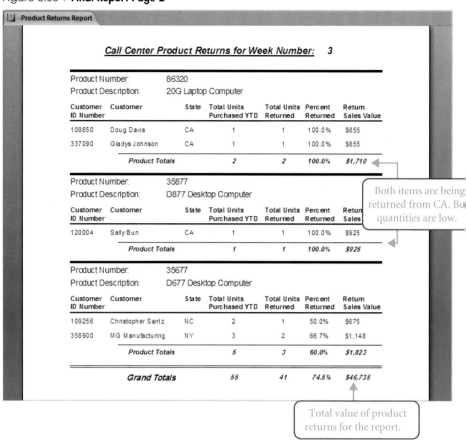

Call Center Product Returns for Week Number: 3

Product Number:	86320					
Product Description:	20G Laptop Computer					

Customer ID Number	Customer	State	Total Units Purchased YTD	Total Units Returned	Percent Returned	Return Sales Value
108650	Doug Davis	CA	1	1	100.0%	$855
337090	Gladys Johnson	CA	1	1	100.0%	$855
	Product Totals		2	2	100.0%	$1,710

Product Number:	35877					
Product Description:	D877 Desktop Computer					

Customer ID Number	Customer	State	Total Units Purchased YTD	Total Units Returned	Percent Returned	Return Sales
120004	Sally Bun	CA	1	1	100.0%	$925
	Product Totals		1	1	100.0%	$925

Both items are being returned from CA. But quantities are low.

Product Number:	35677					
Product Description:	D677 Desktop Computer					

Customer ID Number	Customer	State	Total Units Purchased YTD	Total Units Returned	Percent Returned	Return Sales Value
109256	Christopher Santz	NC	2	1	50.0%	$675
358900	MG Manufacturing	NY	3	2	66.7%	$1,148
	Product Totals		5	3	60.0%	$1,823
	Grand Totals		**55**	**41**	**74.5%**	**$46,735**

Total value of product returns for the report.

>> Comprehensive Project

The purpose of this workshop is to demonstrate the Call Center comprehensive project illustrated in this section of the chapter. I will be demonstrating the tasks in this workshop in the following four videos: **Comp. Project Table Joins**, **Comp. Project Parameter Query**, **Comp. Project Calculated Field**, and **Comp. Project Report**. The name of the video is listed next to each section of tasks. Open the ib_a06_callcenter database before starting this workshop. Complete each section of tasks and then watch the video pertaining to that section.

1. **Adding and Joining Tables in a Query (Video: Comp. Project Table Joins)**

   a. Create a new Select Query and add all five tables contained in the database to the query.

   b. Use the following information to create joins between the tables added to the query:

   i. Call Center Activity by Week table and Product Descriptions table using the Product Number field.

    ii. Call Center Activity by Week table and Customer Detail table using the Customer ID Number field.

    iii. Call Center Activity by Week table and Transaction Code Descriptions table using the Transaction Code field.

    iv. Call Center Activity by Week table and Purchase Activity by Customer table using the Customer ID Number and Product Number fields. You should have two join lines between these two tables.

c. Convert all the joins in the query to Outer Joins. Make sure that you select the option that selects all the records from the Call Center Activity by Week table and only those records that match from the other tables in the query. As a result, the arrows for the Outer Joins should always be pointing away from the Call Center Activity by Week table.

d. Save the query and name it **Call Center Return Data**.

e. Add the following list of fields to the query design grid. Next to each field is the name of the table in which the field is contained.

    i. Week Number: Call Center Activity by Week table

    ii. Service Rep Number: Call Center Activity by Week table

    iii. Customer ID Number: Call Center Activity by Week table

    iv. Customer Name/Organization: Customer Detail table

    v. State of Residence: Customer Detail table

    vi. Product Number: Call Center Activity by Week table

    vii. Product Description: Product Descriptions table

    viii. Transaction Code: Call Center Activity by Week table

    ix. Transaction Description: Transaction Code Descriptions table

    x. Units Purchased YTD: Purchase Activity by Customer

    xi. Purchase Price: Purchase Activity by Customer

    xii. Units Sold/Returned: Call Center Activity by Week table

2. Creating a Parameter Query (Video: Comp. Project Parameter Query)

a. Type the number **2** in the Criteria row of the query design grid for the Transaction Code field.

b. Type the following into the Criteria row of the Week Number field: **[Enter a week number from 1 to 12]**.

c. Save the query and then run it. Type the number **3** in the input box when it opens and then click the **OK** button.

d. Look at the record set for the query. Check that the values in the Transaction Description field all state Defective Return.

e. Switch the query back to **Design View** and save.

3. Adding a Calculated Field (Video: Comp. Project Calculated Field)

a. Type the field name **Value of Returns**, followed by a colon, in the empty column next to the Units Sold/Returned field in the query design grid.

b. Open the Expression Builder.

c. Using the Tables folder on the left side of the Expression Builder, double click the Units/Sold Returned field in the Call Center Activity by Week table.

d. Type an asterisk. Then double-click the Purchase Price field in the Purchase Activity by Customer table.

e. Remember to delete any **<Expr>** symbols that might appear in the formula and then click the **OK** button.

f. Open the **Property Sheet** window for the Return Values field and set the format to Currency.

g. Run the query to check the results of the Value of Returns Value field. Type the number **3** when the parameter input box opens.

h. Save the query and close it.

4. **Constructing the Final Report (Video: Comp. Project Report)**

a. Create a new Access report using the Call Center Return Data query.

b. Add the Report Header and Footer to the design grid of the report and decrease the height of the Report Header section to zero.

c. Set all the margins for the report to 1 inch and Increase the width of the design grid to 6.5 inches.

d. Increase the height of the Page Header section to ½ inch.

e. Open the **Field List** window. Then click and drag the Week Number field from the query field list into the Page Header section of the design grid.

f. Change the description in the label box attached to this field to read `Call Center Product Returns for Week Number:`

g. Format the Week Number field in the Page Header section to an Arial font, 14 point font size, bold, italics, underline, and left alignment. Make these formatting adjustments to both the label and text boxes. Separate the label and text boxes, and increase the size as needed. Position the label and text box so they are centered in the Page Header section.

h. Save the report and name it `Call Center Returns Report`.

i. Add a Group Header and Footer section to the report based on the Product Number field. The groups should be sorted in descending order. Select the **with a footer section** option, and the keep whole group together on one page option in the **Grouping** dialog box.

j. Increase the height of the Product Number Header section to one inch.

k. Add the Product Number and Product Description fields from the Field List to the upper-left side of the Product Number Header section. The fields should be stacked vertically. Format the label and text box for both fields to an Arial font, 12 point font size, and left alignment. Adjust the dimensions of the label and text box, so all data is visible on the report.

l. Draw seven label boxes across the bottom of the Product Number Header section to serve as column headings for the report. Type the following descriptions for the label boxes and set any errors to ignore.

   i. Label box 1: `Customer ID Number`

   ii. Label box 2: `Customer`

   iii. Label box 3: `State`

   iv. Label box 4: `Total Units Purchased YTD`

   v. Label box 5: `Total Units Returned`

   vi. Label box 6: `Percent Returned`

   vii. Label box 7: `Return Sales Value`

m. Make the following format adjustments to the label boxes in letter l.: Arial font, 10 point font size, bold, and left alignment. Adjust the height of label boxes with long descriptions so the wording wraps to two lines.

n. Adjust the height of the Detail section to ¼ inch.

o. Add the following fields from the Field List to the Detail section of the design grid. Align each field under the appropriate label box in the

Product Number Header section. For each field, remove the label box that is attached to the text box and set any errors to ignore. Note that a space should be left in the Detail section under the Percent Returned label box.

  i. Customer ID Number

  ii. Customer Name/Organization

  iii. State of Residence

  iv. Units Purchased YTD

  v. Units Sold/Returned

  vi. Value of Returns

p. Make the following format adjustments to all the text boxes in the Detail section of the design grid: Arial font and font size of 10 points. Align left the Customer ID Number, Customer Name/Organization, State of Residence, and Value of Returns text boxes. Align center the Units Purchased YTD and Units Sold/Returned text boxes. Check the dimensions and positions of the text boxes and make sure that all data is visible and that it is aligned under the column headings.

q. Add a text box in the Detail section under the Percent Returned label box. Delete the label box that is attached to the text box and set any errors to ignore. Add a formula to the text box that divides the Units Sold/Returned field by the Units Purchased YTD date field. Remember to click the **<Field List>** option in the lower-center window of the Expression Builder. Format the result of the formula to a Percentage with 1 decimal place, Arial font, 10 point font size, and center alignment.

r. Increase the height of the Product Number Footer section to ⅜ inch.

s. Add a label box on the left side of the Product Number Footer section under the Customer Name/Organization field in the Detail section. Type the description **Product Totals** in the label box and make the following format adjustments: Arial font, 10 point font size, bold, italics, and left alignment.

t. Increase the height of the Report Footer section to ½ inch.

u. Add a label box to the left side of the Report Footer section and align under the Product Totals label box in the Product Number Footer section. Type the description **Grand Totals** in the label box and format as follows: Arial font, 10 point font size, bold, italics, and right alignment. Set any errors to ignore.

v. Using the **Grouping** dialog box, add totals to the Product Number Footer and Report Footer sections so the following fields are summed on the report:

  i. Units Purchased YTD

  ii. Units Sold/Returned

  iii. Value of Returns

w. Adjust the format of the text boxes in the Product Number Footer and Report Footer sections that were created in step v with bold and italics. Then move all the text boxes and the label boxes 1/8 inch below the top of the Product Number Footer section and Report Footer section. Check the appearance of the totals in the Product Number Footer and Report Footer sections and make any necessary adjustments.

x. Add a text box to the Product Number Footer section and align under the Percent Returned heading in the Product Number Header section. Delete the label box that is attached to the text box and align with the rest of the totals in the Product Number Footer section. Use the Expression Builder to add the following formula to this text box: **=Sum([Units Sold Returned])/Sum([Units Purchased YTD])**.

y. Make the following format adjustments to the text box created in letter x.: Percent number format, one decimal place, Arial font, 10 point font size, bold, italics, and center alignment.

z. Copy the text box created in step x and paste it into the Report Footer section. Align under the Percent Returned heading.

aa. Add the page number to the lower right side of the Page Footer section. Use the N of M format. Then format the page number as follows: Arial font, 10 point font size, bold, italics, and right alignment.

bb. Using the **Grouping** dialog box, sort the data in the Detail section of the report based on the values in the State of Residence field in ascending order.

cc. Add the following lines to the report. The location and width of each line is provided.

    i. Top of Product Number Header section: line width 3 pt

    ii. Bottom of Product Number Header section: line width 2 pt

    iii. Top of Product Number Footer section: line width Hairline

    iv. Top of Report Footer section: 2 lines width Hairline

dd. View the report in **Print Preview** and type `week number` **3** in the parameter input box. After reviewing the report, save and close the report and the database.

≫ Wealth Management Investment Reports

The goal of a wealth management or personal finance firm is to manage investments for their customers so they achieve their financial goals. A financial analyst or financial planner from these firms will develop an investment strategy based on their clients' risk preference. These strategies can range from conservative investments in bonds or mutual funds to the purchase of stocks in public companies. However, what happens when a stock the wealth management firm buys for its customers takes a turn for the worse and starts to decline? A small to medium-sized wealth management firm might manage the investments for a few hundred clients. How does it know who owns the stock and whether the stock should be sold? The answer is databases. Most wealth management firms work with some type of database system to track the investments of their clients. The reports generated from these database systems play a critical role in the buy and sell decisions made by these companies every day.

Exercise

The purpose of this exercise is to construct a report that might be used by a financial analyst in a wealth management firm. The performance of a stock could drastically change over the course of one day. The goal of this project is to create a report that will allow the analyst to enter a stock symbol and show a list of clients that currently own the stock. The decision the analyst will have to make is whether to hold or sell the stock for the client. The report will require the following details for the analyst to make this decision:

- Customer account number and name
- Current price of the stock
- Average price that was paid for the stock
- Current shares owned by the customer

- Current total value of the customer's investment in the stock
- Total dollars paid for all shares owned by the customer
- Difference between the total dollars paid for all shares owned and the current value of those shares.

1. Open the Access database named ib_a06_wealthmanagementdata. Three tables have been imported into this database, which satisfies the project requirements listed previously.

2. Open the Excel file named ib_a06_wealthmanagementdataguide. This file contains definitions and statistics for the tables contained in the database that will be used for this project.

3. Create a new Select Query and add the Client Names, Current Stock Prices, and Stock Ownership by Client tables.

4. Join the Client Names and Current Stock Prices tables to the Stock Ownership by Client table. Use Outer Joins that select *all* records from the Stock Ownership by Client table. Use the information in the Wealth Management Data Guide to identify the primary key in order to properly create these joins.

5. Save the query and name it **Current Stock Value by Client**.

6. Add the following fields to the query design grid. These fields are required to satisfy the requirements of the final report and in some cases might be needed to create calculated fields

   a. Account Number: Stock Ownership by Client table

   b. Client Name: Client Names table

   c. Stock Symbol: Stock Ownership by Client table

   d. Current Price: Current Stock Prices table

   e. Avg Purchase Price: Stock Ownership by Client table

   f. Shares Owned: Stock Ownership by Client table

7. Sort the record set of the query based on the values in the Account Number and Stock Symbol fields in ascending order.

8. Create a parameter query for the Stock Symbol field, which will allow the financial analyst using the report to enter any stock symbol that needs to be evaluated when the report is opened. Type the following in the criteria row of the Stock Symbol field: **[Enter a Stock Symbol]**.

9. Create a calculated field that computes the total value of each client's investment per stock. This will require a formula that multiplies the value in the Avg Purchase Price field by the value in the Shares Owned field. The results of this computed field should be formatted to Currency with zero decimal places. Use the name Total Investment Cost for this calculated field.

10. Create a second calculated field that computes the *current value* of each client's investment, which will require a formula that multiplies the values in the Current Price field by the values in the Shares Owned field. The results of this computed field should be formatted to Currency with zero decimal places. Use the name Current Investment Value for this calculated field.

11. Save the query. Then check the record set of the query. Use the stock symbol SY6 when the parameter input box opens. There should be a total of 17 records in the query, and each client name should appear only one time. Also, check the results of the calculated field to ensure that the formulas are executed properly and that the results are formatted. Close the query after checking the records.

12. Create a new Access report using the Current Stock Value by Client query.

13. Create an Access report with the following requirements. Remember to save your work frequently and name the report **Stock Ownership Report**.

    a. The Report Header and Footer section should be added.

    b. The title of the report should be added to the Report Header section. The title of the report should read **Ownership Status for Stock Symbol:**

    c. The title of the report should show the stock that was selected in the parameter input box. Format the title to an Arial font, font size of 16 points, bold, italics, underline, and right alignment.

    d. Add six label boxes in the Page Header section. These labels will serve as column headings for the report. Formatting for the label boxes should be Arial font, 10 point font size, and bold. The following descriptions should appear in the boxes.

        i. Account Number

        ii. Client Name

        iii. Shares Owned

        iv. Total Investment Cost

        v. Current Investment Value

        vi. Gain/Loss

    e. Add a line across the bottom of the Page Header section and use the 2 pt line width.

    f. Drag matching fields for the five label boxes added in step d from the Field List into the Detail section. Remove the label boxes that are attached to each field and set any errors to Ignore. Format these fields to an Arial font and 10 point font size, and make sure that they are aligned under the label boxes in the Page Header section. Use the stock symbol SY6 when the parameter input box opens when switching to either **Layout View** or **Print Preview**.

    g. Add a text box in the Detail section and align under the **Gain/Loss** label box in the **Page Header** section. Remove the label box that is attached to this text box and create a calculated field that computes the client's gain or loss on the stock. Your formula should subtract the value in the Total Investment Cost field from the value in the Current Investment Value field. Format the results of the formula to Currency, zero decimal places, Arial font, and 10 point font size.

    h. Add report totals to the Report Footer section. For the Gain/Loss column, create a formula that subtracts the sum of the Total Investment Cost column from the sum of the Current Investment Value column. Format the totals to an Arial font, 12 point font size, bold, and italics. Then draw two lines at the top of the Report Footer section using a Hairline width.

    i. Add the date and page number to the Page Footer section.

    j. Sort the data in the report based on the values in the Total Investment Cost column in descending order.

14. The analysts of this wealth management firm recently received news that stock SY6 is expected to drop significantly in price. Run the report you created in step 13 for stock symbol SY6 to identify all clients that own this stock.

15. Are all clients losing money on this stock?

16. What is the total loss on this stock for all clients this firm services?

17. The analyst of this firm also received news that stock SY5 is expecting to increase in price. Close the report and open it again, this time entering symbol **SY5** in the input box. Is the amount of money gained from this stock enough to offset the losses of stock SY6?

18. Save and close the report. Then close the database.

>> What's Wrong with This Database?

Problem

You are working as an analyst in the strategic planning department for a company that runs a chain of specialty stores selling a line of children's products. The product categories include toys, clothes, furniture, and infant products. Your coworker, who is also an analyst in the department, has asked you to look at a sales analysis that he will be presenting to the Vice President of the department. The goal of the analysis is to compare the first 26 weeks of sales data for this year and last year by product category. The company will use this information to identify what categories are declining in sales compared to last year and decide if new promotional marketing strategies should be organized. Your coworker sends you an Access database and asks your opinion regarding the accuracy of the data on the report.

Exercise

The Access database your coworker sent to you is named ib_a06_childrensspecialtystore. Open the database and evaluate the data that is being displayed on the 26 Week Sales Analysis report. Do you think your coworker should be comfortable presenting these results to the vice president of the department? Consider the following points:

1. What query is being used to supply data for the report?

2. Evaluate the construction of the query you identified in point 1. Are primary keys defined for the tables used in the query and are the tables properly joined?

3. Are there any calculated fields in the query? Are they producing valid results?

4. Are there any calculated fields in the report? Are they producing valid results?

5. Is the report professionally formatted and easy to read?

What's wrong with this database? Write a short answer for each point above and fix any errors you find in the ib_a06_childrensspecialtystore database. Make any formatting adjustments to the report that you think will give it a professional appearance and make it easy to read.

We solved our ASN problem by researching the database tables that were maintained by the company. Luckily, the transportation department set up a "fake" store number for any shipments that were made to the grocery company. That is to say, a new store number was added to the system for the purposes of tracking any merchandise that was shipped out of our distribution center to any of the grocery stores. As a result, we linked tables into an Access database and constructed a report showing what shipments were made to each grocery store.

Assignment

The Access database named ib_a06_groceryshipments is very similar to the database that was constructed to solve the ASN problem in the anecdote. Your assignment is to use the tables in this database to construct a report that shows what shipments were made to each grocery store. The following are the requirements for the report.

1. The Excel file named ib_a06_groceryshipmentsdataguide provides information for the tables contained in the ib_a06_groceryshipments database.

2. Construct a report that shows which items were shipped to each grocery store. The report should be grouped based on the locations contained in the Manifest Destination field, which is in the Manifest Destinations table.

3. The store number that was assigned to grocery store shipments is 8333.

4. The report should contain only one week of data. Therefore, set up the report so that you are prompted to enter a week number each time the report is opened. The week number you select should appear in the title of the report.

5. The report should show how many cases and units were shipped for each item. Also, show the total amount of money the grocery company will be charged for each item.

6. The report should show totals for each grocery store and a grand total at the bottom of the report.

7. Use formatting techniques to give this report a professional appearance.

Questions for Discussion

1. Corporate mergers and acquisitions frequently occur in many industries. When a company acquires or merges with another company, what challenges do you think it faces with regard to managing technology and information systems?

2. One idea that was proposed to solve the ASN problem described in the anecdote was to give the grocery company access to the children's retail company's database. This would give the grocery company the capability to query the retailer's database and see what merchandise was shipped to each store. Why do you think both companies were reluctant to use this idea?

The following questions are related to the concepts addressed in this chapter. There are three types of questions: Short Answer, True or False, and Fill in the Blank. If your answer to a True or False question is False, write a short explanation as to why you think the statement is not true.

1. True or False: If you are developing your own database, it is good practice to have the same field of data duplicated in several tables. This reduces the amount of tables you need when creating queries.

2. To use fields from multiple tables in a query, you must _____ the tables.

3. Look at the following figure. Explain how records will be selected from these two tables.

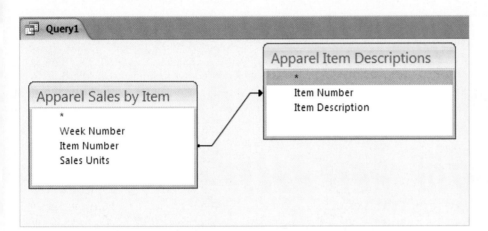

4. What type of join is shown in the figure for question 3?

5. True or False: Access will automatically create join lines between two tables if they both contain fields with the same name.

6. You can open the _____ _____ dialog box by double clicking the join line.

7. Explain when two or more join lines would be required to join two tables.

8. Before using a query to create an Access report, you should check the record set of a query. What three key things should you look for when checking the record set of query, especially if contains multiple tables that are joined together?

9. True or False: The joins created between tables in the **Relationships** window will automatically be created when the tables are added to a query.

10. The relationship between two tables where one identical field is the primary key for both tables is a One to _____ relationship.

11. True or False: If the **Enforce Referential Integrity** option is selected in the **Edit Relationships** dialog box, you can not create a query unless both tables are used.

12. What are two critical pieces of information you will need before selecting tables from a database to construct an Access project?

13. What would you type into the Criteria row in the query design grid for the Category field if you wanted the user to enter a category number between 1 and 10 when the query runs?

14. True or False: You cannot use a parameter query in an Access report because the input box requesting data from the user will not open.

The following exam is designed to test your ability to recognize and execute the Access skills presented in this chapter. Read each question carefully and answer the questions in the order they are listed. You should be able to complete this exam in 60 minutes or less.

1. Open the Access database named ib_a06_skillsexam.

2. Create a new Select Query and add all four tables that are contained in the database.

3. Save the query and name it **Sales Analysis**.

4. Create an Outer Join between the Department Descriptions table and the Plan and Actual Sales by Week table. The Department Number field is the primary key for the Department Descriptions table. The join should select *all* records from the Plan and Actual Sales by Week table.

5. Create an Outer Join between the Category Descriptions table and the Plan and Actual Sales by Week table. The Category Number field is the primary key for the Category Descriptions table. The join should select *all* records from the Plan and Actual Sales by Week table.

6. Join the Plan and Actual Sales by Week table and the Last Year Sales table using an Inner Join. The Week Number, Department Number, and Category Number fields are the primary key for both tables.

7. Add the following fields to the query design grid:

   a. Week Number: Plan and Actual Sales by Week table

   b. Department Number: Plan and Actual Sales by Week table

   c. Department Description: Department Descriptions table

   d. Category Number: Plan and Actual Sales by Week table

   e. Category Description: Category Descriptions table

   f. TY Sales Plan: Plan and Actual Sales by Week table

   g. TY Actual Sales: Plan and Actual Sales by Week table

   h. LY Actual Sales: Last Year Sales table

8. Create a calculated field that subtracts the values in the TY Sales Plan field from the TY Actual Sales field. Name this field **TY Plan vs Actual**.

9. Create a calculated field that subtracts the values in the LY Actual Sales field from the TY Actual Sales field. Name this field **Sales LY vs TY**. Then run, save, and close the query.

10. Create a new Select Query and add the Sales Analysis query. Add the Week Number, Department Number, Department Description, TY Sales Plan, TY Actual Sales, LY Actual Sales, TY Plan vs Actual, and Sales LY vs TY fields to the query design grid.

11. Adjust the query so that fields with text data are grouped and fields with numeric data are summed when the query runs. Then, save the query and name it **Department Sales Analysis**.

12. Create a parameter query on the Department Number field that asks the user to enter a department number when the query runs. The message on the input box for the parameter query should read "Enter a Department number: 10, 20, 50, or 70".

13. Run the query and type department number **50** in the parameter input box. Then save and close the query.

14. Create a new report using the Department Sales Analysis query. Set all margins of the report to 1 inch and set the width of the design grid to 6.5 inches.

15. Add the Report Header and Footer sections to the report.

16. Add the title **Department Sales Results** to the Report Header section. Format the title to an Arial font, 14 point font size, bold, italics, and underline. The title should be centered over the report.

17. Save and name the report **Department Sales Results Report**.

18. Add the Department Number and Department Description fields to the upper-left corner of the Page Header section. Arrange the fields vertically and format to an Arial font, and 12 point font size.

19. Add six label boxes at the bottom of the Page Header section. The following descriptions should appear in the label boxes from left to right. Format the label boxes with an Arial font, 10 point font size, and bold. Set any error to Ignore.

    a. Label box 1: **Week Number**

    b. Label box 2: **TY Sales Plan**

    c. Label box 3: **TY Actual Sales**

    d. Label box 4: **LY Actual Sales**

    e. Label box 5: **Percent Chg Plan vs Actual**

    f. Label box 6: **Percent Chg TY vs LY**

20. Set the height of the Detail section to 3/8 inch.

21. Add four fields from the Field List window to the Detail section. Add matching fields for all label boxes except for the Percent Chg Plan vs Actual and the Percent Chg TY vs LY. Note that because the Department Sales Analysis query is summing results, each field name is preceded by the phrase **SumOf**. The data from these fields should be aligned under the appropriate label boxes and the font should be changed to Arial and the size to 10 points. Remove the label box that is attached to the field and set any errors to Ignore.

22. Add a calculated field to the Detail section for the Percent Chg Plan vs Actual. Your formula should divide the values in the SumOfTY Sales Plan field into the SumOfTY Plan vs Actual field. Format the result of this formula to a percentage, zero decimal places, Arial font, and 10 point font size. The results should be aligned under the Percent Chg Plan vs Actual label box.

23. Add a calculated field to the Detail section for the Percent Chg TY vs LY. Your formula should divide the values in the SumOfLY Actual Sales field into the SumOfSales LY vs TY field. Format the result of this formula to a percentage, zero decimal places, Arial font, and 10 point font size. The results should be aligned under the Percent Chg TY vs LY label box.

24. Add totals to the Report Footer section for each field in the Detail section except for the Week Number field. Format the totals to an Arial font, 12 point font size, bold, and italics. When creating the total Percent Chg Plan vs Actual and Percent Chg TY vs LY for the report, use a percent format with one decimal place. For the other totals, use a standard number format with commas and 0 decimal places. Make sure the totals are aligned under the appropriate column.

25. Add the current date to the upper-left corner of the Page Footer section.

26. Add a line to the bottom of the Page Header section and set the width to 2 pt. Then add two lines to the top of the Report Footer section and set the width to Hairline.

27. View the report in **Print Preview** and make any necessary adjustments to the size and position of any text or label boxes.

28. Save and close the report. Then close the database.

>> Challenge Questions

The following questions are designed to test your ability to apply the Access skills you have learned to complete a business objective. Use your knowledge of Access as well as your creativity to answer these questions. For most questions, there are several possible ways to complete the objective.

1. Open the Access database named ib_a06_wealthmanagementdata. Information regarding the tables contained in the database can be found in the Excel file named ib_a06_wealthmanagementdataguide. Create a report that shows any stocks where the client is currently losing money. Your report should include the following details:

   - The report should be grouped based on the values in the Account Number field. In the group header, show the client's account number and name.
   - For each client, show a list of stocks they own *that are losing money* and the number of shares they own.
   - Show the total cost of the client's investment by multiplying the shares owned by the average purchase price.
   - Show the total loss for each stock by subtracting the total cost of investment from the current value of the investment.
   - Show totals for each group and the overall report.
   - Use formatting techniques to give the report a professional appearance.

2. Open the ib_a06_callcenter database. Associates working in the Call Center are given bonuses based on the number of products they sell. Create a report that shows the product numbers, product descriptions, quantities sold, and total sales value for each associate working in the call center. Include the following details in this report.

   - Your report should show the *total results for all three weeks* of data contained in the Call Center Activity by Week table.
   - The Excel file named ib_a06_callcenterrepnames contains the name of each call center associate. Import this table into the database and show the name and ID number for each Call Center associate on the report.
   - Show sales totals for each associate and for the entire call center.
   - Use formatting techniques to give the report a professional appearance.
   - Figures 6.23 through 6.27 provide information on the tables in this database.

3. Open the Access database named ib_a06_marketingpromotionsdata. Categories 10 and 20 were not included in any of the promotional strategies listed in the Category Promotions TY table. For both categories combined, determine the percent increase or decrease over last year for each of the 26 weeks of data contained in the Category Sales by Week TY table. You will need to compare the 26 weeks of sales data in this table with the data contained in the Category Sales by Week LY table. The goal is to come up with one percentage per week that shows how much both categories combined have increased or decreased in unit sales. Your results should be contained in a query with two fields: Week Number and Percent Chg in Sales.

4. Open the Access database named ib_a06_marketingpromotionsdata. Use the results you calculated in question 3 to show the net change in sales for categories that were promoted in the Category Promotions TY table. Question 3 required you to evaluate the change in sales for categories 10 and 20 combined. Because these categories were not promoted, this percent change in sales will be used as a benchmark to evaluate the sales results of the categories that were promoted. Create a report that shows the percent change in sales this year over last year for the 26 weeks of data contained in the Category Sales by Week TY table. Your report should contain the following:

- Group the report based on the Category Number field and show the category number and category description in the heading of each group.
- Show the Week Number, Unit Sales TY, and Unit Sales LY *for week numbers 1 through 26* for each category. If a category was promoted in a certain week, show the promotional strategy name next to the category description.
- Calculate and show the Percent Gross Change in Sales using the following formula: (Unit Sales TY – Units Sales LY)/Unit Sales LY.
- Calculate and show the Percent Net Sales Change by subtracting the percent change in sales that was calculated in question 3 (this is the benchmark) from the Percent Gross Change in Sales that was calculated in the prior bullet point.
- Show totals for each category and for the entire report.
- Use formatting techniques to give the report a professional appearance.
- Analyze the report and explain how this firm's marketing strategies may have affected the sales results for the categories that were promoted.

≫ POWERPOINT *Quick Reference Guide*

Adding a Line

1. From the **Insert** tab, select **Shapes**. Alternately, from the **Format** tab, select a line from the **Insert Shapes** group.
2. Click on a line from the drop-down list.
3. Return to the slide where you want to draw a line. You will see that the cursor has turned into a cross bow.
4. Position the cross bow where you want to start the line. Hold down the left mouse button, slide your mouse until you've drawn the length of line you want or have connected two objects, and release the mouse button.

PAGE...........................**52**

Applying a Slide Layout

1. To apply a slide layout to a single slide:
   a. Right click on the slide either from the Slide pane or the **Slide/Outline** pane.
   b. Choose a layout.
2. To apply a slide layout to a multiple slides:
   a. Select a range of slides using the **Shift** key or separate slides using the **Ctrl** key.
   b. Right click on any of the selected slides and choose a layout.

PAGE...........................**36**

Changing Bullet or Numbering Locations on a List

1. To increase list level (move the bullets to the right):
   a. Highlight the bullets you wish to move and select the **Increase List Level** icon.
2. To decrease list level (move the bullets to the left):
   a. Highlight the bullets you wish to move and select the **Decrease List Level** icon.

PAGE...........................**45**

Changing the Appearance of a Presentation

From the **Design** tab, you can apply a design template from one of the following PowerPoint libraries:

1. Select the slides whose theme you wish to change.
   a. Select individual slides from **Slide Sorter** view by using the **Ctrl** key.
   b. You do not have to select any particular slide to change the appearance of the entire presentation.
2. From the **Design** tab, right click on a theme.
3. Select either **Apply to All Slides** or **Apply to Selected Slides**.

PAGE...........................**27**

Copy and Paste

1. Highlight the text, text box, or icon to be copied.
2. Click the **Copy** icon in the Ribbon.
3. Place the mouse pointer where the copied data should appear.
4. Click the **Paste** icon in the Ribbon.

PAGE...........................**79**

Copying Consecutive and Nonconsecutive Slides

1. To copy consecutive slides, use the **Shift** key and click on the first and last slide.
2. To copy nonconsecutive slides, use the **Ctrl** key while selecting the slides.

PAGE...........................**103**

Creating Lists of Information

1. Enter your information as phrases or short sentences on separate lines.
2. To create a bulleted list, highlight the lines and select the **Bullets** icon.
3. To create a numbered list, highlight the lines and select the **Numbered List** icon from the Ribbon.

PAGE...........................**44**

Deleting and Rearranging Slides

You can delete or rearrange slides from a presentation from the **Normal** view or **Slide Sorter** view by using the following steps:

1. To delete nonconsecutive slides: Hold down the **Ctrl** key, select the slides to delete, and then use the **Delete** key.
2. To delete consecutive slides: Hold down the **Shift** key, select the first and last slides to delete, and then use the **Delete** key.
3. To rearrange slides: Select the slide, hold down the left mouse button, and drag and drop the slide to the new location.

PAGE...........................**99**

Downloading a Theme from Office Online

1. Go to the **Themes** drop-down list under the **Design** tab and select the **More Themes** on Microsoft Office Online link.
2. You will be connected to the Microsoft Office Web site. Navigate to the page that lists all the available PowerPoint designs.
3. Select Presentations.
4. Select the template of your choice and click the **Download Now** button. A blank slide will appear in the **Slide** pane.
5. After you save the presentation, this theme will be available to you in your **Custom Themes** list.

PAGE...........................**30**

Formatting Data

1. Highlight the text to be formatted.
2. Click the **Home** tab of the Ribbon.
3. Click one of the icons in the **Font** group of the Ribbon or open the **Font** dialog box by clicking the button in the lower-right corner of the **Font** group.
4. If using the **Font** dialog box, click the **OK** button after making a selection.

PAGE **83**

Four-Step Planning Process

Step 1   What are the objectives?
Step 2   Who is the audience?
Step 3   What are the key messages/decisions?
Step 4   How much time do you have?

PAGE **7**

Grouping Shapes

1. Select all the shapes you wish to group.
2. From the **Drawing** group under the **Home** tab, select **Arrange**.
3. Chose **Group** from the drop-down list.

PAGE **52**

Horizontal and Vertical Alignment

1. Highlight a range of text to be formatted.
2. Click the **Home** tab of the Ribbon.
3. Click one of the alignment icons to right justify, left justify, or center the text.

PAGE **85**

How to Change the Font in the Entire Presentation

1. On the **Home** tab, select **Replace Fonts** from the **Editing** group.
2. When you see the options to change the font type across the entire presentation, make changes as desired.

PAGE **83**

How to Select Fonts

1. Highlight the text you wish to change.
2. From the **Font type** drop-down menu, select the new font.
3. The highlighted text font will be changed.

PAGE **80**

Insert a Clip into PowerPoint

1. From the **Insert** tab or **Content** icon, select **Clip**.
2. In the **Search** task pane, in the **Search for** box, type a word or phrase that describes the clip you want.
3. Click **Go**.
4. Choose the clip and either drag it into the slide or place it on the slide by using **Insert** on the drop down box.

PAGE **63**

Inserting a Word Table into PowerPoint

1. In Word, highlight the rows and columns you wish to copy and select **Copy** from the **Home** tab.
2. In PowerPoint, select **Paste** from the **Home** tab.
3. Click **OK** and the rows and columns will be placed on your slide.

PAGE **154**

Inserting an Excel Spreadsheet or Chart into PowerPoint

1. To insert an Excel spreadsheet into a PowerPoint slide, follow these steps:
   a. In Excel, highlight the cells you wish to copy and select **Copy** from the **Home** tab.
   b. In PowerPoint, select **Paste Special** from the **Home** tab and highlight **Microsoft Excel Worksheet Object**.
   c. Click **OK** and the selected cells will be placed on your slide.
2. To insert an Excel chart into a PowerPoint slide, follow these steps:
   a. In Excel, highlight the chart you wish to copy and select **Copy** from the **Home** tab.
   b. In PowerPoint, select **Paste Special** from the **Home** tab and highlight **Microsoft Office Drawing Object**.
   c. Click **OK** and the selected chart will be placed on your slide.

PAGE **153**

Inserting New Slides

1. From the **Home** tab:
   a. Select **New Slide**. You will be prompted to select the slide layout.
2. From the **Slides/Outline** tabs:
   a. Right click on the slide you wish to insert a new slide after.
   b. Select **New Slide**.
   c. The new slide will inherit the same layout which you may go back later and change.

PAGE **40**

Pasting Charts into PowerPoint

1. Activate a chart in an Excel file and click the **Copy** icon.
2. Open a PowerPoint file to a slide where the chart should appear.
3. Click the **Home** tab in the Ribbon.
4. Click the down arrow below the **Paste** icon.
5. Select the **Paste Special** option to open the **Paste Special** dialog box.
6. Select the **Picture (Enhanced Metafile)** option and click the **OK** button in the **Paste Special** dialog box.
7. Adjust the size of the chart by clicking and dragging the sizing handles as needed.

PAGE **57**

Presentation Outline

1. Title
2. Agenda
3. Introduction
4. Body
5. Conclusion

PAGE **9**

Printing Slides

1. Launch a presentation to be printed.
2. Make any necessary page setup adjustments by using the icons in the Ribbon or by opening the **Page Setup** dialog box.
3. Click the **Office Button**.
4. Click the side arrow next to the **Print** option and select **Print Preview** to view the presentation.
5. Click the **Print** icon in the **Print Preview** mode Ribbon.
6. Make any necessary settings in the **Print** dialog box.
7. Click the **OK** button in the **Print** dialog box.

PAGE **134**

Setting Up a Slide Show

Use the options under the **Slide Show** tab to set up any one of the following slide shows:

1. To show all slides from the beginning to the end:
   a. Select the **From Beginning** icon.
2. To show all slides starting from the one currently on the **Slide** pane to the end:

Setting Up a Slide Show (Continued)

   a. Select the **From Current Slide** icon.
3. To create a new custom slide show:
   a. Select the **Custom Slide Show** icon.
   b. Select **New** and give the custom slide show a descriptive name.
   c. Select the slides from the **Slides in presentation** list and click the **Add** button to add them to the **Slides in custom show** list. You can select and add the slides one at a time or select a group of them by using the **Shift** or **Ctrl** keys.
   d. Click the **OK** button to save the custom slide show.
4. To show a specific sequence of slides:
   a. Select the **Set Up Slide Show** icon.
   b. Click on the **From** button under **Show Slides** and enter the range of slides you wish to show.
5. To show all the slides continuously in an unattended mode:
   a. Select the **Set Up Slide Show** icon.
   b. Click on the **Browsed at a kiosk (full screen)** button under **Show type**.
   c. The **Loop continuously until 'Esc'** box directly underneath will automatically be checked and grayed out.

PAGE **125**

Setting Up Slide Transitions

Use the **Transition To This Slide** options under the **Slide Show** tab to set up any one of the following slide shows:

1. Select the slides you wish to apply the transition effect(s) to either from the **Slide Sorter** view or from the **Slides** tab on the left side of the screen.
   a) If you intend to eventually transition all the slides but would like to just test different options on the current slide, you can easily apply your selected transition effects to the entire presentation later.
2. Apply a transition effect from the list.
3. Apply a transition sound and/or transition speed from the pull-down lists.
4. If the presentation is to run unattended, set the timing (in seconds) under **Advance Slide**.
5. If you did not select all the slides in the presentation in step 1, select the **Apply to All** icon.

PAGE **127**

Two Ways to Launch Formatting

1. Select the text and use icons from the **Font** and **Paragraph** groups.
2. Right click on an object and select an option from the context menu.

PAGE............................**86**

Using Rehearse Timings

1. On the **Slide Show** tab, in the **Set Up** group, click **Rehearse Timings**. Be prepared to start delivering your presentation immediately.
2. As you rehearse your presentation:
   a. To move to the next slide, click **Next**.
   b. To temporarily stop recording the time, click **Pause**.
   c. To restart recording the time after pausing, click **Pause**.
   d. To restart recording the time for the current slide, click **Repeat**.
3. After you set the time for the last slide, a message box displays the total time for the presentation and prompts you to do one of the following:
   a. To keep the recorded slide timings, click **Yes**.
   b. To discard the recorded slide timings, click **No**.
4. **Slide Sorter** view appears and displays the time of each slide in your presentation.

PAGE...........................**126**

Which Font Should You Use?

1. Serif: Used for documents and situations in which there is a lot of text. Examples are Times New Roman, Garamond, Century Schoolbook, and Book Antiqua.
2. Sans serif: Used to convey short bursts of information, such as presentations. Examples are Arial, Tahoma, and Verdana.

PAGE............................**80**

⟩⟩ WORD *Quick Reference Guide*

Align Text Center

1. Select the cells to be aligned.
2. Right-click and choose **Cell Alignment**.
3. Select the middle choice.

PAGE..........................**259**

Apply Borders

1. Select the table and right-click on it. Click **Borders and Shading**.
2. Click the **Borders** tab.
3. Change the **Width** to the desired thickness.
4. Click the **Box** in the **Setting** area and return to the document.

PAGE..........................**262**

Applying Styles

1. Place your cursor in the paragraph you want changed or select the text you want changed.
2. Click on the style you wish in the **Styles** group of the **Home** tab.

PAGE..........................**214**

Change Column Widths

1. Click somewhere in the table. (Do not select text or cells).
2. Make sure your Ruler is **On** by looking to see that **Ruler** is checked in the **View** tab.
3. Drag the column width tool to the desired width.

PAGE..........................**255**

Change Font and Font Size

1. Click on the font name in the **Font** group of the **Home** tab of the Ribbon to change the font.
2. Click on the **Font Size** list icon in the **Font** group of the **Home** tab to change the font size.
3. Choose a font size or type in a new font size and press **Enter**.

PAGE..........................**211**

Change Margins

1. Click the **Page Layout** tab on the Ribbon.
2. Click **Margins** in the **Page Setup** group.
3. Choose **Custom Margins** and enter the number of inches for the top, bottom, left, and right margins on the **Margin** tab of the **Page Setup** dialog box.

PAGE..........................**227**

Change Page Orientation

1. Click the **Page Layout** tab.
2. Click **Orientation**.
3. Click **Portrait** or **Landscape**.

PAGE..........................**227**

Changing Save and Print and Display Options

1. Click the **Office Button** menu.
2. Click the **Word Options** button at the bottom of the dialog box.
3. Choose the option category you want to change.
4. Change the option and click **Save Option**.

PAGE..........................**180**

Changing the Default Formatting of Word Documents

1. Click the **Office Button**.
2. Click the **Open** choice.
3. Change **Files of Type** to **Word Template (dotx)**. Word should automatically change the folder to the templates folder.
4. Open the document named Normal.dotx.
5. Make the changes you want to the page margins, fonts, styles, and so on.
6. Save Normal.dotx in the template folder.

PAGE..........................**180**

Clear the Style from Text

1. Click on the **More** button in the **Styles** group of the **Home** tab of the Ruler.
2. Click **Clear Formatting**.

PAGE..........................**208**

Compressing Pictures

1. Choose **Save As** from the **Office Button**.
2. Choose **Save As** from the menu.
3. Click the **Tools** icon.
4. Choose **Compress Pictures**.
5. If necessary, click **Options** to make the appropriate settings.

PAGE..........................**324**

Convert from One Style to Another Style

1. Select the text.
2. Click on the **Style** icon of the **Styles** group of the **Home** tab of the Ribbon to see the current style, which will be outlined.
3. Click on the style you want to use.

PAGE..........................**208**

Convert Text to Table

1. Select the text to be converted.
2. Click the **Insert** tab, the **Table** icon and choose **Convert text to table**.
3. Choose the number of columns, the width of the columns, and the delimiter separating the text.

PAGE..........................**264**

Copy and Paste

1. Select the text you want to copy.
2. Click the **Copy** icon on the **Clipboard** group on the **Home** tab.
3. Place your insertion point where you want the text to be pasted and click to place the blinking cursor.
4. Click the **Paste** icon on the **Clipboard** group on the **Home** tab.

PAGE..........................**186**

Copying Cells from an Excel Spreadsheet into a Word Document

1. Select a range of cells in an Excel file and click the **Copy** icon on the **Home** tab.
2. Open a Word file and place the cursor where the spreadsheet range should appear.
3. Click the **Home** tab in the Ribbon.
4. Click the list box below the **Paste** icon.
5. Select the **Paste Special** option to open the **Paste Special** dialog box.
6. Select the **Picture (Enhanced Metafile)** option and click the **OK** button.

PAGE..........................**344**

Cover Page

1. Press **Ctrl+Enter** at the beginning of the document to create a blank page.
2. Format the text on the cover page.
3. In the **Page Setup** dialog box, on the **Layout** tab, click **Different First Page** under the **Header and Footer** area.

PAGE..........................**239**

Cropping a Graphic

1. Select the graphic you wish to crop.
2. On the **Picture Tools** tab, click **Crop**.
3. Click and drag one or more of the crop bars toward the center of the graphic to the desired cropping.

PAGE..........................**323**

Create a New Style

1. Select a text paragraph with the formatting you wish to become a style.
2. Click on the **More** button in the **Styles** group of the **Home** tab.
3. Click on **Save Selection as a New Quick Style**.
4. Type in a useful name for the new style.

PAGE..........................**211**

Creating an Outline

1. Place your cursor where you want the outline to start.
2. Click the **Multilevel List** icon in the **Paragraph** group on the **Home** tab.
3. Choose one of the list formatting choices that appear.
4. Type the text and press **Enter** to get the next level.
5. Press **Tab** to change the outline level to a sublevel.
6. Press **Shift+Tab** to move back to the previous level.

PAGE..........................**184**

Ensuring the Paragraph Cannot Split across a Page

1. Click on the **Paragraph** dialog box launcher button at the lower-right corner of the **Paragraph** group of the **Home** tab.
2. On the **Paragraph** dialog box, in the **Line and Page Breaks** tab, check **Keep Lines Together**.

PAGE..........................**211**

Find

1. On the **Home** tab, click the **Find** icon on the **Editing** group.
2. Type in the word or words you want to find.
   - To find just one, click **Find Next**.
   - To select them all, click **Find All**.
   - To highlight them all (with a persistent yellow background color), click **Reading Highlight** and choose Highlight All.

PAGE..........................**271**

Find and Replace Invisible Codes

1. On the **Home** tab, click the **Replace** icon on the **Editing** group.
2. Click **<<More>>** and then **Special** and choose the code you want to find or replace.
   - To replace just one, click **Replace**.
   - To replace them all, click **Replace All**.

PAGE..........................**275**

Find and Replace Styles

1. On the **Home** tab, click the **Replace** icon on the **Editing** group.
2. Click **<<More>>** and then **Format** and then **Styles**.
3. In the **Find what:** text box, choose the style you want to find.
4. In the **Replace with:** text box, choose the style you want to replace it with.
   - To replace just one, click **Replace**.
   - To replace them all, click **Replace All**.

PAGE..........................**276**

Insert a Footer

1. Click the **Insert** tab, **Header & Footer** group, and then the **Footer** icon.
2. Choose a **Footer** style or choose **Edit Footer**.
3. Type the text to appear at the bottom of each page.
4. Double click the **Footer** tab to return to the document.

PAGE..........................**237**

Insert a Header

1. Click the **Insert** tab, **Header & Footer** group, and then the **Header** icon.
2. Choose a **Header** style or choose **Edit Header**.
3. Type the text to appear at the top of each page.
4. Double click the **Header** tab to return to the document.

PAGE..........................**237**

Insert a Table

1. Click on the **Insert** tab.
2. Click on the **Table** icon.
3. Select the number of columns and rows by dragging over the same number of cells.

PAGE..........................**254**

Insert a Quick Parts Field

1. Click the **Insert** tab, **Header & Footer** group, and then the **Quick Parts** icon.
2. Choose **Field** and then choose the **Category** of the field you wish to insert.
3. Click the field and any options you wish.
4. Click **OK**.

PAGE..........................**237**

Insert Page Numbers

1. Click the **Insert** tab.
2. Click **Page Numbers**.
3. Choose the location and format for the page numbers.

PAGE..........................**228**

Insert Page Numbers in Document with Footers

1. Open up the footer and place your cursor where you want the page number to appear.
2. On the **Header and Footer** toolbar.
   - Click the **Page Number** icon.
   - Click on **Current Position**.
   - Choose **Plain Number**.
3. Choose **Format Page Numbers** to restart at a different number or to change the format.

PAGE..........................**294**

Insert Section Breaks

1. On the **Page Layout** tab, click **Breaks** on the **Page Setup** group.
2. Choose whether you want a **Continuous, New Page, Odd page, or Even page** section break.
   - **New page** if you need to change page margins, page orientation, headers, footers or page numbers
   - **Odd page** if you want a new section to start on the right side of a two-sided booklet
   - **Continuous** if the new section should not start a new page (often used for columns within a page)

PAGE..........................**286**

Insert Table of Contents

1. Place your cursor where you want the table of contents to appear.
2. Choose **Table of Contents** from the **Table of Contents** group on the **Reference** tab.
3. Choose **Insert Table of Contents Field**. (Do not choose from the Gallery.)
4. Select the number of levels to include (normally two or three) and whether you want page numbers included.
5. If the document is for the Web, ensure that **Use Hyperlinks instead of page numbers** is checked *On*. Otherwise, uncheck it so that it is *Off* and page numbers appear on the screen in the document.

PAGE..........................**298**

Inserting a Caption for a Picture

1. Select the picture.
2. Right-click on the picture and choose **Insert Caption**.
3. Type the phrase you want to appear with the picture.
4. Choose the location of the caption.

PAGE..........................**321**

Inserting a Column into a Table

1. Click in or select a column of a table.
2. Right-click at the same spot and select **Insert**.
3. Click **Insert Columns to the Left** (or **Right**).

PAGE..........................**257**

Inserting a Footnote

1. Place your cursor at the spot where you would like the footnote number to appear.
2. On the **References** tab, click **Insert Footnote**.
3. Type in the text of the footnote.

PAGE..........................**354**

Inserting a Picture

1. Place your cursor where you want the picture to appear.
2. Click the **Insert** tab.
3. Click the **Picture** icon from the **Illustration** group.
4. Change the folder to the location of the picture.
5. Select the file that contains the picture.
6. Click **Insert**.

PAGE..........................**318**

Inserting a Picture of an Access Query into a Word Document

1. In Access, run the query and arrange the window so that it shows just the query results you want to copy.
2. Press **Alt+PrintScreen**.
3. Open a Word file and place the cursor where the query results should appear.
4. Click the **Home** tab in the Ribbon.
5. Click the list box below the **Paste** icon.
6. Select the **Paste Special** option to open the **Paste Special** dialog box.
7. Select the **Picture (Enhanced Metafile)** or **Device Independent Bitmap** option and click the **OK** button.

PAGE..........................**346**

Inserting a Row into a Table

1. Click in or select a row of a table.
2. Right-click at the same spot and select **Insert**.
3. Click **Insert Rows Above** (or **Below**).

PAGE..........................**257**

Inserting a Text Box Around Existing Text

1. Select the text you wish placed in the box.
2. On the **Insert** Ribbon, click **Text Box** from the **Text** group.
3. Click **Draw Text Box**.

PAGE..........................**333**

Inserting an Endnote

1. Place your insertion point in the location you would like the endnote number to appear.
2. On the **References** tab, click **Insert Endnote**.
3. Type in the text of the endnote.

PAGE..........................**354**

Inserting an Excel Chart into Word

1. Activate a chart in an Excel file and click the **Copy** icon on the **Home** tab.
2. Open a Word file and place the cursor where the chart should appear.
3. Click the **Home** tab in the Ribbon.
4. Click the down arrow below the **Paste** icon.
5. Select the **Paste Special** option to open the **Paste Special** dialog box.
6. Select the **Picture (Enhanced Metafile)** option and click the **OK** button in the **Paste Special** dialog box.
7. Adjust the size of the chart by clicking and dragging the sizing handles as needed.

PAGE..........................**343**

Inserting PowerPoint Slide into Word

1. In PowerPoint, with the slide you wish to copy displayed, choose **Save As** from the **Office Menu Button**.
2. Change the file type to JPEG and rename the file.
3. Create one file with **Current Slide Only** or create multiple files with **Every Slide**.
4. In Word, place the insertion point where you want the slide to appear.
5. On the **Insert** tab, click **Picture** and navigate to the folder that contains the file you just exported from PowerPoint.

PAGE..........................**341**

Merge Cells

1. Select the cells to be merged.
2. Right-click and choose **Merge Cells**.

PAGE..........................**259**

Modify a Style

1. Make the formatting change you wish.
2. Right click on the **Stylename** icon in the **Styles** group of the **Home** tab.
3. Choose **Update Stylename to Match Selection**.
4. Alternatively, choose **Modify** and make the changes using the buttons or dialog boxes.

PAGE..........................**222**

Modifying the Indents and Tabs

1. Click and drag one of the **Indent** tools to set the indent.
2. Click the **Tab** tool to the left of the ruler until the type of tab you want to place appears.
3. Click the **Ruler** at the location where you want the tab to appear.
4. Click back into the paragraph and press the **Tab** key to use the tab set.

PAGE..........................**193**

More on Find

1. On the **Find** dialog box, click **More>>**.
   - To limit to whole words, check the **Find whole words only** box.
   - To match capitalization, check **Match case**.
   - To use ? and * as wild-characters, check **Use Wildcards**.
   - To similar sounding words, check **Sounds like**.
   - To find singular and plural as well as different verb tenses, check **Find all word forms**.
   - To find words that start with the letters, check **Match prefix**.
   - To find words that end with the letters, check **Match suffix**.

PAGE..........................**272**

Moving a Picture with Cut and Paste

1. Select the picture and caption.
2. Click **Cut** on the **Home** Ribbon.
3. Scroll to the new location.
4. Click the mouse in the location where you wish the picture to appear.
5. Click **Paste** on the **Home** Ribbon.

PAGE..........................**329**

Moving a Picture with Drag and Drop

1. Select the picture and caption.
2. Click on the text portion and drag the mouse to the location to where you wish the picture to appear.
3. Let go of the mouse button.

PAGE..........................**331**

Paragraph-Level or Text-Level Styles

1. To see if the style is paragraph or text level, click on the **Styles** icon in the **Styles** group of the **Home** tab.
2. Look to see if there is a ¶ for paragraph level or an **a** for text level, or both.

PAGE..........................**220**

Placing Extra Space between Paragraphs

1. Click the **Line Spacing** list icon on the **Paragraph** group of the **Home** tab.
2. Choose **Add Space Before Paragraph**.

PAGE..........................**211**

Repeat Table Header

1. Click in or select the first row of a table.
2. Right-click and select **Table Properties**.
3. Check **Repeat as header row at top of each page**.
4. Uncheck **Allow row to break across pages**.

PAGE..........................**263**

Replace

1. On the **Home** tab, click the **Replace** icon on the **Editing** group.
2. Type in the word or words you want to find.
3. Type in the word or words you want to replace the found word.
   - To replace just one, click **Replace**.
   - To replace them all, click **Replace All**.

PAGE..........................**272**

Resizing a Picture Using Handles

1. Select the picture.
2. Hold down **Ctrl+Shift**.
3. Grab a corner handle of the picture and drag toward the center of the picture until it is the size that you want.

PAGE..........................**322**

Saving a Document Already Named and in the Same Folder

1. Click the **Save** icon on the **Quick Access** menu.

PAGE..........................**188**

Saving a Document to a Different Folder or with a Different Name

1. Click the **Save As** command on the **File** menu.
2. The **Save As** dialog box appears.
3. In the **Save In:** text box, click the list box and navigate to the desired location to which to save the document.
4. If necessary, create a folder by clicking the **New Folder** button, typing the new folder name, and clicking **OK**.
5. In the **File name:** text box, type in a file name and click **Save**.

PAGE..........................**188**

Saving in Word 97-2003 File Format

1. Click the **Office Button**.
2. Point to the List box (the button with the triangle) on the right side of the **Save As** command. Click the **Word 97–2003 Workbook** option on the right side of the **File** menu.
3. Navigate to the desired folder location using the list box to the right of the **Save in:** text box.
4. Type the file name in the **File name:** text box.
5. Click the **Save** button.

PAGE..........................**174**

Selecting a Text Wrapping Option

1. Select the picture.
2. Right-click.
3. Click **Text Wrapping**.
4. Click **In Line With Text** to prevent text wrapping.
5. Click **Tight** if you want the text to wrap around the picture.

PAGE..........................**328**

Selecting Table Components

1. To select a row, move your mouse out into the left margin and drag down next to the row (or rows).
2. To select a cell, hover at the lower-left corner of the cell until the arrow becomes solid pointing toward the cell and then click.
3. To select a column, hover at the top of the column until the arrow becomes solid pointing down. Click.

PAGE.........................**256**

Split Cells

1. Click within the cell you want to split.
2. Right-click in the cell to get the **table option** menu.
3. Choose **Split Cells** and choose two columns.

PAGE.........................**258**

Style Bases and Follow-Ups

1. To see the base and following styles, right click on the button of the style you wish to see from the **Styles** group of the **Home** tab.
2. Choose **Modify**.

PAGE.........................**219**

Unhiding and Modifying the Footer Style

1. Click the **Home** tab.
2. Click the **Show Styles** button at the lower-left corner of the **Styles** group.
3. Click the **Manage Styles** button.
4. Click the **Recommendations** tab.
5. Choose the style you wish to unhide.
6. Click the **Show** button.

PAGE.........................**233**

Unlink Headers and Footers

1. On the **Insert** tab, click **Headers** or **Footers**. Choose **Edit Headers** or **Edit Footers**.
2. Click **Next Section** to go to the next header or footer.
3. Click the **Link to Previous** icon in the **Header & Footers Tools** in the Ribbon to unselect it.

PAGE.........................**292**

Update Table of Contents

1. Place your cursor anywhere in the table of contents.
2. Right-click to get the table of contents option menu.
3. Choose **Update Field**.
4. Choose whether you want page numbers updated or the whole table.

PAGE.........................**300**

Using the Alt Shortcuts

1. Press the **Alt** key.
2. Press the first letter of the tab that contains the command or icon.
3. Press the letters, in sequence, which appear next to the command or icon.

PAGE.........................**176**

Using the Ctrl Shortcuts

1. Hover your mouse over the icon or command to see what the **Ctrl** key shortcut is.
2. Hold down the **Ctrl** key and press the shortcut letter at the same time.

PAGE.........................**176**

Using Word Help

1. Click the **Word Help** icon.
2. Type a term into the input box of the **Help** window and then press the **Enter** key or click the **Search** button.
3. Click a link to see instructions and information related to your topic.

PAGE.........................**177**

Viewing Picture Position

1. Select the picture.
2. Right-click.
3. Choose **Text Wrapping**.
4. Click **More Layout Options**.
5. Choose the **Picture Position** tab.

PAGE.........................**328**

Absolute Reference

1. Identify a cell reference within a formula or function that requires an absolute reference or mixed reference.
2. Type a dollar sign in front of the column letter and row number of a cell reference to apply an absolute reference.
3. Type a dollar sign in front of the column letter or row number to apply a mixed reference.

PAGE..........................**462**

Accounting Format

1. Highlight a range of cells to be formatted.
2. Click the **Home** tab of the Ribbon.
3. Click the **Accounting Number Format** icon $ ▾ . Click the down arrow next to this icon to change the currency symbol.
4. Click the **Increase** or **Decrease Decimal** icons and as needed.

PAGE..........................**405**

Adding Annotations and Objects

1. Activate the chart.
2. Click the **Layout** tab of the **Chart Tools** area on the Ribbon.
3. Click the **Text Box** icon to add an annotation or the **Shapes** icon to add an object. If adding an object, select an option after clicking the **Shapes** icon.
4. Click and drag on the chart to place and set the desired size of the text box or object.
5. Format the text box or object by activating it and right clicking, or using the icons in the **Format** tab of the **Drawing Tools** area on the Ribbon.

PAGE..........................**561**

Adjusting Column Widths

1. Place the cursor between 2 columns.
2. Click and drag to desired width or double click to automatically set to the widest data point.
Or
1. Highlight at least one cell in the columns you want to change.
2. Click the **Home** tab of the Ribbon.
3. Click the **Format** icon.
4. Select **Column Width**.
5. Enter a desired width number in the **Column Width** dialog box.
6. Click the **OK** button.

PAGE..........................**387**

Adjusting Row Heights

1. Place the cursor between 2 rows.
2. Click and drag to desired height or double click to automatically set to the largest data point.
Or
1. Highlight at least one cell in the rows you want to change.
2. Click the **Home** tab of the Ribbon.
3. Click the **Format** icon.
4. Select **Row Height**.
5. Enter a desired height number in the **Row Height** dialog box.
6. Click the **OK** button.

PAGE..........................**387**

AND Function

1. Activate a cell location where the output of the function should appear.
2. Type an equal sign, the function name AND, and an open parenthesis.
3. Create at least one but no more than 30 logical tests. Separate each logical test with a comma. *All* tests must be true to produce a TRUE output.
4. Type a closing parenthesis.
5. Press the **Enter** key.

PAGE..........................**500**

Auto Fill

1. Enter sequential data into at least 2 adjacent cell locations.
2. Highlight all cell locations containing sequential data.
3. Drag the cursor over the **Auto Fill Handle**.
4. When the cursor changes from a white to a black plus sign, click and drag across or down to continue the sequence of data.

PAGE..........................**384**

AutoSum

1. Activate the cell where the output of the function should appear. The cell location should be below or to the right of a range of cells that will be used in the function.
2. Click the **Formulas** tab in the Ribbon.
3. Click the down arrow next to the **AutoSum** icon.
4. Select a function.
5. Press the **Enter** key.

PAGE..........................**457**

Basic Formulas

1. Activate the cell where formula output should appear.
2. Type an equal sign.
3. Type or click a cell location that contains a value that will be used to compute the formula output.
4. Type a math operator (see Figure 3.1).
5. Type or click a second cell location that contains a value that will be used to compute the formula output.
6. Press the **Enter** key.

PAGE..........................**440**

Basic Functions

1. Activate a cell where the output of the function should appear.
2. Type an equal sign.
3. Type the name of the function or double click a function name from the function list.
4. Type an open parenthesis if you typed the function name manually.
5. Type a range or click and drag a range of cells (if you are using specific cells not in a continuous range, type or click each cell and separate with a comma).
6. Type a closing parenthesis.
7. Press the **Enter** key.

PAGE..........................**457**

Borders

1. Highlight a range of cells where lines should appear.
2. Click the **Home** tab of the Ribbon.
3. Click the down arrow in the **Borders** icon.
4. Select a line style and placement option.

Or

1. Highlight a range of cells where lines should appear.
2. Click the **Home** tab of the Ribbon.
3. Click the down arrow in the **Borders** icon and select the **More Borders** option.
4. Select a color and line style on the right side of the window.
5. Select the placement of the line using the locator box or placement icons.
6. Click the **OK** button.

PAGE..........................**408**

Cell Color

1. Highlight range of cells to be colored.
2. Click the **Home** tab of the Ribbon.
3. Click the down arrow of the **Fill Color** icon.
4. Select a color from the palette.

PAGE..........................**409**

Changing the Font Setting for New Workbooks

1. Open a blank Excel workbook.
2. Click the **Office Button**.
3. Click the **Excel Options** button.
4. Click the **Popular** section on the left side of the **Excel Options** dialog box.
5. Select a font style and size in the **When creating new workbooks** section of the **Excel Options** dialog box.
6. Click the **OK** button at the bottom of the dialog box.

PAGE..........................**373**

Complex Formulas

1. Activate the cell where formula output should appear.
2. Type an equal sign.
3. Type or click cell locations or type numeric values if necessary.
4. Use parentheses and math operators where necessary.
5. Check that each opening parenthesis has a closing parenthesis.
6. Press the **Enter** key.

PAGE..........................**448**

Copy and Paste

1. Highlight a cell or range of cells to be copied.
2. Click the **Copy** icon in the Ribbon.
3. Highlight a cell or range of cells where copied data should appear.
4. Click the **Paste** icon in the Ribbon.

PAGE..........................**391**

Creating Charts

1. Highlight a range of cells that contain values that will be used to define the X- and Y-axes of the chart.
2. Click the **Insert** tab on the Ribbon.
3. Click one of the **Chart Type** icons in the **Charts** group on the Ribbon.
4. Select a chart format option based on the needs of your project and the desired visual appearance.
5. Click the **Switch Row/Column** icon (in the **Design** tab) if the data on the X- and Y-axes needs to be reversed.
6. Click the **Move Chart** icon (in the **Design** tab) to move the chart to another existing worksheet or place the chart in a separate chart sheet.
7. Click the **Layout** tab in the **Chart Tools** section on the Ribbon and click the **Chart Title** and/or **Axis Titles** icons to add or adjust boxes for the chart title or axis titles.
8. After adding a title box to the chart, click it twice to type a new title or description.

PAGE..........................**545**

Deleting Columns or Rows

1. Activate one cell in the row or column you want to delete.
2. Click the **Home** tab in the Ribbon.
3. Click the down arrow in the **Delete** icon in the **Cells** group.
4. Select the **Delete Sheet Columns** or **Delete Sheet Rows** options.

PAGE.........................**415**

Deleting Worksheets

1. Activate the worksheet you want to delete by clicking the worksheet tab.
2. Click the **Home** tab of the Ribbon.
3. Click the down arrow in the **Delete** icon in the **Cells** group.
4. Click the **Delete Sheet** option.
5. Check the worksheet carefully to make sure it is okay to delete.
6. Click the **Delete** button at the bottom of the warning box.

PAGE.........................**416**

Editing Data

1. Activate cell containing data.
2. Click in the formula bar.
3. Type edits in the formula bar.
4. Press the **Enter** key.

Or

1. Double click a cell with data.
2. Type edits.
3. Press the **Enter** key.

PAGE.........................**414**

Formatting a Data Series

1. Activate a data series by clicking an image (i.e., bar, marker, pie section) one time. Or click an image a second time to activate a series point.
2. Click the **Format** tab in the **Chart Tools** set of tabs.
3. Click the **Shape Fill** icon and select a color from the palette to change the data series or series point color.
4. Click the **Shape Outline** icon and select a color from the palette, one of the **Weight** options, or one of the **Dashes** options.

PAGE.........................**557**

Formatting Data

1. Highlight a range of cells to be formatted.
2. Click the **Home** tab of the Ribbon.
3. Click one of the icons in the **Font** group of the Ribbon or open the **Format Cells** dialog box by clicking the button in the lower-right corner of the **Font** group.
4. If using the **Format Cells** dialog box, click the **OK** button after making a selection.

PAGE.........................**401**

Formatting Numbers

1. Highlight a range of cells containing numbers to be formatted.
2. Click the **Home** tab of the Ribbon.
3. Click one of the icons in the **Number** group of the Ribbon or open the **Format Cells** dialog box by clicking the button in the lower-right corner of the **Number** group.
4. If using the **Format Cells** dialog box, click the **OK** button after making a selection.

PAGE.........................**406**

Formatting the Plot Area

1. Activate the plot area by clicking it once.
2. Click the **Format** tab in the **Chart Tools** set of tabs.
3. Click the **Shape Fill** icon and select a color from the palette to change the plot area color.
4. Click the **Shape Outline** icon and select a color from the palette, one of the **Weight** options, or one of the **Dashes** options.

PAGE.........................**555**

Formatting Titles and Legends

1. Activate the legend or title by clicking it once.
2. Select any of the format icons in the **Home** tab on the Ribbon and/or the icons in the **Format** tab of the **Chart Tools** area on the Ribbon.
3. To access more detailed formatting controls, click the **Format Selection** icon in the **Format** tab to open the **Format Legend** or **Format Title** dialog box.
4. To edit the wording of a title, click it twice and type any adjustments.
5. To move the legend or titles, click and drag it.
6. To change the size of the legend or titles, click and drag on one of the sizing handles.

PAGE.........................**552**

Formatting X- and Y-Axes Labels

1. Activate the X- or Y-axis by clicking once anywhere along the axis.
2. Select any of the format icons in the **Home** tab on the Ribbon and/or the icons in the **Format** tab of the **Chart Tools** area on the Ribbon.
3. To access more detailed formatting controls such the axis scale, tick marks, or label position, click the **Format Selection** icon in the **Format** tab to open the **Format Axis** dialog box.

PAGE...........................**558**

Freeze Panes

1. Activate a cell that is below the row and to the right of the column you wish to lock in place when scrolling (except cell A1).
2. Click the **View** tab in the Ribbon.
3. Click the **Freeze Panes** icon.
4. Select the **Freeze Panes** option (select the **Unfreeze Panes** option to remove any locked rows and columns).
5. Use the **Freeze Top Row** or **Freeze First Column** options to lock the first column or row.

PAGE...........................**607**

Future Value Function

1. Activate the cell where output should appear.
2. Type an equal sign.
3. Type the function name FV or double click **FV** from the function list.
4. Type an open parenthesis (if you double clicked the function from the function list, this will already be added).
5. Define the following arguments:
   rate: Interest Rate
   nper: Number of Periods or Amount of time
   pmt: Payments (must use a negative sign)
   [pv]: Present Value
   [type]: When payments are made (1 = beginning of year; 0 = end of year)
6. Close the parenthesis.
7. Press the **Enter** key.

PAGE...........................**470**

Hide Columns and Rows

1. Highlight at least one cell in each column or row you want to hide.
2. Click the **Home** tab of the Ribbon.
3. Click the **Format** icon.
4. Select the **Hide & Unhide** option.
5. Select one of the **Hide** options from the submenu.

PAGE...........................**388**

HLookup

1. Activate the cell where output should appear.
2. Type an equal sign, the function name HLookup, and an open parenthesis.
3. Define the following arguments:
   a. **lookup_value**: Cell location that contains the value to be searched in a second worksheet.
   b. **table_array**: Range in a second worksheet or workbook that contains both the lookup value and data for the output of the function (the first row in this range *must* contain the lookup value).
   c. **row_index_num**: Number of rows in the table array range counting from top to bottom that contains data for the output of the function (count the first row as 1).
   d. **range_lookup**: Type the word False to find the exact match to the lookup value. This argument will assume True and look for an approximate match for the lookup value if this argument is not defined.
4. Type a closing parenthesis and press the **Enter** key.
5. Use an absolute reference ($) on the range of the table array segment if copying and pasting the function to other cells. You may also need an absolute reference on the lookup value depending on your project.
6. Check the row index number after pasting to see if any adjustments are necessary.

PAGE...........................**519**

Horizontal and Vertical Alignment

1. Highlight a range of cells to be formatted.
2. Click the **Home** tab of the Ribbon.
3. Click one of the **Vertical Alignment** icons 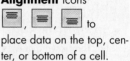 to place data on the top, center, or bottom of a cell.
4. Click one of the **Horizontal Alignment** icons 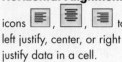 to left justify, center, or right justify data in a cell.

PAGE...........................**403**

IF Functions and Nested IF Functions

1. Activate a cell where the output of the function should appear.
2. Type an equal sign, the function name **IF**, and an open parenthesis.
3. Create a test for the **logical_test** argument.
4. Define an output for the **[value_if_true]** argument (text outputs must be in quotation marks).
5. Define an output for the **[value_if_false]** argument or enter another **IF** function by typing the function name **IF** and an open parenthesis.
6. Type a closing parenthesis. If creating a nested **IF** function, type a closing parenthesis for each **IF** function that you started.
7. Press the **Enter** key.

PAGE...........................**495**

Insert Columns or Rows

1. Activate a cell depending on where a blank column or row should be inserted. Rows are inserted above an active cell; columns are inserted to the left of an active cell.
2. Click the **Home** tab.
3. Click the down arrow in the **Insert** icon in the **Cells** group of the Ribbon.
4. Select **Insert Sheet Rows** or **Insert Sheet Columns**.

PAGE..........................**418**

Insert Function

1. Activate a cell where the output of a function should appear.
2. Click the **Formulas** tab in the Ribbon.
3. Select a function from one of the function category icons in the Function Library or click the **Insert Function** icon.
4. If using the **Insert Function** icon, select a function from the **Insert Function** dialog box and click the **OK** button.
5. Use the input boxes or range finders to define the arguments of the function in the **Function Arguments** dialog box.
6. Click **Help on this function** to see an expanded definition and instructions for building the function.
7. Click the **OK** button at the bottom of the **Function Arguments** dialog box.

PAGE..........................**475**

Inserting Worksheets

1. Click the **Insert Worksheet** tab at the bottom of the Excel screen.

PAGE..........................**419**

Linking Data between Workbooks

1. Open two workbooks.
2. Activate a cell location in the workbook where the data or output of a formula or functions should appear.
3. Type an equal sign, or type an equal sign and the beginning of a formula or function.
4. Click the name of the second workbook in the task bar.
5. Click a **Worksheet** tab that contains the data you wish to display or use in a formula or function.
6. Activate a cell location that contains the data you wish to display or use in a formula or function.
7. Press the **Enter** key, or complete the formula or function and then press the **Enter** key.

PAGE..........................**596**

Linking Data between Worksheets

1. Activate a cell location where the data or output of a formula or functions should appear.
2. Type an equal sign, or type an equal sign and the beginning of a formula or function.
3. Click a **Worksheet** tab that contains the data you wish to display in the first worksheet or use in a formula or function.
4. Activate a cell location that contains the data you wish to display or use in a formula or function.
5. Press the **Enter** key, or complete the formula or function and then press the **Enter** key.

PAGE..........................**595**

Manually Defining a Column Chart

1. Activate a blank cell on a worksheet. A blank column or a blank row must appear between the data on a worksheet and the blank cell that is activated.
2. Select a chart type from the **Insert** tab on the Ribbon.
3. Select a chart format.
4. With the blank chart activated, click the **Select Data Source** icon in the **Design** tab on the Ribbon.
5. Click the **Add** button on the left side of the **Select Data Source** dialog box to add a data series.
6. Define the Series name in the **Edit Series** dialog box with one cell location or type a name in quotation marks.
7. Define the Series values with a range of cells.
8. Click the **OK** button to close the **Edit Series** dialog box.
9. Repeat steps 5–8 to add additional data series if needed.
10. Click the **Edit** button on the right side of the **Select Data Source** dialog box.
11. Use a range of cells to define the Axis Label Range. The descriptions in this cell range will be used for the X-axis labels.
12. Click the **OK** button on the **Axis Labels** dialog box.
13. Click the **OK** button on the **Select Data Source** dialog box.

PAGE..........................**570**

Merge Cells

1. Highlight a range of cells to be merged.
2. Click the **Home** tab of the Ribbon.
3. Click the down arrow of the **Merge & Center** icon and select an option.

PAGE...........................**404**

Moving Data

1. Activate a cell or highlight a range of cells to be moved.
2. Move the cursor to the edge of the cell or range.
3. When the cursor changes to crossed arrows, click and drag.

PAGE...........................**414**

Moving Worksheets

1. Click and drag the worksheet tab.

PAGE...........................**419**

NPV Function

1. Activate cell where the output should appear.
2. Type an equal sign, the function name **NPV**, and an open parenthesis.
3. Define the following arguments:
   a. **rate**: The interest rate that is charged for a loan or a firm's cost to borrow money.
   b. **value1**: The initial investment for starting a new business or in an existing business. You must precede values or cell locations with a negative sign.
   c. **[value(n)]**: Cash generated by the end of the year for a new business or incremental cash generated by an existing business. Use a separate argument to add cash value for each year.
4. Type a closing parenthesis and press the **Enter** key.

PAGE...........................**612**

OR Function

1. Activate a cell location where the output of the function should appear.
2. Type an equal sign, the function name OR, and an open parenthesis.
3. Create at least one but no more than 30 logical tests.
4. Separate each logical test with a comma. Only one test needs to be true to produce a TRUE output.
5. Type a closing parenthesis.
6. Press the **Enter** key.

PAGE...........................**503**

Paste Special

1. Copy a cell or range of cells.
2. Activate the cell where data is to be pasted.
3. Click the down arrow below the **Paste** icon to open the paste options list.
4. Select one of the paste options or select the **Paste Special** option to open the **Paste Special** dialog box.
5. If you are using the **Paste Special** dialog box, select an option and click the **OK** button.

PAGE...........................**443**

Pasting Charts into PowerPoint and Word

1. Activate a chart in an Excel file and click the **Copy** icon.
2. Open a PowerPoint file to a slide where the chart should appear. For a Word document, place the cursor where the chart should appear.
3. Click the **Home** tab in the Ribbon.
4. Click the down arrow below the **Paste** icon.
5. Select the **Paste Special** option to open the **Paste Special** dialog box.
6. Select the **Picture (Enhanced Metafile)** option and click the **OK** button in the **Paste Special** dialog box.
7. Adjust the size of the chart by clicking and dragging the sizing handles as needed.

PAGE...........................**577**

Payment Function

1. Activate a cell where output should appear.
2. Type an equal sign.
3. Type the function name PMT or double click **PMT** from the function list.
4. Type an open parenthesis (if you double clicked the function from the function list, this will already be added).
5. Define the following arguments:
   rate: Interest rate
   nper: Number of payments or period of time
   pv: Present value
   [fv]: Future value
   [type]: When payments are made (1 = beginning of year, 0 = end of year)
6. Close the parenthesis.
7. Press the **Enter** key.

PAGE...........................**474**

Printing Worksheets

1. Activate a worksheet to be printed.
2. Click the **Page Layout** tab of the Ribbon.
3. Make any necessary Page Setup adjustments by using the icons in the Ribbon or by opening the **Page Setup** dialog box.
4. Click the **Office Button**.
5. Click the side arrow next to the **Print** option and select **Print Preview** to view the document.
6. Click the **Print** icon in the **Print Preview** mode Ribbon.
7. Make any necessary settings in the **Print** dialog box.
8. Click the **OK** button in the **Print** dialog box.

PAGE..........................**426**

Renaming a Worksheet Tab

1. Double click the worksheet tab you wish to rename.
2. Type the new name.
3. Press the **Enter** key.

PAGE..........................**419**

Saving in Excel 97-2003 File Format

1. Open an existing Excel workbook or create a new one.
2. Click the **Office Button**.
3. Click the arrow to the right of the **Save As** option.
4. Click the **Excel 97-2003 Workbook** option on the right side of the **File** menu.
5. Select a location and type a file name in the **Save As** dialog box.

PAGE..........................**371**

Scatter Plot Charts

1. Activate a blank cell on a worksheet. A blank column or a blank row must appear between the data on a worksheet and the blank cell that is activated.
2. Click the **Scatter** icon in the **Insert** tab on the Ribbon.
3. Select a chart format.
4. With the blank chart activated, click the **Select Data Source button** icon in the **Design** tab on the Ribbon.
5. Click the **Add** button on the left side of the **Select Data Source** dialog box to add a data series.
6. Define the Series name in the **Edit Series** dialog box with one cell location or type a name in quotation marks.
7. Define the X Series values with a range of cells.
8. Define the Y Series values with a range of cells.
9. Click the **OK** button to close the **Edit Series** dialog box.
10. Repeat steps 5–9 to add additional data series if needed.
11. Click the **OK** button on the **Select Data Source** dialog box.

PAGE..........................**575**

Show Formulas

1. Click the **Formulas** tab of the Ribbon.
2. Click the **Show Formulas** icon.
3. Click the **Show Formulas** icon again to display the formula outputs.

PAGE..........................**449**

Sorting Data (Multiple Levels)

1. Highlight *all* the data on your worksheet that will be sorted.
2. Click the **Data** tab of the Ribbon.
3. Click the **Sort** icon in the Ribbon.
4. Click the **Options** button in the **Sort** dialog box and select the **Sort top to bottom** option if you are sorting a list of items.
5. Click the **OK** button in the **Sort Options** dialog box.
6. Select the **My data has headers** option if column headings are included in the range you highlighted for step 1.
7. Set the **Column**, **Sort On**, and **Order** options for the first sort level.
8. Add other sort levels as needed by clicking the **Add Level** button.
9. Click the **OK** button.

PAGE..........................**394**

Sorting Data (Single Level)

. Activate a cell in the column you wish to use as the basis for sorting your data. The cell you activate must not be blank.

. Make sure there are no blank columns separating data you wish to sort and the column containing the cell you activated in step 1.

. Click the **Data** tab at the top of the Ribbon.

. Click the **Z to A** (descending order) or **A to Z** (ascending order) icon in the **Sort & Filter** section of the Ribbon.

AGE..........................**392**

SUMIF Functions

1. Activate the cell where output should appear.

2. Type an equal sign, the function name **SUMIF**, and an open parenthesis.

3. Define the following arguments:

   a. **range**: A range of cells that will be evaluated by data used to define the **criteria** argument.

   b. **criteria**: A logical test, cell location, value, and so on, that will be searched in the range used to define the **range** argument.

   c. **[sum_range]**: A range of cells containing values that will be summed if the data in the **criteria** argument is found in the range used to define the **range** argument. Define this argument only if the **range** argument does not contain the values that need to be summed.

4. Type a closing parenthesis and press the **Enter** key.

PAGE..........................**600**

Trace Dependents

1. Activate a cell location that is referenced in a formula on a worksheet.

2. Click the **Formulas** tab on the Ribbon.

3. Click the **Trace Dependents** icon.

4. Use the **Remove Arrows** icon to remove the **Trace Dependents** arrow.

PAGE..........................**449**

Trace Precedents

1. Activate a cell location that contains a formula.

2. Click the **Formulas** tab on the Ribbon.

3. Click the **Trace Precedents** icon.

4. Use the **Remove Arrows** icon to remove the **Trace Precedents** arrow.

PAGE..........................**449**

Unhide Columns and Rows

1. Click and drag over to a cell on either side of the hidden column or row.

2. Click the **Home** tab of the Ribbon.

3. Click the **Format** icon.

4. Select the **Hide & Unhide** option.

5. Select one of the **Unhide** options from the submenu.

PAGE..........................**389**

Updating Workbook Links

1. Click the **Options** button in the Security Alert prompt.

2. Select the **Enable this content** option in the **Security Options** dialog box and click the **OK** button.

OR

1. Click the **Data** tab of the Ribbon.

2. Click the **Edit Links** icon.

3. Select the workbook link you wish to update from the **Edit Links** dialog box.

4. Click the **Update Values** button on the right side of the **Edit Links** dialog box.

5. Click the **Close** button at the bottom of the **Edit Links** dialog box.

PAGE..........................**598**

VLookup

1. Activate the cell where the output should appear.
2. Type an equal sign, the function name VLookup, and an open parenthesis.
3. Define the following arguments:
   a. **lookup_value**: Cell location that contains the value to be searched and matched in a second worksheet.
   b. **table_array**: Range in a second worksheet or workbook that contains both the lookup value and data for the output of the function (first column in the range *must* contain the lookup value).
   c. **col_index_num**: Number of columns in the table array range counting from left to right that contains data for the output of the function (count the first column as 1).
   d. **range_lookup**: Type the word False to find an exact match to the lookup value. This argument will assume True and look for an approximate match for the lookup value if this argument is not defined.
4. Type a closing parenthesis and press the **Enter** key.
5. Use an absolute reference ($) on the range used to define the **table_array** argument if pasting the function to other cells.

PAGE..........................**515**

Worksheet Tab Color

1. Click the worksheet tab where the color is to be changed.
2. Place the cursor over the worksheet tab.
3. Right click.
4. Select **Tab Color**.
5. Select a color from the color palette.

PAGE..........................**419**

Wrap Text

1. Highlight a range of cells to be formatted.
2. Click the **Home** tab of the Ribbon.
3. Click the **Wrap Text** icon 📑.

PAGE..........................**403**

Adding a Label Box

1. Open a report in **Design View**.
2. Click the **Design** tab on the Ribbon.
3. Click the **Label** icon in the **Controls** group.
4. Click and drag the dimensions of the label box on the design grid.
5. Adjust the dimensions of the label box by clicking and dragging it.

PAGE..........................**848**

Adding a Query Description

1. Right click a query name in the **Navigation Pane**.
2. Select the **Object Properties** option.
3. Type a description that is no more than 255 characters in the **Description** box.
4. Click the **OK** button.

PAGE..........................**736**

Adding a Report Header and Footer

1. Create a new report or open an existing report in **Design View**.
2. Click the **Arrange** tab in the Ribbon.
3. Click the **Report Header/Footer** icon in the Show/Hide group.

PAGE..........................**845**

Adding Criteria to a Query

1. Click the criteria row of a field.
2. Enter a value or expression using comparison operators.
3. Enter criteria for other fields if necessary.
4. Check your criteria by reading each criteria row one at a time.

PAGE..........................**742**

Adding Custom Fields to Queries

1. Click the first row of an empty column in the design grid of query.
2. Type the name of the new field followed by a colon.
3. Type any numeric or text data after the colon. Any data typed after the colon will appear in every row of the query record set.

PAGE..........................**786**

Adding Data Fields to a Report

1. Open a new or existing report in **Design View**.
2. Open the Field List window by clicking the **Add Existing Fields** icon in the **Design** tab of the Ribbon.
3. Click and drag a field from the **Field List** window into one of the sections in the design grid of a report.
4. Delete the label box that is attached to the field if labels or headings have already been added to the report.
5. Check the alignment and appearance of your data and labels by switching the report to **Layout View**.
6. Make any adjustments to label or text boxes while the report is in **Layout View**.

PAGE..........................**855**

Adding Fields to a Query

1. Add a table or group of tables to a query.
2. Click and drag a field from the table to the first row of the design grid of the query.

OR

1. Click in the first row of any column in the design grid of a query.
2. Click the drop-down arrow.
3. Select a field from the list.
4. Click in the second row to select a table if multiple tables are used in the query.

PAGE..........................**734**

Adding Page Numbers

1. Open a new or existing report in **Design View**.
2. Click the **Design** tab in the Ribbon.
3. Click the **Insert Page Number** icon.
4. Select the desired options in the **Page Number** dialog box and click the **OK** button.
5. Click the Page Number text box in the design grid and choose any desired formatting options.

PAGE..........................**856**

Adjusting Column and Row Widths and Heights

1. Open a table in **Datasheet View**.
2. Place the cursor between two fields or two columns.
3. Click and drag when the cursor changes to double arrows.

PAGE..........................**677**

Adjusting the Width of the Report Design Grid

1. Open a new or existing report in **Design View**.
2. Place the cursor at the right edge of the design grid.
3. When the cursor changes to a double arrow, click and drag to desired width.

PAGE..........................**844**

Calculated Fields

1. Open an existing report in **Design View**.
2. Add a text box to the design grid.
3. Double click the text box to open the **Property Sheet** window.
4. Click the **Data** tab in the **Property Sheet** window.
5. Click the box to the right of the Control Source label.
6. Click the button to the right of the drop-down arrow in the **Control Source** box to open the Expression Builder.
7. Enter a formula or function into the Expression Builder.
8. Click the **OK** button on the Expression Builder.
9. Click the **Format** tab of the **Property Sheet** window to adjust the format of the Text Box producing the calculated results.
10. Close the **Property Sheet** window by clicking the X in the upper-right corner.

PAGE..........................**877**

Changing the Default File Format for New Databases

1. Open a new or existing Access database.
2. Click the **Office Button**.
3. Click the **Access Options** button at the bottom of the **File** menu.
4. Click the **Popular** category on the left side of the **Access Options** dialog box.
5. Click the down arrow of the **Default file format** option and select a format option.
6. Click the **OK** button at the bottom of the **Access Options** dialog box.

PAGE..........................**654**

Changing the Sequence of Fields

1. Open a table in **Design View**.
2. Activate a field by clicking in the box next to the field name.
3. Click and drag the box next to the activated field name to change its position on the table.

OR

1. Open a table in **Datasheet View**.
2. Activate a field by clicking the field name.
3. Click and drag the name of the activated field to change its position on the table.

PAGE..........................**691**

Conditional Formatting

1. Open an existing report in **Design View**.
2. Activate a text box in which the conditional formats will be applied.
3. Click the **Conditional** icon in the **Design** tab of the Ribbon.
4. Check and make necessary adjustments to the Default format settings.
5. Set the first drop-down box in the Condition 1 section to **Field Value Is** if applying formats based on the values or output of a text box.
6. Select a comparison operator in the second box.
7. Enter a value in the box next to the comparison operator.
8. Use the format icons to establish a format setting if the condition is true.
9. Click the **OK** button.

PAGE..........................**878**

Converting a Database to a 2002-2003 File Format

1. Open a database you want to convert to a new file format.
2. Click the **Office Button**.
3. Click the arrow to the right of the **Save As** option.
4. Click the **Access 2002-2003 Database** option on the right side of the **File** menu.
5. Select a location and type a file name in the **Save As** dialog box.
6. Click the **Save** button at the bottom of the **Save As** dialog box.

PAGE...........................**653**

Copying and Pasting Data

1. Copy data from an existing Access table or from an Excel spreadsheet.
2. Open a table in **Datasheet View**.
3. Activate a blank record by clicking the asterisk to the left of the first blank cell.
4. Click the **Home** tab on the Ribbon.
5. Click the **Paste** icon.
6. Click the **Yes** button at the bottom of the Paste Records message.

PAGE...........................**678**

Creating a New Database

1. Launch the Access application.
2. Click the **Blank Database** button.
3. On the right side of your screen, type a name in the **File Name** input box.
4. Click the folder icon next to the **File Name** input box to select a location on your computer or network.
5. Click the **Create** button under the **File Name** input box.

PAGE...........................**651**

Creating a New Query

1. Click the **Create** tab on the Ribbon.
2. Click the **Query Design** icon.
3. Select a table from the **Show Table** dialog box.
4. Click the **Add** button in the **Show Table** dialog box.
5. Click the **Close** button in the **Show Table** dialog box.
6. Research the data contained in the table that is selected for the query.

PAGE...........................**733**

Creating a New Report

1. Click the **Report Design** icon in the **Create** tab of the Ribbon.
2. Click the **Property Sheet** icon in the **Design** tab of the Ribbon.
3. Click the **Data** tab at the top of the **Property Sheet** window.
4. Click the box next to the **Record Source** heading in the **Property Sheet** window.
5. Click the down arrow in the box next to the **Record Source** heading and select a query or table from the list.
6. Close the **Property Sheet** window by clicking the X in the upper-right corner of the window.
7. Click the **Add Existing Fields** icon in the **Design** tab of the Ribbon to open the **Field List** window.

PAGE...........................**842**

Creating a New Table

1. Click the **Create** tab on the Ribbon.
2. Click either the **Table** icon or the **Table Design** icon.

PAGE...........................**667**

Creating Formulas (Calculated Fields)

1. Click the first row of an empty column in the design grid of a Select Query.
2. Type the name of the Calculated Field followed by a colon.
3. Add fields to the formula by using the following syntax: `[Table Name]![Field Name]`.
4. Type the desired mathematical operator.
5. Add another field using the syntax in number 3.
6. If using several fields and operators, use parentheses to control the order in which computations are executed.

PAGE...........................**791**

Crosstab Queries

1. Open a select query in **Design View**.
2. Add any required tables or queries.
3. Convert to a crosstab query by clicking the **Crosstab** icon in the **Design** tab on the Ribbon.
4. Add any required fields.
5. Set the Total row to **Group By** for fields that will be used for either **Row Headings** or **Column Headings**.
6. Select an aggregate function in the Total row for fields where the Crosstab row is set to **Value**.
7. Identify a field as a **Row Heading**, **Column Heading**, or **Value** in the Crosstab row.
8. Run the query.

PAGE..........................**767**

Data Entry

1. Open a table in **Datasheet View**.
2. Activate a cell and type the appropriate text or numeric value. Make sure the data you are typing is compatible with the data type assigned to the field.
3. Use the **Enter**, **Arrow**, or **Tab** keys to enter the data and move to the next cell.

PAGE..........................**676**

Dates

1. Open an existing report in **Design View**.
2. Add a text box in the Page Footer section of the design grid.
3. Open the **Property Sheet** window.
4. Click the Data tab of the Property Sheet window and open the Expression Builder.
5. Type **DATE()** in the upper window of the Expression builder.
6. Click the **OK** button on the Expression Builder.
7. Make any desired formatting adjustments.

PAGE..........................**886**

Defining Indexes

1. Open a table in **Design View**.
2. Click the **Design** tab on the Ribbon.
3. Click the **Indexes** icon to open the **Indexes** dialog box.
4. Type an index name in the far left column of the **Indexes** dialog box.
5. Select a field from the **Field Name** drop-down box.
6. Select **Ascending** or **Descending** in the Sort Order column.
7. Click the X in the upper-right corner to finish the index and close the **Indexes** dialog box.

PAGE..........................**673**

Defining Primary Keys

1. Open a table in **Design View**.
2. Activate a field by clicking the box to the left field name, or click and drag to highlight several fields.
3. Click the **Design** tab on the Ribbob.
4. Click the **Primary Key** icon.

PAGE..........................**674**

Defining Table Relationships

1. Open the **Relationships** window by clicking the **Relationships** icon in the **Database Tools** tab of the Ribbon.
2. Click the **Show Table** icon in the **Design** tab of the Ribbon.
3. Add fields from the **Show Tables** dialog box to the **Relationships** window.
4. Create a join between two tables to open the **Edit Relationships** dialog box.
5. If necessary, create additional joins by clicking the drop-down arrow and selecting fields in the middle of the **Edit Relationships** dialog box.
6. Change the Join Type and enable the **Enforce Referential Integrity** options as needed.
7. Click the **Create** button.
8. Click the **Save** icon in the **Quick Access** toolbar to save the **Relationships** window.
9. Close the **Relationship** window by clicking the **Close** icon in the **Design** tab.

PAGE..........................**917**

Deleting Fields

1. Open a table in **Datasheet View**.
2. Activate a field by clicking the field name or activate one cell in the field to be deleted.
3. Click the **Delete** icon in the **Datasheet** tab on the Ribbon.

PAGE...........................**693**

Deleting Records

1. Open a table in **Datasheet View**.
2. Activate the record(s) to be deleted by clicking and dragging in the box to the left of the record(s).
3. Press the **Delete** key on your keyboard or click the **Delete** icon in the **Home** tab on the Ribbon.

PAGE...........................**693**

Editing Data and Field Names

1. Open a table in **Datasheet View**.
2. Activate the cell that requires data editing and type a new entry.
3. Double click the field name that requires editing and type adjustments.

PAGE...........................**691**

Editing Data Types and Field Properties

1. Open a table in **Design View**.
2. Activate the field that requires editing.
3. Select a new data type if necessary.
4. Make any adjustments to the field properties while the field name or data type for a field is activated.

PAGE...........................**690**

Enabling/Disabling AutoJoin

1. Click the **File** menu icon.
2. Click the **Access Options** button.
3. Click the Object Designers option on the left side of the **Access Options** dialog box.
4. Click the **Enable AutoJoin** option to add or remove the check mark.
5. Click the **OK** button.

PAGE...........................**908**

Exporting Queries to Excel

1. Select a query from the **Navigation Pane**.
2. Click the **External Data** tab on the Ribbon.
3. Click the **Excel** icon in the **Export** group of icons.
4. Click the **Browse** button in the **Export Excel Spreadsheet** dialog box to select a location on your computer or network and change the file name if necessary.
5. Select the appropriate file format in the **Export Excel Spreadsheet** dialog box.
6. Click the **OK** button.
7. Click the **Close** button in the **Save Export Steps** dialog box or save the export steps if you plan to export the same query on a regular basis.

PAGE...........................**746**

Field Names, Data Types, and Field Properties

1. Create a new table in **Design View** or open an existing table in **Design View**.
2. Type field names in the Field Name column.
3. Click in the Data Type column next to the appropriate field name.
4. Click the down arrow and select a data type from the list of options.
5. Click next to one of the field properties in the **Field Properties** box.
6. Click the down arrow next to the appropriate field property and select an option or type the field property setting.
7. Type a description for the field in the Description column.

PAGE...........................**671**

Filter

1. Open a table in **Datasheet View**.
2. Click the down arrow next to the field name that contains the value you wish to filter.
3. Click the **(Select All)** option to remove all check marks.
4. Click next to the value or values that you wish to show in the table.
5. Click the **OK** button.
6. Click the **Toggle Filter** icon in the **Home** tab on the Ribbon to remove the filter.

PAGE...........................**681**

Formatting a Label Box

1. Activate the label box by clicking anywhere inside the border of the box.
2. Click the **Design** tab if a report is opened in **Design View** or click the **Format** tab if a report is opened in **Layout View**.
3. Click any of the formatting icons in the **Font** group.

PAGE...........................**848**

Formatting a Table

1. Open a table in **Datasheet View**.
2. Click the **Home** tab on the Ribbon.
3. Select any of the formatting icons. Note that formats will be applied to the entire table.

PAGE...........................**676**

Formatting Query Fields

1. Click any row in the design grid of the field you need to format.
2. Click the **Design** tab on the Ribbon.
3. Click the **Property Sheet** icon.
4. Type descriptive information in the first row of the **Property Sheet** window.
5. Make any necessary formatting adjustments in the **Property Sheet** window.
6. Click the X in the upper-right corner of the **Property Sheet** window to apply the format settings and close the window.

PAGE...........................**743**

Future Value Function

1. Click in the first row of an empty column in the design grid of a query.
2. Type a name for the calculated field followed by a colon.
3. Click the **Builder** icon in the **Design** tab to open the **Expression Builder**.
4. Double-click the **Functions** folder.
5. Click the **Built in Functions** folder.
6. Click the **Financial** category in the lower center window.
7. Double-click the **FV** option in the lower right window.
8. Define each of the following arguments with numbers or field names:
   a. **rate:** Interest Rate
   b. **nper:** Number of Payments or Period of Time
   c. **pmt:** Amount of money invested or paid
   d. **pv:** Present Value
   e. **due:** When payments are made (1=begin year, 0=end of year)
9. Click the **OK** button.

PAGE...........................**820**

Group and Report Totals

1. Open an existing report in **Design View**.
2. Click the **Group & Sort** icon in the **Design** tab of the Ribbon.
3. Create a group for your report (see Grouping Data).
4. Click the **More** option for one of the Group levels in the **Grouping** dialog box.
5. Click the down arrow next to the **with no totals** option in the **Grouping** dialog box.
6. Select a field and mathematical function at the top of the totals window.
7. Select **Show Grand Total** at the bottom of the totals window when totaling data for an entire report.
8. Select **Show in group footer** at the bottom of the totals window when totaling data at the end of each group.
9. Repeat steps 6 through 8 when adding more than one total to a report.
10. Close the **Grouping** dialog box.

PAGE...........................**883**

Grouping Data

. Open a select query in **Design View**.

. Click the **Design** tab on the Ribbon.

. Click the **Totals** icon to add the Total row to the design grid of the query.

. Click in the Total row for a field that contains duplicate values to be grouped.

. Click the down arrow and select the **Group By** option. Note that this option will already be selected when the Total row is initially added to the query.

. Run the query.

AGE..........................**753**

Grouping Data

. Create a new or open an existing report in **Design View**.

. Click the **Group & Sort** icon in the **Design** tab of the Ribbon.

. Click the **Add a Group** button in the **Grouping** dialog box at the bottom of the design grid.

. Select a field that will be used to create groups of data in a report.

. Select a sort option that will be used to set the order of the groups are displayed on the report.

. Click the **More** option to open additional settings for the group.

. Select the **by entire value** option if you wish to create a new group for each unique value that is contained in the field you selected in number 4.

Grouping Data (Continued)

8. Close the dialog box by clicking the X in the upper-right corner.

PAGE..........................**871**

Hiding Columns

1. Open a table in **Datasheet View**.

2. Activate a field by clicking the field name.

3. Click the **Home** tab on the Ribbon.

4. Click the **More** icon.

5. Select the **Hide Columns** option.

PAGE..........................**677**

IIF Function and Nested IIF Function

1. Click the first row of an empty column in the design grid of a query.

2. Type a name for the calculated field followed by a colon.

3. Click the **Builder** icon in the **Design** tab of the Ribbon to open the **Expression Builder** dialog box.

4. Double-click the **Functions** folder.

5. Click the **Built in Functions** folder.

6. Click the **<All>** category in the lower center window of the **Expression Builder** dialog box.

7. Double-click the **IIF** function in the lower right window in the **Expression Builder** dialog box.

8. Define each of the following arguments:

   a. **expr:** Logical Test
   b. **truepart:** Value to be displayed or result to be calculated if the logical test is true.
   c. **falsepart:** Value to be displayed or result to be calculated if the logical test is false. Add a new **IIF** function to this argument if you are creating a nested **IIF** function.

9. Click the **OK** button.

PAGE..........................**810**

Importing Data

1. Open a blank or existing Access database.

2. Click the **External Data** tab on the Ribbon.

3. Click one of the icons in the **Import** group based on the format of the source data (i.e., if importing data from an Excel workbook, click the **Excel** icon.)

4. Click the **Browse** button in the **Get External Data** dialog box to select a file or database saved on your computer or network.

5. Select the **Import** option in the **Get External Data** dialog box.

6. Click the **OK** button at the bottom of the **Get External Data** dialog box.

7. Follow the steps of the wizard if importing data from an Excel or text file, or select an object from the **Import Objects** dialog box if importing data from another Access database.

8. Select the **Save** option in the **Save Import Steps** dialog box if desired and click the **Close** button, or click the **Close** button to import data without saving the steps.

PAGE..........................**706**

Inserting a Field

1. Open a table in **Design View**.
2. Type a new field name, select a data type, and adjust the field properties.
3. Click and drag the field to the desired sequence in the list of field names.

OR

1. Open a table in **Datasheet View**.
2. Double click the Add New Field placeholder to type a new field name.
3. Use the **Data Type** and **Format** icons in the **Datasheet** tab to select a data type and format for the new field.

PAGE..........................**692**

Joining Tables (Inner Join)

1. Add two or more tables to a new query.
2. Identify a common field between two tables that contain the same data type and serve the same purpose.
3. Click the field name of the common field identified in step 2 in one table and drag it over to the common field name in the second table (it does not matter from which table you click and drag).
4. Add any necessary fields from both tables to the lower grid of the query.

PAGE..........................**908**

Lines

1. Open an existing report in **Design View**.
2. Click the **Line** icon in the **Design** tab of the Ribbon.
3. Click and drag in the desired section on the design grid to add a line to the report.
4. While the line is activated, click the **Line Thickness** icon in the **Design** tab of the Ribbon to change the thickness of the line.
5. Check the position and appearance of the line by switching the report to **Print Preview**.

PAGE..........................**885**

Linking Data

1. Open a blank or existing Access database.
2. Click the **External Data** tab on the Ribbon.
3. Click one of the icons in the **Import** group based on the format of the source data (i.e., if linking data in an Excel workbook, click the **Excel** icon).
4. Click the **Browse** button in the **Get External Data** dialog box to select a file or database saved on your computer or network.
5. Select the **Link** option in the **Get External Data** dialog box.
6. Click the **OK** button at the bottom of the **Get External Data** dialog box.
7. Follow the steps of the wizard if linking to data in an Excel or text file, or select a table from the **Link Tables** dialog box if linking to an Access table.

PAGE..........................**708**

Nested Queries

1. Click the **Create** tab on the Ribbon.
2. Click the **Query Design** icon.
3. Click the **Queries** tab on the **Show Table** dialog box.
4. Select a query and click the **Add** button in the **Show Table** dialog box.
5. Click the **Close** button in the **Show Table** dialog box.
6. Research the construction and record set of the query that is selected to identify any fields that contain duplicate values.

PAGE..........................**761**

Opening the Expression Builder

1. Click the first row of any column in the design grid of query.
2. Click the **Design** tab in the Ribbon.
3. Click the **Builder** icon.

PAGE..........................**795**

Opening the Zoom Window

1. Click the first row of any column in the design grid of a Select Query.
2. Right click to open a menu of options.
3. Select **Zoom** from the menu.
4. If the **Zoom** window is opened when clicking in a column that contains a field or formula, the contents of the column will be displayed in the window.

PAGE..........................**791**

Outer Joins

1. Create a join line between two tables.
2. Open the **Join Properties** dialog box by double clicking the join line.
3. Select option 2 or 3 in the lower area of the **Join Properties** dialog box, depending on the table in which you want to select all records.

PAGE..........................**912**

Parameter Queries

1. Create a new Select Query.
2. Add fields to the query design grid.
3. Choose a field that you want the user to define when the query is run.
4. Type a phrase in brackets [in the criteria row of the field that the user will define. This phrase should tell the user which type of value should be entered in the input box.
5. Run the query to check the appearance of the input box.

PAGE..........................**929**

Payment Function

1. Click in the first row of an empty column in the design grid of a query.
2. Type a name for the calculated field followed by a colon.
3. Click the **Builder** icon in the **Design** tab of the Ribbon to open the **Expression Builder**.
4. Double-click the **Functions** folder.
5. Click the **Built in Functions** folder.
6. Click the **Financial** category in the lower center window.
7. Double-click the **Pmt** function in the lower right window.
8. Define each of the following arguments with numbers or field names:
   a. **rate** = Interest Rate
   b. **nper** = Number of Payments or Period of Time
   c. **pv** = Present Value
   d. **fv** = Future Value
   e. **due** = When payments are made (1=begin year, 0=end of year)
9. Click the **OK** button.

PAGE..........................**824**

Printing Tables

1. Open a table in **Datasheet** view.
2. Click the **File** icon.
3. Click the arrow next to the **Print** option.
4. Click the **Print Preview** option on the right side of the menu.
5. Use the icons in the **Page Layout** group on the Ribbon to make any necessary adjustments.
6. Click the **Print** icon on the Ribbon.

PAGE..........................**709**

Renaming a Query

1. Right click a query name in the **Navigation Pane.**
2. Select the **Rename** option from the menu.
3. Type a new name.
4. Press the **Enter** key.

PAGE...........................**736**

Report Margins and Orientation

1. Create a new report or open an existing report in **Design View**.
2. Click the **Page Setup** tab in the Ribbon.
3. Use the icons or open the **Page Setup** dialog box by clicking the **Page Setup** icon.
4. Click the **OK** button if making any adjustments in the **Page Setup** dialog box.

PAGE...........................**844**

Sorting Data

1. Open an existing report in **Design View**.
2. Click the **Group & Sort** icon in the **Design** tab of the Ribbon.
3. Click the **Add a Sort** button.
4. Select a field from the field window that will be used as a basis to sort the data in the Detail section.
5. Choose a sort order to the right of the field name in the **Sort by** level.
6. Close the dialog box by clicking the X in the upper-right corner.

PAGE...........................**873**

Sorting Query Record Sets

1. Click the Sort row of the field that will be used to sort the record set of the query.
2. Click the drop-down arrow and select either **Ascending** or **Descending**.

PAGE...........................**743**

Using Aggregate Function

1. Open a select query in **Design View**.
2. Click the **Design** tab on the Ribbon.
3. Click the **Totals** icon to add the Total row to the design grid of the query.
4. Identify any fields that contain duplicate values. Applying an aggregate function to a field with duplicate values could produce erroneous results.
5. Choose an aggregate function by clicking the down arrow in the Total row under the appropriate field.
6. Run the query.

PAGE...........................**757**

>> Glossary

Absolute Reference This cell reference does not change when it is pasted to another cell location on a worksheet.

Add Space Before Paragraph A way of adding space between paragraphs that doesn't increase the line spacing within paragraphs.

Aggregate Functions Access functions used for conducting mathematical summaries of the data contained in a field.

Align Left An icon that aligns text and objects to the left edge of the placeholder box. This alignment is usually used with text and paragraphs.

Align Right An icon that aligns text and objects to the right edge of the placeholder box. Labels commonly use this alignment.

Alignment How data appears in a cell.

Anchor A spot which serves as a reference point for location of the graphic. When the graphic is selected, the reference point spot appears in the form of an anchor.

Animation A special visual or sound effect added to text or an object.

Argument The parts of a mathematical function that must be defined in order to produce a result.

Arrange All A function that tiles presentations, or arranges them side by side, which makes it easier to perform these tasks.

Ascending Order Sorted in the order of lowest to highest.

Author The contents of the program field called Author when the file was created. The Author's name is requested the first time a Microsoft Office program runs. It does not change if the file is opened in a different environment.

Auto Fill Automatically completes a set of data points that are in sequential order, such as numbers, years, months, or days of the week.

AutoFit Selection This option automatically changes the width of a column to fit the width of the longest entered data.

AutoJoin Creates a join line when a field in one table is designated as the primary key and a field with an identical name and data type appears in a second table.

Based On A phrase that refers to the foundation style of another style. Style formatting either adds to or subtracts from the style it is *based on*.

Basic Formula Any equation that consists of two variables separated by a mathematical operator such as + (addition), - (subtraction), and so on.

Basic Shapes A group of ready-made simple shapes, such as circles and stars, used to present qualitative information; help the audience understand large amounts of information more quickly than if they were just looking at text.

Bitmapped A format used by Microsoft that does not compress any of the graphic information within a graphic.

BMP Bitmapped graphic format. A format developed by Microsoft for Windows graphics that doesn't normally include compression algorithms, so the files are extremely large.

Borders and Shading Refer to the lines around the cells of a table or to the color of the background of each cell in the table.

Borders An Excel icon that provides several options for adding lines to a worksheet.

Built-in Styles Formatting that is pre-existing in the Normal template of Word.

Bullet points Small icons, such as circles or squares, that indicate the start of a bullet.

Bulleted list A list that separates each line with bullets, which are symbols that precede each sentence or phrase. They are created in PowerPoint by entering text after the bullet points, using the default bullet location and style that came with the slide layout.

Bullets Short phrases used in business presentations to summarize points and list key messages.

Button A clickable object with an icon on it that provides some command or function in Word.

Calculated field A custom field that contains the results of a formula or function.

Caption A description of what is depicted by the graphic, usually just above or just below the picture or table in a document.

Cell Location In Excel, the column letter followed by the row number.

Cell Reference A cell location that is used in a formula or function. Math calculations will use the value that is placed in this cell location to produce an output. This allows Excel to produce new mathematical outputs when one or more inputs are changed.

Cell In Excel, the intersection of a row and a column.

Center An icon that places text and objects in the middle of the placeholder box. This alignment is used mainly for headings and titles.

Chart Legend The reference area of a chart showing which color relates to each data series or category that is displayed in the chart plot area.

Chart Sheet A dedicated worksheet for a chart.

Chart Tool Chart which displays data using lines and markers. Used for showing trends or comparing trends over time.

Charts Form used to convey information visually and quickly; examples include pie, column, line, and bar charts.

Clear Formatting The command to delete any named styles and return the selected text to the Normal style.

Clip Art Collection of images that can be used in a presentation.

Clipboard panel Contains the Cut, Copy and Paste commands.

Clipboard A temporary workspace where the information you cut or copied is placed to reuse however many times you would like. The contents of the Clipboard are erased when you save your presentation.

Column (on the Insert menu) A definition whereby information can continue on in another perpendicular area of the page when text does not extend across the entire page as a column in a newspaper or magazine article.

Column Chart Chart which displays data in vertical bars. Used mostly to compare data.

Column Width The width of a column which is adjusted to show text or numeric data that is entered into a cell.

Columns (in a table) Information vertically aligned within a table.

Complex Formula Any equation that consists of more than two variables and requires two or more mathematical operators.

Compression A method of storing electronic data that minimize the amount of space necessary to store graphics.

Conditional formatting A feature used to highlight critical information on a business report. May be used to change the appearance of data in a report depending on the value or output.

Constraint key When resizing a graphic, holding Ctrl+Shift will prevent the graphic from changing height and width disproportionately.

Content sensitive menu See *Option Menu*.

Content Graphics, charts, and diagrams placed in a PowerPoint presentation.

Contextual formatting When text or content is selected, PowerPoint displays a small, semitransparent toolbar called the Mini toolbar. The Mini toolbar displays only those formatting options that are applicable to the object selected.

Copy Creates a duplicate of the object from the slide and places it on the Clipboard for later use.

Crop To cut off the edges of a graphic.

Cross-reference When you refer to a picture or table within a document with a dynamic field that changes based upon the caption of the picture or table. For example, if you use cross-reference to refer to Figure #2, and then insert a new figure prior to it, both the caption and the cross-reference will automatically change to Figure #3.

Custom fields Formulas and functions created in Access by adding a new field to the design grid of a query. Can show a specific data value typed into the first row of the query design grid, such as a constant (number), a word, a date, a letter, or the result of a formula or function. Created in the query and *not* included in a table.

Custom Margins The command to change the margins to a specified number.

Cut Removes an object from the slide and places it on the Clipboard for later use.

Data Catalog See Data Dictionary.

Data Dictionary (Data Catalog) A document that is usually maintained by a company's information systems division and contains a list of tables that are designed and maintained for the firm's business managers. A well-constructed data dictionary will provide the purpose of each table, the definition of each field, the index for the table, and the primary key.

Data Entry The most basic and fundamental Excel skill: typing information into a cell.

Data Marts See Data Warehouses.

Data Series Refers to the image that appears on the chart, which is representing a category of values.

Data Type The type of data that is contained in a database field. Setting a data type for a field ensures all values in the field are consistent.

Data Warehouses (Data Marts) Systems that contain data relating to a specific business area, such as marketing, logistics, or sales and inventory.

Data Numbers, letters, or words related to a specific subject or topic. For example, numbers representing sales results or names of products. Data is usually processed or used in calculations to produce meaningful information.

Database A central location where data is collected and stored electronically in tables. A database might contain or several tables of data.

Datasheet View When the data contained in a database is visible. This is also a command in Access which is used to inspect the data values that are contained in a table.

Decrease List Level In PowerPoint, function that moves the bullet to the left. It also changes the bullet type and text size (usually makes the text larger in size).

Default The choice that is selected if no other specific choice is made. For example, the default font might be Cabrini.

Descending Order Sorted in the order of highest to lowest.

Design Tab Option that displays all available PowerPoint templates.

Design View When the design settings of a table are visible. This is also a command in Access which is used to inspect, set, or adjust the design settings of a table.

Desktop publishing The ability for anyone with a computer and a printer to "typeset" their own newspapers, newsletters, brochures, documents, books, articles, and manuals instead of sending documents to a typesetter to painstakingly lay out letters on a press to be printed (as was done before computers and word processors).

Document A generic category for files written with word processors.

Dots per Inch (DPI) The measure of picture resolution on a printer. A low quality printer will print 300 dots per inch, whereas a high quality printer will print up to 1200 dots per inch.

Drag and drop A method of copying or moving text and graphics without using the menu, Ribbon, or toolbars. Once selected, you can click on the selection and drag it to a new location. Wherever you let go of the mouse, the selection *drops*.

Embedded Chart The column chart created to display other data.

Endnotes Same as footnote, except that the text is at the end of the book or chapter instead of at the bottom of each page.

Entity Integrity The requirement of critical data to be entered in or order for a record to be added to a table. The absence of data in certain fields will prevent a record from being added to a table.

Export To convert a document or object from one format to another.

Expression Builder An Access tool that enables the user to create a formula in the design grid of a query using a point-and-click method. This eliminates the risk of spelling errors when adding fields to a formula.

Field A column of data in a database table. Fields contain one consistent type of data such as numbers, currency values, text descriptions, etc.

Field Automatically updating snippets of text. For example, SaveDate, PrintDate, Page, Title, Author, LastSavedBy.

Field Properties The storage capacity and format for the data type assigned to a field. For Currency values, the field properties would contain the monetary symbol (dollars or euros) and the decimal places.

Field Size The storage capacity assigned for a field of data in a table. For text data types, a specific number of characters is used to set the storage limitations of a field.

File extension The letters that appear after the period in a file name, such as .doc or .docx.

Fill Color A formatting technique used to change the color of the cells in a worksheet; makes titles and column heading stand out.

Find and Replace A procedure that will find the letters you enter in the **Find what:** box and replace them with the letters you enter in the **Replace with:** box.

First Capital An attribute that capitalizes the first letter of a word or phrase. (Not to be confused with Title case, which capitalizes the first letter of every word in a phrase.)

Following Paragraph A phrase that refers to what other style should follow the current style. If a paragraph is created by pressing **Enter,** then the *following paragraph* style will become the style of that paragraph.

Font color The palette of colors to choose from.

Font dialog box Instead of clicking on individual icons, you can use this dialog box to apply multiple formats to selected text from one screen.

Font panel Provides many text formatting options that you can use to make your slides look professional; located on Home tab.

Font style Applies to text. Default is Regular. Additional styles that can be applied are Italic and Bold.

Font A font, also referred to as a type or typeface, is a graphic design applied to all numerals, symbols, and alphabetic characters. Fonts fall into one of the following visual categories: Serif and Sans serif.

Footers The text that appears at the bottom of all the pages of a section of a document. Used to display items such as the page number, file name, or worksheet tab name at the bottom of a printed document.

Footnotes The text at the bottom of a page that contains references for your sources or parenthetical comments about the topic. Footnotes are usually numbers, and the point to which they refer is a superscripted number at the end of the related word or phrase.

Foreign key A field used to create a join between two tables.

Formatted Text RTF or Rich Text Format. A format developed by IBM in the early days of word processing to store both text and simple formatting.

Formatting Excel commands used to enhance the visual appearance of a spreadsheet; can transform the appearance of a basic spreadsheet into a professional-looking document and guide the reader's attention to the most critical information, which enables a business manager to scan a spreadsheet efficiently and identify the most important information required to make key decisions.

Formula Auditing Contains features that can be used for viewing and checking all formulas in a worksheet.

Formula Bar Used to change data after it has been typed into a cell location; always shows the contents of an active cell.

Function Used for specific types of mathematical, text, and date calculations.

Future Value (FV) Used to calculate the future value of an investment given a certain period of time, investment value, and interest rate.

GIF Graphic Interchange Format. One of the first graphic formats, used most commonly for color drawings that allow transparency and animation.

Graphics Visual aids such as shapes, pictures, and other non-text images within a document. Used to enhance a PowerPoint presentation and to make it more visually appealing.

Gridlines Horizontal and vertical lines that are visible on an Excel worksheet. Print settings are required for these lines to appear on a printed document. Also, the vertical and horizontal lines in the plot area of a chart.

Group To associate shapes together as one large shape. Allows you to manipulate them (move, rotate, or resize) as though they were a single object.

Handles Little squares or circles that appear on each edge and corner of a selected object. The appearance of handles indicates that the object has been selected, and can be moved or resized.

Handouts Miniature snapshots of your slides condensed onto a page. Their use offers two main benefits: The audience can have something to take with them or jot notes on, and because the slides are captured in snapshots, less paper is used.

Header The area at the top of a printed document. Usually contains items such as the date, description of the document, or the file name.

HLookup Is identical to the VLookup function; however, it looks horizontally across the first row of a range of cells to find a lookup value instead of vertically down a column.

Horizontal Alignment To center- or right-justify data in a cell.

HTML HyperText Markup Language. The formatting language used by most web pages.

Icons A picture that normally appears on command buttons. Arranged in related groups and used to activate any Excel command.

Increase List Level A PowerPoint function that moves the bullet to the right. It may also change the bullet type and text size (usually smaller).

Indent A paragraph "margin" relative to the page margin. An indent can be first line, hanging, left, or right.

Index Used to determine how data is organized or sequenced in a table. Tables are indexed to increase the speed and efficiency of selecting data using a query.

Information Data that has been collected and processed in a meaningful way to produce intelligence about a specific topic or subject. For example, the collection of stock prices over several months can produce trend information indicating if a company is increasing or decreasing its value for shareholders.

Inner Join Sometimes referred to as a Simple Join or an Equal Join, an Inner Join will display data in the record set of a query where the value in both fields used to create the join line are identical.

Join Used to combine data from two or more tables or queries (if creating a nested query).

JPEG Joint Photographic Experts Group graphic format. A format developed specifically for photographs that enables differing amounts of compression. More compression means lower quality, but for screen applications such as the web, lower quality is not necessarily a problem.

Jumping graphic When a graphic jumps unexpectedly to a new location. An annoying problem in Word that usually occurs when the relative position of a graphic does not fit on the current page.

Justify An icon that aligns text to both the left and right edges of the placeholder box, adding extra spaces where needed to create the effect.

Keep Lines Together A way of ensuring that a paragraph doesn't split across a page break; also prevents text wrapping around pictures.

Landscape The orientation of a paper printed lengthwise, with 8H inches down the side and 11 inches across the top (for a standard-sized paper).

LastSavedBy The contents of the Author field of the current environment. Whereas the Author's name is normally saved when the file was created, LastSavedBy is changed each time the file is saved.

Layout Refers to the way elements are arranged on a slide. A layout contains predetermined placeholders for information.

LCD Projectors Devices utilized for displaying video images or data. They are the modern-day equivalent of slide projectors and overhead projectors.

Leader line A row of dots or dashes that connects a word to another word or number.

Line Chart Chart which displays data using lines and markers. Used for showing trends or comparing trends over time.

Lines Connect shapes and indicate a flow or sequence.

Linking (Excel) A cell reference which displays the contents of a cell in another worksheet or workbook. Often used when constructing spreadsheets for financial planning or accounting.

List box The little arrow or triangle that brings up a list of options or choices.

Logical Function A function that can be used to evaluate data and provide an output based on the results of a test.

Logical Test A test that uses comparison operators to evaluate the contents of a cell based on the contents of another cell location, a formula, constant, or text.

Lookup Function A function that looks for a value that exists in one worksheet, in a second worksheet or workbook and returns another value based on settings that you define.

Lossless The ability of a graphic compression format to retain all the information about a digital graphic. A lossless format results in a higher quality picture.

Lossy The loss of some digital media information about a graphic, usually due to compression. The lossier the compression format, the lower the quality of the graphic.

Manage Styles A dialog box used to unhide and modify all the styles of a document.

Margin The space on the left, right, top, and bottom of a printed document.

Match case During a **Find** procedure, you can choose to find only those words that match uppercase letters for uppercase letters and lowercase letters for lowercase letters. For example, *Hello* matches case with *Hello*, but not *hello* or *HELLO*.

Mathematical Operator Such as + (addition), - (subtraction), and so on.

Merge Cells Enables users to create one big cell out of several smaller cells; commonly used to center a title at the top of a spreadsheet.

Microsoft Graphic Object A format used by Microsoft when pasting Excel graphs into a Word document. This format attempts to retain the individual objects within the graphic, and often does not look as good as a simple picture that does not contain individual objects within a group.

Mixed Reference When a dollar sign appears before either the column letter or row number of a cell location.

Movies Streaming video files in formats such as .mpg, .avi.

Multilevel List An outline format that requires different levels of indents and line numbers or letters.

Nested Queries Queries that select data from existing queries.

New Presentation window Blank window in PowerPoint where you can create your presentation in a number of ways.

New Quick Style The command to create a new style based on the format of the selected text.

Normal template A file stored in the user's Template folder called Normal that controls the formatting for the initial file that opens up when you launch Word 2007.

Normal view The main editing view, where you write and design your presentation.

Normal The name of the default style of text in Word.

Numbered lists Work well when explaining procedures or presenting information that has some order or priority associated with it. Numbered lists label items using: Cardinal numbers (1, 2, 3, etc.); Roman numerals (I, II, III, etc.); and Alphabet (A, B, C, etc.).

Objects The components of an Access database that include Tables, Queries, Reports, and Forms.

Option menu (or Context Sensitive menu) The menu that appears when you right-click an object.

Orientation Either a *Portrait* or *Landscape* orientation for a document.

Orphan The last word that appears by itself on a line at the end of a paragraph.

Outer Join Sometimes referred to as a Left Join, Right Join, or One Way Join. When used, a query will select all records from one table and only the matching records from a second table.

Page Footer The section of a report that shows any labels or data at the bottom of each page of reportReport FooterDisplays text from a label box or data from a text box on the last page of the report.

Page Header Descriptive information that appears at the top of every page of a report.

Page Layout The Ribbon tab on which margins, section attributes, headers, and footers that appear on each page are modified.

Page Numbers The feature that automatically updates page numbers so that the document repaginates.

Paragraph dialog box Instead of clicking on individual icons, you can use this dialog box to apply multiple formats to selected text from one screen.

Paragraph mark An invisible code at the end of the paragraph inserted into the document when you press the **Enter** key. It can be represented with a ¶ symbol on the screen or with a ^p in the **Find what:** or **Replace with:** box.

Paragraph panel Provides many formatting options that are most commonly used to organize multiple lines or paragraphs of information.

Paragraph-Level Style A type of style that is applied to an entire paragraph rather than just the text within the paragraph. A paragraph-level style is stored within the paragraph mark at the end of the paragraph.

Paragraph Multiple lines of information in a PowerPoint presentation.

Parameter query A query that requests a value from the user that will be used in the criteria row for a particular field.

Parenthetical Text or graphics which are not the main topic, but are related to the main topic.

Paste Special Commands used to selectively paste contents that have been copied. An extra option under Paste that allows you to insert objects and retain the attributes from the tool they were created in.

Paste Inserts an object from the Clipboard.

Path The location of a file, usually preceding the filename. For example C:\My Documents\Wordfiles\Myletter.docx is a path and filename.

Payment (PMT) Function used to determine the payments of a mortgage or lease payments.

Picture Enhanced Metafile A 32-bit graphic format used by Microsoft that pastes an object as a simple picture. A Picture Enhanced Metafile can be resized or cropped just like any other picture.

Pictures Digital images in file formats such as .tif, .jpg, .bmp, .png.

Pie Chart Used to show a percent-to-total comparison for various data categories.

Pitch A width measurement, usually applied to fixed-width fonts. The number of letters that can fit within one inch. A 12-pitch font can fit 12 letters within one inch.

Pixelate What happens to a picture when you can visually see individual pixels. To pixelate is an indication of poor quality.

Pixels per Inch (PPI) The measure of picture resolution on a screen. A computer screen has thousands of dots called pixels. The more pixels, the higher the resolution.

Plot Area Area of a chart used to display a data series.

PNG Portable Network Graphics format. Developed specifically for web applications, but not yet supported in all graphics programs.

Point A height measurement, usually applied to fonts of variable widths. There are 72 points in an inch.

Portrait The orientation of a paper printed lengthwise, with 8H inches across the top and 11 inches down the side (for a standard-sized paper).

Present Value (PV) Is used when a one-time investment is made to an account.

Preview Viewing a worksheet before printing.

Primary Key A field or number of fields in a table that makes every record unique.

Print Area Icon to use if you want to print only a portion of a worksheet.

Print Titles Duplicates the column headings or row headings of a worksheet on each page that is printed.

PrintScreen or Prt Scrn A key on the keyboard that, when used in conjunction with the Ctrl or Alt keys, will send a picture of the screen to the operating system clipboard so that it can be pasted into a document.

Propagating Field Properties Maintains the format properties of a field in all Access objects. This command is typically used when editing the field properties of a table.

Property Update Options Options that appear when editing the design settings of a table. These options appear when the field properties of an existing table are changed.

Qualitative Information that is descriptive and narrative. Qualitative information is sometimes considered to be subjective.

Quantitative Information that is described using numbers and units of measurement. Quantitative information is considered to be objective.

Query A file that stores the condition you defined to determine which information from the database will be displayed.

Query A term synonymous with the word *question*; often referred to as a tool that asks an Access table "questions."

Quick Access Toolbar Contains a few commonly used icons, such as Save and Undo.

Quick Parts Microsoft's name for many different kinds of automatically entered text including fields, predefined headers, predefined footers, preformatted page numbers, or user-defined text snippets.

Quick Styles Collections of formatting options (colors, fonts, and effects combinations.)

Range In Excel, a group of cells on a worksheet; noted by any two cell locations separated by a colon.

Reading Highlight During a **Find** procedure, instead of *selecting* the letters found in the document, you can choose to *highlight* the letters with a yellow background.

Record Set In regards to an Access query, a temporary display of the records that were selected from the table.

Record One row of a database table. A record from a database table contains related values from each field in the table.

Rectangles Shape that is useful for presenting qualitative information.

Referential integrity Ensures that the common field used to join two tables always contains identical values.

3-D Reference Using cell referencing to link data between two worksheets or workbooks.

Refresh (Excel) Once the workbook links are updated.

Relational Database Management system (RDBMS) A system used to electronically collect and store data in several tables. The system is typically used to retrieve data for processing and reporting information.

Relative Referencing Adjusts any cell references when a formula is copied and pasted to a new location on a worksheet.

Repeating header row Enables the first row of a table to repeat at the top of the next page if the table gets split across a page break.

Report Design Option used when creating an Access report from scratch.

Report Details The section of a report that contains numeric or text data in columns.

Report Header Usually used for creating the title of a report.

Ribbon Area at the top of the screen in the new Office interface that contains groups of buttons for accessing the features and functions of Word 2007.

Row Height Used to set a specific height for a row or group of rows.

Ruler Area at the top of the document below the Ribbon that indicates what the margins, indents, and tab settings are for the current paragraph.

Sans serif These fonts have straight letters. They are crisp and more defined, and they are used in situations in which there is not too much text (titles, phrases, short pieces of text) and where the content needs to be read from a distance. As such, sans-serif fonts are recommended for all text within a PowerPoint presentation.

Scale To manually reduce or enlarge the printed appearance of a worksheet.

Section Break, Section Code, or Section Break Code A defined code in the document that sets up an alternative page margin, headers and footers, columns, and page numbers.

Security Alert This prompt informs you that data is being linked to an external workbook and gives you the option of updating these links.

Select Query The most fundamental type of query in Access. It is primarily used for selecting and adding computations to data extracted from a table.

Series Point The method used to format the data series of a chart.

Serif These fonts have little curls at the end of each letter. They are used mainly for lengthy documents.

Sizing Handle Used to change the size of an object such as charts, chart components, text boxes, etc.

Slide Sorter Displays all the slides in the presentation in thumbnail form.

Slides Individual pages within a PowerPoint presentation.

SmartArt Graphics Prebuilt diagrams such as lists, process charts, hierarchies, and pyramids used to represent relationships.

Sorting Used to rearrange data in a specific sequence or rank that enables business managers to assess information efficiently and make key decisions.

Speaker Notes Additional text associated with each PowerPoint slide that can be printed and used for reference.

Spelling A feature, found in the Review tab, used to locate misspellings and suggest alternate, correct spellings. Sometimes referred to as Spell Check.

Split cell Creating two cells out of a single cell.

Spreadsheet In its most basic form, Excel is an electronic version of a paper.

Stack Column Chart Shows the proportion or percentage that each category contributes to a total and can be used to show how this relationship changes over time.

Status Bar Area at the bottom of the Excel screen which shows items such as the Zoom slider and view icons.

Styles A combination of formatting that can be saved under a name and applied quickly and easily.

Tab (1) Appears at the top of the Ribbon or dialog box to enable you to choose different groups and functions.

Tab (2) The location for a "stopping place" on a line that becomes active when you press the Tab key on the keyboard. A tab can be left, right, center, decimal, or bar.

Tab (3) A key on the keyboard that enables you to move between objects in a dialog box or activate a tab stop when typing.

Table options menu The menu that appears when you right–click on one of the objects in a table.

Table properties A dialog box that enables the formatting and configuration of a table.

Tables (1) A defined grid, with or without borderlines, that presents information horizontally and vertically in columns and rows. You can summarize, categorize, and compare information easily using tables; consequently, they are used a great deal in presentations across almost all areas of business.

Tables (2) Where data is collected and stored in a database system. It is also one of the objects available in Access.

Templates A file that contains the styles in a presentation, including the type and size of bullets and fonts; placeholder sizes and positions; background design and fill color schemes. In Word, a set up or configuration file upon which a new document is based.

Text-Level Style A style that can be applied to an entire paragraph or to just the text within the paragraph, or both. A text-level style is stored within the individual letters to which it is applied but cannot contain paragraph-level formatting.

Text (1) In Access, a data type used to define a field in a table. Text values are not numeric and can not be used in mathematical calculations.

Text (2) Letters, numbers, and special characters.

Theme A prebuilt PowerPoint format that already has design elements (colors, fonts, graphics) applied to it. When a theme is selected, the format is automatically applied to all the slides in the presentation.

Thesaurus A feature found in the Review tab that suggests alternate words (synonyms). Used to prevent the overuse of a certain word within a PowerPoint presentation or Word document.

Thumbnails A thumbnail is a smaller representation of a pictureoften used on web sites or in file listings to show what a picture looks like without having to show the full-sized picture (which would slow down the webpage or file listing).

TIFF Tag Interchange File Format. A format developed by Adobe that stores all the source information of a bitmap but can be compressed (though is still a very large file).

Title The contents of the document property field called Title. (Not to be confused with filename, which is what you name the document when you are saving it.)

Transition An effect that specifies how the screen changes as you move from one slide to another.

Transparency The ability to see something under a certain area of the drawing.

Transposed Data that has been reversed in its orientation on a worksheet (i.e. numbers in a column are displayed in a row). Also, the reversing of digits in a number.

Typewriter A precomputer device on which people typed letters and documents on paper.

Unbound control A text box that is not associated to a field in a query or table.

Unformatted Text Text with no formatting at all. Bold, underline, italic—anything that formats the numbers, letters, or paragraphs will be gone

Unformatted Unicode Text Same as Unformatted Text, but a smaller character set designed to be internationally compatible.

Vertical Alignment To place data on the top, center, or bottom of a cell.

VLookup A lookup function used mostly to display data from one worksheet or workbook into another.

What If Scenario Used by business managers to understand how potential outcomes will affect the decisions they make.

Whitespace A page designer phrase that indicates how much of the page does not have text or graphics on it

Widow The end of a line that splits across a page break

Windows Enhanced Metafile An older format similar to the Picture Enhanced Metafile, but one that works within 16-bit graphic programs.

Word options General settings for saving and printing and user information associated with an installation of Word.

WordArt Formatting options that allow you to insert text that is formatted as pictures.

Workbook The entire Excel file that contains a collection of worksheets.

Worksheet One page of an Excel file or workbook.

Wrap Text Automatically expands the row height and creates a second line to fit long entries.

Wrapping text A way of placing a graphic within a document that allows surrounding text to flow around it.

X-Axis The bottom horizontal axis of a chart.

Y-Axis The vertical axis of a chart. Usually appears along the left side of a chart.

» Index